WASAFF

The Norton Reader
Fourteenth Edition

BRIEF CONTENTS

CONTENTS

SEE ALSO

Profiles 87

GENDER AND HUMAN NATURE   164

CULTURAL ANALYSIS   200

FOOD 274

See Also

Sports   320

Language and Communication   458

MEDIA AND TECHNOLOGY   572

ETHICS 637

SEE ALSO

HISTORY AND POLITICS 750

SEE ALSO

religions, history, geography, education, orature and literature, and the
conscious elevation of the language of the colonizer."

See Also

PHILOSOPHY AND RELIGION 947

PREFACE

The Norton Reader began as an attempt to introduce students to the essay as a genre, and to create an anthology of excellent nonfiction writing. This new edition continues that tradition, offering a wide selection of essays on a broad range of subjects, and including examples of the kinds of writing students are most assigned, from profiles and arguments to narratives and analyses. With 155 selections in the Full Edition and ninety-five in the Shorter Edition, *The Norton Reader* offers depth, breadth, and variety for teaching the essay as it's developed over time, including selections from the classic to contemporary.

And always, *The Norton Reader* has aimed to uphold a tradition of anthologizing excellent prose, starting with Arthur Eastman, the founding editor, who insisted that essays be selected for the quality of their writing. As he put it, "Excellence would be their pillar of smoke by day, of fire by night." With this vision, the original editors of *The Norton Reader* chose classic essays that appealed to modern readers and that are now recognized as comprising the essay canon. We have aimed to continue this practice, yet have also adapted the *Reader* to new pedagogies and have updated it by adding new writers whose work appeals to new generations of student readers. We believe that the essays in this volume are well-written, focus on topics that matter, and demonstrate what all of us tell our students about good writing.

The fourteenth edition marks *The Norton Reader*'s fiftieth anniversary and introduces a new general editor, Melissa A. Goldthwaite of Saint Joseph's University, who follows Arthur Eastman (editor of the first through eighth editions) and Linda Peterson (editor of the ninth through thirteenth editions).

HIGHLIGHTS OF THE FOURTEENTH EDITION

- New contemporary essays by authors as diverse as Alison Bechdel, Christopher Hitchens, Marion Nestle, Jane McGonigal, and Joyce Carol Oates, among others.

- Canonical essays by Toni Morrison, Virginia Woolf, Henry David Thoreau, Martin Luther King Jr., E. B. White, Maya Angelou, and others.

- Unique coverage of both themes and genres. Thematic chapters on education, media and technology, gender, language, food, ethics, history, and the environment, among others, introduce important academic ideas and civic conversations, while genre chapters provide examples of cultural analysis, arguments, profiles, and other kinds of writing.

- A newly designed website, nortonreader.com, that makes *The Norton Reader* uniquely searchable and easy to use. Search for readings by theme, genre, rhetorical mode, author, year, type of publication, and keyword—or any combination. With this flexibility, teachers can build a syllabus around any of these categories, and students can easily find readings that they will use as sources for their own writing. The site also features biographical notes about the authors and a short excerpt from each reading.

- Apparatus to provide just enough detail—but not so much as to overwhelm the essays themselves. Contextual notes indicate when and where the essay was written; annotations explain unfamiliar persons, events, and concepts; and study questions for all essays prompt analysis and discussion.

- Biographical information located at the end of the volume lets you choose if and when you want to find out more about the authors.

- Four expanded indexes that organize the readings according to date of publication, genre, rhetorical mode, and theme. This helps meet crucial goals of the WPA Outcomes Statement, which urges that students learn to write in several genres, identify conventions of format and structure, and understand how genres shape reading and writing.

NEW TO THIS EDITION

- Fifty-seven new selections (thirty-one in the Shorter Edition), including essays from American, Mexican, Kenyan, Canadian, Chinese, Indian, English, Korean, and Russian writers.

- Two new and two completely revised chapters. Chapters on "Food" and "Sports" are new to this edition and feature writing by Marion Nestle, Julia Child, Roger Angell, Joe Posnanski, and David Halberstam. Completely revised chapters on "Media and Technology" and "Science" introduce essays on everything from social media and gaming to medical ethics and scientific inquiry.

- The table of contents now cross-lists readings, making it easy to locate all the selections that address a particular theme or genre.

- More visuals than ever (over 100)—photographs, drawings, graphs, and other illustrations—that accompanied the essays when they were first published, including a full chapter from Alison Bechdel's graphic memoir *Fun Home*, a drawing by Lynda Barry, and photographs included in Julia Child's memoir. We hope that these images will encourage readers to think about the intersection of the visual and the verbal in modern culture, and the ways in which images enrich, highlight, and sometimes challenge the written text.

ACKNOWLEDGMENTS

Linda Peterson began her association with *The Norton Reader* in 1989 when the house editor for the book, Julia Reidhead, invited Linda to write a review of the seventh edition. In her fifteen-page review, Linda praised the many positive aspects of the book and made specific suggestions for new editions: that it provide support for different writing pedagogies, including writing across the curriculum; that it invite students to practice the same kinds of writing represented in the book; and that it include a chapter on "Nature and the Environment." On the strength of this review and her reputation as a teacher and scholar, Linda was invited to join the editorial team for the eighth edition—in which her suggestions would be implemented and later refined in subsequent editions. She expertly served as the general editor of the ninth through thirteenth editions, leading and guiding by example, expanding the range of genres and diversity of essays and authors included, increasing the pedagogical support for student writing in association with the book, and inviting new editors to collaborate with her in the process. Her intelligence, diligence, and insight shaped seven editions of this book, including the fourteenth edition. After a multi-year battle with cancer, Linda Peterson died on June 25, 2015. We will miss her, her collaboration and dependability, her friendship and example. We dedicate this edition to her and in her memory.

The editors would like to express appreciation and thanks to the many teachers who provided reviews and invaluable feedback: Sadaf Alam (San Jacinto College), Deborah Bertsch (Columbus State Community College), Patricia Bjorklund (Southeastern Community College), Jessica Brown (City College of San Francisco), Lee Carmouche (Houston Community College), Jessie Casteel (San Jacinto Community College), James M. Chesbro (Fairfield University), Delicia Daniels (Houston Community College), Gita DasBender (Seton Hall University), Syble Davis (Houston Community College), Michael DeStefano (Fairfield University), Michael Duffy (Moorpark College), Charles Ellenbogen (John F. Kennedy—Eagle Academy), Craig Fehrman (Indiana University), Rebecca Fleming (Columbus State Community College), Lori Franklin (Northern New Mexico College), David Gorin (Yale University), Stacey Higdon (Houston Community College), Sonya Huber (Fairfield University), John Isles (City College of San Francisco), Crystal Johnson (Houston Community College), Kristi Krumnow (San Jacinto College), John Kwist (Georgia Highlands College), Susanna Lankheet (Lake Michigan College), Andrea Laurencell Sheridan (SUNY Orange), Jessica Lindberg (Georgia Highlands College), Iswari Pandey (California State University at Northridge), Rolf Potts, Sonya Prince (San Jacinto College), Mark Ridge (Rust College), Guy Shebat (Youngstown State University), and Kim Shirkhani (Yale University)

We also thank Shuli Traub for her expert project editing; Katharine Ings for her copyediting; Lynne Cannon Menges for her proofreading; and Michael Fleming for his work on the author biographies that appear in the back of the book. At Norton we thank Katie Callahan, Rebecca Homiski, Ashley Horna, and Claire Wallace for their help with editing and production; Erica Wnek, Cliff Landesman, Patrick Cartelli, Morgan Miranda, Livern Chin, Marie McHale, Denise Shanks, and Ava Bramson for their work on the website; Megan Jackson, Margaret Gorenstein, Stephanie Romeo, and Rona Tuccillo for their help with permissions; Debra Morton Hoyt and Tiani Kennedy for their work on the new cover design; and our editors past and present: Jennifer Bartlett, Carol Hollar-Zwick, Julia Reidhead, and Marilyn Moller. A special thanks to our new editor Ariella Foss, who guided this edition from conception through production with admirable patience, efficiency, and intelligence.

INTRODUCTION
Reading and Writing with The Norton Reader

Reading with a Writer's Eye

How do specific people, experiences, and environments help shape identity? How might we live and eat in more sustainable ways? How do sports influence our lives and culture? If technology inevitably shapes us, how might we use it to solve some of the world's greatest problems? How might we listen, view art, and understand one another better? These are just a few of the questions and issues explored by essays in *The Norton Reader*. Whether you read many or just a few of the selections, we hope that you will find them thought provoking. We also hope you will use them to inform and improve your own writing—in this anthology you will find readings that model a wide range of genres and styles from a diverse group of writers.

The more than 150 pieces collected here come from a variety of publications, from graphic novels and daily newspapers to blogs, online magazines, science journals, and books. In an anthology like *The Norton Reader*, all of these selections appear in the same format, with the same typeface and layout; most have annotations to explain references and allusions; and all have questions to urge you to think about major issues and themes.

To help in the reading process, we provide information about the context in which the essay first appeared. We also suggest, in this introduction, some ways of reading essays that will help you with your own writing. Among the goals of a college anthology like this one are helping to make your reading enrich, inspire, and improve your writing.

When you begin reading an essay that your instructor assigns, ask yourself some or all of the following questions. These questions—about the audience, the author and his or her purpose, and the genre—will help you understand the essay, consider its original context, analyze its meaning, recognize its organization and rhetorical strategies, and imagine how you might use similar strategies for your own writing.

WHO IS THE AUDIENCE?

An *audience* consists of those to whom the essay is directed—the people who read the article, listen to the speech, or view the text. The question about audience might be posed in related ways: For whom did the author write? What readers does the author hope to reach? What readers did he or she actually reach?

Sometimes the audience is national or international, as in an editorial for a newspaper like the *Washington Post* or the *New York Times*. Often, the

audience shares a common interest, as the readers of an environmental magazine might do or the buyers of books on food or history. To help you understand the original audience for each essay, we provide *contextual notes* at the
bottom of the first page of each essay. Contextual notes give information about
when and where the essay first appeared and, if it began as a talk, when and
where it was delivered and to what audience. As editors, we could swamp you
with information about publication and authorship, but we prefer to include
more essays and keep contextual information focused on the original audience
and publication context—that is, on where the essay appeared, who read it,
and (if we know) what reaction it received.

For example, the contextual note for Chris Wiewiora's "This Is Tossing"
(p. 316) tells you that it appeared in *MAKE*, a small-circulation magazine that
attracts readers who enjoy fiction, essays, and poetry. In contrast, Dan Barber's
"What Farm-to-Table Got Wrong" (p. 400) appeared as an op-ed in the *New
York Times*, a daily newspaper with a huge national readership. Wiewiora could
assume that his audience would like reading personal memoirs, whereas Barber knew that he needed to speak to a large, diverse national audience of people
holding different opinions on matters of education, politics, religion, and the
environment. Knowing these audiences gives a window into the writers' choices,
strategies, and styles.

Wiewiora begins in the present tense, putting the reader in the moment:

> It's 10AM. An hour before Lazy Moon Pizzeria opens. You have an hour—
> this hour—to toss. You're supposed to have 11 pies by 11AM. One hour.

He puts the reader in the place of the dough tosser, providing a sense of purpose and urgency.

Barber, too, begins by putting the reader in a specific moment:

> It's spring again. Hip deep in asparagus—and, soon enough, tomatoes and
> zucchini—farm-to-table advocates finally have something from the farm to
> put on the table. . . . Today, almost 80 percent of Americans say sustain-
> ability is a priority when purchasing food. The promise of this kind of
> majority is that eating local can reshape landscapes and drive lasting change.
>   Except it hasn't.

But unlike Wiewiora, who keeps his reader in the position of dough tosser,
Barber quickly moves to his main argument: that the farm-to-table movement
has not created sustainable changes in the American food system. The expectations of the two different audiences explain, in part, the writers' different
approaches and styles.

Sometimes contextual notes give information about where the selection was
published and how it was received—another way to understand the audience.
Maya Angelou's "Graduation" (p. 45) comes from her autobiography *I Know
Why the Caged Bird Sings* (1969); Angelou then continued writing her life story
in six sequential volumes, most recently *Mom & Me & Mom* (2013)—a sequence
that testifies to her book's success and its appeal to a wide variety of readers.

In each contextual note, we try to explain a little about the magazines, news-papers, and books that published these essays—whether it's *MAKE*, a small literary journal published twice a year; the *New York Times Magazine*, a Sun-day supplement of the daily newspaper; or *I Know Why the Caged Bird Sings*, a freestanding book.

WHO IS THE AUTHOR?

If the audience consists of those who read the essays, the *author* is the person who writes them. Through their writing, authors tend to introduce themselves to their audiences, revealing personal experiences, preferences, and beliefs that bear on the subject at hand. In "We Do Abortions Here: A Nurse's Story" (p. 709), the title gives us an important fact about the author Sallie Tisdale and her perspective: she is a nurse and has seen abortions up close. In "Who Shot Johnny?" (p. 270), Debra Dickerson introduces herself directly to her readers in the opening paragraph:

> I am unrepentant and vocal about having gained admittance to Harvard through affirmative action; I am a feminist, stoic about my marriage chances as a well-educated, 36-year-old black woman who won't pretend to need help taking care of herself.

Who the author is—where she comes from, what her background is, what her educational and professional experience are—becomes part of Dickerson's story, and it influences her perspective on the random shooting of her nephew, the subject of her essay.

Not all authors are as direct as Tisdale or Dickerson. You don't really need to know that Brian Doyle is editor of *Portland Magazine* and the author of sev-eral novels to appreciate his meditation on hearts—from those belonging to tiny hummingbirds to huge whales to humans—in "Joyas Voladoras" (p. 526). Nor do you need to know that David Halberstam, author of "Jordan's Moment" (p. 361), wrote about the Vietnam War and the civil rights movement before becoming a sports journalist. Such biographical facts are interesting but not essential to understanding the essays included.

Because we believe that essayists prefer to introduce themselves and reveal details of personality and experience that they consider most relevant, we do not preface each essay with a biographical note. We think they, as authors, should step forward and we, as editors, should stand back and let them speak. But if you want to learn more about the writer of an essay, you can check the "Author Biographies" section at the end of the book. Putting this information at the end of the book gives you a choice. You may already know something about an author and not wish to consult this section, or you may wish to know more about an author before you read his or her writing. Or you may just pre-fer to encounter the authors on their own terms, letting them identify them-selves within the essay. Sometimes knowing who authors are and where their voices come from help readers grasp what they say—but sometimes it doesn't.

WHAT IS THE RHETORICAL CONTEXT AND PURPOSE?

The *rhetorical context*, sometimes called *rhetorical situation* or *rhetorical occasion*, refers to the context—social, political, biographical, historical—in which writing takes place and becomes public. The term *purpose*, in a writing class, refers to the author's goal—whether to inform, to persuade, to entertain, to analyze, or to do something else through the essay. We could also pose this question as follows: what goals did the writer have in composing and publishing the essay? What effect did the author wish to have on the audience?

For some selections, the rhetorical context is indicated by the *title*. Abraham Lincoln's "Second Inaugural Address" (p. 801) and John F. Kennedy's "Inaugural Address" (p. 803) were speeches that marked the beginning of their presidencies. An inauguration represents a significant moment in a leader's—and the nation's—life. The speech given on such an occasion requires a statement of the president's goals for the next four years. In addition to the title, you can discover more about the rhetorical context of a president's inaugural speech in the *opening paragraphs*. Lincoln, for example, refers back to his first inaugural address and the "impending civil war"; then he acknowledges that the war continues and that he prays "this mighty scourge of war may speedily pass away." In the midst of the American Civil War, Lincoln knows that he must, as president, address the political conflict that faces the nation, offer hope for its resolution, and set the moral tone for the aftermath. That's his purpose.

Like the presidential speech, many essays establish the rhetorical context in their opening paragraphs. Editorials and op-eds begin with a "hook"—an opening reference to the issue at hand or the news report under consideration. You might even say that the editorial writer "creates" the rhetorical context and shows us her purpose straight away. In her op-ed "Get a Knife, Get a Dog, but Get Rid of Guns" (p. 384), Molly Ivins begins with "Guns. Everywhere guns"—letting her readers know that she's addressing the controversial topic of gun control and establishing her position right up front (she's pro-control). Ivins's main purpose is to persuade others to adopt her position, but another purpose is, through humor, to amuse her readers and poke fun at the anti-control group. Jo-Ann Pilardi's "Immigration Problem Is about Us, Not Them" (p. 386) reveals, in its title, her rhetorical purpose: to reconsider the immigration debate. In her opening paragraphs, Pilardi reminds us of the social and political context:

> The immigration debates always focus on small brown bodies jumping fences and scooting through the brush of our Southwestern states (land that was Mexico about 150 years ago).
>   Our self-righteous anger at those brown bodies is fueled by our narrow use of the word "illegal"—a term reserved only for those immigrant workers.

Even if you haven't followed newspaper reports about immigration, you can tell from this opening that the writer is engaging a highly contested debate concerning immigrants who cross the U.S.-Mexico border and enter the United States. Pilardi's purpose is to disrupt the us/them thinking that hinders fruitful discussion of the issue.

If an essay does not establish a rhetorical context in its opening paragraphs, you can find additional information in the *contextual note* (described above) or in the *annotations* to each essay (described below). For example, the contextual note for Wallace Stegner's "Wilderness Letter" (p. 544) is:

> Written when the United States Congress was debating the creation of a National Wilderness Preservation System which, when passed in 1964, recognized wilderness as "an area where the earth and its community of life are untrammeled by man, where man himself is a visitor who does not remain." In this letter, Wallace Stegner writes to David E. Pesonen, who chaired the Outdoor Resources Review Commission, which determined the needs of Americans for outdoor recreation spaces. This letter was later included as a "coda" in *The Sound of Mountain Water* (1969), a collection of essays, letters, and speeches concerning the American West's environment, history, and culture.

The annotations (footnotes marked with small numerals) give further clues. For instance, the first annotation of that essay, which footnotes *Brave New World* in the third paragraph, tells us that this title is an "allusion to the dystopian novel by Aldous Huxley about a future totalitarian society in which all aspects of human life are controlled and conditioned." If you were not already familiar with this book, the annotation helps you understand the extent of Stegner's fear, namely that a lack of environmental preservation could lead to the dystopia that Huxley describes. Both the contextual note and annotation provide information on the role of the United States Congress in creating a National Wilderness Preservation System and the degree of Stegner's concern.

Here is some additional information about *annotations* and how to use them as you read an essay: the annotations are explanatory footnotes—a common feature of a textbook. When the original authors wrote the footnotes themselves, we indicate that in the text. In Gloria Anzaldúa's essay, for example, we note that all footnotes are the author's (p. 471). This tells you that the author wished to cite an expert, add information, or send the reader to another source. In most cases, however, we have written the footnotes to help with difficult words, allusions, and references. We provide information about people, places, works, theories, and other unfamiliar things that the original audience may have known. For example, for Maya Angelou's "Graduation" (p. 45) we give an annotation for Gabriel Prosser and Nat Turner, but not Abraham Lincoln and Christopher Columbus. Many of Angelou's readers would have known that Prosser and Turner were executed leaders of slave rebellions in the nineteenth century. But because not all readers today know (or remember) this part of American history, we add a footnote.

Here's a final important point: Annotation, while it facilitates the making of meaning in reading, can never take its place. Reading is an active process. Experienced readers take responsibility for that action—reading critically, constructing meaning, interpreting what they read. If our annotations help you read critically, then use them; if they interfere, then just continue reading the main text and skip over them.

WHAT IS THE GENRE AND ITS CONVENTIONS?

Genre is a term used by composition and literature teachers to refer to kinds of writing that are expected to have common features and certain conventions of style, presentation, and subject matter. Essay genres include the memoir and the profile, the visual analysis and the op-ed, the literacy narrative and the parable, among others. For the essay, *genre* partially determines the form's content and organization, but it should never do so in a "cookie-cutter" way.

Conventions are practices or customs commonly used in a genre—like a handshake for a social introduction or a eulogy at a funeral. Genre and convention are linked concepts, the one implying the other. Articles in a scientific journal (a genre) begin with a title and an abstract (conventions) and include sections about the methodology and the results (also conventions). Op-eds, by convention, begin with a "hook"; profiles of people or places include a physical description of the subject; literacy narratives include a key episode in the acquisition of reading or writing skills. But in reading and writing essays, conventions should not be thought of as rigid rules; rather, they should be seen as guidelines, strategies, or special features.

As you read an essay, think about its form: what it includes, how the writer presents the subject, what features seem distinctive. If you read a pair or group of essays assigned by your teacher, you might ask yourself whether they represent the same genre or are noticeably different. If they are the same, you will recognize similar features; if they are different, you will notice less overlap.

The Norton Reader includes four categories of genres, some of which overlap in particular cases:

- **Narrative genres**, which tell stories and include personal essays, memoirs, graphic memoirs, and literacy narratives.

- **Descriptive genres**, which give details about how a person, place, or thing looks, sounds, and feels, often in a larger framework. These include profiles of people and places, essays about nature and the environment, reportage, and pieces of humor and satire.

- **Analytic genres**, which examine texts, images, and cultural objects and trends. They include reflection, textual analysis, visual analysis, and cultural analysis.

- **Argumentative genres**, which take positions and use reasons and evidence to support them. These include evaluations and reviews, proposals, op-eds, speeches, and parables.

For more detailed information on some of the common genres included in *The Norton Reader* and some features to consider as you read and write, see pp. li–lxii.

What Are Rhetorical Strategies?

Writers use a range of strategies in order to develop and organize their material. Here are some of the most common rhetorical strategies:

- **Describing**, which appeals to the senses to describe something or someone.
- **Narrating**, which provides an account of actions or events that occur over a period of time.
- **Exemplifying**, which provides examples to illustrate a claim or idea.
- **Classifying and dividing**, which groups people or things on the basis of shared qualities.
- **Explaining or analyzing a process**, which breaks a process or concept into its component parts.
- **Comparing and contrasting**, which analyzes the similarities and differences between or among people, places, things, or ideas.
- **Defining**, which attempts to give the essential meaning of something.
- **Analyzing cause and effect**, which analyzes the reasons something happened (cause) and determines the results (effect).
- **Making an argument**, which makes a claim and provides evidence to support that claim.

Sometimes authors use rhetorical strategies to structure an entire piece. Garrison Keillor, for example, uses process analysis to explain "How to Write a Letter" (p. 505) and uses exemplification in "Postcards" (p. 508). But writers most often use a combination of rhetorical strategies to develop and present their ideas. For example, Maya Angelou in "Graduation" (p. 45) blends narration and description as she tells the story of her graduation from high school. And Gwendolyn Anne Smith uses narration and definition, as well as classification and division, to make an argument in "We're All Someone's Freak" (p. 184). As you read the essays included in *The Norton Reader*, notice how the writers develop and organize their material—and see if you can get ideas for your own writing. For more details on rhetorical strategies, see pp. lxiii–lxvii.

Strategies for Critical Reading

The previous pages gave an overview of different questions to consider when reading, from thinking about the intended audience to recognizing genres and rhetorical strategies. Here we offer some general tips for approaching the reading your instructor assigns.

Preview the essay

Think about the essay's title, read its opening paragraph, skim the topic sentences (usually, the first sentence of each paragraph). Look at the contextual note on the first page, and try to imagine the experience, issue, or debate that motivated the essayist to write. Previewing is a technique widely used for college reading, but not all writing teachers encourage it. Some teachers encourage previewing, explaining that it helps readers focus on key issues; other teachers discourage previewing, pointing out that a good essay—like a good novel or movie—can be ruined by knowing the ending.

Annotate in the margin

As you read, note points that seem interesting and important, forecast issues that you think the writer will address, and pose questions of your own. Imagine that you're having a conversation with the author. Respond to his or her ideas with some of your own. Most essayists want active readers who think about what the essay says, implies, and urges as a personal response or course of action. Similarly, note points that you don't understand or that you find ambiguous. Puzzling over a sentence or a passage with your classmates can lead to crucial points of debate. Mark your queries and use them to energize class discussion.

Analyze any illustrations

Many of the essays in *The Norton Reader* include illustrations from their original publications. Think about how the essays and the images "speak" to each other. Consider whether the images enrich, highlight, or possibly challenge the essay. Does the image primarily illustrate the essay, or does it emphasize a feature unexplained by the essayist? Does the image enrich and make clearer one aspect of the writing, or does it minimize certain aspects of the subject, perhaps aspects you find important? What do you see in the images that the essayist discusses or explains? What do you see that he or she overlooks or minimizes? Thinking about images can help you clarify the author's argument or reveal points the author may have missed.

Summarize the essay

Write a summary of the essay. Begin by making a list of its key points and identifying the evidence used in support of each; then try to state briefly, in your own words, the "gist" or core of the essay. The goal is to condense the argument and evidence, while remaining faithful to the author's meaning. Your summary will be useful when you discuss the essay in class or write about it in a paper.

Keep a reading journal

Buy a class notebook or keep an electronic journal for reflections on the essays you read. For each essay, take notes, record your responses, write questions about what puzzles you and what you might want to write about in an essay of your own. Write down sentences or passages that you like and that you might want to use as models for your writing. You may also want to list questions that the essayist raises and answers, as well as write down questions that you think the essayist has overlooked.

Use the study questions

Review the questions that follow each essay in *The Norton Reader* and think about the issues—the subject, the structure, the language—that they cover. We include these questions to help you become an active reader, to focus attention on key issues, and sometimes to make suggestions for doing or writing something.

- Some questions ask you to locate or mark the essays' structural features, the patterns that undergird and clarify meaning. Narrative, description, exposition, persuasion, and argument follow conventional shapes—or distort them—and your ability to recognize these shapes will improve your comprehension.

- Other questions ask you to paraphrase meanings or extend them—that is, to express the meaning in your own words, to amplify points by providing your own examples, or to reframe points by connecting them with points in other essays.

- Still other questions ask you to notice special features or conventions that contribute to meaning: the author's choice of title, the author's voice (or persona), the author's assumptions about audience (and how the author speaks to the audience), and the author's choice of style and forms of expression.

- At least one question, usually the last, asks you to write. Sometimes we ask you to demonstrate comprehension by writing about something from your experience or reading that extends an essay and enforces its argument. Sometimes, we invite you to express disagreement or dissent by writing about something from your experience or knowledge that qualifies the author's argument or calls it into question. The final question may ask you to compare or contrast two authors' positions—especially when their positions seem opposed. Or we may ask you to adapt one of the essay's rhetorical strategies to a topic of your own choice and to make the essay even more your own by basing it on personal experience.

Reread the essay

If possible, read the essay a second time before you discuss it with your peers or write about it in an essay of your own. If you're short on time, reread the key passages and paragraphs that you marked in marginal notes. Ask yourself what you see the second time that you didn't register on first reading.

Reading need not be only a private activity; it can also become communal and cooperative. Writing down your thoughts or taking part in conversations with others can clarify your own and others' interpretation of the essays. What interests and motives does each reader bring to particular essays? What are responsive and responsible readings? Are there irresponsible readings, and how do we decide? All these questions—and others—can emerge as private reading moves into the more public arena of the classroom.

Readers write, writers read. Making meaning by writing is the flip side of making it by reading, and we hope to engage you in both processes. But in neither process are meanings passed from hand to hand like nickels, dimes, and quarters. Instead, they are constructed—as a quilt or a house or an institution. We hope that these suggestions for reading will lead you to engaged and fruitful writing.

Writing in Academic Contexts

Not too long ago, a college composition class usually involved more one-way communication. Teachers gave out assignments and students wrote essays and handed them in for a grade. Teachers would generally read them once and hand them back with the errors circled and a grade. Times have changed. Now teachers still give out writing assignments, but students do them in stages, as drafts, and teachers often review them more than once. Papers might be reviewed at a tutorial session at the Writing Center, and drafts-in-process are often read by other class members, who are encouraged to give the writer frank, helpful responses about much more than the grammar, spelling, and punctuation. Today's students often get a great deal more feedback on their writing *before* it's handed in for a grade.

Additionally, the audience for student writing has changed. Papers are no longer always written to an audience of one, a "teacher as examiner." For some time now, students have been writing for peers outside of class and for larger communities as well. They have been creating blogs, wikis, and websites with a variety of public audiences and uses. Today's students often do a great deal of writing outside of their class assignments. Finally, many writing courses today employ a portfolio approach, in which a term's worth of student papers are kept together and selectively submitted at the end, with a substantive cover letter or essay in which students reflect on their writing over the course of the semester.

Much of the writing you will do in a composition course will start with an assignment from your instructor. Perhaps you will be asked to respond to some of the essays in *The Norton Reader*—to expand on something a writer has said; to agree, disagree, or both with a claim a writer has made; or to do some research to extend an author's argument and say something new about it. Or, you may be assigned a particular genre or kind of writing—a literacy narrative, a profile of a person or place, a visual or textual analysis, or an argumentative paper—and asked to use selections in this book as models of these kinds of writing. We have selected the readings because they are full of important ideas you can react to, either by agreeing or disagreeing, and also because the essays represent excellent examples of good writers at their best.

What follows is a brief guide for writing with *The Norton Reader*. We'll look at knowing your purpose, addressing your audience, finding a subject, determining what genre to employ, using rhetorical strategies, and understanding the writing process.

KNOWING YOUR PURPOSE

Your *purpose* is, put simply, the goal for your writing. What do you want to achieve? What points do you want to make? What idea or cause motivates you to write? Anything you can do to sharpen your thinking and infuse your writing with a clear sense of purpose will be for the better: you will find it easier to stay focused and help your readers see your key point and main ideas about your subject.

What are some common purposes writers have? The authors of the essays in *The Norton Reader* had informing, persuading, entertaining, or expressing as some of their purposes. So, too, your writing will have a primary purpose, usually defined in an assignment by words such as "explain," "describe," "analyze," "argue." Each is a signal about the purpose for your writing.

For instance, if an assignment asks you to *analyze* the persuasiveness of Molly Ivins's "Get a Knife, Get a Dog, but Get Rid of Guns" (p. 384), then your purpose is to explain the claims Ivins makes, examine the evidence she uses to support them, discuss points or perspectives she might have included, and develop a thesis about the reasons for the essay's persuasiveness. If an assignment asks you to *argue* for or against Ivins's claim about gun ownership, then your purpose is to take a side, defending or refuting her claims and using evidence from your own knowledge and from reputable sources to support your argument.

Use these questions to think about your purpose for writing:

- What does the assignment ask you to do? Is the goal to inform readers, entertain them, argue a point, or express an idea or feeling? Beyond a general purpose, what does the assignment require in terms of a specific purpose?

- How does your purpose affect your choice of a subject? What do you know about the subject? How can you find out more about this subject?

- How can you connect to your readers? What will they want or need to know? How do you want them to respond to your writing?

ADDRESSING YOUR AUDIENCE

Just as the authors in *The Norton Reader* aimed their essays at different *audiences*—readers of books, large newspapers, magazines, small journals, and scholarly publications, as well as activists, ordinary citizens, and churchgoers—so you need to imagine your audience as you write. Too wide an audience—"the general public"—and you run the risk of making your essay too diffuse, trying to reach everyone. Too narrow an audience—"my friend Zach"—and you run the risk of being too specific.

How can you imagine an audience of your own? One way is to look around your writing classroom: that's your immediate audience, the people who are taking the course with you and your instructor. Another way is to think about your home community: your family, your neighbors, and the people of your town or city. If you're taking an online class, what do you know about your classmates as a result of web-based discussions or drafts they've shared? Think of your audience as readers like yourself, with some of the same knowledge of the world and some of the same tastes. Consider your audience's range of reference: historical events they have witnessed firsthand, movies and TV shows they know about or have seen, and the books they have read or heard of. Think of them as willing to be convinced by whatever you write, but in need of good evidence.

Inevitably, some writers find that imagining an audience made only of class members seems too restrictive. That's fine; feel free to invoke another audience, say, a group of people who share a certain passion, perhaps for a team, a sport, a game, or a type of music or film. (But remember to take into account your instructor, who may need some filling in about the special knowledge you share with your audience.)

Use these questions to guide you in thinking about audience:

- What readers are you hoping to reach?

- What information can you assume your readers know? What information do you need to explain?

- In what ways will you need to adjust the style of your writing—the language, tone, sentence structure and complexity, and examples—to meet the needs of your audience?

FINDING A SUBJECT

Like the audience and purpose for your writing, the *subject* of your writing— what you write about—will often be assigned by your instructor. Some assignments are very specific, such as this study question following Stephen King's "On Writing" (p. 493): "Write about a time someone responded to your writing in a way that helped you learn to be a better writer. What kinds of comments and edits did that person make? Why was that response helpful to you?" Other assignments may be more general, such as the following study question on Scott Russell Sanders's profile of his father, "Under the Influence" (p. 87): "Drawing on your memories of a friend or family member, write an essay about a problem that person had and its effect on your life." This broader assignment requires you to determine the person you wish to discuss, the problem you wish to analyze, and the larger effect the person and problem had on your life.

Some assignments give you even more leeway in choosing a subject, leaving you with the inevitable question "What should I write about?" In this case, write about what you know or care about, drawing on knowledge you've already gleaned about a subject from personal experience, your reading, or research. Your knowledge does not have to be totally new, but your perspective on a subject needs to come from you—a real person writing about a subject that matters.

How do you find what you know or care about? One way is to raise questions about an essay you've read:

- What is the author's main point? Do you agree or disagree with the main point?

- Has the author said enough about the subject? What gaps or omissions do you see, if any? Are there sentences or paragraphs that you could expand into an essay of your own?

- Are the author's examples and evidence convincing? If not, why not? Can you provide a more compelling example, additional evidence, or a counterexample?

- Does this reading "speak" to anything else you've read in *The Norton Reader*? Can you explain how this reading connects to the other? Do the readings agree or disagree?

- Is this reading true to your own experience? Has anything like this happened to you, or have you ever observed anything like this?

You can also choose a subject by reflecting on your own experience:

- Has someone you know affected your life in some way—by teaching you, by serving as an example (good or bad), or by changing your attitude?

- Is there a place that you can describe to others, telling them what makes it unique or special to you?

- Is there a subject you feel strongly about, something you believe others need to learn about—for example, a program on your campus or in your neighborhood, a controversial item of national significance, or a matter of global importance?

- Have you had an experience that has taught you something valuable, influenced the way you live, or made you think differently about life, school, work, family, or friends? Readers will be interested in the details of the experience, including how it affected you and what you have learned.

DETERMINING A GENRE

Like the purpose, audience, and subject of your writing, the *genre* of your writing may be prescribed in your instructor's assignment. *The Norton Reader* contains a variety of essay genres. What follows is an explanation of narrative, descriptive, analytic, and argumentative genres, and the subcategories within them.

Narrative genres

Narrative genres tell a story, using vivid details about people, events, and conflicts or crises. They also reflect on the meaning of the stories, offering the reader an interpretation or explanation of what occurred. Common narrative genres include the memoir, personal essay, and literacy narrative.

Memoir   Memoirs are first-person accounts of important events or people from an author's life. They include selected details and descriptions that show how the author feels about and remembers the events or people. Often, memoirs are book-length reflections that span a number of years in the author's life. *The Norton Reader* includes several selections from longer memoirs: Annie Dillard's remembrances of her mother from *An American Childhood* (p. 98), Maya Angelou's chapters on her high school graduation and on an important boxing match from *I Know Why the Caged Bird Sings* (p. 45 and p. 371), Langston Hughes's account of a memorable experience in church from *The Big Sea* (p. 947), Julia Child's recollection of her education at Le Cordon Bleu from *My Life in France* (p. 296), and Alison Bechdel's memories of her relationship with her father, which she depicts in graphic form in *Fun Home* (p. 12).

Memoirs can also be essay-length reflections on a significant event or person; such memoirs are also considered personal essays. If you are asked to write a memoir for class, it will likely be one of these shorter pieces, perhaps one in which you narrate an event or series of events that helped shaped you or your understanding of yourself. You might choose to write such a memoir in a series of present-tense vignettes, as Alice Walker does in "Beauty: When the Other Dancer Is the Self" (p. 74).

Another form of autobiographical writing, the *graphic memoir* renders the author's experience in visual and textual form. This form often includes a narrative storyline, dialogue, and drawings that emphasize elements of the story or sometimes provide information not directly available in the written narrative. In the selection from *Fun Home* (p. 12), Alison Bechdel uses narrative and drawings to show features of the home in which she was reared and to reveal and reflect upon her relationship with her father. When you read graphic memoirs, and if you choose to create your own, pay close attention to the ways in which images and words are connected—and whether one feature of the text provides information not included elsewhere.

Personal essay   Personal essays focus on a significant personal experience in the writer's past and draw out the meaning as the writer tells the story and reflects on the experience. Sometimes a personal essay is called *memoir* or *autobiographical essay*. Its key features include a dramatic event or episode; vivid details and narration; and an interweaving of narration with reflection on and interpretation of the essayist's experience.

If you are assigned Alice Walker's "Beauty: When the Other Dancer Is the Self" (p. 74) or George Orwell's "Shooting an Elephant" (p. 750), you will immediately spot the dramatic event. For Walker, it is the day a BB pellet strikes her eye and causes "a glob of whitish scar tissue, a hideous cataract." For Orwell, it is the day when he, a young British official in Burma, must shoot an elephant that has gone "must." Walker introduces the drama in two italicized sentences: *It was great fun being cute. But then, one day, it ended.* In the remainder of the essay she reflects on how the injury affected her sense of self, her identity. Orwell builds up to the dramatic moment more slowly, taking us through the thoughts and events that lead to his pulling the trigger. As he tells his story, Orwell reflects on the motivations for his action and reaches a point of insight:

> And it was at this moment, as I stood there with the rifle in my hands, that I first grasped the hollowness, the futility of the white man's dominion in the East.

These two essayists handle the conventions of their personal essays differently, with different narrative styles and different pacing, but they both focus on a significant event and draw out its significance in the course of the essay.

Literacy narrative   A subcategory of the personal essay, the *literacy narrative* focuses on learning to read or write. Like other narrative genres, it uses personal experience, requires vivid details, and gives a clear indication of the narrative's significance. Teachers frequently assign this genre in composition courses, for reading or writing or both.

If you read Frederick Douglass's "Learning to Read" (p. 404) or Benjamin Franklin's "Learning to Write" (p. 484), you will encounter two classic versions of the literacy narrative. For Douglass, a slave, reading was a forbidden, illegal activity, so to learn to read he was "compelled to resort to various stratagems," as he phrases it. Douglass's literacy narrative includes rich details about his life as a slave, the strategies he used to acquire literacy, and the essential value that reading held for someone who did not want to remain *"a slave for life."* For Franklin, a young man trained as a printer, writing became a means to raise himself in his social and professional world, and his narrative explains some of the tactics that allowed him to succeed. As you read Douglass or Franklin, watch for the details they choose to include and the anecdotes they recount as important to their stories. Other literacy narratives in *The Norton Reader* include Eudora Welty's "Clamorous to Learn" (p. 409), Gerald Graff's "Hidden Intellectualism" (p. 418), and Richard Rodriguez's "Aria" (p. 465), which illustrate with fascinating, sometimes painful, details the meaning of reading, writing, and education in American culture.

Descriptive genres

Descriptive genres let the reader know how a person, place, or thing looks, sounds, feels, or maybe even smells. But they do more: they give a dominant impression, interpret a person's actions, offer a reflection on the significance of place, or in some other way put the objective details into a larger framework.

Descriptive genres in *The Norton Reader* include the profile of a person, profile of a place, nature writing, reportage, and humor and satire.

Profile of a person   The *profile of a person* features an individual or a group of people and uses firsthand knowledge, interviews, and/or research to present its subject. Since readers like to read about interesting subjects, it is sometimes assumed that the person must be interesting beforehand. But, really, it's the writer who makes the person interesting by discovering special characteristics or qualities through interviews or observation; by finding an interesting angle from which to present the subject; and by including engaging details, anecdotes, or dialogue to enliven the portrait.

Profiles can be freestanding essays or parts of books. Tom Wolfe's "Yeager" (p. 114) is a portrait of the astronaut Chuck Yeager and part of a book about the first American astronauts in space, *The Right Stuff*. When you read this essay, you will see that Wolfe does not begin with date of birth, place of birth, parents, and education (though those details eventually make it into the profile). Instead, Wolfe lets us *hear* Yeager's voice by imitating its sound and style. Then Wolfe suggests the importance of Yeager's place in American aviation by describing how every American pilot tries to imitate this man with "the right stuff." The profile features tales about Yeager's daring, often reckless, escapades—even as it narrates the story of how Yeager made history by breaking the sound barrier.

Profiles about family members can be difficult. Even if an essayist loves his or her parents, not every reader will find someone else's parents distinctive, memorable, or worth reading about. So it takes vivid details, humorous (or chilling) stories, and a bit of distance for the family profile to succeed. Annie Dillard *makes* her mother memorable in "An American Childhood" (p. 98) by recalling idiosyncratic stories and sayings, including the line "Terwilliger bunts one" that amuses and annoys her mother. Scott Russell Sanders remembers many characteristic episodes about his father. His profile, titled "Under the Influence" (p. 87), begins: "My father drank." Both of these writers had ordinary parents, but they make them seem extraordinary by the vividness of their memories, the special angles they take, and the overarching perspective on their parents' characters that they bring to the essay.

Profile of a place   Places can also become the focus of a profile. The features of a *profile of a place* involve discovering the special characteristics or qualities of the place; finding an interpretive framework in which to present it; and including engaging details, anecdotes, or dialogue to enliven the essay. Since places can't speak, the essayist must speak for them and say enough about them to make them come alive.

Essayists re-create places through description. Ian Frazier, in "Take the F" (p. 151), uses a subway line (the F Sixth Avenue Local) to locate his Brooklyn neighborhood on the New York City grid, but he also engages the five senses—sight, sound, smell, taste, and touch—to give non-New Yorkers a feel for the place.

E. B. White describes a place far different than Brooklyn, New York. In "Once More to the Lake" (p. 158) he recalls a place in Maine where he spent time both as a child and as an adult, using lists such as the following one:

> ... the fade-proof lake, the woods unshatterable, the pasture with the sweetfern and the juniper forever and ever, summer without end; this was the background, and the life along the shore was the design, the cottages with their innocent and tranquil design, their tiny docks with the flagpole and the American flag floating against the white clouds in the blue sky, the little paths over the roots of the trees leading from camp to camp and the paths leading back to the outhouses and the can of lime for sprinkling, and at the souvenir counters at the store the miniature birch-bark canoes and the post cards that showed things looking a little better than they looked.

He also uses comparisons and contrasts to show how this place has changed and how it has remained the same over the course of decades.

If a profile includes both person and place, as White's essay does, it is what the writer Anne Fadiman calls a "Character in Context" piece. Many times, we learn about a person by seeing him or her in a characteristic space; the place defines the person, the person defines the place. N. Scott Momaday's "The Way to Rainy Mountain" (p. 136) gives us a sacred place of the Kiowas, an old landmark that they called "Rainy Mountain." Yet his profile is also about his grandmother, Abo, whom he associates with the sacred mountain:

> Her forebears came down from the high country in western Montana nearly three centuries ago. They were mountain people, a mysterious tribe of hunters whose language has never been positively classified in any major group.

To understand the significance of Momaday's return to Rainy Mountain, we must understand the mountain's associations with his grandmother. And vice versa: to understand Abo's significance to her grandson, we must understand the meaning of Rainy Mountain to the Kiowa.

Nature writing   Nature writing can refer generally to any writing about nature and can be a profile of a place or some part of the natural world, such as plants or animals. (Think of it as profiling not a person but the desert, a bear, a dragonfly, or a weed.) You will find some of these essays in the "Nature and Environment" chapter of this book.

In "Under the Snow" (p. 521) John McPhee focuses on a wildlife biologist, Gary Alt, who studies bears; as he describes Alt's research, McPhee includes many scientific facts about the life cycle of bears, including their breeding and feeding practices, their natural habitat, and hibernation patterns. In "Joyas Voladoras" (p. 526) Brian Doyle, too, writes about parts of the natural world. But Doyle's purpose is to consider the hearts of birds and mammals and their metaphorical significance, including the human heart with its capacity to be "bruised and scarred, scored and torn, repaired by time and will, patched by force of character."

Many kinds of writing about nature and the environment in *The Norton Reader* raise questions about science and human nature. Look for them in David Foster Wallace's "Consider the Lobster" (p. 697), Henry David Thoreau's "The Battle of the Ants" (p. 770), and Edward Abbey's "The Great American Desert" (p. 535).

Reportage *Reportage* often includes analysis and evaluation and makes an argument, but its primary purpose is to relate information. *The Norton Reader* focuses on reports that inform readers about a particular topic or issue, and there are many essays that do just that. In his essay "Fremont High School" (p. 423) Jonathan Kozol goes inside one high school in California and relates to his readers what he learns, from the needs of the students to the condition of the school and its amenities. In the process, he also argues that more needs to be done to address the deplorable conditions of many public schools in the United States.

Humor and satire Both *humor* and *satire* use hyperbole and far-fetched comparisons or descriptions to make a larger point. Sometimes the point is to show the abuses of a government or political policy, as in the case of Jonathan Swift's "A Modest Proposal" (p. 756), which offers that the poor sell their children as food to the rich to fix Ireland's depressed economy. Other times the purpose is to show a different kind of irony, as Dan Barry does in "Back When a Chocolate Puck Tasted, Guiltily, Like America" (p. 307), when he uses unsavory comparisons between snack cakes and inedible objects. He uses these comparisons even as he describes the appeal and pleasure of eating "faux-chocolate, crème-filled, Bloomberg-infuriating, chemical-rich, bad-for-me, really-really-bad-for-me, all-but-extinct Ring Dings."

Humor and satire can be used in any genre of writing. Molly Ivins uses humor in her op-ed "Get a Knife, Get a Dog, but Get Rid of Guns" (p. 384) when she proposes that people use knives for protection rather than guns because knives "promote physical fitness" since "you have to catch up with someone in order to stab him." Mark Twain uses humor and satire in his speech "Advice to Youth" (p. 637), both providing advice and undermining it: "Always obey your parents, when they are present."

Some writers use self-deprecating humor, as Nancy Mairs and JJ Goode do in their personal essays (p. 64; p. 280) when they describe the serious yet sometimes humorous challenges of living with a disability. Such uses of humor can make a reader more receptive to a writer or speaker, showing that even those addressing serious topics can have a good laugh.

Humor and satire often push the limits of what is acceptable or expected in communication. Since what's funny to one person might be offensive to others, if you use humor in your writing, be aware of potential consequences. Humor can make audiences more receptive to you, but it can also make audiences less receptive if you unintentionally offend someone you're trying to persuade. Of course, writers of satire often intentionally ridicule and shame with the purpose of improvement or change. Still, having your teacher, classmates, or friends read drafts of your humorous and satirical writing can help you gauge responses, making sure your humor has the intended effect.

Analytic genres

Analytic genres carefully and methodically examine a text, an image, a cultural object, or a social trend by breaking it into parts, closely reading its components, and noting how the parts work in relation to the whole. In *The Norton Reader* you will find examples of reflection, textual analysis, visual analysis, and cultural analysis.

Reflection   *Reflection* is a form of personal analysis, exploring the ways an experience, practice, idea, or event relates to you and what you can learn from it. Reflection can be done in response to your reading, a past event or series of events, or something you or someone else has done. For example, your teacher might ask you to reflect on your writing process for a specific assignment, to think about what you learned from the process and what you might do differently for the next assignment. Or your teacher might ask you to write a cover letter for a final portfolio of your work for the entire term; in this type of reflection, you might consider why you chose the pieces you did, how you revised those assignments, what you did well, and what you could have done differently. You might also be asked to write a reflection essay on a selection you've read for class and to consider how you made sense of the author's position or ideas in the context of your own experience, ideas, or other reading.

Reflection is also a part of writing a personal essay or a literacy narrative, and you will see many examples of reflection in *The Norton Reader*, especially in "Personal Accounts" and "Education." In "Under the Influence" (p. 87), Scott Russell Sanders reflects on the effects of having an alcoholic father, "trying to understand the corrosive mixture of helplessness, responsibility, and shame." In "Salvation" (p. 947), Langston Hughes reflects on a childhood experience in church, contemplating why he pretended to have an experience he didn't have. In "On Being a Cripple" (p. 64), Nancy Mairs reflects on her life with multiple sclerosis. In each of these examples, the author chooses one aspect of experience and seeks to make sense of it through writing, offering readers an interpretation of that experience.

At times, reflection is also a part of writing an argument. In "Is Google Making Us Stupid?" (p. 572), Nicholas Carr starts by reflecting on his own experience of reading online before moving to accounts of other people's experiences and studies of the effects of online reading. In "An Animal's Place" (p. 681), Michael Pollan reflects on his experience of eating steak while reading *Animal Liberation* before he makes an argument about the ethics of farming and eating animals. In such cases, reflection provides a context for the argument and helps establish the author's purpose and ethos or character.

Textual analysis   Also called *close reading, textual analysis* focuses on written words. It examines words and phrases for explicit and implicit meanings; it looks for similes (comparisons using *like* or *as*) and metaphors (comparisons without explicit connectors) to reveal patterns of association and meanings; and it interprets the whole text on the basis of these methodical, individual observations.

The *text* may be anything from the Bible or Koran, to poems and novels, to ads, billboards, or official memos.

In "When the King Saved God" (p. 956), Christopher Hitchens combines historical narrative and textual analysis. He considers interpretations of key words and phrases in the Bible and the meaning and effects of different interpretations. He writes:

> For example, in Isaiah 7:14 it is stated that, "behold, a virgin shall conceive, and bear a son, and shall call his name Immanuel." This is the scriptural warrant and prophesy for the impregnation of the Virgin Mary by the Holy Ghost. But the original Hebrew wording refers only to the pregnancy of an *almah*, or young woman. If the Hebrew language wants to identify virginity, it has other terms in which to do so. The implications are not merely textual. To translate is also to interpret; or indeed, to lay down the law.

In his analysis, Hitchens examines the importance of language to the development and sustenance of culture, using examples from the King James Version of the Bible to illustrate his claims.

Leslie Jamison, too, writes about interpreting texts. In "Mark My Words. Maybe." (p. 458), she considers the ways in which other people interpret her tattoo, a translation of a quotation from "Terence, the Roman playwright. In the original Latin, it reads: homo sum: humani nil a me alienum puto." Jamison's arm tattoo reads: "I am human: nothing human is alien to me." Throughout the essay, she relays other people's responses to her tattoo and how it has come to have multiple meanings to her.

Visual analysis Like textual analysis, *visual analysis* looks for explicit and implicit meanings; searches for patterns of association; and interprets the whole object on the basis of these methodical, individual observations. Instead of a written text, visual analysis focuses on an image, a photograph, a painting, or another phenomenon.

Some visual analyses have as their goal the explanation of the image itself. In *Understanding Comics* (p. 921), Scott McCloud draws a teacher figure in the left-hand frame to explain the function of pictures and how they relate to words in a comic strip. In effect, he creates images and embeds visual analysis within the same piece. In "Song Schematics" (p. 943), Michael Hamad creates a visual essay to analyze a different sensory process: listening to music. He arranges words and symbols on the page to analyze the process of listening to a Phish song—and his essay invites a visual analysis by readers.

In *The Norton Reader* you will find essays that combine textual and visual analysis or that use images to trigger both kinds of analysis. (Watch for essays that include photographs, drawings, graphs, and other visual material.) In N. Scott Momaday's "The Way to Rainy Mountain" (p. 136) and Annie Leonard's "The Story of Bottled Water: A Footnoted and Annotated Script" (p. 200), the authors provide images to accompany their prose: in Momaday's case, his father's drawings; in Leonard's, drawings that emphasize problems created or exacerbated by the bottled water industry. These images enrich the primary analyses of the authors by underscoring key points and adding visual evidence to their arguments.

Cultural analysis   This genre, called both *cultural analysis* and *cultural critique*, takes an object, trend, fad, or other phenomenon as the subject of its analysis. It uses the strategies of textual and visual analysis described above, adding personal response and research, if desirable, to explain and interpret. Examples of this form appear in the chapter "Cultural Analysis."

What kinds of cultural objects and trends do essayists analyze? Almost anything and everything, it seems. Malcolm Gladwell in "Java Man" (p. 232) chooses caffeine as his subject, Annie Leonard takes on bottled water in "The Story of Bottled Water: A Footnoted and Annotated Script" (p. 200), and Tom Bissell considers video games in "Extra Lives: Why Video Games Matter" (p. 214). The scholar Henry Louis Gates Jr. analyzes hairstyles popular in his youth (p. 245)—how they were created; how movie stars, singers, and black icons popularized them; and why the styles remain so important for him.

Other essayists analyze trends or social practices. Jessica Mitford, for example, looks at the funeral industry, taking an outsider perspective. In "Behind the Formaldehyde Curtain" (p. 238), Mitford engages many different strategies in making her analysis—from "the arrival of the corpse at the mortuary" to the process of embalming to the presentation of the body for open-casket viewing. Her goal is to debunk the "American way of death," as she calls it, and to show how the undertaker has assumed the place formerly held by the clergyman. In "The Case for Single-Child Families" (p. 223), Bill McKibben considers a different practice: having children. He argues that "we live in an era—maybe only a brief one, maybe only for a few generations—when parenting a bunch of kids clashes with the good of the planet," and he analyzes the cultural pressure to procreate.

Argumentative genres

Forms of modern argument have their roots in classical Greece and Rome— that is, they go back at least 2,500 years. The Greek philosopher Aristotle held that there were really only two essential parts of an argument: (1) the statement of the case, and (2) the proof of the case. But he conceded that in practice most orators added two other parts: an introduction and a conclusion.

Roman rhetoricians like Quintillian refined and expanded this simple Aristotelian approach to include five or six parts:

(1) *exordium*: the introduction

(2) *narratio*: the statement or exposition of the case under discussion

(3) *divisio*: the outline of the points or steps in the argument

(4) *confirmatio*: the proof of the case (sometimes called *probatio*)

(5) *confutatio*: the refutation of opposing arguments

(6) *peroratio*: the conclusion

Yet Roman rhetoricians also acknowledged that, for any given argument, orators might want to omit parts. (They might, for example, omit *divisio* if the steps of the argument were simple.) And orators would often rearrange the parts of their speeches. They might, for instance, refute an opponent's arguments before advancing their own case.

Unless you participate in a debating society, you—like most modern college students—won't see this formal version of classical argument very often. In "The Declaration of Independence" (p. 773), however, Thomas Jefferson used the tactics of classical rhetoric as revived in the eighteenth century. Today, we hear its legacy in public speeches and see traces of it in newspaper editorials. The Greek and Roman philosophers weren't so much prescribing a genre as they were describing common argumentative practices. It makes sense that, if you want to argue your case effectively, you need to introduce it, outline the key points, present your evidence, and refute your opponent's position—all the steps they described. You will find these steps in the argumentative genres considered below: evaluations and reviews, proposals, op-eds, speeches, and parables.

Evaluation and review *Evaluations* and *reviews* combine analysis and argument, using clear criteria as the basis for evaluation. When you write an evaluation, you make and support an argument about quality, whether something is good or bad, effective or ineffective. The criteria the author uses depends on the subject being analyzed. For example, in analyzing a website, you might focus on design and usability. Is it easy to navigate? Do the organization and design fit the content of the site? Are the visuals appropriate to the subject? In reviewing a restaurant, you might evaluate the quality of the food and service, the value and price, and the atmosphere and décor. In "Extra Lives: Why Video Games Matter" (p. 214), Tom Bissell reviews the video game *Fallout 3*, evaluating visual features, the choices it offers, its tutorial, and its narrative structure. Although he finds much to critique about the game, he argues that it is "a game of profound stylishness, sophistication, and intelligence."

In "Utopian Dream: A New Farm Bill" (p. 274), Marion Nestle evaluates a piece of legislation, the farm bill, using nutrition, health, and the environment as criteria. She takes a clear stance: "Beyond providing an abundance of inexpensive food, the current farm bill addresses practically none of the other goals." She then details the ways the farm bill falls short, providing background information and evidence to support her assessment.

Proposal Evaluation and review often provide the groundwork for a *proposal*. A proposal includes a clear statement of what is being proposed, a plan for action, and an explanation of desired outcomes. Marion Nestle's evaluation of the farm bill leads her to propose goals for a new farm bill, one that will support farmers and farm workers, the environment, and human health. Although Nestle doesn't provide a fully developed proposal (she doesn't offer a new farm bill), she does propose guidelines and goals for new legislation.

Your instructor may ask you to write a proposal for a long paper or project that you will undertake. If so, you will likely do a review of other essays, books, or articles on your topic before proposing your own project, one that will be different from the literature you've reviewed. Another kind of proposal you might be assigned is to define a problem and its effects and then to propose a workable solution or approach to that problem.

Op-ed   This genre focuses on issues of public interest and encourages ordinary citizens to contribute their perspectives, opinions, and arguments to the public debate. *Op-eds* begin with a "hook"—a link to a recent event or news article that grabs readers' attention—as the introduction. Specific features, or conventions, include a forthright statement of position, evidence in support, often a counterargument or rebuttal of the opposition, and sometimes a formal conclusion.

Brent Staples's "Why Colleges Shower Their Students with A's" (p. 388) features most of these conventions. Staples begins by citing the principle of a famous economist, Milton Friedman, to the effect that superior products flourish and shabby ones die out. But Staples refutes this principle when applied to colleges and argues that, in fact, colleges are giving too many A's and thus "stoking grade inflation and devaluing degrees." When you read Staples's op-ed, note how he puts forward his evidence, then rebuts a common argument of his opposition:

> The argument that grades are rising because students are better prepared is simply not convincing. The evidence suggests that students and parents are demanding—and getting—what they think of as their money's worth.

Staples wraps up with some proposals to remedy grade inflation and a final stab at parents and students who are "addicted to counterfeit excellence." Although he no doubt wrote from the evidence he had gathered and the conclusion he had independently reached, you will discover that Staples uses five of the six parts of the "formal" classical argument—all but number 3.

Speech   Because *speeches* derive directly, if also distantly, from the classical tradition of argument, they often show its formal features. Many speechwriters introduce the issue at hand, state their position, offer evidence in support and counterarguments against, and sum up—sometimes with a high rhetorical flourish. These modern tactics are based on the older classical conventions.

Elizabeth Cady Stanton, the nineteenth-century feminist, shows her knowledge of American public oratory in "Declaration of Sentiments and Resolutions" (p. 784). Stanton's declaration, presented at the first U.S. women's rights convention, is modeled on Thomas Jefferson's seminal American "The Declaration of Independence" (p. 773). A century later, Martin Luther King Jr., one of the great civil rights leaders and orators of modern America, continues the tradition in "Letter from Birmingham Jail" (p. 806). He makes the case for civil disobedience, taking his audience through the steps of his thinking and quietly refuting those who disagree. It is no coincidence that these important American speeches and documents use the formal conventions of argument: in so doing, the speakers demonstrate their education, ability, and right to debate the pressing issues of their day.

Parable   A *parable* is a story that illustrates a point, poses or answers a question, or suggests a lesson. A parable can imply an argument—though it does not make that argument directly or simply. The word *parable* means "thrown beside," and there's a sense in which any attempt to interpret a parable too specifically will always just miss the mark: the form is too complex to be reduced to a single meaning or simple moral. It is worth considering the parable as an alternative form of argument—a genre a writer might use when more formal arguments won't quite work. Feminists, for example, sometimes turn to the parable when they find that masculine logic fails to grasp an issue. Native Americans, including Chief Seattle, have traditionally used the parable to refute the wrong-headed logic of white Americans.

Most religious traditions include parables—such as those told by Jesus or the Zen parables we include in "Philosophy and Religion." In the Zen parable "Muddy Road" (p. 996) there's a literal-minded character, Ekido, who lives strictly by the rules, and a more knowing character, Tanzan, who has deeper wisdom. Ekido knows that a monk is supposed to avoid women, so he chastises Tanzan for picking up a "lovely girl in a silk kimono and sash" and carrying her across a muddy intersection. Tanzan responds with a question: "I left the girl there. Are you still carrying her?" Tanzan's question suggests that it's not the literal touching of a woman that matters. What matters is sexual desire. By carrying the image of the girl in his mind and brooding on it, Ekido is harboring desire within his heart, perhaps giving it space to grow. The parable is about the complexities of human desire—but it's hard to argue Tanzan's position without using many more words and perhaps being less effective. The parable—a narrative with a probing final twist—does the trick.

As you read arguments in various chapters of *The Norton Reader*, consider where and why authors use conventions of argument and where and why they turn to conventions often associated with other genres. In the end, the goal is to make an effective argument, to convince the reader of the validity of your evidence, or urge the listener to take a prescribed course of action.

If you have some leeway in choosing the genre in which you will write, consider what genre best fits your purpose, audience, and subject:

- What goal do you have for your writing? What genre is most appropriate for that goal?

- Who will read your writing? What genre will best convey the point of your writing to your readers?

- What are you writing about? What genre is well-suited to your subject?

To gain more understanding of these genres, read plenty of examples, analyze the forms and strategies they use, and then try out a genre on your own. There's no better way to understand how a genre works than to try your hand at writing it.

USING RHETORICAL STRATEGIES

As you plan your essay, you will want to think about the *rhetorical strategies* by which you will present your ideas and evidence to readers. These strategies, sometimes called *rhetorical modes* or *techniques*, help a writer organize evidence, connect facts into a sequence, and provide clusters of information necessary for conveying a purpose or an argument. You might choose to *analyze* the cause of an outcome; *compare* one thing to another; *classify* your facts into categories; *define* a key term; *describe* a person, place, or phenomenon; *explain* how a process works; or *narrate* a pertinent event or experience.

Sometimes, the writing assignment that your instructor gives will determine the strategy: for example, an assignment to compare Alice Walker's "Beauty: When the Other Dancer Is the Self" (p. 74) to Nancy Mairs's "On Being a Cripple" (p. 64) will require that you use a compare/contrast strategy. Similarly, the title of an essay or a study question might imply a rhetorical strategy: for example, Garrison Keillor's title, "How to Write a Letter" (p. 505), suggests a "process" essay. One of the study questions asks you to "Make a list of the suggestions that seem most helpful" and then goes on to ask, "Why might Keillor have included the other, less practical suggestions?" Here you'll need to write a list, not a paragraph, and then decide which are practical suggestions and which aren't for the process of writing a letter—an assignment you might be given.

Many essays use a mix of strategies. You might want to define a key term in an opening paragraph, narrate a story to make a point in the next paragraph, and analyze cause and effect in yet another. Except for very short pieces, most writers use several rhetorical strategies in an essay, choosing the ones that best fit their material.

Following are some rhetorical strategies that you will encounter in *The Norton Reader* and that you will want to use in your own writing.

Describing

When writers describe a person, place, or thing, they indicate what it looks like and often how it feels, smells, sounds, or tastes. As a strategy, describing involves showing rather than telling, helping readers see rather than giving them a formal definition, making the subject come alive rather than remaining abstract. When you describe, you want to choose precise verbs, specific nouns, vivid adjectives—unless your subject is dullness itself.

As a writer, you will use description in many kinds of assignments: in profiles of people and places to provide a key to their essence, in visual analysis to reveal the crucial features of a painting or photograph, in cultural critique to highlight the features of the object or phenomenon you will analyze, and in scientific lab reports to give details of an experiment. Almost no essay can be written without at least some description, and many essays rely on this strategy as a fundamental technique. In *The Norton Reader* you will find study questions in almost every section that ask you to describe: "Describe a 'treasure' someone found and held on to," "Take a flower or tree and write a close-up description of it," "Describe some particular experience that raises a large social question"—these are just a few examples of writing assignments that ask for description.

Narrating

Narrating may be the most fundamental of all rhetorical strategies. We tell stories about ourselves, about our families, and about friends and neighbors. We tell stories to make a point, to illustrate an argument, to offer evidence or counterevidence, and sometimes even to substitute for an argument. As these uses suggest, narrating appears in many genres: from memoirs and biographies, to op-eds, formal speeches, and parables. Narrating is basic to essay writing.

As you plan a paragraph or segment of narration, think about sequence: the order in which the events occurred (chronological order) or an order in which the events might be most dramatically presented (reverse chronological order or the present moment with flashback). Often, sequential order is easier for the reader to comprehend, but sometimes beginning *in medias res* (at the present moment *in the middle of things*) and then flashing back to the past creates a more compelling story. Consider incorporating time markers—not only dates, but also sequential phrases: early one evening, later that night, the next morning. And use transitions and transitional words: first, then, meanwhile, later, finally. When you've finished narrating your event or episode, reread it and ask: What have I left out that the reader needs to know? What might I omit because the reader doesn't need to know it?

Exemplifying

Exemplification involves a main idea and either an extended example or a series of examples that illustrate that idea. In "Postcards" (p. 508), Garrison Keillor structures his essay in short sections that mimic the conventions of writing postcards. Each section provides an example of what a person might write on the back of a postcard, thus exemplifying conventions of that form of writing. Often, exemplification is combined with other rhetorical modes of development, as is the case in Henry Louis Gates Jr.'s essay "In the Kitchen" (p. 245). Much of Gates's essay involves narration and description as he reflects on different hairstyles, processes, and products in African American culture. Yet he also provides numerous examples—especially of African American celebrities—in order to illustrate his ideas.

Classifying and dividing

Classifying and dividing involves either putting things into groups or dividing up a large block into smaller units. While this strategy might seem better suited to a biology lab than to a writing class, in fact it works well for organizing facts that seem chaotic or for handling big topics that at first glance seem overwhelming. Classifying and dividing allow the writer—and the reader—to get control of a big topic and break it into smaller units of analysis.

How does William Zinsser organize "College Pressures" (p. 437)? He identifies and classifies four kinds of pressures on college students: "economic pressure, parental pressure, peer pressure, and self-induced pressure." How does the composer Aaron Copland discuss "How We Listen" (p. 938)? He divides his essay—and the modes of listening to music—into three "planes" or levels of listening. This basic division helps the writer explain the different goals and experiences that listeners bring to a piece of music. Dividing goals into levels allows the writer to manage a difficult, abstract topic and to lead the reader from the simpler to the more complex level of listening.

You will find that classifying and dividing is helpful in writing all genres of analysis: textual, visual, and cultural. You will also find that it can help in argumentative genres because it enables you, as a writer or speaker, to break down a complex argument into parts or to group pieces of evidence into similar categories.

Explaining or analyzing a process

With this rhetorical strategy, the writer explains how something is done: from everyday processes like how to write a letter, how to play basketball, or how to toss a pizza, to unusual or extreme processes like how to embalm a corpse or how to face death. Sometimes, writers use this strategy in historical essays to show how something was done in the past. As these examples suggest, explaining a process can be useful in a range of genres: from a literacy narrative that explains learning to read, to a cultural analysis that treats the funeral industry, to a philosophical essay that explores the meaning and purpose of death and dying.

To make a process accessible to the reader, you will need to identify the main steps or stages and then explain them in order, one after the other. Sequence matters. In preparing to write a paragraph explaining a process, it might help to list the steps as a flowchart or as a cookbook recipe—and then turn your list into a paragraph (or more) of fully elaborated prose.

Comparing and contrasting

Comparisons look for similarities between things; contrasts look for differences. In most uses of this rhetorical strategy, you will want to consider both similarities and differences—that is, you will want to compare *and* contrast. That's because most things worth comparing have something in common, even if they also have significant differences. You may end up finding more similarities than differences, or vice versa, but when using this strategy, think about both.

Comparison-contrast may be used for a single paragraph or for an entire essay. It tends to be set up in one of two ways: block or point-by-point. In the block technique, the writer gives all the information about one item and then follows with all the information about the other. Think of it as giving all the A's, then all the B's. Usually, the order of the information is the same for both. In the point-by-point technique, the writer focuses on specific points of comparison, alternating A, B, A, B, A, B, and so on until the main points have been covered.

Comparing and contrasting is an excellent strategy to use in writing a report, making an argument in an op-ed, or giving a speech to persuade your audience to take a specific course of action. You can set forth the pros and cons of different programs, political policies, or courses of action, leading up to the recommendation you endorse and believe is the more effective.

Defining

Defining involves telling your reader what something means—and what it does not. It involves saying what something is—and what it is not. As a strategy, defining means making sure you—and your readers—understand what you mean by a key term. It may mean redefining a common term to have a more precise meaning or giving nuance to a term that is commonly used too broadly. Defining and redefining are great strategies to use in argumentative writing; they help the writer reshape the thinking of the audience and see a concept in a new light.

This rhetorical strategy is not as simple as looking up a word in a dictionary, though often that is a good place to begin—you may discover that a word or term meant something one hundred years ago that it no longer means, or that its meaning varies from one context to another. Citing one of these definitions can help in composing your essay. But defining as a rhetorical strategy may also include giving examples or providing descriptions.

Analyzing cause and effect

Focusing on causes helps a writer think about why something happened; focusing on effects helps a writer think about what might happen or has happened already. Cause is oriented toward the future; effect looks back to the past. But you can use this strategy by working in either direction: from present to future, or from present to the past.

If you were writing about global warming and intending to show its harmful effects, you might lay out your evidence in this sequence:

Cause → leads to → these effects.

If you were writing about a student's actions and trying to identify the pressures that led to those actions, you might reverse the direction:

Effect ← are the result of ← these causes.

Analyzing a cause (or causes) is a crucial strategy for genres such as cultural analysis and op-eds. But you can also use it in a personal essay or reflection, where you might analyze the effects of a childhood experience on your later life, or in a profile of a person, where you might seek the sources (the causes) of the person's adult personality or achievements.

Making an argument

Argument requires you take a position on a topic of debate. That is, you need to choose a topic and make a claim about which reasonable people might disagree. Once you take a position on the question or issue at hand, you need to support that position and answer potential objections from those who would disagree with you. Support for an argument can come in many forms—quotations from experts, statistics, facts—but all these forms of evidence must be interpreted, not simply dropped in. Often, after making an argument, a writer proposes a better alternative.

In "What Farm-to-Table Got Wrong" (p. 400), Dan Barber argues that the farm-to-table movement has not "reworked the economic and political forces that dictate how our food is grown and raised." He provides support for his claim through statistics and through expert opinion by interviewing a farmer. He proposes, instead of farm-to-table practices that he once supported, a diversified diet and deeper understanding of how agriculture works.

STRATEGIES FOR WRITING

If you were to watch a writer at work, either yourself or someone else, you might see that the task of writing often occurs in stages in what is often referred to as the *writing process.* You generate ideas, write a draft, revise the draft (sometimes once, often many times), edit (make sentence- or word-level changes), and finally, proofread (check to see that the grammar, spelling, and formatting are correct). Along the way, you develop a main point and find examples and evidence to support that point. The next few pages will walk you through these different stages of the writing process.

Generate ideas

For many people, the hardest part of writing is looking at the blank page or empty screen. What can you say? How can you even get started? Sometimes your task is made easier when your instructor gives you a specific assignment or asks a particular question. In the next pages, we'll follow one student as she develops an essay responding to Brent Staples's "Why Colleges Shower Their Students with A's" (p. 388). Her instructor assigned the following study question:

> How broad is Staples's range of examples? Would he need to adjust his position if he considered other colleges? Write an analysis of the situation at your college either to confirm or to contest Staples's argument.

The student knew she had to analyze Staples's range of examples and so began gathering ideas by rereading his essay. She noted that he cites only three colleges by name—the University of Pennsylvania, the University of Phoenix, and Duke University—and decided to do research on her own campus. Her instructor directed her to the Office of Institutional Research, which supplied her with a summary of grade distribution at her college. The summary showed that 30 percent of grades were A's, 45 percent were B's, and 25 percent were C's or below. The evidence her research produced did not seem particularly odd to her; it was about what she expected, and it refuted Staples's claim that "colleges shower their students with A's." Notice this student's process for generating ideas and getting started: she began with the question in *The Norton Reader*, reread the essay, conducted research, and discovered hard evidence that did not support Staples's claim. In fact, she developed a claim of her own, a counterclaim to Staples's.

Sometimes, the assignment is more open-ended, such as this study question following Nancy Mairs's "On Being a Cripple" (p. 64):

> Mairs deliberately chooses to call herself a "cripple." Select a person or group that deliberately chooses its own name or description and explain in an essay the rationale behind the choice.

You can respond to this assignment by examining your own memory for stories you've heard, incidents you've witnessed, or people you've met, or you may need to do some research in order to have enough to say. Use one or more of the following techniques to mine your memory or generate ideas:

- Freewrite for several minutes to discover what you already know and think about a subject.

- Group or cluster related ideas.

- Read some articles about the subject. Take notes on what you read.

- Ask questions about the subject, starting with *who, what, when, why,* and *how.*

Different writers develop different ways of finding their material, so experiment with a variety of techniques until you discover one or more that work for you.

Develop a main point or thesis

Most writing in college courses needs a central claim, often called a *thesis*. Most papers contain a thesis statement, often stated in the introduction, that tells readers the main point that will be supported, developed, and extended in the body of the paper.

Sometimes the thesis statement will be an arguable claim supported by evidence, such as Brent Staples's thesis, which falls at the end of the first paragraph of his op-ed: "Faced with demanding consumers and stiff competition, colleges have simply issued more and more A's, stoking grade inflation and devaluing degrees." The student who responded to Staples's essay also developed a thesis statement, narrowing a broad initial claim—"Staples is wrong about colleges showering their students with A's"—to a specific, arguable claim—"For most students at Central College, however, Staples is wrong: 70 percent of students on this campus are not being showered with A's." Her thesis statement is good because it emerges from the research she has carried out on her own campus.

At other times, the main point of your writing won't be stated so plainly. Instead, it will be implied or evident to the reader, but you won't be trying to argue a claim with evidence. If you're writing in a narrative or descriptive genre, for example, you'll have a main point, of course, particularly if you're writing a historical narrative or creating a profile of a person or place. You will make a claim about the reasons something happened or about the reasons for a person's or place's distinctive characteristics, as Scott Russell Sanders does in "Under the Influence" (p. 87):

> My father drank. He drank as a gut-punched boxer gasps for breath, as a starving dog gobbles food—

Those two sentences, in which Sanders uses similes to describe his father, paint an unflattering picture of his character. The reader can assume that Sanders does not look favorably upon drinking.

Gather evidence

What counts as adequate evidence for your claim or thesis? The student who responded to Brent Staples's "Why Colleges Shower Their Students with A's" was not convinced by the evidence Staples used and found evidence that refuted his claim. Her argument would have been even stronger if she had looked for other sources, such as published survey results and reports of grade distribution at other colleges, to find out whether Staples's claim or her hunch was more accurate.

In other kinds of writing, evidence is drawn more often from personal experience than from secondary sources. In a literacy narrative, for example, the evidence will be in the examples and details of the story you tell about a formative time in your education. In a profile of a person, the evidence will also take the form of examples—the descriptive details about the person's personality, accomplishments, talents, weaknesses, looks, and behavior; anecdotes or stories about the person's life; or testimony from people who've observed the person closely. Evidence is also often drawn directly from reading. In a textual analysis, the evidence will be examples that demonstrate the text's structure, style, and language.

Organize your ideas

How you organize your ideas in a piece of writing depends to a large extent on your genre and purpose. N. Scott Momaday organizes "The Way to Rainy Mountain" (p. 136) as a journey to his grandmother's house and his native Kiowa homeland, narrating his trip in simple past tense ("I returned to Rainy Mountain in July") and interspersing family history and Native American lore as he progresses (as in the legend of the Big Dipper, where Momaday comments that "the Kiowas have kinsmen in the night sky"). Marion Nestle organizes "Utopian Dream: A New Farm Bill" (p. 274) by using clear headings and subheadings. First she provides context for her argument, explains what is wrong with the current farm bill, describes the health implications of the farm bill, and then proposes suggestions for its improvement.

For many of the essays you write in college, you will use the familiar format of an introduction, body, and conclusion, with separate paragraphs in the body for each major piece of evidence. The introduction often connects your ideas to what your readers already know and seeks to interest them in what you have to say. For instance, the student writing in response to Brent Staples's op-ed began her essay this way:

> The notion of grade inflation has been in the air for the past decade. Critics have complained that today's students are receiving far too many A's and not enough C's, D's, and F's. Things were different in the past, these critics say; grades really meant something back when the critics went to college; today's college students have it far too easy. In his recent op-ed piece, Brent Staples struck the familiar theme when he claimed to explain why colleges nowadays "shower" their students with A's. For most students at Central College, however, Staples is wrong: 70 percent of students on this campus are not being showered with A's.

In the body of an essay, you may want to place your most compelling piece of evidence first, or you may want it to come last to tie matters up for the reader. (But don't hide your best bit of evidence by placing it in the middle.) The student who wrote in response to Staples decided to use the body of her essay to present anecdotal evidence from her roommates, informal survey results from classmates about their grades, and finally the results of her research at the Office of Institutional Research. Whatever type of organization you choose, try the ideas out and write a different outline for each type of placement to see which works more successfully.

In the conclusion, you try to wrap things up, finish off your line of reasoning, and send your readers off with a final thought. Brent Staples ends "Why Colleges Shower Their Students with A's" with a predication:

> Addicted to counterfeit excellence, colleges, parents and students are unlikely to give it up. As a consequence, diplomas will become weaker and more ornamental as the years go by.

That's a fine way to conclude. Our student writer, responding to Staples, takes a different approach in her conclusion:

> Those of us who work hard and study at Central College note that we have never been "showered" with A's. We study at a place where high grades remain difficult to earn, and our situation makes me wonder whether Staples gathered only the evidence he wanted to find. Had he considered other colleges, he would not have made such a sweeping assertion.

Write multiple drafts

Even the most experienced writers know they can't do everything at once: find or invent material, assess its usefulness, arrange it in paragraphs, and write it out in well-formed sentences. If you try to produce a good essay at one sitting, in a single draft, you are likely to thin out your material, lock yourself into a structure that may not work and that you don't have time to change, and write sentences that won't fully convey your meaning or intention. In the end, writing a few drafts—in short periods spaced over more than a day—will produce a better essay, one that is thoughtful and deserving of a respectable grade. Here are some tips for drafting in stages:

- Get started by composing a rough draft or small sections of a draft. Don't feel obliged to start with the introduction and write straight through to the conclusion. If you don't know where to begin, write a section you know you want to include, then move to another. As you compose, you will begin to find out what you mean, what is important to your argument, what is missing, and what needs to be revised. Think of composing a rough draft as a way of discovering what you want to say.

- If you get stuck, try focused freewriting. That is, write all you can in response to a particular point or about a particular idea, not stopping for five minutes. After you're done, read what you've written, looking for your thoughts on the subject. You may have come up with key notions or put yourself in touch with useful ideas.

- Write a single paragraph for each key piece of evidence you have to support your thesis. Later on you can refine these paragraphs, combining some and breaking up others.

- At any point in this process, print out a clean version of your draft, read it through, and make changes. Add to, subtract from, rearrange, and revise the parts of your essay.

Acknowledge the words and ideas of others

Your writing should reflect your own thinking, of course, but you'll often incorporate the ideas and actual words of others. Synthesizing and citing the work of others will show your readers that you have consulted reputable sources and will make readers more open to your argument. It may help you to think of anything you write as part of a dialogue you are having with other writers and scholars; just be sure to credit the other writers and scholars whose words and ideas you borrow, so your readers can follow the dialogue and know who said what.

When you cite information from another source in your writing, you must credit the source. First, give the author credit by acknowledging his or her work in your text. If you cite someone's exact words, put them in quotation marks, or, if you quote more than five lines, indent them without quotation marks. Tell your readers where you got the words by including the author's name in your text and putting the page number of the book or article in parentheses right after the quote. Here is an example of a direct quotation with appropriate citation:

> Staples argues that the rise of part-time instructors is partially responsible for grade inflation: "Writing in the last issue of the journal *Academe*, two part-timers suggest that students routinely corner adjuncts, threatening to complain if they do not turn C's into A's" (389).

If you paraphrase a source, that is, if you use another person's idea but not the exact words, you still need to cite the source of that idea, even though you have expressed it in your own words. Here is an example of a paraphrase:

> Staples dismisses the argument that grades are getting higher because of students' better preparation (389).

At the end of your paper on a separate page, list all the sources you have quoted and paraphrased. Many style guides provide directions for formatting source material. The guide used most frequently in English classes is the *MLA Handbook for Writers of Research Papers*, Seventh Edition (2009), published by the Modern Language Association. At the end of each essay, we have included an MLA citation so that you can easily cite the essays you've used in your paper.

Sometimes writers in a hurry are tempted to absorb others' writing wholesale into their papers. This is *plagiarism*. Plagiarism is unethical because it involves the theft of another writer's words and ideas; in college courses, it is a guarantee of failure when discovered. Avoid plagiarizing at all costs. If you have fallen behind on a writing assignment, tell your instructor. You will often find that he or she will accept a late submission, and even if you are graded down for submitting the paper late, that is better than using others' ideas and words without attribution.

Get responses and revise

Although writers can and often do compose and revise alone, we all need helpful responses, whether from professional editors, classmates, or friends. Many writing classes encourage that process, teaching students to draft and revise independently but also enabling them to put less-than-final drafts forward for responses from the instructor and fellow students. Examples and arguments that seem clear to the writer may seem forced or exaggerated to another reader. In peer groups, listen to readers who disagree with you, who find your position slanted, overstated, or not fully convincing. Be responsive to their comments, and qualify interpretations or further explain points that they do not understand.

Here are some all-purpose questions that you can use to review a draft on your own or in a peer group. Whether you're talking with classmates face-to-face in small groups or responding in writing electronically, the questions should probably be asked in the order below, since they move from larger elements to smaller ones.

Introduction   Treat the introduction as a promise by asking, "Does this essay keep the promises the introduction makes?" If it doesn't, either the introduction or the essay needs to be revised. Try to determine where the problem lies: Is the introduction off track? Does one or more of the paragraphs wander off the topic? Does the introduction promise an organization that isn't followed?

Content   Does this essay include enough material? As you read your own work and that of your classmates, look for examples and details that transmit meaning and engage your interest, understanding, and imagination. Check for adequate and persuasive evidence and multiple illustrative examples that clarify main points. If you or your readers think you need more evidence, examples, or information, revise accordingly.

Evidence and source material Does the essay interpret its material clearly and connect its examples to the main argument? Your essay, and those you read as a peer reviewer, should specify the meanings of the examples you use; don't expect the examples to speak for themselves. A case in point is the use of quotations. How many are there? How necessary are they? How well are they integrated? What analysis or commentary follows each? Watch for quotations that are simply dropped in, without enough introduction or "placing" so that the reader can understand their significance. Quotations should be well integrated, clearly explaining who is speaking, where the voice is coming from, and what to attend to.

Organization and transitions   Are the main and supporting points of this essay well-organized? Writing puts readers in possession of material in a temporal order: that is, readers read from start to finish. Sometimes material that appears near the end of an essay might work better near the beginning; sometimes material that appears near the beginning might better be postponed. Pay attention to transitions between and within paragraphs; if they are unclear, the difficulty may lie in the organization of the material.

Tone   Is the tone of the essay appropriate for its purpose and its audience? Whether the tone is lighthearted, serious, reasoned, funny, enraged, thoughtful, or anything else, it needs to be appropriate to the purpose of the essay and sensitive to the expectations of the audience. Be aware of how formal your writing should be and whether contractions, abbreviations, and slang are acceptable.

Sentences   Which sentences unfold smoothly and which sentences might cause readers to stumble? If working in a group, ask your classmates to help you rephrase a sentence or write the thought in new words. Remember, you're trying to reach readers just like your peers, so take their questions and reactions seriously.

Learning to be a responsive reader of essays in *The Norton Reader* can teach you to respond helpfully to the essays of peer writers in your composition class—and to improve your own. Large and small elements of the composing process are reciprocal. Learn to work back and forth among wholes and parts, sections and paragraphs, introductions and conclusions. As shape and meaning come together, you can begin to refine smaller elements: sentences, phrases, specific words. You can qualify your assertions, complicate your generalizations, and tease out the implications of your examples.

Edit, proofread, and format the final draft

After you have revised the structure of your writing, you should devote time to editing and proofreading. This work is best done after giving the paper a rest and coming to it afresh. You may be tempted to move directly to the proofreading stage, thus shortchanging the larger, more important revision work described above. So long as the larger elements of an essay need repair, it's too soon to work on the smaller ones, so save the tinkering for last. When you're satisfied with the overall shape of your essay, turn to the work of tightening your writing by eliminating unnecessary repetition and awkward phrases; correcting grammar, punctuation, and spelling; and putting your work in its final form. Be sure you know what style and format your work should take, be it that of an academic paper with set margins, double-spacing, and a works cited page, or some other format. Ask your instructor if you are unsure about any of these, and make the necessary changes. Then, like other writers, you will need to stop—not because there isn't more to be done but because you have other things to do.

THE NORTON READER
Fourteenth Edition

PERSONAL
ACCOUNTS

JOAN DIDION   *On Going Home*

I AM HOME for my daughter's first birthday. By "home" I do not mean the house in Los Angeles where my husband and I and the baby live, but the place where my family is, in the Central Valley of California. It is a vital although troublesome distinction. My husband likes my family but is uneasy in their house, because once there I fall into their ways, which are difficult, oblique, deliberately inarticulate, not my husband's ways. We live in dusty houses ("D-U-S-T," he once wrote with his finger on surfaces all over the house, but no one noticed it) filled with mementos quite without value to him (what could the Canton dessert plates mean to him? how could he have known about the assay scales, why should he care if he did know?), and we appear to talk exclusively about people we know who have been committed to mental hospitals, about people we know who have been booked on drunk-driving charges, and about property, particularly about property, land, price per acre and C-2 zoning and assessments and freeway access. My brother does not understand my husband's inability to perceive the advantage in the rather common real-estate transaction known as "sale-leaseback," and my husband in turn does not understand why so many of the people he hears about in my father's house have recently been committed to mental hospitals or booked on drunk-driving charges. Nor does he understand that when we talk about sale-leasebacks and right-of-way condemnations we are talking in code about the things we like best, the yellow fields and the cottonwoods and the rivers rising and falling and the mountain roads closing when the heavy snow comes in. We miss each other's points, have another drink and regard the fire. My brother refers to my husband, in his presence, as "Joan's husband." Marriage is the classic betrayal.

Or perhaps it is not any more. Sometimes I think that those of us who are now in our thirties were born into the last generation to carry the burden of "home," to find in family life the source of all tension and drama. I had by all objective accounts a "normal" and a "happy" family situation, and yet I was almost thirty years old before I could talk to my family on the telephone without crying after I had hung up. We did not fight. Nothing was wrong. And yet some nameless anxiety colored the emotional charges between me and the place

From Slouching towards Bethlehem *(1968), Joan Didion's first work of nonfiction, which includes essays analyzing American culture in the 1960s.*

that I came from. The question of whether or not you could go home again was a very real part of the sentimental and largely literary baggage with which we left home in the fifties; I suspect that it is irrelevant to the children born of the fragmentation after World War II. A few weeks ago in a San Francisco bar I saw a pretty young girl on crystal[1] take off her clothes and dance for the cash prize in an "amateur-topless" contest. There was no particular sense of moment about this, none of the effect of romantic degradation, of "dark journey," for which my generation strived so assiduously. What sense could that girl possibly make of, say, *Long Day's Journey into Night?*[2] Who is beside the point?

That I am trapped in this particular irrelevancy is never more apparent to me than when I am home. Paralyzed by the neurotic lassitude engendered by meeting one's past at every turn, around every corner, inside every cupboard, I go aimlessly from room to room. I decide to meet it head-on and clean out a drawer, and I spread the contents on the bed. A bathing suit I wore the summer I was seventeen. A letter of rejection from *The Nation*, an aerial photograph of the site for a shopping center my father did not build in 1954. Three teacups hand-painted with cabbage roses and signed "E.M.," my grandmother's initials. There is no final solution for letters of rejection from *The Nation* and teacups hand-painted in 1900. Nor is there any answer to snapshots of one's grandfather as a young man on skis, surveying around Donner Pass in the year 1910. I smooth out the snapshot and look into his face, and do and do not see my own. I close the drawer, and have another cup of coffee with my mother. We get along very well, veterans of a guerrilla war we never understood.

Days pass. I see no one. I come to dread my husband's evening call, not only because he is full of news of what by now seems to me our remote life in Los Angeles, people he has seen, letters which require attention, but because he asks what I have been doing, suggests uneasily that I get out, drive to San Francisco or Berkeley. Instead I drive across the river to a family graveyard. It has been vandalized since my last visit and the monuments are broken, overturned in the dry grass. Because I once saw a rattlesnake in the grass I stay in the car and listen to a country-and-Western station. Later I drive with my father to a ranch he has in the foothills. The man who runs his cattle on it asks us to the roundup, a week from Sunday, and although I know that I will be in Los Angeles I say, in the oblique way my family talks, that I will come. Once home I mention the broken monuments in the graveyard. My mother shrugs.

5   I go to visit my great-aunts. A few of them think now that I am my cousin, or their daughter who died young. We recall an anecdote about a relative last seen in 1948, and they ask if I still like living in New York City. I have lived in Los Angeles for three years, but I say that I do. The baby is offered a horehound drop, and I am slipped a dollar bill "to buy a treat." Questions trail off, answers are abandoned, the baby plays with the dust motes in a shaft of afternoon sun.

It is time for the baby's birthday party: a white cake, strawberry-marshmallow ice cream, a bottle of champagne saved from another party. In the eve-

1. Methamphetamine.
2. Tragedy by playwright Eugene O'Neill (1950), based on the shame and deception that haunted his own family.

ning, after she has gone to sleep, I kneel beside the crib and touch her face, where it is pressed against the slats, with mine. She is an open and trusting child, unprepared for and unaccustomed to the ambushes of family life, and perhaps it is just as well that I can offer her little of that life. I would like to give her more. I would like to promise her that she will grow up with a sense of her cousins and of rivers and of her great-grandmother's teacups, would like to pledge her a picnic on a river with fried chicken and her hair uncombed, would like to give her *home* for her birthday, but we live differently now and I can promise her nothing like that. I give her a xylophone and a sundress from Madeira, and promise to tell her a funny story.

MLA CITATION

Didion, Joan. "On Going Home." 1968. *The Norton Reader: An Anthology of Nonfiction.* Ed. Melissa A. Goldthwaite et al. 14th ed. New York: Norton, 2016. 1–3. Print.

QUESTIONS

1. Joan Didion speaks of herself at home as "paralyzed by the neurotic lassitude engendered by meeting one's past at every turn" (paragraph 3). What about the essay helps explain these feelings?

2. Consider the metaphors Didion uses to describe the relationship she has with her family (for example, "guerrilla warfare" in paragraph 3), and the body language she uses to describe interactions with family members (for example, "My mother shrugs" in paragraph 4). Based on your analysis of Didion's use of language, how would you characterize her family relationships?

3. In paragraph 6 Didion says she would like to give her daughter "*home* for her birthday, but we live differently now." In an essay, explain whether or not you think parents today can give their children "home." Include examples to support your argument.

CHANG-RAE LEE   *Coming Home Again*

Whook my mother began using the electronic pump that fed her liquids and medication, we moved her to the family room. The bedroom she shared with my father was upstairs, and it was impossible to carry the machine up and down all day and night. The pump itself was attached to a metal stand on casters, and she pulled it along wherever she went. From anywhere in the house, you could hear the sound of the wheels clicking out a steady time over the grout lines of the slate-tiled foyer, her main thoroughfare to the bathroom and the kitchen.

Published in the New Yorker *(1995), a weekly magazine of "reportage, commentary, criticism, essays, fiction, satire, cartoons, and poetry."*

Sometimes you would hear her halt after only a few steps, to catch her breath or steady her balance, and whatever you were doing was instantly suspended by a pall of silence.

I was usually in the kitchen, preparing lunch or dinner, poised over the butcher block with her favorite chef's knife in my hand and her old yellow apron slung around my neck. I'd be breathless in the sudden quiet, and, having ceased my mincing and chopping, would stare blankly at the brushed sheen of the blade. Eventually, she would clear her throat or call out to say she was fine, then begin to move again, starting her rhythmic *ka-jug*; and only then could I go on with my cooking, the world of our house turning once more, wheeling through the black.

I wasn't cooking for my mother but for the rest of us. When she first moved downstairs she was still eating, though scantily, more just to taste what we were having than from any genuine desire for food. The point was simply to sit together at the kitchen table and array ourselves like a family again. My mother would gently set herself down in her customary chair near the stove. I sat across from her, my father and sister to my left and right, and crammed in the center was all the food I had made—a spicy codfish stew, say, or a casserole of gingery beef, dishes that in my youth she had prepared for us a hundred times.

It had been ten years since we'd all lived together in the house, which at fifteen I had left to attend boarding school in New Hampshire. My mother would sometimes point this out, by speaking of our present time as being "just like before Exeter," which surprised me, given how proud she always was that I was a graduate of the school.

5   My going to such a place was part of my mother's not so secret plan to change my character, which she worried was becoming too much like hers. I was clever and able enough, but without outside pressure I was readily given to sloth and vanity. The famous school—which none of us knew the first thing about—would prove my mettle. She was right, of course, and while I was there I would falter more than a few times, academically and otherwise. But I never thought that my leaving home then would ever be a problem for her, a private quarrel she would have even as her life waned.

Now her house was full again. My sister had just resigned from her job in New York City, and my father, who typically saw his psychiatric patients until eight or nine in the evening, was appearing in the driveway at four-thirty. I had been living at home for nearly a year and was in the final push of work on what would prove a dismal failure of a novel. When I wasn't struggling over my prose, I kept occupied with the things she usually did—the daily errands, the grocery shopping, the vacuuming and the cleaning, and, of course, all the cooking.

When I was six or seven years old, I used to watch my mother as she prepared our favorite meals. It was one of my daily pleasures. She shooed me away in the beginning, telling me that the kitchen wasn't my place, and adding, in her half-proud, half-deprecating way, that her kind of work would only serve to weaken me. "Go out and play with your friends," she'd snap in Korean, "or better yet, do your reading and homework." She knew that I had already done both, and that as the evening approached there was no place to go save her small and tidy kitchen, from which the clatter of her mixing bowls and pans would ring through the house.

I would enter the kitchen quietly and stand beside her, my chin lodging upon the point of her hip. Peering through the crook of her arm, I beheld the movements of her hands. For *kalbi*,[1] she would take up a butchered short rib in her narrow hand, the flinty bone shaped like a section of an airplane wing and deeply embedded in gristle and flesh, and with the point of her knife cut so that the bone fell away, though not completely, leaving it connected to the meat by the barest opaque layer of tendon. Then she methodically butterflied the flesh, cutting and unfolding, repeating the action until the meat lay out on her board, glistening and ready for seasoning. She scored it diagonally, then sifted sugar into the crevices with her pinched fingers, gently rubbing in the crystals. The sugar would tenderize as well as sweeten the meat. She did this with each rib, and then set them all aside in a large shallow bowl. She minced a half-dozen cloves of garlic, a stub of gingerroot, sliced up a few scallions, and spread it all over the meat. She wiped her hands and took out a bottle of sesame oil, and, after pausing for a moment, streamed the dark oil in two swift circles around the bowl. After adding a few splashes of soy sauce, she thrust her hands in and kneaded the flesh, careful not to dislodge the bones. I asked her why it mattered that they remain connected. "The meat needs the bone nearby," she said, "to borrow its richness." She wiped her hands clean of the marinade, except for her little finger, which she would flick with her tongue from time to time, because she knew that the flavor of a good dish developed not at once but in stages.

Whenever I cook, I find myself working just as she would, readying the ingredients—a mash of garlic, a julienne of red peppers, fantails of shrimp—and piling them in little mounds about the cutting surface. My mother never left me any recipes, but this is how I learned to make her food, each dish coming not from a list or a card but from the aromatic spread of a board.

I've always thought it was particularly cruel that the cancer was in her stomach, and that for a long time at the end she couldn't eat. The last meal I made for her was on New Year's Eve, 1990. My sister suggested that instead of a rib roast or a bird, or the usual overflow of Korean food, we make all sorts of finger dishes that our mother might fancy and pick at. 10

We set the meal out on the glass coffee table in the family room. I prepared a tray of smoked-salmon canapés,[2] fried some Korean bean cakes, and made a few other dishes I thought she might enjoy. My sister supervised me, arranging the platters, and then with some pomp carried each dish in to our parents. Finally, I brought out a bottle of champagne in a bucket of ice. My mother had moved to the sofa and was sitting up, surveying the low table. "It looks pretty nice," she said. "I think I'm feeling hungry."

This made us all feel good, especially me, for I couldn't remember the last time she had felt any hunger or had eaten something I cooked. We began to

1. Korean-style beef ribs.
2. Appetizers, usually toast, crackers, or bread slices with toppings.

eat. My mother picked up a piece of salmon toast and took a tiny corner in her mouth. She rolled it around for a moment and then pushed it out with the tip of her tongue, letting it fall back onto her plate. She swallowed hard, as if to quell a gag, then glanced up to see if we had noticed. Of course we all had. She attempted a bean cake, some cheese, and then a slice of fruit, but nothing was any use.

She nodded at me anyway, and said, "Oh, it's very good." But I was already feeling lost and I put down my plate abruptly, nearly shattering it on the thick glass. There was an ugly pause before my father asked me in a weary, gentle voice if anything was wrong, and I answered that it was nothing, it was the last night of a long year, and we were together, and I was simply relieved. At midnight, I poured out glasses of champagne, even one for my mother, who took a deep sip. Her manner grew playful and light, and I helped her shuffle to her mattress, and she lay down in the place where in a brief week she was dead.

My mother could whip up most anything, but during our first years of living in this country we ate only Korean foods. At my harangue-like behest, my mother set herself to learning how to cook exotic American dishes. Luckily, a kind neighbor, Mrs. Churchill, a tall, florid young woman with flaxen hair, taught my mother her most trusted recipes. Mrs. Churchill's two young sons, palish, weepy boys with identical crew cuts, always accompanied her, and though I liked them well enough, I would slip away from them after a few minutes, for I knew that the real action would be in the kitchen, where their mother was playing guide. Mrs. Churchill hailed from the state of Maine, where the finest Swedish meatballs and tuna casserole and angel food cake in America are made. She readily demonstrated certain techniques—how to layer wet sheets of pasta for a lasagna or whisk up a simple roux,[3] for example. She often brought gift shoeboxes containing curious ingredients like dried oregano, instant yeast, and cream of mushroom soup. The two women, though at ease and jolly with each other, had difficulty communicating, and this was made worse by the often confusing terminology of Western cuisine ("corned beef," "deviled eggs"). Although I was just learning the language myself, I'd gladly play the interlocutor, jumping back and forth between their places at the counter, dipping my fingers into whatever sauce lay about.

15   I was an insistent child, and, being my mother's firstborn, much too prized. My mother could say no to me, and did often enough, but anyone who knew us—particularly my father and sister—could tell how much the denying pained her. And if I was overconscious of her indulgence even then, and suffered the rushing pangs of guilt that she could inflict upon me with the slightest wounded turn of her lip, I was too happily obtuse and venal to let her cease. She reminded me daily that I was her sole son, her reason for living, and that if she were to lose me, in either body or spirit, she wished that God would mercifully smite her, strike her down like a weak branch.

In the traditional fashion, she was the house accountant, the maid, the

3. Thickening agent for sauces and soups.

launderer, the disciplinarian, the driver, the secretary, and, of course, the cook. She was also my first basketball coach. In South Korea, where girls' high school basketball is a popular spectator sport, she had been a star, the point guard for the national high school team that once won the all-Asia championships. I learned this one Saturday during the summer, when I asked my father if he would go down to the schoolyard and shoot some baskets with me. I had just finished the fifth grade, and wanted desperately to make the middle school team the coming fall. He called for my mother and sister to come along. When we arrived, my sister immediately ran off to the swings, and I recall being annoyed that my mother wasn't following her. I dribbled clumsily around the key, on the verge of losing control of the ball, and flung a flat shot that caromed wildly off the rim. The ball bounced to my father, who took a few not so graceful dribbles and made an easy layup. He dribbled out and then drove to the hoop for a layup on the other side. He rebounded his shot and passed the ball to my mother, who had been watching us from the foul line. She turned from the basket and began heading the other way.

"*Um-mah*,"[4] I cried at her, my exasperation already bubbling over, "the basket's over *here!*"

After a few steps she turned around, and from where the professional three-point line must be now, she effortlessly flipped the ball up in a two-handed set shot, its flight truer and higher than I'd witnessed from any boy or man. The ball arced cleanly into the hoop, stiffly popping the chain-link net. All afternoon, she rained in shot after shot, as my father and I scrambled after her.

When we got home from the playground, my mother showed me the photograph album of her team's championship run. For years I kept it in my room, on the same shelf that housed the scrapbooks I made of basketball stars, with magazine clippings of slick players like Bubbles Hawkins and Pistol Pete and George (the Iceman) Gervin.

It puzzled me how much she considered her own history to be immaterial, 20 and if she never patently diminished herself, she was able to finesse a kind of self-removal by speaking of my father whenever she could. She zealously recounted his excellence as a student in medical school and reminded me, each night before I started my homework, of how hard he drove himself in his work to make a life for us. She said that because of his Asian face and imperfect English, he was "working two times the American doctors." I knew that she was building him up, buttressing him with both genuine admiration and her own brand of anxious braggadocio, and that her overarching concern was that I might fail to see him as she wished me to—in the most dawning light, his pose steadfast and solitary.

In the year before I left for Exeter, I became weary of her oft-repeated accounts of my father's success. I was a teenager, and so ever inclined to be dismissive and bitter toward anything that had to do with family and home. Often enough, my mother was the object of my derision. Suddenly, her life seemed so small to me. She was there, and sometimes, I thought, *always* there,

4. Korean for "mommy."

as if she were confined to the four walls of our house. I would even complain about her cooking. Mostly, though, I was getting more and more impatient with the difficulty she encountered in doing everyday things. I was afraid for her. One day, we got into a terrible argument when she asked me to call the bank, to question a discrepancy she had discovered in the monthly statement. I asked her why she couldn't call herself. I was stupid and brutal, and I knew exactly how to wound her.

"Whom do I talk to?" she said. She would mostly speak to me in Korean, and I would answer in English.

"The bank manager, who else?"

"What do I say?"

"Whatever you want to say."

"Don't speak to me like that!" she cried.

"It's just that you should be able to do it yourself," I said.

"You know how I feel about this!"

"Well, maybe then you should consider it *practice*," I answered lightly, using the Korean word to make sure she understood.

Her face blanched, and her neck suddenly became rigid, as if I were throttling her. She nearly struck me right then, but instead she bit her lip and ran upstairs. I followed her, pleading for forgiveness at her door. But it was the one time in our life that I couldn't convince her, melt her resolve with the blandishments of a spoiled son.

When my mother was feeling strong enough, or was in particularly good spirits, she would roll her machine into the kitchen and sit at the table and watch me work. She wore pajamas day and night, mostly old pairs of mine.

She said, "I can't tell, what are you making?"

"*Mahn-doo*[5] filling."

"You didn't salt the cabbage and squash."

"Was I supposed to?"

"Of course. Look, it's too wet. Now the skins will get soggy before you can fry them."

"What should I do?"

"It's too late. Maybe it'll be OK if you work quickly. Why didn't you ask me?"

"You were finally sleeping."

"You should have woken me."

"No way."

She sighed, as deeply as her weary lungs would allow.

"I don't know how you were going to make it without me."

"I don't know, either. I'll remember the salt next time."

"You better. And not too much."

We often talked like this, our tone decidedly matter-of-fact, chin up, just this side of being able to bear it. Once, while inspecting a potato fritter batter I was making, she asked me if she had ever done anything that I wished she

---

5. Korean dumplings, usually filled with cabbage and meat.

hadn't done. I thought for a moment, and told her no. In the next breath, she wondered aloud if it was right of her to have let me go to Exeter, to live away from the house while I was so young. She tested the batter's thickness with her finger and called for more flour. Then she asked if, given a choice, I would go to Exeter again.

I wasn't sure what she was getting at, and I told her that I couldn't be certain, but probably yes, I would. She snorted at this and said it was my leaving home that had once so troubled our relationship. "Remember how I had so much difficulty talking to you? Remember?"

She believed back then that I had found her more and more ignorant each time I came home. She said she never blamed me, for this was the way she knew it would be with my wonderful new education. Nothing I could say seemed to quell the notion. But I knew that the problem wasn't simply the *education*; the first time I saw her again after starting school, barely six weeks later, when she and my father visited me on Parents Day, she had already grown nervous and distant. After the usual campus events, we had gone to the motel where they were staying in a nearby town and sat on the beds in our room. She seemed to sneak looks at me, as though I might discover a horrible new truth if our eyes should meet.

My own secret feeling was that I had missed my parents greatly, my mother especially, and much more than I had anticipated. I couldn't tell them that these first weeks were a mere blur to me, that I felt completely overwhelmed by all the studies and my much brighter friends and the thousand irritating details of living alone, and that I had really learned nothing, save perhaps how to put on a necktie while sprinting to class. I felt as if I had plunged too deep into the world, which, to my great horror, was much larger than I had ever imagined.

I welcomed the lull of the motel room. My father and I had nearly dozed   50
off when my mother jumped up excitedly, murmured how stupid she was, and hurried to the closet by the door. She pulled out our old metal cooler and dragged it between the beds. She lifted the top and began unpacking plastic containers, and I thought she would never stop. One after the other they came out, each with a dish that traveled well—a salted stewed meat, rolls of Korean-style sushi. I opened a container of radish kimchi[6] and suddenly the room bloomed with its odor, and I reveled in the very peculiar sensation (which perhaps only true kimchi lovers know) of simultaneously drooling and gagging as I breathed it all in. For the next few minutes, they watched me eat. I'm not certain that I was even hungry. But after weeks of pork parmigiana and chicken patties and wax beans, I suddenly realized that I had lost all the savor in my life. And it seemed I couldn't get enough of it back. I ate and I ate, so much and so fast that I actually went to the bathroom and vomited. I came out dizzy and sated with the phantom warmth of my binge.

And beneath the face of her worry, I thought, my mother was smiling.

From that day, my mother prepared a certain meal to welcome me home. It was always the same. Even as I rode the school's shuttle bus from Exeter to Logan airport, I could already see the exact arrangement of my mother's table.

6. Spicy Korean relish.

I knew that we would eat in the kitchen, the table brimming with plates. There was the *kalbi*, of course, broiled or grilled depending on the season. Leaf lettuce, to wrap the meat with. Bowls of garlicky clam broth with miso and tofu and fresh spinach. Shavings of cod dusted in flour and then dipped in egg wash and fried. Glass noodles with onions and shiitake. Scallion-and-hot-pepper pancakes. Chilled steamed shrimp. Seasoned salads of bean sprouts, spinach, and white radish. Crispy squares of seaweed. Steamed rice with barley and red beans. Homemade kimchi. It was all there—the old flavors I knew, the beautiful salt, the sweet, the excellent taste.

After the meal, my father and I talked about school, but I could never say enough for it to make any sense. My father would often recall his high school principal, who had gone to England to study the methods and traditions of the public schools, and regaled students with stories of the great Eton man. My mother sat with us, paring fruit, not saying a word but taking everything in. When it was time to go to bed, my father said good night first. I usually watched television until the early morning. My mother would sit with me for an hour or two, perhaps until she was accustomed to me again, and only then would she kiss me and head upstairs to sleep.

55   During the following days, it was always the cooking that started our conversations. She'd hold an inquest over the cold leftovers we ate at lunch, discussing each dish in terms of its balance of flavors or what might have been prepared differently. But mostly I begged her to leave the dishes alone. I wish I had paid more attention. After her death, when my father and I were the only ones left in the house, drifting through the rooms like ghosts, I sometimes tried to make that meal for him. Though it was too much for two, I made each dish anyway, taking as much care as I could. But nothing turned out quite right—not the color, not the smell. At the table, neither of us said much of anything. And we had to eat the food for days.

I remember washing rice in the kitchen one day and my mother's saying in English, from her usual seat, "I made a big mistake."

"About Exeter?"

"Yes. I made a big mistake. You should be with us for that time. I should never let you go there."

"So why did you?" I said.

60   "Because I didn't know I was going to die."

I let her words pass. For the first time in her life, she was letting herself speak her full mind, so what else could I do?

"But you know what?" she spoke up. "It was better for you. If you stayed home, you would not like me so much now."

I suggested that maybe I would like her even more.

She shook her head. "Impossible."

65   Sometimes I still think about what she said, about having made a mistake. I would have left home for college, that was never in doubt, but those years I was away at boarding school grew more precious to her as her illness progressed. After many months of exhaustion and pain and the haze of the drugs, I thought that her mind was beginning to fade, for more and more it seemed that she

was seeing me again as her fifteen-year-old boy, the one she had dropped off in New Hampshire on a cloudy September afternoon.

I remember the first person I met, another new student, named Zack, who walked to the welcome picnic with me. I had planned to eat with my parents—my mother had brought a coolerful of food even that first day—but I learned of the cookout and told her that I should probably go. I wanted to go, of course. I was excited, and no doubt fearful and nervous, and I must have thought I was only thinking ahead. She agreed wholeheartedly, saying I certainly should. I walked them to the car, and perhaps I hugged them, before saying goodbye. One day, after she died, my father told me what happened on the long drive home to Syracuse.

He was driving the car, looking straight ahead. Traffic was light on the Massachusetts Turnpike, and the sky was nearly dark. They had driven for more than two hours and had not yet spoken a word. He then heard a strange sound from her, a kind of muffled chewing noise, as if something inside her were grinding its way out.

"So, what's the matter?" he said, trying to keep an edge to his voice.

She looked at him with her ashen face and she burst into tears. He began to cry himself, and pulled the car over onto the narrow shoulder of the turnpike, where they stayed for the next half hour or so, the blank-faced cars droning by them in the cold, onrushing night.

Every once in a while, when I think of her, I'm driving alone somewhere   70
on the highway. In the twilight, I see their car off to the side, a blue Olds coupe with a landau top, and as I pass them by I look back in the mirror and I see them again, the two figures huddling together in the front seat. Are they sleeping? Or kissing? Are they all right?

MLA CITATION

Lee, Chang-rae. "Coming Home Again." 1995. *The Norton Reader: An Anthology of Nonfiction.* Ed. Melissa A. Goldthwaite et al. 14th ed. New York: Norton, 2016. 3–11. Print.

QUESTIONS

1. Because Chang-rae Lee begins his essay at a late stage of his mother's illness, he often flashes back to earlier points in their relationship. Mark the flashbacks in the text and explain the purpose of each.

2. Details of food and cooking appear throughout the essay—for example, in paragraphs 8–9, 11–13, and 32–36. Besides giving us a flavor of Korean food, what function do these details serve?

3. Lee titles his essay "Coming Home Again," whereas Joan Didion titles hers "On Going Home" (pp. 1–3). What different connotations do "coming home" and "going home" suggest? How do these differences emerge in the personal accounts of each writer?

4. Write a personal essay about "coming home" or "going home."

ALISON BECHDEL
from *Fun Home*

OLD FATHER, OLD ARTIFICER

From Fun Home: A Family Tragicomic (2006), *a graphic memoir that chronicles Alison Bechdel's childhood and relationship with her father.*

LIKE MANY FATHERS, MINE COULD OCCASIONALLY BE PREVAILED ON FOR A SPOT OF "AIRPLANE."

AS HE LAUNCHED ME, MY FULL WEIGHT WOULD FALL ON THE PIVOT POINT BETWEEN HIS FEET AND MY STOMACH.

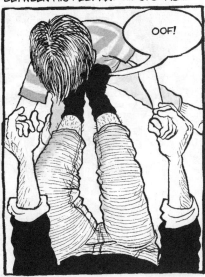

OOF!

IT WAS A DISCOMFORT WELL WORTH THE RARE PHYSICAL CONTACT, AND CERTAINLY WORTH THE MOMENT OF PERFECT BALANCE WHEN I SOARED ABOVE HIM.

IN THE CIRCUS, ACROBATICS WHERE ONE PERSON LIES ON THE FLOOR BALANCING ANOTHER ARE CALLED "ICARIAN GAMES."

CONSIDERING THE FATE OF ICARUS[1] AFTER HE FLOUTED HIS FATHER'S ADVICE AND FLEW SO CLOSE TO THE SUN HIS WINGS MELTED, PERHAPS SOME DARK HUMOR IS INTENDED.

BUT BEFORE HE DID SO, HE MANAGED TO GET QUITE A LOT DONE.

HIS GREATEST ACHIEVEMENT, ARGUABLY, WAS HIS MONOMANIACAL RESTORATION OF OUR OLD HOUSE.

1. Son of Daedalus in Greek mythology. Daedalus crafted wings made of feathers and wax for himself and his son Icarus so they could escape from Crete, where they had been imprisoned in the Labyrinth (which Daedalus had created) by King Minos. Daedalus warned Icarus not to fly too close to the sun, which could cause his wings to melt, but Icarus did not heed his father's warning. When he flew too close to the sun, his wings failed and he drowned.

WHEN OTHER CHILDREN CALLED OUR HOUSE A MANSION, I WOULD DEMUR. I RESENTED THE IMPLICATION THAT MY FAMILY WAS RICH, OR UNUSUAL IN ANY WAY.

IN FACT, WE WERE UNUSUAL, THOUGH I WOULDN'T APPRECIATE EXACTLY HOW UNUSUAL UNTIL MUCH LATER. BUT WE WERE NOT RICH.

THE GILT CORNICES, THE MARBLE FIREPLACE, THE CRYSTAL CHANDELIERS, THE SHELVES OF CALF-BOUND BOOKS--THESE WERE NOT SO MUCH BOUGHT AS PRODUCED FROM THIN AIR BY MY FATHER'S REMARKABLE LEGERDEMAIN.

MY FATHER COULD SPIN GARBAGE...   ...INTO GOLD.

HE COULD TRANSFIGURE A ROOM WITH   HE COULD CONJURE AN ENTIRE, FINISHED
THE SMALLEST OFFHAND FLOURISH.   PERIOD INTERIOR FROM A PAINT CHIP.

HE WAS AN ALCHEMIST OF APPEARANCE, A SAVANT OF SURFACE, A DAEDALUS² OF DECOR.

2. Master craftsman in Greek mythology who created the Labyrinth on the island of
Crete.

FOR IF MY FATHER WAS ICARUS, HE WAS ALSO DAEDALUS--THAT SKILLFUL ARTIFICER, THAT MAD SCIENTIST WHO BUILT THE WINGS FOR HIS SON AND DESIGNED THE FAMOUS LABYRINTH...

THIS IS THE WALLPAPER FOR MY ROOM?

...AND WHO ANSWERED NOT TO THE LAWS OF SOCIETY, BUT TO THOSE OF HIS CRAFT.

BUT I **HATE** PINK! I **HATE** FLOWERS!

TOUGH TITTY.

HISTORICAL RESTORATION WASN'T HIS JOB.

(TWELFTH-GRADE ENGLISH)

ARCHI-TECTURAL DIGEST

IT WAS HIS PASSION. AND I MEAN PASSION IN EVERY SENSE OF THE WORD.

LIBIDINAL. MANIC. MARTYRED.

OUR GOTHIC REVIVAL HOUSE HAD BEEN BUILT DURING THE SMALL PENNSYLVANIA TOWN'S ONE BRIEF MOMENT OF WEALTH, FROM THE LUMBER INDUSTRY, IN 1867.

BUT LOCAL FORTUNES HAD DECLINED STEADILY FROM THAT POINT, AND WHEN MY PARENTS BOUGHT THE PLACE IN 1962, IT WAS A SHELL OF ITS FORMER SELF.

THE SHUTTERS AND SCROLLWORK WERE GONE. THE CLAPBOARDS HAD BEEN SHEATHED WITH SCABROUS SHINGLES.

THE BARE LIGHTBULBS REVEALED DINGY WARTIME WALLPAPER AND WOODWORK PAINTED PASTEL GREEN.

ALL THAT WAS LEFT OF THE HOUSE'S LUMBER-ERA GLORY WERE THE EXUBERANT FRONT PORCH SUPPORTS.

BUT OVER THE NEXT EIGHTEEN YEARS, MY FATHER WOULD RESTORE THE HOUSE TO ITS ORIGINAL CONDITION, AND THEN SOME.

HE WOULD PERFORM, AS DAEDALUS DID, DAZZLING DISPLAYS OF ARTFULNESS.

3. A 1946 film starring actors James Stewart and Donna Reed that has become a classic Christmas movie in the United States.

BUT IN THE MOVIE WHEN JIMMY STEWART COMES HOME ONE NIGHT AND STARTS YELLING AT EVERYONE...

...IT'S OUT OF THE ORDINARY.

DAEDALUS, TOO, WAS INDIFFERENT TO THE HUMAN COST OF HIS PROJECTS.

HE BLITHELY BETRAYED THE KING, FOR EXAMPLE, WHEN THE QUEEN ASKED HIM TO BUILD HER A COW DISGUISE SO SHE COULD SEDUCE THE WHITE BULL.

INDEED, THE RESULT OF THAT SCHEME--A HALF-BULL, HALF-MAN MONSTER--INSPIRED DAEDALUS'S GREATEST CREATION YET.

HE HID THE MINOTAUR[4] IN THE LABYRINTH-- A MAZE OF PASSAGES AND ROOMS OPENING ENDLESSLY INTO ONE ANOTHER...

...AND FROM WHICH, AS STRAY YOUTHS AND MAIDENS DISCOVERED TO THEIR PERIL...

...ESCAPE WAS IMPOSSIBLE.

THEN THERE ARE THOSE FAMOUS WINGS. WAS DAEDALUS REALLY STRICKEN WITH GRIEF WHEN ICARUS FELL INTO THE SEA?

OR JUST DISAPPOINTED BY THE DESIGN FAILURE?

4. Mythical creature with the body of a man and head of a bull.

SOMETIMES, WHEN THINGS WERE GOING WELL, I THINK MY FATHER ACTUALLY ENJOYED HAVING A FAMILY.

AND OF COURSE, MY BROTHERS AND I WERE FREE LABOR. DAD CONSIDERED US EXTENSIONS OF HIS OWN BODY, LIKE PRECISION ROBOT ARMS.

OR AT LEAST, THE AIR OF AUTHENTICITY WE LENT TO HIS EXHIBIT. A SORT OF STILL LIFE WITH CHILDREN.

PUT HOT, SOAPY WATER IN THE SINK AND GET SOME CLEAN RAGS.

IN THIS REGARD, IT WAS LIKE BEING RAISED NOT BY JIMMY BUT BY MARTHA STEWART.[5]

IN THEORY, HIS ARRANGEMENT WITH MY MOTHER WAS MORE COOPERATIVE.

IN PRACTICE, IT WAS NOT.

WHAT DO YOU THINK OF THIS GAS CHANDELIER?

BORDELLO.

AUCTION CATALOG

5. TV personality, author, and businesswoman (b. 1941) whose TV shows, books, and magazine provide advice for crafting, decorating, cooking, and entertaining.

WE EACH RESISTED IN OUR OWN WAYS, BUT IN THE END WE WERE EQUALLY POWERLESS BEFORE MY FATHER'S CURATORIAL ONSLAUGHT.

MY BROTHERS AND I COULDN'T COMPETE WITH THE ASTRAL LAMPS AND GIRANDOLES AND HEPPLEWHITE SUITE CHAIRS. THEY WERE PERFECT.

I GREW TO RESENT THE WAY MY FATHER TREATED HIS FURNITURE LIKE CHILDREN, AND HIS CHILDREN LIKE FURNITURE.

MY OWN DECIDED PREFERENCE FOR THE UNADORNED AND PURELY FUNCTIONAL EMERGED EARLY.

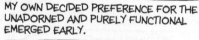

I WAS SPARTAN TO MY FATHER'S ATHENIAN.   MODERN TO HIS VICTORIAN.

BUTCH TO HIS NELLY.   UTILITARIAN TO HIS AESTHETE.

I DEVELOPED A CONTEMPT FOR USE-
LESS ORNAMENT. WHAT FUNCTION WAS
SERVED BY THE SCROLLS, TASSELS, AND
BRIC-A-BRAC THAT INFESTED OUR HOUSE?

IF ANYTHING, THEY OBSCURED FUNCTION.
THEY WERE EMBELLISHMENTS IN THE
WORST SENSE.

PLING
KLINK

THEY WERE LIES.

INCIPIENT
YELLOW
LUNG
DISEASE

MY FATHER BEGAN TO SEEM MORALLY
SUSPECT TO ME LONG BEFORE I KNEW
THAT HE ACTUALLY HAD A DARK SECRET.

MOM SAYS
HURRY UP.

"BRONZING
STICK"

HE USED HIS SKILLFUL ARTIFICE NOT TO MAKE THINGS, BUT TO MAKE THINGS APPEAR
TO BE WHAT THEY WERE NOT.

MASS WILL BE
OVER BEFORE WE
GET THERE.

THAT IS TO SAY,
IMPECCABLE.

HE APPEARED TO BE AN IDEAL HUSBAND AND FATHER, FOR EXAMPLE.

BUT WOULD AN IDEAL HUSBAND AND FATHER HAVE SEX WITH TEENAGE BOYS?

IT'S TEMPTING TO SUGGEST, IN RETRO-SPECT, THAT OUR FAMILY WAS A SHAM.

THAT OUR HOUSE WAS NOT A REAL HOME AT ALL BUT THE SIMULACRUM OF ONE, A MUSEUM.

YET WE REALLY WERE A FAMILY, AND WE REALLY DID LIVE IN THOSE PERIOD ROOMS.

I CAN'T FIND THE SCISSORS!

LOOK IN THE CHIPPEN-DALE.

STILL, SOMETHING VITAL WAS MISSING.

WELL?

ME, AGE 4

MY BROTHER CHRISTIAN, AGE 3

AN ELASTICITY, A MARGIN FOR ERROR.

HOW DID THIS VASE GET SO CLOSE TO THE EDGE OF THE TABLE?

BUT I DIDN'T DO ANYTHING!

MOST PEOPLE, I IMAGINE, LEARN TO ACCEPT THAT THEY'RE NOT PERFECT.

BUT AN IDLE REMARK ABOUT MY FATHER'S TIE OVER BREAKFAST COULD SEND HIM INTO A TAILSPIN.

PEACE, MAN.

MY MOTHER ESTABLISHED A RULE.

IF WE COULDN'T CRITICIZE MY FATHER, SHOWING AFFECTION FOR HIM WAS AN EVEN DICIER VENTURE.

HAVING LITTLE PRACTICE WITH THE GESTURE, ALL I MANAGED WAS TO GRAB HIS HAND AND BUSS THE KNUCKLES LIGHTLY...

...AS IF HE WERE A BISHOP OR AN ELEGANT LADY, BEFORE RUSHING FROM THE ROOM IN EMBARRASSMENT.

THIS EMBARRASSMENT ON MY PART WAS A TINY SCALE MODEL OF MY FATHER'S MORE FULLY DEVELOPED SELF-LOATHING.

HIS SHAME INHABITED OUR HOUSE AS PERVASIVELY AND INVISIBLY AS THE AROMATIC MUSK OF AGING MAHOGANY.

IN FACT, THE METICULOUS, PERIOD INTERIORS WERE EXPRESSLY DESIGNED TO CONCEAL IT.

MIRRORS, DISTRACTING BRONZES, MULTIPLE DOORWAYS. VISITORS OFTEN GOT LOST UPSTAIRS.

GRACIOUS, I ALMOST WALKED RIGHT INTO THIS!

MY MOTHER, MY BROTHERS, AND I KNEW OUR WAY AROUND WELL ENOUGH, BUT IT WAS IMPOSSIBLE TO TELL IF THE MINOTAUR LAY BEYOND THE NEXT CORNER.

AND THE CONSTANT TENSION WAS HEIGHTENED BY THE FACT THAT SOME ENCOUNTERS COULD BE QUITE PLEASANT.

HIS BURSTS OF KINDNESS WERE AS INCANDESCENT AS HIS TANTRUMS WERE DARK.

ALTHOUGH I'M GOOD AT ENUMERATING MY FATHER'S FLAWS, IT'S HARD FOR ME TO SUSTAIN MUCH ANGER AT HIM.

I EXPECT THIS IS PARTLY BECAUSE HE'S DEAD, AND PARTLY BECAUSE THE BAR IS LOWER FOR FATHERS THAN FOR MOTHERS.

MY MOTHER MUST HAVE BATHED ME HUNDREDS OF TIMES. BUT IT'S MY FATHER RINSING ME OFF WITH THE PURPLE METAL CUP THAT I REMEMBER MOST CLEARLY.

THE SUFFUSION OF WARMTH AS THE HOT WATER SLUICED OVER ME...

...THE SUDDEN, UNBEARABLE COLD OF ITS ABSENCE.

WAS HE A GOOD FATHER? I WANT TO SAY, "AT LEAST HE STUCK AROUND." BUT OF COURSE, HE DIDN'T.

IT'S TRUE THAT HE DIDN'T KILL HIMSELF UNTIL I WAS NEARLY TWENTY.

BUT HIS ABSENCE RESONATED RETRO-ACTIVELY, ECHOING BACK THROUGH ALL THE TIME I KNEW HIM.

MAYBE IT WAS THE CONVERSE OF THE WAY AMPUTEES FEEL PAIN IN A MISSING LIMB.

HE REALLY WAS THERE ALL THOSE YEARS, A FLESH-AND-BLOOD PRESENCE STEAMING OFF THE WALLPAPER, DIGGING UP THE DOGWOODS, POLISHING THE FINIALS...

...SMELLING OF SAWDUST AND SWEAT AND DESIGNER COLOGNE.

BUT I ACHED AS IF HE WERE ALREADY GONE.

MLA CITATION

Bechdel, Alison. *Fun Home*. 2006. *The Norton Reader: An Anthology of Nonfiction*.
    Ed. Melissa A. Goldthwaite et al. 14th ed. New York: Norton, 2016. 12–33.
    Print.

QUESTIONS

1. Alison Bechdel compares her father to both Daedalus and Icarus from Greek
mythology. She also mentions Daedalus's Labyrinth and the Minotaur. Trace the
references to the Daedalus and Icarus myths throughout. What is Bechdel trying
to get across about her father by making these comparisons?

2. Consider Bechdel's use of foreshadowing. For example, in panel 4, she writes,
". . . it was not me but my father who was to plummet from the sky," and in panel 8
she states that her family was unusual, though she "wouldn't appreciate exactly how
unusual until much later." What was her father's secret? Where does she reveal it?

3. In a graphic memoir, the images are as important as the words. What do you
learn from Bechdel's images that you might not have picked up from her words?

4. Write a piece about a person or a place (or both). Like Bechdel, use allusions to
myth or some other well-known story. If you are comfortable drawing, consider making your text a graphic essay.

DAVID SEDARIS   *Loggerheads*

THE THING ABOUT HAWAII, at least the part that is
geared toward tourists, is that it's exactly what it
promises to be. Step off the plane and someone places
a lei around your neck, as if it were something you had
earned—an Olympic medal for sitting on your ass.
Raise a hand above your shoulder and, no matter
where you are, a drink will appear: something served in a hollowed-out pine-
apple, or perhaps in a coconut that's been sawed in half. Just like in the time
before glasses! you think.

Volcanic craters, waterfalls, and those immaculate beaches—shocking
things when you're coming from Europe. At the spot that Hugh and I go to in
Normandy, you'll find, in place of sand, speckled stones the size of potatoes.
The water runs from glacial to heart attack and is tinted the color of iced tea.
Then there's all the stuff floating in it: not man-made garbage but sea garbage—
scum and bits of plant life, all of it murky and rotten-smelling.

The beaches in Hawaii look as if they'd been bleached; that's how white
the sand is. The water is warm—even in winter—and so clear that you can see

Published in the New Yorker *(2009), a weekly magazine of "reportage, commentary, criticism, essays, fiction, satire, cartoons, and poetry."*

not just your toes but the corns cleaving, barnacle-like, to the sides of them. On Maui, one November, Hugh[1] and I went swimming, and turned to find a gigantic sea turtle coming up between us. As gentle as a cow she was, and with a cow's dopey, almost lovesick expression on her face. That, to me, was worth the entire trip, worth my entire life, practically. For to witness majesty, to find yourself literally touched by it—isn't that what we've all been waiting for?

I had a similar experience a few years later, and again with Hugh. We were in Japan, walking through a national forest in a snowstorm, when a monkey the height of a bar stool brushed against us. His fur was a dull silver, the color of dishwater, but he had this beet-red face, set in a serious, almost solemn expression. We saw it full on when he turned to briefly look at us. Then he shrugged and ambled off over a footbridge.

"Jesus Christ!" I said. Because it was too much: the forest, the snowstorm,   5
and now this. Monkeys were an attraction in that part of the country. We expected to see them at some point, but I thought they'd be fenced in. As with the sea turtle, part of the thrill was the feeling of being accepted, which is to say, not feared. It allowed you to think that you and this creature had a special relationship, a juvenile thought, but one that brings with it a definite comfort. Well, monkeys like me, I'd find myself thinking during the next few months, whenever I felt lonely or unappreciated. Just as, in the months following our trip to Hawaii, I thought of the sea turtle. With her, though, my feelings were a bit more complicated, and, instead of believing that we had bonded, I'd wonder that she could ever have forgiven me.

The thing between me and sea turtles started in the late sixties, and involved my best friend from grade school, a boy I'll call Shaun (some of the names in this story have been changed), who lived down the street from me in Raleigh. What brought us together was a love of nature, or, more specifically, of catching things, and unintentionally killing them. We started when I was in the fourth grade, which would have made me ten, I guess. It's different for everyone, but at that age, though I couldn't have said that I was gay, I knew that I was not like the other boys in my class or my Scout troop. While they welcomed male company, I shrank from it, dreaded it, feeling like someone forever trying to pass, someone who would eventually be found out, and be expelled from polite society. Is this how a normal boy would swing his arms? I'd ask myself, standing before the full-length mirror in my parents' bedroom. Is this how he'd laugh? *Is this what he would find funny?* It was like doing an English accent. The more concentrated the attempt, the more self-conscious and unconvincing I became.

With Shaun, though, I could almost be myself. This didn't mean that we were alike, only that he wasn't paying that much attention. Childhood, for him, seemed something to be endured, passed through like a tiresome stretch of road. Ahead of this was the good stuff, and, looking at him from time to time, at the way he had of staring off, of boring a hole into the horizon, you got the

1. David Sedaris's partner.

sense that he could not only imagine it but see it: this great, grownup life, waiting on the other side of sixteen.

Apart from an interest in wildlife, the two of us shared an identity as transplants. My family was from the North, and the Taylors were from the Midwest. Shaun's father, Hank, was a psychiatrist, and sometimes gave his boys and me tests, the type for which there were, he assured us, "no right answers." He and his wife were younger than my parents, and they seemed it, not just in their dress but in their eclectic tastes—records by Donovan and Moby Grape shelved among the Schubert. Their house had real hardcover books in it, and you often saw them lying open on the sofa, the words still warm from being read.

In a neighborhood of stay-at-home moms, Shaun's mother worked. A public-health nurse, she was the one you went to if you woke up with yellow eyes, or had jammed a piece of caramel corn too far into your ear. "Oh, you're fine," Jean would say, for that was what she wanted us to call her, not Mrs. Taylor. With her high cheekbones and ever so slightly turned-down mouth, she brought to mind a young Katharine Hepburn.[2] Other mothers might be pretty, might, in their twenties or early thirties, *pause* at beauty, but Jean was clearly parked there for a lifetime. You'd see her in her flower bed, gardening gloves hanging from the waistband of her slacks like someone clawing to get out, and you just had to wish she was your mom instead.

10   The Taylor children had inherited their mother's good looks, especially Shaun. Even as a kid, he seemed at home in his skin—never cute, just handsome, blond hair like a curtain drawn over half his face. The eye that looked out from the uncurtained side was cornflower blue, and excelled at spotting wounded or vulnerable animals. While the other boys in our neighborhood played touch football in the street, Shaun and I searched the woods behind our houses. I drew the line at snakes, but anything else was brought home, and imprisoned in our ten-gallon aquariums. Lizards, toads, baby birds: they all got the same diet—raw hamburger meat—and, with few exceptions, they all died within a few weeks.

"Menu-wise, it might not hurt you to branch out a little," my mother once said, in reference to my captive luna moth. It was the size of a paperback novel, a beautiful mint green, but not much interested in ground chuck. "Maybe you could feed it some, I don't know, flowers or something."

Like she knew.

The best-caught creature belonged to Shaun's younger brother, Chris, who'd found an injured flying squirrel and kept him, uncaged, in his bedroom. The thing was no bigger than a hamster, and when he glided from the top bunk to the dresser his body flattened out, making him look like an empty hand puppet. The only problem was the squirrel's disposition, his one-track mind. You wanted him to cuddle, or to ride sentry on your shoulder, but he refused to relax. *I've got to get out of here*, you could sense him thinking, as he clawed, desperate and wild-eyed, at the windowpane, or tried to squeeze himself underneath

2. American film, TV, and theater actor (1907–2003).

the door. He made it out eventually, and though we all hoped he'd return for meals, and become a kind of part-time pet, he never did.

Not long after the squirrel broke free, Jean took her boys and me for a weekend on the North Carolina coast. It was mid-October, the start of the sixth grade, and the water was too chilly to swim in. On the Sunday that we were to head back home, Shaun and I got up at dawn and took a walk with our nets. We were hunting for ghost crabs when, in the distance, we made out these creatures, moving blockily, like windup toys on an unsteady surface. On closer inspection, we saw that they were baby sea turtles, dozens of them, digging out from under the sand, and stumbling toward the ocean.

An adult might have carried them into the surf, or held at bay the predatory gulls, but we were twelve, so while I scooped the baby turtles into a pile, Shaun ran back and got the trash cans from our hotel room. 15

We might have walked off with the whole lot, but they seemed pretty miserable, jumbled atop one another. Thus, in the end, we took only ten, which meant five apiece.

The great thing about the sea turtles, as opposed to, say, flying squirrels, was that they would grow exponentially—meaning, what, fifty, a hundred times their original size? When we got them, each one called to mind a plastic coin purse, the oval sort handed out by banks and car dealerships. Then there were the flippers and, of course, the heads, which were bald and beaky, like a newly hatched bird's. Since the death of a traumatized mole pried from the mouth of our cat, Samantha, my aquarium had sat empty and was therefore ready for some new tenants. I filled it with a jug of ocean water that I'd brought from the beach, then threw in a conch shell and a couple of sand dollars, to make it more homey. The turtles swam the short distance from one end of the tank to the other, and then they batted at the glass with their flippers, unable to understand that this was it—the end of the road. What they needed, it seemed, was something to eat.

"Mom, do we have any raw hamburger?"

Looking back, you'd think that someone would have said something—sea turtles, for God's sakes!—but maybe they weren't endangered yet. Animal cruelty hadn't been invented, either. The thought that a non-human being had *physical* feelings, let alone the wherewithal to lose hope, was outlandish and alien, like thinking that paper had relatives. Then, too, when it comes to eliciting empathy, it's the back of the line for reptiles and amphibians, creatures with, face it, not much in the way of a personality. Even giving them names didn't help, as playing with Shelly was no different from playing with Pokyhontus; "playing," in this case, amounting to placing them on my desk and watching them toddle over the edge.

It was good to know that in the house down the street Shaun's turtles 20 weren't faring much better. The hamburger meat we'd put in our aquariums went uneaten, and within a short time it spoiled, and started stinking up our rooms. I emptied my tank, and in the absence of seawater I made my own, with plain old tap water and salt.

"I'm not sure that that's going to work," my mother said. She was standing in my doorway with a cigarette in one hand and an ashtray in the other. Recent experiments with a home-frosting kit had dried out and broken her already brittle hair. What was left she'd covered with a scarf, a turquoise one, that looked great when she had a tan but not so great when she didn't. "Doesn't ocean water have nutrients in it or something?"

"I dunno."

She looked at the turtles, unhappily dragging themselves across my bedspread. "Well, if you want to find out, I'm taking Lisa to the library this Saturday."

I'd hoped to spend my weekend outside, but then it rained, and my father hogged the TV for one of his football games. It was either go to the library or stay home and die of boredom, so I got into the car, groaning at the unfairness of it all. My mother dropped my sister and me downtown, and then she went to do some shopping, promising to return in a few hours.

25   It wasn't much to look at, our public library. I later learned that it used to be a department store, and that made sense: the floor-to-ceiling windows were right for mannequins, and you could easily imagine dress shirts where the encyclopedias were, wigs in place of the magazines. I remember that in the basement there were two rest rooms, one marked "Men" and the other marked "Gentleman." Inside each was a toilet, a sink, and a paper-towel dispenser, meaning that whichever you chose you got pretty much the same treatment. Thus, it came down to how you saw yourself: as regular, or fancy. On the day I went to research turtles, I saw myself as fancy, and so I opened the door marked "Gentleman." What happened next happened very quickly. Two men, both black, turned their heads in my direction. One was standing with his pants and underwear pulled down past his knees, and as he bent to yank them up the other man, who'd been kneeling before him, and who also had his pants lowered, covered his face with his hand, and let out a little cry.

"Oh," I told them. "I'm sorry."

I backed, shaken, out of the room, and just as the door had closed behind me it swung open again. Then the pair spilled out, that flying-squirrel look in their eyes. The stairs were at the end of a short hall, and they took them two at a time, the slower man turning his head, just briefly, and looking at me as if I held a gun. When I saw that he was afraid of me, I felt powerful. Then I wondered how I might use that power.

My first instinct was to tell on them—not because I wanted the two punished but because I would have liked the attention. "Are you all right?" the librarian would have asked. "And these were Negroes, you say? Quick, somebody, get this young man a glass of water or, better yet, a Coke. Would you like a Coke while we wait for the police?"

And, in my feeblest voice, I would have said, "Yes."

30   Then again, it could so easily backfire. The men were doing something indecent, and recognizing it as such meant that I had an eye for it. That I, too, was suspect. And wasn't I?

In the end, I told no one. Not even Lisa.

"So did you find out what kind of turtles they are?" my mother asked as we climbed back into the car.

"Sea turtles," I told her.

"Well, we *know* that."

"No, I mean, that's what they're called, 'sea turtles.'"   35

"And what do they eat?"

I looked out the rain-streaked window. "Hamburger."

My mother sighed. "Have it your way."

It took a few weeks for my first turtle to die. The water in the tank had again grown murky with spoiled, uneaten beef, but there was something else as well, something I couldn't begin to identify. The smell that developed in the days after Halloween, this deep, swampy funk, was enough to make your eyes water. It was as if the turtles' very souls were rotting, yet still they gathered in the corner of their tank, determined to find the sea. At night, I would hear their flippers against the glass, and think about the Negroes in the Gentleman's room, wondering what would become of them—what, by extension, would become of me? Would I, too, have to live on the run? Afraid of even a twelve-year-old?

One Friday in early November, my father paid a rare visit to my room. In   40
his hand was a glass of gin, his standard, after-work cocktail, mixed with a little water, and garnished with a lemon peel. I normally liked the smell of it, but today the aquarium won. He regarded it briefly and, wincing at the stench, removed two tickets from his jacket pocket. "They're for a game," he told me.

"A game?"

"Football," he said. "I thought we could go tomorrow afternoon."

"But tomorrow I have to write a report."

"Write it on Sunday."

I'd never expressed any interest in football. Never played it with the kids   45
on the street, never watched it on TV, never touched the helmet I'd received the previous Christmas. "Why not take Lisa?" I asked.

"Because you're my son, that's why."

I looked at the holocaust taking place in my aquarium. "Do I have to?"

If I were to go to a game today, I'd certainly find something to enjoy: the food, the noise, the fans marked up with paint. It would be an experience. At the time, though, it threw me into a panic. Which team am I supposed to care about? I asked myself as we settled into our seats. How am I supposed to react if somebody scores a point? The thing about sports, at least for guys, is that nobody ever defines the rules, not even in gym class. Asking what a penalty means is like asking who Jesus was. It's one of those things you're just supposed to know, and if you don't there's something seriously wrong with you.

Two of the popular boys from my school were standing against a railing a few rows ahead of us, and when I stupidly pointed them out to my father he told me to go and say hello to them.

How to explain that looking at them, even from this distance, was pushing   50
it. Addressing them, it followed, was completely out of the question. People had

their places, and to not understand that, to act in violation of it, demoted you
from a nature nut to something even lower, a complete untouchable, basically.
"That's all right," I said. "They don't really know who I am."

"Aw, baloney. Go over and talk to them."

"No, really."

"Do you want me to drag you over there?"

As I dug in, I thought of the turtles. All they'd ever wanted was to live in the
ocean—that was it, their entire wish list, and instead I'd decided they'd be better off in my bedroom. Just as my dad had decided that I'd be better off at the
football game. If I could have returned them to the beach, I would have, though
I knew it was already too late. In another few days they would start going blind.
Then their shells would soften, and they'd just sort of melt away, like soap.

55   "Are you going over there or aren't you?" my dad said.

When the last turtle died and was pitched into the woods behind my house,
Shaun and I took up bowling, the only sport I was ever half decent at. The Western Lanes was a good distance away, and when our parents wouldn't drive us
we rode our bikes, me with a transistor radio attached by rubber bands to my
handlebars. We were just thinking of buying our own bowling shoes, when
Shaun's mother and father separated. Hank took an apartment in one of the
new complexes, and a few months later, not yet forty years old, he died.

"Died of what?" I asked.

"His heart stopped beating" was the answer Shaun gave me.

"Well, sure," I said. "But doesn't *every* dead person's heart stop beating?
There must have been something else going on."

60   "His heart stopped beating."

Following the funeral, there was a reception at the Taylors' house. Shaun
and I spent most of it on the deck off his living room, him firing his BB gun
into the woods with that telescopic look in his eye. After informing me that his
father's heart had stopped beating, he never said another word about him. I
never saw Shaun cry, or buckle at the knees, or do any of the things that I would
have done. Drama-wise, it was the chance of a lifetime, but he wasn't having
any of it. From the living room, I could hear my father talking to Jean. "What
with Hank gone, the boys are going to need a positive male influence in their
lives," he said. "That being the case I'll be happy to, well, happy to—"

"Ignore them," my mother cut in. "Just like he does with his own damn kids."
And Jean laughed. "Oh, Sharon."

Eighteen years passed before I learned what had really happened to Shaun's
father. By then I was living in Chicago. My parents were still in Raleigh, and
several times a week I'd talk to my mother on the phone. I don't remember how
the subject came up, but after she told me I was stunned.

65   "Did Shaun know?" I asked.

"I'm sure he did," my mother said, and although I hadn't seen or spoken to
him since high school, I couldn't help but feel a little betrayed. If you can't tell
your best friend that your dad essentially drank himself to death, who *can* you
tell? It's a lot to hold in at that age, but then I guess we all had our secrets.

It was after talking to my mom on the phone that I finally went to the library and looked up those turtles: loggerheads is what they were called. When mature, they can measure three and a half feet long. A female might reach four hundred pounds, and, of all the eggs she lays in a lifetime, only one in a thousand will make it to adulthood. Pretty slim odds when, by "making it," you mean simply surviving.

Before the reception ended that day, Shaun handed his BB gun to me. My father was watching from the living-room window, and intercepted me just as I raised it to my shoulder.

"Oh, no you don't. You're going to put somebody's eye out."

"Somebody like a bird?" I said. "We're firing into the woods, not into the house."   70

"I don't give a damn where you're aiming."

I handed the rifle back to Shaun, and, as he brushed the hair from his eyes and peered down the scope, I tried to see what I imagined he did: a life on the other side of this, something better, perhaps even majestic, waiting for us to grow into it.

MLA CITATION

Sedaris, David. "Loggerheads." 2009. *The Norton Reader: An Anthology of Nonfiction.* Ed. Melissa A. Goldthwaite et al. 14th ed. New York: Norton, 2016. 34–41. Print.

QUESTIONS

1. David Sedaris writes about both childhood and more recent experiences with animals. How do those experiences differ? In what ways has his understanding of animals changed?

2. Sedaris considers both power and fear in this essay. For example, he recalls, "When I saw that he was afraid of me, I felt powerful" (paragraph 27). Look for other places in the essay where the themes of power and fear are present. How does Sedaris portray the relationship between power and fear throughout?

3. Write a personal essay that demonstrates the difference between your childhood and adult understanding of something or someone.

ZORA NEALE HURSTON *How It Feels to Be Colored Me*

I AM COLORED but I offer nothing in the way of extenuating circumstances except the fact that I am the only Negro in the United States whose grandfather on the mother's side was not an Indian chief.

I remember the very day that I became colored. Up to my thirteenth year I lived in the little Negro town of Eatonville, Florida. It is exclusively a colored town. The only white people I knew passed through the town going to or coming from Orlando. The native whites rode dusty horses, the Northern tourists chugged down the sandy village road in automobiles. The town knew the Southerners and never stopped cane chewing[1] when they passed. But the Northerners were something else again. They were peered at cautiously from behind curtains by the timid. The more venturesome would come out on the porch to watch them go past and got just as much pleasure out of the tourists as the tourists got out of the village.

The front porch might seem a daring place for the rest of the town, but it was a gallery seat for me. My favorite place was atop the gate-post. Proscenium box for a born first-nighter. Not only did I enjoy the show, but I didn't mind the actors knowing that I liked it. I usually spoke to them in passing. I'd wave at them and when they returned my salute, I would say something like this: "Howdy-do-well-I-thank-you-where-you-goin'?" Usually automobile or the horse paused at this, and after a queer exchange of compliments, I would probably "go a piece of the way" with them, as we say in farthest Florida. If one of my family happened to come to the front in time to see me, of course negotiations would be rudely broken off. But even so, it is clear that I was the first "welcome-to-our-state" Floridian, and I hope the Miami Chamber of Commerce will please take notice.

During this period, white people differed from colored to me only in that they rode through town and never lived there. They liked to hear me "speak pieces" and sing and wanted to see me dance the parse-me-la, and gave me generously of their small silver for doing these things, which seemed strange to me for I wanted to do them so much that I needed bribing to stop. Only they didn't know it. The colored people gave no dimes. They deplored any joyful tendencies in me, but I was their Zora nevertheless. I belonged to them, to the nearby hotels, to the county—everybody's Zora.

5   But changes came in the family when I was thirteen, and I was sent to school in Jacksonville. I left Eatonville, the town of the oleanders,[2] as Zora. When I disembarked from the river-boat at Jacksonville, she was no more. It

Originally published in the political magazine World Tomorrow *(1928), just as Zora Neale Hurston was graduating from Barnard College; collected and reprinted in* I Love Myself When I Am Laughing . . . and Then Again When I Am Looking Mean and Impressive *(1973), a volume of Hurston's writings edited by Alice Walker.*

1. Chewing sugarcane.
2. Fragrant tropical flowers, common in the South.

seemed that I had suffered a sea change. I was not Zora of Orange County any more, I was now a little colored girl. I found it out in certain ways. In my heart as well as in the mirror, I became a fast brown—warranted not to rub nor run.

But I am not tragically colored. There is no great sorrow dammed up in my soul, nor lurking behind my eyes. I do not mind at all. I do not belong to the sobbing school of Negrohood who hold that nature somehow has given them a lowdown dirty deal and whose feelings are all hurt about it. Even in the helter-skelter skirmish that is my life, I have seen that the world is to the strong regardless of a little pigmentation more or less. No, I do not weep at the world—I am too busy sharpening my oyster knife.[3]

Someone is always at my elbow reminding me that I am the granddaughter of slaves. It fails to register depression with me. Slavery is sixty years in the past. The operation was successful and the patient is doing well, thank you. The terrible struggle[4] that made me an American out of a potential slave said "On the line!" The Reconstruction said "Get set!"; and the generation before said "Go!" I am off to a flying start and I must not halt in the stretch to look behind and weep. Slavery is the price I paid for civilization, and the choice was not with me. It is a bully adventure and worth all that I have paid through my ancestors for it. No one on earth ever had a greater chance for glory. The world to be won and nothing to be lost. It is thrilling to think—to know that for any act of mine, I shall get twice as much praise or twice as much blame. It is quite exciting to hold the center of the national stage, with the spectators not knowing whether to laugh or to weep.

The position of my white neighbor is much more difficult. No brown specter pulls up a chair beside me when I sit down to eat. No dark ghost thrusts its leg against mine in bed. The game of keeping what one has is never so exciting as the game of getting.

I do not always feel colored. Even now I often achieve the unconscious Zora of Eatonville before the Hegira.[5] I feel most colored when I am thrown against a sharp white background.

For instance at Barnard. "Beside the waters of the Hudson"[6] I feel my race.   10
Among the thousand white persons, I am a dark rock surged upon, and overswept, but through it all, I remain myself. When covered by the waters, I am; and the ebb but reveals me again.

Sometimes it is the other way around. A white person is set down in our midst, but the contrast is just as sharp for me. For instance, when I sit in the drafty

3. Cf. the popular expression "The world is my oyster."
4. The Civil War. The Reconstruction was the period immediately following the war; one of its effects was that northern educators came South to teach newly freed slaves.
5. Journey undertaken away from a dangerous situation into a more highly desirable one (literally, the flight of Muhammad from Mecca in 622 c.e.).
6. Barnard, an American women's college in New York City, located near the Hudson River; cf. the psalmist's "by the waters of Babylon."

basement that is The New World Cabaret with a white person, my color comes. We enter chatting about any little nothing that we have in common and are seated by the jazz waiters. In the abrupt way that jazz orchestras have, this one plunges into a number. It loses no time in circumlocutions, but gets right down to business. It constricts the thorax and splits the heart with its tempo and narcotic harmonies. This orchestra grows rambunctious, rears on its hind legs and attacks the tonal veil with primitive fury, rending it, clawing it until it breaks through to the jungle beyond. I follow those heathen—follow them exultingly. I dance wildly inside myself; I yell within, I whoop; I shake my assegai[7] above my head, I hurl it true to the mark *yeeeeooww*! I am in the jungle and living in the jungle way. My face is painted red and yellow and my body is painted blue. My pulse is throbbing like a war drum. I want to slaughter something— give pain, give death to what, I do not know. But the piece ends. The men of the orchestra wipe their lips and rest their fingers. I creep back slowly to the veneer we call civilization with the last tone and find the white friend sitting motionless in his seat, smoking calmly.

"Good music they have here," he remarks, drumming the table with his fingertips.

Music. The great blobs of purple and red emotion have not touched him. He has only heard what I felt. He is far away and I see him but dimly across the ocean and the continent that have fallen between us. He is so pale with his whiteness then and I am *so* colored.

At certain times I have no race, I am *me*. When I set my hat at a certain angle and saunter down Seventh Avenue, Harlem City, feeling as snooty as the lions in front of the Forty-Second Street Library, for instance. So far as my feelings are concerned, Peggy Hopkins Joyce on the Boule Mich[8] with her gorgeous raiment, stately carriage, knees knocking together in a most aristocratic manner, has nothing on me. The cosmic Zora emerges. I belong to no race nor time. I am the eternal feminine with its string of beads.

15   I have no separate feeling about being an American citizen and colored. I am merely a fragment of the Great Soul that surges within the boundaries. My country, right or wrong.

Sometimes, I feel discriminated against, but it does not make me angry. It merely astonishes me. How *can* any deny themselves the pleasure of my company? It's beyond me.

But in the main, I feel like a brown bag of miscellany propped against a wall. Against a wall in company with other bags, white, red and yellow. Pour out the contents, and there is discovered a jumble of small things priceless and worthless. A first-water diamond, an empty spool, bits of broken glass, lengths of string, a key to a door long since crumbled away, a rusty knife-blade, old shoes saved for a road that never was and never will be, a nail bent under the weight

7. South African hunting spear.

8. Peggy Hopkins Joyce (1893–1957), American beauty and fashion-setter of the twenties; Boule Mich, Boulevard Saint-Michel, a fashionable Parisian street.

of things too heavy for any nail, a dried flower or two still a little fragrant. In your hand is the brown bag. On the ground before you is the jumble it held—so much like the jumble in the bags, could they be emptied, that all might be dumped in a single heap and the bags refilled without altering the content of any greatly. A bit of colored glass more or less would not matter. Perhaps that is how the Great Stuffer of Bags filled them in the first place—who knows?

MLA CITATION

Hurston, Zora Neale. "How It Feels to Be Colored Me." 1928. *The Norton Reader: An Anthology of Nonfiction*. Ed. Melissa A. Goldthwaite et al. 14th ed. New York: Norton, 2016. 42–45. Print.

QUESTIONS

1. From the beginning Zora Neale Hurston startles us: "I remember the very day that I became colored" (paragraph 2). Why does Hurston insist that one *becomes* colored? What happened on that day to make her so?

2. Each section of Hurston's essay explores a different possible identity, some based on skin color, others emphasizing history, culture, or gender. What does Hurston accomplish by such an approach?

3. The final paragraph introduces a key simile: "like a brown bag of miscellany propped against a wall." How does Hurston develop this simile? What does she mean by it?

4. Like Nancy Mairs in "On Being a Cripple" (pp. 64–73), Hurston chooses a label, "colored me," to explore questions of personal identity. Compare Hurston's use of "colored" with Mairs's use of "cripple."

MAYA ANGELOU   *Graduation*

THE CHILDREN IN STAMPS[1] trembled visibly with anticipation. Some adults were excited too, but to be certain the whole young population had come down with graduation epidemic. Large classes were graduating from both the grammar school and the high school. Even those who were years removed from their own day of glorious release were anxious to help with preparations as a kind of dry run. The junior students who were moving into the vacating classes'

From I Know Why the Caged Bird Sings *(1969), the first volume of Maya Angelou's autobiography of growing up in a segregated southern town. After its success, Angelou continued her life story in seven sequential volumes, ending with* Mom & Me & Mom *(2013).*

1. Town in Arkansas.

chairs were tradition-bound to show their talents for leadership and management. They strutted through the school and around the campus exerting pressure on the lower grades. Their authority was so new that occasionally if they pressed a little too hard it had to be overlooked. After all, next term was coming, and it never hurt a sixth grader to have a play sister in the eighth grade, or a tenth-year student to be able to call a twelfth grader Bubba. So all was endured in a spirit of shared understanding. But the graduating classes themselves were the nobility. Like travelers with exotic destinations on their minds, the graduates were remarkably forgetful. They came to school without their books or tablets or even pencils. Volunteers fell over themselves to secure replacements for the missing equipment. When accepted, the willing workers might or might not be thanked, and it was of no importance to the pregraduation rites. Even teachers were respectful of the now quiet and aging seniors, and tended to speak to them, if not as equals, as beings only slightly lower than themselves. After tests were returned and grades given, the student body, which acted like an extended family, knew who did well, who excelled, and what piteous ones had failed.

Unlike the white high school, Lafayette County Training School distinguished itself by having neither lawn, nor hedges, nor tennis court, nor climbing ivy. Its two buildings (main classrooms, the grade school and home economics) were set on a dirt hill with no fence to limit either its boundaries or those of bordering farms. There was a large expanse to the left of the school which was used alternately as a baseball diamond or basketball court. Rusty hoops on swaying poles represented the permanent recreational equipment, although bats and balls could be borrowed from the P.E. teacher if the borrower was qualified and if the diamond wasn't occupied.

Over this rocky area relieved by a few shady tall persimmon trees the graduating class walked. The girls often held hands and no longer bothered to speak to the lower students. There was a sadness about them, as if this old world was not their home and they were bound for higher ground. The boys, on the other hand, had become more friendly, more outgoing. A decided change from the closed attitude they projected while studying for finals. Now they seemed not ready to give up the old school, the familiar paths and classrooms. Only a small percentage would be continuing on to college—one of the South's A & M (agricultural and mechanical) schools, which trained Negro youths to be carpenters, farmers, handymen, masons, maids, cooks and baby nurses. Their future rode heavily on their shoulders, and blinded them to the collective joy that had pervaded the lives of the boys and girls in the grammar school graduating class.

Parents who could afford it had ordered new shoes and readymade clothes for themselves from Sears and Roebuck or Montgomery Ward. They also engaged the best seamstresses to make the floating graduating dresses and to cut down secondhand pants which would be pressed to a military slickness for the important event.

5   Oh, it was important, all right. Whitefolks would attend the ceremony, and two or three would speak of God and home, and the Southern way of life, and

Mrs. Parsons, the principal's wife, would play the graduation march while the lower-grade graduates paraded down the aisles and took their seats below the platform. The high school seniors would wait in empty classrooms to make their dramatic entrance.

In the Store I was the person of the moment. The birthday girl. The center. Bailey[2] had graduated the year before, although to do so he had had to forfeit all pleasures to make up for his time lost in Baton Rouge.

My class was wearing butter-yellow piqué dresses, and Momma launched out on mine. She smocked the yoke into tiny crisscrossing puckers, then shirred the rest of the bodice. Her dark fingers ducked in and out of the lemony cloth as she embroidered raised daisies around the hem. Before she considered herself finished she had added a crocheted cuff on the puff sleeves, and a pointy crocheted collar.

I was going to be lovely. A walking model of all the various styles of fine hand sewing and it didn't worry me that I was only twelve years old and merely graduating from the eighth grade. Besides, many teachers in Arkansas Negro schools had only that diploma and were licensed to impart wisdom.

The days had become longer and more noticeable. The faded beige of former times had been replaced with strong and sure colors. I began to see my classmates' clothes, their skin tones, and the dust that waved off pussy willows. Clouds that lazed across the sky were objects of great concern to me. Their shiftier shapes might have held a message that in my new happiness and with a little bit of time I'd soon decipher. During that period I looked at the arch of heaven so religiously my neck kept a steady ache. I had taken to smiling more often, and my jaws hurt from the unaccustomed activity. Between the two physical sore spots, I suppose I could have been uncomfortable, but that was not the case. As a member of the winning team (the graduating class of 1940) I had outdistanced unpleasant sensations by miles. I was headed for the freedom of open fields.

Youth and social approval allied themselves with me and we trammeled   10
memories of slights and insults. The wind of our swift passage remodeled my features. Lost tears were pounded to mud and then to dust. Years of withdrawal were brushed aside and left behind, as hanging ropes of parasitic moss.

My work alone had awarded me a top place and I was going to be one of the first called in the graduating ceremonies. On the classroom blackboard, as well as on the bulletin board in the auditorium, there were blue stars and white stars and red stars. No absences, no tardinesses, and my academic work was among the best of the year. I could say the preamble to the Constitution even faster than Bailey. We timed ourselves often: "We the people of the United States in order to form a more perfect union . . ." I had memorized the Presidents of the United States from Washington to Roosevelt in chronological as well as alphabetical order.

---

2. Author's brother.

My hair pleased me too. Gradually the black mass had lengthened and thickened, so that it kept at last to its braided pattern, and I didn't have to yank my scalp off when I tried to comb it.

Louise and I had rehearsed the exercises until we tired out ourselves. Henry Reed was class valedictorian. He was a small, very black boy with hooded eyes, a long, broad nose and an oddly shaped head. I had admired him for years because each term he and I vied for the best grades in our class. Most often he bested me, but instead of being disappointed I was pleased that we shared top places between us. Like many Southern Black children, he lived with his grandmother, who was as strict as Momma and as kind as she knew how to be. He was courteous, respectful and soft-spoken to elders, but on the playground he chose to play the roughest games. I admired him. Anyone, I reckoned, sufficiently afraid or sufficiently dull could be polite. But to be able to operate at a top level with both adults and children was admirable.

His valedictory speech was entitled "To Be or Not to Be." The rigid tenth-grade teacher had helped him write it. He'd been working on the dramatic stresses for months.

15   The weeks until graduation were filled with heady activities. A group of small children were to be presented in a play about buttercups and daisies and bunny rabbits. They could be heard throughout the building practicing their hops and their little songs that sounded like silver bells. The older girls (non-graduates, of course) were assigned the task of making refreshments for the night's festivities. A tangy scent of ginger, cinnamon, nutmeg and chocolate wafted around the home economics building as the budding cooks made samples for themselves and their teachers.

In every corner of the workshop, axes and saws split fresh timber as the woodshop boys made sets and stage scenery. Only the graduates were left out of the general bustle. We were free to sit in the library at the back of the building or look in quite detachedly, naturally, on the measures being taken for our event.

Even the minister preached on graduation the Sunday before. His subject was, "Let your light so shine that men will see your good works and praise your Father, Who is in Heaven." Although the sermon was purported to be addressed to us, he used the occasion to speak to backsliders, gamblers and general ne'er-do-wells. But since he had called our names at the beginning of the service we were mollified.

Among Negroes the tradition was to give presents to children going only from one grade to another. How much more important this was when the person was graduating at the top of the class. Uncle Willie and Momma had sent away for a Mickey Mouse watch like Bailey's. Louise gave me four embroidered handkerchiefs. (I gave her crocheted doilies.) Mrs. Sneed, the minister's wife, made me an undershirt to wear for graduation, and nearly every customer gave me a nickel or maybe even a dime with the instruction "Keep on moving to higher ground," or some such encouragement.

Amazingly the great day finally dawned and I was out of bed before I knew it. I threw open the back door to see it more clearly, but Momma said, "Sister, come away from that door and put your robe on."

I hoped the memory of that morning would never leave me. Sunlight was   20
itself young, and the day had none of the insistence maturity would bring it in a few hours. In my robe and barefoot in the backyard, under cover of going to see about my new beans, I gave myself up to the gentle warmth and thanked God that no matter what evil I had done in my life He had allowed me to live to see this day. Somewhere in my fatalism I had expected to die, accidentally, and never have the chance to walk up the stairs in the auditorium and gracefully receive my hard-earned diploma. Out of God's merciful bosom I had won reprieve.

Bailey came out in his robe and gave me a box wrapped in Christmas paper. He said he had saved his money for months to pay for it. It felt like a box of chocolates, but I knew Bailey wouldn't save money to buy candy when we had all we could want under our noses.

He was as proud of the gift as I. It was a soft-leather-bound copy of a collection of poems by Edgar Allan Poe, or, as Bailey and I called him, "Eap." I turned to "Annabel Lee" and we walked up and down the garden rows, the cool dirt between our toes, reciting the beautifully sad lines.

Momma made a Sunday breakfast although it was only Friday. After we finished the blessing, I opened my eyes to find the watch on my plate. It was a dream of a day. Everything went smoothly and to my credit, I didn't have to be reminded or scolded for anything. Near evening I was too jittery to attend to chores, so Bailey volunteered to do all before his bath.

Days before, we had made a sign for the Store, and as we turned out the lights Momma hung the cardboard over the doorknob. It read clearly: CLOSED. GRADUATION.

My dress fitted perfectly and everyone said that I looked like a sunbeam in   25
it. On the hill, going toward the school, Bailey walked behind with Uncle Willie, who muttered, "Go on, Ju." He wanted him to walk ahead with us because it embarrassed him to have to walk so slowly. Bailey said he'd let the ladies walk together, and the men would bring up the rear. We all laughed, nicely.

Little children dashed by out of the dark like fireflies. Their crepe-paper dresses and butterfly wings were not made for running and we heard more than one rip, dryly, and the regretful "uh uh" that followed.

The school blazed without gaiety. The windows seemed cold and unfriendly from the lower hill. A sense of ill-fated timing crept over me, and if Momma hadn't reached for my hand I would have drifted back to Bailey and Uncle Willie, and possibly beyond. She made a few slow jokes about my feet getting cold, and tugged me along to the now-strange building.

Around the front steps, assurance came back. There were my fellow "greats," the graduating class. Hair brushed back, legs oiled, new dresses and pressed pleats, fresh pocket handkerchiefs and little handbags, all homesewn. Oh, we were up to snuff, all right. I joined my comrades and didn't even see my family go in to find seats in the crowded auditorium.

The school band struck up a march and all classes filed in as had been rehearsed. We stood in front of our seats, as assigned, and on a signal from the choir director, we sat. No sooner had this been accomplished than the band started to play the national anthem. We rose again and sang the song, after which we recited the pledge of allegiance. We remained standing for a brief minute before the choir director and the principal signaled to us, rather desperately I thought, to take our seats. The command was so unusual that our carefully rehearsed and smooth-running machine was thrown off. For a full minute we fumbled for our chairs and bumped into each other awkwardly. Habits change or solidify under pressure, so in our state of nervous tension we had been ready to follow our usual assembly pattern: the American national anthem, then the pledge of allegiance, then the song every Black person I knew called the Negro National Anthem. All done in the same key, with the same passion and most often standing on the same foot.

30   Finding my seat at last, I was overcome with a presentiment of worse things to come. Something unrehearsed, unplanned, was going to happen, and we were going to be made to look bad. I distinctly remember being explicit in the choice of pronoun. It was "we," the graduating class, the unit, that concerned me then.

The principal welcomed "parents and friends" and asked the Baptist minister to lead us in prayer. His invocation was brief and punchy, and for a second I thought we were getting on the high road to right action. When the principal came back to the dais, however, his voice had changed. Sounds always affected me profoundly and the principal's voice was one of my favorites. During assembly it melted and lowed weakly into the audience. It had not been in my plan to listen to him, but my curiosity was piqued and I straightened up to give him my attention.

He was talking about Booker T. Washington, our "late great leader," who said we can be as close as the fingers on the hand, etc. . . . Then he said a few vague things about friendship and the friendship of kindly people to those less fortunate than themselves. With that his voice nearly faded, thin, away. Like a river diminishing to a stream and then to a trickle. But he cleared his throat and said, "Our speaker tonight, who is also our friend, came from Texarkana to deliver the commencement address, but due to the irregularity of the train schedule, he's going to, as they say, 'speak and run.'" He said that we understood and wanted the man to know that we were most grateful for the time he was able to give us and then something about how we were willing always to adjust to another's program, and without more ado—"I give you Mr. Edward Donleavy."

Not one but two white men came through the door off-stage. The shorter one walked to the speaker's platform, and the tall one moved to the center seat and sat down. But that was our principal's seat, and already occupied. The dislodged gentleman bounced around for a long breath or two before the Baptist minister gave him his chair, then with more dignity than the situation deserved, the minister walked off the stage.

Donleavy looked at the audience once (on reflection, I'm sure that he wanted only to reassure himself that we were really there), adjusted his glasses and began to read from a sheaf of papers.

He was glad "to be here and to see the work going on just as it was in the   35
other schools."

At the first "Amen" from the audience I willed the offender to immediate death by choking on the word. But Amens and Yes, sirs began to fall around the room like rain through a ragged umbrella.

He told us of the wonderful changes we children in Stamps had in store. The Central School (naturally, the white school was Central) had already been granted improvements that would be in use in the fall. A well-known artist was coming from Little Rock to teach art to them. They were going to have the newest microscopes and chemistry equipment for their laboratory. Mr. Donleavy didn't leave us long in the dark over who made these improvements available to Central High. Nor were we to be ignored in the general betterment scheme he had in mind.

He said that he had pointed out to people at a very high level that one of the first-line football tacklers at Arkansas Agricultural and Mechanical College had graduated from good old Lafayette County Training School. Here fewer Amens were heard. Those few that did break through lay dully in the air with the heaviness of habit.

He went on to praise us. He went on to say how he had bragged that "one of the best basketball players at Fisk sank his first ball right here at Lafayette County Training School."

The white kids were going to have a chance to become Galileos and   40
Madame Curies and Edisons and Gauguins, and our boys (the girls weren't even in on it) would try to be Jesse Owenses and Joe Louises.

Owens and the Brown Bomber were great heroes in our world, but what school official in the white-goddom of Little Rock had the right to decide that those two men must be our only heroes? Who decided that for Henry Reed to become a scientist he had to work like George Washington Carver, as a bootblack, to buy a lousy microscope? Bailey was obviously always going to be too small to be an athlete, so which concrete angel glued to what country seat had decided that if my brother wanted to become a lawyer he had to first pay penance for his skin by picking cotton and hoeing corn and studying correspondence books at night for twenty years?

The man's dead words fell like bricks around the auditorium and too many settled in my belly. Constrained by hard-learned manners I couldn't look behind me, but to my left and right the proud graduating class of 1940 had dropped their heads. Every girl in my row had found something new to do with her handkerchief. Some folded the tiny squares into love knots, some into triangles, but most were wadding them, then pressing them flat on their yellow laps.

On the dais, the ancient tragedy was being replayed. Professor Parsons sat, a sculptor's reject, rigid. His large, heavy body seemed devoid of will or willingness, and his eyes said he was no longer with us. The other teachers examined the flag (which was draped stage right) or their notes, or the windows which opened on our now-famous playing diamond.

Graduation, the hush-hush magic time of frills and gifts and congratulations and diplomas, was finished for me before my name was called. The accomplishment was nothing. The meticulous maps, drawn in three colors of ink, learning and spelling decasyllabic words, memorizing the whole of *The Rape of Lucrece*[3]—it was for nothing. Donleavy had exposed us.

45   We were maids and farmers, handymen and washerwomen, and anything higher that we aspired to was farcical and presumptuous.

Then I wished that Gabriel Prosser and Nat Turner[4] had killed all whitefolks in their beds and that Abraham Lincoln had been assassinated before the signing of the Emancipation Proclamation, and that Harriet Tubman[5] had been killed by that blow on her head and Christopher Columbus had drowned in the *Santa Maria*.

It was awful to be a Negro and have no control over my life. It was brutal to be young and already trained to sit quietly and listen to charges brought against my color with no chance of defense. We should all be dead. I thought I should like to see us all dead, one on top of the other. A pyramid of flesh with the whitefolks on the bottom, as the broad base, then the Indians with their silly tomahawks and teepees and wigwams and treaties, the Negroes with their mops and recipes and cotton sacks and spirituals sticking out of their mouths. The Dutch children should all stumble in their wooden shoes and break their necks. The French should choke to death on the Louisiana Purchase (1803) while silkworms ate all the Chinese with their stupid pigtails. As a species, we were an abomination. All of us.

Donleavy was running for election, and assured our parents that if he won we could count on having the only colored paved playing field in that part of Arkansas. Also—he never looked up to acknowledge the grunts of acceptance—also, we were bound to get some new equipment for the home economics building and the workshop.

He finished, and since there was no need to give any more than the most perfunctory thank-you's, he nodded to the men on the stage, and the tall white man who was never introduced joined him at the door. They left with the attitude that now they were off to something really important. (The graduation ceremonies at Lafayette County Training School had been a mere preliminary.)

3. A 1,855-line narrative poem (1594) by the playwright William Shakespeare, which recounts the story of the daughter of a Roman prefect. When she was defiled, she stabbed herself in the presence of her father and her husband.

4. Gabriel Prosser (c. 1776–1800) and Nat Turner (1800–1831), executed leaders of slave rebellions in Virginia.

5. Black abolitionist (c. 1822–1913), known for her work on the Underground Railroad, which brought slaves to free states through a network of secret paths and routes.

The ugliness they left was palpable. An uninvited guest who wouldn't leave.   50
The choir was summoned and sang a modern arrangement of "Onward, Christian Soldiers," with new words pertaining to graduates seeking their place in the
world. But it didn't work. Elouise, the daughter of the Baptist minister,
recited "Invictus,"[6] and I could have cried at the impertinence of "I am the
master of my fate, I am the captain of my soul."

My name had lost its ring of familiarity and I had to be nudged to go and
receive my diploma. All my preparations had fled. I neither marched up to the
stage like a conquering Amazon, nor did I look in the audience for Bailey's nod
of approval. Marguerite Johnson, I heard the name again, my honors were read,
there were noises in the audience of appreciation, and I took my place on the
stage as rehearsed.

I thought about colors I hated: ecru, puce, lavender, beige and black.

There was shuffling and rustling around me, then Henry Reed was giving
his valedictory address, "To Be or Not to Be." Hadn't he heard the white-folks?
We couldn't *be,* so the question was a waste of time. Henry's voice came out
clear and strong. I feared to look at him. Hadn't he got the message? There was
no "nobler in the mind" for Negroes because the world didn't think we had
minds, and they let us know it. "Outrageous fortune"? Now, that was a joke.
When the ceremony was over I had to tell Henry Reed some things. That is, if
I still cared. Not "rub," Henry, "erase." "Ah, there's the erase." Us.

Henry had been a good student in elocution. His voice rose on tides of
promise and fell on waves of warnings. The English teacher had helped him to
create a sermon winging through Hamlet's soliloquy. To be a man, a doer, a
builder, a leader, or to be a tool, an unfunny joke, a crusher of funky toad-
stools. I marveled that Henry could go through with the speech as if we had a
choice.

I had been listening and silently rebutting each sentence with my eyes   55
closed; then there was a hush, which in an audience warns that something
unplanned is happening. I looked up and saw Henry Reed, the conservative,
the proper, the A student, turn his back to the audience and turn to us (the
proud graduating class of 1940) and sing, nearly speaking,

> "Lift ev'ry voice and sing
> Till earth and heaven ring
> Ring with the harmonies of Liberty . . ."

It was the poem written by James Weldon Johnson. It was the music composed
by J. Rosamond Johnson. It was the Negro national anthem. Out of habit we
were singing it.

Our mothers and fathers stood in the dark hall and joined the hymn of
encouragement. A kindergarten teacher led the small children onto the stage

6. Inspirational poem (1888) by William Ernest Henley, once very popular for occasions such as this one.

and the buttercups and daisies and bunny rabbits marked time and tried to follow:

> "Stony the road we trod
> Bitter the chastening rod
> Felt in the days when hope, unborn, had died.
> Yet with a steady beat
> Have not our weary feet
> Come to the place for which our fathers sighed?"

Each child I knew had learned that song with his ABC's and along with "Jesus Loves Me This I Know." But I personally had never heard it before. Never heard the words, despite the thousands of times I had sung them. Never thought they had anything to do with me.

On the other hand, the words of Patrick Henry had made such an impression on me that I had been able to stretch myself tall and trembling and say, "I know not what course others may take, but as for me, give me liberty or give me death."

And now I heard, really for the first time:

> "We have come over a way that with tears
>   has been watered,
> We have come, treading our path through
>   the blood of the slaughtered."

60   While echoes of the song shivered in the air, Henry Reed bowed his head, said "Thank you," and returned to his place in the line. The tears that slipped down many faces were not wiped away in shame.

We were on top again. As always, again. We survived. The depths had been icy and dark, but now a bright sun spoke to our souls. I was no longer simply a member of the proud graduating class of 1940; I was a proud member of the wonderful, beautiful Negro race.

Oh, Black known and unknown poets, how often have your auctioned pains sustained us? Who will compute the lonely nights made less lonely by your songs, or the empty pots made less tragic by your tales?

If we were a people much given to revealing secrets, we might raise monuments and sacrifice to the memories of our poets, but slavery cured us of that weakness. It may be enough, however, to have it said that we survive in exact relationship to the dedication of our poets (include preachers, musicians and blues singers).

MLA CITATION

Angelou, Maya. "Graduation." 1969. *The Norton Reader: An Anthology of Nonfiction.*
    Ed. Melissa A. Goldthwaite et al. 14th ed. New York: Norton, 2016. 45–54. Print.

QUESTIONS

1. Presumably, all of Maya Angelou's readers would have witnessed a graduation ceremony and brought their memories to her essay. How does she fulfill the read-

back of the refrigerator for six months or so before discarding it. Characteristic of this type are the reused jars and margarine tubs to which the remains are committed. I avoid ethnic foods I am unfamiliar with. If I do not know what it is supposed to look like when it is good, I cannot be certain I will be able to tell if it is bad.

No matter how careful I am I still get dysentery at least once a month, oftener in warm weather. I do not want to paint too romantic a picture. Dumpster diving has serious drawbacks as a way of life. 30

I learned to scavenge gradually, on my own. Since then I have initiated several companions into the trade. I have learned that there is a predictable series of stages a person goes through in learning to scavenge.

At first the new scavenger is filled with disgust and self-loathing. He is ashamed of being seen and may lurk around, trying to duck behind things, or he may try to dive at night. (In fact, most people instinctively look away from a scavenger. By skulking around, the novice calls attention to himself and arouses suspicion. Diving at night is ineffective and needlessly messy.)

Every grain of rice seems to be a maggot. Everything seems to stink. He can wipe the egg yolk off the found can, but he cannot erase from his mind the stigma of eating garbage.

That stage passes with experience. The scavenger finds a pair of running shoes that fit and look and smell brand-new. He finds a pocket calculator in perfect working order. He finds pristine ice cream, still frozen, more than he can eat or keep. He begins to understand: People throw away perfectly good stuff, a lot of perfectly good stuff.

At this stage, Dumpster shyness begins to dissipate. The diver, after all, has the last laugh. He is finding all manner of good things that are his for the taking. Those who disparage his profession are the fools, not he. 35

He may begin to hang on to some perfectly good things for which he has neither a use nor a market. Then he begins to take note of the things that are not perfectly good but are nearly so. He mates a Walkman with broken earphones and one that is missing a battery cover. He picks up things that he can repair.

At this stage he may become lost and never recover. Dumpsters are full of things of some potential value to someone and also of things that never have much intrinsic value but are interesting. All the Dumpster divers I have known come to the point of trying to acquire everything they touch. Why not take it, they reason, since it is all free? This is, of course, hopeless. Most divers come to realize that they must restrict themselves to items of relatively immediate utility. But in some cases the diver simply cannot control himself. I have met several of these pack-rat types. Their ideas of the values of various pieces of junk verge on the psychotic. Every bit of glass may be a diamond, they think, and all that glisters, gold.

I tend to gain weight when I am scavenging. Partly this is because I always find far more pizza and doughnuts than water-packed tuna, nonfat yogurt, and fresh vegetables. Also I have not developed much faith in the reliability of Dumpsters as a food source, although it has been proven to me many times. I tend to eat as if I have no idea where my next meal is coming from. But mostly I just hate to see food go to waste and so I eat much more than I should. Something like this drives the obsession to collect junk.

As for collecting objects, I usually restrict myself to collecting one kind of small object at a time, such as pocket calculators, sunglasses, or campaign buttons. To live on the street I must anticipate my needs to a certain extent: I must pick up and save warm bedding I find in August because it will not be found in Dumpsters in November. As I have no access to health care, I often hoard essential drugs, such as antibiotics and antihistamines. (This course can be recommended only to those with some grounding in pharmacology. Antibiotics, for example, even when indicated are worse than useless if taken in insufficient amounts.) But even if I had a home with extensive storage space, I could not save everything that might be valuable in some contingency.

40   I have proprietary feelings about my Dumpsters. As I have mentioned, it is no accident that I scavenge from ones where good finds are common. But my limited experience with Dumpsters in other areas suggests to me that even in poorer areas, Dumpsters, if attended with sufficient diligence, can be made to yield a livelihood. The rich students discard perfectly good kiwifruit; poorer people discard perfectly good apples. Slacks and Polo shirts are found in the one place; jeans and T-shirts in the other. The population of competitors rather than the affluence of the dumpers most affects the feasibility of survival by scavenging. The large number of competitors is what puts me off the idea of trying to scavenge in places like Los Angeles.

Curiously, I do not mind my direct competition, other scavengers, so much as I hate the can scroungers.

People scrounge cans because they have to have a little cash. I have tried scrounging cans with an able-bodied companion. Afoot a can scrounger simply cannot make more than a few dollars a day. One can extract the necessities of life from the Dumpsters directly with far less effort than would be required to accumulate the equivalent value in cans. (These observations may not hold in places with container redemption laws.)

Can scroungers, then, are people who must have small amounts of cash. These are drug addicts and winos, mostly the latter because the amounts of cash are so small. Spirits and drugs do, like all other commodities, turn up in Dumpsters and the scavenger will from time to time have a half bottle of a rather good wine with his dinner. But the wino cannot survive on these occasional finds; he must have his daily dose to stave off the DTs. All the cans he can carry will buy about three bottles of Wild Irish Rose.

I do not begrudge them the cans, but can scroungers tend to tear up the Dumpsters, mixing the contents and littering the area. They become so specialized that they can see only cans. They earn my contempt by passing up change, canned goods, and readily hockable items.

45   There are precious few courtesies among scavengers. But it is common practice to set aside surplus items: pairs of shoes, clothing, canned goods, and such. A true scavenger hates to see good stuff go to waste, and what he cannot use he leaves in good condition in plain sight.

Can scroungers lay waste to everything in their path and will stir one of a pair of good shoes to the bottom of a Dumpster, to be lost or ruined in the muck. Can scroungers will even go through individual garbage cans, something I have never seen a scavenger do.

Individual garbage cans are set out on the public easement only on garbage days. On other days going through them requires trespassing close to a dwelling. Going through individual garbage cans without scattering litter is almost impossible. Litter is likely to reduce the public's tolerance of scavenging. Individual cans are simply not as productive as Dumpsters; people in houses and duplexes do not move so often and for some reason do not tend to discard as much useful material. Moreover, the time required to go through one garbage can that serves one household is not much less than the time required to go through a Dumpster that contains the refuse of twenty apartments.

But my strongest reservation about going through individual garbage cans is that this seems to me a very personal kind of invasion to which I would object if I were a householder. Although many things in Dumpsters are obviously meant never to come to light, a Dumpster is somehow less personal.

I avoid trying to draw conclusions about the people who dump in the Dumpsters I frequent. I think it would be unethical to do so, although I know many people will find the idea of scavenger ethics too funny for words.

Dumpsters contain bank statements, correspondence, and other documents, just as anyone might expect. But there are also less obvious sources of information. Pill bottles, for example. The labels bear the name of the patient, the name of the doctor, and the name of the drug. AIDS drugs and antipsychotic medicines, to name but two groups, are specific and are seldom prescribed for any other disorders. The plastic compacts for birth-control pills usually have complete label information.

Despite all of this sensitive information, I have had only one apartment resident object to my going through the Dumpster. In that case it turned out the resident was a university athlete who was taking bets and who was afraid I would turn up his wager slips.

Occasionally a find tells a story. I once found a small paper bag containing some unused condoms, several partial tubes of flavored sexual lubricants, a partially used compact of birth-control pills, and the torn pieces of a picture of a young man. Clearly she was through with him and planning to give up sex altogether.

Dumpster things are often sad—abandoned teddy bears, shredded wedding books, despaired-of sales kits. I find many pets lying in state in Dumpsters. Although I hope to get off the streets so that Lizbeth can have a long and comfortable old age, I know this hope is not very realistic. So I suppose when her time comes she too will go into a Dumpster. I will have no better place for her. And after all, it is fitting, since for most of her life her livelihood has come from the Dumpster. When she finds something I think is safe that has been spilled from a Dumpster, I let her have it. She already knows the route around the best ones. I like to think that if she survives me she will

50

have a chance of evading the dog catcher and of finding her sustenance on the route.

Silly vanities also come to rest in the Dumpsters. I am a rather accomplished needleworker. I get a lot of material from the Dumpsters. Evidently sorority girls, hoping to impress someone, perhaps themselves, with their mastery of a womanly art, buy a lot of embroider-by-number kits, work a few stitches horribly, and eventually discard the whole mess. I pull out their stitches, turn the canvas over, and work an original design. Do not think I refrain from chuckling as I make gifts from these kits.

55   I find diaries and journals. I have often thought of compiling a book of literary found objects. And perhaps I will one day. But what I find is hopelessly commonplace and bad without being, even unconsciously, camp. College students also discard their papers. I am horrified to discover the kind of paper that now merits an A in an undergraduate course. I am grateful, however, for the number of good books and magazines the students throw out.

In the area I know best I have never discovered vermin in the Dumpsters, but there are two kinds of kitty surprise. One is alley cats whom I meet as they leap, claws first, out of Dumpsters. This is especially thrilling when I have Lizbeth in tow. The other kind of kitty surprise is a plastic garbage bag filled with some ponderous, amorphous mass. This always proves to be used cat litter.

City bees harvest doughnut glaze and this makes the Dumpster at the doughnut shop more interesting. My faith in the instinctive wisdom of animals is always shaken whenever I see Lizbeth attempt to catch a bee in her mouth, which she does whenever bees are present. Evidently some birds find Dumpsters profitable, for birdie surprise is almost as common as kitty surprise of the first kind. In hunting season all kinds of small game turn up in Dumpsters, some of it, sadly, not entirely dead. Curiously, summer and winter, maggots are uncommon.

The worst of the living and near-living hazards of the Dumpsters are the fire ants. The food they claim is not much of a loss, but they are vicious and aggressive. It is very easy to brush against some surface of the Dumpster and pick up half a dozen or more fire ants, usually in some sensitive area such as the underarm. One advantage of bringing Lizbeth along as I make Dumpster rounds is that, for obvious reasons, she is very alert to ground-based fire ants. When Lizbeth recognizes a fire-ant infestation around our feet, she does the Dance of the Zillion Fire Ants. I have learned not to ignore this warning from Lizbeth, whether I perceive the tiny ants or not, but to remove ourselves at Lizbeth's first pas de bourée. All the more so because the ants are the worst in the summer months when I wear flip-flops if I have them. (Perhaps someone will misunderstand this. Lizbeth does the Dance of the Zillion Fire Ants when she recognizes more fire ants than she cares to eat, not when she is being bitten. Since I have learned to react promptly, she does not get bitten at all. It is the isolated patrol of fire ants that falls in Lizbeth's range that deserves pity. She finds them quite tasty.)

By far the best way to go through a Dumpster is to lower yourself into it. Most of the good stuff tends to settle at the bottom because it is usually weightier than the rubbish. My more athletic companions have often demonstrated to me that they can extract much good material from a Dumpster I have already been over.

To those psychologically or physically unprepared to enter a Dumpster, I recommend a stout stick, preferably with some barb or hook at one end. The hook can be used to grab plastic garbage bags. When I find canned goods or other objects loose at the bottom of a Dumpster, I lower a bag into it, roll the desired object into the bag, and then hoist the bag out—a procedure more easily described than executed. Much Dumpster diving is a matter of experience for which nothing will do except practice. 60

Dumpster diving is outdoor work, often surprisingly pleasant. It is not entirely predictable; things of interest turn up every day and some days there are finds of great value. I am always very pleased when I can turn up exactly the thing I most wanted to find. Yet in spite of the element of chance, scavenging more than most other pursuits tends to yield returns in some proportion to the effort and intelligence brought to bear. It is very sweet to turn up a few dollars in change from a Dumpster that has just been gone over by a wino.

The land is now covered with cities. The cities are full of Dumpsters. If a member of the canine race is ever able to know what it is doing, then Lizbeth knows that when we go around to the Dumpsters, we are hunting. I think of scavenging as a modern form of self-reliance. In any event, after having survived nearly ten years of government service, where everything is geared to the lowest common denominator, I find it refreshing to have work that rewards initiative and effort. Certainly I would be happy to have a sinecure again, but I am no longer heartbroken that I left one.

I find from the experience of scavenging two rather deep lessons. The first is to take what you can use and let the rest go by. I have come to think that there is no value in the abstract. A thing I cannot use or make useful, perhaps by trading, has no value however rare or fine it may be. I mean useful in a broad sense—some art I would find useful and some otherwise.

I was shocked to realize that some things are not worth acquiring, but now I think it is so. Some material things are white elephants that eat up the possessor's substance. The second lesson is the transience of material being. This has not quite converted me to a dualist, but it has made some headway in that direction. I do not suppose that ideas are immortal, but certainly mental things are longer lived than other material things.

Once I was the sort of person who invests objects with sentimental value. Now I no longer have those objects, but I have the sentiments yet. 65

Many times in our travels I have lost everything but the clothes I was wearing and Lizbeth. The things I find in Dumpsters, the love letters and rag dolls of so many lives, remind me of this lesson. Now I hardly pick up a thing without envisioning the time I will cast it aside. This I think is a healthy state of mind. Almost everything I have now has already been cast out at least once, proving that what I own is valueless to someone.

Anyway, I find my desire to grab for the gaudy bauble has been largely sated. I think this is an attitude I share with the very wealthy—we both know there

is plenty more where what we have came from. Between us are the rat-race millions who nightly scavenge the cable channels looking for they know not what.

I am sorry for them.

MLA CITATION

Eighner, Lars. "On Dumpster Diving." 1993. *The Norton Reader: An Anthology of
Nonfiction*. Ed. Melissa A. Goldthwaite et al. 14th ed. New York: Norton, 2016.
55–64. Print.

QUESTIONS

1. How does Lars Eighner organize his essay? What might such an organization
imply?

2. Eighner's simple, understated tone suggests that anyone can adapt to Dumpster
diving with a little practice. Why do you think he uses such a tone?

3. Write about someone who, as Eighner criticizes in his closing paragraphs, "invests
objects with sentimental value" (paragraph 65). Let your description reveal whether
or not you agree with Eighner.

NANCY MAIRS   *On Being a Cripple*

> To escape is nothing. Not to escape is nothing.
> —LOUISE BOGAN

THE OTHER DAY I was thinking of writing an essay
on being a cripple. I was thinking hard in one of
the stalls of the women's room in my office building,
as I was shoving my shirt into my jeans and tugging up
my zipper. Preoccupied, I flushed, picked up my book
bag, took my cane down from the hook, and unlatched
the door. So many movements unbalanced me, and as I pulled the door open I
fell over backward, landing fully clothed on the toilet seat with my legs splayed
in front of me: the old beetle-on-its-back routine. Saturday afternoon, the
building deserted, I was free to laugh aloud as I wriggled back to my feet, my
voice bouncing off the yellowish tiles from all directions. Had anyone been
there with me, I'd have been still and faint and hot with chagrin. I decided
that it was high time to write the essay.

First, the matter of semantics. I am a cripple. I choose this word to name
me. I choose from among several possibilities, the most common of which are
"handicapped" and "disabled." I made the choice a number of years ago, with-

From Plaintext *(1986), Nancy Mairs's book of personal essays about life with multiple
sclerosis.*

out thinking, unaware of my motives for doing so. Even now, I'm not sure what those motives are, but I recognize that they are complex and not entirely flattering. People—crippled or not—wince at the word "cripple," as they do not at "handicapped" or "disabled." Perhaps I want them to wince. I want them to see me as a tough customer, one to whom the fates/gods/viruses have not been kind, but who can face the brutal truth of her existence squarely. As a cripple, I swagger.

But, to be fair to myself, a certain amount of honesty underlies my choice. "Cripple" seems to me a clean word, straightforward and precise. It has an honorable history, having made its first appearance in the Lindisfarne Gospel[1] in the tenth century. As a lover of words, I like the accuracy with which it describes my condition: I have lost the full use of my limbs. "Disabled," by contrast, suggests any incapacity, physical or mental. And I certainly don't like "handicapped," which implies that I have deliberately been put at a disadvantage, by whom I can't imagine (my God is not a Handicapper General), in order to equalize chances in the great race of life. These words seem to me to be moving away from my condition, to be widening the gap between word and reality. Most remote is the recently coined euphemism "differently abled," which partakes of the same semantic hopefulness that transformed countries from "undeveloped" to "underdeveloped," then to "less developed," and finally to "developing" nations. People have continued to starve in those countries during the shift. Some realities do not obey the dictates of language.

Mine is one of them. Whatever you call me, I remain crippled. But I don't care what you call me, so long as it isn't "differently abled," which strikes me as pure verbal garbage designed, by its ability to describe anyone, to describe no one. I subscribe to George Orwell's thesis that "the slovenliness of our language makes it easier for us to have foolish thoughts."[2] And I refuse to participate in the degeneration of the language to the extent that I deny that I have lost anything in the course of this calamitous disease; I refuse to pretend that the only differences between you and me are the various ordinary ones that distinguish any one person from another. But call me "disabled" or "handicapped" if you like. I have long since grown accustomed to them; and if they are vague, at least they hint at the truth. Moreover, I use them myself. Society is no readier to accept crippledness than to accept death, war, sex, sweat, or wrinkles. I would never refer to another person as a cripple. It is the word I use to name only myself.

I haven't always been crippled, a fact for which I am soundly grateful. To   5
be whole of limb is, I know from experience, infinitely more pleasant and useful than to be crippled; and if that knowledge leaves one open to bitterness at my loss, the physical soundness I once enjoyed (though I did not enjoy it half enough) is well worth the occasional stab of regret. Though never any good at

1. Illustrated manuscript of the four gospels of the New Testament (c. 700 C.E.) done by Irish monks; English commentaries were added in the tenth century.
2. Quotation from "Politics and the English Language" (1946) by George Orwell, British essayist and novelist; see pp. 510–19.

sports, I was a normally active child and young adult. I climbed trees, played hopscotch, jumped rope, skated, swam, rode my bicycle, sailed. I despised team sports, spending some of the wretchedest afternoons of my life, sweaty and humiliated, behind a field-hockey stick and under a basketball hoop. I tramped alone for miles along the bridle paths that webbed the woods behind the house I grew up in. I swayed through countless dim hours in the arms of one man or another under the scattered shot of light from mirrored balls, and gyrated through countless more as Tab Hunter and Johnny Mathis[3] gave way to the Rolling Stones, Creedence Clearwater Revival, Cream. I walked down the aisle. I pushed baby carriages, changed tires in the rain, marched for peace.

When I was twenty-eight I started to trip and drop things. What at first seemed my natural clumsiness soon became too pronounced to shrug off. I consulted a neurologist, who told me that I had a brain tumor. A battery of tests, increasingly disagreeable, revealed no tumor. About a year and a half later I developed a blurred spot in one eye. I had, at last, the episodes "disseminated in space and time" requisite for a diagnosis: multiple sclerosis. I have never been sorry for the doctor's initial misdiagnosis, however. For almost a week, until the negative results of the tests were in, I thought that I was going to die right away. Every day for the past nearly ten years, then, has been a kind of gift. I accept all gifts.

Multiple sclerosis is a chronic degenerative disease of the central nervous system, in which the myelin that sheathes the nerves is somehow eaten away and scar tissue forms in its place, interrupting the nerves' signals. During its course, which is unpredictable and uncontrollable, one may lose vision, hearing, speech, the ability to walk, control of bladder and/or bowels, strength in any or all extremities, sensitivity to touch, vibration, and/or pain, potency, coordination of movements—the list of possibilities is lengthy and, yes, horrifying. One may also lose one's sense of humor. That's the easiest to lose and the hardest to survive without.

In the past ten years, I have sustained some of these losses. Characteristic of MS are sudden attacks, called exacerbations, followed by remissions, and these I have not had. Instead, my disease has been slowly progressive. My left leg is now so weak that I walk with the aid of a brace and a cane; and for distances I use an Amigo, a variation on the electric wheelchair that looks rather like an electrified kiddie car. I no longer have much use of my left hand. Now my right side is weakening as well. I still have the blurred spot in my right eye. Overall, though, I've been lucky so far. My world has, of necessity, been circumscribed by my losses, but the terrain left me has been ample enough for me to continue many of the activities that absorb me: writing, teaching, raising children and cats and plants and snakes, reading, speaking publicly about MS and depression, even playing bridge with people patient and honorable enough to let me scatter cards every which way without sneaking a peek.

Lest I begin to sound like Pollyanna, however, let me say that I don't like having MS. I hate it. My life holds realities—harsh ones, some of them—that

---

3. Hunter (b. 1931), American actor and singer popular in the 1960s; Mathis (b. 1935), American singer popular in the 1950s and 1960s and well known for his love ballads.

no right-minded human being ought to accept without grumbling. One of them is fatigue. I know of no one with MS who does not complain of bone-weariness; in a disease that presents an astonishing variety of symptoms, fatigue seems to be a common factor. I wake up in the morning feeling the way most people do at the end of a bad day, and I take it from there. As a result, I spend a lot of time *in extremis*[4] and, impatient with limitation, I tend to ignore my fatigue until my body breaks down in some way and forces rest. Then I miss picnics, dinner parties, poetry readings, the brief visits of old friends from out of town. The offspring of a puritanical tradition of exceptional venerability, I cannot view these lapses without shame. My life often seems a series of small failures to do as I ought.

I lead, on the whole, an ordinary life, probably rather like the one I would have led had I not had MS. I am lucky that my predilections were already solitary, sedentary, and bookish—unlike the world-famous French cellist I have read about, or the young woman I talked with one long afternoon who wanted only to be a jockey. I had just begun graduate school when I found out something was wrong with me, and I have remained, interminably, a graduate student. Perhaps I would not have if I'd thought I had the stamina to return to a full-time job as a technical editor; but I've enjoyed my studies.

In addition to studying, I teach writing courses. I also teach medical students how to give neurological examinations. I pick up freelance editing jobs here and there. I have raised a foster son and sent him into the world, where he has made me two grandbabies, and I am still escorting my daughter and son through adolescence. I go to Mass every Saturday. I am a superb, if messy, cook. I am also an enthusiastic laundress, capable of sorting a hamper full of clothes into five subtly differentiated piles, but a terrible housekeeper. I can do italic writing and, in an emergency, bathe an oil-soaked cat. I play a fiendish game of Scrabble. When I have the time and the money, I like to sit on my front steps with my husband, drinking Amaretto and smoking a cigar, as we imagine our counterparts in Leningrad and make sure that the sun gets down once more behind the sharp childish scrawl of the Tucson Mountains.

This lively plenty has its bleak complement, of course, in all the things I can no longer do. I will never run again, except in dreams, and one day I may have to write that I will never walk again. I like to go camping, but I can't follow George and the children along the trails that wander out of a campsite through the desert or into the mountains. In fact, even on the level I've learned never to check the weather or try to hold a coherent conversation: I need all my attention for my wayward feet. Of late, I have begun to catch myself wondering how people can propel themselves without canes. With only one usable hand, I have to select my clothing with care not so much for style as for ease of ingress and egress, and even so, dressing can be laborious. I can no longer do fine stitchery, pick up babies, play the piano, braid my hair. I am immobilized by acute attacks of depression, which may or may not be physiologically related to MS but are certainly its logical concomitant.

10

---

4. Latin for "in the last straits." Here it means "at the limits of endurance."

These two elements, the plenty and the privation, are never pure, nor are the delight and wretchedness that accompany them. Almost every pickle that I get into as a result of my weakness and clumsiness—and I get into plenty—is funny as well as maddening and sometimes painful. I recall one May afternoon when a friend and I were going out for a drink after finishing up at school. As we were climbing into opposite sides of my car, chatting, I tripped and fell, flat and hard, onto the asphalt parking lot, my abrupt departure interrupting him in mid-sentence. "Where'd you go?" he called as he came around the back of the car to find me hauling myself up by the door frame. "Are you all right?" Yes, I told him, I was fine, just a bit rattly, and we drove off to find a shady patio and some beer. When I got home an hour or so later, my daughter greeted me with "What have you done to yourself?" I looked down. One elbow of my white turtleneck with the green froggies, one knee of my white trousers, one white kneesock were blood-soaked. We peeled off the clothes and inspected the damage, which was nasty enough but not alarming. That part wasn't funny: The abrasions took a long time to heal, and one got a little infected. Even so, when I think of my friend talking earnestly, suddenly, to the hot thin air while I dropped from his view as though through a trap door, I find the image as silly as something from a Marx Brothers movie.

I may find it easier than other cripples to amuse myself because I live propped by the acceptance and the assistance and, sometimes, the amusement of those around me. Grocery clerks tear my checks out of my checkbook for me, and sales clerks find chairs to put into dressing rooms when I want to try on clothes. The people I work with make sure I teach at times when I am least likely to be fatigued, in places I can get to, with the materials I need. My students, with one anonymous exception (in an end-of-the-semester evaluation), have been unperturbed by my disability. Some even like it. One was immensely cheered by the information that I paint my own fingernails; she decided, she told me, that if I could go to such trouble over fine details, she could keep on writing essays. I suppose I became some sort of bright-fingered muse. She wrote good essays, too.

15   The most important struts in the framework of my existence, of course, are my husband and children. Dismayingly few marriages survive the MS test, and why should they? Most twenty-two- and nineteen-year-olds, like George and me, can vow in clear conscience, after a childhood of chicken pox and summer colds, to keep one another in sickness and in health so long as they both shall live. Not many are equipped for catastrophe: the dismay, the depression, the extra work, the boredom that a degenerative disease can insinuate into a relationship. And our society, with its emphasis on fun and its association of fun with physical performance, offers little encouragement for a whole spouse to stay with a crippled partner. Children experience similar stresses when faced with a crippled parent, and they are more helpless, since parents and children can't usually get divorced. They hate, of course, to be different from their peers, and the child whose mother is tacking down the aisle of a school auditorium packed with proud parents like a Cape Cod dinghy in a stiff breeze jolly well stands out in a crowd. Deprived of legal divorce, the child can at least deny the

mother's disability, even her existence, forgetting to tell her about recitals and PTA meetings, refusing to accompany her to stores or church or the movies, never inviting friends to the house. Many do.

But I've been limping along for ten years now, and so far George and the children are still at my left elbow, holding tight. Anne and Matthew vacuum floors and dust furniture and haul trash and rake up dog droppings and button my cuffs and bake lasagna and Toll House cookies with just enough grumbling so I know that they don't have brain fever. And far from hiding me, they're forever dragging me by racks of fancy clothes or through teeming school corridors, or welcoming gaggles of friends while I'm wandering through the house in Anne's filmy pink babydoll pajamas. George generally calls before he brings someone home, but he does just as many dumb thankless chores as the children. And they all yell at me, laugh at some of my jokes, write me funny letters when we're apart—in short, treat me as an ordinary human being for whom they have some use. I think they like me. Unless they're faking. . . .

Faking. There's the rub. Tugging at the fringes of my consciousness always is the terror that people are kind to me only because I'm a cripple. My mother almost shattered me once, with that instinct mothers have—blind, I think, in this case, but unerring nonetheless—for striking blows along the fault-lines of their children's hearts, by telling me, in an attack on my selfishness, "We all have to make allowances for you, of course, because of the way you are." From the distance of a couple of years, I have to admit that I haven't any idea just what she meant, and I'm not sure that she knew either. She was awfully angry. But at the time, as the words thudded home, I felt my worst fear, suddenly realized. I could bear being called selfish: I am. But I couldn't bear the corroboration that those around me were doing in fact what I'd always suspected them of doing, professing fondness while silently putting up with me because of the way I am. A cripple. I've been a little cracked ever since.

Along with this fear that people are secretly accepting shoddy goods comes a relentless pressure to please—to prove myself worth the burdens I impose, I guess, or to build a substantial account of goodwill against which I may write drafts in times of need. Part of the pressure arises from social expectations. In our society, anyone who deviates from the norm had better find some way to compensate. Like fat people, who are expected to be jolly, cripples must bear their lot meekly and cheerfully. A grumpy cripple isn't playing by the rules. And much of the pressure is self-generated. Early on I vowed that, if I had to have MS, by God I was going to do it well. This is a class act, ladies and gentlemen. No tears, no recriminations, no faintheartedness.

One way and another, then, I wind up feeling like Tiny Tim,[5] peering over the edge of the table at the Christmas goose, waving my crutch, piping down God's blessing on us all. Only sometimes I don't want to play Tiny Tim. I'd rather be Caliban,[6] a most scurvy monster. Fortunately, at home no one much

5. Crippled, frail young boy saved by Ebenezer Scrooge's generosity in Charles Dickens's novel *A Christmas Carol* (1843).
6. Son of the witch Sycorax in William Shakespeare's play *The Tempest* (c. 1611).

cares whether I'm a good cripple or a bad cripple as long as I make vichyssoise with fair regularity. One evening several years ago, Anne was reading at the dining-room table while I cooked dinner. As I opened a can of tomatoes, the can slipped in my left hand and juice spattered me and the counter with bloody spots. Fatigued and infuriated, I bellowed, "I'm so sick of being crippled!" Anne glanced at me over the top of her book. "There now," she said, "do you feel better?" "Yes," I said, "yes, I do." She went back to her reading. I felt better. That's about all the attention my scurviness ever gets.

20   Because I hate being crippled, I sometimes hate myself for being a cripple. Over the years I have come to expect—even accept—attacks of violent self-loathing. Luckily, in general our society no longer connects deformity and disease directly with evil (though a charismatic once told me that I have MS because a devil is in me) and so I'm allowed to move largely at will, even among small children. But I'm not sure that this revision of attitude has been particularly helpful. Physical imperfection, even freed of moral disapprobation, still defies and violates the ideal, especially for women, whose confinement in their bodies as objects of desire is far from over. Each age, of course, has its ideal, and I doubt that ours is any better or worse than any other. Today's ideal woman, who lives on the glossy pages of dozens of magazines, seems to be between the ages of eighteen and twenty-five; her hair has body, her teeth flash white, her breath smells minty, her underarms are dry; she has a career but is still a fabulous cook, especially of meals that take less than twenty minutes to prepare; she does not ordinarily appear to have a husband or children; she is trim and deeply tanned; she jogs, swims, plays tennis, rides a bicycle, sails, but does not bowl; she travels widely, even to out-of-the-way places like Finland and Samoa, always in the company of the ideal man, who possesses a nearly identical set of characteristics. There are a few exceptions. Though usually white and often blonde, she may be black, Hispanic, Asian, or Native American, so long as she is unusually sleek. She may be old, provided she is selling a laxative or is Lauren Bacall. If she is selling a detergent, she may be married and have a flock of strikingly messy children. But she is never a cripple.

Like many women I know, I have always had an uneasy relationship with my body. I was not a popular child, largely, I think now, because I was peculiar: intelligent, intense, moody, shy, given to unexpected actions and inexplicable notions and emotions. But as I entered adolescence, I believed myself unpopular because I was homely: my breasts too flat, my mouth too wide, my hips too narrow, my clothing never quite right in fit or style. I was not, in fact, particularly ugly, old photographs inform me, though I was well off the ideal; but I carried this sense of self-alienation with me into adulthood, where it regenerated in response to the depredations of MS. Even with my brace I walk with a limp so pronounced that, seeing myself on the videotape of a television program on the disabled, I couldn't believe that anything but an inchworm could make progress humping along like that. My shoulders droop and my pelvis thrusts forward as I try to balance myself upright, throwing my frame into a bony S. As a result of contractures, one shoulder is higher than the other and I carry one arm bent in front of me, the fingers curled into a claw. My left arm and leg have wasted into pipe-stems, and I try always to keep them covered.

down on her, knowing that if she dies, I cannot live. She is being treated with warm oils and hot bricks held against her cheek. Finally a doctor comes. But I must go back to my grandparents' house. The weeks pass but I am hardly aware of it. All I know is that my mother might die, my father is not so jolly, my brothers still have their guns, and I am the one sent away from home.

"You did not change," they say.

Did I imagine the anguish of never looking up?

I am twelve. When relatives come to visit I hide in my room. My cousin Brenda, just my age, whose father works in the post office and whose mother is a nurse, comes to find me. "Hello," she says. And then she asks, looking at my recent school picture, which I did not want taken, and on which the "glob," as I think of it, is clearly visible, "You still can't see out of that eye?"

"No," I say, and flop back on the bed over my book.

That night, as I do almost every night, I abuse my eye. I rant and rave at   30
it, in front of the mirror. I plead with it to clear up before morning. I tell it I hate and despise it. I do not pray for sight. I pray for beauty.

"You did not change," they say.

I am fourteen and baby-sitting for my brother Bill, who lives in Boston. He is my favorite brother and there is a strong bond between us. Understanding my feelings of shame and ugliness he and his wife take me to a local hospital, where the "glob" is removed by a doctor named O. Henry. There is still a small bluish crater where the scar tissue was, but the ugly white stuff is gone. Almost immediately I become a different person from the girl who does not raise her head. Or so I think. Now that I've raised my head I win the boyfriend of my dreams. Now that I've raised my head I have plenty of friends. Now that I've raised my head classwork comes from my lips as faultlessly as Easter speeches did, and I leave high school as valedictorian, most popular student, and *queen,* hardly believing my luck. Ironically, the girl who was voted most beautiful in our class (and was) was later shot twice through the chest by a male companion, using a "real" gun, while she was pregnant. But that's another story in itself. Or is it?

"You did not change," they say.

It is now thirty years since the "accident." A beautiful journalist comes to visit and to interview me. She is going to write a cover story for her magazine that focuses on my latest book. "Decide how you want to look on the cover," she says. "Glamorous, or whatever."

Never mind "glamorous," it is the "whatever" that I hear. Suddenly all I can   35
think of is whether I will get enough sleep the night before the photography session: if I don't, my eye will be tired and wander, as blind eyes will.

At night in bed with my lover I think up reasons why I should not appear on the cover of a magazine. "My meanest critics will say I've sold out," I say. "My family will now realize I write scandalous books."

"But what's the real reason you don't want to do this?" he asks.

"Because in all probability," I say in a rush, "my eye won't be straight."

"It will be straight enough," he says. Then, "Besides, I thought you'd made your peace with that."

40   And I suddenly remember that I have.

I remember:

I am talking to my brother Jimmy, asking if he remembers anything unusual about the day I was shot. He does not know I consider that day the last time my father, with his sweet home remedy of cool lily leaves, chose me, and that I suffered and raged inside because of this. "Well," he says, "all I remember is standing by the side of the highway with Daddy, trying to flag down a car. A white man stopped, but when Daddy said he needed somebody to take his little girl to the doctor, he drove off."

I remember:

I am in the desert for the first time. I fall totally in love with it. I am so overwhelmed by its beauty, I confront for the first time, consciously, the meaning of the doctor's words years ago: "Eyes are sympathetic. If one is blind, the other will likely become blind too." I realize I have dashed about the world madly, looking at this, looking at that, storing up images against the fading of the light. *But I might have missed seeing the desert!* The shock of that possibility— and gratitude for over twenty-five years of sight—sends me literally to my knees. Poem after poem comes—which is perhaps how poets pray.

On Sight

I am so thankful I have seen
The Desert
And the creatures in the desert
And the desert Itself.

The desert has its own moon
Which I have seen
With my own eye.
There is no flag on it.

Trees of the desert have arms
All of which are always up
That is because the moon is up
The sun is up

Also the sky
The stars
Clouds
None with flags.

If there were flags, I doubt
the trees would point.
Would you?

But mostly, I remember this: 45

I am twenty-seven, and my baby daughter is almost three. Since her birth I have worried about her discovery that her mother's eyes are different from other people's. Will she be embarrassed? I think. What will she say? Every day she watches a television program called "Big Blue Marble." It begins with a picture of the earth as it appears from the moon. It is bluish, a little battered-looking, but full of light, with whitish clouds swirling around it. Every time I see it I weep with love, as if it is a picture of Grandma's house. One day when I am putting Rebecca down for her nap, she suddenly focuses on my eye. Something inside me cringes, gets ready to try to protect myself. All children are cruel about physical differences, I know from experience, and that they don't always mean to be is another matter. I assume Rebecca will be the same.

But no-o-o-o. She studies my face intently as we stand, her inside and me outside her crib. She even holds my face maternally between her dimpled little hands. Then, looking every bit as serious and lawyerlike as her father, she says, as if it may just possibly have slipped my attention: "Mommy, there's a *world* in your eye." (As in, "Don't be alarmed, or do anything crazy.") And then, gently, but with great interest: "Mommy, where did you *get* that world in your eye?"

For the most part, the pain left then. (So what, if my brothers grew up to buy even more powerful pellet guns for their sons and to carry real guns themselves. So what, if a young "Morehouse man"[1] once nearly fell off the steps of Trevor Arnett Library because he thought my eyes were blue.) Crying and laughing I ran to the bathroom, while Rebecca mumbled and sang herself off to sleep. Yes indeed, I realized, looking into the mirror. There *was* a world in my eye. And I saw that it was possible to love it: that in fact, for all it had taught me of shame and anger and inner vision, I *did* love it. Even to see it drifting out of orbit in boredom, or rolling up out of fatigue, not to mention floating back at attention in excitement (bearing witness, a friend has called it), deeply suitable to my personality, and even characteristic of me.

That night I dream I am dancing to Stevie Wonder's[2] song "Always" (the name of the song is really "As," but I hear it as "Always"). As I dance, whirling and joyous, happier than I've ever been in my life, another bright-faced dancer joins me. We dance and kiss each other and hold each other through the night. The other dancer has obviously come through all right, as I have done. She is beautiful, whole and free. And she is also me.

1. Student at Morehouse College in Atlanta, Georgia.
2. Singer, songwriter, and music producer (b. 1950).

MLA CITATION

Walker, Alice. "Beauty: When the Other Dancer Is the Self." 1983. *The Norton Reader: An Anthology of Nonfiction.* Ed. Melissa A. Goldthwaite et al. 14th ed. New York: Norton, 2016. 74–79. Print.

QUESTIONS

1. From paragraph 12 onward, Alice Walker refers to the "accident." Why does she put the word in quotation marks? To what extent has Walker made peace with the "accident" and its consequences?

2. Walker writes her essay by selecting particular moments in her life. What are these moments and what do they tell us about Walker's theme?

3. What is the effect of ending the essay by recounting a dream? How does the dream relate to the essay's title?

4. Write an essay comparing and contrasting Walker's essay and Nancy Mairs's "On Being a Cripple" (pp. 64–73). Consider especially the two authors' responses and attitudes toward injury or illness.

JOEY FRANKLIN   *Working at Wendy's*

I T'S 8:45 P.M., and I am standing in front of the counter at Wendy's. It smells of French fries and mop water. In my right hand I hold my résumé. I don't know if I need a résumé to apply for the Wendy's night shift, but I bring it anyway. It anchors me as I drift toward the sixteen-year-old kid behind the counter and ask to speak to his manager.

"One mandarin orange salad?" the boy asks.

"Uh, no. Actually, I'd like to speak to the *manager.*" As the cashier retreats to the back of the store, I recognize a large kid with curly hair working the fryer—he used to play football with some of the members of my Boy Scout troop. He looks up at me, and I avert my eyes. Part of me wants to turn around and leave before the manager comes out. A couple in their twenties walks into the restaurant behind me. I step away from the counter and pretend to read the menu, holding my résumé close to my chest. The urge to leave increases. Just then the manager comes out and asks, "You here about the night shift?"

As I hand the manager my résumé, I realize it is a mistake. He doesn't want to know my service experience, or my academic references, or my GPA. All he wants to know is if I can spell my name correctly.

5   "Er, the application is over there," the manager says, handing me back my résumé and pointing to a file folder mounted on the wall next to the counter. I take the application to an empty table in the corner of the restaurant and hunch over it, wishing I had a drink, or a hamburger, or something to put on the table beside me.

Joey Franklin wrote this essay when he was an English major at Brigham Young University in Provo, Utah. It was published in Twentysomething Essays by Twentysomething Writers *(2006), a collection of writings from the winners of a national contest organized by the publishing company Random House.*

The next day I go for an interview with the hiring manager. I sit down at a table in the lobby and answer two questions: "What hours do you want to work?" and "When can you start?"

When he was sixteen, my brother, Josh, got his first job at McDonald's. He lasted two weeks before deciding the greasy uniform and salty mop water weren't worth $5.25 an hour. His manager used to show off rejected applications to the other employees in the back of the store. Most were high school dropouts looking for spending money, but a few had college degrees. One application was from a doctor who had recently left his practice because he "couldn't handle the mortality rate."

I think about that doctor now as I sit in a small back room at Wendy's. I have just watched thirty minutes of training videos about customer service, floor mopping, heavy lifting, and armed robbery. Chelsea, the training manager, hands me two neatly folded uniforms and a brand-new hat. Holding the hat in my hand, I look out into the kitchen at my new coworkers. At the fryer is the large high school kid I remember from the night before. A skinny brown-haired Asian-looking boy who must be about nineteen years old is washing dishes. Two girls are at the front of the store taking orders, and the manager is on the phone with an angry customer. "Can I do this?" I ask myself, and put on my hat.

Chelsea is pregnant. During our training session, I guess she is about six months along. It turns out she is due in three days. "This is my last week on the day shift," she says. "After the baby is born, I'll be back on nights." This is her first child, she explains, and says she is looking forward to being a mom. She smiles as she pats her stomach and asks about my son.

"Eighteen months," I tell her, "a real handful." I explain that I want to work nights so I can take care of my son during the day while my wife finishes her last semester of college. I ask about the pay, but I already know her answer. "We start at five-seventy-five," she says, "but the night guys get six." I ask her what she thinks about $7. She says she'll see what she can do.

Chelsea trains me on Tuesday and goes into labor on Wednesday. I don't see her again for three weeks.

Kris Livingston's mom ran the register at the Taco Bell on the corner of Lombard Street and Allen Boulevard in a poorer section of Beaverton, Oregon. Her name was Dawn. She was divorced and had three boys. She shared a three-bedroom apartment with another single mom and her own five children. They listened to Snoop Dogg and Ice-T, drank forty-ounce malt liquors, and walked over two miles round-trip every Saturday to watch the neighborhood boys play basketball at Schiffler Park.

On welfare-check days, Dawn went grocery shopping and brought home twelve-packs of Pepsi, stacks of frozen steaks, crinkly bags of potato chips, several gallons of 2-percent milk, and bag after bag of Malt-O-Meal cereal. The week before welfare checks came, they ate eggs and instant ramen—lots of ramen.

Her son Kris was my best friend in sixth grade. We often walked to Taco Bell together to visit his mother. She usually bought us a taco while we sat in a booth in the corner of the store and talked about bicycles, girls, and football. Once, on the way home from visiting his mom, Kris said, "She used to sell drugs, you know. We had plenty of money, and nobody thought she was a bad mom then."

15   My first night on the job, I work with Dave. He is seventeen years old, five-ten, and keeps his hair short, like a soldier. He goes to an alternative high school if he wakes up in time and is looking forward to enlisting in the military when he turns eighteen. His dad, who recently remarried and moved, told Dave he would have to find his own place to live. When Dave isn't sleeping on his friends' couches, he lives in his car, a 1982 Volkswagen Rabbit with a hole in the floor just beneath the gas pedal.

Dave works with me a few nights a week and knows the business well. He's quick with a mop, can make all the sandwiches blindfolded, and has the entire computer memorized. When he's not working, he hangs out in the restaurant lobby trying to steal Frosties and old fries when no one is looking. The manager says she will give him food if he needs it and asks that he not steal anymore. "Asking gets you nowhere," he says, and keeps stealing.

Because I live just two blocks from the store, I recognize a disproportionate number of the late-night drive-through customers. Mostly, I see parents of the scouts I work with, or other scout leaders, and occasionally a friend from school. When they pull up to the window and see me in the Wendy's hat and head-phones, the following conversation ensues:

"Joey, I didn't know you worked here! How's it going?"

"Good, good. Just flipping burgers."

20   "Hey, you've got to do what you've got to do."

Then I explain the job is temporary, and it's the only job in town that allows me to work at night so I can watch my son during the day while my wife fin-ishes school. I tell them in another month I'll be back in school and working at a better-paying, less humiliating campus job.

One evening a fellow scout leader comes through, and after an exchange similar to the one described above, he says, "Hey, more power to ya. I know a lot of people who think they're above that." He thanks me as I hand him his triple cheeseburger, and he drives around the corner and out of sight.

At 250 pounds, Danny really fills out his uniform. He played varsity football for the local high school, has earned his Eagle Scout award, and knows his way around a car engine. On several occasions he has changed spark plugs, jumped batteries, and even replaced brakes on the cars of fellow employees, usually right in the store parking lot.

Wendy's is the first job Danny has ever had. With six months' experience, he is the senior employee and is being considered for a management position. He brings in about $1,000 a month, much of which he gives to his grandmother. At closing, he always saves the good salads for me and talks the manager into letting me go home early. He likes listening to Metallica, working on his Trans Am, and talking with Tonya, a high school junior who also works at the store.

While I'm washing my hands in the bathroom at work, a well-groomed twenty-   25
something man standing at the sink next to me starts a conversation. "Do you like working the night shift?" he asks.

"It's not bad," I say, shaking my wet hands over the sink.

"How long have you worked here?"

"Two weeks."

"Have you ever thought about college?" he asks. I want to tell him I'm in the top 5 percent of students at my college, that I am two semesters away from graduating, and that I'm on my way to grad school to get a Ph.D. in English literature. Instead, I shrug and tell him the same line I tell everyone: "Oh yeah, I'm just working here until my wife finishes." He doesn't believe me. To him, I look like another wasted life, another victim. He thinks I got my girlfriend pregnant, that I never graduated from high school, that I can't do any better than flip burgers at two in the morning. He feels sorry for my kids.

"I only applied here because I knew I would get hired," says Sara the first night   30
I work with her. She is a nineteen-year-old single mother with a sixteen-month-old boy. She is very tall and wears her long brown hair in a ponytail pulled through the hole in the back of her Wendy's hat. I ask her why she needed a job so bad.

"I had to get one," she tells me. "My parole officer said it was the only way to stay out of jail." I start at this and then ask, "Why were you in jail?"

"Drugs," she says, and pauses, testing me. "I was wearing my boyfriend's jacket, and the cops found a heroin pipe in the pocket." I ask how long she was in jail. "One year," she tells me. "I just got out a month ago."

When I was in fifth grade, my dad got a job delivering pizza. As an eleven-year-old, pivoting on that blurry edge between boyhood and adolescence, I found myself bragging to my friends about the prospect of free pizza and then wishing I hadn't told them anything about my father's job. He worked a few nights a week, and when he came home, his uniform smelled like steaming cardboard and burnt cheese, but he always brought home pizza.

Oren is nineteen years old and works at Wendy's to pay for a cell-phone bill and to get out of the house. His parents are devout Mormons and think he is a disgrace to their entire family. He wants to sell marijuana because he believes he can do nothing else. "I don't do anything well," he tells me one night while washing dishes. "I don't know what I want to do with my life." He asks Sara to find some pot for him to sell.

Oren's mother is Japanese, born and raised, and speaks to her children in   35
her native tongue. That means Oren speaks Japanese and has family connections in Japan.

Oren also owns an AK-47 and likes to go up into the canyons and shoot jackrabbits. He showed me a picture once of a rabbit carcass out in the desert, its innards all blown out and dangling for the camera.

Tonight, while working the grill, Danny tells me he has never been on a date. "Girls don't like me," he says as he flips a row of sizzling, square quarter-pound patties. I can tell he believes it. Danny, by his own admission, is the kind of guy whom girls like for support. He is a gentleman, he asks thoughtful questions, and he's always willing to talk. He thinks his weight and his scruff turn girls off. He tells me he is going to ask Tonya to a movie this weekend but isn't sure she'll say yes. Later, Tonya comes into the store, and Danny disappears with her for a few minutes out in the lobby. He comes back with a large smile on his face and says, "I've got a date this weekend, can you work for me?"

I don't like when Dave works the front line with me. I can't make sandwiches very fast yet, and he gets tired of waiting. More than once he pushes me aside to finish an order. If he sees me hesitate on a step, he barks at me, "Red, green, red, green! Ketchup, pickle, tomato, lettuce! Come on, Joe, it's not that hard."

Later, while I'm mopping the floor at closing, Dave comes by and takes the mop from my hand. "Like this," he says, scrubbing the tile vigorously. He thrusts the mop back in my hands and walks away, rolling his eyes.

40   Chelsea is back at work tonight for the first time since having her baby. She appears fairly happy, and I am surprised at how well adjusted she seems to being a working mom. The phone rings several times, and Chelsea takes the calls in her office. She tells me her husband has lots of questions about putting the baby to bed. After the lobby closes, Chelsea disappears into the bathroom for nearly half an hour. This happens every time I work with her. I wonder if she is sick. Then I notice the breast pump in a case on her desk. Another employee tells me Chelsea has been expressing milk in one of the bathroom stalls on her breaks.

Danny and Tonya have been dating for two weeks. He shows up for his shift an hour early to see her before she gets off. They sit in the lobby holding hands and talking for almost the entire hour. When they're not in the store together, she sends text messages to his phone, which I catch him reading while he stands at the grill.

Tonight Danny approaches me while I'm opening boxes of French fries. He wants advice on how to ask Tonya to her junior prom. "I want to do something romantic," he says. I suggest Shakespeare's eighteenth sonnet. He has never heard of it. "'Shall I compare thee to a summer's day . . .'" I recite. "She'll love it." I print off the sonnet at home and bring it to work for him the next day. He writes it in a card and delivers it with flowers. Two weeks later, in a rented tux at Tonya's junior prom, Danny gets his first kiss.

I call my dad tonight. He asks about school, about my son, and about work. I tell him about Wendy's.

"What? Who?" he says.

"Me. I got a job at Wendy's." Long pause. "I needed a job I could do at   45
night." More silence. "It's not so bad." Still silence. "I work from nine P.M. to
one A.M. a few nights a week."

Just when I think the line must be disconnected, Dad clears his throat and
asks, "What happened to your computer job?"

"The guy ran out of work for me."

"Oh." More silence. I imagine he looks around the room to make sure no
one is listening before he says, "Wendy's? When did that happen?" I want to
tell him that it didn't *happen,* that it wasn't an accident, but I am stuck wondering how to make him understand, and at the same time wondering why I
should have to explain anything at all. I wonder what his reaction would be if
I had chosen to get more student loans instead of the part-time job. I choose to
say nothing. Then I offer him my employee discount on fries next time he is in
town. He says he'll take me up on it.

When I come into the store tonight, Dave is talking loudly to some employees
gathered in the lobby. I ask what all the laughing is about. They tell me that
last night Dave and Oren siphoned all the gas out of Dave's stepmother's four-
wheeler, and then they urinated on her car handles.

Everyone dreads working with Chelsea. When she is not in her office counting   50
the till or on the phone with her husband, she sits on the front counter and
complains about her mother-in-law. She does very little to help prep the store
for closing, and we rarely get out before two A.M.

Tonight she tells me about her mother-in-law's most recent visit. "I cleaned
the house for hours before she came," Chelsea says, nursing a Diet Coke.
"And the first thing she says when she gets there is how disgusting the place
looks. She won't even eat my cooking." According to Chelsea, her mother-in-
law has hated her ever since she got engaged. She wouldn't even visit except
that Chelsea has a baby now, and the mother-in-law feels obligated. Chelsea's
mother-in-law is disappointed that she is still working. "A mother's place is in
the home," she says to Chelsea. "Your kids will be ruined."

Tonight Waymon Hamilton comes through the drive-up window with his family.
Waymon lives around the corner from me, and his two sons are in my scout
troop, but they spend most of their free time traveling around the state playing
premier Little League baseball. They order a few value meals, some drinks, and
they ask how I'm doing. There is no hint of concern or condolence in their
voices, and I appreciate it.

I hand them their food and watch them drive away. Most people know Waymon the way I know him, as a dedicated father who works hard at a thankless
job to provide for his family. His unassuming nature and warm smile are what
I see when I think about him. Few people know him as the fleet-footed running
back who helped Brigham Young University win Holiday Bowls in 1981
and 1983. Few people know he holds several BYU scoring records, including

second place for touchdowns in a season, third in career touchdowns, and fifth for both season and career points scored. I didn't even know he played college football until someone mentioned it at a scout meeting. I once worked all day with Waymon, putting in a new driveway for a neighbor, and he never mentioned his football days once. He told me about his boys, about teaching public school in California, and about pouring lots of concrete.

After the store closes, I come home, take off my uniform, and climb into bed with my wife. She rolls over, tells me she loves me, and murmurs something about the smell of French fries. I kiss her on the cheek and close my eyes. It is winter, but the house is warm. My son is asleep in the next room. There is food in the fridge, and I have a job that pays an honest wage. In the morning I will make breakfast and send my wife off to school. And then, after the dishes are done, if the weather permits, my son and I will take a walk to the park.

MLA CITATION

Franklin, Joey. "Working at Wendy's." 2006. *The Norton Reader: An Anthology of Nonfiction.* Ed. Melissa A. Goldthwaite et al. 14th ed. New York: Norton, 2016. 80–86. Print.

QUESTIONS

1. What is Joey Franklin's attitude toward working at Wendy's? How does he demonstrate it? In answering these questions, look especially at the conclusion of the essay and at the details he chooses about how others respond to him.

2. Franklin uses considerable detail to develop his coworkers as characters (see paragraph 13 for an example). Which details do you find especially effective? Why?

3. Most of this essay is written in the present tense (with past-tense reflections about former jobs held by family members). What is the effect of Franklin's use of this verb tense? How would the essay differ if he wrote the entire essay in past tense?

4. Write an essay about a job you've held. Use dialogue and details to develop characters.

PROFILES

SCOTT RUSSELL SANDERS *Under the Influence*

MY FATHER DRANK. He drank as a gut-punched boxer gasps for breath, as a starving dog gobbles food— compulsively, secretly, in pain and trembling. I use the past tense not because he ever quit drinking but because he quit living. That is how the story ends for my father, age sixty-four, heart bursting, body cooling and forsaken on the linoleum of my brother's trailer. The story continues for my brother, my sister, my mother, and me, and will continue so long as memory holds.

In the perennial present of memory, I slip into the garage or barn to see my father tipping back the flat green bottles of wine, the brown cylinders of whiskey, the cans of beer disguised in paper bags. His Adam's apple bobs, the liquid gurgles, he wipes the sandy-haired back of a hand over his lips, and then, his bloodshot gaze bumping into me, he stashes the bottle or can inside his jacket, under the workbench, between two bales of hay, and we both pretend the moment has not occurred.

"What's up, buddy?" he says, thick-tongued and edgy.

"Sky's up," I answer, playing along.

"And don't forget prices," he grumbles. "Prices are always up. And taxes." 5

In memory, his white 1951 Pontiac with the stripes down the hood and the Indian head on the snout jounces to a stop in the driveway; or it is the 1956 Ford station wagon, or the 1963 Rambler shaped like a toad, or the sleek 1969 Bonneville that will do 120 miles per hour on straightaways; or it is the robin's-egg blue pickup, new in 1980, battered in 1981, the year of his death. He climbs out, grinning dangerously, unsteady on his legs, and we children interrupt our game of catch, our building of snow forts, our picking of plums, to watch in silence as he weaves past into the house, where he slumps into his overstuffed chair and falls asleep. Shaking her head, our mother stubs out the cigarette he has left smoldering in the ashtray. All evening, until our bedtimes, we tiptoe past him, as past a snoring dragon. Then we curl in our fearful sheets, listening. Eventually he wakes with a grunt, Mother slings accusations at him, he snarls back, she yells, he growls, their voices clashing. Before long, she retreats to their bedroom, sobbing—not from the blows of fists, for he never strikes her, but from the force of words.

Originally published in Harper's Magazine *(1989), an American monthly covering politics, society, culture, and the environment.*

Left alone, our father prowls the house, thumping into furniture, rummaging in the kitchen, slamming doors, turning the pages of the newspaper with a savage crackle, muttering back at the late-night drivel from television. The roof might fly off, the walls might buckle from the pressure of his rage. Whatever my brother and sister and mother may be thinking on their own rumpled pillows, I lie there hating him, loving him, fearing him, knowing I have failed him. I tell myself he drinks to ease an ache that gnaws at his belly, an ache I must have caused by disappointing him somehow, a murderous ache I should be able to relieve by doing all my chores, earning A's in school, winning baseball games, fixing the broken washer and the burst pipes, bringing in money to fill his empty wallet. He would not hide the green bottles in his tool box, would not sneak off to the barn with a lump under his coat, would not fall asleep in the daylight, would not roar and fume, would not drink himself to death, if only I were perfect.

I am forty-two as I write these words, and I know full well now that my father was an alcoholic, a man consumed by disease rather than by disappointment. What had seemed to me a private grief is in fact a public scourge. In the United States alone some ten or fifteen million people share his ailment, and behind the doors they slam in fury or disgrace, countless other children tremble. I comfort myself with such knowledge, holding it against the throb of memory like an ice pack against a bruise. There are keener sources of grief: poverty, racism, rape, war. I do not wish to compete for a trophy in suffering. I am only trying to understand the corrosive mixture of helplessness, responsibility, and shame that I learned to feel as the son of an alcoholic. I realize now that I did not cause my father's illness, nor could I have cured it. Yet for all this grown-up knowledge, I am still ten years old, my own son's age, and as that boy I struggle in guilt and confusion to save my father from pain.

Consider a few of our synonyms for *drunk*: tipsy, tight, pickled, soused, and plowed; stoned and stewed, lubricated and inebriated, juiced and sluiced; three sheets to the wind, in your cups, out of your mind, under the table; lit up, tanked up, wiped out; besotted, blotto, bombed, and buzzed; plastered, polluted, putrified; loaded or looped, boozy, woozy, fuddled, or smashed; crocked and shit-faced, corked and pissed, snockered and sloshed.

10   It is a mostly humorous lexicon, as the lore that deals with drunks—in jokes and cartoons, in plays, films, and television skits—is largely comic. Aunt Matilda nips elderberry wine from the sideboard and burps politely during supper. Uncle Fred slouches to the table glassy-eyed, wearing a lamp shade for a hat and murmuring, "Candy is dandy but liquor is quicker." Inspired by cocktails, Mrs. Somebody recounts the events of her day in a fuzzy dialect, while Mr. Somebody nibbles her ear and croons a bawdy song. On the sofa with Boyfriend, Daughter giggles, licking gin from her lips, and loosens the bows in her hair. Junior knocks back some brews with his chums at the Leopard Lounge and stumbles home to the wrong house, wonders foggily why he cannot locate his pajamas, and crawls naked into bed with the ugliest girl in school. The family dog

slurps from a neglected martini and wobbles to the nursery, where he vomits in Baby's shoe.

It is all great fun. But if in the audience you notice a few laughing faces turn grim when the drunk lurches on stage, don't be surprised, for these are the children of alcoholics. Over the grinning mask of Dionysus,[1] the leering mask of Bacchus,[2] these children cannot help seeing the bloated features of their own parents. Instead of laughing, they wince, they mourn. Instead of celebrating the drunk as one freed from constraints, they pity him as one enslaved. They refuse to believe *in vino veritas*,[3] having seen their befuddled parents skid away from truth toward folly and oblivion. And so these children bite their lips until the lush staggers into the wings.

My father, when drunk, was neither funny nor honest; he was pathetic, frightening, deceitful. There seemed to be a leak in him somewhere, and he poured in booze to keep from draining dry. Like a torture victim who refuses to squeal, he would never admit that he had touched a drop, not even in his last year, when he seemed to be dissolving in alcohol before our very eyes. I never knew him to lie about anything, ever, except about this one ruinous fact. Drowsy, clumsy, unable to fix a bicycle tire, throw a baseball, balance a grocery sack, or walk across the room, he was stripped of his true self by drink. In a matter of minutes, the contents of a bottle could transform a brave man into a coward, a buddy into a bully, a gifted athlete and skilled carpenter and shrewd businessman into a bumbler. No dictionary of synonyms for *drunk* would soften the anguish of watching our prince turn into a frog.

Father's drinking became the family secret. While growing up, we children never breathed a word of it beyond the four walls of our house. To this day, my brother and sister rarely mention it, and then only when I press them. I did not confess the ugly, bewildering fact to my wife until his wavering walk and slurred speech forced me to. Recently, on the seventh anniversary of my father's death, I asked my mother if she ever spoke of his drinking to friends. "No, no, never," she replied hastily. "I couldn't bear for anyone to know."

The secret bores under the skin, gets in the blood, into the bone, and stays there. Long after you have supposedly been cured of malaria, the fever can flare up, the tremors can shake you. So it is with the fevers of shame. You swallow the bitter quinine[4] of knowledge, and you learn to feel pity and compassion toward the drinker. Yet the shame lingers in your marrow, and, because of the shame, anger.

For a long stretch of my childhood we lived on a military reservation in Ohio, 15
an arsenal where bombs were stored underground in bunkers, vintage airplanes

1. Greek name for the god of wine and intoxication.
2. Roman name for the god of wine and intoxication.
3. Latin for "in wine is truth."
4. Drug used to treat malaria, made from the bark of the South American cinchona tree.

burst into flames, and unstable artillery shells boomed nightly at the dump. We had the feeling, as children, that we played in a mine field, where a heedless footfall could trigger an explosion. When Father was drinking, the house, too, became a mine field. The least bump could set off either parent.

The more he drank, the more obsessed Mother became with stopping him. She hunted for bottles, counted the cash in his wallet, sniffed at his breath. Without meaning to snoop, we children blundered left and right into damning evidence. On afternoons when he came home from work sober, we flung ourselves at him for hugs, and felt against our ribs the telltale lump in his coat. In the barn we tumbled on the hay and heard beneath our sneakers the crunch of buried glass. We tugged open a drawer in his workbench, looking for screwdrivers or crescent wrenches, and spied a gleaming six-pack among the tools. Playing tag, we darted around the house just in time to see him sway on the rear stoop and heave a finished bottle into the woods. In his good night kiss we smelled the cloying sweetness of Clorets, the mints he chewed to camouflage his dragon's breath.

I can summon up that kiss right now by recalling Theodore Roethke's[5] lines about his own father in "My Papa's Waltz":

> The whiskey on your breath
> Could make a small boy dizzy;
> But I hung on like death:
> Such waltzing was not easy.

Such waltzing was hard, terribly hard, for with a boy's scrawny arms I was trying to hold my tipsy father upright.

For years, the chief source of those incriminating bottles and cans was a grimy store a mile from us, a cinder block place called Sly's, with two gas pumps outside and a moth-eaten dog asleep in the window. A strip of flypaper, speckled the year round with black bodies, coiled in the doorway. Inside, on rusty metal shelves or in wheezing coolers, you could find pop and Popsicles, cigarettes, potato chips, canned soup, raunchy postcards, fishing gear, Twinkies, wine, and beer. When Father drove anywhere on errands, Mother would send us kids along as guards, warning us not to let him out of our sight. And so with one or more of us on board, Father would cruise up to Sly's, pump a dollar's worth of gas or plump the tires with air, and then, telling us to wait in the car, he would head for that fly-spangled doorway.

Dutiful and panicky, we cried, "Let us go in with you!"

20   "No," he answered. "I'll be back in two shakes."

"Please!"

"No!" he roared. "Don't you budge, or I'll jerk a knot in your tails!"

So we stayed put, kicking the seats, while he ducked inside. Often, when he had parked the car at a careless angle, we gazed in through the window and saw Mr. Sly fetching down from a shelf behind the cash register two green pints

5. American poet (1908–1963) whose father also drank a lot.

of Gallo wine. Father swigged one of them right there at the counter, stuffed the other in his pocket, and then out he came, a bulge in his coat, a flustered look on his red face.

Because the Mom and Pop who ran the dump were neighbors of ours, living just down the tar-blistered road, I hated them all the more for poisoning my father. I wanted to sneak in their store and smash the bottles and set fire to the place. I also hated the Gallo brothers, Ernest and Julio, whose jovial faces shone from the labels of their wine, labels I would find, torn and curled, when I burned the trash. I noted the Gallo brothers' address, in California, and I studied the road atlas to see how far that was from Ohio, because I meant to go out there and tell Ernest and Julio what they were doing to my father, and then, if they showed no mercy, I would kill them.

While growing up on the back roads and in the country schools and cramped   25
Methodist churches of Ohio and Tennessee, I never heard the word *alcoholism*, never happened across it in books or magazines. In the nearby towns, there were no addiction treatment programs, no community mental health centers, no Alcoholics Anonymous chapters, no therapists. Left alone with our grievous secret, we had no way of understanding Father's drinking except as an act of will, a deliberate folly or cruelty, a moral weakness, a sin. He drank because he chose to, pure and simple. Why our father, so playful and competent and kind when sober, would choose to ruin himself and punish his family, we could not fathom.

Our neighborhood was high on the Bible, and the Bible was hard on drunkards. "Woe to those who are heroes at drinking wine, and valiant men in mixing strong drink," wrote Isaiah. "The priest and the prophet reel with strong drink, they are confused with wine, they err in vision, they stumble in giving judgment. For all tables are full of vomit, no place is without filthiness." We children had seen those fouled tables at the local truck stop where the notorious boozers hung out, our father occasionally among them. "Wine and new wine take away the understanding," declared the prophet Hosea. We had also seen evidence of that in our father, who could multiply seven-digit numbers in his head when sober, but when drunk could not help us with fourth-grade math. Proverbs warned: "Do not look at wine when it is red, when it sparkles in the cup and goes down smoothly. At the last it bites like a serpent, and stings like an adder. Your eyes will see strange things, and your mind utter perverse things." Woe, woe.

Dismayingly often, these biblical drunkards stirred up trouble for their own kids. Noah made fresh wine after the flood, drank too much of it, fell asleep without any clothes on, and was glimpsed in the buff by his son Ham, whom Noah promptly cursed. In one passage—it was so shocking we had to read it under our blankets with flashlights—the patriarch Lot fell down drunk and slept with his daughters. The sins of the fathers set their children's teeth on edge.

Our ministers were fond of quoting St. Paul's pronouncement that drunkards would not inherit the kingdom of God. These grave preachers assured us that the wine referred to during the Last Supper was in fact grape juice. Bible and sermons and hymns combined to give us the impression that Moses should have brought down from the mountain another stone tablet, bearing the Eleventh Commandment: Thou shalt not drink.

The scariest and most illuminating Bible story apropos of drunkards was the one about the lunatic and the swine. Matthew, Mark, and Luke each told a version of the tale. We knew it by heart: When Jesus climbed out of his boat one day, this lunatic came charging up from the graveyard, stark naked and filthy, frothing at the mouth, so violent that he broke the strongest chains. Nobody would go near him. Night and day for years this madman had been wailing among the tombs and bruising himself with stones. Jesus took one look at him and said, "Come out of the man, you unclean spirits!" for he could see that the lunatic was possessed by demons. Meanwhile, some hogs were conveniently rooting nearby. "If we have to come out," begged the demons, "at least let us go into those swine." Jesus agreed. The unclean spirits entered the hogs, and the hogs rushed straight off a cliff and plunged into a lake. Hearing the story in Sunday school, my friends thought mainly of the pigs. (How big a splash did they make? Who paid for the lost pork?) But I thought of the redeemed lunatic, who bathed himself and put on clothes and calmly sat at the feet of Jesus, restored—so the Bible said—to "his right mind."

30   When drunk, our father was clearly in his wrong mind. He became a stranger, as fearful to us as any graveyard lunatic, not quite frothing at the mouth but fierce enough, quick-tempered, explosive; or else he grew maudlin and weepy, which frightened us nearly as much. In my boyhood despair, I reasoned that maybe he wasn't to blame for turning into an ogre. Maybe, like the lunatic, he was possessed by demons. I found support for my theory when I heard liquor referred to as "spirits," when the newspapers reported that somebody had been arrested for "driving under the influence," and when church ladies railed against that "demon drink."

If my father was indeed possessed, who would exorcise him? If he was a sinner, who would save him? If he was ill, who would cure him? If he suffered, who would ease his pain? Not ministers or doctors, for we could not bring ourselves to confide in them; not the neighbors, for we pretended they had never seen him drunk; not Mother, who fussed and pleaded but could not budge him; not my brother and sister, who were only kids. That left me. It did not matter that I, too, was only a child, and a bewildered one at that. I could not excuse myself.

On first reading a description of delirium tremens—in a book on alcoholism I smuggled from the library—I thought immediately of the frothing lunatic and the frenzied swine. When I read stories or watched films about grisly metamorphoses—Dr. Jekyll becoming Mr. Hyde,[6] the mild husband changing into a werewolf, the kindly neighbor taken over by a brutal alien—I could not help

6. London physician and his evil alter ego, in Robert Louis Stevenson's novella *The Strange Case of Dr. Jekyll and Mr. Hyde* (1886).

seeing my own father's mutation from sober to drunk. Even today, knowing better, I am attracted by the demonic theory of drink, for when I recall my father's transformation, the emergence of his ugly second self, I find it easy to believe in possession by unclean spirits. We never knew which version of Father would come home from work, the true or the tainted, nor could we guess how far down the slope toward cruelty he would slide.

How far a man *could* slide we gauged by observing our back-road neighbors—the out-of-work miners who had dragged their families to our corner of Ohio from the desolate hollows of Appalachia, the tight-fisted farmers, the surly mechanics, the balked and broken men. There was, for example, whiskey-soaked Mr. Jenkins, who beat his wife and kids so hard we could hear their screams from the road. There was Mr. Lavo the wino, who fell asleep smoking time and again, until one night his disgusted wife bundled up the children and went outside and left him in his easy chair to burn; he awoke on his own, staggered out coughing into the yard, and pounded her flat while the children looked on and the shack turned to ash. There was the truck driver, Mr. Sampson, who tripped over his son's tricycle one night while drunk and got so mad that he jumped into his semi and drove away, shifting through the dozen gears, and never came back. We saw the bruised children of these fathers clump onto our school bus, we saw the abandoned children huddle in the pews at church, we saw the stunned and battered mothers begging for help at our doors.

Our own father never beat us, and I don't think he ever beat Mother, but he threatened often. The Old Testament Yahweh was not more terrible in his wrath. Eyes blazing, voice booming, Father would pull out his belt and swear to give us a whipping, but he never followed through, never needed to, because we could imagine it so vividly. He shoved us, pawed us with the back of his hand, as an irked bear might smack a cub, not to injure, just to clear a space. I can see him grabbing Mother by the hair as she cowers on a chair during a nightly quarrel. He twists her neck back until she gapes up at him, and then he lifts over her skull a glass quart bottle of milk, the milk running down his forearm; and he yells at her, "Say just one more word, one goddamn word, and I'll shut you up!" I fear she will prick him with her sharp tongue, but she is terrified into silence, and so am I, and the leaking bottle quivers in the air, and milk slithers through the red hair of my father's uplifted arm, and the entire scene is there to this moment, the head jerked back, the club raised.

When the drink made him weepy, Father would pack a bag and kiss each   35
of us children on the head, and announce from the front door that he was moving out. "Where to?" we demanded, fearful each time that he would leave for good, as Mr. Sampson had roared away for good in his diesel truck. "Someplace where I won't get hounded every minute," Father would answer, his jaw quivering. He stabbed a look at Mother, who might say, "Don't run into the ditch before you get there," or, "Good riddance," and then he would slink away. Mother watched him go with arms crossed over her chest, her face closed like the lid on a box of snakes. We children bawled. Where could he go? To the truck stop, that den of iniquity? To one of those dark, ratty flophouses in town? Would he wind up sleeping under a railroad bridge or on a park bench or in a cardboard

box, mummied in rags, like the bums we had seen on our trips to Cleveland and Chicago? We bawled and bawled, wondering if he would ever come back.

He always did come back, a day or a week later, but each time there was a sliver less of him.

In Kafka's[7] *The Metamorphosis*, which opens famously with Gregor Samsa waking up from uneasy dreams to find himself transformed into an insect, Gregor's family keep reassuring themselves that things will be just fine again, "When he comes back to us." Each time alcohol transformed our father, we held out the same hope, that he would really and truly come back to us, our authentic father, the tender and playful and competent man, and then all things would be fine. We had grounds for such hope. After his weepy departures and chapfallen returns, he would sometimes go weeks, even months without drinking. Those were glad times. Joy banged inside my ribs. Every day without the furtive glint of bottles, every meal without a fight, every bedtime without sobs encouraged us to believe that such bliss might go on forever.

Mother was fooled by just such a hope all during the forty-odd years she knew this Greeley Ray Sanders. Soon after she met him in a Chicago delicatessen on the eve of World War II and fell for his butter-melting Mississippi drawl and his wavy red hair, she learned that he drank heavily. But then so did a lot of men. She would soon coax or scold him into breaking the nasty habit. She would point out to him how ugly and foolish it was, this bleary drinking, and then he would quit. He refused to quit during their engagement, however, still refused during the first years of marriage, refused until my sister came along. The shock of fatherhood sobered him, and he remained sober through my birth at the end of the war and right on through until we moved in 1951 to the Ohio arsenal, that paradise of bombs. Like all places that make a business of death, the arsenal had more than its share of alcoholics and drug addicts and other varieties of escape artists. There I turned six and started school and woke into a child's flickering awareness, just in time to see my father begin sneaking swigs in the garage.

He sobered up again for most of a year at the height of the Korean War, to celebrate the birth of my brother. But aside from that dry spell, his only breaks from drinking before I graduated from high school were just long enough to raise and then dash our hopes. Then during the fall of my senior year—the time of the Cuban missile crisis, when it seemed that the nightly explosions at the munitions dump and the nightly rages in our household might spread to engulf the globe—Father collapsed. His liver, kidneys, and heart all conked out. The doctors saved him, but only by a hair. He stayed in the hospital for weeks, going through a withdrawal so terrible that Mother would not let us visit him. If he wanted to kill himself, the doctors solemnly warned him, all he had to do was hit the bottle again. One binge would finish him.

40   Father must have believed them, for he stayed dry the next fifteen years. It was an answer to prayer, Mother said, it was a miracle. I believe it was a reflex

---

7. Franz Kafka (1883–1924), Prague-born novelist and short-story writer.

of fear, which he sustained over the years through courage and pride. He knew a man could die from drink, for his brother Roscoe had. We children never laid eyes on doomed Uncle Roscoe, but in the stories Mother told us he became a fairy-tale figure, like a boy who took the wrong turning in the woods and was gobbled up by the wolf.

The fifteen-year dry spell came to an end with Father's retirement in the spring of 1978. Like many men, he gave up his identity along with his job. One day he was a boss at the factory, with a brass plate on his door and a reputation to uphold; the next day he was a nobody at home. He and Mother were leaving Ontario, the last of the many places to which his job had carried them, and they were moving to a new house in Mississippi, his childhood stomping grounds. As a boy in Mississippi, Father sold Coca-Cola during dances while the moonshiners peddled their brew in the parking lot; as a young blade, he fought in bars and in the ring, seeking a state Golden Gloves championship; he gambled at poker, hunted pheasants, raced motorcycles and cars, played semiprofessional baseball, and, along with all his buddies—in the Black Cat Saloon, behind the cotton gin, in the woods—he drank. It was a perilous youth to dream of recovering.

After his final day of work, Mother drove on ahead with a car full of begonias and violets, while Father stayed behind to oversee the packing. When the van was loaded, the sweaty movers broke open a six-pack and offered him a beer.

"Let's drink to retirement!" they crowed. "Let's drink to freedom! to fishing! hunting! loafing! Let's drink to a guy who's going home!"

At least I imagine some such words, for that is all I can do, imagine, and I see Father's hand trembling in midair as he thinks about the fifteen sober years and about the doctors' warning, and he tells himself *God damnit, I am a free man,* and *Why can't a free man drink one beer after a lifetime of hard work?* and I see his arm reaching, his fingers closing, the can tilting to his lips. I even supply a label for the beer, a swaggering brand that promises on television to deliver the essence of life. I watch the amber liquid pour down his throat, the alcohol steal into his blood, the key turn in his brain.

Soon after my parents moved back to Father's treacherous stomping ground, my wife and I visited them in Mississippi with our five-year-old daughter. Mother had been too distraught to warn me about the return of the demons. So when I climbed out of the car that bright July morning and saw my father napping in the hammock, I felt uneasy, for in all his sober years I had never known him to sleep in daylight. Then he lurched upright, blinked his bloodshot eyes, and greeted us in a syrupy voice. I was hurled back helpless into childhood.

"What's the matter with Papaw?" our daughter asked.

"Nothing," I said. "Nothing!"

Like a child again, I pretended not to see him in his stupor, and behind my phony smile I grieved. On that visit and on the few that remained before his death, once again I found bottles in the workbench, bottles in the woods. Again his hands shook too much for him to run a saw, to make his precious miniature furniture, to drive straight down back roads. Again he wound up in the ditch, in the hospital, in jail, in treatment centers. Again he shouted and wept. Again he lied. "I never touched a drop," he swore. "Your mother's making it up."

I no longer fancied I could reason with the men whose names I found on the bottles—Jim Beam, Jack Daniels—nor did I hope to save my father by burning down a store. I was able now to press the cold statistics about alcoholism against the ache of memory: ten million victims, fifteen million, twenty. And yet, in spite of my age, I reacted in the same blind way as I had in childhood, ignoring biology, forgetting numbers, vainly seeking to erase through my efforts whatever drove him to drink. I worked on their place twelve and sixteen hours a day, in the swelter of Mississippi summers, digging ditches, running electrical wires, planting trees, mowing grass, building sheds, as though what nagged at him was some list of chores, as though by taking his worries on my shoulders I could redeem him. I was flung back into boyhood, acting as though my father would not drink himself to death if only I were perfect.

50   I failed of perfection; he succeeded in dying. To the end, he considered himself not sick but sinful. "Do you want to kill yourself?" I asked him. "Why not?" he answered. "Why the hell not? What's there to save?" To the end, he would not speak about his feelings, would not or could not give a name to the beast that was devouring him.

In silence, he went rushing off the cliff. Unlike the biblical swine, however, he left behind a few of the demons to haunt his children. Life with him and the loss of him twisted us into shapes that will be familiar to other sons and daughters of alcoholics. My brother became a rebel, my sister retreated into shyness, I played the stalwart and dutiful son who would hold the family together. If my father was unstable, I would be a rock. If he squandered money on drink, I would pinch every penny. If he wept when drunk—and only when drunk—I would not let myself weep at all. If he roared at the Little League umpire for calling my pitches balls, I would throw nothing but strikes. Watching him flounder and rage, I came to dread the loss of control. I would go through life without making anyone mad. I vowed never to put in my mouth or veins any chemical that would banish my everyday self. I would never make a scene, never lash out at the ones I loved, never hurt a soul. Through hard work, relentless work, I would achieve something dazzling—in the classroom, on the basketball floor, in the science lab, in the pages of books—and my achievement would distract the world's eyes from his humiliation. I would become a worthy sacrifice, and the smoke of my burning would please God.

It is far easier to recognize these twists in my character than to undo them. Work has become an addiction for me, as drink was an addiction for my father. Knowing this, my daughter gave me a placard for the wall: WORKAHOLIC. The labor is endless and futile, for I can no more redeem myself through work than I could redeem my father. I still panic in the face of other people's anger, because his drunken temper was so terrible. I shrink from causing sadness or disappointment even to strangers, as though I were still concealing the family shame. I still notice every twitch of emotion in the faces around me, having learned as a child to read the weather in faces, and I blame myself for their least pang of unhappiness or anger. In certain moods I blame myself for everything. Guilt burns like acid in my veins.

I am moved to write these pages now because my own son, at the age of ten, is taking on himself the griefs of the world, and in particular the griefs of his father. He tells me that when I am gripped by sadness he feels responsible; he feels there must be something he can do to spring me from depression, to fix my life. And that crushing sense of responsibility is exactly what I felt at the age of ten in the face of my father's drinking. My son wonders if I, too, am possessed. I write, therefore, to drag into the light what eats at me—the fear, the guilt, the shame—so that my own children may be spared.

I still shy away from nightclubs, from bars, from parties where the solvent is alcohol. My friends puzzle over this, but it is no more peculiar than for a man to shy away from the lions' den after seeing his father torn apart. I took my own first drink at the age of twenty-one, half a glass of burgundy. I knew the odds of my becoming an alcoholic were four times higher than for the sons of nonalcoholic fathers. So I sipped warily.

I still do—once a week, perhaps, a glass of wine, a can of beer, nothing   55
stronger, nothing more. I listen for the turning of a key in my brain.

MLA CITATION

Sanders, Scott Russell. "Under the Influence." 1989. *The Norton Reader: An Anthology of Nonfiction*. Ed. Melissa A. Goldthwaite et al. 14th ed. New York: Norton, 2016. 87–97. Print.

QUESTIONS

1. Scott Russell Sanders frequently punctuates his memories of his father with information from other sources—dictionaries, medical encyclopedias, poems and short stories, the Bible. What function do these sources perform? How do they enlarge and enrich Sanders's essay?

2. Why does Sanders conclude his essay with paragraphs 53–55? What effect do they create that would be lost without them?

3. Drawing on your memories of a friend or family member, write an essay about a problem that person had and its effect on your life.

ANNIE DILLARD   from *An American Childhood*

O NE SUNDAY AFTERNOON Mother wandered through our kitchen, where Father was making a sandwich and listening to the ball game. The Pirates were playing the New York Giants at Forbes Field. In those days, the Giants had a utility infielder named Wayne Terwilliger. Just as Mother passed through, the radio announcer cried—with undue drama—"Terwilliger bunts one!"

"Terwilliger bunts one?" Mother cried back, stopped short. She turned. "Is that English?"

"The player's name is Terwilliger," Father said. "He bunted."

"That's marvelous," Mother said. "'Terwilliger bunts one.' No wonder you listen to baseball. 'Terwilliger bunts one.'"

5   For the next seven or eight years, Mother made this surprising string of syllables her own. Testing a microphone, she repeated, "Terwilliger bunts one"; testing a pen or a typewriter, she wrote it. If, as happened surprisingly often in the course of various improvised gags, she pretended to whisper something else in my ear, she actually whispered, "Terwilliger bunts one." Whenever someone used a French phrase, or a Latin one, she answered solemnly, "Terwilliger bunts one." If Mother had had, like Andrew Carnegie, the opportunity to cook up a motto for a coat of arms, hers would have read simply and tellingly, "Terwilliger bunts one." (Carnegie's was "Death to Privilege.")

She served us with other words and phrases. On a Florida trip, she repeated tremulously, "That . . . is a royal poinciana." I don't remember the tree; I remember the thrill in her voice. She pronounced it carefully, and spelled it. She also liked to say "portulaca."

The drama of the words "Tamiami Trail" stirred her, we learned on the same Florida trip. People built Tampa on one coast, and they built Miami on another. Then—the height of visionary ambition and folly—they piled a slow, tremendous road through the terrible Everglades to connect them. To build the road, men stood sunk in muck to their armpits. They fought off cottonmouth moccasins and six-foot alligators. They slept in boats, wet. They blasted muck with dynamite, cut jungle with machetes; they laid logs, dragged drilling machines, hauled dredges, heaped limestone. The road took fourteen years to build up by the shovelful, a Panama Canal in reverse, and cost hundreds of lives from tropical, mosquito-carried diseases. Then, capping it all, some genius thought of the word Tamiami: they called the road from Tampa to Miami, this very road under our spinning wheels, the Tamiami Trail. Some called it Alligator Alley. Anyone could drive over this road without a thought.

Hearing this, moved, I thought all the suffering of road building was worth it (it wasn't my suffering), now that we had this new thing to hang these new

From An American Childhood (1987), Annie Dillard's memoir of growing up in Pittsburgh in the 1950s.

words on—Alligator Alley for those who liked things cute, and, for connois-
seurs like Mother, for lovers of the human drama in all its boldness and terror,
the Tamiami Trail.

Back home, Mother cut clips from reels of talk, as it were, and played
them back at leisure. She noticed that many Pittsburghers confuse "leave"
and "let." One kind relative brightened our morning by mentioning why she'd
brought her son to visit: "He wanted to come with me, so I left him." Mother
filled in Amy and me on locutions we missed. "I can't do it on Friday," her
pretty sister told a crowded dinner party, "because Friday's the day I lay in the
stores."

(All unconsciously, though, we ourselves used some pure Pittsburghisms.   10
We said "tele pole," pronounced "telly pole," for that splintery sidewalk post I
loved to climb. We said "slippy"—the sidewalks are "slippy." We said, "That's
all the farther I could go." And we said, as Pittsburghers do say, "This glass
needs washed," or "The dog needs walked"—a usage our father eschewed; he
knew it was not standard English, nor even comprehensible English, but he
never let on.)

"Spell 'poinsettia,'" Mother would throw out at me, smiling with pleasure.
"Spell 'sherbet.'" The idea was not to make us whizzes, but, quite the contrary,
to remind us—and I, especially, needed reminding—that we didn't know it all
just yet.

"There's a deer standing in the front hall," she told me one quiet evening
in the country.

"Really?"

"No. I just wanted to tell you something once without your saying, 'I know.'"

Supermarkets in the middle 1950s began luring, or bothering, customers by   15
giving out Top Value Stamps or Green Stamps. When, shopping with Mother,
we got to the head of the checkout line, the checker, always a young man, asked,
"Save stamps?"

"No," Mother replied genially, week after week, "I build model airplanes."
I believe she originated this line. It took me years to determine where the
joke lay.

Anyone who met her verbal challenges she adored. She had surgery on one
of her eyes. On the operating table, just before she conked out, she appealed
feelingly to the surgeon, saying, as she had been planning to say for weeks, "Will
I be able to play the piano?" "Not on me," the surgeon said. "You won't pull
that old one on me."

It was, indeed, an old one. The surgeon was supposed to answer, "Yes, my
dear, brave woman, you will be able to play the piano after this operation," to
which Mother intended to reply, "Oh, good, I've always wanted to play the
piano." This pat scenario bored her; she loved having it interrupted. It must
have galled her that usually her acquaintances were so predictably unalert; it
must have galled her that, for the length of her life, she could surprise everyone so continually, so easily, when she had been the same all along. At any rate,
she loved anyone who, as she put it, saw it coming, and called her on it.

She regarded the instructions on bureaucratic forms as straight lines. "Do you advocate the overthrow of the United States government by force or violence?" After some thought she wrote, "Force." She regarded children, even babies, as straight men. When Molly learned to crawl, Mother delighted in buying her gowns with drawstrings at the bottom, like Swee'pea's,[1] because, as she explained energetically, you could easily step on the drawstring without the baby's noticing, so that she crawled and crawled and crawled and never got anywhere except into a small ball at the gown's top.

20   When we children were young, she mothered us tenderly and dependably; as we got older, she resumed her career of anarchism. She collared us into her gags. If she answered the phone on a wrong number, she told the caller, "Just a minute," and dragged the receiver to Amy or me, saying, "Here, take this, your name is Cecile," or, worse, just, "It's for you." You had to think on your feet. But did you want to perform well as Cecile, or did you want to take pity on the wretched caller?

During a family trip to the Highland Park Zoo, Mother and I were alone for a minute. She approached a young couple holding hands on a bench by the seals, and addressed the young man in dripping tones: "Where have you been? Still got those baby-blue eyes; always did slay me. And this"—a swift nod at the dumbstruck young woman, who had removed her hand from the man's—"must be the one you were telling me about. She's not so bad, really, as you used to make out. But listen, you know how I miss you, you know where to reach me, same old place. And there's Ann over there—see how she's grown? See the blue eyes?"

And off she sashayed, taking me firmly by the hand, and leading us around briskly past the monkey house and away. She cocked an ear back, and both of us heard the desperate man begin, in a high-pitched wail, "I swear, I never saw her before in my life. . . ."

On a long, sloping beach by the ocean, she lay stretched out sunning with Father and friends, until the conversation gradually grew tedious, when without forethought she gave a little push with her heel and rolled away. People were stunned. She rolled deadpan and apparently effortlessly, arms and legs extended and tidy, down the beach to the distant water's edge, where she lay at ease just as she had been, but half in the surf, and well out of earshot.

She dearly loved to fluster people by throwing out a game's rules at whim—when she was getting bored, losing in a dull sort of way, and when everybody else was taking it too seriously. If you turned your back, she moved the checkers around on the board. When you got them all straightened out, she denied she'd touched them; the next time you turned your back, she lined them up on the rug or hid them under your chair. In a betting rummy game called Michigan, she routinely played out of turn, or called out a card she didn't hold, or counted backward, simply to amuse herself by causing an uproar and watching

---

1. Infant in the comic strip *Popeye* (first appearance: 1929) by Elzie Crisler Segar.

the rest of us do double takes and have fits. (Much later, when serious suitors came to call, Mother subjected them to this fast card game as a trial by ordeal; she used it as an intelligence test and a measure of spirit. If the poor man could stay a round without breaking down or running out, he got to marry one of us, if he still wanted to.)

She excelled at bridge, playing fast and boldly, but when the stakes were low and the hands dull, she bid slams for the devilment of it, or raised her opponents' suit to bug them, or showed her hand, or tossed her cards in a handful behind her back in a characteristic swift motion accompanied by a vibrantly innocent look. It drove our stolid father crazy. The hand was over before it began, and the guests were appalled. How do you score it, who deals now, what do you do with a crazy person who is having so much fun? Or they were down seven, and the guests were appalled. "Pam!" "Dammit, Pam!" He groaned. What ails such people? What on earth possesses them? He rubbed his face.

She was an unstoppable force; she never let go. When we moved across town, she persuaded the U.S. Post Office to let her keep her old address—forever—because she'd had stationery printed. I don't know how she did it. Every new post office worker, over decades, needed to learn that although the Doaks' mail is addressed to here, it is delivered to there.

Mother's energy and intelligence suited her for a greater role in a larger arena—mayor of New York, say—than the one she had. She followed American politics closely; she had been known to vote for Democrats. She saw how things should be run, but she had nothing to run but our household. Even there, small minds bugged her; she was smarter than the people who designed the things she had to use all day for the length of her life.

"Look," she said. "Whoever designed this corkscrew never used one. Why would anyone sell it without trying it out?" So she invented a better one. She showed me a drawing of it. The spirit of American enterprise never faded in Mother. If capitalizing and tooling up had been as interesting as theorizing and thinking up, she would have fired up a new factory every week, and chaired several hundred corporations.

"It grieves me," she would say, "it grieves my heart," that the company that made one superior product packaged it poorly, or took the wrong tack in its advertising. She knew, as she held the thing mournfully in her two hands, that she'd never find another. She was right. We children wholly sympathized, and so did Father; what could she do, what could anyone do, about it? She was Samson in chains.[2] She paced.

She didn't like the taste of stamps so she didn't lick stamps; she licked the corner of the envelope instead. She glued sandpaper to the sides of kitchen drawers, and under kitchen cabinets, so she always had a handy place to strike a match. She designed, and hounded workmen to build against all norms, doubly wide kitchen counters and elevated bathroom sinks. To splint a finger, she

25

30

2. Israelite judge who fought the Philistines, to whom he was betrayed by Delilah, his lover.

stuck it in a lightweight cigar tube. Conversely, to protect a pack of cigarettes, she carried it in a Band-Aid box. She drew plans for an over-the-finger tooth-brush for babies, an oven rack that slid up and down, and—the family favorite—Lendalarm. Lendalarm was a beeper you attached to books (or tools) you loaned friends. After ten days, the beeper sounded. Only the rightful owner could silence it.

She repeatedly reminded us of P. T. Barnum's dictum: You could sell any-thing to anybody if you marketed it right. The adman who thought of making Americans believe they needed underarm deodorant was a visionary. So, too, was the hero who made a success of a new product, Ivory soap. The executives were horrified, Mother told me, that a cake of this stuff floated. Soap wasn't supposed to float. Anyone would be able to tell it was mostly whipped-up air. Then some inspired adman made a leap: Advertise that it floats. Flaunt it. The rest is history.

She respected the rare few who broke through to new ways. "Look," she'd say, "here's an intelligent apron." She called upon us to admire intelligent con-trol knobs and intelligent pan handles, intelligent andirons and picture frames and knife sharpeners. She questioned everything, every pair of scissors, every knitting needle, gardening glove, tape dispenser. Hers was a restless mental vigor that just about ignited the dumb household objects with its force.

Torpid conformity was a kind of sin; it was stupidity itself, the mighty stream against which Mother would never cease to struggle. If you held no minority opinions, or if you failed to risk total ostracism for them daily, the world would be a better place without you.

Always I heard Mother's emotional voice asking Amy and me the same few questions: Is that your own idea? Or somebody else's? "*Giant* is a good movie," I pronounced to the family at dinner. "Oh, really?" Mother warmed to these occasions. She all but rolled up her sleeves. She knew I hadn't seen it. "Is that your considered opinion?"

35   She herself held many unpopular, even fantastic, positions. She was scath-ingly sarcastic about the McCarthy hearings[3] while they took place, right on our living-room television; she frantically opposed Father's wait-and-see calm. "We don't know enough about it," he said. "I do," she said. "I know all I need to know."

She asserted, against all opposition, that people who lived in trailer parks were not bad but simply poor, and had as much right to settle on beautiful land, such as rural Ligonier, Pennsylvania, as did the oldest of families in the finest of hidden houses. Therefore, the people who owned trailer parks, and sought zoning changes to permit trailer parks, needed our help. Her profound belief that the country-club pool sweeper was a person, and that the department-store

3. In televised hearings in 1954, the United States Army accused Wisconsin senator Joseph R. McCarthy of improperly seeking preferential treatment for a former col-league then in the service. Senator McCarthy, widely known as a Communist hunter, accused the Army of covering up certain espionage action, which led to the senator's loss of public favor. He was officially condemned by the Senate in December 1954.

saleslady, the bus driver, telephone operator, and housepainter were people, and even in groups the steelworkers who carried pickets and the Christmas shoppers who clogged intersections were people—this was a conviction common enough in democratic Pittsburgh, but not altogether common among our friends' parents, or even, perhaps, among our parents' friends.

Opposition emboldened Mother, and she would take on anybody on any issue—the chairman of the board, at a cocktail party, on the current strike; she would fly at him in a flurry of passion, as a songbird selflessly attacks a big hawk.

"Eisenhower's going to win," I announced after school. She lowered her magazine and looked me in the eyes: "How do you know?" I was doomed. It was fatal to say, "Everyone says so." We all knew well what happened. "Do you consult this Everyone before you make your decisions? What if Everyone decided to round up all the Jews?" Mother knew there was no danger of cowing me. She simply tried to keep us all awake. And in fact it was always clear to Amy and me, and to Molly when she grew old enough to listen, that if our classmates came to cruelty, just as much as if the neighborhood or the nation came to madness, we were expected to take, and would be each separately capable of taking, a stand.

MLA CITATION

Dillard, Annie. "An American Childhood." 1987. *The Norton Reader: An Anthology of Nonfiction*. Ed. Melissa A. Goldthwaite et al. 14th ed. New York: Norton, 2016. 98–103. Print.

QUESTIONS

1. Annie Dillard piles up examples in this excerpt, barely creating transitions between them. What do the many examples add up to? What is the overall point she wishes to make?

2. When this piece was originally published in Dillard's *An American Childhood*, the chapter had no title. If you could title this piece, what would that title be? Why?

3. Dillard, like Scott Russell Sanders in "Under the Influence" (pp. 87–97), writes about a parent. Compare the two essays. How do they differ? How are they similar?

4. Do some freewriting about one of your parents or someone important in your life when you were a child. Like Dillard, use as many specific examples as possible to communicate that person's character and personality.

David James Duncan   *The Mickey Mantle Koan*

(for my mother)

On April 6, 1965, my brother Nicholas John Duncan died of what his surgeons called "complications" after three unsuccessful open-heart operations. He was seventeen at the time—four years my elder to the very day. He'd been the fastest sprinter in his high school class till the valve in his heart began to close, but he was so bonkers about baseball that he'd preferred playing a mediocre JV shortstop to starring at varsity track. As a ballplayer he was a competent fielder, had a strong and fairly accurate arm and stole bases with ease—when he reached them. But no matter how much he practiced or what stances, grips or self-hypnotic tricks he tried, he lacked the hand-eye magic that consistently lays bat-fat against ball, and remained one of the weakest hitters on his team.

John lived his entire life on the outskirts of Portland, Oregon—650 miles from the nearest Major League team—and in franchiseless cities in the fifties and early sixties there were really just two types of fans: those who thought the Yankees stood for everything right with America, and those who thought they stood for everything wrong with it. My brother was an extreme manifestation of the former type. He conducted a one-man campaign to notify the world that Roger Maris's sixty-one homers in '61 came in three fewer at-bats than Babe Ruth's sixty in '27. He maintained—all statistical evidence to the contrary—that Clete Boyer was a better third baseman than his brother, Ken, simply because Clete was a Yankee. He combed the high school every October for fools willing to bet against Whitey Ford in the World Series, and if he couldn't find one there he knew he'd find one at home: me. He tried to enhance our games of catch by portraying the first two-thirds of Kubek to Richardson to Skowron double plays, but the intensity of his Kubek for some reason caused his Richardson to imagine my "Moose" to be the genuine six-four article—so off the ball would sail into the neighbor's apple orchard. He may not have been the only kid on the block who considered Casey Stengel the greatest sage since Solomon,[1] but I'm sure he was the only one who considered Yogi Berra the second greatest. And though he would concede that Ted Williams, and later Willie Mays, had slightly more productive careers than Mickey Mantle, even this was for a pro-Yankee reason: Mantle was his absolute hero, but his tragic hero. The Mick, my brother maintained, was the greatest raw talent of all time. He was one to whom great gifts were given, from whom great gifts had been ripped

Published in Harper's Magazine *(1992), an American monthly covering politics, society, culture, and the environment. This essay was also included in David James Duncan's collection* River Teeth: Stories and Writings *(1995).*

1. In the Bible, King of Israel and son of David, known for his wisdom.

away, and the more scarred his knees became, the more frequently he fanned, the more flagrant his limp and apologetic his smile, the more John revered him. And toward this single Yankee I too was able to feel a touch of reverence, if only because, on the subject of scars, I considered my brother an unimpeachable authority: he'd worn one from the time he was eight, compliments of the Mayo Clinic, that wrapped clear around his chest in a wavy line, like stitching round a clean white baseball.[2]

Yankees aside, John and I had more in common than a birthday. We bickered regularly with our middle brother and little sister but almost never with each other. We were both bored, occasionally to insurrection, by schoolgoing, church-going and any game or sport that didn't involve a ball. We both preferred, as a mere matter of style, Indians to cowboys, knights of the road to Knights of Columbus,[3] Buster Keaton to Charlie Chaplin, Gary Cooper to John Wayne, deadbeats to brown-nosers, and even brown-nosers to Elvis Presley. We shared a single devil's food chocolate cake on our joint birthday, invariably annihilating the candle flames with a tandem blowing effort, only to realize that we'd once again forgotten to make a wish. And whenever the parties were over or the house was stuffy, the parents cranky or the TV insufferably dumb, whenever we were restless, punchy or just feeling the "nuthin' to do" feeling, catch—with a hardball—was the nuthin' John and I chose to do.

We were not exclusive, or not by intention: our father and middle brother and an occasional cousin or friend would join us now and then. But something in most people's brains or bloodstreams sent them bustling off to more industrious endeavors before the real rhythm of the thing ever took hold. Genuine catch-playing occurs in a double-limbo between busyness and idleness, and between the imaginary and the real. As with any contemplative pursuit, it takes time, and the ability to forget time, to slip into this dual limbo, and to discover (i.e. lose) oneself in the music of the game.

It helps to have a special spot to play. Ours was a shaded, ninety-foot corridor between one neighbor's apple orchard and the other's stand of old-growth Douglas firs, on a stretch of lawn so lush and mossy it sucked the heat out of even the hottest grounders. I always stood in the north, John in the south. When I had to chase his wild throws into the orchard I'd sometimes hide the ball in my shirt and fire back a Gravenstein,[4] leaving him to judge, while it was in the air, whether it was fit to catch and eat or an overripe rotter about to splatter in

5

---

2. All baseball players mentioned in this paragraph played with the New York Yankees in the 1950s and 1960s, with the exception of Babe Ruth, who played for the Yankees in the 1920s and 1930s; Ted Williams, who played for the Boston Red Sox in the 1940s and 1950s; and Willie Mays, who played for the New York and San Francisco Giants, in the 1950s and 1960s.

3. Knights of the road, term used for both vagrants and commercial truck drivers; Knights of Columbus, Catholic fraternal service organization that helps those in need.

4. Kind of apple.

his mitt. When he chased my dud pegs into the firs, he'd give me an innocent, uncomplaining smile as he trotted back into position—then rifle a cone, dirt clod or stone at my head.

But these antics were the exception. The deep shade, the two-hundred-foot firs, the mossy footing and fragrance of apples all made it a setting more conducive to mental-vacationing than to any kind of disciplined effort, so a vigorous serenity was the rule. We might call balls and strikes for an imaginary inning or two, throw each other a few pop-ups or grounders or maybe count the number of errorless catches and throws we could make (three-hundreds were common, and our record was high in the eight-hundreds). But as our movements became fluid and the throws brisk and accurate, the pretense of practice would inevitably fade, and we'd just aim for the chest and fire, *hisssss pop! hisssss pop!* till a meal, a duty or total darkness forced us to recall that this is the world in which even timeless pursuits come to an end.

Our talk must have seemed strange to eavesdroppers. We lived in our bodies during catch, and our minds and mouths, though still operative, were just along for the ride. Most of the noise I made was with the four or five pieces of Bazooka I was invariably working over, though once the gum lost its sugar I'd sometimes narrate our efforts in a stream-of-doggerel play-by-play. My brother's speech was a bit more coherent, but of no greater didactic intent: he poured out idle litanies of Yankee worship or even idler braggadocio à la Dizzy Dean,[5] all of it artfully spiced with spat sunflower-seed husks.

Dan Jenkins[6] defined the catch-player perfectly when he spoke of athletes who "mostly like to stand around, chew things, spit and scratch their nuts." Not too complimentary a definition, perhaps, yet from the catch-playing point of view, what are the alternatives? Why run around wrecking the world for pay when you could be standing in one place transcending time? Why chew Rolaids, swallow your spit and feel too inhibited to scratch where it itches when you could be chewing Day's Work or Double Bubble, shooting end-over-enders, easing the itch and firing off hisses and pops? Whatever he really meant, Yogi Berra defended catch-players best. He said: "If you can't copy 'em, don't imitate 'em."[7]

But one day, when we were sixteen and twelve respectively, my big brother surprised me out there in our corridor. Snagging a low throw, he closed his mitt round the ball, stuck it under his arm, stared off into the trees and got serious for a minute. All his life, he said, he'd struggled to be a shortstop and a hitter,

5. Nickname of Jay Hanna Dean (1910–1974), Major League Baseball player mainly in the 1930s until injuries shortened his career. He then went into sports broadcasting and was known for using the word "ain't" and mispronouncing or using made-up words.

6. Sportswriter (b. 1929) who wrote for many publications, including *Sports Illustrated* and *Golf Digest*.

7. Reversal of Yogi Berra's statement, "If you can't imitate him, don't copy him."

to pretend that I wasn't hurting, that I hadn't expected or wanted any more from the ball than I got, that I'd harbored no desire for any sort of sign, any imprimatur, any flicker of recognition from an Above or a Beyond.

I then began falling to pieces, for lack of that sign.

The bad thing about falling to pieces is that it hurts. The good thing about it is that once you're lying there in shards you've got nothing left to protect, and so have no reason not to be honest. I got honest with Mantle's baseball: I finally picked the thing up, read it once more and admitted for the first time that I was *pissed*. As is always the case with arriving baseballs, timing is the key—and this cheery orb was inscribed on the day its recipient lay dying and arrived on the day he was being embalmed! This was *not* a "harmless coincidence." It was the shabbiest, most embittering joke that Providence had ever played on me. My best friend and brother was dead, dead, dead, Mantle's damned ball and best wishes made that loss far less tolerable, and *that*, I told myself, really *was* all there was to it.

I hardened my heart, quit the baseball team, went out for golf. I practiced like a zealot, cheated like hell, kicked my innocuous, naive little opponents all over the course. I sold my beautiful inherited mitt for a pittance.

But, as is usual in baseball stories, that wasn't all there was to it.

I'd never heard of Zen koans at the time, and Mickey Mantle is certainly no *roshi*.[13] But baseball and Zen are two things that Americans and Japanese have each imported without embargo; and *roshis* are men famous for hitting things hard with a big wooden stick; and a koan is a perfectly nonsensical or nonsequacious statement given by an old pro (*roshi*) to a rookie (layman or monk); and the stress of living with and meditating upon one of these mind-numbing pieces of nonsense is said to eventually prove illuminating. So I know of no better way to describe what the message on the ball became for me than to call it a koan.

In the first place, the damned thing's batteries just wouldn't run down. For weeks, months, *years*, every time I saw those ten blithe, blue-inked words they knocked me off balance like a sudden shove from behind. They were an emblem of all the false assurances of surgeons, all the futile prayers of preachers, all the hollowness of good-guys-can't-lose baseball stories I'd ever heard or read. They were graffiti scrawled across my brother's ruined chest. They were a throw I'd never catch. And yet—REACH, the ball said, THE SIGN OF QUALITY. So year after year I kept trying, kept struggling to somehow answer the koan.

I hit adolescence, enrolled in the school of pain-without-dignity called "puberty," nearly flunked, then graduated almost without noticing. In the process I discovered that there was life after baseball, that America was not the Good Guy, that Jesus was not a Christian and that some girls, contrary to my boyhood opinion, were nothing like 95 percent Crud; I discovered Europe and metaphysics, high lakes and wilderness, black tea, rock, Bach, trout streams, the Orient, my life's work and a hundred other grown-up tools and toys. But

25

30

13. Respected older teacher in Zen Buddhism.

amid these maturations and transformations there was an unwanted constant: in the presence of that confounded ball, I remained thirteen years old. One peek at the "Your Pal" koan and whatever maturity or equanimity I possessed was repossessed, leaving me irked as any stumped monk or slumping slugger.

It took four years to solve the riddle on the ball. It was autumn when it happened—the same autumn during which I'd grown a little older than my big brother would ever be. As often happens with koan solutions, I wasn't even thinking about the ball when it came. As is also the case with koans, I can't possibly paint in words the impact of the response, the instantaneous healing that took place or the ensuing sense of lightness and release. But I'll say what I can.

The solution came during a fit of restlessness brought on by a warm Indian summer evening. I'd just finished watching the Miracle Mets blitz the Orioles in the World Series and was standing alone in the living room, just staring out at the yard and fading sunlight, feeling a little stale and fidgety, when I realized that these were just the sort of fidgets I'd never had to suffer when John was alive—because we'd always work our way through them with a long game of catch. With that thought, and at that moment, I simply saw my brother catch, then throw a baseball. It occurred in neither an indoors nor an outdoors. It lasted a couple of seconds, no more. But I saw him so clearly, and he then vanished so completely, that my eyes blurred, my throat and chest ached, and I didn't need to see Mantle's baseball to realize exactly what I'd wanted from it all along:

From the moment I'd first laid eyes on it, all I'd wanted was to take that immaculate ball out to our corridor on an evening just like this one, to take my place near the apples in the north and to find my brother waiting beneath the immense firs to the south. All I'd wanted was to pluck that too-perfect ball off its pedestal and proceed, without speaking, to play catch so long and hard that the grass stains and nicks and the sweat of our palms would finally obliterate every last trace of Mantle's blue ink, till all he would have sent us was a grass-green, earth-brown, beat-up old baseball. Beat-up old balls were all we'd ever had anyhow. They were all we'd ever needed. The dirtier they were, the more frayed the skin and stitching, the louder they'd hissed and the better they'd curved. And remembering this—recovering in an instant the knowledge of how little we'd needed in order to be happy—my grief for my brother became palpable, took on shape and weight, color and texture, even an odor: the measure of my loss was precisely the difference between one of the beat-up, earth-colored, grass-scented balls that had given us such happiness, and this antiseptic-smelling, sad-making icon ball on its bandage-box pedestal. And as I felt this—as I stood there palpating my grief, shifting it round like a throwing stone in my hand—I suddenly fell through a floor inside myself, landing in a deeper, brighter chamber just in time to feel something or someone tell me, *But who's to say we need even an old ball to be happy? Who's to say we couldn't do with less? Who's to say we couldn't still be happy—with no ball at all?*

And with that, the koan was solved.

35   I can't explain why this felt like a complete solution. Reading the bare words, two decades later, they don't look like much of a solution. But a koan

answer is not a verbal or a literary or even a personal experience. It's a spiritual experience. And a boy, a man, a "me," does not have spiritual experiences: only the spirit has spiritual experiences. That's why churches so soon become bandage boxes propping up antiseptic icons that lost all value the instant they were removed from the greens and browns of grass and dirt and life. It's also why a good Zen monk always states a koan solution in the barest possible terms. "No ball at all!" is, perhaps, all I should have written about this thing—because then no one would have an inkling of what was meant, and so could form no misconceptions, and the immediacy and integrity and authority of the experience would be safely locked away. ("If you can't copy 'em, don't imitate 'em.") But it's a time-honored tradition, in baseball, to interview the bubbling, burbling athlete when the game is done. So I've bubbled and burbled.

This has gotten a bit iffy for a sports story. But jocks die, and then what? The brother I played a thousand games of catch with is dead, and so will I be, and unless you're one hell of an athlete, so will you be. In the face of this fact I find it more than a little consoling to recall my encounter, one October day, with an unspeakable spark in me that needs *nothing*—not even a dog-eared ball—to be happy. From that day forward the relic on the mantel lost its irksome overtones and became an autographed ball—nothing more, nothing less. It lives in my study now, beside an old beater ball my brother and I wore out, and it gives me a satisfaction I can't explain to sit back now and then and compare the two—though I'd still gladly trash the white one for a good game of catch.

As for the ticklish timing of its arrival, I only recently learned a couple of facts that shed some light. First I discovered—in a copy of the old letter my mother wrote to Mantle—that she'd made it clear that my brother was dying. So the Mick had signed the ball knowing perfectly well what the situation might be when it arrived. Second, I found out that my mother actually went ahead and showed the ball to my brother. True, he was embalmed when she did this. But what was embalmed, the koan taught me, wasn't all of him. And I've no reason to assume that the unembalmed part had changed much, so far. It should be remembered, then, that while he lived my brother was more than a little vain, that he'd been compelled by his death to leave a handsome head of auburn hair behind, and that when my mother and Mantle's baseball arrived at the funeral parlor, that hair was being prepared for an open-casket funeral by a couple of cadaverous-looking yahoos whose oily manners, hair and clothes made it plain they didn't know Kookie Kookson from Roger Maris or Solid Cool from Kool-Aid. What if this pair took it into their heads to spruce John up for the Hereafter with a Bible Camp cut? Worse yet, what if they tried to show what sensitive, accommodating artists they were and decked him out like a damned Elvis the Pelvis *greaser*? I'm not trying to be morbid here. I'm trying to state the facts. "The Bod" my brother had so delighted in grooming was about to be seen for the last time by all his buddies, his family and a girlfriend who was only 1.5 percent Crud, and the part of the whole ensemble he'd been most fastidious about—the coiffure—was completely out of his control! He *needed* "Best Wishes." He needed a "Pal." Preferably one with a comb.

Enter my mother—who took one look at what the two rouge-and-casket-wallahs were doing to the hair, said "No no no!" produced a snapshot, told them, "He wants it *exactly* like this," sat down to critique their efforts and kept on critiquing till in the end you'd have thought John had dropped in to groom himself.

Only then did she ask them to leave. Only then did she pull the autographed ball from her purse, share it with her son, read him the inscription.

40   As is always the case with arriving baseballs, timing is the key. Thanks to the timing that has made the Mick a legend, my brother, the last time we all saw him, looked completely himself.

I return those best wishes to my brother's pal.

MLA CITATION

Duncan, David James. "The Mickey Mantle Koan." 1992. *The Norton Reader: An Anthology of Nonfiction*. Ed. Melissa A. Goldthwaite et al. 14th ed. New York: Norton, 2016. 104–14. Print.

QUESTIONS

1. David James Duncan includes a list in paragraph 3 to show his and his brother John's preferences. In paragraph 14 he includes other lists describing John. What do these lists tell you about John? How do they reveal his character?

2. The autographed baseball functions as a symbol in this essay. What does it symbolize? In what way did the ball from Mickey Mantle serve another purpose even though John did not see the ball when he was alive?

3. Write an essay about someone you know well. As Duncan does, include lists of specific qualities and preferences that reveal that person's character. Also include anecdotes to provide a greater understanding of that person.

TOM WOLFE   *Yeager*

ANYONE WHO TRAVELS VERY MUCH ON AIRLINES in the United States soon gets to know the voice of *the airline pilot*. . . . coming over the intercom . . . with a particular drawl, a particular folksiness, a particular down-home calmness that is so exaggerated it begins to parody itself (nevertheless!—it's reassuring) . . . the voice that tells you, as the airliner is caught in thunderheads and goes bolting up and down a thousand feet at a single gulp, to check your seat belts because "it might get a little choppy" . . . the voice that tells you (on a flight from Phoenix

From The Right Stuff (1979), *Tom Wolfe's account of American test pilots and the first U.S. astronauts, which was made into a 1983 movie. "Yeager" refers to Chuck Yeager, a famous Air Force general and an accomplished pilot.*

preparing for its final approach into Kennedy Airport, New York, just after dawn): "Now, folks, uh . . . this is the captain. . . . ummmm . . . We've got a little ol' red light up here on the control panel that's tryin' to tell us that the *landin'* gears're not . . . uh . . . *lockin'* into position when we lower 'em . . . Now . . . *I* don't believe that little ol' red light knows what it's *talkin'* about—I believe it's that little ol' red light that iddn' workin' right" . . . faint chuckle, long pause, as if to say, *I'm not even sure all this is really worth going into—still, it may amuse you* . . . "But . . . I guess to play it by the rules, we oughta *humor* that little ol' light. . . . so we're gonna take her down to about, oh, two or three hundred feet over the runway at Kennedy, and the folks down there on the ground are gonna see if they caint give us a *vi*sual inspection of those ol' landin' gears"—with which he is obviously on intimate ol'-buddy terms, as with every other working part of this mighty ship—"and if I'm right . . . they're gonna tell us everything is copa*ce*tic all the way aroun' an' we'll jes take her on in" . . . and, after a couple of low passes over the field, the voice returns: "Well, folks, those folks down there on the ground—it must be too early for 'em or somethin'—I 'spect they still got the *sleep*ers in their eyes. . . . 'cause they say they caint tell if those ol' landin' gears are all the way down or not . . . But, you know, up here in the cockpit we're convinced they're all the way down, so we're jes gonna take her on in. . . . And oh" . . . (*I almost forgot*) . . . "while we take a little swing out over the ocean an' empty some of that surplus fuel we're not gonna be needin' anymore—that's what you might be seein' comin' out of the wings—our lovely little ladies . . . if they'll be so kind . . . they're gonna go up and down the aisles and show you how we do what we call 'assumin' the position'" . . . another faint chuckle (*We do this so often, and it's so much fun, we even have a funny little name for it*) . . . and the stewardesses, a bit grimmer, by the looks of them, than *that voice,* start telling the passengers to take their glasses off and take the ballpoint pens and other sharp objects out of their pockets, and they show them *the position,* with the head lowered. . . . while down on the field at Kennedy the little yellow emergency trucks start roaring across the field—and even though in your pounding heart and your sweating palms and your broiling brainpan you *know* this is a critical moment in your life, you still can't quite bring yourself to be*lieve* it, because if it were . . . how could *the captain,* the man who knows the actual situation most intimately . . . how could he keep on drawlin' and chucklin' and driftin' and lollygaggin' in that particular voice of his—

Well!—who doesn't know that voice! And who can forget it!—even after he is proved right and the emergency is over.

That particular voice may sound vaguely Southern or Southwestern, but it is specifically Appalachian in origin. It originated in the mountains of West Virginia, in the coal country, in Lincoln County, so far up in the hollows that, as the saying went, "they had to pipe in daylight." In the late 1940's and early 1950's this up-hollow voice drifted down from on high, from over the high desert of California, down, down, down, from the upper reaches of the Brotherhood into all phases of American aviation. It was amazing. It was *Pygmalion*[1]

---

1. Play (1912) by George Bernard Shaw, in which a teacher of phonetics attempts to transform a Cockney flower girl into an elegant lady by means of transforming her speech.

in reverse. Military pilots and then, soon, airline pilots, pilots from Maine and Massachusetts and the Dakotas and Oregon and everywhere else, began to talk in that poker-hollow West Virginia drawl, or as close to it as they could bend their native accents. It was the drawl of the most righteous of all the possessors of the right stuff: Chuck Yeager.

Yeager had started out as the equivalent, in the Second World War, of the legendary Frank Luke of the 27th Aero Squadron in the First. Which is to say, he was the boondocker, the boy from the back country, with only a high-school education, no credentials, no cachet or polish of any sort, who took off the feedstore overalls and put on a uniform and climbed into an airplane and lit up the skies over Europe.

5   Yeager grew up in Hamlin, West Virginia, a town on the Mud River not far from Nitro, Hurricane Whirlwind, Salt Rock, Mud, Sod, Crum, Leet, Dollie, Ruth, and Alum Creek. His father was a gas driller (drilling for natural gas in the coalfields), his older brother was a gas driller, and he would have been a gas driller had he not enlisted in the Army Air Force in 1941 at the age of eighteen. In 1943, at twenty, he became a flight officer, i.e., a non-com who was allowed to fly, and went to England to fly fighter planes over France and Germany. Even in the tumult of the war Yeager was somewhat puzzling to a lot of other pilots. He was a short, wiry, but muscular little guy with dark curly hair and a tough-looking face that seemed (to strangers) to be saying: "You best not be lookin' me in the eye, you peckerwood, or I'll put four more holes in your nose." But that wasn't what was puzzling. What was puzzling was the way Yeager talked. He seemed to talk with some older forms of English elocution, syntax, and conjugation that had been preserved up-hollow in the Appalachians. There were people up there who never said they disapproved of anything, they said: "I don't hold with it." In the present tense they were willing to *help* out, like anyone else; but in the past tense they only *holped*. "H'it weren't nothin' I hold with, but I holped him out with it, anyways."

In his first eight missions, at the age of twenty, Yeager shot down two German fighters. On his ninth he was shot down over German-occupied French territory, suffering flak wounds; he bailed out, was picked up by the French underground, which smuggled him across the Pyrenees into Spain disguised as a peasant. In Spain he was jailed briefly, then released, whereupon he made it back to England and returned to combat during the Allied invasion of France. On October 12, 1944, Yeager took on and shot down five German fighter planes in succession. On November 6, flying a propeller-driven P-51 Mustang, he shot down one of the new jet fighters the Germans had developed, the Messerschmitt-262, and damaged two more, and on November 20 he shot down four FW-190s. It was a true Frank Luke–style display of warrior fury and personal prowess. By the end of the war he had thirteen and a half kills. He was twenty-two years old.

In 1946 and 1947 Yeager was trained as a test pilot at Wright Field in Dayton. He amazed his instructors with his ability at stunt-team flying, not to mention the unofficial business of hassling. That plus his up-hollow drawl had everybody saying, "He's a natural-born stick 'n' rudder man." Nevertheless, there was something extraordinary about it when a man so young, with so little experience in flight test, was selected to go to Muroc Field in California for the XS-1 project.

Muroc was up in the high elevations of the Mojave Desert. It looked like some fossil landscape that had long since been left behind by the rest of terrestrial evolution. It was full of huge dry lake beds, the biggest being Rogers Lake. Other than sagebrush the only vegetation was Joshua trees, twisted freaks of the plant world that looked like a cross between cactus and Japanese bonsai. They had a dark petrified green color and horribly crippled branches. At dusk the Joshua trees stood out in silhouette on the fossil wasteland like some arthritic nightmare. In the summer the temperature went up to 110 degrees as a matter of course, and the dry lake beds were covered in sand, and there would be windstorms and sandstorms right out of a Foreign Legion movie. At night it would drop to near freezing, and in December it would start raining, and the dry lakes would fill up with a few inches of water, and some sort of putrid prehistoric shrimps would work their way up from out of the ooze, and sea gulls would come flying in a hundred miles or more from the ocean, over the mountains, to gobble up these squirming little throwbacks. A person had to see it to believe it: flocks of sea gulls wheeling around in the air out in the middle of the high desert in the dead of winter and grazing on antediluvian crustaceans in the primordial ooze.

When the wind blew the few inches of water back and forth across the lake beds, they became absolutely smooth and level. And when the water evaporated in the spring, and the sun baked the ground hard, the lake beds became the greatest natural landing fields ever discovered, and also the biggest, with miles of room for error. That was highly desirable, given the nature of the enterprise at Muroc.

Besides the wind, sand, tumbleweed, and Joshua trees, there was nothing at Muroc except for two quonset-style hangars, side by side, a couple of gasoline pumps, a single concrete runway, a few tarpaper shacks, and some tents. The officers stayed in the shacks marked "barracks," and lesser souls stayed in the tents and froze all night and fried all day. Every road into the property had a guardhouse on it manned by soldiers. The enterprise the Army had undertaken in this godforsaken place was the development of supersonic jet and rocket planes.

At the end of the war the Army had discovered that the Germans not only had the world's first jet fighter but also a rocket plane that had gone 596 miles an hour in tests. Just after the war a British jet, the Gloster Meteor, jumped the official world speed record from 469 to 606 in a single day. The next great plateau would be Mach 1, the speed of sound, and the Army Air Force considered it crucial to achieve it first.

The speed of sound, Mach 1, was known (thanks to the work of the physicist Ernst Mach) to vary at different altitudes, temperatures, and wind speeds. On a calm 60-degree day at sea level it was about 760 miles an hour, while at 40,000 feet, where the temperature would be at least sixty below, it was about

660 miles an hour. Evil and baffling things happened in the transonic zone, which began at about .7 Mach. Wind tunnels choked out at such velocities. Pilots who approached the speed of sound in dives reported that the controls would lock or "freeze" or even alter their normal functions. Pilots had crashed and died because they couldn't budge the stick. Just last year Geoffrey de Havilland, son of the famous British aircraft designer and builder, had tried to take one of his father's DH 108s to Mach 1. The ship started buffeting and then disintegrated, and he was killed. This led engineers to speculate that the shock waves became so severe and unpredictable at Mach 1, no aircraft could survive them. They started talking about "the sonic wall" and "the sound barrier."

So this was the task that a handful of pilots, engineers, and mechanics had at Muroc. The place was utterly primitive, nothing but bare bones, bleached tarpaulins, and corrugated tin rippling in the heat with caloric waves; and for an ambitious young pilot it was perfect. Muroc seemed like an outpost on the dome of the world, open only to a righteous few, closed off to the rest of humanity, including even the Army Air Force brass of command control, which was at Wright Field. The commanding officer at Muroc was only a colonel, and his superiors at Wright did not relish junkets to the Muroc rat shacks in the first place. But to pilots this prehistoric throwback of an airfield became . . . shrimp heaven! the rat-shack plains of Olympus!

Low Rent Septic Tank Perfection . . . yes; and not excluding those traditional essentials for the blissful hot young pilot: Flying & Drinking and Drinking & Driving.

15   Just beyond the base, to the southwest, there was a rickety windblown 1930's-style establishment called Pancho's Fly Inn, owned, run, and bartended by a woman named Pancho Barnes. Pancho Barnes wore tight white sweaters and tight pants, after the mode of Barbara Stanwyck in *Double Indemnity*.[2] She was only forty-one when Yeager arrived at Muroc, but her face was so weatherbeaten, had so many hard miles on it, that she looked older, especially to the young pilots at the base. She also shocked the pants off them with her vulcanized tongue. Everybody she didn't like was an old bastard or a sonofabitch. People she liked were old bastards and sonsabitches, too. "I tol' 'at ol' bastard to get 'is ass on over here and I'd g'im a drink." But Pancho Barnes was anything but Low Rent. She was the granddaughter of the man who designed the old Mount Lowe cable-car system, Thaddeus S. C. Lowe. Her maiden name was Florence Leontine Lowe. She was brought up in San Marino, which adjoined Pasadena and was one of Los Angeles' wealthiest suburbs, and her first husband—she was married four times—was the pastor of the Pasadena Episcopal Church, the Rev. C. Rankin Barnes. Mrs. Barnes seemed to have few of the conventional community interests of a Pasadena matron. In the late 1920's, by boat and plane, she ran guns for Mexican revolutionaries and picked up the nickname Pancho. In 1930 she broke Amelia Earhart's[3] air-speed record for women. Then she barnstormed around the country as the featured performer

2. Film (1944) featuring a femme fatale housewife played by Stanwyck (1907–1990).
3. Pioneering aviator (1897–1937) and the first woman to fly solo across the Atlantic Ocean.

of "Pancho Barnes's Mystery Circus of the Air." She always greeted her public in jodhpurs and riding boots, a flight jacket, a white scarf, and a white sweater that showed off her terrific Barbara Stanwyck chest. Pancho's desert Fly Inn had an airstrip, a swimming pool, a dude ranch corral, plenty of acreage for horseback riding, a big old guest house for the lodgers, and a connecting building that was the bar and restaurant. In the barroom the floors, the tables, the chairs, the walls, the beams, the bar were of the sort known as extremely weatherbeaten, and the screen doors kept banging. Nobody putting together such a place for a movie about flying in the old days would ever dare make it as dilapidated and generally go-to-hell as it actually was. Behind the bar were many pictures of airplanes and pilots, lavishly autographed and inscribed, badly framed and crookedly hung. There was an old piano that had been dried out and cracked to the point of hopeless desiccation. On a good night a huddle of drunken aviators could be heard trying to bang, slosh, and navigate their way through old Cole Porter[4] tunes. On average nights the tunes were not that good to start with. When the screen door banged and a man walked through the door into the saloon, every eye in the place checked him out. If he wasn't known as somebody who had something to do with flying at Muroc, he would be eyed like some lame goddamned mouseshit sheepherder from *Shane*.[5]

The plane the Air Force wanted to break the sound barrier with was called the X-1 at the outset and later on simply the X-1. The Bell Aircraft Corporation had built it under an Army contract. The core of the ship was a rocket of the type first developed by a young Navy inventor, Robert Truax, during the war. The fuselage was shaped like a 50-caliber bullet—an object that was known to go supersonic smoothly. Military pilots seldom drew major test assignments; they went to highly paid civilians working for the aircraft corporations. The prime pilot for the X-1 was a man whom Bell regarded as the best of the breed. This man looked like a movie star. He looked like a pilot from out of *Hell's Angels*.[6] And on top of everything else there was his name: Slick Goodlin.

The idea in testing the X-1 was to nurse it carefully into the transonic zone, up to seven-tenths, eight-tenths, nine-tenths the speed of sound (.7 Mach, .8 Mach, .9 Mach) before attempting the speed of sound itself, Mach 1, even though Bell and the Army already knew the X-1 had the rocket power to go to Mach 1 and beyond, if there *was* any *beyond*. The consensus of aviators and engineers, after Geoffrey de Havilland's death, was that the speed of sound was an absolute, like the firmness of the earth. The sound barrier was a farm you could buy in the sky. So Slick Goodlin began to probe the transonic zone in the X-1, going up to .8 Mach. Every time he came down he'd have a riveting tale to tell. The buffeting, it was so fierce—and the listeners, their imaginations aflame, could practically see poor Geoffrey de Havilland disintegrating in

4. American composer of popular music (1891–1964), including Broadway show tunes.
5. Classic Western movie (1953).
6. Movie (1930) about aviation during World War I.

midair. And the goddamned aerodynamics—and the listeners got a picture of a man in ballroom pumps skidding across a sheet of ice, pursued by bears. A controversy arose over just how much bonus Slick Goodlin should receive for assaulting the dread Mach 1 itself. Bonuses for contract test pilots were not unusual; but the figure of $150,000 was now bruited about. The Army balked, and Yeager got the job. He took it for $283 a month, or $3,396 a year; which is to say, his regular Army captain's pay.

The only trouble they had with Yeager was in holding him back. On his first powered flight in the X-1 he immediately executed an unauthorized zero-g roll with a full load of rocket fuel, then stood the ship on its tail and went up to .85 Mach in a vertical climb, also unauthorized. On subsequent flights, at speeds between .85 Mach and .9 Mach, Yeager ran into most known airfoil problems—loss of elevator, aileron, and rudder control, heavy trim pressures, Dutch rolls, pitching and buffeting, the lot—yet was convinced, after edging over .9 Mach, that this would all get better, not worse, as you reached Mach 1. The attempt to push beyond Mach 1—"breaking the sound barrier"—was set for October 14, 1947. Not being an engineer, Yeager didn't believe the "barrier" existed.

October 14 was a Tuesday. On Sunday evening, October 12, Chuck Yeager dropped in at Pancho's, along with his wife. She was a brunette named Glennis, whom he had met in California while he was in training, and she was such a number, so striking, he had the inscription "Glamorous Glennis" written on the nose of his P-51 in Europe and, just a few weeks back, on the X-1 itself. Yeager didn't go to Pancho's and knock back a few because two days later the big test was coming up. Nor did he knock back a few because it was the weekend. No, he knocked back a few because night had come and he was a pilot at Muroc. In keeping with the military tradition of Flying & Drinking, that was what you did, for no other reason than that the sun had gone down. You went to Pancho's and knocked back a few and listened to the screen doors banging and to other aviators torturing the piano and the nation's repertoire of Familiar Favorites and to lonesome mouseturd strangers wandering in through the banging doors and to Pancho classifying the whole bunch of them as old bastards and miserable peckerwoods. That was what you did if you were a pilot at Muroc and the sun went down.

20   So about eleven Yeager got the idea that it would be a hell of a kick if he and Glennis saddled up a couple of Pancho's dude-ranch horses and went for a romp, a little rat race, in the moonlight. This was in keeping with the military tradition of Flying & Drinking and Drinking & Driving, except that this was prehistoric Muroc and you rode horses. So Yeager and his wife set off on a little proficiency run at full gallop through the desert in the moonlight amid the arthritic silhouettes of the Joshua trees. Then they start racing back to the corral, with Yeager in the lead and heading for the gateway. Given the prevailing conditions, it being nighttime, at Pancho's, and his head being filled with a black sandstorm of many badly bawled songs and vulcanized oaths, he sees too late that the gate has been closed. Like many a hard-driving midnight pilot before him, he does not realize that he is not equally gifted in the control of all

forms of locomotion. He and the horse hit the gate, and he goes flying off and lands on his right side. His side hurts like hell.

The next day, Monday, his side still hurts like hell. It hurts every time he moves. It hurts every time he breathes deep. It hurts every time he moves his right arm. He knows that if he goes to a doctor at Muroc or says anything to anybody even remotely connected with his superiors, he will be scrubbed from the flight on Tuesday. They might even go so far as to put some other miserable peckerwood in his place. So he gets on his motorcycle, an old junker that Pancho had given him, and rides over to see a doctor in the town of Rosamond, near where he lives. Every time the goddamned motorcycle hits a pebble in the road, his side hurts like a sonofabitch. The doctor in Rosamond informs him he has two broken ribs and he tapes them up and tells him that if he'll just keep his right arm immobilized for a couple of weeks and avoid any physical exertion or sudden movements, he should be all right.

Yeager gets up before daybreak on Tuesday morning—which is supposed to be the day he tries to break the sound barrier—and his ribs still hurt like a sonofabitch. He gets his wife to drive him over to the field, and he has to keep his right arm pinned down to his side to keep his ribs from hurting so much. At dawn, on the day of a flight, you could hear the X-1 screaming long before you got there. The fuel for the X-1 was alcohol and liquid oxygen, oxygen converted from a gas to a liquid by lowering its temperature to 297 degrees below zero. And when the lox, as it was called, rolled out of the hoses and into the belly of the X-1, it started boiling off and the X-1 started steaming and screaming like a teakettle. There's quite a crowd on hand, by Muroc standards. . . . perhaps nine or ten souls. They're still fueling the X-1 with the lox, and the beast is wailing.

The X-1 looked like a fat orange swallow with white markings. But it was really just a length of pipe with four rocket chambers in it. It had a tiny cockpit and a needle nose, two little straight blades (only three and a half inches thick at the thickest part) for wings, and a tail assembly set up high to avoid the "sonic wash" from the wings. Even though his side was throbbing and his right arm felt practically useless, Yeager figured he could grit his teeth and get through the flight—except for one specific move he had to make. In the rocket launches, the X-1, which held only two and a half minutes' worth of fuel, was carried up to twenty-six thousand feet underneath a B-29. At seven thousand feet, Yeager was to climb down a ladder from the bomb bay of the B-29 to the open doorway of the X-1, hook up to the oxygen system and the radio microphone and earphones, and put his crash helmet on and prepare for the launch, which would come at twenty-five thousand feet. This helmet was a homemade number. There had never been any such thing as a crash helmet before, except in stunt flying. Throughout the war pilots had used the old skin-tight leather helmet-and-goggles. But the X-1 had a way of throwing the pilot around so violently that there was danger of getting knocked out against the walls of the cockpit. So Yeager had bought a big leather football helmet—there were no plastic ones at the time—and he butchered it with a hunting knife until he carved the right kind of holes in it, so that it would fit down over his regular flying helmet and the earphones and the oxygen rig. Anyway, then his flight engineer, Jack Ridley, would climb down the ladder, out in the breeze, and shove into place the cockpit door, which had to be lowered out of the belly of the B-29 on a chain. Then Yeager had to push a handle to lock the door airtight. Since the X-1's cockpit was minute, you had to push the handle with your right hand. It took quite a shove. There was no way you could move into position to get enough leverage with your left hand.

Out in the hangar Yeager makes a few test shoves on the sly, and the pain is so incredible he realizes that there is no way a man with two broken ribs is going to get the door closed. It is time to confide in somebody, and the logical man is Jack Ridley. Ridley is not only the flight engineer but a pilot himself and a good old boy from Oklahoma to boot. He will understand about Flying & Drinking and Drinking & Driving through the goddamned Joshua trees. So Yeager takes Ridley off to the side in the tin hangar and says: Jack, I got me a little ol' problem here. Over at Pancho's the other night I sorta . . . dinged my goddamned ribs. Ridley says, Whattya mean . . . *dinged?* Yeager says, Well, I guess you might say I damned near like to . . . *broke* a coupla the sonsabitches. Whereupon Yeager sketches out the problem he foresees.

25   Not for nothing is Ridley the engineer on this project. He has an inspiration. He tells a janitor named Sam to cut him about nine inches off a broom handle. When nobody's looking, he slips the broomstick into the cockpit of the X-1 and gives Yeager a little advice and counsel.

So with that added bit of supersonic flight gear Yeager went aloft.

At seven thousand feet he climbed down the ladder into the X-1's cockpit, clipped on his hoses and lines, and managed to pull the pumpkin football helmet over his head. Then Ridley came down the ladder and lowered the door into place. As Ridley had instructed, Yeager now took the nine inches of broomstick and slipped it between the handle and the door. This gave him just enough mechanical advantage to reach over with his left hand and whang the thing shut. So he whanged the door shut with Ridley's broomstick and was ready to fly.

At 26,000 feet the B-29 went into a shallow dive, then pulled up and released Yeager and the X-1 as if it were a bomb. Like a bomb it dropped and shot forward (at the speed of the mother ship) at the same time. Yeager had been launched straight into the sun. It seemed to be no more than six feet in front of him, filling up the sky and blinding him. But he managed to get his bearings and set off the four rocket chambers one after the other. He then experienced something that became known as the ultimate sensation in flying: "booming and zooming." The surge of the rockets was so tremendous, forced him back into his seat so violently, he could hardly move his hands forward the few inches necessary to reach the controls. The X-1 seemed to shoot straight up in an absolutely perpendicular trajectory, as if determined to snap the hold of gravity via the most direct route possible. In fact, he was only climbing at the 45-degree angle called for in the flight plan. At about .87 Mach the buffeting started.

On the ground the engineers could no longer see Yeager. They could only hear . . . that poker-hollow West Virginia drawl.

"Had a mild buffet there . . . jes the usual instability . . ." 30

Jes the usual instability?

Then the X-1 reached the speed of .96 Mach, and that incredible caint-hardlyin' aw-shuckin' drawl said:

"Say, Ridley . . . make a note here, will ya?" *(if you ain't got nothin' better to do)* ". . . elevator effectiveness *re*gained."

Just as Yeager had predicted, as the X-1 approached Mach 1, the stability improved. Yeager had his eyes pinned on the machometer. The needle reached .96, fluctuated, and went off the scale.

And on the ground they heard . . . that voice: 35

"Say, Ridley . . . make another note, will ya?" *(if you ain't too bored yet)* ". . . there's somethin' wrong with this ol' machometer. . . ." (faint chuckle) ". . . it's gone kinda screwy on me. . . ."

And in that moment, on the ground, they heard a boom rock over the desert floor—just as the physicist Theodore von Kármán had predicted many years before.

Then they heard Ridley back in the B-29: "If it is, Chuck, we'll fix it. Personally I think you're seeing things."

Then they heard Yeager's poker-hollow drawl again:

"Well, I guess I am, Jack. . . . And I'm still goin' upstairs like a bat." 40

The X-1 had gone through "the sonic wall" without so much as a bump. As the speed topped out at Mach 1.05, Yeager had the sensation of shooting straight through the top of the sky. The sky turned a deep purple and all at once the stars and the moon came out—and the sun shone at the same time. He had reached a layer of the upper atmosphere where the air was too thin to contain reflecting dust particles. He was simply looking out into space. As the X-1 nosed over at the top of the climb, Yeager now had seven minutes of . . . Pilot Heaven . . . ahead of him. He was going faster than any man in history, and it was almost silent up here, since he had exhausted his rocket fuel, and he was so high in such a vast space that there was no sensation of motion. He was master of the sky. His was a king's solitude, unique and inviolate, above the dome of the world. It would take him seven minutes to glide back down and land at Muroc. He spent the time doing victory rolls and wing-over-wing aerobatics while Rogers Lake and the High Sierras spun around below.

MLA CITATION

Wolfe, Tom. "Yeager." 1979. *The Norton Reader: An Anthology of Nonfiction.* Ed. Melissa A. Goldthwaite et al. 14th ed. New York: Norton, 2016. 114–23. Print.

QUESTIONS

1. Before recounting Yeager's personal history or the story of breaking the sound barrier, Tom Wolfe begins with the voice of an airline pilot. Why does he begin this way? What connection does the first paragraph have with the rest of the essay?

2. Wolfe interweaves Yeager's personal history with a more public, official history of the space program. Make a flowchart or diagram to show how this interweaving works.

3. Write an essay that interweaves some part of your personal history with some larger, public story.

VIRGINIA WOOLF *Ellen Terry*

WHEN SHE CAME ON TO THE STAGE as Lady Cicely in *Captain Brassbound's Conversion*, the stage collapsed like a house of cards and all the limelights were extinguished. When she spoke it was as if someone drew a bow over a ripe, richly seasoned 'cello; it grated, it glowed, and it growled. Then she stopped speaking. She put on her glasses. She gazed intently at the back of a settee. She had forgotten her part. But did it matter? Speaking or silent, she was Lady Cicely—or was it Ellen Terry? At any rate, she filled the stage and all the other actors were put out, as electric lights are put out in the sun.

Yet this pause when she forgot what Lady Cicely said next was significant. It was a sign not that she was losing her memory and past her prime, as some said. It was a sign that Lady Cicely was not a part that suited her. Her son, Gordon Craig, insists that she only forgot her part when there was something uncongenial in the words, when some speck of grit had got into the marvellous machine of her genius. When the part was congenial, when she was Shakespeare's Portia, Desdemona, Ophelia,[1] every word, every comma was consumed. Even her eyelashes acted. Her body lost its weight. Her son, a mere boy, could lift her in his arms. 'I am not myself,' she said. 'Something comes upon me. . . . I am always-in-the-air, light and bodiless.' We, who can only remember her as Lady Cicely on the little stage at the Court Theatre, only remember what, compared with her Ophelia or her Portia, was as a picture postcard compared with the great Velasquez[2] in the gallery.

Known for her novels, Virginia Woolf (1882–1941) was also a literary critic and essayist; this selection was written in 1941 and later published in Woolf's collections of writings The Moment and Other Essays *(1947). Ellen Terry (1847–1928) was an actor who made her stage debut at the age of nine and celebrated her fiftieth anniversary on the stage in 1906, the year she starred in* Captain Brassbound's Conversion *(1900), a play that George Bernard Shaw wrote with Terry in mind for the female lead as Lady Cicely.*

1. William Shakespeare (1564–1616), English playwright; Portia is a character in his play *The Merchant of Venice* (c. 1596), Desdemona is a character in *Othello* (c. 1604), and Ophelia is a character in *Hamlet* (c. 1600).
2. Diego Rodríguez de Silva y Velázquez (1599–1660), Spanish painter known for his powerful larger-than-life portraits.

It is the fate of actors to leave only picture postcards behind them. Every night when the curtain goes down the beautiful coloured canvas is rubbed out. What remains is at best only a wavering, insubstantial phantom—a verbal life on the lips of the living. Ellen Terry was well aware of it. She tried herself, overcome by the greatness of Irving[3] as Hamlet and indignant at the caricatures of his detractors, to describe what she remembered. It was in vain. She dropped her pen in despair. 'Oh God, that I were a writer!' she cried. 'Surely a *writer* could not string words together about Henry Irving's Hamlet and say *nothing, nothing*.' It never struck her, humble as she was, and obsessed by her lack of book learning, that she was, among other things, a writer. It never occurred to her when she wrote her autobiography, or scribbled page after page to Bernard Shaw late at night, dead tired after a rehearsal, that she was 'writing'. The words in her beautiful rapid hand bubbled off her pen. With dashes and notes of exclamation she tried to give them the very tone and stress of the spoken word. It is true, she could not build a house with words, one room opening out of another, and a staircase connecting the whole. But whatever she took up became in her warm, sensitive grasp a tool. If it was a rolling-pin, she made perfect pastry. If it was a carving knife, perfect slices fell from the leg of mutton. If it were a pen, words peeled off, some broken, some suspended in mid-air, but all far more expressive than the tappings of the professional typewriter.

With her pen then at odds and ends of time she has painted a self-portrait. It is not an Academy portrait, glazed, framed, complete. It is rather a bundle of loose leaves upon each of which she has dashed off a sketch for a portrait— here a nose, here an arm, here a foot, and there a mere scribble in the margin. The sketches done in different moods, from different angles, sometimes contradict each other. The nose cannot belong to the eyes; the arm is out of all proportion to the foot. It is difficult to assemble them. And there are blank pages, too. Some very important features are left out. There was a self she did not know, a gap she could not fill. Did she not take Walt Whitman's words for a motto? 'Why, even I myself, I often think, know little or nothing of my real life. Only a few hints—a few diffused faint clues and indirections . . . I seek. . . . to trace out here.'[4]

Nevertheless, the first sketch is definite enough. It is the sketch of her   5
childhood. She was born to the stage. The stage was her cradle, her nursery. When other little girls were being taught sums and pot-hooks she was being cuffed and buffeted into the practice of her profession. Her ears were boxed, her muscles suppled. All day she was hard at work on the boards. Late at night when other children were safe in bed she was stumbling along the dark streets wrapped in her father's cloak. And the dark street with its curtained windows was nothing but a sham to that little professional actress, and the rough-and-tumble life on the boards was her home, her reality. 'It's all such sham there', she wrote—meaning by 'there' what she called 'life lived in

3. Henry Irving (1838–1905), English tragedian who performed with Terry.
4. From *Leaves of Grass* (1900), a collection of poems by Walt Whitman.

houses'—'sham—cold—hard—pretending. It's not sham here in our theatre—here all is real, warm and kind—we live a lovely spiritual life here.'

That is the first sketch. But turn to the next page. The child born to the stage has become a wife. She is married at sixteen to an elderly famous painter.[5] The theatre has gone; its lights are out and in its place is a quiet studio in a garden. In its place is a world full of pictures and 'gentle artistic people with quiet voices and elegant manners'. She sits mum in her corner while the famous elderly people talk over her head in quiet voices. She is content to wash her husband's brushes; to sit to him; to play her simple tunes on the piano to him while he paints. In the evening she wanders over the Downs[6] with the great poet, Tennyson.[7] 'I was in Heaven', she wrote. 'I never had one single pang of regret for the theatre.' If only it could have lasted! But somehow—here a blank page intervenes—she was an incongruous element in that quiet studio. She was too young, too vigorous, too vital, perhaps. At any rate, the marriage was a failure.

And so, skipping a page or two, we come to the next sketch. She is a mother now. Two adorable children claim all her devotion. She is living in the depths of the country, in the heart of domesticity. She is up at six. She scrubs, she cooks, she sews. She teaches the children. She harnesses the pony. She fetches the milk. And again she is perfectly happy. To live with children in a cottage, driving her little cart about the lanes, going to church on Sunday in blue and white cotton—that is the ideal life! She asks no more than that it shall go on like that for ever and ever. But one day the wheel comes off the pony cart. Huntsmen in pink leap over the hedge. One of them dismounts and offers help. He looks at the girl in a blue frock and exclaims; 'Good God! It's Nelly!' She looks at the huntsman in pink and cries, 'Charles Reade!'[8] And, so, all in a jiffy, back she goes to the stage, and to forty pounds a week. For—that is the reason she gives—the bailiffs are in the house. She must make money.

At this point a very blank page confronts us. There is a gulf which we can only cross at a venture. Two sketches face each other; Ellen Terry in blue cotton among the hens; Ellen Terry robed and crowned as Lady Macbeth[9] on the stage of the Lyceum. The two sketches are contradictory yet they are both of the same woman. She hates the stage; yet she adores it. She worships her children; yet she forsakes them. She would like to live for ever among pigs and ducks in the open air; yet she spends the rest of her life among actors and actresses in the limelight. Her own attempt to explain the discrepancy is hardly convincing. 'I have always been more woman than artist', she says. Irving put the theatre first. 'He had none of what I may call my bourgeois qualities—the love of being in love, the love of a home, the dislike of solitude.' She tries to persuade

---

5. G. F. Watts (1817–1904), an English painter, was forty-seven when he married Terry—not elderly but more than twice her age.

6. Grassy hill on the Isle of Wight in southern England.

7. Alfred Tennyson (1809–1892), English poet.

8. English novelist and playwright (1814–1884) who convinced Terry to return to the stage in 1874 and act in his drama *The Wandering Heir* (1875).

9. Character in William Shakespeare's *The Tragedy of Macbeth* (c. 1606).

us that she was an ordinary woman enough; a better hand at pastry than most; an adept at keeping house; with an eye for colour, a taste for furniture, and a positive passion for washing children's heads. If she went back to the stage it was because—well, what else could she do when the bailiffs were in the house?

This is the little sketch that she offers us to fill in the gap between the two Ellen Terrys—Ellen the mother, and Ellen the actress. But here we remember her warning: 'Why, even I myself know little or nothing of my real life.' There was something in her that she did not understand; something that came surging up from the depths and swept her away in its clutches. The voice she heard in the lane was not the voice of Charles Reade; nor was it the voice of the bailiffs. It was the voice of her genius; the urgent call of something that she could not define, could not suppress, and must obey. So she left her children and followed the voice back to the stage, back to the Lyceum, back to a long life of incessant toil, anguish, and glory.

But, having gazed at the full-length portrait of Ellen Terry as Sargent[10] painted her, robed and crowned as Lady Macbeth, turn to the next page. It is done from another angle. Pen in hand, she is seated at her desk. A volume of Shakespeare lies before her. It is open at *Cymbeline*,[11] and she is making careful notes in the margin. The part of Imogen presents great problems. She is, she says, 'on the rack' about her interpretation. Perhaps Bernard Shaw can throw light upon the question? A letter from the brilliant young critic of the *Saturday Review*[12] lies beside Shakespeare. She has never met him, but for years they have written to each other, intimately, ardently, disputatiously, some of the best letters in the language. He says the most outrageous things. He compares dear Henry to an ogre, and Ellen to a captive chained in his cage. But Ellen Terry is quite capable of holding her own against Bernard Shaw. She scolds him, laughs at him, fondles him, and contradicts him. She has a curious sympathy for the advanced views that Henry Irving abominated. But what suggestions has the brilliant critic to make about Imogen? None apparently that she has not already thought for herself. She is as close and critical a student of Shakespeare as he is. She has studied every line, weighed the meaning of every word; experimented with every gesture. Each of those golden moments when she becomes bodyless, not herself, is the result of months of minute and careful study. 'Art', she quotes, 'needs that which we can give her, I assure you.' In fact this mutable woman, all instinct, sympathy, and sensation, is as painstaking a student and as careful of the dignity of her art as Flaubert[13] himself.

But once more the expression on that serious face changes. She works like a slave—none harder. But she is quick to tell Mr. Shaw that she does not work with her brain only. She is not in the least clever. Indeed, she is happy she tells him, '*not to be clever*'. She stresses the point with a jab of her pen. 'You clever people', as she calls him and his friends, 'miss so much, mar so much. As for

10. John Singer Sargent (1856–1925), American painter.
11. Play (c. 1611) by William Shakespeare.
12. Weekly magazine started in 1924; it was published until the early 1980s.
13. Gustave Flaubert (1821–1880), French novelist.

education, she never had a day's schooling in her life. As far as she can see, but the problem baffles her, the main-spring of her art is imagination. Visit mad-houses, if you like; take notes; observe; study endlessly. But first, imagine. And so she takes her part away from the books out into the woods. Rambling down grassy rides, she lives her part until she is it. If a word jars or grates, she must re-think it, rewrite it. Then when every phrase is her own, and every gesture spontaneous, out she comes on to the stage and is Imogen, Ophelia, Desdemona.

But is she, even when the great moments are on her, a great actress? She doubts it. 'I cared more for love and life', she says. Her face, too, has been no help to her. She cannot sustain emotion. Certainly she is not a great tragic actress. Now and again, perhaps, she has acted some comic part to perfection. But even while she analyses herself, as one artist to another, the sun slants upon an old kitchen chair. 'Thank the Lord for my eyes!' she exclaims. What a world of joy her eyes have brought her! Gazing at the old 'rush-bottomed, sturdy-legged, and wavy-backed' chair, the stage is gone, the limelights are out, the famous actress is forgotten.

Which, then, of all these women is the real Ellen Terry? How are we to put the scattered sketches together? Is she mother, wife, cook, critic, actress, or should she have been, after all, a painter? Each part seems the right part until she throws it aside and plays another. Something of Ellen Terry it seems overflowed every part and remained unacted. Shakespeare could not fit her; not Ibsen;[14] nor Shaw. The stage could not hold her; nor the nursery. But there is, after all, a greater dramatist than Shakespeare, Ibsen, or Shaw. There is Nature. Hers is so vast a stage and so innumerable a company of actors, that for the most part she fobs them off with a tag or two. They come on and they go off without breaking the ranks. But now and again Nature creates a new part, an original part. The actors who act that part always defy our attempts to name them. They will not act the stock parts—they forget the words, they improvise others of their own. But when they come on the stage falls like a pack of cards and the limelights are extinguished. That was Ellen Terry's fate—to act a new part. And thus while other actors are remembered because they were Hamlet, Phèdre, or Cleopatra,[15] Ellen Terry is remembered because she was Ellen Terry.

14. Henrik Ibsen (1828–1906), Norwegian playwright.

15. Phèdre, character in Jean Baptiste Racine's *Phèdre* (1677); Cleopatra (69 B.C.E.–30 B.C.E.), pharaoh of Ancient Egypt who was known for her beauty; she is depicted in William Shakespeare's *Antony and Cleopatra* (c. 1606) and in George Bernard Shaw's *Caesar and Cleopatra* (1898).

MLA CITATION

Woolf, Virginia. "Ellen Terry." 1947. *The Norton Reader: An Anthology of Nonfiction.* Ed. Melissa A. Goldthwaite et al. 14th ed. New York: Norton, 2016. 124–28. Print.

QUESTIONS

1. In this profile of Ellen Terry, what Virginia Woolf does not include is as interesting as what she does include. She does not include a list of Terry's accomplishments, her honors, or reviews of her acting. How does Woolf persuade readers of Terry's importance? What does she want us to know of Terry beyond her acting?

2. Much of this essay takes the form of descriptions of actual photographs and imagined drawings. What does this technique help Woolf convey about Terry? How is it effective?

3. Write a profile of someone who is famous. As Woolf does, try to give readers a picture of that person's personality—not just his or her professional accomplishments.

TONI MORRISON   *Strangers*

I AM IN THIS RIVER PLACE—newly mine—walking in the yard when I see a woman sitting on the seawall at the edge of a neighbor's garden. A homemade fishing pole arcs into the water some twenty feet from her hand. A feeling of welcome washes over me. I walk toward her, right up to the fence that separates my place from the neighbor's, and notice with pleasure the clothes she wears: men's shoes, a man's hat, a well-worn colorless sweater over a long black dress. The woman turns her head and greets me with an easy smile and a "How you doing?" She tells me her name (Mother Something) and we talk for some time—fifteen minutes or so—about fish recipes and weather and children. When I ask her if she lives there, she answers no. She lives in a nearby village, but the owner of the house lets her come to this spot any time she wants to fish, and she comes every week, sometimes several days in a row when the perch or catfish are running and even if they aren't because she likes eel, too, and they are always there. She is witty and full of the wisdom that older women always seem to have a lock on. When we part, it is with an understanding that she will be there the next day or very soon after and we will visit again. I imagine more conversations with her. I will invite her into my house for coffee, for tales, for laughter. She reminds me of someone, something. I imagine a friendship, casual, effortless, delightful.

She is not there the next day. She is not there the following days, either. And I look for her every morning. The summer passes, and I have not seen her at all. Finally, I approach the neighbor to ask about her and am bewildered to learn that the neighbor does not know who or what I am talking about. No old

Toni Morrison wrote this essay to introduce A Kind of Rapture *(1998), a book of photographs that Robert Bergman took while traveling by car through the United States.*

woman fished from her wall—ever—and none had permission to do so. I decide that the fisherwoman fibbed about the permission and took advantage of the neighbor's frequent absences to poach. The fact of the neighbor's presence is proof that the fisherwoman would not be there. During the months following, I ask lots of people if they know Mother Something. No one, not even people who have lived in nearby villages for seventy years, has ever heard of her.

I feel cheated, puzzled, but also amused, and wonder off and on if I have dreamed her. In any case, I tell myself, it was an encounter of no value other than anecdotal. Still. Little by little, annoyance then bitterness takes the place of my original bewilderment. A certain view from my windows is now devoid of her, reminding me every morning of her deceit and my disappointment. What was she doing in that neighborhood, anyway? She didn't drive, had to walk four miles if indeed she lived where she said she did. How could she be missed on the road in that hat, those awful shoes? I try to understand the intensity of my chagrin, and why I am missing a woman I spoke to for fifteen minutes. I get nowhere except for the stingy explanation that she had come into my space (next to it, anyway—at the property line, at the edge, just at the fence, where the most interesting things always happen), and had implied promises of female camaraderie, of opportunities for me to be generous, of protection and protecting. Now she is gone, taking with her my good opinion of myself, which, of course, is unforgivable.

Isn't that the kind of thing that we fear strangers will do? Disturb. Betray. Prove they are not like us. That is why it is so hard to know what to do with them. The love that prophets have urged us to offer the stranger is the same love that Jean-Paul Sartre[1] could reveal as the very mendacity of Hell. The signal line of *No Exit*, "*L'enfer, c'est les autres*," raises the possibility that "other people" are responsible for turning a personal world into a public hell. In the admonition of a prophet and the sly warning of an artist, strangers as well as the beloved are understood to tempt our gaze, to slide away or to stake claims. Religious prophets caution against the slide, the looking away; Sartre warns against love as possession.

5   The resources available to us for benign access to each other, for vaulting the mere blue air that separates us, are few but powerful: language, image, and experience, which may involve both, one, or neither of the first two. Language (saying, listening, reading) can encourage, even mandate, surrender, the breach of distances among us, whether they are continental or on the same pillow, whether they are distances of culture or the distinctions and indistinctions of age or gender, whether they are the consequences of social invention or biology. Image increasingly rules the realm of shaping, sometimes becoming, often contaminating, knowledge. Provoking language or eclipsing it, an image can determine not only what we know and feel but also what we believe is worth knowing about what we feel.

These two godlings, language and image, feed and form experience. My instant embrace of an outrageously dressed fisherwoman was due in part to an

1. French existentialist philosopher (1905–1980). The line in Sartre's 1944 play *No Exit* is usually translated as "Hell is other people."

image on which my representation of her was based. I immediately sentimentalized and appropriated her. I owned her or wanted to (and I suspect she glimpsed it). I had forgotten the power of embedded images and stylish language to seduce, reveal, control. Forgot, too, their capacity to help us pursue the human project—which is to remain human and to block the dehumanization of others.

But something unforeseen has entered into this admittedly oversimplified menu of our resources. Far from our original expectations of increased intimacy and broader knowledge, routine media presentations deploy images and language that narrow our view of what humans look like (or ought to look like) and what in fact we are like. Succumbing to the perversions of media can blur vision, resisting them can do the same. I was clearly and aggressively resisting such influences in my encounter with the fisherwoman. Art as well as the market can be complicit in the sequestering of form from formula, of nature from artifice, of humanity from commodity. Art gesturing toward representation has, in some exalted quarters, become literally beneath contempt. The concept of what it is to be human has altered, and the word *truth* needs quotation marks around it so that its absence (its elusiveness) is stronger than its presence.

Why would we want to know a stranger when it is easier to estrange another? Why would we want to close the distance when we can close the gate? Appeals in arts and religion for comity in the Common Wealth are faint.

It took some time for me to understand my unreasonable claims on that fisherwoman. To understand that I was longing for and missing some aspect of myself, and that there are no strangers. There are only versions of ourselves, many of which we have not embraced, most of which we wish to protect ourselves from. For the stranger is not foreign, she is random, not alien but remembered; and it is the randomness of the encounter with our already known—although unacknowledged—selves that summons a ripple of alarm. That makes us reject the figure and the emotions it provokes—especially when these emotions are profound. It is also what makes us want to own, govern, administrate the Other. To romance her, if we can, back into our own mirrors. In either instance (of alarm or false reverence), we deny her personhood, the specific individuality we insist upon for ourselves.

Robert Bergman's radiant portraits of strangers provoked this meditation. 10 Occasionally, there arises an event or a moment that one knows immediately will forever mark a place in the history of artistic endeavor. Bergman's portraits represent such a moment, such an event. In all its burnished majesty his gallery refuses us unearned solace, and one by one by one the photographs unveil *us*, asserting a beauty, a kind of rapture, that is as close as can be to a master template of the singularity, the community, the unextinguishable sacredness of the human race.

MLA CITATION

Morrison, Toni. "Strangers." 1998. *The Norton Reader: An Anthology of Nonfiction.* Ed. Melissa A. Goldthwaite et al. 14th ed. New York: Norton, 2016. 129–31. Print.

QUESTIONS

1. In his book *A Kind of Rapture*, Robert Bergman included photographs of people he encountered on the streets of America. Why does Toni Morrison not dwell on this fact?

2. In paragraphs 1–3 Morrison relates a story about a woman she sees fishing near her property; later in the essay she expresses regret, even guilt, that her story "sentimentalized and appropriated" the woman (paragraphs 6–7). What does Morrison mean by this self-criticism? Do you agree that it may be ethically wrong to create stories about the strangers we see?

3. Write an essay in which you describe and reflect on an encounter you have had with a stranger.

JUDITH ORTIZ COFER   *More Room*

MY GRANDMOTHER'S HOUSE is like a chambered nautilus; it has many rooms, yet it is not a mansion. Its proportions are small and its design simple. It is a house that has grown organically, according to the needs of its inhabitants. To all of us in the family it is known as *la casa de Mamá*.[1] It is the place of our origin; the stage for our memories and dreams of Island life.

I remember how in my childhood it sat on stilts; this was before it had a downstairs. It rested on its perch like a great blue bird, not a flying sort of bird, more like a nesting hen, but with spread wings. Grandfather had built it soon after their marriage. He was a painter and housebuilder by trade, a poet and meditative man by nature. As each of their eight children were born, new rooms were added. After a few years, the paint did not exactly match, nor the materials, so that there was a chronology to it, like the rings of a tree, and Mamá could tell you the history of each room in her *casa*, and thus the genealogy of the family along with it.

Her room is the heart of the house. Though I have seen it recently, and both woman and room have diminished in size, changed by the new perspective of my eyes, now capable of looking over countertops and tall beds, it is not this picture I carry in my memory of Mamá's *casa*. Instead, I see her room as a queen's chamber where a small woman loomed large, a throne-room with a massive four-poster bed in its center which stood taller than a child's head. It was on this bed where her own children had been born that the smallest grandchildren were allowed to take naps in the afternoons; here too was where

From Judith Ortiz Cofer's book, Silent Dancing: A Partial Remembrance of a Puerto Rican Childhood *(1990), which won the 1991 PEN/Martha Albrand Special Citation for Nonfiction.*

1. Spanish for "Mama's house." All translations that follow are of Spanish words.

Mamá secluded herself to dispense private advice to her daughters, sitting on the edge of the bed, looking down at whoever sat on the rocker where generations of babies had been sung to sleep. To me she looked like a wise empress right out of the fairy tales I was addicted to reading.

Though the room was dominated by the mahogany four-posters, it also contained all of Mamá's symbols of power. On her dresser instead of cosmetics there were jars filled with herbs: *yerba buena, yerba mala,*[2] the making of purgatives and teas to which we all subjected during childhood crises. She had a steaming cup for anyone who could not, or would not, get up to face life on any given day. If the acrid aftertaste of her cures for malingering did not get you out of bed, then it was time to call *el doctor.*

And there was the monstrous chifforobe she kept locked with a little golden   5
key she did not hide. This was a test of her dominion over us; though my cousins and I wanted a look inside that massive wardrobe more than anything, we never reached for that little key lying on top of her Bible on the dresser. This was also where she placed her earrings and rosary at night. God's word was her security system. This chifforobe was the place where I imagined she kept jewels, satin slippers, and elegant sequined, silk gowns of heart-breaking fineness. I lusted after those imaginary costumes. I had heard that Mamá had been a great beauty in her youth, and the belle of many balls. My cousins had other ideas as to what she kept in that wooden vault: its secret could be money (Mamá did not hand cash to strangers, banks were out of the question, so there were stories that her mattress was stuffed with dollar bills, and that she buried coins in jars in her garden under rosebushes, or kept them in her inviolate chifforobe); there might be that legendary gun salvaged from the Spanish-American conflict over the Island. We went wild over suspected treasures that we made up simply because children have to fill locked trunks with something wonderful.

On the wall above the bed hung a heavy silver crucifix. Christ's agonized head hung directly over Mamá's pillow. I avoided looking at this weapon suspended over where her head would lay; and on the rare occasions when I was allowed to sleep on that bed, I scooted down to the safe middle of the mattress, where her body's impression took me in like a mother's lap. Having taken care of the obligatory religious decoration with a crucifix, Mamá covered the other walls with objects sent to her over the years by her children in the States. *Los Nueva Yores*[3] were represented by, among other things, a postcard of Niagara Falls from her son Hernán, postmarked, Buffalo, N.Y. In a conspicuous gold frame hung a large color photograph of her daughter Nena, her husband and their five children at the entrance to Disneyland in California. From us she had gotten a black lace fan. Father had brought it to her from a tour of duty with the Navy in Europe (on Sundays she would remove it from its hook on the wall to fan herself at Sunday mass). Each year more items were added as the family grew and dispersed, and every object in the room had a story attached to it, a *cuento*[4] which Mamá would

2. "Good herbs, bad herbs."
3. "The New Yorkers."
4. "Tale."

bestow on anyone who received the privilege of a day alone with her. It was almost worth pretending to be sick, though the bitter herb purgatives of the body were a big price to pay for the spirit revivals of her story-telling.

Mamá slept alone on her large bed, except for the times when a sick grand-child warranted the privilege, or when a heartbroken daughter came home in need of more than herbal teas. In the family there is a story about how this came to be.

When one of the daughters, my mother or one of her sisters, tells the *cuento* of how Mamá came to own her nights, it is usually preceded by the qualifica-tions that Papá's exile from his wife's room was not a result of animosity between the couple, but that the act had been Mamá's famous bloodless coup for her personal freedom. Papá was the benevolent dictator of her body and her life who had had to be banished from her bed so that Mamá could better serve her family. Before the telling, we had to agree that the old man was not to blame. We all recognized that in the family Papá was as an *alma de Dios*,[5] a saintly, soft-spoken presence whose main pleasures in life, such as writing poetry and reading the Spanish large-type editions of *Reader's Digest*, always took place outside the vortex of Mamá's crowded realm. It was not his fault, after all, that every year or so he planted a babyseed in Mamá's fertile body, keeping her from leading the active life she needed and desired. He loved her and the babies. Papá composed odes and lyrics to celebrate births and anniver-saries and hired musicians to accompany him in singing them to his family and friends at extravagant pig-roasts he threw yearly. Mamá and the oldest girls worked for days preparing the food. Papá sat for hours in his painter's shed, also his study and library, composing the songs. At these celebrations he was also known to give long speeches in praise of God, his fecund wife, and his beloved island. As a middle child, my mother remembers these occasions as a time when the women sat in the kitchen and lamented their burdens, while the men feasted out in the patio, their rum-thickened voice rising in song and praise for each other, *compañeros* all.[6]

It was after the birth of her eighth child, after she had lost three at birth or in infancy, that Mamá made her decision. They say that Mamá had had a special way of letting her husband know that they were expecting, one that had begun when, at the beginning of their marriage, he had built her a house too confining for her taste. So, when she discovered her first pregnancy, she supposedly drew plans for another room, which he dutifully executed. Every time a child was due, she would demand, *more space, more space*. Papá acceded to her wishes, child after child, since he had learned early that Mamá's renowned temper was a thing that grew like a monster along with a new belly. In this way Mamá got the house that she wanted, but with each child she lost in heart and energy. She had knowledge of her body and perceived that if she had any more children, her dreams and her plans would have to be permanently forgotten,

5. Literally, "soul of God"; "a thoroughly good person."
6. "Companions."

because she would be a chronically ill woman, like Flora with her twelve children: asthma, no teeth, in bed more than on her feet.

And so, after my youngest uncle was born, she asked Papá to build a large   10
room at the back of the house. He did so in joyful anticipation. Mamá had asked him special things this time: shelves on the walls, a private entrance. He thought that she meant this room to be a nursery where several children could sleep. He thought it was a wonderful idea. He painted it his favorite color, sky blue, and made large windows looking out over a green hill and the church spires beyond. But nothing happened. Mamá's belly did not grow, yet she seemed in a frenzy of activity over the house. Finally, an anxious Papá approached his wife to tell her that the new room was finished and ready to be occupied. And Mamá, they say, replied: "Good, it's for *you*."

And so it was that Mamá discovered the only means of birth control available to a Catholic woman of her time: sacrifice. She gave up the comfort of Papá's sexual love for something she deemed greater: the right to own and control her body, so that she might live to meet her grandchildren—me among them—so that she could give more of herself to the ones already there, so that she could be more than a channel for other lives, so that even now that time has robbed her of the elasticity of her body and of her amazing reservoir of energy, she still emanates the kind of joy that can only be achieved by living according to the dictates of one's own heart.

MLA CITATION

Cofer, Judith Ortiz. "More Room." 1990. *The Norton Reader: An Anthology of Nonfiction.* Ed. Melissa A. Goldthwaite et al. New York: Norton, 2016. 132–35. Print.

Qᴜᴇsᴛɪᴏɴs

1. At the end of the essay, Judith Ortiz Cofer explains in fairly direct terms why her grandmother wanted "more room." Why do you think she uses narration as the primary mode in the rest of the essay? What does she gain by first narrating, then explaining?

2. Cofer uses many similes (comparisons with "like" or "as") and metaphors (comparisons without specific connectors)—for example, in paragraph 1 she says that her grandmother's house was "like a chambered nautilus" and in paragraph 5 that her grandmother's Bible was "her security system." Discuss the use of one or two such comparisons that you find particularly effective.

3. What are the possible meanings of the title?

4. Write about a favorite or mysterious place you remember from childhood.

N. Scott Momaday   *The Way to Rainy Mountain*

A SINGLE KNOLL RISES out of the plain in Oklahoma, north and west of the Wichita Range. For my people, the Kiowas, it is an old landmark, and they gave it the name Rainy Mountain. The hardest weather in the world is there. Winter brings blizzards, hot tornadic winds arise in the spring, and in summer the prairie is an anvil's edge. The grass turns brittle and brown, and it cracks beneath your feet. There are green belts along the rivers and creeks, linear groves of hickory and pecan, willow and witch hazel. At a distance in July or August the steaming foliage seems almost to writhe in fire. Great green and yellow grasshoppers are everywhere in the tall grass, popping up like corn to sting the flesh, and tortoises crawl about on the red earth, going nowhere in the plenty of time. Loneliness is an aspect of the land. All things in the plain are isolate; there is no confusion of objects in the eye, but *one* hill or *one* tree or *one* man. To look upon that landscape in the early morning, with the sun at your back, is to lose the sense of proportion. Your imagination comes to life, and this, you think, is where Creation was begun.

I returned to Rainy Mountain in July. My grandmother had died in the spring, and I wanted to be at her grave. She had lived to be very old and at last infirm. Her only living daughter was with her when she died, and I was told that in death her face was that of a child.

I like to think of her as a child. When she was born, the Kiowas were living the last great moment of their history. For more than a hundred years they had controlled the open range from the Smoky Hill River to the Red, from the headwaters of the Canadian to the fork of the Arkansas and Cimarron. In alliance with the Comanches, they had ruled the whole of the southern Plains. War was their sacred business, and they were among the finest horsemen the world has ever known. But warfare for the Kiowas was preeminently a matter of disposition rather than of survival, and they never understood the grim, unrelenting advance of the U.S. Cavalry. When at last, divided and ill-provisioned, they were driven onto the Staked Plains in the cold rains of autumn, they fell into panic. In Palo Duro Canyon they abandoned their crucial stores to pillage

First published in 1967 in the Reporter, *a now defunct small-circulation American magazine; reprinted in* The Way to Rainy Mountain *(1969), N. Scott Momaday's book about the west. The illustrations were drawn by the author's father, Al Momaday.*

and had nothing then but their lives. In order to save themselves, they surrendered to the soldiers at Fort Sill and were imprisoned in the old stone corral that now stands as a military museum. My grandmother was spared the humiliation of those high gray walls by eight or ten years, but she must have known from birth the affliction of defeat, the dark brooding of old warriors.

Her name was Aho, and she belonged to the last culture to evolve in North America. Her forebears came down from the high country in western Montana nearly three centuries ago. They were a mountain people, a mysterious tribe of hunters whose language has never been positively classified in any major group. In the late seventeenth century they began a long migration to the south and east. It was a journey toward the dawn, and it led to a golden age. Along the way the Kiowas were befriended by the Crows, who gave them the culture and religion of the Plains. They acquired horses, and their ancient nomadic spirit was suddenly free of the ground. They acquired Tai-me, the sacred Sun Dance doll, from that moment the object and symbol of their worship, and so shared in the divinity of the sun. Not least, they acquired the sense of destiny, therefore courage and pride. When they entered upon the southern Plains they had been transformed. No longer were they slaves to the simple necessity of survival; they were a lordly and dangerous society of fighters and thieves, hunters and

priests of the sun. According to their origin myth, they entered the world through a hollow log. From one point of view, their migration was the fruit of an old prophecy, for indeed they emerged from a sunless world.

5   Although my grandmother lived out her long life in the shadow of Rainy Mountain, the immense landscape of the continental interior lay like memory in her blood. She could tell of the Crows, whom she had never seen, and of the Black Hills, where she had never been. I wanted to see in reality what she had seen more perfectly in the mind's eye, and traveled fifteen hundred miles to begin my pilgrimage.

Yellowstone, it seemed to me, was the top of the world, a region of deep lakes and dark timber, canyons and waterfalls. But, beautiful as it is, one might have the sense of confinement there. The skyline in all directions is close at hand, the high wall of the woods and deep cleavages of shade. There is a perfect freedom in the mountains, but it belongs to the eagle and the elk, the badger and the bear. The Kiowas reckoned their stature by the distance they could see, and they were bent and blind in the wilderness.

Descending eastward, the highland meadows are a stairway to the plain. In July the inland slope of the Rockies is luxuriant with flax and buckwheat, stonecrop and larkspur. The earth unfolds and the limit of the land recedes. Clusters of trees, and animals grazing far in the distance, cause the vision to reach away and wonder to build upon the mind. The sun follows a longer course in the day, and the sky is immense beyond all comparison. The great billowing clouds that sail upon it are the shadows that move upon the grain like water, dividing light. Farther down, in the land of the Crows and Blackfeet, the plain is yellow. Sweet clover takes hold of the hills and bends upon itself to cover and seal the soil. There the Kiowas paused on their way; they had come to the place where they must change their lives. The sun is at home on the plains. Precisely there does it have the certain character of a god. When the Kiowas came to the land of the Crows, they could see the dark lees of the hills at dawn across the Bighorn River, the profusion of light on the grain shelves, the oldest deity ranging after the solstices. Not yet would they veer southward to the caldron of the land that lay below; they must wean their blood from the northern winter and hold the mountains a while longer in their view. They bore Tai-me in procession to the east.

A dark mist lay over the Black Hills, and the land was like iron. At the top of a ridge I caught sight of Devil's Tower upthrust against the gray sky as if in the birth of time the core of the earth had broken through its crust and the motion of the world was begun. There are things in nature that engender an awful quiet in the heart of man; Devil's Tower is one of them. Two centuries ago, because they could not do otherwise, the Kiowas made a legend at the base of the rock. My grandmother said:

> Eight children were there at play, seven sisters and their brother. Suddenly the boy was struck dumb; he trembled and began to run upon his hands and feet. His fingers became claws, and his body was covered with fur. Directly there was a bear where the boy had been. The sisters were terrified; they ran, and the bear after them. They came to the stump of a great tree, and the tree spoke to them. It bade them climb upon it, and as they did so it began to rise into the air. The bear came to kill them, but they were just beyond its reach. It reared against the tree and scored the bark all around with its claws. The seven sisters were borne into the sky, and they became the stars of the Big Dipper.

From that moment, and so long as the legend lives, the Kiowas have kinsmen in the night sky. Whatever they were in the mountains, they could be no more. However tenuous their well-being, however much they had suffered and would suffer again, they had found a way out of the wilderness.

My grandmother had a reverence for the sun, a holy regard that now is all but gone out of mankind. There was a wariness in her, and an ancient awe. She was a Christian in her later years, but she had come a long way about, and she never forgot her birthright. As a child she had been to the Sun Dances; she had taken part in those annual rites, and by them she had learned the restoration of her people in the presence of Tai-me. She was about seven when the last Kiowa Sun Dance was held in 1887 on the Washita River above Rainy Mountain Creek. The buffalo were gone. In order to consummate the ancient sacrifice—to impale the head of a buffalo bull upon the medicine tree—a delegation of old men journeyed into Texas, there to beg and barter for an animal from the Goodnight herd. She was ten when the Kiowas came together for the last time as a living Sun Dance culture. They could find no buffalo; they had to hang an old hide from the sacred tree. Before the dance could begin, a company of soldiers rode out from Fort Sill under orders to disperse the tribe. Forbidden without cause the essential act of their faith, having seen the wild herds slaughtered and left to rot upon the ground, the Kiowas backed away forever from the medicine tree. That was July 20, 1890, at the great bend of the Washita. My grandmother was there. Without bitterness, and for as long as she lived, she bore a vision of deicide.

10   Now that I can have her only in memory, I see my grandmother in the several postures that were peculiar to her: standing at the wood stove on a winter morning and turning meat in a great iron skillet; sitting at the south window, bent above her beadwork, and afterwards, when her vision failed, looking down for a long time into the fold of her hands; going out upon a cane, very slowly as she did when the weight of age came upon her; praying. I remember her most often at prayer. She made long, rambling prayers out of suffering and hope, having seen many things. I was never sure that I had the right to hear, so exclusive were they of all mere custom and company. The last time I saw her she prayed standing by the side of her bed at night, naked to the waist, the light of a kerosene lamp moving upon her dark skin. Her long, black hair, always drawn and braided in the day, lay upon her shoulders and against her breasts like a shawl. I do not speak Kiowa, and I never understood her prayers, but there was something inherently sad in the sound, some merest hesitation upon the syllables of sorrow. She began in a high and descending pitch, exhausting her breath to silence; then again and again—and always the same intensity of effort, of something that is, and is not, like urgency in the human voice. Transported so in the dancing light among the shadows of her room, she seemed beyond the reach of time. But that was illusion; I think I knew then that I should not see her again.

Houses are like sentinels in the plain, old keepers of the weather watch. There, in a very little while, wood takes on the appearance of great age. All colors wear soon away in the wind and rain, and then the wood is burned gray and the grain appears and the nails turn red with rust. The windowpanes are black and opaque; you imagine there is nothing within, and indeed there are many ghosts, bones given up to the land. They stand here and there against the sky, and you approach them for a longer time than you expect. They belong in the distance; it is their domain.

Once there was a lot of sound in my grandmother's house, a lot of coming and going, feasting and talk. The summers there were full of excitement and reunion. The Kiowas are a summer people; they abide the cold and keep to themselves, but when the season turns and the land becomes warm and vital they cannot hold still; an old love of going returns upon them. The aged visitors who came to my grandmother's house when I was a child were made of lean and leather, and they bore themselves upright. They wore great black hats and bright ample shirts that shook in the wind. They rubbed fat upon their hair and wound their braids with strips of colored cloth. Some of them painted their faces and carried the scars of old and cherished enmities. They were an old council of warlords, come to remind and be reminded of who they were. Their wives and daughters served them well. The women might indulge themselves; gossip was at once the mark and compensation of their servitude. They made loud and elaborate talk among themselves, full of jest and gesture, fright and false alarm. They went abroad in fringed and flowered shawls, bright beadwork and German silver. They were at home in the kitchen, and they prepared meals that were banquets.

There were frequent prayer meetings, and great nocturnal feasts. When I was a child I played with my cousins outside, where the lamplight fell upon the ground and the singing of the old people rose up around us and carried away into the darkness. There were a lot of good things to eat, a lot of laughter and surprise. And afterwards, when the quiet returned, I lay down with my grandmother and could hear the frogs away by the river and feel the motion of the air.

Now there is a funeral silence in the rooms, the endless wake of some final word. The walls have closed in upon my grandmother's house. When I returned to it in mourning, I saw for the first time in my life how small it was. It was late at night, and there was a white moon, nearly full. I sat for a long time on the stone steps by the kitchen door. From there I could see out across the land; I could see the long row of trees by the creek, the low light upon the rolling plains, and the stars of the Big Dipper. Once I looked at the moon and caught sight of a strange thing. A cricket had perched upon the handrail, only a few inches away from me. My line of vision was such that the creature filled the moon like a fossil. It had gone there, I thought, to live and die, for there, of all places, was its small definition made whole and eternal. A warm wind rose up and purled like the longing within me.

The next morning I awoke at dawn and went out on the dirt road to Rainy   15
Mountain. It was already hot, and the grasshoppers began to fill the air. Still, it was early in the morning, and the birds sang out of the shadows. The long yellow grass on the mountain shone in the bright light, and a scissortail hied above the land. There, where it ought to be, at the end of a long and legendary way, was my grandmother's grave. Here and there on the dark stones were ancestral names. Looking back once, I saw the mountain and came away.

MLA CITATION

Momaday, N. Scott. "The Way to Rainy Mountain." 1967. *The Norton Reader: An Anthology of Nonfiction.* Ed. Melissa A. Goldthwaite et al. 14th ed. New York: Norton, 2016. 136–41. Print.

QUESTIONS

1. Throughout this essay, N. Scott Momaday uses similes (comparisons with "like" or "as") and metaphors (comparisons without specific connectors). Which comparisons were most helpful in aiding your understanding? Which comparison was most surprising?

2. Momaday connects personal and cultural history to a particular place. Find another essay, either in "Profiles" or "Nature and the Environment," that makes similar connections. Write a comparison of the two essays.

3. In paragraph 10, Momaday describes the roles that women played in his grand-mother's Kiowa culture. Consider the roles women played in your grandmother's generation and culture; perhaps ask your mother or grandmother about their experiences. To what extent have those roles remained the same or changed in your generation? Write an essay based on your conversations with older family members and your own personal knowledge.

JHUMPA LAHIRI   *Rhode Island*

RHODE ISLAND IS NOT AN ISLAND. Most of it is attached to the continental United States, tucked into a perfect-looking corner formed by the boundaries of Connecticut to the west and Massachusetts above. The rest is a jagged confusion of shoreline: delicate slivers of barrier beach, numerous inlets and peninsulas, and a cluster of stray puzzle pieces, created by the movement of glaciers, nestled in the Narragansett Bay. The tip of Watch Hill, in the extreme southwest, extends like a curving rib bone into the Atlantic Ocean. The salt ponds lining the edge of South Kingstown,[1] where I grew up, resemble the stealthy work of insects who have come into contact with nutritious, antiquated paper.

In 1524, Giovanni Verrazzano[2] thought that the pear-shaped contours of Block Island, nine miles off the southern coast, resembled the Greek island of Rhodes. In 1644, subsequent explorers, mistaking one of Rhode Island's many attendant islands—there are over thirty of them—for another, gave the same name to Aquidneck Island, famous for Newport, and it has now come to represent the state as a whole. Though the name is misleading it is also apt, for despite Rhode Island's physical connection to the mainland, a sense of insularity prevails. Typical to many island communities, there is a combination of those who come only in the warm months, for the swimming and the clamcakes, and those full-time residents who seem never to go anywhere else. Jacqueline Kennedy Onassis and Cornelius Vanderbilt[3] were among Rhode Island's

Published in State by State: A Panoramic Portrait of America (2008), *a collection edited by Matt Weiland and Sean Wilsey to show the regional diversity of the United States. All fifty contributors wrote about their home states, exploring the intersections of personal, regional, and national history.*

1. Small town in the southern part of the state and home to the University of Rhode Island.
2. Italian explorer (1485–1528) working for King Francis I of France, who sailed the North American coast between South Carolina and Newfoundland.
3. Jacqueline Kennedy Onassis (1929–1994), wife of U.S. president John Fitzgerald Kennedy and later of Greek shipping magnate Aristotle Onassis; Cornelius Vanderbilt (1794–1877), American multimillionaire who made his wealth from steamships and railroads, and built "The Breakers," a summer house in Newport, Rhode Island.

summer people. Given its diminutive proportions there is a third category: those who pass through without stopping. Forty-eight miles long and thirty-seven wide, it is a brief, unavoidable part of the journey by train between Boston and New York and also, if one chooses to take I-95, by car.

Historically it has harbored the radical and the seditious, misfits and minorities. Roger Williams, the liberal theologian who is credited with founding Rhode Island in 1636, was banished from the Massachusetts Bay Colony by, among others, Nathaniel Hawthorne's great grandfather.[4] Williams's unorthodox views on matters religious and otherwise made him an enemy of the Puritans. He eventually became and remained until his death a Seeker, rejecting any single body of doctrine and respecting the good in all branches of faith. Rhode Island, the thirteenth of the original thirteen colonies, had the greatest degree of self-rule, and was the first to renounce allegiance to King George in 1776. The Rhode Island Charter of 1663 guaranteed "full liberty in religious concernments," and, to its credit, the state accommodated the nation's first Baptists, its first Quakers, and is the site of its oldest synagogue, dedicated in 1763. A different attitude greeted the indigenous population, effectively decimated by 1676 in the course of King Philip's War.[5] Rhode Island is the only state that continues to celebrate, the second Monday of every August, VJ Day, which commemorates the surrender of Japan after the bombings of Hiroshima and Nagasaki. On a lesser but also disturbing note, it has not managed to pass the bottle bill, which means that all those plastic containers of Autocrat Coffee Syrup, used to make coffee milk (Rhode Island's official beverage), are destined for the purgatory of landfills.

Though I was born in London and have Indian parents, Rhode Island is the reply I give when people ask me where I am from. My family came in the summer of 1970, from Cambridge, Massachusetts, so that my father could begin work as a librarian at the University of Rhode Island. I had just turned three years old. URI is located in the village of Kingston, a place originally called Little Rest. The name possibly stems from accounts of Colonial troops pausing on their way to fight the Narragansett tribe on the western banks of Worden Pond, an event known as the Great Swamp Massacre.[6] We lived on Kingston's main historic tree-lined drag, in a white house with a portico and black shutters. It had been built in 1829 (a fact stated by a plaque next to the front door) to contain the law office of Asa Potter, who was at one point Rhode Island's secretary of state, and whose main residence was the larger, more spectacular house next door. After Asa Potter left Rhode Island to work in a bank in New

---

4. Roger Williams (c. 1603–1683) was banished by Colonel John Hawthorne (1641–1717), the judge most famous for presiding over the Salem witch trials in 1692. His descendant was the novelist Nathaniel Hawthorne (1804–1864).

5. King Philip's War (1675–1676), sometimes called Metacom's Rebellion after the Native American leader whom the English called "King Philip," was fought between the Native American inhabitants of New England and the English settlers.

6. Pivotal battle in King Philip's War, fought in November 1675 between the colonial militia and the Narragansett tribe.

York, the house became the site of a general store, with a tailor's shop at the front. By 1970 it was an apartment house owned by a fellow Indian, a professor of mathematics named Dr. Suryanarayan.

5   My family was a hybrid; year-rounders who, like the summer people, didn't fundamentally belong. We rented the first floor of the house; an elderly American woman named Miss Tay lived above us, alone, and her vulnerable, solitary presence was a constant reminder, to my parents, of America's harsh ways. A thick iron chain threaded through wooden posts separated us from our neighbors, the Fishers. A narrow path at the back led to a brown shingled shed I never entered. Hanging from one of the outbuildings on the Fishers' property was an oxen yoke, an icon of old New England agriculture, at once elegant and menacing, that both intrigued and scared me as a child. Its bowed shape caused me to think it was a weapon, not merely a restraint. Until I was an adult, I never knew exactly what it was for.

Kingston in those days was a mixture of hippies and Yankees and professors and students. The students arrived every autumn, taking up all the parking spaces, crowding the tables in the Memorial Union with their trays of Cokes and French fries, one year famously streaking on the lawn outside a fraternity building. After commencement in May, things were quiet again, to the point of feeling deserted. I imagine this perpetual ebb and flow, segments of the population ritually coming and going, made it easier for my foreign-born parents to feel that they, too, were rooted to the community in some way. Apart from the Suryanarayans, there were a few other Indian families, women other than my mother in saris walking now and then across the quad. My parents sought them out, invited them over for Bengali[7] dinners, and consider a few of these people among their closest friends today.

The gravitational center of Kingston was, and remains, the Kingston Congregational Church ("King Kong" to locals), where my family did not worship but where I went for Girl Scout meetings once a week, and where my younger sister eventually had her high-school graduation party. Across the street from the church, just six houses down from ours, was the Kingston Free Library. It was constructed as a courthouse, and also served as the state house between 1776 and 1791. The building's staid Colonial bones later incorporated Victorian flourishes, including a belfry and a mansard roof. If you stand outside and look up at a window to the right on the third floor, three stern white life-sized busts will stare down at you through the glass. They are thought to be likenesses of Abraham Lincoln, Oliver Wendell Holmes, and John Greenleaf Whittier.[8] For many years now, the bust of Lincoln has worn a long red-and-white striped hat, *Cat in the Hat*[9]-style, on its head.

From my earliest memories I was obsessed with the library, with its creaky, cramped atmosphere and all the things it contained. The books used to live on

---

7. From the historic region now in northern India and southern Bangladesh.

8. Abraham Lincoln (1809–1865), president of the United States during the Civil War; Oliver Wendell Holmes (1841–1935), legal theorist and associate justice of the U.S. Supreme Court from 1902 until 1932; John Greenleaf Whittier (1807–1892), American Quaker poet.

9. Children's book (1957) that launched the career of Dr. Seuss.

varnished wooden shelves, the modest card catalog contained in two bureau-sized units, sometimes arranged back to back. Phyllis Goodwin, then and for decades afterward the children's librarian, conducted the story hours I faith-fully attended when I was little, held upstairs in a vaulted space called Potter Hall. Light poured in through enormous windows on three sides, and Asa Pot-ter's portrait, predominantly black apart from the pale shade of his face, pre-sided over the fireplace. Along with Phyllis there were two other women in charge of the library—Charlotte Schoonover, the director, and Pam Stoddard. Charlotte and Pam, roughly my mother's generation, were friends, and they both had sons about my age. For many years, Charlotte, Pam, and Phyllis rep-resented the three graces to me, guardians of a sacred place that seemed both to represent the heart of Kingston and also the means of escaping it. They liked to play Corelli or Chopin on the little tape recorder behind the desk, but ordered Patti Smith's *Horses* for the circulating album collection.[10]

When I was sixteen I was hired to work as a page at the library, which meant shelving books, working at the circulation desk, and putting plastic wrap-pers on the jackets of new arrivals. A lot of older people visited daily, to sit at a table with an arrangement of forsythia or cattails at the center, and read the newspaper. I remember a tall, slightly harried mother with wire-rimmed glasses who would come every two weeks with many children behind her and a large canvas tote bag over her shoulder, which she would dump out and then fill up again with more volumes of *The Borrowers* and Laura Ingalls Wilder[11] for the next round of collective reading. Jane Austen was popular with the patrons, enough for me to remember that the books had red cloth covers. I was an unhappy adolescent, lacking confidence, boyfriends, a proper sense of myself. When I was in the library it didn't matter. I took my cue from the readers who came and went and understood that books were what mattered, that they were above high school, above an adolescent's petty trials, above life itself.

By this time we no longer lived in Kingston. We had moved, when I was eight and my sister was one, to a house of our own. I would have preferred to stay in Kingston and live in an enclave called Biscuit City, not only because of the name but because it was full of professors and their families and had a laid-back, intellectual feel. Instead we moved to a town called Peace Dale, exactly one mile away. Peace Dale was a former mill town, an area where the univer-sity didn't hold sway. Our housing development, called Rolling Acres, was a leafy loop of roads without sidewalks. The turn into the neighborhood, off the main road, is between a John Deere showroom[12] and a bingo hall. Our house, a style called Colonial Garrison according to the developer's brochure, was historical

10

---

10. Arcangelo Corelli (1653–1713), Italian composer; Frédéric François Chopin (1810–1849), Polish composer and pianist; Patti Smith (b. 1946), American musician, poet, and visual artist.

11. *The Borrowers* (1952), the first in a series of children's books by Mary Norton about little people who live in the houses of big people and "borrow" things; Laura Ingalls Wilder (1867–1957), author of the popular "Little House" series for children.

12. For the sale of John Deere tractors and other agricultural equipment.

in name only. In 1975 it was built before our eyes—the foundation dug, concrete poured, pale yellow vinyl siding stapled to the exterior.

After we moved into that house, something changed; whether it was my growing older or the place itself, I was aware that the world immediately outside our door, with its red-flagged mailboxes and children's bicycles left overnight on well-seeded grass, was alien to my parents. Some of our neighbors were friendly. Others pretended we were not there. I remember hot days when the mothers of my American friends in the neighborhood would lie in their bikinis on reclining chairs, chatting over wine coolers as my friends and I ran through a sprinkler, while my fully dressed mother was alone in our house, deep-frying a carp or listening to Bengali folk songs. In Rolling Acres we became car-bound. We couldn't walk, as we had been able to do in Kingston, to see a movie on campus, or buy milk and bread at Evan's Market, or get stamps at the post office. While one could walk (or run or bike) endlessly around the looping roads of Rolling Acres, without a car we were cut off from the rest of the world. When my parents first moved to Rhode Island, I think they both assumed that it was an experiment, just another port of call on their unfolding immigrant journey. The fact that they now owned a house, along with my father getting tenure, brought the journey to a halt. Thirty-seven years later, my parents still live there. The Little Rest they took in 1970 has effectively become the rest of their lives.

The sense of the environment radically shifting from mile to mile holds true throughout Rhode Island, almost the way life can vary block by block in certain cities. In South Kingstown alone there is a startling mixture of the lovely and the ugly—of resort, rural, and run-of-the-mill. There are strip malls, most of them radiating from a frenetic intersection called Dale Carlia corner, and no one who lives in my town can avoid negotiating its many traffic lights and lanes on a regular basis. There are countless housing developments, filled with energy-efficient split-levels when I was growing up, these days with McMansions. There are several Dunkin' Donut shops (Rhode Island has more per capita than any other state). There are also quiet farms where horses graze, and remote, winding roads through woods, flanked by low stone walls. There are places to buy antiques and handmade pottery. Along South Road is a sloping, empty field that resembles the one where Wyeth painted Christina's World.[13] There is a house on Route 108, just after the traffic light on 138, with the most extraordinary show of azaleas I have ever seen. And then, of course, there are the beaches.

We did not live on the ocean proper, but it was close enough, about five miles away. The ocean was where we took all our visitors from Massachusetts (which was where the majority of my parents' Bengali friends lived), either to Scarborough, which is the state beach, or to Point Judith Light. They used to sit on the grassy hill speaking a foreign tongue, sometimes bringing a picnic of packaged white bread and a pot of aloo dum.[14] On the way back they liked to

13. Andrew Wyeth (1917–2009), Maine artist whose most famous work, Christina's World (1948), shows a woman in a field of golden grass struggling to reach a farmhouse at the top of the hill.
14. Potato curry.

stop in the fishing village of Galilee, where the parking lots of the shops and restaurants were covered with broken seashells. They did not go to eat stuffies, a local delicacy made from quahogs and bread crumbs, but to see if the daily catch included any butterfish or mackerel, to turn into a mustard curry at home. Occasionally my mother's best friend from Massachusetts, Koely Das, wanted to get lobsters or crabs, but these, too, received the curry treatment, a far, fiery cry from a side of melted butter.

The Atlantic I grew up with lacks the color and warmth of the Caribbean, the grandeur of the Pacific, the romance of the Mediterranean. It is generally cold, and full of rust-colored seaweed. Still, I prefer it. The waters of Rhode Island, as much a part of the state's character, if not more, as the land, never asked us questions, never raised a brow. Thanks to its very lack of welcome, its unwavering indifference, the ocean always made me feel accepted, and to my dying day, the seaside is the only place where I can feel truly and recklessly happy.

My father, a global traveler, considers Rhode Island paradise. For nearly four   15 decades he has dedicated himself there to a job he loves, rising through the ranks in the library's cataloging department to become its head. But in addition to the job, he loves the place. He loves that it is quiet, and moderate, and is, in the great scheme of things, uneventful. He loves that he lives close to his work, and that he does not have to spend a significant portion of his life sitting in a car on the highway, or on a crowded subway, commuting. (Lately, because my parents have downsized to one car, he has begun to take a bus, on which he is frequently the sole passenger.) Though Rhode Island is a place of four proper seasons, he loves that both winters and summers, tempered by the ocean breezes, are relatively mild. He loves working in his small garden, and going once a week to buy groceries, coupons in hand, at Super Stop&Shop. In many ways he is a spiritual descendant of America's earliest Puritan settlers: thrifty, hard-working, plain in his habits. Like Roger Williams, he is something of a Seeker, aloof from organized religions but appreciating their philosophical worth. He also embodies the values of two of New England's greatest thinkers, demonstrating a profound lack of materialism and self-reliance that would have made Thoreau and Emerson proud.[15] "The great man is he who in the midst of the crowd keeps with perfect sweetness the independence of solitude," Emerson wrote. This is the man who raised me.

My mother, a gregarious and hard-wired urbanite, has struggled; to hear her recall the first time she was driven down from Massachusetts, along I-95 and then a remote, lightless stretch of Route 138, is to understand that Rhode Island was and in many ways remains the heart of darkness for her. She stayed at home to raise me and my sister, frequently taking in other children as well, but apart from a stint as an Avon Lady she had no job. In 1987, when my sister was a teenager, my mother finally ventured out, directing a day care and also

15. Henry David Thoreau (1817–1862), American writer; see "The Battle of the Ants" (pp. 770–72) and "Where I Lived, and What I Lived For" (pp. 967–75); Ralph Waldo Emerson (1803–1882), American writer and philosopher.

working as a classroom assistant at South Road Elementary School, which both my sister and I had attended. One day, after she'd been working at the school for a decade, she started to receive anonymous hate mail. It came in the form of notes placed in her mailbox at school, and eventually in her coat pocket. There were nine notes in total. The handwriting was meant to look like a child's awkward scrawl. The content was humiliating, painful to recount. "Go back to India," one of them said. "Many people here do not like to see your face," read another. By then my mother had been a resident of Rhode Island for twenty-seven years. In Rhode Island she had raised two daughters, given birth to one. She had set up a home and potted geraniums year after year and thrown hundreds of dinner parties for her ever-expanding circle of Bengali friends. In Rhode Island she had renounced her Indian passport for an American one, pledged allegiance to the flag. My mother was ashamed of the notes, and for a while, hoping they would stop, she kept them to herself.

The incident might make a good start to a mystery novel, the type that always flew out of the Kingston Free Library: poison-pen letters appearing in a quaint, sleepy town. But there was nothing cozily intriguing about the cold-blooded correspondence my mother received. After finding the note in her coat pocket (it was February, recess time, and she had been expecting to pull out a glove), she told the school principal, and she also told my family what was going on. In the wake of this incident, many kind people reached out to my mother to express their outrage on her behalf, and for each of those nine notes, she received many sympathetic ones, including words of support from the former president of the university, Francis Horn. The majority of these people were Americans; one of the things that continues to upset my mother was that very few members of Rhode Island's Indian community, not insignificant by then, were willing to stand by her side. Some resented my mother for creating controversy, for drawing attention to their being foreign, a fact they worked to neutralize. Others told her that she might not have been targeted if she had worn skirts and trousers instead of saris and bindis. Meetings were held at the elementary school, calling for increased tolerance and sensitivity. The story was covered by the *Providence Journal-Bulletin* and the local television news. Montel Williams called our house, wanting my mother to appear on his show (she declined). A detective was put on the case, but the writer of the notes never came forward, was never found. Over ten years have passed. South Road School has shut down, for reasons having nothing to do with what happened to my mother. She worked for another school, part of the same system, in West Kingston, and has recently retired.

I left Rhode Island at eighteen to attend college in New York City, which is where, following a detour up to Boston, I continue to live. Because my parents still live in Rhode Island I still visit, though the logistics of having two small children mean they come to me these days more often than I go to them. I was there in August 2007. My parents, children, sister, and I had just been to Vermont, renting a cabin on a lake. There was a screened-in porch, a Modern Library first edition of *To the Lighthouse*[16] in the bookcase, and a severe mouse

16. Novel (1927) by Virginia Woolf set in a summer house by the sea.

problem in the kitchen. In the end the mice drove us away, and during the long drive back to my parents' house, I was aware how little Vermont and Rhode Island, both New England states, have in common. Vermont is dramatically northern, rural, mountainous, landlocked. Rhode Island is flat, briny, more densely populated. Vermont is liberal enough to sanction gay marriage but feels homogenous, lacking Rhode Island's deep pockets of immigration from Ireland, Portugal, and Italy. Rhode Island's capital, Providence, was run for years by a Republican Italian, Buddy Cianci. In 1984 he was convicted of kidnapping his then-estranged wife's boyfriend, beating him with a fire log, and burning him with a lighted cigarette. In 1991 he ran again for mayor, and the citizens of Rhode Island handed him 97 percent of the vote.

It was hotter in Rhode Island than it had been in Vermont. The Ghiorse Beach Factor, courtesy of John Ghiorse, the meteorologist on Channel 10, was a perfect 10 for the weekend we were there. On my way to buy sunscreen at the CVS pharmacy in Kingston, I stopped by the library, excited to see the sign outside indicating that the summer book sale was still going on. The library has been expanded and renovated since I worked there, the circulation desk much larger now and facing the entering visitor, with a computer system instead of the clunky machine that stamped due date cards. The only familiar thing, apart from the books, was Pam. "Just the dregs," she warned me about the book sale. As we were catching up, an elderly couple with British accents approached. "Excuse me," the woman interrupted. "Can you recommend something decent? I'm tired of murder mysteries and people being killed. I just want to hear a decent family story." Pam led her away to the books on tape section, and I went upstairs to Potter Hall to look at the sale. It was just the dregs, as Pam had said, but I managed to find a few things I'd always meant to read—a paperback copy of Donna Tartt's *The Secret History*, and *Monkeys* by Susan Minot. The curtained stage that used to be at one end of the room, on which I had performed, among other things, the role of the Queen of Hearts in *Alice in Wonderland*, was gone, so that the space seemed even bigger. The grand piano was still there, but Asa Potter's portrait was at the Museum of Fine Arts in Boston, Pam later explained, for repairs. She told me she was thinking of retiring soon, and that Phyllis, who had retired long before, had discovered a late-blooming talent for portrait painting. "It's a quirky place," Pam reflected when I asked her about Rhode Island, complaining, "There's no zoning. No united front." And practically in the same breath, proudly: "Kingston is the melting pot of the state."

In the afternoon I took my children, along with my mother and sister, to   20
Scarborough. The beach was packed, the tide high and rough. As soon as we set down our things, a wave hit us, forcing us to pick up a drenched blanket and move. Scarborough is a large beach with a paved parking lot that feels even larger. The parking lot itself is also useful in the off-season, for learning how to drive. Scarborough lacks the steep, dramatic dunes and isolated aura of lower Cape Cod, a stretch of New England coastline I have come, in my adult life, to love more than the beach of my childhood. The sand at Scarborough is extremely fine and gray and, when moist, resembles wet ash. A large tide pool had formed that day, and it was thick with young muddied children lying on their bellies, pretending to swim. My son darted off to chase seagulls. The breeze blew

impressively in spite of the sultry weather, justifying Ghiorse's ten out of ten. In the distance I could see Point Judith Light. The giant billboard for Copper-tone, the Dr. T. J. Eckleburg of my youth,[17] has vanished, but I imagined it was still there—the model's toasted bikini-clad seventies body sprawled regally, indifferently, above the masses.

An announcement on the loudspeaker informed us that a little girl was lost, asking her to meet her mother under the flag on the boardwalk. Another announcement followed: The men's hot water showers were temporarily out of service. The population was democratic, unpretentious, inclusive: ordinary bod-ies of various sizes and shades, the shades both genetic and cultivated, reading paperback bestsellers and reaching into big bags of chips. I saw no *New Yorker* magazines being read, no heirloom tomato sandwiches or organic peaches being consumed. A trio of deeply tanned adolescent boys tripped past, collectively courting, one could imagine, the same elusive girl. The sun began to set, and within an hour the crowd had thinned to the point where a man started to drag his metal detector through the sand, and the only kids in the tide pool were my own. As we were getting up to go, our bodies sticky with salt, it occurred to me that Scarborough Beach on a summer day is one of the few places that is not a city but still manages, reassuringly, to feel like one. Two days later, I headed home with my sister and my children to Brooklyn. On our way through West Kingston to catch the highway, a lone green truck selling Dell's, Rhode Island's beloved frozen lemonade, beckoned at an otherwise desolate intersection, but my sister and I drove on, accepting the fact that we would not taste Dell's for another year.

As long as my mother and father live, I will continue to visit Rhode Island. They are, respectively, in their late sixties and seventies now, and each time I drive by the local funeral home in Wakefield, I try to prepare myself. Just after I'd finished a draft of this essay, early one November morning, my mother had a heart attack at home. An Indian doctor at Rhode Island Hospital, Arun Singh, performed the bypass operation that has saved her life. When I was a child, I remember my mother often wondering who, in the event of an emergency or other crisis, would come running to help us. During the weeks when I feared she might slip away, everyone did. Our mailbox was stuffed with get-well cards from my mother's students, the refrigerator stuffed with food from her friends. My father's colleagues at the library took up a collection to buy my family Thanks-giving dinner. Our next door neighbor, Mrs. Hyde, who had seen the ambulance pulling up to our house, crossed over to our yard as I was heading to the hospital one day, and told me she'd said a special prayer for my mother at her church.

Due to my parents' beliefs, whenever and wherever they do die, they will not be buried in Rhode Island soil. The house in Rolling Acres will belong to other people; there will be no place there to pay my respects. At the risk of pre-dicting the future, I can see myself, many years from now, driving up I–95, on

17. Lahiri alludes to a billboard in F. Scott Fitzgerald's novel *The Great Gatsby* (1925), which shows the eyes of Dr. T. J. Eckleburg, "blue and gigantic—their irises are one yard high."

my way to another vacation on the Cape. We will cross the border after Connecticut, turn off at exit 3A for Kingston, and then continue along an alternative, prettier route that will take us across Jamestown and over the Newport Bridge, where the sapphire bay spreads out on either side, a breathtaking sight that will never grow old. There will no longer be a reason to break the journey in Little Rest. Like many others, we will pass through without stopping.

MLA CITATION

Lahiri, Jhumpa. "Rhode Island." 2008. *The Norton Reader: An Anthology of Nonfiction.* Ed. Melissa A. Goldthwaite et al. 14th ed. New York: Norton, 2016. 142–51. Print.

QUESTIONS

1. One purpose of the collection in which Jhumpa Lahiri's essay appeared is to show the diversity of the fifty American states. How does Lahiri achieve this purpose? What details does she provide that are unique to Rhode Island or New England?

2. Lahiri is a novelist who alludes to other authors and their writing. Choose one allusion to a novel or short story, and explain how this reference enriches Lahiri's narrative.

3. Lahiri gives both her personal history and a brief history of the state in which she grew up. What connections might be drawn between the personal and the regional? Consider both the explicit and implicit connections.

4. Write an account of the region or state in which you grew up, integrating some of its history with your personal experience.

IAN FRAZIER   *Take the F*

BROOKLYN, NEW YORK, has the undefined, hard-to-remember shape of a stain. I never know what to tell people when they ask me where in it I live. It sits at the western tip of Long Island at a diagonal that does not conform neatly to the points of the compass. People in Brooklyn do not describe where they live in terms of north or west or south. They refer instead to their neighborhoods and to the nearest subway lines. I live on the edge of Park Slope, a neighborhood by the crest of a low ridge that runs through the borough. Prospect Park is across the street. Airplanes in the landing pattern for LaGuardia

First published as "Letter from Brooklyn" in the New Yorker *(1995), a weekly magazine of "reportage, commentary, criticism, essays, fiction, satire, cartoons, and poetry," to which Ian Frazier is a regular contributor; later included in his book* Gone to New York: Adventures in the City *(2005).*

Airport sometimes fly right over my building; every few minutes, on certain sunny days, perfectly detailed airplane shadows slide down my building and up the building opposite in a blink. You can see my building from the plane—it's on the left-hand side of Prospect Park, the longer patch of green you cross after the expanse of Green-Wood Cemetery.

We moved to a co-op apartment in a four-story building a week before our daughter was born. She is now six. I grew up in the country and would not have expected ever to live in Brooklyn. My daughter is a city kid, with less sympathy for certain other parts of the country. When we visited Montana, she was disappointed by the scarcity of pizza places. I overheard her explaining—she was three or four then—to a Montana kid about Brooklyn. She said, "In Brooklyn, there is a lot of broken glass, so you have to wear shoes. And, there is good pizza." She is stern in her judgment of pizza. At the very low end of the pizza-ranking scale is some pizza she once had in New Hampshire, a category now called New Hampshire pizza. In the middle is some okay pizza she once had at the Bronx Zoo, which she calls zoo pizza. At the very top is the pizza at the pizza place where the big kids go, about two blocks from our house.

Our subway is the F train. It runs under our building and shakes the floor. The F is generally a reliable train, but one spring as I walked in the park I saw emergency vehicles gathered by a concrete-sheathed hole in the lawn. Firemen lifted a metal lid from the hole and descended into it. After a while, they reappeared, followed by a few people, then dozens of people, then a whole lot of people—passengers from a disabled F train, climbing one at a time out an exit shaft. On the F, I sometimes see large women in straw hats reading a newspaper called the *Caribbean Sunrise*, and Orthodox Jews bent over Talmudic texts[1] in which the footnotes have footnotes, and groups of teenagers wearing identical red bandannas with identical red plastic baby pacifiers in the corners of their mouths, and female couples in porkpie hats, and young men with the silhouettes of the Manhattan skyline razored into their short side hair from one temple around to the other, and Russian-speaking men with thick wrists and big wristwatches, and a hefty, tall woman with long, straight blond hair who hums and closes her eyes and absently practices cello fingerings on the metal subway pole. As I watched the F train passengers emerge among the grass and trees of Prospect Park, the faces were as varied as usual, but the expressions of indignant surprise were all about the same.

Just past my stop, Seventh Avenue, Manhattan-bound F trains rise from underground to cross the Gowanus Canal. The train sounds different—lighter, quieter—in the open air. From the elevated tracks, you can see the roofs of many houses stretching back up the hill to Park Slope, and a bumper crop of rooftop graffiti, and neon signs for Eagle Clothes and Kentile Floors, and flat expanses of factory roofs where seagulls stand on one leg around puddles in the sagging spots. There are fuel-storage tanks surrounded by earthen barriers, and slag piles, and conveyor belts leading down to the oil-slicked waters of

---

1. Rabbinic discussions of law, ethics, philosophy, and history collected in the Talmud, a key text of Judaism.

the canal. On certain days, the sludge at the bottom of the canal causes it to bubble. Two men fleeing the police jumped in the canal a while ago; one made it across, the other quickly died. When the subway doors open at the Smith–Ninth Street stop, you can see the bay and sometimes smell the ocean breeze. This stretch of elevated is the highest point of the New York subway system. To the south you can see the Verrazano-Narrows Bridge, to the north the World Trade towers. For just a few moments, the Statue of Liberty appears between passing buildings. Pieces of a neighborhood—laundry on clotheslines, a standup swimming pool, a plaster saint, a satellite dish, a rectangle of lawn—slide by like quickly dealt cards. Then the train descends again; growing over the wall just before the tunnel is a wisteria bush, which blooms pale blue every May.

I have spent days, weeks on the F train. The trip from Seventh Avenue to midtown Manhattan is long enough so that every ride can produce its own minisociety of riders, its own forty-minute Ship of Fools.[2] Once a woman an arm's length from me on a crowded train pulled a knife on a man who threatened her. I remember the argument and the principals, but mostly I remember the knife—its flat, curved wood-grain handle inlaid with brass fittings at each end, its long, tapered blade. Once a man sang the words of the Lord's Prayer to a mournful, syncopated tune, and he fitted the mood of the morning so exactly that when he asked for money at the end the riders reached for their wallets and purses as if he'd pulled a gun. Once a big white kid with some friends was teasing a small old Hispanic lady, and when he got off the train I looked at him through the window and he slugged it hard next to my face. Once a thin woman and a fat woman sitting side by side had a long and loud conversation about someone they intended to slap silly: "Her butt be in the *hospital!*" "Bring out the ar-*tillery!*" The terminus of the F in Brooklyn is at Coney Island, not far from the beach. At an off hour, I boarded the train and found two or three passengers and, walking around on the floor, a crab. The passengers were looking at the crab. Its legs clicked on the floor like varnished fingernails. It moved in this direction, then that, trying to get comfortable. It backed itself under a seat, against the wall. Then it scooted out just after some new passengers had sat down there, and they really screamed. Passengers at the next stop saw it and laughed. When a boy lifted his foot as if to stomp it, everybody cried, "Noooh!" By the time we reached Jay Street–Borough Hall,[3] there were maybe a dozen of us in the car, all absorbed in watching the crab. The car doors opened and a heavyset woman with good posture entered. She looked at the crab; then, sternly, at all of us. She let a moment pass. Then she demanded, "*Whose* is *that?*" A few stops later, a short man with a mustache took a manila envelope, bent down, scooped the crab into it, closed it, and put it in his coat pocket.

The smells in Brooklyn: coffee, fingernail polish, eucalyptus, the breath from laundry rooms, pot roast, Tater Tots. A woman I know who grew up here says

2. Ancient Western allegory depicting a ship with human passengers who are mad, frivolous, or witlessly ignorant of their fate.

3. Station on the New York City subway system.

she moved away because she could not stand the smell of cooking food in the hallway of her parents' building. I feel just the opposite. I used to live in a converted factory above an army-navy store, and I like being in a place that smells like people live there. In the mornings, I sometimes wake to the smell of toast, and I still don't know exactly whose toast it is. And I prefer living in a borough of two and a half million inhabitants, the most of any borough in the city. I think of all the rural places, the pine-timbered canyons and within-commuting-distance farmland, that we are preserving by not living there. I like the immensities of the borough, the unrolling miles of Eastern Parkway and Ocean Parkway and Linden Boulevard, and the disheveled outlying parks strewn with tree limbs and with shards of glass held together by liquor bottle labels, and the tough bridges—the Williamsburg and the Manhattan—and the gentle Brooklyn Bridge. And I like the way the people talk; some really do have Brooklyn accents, really do say "dese" and "dose." A week or two ago, a group of neighbors stood on a street corner watching a peregrine falcon on a building cornice contentedly eating a pigeon it had caught, and the sunlight came through its tail feathers, and a woman said to a man, "Look at the tail, it's so ah-range," and the man replied, "Yeah, I soar it." Like many Americans, I fear living in a nowhere, in a place that is no-place; in Brooklyn, that doesn't trouble me at all.

Everybody, it seems, is here. At Grand Army Plaza, I have seen traffic tie-ups caused by Haitians and others rallying in support of President Aristide,[4] and by St. Patrick's Day parades, and by Jews of the Lubavitcher sect celebrating the birthday of their Grand Rebbe with a slow procession of ninety-three motor homes—one for each year of his life. Local taxis have bumper stickers that say "Allah Is Great"; one of the men who made the bomb that blew up the World Trade Center used an apartment just a few blocks from me. When an election is held in Russia, crowds line up to cast ballots at a Russian polling place in Brighton Beach. A while ago, I volunteer-taught reading at a public elementary school across the park. One of my students, a girl, was part Puerto Rican, part Greek, and part Welsh. Her looks were a lively combination, set off by sea-green eyes. I went to a map store in Manhattan and bought maps of Puerto Rico, Greece, and Wales to read with her, but they didn't interest her. A teacher at the school was directing a group of students to set up chairs for a program in the auditorium, and she said to me, "We have a problem here— each of these kids speaks a different language." She asked the kids to tell me where they were from. One was from Korea, one from Brazil, one from Poland, one from Guyana, one from Taiwan. In the program that followed, a chorus of fourth and fifth graders sang "God Bless America," "You're a Grand Old Flag," and "I'm a Yankee-Doodle Dandy."

People in my neighborhood are mostly white, and middle class or above. People in neighborhoods nearby are mostly not white, and mostly middle class or below. Everybody uses Prospect Park. On summer days, the park teems with sound—the high note is kids screaming in the water sprinklers at the

4. Jean-Bertrand Aristide (b. 1953), president of Haiti briefly in 1991, and again from 1994 to 1996 and 2001 to 2004.

playground, the midrange is radios and tape players, and the bass is idling or speeding cars. People bring lawn furniture and badminton nets and coolers, and then they barbecue. Charcoal smoke drifts into the neighborhood. Last year, local residents upset about the noise and litter and smoke began a campaign to outlaw barbecuing in the park. There was much unfavorable comment about "the barbecuers." Since most of the barbecuers, as it happens, are black or Hispanic, the phrase "Barbecuers Go Home," which someone spray-painted on the asphalt at the Ninth Street entrance to the park, took on a pointed, unkind meaning. But then park officials set up special areas for barbecuing, and the barbecuers complied, and the controversy died down.

Right nearby is a shelter for homeless people. Sometimes people sleep on the benches along the park, sometimes they sleep in the foyer of our building. Once I went downstairs, my heart pounding, to evict a homeless person who I had been told was there. The immediate, unquestioning way she left made me feel bad; later I always said "Hi" to her and gave her a dollar when I ran into her. One night, late, I saw her on the street, and I asked her her last name (by then I already knew her first name) and for a moment she couldn't recall it. At this, she shook her head in mild disbelief.

There's a guy I see on a bench along Prospect Park West all the time. Once 10 I walked by carrying my year-old son, and the man said, "Someday he be carrying you." At the local copy shop one afternoon, a crowd was waiting for copies and faxes when a man in a houndstooth fedora came in seeking signatures for a petition to have the homeless shelter shut down. To my surprise, and his, the people in the copy shop instantly turned on him. "I suppose because they're poor they shouldn't even have a place to sleep at night," a woman said as he backed out the door. On the park wall across the street from my building, someone has written in black marker:

COPS PROTECT CITIZENS
WHO PROTECT US FROM COPS.

Sometimes I walk from my building downhill and north, along the Brooklyn waterfront, where cargo ships with scuffed sides and prognathous bows lean overhead. Sometimes I walk by the Brooklyn Navy Yard, its docks now too dormant to attract saboteurs, its long expanses of chain-link fence tangled here and there with the branches of ailanthus trees growing through. Sometimes I head southwest, keeping more or less to the high ground—Bay Ridge—along Fifth Avenue, through Hispanic neighborhoods that stretch in either direction as far as you can see, and then through block after block of Irish. I follow the ridge to its steep descent to the water at the Verrazano Narrows; Fort Hamilton, an army post dating from 1814, is there, and a small Episcopal church called the Church of the Generals. Robert E. Lee once served as a vestryman of this church, and Stonewall Jackson was baptized here. Today the church is in the shade of a forest of high concrete columns supporting an access ramp to the Verrazano-Narrows Bridge.

Sometimes I walk due south, all the way out Coney Island Avenue. In that direction, as you approach the ocean, the sky gets bigger and brighter, and the buildings seem to flatten beneath it. Dry cleaners advertise "Tallis[5] Cleaned Free with Every Purchase Over Fifteen Dollars." Then you start to see occasional lines of graffiti written in Cyrillic.[6] Just past a Cropsey Avenue billboard welcoming visitors to Coney Island is a bridge over a creek filled nearly to the surface with metal shopping carts that people have tossed there over the years. A little farther on, the streets open onto the beach. On a winter afternoon, bundled-up women sit on the boardwalk on folding chairs around a portable record player outside a restaurant called Gastronom Moscow. The acres of trash-dotted sand are almost empty. A bottle of Peter the Great vodka lies on its side, drops of water from its mouth making a small depression in the sand. A man with trousers rolled up to his shins moves along the beach, chopping at driftwood with an axe. Another passerby says, "He's vorking hard, that guy!" The sunset unrolls light along the storefronts like tape. From the far distance, little holes in the sand at the water's edge mark the approach of a short man wearing hip boots and earphones and carrying a long-handled metal detector. Treasure hunters dream of the jewelry that people must have lost here over the years. Some say that this is the richest treasure beach in the Northeast. The man stops, runs the metal detector again over a spot, digs with a clamming shovel, lifts some sand, brushes through it with a gloved thumb, discards it. He goes on, leaving a trail of holes behind him.

I like to find things myself, and I always try to keep one eye on the ground as I walk. So far I have found seven dollars (a five and two ones), an earring in the shape of a strawberry, several personal notes, a matchbook with a 900 number to call to hear "prison sex fantasies," and two spent .25-caliber shells. Once on Carroll Street, I saw a page of text on the sidewalk, and I bent over to read it. It was page 191 from a copy of Anna Karenina.[7] I read the whole page. It described Vronsky leaving a gathering and riding off in a carriage. In a great book, the least fragment is great. I looked up and saw a woman regarding me closely from a few feet away. "You're reading," she said wonderingly. "From a distance, I t'ought you were watchin' ants."

My favorite place to walk is the Brooklyn Botanic Garden, not more than fifteen minutes away. It's the first place I take out-of-towners, who may not associate Brooklyn with flowers. In the winter, the garden is drab as pocket lint, and you can practically see all the way through from Flatbush Avenue to Washington Avenue. But then in February or March a few flowerings begin, the snowdrops and the crocuses, and then the yellow of the daffodils climbs Daffodil Hill, and then the magnolias—star magnolias, umbrella magnolias, saucer magnolias— go off all at once, and walking among them is like flying through cumulus clouds. Then the cherry trees blossom, some a soft and glossy red like makeup, others pink as a dessert, and crowds fill the paths on weekends and stand in front of the blossoms in their best clothes and have their pictures taken. Security guards

5. Jewish prayer shawl.
6. Alphabet used for Russian and other Slavic languages.
7. Novel by the Russian writer Leo Tolstoy, published in serial installments between 1873 and 1877.

tell people, "No eating, no sitting on the grass—this is a garden, not a park." There are traffic jams of strollers and kids running loose. One security guard jokes into his radio, "There's a pterodactyl on the overlook!" In the pond in the Japanese Garden, ducks lobby for pieces of bread. A duck quacks, in Brooklynese, "Yeah, yeah, yeah," having heard it all before.

Then the cherry blossoms fall, they turn some paths completely pink next to the grass's green, and the petals dry, and people tread them into a fine pink powder. Kids visit on end-of-school-year field trips, and teachers yell, "Shawon, get back on line!" and boys with long T-shirts printed from neck to knee with an image of Martin Luther King's face run by laughing and swatting at one another. The yellow boxes that photographic film comes in fall on the ground, and here and there an empty bag of Crazy Calypso potato chips. The lilacs bloom, each bush with a scent slightly different from the next, and yellow tulips fill big round planters with color so bright it ascends in a column, like a searchlight beam. The roses open on the trellises in the Rose Garden and attract a lively air traffic of bees, and June wedding parties, brides and grooms and their subsidiaries, adjust themselves minutely for photographers there. A rose called the Royal Gold smells like a new bathing suit and is as yellow.

In our building of nine apartments, two people have died and six have been born since we moved in. I like our neighbors—a guy who works for Off-Track Betting, a guy who works for the Department of Correction, a woman who works for Dean Witter, an in-flight steward, a salesperson of subsidiary rights at a publishing house, a restaurant manager, two lawyers, a retired machinist, a Lebanese-born woman of ninety-five—as well as any I've ever had. We keep track of the bigger events in the building with the help of Chris, our downstairs neighbor. Chris lives on the ground floor and often has conversations in the hall while her foot props her door open. When our kids are sick, she brings them her kids' videos to watch, and when it rains she gives us rides to school. One year, Chris became pregnant and had to take a blood-thinning medicine and was in and out of the hospital. Finally, she had a healthy baby and came home, but then began to bleed and didn't stop. Her husband brought the baby to us about midnight and took Chris to the nearest emergency room. Early the next morning, the grandmother came and took the baby. Then for two days nobody heard anything. When we knocked on Chris's door we got no answer and when we called we got an answering machine. The whole building was expectant, spooky, quiet. The next morning I left the house and there in the foyer was Chris. She held her husband's arm, and she looked pale, but she was returning from the hospital under her own steam. I hugged her at the door, and it was the whole building hugging her. I walked to the garden seeing glory everywhere. I went to the Rose Garden and took a big Betsy McCall rose to my face and breathed into it as if it were an oxygen mask.

15

MLA CITATION

Frazier, Ian. "Take the F." 1995. *The Norton Reader: An Anthology of Nonfiction*. Ed. Melissa A. Goldthwaite et al. 14th ed. New York: Norton, 2016. 151–57. Print.

Questions

1. According to Ian Frazier, Brooklynites identify themselves by neighborhood and subway line (paragraph 1). In addition to his subway line, how does Frazier describe where he lives? What techniques help him present his Brooklyn neighborhood to readers who are nonresidents?

2. Frazier engages all of the senses—sight, sound, smell, taste, and touch—to portray his Brooklyn home. Choose one example of each that stands out to you. How do these examples create a sense of place?

3. Like Jhumpa Lahiri in "Rhode Island" (pp. 142–51), Frazier wishes to establish the uniqueness of his home. What features seem to be unique? What features seem universal? What relation do you see between the unique and the universal?

4. Write an essay about your neighborhood, using techniques identified in questions 1 and 2.

E. B. White   *Once More to the Lake*

ONE SUMMER, ALONG ABOUT 1904, my father rented a camp on a lake in Maine and took us all there for the month of August. We all got ringworm from some kittens and had to rub Pond's Extract on our arms and legs night and morning, and my father rolled over in a canoe with all his clothes on; but outside of that the vacation was a success and from then on none of us ever thought there was any place in the world like that lake in Maine. We returned summer after summer—always on August 1st for one month. I have since become a salt-water man, but sometimes in summer there are days when the restlessness of the tides and the fearful cold of the sea water and the incessant wind which blows across the afternoon and into the evening make me wish for the placidity of a lake in the woods. A few weeks ago this feeling got so strong I bought myself a couple of bass hooks and a spinner and returned to the lake where we used to go, for a week's fishing and to revisit old haunts.

I took along my son, who had never had any fresh water up his nose and who had seen lily pads only from train windows. On the journey over to the lake I began to wonder what it would be like. I wondered how time would have marred this unique, this holy spot—the coves and streams, the hills that the sun set behind, the camps and the paths behind the camps. I was sure the tarred road would have found it out and I wondered in what other ways it would be

Originally appeared in "One Man's Meat," E. B. White's column for Harper's Magazine *(1941), an American monthly covering politics, society, culture, and the environment; later included in* One Man's Meat *(1942), a collection of his columns about life on a Maine saltwater farm, and then in* Essays of E. B. White *(1977).*

and wrung them out. Languidly, and with no thought of going in, I watched him, his hard little body, skinny and bare, saw him wince slightly as he pulled up around his vitals the small, soggy, icy garment. As he buckled the swollen belt suddenly my groin felt the chill of death.

MLA CITATION

White, E. B. "Once More to the Lake." 1941. *The Norton Reader: An Anthology of Nonfiction*. Ed. Melissa A. Goldthwaite et al. 14th ed. New York: Norton, 2016. 158–63. Print.

QUESTIONS

1. E. B. White includes many details to describe his impressions of the lake when he went there as a child and when he returns as an adult—for example, about the road, the dragonfly, and the boat's motor. What are some other details, and what do they tell us about what has changed or stayed the same?

2. White's last sentence often surprises readers. Go back through the essay and pick out sections, words, or phrases that seem to prepare for the ending.

3. Write about revisiting a place that has special meaning for you, including details of your early memories and reflections on your more recent visit.

GENDER AND HUMAN NATURE

ANNA QUINDLEN   *Between the Sexes, a Great Divide*

PERHAPS WE ALL HAVE THE SAME MEMORY of the first boy-girl party we attended. The floors were waxed, the music loud, the air thick with the smell of cologne. The boys stood on one side of the room and the girls on the other, each affecting a nonchalance belied by the shuffling male loafers and the occasional high birdlike sound of a female giggle.

Eventually, one of the taller, better-looking boys, perhaps dogged by two slightly shorter, squeakier acolytes, would make the big move across the chasm to ask the cutest girl to dance. Eventually, one of the girls would brave the divide to start a conversation on the other side. We would immediately develop a certain opinion of that girl, so that for the rest of our school years together, pajama parties would fairly crackle when she was not there.

None of us would consciously know it then, but what we were seeing, that great empty space in the center of the floor as fearful as a trapdoor, was the great division between the sexes. It was wonderful to think of the time when it would no longer be there, when the school gym would be a great meeting ground in which we would mingle freely, girl and boy, boy and girl, person to person, all alike. And maybe that's going to happen sometime in my lifetime, but I can't say I know when.

I've thought about this for some time, because I've written some loving things about men, and some nasty things too, and I meant them all. And I've always been a feminist, and I've been one of the boys as well, and I've given both sides a pretty good shot. I've spent a lot of time telling myself that men and women are fundamentally alike, mainly in the service of arguing that women should not only be permitted but be welcomed into a variety of positions and roles that only men occupied.

5   And then something happens, a little thing usually, and all I can see is that great shiny space in the middle of the dance floor where no one ever meets. "I swear to God we are a different species," one of my friends said on the telephone recently. I can't remember whether the occasion was a fight with her

Anna Quindlen wrote this essay for the op-ed column "Hers" that ran in the New York Times *(1988). The column was a forum for women to write about topics that mattered to them and to women in general.*

husband, a scene at work or a contretemps with a mutual male friend of ours. No matter. She's said it before and she'll say it again, just like all my other friends have said it to me, and I to them. Men are the other.

We are the other, too, of course. That's why we want to believe so badly that there are no others at all, because over the course of human history being other has meant being symbols of divinity, evil, carnal degeneration, perfect love, fertility and death, to name a few. And anybody who has ever been a symbol knows that it's about as relaxing as sitting on a piece of Louis XV furniture. It is also true that over the course of history, we have been subordinate to others, symbols of weakness, dependency and emotions run amok.

Yet isn't it odd that I feel that the prejudice is somehow easier to deal with than the simple difference? Prejudice is evil and can be fought, while difference simply is. I live with three males, one husband and two sons, and occasionally I realize with great clarity that they are gazing across a divide at me, not because of big differences among us, but because of small ones.

The amaryllis bulb haunts me. "Why did you put an onion in a pot in the bathroom?" my elder son asked several months ago. I explained that it was not an onion but an amaryllis bulb and that soon it would grow into fabulous flowers. "What is that thing in the bathroom?" his father said later the same day. Impatiently I explained again. A look flashed between them, and then the littlest boy, too. Mom. Weird. Women.

Once I would have felt anger flame inside me at that. But I've done the same so many times now. On the telephone a friend and I will be commiserating about the failure of our husbands to listen when we talk, or their inexorable linear thinking, or their total blindness to the use and necessity of things like amaryllis bulbs. One of us will sigh, and the other will know what the sigh means. Husband. Strange. Men. Is it any wonder that our relationships are so often riddled with misunderstandings and disappointments?

In the children you can see the beginnings, even though we raise them in 10 households in which mothers do things fathers once did, and vice versa. Children try to nail down the world, and themselves, early on and in a very primitive and real way. I remember a stage with my elder son in which, going through the supermarket or walking down the street, he would pin me down on each person walking by, and on such disparate cultural influences as Vanna White and Captain Kangaroo,[1] by demanding that I tell him which genitalia category they fell in. Very soon, he got the idea: us and them, him and her. It was all very well to say that all people are the same inside (even if I had believed it) but he thought the outside was very important, too, and it helped him classify the world.

I must never forget, I suppose, that even in the gym, with all that space between us, we still managed to pick partners and dance. It's the dance that's important,

---

1. White (b. 1957), best known as the hostess of the TV game show *Wheel of Fortune* (since 1982); Captain Kangaroo (1955–1985), title character played by Bob Keeshan (1927–2004) of the children's TV show by the same name.

not the difference. (I shouldn't leave out who leads and who follows. But I speak to that from a strange perspective, since any man who has ever danced with me can attest to the fact that I have never learned to follow.)

I have just met the dance downstairs. My elder son has one of his best friends over, and he does not care that she is a girl, and she does not care that he is a boy. But she is complaining that he is chasing her with the plastic spider and making her scream, and he is grinning maniacally because that is just exactly the response he is looking for, and they are both having a great time. Two children, raised in egalitarian households in the 1980s. Between them the floor already stretches, an ocean to cross before they can dance uneasily in one another's arms.

MLA CITATION

Quindlen, Anna. "Between the Sexes, a Great Divide." 1988. *The Norton Reader: An Anthology of Nonfiction*. Ed. Melissa A. Goldthwaite et al. 14th ed. New York: Norton, 2016. 164–66. Print.

QUESTIONS

1. Note the places in this essay where Anna Quindlen, after describing "the first boy-girl party we attended" (paragraph 1), returns to it. How does she turn this moment into an observation about the differences between men and women?

2. Quindlen writes about two genders—male and female—but some recent theorists describe multiple genders. Read Gwendolyn Ann Smith's "We're All Someone's Freak" (pp. 184–87) and compare Quindlen's classification to hers. What changes when new categories are added? What problems persist?

3. As Quindlen does with the "boy-girl party" in this essay, describe a memorable event and turn it into a greater observation about an issue important to you.

PAUL THEROUX   *Being a Man*

THERE IS A PATHETIC SENTENCE in the chapter "Fetishism" in Dr. Norman Cameron's book *Personality Development and Psychopathology*. It goes, "Fetishists are nearly always men; and their commonest fetish is a woman's shoe." I cannot read that sentence without thinking that it is just one more awful thing about being a man—and perhaps it is an important thing to know about us.

I have always disliked being a man. The whole idea of manhood in America is pitiful, in my opinion. This version of masculinity is a little like having to wear an ill-fitting coat for one's entire life (by contrast, I imagine femininity

From Sunrise with Seamonsters *(1985), Paul Theroux's collection of essays.*

to be an oppressive sense of nakedness). Even the expression "Be a man!" strikes me as insulting and abusive. It means: Be stupid, be unfeeling, obedient, soldierly and stop thinking. Man means "manly"—how can one think about men without considering the terrible ambition of manliness? And yet it is part of every man's life. It is a hideous and crippling lie; it not only insists on difference and connives at superiority, it is also by its very nature destructive—emotionally damaging and socially harmful.

The youth who is subverted, as most are, into believing in the masculine ideal is effectively separated from women and he spends the rest of his life finding women a riddle and a nuisance. Of course, there is a female version of this male affliction. It begins with mothers encouraging little girls to say (to other adults) "Do you like my new dress?" In a sense, little girls are traditionally urged to please adults with a kind of coquettishness, while boys are enjoined to behave like monkeys toward each other. The nine-year-old coquette proceeds to become womanish in a subtle power game in which she learns to be sexually indispensable, socially decorative and always alert to a man's sense of inadequacy.

Femininity—being lady-like—implies needing a man as witness and seducer; but masculinity celebrates the exclusive company of men. That is why it is so grotesque; and that is also why there is no manliness without inadequacy—because it denies men the natural friendship of women.

It is very hard to imagine any concept of manliness that does not belittle women, and it begins very early. At an age when I wanted to meet girls—let's say the treacherous years of thirteen to sixteen—I was told to take up a sport, get more fresh air, join the Boy Scouts, and I was urged not to read so much. It was the 1950s and if you asked too many questions about sex you were sent to camp—boy's camp, of course: the nightmare. Nothing is more unnatural or prison-like than a boy's camp, but if it were not for them we would have no Elks' Lodges, no pool rooms, no boxing matches, no Marines.

And perhaps no sports as we know them. Everyone is aware of how few in number are the athletes who behave like gentlemen. Just as high school basketball teaches you how to be a poor loser, the manly attitude toward sports seems to be little more than a recipe for creating bad marriages, social misfits, moral degenerates, sadists, latent rapists and just plain louts. I regard high school sports as a drug far worse than marijuana, and it is the reason that the average tennis champion, say, is a pathetic oaf.

Any objective study would find the quest for manliness essentially right-wing, puritanical, cowardly, neurotic and fueled largely by a fear of women. It is also certainly philistine. There is no book-hater like a Little League coach. But indeed all the creative arts are obnoxious to the manly ideal, because at their best the arts are pursued by uncompetitive and essentially solitary people. It makes it very hard for a creative youngster, for any boy who expresses the desire to be alone seems to be saying that there is something wrong with him.

It ought to be clear by now that I have something of an objection to the way we turn boys into men. It does not surprise me that when the President of the United States has his customary weekend off he dresses like a cowboy—it is both a measure of his insecurity and his willingness to please. In many ways,

American culture does little more for a man than prepare him for modeling clothes in the L. L. Bean catalog. I take this as a personal insult because for many years I found it impossible to admit to myself that I wanted to be a writer. It was my guilty secret, because being a writer was incompatible with being a man.

There are people who might deny this, but that is because the American writer, typically, has been so at pains to prove his manliness that we have come to see literariness and manliness as mingled qualities. But first there was a fear that writing was not a manly profession—indeed, not a profession at all. (The paradox in American letters is that it has always been easier for a woman to write and for a man to be published.) Growing up, I had thought of sports as wasteful and humiliating, and the idea of manliness was a bore. My wanting to become a writer was not a flight from that oppressive roleplaying, but I quickly saw that it was at odds with it. Everything in stereotyped manliness goes against the life of the mind. The Hemingway personality is too tedious to go into here, and in any case his exertions are well known, but certainly it was not until this aberrant behavior was examined by feminists in the 1960s that any male writer dared question the pugnacity in Hemingway's fiction. All the bullfighting and arm wrestling and elephant shooting diminished Hemingway as a writer, but it is consistent with a prevailing attitude in American writing: one cannot be a male writer without first proving that one is a man.

10   It is normal in America for a man to be dismissive or even somewhat apologetic about being a writer. Various factors make it easier. There is a heartiness about journalism that makes it acceptable—journalism is the manliest form of American writing and, therefore, the profession the most independent-minded women seek (yes, it is an illusion, but that is my point). Fiction-writing is equated with a kind of dispirited failure and is only manly when it produces wealth— money is masculinity. So is drinking. Being a drunkard is another assertion, if misplaced, of manliness. The American male writer is traditionally proud of his heavy drinking. But we are also a very literal-minded people. A man proves his manhood in America in old-fashioned ways. He kills lions, like Hemingway; or he hunts ducks, like Nathanael West; or he makes pronouncements like, "A man should carry enough knife to defend himself with," as James Jones once said to a *Life* interviewer. Or he says he can drink you under the table. But even tiny drunken William Faulkner loved to mount a horse and go fox hunting, and Jack Kerouac roistered up and down Manhattan in a lumberjack shirt (and spent every night of *The Subterraneans* with his mother in Queens). And we are familiar with the lengths to which Norman Mailer is prepared, in his endearing way, to prove that he is just as much a monster as the next man.[1]

When the novelist John Irving was revealed as a wrestler, people took him to be a very serious writer; and even a bubble reputation like Erich (*Love Story*) Segal's was enhanced by the news that he ran the marathon in a respectable

---

1. Writers named in this paragraph and the next are twentieth-century Americans whose personal lives may be seen as conforming (or not conforming, in the cases of Oates and Didion) to stereotypical ideas of masculinity.

time. How surprised we would be if Joyce Carol Oates were revealed as a sumo wrestler or Joan Didion active in pumping iron. "Lives in New York City with her three children" is the typical woman writer's biographical note, for just as the male writer must prove he has achieved a sort of muscular manhood, the woman writer—or rather her publicists—must prove her motherhood.

There would be no point in saying any of this if it were not generally accepted that to be a man is somehow—even now in feminist-influenced America—a privilege. It is on the contrary an unmerciful and punishing burden. Being a man is bad enough; being manly is appalling (in this sense, women's lib has done much more for men than for women). It is the sinister silliness of men's fashions, and a clubby attitude in the arts. It is the subversion of good students. It is the so-called Dress Code of the Ritz-Carlton Hotel in Boston, and it is the institutionalized cheating in college sports. It is the most primitive insecurity.

And this is also why men often object to feminism but are afraid to explain why: of course women have a justified grievance, but most men believe—and with reason—that their lives are just as bad.

MLA CITATION

Theroux, Paul. "Being a Man." 1985. *The Norton Reader: An Anthology of Nonfiction.* Ed. Melissa A. Goldthwaite et al. 14th ed. New York: Norton, 2016. 166–69. Print.

QUESTIONS

1. In this essay, Paul Theroux makes many negative statements about being a man and being manly. Do you agree with his assessment of what it means to be a man or to be manly? Why or why not?

2. In paragraph 2, Theroux uses similes to describe his feelings about masculinity and femininity: he claims that "masculinity is . . . like having to wear an ill-fitting coat for one's entire life" and imagines "femininity to be an oppressive sense of nakedness." Write two similes, one describing your sense of what it is to be conventionally masculine, the other describing your sense of what it is to be feminine. How do your similes supplement, or differ from, Theroux's?

3. In paragraph 6, Theroux says he regards "high school sports as a drug far worse than marijuana." Consider his attitude toward sports throughout the essay. How does his sense of sports compare to yours? Explain the differences and similarities in a brief essay.

SOJOURNER TRUTH *Ain't I a Woman?*

1851 VERSION

I WANT TO SAY A FEW WORDS about this matter. I am a woman's rights [sic]. I have as much muscle as any man, and can do as much work as any man. I have plowed and reaped and husked and chopped and mowed, and can any man do more than that? I have heard much about the sexes being equal. I can carry as much as any man, and can eat as much too, if I can get it. I am as strong as any man that is now. As for intellect, all I can say is, if a woman have a pint, and a man a quart—why can't she have her little pint full? You need not be afraid to give us our rights for fear we will take too much,—for we can't take more than our pint'll hold. The poor men seems to be all in confusion, and don't know what to do. Why children, if you have woman's rights, give it to her and you will feel better. You will have your own rights, and they won't be so much trouble. I can't read, but I can hear. I have heard the bible and have learned that Eve caused man to sin. Well, if woman upset the world, do give her a chance to set it right side up again. The Lady has spoken about Jesus, how he never spurned woman from him, and she was right. When Lazarus died, Mary and Martha came to him with faith and love and besought him to raise their brother. And Jesus wept and Lazarus came forth. And how came Jesus into the world? Through God who created him and the woman who bore him. Man, where was your part? But the women are coming up blessed be God and a few of the men are coming up with them. But man is in a tight place, the poor slave is on him, woman is coming on him, he is surely between a hawk and a buzzard.

MLA CITATION

Truth, Sojourner. "Ain't I a Woman?" 1851. *The Norton Reader: An Anthology of Nonfiction.* Ed. Melissa A. Goldthwaite et al. 14th ed. New York: Norton, 2016. 170. Print.

Sojourner Truth (c. 1797–1883), born Isabella Baumfree, was an African American abolitionist and women's rights activist. On May 28, 1851, at the Women's Rights Convention in Akron, Ohio, Truth delivered an extemporaneous speech that is most often titled "Ain't I a Woman?" Since what was passed down is a reported version of what Truth said, the speech is a composite of her words and the recollections of two individuals who witnessed it. Two versions appear here—the first recorded version of the speech reported by editor Marius Robinson in the Anti-Slavery Bugle *in 1851 and another more famous version published by the abolitionist, writer, and speaker Frances Dana Gage in the* National Anti-Slavery Standard *on May 2, 1863.*

1863 Version

WELL, CHILDREN, WHERE THERE IS SO MUCH RACKET there must be something out of kilter. I think that 'twixt the negroes of the South and the women at the North, all talking about rights, the white men will be in a fix pretty soon. But what's all this here talking about?

That man over there says that women need to be helped into carriages, and lifted over ditches, and to have the best place everywhere. Nobody ever helps me into carriages, or over mud-puddles, or gives me any best place! And ain't I a woman? Look at me! Look at my arm! I have ploughed and planted, and gathered into barns, and no man could head me! And ain't I a woman? I could work as much and eat as much as a man—when I could get it—and bear the lash as well! And ain't I a woman? I have borne thirteen children, and seen most all sold off to slavery, and when I cried out with my mother's grief, none but Jesus heard me! And ain't I a woman?

Then they talk about this thing in the head; what's this they call it? [member of audience whispers, "intellect"] That's it, honey. What's that got to do with women's rights or negroes' rights? If my cup won't hold but a pint, and yours holds a quart, wouldn't you be mean not to let me have my little half measure full?

Then that little man in black there, he says women can't have as much rights as men, 'cause Christ wasn't a woman! Where did your Christ come from? Where did your Christ come from? From God and a woman! Man had nothing to do with Him.

If the first woman God ever made was strong enough to turn the world upside down all alone, these women together ought to be able to turn it back, and get it right side up again! And now they is asking to do it, the men better let them.

Obliged to you for hearing me, and now old Sojourner ain't got nothing more to say.

5

MLA CITATION

Truth, Sojourner. "Ain't I a Woman?" 1863. *The Norton Reader: An Anthology of Nonfiction.* Ed. Melissa A. Goldthwaite et al. 14th ed. New York: Norton, 2016. 171. Print.

Questions

1. Sojourner Truth uses both comparison and contrast to develop her speech. How does she compare herself to a man? In what ways does she believe she is not like a man? What do these similarities and differences tell us about how she understands gender?

2. Discuss Truth's use of the Bible to challenge the limitations others try to impose on her. How does her use of biblical allusions support her argument?

3. Compare the two versions of this speech. What similar elements are included in both versions? What significant differences are there? Write an essay about these similarities and differences. Explain why one version is better than the other or why both are equally important.

AMY CUNNINGHAM *Why Women Smile*

AFTER SMILING BRILLIANTLY for nearly four decades, I now find myself trying to quit. Or, at the very least, seeking to lower the wattage a bit.

Not everyone I know is keen on this. My smile has gleamed like a cheap plastic night-light so long and so reliably that certain friends and relatives worry that my mood will darken the moment my smile dims. "Gee," one says, "I associate you with your smile. It's the essence of you. I should think you'd want to smile more!" But the people who love me best agree that my smile—which springs forth no matter where I am or how I feel—hasn't been serving me well. Said my husband recently, "Your smiling face and unthreatening demeanor make people like you in a fuzzy way, but that doesn't seem to be what you're after these days."

Smiles are not the small and innocuous things they appear to be: Too many of us smile in lieu of showing what's really on our minds. Indeed, the success of the women's movement might be measured by the sincerity—and lack of it—in our smiles. Despite all the work we American women have done to get and maintain full legal control of our bodies, not to mention our destinies, we still don't seem to be fully in charge of a couple of small muscle groups in our faces.

We smile so often and so promiscuously—when we're angry, when we're tense, when we're with children, when we're being photographed, when we're interviewing for a job, when we're meeting candidates to employ—that the Smiling Woman has become a peculiarly American archetype. This isn't entirely a bad thing, of course. A smile lightens the load, diffuses unpleasantness, redistributes nervous tension. Women doctors smile more than their male counterparts, studies show, and are better liked by their patients.

5   Oscar Wilde's[1] old saw that "a woman's face is her work of fiction" is often quoted to remind us that what's on the surface may have little connection to what we're feeling. What is it in our culture that keeps our smiles on automatic pilot? The behavior seems to be an equal blend of nature and nurture. Research has demonstrated that since females often mature earlier than males and are less irritable, girls smile more than boys from the very beginning. But by adolescence, the differences in the smiling rates of boys and girls are so robust that it's clear the culture has done more than its share of the dirty work. Just think of the mothers who painstakingly embroidered the words ENTER SMILING on little samplers, and then hung their handiwork on doors by golden chains. Translation: "Your real emotions aren't welcome here."

Clearly, our instincts are another factor. Our smiles have their roots in the greetings of monkeys, who pull their lips up and back to show their fear of

Many of Amy Cunningham's writings have appeared in wide-circulation magazines aimed at women, like this one from Lear's *Magazine (1993), which was published from 1988 to 1994 and whose slogan was "For the Woman Who Wasn't Born Yesterday."*

1. Irish-born Victorian dramatist (1854–1900).

attack, as well as their reluctance to vie for a position of dominance. And like the opossum caught in the light by the clattering garbage cans, we, too, flash toothy grimaces when we make major mistakes. By declaring ourselves non-threatening, our smiles provide an extremely versatile means of protection.

Our earliest baby smiles are involuntary reflexes having only the vaguest connection to contentment or comfort. In short, we're genetically wired to pull on our parents' heartstrings. As Desmond Morris explains in *Babywatching*, this is our way of attaching ourselves to our caretakers, as truly as baby chimps clench their mothers' fur. Even as babies we're capable of projecting onto others (in this case, our parents) the feelings we know we need to get back in return.

Bona fide social smiles occur at two-and-a-half to three months of age, usually a few weeks after we first start gazing with intense interest into the faces of our parents. By the time we are six months old, we are smiling and laughing regularly in reaction to tickling, feedings, blown raspberries, hugs, and peeka-boo games. Even babies who are born blind intuitively know how to react to pleasurable changes with a smile, though their first smiles start later than those of sighted children.

Psychologists and psychiatrists have noted that babies also smile and laugh with relief when they realize that something they thought might be dangerous is not dangerous after all. Kids begin to invite their parents to indulge them with "scary" approach-avoidance games; they love to be chased or tossed up into the air. (It's interesting to note that as adults, we go through the same gosh-that's-shocking-and-dangerous-but-it's-okay-to-laugh-and-smile cycles when we listen to raunchy stand-up comics.)

From the wilds of New Guinea to the sidewalks of New York, smiles are   10
associated with joy, relief, and amusement. But smiles are by no means limited to the expression of positive emotions: People of many different cultures smile when they are frightened, embarrassed, angry, or miserable. In Japan, for instance, a smile is often used to hide pain or sorrow.

Psychologist Paul Ekman, the head of the University of California's Human Interaction Lab in San Francisco, has identified 18 distinct types of smiles, including those that show misery, compliance, fear, and contempt. The smile of true merriment, which Dr. Ekman calls the Duchenne Smile, after the 19th century French doctor who first studied it, is characterized by heightened circulation, a feeling of exhilaration, and the employment of two major facial muscles: the zygomaticus major of the lower face, and the orbicularis oculi, which crinkles the skin around the eyes. But since the average American woman's smile often has less to do with her actual state of happiness than it does with the social pressure to smile no matter what, her baseline social smile isn't apt to be a felt expression that engages the eyes like this. Ekman insists that if people learned to read smiles, they could see the sadness, misery, or pain lurking there, plain as day.

Evidently, a woman's happy, willing deference is something the world wants visibly demonstrated. Woe to the waitress, the personal assistant or receptionist, the flight attendant, or any other woman in the line of public service whose smile is not offered up to the boss or client as proof that there are no storm clouds—no kids to support, no sleep that's been missed—rolling into the sunny workplace landscape. Women are expected to smile no matter where they line up on the social, cultural, or economic ladder: College professors are criticized for not smiling, political spouses are pilloried for being too serious, and women's roles in films have historically been smiling ones. It's little wonder that men on the street still call out, "Hey, baby, smile! Life's not *that* bad, is it?" to women passing by, lost in thought.

A friend remembers being pulled aside by a teacher after class and asked, "What is wrong, dear? You sat there for the whole hour looking so sad!" "All I could figure," my friend says now, "is that I wasn't smiling. And the fact that *she* felt sorry for me for looking normal made me feel horrible."

Ironically, the social laws that govern our smiles have completely reversed themselves over the last 2,000 years. Women weren't always expected to seem animated and responsive; in fact, immoderate laughter was once considered one of the more conspicuous vices a woman could have, and mirth was downright sinful. Women were kept apart, in some cultures even veiled, so that they couldn't perpetuate Eve's seductive, evil work. The only smile deemed appropriate on a privileged woman's face was the serene, inward smile of the Virgin Mary at Christ's birth, and even that expression was best directed exclusively at young children. Cackling laughter and wicked glee were the kinds of sounds heard only in hell.

15   What we know of women's facial expressions in other centuries comes mostly from religious writings, codes of etiquette, and portrait paintings. In 15th century Italy, it was customary for artists to paint lovely, blank-faced women in profile. A viewer could stare endlessly at such a woman, but she could not gaze back. By the Renaissance, male artists were taking some pleasure in depicting women with a semblance of complexity, Leonardo da Vinci's *Mona Lisa*, with her veiled enigmatic smile, being the most famous example.

The Golden Age of the Dutch Republic marks a fascinating period for studying women's facial expressions. While we might expect the drunken young whores of Amsterdam to smile devilishly (unbridled sexuality and lasciviousness were *supposed* to addle the brain), it's the faces of the Dutch women from fine families that surprise us. Considered socially more free, these women demonstrate a fuller range of facial expressions than their European sisters. Frans Hals's 1622 portrait of Stephanus Geraerdt and Isabella Coymans, a married couple, is remarkable not just for the full, friendly smiles on each face, but for the frank and mutual pleasure the couple take in each other.

In the 1800s, sprightly, pretty women began appearing in advertisements for everything from beverages to those newfangled Kodak Land cameras. Women's faces were no longer impassive, and their willingness to bestow status, to offer, proffer, and yield, was most definitely promoted by their smiling images. The culture appeared to have turned the smile, originally a bond shared between intimates, into a socially required display that sold capitalist ideology as well as kitchen appliances. And female viewers soon began to emulate these highly idealized pictures. Many longed to be more like her, that perpetually smiling female. She seemed so beautiful. So content. So whole.

By the middle of the 19th century, the bulk of America's smile burden was falling primarily to women and African-American slaves, providing a very portable means of protection, a way of saying, "I'm harmless. I won't assert myself here." It reassured those in power to see signs of gratitude and contentment in the faces of subordinates. As long ago as 1963, adman David Ogilvy declared the image of a woman smiling approvingly at a product clichéd, but we've yet to get the message. Cheerful Americans still appear in ads today, smiling somewhat less disingenuously than they smiled during the middle of the century, but smiling broadly nonetheless.

Other countries have been somewhat reluctant to import our "Don't worry, be happy" American smiles. When McDonald's opened in Moscow not long ago and when EuroDisney debuted in France last year, the Americans involved in both business ventures complained that they couldn't get the natives they'd employed to smile worth a damn.

Europeans visiting the United States for the first time are often surprised   20
at just how often Americans smile. But when you look at our history, the relentless good humor (or, at any rate, the pretense of it) falls into perspective. The American wilderness was developed on the assumption that this country had a shortage of people in relation to its possibilities. In countries with a more rigid class structure or caste system, fewer people are as captivated by the idea of quickly winning friends and influencing people. Here in the States, however, every stranger is a potential associate. Our smiles bring new people on board. The American smile is a democratic version of a curtsy or doffed hat, since, in this land of free equals, we're not especially formal about the ways we greet social superiors.

The civil rights movement never addressed the smile burden by name, but activists worked on their own to set new facial norms. African-American males stopped smiling on the streets in the 1960s, happily aware of the unsettling effect this action had on the white population. The image of the simpleminded, smiling, white-toothed black was rejected as blatantly racist, and it gradually retreated into the distance. However, like the women of Sparta and the wives of samurai, who were expected to look happy upon learning their sons or husbands had died in battle, contemporary American women have yet to unilaterally declare their faces their own property.

For instance, imagine a woman at a morning business meeting being asked if she could make a spontaneous and concise summation of a complicated project she's been struggling to get under control for months. She might draw the end of her mouth back and clench her teeth—*Eek!*—in a protective response, a polite, restrained expression of her surprise, not unlike the expression of a conscientious young schoolgirl being told to get out paper and pencil for a pop quiz. At the same time, the woman might be feeling resentful of the supervisor who sprang the request, but she fears taking that person on. So she holds back a comment. The whole performance resolves in a weird grin collapsing into a nervous smile that conveys discomfort and unpreparedness. A pointed remark by way of explanation or self-defense might've worked better for her—but her mouth was otherwise engaged.

We'd do well to realize just how much our smiles misrepresent us, and swear off for good the self-deprecating grins and ritual displays of deference. Real smiles have beneficial physiological effects, according to Paul Ekman. False ones do nothing for us at all.

"Smiles are as important as sound bites on television," insists producer and media coach Heidi Berenson, who has worked with many of Washington's most famous faces. "And women have always been better at understanding this than men. But the smile I'm talking about is not a cutesy smile. It's an authoritative smile. A genuine smile. Properly timed, it's tremendously powerful."

25   To limit a woman to one expression is like editing down an orchestra to one instrument. And the search for more authentic means of expression isn't easy in a culture in which women are still expected to be magnanimous smilers, helpmates in crisis, and curators of everybody else's morale. But change is already floating in the high winds. We see a boon in assertive female comedians who are proving that women can *dish out* smiles, not just wear them. Actress Demi Moore has stated that she doesn't like to take smiling roles. Nike is running ads that show unsmiling women athletes sweating, reaching, pushing themselves. These women aren't overly concerned with issues of rapport; they're not being "nice" girls—they're working out.

If a woman's smile were truly her own, to be smiled or not, according to how the *woman* felt, rather than according to what someone else needed, she would smile more spontaneously, without ulterior, hidden motives. As Rainer Maria Rilke wrote in *The Journal of My Other Self*, "Her smile was not meant to be seen by anyone and served its whole purpose in being smiled."

That smile is my long-term aim. In the meantime, I hope to stabilize on the smile continuum somewhere between the eliciting grin of Farrah Fawcett and the haughty smirk of Jeane Kirkpatrick.[2]

2. Fawcett (1947–2009), TV star and pinup girl of the 1970s, famous for her feathered hair; Kirkpatrick (1926–2006), American educator, diplomat, and U.S. ambassador to the United Nations under Ronald Reagan, from 1981 to 1985.

MLA CITATION

Cunningham, Amy. "Why Women Smile." 1993. *The Norton Reader: An Anthology of Nonfiction*. Ed. Melissa A. Goldthwaite et al. 14th ed. New York: Norton, 2016. 172–76. Print.

QUESTIONS

1. Have you or people you know ever been urged to smile or to smile more? How was the advice given? What do you think the motive was?

2. Collect some observational data on the way men and women interact with strangers and see if you can confirm any part of Amy Cunningham's essay.

3. Several years after Cunningham wrote "Why Women Smile," she discovered new research on smiling (see below, "All Smiles Now," an entry that Cunningham posted in 2006 on her blog *Chattering Minds* at beliefnet.com). This research has made her change her view on women's smiles. Write a brief account of what these changes are and what new evidence they reflect.

4. Do you think that Paul Ekman's research on Buddhist monks fully applies to American women and their smiles? What issues remain? Write about the issues in an essay that draws on your own experience and observation.

ALL SMILES NOW

I once wrote an essay called "Why Women Smile" for the women's magazine *Lear's*. More than fifteen years later, I'm still receiving checks from academic presses planning to re-run the article because, apparently, it "teaches well" in first-year college writing classes. . . .

But here's the quandary: I now know that a whole chunk of my article is incorrect. . . . For my research at the time, I interviewed a noted psychologist and facial expression expert Paul Ekman. I remember that when the piece was published, Ekman didn't seem so thrilled with it. He didn't write me back. I now know that's because he had been trying to tell me that he was conceiving of the human smile in a new way and that the feminists who thought women should smile less weren't approaching smiles from the right perspective. But I couldn't hear him. Ekman then was just a short time from researching Tibetan monks and the Dalai Lama's smiling meditations. He was on his way to sub-stantiating that smiles—even fake plastered-on smiles—can indeed lift our moods and keep us happier. So actually, smiling women have had the right idea all along.

But I was so attached to the notion that feminine niceness was some kind of pathology that I couldn't hear what Ekman was telling me. Indeed, I couldn't imagine that if you smiled while seated quietly in meditation, you would spread the energy of cheer throughout the world and rise up feeling better. I couldn't conceive of the topic spiritually.

Since then, Ekman has published his findings. And my melancholy little prose piece (which my mother always hated anyway) is out there like the Ener-gizer Bunny banging its drum. So until I can make this wrong a right, do me a favor: Smile freely and broadly. Get happy.

ROXANE GAY   *A Tale of Three Coming Out Stories*

W E ARE STILL IN THAT TIME in our history when public figures come out of invisible closets largely
built by a public insatiable in its desire to know all
the intimate details of the private lives of very public
people.

We want to know everything. In this information
age, we are inundated with information, so now we feel entitled. We also like
taxonomy, classification, definition. Are you a man or a woman? Are you a
Democrat or a Republican? Are you married or single? Are you gay or straight?
We don't know what to do when we don't know the answers to these questions or, worse, when the answers to these questions do not fall neatly into a
category.

When public figures don't provide outward evidence of their sexuality, our
desire to classify intensifies. Any number of celebrities are dogged by "gay
rumors" because we cannot quite place them into a given category. We act like
placing these people in categories will have some impact on our lives, or that
creating these categories is our responsibility, when, most of the time, such taxonomy won't change anything at all. For example, there is nothing in my life
that is impacted by knowing Ricky Martin[1] is gay. The only thing satisfied by
that information is my curiosity.

Sometimes, this zeal to classify has resulted in public figures being outed
against their will. In particular, politicians who have gone on record for legislation that suppresses civil rights have found themselves in the glare of the spotlight. Congressman Edward Schrock was outed in 2004 because he voted for
the Marriage Protection Act.[2] There have been many others. When people have
been forcibly outed, those doing the outing have said they were acting for
the greater good or working to reveal hypocrisy, as if the right to privacy and
the right to determine if and when to come out is only afforded to those who
are infallible.

5   This is, in part, a matter of privacy. What information do we have the right
to keep to ourselves? What boundaries are we allowed to maintain in our personal lives? What do we have a right to know about the lives of others? When
do we have a right to breach the boundaries others have set for themselves?

This essay first appeared in the Rumpus *(2012), an online source for "essays, reviews, interviews, advice, music, film and poetry." It was reprinted in Roxane Gay's essay collection,*
Bad Feminist *(2014).*

1. Puerto Rican singer, author, and actor (b. 1971).

2. Schrock (b. 1941), congressman from Virginia, resigned from office when rumors
circulated that he was secretly soliciting sex with men while publicly opposing rights
for same-sex couples; Marriage Protection Act (2003), unsuccessful attempt to reinforce the Defense of Marriage Act (1996), a U.S. federal law that once protected the
rights of states to refuse to recognize same-sex marriages approved in other states.

People with high public profiles are allowed very few boundaries. In exchange for the erosion of privacy, they receive fame and/or fortune and/or power. Is this a fair price? Are famous people aware of how they are sacrificing privacy when they ascend to a position of cultural prominence?

There are many ways we have surrendered privacy in the information age. We willingly disclose what we've eaten for breakfast, where we spent last night and with whom, and all manner of trivial information. We submit personal information when registering for social media accounts and when making purchases online. We often surrender this information without question or reflection. These disclosures come so freely because we've long been conditioned to share too much with too many.

In his book *Privacy*, Garret Keizer explores privacy through a series of essays that consider privacy legally, from the feminist perspective, through the lens of class, and more. He demonstrates a real concern for how little privacy we have, how cavalier we can be with our privacy, and how unthinkingly we might infringe on the privacy of others. He says,

> We speak of privacy as a right but we might also think of it as a test, as a canary in the mine[3] of our civilization. It lives or dies to the extent that we remain willing to believe that the human person, body and soul—our blood relative in his or her flesh, and beyond reduction in his or her grandeur and nobility—is sacred, endowed with inalienable rights, and a microcosm of us all.

We tend to forget that culturally prominent figures are as sacred to those they love as the people closest to us. We tend to forget that they are flesh and blood. We assume that as they rise to prominence, they shed their inalienable rights. We do this without question.

One of the most striking arguments Keizer makes is that privacy and class are intrinsically bound together. He asserts that people with privilege have more access to privacy than people who don't. Keizer notes, "Social class is defined in large part by the degree of freedom one has to move from private space to public space, and by the amount of time one spends in relative privacy."

This relationship between privacy and privilege extends to race, gender, and sexuality. When a woman is pregnant, for example, there's increasingly less privacy because, as she reaches full term, her condition becomes more and more visible. Keizer remarks, with regard to pregnant women, that

> her condition is an unequivocally public statement of a very private experience, begun in circumstances of intimacy and continued within the sanctum of her own body—yet there is no hiding it for her, nor any denying the feeling we have that somehow she belongs to us, that she embodies our collective future and represents our individual pasts.

---

3. Expression for danger. It originated with coal miners using canaries to detect noxious, odorless gas such as carbon monoxide. If the canary died, the miners knew they were in danger.

Any time your body represents some kind of difference, your privacy is compromised to some degree. A surfeit of privacy is just one more benefit the privileged class enjoys and often takes for granted.

Heterosexuals take the privacy of their sexuality for granted. They can date, marry, and love whom they choose without needing to disclose much of anything. If they do choose to disclose, there are rarely negative consequences.

In recent years, celebrities have started coming out with little fanfare by way, perhaps, of an interview where a man might casually mention his male partner or refer to himself as a gay man, or a woman might thank her partner in an award acceptance speech. The public reacts when celebrities come out quietly, but the spectacle is somewhat muted. When celebrities come out in this manner, they are generally saying, "This is simply one more thing you now know about me."

In July 2012, popular journalist Anderson Cooper came out of one of those invisible closets built by someone else's hands in an e-mail to the *Daily Beast's* Andrew Sullivan, who published the message on his blog.

15   Cooper wrote:

> The fact is, I'm gay, always have been, always will be, and I couldn't be any more happy, comfortable with myself, and proud.
> I have always been very open and honest about this part of my life with my friends, my family, and my colleagues. In a perfect world, I don't think it's anyone else's business, but I do think there is value in standing up and being counted.

There was a range of responses to Cooper's coming out. Many people shrugged and said Cooper's sexuality was presumed, an open secret. Others insisted it was important and even necessary for Cooper to come out and to, as he puts it, stand up and be counted.

This is often what is said when public figures do or do not come out in this day and age: there is a greater obligation that must be met beyond what that person might ordinarily choose to meet. We make these demands, though, without considering how much less privacy that person might have as a public figure who is also part of an underrepresented group. I am not suggesting that we cry for the celebrity who enjoys a lush lifestyle; I am saying we should give thought to the celebrity who would prefer to keep his marriage to a man private for whatever reason, but isn't allowed that right, a right that is, for heterosexuals, inalienable.

In *Privacy*, Keizer notes, "The public obligations of prominently powerful people can also constrain their private lives." We see these constraints time and again when celebrities and other prominent figures sidestep questions about their personal lives they are unwilling to answer. They may be hesitant for any number of reasons—protecting their privacy, protecting their careers and social standing, protecting loved ones. The public rarely seems to care about those reasons. They—we—need to know.

At the same time, we live in a complex cultural climate, one where seventeen states allow same-sex marriage but twenty-nine states have constitutions forbidding marriage equality.[4] Things are improving, but we are inching too slowly to equal rights for all. The world we live in is not as progressive as we need it to be. When a celebrity comes out, it is still news. The coming out is still culturally significant. When a man like Anderson Cooper comes out, it's a step forward in achieving civil rights for everyone. At the very least, it is one more person saying, "I am here. I matter. I demand to be recognized." Cooper is, by many standards, the "right kind of gay"—white, handsome, successful, masculine. Many celebrities who have successfully come out in recent years fit that profile—Neil Patrick Harris, Matt Bomer, Zachary Quinto, and so on. These men are held up as examples—not too flamboyant, not *too* gay.

Still, prominent gay people need to stand up and be counted because the word "gay" is still used as a slur. Nine out of ten LGBT teenagers report being bullied at school. LGBT youth are two to three times more likely to commit suicide. The bullying and harassment of LGBT youth are so pervasive that, in 2010, Dan Savage[5] and his partner, Terry Miller, created a YouTube video to show LGBT youth how life can, indeed, get better beyond the torments of adolescence. That video spawned countless other videos and a foundation dedicated to continuing this project of showing LGBT youth there is a light at the end of an often very dark tunnel.

Celebrities like Cooper also need to stand up and be counted because there is only a handful of states where gay marriage is legal.[6] It was only in 2013 that the Supreme Court invalidated the Defense of Marriage Act, passed in 1996. The Defense of Marriage Act denied gay couples 1,138 federally preserved rights afforded to heterosexual couples. More than twenty states have constitutional provisions explicitly defining marriage as a union between a man and a woman. There are states where LGBT people cannot adopt children. Depending on where they live, members of the LGBT community may lose their jobs because of their sexual orientation. They may face ostracism from family, friends, and community. Things get better, perhaps, but slowly and certainly not universally.

LGBT people are the victims of hate crimes. There is the young lesbian couple in Texas, Mary Kristene Chapa and Mollie Olgin, who were both shot in the head by an unknown assailant and left to die. A gay couple in northeast DC was attacked two blocks from their apartment by three assailants who were shouting homophobic slurs. One, Michael Hall, was hospitalized; he had no health insurance and had a fractured jaw. In Edmond, Oklahoma, a gay man's car was vandalized with a homophobic slur and set on fire. In Indianapolis, Indiana, there was a drive-by shooting of a gay bar. Hate is everywhere.

20

4. When this essay was published in 2012, gay marriage was legal in just nine states. In June 2015, the Supreme Court ruled in *Obergefell v. Hodges* that, in accordance with the Fourteenth Amendment to the U.S. Constitution, marriage is a fundamental right guaranteed to same-sex couples.

5. American sex columnist and author (b. 1964).

6. Cf. footnote 4.

It gets better, sort of. It gets better unless you're in the wrong place at the wrong time. Sometimes the wrong place is your home, the one place where you should be able to feel safe no matter what the world is like.

Sally Ride, the first woman astronaut, who died in July 2012 at the age of sixty-one, was survived by her female partner of twenty-seven years. At the time of her death, Ride's widow was not able to receive the federal benefits normally given to a surviving spouse. Sally Ride was able to fly into space and reach the stars, but here on earth, her long-term relationship went largely unrecognized. The 2012 Republican presidential hopeful Mitt Romney tweeted, "Sally Ride ranks among the greatest pioneers. I count myself among the millions of Americans she inspired with her travel to space." Music group the Mountain Goats replied, "Kind of despicable and grotesque that her partner of twenty-seven years will be denied her federal benefits, don't you think?" Despicable and grotesque, indeed, but in her death, Sally Ride stood up and was counted. She became even more of a hero than she already was.

25   It's a problem, though, that there's a right kind of gay, that there are LGBT people who are warmly encouraged to step out of the closet while others who don't fit certain parameters go largely ignored. It's easy enough for a man like Anderson Cooper, living in fairly liberal New York City, to come out. He will likely continue to be very successful. He has a supportive family and a welcoming community to embrace him. Coming out stories for everyday people are often far different, complicated and difficult. We forget what it's like to come out in the so-called flyover states. It's not easy.

In July 2012, musician Frank Ocean, a celebrity with a lower profile than Cooper but with, perhaps, more to lose, came out via Tumblr as having once loved a man by sharing some of the liner notes for his critically acclaimed album *Channel Orange*. Once again, cultural observers noted that Ocean's coming out was significant.

As a black man coming out as gay or bisexual, particularly as part of the notoriously homophobic R&B and hip-hop community, Ocean was taking a bold step, a risk. He was trusting that his music would transcend the prejudices of his audience. So far, that risk seems to have paid off. Many celebrities vocalized their support of Ocean, including Russell Simmons, Beyoncé, 50 Cent, and others. He is standing up to be counted. *Channel Orange* was a critical and commercial success.

Of course, Ocean is also part of the Odd Future collective. His friend and collaborator Tyler, the Creator's debut album, *Goblin*, contains 213 gay slurs. Tyler, the Creator continues to assert he's not homophobic with that old canard of having gay friends. He stepped up his defense by also claiming his gay fans were totally fine with his use of the term "faggot" over and over and over— immunity by association. I do not know the man. Maybe he is homophobic, maybe he isn't. I do know he doesn't think about language very carefully. He believes that just because you can say something, you should. He is not shamed by using slurs 213 times on one album, no matter how that frequency reflects a lack of imagination.

For every step forward, there is some asshole shoving progress back.

Despite our complex cultural climate and what needs to be done for the   30
greater good, it is still an unreasonable burden that someone who is marginalized must bear an extra set of responsibilities. It is unfair that prominent cultural figures who come out have to forge these inroads on our behalf; they carry
the hopes of so many on their shoulders. They stand up and are counted so that
someday things might actually be better for everyone, everywhere, not just the
camera- or radio-ready celebrities for whom coming out is far easier than most.

I am reminded of the Iowa lesbian couple whose son, Zach Wahls, testified in
2011 before the Iowa House Judiciary Committee about how a child raised by two
women turns out. He spoke in support of gay marriage in Iowa. He was passionate
and eloquent and a real credit to his parents. The video clip of his testimony was
shared across the Internet. Every time I saw it I was both thrilled and angry—
angry because queer people always have to fight so much harder for a fraction of
the recognition. No one ever asks heterosexual parents to ensure that their children are models of citizenry. The bar for queer parents is unfairly, unnecessarily
high, but young men like this one keep vaulting that bar nonetheless.

Perhaps we expect gay public figures and other prominent queer people to
come out, to stand and be counted, so they can do the work we're unwilling
to do to change the world, to carry the burdens we are unwilling to shoulder, to
take the stands we are unwilling to make. As individuals, we may not be able to
do much, but when we're silent when someone uses the word "gay" as an insult,
we are falling short. When we don't vote to support equal marriage rights for all,
we are falling short. When we support musicians like Tyler, the Creator, we
are falling short. We are failing our communities. We are failing civil rights.
There are injustices great and small, and even if we can only fight the small
ones, at least we are fighting.

Too often, we fail to ask ourselves what sacrifices we will make for the
greater good. What stands will we take? We expect *role models* to model the
behaviors we are perfectly capable of modeling ourselves. We know things are
getting better. We know we have far to go. In *Privacy*, Keizer also says, "The plu-
rality of intrusions on our privacy has the cumulative effect of inducing a sense of
helplessness." We are willing—even anxious—to see prominent figures in a state
of helplessness as they sacrifice their privacy for the greater good. How helpless
are *we* willing to be for the greater good? That question interests me most.

MLA CITATION

Gay, Roxane. "A Tale of Three Coming Out Stories." 2012. *The Norton Reader: An
Anthology of Nonfiction*. Ed. Melissa A. Goldthwaite et al. 14th ed. New York:
Norton, 2016. 178–83. Print.

QUESTIONS

1. Compare the similarities and differences among the "three coming out stories"
referred to in the title of Roxane Gay's essay. What do the lives of Sally Ride, Anderson Cooper, and Frank Ocean, as described in this essay, tell us about the process
of publicly declaring one's sexual orientation?

2. Throughout the essay, Gay discusses the balance between privacy and the disclosure of personal information for the greater good. She ends her essay with a question for those of us who are not celebrities: "How helpless are *we* willing to be for the greater good?" (paragraph 33). When, if ever, might it serve the greater good to give up some privacy?

3. Research one of the news stories Gay references here (e.g., the hate crimes listed in paragraph 22, or the testimony referred to in paragraph 31). In an essay, compare how several different news outlets treat the same story. What do those differences suggest about how attitudes toward sexual orientation differ based on region or political affiliation?

GWENDOLYN ANN SMITH   *We're All Someone's Freak*

BEING TRANSGENDER GUARANTEES you will upset someone. People get upset with transgender people who choose to inhabit a third gender space rather than "pick a side." Some get upset at transgender people who do not eschew their birth histories. Others get up in arms with those who opted out of surgical options, instead living with their original equipment. Ire is raised at those who transition, then transition again when they decide that their initial change was not the right answer for them. Heck, some get their dander up simply because this or that transgender person simply is not "trying hard enough" to be a particular gender, whatever that means. Some are irked that the Logo program *RuPaul's Drag Race* shows a version of transgender life different from their own. Meanwhile, all around are those who have decided they aren't comfortable with the lot of us, because we dared to change from one gender expression or identity to some other.

To hell with that.

You see, I have learned not only that I have to do what I have to do to be happy regardless of the struggles I may face, but also that I am the only person responsible for my own comfort or discomfort about my gender. I may wrinkle my nose about what someone else might do, but ultimately what others do cannot change who I am.

I had an unusual request from a friend of mine some time back: I was asked not to mention that I was a friend of hers. You see, I'm transgender. More than this, it's hardly a secret that I'm transgender—I am professionally transgender, as well as the founder of Trans Day of Remembrance. Her fear was that if someone knew that I knew her, then it would automatically be assumed that she was transgender, too.

5   It was a difficult thing to hear that my very existence was perceived as being enough to harm a person I called a friend. I try to harm no one in my daily

This essay first appeared in the Bay Area Reporter *(2006), a free weekly newspaper based in San Francisco, California, that caters to the LGBT community; it was reprinted in* Gender Outlaws: The Next Generation *(2010), a volume edited by Kate Bornstein and S. Bear Bergman that "collects and contextualizes the work of this generation's trans and genderqueer forward thinkers."*

affairs—yet here I was, being told that all I need to do to cause someone difficulty is to call them a friend.

I asked many of my friends who are transgender, in the wake of this incident, if they too would be uncomfortable being identified publicly as friends of mine. I consider these people close friends, I said, and still if this inadvertent outing would cause them trouble, I promised I would disclaim them immediately. Oddly, no one else seemed all that perturbed. I did not address this with my non-transgender friends, but maybe I should; presumably it will be a great shock to discover that merely being acquainted with me has the potential to cast doubt on their birth gender.

One of the first lessons I was taught at some of my earliest transgender support group meetings (more years ago than I usually would wish to admit) was that being in a group of transgender people exponentially raises the risk of being read as transgender. If you want to remain hidden, I was told, avoid others like you. Large group events would always require remote locations where we could all be hidden away; the concept of meeting with your transgender siblings just anywhere was taboo. This was a world just a step away from secret handshakes and coded catch-phrases.

Much later, I learned that this divide-and-conquer strategy had been common in the older, university-based transsexuality programs of the 1970s. Associating with other transgender people could get you drummed out of the program. After all, you were supposed to be associating with those in your preferred gender, making strides down the road to Normal, not hanging about with others trying to take paths similar to yours.

While those gatekeeping systems are long gone, their survivors live on. Worse, these individuals, themselves transsexual, perpetuate the enforcement of the system they were required to navigate. If you don't fit the gender-norming rules they were expected to observe, you are a subject of derision, worthy of little more than the ridicule of your would-be peers. They have learned to construct a hierarchical order of who is acceptable and who is not.

Let me break it down this way: some lesbians and gays feel that their issues are more important than transgender issues, because transgender people are freaks. Some transgender people—often, but not only, transsexuals—view transsexual issues as more important than the issues of, say, cross-dressers. Some among the more genderqueer portions of our community look down upon those who opt to live in a more "normatively gendered" space. There are even groups that cross-dressers feel superior to: sissies, drag kings and queens, "little girls," and so on. Yes, I'm sure that we could follow even each of these groups and find that, eventually, everyone has someone they view as a freak.

This is a human phenomenon, and one which occurs especially, it seems, among marginalized groups. Trekkers versus trekkies versus people in Klingon costumes, or furries versus fursuiters versus, oh, plushies. I'm sure if I looked at model railroaders, I'd probably find that HO gauge fans look down at N scale,[1] or something like that. The taxonomies are endless, often circular, and

10

---

1. Names of scales—or sizes—of model trains; the scale refers to the train's relationship to life-scale measurements.

are usually graded to a fineness that would be invisible to any outsider. We just want to identify the "real" freaks, so we can feel closer to normal. In reality, not a single one of us is so magically normative as to claim the right to separate out the freaks from everyone else. We are all freaks to someone. Maybe even—if we're honest—to ourselves.

In the end, we find ourselves with one of two choices: do we push others like us away, to best fit in? Or do we seek out our kin, for comfort and company? For that matter, if we are all someone's "freak", does this mean we are all each other's "normal" too—and worthy of embrace?

These are questions I have asked myself, time and time again. I confess to having a phase during which I did not associate with other transgender people, for fear I would be guilty by association, or even get "tranny cooties." Maybe I was afraid I would see things in my own being I was not ready to face, or was afraid of challenging my own assumptions. I found it to be a very limiting way to live, and have chosen to embrace those I might see as my siblings.

Yes, even those who might be having a hard time embracing me.

15   This isn't to say that there's no such thing as defamation, or that everything is acceptable. Far from it. There is always a need to watch for attacks on us as a whole. We can't ignore right-wing demagogues who insist that the word of the doctor who proclaims a child's sex at birth somehow holds more sway over the reality of the body than the word of the person who inhabits it. Yet just as anyone can call me whatever they want it is up to me to decide whether I care to answer. More than this, it should be irrelevant to me what any other transgender person opts to do. Their action does not somehow change who I am. It cannot.

I know what I am. I know that I've chosen to identify as a transgender woman, and that I am—by and large—happy with where I am in this world. I'm far from perfect, and I could give you a list as long as my arms of the things I'd love to change. Nevertheless, I am still here, and I am still me, and no one can change that without my permission.

At the same time, even though I am happy to identify as a transgender woman, I also applaud those who are seeking to redefine the notions of gender and are carving out spaces of their own. My own comfort is such that I'm glad to see other people out there challenging the assumptions and to know that their challenges do not necessarily pose a threat to my beliefs. Who knows—maybe my beliefs could stand a good challenge once in a while, and they might end up broader than they were before.

We live in a world of incredible variations, where there are some 200,000 species of moths and butterflies to be found in this planet, where one can find snowy ice caps and boiling cauldrons of lava, and where biodiversity is the very thing that keeps the whole complex system in tune. The notion of classifying things and then claiming that only this or that is a *proper* version of some being is a distinctly human construct, full of arrogance and hubris. When those of us who are gender outlaws of any stripe seek to set definitions on our realness, to determine who is somehow "normal" amongst us, it seems all the more crazy.

I assume it is some sort of human failing that makes us always need to shun someone who we perceive as "more different than thou." Some simply need

bridges of muscles and columns of bones. They think of jobs and joys of a different kind, perhaps even if they are engineers.

> Jack and Jill went up the hill
> To fetch a pail of water,
> Jack fell down and broke his crown
> And Jill came tumbling after.

The natural fragileness of things comes to be forgotten, for we have learned to take it easy on the man-made world. We do not pile too high or reach too far. We make our pencil points sharper, but we do not press as hard. We learn to write without snap, and the story of our life goes smoothly, but quickly becomes dull. (Everyone wishes secretly to be the writer pushing the pencil to its breaking point.) We feel it in our bones as we grow old and then we remember how brittle but exhilarating life can be. And we extend ourselves beyond our years and break our bones again, thinking what the hell. We have wisdom and we understand the odds and probabilities. We know that nothing is forever.

> Three wise men of Gotham
> Went to sea in a bowl:
> If the vessel had been stronger,
> My song would be longer.

As if it were not enough that the behavior of our very bodies accustoms us to the limitations of engineering structures, our language itself is ambiguous about the daily trials to which life and limb are subjected. Both human beings and inhuman beams are said to be under stress and strain that may lead to fatigue if not downright collapse. Breakdowns of man and machine can occur if they are called upon to carry more than they can bear. The anthropomorphic language of engineering is perhaps no accident since man is not only the archetypal machine but also the Ur-structure.

Furniture is among the oldest of inanimate engineering structures designed to carry a rather well-defined load under rather well-defined circumstances. We are not surprised that furniture used beyond its intended purpose is broken, and we readily blame the child who abuses the furniture rather than the designer of the furniture or the furniture itself when it is abused. Thus a chair must support a person in a sitting position, but it might not be expected to survive a brawl in a saloon. A bed might be expected to support a recumbent child, a small rocking chair only a toddler. But the child's bed would not necessarily be considered badly designed if it collapsed under the child's wild use of it as a trampoline, and a child's chair cannot be faulted for breaking under the weight of a heavier child using it as a springboard. The arms and legs of chairs, the heads and feet of beds, just like those of the people whom they serve, cannot be expected to be strong without limit.

Mother Goose is as full of structural failures as human history. The nursery rhymes acknowledge the limitations of the strength of the objects man builds as readily as fairy tales recognize the frailties of human nature. The story of Goldilocks and the Three Bears teaches us how we can unwittingly proceed from engineering success to failure. Papa Bear's chair is so large and so hard and so unyielding under the weight of Goldilocks that apparently without thinking she gains a confidence in the strength of all rocking chairs. Goldilocks next tries Mama Bear's chair, which is not so large but is softer, perhaps because it is built with a lighter wood. Goldilocks finds this chair too soft, however, too yielding in the cushion. Yet it is strong enough to support her. Thus the criterion of strength becomes less a matter of concern than the criteria of "give" and comfort, and Goldilocks is distracted by her quest for a comfortable chair at the expense of one sufficiently strong. Finally Goldilocks approaches Baby Bear's chair, which is apparently stiffer but weaker than Mama Bear's, with little if any apprehension about its safety, for Goldilocks' experience is that all chairs are overdesigned. At first the smallest chair appears to be "just right," but, as with all marginal engineering designs, whether chairs or elevated walkways, the chair suddenly gives way under Goldilocks and sends her crashing to the floor.

The failure of the chair does not keep Goldilocks from next trying beds without any apparent concern for their structural integrity. When Papa Bear's bed is too hard and Mama's is too soft, Goldilocks does not seem to draw a parallel with the chairs. She finds Baby Bear's bed "just right" and falls asleep in it without worrying about its collapsing under her. One thing the fairy tale implicitly teaches us as children is to live in a world of seemingly capricious structural failure and success without anxiety. While Goldilocks may worry about having broken Baby Bear's chair, she does not worry about all chairs and beds breaking. According to Bruno Bettelheim, the tale of Goldilocks and the Three Bears lacks some of the important features of a true fairy tale, for in it there is neither recovery nor consolation, there is no resolution of conflict, and Goldilocks' running away from the bears is not exactly a happy ending. Yet there is structural recovery and consolation in that the bed does not break, and there is thereby a structural happy ending.

If the story of Goldilocks demonstrates how the user of engineering products can be distracted into overestimating their strength, the story of the Three Little Pigs shows how the designer can underestimate the strength his structure may need in an emergency or, as modern euphemisms would put it, under extreme load or hypothetical accident conditions. We recall that each of the three pigs has the same objective: to build a house. It is implicit in the mother pig's admonishment as they set out that their houses not only will have to shelter the little pigs from ordinary weather, but must also stand up against any extremes to which the Big Bad Wolf may subject them.

15   The three little pigs are all aware of the structural requirements necessary to keep the wolf out, but they differ in their beliefs of how severe a wolf's onslaught can be, and some of the pigs would like to get by with the least work and the most play. Thus the individual pigs make different estimates of how

strong their houses must be, and each reaches a different conclusion about how much strength he can sacrifice to availability of materials and time of construction. That each pig thinks he is building his house strong enough is demonstrated by the first two pigs dancing and singing, "Who's afraid of the Big Bad Wolf." They think their houses are safe enough and that their brother laboring over his brick house has overestimated the strength of the wolf and overdesigned his structure. Finally, when the third pig's house is completed, they all dance and sing their assurances. It is only the test of the wolf's full fury that ultimately proves the third pig correct. Had the wolf been a bugaboo, all three houses might have stood for many a year and the first two pigs never been proven wrong.

Thus the nursery rhymes, riddles, and fairy tales of childhood introduce us to engineering. From lullabies that comfort us even as they sing of structural failure to fairy tales that teach us that we can build our structures so strong that they can withstand even the huffing and puffing of a Big Bad Wolf, we learn the rudiments and the humanness of engineering.

Our own bodies, the oral tradition of our language and our nursery rhymes, our experiences with blocks and sand, all serve to accustom us to the idea that structural failure is part of the human condition. Thus we seem to be preconditioned, or at least emotionally prepared, to expect bridges and dams, buildings and boats, to break now and then. But we seem not at all resigned to the idea of major engineering structures having the same mortality as we. Somehow, as adults who forget their childhood, we expect our constructions to have evolved into monuments, not into mistakes. It is as if engineers and nonengineers alike, being human, want their creations to be superhuman. And that may not seem to be an unrealistic aspiration, for the flesh and bone of steel and stone can seem immortal when compared with the likes of man.

MLA CITATION

Petroski, Henry. "Falling Down Is Part of Growing Up." 1985. *The Norton Reader: An Anthology of Nonfiction.* Ed. Melissa A. Goldthwaite et al. 14th ed. New York: Norton, 2016. 187–93. Print.

QUESTIONS

1. Henry Petroski begins his essay with a metaphor: "We are all engineers of sorts, for we all have the principles of machines and structures in our bones." Does he convince you of his point by the end of the essay? How are we like and not like engineers and the structures they build?

2. Petroski intersperses his prose with excerpts from nursery rhymes, riddles, and fairy tales. Do you find this technique effective? Why or why not? In what ways do the different texts reinforce each other?

3. Describe a time when you or someone you know overstressed his or her body or a piece of furniture. Incorporate excerpts of your favorite rhymes, fairy tales, poems, or songs in your essay.

Elisabeth Kübler-Ross   *On the Fear of Death*

> Let me not pray to be sheltered from
>   dangers but to be fearless in facing them.
> Let me not beg for the stilling of
>   my pain but for the heart to conquer it.
> Let me not look for allies in life's
>   battlefield but to my own strength.
> Let me not crave in anxious fear to
>   be saved but hope for the patience to
>   win my freedom.
> Grant me that I may not be a
>   coward, feeling your mercy in my
>   success alone; but let me find the grasp
>   of your hand in my failure.
>   —Rabindranath Tagore,
>   *Fruit-Gathering*

EPIDEMICS HAVE TAKEN A GREAT TOLL OF LIVES in past generations. Death in infancy and early childhood was frequent and there were few families who didn't lose a member of the family at an early age. Medicine has changed greatly in the last decades. Widespread vaccinations have practically eradicated many illnesses, at least in western Europe and the United States. The use of chemotherapy, especially the antibiotics, has contributed to an ever decreasing number of fatalities in infectious diseases. Better child care and education has effected a low morbidity and mortality among children. The many diseases that have taken an impressive toll among the young and middle-aged have been conquered. The number of old people is on the rise, and with this fact come the number of people with malignancies and chronic diseases associated more with old age.

Pediatricians have less work with acute and life-threatening situations as they have an ever increasing number of patients with psychosomatic disturbances and adjustment and behavior problems. Physicians have more people in their waiting rooms with emotional problems than they have ever had before, but they also have more elderly patients who not only try to live with their decreased physical abilities and limitations but who also face loneliness and isolation with all its pains and anguish. The majority of these people are not seen by a psychiatrist. Their needs have to be elicited and gratified by other professional people, for instance, chaplains and social workers. It is for them that I am trying to outline the changes that have taken place in the last few decades, changes that are ultimately responsible for the increased fear of death, the rising number of emotional problems, and the greater need for understanding of and coping with the problems of death and dying.

A chapter from Elisabeth Kübler-Ross's celebrated book, On Death and Dying *(1969), which traces the "stages of grief"—denial, anger, bargaining, depression, and acceptance— through which a dying person passes when faced with a terminal illness.*

When we look back in time and study old cultures and people, we are impressed that death has always been distasteful to man and will probably always be. From a psychiatrist's point of view this is very understandable and can perhaps best be explained by our basic knowledge that, in our unconscious, death is never possible in regard to ourselves. It is inconceivable for our unconscious to imagine an actual ending of our own life here on earth, and if this life of ours has to end, the ending is always attributed to a malicious intervention from the outside by someone else. In simple terms, in our unconscious mind we can only be killed; it is inconceivable to die of a natural cause or of old age. Therefore death in itself is associated with a bad act, a frightening happening, something that in itself calls for retribution and punishment.

One is wise to remember these fundamental facts as they are essential in understanding some of the most important, otherwise unintelligible communications of our patients.

The second fact that we have to comprehend is that in our unconscious   5
mind we cannot distinguish between a wish and a deed. We are all aware of some of our illogical dreams in which two completely opposite statements can exist side by side—very acceptable in our dreams but unthinkable and illogical in our wakening state. Just as our unconscious mind cannot differentiate between the wish to kill somebody in anger and the act of having done so, the young child is unable to make this distinction. The child who angrily wishes his mother to drop dead for not having gratified his needs will be traumatized greatly by the actual death of his mother—even if this event is not linked closely in time with his destructive wishes. He will always take part or the whole blame for the loss of his mother. He will always say to himself—rarely to others—"I did it, I am responsible, I was bad, therefore Mommy left me." It is well to remember that the child will react in the same manner if he loses a parent by divorce, separation, or desertion. Death is often seen by a child as an impermanent thing and has therefore little distinction from a divorce in which he may have an opportunity to see a parent again.

Many a parent will remember remarks of their children such as, "I will bury my doggy now and next spring when the flowers come up again, he will get up." Maybe it was the same wish that motivated the ancient Egyptians to supply their dead with food and goods to keep them happy and the old American Indians to bury their relatives with their belongings.

When we grow older and begin to realize that our omnipotence is really not so omnipotent, that our strongest wishes are not powerful enough to make the impossible possible, the fear that we have contributed to the death of a loved one diminishes—and with it the guilt. The fear remains diminished, however, only so long as it is not challenged too strongly. Its vestiges can be seen daily in hospital corridors and in people associated with the bereaved.

A husband and wife may have been fighting for years, but when the partner dies, the survivor will pull his hair, whine and cry louder and beat his chest in regret, fear and anguish, and will hence fear his own death more than before, still believing in the law of talion—an eye for an eye, a tooth for a tooth—"I am responsible for her death, I will have to die a pitiful death in retribution."

Maybe this knowledge will help us understand many of the old customs and rituals which have lasted over the centuries and whose purpose is to diminish the anger of the gods or the people as the case may be, thus decreasing the anticipated punishment. I am thinking of the ashes, the torn clothes, the veil, the *Klage Weiber*[1] of the old days—they are all means to ask you to take pity on them, the mourners, and are expressions of sorrow, grief, and shame. If someone grieves, beats his chest, tears his hair, or refuses to eat, it is an attempt at self-punishment to avoid or reduce the anticipated punishment for the blame that he takes on the death of a loved one.

10   This grief, shame, and guilt are not very far removed from feelings of anger and rage. The process of grief always includes some qualities of anger. Since none of us likes to admit anger at a deceased person, these emotions are often disguised or repressed and prolong the period of grief or show up in other ways. It is well to remember that it is not up to us to judge such feelings as bad or shameful but to understand their true meaning and origin as something very human. In order to illustrate this I will again use the example of the child— and the child in us. The five-year-old who loses his mother is both blaming himself for her disappearance and being angry at her for having deserted him and for no longer gratifying his needs. The dead person then turns into something the child loves and wants very much but also hates with equal intensity for this severe deprivation.

The ancient Hebrews regarded the body of a dead person as something unclean and not to be touched. The early American Indians talked about the evil spirits and shot arrows in the air to drive the spirits away. Many other cultures have rituals to take care of the "bad" dead person, and they all originate in this feeling of anger which still exists in all of us, though we dislike admitting it. The tradition of the tombstone may originate in this wish to keep the bad spirits deep down in the ground, and the pebbles that many mourners put on the grave are left-over symbols of the same wish. Though we call the firing of guns at military funerals a last salute, it is the same symbolic ritual as the Indian used when he shot his spears and arrows into the skies.

I give these examples to emphasize that man has not basically changed. Death is still a fearful, frightening happening, and the fear of death is a universal fear even if we think we have mastered it on many levels.

What has changed is our way of coping and dealing with death and dying and our dying patients.

Having been raised in a country in Europe where science is not so advanced, where modern techniques have just started to find their way into medicine, and where people still live as they did in this country half a century ago, I may have had an opportunity to study a part of the evolution of mankind in a shorter period.

15   I remember as a child the death of a farmer. He fell from a tree and was not expected to live. He asked simply to die at home, a wish that was granted without questioning. He called his daughters into the bedroom and spoke with each one of them alone for a few moments. He arranged his affairs quietly, though he was

---

1. German for "wailing wives."

in great pain, and distributed his belongings and his land, none of which was to be split until his wife should follow him in death. He also asked each of his children to share in the work, duties, and tasks that he had carried on until the time of the accident. He asked his friends to visit him once more, to bid good-bye to them. Although I was a small child at the time, he did not exclude me or my siblings. We were allowed to share in the preparations of the family just as we were permitted to grieve with them until he died. When he did die, he was left at home, in his own beloved home which he had built, and among his friends and neighbors who went to take a last look at him where he lay in the midst of flowers in the place he had lived in and loved so much. In that country today there is still no make-believe slumber room, no embalming, no false makeup to pretend sleep. Only the signs of very disfiguring illnesses are covered up with bandages and only infectious cases are removed from the home prior to the burial.

Why do I describe such "old-fashioned" customs? I think they are an indication of our acceptance of a fatal outcome, and they help the dying patient as well as his family to accept the loss of a loved one. If a patient is allowed to terminate his life in the familiar and beloved environment, it requires less adjustment for him. His own family knows him well enough to replace a sedative with a glass of his favorite wine; or the smell of a home-cooked soup may give him the appetite to sip a few spoons of fluid which, I think, is still more enjoyable than an infusion. I will not minimize the need for sedatives and infusions and realize full well from my own experience as a country doctor that they are sometimes life-saving and often unavoidable. But I also know that patience and familiar people and foods could replace many a bottle of intravenous fluids given for the simple reason that it fulfills the physiological need without involving too many people and/or individual nursing care.

The fact that children are allowed to stay at home where a fatality has stricken and are included in the talk, discussions, and fears gives them the feeling that they are not alone in the grief and gives them the comfort of shared responsibility and shared mourning. It prepares them gradually and helps them view death as part of life, an experience which may help them grow and mature.

This is in great contrast to a society in which death is viewed as taboo, discussion of it is regarded as morbid, and children are excluded with the presumption and pretext that it would be "too much" for them. They are then sent off to relatives, often accompanied with some unconvincing lies of "Mother has gone on a long trip" or other unbelievable stories. The child senses that something is wrong, and his distrust in adults will only multiply if other relatives add new variations of the story, avoid his questions or suspicions, shower him with gifts as a meager substitute for a loss he is not permitted to deal with. Sooner or later the child will become aware of the changed family situation and, depending on the age and personality of the child, will have an unresolved grief and regard this incident as a frightening, mysterious, in any case very traumatic experience with untrustworthy grownups, which he has no way to cope with.

It is equally unwise to tell a little child who lost her brother that God loved little boys so much that he took little Johnny to heaven. When this little girl grew up to be a woman she never solved her anger at God, which resulted in a psychotic depression when she lost her own little son three decades later.

20   We would think that our great emancipation, our knowledge of science and of man, has given us better ways and means to prepare ourselves and our families for this inevitable happening. Instead the days are gone when a man was allowed to die in peace and dignity in his own home.

The more we are making advancements in science, the more we seem to fear and deny the reality of death. How is this possible?

We use euphemisms, we make the dead look as if they were asleep, we ship the children off to protect them from the anxiety and turmoil around the house if the patient is fortunate enough to die at home, we don't allow children to visit their dying parents in the hospitals, we have long and controversial discussions about whether patients should be told the truth—a question that rarely arises when the dying person is tended by the family physician who has known him from delivery to death and who knows the weaknesses and strengths of each member of the family.

I think there are many reasons for this flight away from facing death calmly. One of the most important facts is that dying nowadays is more gruesome in many ways, namely, more lonely, mechanical, and dehumanized; at times it is even difficult to determine technically when the time of death has occurred.

Dying becomes lonely and impersonal because the patient is often taken out of his familiar environment and rushed to an emergency room. Whoever has been very sick and has required rest and comfort especially may recall his experience of being put on a stretcher and enduring the noise of the ambulance siren and hectic rush until the hospital gates open. Only those who have lived through this may appreciate the discomfort and cold necessity of such transportation which is only the beginning of a long order—hard to endure when you are well, difficult to express in words when noise, light, pumps, and voices are all too much to put up with. It may well be that we might consider more the patient under the sheets and blankets and perhaps stop our well-meant efficiency and rush in order to hold the patient's hand, to smile, or to listen to a question. I include the trip to the hospital as the first episode in dying, as it is for many. I am putting it exaggeratedly in contrast to the sick man who is left at home— not to say that lives should not be saved if they can be saved by a hospitalization but to keep the focus on the patient's experience, his needs and his reactions.

25   When a patient is severely ill, he is often treated like a person with no right to an opinion. It is often someone else who makes the decision if and when and where a patient should be hospitalized. It would take so little to remember that the sick person too has feelings, has wishes and opinions, and has—most important of all—the right to be heard.

Well, our presumed patient has now reached the emergency room. He will be surrounded by busy nurses, orderlies, interns, residents, a lab technician perhaps who will take some blood, an electrocardiogram technician who takes the cardiogram. He may be moved to X-ray and he will overhear opinions of his condition and discussions and questions to members of the family. He slowly but surely is beginning to be treated like a thing. He is no longer a person. Decisions are made often without his opinion. If he tries to rebel he will be sedated and after hours of waiting and wondering whether he has the strength, he will be wheeled into the operating room or intensive treatment unit and become an object of great concern and great financial investment.

He may cry for rest, peace, and dignity, but he will get infusions, transfusions, a heart machine, or tracheotomy if necessary. He may want one single person to stop for one single minute so that he can ask one single question—but he will get a dozen people around the clock, all busily preoccupied with his heart rate, pulse, electrocardiogram or pulmonary functions, his secretions or excretions but not with him as a human being. He may wish to fight it all but it is going to be a useless fight since all this is done in the fight for his life, and if they can save his life they can consider the person afterwards. Those who consider the person first may lose precious time to save his life! At least this seems to be the rationale or justification behind all this—or is it? Is the reason for this increasingly mechanical, depersonalized approach our own defensiveness? Is this approach our own way to cope with and repress the anxieties that a terminally or critically ill patient evokes in us? Is our concentration on equipment, on blood pressure our desperate attempt to deny the impending death which is so frightening and discomforting to us that we displace all our knowledge onto machines, since they are less close to us than the suffering face of another human being which would remind us once more of our lack of omnipotence, our own limits and failures, and last but not least perhaps our own mortality?

Maybe the question has to be raised: Are we becoming less human or more human?

[I]t is clear that whatever the answer may be, the patient is suffering more—not physically, perhaps, but emotionally. And his needs have not changed over the centuries, only our ability to gratify them.

MLA CITATION

Kübler-Ross, Elisabeth. "On the Fear of Death." 1969. *The Norton Reader: An Anthology of Nonfiction.* Ed. Melissa A. Goldthwaite et al. 14th ed. New York: Norton, 2016. 194–99. Print.

QUESTIONS

1. Elisabeth Kübler-Ross incorporates various kinds of evidence—experience, observation, and reading—in this essay. Mark these kinds of evidence and describe how she integrates them into her text.

2. Kübler-Ross attends to the needs of the living and the rights of the dying. Describe where and how she addresses each and how she presents the conflicts, actual and potential, between them.

3. In paragraphs 24–27 Kübler-Ross describes the experience of being in an ambulance, emergency room, and hospital from a patient's point of view. What does this shift in point of view contribute to the essay?

4. Imagine a situation in which a child or children are not isolated from death. What might be the consequences? Using this situation and its possible consequences, write an essay in which you agree, disagree, or both with Kübler-Ross's views.

CULTURAL ANALYSIS

ANNIE LEONARD   *The Story of Bottled Water:*
A Footnoted and Annotated Script

O
NE OF THE PROBLEMS with trying to use less stuff is that sometimes we feel like we really need it. What if you live in a city like, say, Cleveland and you want a glass of water? Are you going to take your chances and get it from the city tap? Or should you reach for a bottle of water that comes from the pristine rainforests of . . . Fiji?

Well, Fiji brand water thought the answer to this question was obvious. So they built a whole ad campaign around it. It turned out to be one of the dumbest moves in advertising history.[1]

See, the city of Cleveland didn't like being the butt of Fiji's joke, so they did some tests and guess what? These tests showed a glass of Fiji water is lower quality, it loses taste tests against Cleveland tap, and costs thousands of times more.[2]

This story is typical of what happens when you test bottled water against tap water.

5   Is it cleaner? Sometimes, sometimes not: in many ways, bottled water is less regulated than tap.[3]

Is it tastier? In taste tests across the country, people consistently choose tap over bottled water.[4]

These bottled water companies say they're just meeting consumer demand— but who would demand a less sustainable, less tasty, way more expensive product,

A script of Annie Leonard's eight-minute video The Story of Bottled Water, *which was first released on March 22, 2010, to celebrate World Water Day. The video and script can be accessed through the website of Leonard's organization The Story of Stuff Project (storyofstuff.org/movies/story-of-bottled-water), which is dedicated to creating "a more healthy and just planet." The organization is committed to informing people about the ways they produce, use, and discard all the "stuff" in their lives. This script belongs to one of many videos available on the website, and the images are stills taken from the video. Leonard includes multiple footnotes, which appear at the end of this reading.*

especially one you can get almost free in your kitchen? Bottled water costs about 2,000 times more than tap water.[5] Can you imagine paying 2,000 times the price of anything else? How about a $10,000 sandwich?

Yet people in the U.S. buy more than half a billion bottles of water every week. That's enough to circle the globe more than 5 times.[6] How did this come to be? Well it all goes back to how our materials economy works and one of its key drivers, which is known as manufactured demand.[7]

If companies want to keep growing, they have to keep selling more and more stuff. In the 1970s giant soft drink companies got worried as their growth projections started to level off.[8] There's only so much soda a person can drink. Plus it wouldn't be long before people began realizing that soda is not that healthy and turned back to—gasp—drinking tap water.

Well, the companies found their next big idea in a silly designer product that most people laughed at as a passing yuppie fad.[9] Water is free, people said back then, what will they sell us next, air?[10]

So how do you get people to buy this fringe product? Simple: You manufacture demand. How do you do that? Well, imagine you're in charge of a bottled water company.

Since people aren't lining up to trade their hard earned money for your unnecessary product, you make them feel scared and insecure if they *don't* have it.[11] And that's exactly what the bottled water industry did. One of their first marketing tactics was to scare people about tap water, with ads like Fiji's Cleveland campaign.

"When we're done," one top water exec said, "tap water will be relegated to showers and washing dishes."[12]

Next, you hide the reality of your product behind images of pure fantasy. Have you ever noticed how bottled water tries to seduce us with pictures of mountain streams and pristine nature? But guess where a third of all bottled water in the U.S. actually comes from? The tap! Pepsi's Aquafina and Coke's Dasani are two of the many brands that are really filtered tap water.[13]

But the pristine nature lie goes much deeper. In a recent full page ad, Nestlé said: "bottled water is the most environmentally responsible consumer product in the world."[14] What?!

They're trashing the environment all along the product's life cycle. Exactly how is that environmentally responsible?

The problems start here with extraction and production where oil is used to make water bottles.[15] Each year, making the plastic water bottles used in the U.S. takes enough oil and energy to fuel a million cars.[16]

All that energy spent to make the bottle, even more to ship it around the planet, and then we drink it in about 2 minutes?[17] That brings us to the big problem at the other end of the life cycle—disposal.

What happens to all these bottles when we're done? Eighty percent end up in landfills, where they will sit for thousands of years,[18] or in incinerators, where they are burned, releasing toxic pollution.[19] The rest gets collected for recycling.

20   I was curious about where the plastic bottles that I put in recycling bins go. I found out that shiploads were being sent to India.[20] So, I went there. I'll never forget riding over a hill outside Madras where I came face to face with a mountain of plastic bottles from California. Real recycling would turn these bottles back into bottles. But that wasn't what was happening here. Instead these bottles were slated to be downcycled,[21] which means turning them into lower quality products that would just be chucked later. The parts that couldn't be downcycled were thrown away there; shipped all the way to India just to be dumped in someone else's backyard.

If bottled water companies want to use mountains on their labels, it'd be more accurate to show one of those mountains of plastic waste.

Scaring us, seducing us, and misleading us—these strategies are all core parts of manufacturing demand.

Once they've manufactured all this demand, creating a new multibillion dollar market,[22] they defend it by beating out the competition. But in this case, the competition is our basic human right to clean, safe drinking water.[23]

Pepsi's Vice Chairman publicly said "the biggest enemy is tap water!"[24] They want us to think it's dirty and bottled water is the best alternative.

25   In many places, public water is polluted thanks to polluting industries like the plastic bottle industry![25] And these bottled water guys are all too happy to offer their expensive solution[26] which keeps us hooked on their product.

It's time we took back the tap.

That starts with making a personal commitment to not buy or drink bottled water unless the water in your community is truly unhealthy.[27] Yes, it takes a bit of foresight to grab a reusable bottle[28] on the way out, but I think we can handle it.

Then take the next step—join a campaign that's working for real solutions, like demanding investment in clean tap water for all. In the U.S. tap water is underfunded by $24 billion,[29] partly because people believe drinking water only comes from a bottle! Around the world, a billion people don't have access to clean water right now.[30] Yet cities all over are spending millions of dollars to deal with all the plastic bottles we throw out.[31] What if we spent that money improving our water systems or better yet, preventing pollution to begin with?

There are many more things we can do to solve this problem. Lobby your city officials to bring back drinking fountains.[32] Work to ban the purchase of bottled water by your school, organization or entire city.[33]

30   This is a huge opportunity for millions of people to wake up and protect our wallets, our health and the planet. The good news is: it's already started.

Bottled water sales have begun to drop[34] while business is booming for safe refillable water bottles.[35] Yay!

Restaurants are proudly serving "tap"[36] and people are choosing to pocket the hundred or thousands of dollars they would otherwise be wasting on bottled water. Carrying bottled water is on its way to being as cool as smoking while pregnant. We know better now.

The bottled water industry is getting worried because the jig is up. We're not buying into their manufactured demand anymore. We'll choose our own demands, thank you very much, and we're demanding clean, safe water for all.

Notes

1. Fiji's ad ran in national magazines with the tagline, "The label says Fiji because it's not bottled in Cleveland," and as you'd expect, the city of Cleveland was not happy. CNNMoney.com ranked it #20 in their 101 Dumbest Moments in Business. To be fair, Fiji president Edward Cochran grew up near Cleveland, and said, "It is only a joke. We had to pick some town." But actually, Fiji, you didn't have to pick on some town. Picking on our public water systems isn't cool. Why don't you go beat up a hospital? [Editors' note: Cleveland's polluted Cuyahoga River caught fire in 1969, an event that helped lead to the Clean Water Act of 1972.]

2. After seeing the offensive ad, Cleveland's public utilities director Julius Ciaccia decided to put the two waters to the test; according to the Associated Press, the results found 6.31 micrograms of arsenic per liter in the Fiji bottle. Cleveland tap water, on the other hand, had no measurable arsenic. After safety comes taste: Cleveland's NewsChannel5 held a blind taste test. The result? Testers preferred Cleveland water. "I never had Fiji Water. I thought Cleveland was much more refreshing," one tennis player told reporters. "Just not as good as I thought it would be and not worth the price," one man said.

3. Municipal water in the U.S. is regulated by the Environmental Protection Agency, which does frequent testing, as do local authorities. The federal Safe Drinking Water Act empowers EPA to require water testing by certified laboratories and that violations be reported within a specified time frame. Public water systems must also provide reports to customers about their water, noting its source, evidence of contaminants and compliance with regulations.

The Food and Drug Administration, on the other hand, regulates bottled water as a food and cannot require certified lab testing or violation reporting. FDA monitors the labeling of bottled water, but the bottlers themselves are responsible for testing—kind of like the fox guarding the henhouse. Furthermore, FDA doesn't require bottled water companies to disclose where the water came from, how it was treated or what contaminants it contains. For a good article on the topic, see *The New York Times,* "Fewer Regulations for Bottled Water Than Tap, GAO Says," at http://www.nytimes.com /gwire/2009/07/09/09greenwire-fewer-regulations-for-bottled-water-than-tap-g-33331 .html

In a survey of 188 brands of bottled water, the Environmental Working Group (EWG) found only two providing such information about its product to customers. Based on extensive research and testing, EWG developed a "bottled water scorecard" where you can compare brands, and learn more about the process of testing, labeling, and marketing bottled water.

4. In February, 2006, *The New York Times* submitted six bottled waters (a mix of domestic and imported, natural and purified) and one sample of New York City tap water for chemical analysis. Minerals like magnesium, calcium and even arsenic in trace amounts are expected in water, and nothing out of the ordinary turned up. In a bacteriological examination, six came back with results well within the parameters defined by the EPA. But one bottled spring water showed much higher levels of unspecified bacteria and was labeled "substandard for drinking water." Because only one bottle was tested, the brand was not named.

The Times then brought in its heavy hitters: the Restaurant Reviewers. In a blind tasting, *The Times* Dining staff sampled nine still waters: New York tap; Biota, a new Colorado spring water in a biodegradable bottle; Poland Spring from Maine; Aquafina, from Pepsi, the country's best seller; Dasani, from Coca-Cola; Saratoga, a natural mineral water from upstate New York; Smartwater, "vapor-distilled and electrolyte-enhanced"; Fiji, artesian water from the South Pacific (artesian water comes from a deep underground source, such as an aquifer, that has no contact with surface air); and Penta, an "ultrapremium" water. None was universally disliked.

"We found that we were able to distinguish among two main types of water," says the *New York Times* report. Natural spring, mineral and artesian waters, which have "a velvety feel across the tongue and a slightly flatter flavor," and "purified waters, including tap water."

Corporate Accountability International's "Think Outside the Bottle" Campaign has held countless taste tests comparing bottled water to tap water, and the results generally favor the tap. But ultimately, the point isn't whether one tastes better than the other—it's how our taste, and our tastes, are shaped by advertising, rather than by what's good for us.

5. The consumer advocacy group Food & Water Watch offers this assessment, from their Take Back the Tap report (http://www.foodandwaterwatch.org/water/pubs/reports /take-back-the-tap): "A quick calculation comparing the average cost of one gallon of tap water . . . [to] one gallon of commercial bottled water comes out to: Tap water: $0.002 per gallon; bottled water: ranges from $0.89 to $8.26 per gallon." Here's how they break this out: "Pepsi's Aquafina brand, which is nothing more than tap water further purified, registered $425.7 million in sales in 2005, followed by Coca-Cola's Dasani bottled tap water with a sales tally of $346.1 million. Meanwhile, Nestlé's Poland Spring brand, which does come from spring sources, rang up sales of $199.7 million. That all pencils out to bottled water costing consumers 240 to 10,000 times more per gallon than tap water that is as good, or better, and far more monitored." *Fortune* magazine writer Marc Gunther paid $1.57 for a 20-ounce bottle of Aquafina, Pep-

si's bottled tap water, and spent $3.05 for one gallon (128 ounces) of gas. A bit of math shows that his bottled water bill amounted to $10.05 per gallon: big profits for the bottlers. By comparison, most Americans pay about $2 per 1,000 gallons for municipal water service."

6. In the intro to his book, *Bottled and Sold: The Story Behind Our Obsession with Bottled Water* (2010), Peter Gleick offers the figures like this: ". . . every second of every day in the United States, a thousand people buy and open up a plastic bottle of commercially produced water, and every second of every day in the United States, a thousand plastic bottles are thrown away. Eighty-five million bottles a day. More than thirty billion bottles a year at a cost to consumers of tens of billions of dollars."

To get back to Annie's number, that eighty-five million bottles a day, times seven days a week, gives us 595 million bottles a week. We asked the experts to do a little more math for us, and here's what they came up with. Renee Sharp, Director of the California Office of the Environmental Working Group offered the following calculation: "Assuming each bottle is 8 inches high, which is the height of the 20 fl. oz. Aquafina bottle I have on my desk for just this reason, 1 billion bottles would circle the globe 5.4 times, or would span the distance between Los Angeles and Tokyo 23 times." Peter Gleick of the Pacific Institute says, "I also calculated that the bottles would circle the Earth 5 times. But I assumed 600 million bottles (which I think is a more accurate number than a billion) and 12 inches high each (I didn't have a bottle on my desk to measure. . . .)." The 600 million 12-inch bottles is more akin to Annie's "more than half a billion bottles every week" being "enough to circle the globe more than 5 times."

You know, when you're talking about numbers this big and planets this fragile, unique, and essential to supporting all life, it's good to consult a variety of sources. . . .

7. Manufactured demand is a desire for something that didn't just develop naturally but was stoked by some outside force. Manufacturing demand is a core strategy of today's consumer economy. In order to get people to keep buying stuff, when most of us have plenty of stuff already, companies manufacture demand so we feel like we need ever more and ever newer clothes, cars, toasters, furniture, shoes. . . . everything. I mean, it's not like any of us just woke up and said "I need, really need, a new cell phone to replace my perfectly functional one" or "I really need a 15th pair of shoes."

The main tool to promote manufactured demand is advertising. In the past, advertising served to make announcements ("just arrived!") and then to distinguish products from one another; advertising's main role these days is to manufacture demand: to convince us we will be more successful, more happy, more loved if we just had a new (insert any consumer good here).

Now sometimes we really do need something, but a real need is different than manufactured demand. And manufactured demand has become so omnipresent that sometimes we get confused. It's not just bottled water; it's all over the place. Look around. Next time you're about to lay out some hard-earned cash for something, stop for a minute and ask yourself: do I really need this or am I responding to the bombardment of messages convincing me I need this?

Our friends at Polaris Institute tell us, "The real market value of bottled water lies in its perceived social value, a perception companies have worked hard to create. Between 10% to 15% of the price of a bottle of water goes to cover advertising costs." This means we're actually paying to be manipulated by advertising.

8. An article in the *Financial Times* of May 5, 1983, titled "Marketing: Coke plugs market gap," describes the trend, in part:

"Never-a-place for the faint-hearted, the U.S. soft drinks industry is today locked in a competitive battle which could prove to be just too much for some of the weaker contestants. The latest sally comes from the strongest of them all, Coca-Cola. This time last year, Coke had only two cola products on the market: after the launch of three new products this week, it now has six.

The proliferation of brands in this way has become common in the industry, probably because the overall growth in the market place is not what it was. U.S. soft drink consumption, which was rising at an annual 6 percent or more until the late 1970s, has been increasing at less than 3 percent a year since 1980, and, as a result, the manufacturers are hunting for growth at each other's expense.

Coke had a big success with last year's new product, Diet Coke, which it is now launching in the UK with a [1.5 million pounds] ad campaign starting this month. . . . It is now moving into another segment of the market which is being expanded by health conscious Americans—caffeine free colas."

9. Those of you old folks in the audience (that's Generation X and beyond) may recall Orson Welles, circa 1977, gushing on television about "a place in the south of France where there is a spring, and its name is Perrier." That was the first ever television ad for bottled water, and thus began one of the most baffling cons in modern consumerism. The sad fact, though, is that it wasn't a passing yuppie fad: in the three years following that ad, American sales of Perrier went up more than 3,000 percent. Speaking to the *New York Times* for an article of February 15, 2006 ("There Must be Something in the Water"), New York resident Johanna Raymond recalled, ''I remember thousands of us running in Perrier t-shirts in the 1979 marathon. Perrier was the coolest thing then. It was more than water."

10. Another retro reference: in the 1987 screwball comedy *Spaceballs*, Mel Brooks pops open a can of Perri-Air, brings it to his nose and takes a deep breath of the pure oxygen. Twenty years later, it just goes to show that reality is stranger than science fiction.

11. When Fiji's ad said, "It's not bottled in Cleveland," the underlying message was, "because Cleveland's water is dirty and dangerous." Which is, in fact, not true, but this was the message that the bottled water industry had planted in our collective imaginations.

Polaris Institute breaks it down: "Wherever there are incidents of contamination or disruption in municipal water systems, companies have been quick to respond with the promise of security, playing on fears about the spread of germs and toxins and a growing lack of faith in governments' ability to provide security through reliable public services."

It's curious to note that the marketing of bottled water took off in North America in the 1990s, precisely when cigarette smoking, the fast food industry and the soft drink industry were coming under fire for promoting unhealthy lifestyles. By using images of waterfalls and pristine mountain springs, by associating bottled water with a healthy lifestyle, and by turning it into a status symbol, the bottled water industry has been successful at creating a mass market for their product. A variety of marketing techniques are used to associate bottled water with images of "activity," "health," "relaxation," and "pureness."

In her book *Bottlemania* (2008), Elizabeth Royte refers to ads for Glaceau water "which ask, 'Who Approved Your Water?' The copy claims that tap water is 'rejected by Mother Nature'; springwater is approved by nature 'for potty training animals' (accompanied by an ideogram of a fish pooping); and purified water is approved by the FDA, but 'investigated by the FBI' (with an ideogram of a belching factory)." (Royte, *Bottlemania*, 34). In *Bottled and Sold: The Story Behind Our Obsession with Bottled Water*, Peter Gleick tells of an ad received in the mail from Royal Spring, a Texas bottled water company, that said "Americans no longer trust their tap water. . . . Clearly people are more worried than ever about what comes out of their taps." (Gleick, *Bottled and Sold*, 7). It is these kinds of underhanded marketing techniques that lead us to believe that tap water is dangerous and deadly, often despite any legitimate evidence. As it turns out, from the big picture perspective, if you take into account the real harm from pollution and waste that can be traced directly to the beverage industry, the real danger lies with them. . . .

12. The quote is from Susan D. Wellington, president of the Quaker Oats Company's United States beverage division, which makes Gatorade, speaking before industry analysts in 2000. (See Gleick, *Bottled and Sold*, 7).

13. An article of July 27, 2007 on CNN.Money.com said: "Pepsi-Cola announced Friday that the labels of its Aquafina brand bottled water will be changed to make it clear the product is tap water. The new bottles will say, 'The Aquafina in this bottle is purified water that originates from a public water source,' or something similar, PepsiCola North America spokeswoman Nicole Bradley told CNN. CocaCola does not have plans to change the labeling on its Dasani brand bottled water, a company spokesman told CNN, despite the fact the water also comes from a public water supply."

Now, the companies go to great length to tell you that, while their water originates from a public water source, it is more than "just filtered tap water." They boast proprietary, state-of-the-art, multi-stage filtration processes and esoteric references to mineral additives that make their water more than just water, and certainly better than tap. But, as Tony Clarke of Canada's Polaris Institute points out in his book, *Inside the Bottle* (2005), "unlike other resource production processes, where raw materials like timber, minerals, and oil are transformed into new products, bottled water is different. Bottled water is about 'turning water into water.'" (*Inside the Bottle*, 54).

14. The ad ran in Canada's *Globe and Mail*, October 20, 2008, page E7. The ad caused such a stir among environmentalists that it merited an entire article in *This Magazine* titled "'Environmentally friendly' Bottled Water? No such thing." The article concludes with a sharp observation by Meera Karunananthan, the national water campaigner for the Council of Canadians: "When the carbon footprint of drinking out of your tap is zero, you can't deny that the environmental impact of bottled water is more harmful."

In fact, to say that tap water (or anything, for that matter) has no carbon footprint might be an exaggeration, but a recent study commissioned by the Oregon Department of Environmental Quality called "Life Cycle Assessment of Drinking Water Delivery Systems: Bottled Water, Tap Water and Home/Office Delivery Water" (http://www.deq .state.or.us/lq/sw/wasteprevention/drinkingwater.htm) concludes that "consuming water from the tap in an average reusable bottle, even if washed frequently in a highly inefficient dishwasher, reduces energy consumption by 85 percent and greenhouse gases by 79 percent. . . . Even the best performing bottled water scenario has global warming effects 46 times greater than the best performing tap water scenario." Which is to say, choosing tap water is not only good for your budget, it's an important way to reduce global warming.

15. Most plastic water bottles are made of PET plastic, or polyethylene terephthalate, which is made from crude oil. The invention of PET in the 1970s made the portable water bottle possible. While plastic is everywhere because it is probably the most convenient material ever made, it comes at a high price. Back in 1993, the Glass Packaging Institute put out a report comparing glass and plastic, in which they noted that, "The production of the organic chemical industry has increased by a factor of ten over the past 40 years, a rate which has far outstripped total industrial production. In the U.S., plastics production has increased from 6 billion pounds in 1960 to 58 billion pounds in 1989. A major consumer of plastic production is the packaging industry, and containers account for nearly half of the total packaging material sales." (And this was before the bottled water boom. . . .)

The report goes on: "The post-war boom in plastic and other petrochemicals has led to an enormous rise in the volume and toxicity of hazardous chemicals and wastes in the environment. The number of chemicals used and released that are known to cause cancer, birth defects and damage to reproductive systems has increased dramatically." (*Advantage Glass! Switching to Plastic Is an Environmental Mistake,* by Henry S. Cole, Ph.D. and Kenneth A. Brown, 1993, 60).

So much for bottled water being healthy. . . .

16. The Pacific Institute breaks it down like this: "Because bottled water required approximately 1 million tons of PET in 2006, those bottles required roughly 100 billion MJ of energy. A barrel of oil contains around 6,000 MJ, so producing those bottles required the equivalent of around 17 million barrels of oil. This is enough energy to fuel one million American cars for one year."

17. Two minutes, three minutes, four minutes, whatever . . . The point is, it takes A LOT of energy and resources to produce a plastic bottle that is meant to be used exactly ONCE. In *The Story of Stuff* Annie talks about "planned obsolescence": "Planned obsolescence is another word for 'designed for the dump.' It means they actually make stuff that is designed to be useless as quickly as possible so we will chuck it and go buy a new one. It's obvious with stuff like plastic bags and coffee cups, but now it's even big stuff: mops, DVDs, cameras, barbeques even, everything!" A couple of Annie's favorite books on the topic are *The Waste Makers* (1960) by Vance Packard, and *Made to Break* (2006) by Giles Slade.

18. According to the Container Recycling Institute (http://www.container-recycling .org/), in fact, 90 percent of PET bottles end up in landfills, where they take between 450 and 1000 years to break down.

In addition, a 2004 report from the Container Recycling Institute (*The 10¢ Incentive to Recycle,* by Jenny Gitlitz and Pat Franklin, CRI, 2004) tells us that "Beverage containers make up 4.4 percent of the waste stream and 40 to 60 percent of roadside litter," and goes on to say that "While municipal curbside recycling programs rippled nationally during the 1990s, they have been unable to keep up with increasing sales of single-serving beverages and away-from-home consumption of food and drinks. An estimated 118 billion beverage bottles and cans were landfilled, littered, or incinerated in 2002—83 percent more than were wasted in 1992, and more than twice the amount wasted in 1982."

19. Some good facts on incinerators can be found at http://www.zerowasteamerica.org /Incinerators.htm. To get more in-depth, see *Incineration: A Dying Technology* by Neil Tangri (2003); *Gone Tomorrow* by Heather Rogers (2005); "Landfills Are Dangerous" in Rachel's *Democracy and Health News* (1998); and *Incineration and Human Health* by Pat Costner, Paul Johnston, Michelle Allsopp (2001).

20. Annie wrote about one such case way back in 1994 in *Multinational Monitor:*

> Indian environmentalists, working with investigators from Greenpeace's International Toxic Trade Project, have discovered that Pepsi is involved in both producing and disposing of plastic waste in India. Under Pepsi's two-part scheme, plastic for single-use disposal bottles will be manufactured in India and exported to the United States and Europe, while the toxic by-products of the plastic production process will stay in India. Used plastic bottles will then be returned from these countries to India.
>
> India will bear the burden of environmental and health impacts from plastic production and plastic waste, while consumers in industrialized countries will be able to continue using and disposing of massive quantities of unsustainable and unnecessary beverage packaging without absorbing the true costs—financial, health and environmental. In short, India gets shafted at both ends, while industrialized country consumers receive all the benefits.

Activists first learned of Pepsi's waste exports to India through U.S. Customs Department Data. Greenpeace researchers discovered records listing Pepsi as the exporter of about 4,500 tons of plastic scrap in 23 shipments during 1993.

The U.S. Customs records indicated that all of the waste exports were destined for the southern Indian city of Madras. All of the shipments left from the U.S. West Coast: eight shipments from San Francisco, two shipments from Long Beach, ten from Los Angeles, and three from Oakland. The most frequently used shipping lines for these waste shipments were OOCL and Presidential.

Much of the waste was dumped at the site of a factory owned by Futura Industries in Tiruvallur, outside of Madras. "As we came over the hill in our auto-rickshaw, we saw a mountain of plastic waste," recounts Madras environmentalist Satish Vangal, one of the researchers who discovered the site. "Piles and piles of used soda bottles stacked behind a wall. When we got closer to the factory, we found many bottles and plastic scrap along the road and blowing in the wind. Every bottle we saw said 'California Redemption Value.' They were all from California's recycling program and now they are sitting in a pile in India!" explains Vangal. "We have enough problems dealing with our own plastic wastes; why should we import other peoples's rubbish?"

Pepsi officials in the United States acknowledge the waste is exported to India, but claim it is all recycled. Futura officials also say the waste is imported, but they admit that much of it is not actually recycled. The senior manager of the Futura plant, Dr. L.R. Subbaraman, estimated that 60 to 70 percent of the waste can be processed at his factory, but the rest is either too contaminated with residual materials or other garbage that arrives mixed in with the shipment, or is the wrong type of plastic. Subbaraman refused to disclose the fate of the waste which cannot be reprocessed at the plant.

Subbaraman reports that Futura has imported a total of 10,000 metric tons of plastic waste from Pepsi and other companies since 1992. If only 60 to 70 percent could be processed within the Futura plant, 3,000 to 4,000 metric tons of plastic garbage have been imported which were not recyclable. A visit to the back of the plant revealed a massive pile of plastic discards.

Find Annie's entire article at: http://www.mindfully.org/Pesticide/Dumping-Pepsi-Plastic-India94.htm

21. Most plastic "recycling" is actually "downcycling." In *Cradle to Cradle: Remaking the Way We Make Things* (2002) architect William McDonough and chemist Michael Braungart tell us that when most plastics are recycled, they are mixed with different plastics to produce a hybrid of lower quality, which is then molded into something amorphous and cheap, such as a park bench or a speed bump. This tells us that even something as "environmentally friendly" as recycling still does not really bring about sustainable use of resources, it just moves our waste around the built environment in ever-more degraded forms. Even worse, McDonough and Braungart say that "Downcycling can actually increase contamination of the biosphere" (*Cradle to Cradle*, 57), because the process releases toxins, and because "downcycled materials of all kinds are materially less rigorous than their predecessors, more chemicals are often added to make the materials useful again."

22. When numbers get this big, they're hard to track, but here are a few: The U.S. Census Bureau reports that Americans drank 23.2 gallons of bottled water per capita in 2004, up from only 2.7 gallons in 1980. Another report says we drink less, but still a lot: "The average American drinks approximately 14 gallons of bottled water a year. Assuming a population of 250 million, this comes to a staggering 13 billion liters (13 Gl=13 gigaliters)." USEPA quotes the Beverage Marketing Corporation of 2004 (http://www.epa. gov/ogwdw000/faq/pdfs/fs_healthseries_bottlewater.pdf) to tell us that

"Bottled water is the fastest growing drink choice in the United States, and Americans spend billions of dollars each year to buy it." One report (http://www.fastcompany. com /magazine/117/features-message-in-a-bottle.html) tells us that in 2007, Americans spent more money on bottled water than on iPods or movie tickets: $15 Billion.

23. If asked, "Is water a human right?" most of us would say "Of course!" without blinking an eye. And it is. . . . sort of. But because "human rights" is a big complicated field of legal and technical concerns, it can get a little . . . sticky. The Universal Declaration of Human Rights, the founding document of modern human rights law, for example, says nothing specifically about water. When it was written in the 1940s it would've been hard to imagine companies buying and selling water in a way that denied it to anyone, so making water a human right would have seemed as silly as making air a human right. The document does say we all have the right to life, to health, to dignity, security, etc. . . . But nothing about water. Of course, without water, there's no life, health, dignity, or security, so . . . The Universal Declaration protected what are called "political rights." Only later did it become clear that we needed protections also of what are called "economic, social, and cultural rights." In 2002, partly in response to growing concerns that poor people worldwide were being forced to pay for water or go without, the United Nations Committee on Economic, Social, and Cultural Rights wrote General Comment No.15, which is now considered the definitive and official interpretation of human rights laws regarding water.

For those of you who may not have time to read the whole thing, the gist of General Comment 15 is in its introductory paragraph: "the human right to water entitles everyone to sufficient, safe, acceptable, physically accessible and affordable water for personal and domestic uses." It notes that the right to water has been recognized in a wide range of international documents and reaffirms the fundamental importance of the right stating that: "the human right to water is indispensable for leading a life in human dignity. It is a prerequisite for the realization of other human rights."

24. This quote is from Robert S. Morrison, quoted in 2000, shortly before he was made chairman of Pepsico's North American Beverage and Food division. The full quote is: "The biggest enemy is tap water. . . . We're not against water—it just has its place. We think it's good for irrigation and cooking." Both this and the earlier citation, from Susan D. Wellington, are cited in a letter to the *New York Times* by Peter Gleick of the Pacific Institute and in Peter Gleick's book, *Bottled and Sold: The Story Behind Our Obsession with Bottled Water.*

25. . . . and the oil industry . . . and the mining industry . . . and big agribusiness . . . That is to say, the manufacturing of demand that we associate with bottled water leads to pollution such as that Annie wrote about back in 1994 (http://www.mindfully.org /Pesticide/Dumping-Pepsi-Plastic-India94.htm) and stunning pollution disasters like the great Pacific garbage patch, a floating dump the size of Texas, containing shoes, toys, bags, pacifiers, wrappers, toothbrushes, and bottles—approximately 3.5 million tons of trash—out in the ocean midway between Hawaii and San Francisco (http:// www.greatgarbagepatch.org/). The same "manufactured demand" leads to massive overconsumption of fossil fuels and the pollution it causes (http://chevrontoxico.com/), an industrial system of agriculture that leaves toxic pollution in its wake and mining for energy and mineral demand that is way out of control.

That is to say, bottled water is a big problem. . . . But it is also a symptom of a much bigger problem: using too much stuff, and leaving too much waste.

26. We've already covered the "expensive" part; for some critical thinking on the "solution" part, see the next footnote. . . .

27. At the heart of the water issue is the fact that literally billions of people around the world—including in parts of the U.S. and other rich countries—do not have access to safe

drinking water. The causes are complex, including both man-made political and economic causes, and natural causes; in short, it might be the water, it might be the pipes—or it might be the lack of water or the lack of pipes. In either case, selling bottled water (or even giving it away as some companies and organizations do as part of relief efforts in emergencies), will not fix the problem. The real fix is more public investment in water infrastructure, and community control of that infrastructure to ensure that the poorest and most vulnerable communities have their needs met. Even in places where both tourists and locals are urged to "not drink the water," the long-term solution is not to avoid tap water—but to make the tap water safe to drink. Yes, this solution will cost money, but at least it's an investment in something permanent, and that benefits everyone.

28. . . . or mug . . . or mason jar . . . or sippy cup . . . or . . . With all the empty containers in your kitchen and all the good water flowing from the tap, there's no reason not to carry one.

29. By "underfunded," we mean the difference between what is currently spent and is projected to be spent on water infrastructure investment, and what will actually need to be spent during that same time period to keep service levels roughly comparable to desirable past and current service levels.

The $24 billion projection is based on the rough averaging of two water infrastructure investment gap analyses conducted by the EPA (U.S. Environmental Protection Agency, "The Clean Water and Drinking Water Infrastructure Gap Analysis," September 2002, EPA 816-R-02-020, 50) and by the Water Infrastructure Network, a coalition of labor, environment and water utility officials (see Water Infrastructure Network, Clean & Safe Water for the 21st Century, A Renewed National Commitment to Water and Wastewater Infrastructure, April 2000).

For a more detailed explanation, see the Congressional Research Service's 2008 report, "Water Infrastructure Needs and Investment: Review and Analysis of Key Issues" (http://fas.org/sgp/crs/homesec/RL31116.pdf).

30. More precisely, 1.2 billion people lack access to safe water and 2.6 billion lack access to sanitation, according to the UN Development Program's 2006 Human Development Report (http://hdr.undp.org/en/reports/global/hdr2006/).

31. Bill Sheehan, Director of the Product Policy Institute (http://www.productpolicy .org/), says "Three-quarters of the waste material that local governments are responsible for managing in North America is products and packaging; the costs of collecting PET bottles alone runs about $900 per ton. That amounts to welfare for the makers of products and packaging. Citizens and their governments would be better served if those funds were supporting schools, police and parks, and other services that the market cannot or will not provide, like public water fountains. . . . In a time of tight budgets many local governments are asking why taxpayers and ratepayers, and not producers and consumers, are the ones paying to pick up products and associated packaging 'designed for the dump.' The costs of recycling and litter clean up should be the responsibility of producers and included in the purchase price."

32. Anyone remember water fountains? Coincidentally, just before the bottled water craze hit, it was taken for granted that public fountains were part of any public building: schools, offices, sports stadiums, parks. Where did they go?

Meanwhile, in the U.S., many state building codes mandate that there be one source of public water for every 1,000 people the building has capacity for. This came up in recent news in two cases. In Cleveland (why always Cleveland?), the new sports arena that hosts the Cleveland Cavaliers basketball team removed its drinking water fountains. The only way for thirsty fans to get water was to wait in line at the concessions counter for a free small cup or pay $4 for bottled water—or try to drink water from the bathroom faucets. As Peter Gleick of Pacific Institute wrote, "This wasn't the first time a sports arena ran into trouble over water fountains. In September 2007, the University of Central Florida opened its brand new 45,000 seat football stadium with a sell-out crowd on hand to watch the UCF Knights battle the Texas Longhorns. The loser? The fans. With temperatures near 100 degrees the crowd found out the hard way that the stadium had been built without a single drinking fountain (in apparent violation of building codes). Security concerns kept out personal water bottles. And the only water available (other than the taps in the bathrooms) was $3 bottled water, which quickly sold out. Eighteen people were taken to local hospitals and sixty more were treated by campus medical personnel for heat-related illnesses. After a massive public brouhaha, the university quickly retrofitted the stadium with water fountains."

The public fountains were brought back at the Cleveland Cavaliers' stadium, too. The lesson? We like our drinking fountains; in fact, we don't just like them. . . . We need them for public health and safety. The other lesson? When people organize to take back our right to public water . . . we win.

33. Bottled water bans are spreading faster than we can count. The Polaris Institute in Canada says that as of December 2009, 72 municipalities from 8 provinces and 2 territories had implemented restrictions on bottled water. In the U.S., San Francisco, Minneapolis, Seattle, and Salt Lake City have all banned bottled water at city functions as a way of reducing budgets while promoting their cities' highly drinkable tap water (and these are just the big cities). At the 75th annual Conference of Mayors the mayors of these three cities introduced a resolution to ban bottled water in city functions nationwide.

34. The Beverage Marketing Corp. documents sales trends of bottled water, soft drinks, fruit juice and many other kinds of drinks. Its data shows that bottled water sales fell 1 percent in 2008 to 8.7 billion gallons, down from 8.8 billion gallons in 2007. In 2009, the company reported, sales remained depressed, on a par with 2008. The biggest hit was taken by Nestle, the Swiss company that is the world's biggest seller of bottled water under such brand names as Perrier, Poland Springs, San Pellegrino and Deer Park. The company reported that the volume of its bottled water sales fell 3.7 percent in the first half of 2009. A report by the Worldwatch Institute (http://www.worldwatch .org/node/5878) gives the details.

Behind the story are some grisly details of what an industry does when its market share is under threat. Richard Girard of Polaris Institute wrote an in-depth article on that topic.

35. Many companies now sell safe, easy-to-clean, lightweight drinking water bottles; we found a pretty hefty selection available here: http://www.reusablebags.com/store/bottles accessories-c-19.html. Our partners at Food & Water Watch and Corporate Accountability International offer sleek, stainless steel water bottles to their members.

36. Food & Water Watch, which has been supporting restaurants nationwide in making the switch back to good old tapwater, even offers a handy guide to the topic: http:// www.foodandwaterwatch.org/water/bottled/restaurants

MLA CITATION

Leonard, Annie. "The Story of Bottled Water." 2010. *The Norton Reader: An Anthology of Nonfiction*. Ed. Melissa A. Goldthwaite et al. 14th ed. New York: Norton, 2016. 200–12. Print.

QUESTIONS

1. Why, Annie Leonard wonders, do consumers buy so much bottled water when it is far more expensive, and arguably less tasty and healthy, than ordinary tap water?

How does Leonard answer this question? What assumptions about consumers does her answer imply? Can you imagine other possible answers to her question?

2. The footnotes to Leonard's piece are much longer than the main text itself. Why do you think Leonard and her staff at The Story of Stuff Project decided to document the text so heavily, filling it with references to websites, books, and articles? Compare the style in which the footnotes are written to the style of the main text. Is there a style you prefer? Why or why not?

3. Leonard wants to persuade her audience to change a deep-seated habit, to give up bottled water and "[take] back the tap" (paragraph 26). To this end, she develops her argument in stages. Trace the stages of her argument. Is her approach effective? Why or why not?

4. This piece is a "footnoted and annotated script" of Leonard's short animated documentary *The Story of Bottled Water*, available at storyofstuff.org/movies/story-of-bottled-water. Watch the movie and then re-read the printed text. How would you characterize its style? How is its style related to its origin as a movie? Did watching the movie change your response to Leonard's argument? If so, how?

5. Write a script for a short movie of your own, modeled on Leonard's, addressing an issue you care about deeply. Consider including footnotes to provide additional information for your readers.

TOM BISSELL   *Extra Lives:*
                      Why Video Games Matter

S
OMEDAY MY CHILDREN WILL ASK ME where I was and what I was doing when the United States elected its first black president. I could tell my children— who are entirely hypothetical; call them Kermit and Hussein[1]—that I was home at the time and, like hundreds of millions of other Americans, watching television. This would be a politician's answer, which is to say, factual but inaccurate in every important detail. Because Kermit and Hussein deserve an honestly itemized answer, I will tell them that, on November 4, 2008, their father was living in Tallinn, Estonia, where the American Election Day's waning hours were a cold, salmon-skied November 5 morning. My intention that day was to watch CNN International until the race was called. I will then be forced to tell Kermit and Hussein about what else happened on November 4, 2008.

The postapocalyptic video game *Fallout 3* had been officially released to the European market on October 30, but in Estonia it was nowhere to be found. For several weeks, Bethesda Softworks, *Fallout 3's* developer, had been posting online a series of promotional gameplay videos, which I had been watching and rewatching with fetish-porn avidity. I left word with Tallinn's best game store: *Call me the moment* Fallout 3 *arrives.* In the late afternoon of November 4, they finally rang. When I slipped the game into the tray of my Xbox 360, the first polls were due to close in America in two hours. One hour of *Fallout 3,* I told myself. Maybe two. Absolutely no more than three. Seven hours later, blinking and dazed, I turned off my Xbox 360, checked in with CNN, and discovered that the acceptance speech had already been given.

And so, my beloved Kermit, my dear little Hussein, at the moment America changed forever, your father was wandering an ICBM[2]-denuded wasteland, nervously monitoring his radiation level, armed only with a baseball bat, a 10mm pistol, and six rounds of ammunition, in search of a vicious gang of mohawked marauders who were 100 percent bad news and totally had to be dealt with. Trust Daddy on this one.

This essay is taken from a chapter of Tom Bissell's book Extra Lives: Why Video Games Matter *(2010). In addition to being an author and journalist, Bissell is an avid gamer who has written scripts for several video games.*

1. Kermit, name of a son, grandson, and great-grandson of President Theodore Roosevelt (1858–1919), now associated with Kermit the Frog, a puppet created by Jim Henson (1936–1990); Hussein, name that recalls Saddam Hussein (1937–2006), the president of Iraq who was deposed near the beginning of the Iraq War (2003–2011) and subsequently executed; also the middle name of Barack Hussein Obama (b. 1961), forty-fourth president of the United States.
2. Intercontinental Ballistic Missile.

Fallout 3 poster promoting the game's release.

Fallout 3 was Bethesda's first release since 2006's *The Elder Scrolls IV: Oblivion*. Both games fall within a genre known by various names: the open-world or sandbox or free-roaming game. This genre is superintended by a few general conventions, which include the sensation of being inside a large and disinterestedly functioning world, a main story line that can be abandoned for subordinate story lines (or for no purpose at all), large numbers of supporting characters with whom meaningful interaction is possible, and the ability to customize (or pimp, in the parlance of our time) the game's player-controlled central character. The pleasures of the open-world game are ample, complicated, and intensely private; their potency is difficult to explain, sort of like religion, of which these games become, for many, an aspartame form. Because of the freedom they grant gamers, the narrative- and mission-generating manner in which they reward exploration, and their convincing illusion of endlessness, the best open-world games tend to become leisure-time-eating viruses. As incomprehensible as it may seem, I have somehow spent more than two hundred hours playing *Oblivion*. I know this because the game keeps a running tally of the total time one has spent with it.

It is difficult to describe *Oblivion* without atavistic fears of being savaged   5
by the same jean-jacketed dullards who in 1985 threw my *Advanced Dungeons & Dragons Monster Manual II* into Lake Michigan (That I did not even play D&D, and only had the book because I liked to look at the pictures, left my assailants unmoved.) As to what *Oblivion* is about, I note the involvement of orcs and a "summon skeleton" spell and leave it at that. So: two hundred hours playing *Oblivion*? How is that even possible? I am not actually sure. Completing the game's narrative missions took a fraction of that time, but in the world of *Oblivion* you can also pick flowers, explore caves, dive for treasure, buy houses, bet

on gladiatorial arena fights, hunt bear, and read books. *Oblivion* is less a game than a world that best rewards full citizenship, and for a while I lived there and claimed it. At the time I was residing in Rome on a highly coveted literary fellowship, surrounded by interesting and brilliant people, and quite naturally mired in a lagoon of depression more dreadfully lush than any before or since. I would be lying if I said *Oblivion* did not, in some ways, aggravate my depression, but it also gave me something with which to fill my days other than piranhic self-hatred. It was an extra life; I am grateful to have had it.

When Bethesda announced that it had purchased the rights to develop *Fallout 3* from the defunct studio Interplay, the creators of the first two *Fallout* games, many were doubtful. How would the elvish imaginations behind *Oblivion* manage with the rather different milieu of an annihilated twenty-third-century America? The first *Fallout* games, which were exclusive to the personal computer, were celebrated for their clever satire and often freakishly exaggerated violence. *Oblivion* is about as satirical as a colonoscopy, and the fighting in the game, while not unviolent, is often weirdly inert.

Bethesda released *Fallout 3*'s first gameplay video in the summer of 2008. In it, Todd Howard, the game's producer, guides the player-controlled character into a disorientingly nuked Washington, D.C., graced with just enough ravaged familiarities—among which a pummeled Washington Monument stands out—to be powerfully unsettling. Based on these few minutes, *Fallout 3* appeared guaranteed to take its place among the most visually impressive games ever made. When Bethesda posted a video showcasing *Fallout 3*'s in-game combat—a brilliant synthesis of trigger-happy first-person-style shooting and the more deliberative, turn-based tactics of the traditional role-playing video game, wherein you attack, suffer your enemy's counterattack, counterattack yourself, and so on, until one of you is dead—many could not believe the audacity of its cartoon-Peckinpah[3] violence. Much of it was rendered in a slo-mo as disgusting as it was oddly beautiful: skulls exploding into the distinct flotsam of eyeballs, gray matter, and upper vertebrae; limbs liquefying into constellations of red pearls; torsos somersaulting through the air. The consensus was a bonfire of the skepticisms:[4] *Fallout 3* was going to be fucking awesome.

Needless to say, the first seven hours I spent with the game were distinguished by a bounty of salutary things. Foremost among them was how the world of *Fallout 3* looked. The art direction in a good number of contemporary big-budget video games has the cheerful parasitism of a tribute band. Visual inspirations are perilously few: Forests will be Tolkienishly[5] enchanted; futuristic industrial zones will be mazes of predictably grated metal catwalks; gunfights will erupt amid rubble- and car-strewn boulevards on loan from a thousand war-movie sieges. Once video games shed their distinctive vector-

---

3. Sam Peckinpah (1925–1984), American film director and screenwriter known for his violent Westerns.

4. Allusion to "bonfire of the vanities," a term for the burning of items deemed sinful by religious authorities.

5. Allusion to J. R. R. Tolkien (1892–1973), British philologist and fantasy writer.

The player-controlled character of *Fallout 3* in a futuristic Washington, D.C.

graphic and primary-color 8-bit origins, a commercially ascendant subset of game slowly but surely matured into what might well be the most visually derivative popular art form in history. *Fallout 3* is the rare big-budget game to begin rather than end with its derivativeness.

It opens in 2277, two centuries after a nuclear conflagration between the United States and China. Chronologically speaking, the world this Sino-American war destroyed was of late-twenty-first-century vintage, and yet its ruins are those of the gee-whiz futurism popular during the Cold War. *Fallout 3's* Slinky-armed sentry Protectrons, for instance, are knowing plagrarisms of *Forbidden Planet's* Robby the Robot,[6] and the game's many specimens of faded prewar advertising mimic the nascent slickness of 1950s-era graphic design. *Fallout 3* bravely takes as its aesthetic foundation a future that is both six decades old and one of the least convincing ever conceptualized. The result is a fascinating past-future never-never-land weirdness that infects the game's every corner: *George Jetson Beyond Thunderdome.*[7]

What also impressed me about *Fallout 3* was the buffet of choices set out by its early stages. The first settlement one happens upon, Megaton, has been   10

6. Multilingual robotic hero first introduced in the science-fiction film *Forbidden Planet* (1956).

7. Never-never-land, allusion to Neverland, island home of the fictional character Peter Pan; George Jetson, father of a futuristic family in the cartoon *The Jetsons* (1962–1963); *Mad Max: Beyond Thunderdome* (1985), sequel to the postapocalyptic Australian film *Mad Max* (1979).

built around an undetonated nuclear warhead, which a strange religious cult native to the town actually worships. Megaton can serve as base of operations or be wiped off the face of the map shortly after one's arrival there by detonating its nuke in exchange for a handsome payment. I spent quite a while poking around Megaton and getting to know its many citizens. What this means is that the first several hours I spent inside *Fallout 3* were, in essence, optional. Even for an open-world game, this suggests an awesome range of narrative variability. (Eventually, of course, I made the time to go back and nuke the place.)

Fallout 3, finally, looks beautiful. Most modern games—even shitty ones—look beautiful. Taking note of this is akin to telling the chef of a Michelin-starred restaurant that the tablecloths were lovely. Nonetheless, at one point in *Fallout 3* I was running up the stairs of what used to be the Dupont Circle Metro station and, as I turned to bash in the brainpan of a radioactive ghoul, noticed the playful, lifelike way in which the high-noon sunlight streaked along the grain of my sledgehammer's wooden handle. During such moments, it is hard not to be startled—even moved—by the care poured into the game's smallest atmospheric details.

Despite all this, I had problems with *Fallout 3*, and a number of these problems seem to me emblematic of the intersection at which games in general currently find themselves stalled. Take, for instance, *Fallout 3*'s tutorial. One feels for game designers: It would be hard to imagine a formal convention more inherently bizarre than the video-game tutorial. Imagine that, every time you open a novel, you are forced to suffer through a chapter in which the characters do nothing but talk to one another about the physical mechanics of how one goes about reading a book. Unfortunately, game designers do not really have a choice. Controller schemas change, sometimes drastically, from game to game, and designers cannot simply banish a game's relevant instructions to a directional booklet: That would be a violation of the interactive pact between game and gamer. Many games thus have to come up with a narratively plausible way in which one's controlled character engages in activity comprehensive enough to be instructive but not so intense as to involve a lot of failure. Games with a strong element of combat almost always solve this dilemma by opening with some sort of indifferently conceived boot-camp exercise or training round.

Fallout 3's tutorial opens, rather more ambitiously, with your character's birth, during which you pick your race and gender (if given the choice, I always opt for a woman, for whatever reason) and design your eventual appearance (probably this is the reason). The character who pulls you from your mother's birth canal is your father, whose voice is provided by Liam Neeson.[8] (Many games attempt to class themselves up with early appearances by accomplished

8. Irish film actor (b. 1952).

actors; Patrick Stewart's[9] platinum larynx served this purpose in *Oblivion*.) Now, aspects of *Fallout 3's* tutorial are brilliant: When you learn to walk as a baby, you are actually learning how to move within the game; you decide whether you want your character to be primarily strong, intelligent, or charismatic by reading a children's book; and, when the tutorial flashes forward to your tenth birthday party, you learn to fire weapons when you receive a BB gun as a gift. The tutorial flashes forward again, this time to a high school classroom, where you further define your character by answering ten aptitude-test-style questions. What is interesting about this is that it allows you to customize your character *indirectly* rather than directly, and many of the questions (one asks what you would do if your grandmother ordered you to kill someone) are morbidly amusing. While using an in-game aptitude test as a character-design aid is not exactly a new innovation, *Fallout 3* provides the most streamlined, narratively economical, and interactively inventive go at it yet.

By the time I was taking this aptitude test, however, I was a dissident citizen of Vault 101, the isolated underground society in which *Fallout 3* proper begins. My revolt was directed at a few things. The first was *Fallout 3's* dialogue, some of it so appalling ("Oh, James, we did it. A daughter. Our beautiful daughter") as to make Stephenie Meyer look like Ibsen.[10] The second was *Fallout 3's* addiction to trust-shattering storytelling redundancy, such as when your father announces, "I can't believe you're already ten," at what is clearly established as your tenth birthday party. The third, and least forgivable, was *Fallout 3's* Jell-O-mold characterization: In the game's first ten minutes you exchange gossip with the spunky best friend, cower beneath the megalomaniacal leader, and gain the trust of the goodhearted cop. Vault 101 even has a resident cadre of hoodlums, the Tunnel Snakes, whose capo resembles a malevolent Fonz.[11] Even with its backdrop of realized Cold War futurism, a greaser-style youth gang in an underground vault society in the year 2277 is the working definition of a dumb idea. During the tutorial's final sequence, the Tunnel Snakes' leader, your tormentor since childhood, requests your help in saving his mother from radioactive cockroaches (long story), a reversal of such tofu drama that, in my annoyance, I killed him, his mother, and then everyone else I could find in Vault 101, with the most perversely satisfying weapon I had on hand: a baseball bat. Allowing your decisions to establish for your character an in-game identity as a skull-crushing monster, a saint of patience, or some mixture thereof is another attractive feature of *Fallout 3*. These pretensions to morality, though, suddenly bored me, because they were

---

9. English stage, TV, and film actor (b. 1940).

10. Meyer (b. 1973), young-adult fiction writer and author of the *Twilight* series of vampire romance novels (2005–2008); Henrik Ibsen (1828–1906), Norwegian playwright, considered by many to have revolutionized modern drama.

11. Nickname of Arthur Fonzarelli, a character in the TV sitcom *Happy Days* (1974–1984).

occurring in a universe that had been designed by geniuses and written by Ed Wood Jr.[12]

15   Had I really waited a year for this? And was I really missing a cardinal event in American history to keep playing it? I had, and I was, and I could not really explain why.

What I know is this: If I were reading a book or watching a film that, every ten minutes, had me gulping a gallon of aesthetic Pepto, I would stop reading or watching. Games, for some reason, do not have this problem. Or rather, their problem is not having this problem. I routinely tolerate in games crudities I would never tolerate in any other form of art or entertainment. For a long time my rationalization was that, provided a game was fun to play, certain failures could be overlooked. I came to accept that games were generally incompetent with almost every aspect of what I would call traditional narrative. In the last few years, however, a dilemma has become obvious. Games have grown immensely sophisticated in any number of ways while at the same time remaining stubbornly attached to aspects of traditional narrative for which they have shown little feeling. Too many games insist on telling stories in a manner in which some facility with plot and character is fundamental to—and often even determinative of—successful storytelling.

The counterargument to all this is that games such as *Fallout 3* are more about the world in which the game takes place than the story concocted to govern one's progress through it. It is a fair point, especially given how beautifully devastated and hypnotically lonely the world of *Fallout 3* is. But if the world is paramount, why bother with a story at all? Why not simply cut the ribbon on the invented world and let gamers explore it? The answer is that such a game would probably not be very involving. Traps, after all, need bait. In a narrative game, story and world combine to create an experience. As the game designer Jesse Schell writes in *The Art of Game Design*, "The game is not the experience. The game enables the experience, but it *is not the experience.*" In a world as large as that of *Fallout 3*, which allows for an experience framed in terms of wandering and lonesomeness, story provides, if nothing else, badly needed direction and purpose. Unless some narrative game comes along that radically changes gamer expectation, stories, with or without Super Mutants, will continue to be what many games will use to harness their uniquely extravagant brand of fictional absorption.

I say this in full disclosure: The games that interest me the most are the games that choose to tell stories. Yes, video games have always told some form of story. PLUMBER'S GIRLFRIEND CAPTURED BY APE![13] is a story, but it is a rudimentary fairytale story without any of the proper fairytale's evocative nuances and dreads. Games are often compared to films, which would seem to make

---

12. American director (1924–1978) of "B" movies such as *Plan 9 from Outer Space* (1958) and known among his cult following as the "worst director of all time."

13. Allusion to *Donkey Kong*, an arcade game introduced in 1981 that is credited with introducing storytelling to video games.

sense, given their many apparent similarities (both are scored, both have actors, both are cinematographical, and so on). Upon close inspection comparison falls leprously apart. In terms of storytelling, they could not be more different. Films favor a compressed type of storytelling and are able to do this because they have someone deciding where to point the camera. Games, on the other hand, contain more than most gamers can ever hope to see, and the person deciding where to point the camera is, in many cases, you—and you might never even see the "best part." The best part of looking up at a night sky, after all, is not any one star but the infinite possibility of what is between stars. Games often provide an approximation of this feeling, with the difference that you can find out what is out there. Teeming with secrets, hidden areas, and surprises that may pounce only on the second or third (or fourth) playthrough—I still laugh to think of the time I made it to an isolated, hard-to-find corner of *Fallout 3's* Wasteland and was greeted by the words FUCK YOU spray-painted on a rock— video games favor a form of storytelling that is, in many ways, completely unprecedented. The conventions of this form of storytelling are only a few decades old and were created in a formal vacuum by men and women who still walk among us. There are not many mediums whose Dantes and Homers one can ring up and talk to.[14] With games, one can.

I am uninterested in whether games are better or worse than movies or novels or any other form of entertainment. More interesting to me is what games *can* do and how they make me feel while they are doing it. Comparing games to other forms of entertainment only serves as a reminder of what games are not. Storytelling, however, does not belong to film any more than it belongs to the novel. Film, novels, and video games are separate economies in which storytelling is the currency. The problem is that video-game storytelling, across a wide spectrum of games, too often feels counterfeit, and it is easy to tire of laundering the bills.

It should be said that *Fallout 3* gets much better as you play through it. A few of its set pieces (such as stealing the Declaration of Independence from a ruined National Archives, which is protected by a bewigged robot programmed to believe itself to be Button Gwinnett,[15] the Declaration's second signatory) are as gripping as any fiction I have come across. But it cannot be a coincidence that every scene involving human emotion (confronting a mind-wiped android who believes he is human, watching as a character close to you suffocates and dies) is at best unaffecting and at worst risible. Can it really be a surprise that deeper human motivations remain beyond the reach of something that regards character as the assignation of numerical values to hypothetical abilities and characteristics?

20

---

14. Dante Alighieri (1265–1321), Italian poet who wrote the *Divine Comedy*; Homer (unknown), ancient Greek poet to whom the epics the *Iliad* and the *Odyssey* are traditionally attributed.
15. Georgia delegate (1735–1777) to the Second Continental Congress in Philadelphia.

Viewed as a whole, *Fallout* 3 is a game of profound stylishness, sophistication, and intelligence—so much so that every example of Etch A Sketch[16] characterization, every stone-shoed narrative pivot, pains me. When we say a game
is sophisticated, are we grading on a distressingly steep curve? Or do we need
a new curve altogether? Might we really mean that the game in question only
occasionally insults one's intelligence? Or is this kind of intelligence, at least
when it comes to playing games, beside the point? How is it, finally, that I keep
returning to a form of entertainment that I find so uniquely frustrating? To what
part of me do games speak, and on which frequency?

16. Iconic drawing toy.

MLA CITATION

Bissell, Tom. "Extra Lives: Why Video Games Matter." 2010. *The Norton Reader: An
     Anthology of Nonfiction.* Ed. Melissa A. Goldthwaite et al. 14th ed. New York:
     Norton, 2016. 214–22. Print.

QUESTIONS

1. A common objection to video games is that they encourage violence. How do
you think Tom Bissell would respond to this objection? How does he treat violence
in his essay?

2. Bissell asserts, "The pleasures of the open-world game are ample, complicated,
and intensely private; their potency is difficult to explain" (paragraph 4). What sorts
of pleasures does Bissell find in games? How are these pleasures connected or in
tension with each other? How, in his prose style and manner of arguing, does Bissell wrestle with the difficulty of explaining these pleasures?

3. In sharing his responses to *Fallout* 3 and *Oblivion,* Bissell is also teaching us
how to experience, interpret, and appreciate video games ourselves. Scott McCloud
in "Understanding Comics" (pp. 921–26), Susan Sontag in "A Century of Cinema"
(pp. 927–34), and Aaron Copland in "How We Listen" (pp. 938–42) endeavor to do
the same for art forms they care about: comics, cinema, and music. Choose one of
these essays to compare and contrast with Bissell's essay. How are they similar?
How are they different?

4. Bissell concludes his essay with a series of questions. What is the effect of this
gesture? Write an essay that responds to these questions. If you are a gamer, consider relating your own experiences to Bissell's. If not, consider interviewing a gamer
or writing about an activity that is important to you.

BILL McKIBBEN   *The Case for Single-Child Families*

THE BUILDING WAS NONDESCRIPT; four stories of modern concrete just down the street from Ottawa's Civic Hospital. The receptionist greeted me politely, told me the doctor was running a little late. And so I sat on the couch next to the old and dog-eared magazines and read one more time the list of questions Dr. Phil McGuire wanted his vasectomy patients to answer before he performed The Procedure:

"What would you and your partner feel if you were told tomorrow that she was pregnant? Joy? Despair? Resignation? What about in five years?

"Would you want the chance to have children with another partner if your current relationship ended through separation or death?

"Would you want to have the chance to have more children if one or more of your children died?

"Would more children be in your picture now if your financial circum-   5 stances improved significantly?"

These are tougher questions than you usually get asked in a doctor's office. If you have heart disease, you have to choose *what* to do; it's rare to have to choose, until the very end, whether you want to do *anything at all*. But I could have gotten up and left, no harm done. I have one child. I'd decided to have no more. But this seemed so final.

Then Dr. McGuire came in, wearing khakis, old Nikes, an earring, a plaid shirt. So far that day, he said, he'd done nine vasectomies, pruned branches of nine family trees. He was calm, gentle—sweet. "I had a couple this morning who'd had one child when they were in their 30s, spent the next ten years trying to have another, and failed. Now they were in their early 40s and just couldn't conceive of conceiving again, so they wanted some insurance." He'd had a police officer, and a guy who builds Web pages, and several couples in their early 30s, each with two kids.

And he'd talked with all of them. "I try to protect people if I don't think they're ready," he said. "I'm a general practitioner and I've seen so many women come in who are unexpectedly pregnant, and completely delighted about it." But when people have made up their minds, he's ready to help—he's done 1,100 vasectomies, more and more each year. "Someday I hope to have a clinic just devoted to vasectomies—a fish tank and all the hunting and fishing and outdoors magazines," he said.

I'd come to him because Ottawa is not far from my home, because I could afford him (he charged just over $200, less than most American operations), and because I could tell from his Web site (www.ottawa-vas.com) that he

First published in the Christian Century *(1998), a Protestant magazine with a stated mission to nurture faith and examine issues of politics, culture, and theology. This essay was also included in* Maybe One: A Personal and Environmental Argument for Single-Child Families *(1998), a book that extends Bill McKibben's work as an environmental writer.*

thought pretty deeply about the whole issue. He had a sense of humor (his toll-free number is 1-800-LASTKID), but he also had a sense of purpose. "Sometimes I turn people down," he said. "But it's so much safer than having a woman get a tubal ligation, which is a big operation inside a major body cavity with general anaesthesia."

10   So I sat on the table and pulled my pants down around my ankles. He swabbed my scrotum with iodine ("The iodine needs to be a little warm—the last thing we want is any shrinkage before we start") and then injected a slug of anaesthetic into each side of my testicles. Yes, it was a needle down there, but no, it didn't hurt much—by chance I'd spent the previous afternoon in the dentist's chair, and this was much less painful. (And no flossing!) He cut a small hole in my scrotum, and with a forceps pulled out the vas deferens, the tube that carried sperm to my penis. Then he cauterized it and put it back inside, repeating the procedure on the other side. I could feel a little tugging, nothing more. The wound was so small it didn't require stitches, or even a Band-Aid. For a few days, he said, my groin would be a little sore. After that it would take 20 ejaculations or so to drain the last of the sperm already in my system. And that would be that. In evolutionary terms, I'd be out of business.

It's easy for me to explain why I was lying on the table at the Ottawa Vasectomy Clinic: all I need is a string of statistics. In one recent study, condoms broke 4.8 percent of the time that they were used. Sixty percent of all pregnancies in the U.S. are unintended—60 percent. That doesn't mean all those children are unwanted; half just come when their parents weren't planning on it. But half end in abortion. In fact, six in ten women having abortions did so because their contraceptives failed; among typical couples, 18 percent using diaphragms and 12 percent using condoms managed to get pregnant. And no one's doing much to improve the situation—a nation that spends $600 million developing new cosmetics and fragrances each year has exactly one pharmaceutical company still conducting research on improved methods of birth control. So if I was serious about stopping at one child, this was where I belonged. For my wife, Sue, getting sterilized would have meant a real operation, real risk; for me it meant a bag of ice on my lap as I drove home. It all added up.

Not that we'd come to our decision to have one child easily. Although my work on environmental issues keeps bringing population questions front and center, I have avoided the issue of population for years. I know that by 2050 there will be almost 50 percent more Americans (and nearly 100 percent more human beings) than there are now. I know that in the last ten or 20 or 30 years, our impact has grown so much that we're changing even those places we don't inhabit—changing the way the weather works, changing the plants and animals that live at the poles and deep in the jungle.

I am convinced, too, that simplifying lifestyles alone, although crucial, will not do enough to reduce our impact in the next 50 years. Americans' lifestyles are just so "big." During the next decade India and China will each add to the planet about ten times as many people as the U.S., but the stress on the natural world by those new Americans may exceed that from the new Indians and Chinese combined. My five-year-old daughter has already used more stuff and added more waste to the environment than many of the world's residents do in a lifetime.

When Sue and I faced the issue of how many children to have, these abstract issues of population became personal and practical. What about Sophie? Would being an only child damage her spirit and mind? I explored the myths surrounding "the only child," and the clichés about one child being spoiled and overly dependent. Although these questions are emotionally charged and complex, every bit of research in recent decades shows that only kids do just fine—that they achieve as much and are as well adjusted as children with siblings. So that wasn't the hitch.

Along with doing all the research, however, I had to confront the deeply   15
ingrained sense in many of us that there's something inherently selfish about not being willing to have children. It's not as strong as the sense of selfishness that can attach itself to abortion, but it's there nonetheless, and particularly strong, I think, in people of faith. It's the relic of our long theological wrestle with the issue of birth control. And it is not easily dismissed. Condoms may not be sinful, but selfishness must be, if anything is. The children of small families are no more selfish than any other kids—but are the parents?

In a consumer society, where we've been drilled relentlessly in selfishness, it's a peril to take seriously. In her book *Beyond Motherhood*, Jeanne Safer interviews dozens of men and women who have decided against children. I have no wish to judge them, for it's often an honorable decision, and people should not bear children if they feel they can't cope with them. On the other hand, I have no wish to *become* them. They are selfish, and proudly; one New York literary agent describes herself as "an advocate of selfishness." Safer says she herself felt her biological clock ticking, but heard other clocks as well:

> My practice is just starting to take off—I'll lose all the momentum if I cut back to part-time. That summer I thought, it'll have to wait until after we get back from Bali and I'm no longer taking medication to prevent malaria. And what about the trip to Turkey we want to take next summer.

She was, she said, "particularly aware that children would change my marriage drastically. . . . Parenthood, I believed, would certainly spell the end of our nightly candlelit sandalwood-scented bubble baths complete with silly bath toys, where we played like children in a deliciously adult incarnation." Not only that, "I realized that having a child of my own would force me to spend a great deal of time doing things I'd disliked; I'd never been crazy about children's birthday parties when I'd attended them years earlier, and a trip to the circus is my idea of purgatory."

Safer found many like-minded folk. Sandra Singer, for instance, a photographer who moonlights as a belly dancer to "guarantee her allure" and who insists that "I've seen too many women who have children lose their sexuality as well as their identity. They let their bodies go, and they complain about their husband's sexual advances. I complain about the lack."

Safer reconciles herself to her decision not to have kids, and celebrates by giving her own belly-dancing performance. "Working through feelings about motherhood had unleashed hidden reserves of creativity and femininity, and I emerged liberated, energized and strong," she reports. In fact one night she dreams of a cantaloupe growing on a vine in her parents' garden in the middle of winter: "The cantaloupe was myself, the fruit of my parents' loins, which, though barren in the biological sense, was ripening out of season."

20   It's wrong to ridicule such attitudes, at least in a culture that still assigns the work of raising kids mostly to women and allows men to continue their careers at full tilt. Sometimes people have to rescue themselves; in Toni Morrison's novel *Sula*, the heroine won't marry or bear children in order to preserve her "Me-ness." When her grandmother wants her to have babies to "settle" her, Sula says, "I don't want to make somebody else. I want to make myself." Often it's women from very poor backgrounds who decide to remain childless, realizing that it's their best hope for upward mobility against strong odds; in a 1985 study of poor Southern high school students, the 16 percent who wanted no children were the ones with the loftiest ambitions, the ambitions that in other contexts we want such children to have.

But it's also possible to understand the concern of popes and rabbis and just ordinary folk that, for some people, the decision to have no children or a small family represents a decision to indulge yourself without a thought for anyone else, a decision to take sandalwood-scented candlelit baths without the danger that there might be stray Legos left in the tub to poke you in the backside.

Theologian Gilbert Meilaender quotes one young man who says, "When you have children, the focus changes from the couple to the kids. Suddenly everything is done for them. Well, I'm 27, I've used up a good portion of my life already. Why should I want to sacrifice for someone who's still got his whole life ahead of him?" Such an attitude is, among other things, environmentally problematic; even if this fellow has no kids, thereby sparing the planet some burden, he seems unlikely to do much else to ensure its future—he's the same guy who's going to be voting against gas taxes and demanding the right to drive his Suburban into the overheated sunset.

John Ryan, an American Catholic theologian of the first half of the 20th century, made this argument most powerfully. A man of impeccable progressive credentials, Ryan was known as "the Right Reverend New Dealer" for his unwavering support of the Roosevelt administration.[1] But this same John Ryan also wanted everyone who married to have many children, not simply as proof that they weren't using birth control but because he thought that raising large families makes people better human beings.

Ryan argued that supporting large families demands "forms of discipline necessary for the successful life," a life "accomplished only at the cost of continuous and considerable sacrifice, of compelling ourselves to do without the immediate and pleasant goods for the sake of remote and permanent goods." One of eleven children himself, Ryan thought that most people practicing birth

1. The New Deal (1933–39) was an array of social and economic programs enacted during the presidency of Franklin Delano Roosevelt (1882–1945) in response to the Great Depression.

control would be doing it from a "decadent" frame of mind; that bachelors were not building the kind of character necessary to contribute to the common good of society. Not only that, those with few children might become too wealthy, which was as dangerous as being too poor. In the words of ethicist John Berkman, "He was appealing to hard work, and building character, and he thought that was best achieved for most people in the context of having a large family."

This pragmatic argument comes straight from the American sense of purpose. And it is by no means a negligible or stupid argument: successfully raising a large brood of well-adjusted children is a great accomplishment, one that cannot help but change and deepen the parents. You emerge different people when you spend your life focusing, as good parents must, on *someone else's* well-being. If maturity is the realization that you are not at the center of the world, then the most time-honored way to become mature is to be a parent many times over, and a good one. Not just because parenting is tough, but also because it's so joyful, because it shows you that real transcendent pleasure comes from putting someone else first. It teaches you how dull self-absorption can be.

Such lessons don't always take, of course. As essayist Katha Pollitt points out, the tendency to ascribe "particular virtues—compassion, patience, common sense, nonviolence—to mothers" is an overdone, and in some ways oppressive, cliché; telling yourself that toilet training a string of two-year-olds is good for your soul may keep you away from other worlds. And in a country where incredible numbers of fathers walk away from their kids, you could argue that fatherhood seems to barely dent the culture's pervasive selfishness. And yet when I think of my circle of friends and acquaintances, the single most common route to maturity has been through raising children, often lots of them.

The problem, of course, is that now we live in an era—maybe only a brief one, maybe only for a few generations—when parenting a bunch of kids clashes with the good of the planet. So is there a different way to achieve some of that maturity, with no children or only a single child to change your life? It's not that one kid won't alter most things in your life; he or she will. But Ryan was right—it's not the total commitment that comes with a large brood. Your career or a calling continues, however hobbled you may sometimes be. Alice Walker, in a pithy essay titled "*One* Child of One's Own," called her single daughter a "meaningful digression," and that's right in many ways; if she had borne five children, she probably wouldn't have been writing many books. But those books represent a serious attempt at maturity in another way, and perhaps that's a clue. We need to find ways to be adults, grownups, *people who focus on others*, without being parents of large families.

In the weeks leading up to the 1994 Cairo Conference on population, the pope led the fight against many of the provisions in the draft documents for that conclave. Though I disagreed with some of his stands, I found much of his language powerful and intriguing. The Catholic Church, he said, does not support "an ideology of fertility at all costs," but instead an ethic in which the decision "whether or not to have a child" is not "motivated by selfish or carelessness, but by a prudent, conscious generosity that weighs the possibilities and circumstances." True, he added that such an ethic "gives priority to the

25

welfare of the unborn child," but several weeks later, arguing that radical individualism and "a sexuality apart from ethical references" was inhuman, he
called for a "culture of responsible procreation."

In those words, and the words of many others, I think we can see the outline of an ethic that avoids self-indulgence yet does not deny the physical facts
of a planet with 6 billion people who may soon nearly double their numbers—a
planet that grows hotter, stormier and less stable by the day, a planet where
huge swaths of God's creation are being wiped out by the one species told to
tend this particular garden. I don't pretend it is an ethic that can be embraced
by the Vatican, or the Hasidim; but I do think it is an ethic that might undergird a more sustainable world.

30   The beginning of Genesis contains the fateful command, repeated elsewhere in the Hebrew Bible, to "be fruitful and multiply, and fill the earth." That
this was the first commandment gave it special priority. And it was biological,
too, a command that echoed what our genes already shouted.

But there is something else unique about it—it is the first commandment we
have fulfilled. There's barely a habitable spot on the planet without a human
being; in our lifetimes we've filled every inch of the planet with our presence.
Everywhere the temperature climbs, the ultraviolet penetrates more deeply. In
furthest Alaska, always our national metaphor for emptiness, the permafrost
now melts at a rapid pace, trees move on to the tundra, insects infest forests in
record numbers, and salmon turn back down streams because the water's gotten
too warm to spawn. "There's been a permanent and significant climate regime
shift," says an Alaskan scientist. "There has been nothing like this in the record."
There's not a creature anywhere on earth whose blood doesn't show the presence
of our chemicals, not an ocean that isn't higher because of us. For better and for
worse, we are everywhere. We can check this commandment off the list.

And we can check it off for happier reasons as well. There's no denying
that we've done great environmental damage, but it's also true that we've spread
wondrous and diverse cultures, full of love and song, across the wide earth.
We should add a holiday to the calendar of every church to celebrate this
achievement.

But when you check something off a list, you don't just throw the list away.
You look further down the list, see what comes next. And the list, of course, is
long. The Gospels, the Torah, the Koran and a thousand other texts sacred and
profane give us plenty of other goals toward which to divert some of the energy
we've traditionally used in raising large families, goals on which we've barely
begun. Feed the hungry, clothe the naked, comfort the oppressed; love your
neighbor as yourself; heal the earth. We live on a planet where 3 billion people
don't have clean water, where species die by the score each day, where kids grow
up without fathers, where violence overwhelms us, where people judge each
other by the color of their skin, where a hypersexualized culture poisons the
adolescence of girls, where old people and young people need each other's support. And the energy freed by having smaller families may be some of the energy
needed to take on these next challenges. To really take them on, not just to
announce that they're important, or to send a check, or to read an article, but
to make them central to our lives.

I have one child; she is the light of my life; she makes me care far more about the future than I used to. And I have one child; so even after my work I have some time, money and energy left to do other things. I get to work on Adirondack conservation issues and assist those who are fighting global warming; I've helped my wife start a new school in our town; I can teach Sunday school and help run a nationwide effort to decommercialize Christmas and sit on the board of the local college. (And I belly dance too, though in my case it's hiking, cross-country skiing, mountain biking.) If I had three kids, I would still do those things, but less of them; either that, or my work would come at their expense. As it is, once in a while I'm stretched too thin and don't see Sophie for a day, and that reminds me to slow down, to find the real center of my life. But I want to get further down that list.

So the pope strikes me as largely right in his reasoning if not his conclusions. Radical individualism is inhuman. Living as if you were the most important thing on earth is, literally, blasphemy; recreational sex may not bother me, but recreational life does. Our decisions should be motivated "not by selfishness or carelessness, but by a prudent conscious generosity." It's just that at the end of the twentieth century, on this planet, the signs of the times point me in the direction of the kinds of caring, the ways of maturing, that come with small, not large, families.

The church should not find that argument so foreign. Priests are celibate at least in part because it allows them to make Christ their bride, to devote all their energies to the other tasks set before us on this earth. And the wisdom of that argument is proved daily in a million places around the globe where committed priests and nuns take on the hardest and dirtiest challenges the earth has to offer. If we now have plenty of people to guarantee our survival as a race, and if lots more people may make that survival harder, then it's time to follow the lead of those clerics a little—not to embrace celibacy necessarily, but to love your child to pieces, and with whatever you have left to start working your way down the list.

And the same logic should make it clear, of course, that all sorts of other kinds of people—childless gay people, infertile people, people who do not feel called to parenthood—can become every bit as mature (or immature) as a parent of six, as long as they can find some substitute discipline for repeatedly placing someone or something else at the center of their lives.

Sometimes those disciplines are quiet and private, sometimes public. In Allan Gurganus's novel *Plays Well with Others*, his main character describes taking care of one friend after another as they succumbed to AIDS—describes the almost hydraulic outpouring of love it took to tend them. "My own loved ones were not brought into the world by me, but only, in my company, let out of it," he writes. His own obituary, he knows, will show that he left "no immediate survivors." "And yet I feel I've earned a family too." More so, of course, than many parents.

When she began studying the differences between pro-choice and pro-life advocates in the abortion dispute, Kristin Luker noticed something interesting. It was true that they differed over the morality of terminating pregnancy, but those differences were the product of other, more fundamental splits in their view of the world. They felt differently about God, about the role of women and, most interestingly, they felt very differently about the nature of planning.

40   Pro-choice activists, she observed, were almost obsessed with planning for their children, trying to give them "maximum parental guidance and every possible advantage," while parents active in the antiabortion movement "tend to be *laissez-faire* individualists in their attitude" toward child-rearing. "Pro-life people," she wrote, "believe that one becomes a parent by *being* a parent; parenthood is for them a 'natural' rather than a social role. The values implied by the in-vogue term 'parenting' (as in parenting classes) are alien to them." One woman she interviewed said, "I think people are foolish to worry about things in the future. The future takes care of itself." Too much planning, including too much family planning, means "playing God."

One of my favorite magazines comes from a small Ohio town. Called *Plain*, it is edited (and its type hand-set) by "conservative" Quakers, which is to say a group of men and women who live more or less in the fashion of Old Order Amish. The magazine recently reprinted a dinner conversation about the subject of family planning. The participants, each of them the parent of four children, were discussing their unease with contraception, and in terms very reminiscent of Luker's study:

> Miriam: It breeds the mentality that "I want what I want, when I want."
>
> Scott: It leads back to self-seeking, which eventually knows no bounds.
>
> Marvin: Actually, it leads to a bottom-line refusal to accept God's will for our lives.
>
> Scott: I think that one of the things Mary Ann and I have learned along the way, and which has further separated us from the mainstream culture, is the realization that we can always make room for one more. Because the room to be made is in our hearts.

That way of seeing the world attracts me—there is in its spontaneity and confidence something of real beauty. It offers a kind of freedom. Not the freedom of unlimited options that we've come to idolize, but a freedom from constant worrying and fretting. Sometimes I hate the calculator instinct in me, the part of me that constantly weighs benefits and risks, the part that keeps me safe and solvent at the expense of experience. There is something incredibly attractive about the mystery of the next child, and the next; I'd love to meet them. I'd love to leave it to God, or to chance, or to biology, or to destiny, or to the wind. Part of me thinks that those conservative Quakers, those pro-lifers, are unequivocally right.

The trouble is, there are now other ways to play God in this world, and not planning is one of them.

This was not always the case. In the Book of Job, God appears as a taunting voice from the whirlwind: "Where were you when I laid the foundations of the earth?" God asks Job. "Who shut up the sea with doors . . . and said here shall thy proud waves be stayed? . . . Who has cleft a channel for the torrents of rain, and a way for the thunderbolt?" Job has no way to reply, and no need; the earth is infinitely bigger than he; how absurd he would look standing at the edge of the sea and trying to whistle up the waves. God—the world—was huge, and we were tiny. Creation dwarfed us.

But now there are so many of us, and we have done such a poor job of planning for our numbers, that for the first time we can answer God back. We can say: we set the boundaries of the ocean. If we keep heating the planet at our current pace, the seas will rise two feet in the next century. Every one foot will bring the water 90 feet further inland across the typical American beach, drowning wetland and marsh. It's our lack of planning that changes the rainfall, that means more severe storms and worse flooding. It's not an "act of God." It's an act of us.

We no longer have the luxury of not planning; we're simply too big. We   45
dominate the earth. When people first headed west across the plains, they didn't need a zoning board; now Californians try to channel and control growth lest they choke on it. In a crowded world, not planning has as many consequences as planning. This is a special time, and that turns everything on its head.

MLA CITATION

McKibben, Bill. "The Case for Single-Child Families." 1998. *The Norton Reader: An Anthology of Nonfiction*. Ed. Melissa A. Goldthwaite et al. 14th ed. New York: Norton, 2016. 223–31. Print.

QUESTIONS

1. Bill McKibben tells of how his five-year-old daughter Sophie "has already used more stuff and added more waste to the environment than many of the world's residents do in a lifetime" (paragraph 13). Make an inventory of how much "stuff" you use in an average week, and then discuss whether your inventory proves McKibben's point.

2. McKibben's essay was originally published in the *Christian Century*, a magazine that addresses political and cultural topics from a Christian perspective. Consider the role of faith and religion in McKibben's argument. How might his argument differ if it were written from a purely secular perspective?

3. McKibben ends his essay by stating, "This is a special time, and that turns everything on its head." How does he demonstrate that this is "a special time"? Do you agree with him? In what sense does his argument depend on this being "a special time"?

4. Like McKibben, Chief Seattle (p. 543) and Wallace Stegner (pp. 544–49) also argue that we have a responsibility to care for the earth. But Chief Seattle was writing in 1855 and Stegner in 1960. Write an essay comparing and contrasting McKibben's essay to one or both of these older pieces.

MALCOLM GLADWELL   *Java Man*

THE ORIGINAL COCA-COLA was a late-nineteenth-century concoction known as Pemberton's French Wine Coca, a mixture of alcohol, the caffeine-rich kola nut, and coca, the raw ingredient of cocaine. In the face of social pressure, first the wine and then the coca were removed, leaving the more banal modern beverage in its place: carbonated, caffeinated sugar water with less kick to it than a cup of coffee. But is that the way we think of Coke? Not at all. In the nineteen-thirties, a commercial artist named Haddon Sundblom had the bright idea of posing a portly retired friend of his in a red Santa Claus suit with a Coke in his hand, and plastering the image on billboards and advertisements across the country. Coke, magically, was reborn as caffeine for children, caffeine without any of the weighty adult connotations of coffee and tea. It was—as the ads with Sundblom's Santa put it—"the pause that refreshes." It added life. It could teach the world to sing.

One of the things that have always made drugs so powerful is their cultural adaptability, their way of acquiring meanings beyond their pharmacology. We think of marijuana, for example, as a drug of lethargy, of disaffection. But in Colombia, the historian David T. Courtwright points out in "Forces of Habit," "peasants boast that cannabis helps them to *quita el cansancio* or reduce fatigue; increase their *fuerza* and *ánimo*, force and spirit; and become *incansable*, tireless." In Germany right after the Second World War, cigarettes briefly and suddenly became the equivalent of crack cocaine. "Up to a point, the majority of the habitual smokers preferred to do without food even under extreme conditions of nutrition rather than to forgo tobacco," according to one account of the period. "Many housewives . . . bartered fat and sugar for cigarettes." Even a drug as demonized as opium has been seen in a more favorable light. In the eighteen-thirties, Franklin Delano Roosevelt's grandfather Warren Delano II made the family fortune exporting the drug to China, and Delano was able to sugar-coat his activities so plausibly that no one ever accused his grandson of being the scion of a drug lord. And yet, as Bennett Alan Weinberg and Bonnie K. Bealer remind us in their marvellous book "The World of Caffeine," there is no drug quite as effortlessly adaptable as caffeine, the Zelig of chemical stimulants.

At one moment, in one form, it is the drug of choice of café intellectuals and artists; in another, of housewives; in another, of Zen monks; and, in yet another, of children enthralled by a fat man who slides down chimneys. King Gustav III, who ruled Sweden in the latter half of the eighteenth century, was so convinced of the particular perils of coffee over all other forms of caffeine

First published in the New Yorker (2001), a weekly magazine of "reportage, commentary, criticism, essays, fiction, satire, cartoons, and poetry," to which Malcolm Gladwell has been a regular contributor.

that he devised an elaborate experiment. A convicted murderer was sentenced to drink cup after cup of coffee until he died, with another murderer sentenced to a lifetime of tea drinking, as a control. (Unfortunately, the two doctors in charge of the study died before anyone else did; then Gustav was murdered; and finally the tea drinker died, at eighty-three, of old age—leaving the original murderer alone with his espresso, and leaving coffee's supposed toxicity in some doubt.) Later, the various forms of caffeine began to be divided up along sociological lines. Wolfgang Schivelbusch, in his book "Tastes of Paradise," argues that, in the eighteenth century, coffee symbolized the rising middle classes, whereas its great caffeinated rival in those years—cocoa, or, as it was known at the time, chocolate—was the drink of the aristocracy. "Goethe, who used art as a means to lift himself out of his middle class background into the aristocracy, and who as a member of a courtly society maintained a sense of aristocratic calm even in the midst of immense productivity, made a cult of chocolate, and avoided coffee," Schivelbusch writes. "Balzac, who despite his sentimental allegiance to the monarchy, lived and labored for the literary marketplace and for it alone, became one of the most excessive coffee-drinkers in history. Here we see two fundamentally different working styles and means of stimulation—fundamentally different psychologies and physiologies." Today, of course, the chief cultural distinction is between coffee and tea, which, according to a list drawn up by Weinberg and Bealer, have come to represent almost entirely opposite sensibilities:

Coffee Aspect	Tea Aspect
Male	Female
Boisterous	Decorous
Indulgence	Temperance
Hardheaded	Romantic
Topology	Geometry
Heidegger	Carnap
Beethoven	Mozart
Libertarian	Statist
Promiscuous	Pure

That the American Revolution began with the symbolic rejection of tea in Boston Harbor, in other words, makes perfect sense. Real revolutionaries would naturally prefer coffee. By contrast, the freedom fighters of Canada, a hundred years later, were most definitely tea drinkers. And where was Canada's autonomy won? Not on the blood-soaked fields of Lexington and Concord but in the genteel drawing rooms of Westminster, over a nice cup of Darjeeling and small, triangular cucumber sandwiches.

All this is a bit puzzling. We don't fetishize the difference between salmon eaters and tuna eaters, or people who like their eggs sunny-side up and those who like them scrambled. So why invest so much importance in the way people prefer their caffeine? A cup of coffee has somewhere between a hundred and two hundred and fifty milligrams; black tea brewed for four minutes has

5

between forty and a hundred milligrams. But the disparity disappears if you consider that many tea drinkers drink from a pot, and have more than one cup. Caffeine is caffeine. "The more it is pondered," Weinberg and Bealer write, "the more paradoxical this duality within the culture of caffeine appears. After all, both coffee and tea are aromatic infusions of vegetable matter, served hot or cold in similar quantities; both are often mixed with cream or sugar; both are universally available in virtually any grocery or restaurant in civilized society; and both contain the identical psychoactive alkaloid stimulant, caffeine."

It would seem to make more sense to draw distinctions based on the way caffeine is metabolized rather than on the way it is served. Caffeine, whether it is in coffee or tea or a soft drink, moves easily from the stomach and intestines into the bloodstream, and from there to the organs, and before long has penetrated almost every cell of the body. This is the reason that caffeine is such a wonderful stimulant. Most substances can't cross the blood-brain barrier, which is the body's defensive mechanism, preventing viruses or toxins from entering the central nervous system. Caffeine does so easily. Within an hour or so, it reaches its peak concentration in the brain, and there it does a number of things—principally, blocking the action of adenosine, the neuromodulator that makes you sleepy, lowers your blood pressure, and slows down your heartbeat. Then, as quickly as it builds up in your brain and tissues, caffeine is gone—which is why it's so safe. (Caffeine in ordinary quantities has never been conclusively linked to serious illness.)

But how quickly it washes away differs dramatically from person to person. A two-hundred-pound man who drinks a cup of coffee with a hundred milligrams of caffeine will have a maximum caffeine concentration of one milligram per kilogram of body weight. A hundred-pound woman having the same cup of coffee will reach a caffeine concentration of two milligrams per kilogram of body weight, or twice as high. In addition, when women are on the Pill, the rate at which they clear caffeine from their bodies slows considerably. (Some of the side effects experienced by women on the Pill may in fact be caffeine jitters caused by their sudden inability to tolerate as much coffee as they could before.) Pregnancy reduces a woman's ability to process caffeine still further. The half-life of caffeine in an adult is roughly three and a half hours. In a pregnant woman, it's eighteen hours. (Even a four-month-old child processes caffeine more efficiently.) An average man and woman sitting down for a cup of coffee are thus not pharmaceutical equals: in effect, the woman is under the influence of a vastly more powerful drug. Given these differences, you'd think that, instead of contrasting the caffeine cultures of tea and coffee, we'd contrast the caffeine cultures of men and women.

But we don't, and with good reason. To parse caffeine along gender lines does not do justice to its capacity to insinuate itself into every aspect of our lives, not merely to influence culture but even to create it. Take coffee's reputation as the "thinker's" drink. This dates from eighteenth-century Europe, where coffeehouses played a major role in the egalitarian, inclusionary spirit that was then sweeping the continent. They sprang up first in London, so alarming Charles II that in 1676 he tried to ban them. It didn't work. By 1700, there were hundreds of coffeehouses in London, their subversive spirit best captured by a couplet from a comedy of the period: "In a coffeehouse just now among the rabble I bluntly asked, which is the treason table." The movement then spread to Paris, and by the end of the eighteenth century coffeehouses numbered in the hundreds— most famously; the Café de la Régence, near the Palais Royal, which counted among its customers Robespierre, Napoleon, Voltaire, Victor Hugo, Théophile Gautier, Rousseau, and the Duke of Richelieu.[1] Previously, when men had gathered together to talk in public places, they had done so in bars, which drew from specific socioeconomic niches and, because of the alcohol they served, created a specific kind of talk. The new coffeehouses, by contrast, drew from many different classes and trades, and they served a stimulant, not a depressant. "It is not extravagant to claim that it was in these gathering spots that the art of conversation became the basis of a new literary style and that a new ideal of general education in letters was born," Weinberg and Bealer write.

It is worth nothing, as well, that in the original coffeehouses nearly everyone smoked, and nicotine also has a distinctive physiological effect. It moderates mood and extends attention, and, more important, it doubles the rate of caffeine metabolism: it allows you to drink twice as much coffee as you could otherwise. In other words, the original coffeehouse was a place where men of all types could sit all day; the tobacco they smoked made it possible to drink coffee all day; and the coffee they drank inspired them to talk all day. Out of this came the Enlightenment. (The next time we so perfectly married pharmacology and place, we got Joan Baez.)[2]

In time, caffeine moved from the café to the home. In America, coffee   10 triumphed because of the country's proximity to the new Caribbean and Latin American coffee plantations, and the fact that throughout the nineteenth century duties were negligible. Beginning in the eighteen-twenties, Courtwright tells us, Brazil "unleashed a flood of slave-produced coffee. American per capita consumption, three pounds per year in 1830, rose to eight pounds by 1859."

What this flood of caffeine did, according to Weinberg and Bealer, was to abet the process of industrialization—to help "large numbers of people to coordinate their work schedules by giving them the energy to start work at a given time and continue it as long as necessary." Until the eighteenth century, it must be remembered, many Westerners drank beer almost continuously, even beginning their day with something called "beer soup." (Bealer and Weinberg helpfully provide the following eighteenth-century German recipe: "Heat the beer in a saucepan; in a separate small pot beat a couple of eggs. Add a chunk of butter to the hot beer. Stir in some cool beer to cool it, then pour over the eggs.

1. French politicians, authors, or nobility.
2. American folksinger and political activist (b. 1941).

Add a bit of salt, and finally mix all the ingredients together, whisking it well to keep it from curdling.") Now they began each day with a strong cup of coffee. One way to explain the industrial revolution is as the inevitable consequence of a world where people suddenly preferred being jittery to being drunk. In the modern world, there was no other way to keep up. That's what Edison[3] meant when he said that genius was ninety-nine per cent perspiration and one per cent inspiration. In the old paradigm, working with your mind had been associated with leisure. It was only the poor who worked hard. (The quintessential pre-industrial narrative of inspiration belonged to Archimedes,[4] who made his discovery, let's not forget, while taking a bath.) But Edison was saying that the old class distinctions no longer held true—that in the industrialized world there was as much toil associated with the life of the mind as there had once been with the travails of the body.

In the twentieth century, the professions transformed themselves accordingly: medicine turned the residency process into an ordeal of sleeplessness, the legal profession borrowed a page from the manufacturing floor and made its practitioners fill out time cards like union men. Intellectual heroics became a matter of endurance. "The pace of computation was hectic," James Gleick writes of the Manhattan Project[5] in "Genius," his biography of the physicist Richard Feynman. "Feynman's day began at 8:30 and ended fifteen hours later. Sometimes he could not leave the computing center at all. He worked through for thirty-one hours once and the next day found that an error minutes after he went to bed had stalled the whole team. The routine allowed just a few breaks." Did Feynman's achievements reflect a greater natural talent than his less productive forebears had? Or did he just drink a lot more coffee? Paul Hoffman, in "The Man Who Loved Only Numbers," writes of the legendary twentieth-century mathematician Paul Erdös that "he put in nineteen-hour days, keeping himself fortified with 10 to 20 milligrams of Benzedrine or Ritalin, strong espresso and caffeine tablets. 'A mathematician,' Erdös was fond of saying, 'is a machine for turning coffee into theorems.'" Once, a friend bet Erdös five hundred dollars that he could not quit amphetamines for a month. Erdös took the bet and won, but, during his time of abstinence, he found himself incapable of doing any serious work. "You've set mathematics back a month," he told his friend when he collected, and immediately returned to his pills.

Erdös's unadulterated self was less real and less familiar to him than his adulterated self, and that is a condition that holds, more or less, for the rest of society as well. Part of what it means to be human in the modern age is that we have come to construct our emotional and cognitive states not merely from the inside out—with thought and intention—but from the outside in, with chemical additives. The modern personality is, in this sense, a synthetic creation: skillfully regulated and medicated and dosed with caffeine so that we

3. Thomas Alva Edison (1847–1931), American inventor.

4. Greek mathematician and inventor (c. 290–80 B.C.E.–c. 212 B.C.E.).

5. Project that built the atomic bomb.

can always be awake and alert and focussed when we need to be. On a bet, no doubt, we could walk away from caffeine if we had to. But what would be the point? The lawyers wouldn't make their billable hours. The young doctors would fall behind in their training. The physicists might still be stuck out in the New Mexico desert. We'd set the world back a month.

That the modern personality is synthetic is, of course, a disquieting notion. When we talk of synthetic personality—or of constructing new selves through chemical means—we think of hard drugs, not caffeine. Timothy Leary used to make such claims about LSD, and the reason his revolution never took flight was that most of us found the concept of tuning in, turning on, and dropping out to be a bit creepy. Here was this shaman, this visionary—and yet, if his consciousness was so great, why was he so intent on altering it? More important, what exactly were we supposed to be tuning in to? We were given hints, with psychedelic colors and deep readings of "Lucy in the Sky with Diamonds," but that was never enough. If we are to re-create ourselves, we would like to know what we will become.

Caffeine is the best and most useful of our drugs because in every one of its forms it can answer that question precisely. It is a stimulant that blocks the action of adenosine, and comes in a multitude of guises, each with a ready-made story attached, a mixture of history and superstition and whimsy which infuses the daily ritual of adenosine blocking with meaning and purpose. Put caffeine in a red can and it becomes refreshing fun. Brew it in a teapot and it becomes romantic and decorous. Extract it from little brown beans and, magically, it is hardheaded and potent. "There was a little known Russian émigré, Trotsky by name, who during World War I was in the habit of playing chess in Vienna's Café Central every evening," Bealer and Weinberg write, in one of the book's many fascinating café yarns:

> A typical Russian refugee, who talked too much but seemed utterly harmless, indeed, a pathetic figure in the eyes of the Viennese. One day in 1917 an official of the Austrian Foreign Ministry rushed into the minister's room, panting and excited, and told his chief, "Your excellency . . . Your excellency . . . Revolution has broken out in Russia." The minister, less excitable and less credulous than his official, rejected such a wild claim and retorted calmly, "Go away. . . . Russia is not a land where revolutions break out. Besides, who on earth would make a revolution in Russia? Perhaps Herr Trotsky from the Café Central?"

The minister should have known better. Give a man enough coffee and he's capable of anything.

MLA CITATION

Gladwell, Malcolm. "Java Man." 2001. *The Norton Reader: An Anthology of Nonfiction.* Ed. Melissa A. Goldthwaite et al. 14th ed. New York: Norton, 2016. 232–37. Print.

QUESTIONS

1. How serious do you think Malcolm Gladwell is when he says that we're all drugged on caffeine? How can you tell?

2. Gladwell creates a binary between coffee and tea. Describe another binary between two closely similar forms—such as seashore vs. mountains; Coke vs. Pepsi; skis vs. snowboards. How do binaries work? What limitations do you see in the binary you created or in Gladwell's?

3. Gladwell offers several hypotheses for caffeine's success as the drug of choice for the modern world. Which one do you find most persuasive, and why?

4. Write a description of some of the rituals that you or someone you know indulges in with coffee or tea.

JESSICA MITFORD   *Behind the Formaldehyde Curtain*

T HE DRAMA BEGINS TO UNFOLD with the arrival of the corpse at the mortuary.

Alas, poor Yorick![1] How surprised he would be to see how his counterpart of today is whisked off to a funeral parlor and is in short order sprayed, sliced, pierced, pickled, trussed, trimmed, creamed, waxed, painted, rouged and neatly dressed—transformed from a common corpse into a Beautiful Memory Picture. This process is known in the trade as embalming and restorative art, and is so universally employed in the United States and Canada that the funeral director does it routinely, without consulting corpse or kin. He regards as eccentric those few who are hardy enough to suggest that it might be dispensed with. Yet no law requires embalming, no religious doctrine commends it, nor is it dictated by considerations of health, sanitation, or even of personal daintiness. In no part of the world but in Northern America is it widely used. The purpose of embalming is to make the corpse presentable for viewing in a suitably costly container; and here too the funeral director routinely, without first consulting the family, prepares the body for public display.

Is all this legal? The processes to which a dead body may be subjected are after all to some extent circumscribed by law. In most states, for instance, the signature of next of kin must be obtained before an autopsy may be performed, before the deceased may be cremated, before the body may be turned over to a

---

From The American Way of Death *(1963), an exposé of the funeral industry, which was revised and updated by Jessica Mitford as* The American Way of Death Revisited *(1998) just before her death in 1996.*

1. Hamlet says this upon seeing the skull of the court clown he had known as a child. From *Hamlet* (c. 1606), a play by William Shakespeare.

medical school for research purposes; or such provision must be made in the decedent's will. In the case of embalming, no such permission is required nor is it ever sought. A textbook, *The Principles and Practices of Embalming,* comments on this: "There is some question regarding the legality of much that is done within the preparation room." The author points out that it would be most unusual for a responsible member of a bereaved family to instruct the mortician, in so many words, to "embalm" the body of a deceased relative. The very term "embalming" is so seldom used that the mortician must rely upon custom in the matter. The author concludes that unless the family specifies otherwise, the act of entrusting the body to the care of a funeral establishment carries with it an implied permission to go ahead and embalm.

Embalming is indeed a most extraordinary procedure, and one must wonder at the docility of Americans who each year pay hundreds of millions of dollars for its perpetuation, blissfully ignorant of what it is all about, what is done, how it is done. Not one in ten thousand has any idea of what actually takes place. Books on the subject are extremely hard to come by. They are not to be found in most libraries or bookshops.

In an era when huge television audiences watch surgical operations in   5
the comfort of their living rooms, when, thanks to the animated cartoon, the geography of the digestive system has become familiar territory even to the nursery school set, in a land where the satisfaction of curiosity about almost all matters is a national pastime, the secrecy surrounding embalming can, surely, hardly be attributed to the inherent gruesomeness of the subject. Custom in this regard has within this century suffered a complete reversal. In the early days of American embalming, when it was performed in the home of the deceased, it was almost mandatory for some relative to stay by the embalmer's side and witness the procedure. Today, family members who might wish to be in attendance would certainly be dissuaded by the funeral director. All others, except apprentices, are excluded by law from the preparation room.

A close look at what does actually take place may explain in large measure the undertaker's intractable reticence concerning a procedure that has become his major *raison d'être.*[2] Is it possible he fears that public information about embalming might lead patrons to wonder if they really want this service? If the funeral men are loath to discuss the subject outside the trade, the reader may, understandably, be equally loath to go on reading at this point. For those who have the stomach for it, let us part the formaldehyde curtain. . . .

The body is first laid out in the undertaker's morgue—or rather, Mr. Jones is reposing in the preparation room—to be readied to bid the world farewell.

The preparation room in any of the better funeral establishments has the tiled and sterile look of a surgery, and indeed the embalmer-restorative artist who does his chores there is beginning to adopt the term "dermasurgeon" (appropriately corrupted by some mortician-writers as "demi-surgeon") to describe his calling. His equipment, consisting of scalpels, scissors, augers,

2. French for "reason for being."

forceps, clamps, needles, pumps, tubes, bowls and basins, is crudely imitative of the surgeon's, as is his technique, acquired in a nine- or twelve-month post-high-school course in an embalming school. He is supplied by an advanced chemical industry with a bewildering array of fluids, sprays, pastes, oils, powders, creams, to fix or soften tissue, shrink or distend it as needed, dry it here, restore the moisture there. There are cosmetics, waxes and paints to fill and cover features, even plaster of Paris to replace entire limbs. There are ingenious aids to prop and stabilize the cadaver: a Vari-Pose Head Rest, the Edwards Arm and Hand Positioner, the Repose Block (to support the shoulders during the embalming), and the Throop Foot Positioner, which resembles an old-fashioned stocks.

Mr. John H. Eckels, president of the Eckels College of Mortuary Science, thus describes the first part of the embalming procedure: "In the hands of a skilled practitioner, this work may be done in a comparatively short time and without mutilating the body other than by slight incision—so slight that it scarcely would cause serious inconvenience if made upon a living person. It is necessary to remove the blood, and doing this not only helps in the disinfecting, but removes the principal cause of disfigurements due to discoloration."

10   Another textbook discusses the all-important time element: "The earlier this is done, the better, for every hour that elapses between death and embalming will add to the problems and complications encountered. . . ." Just how soon should one get going on the embalming? The author tells us, "On the basis of such scanty information made available to this profession through its rudimentary and haphazard system of technical research, we must conclude that the best results are to be obtained if the subject is embalmed before life is completely extinct—that is, before cellular death has occurred. In the average case, this would mean within an hour after somatic death." For those who feel that there is something a little rudimentary, not to say haphazard, about this advice, a comforting thought is offered by another writer. Speaking of fears entertained in early days of premature burial, he points out, "One of the effects of embalming by chemical injection, however, has been to dispel fears of live burial." How true; once the blood is removed, chances of live burial are indeed remote.

To return to Mr. Jones, the blood is drained out through the veins and replaced by embalming fluid pumped in through the arteries. As noted in *The Principles and Practices of Embalming*, "every operator has a favorite injection and drainage point—a fact which becomes a handicap only if he fails or refuses to forsake his favorites when conditions demand it." Typical favorites are the carotid artery, femoral artery, jugular vein, subclavian vein. There are various choices of embalming fluid. If Flextone is used, it will produce a "mild, flexible rigidity. The skin retains a velvety softness, the tissues are rubbery and pliable. Ideal for women and children." It may be blended with B. and G. Products Company's Lyf-Lyk tint, which is guaranteed to reproduce "nature's own skin texture. . . . the velvety appearance of living tissue." Suntone comes in three separate tints: Suntan; Special Cosmetic Tint, a pink shade "especially indicated for young female subjects"; and Regular Cosmetic Tint, moderately pink.

About three to six gallons of a dyed and perfumed solution of formaldehyde, glycerin, borax, phenol, alcohol and water is soon circulating through Mr. Jones, whose mouth has been sewn together with a "needle directed upward between the upper lip and gum and brought out through the left nostril," with the corners raised slightly "for a more pleasant expression." If he should be bucktoothed, his teeth are cleaned with Bon Ami and coated with colorless nail polish. His eyes, meanwhile, are closed with flesh-tinted eye caps and eye cement.

The next step is to have at Mr. Jones with a thing called a trocar. This is a long, hollow needle attached to a tube. It is jabbed into the abdomen, poked around the entrails and chest cavity, the contents of which are pumped out and replaced with "cavity fluid." This done, and the hole in the abdomen sewn up, Mr. Jones's face is heavily creamed (to protect the skin from burns which may be caused by leakage of the chemicals), and he is covered with a sheet and left unmolested for a while. But not for long—there is more, much more, in store for him. He has been embalmed, but not yet restored, and the best time to start the restorative work is eight to ten hours after embalming, when the tissues have become firm and dry.

The object of all this attention to the corpse, it must be remembered, is to make it presentable for viewing in an attitude of healthy repose. "Our customs require the presentation of our dead in the semblance of normality. . . . unmarred by the ravages of illness, disease or mutilation," says Mr. J. Sheridan Mayer in his *Restorative Art*. This is rather a large order since few people die in the full bloom of health, unravaged by illness and unmarked by some disfigurement. The funeral industry is equal to the challenge: "In some cases the gruesome appearance of a mutilated or disease-ridden subject may be quite discouraging. The task of restoration may seem impossible and shake the confidence of the embalmer. This is the time for intestinal fortitude and determination. Once the formative work is begun and affected tissues are cleaned or removed, all doubts of success vanish. It is surprising and gratifying to discover the results which may be obtained."

The embalmer, having allowed an appropriate interval to elapse, returns to   15
the attack, but now he brings into play the skill and equipment of sculptor and cosmetician. Is a hand missing? Casting one in plaster of Paris is a simple matter. "For replacement purposes, only a cast of the back of the hand is necessary; this is within the ability of the average operator and is quite adequate." If a lip or two, a nose or an ear should be missing, the embalmer has at hand a variety of restorative waxes with which to model replacements. Pores and skin texture are simulated by stippling with a little brush, and over this cosmetics are laid on. Head off? Decapitation cases are rather routinely handled. Ragged edges are trimmed, and head joined to torso with a series of splints, wires and sutures. It is a good idea to have a little something at the neck—a scarf or a high collar—when time for viewing comes. Swollen mouth? Cut out tissue as needed from inside the lips. If too much is removed, the surface contour can easily be restored by padding

with cotton. Swollen necks and cheeks are reduced by removing tissue through vertical incisions made down each side of the neck. "When the deceased is casketed, the pillow will hide the suture incisions. . . . as an extra precaution against leakage, the suture may be painted with liquid sealer."

The opposite condition is more likely to present itself—that of emaciation. His hypodermic syringe now loaded with massage cream, the embalmer seeks out and fills the hollowed and sunken areas by injection. In this procedure the backs of the hands and fingers and the under-chin area should not be neglected.

Positioning the lips is a problem that recurrently challenges the ingenuity of the embalmer. Closed too tightly, they tend to give a stern, even disapproving expression. Ideally, embalmers feel, the lips should give the impression of being ever so slightly parted, the upper lip protruding slightly for a more youthful appearance. This takes some engineering, however, as the lips tend to drift apart. Lip drift can sometimes be remedied by pushing one or two straight pins through the inner margin of the lower lip and then inserting them between the two front upper teeth. If Mr. Jones happens to have no teeth, the pins can just as easily be anchored in his Armstrong Face Former and Denture Replacer. Another method to maintain lip closure is to dislocate the lower jaw, which is then held in its new position by a wire run through holes which have been drilled through the upper and lower jaws at the midline. As the French are fond of saying, *il faut souffrir pour être belle.*[3]

If Mr. Jones has died of jaundice, the embalming fluid will very likely turn him green. Does this deter the embalmer? Not if he has intestinal fortitude. Masking pastes and cosmetics are heavily laid on, burial garments and casket interiors are color-correlated with particular care, and Jones is displayed beneath rose-colored lights. Friends will say "How *well* he looks." Death by carbon monoxide, on the other hand, can be rather a good thing from the embalmer's viewpoint: "One advantage is the fact that this type of discoloration is an exaggerated form of a natural pink coloration." This is nice because the healthy glow is already present and needs but little attention.

The patching and filling completed, Mr. Jones is now shaved, washed and dressed. Cream-based cosmetic, available, in pink, flesh, suntan, brunette and blond, is applied to his hands and face, his hair is shampooed and combed (and, in the case of Mrs. Jones, set), his hands manicured. For the horny-handed son of toil special care must be taken; cream should be applied to remove ingrained grime, and the nails cleaned. "If he were not in the habit of having them manicured in life, trimming and shaping is advised for better appearance—never questioned by kin."

20   Jones is now ready for casketing (this is the present participle of the verb "to casket"). In this operation his right shoulder should be depressed slightly "to turn the body a bit to the right and soften the appearance of lying flat on the back." Positioning the hands is a matter of importance, and special rubber positioning blocks may be used. The hands should be cupped slightly for a more lifelike, relaxed appearance. Proper placement of the body requires a delicate

3. French for "It is necessary to suffer to be beautiful."

sense of balance. It should lie as high as possible in the casket, yet not so high that the lid, when lowered, will hit the nose. On the other hand, we are cautioned, placing the body too low "creates the impression that the body is in a box."

Jones is next wheeled into the appointed slumber room where a few last touches may be added—his favorite pipe placed in his hand or, if he was a great reader, a book propped into position. (In the case of little Master Jones a Teddy bear may be clutched.) Here he will hold open house for a few days, visiting hours 10 A.M. to 9 P.M.

All now being in readiness, the funeral director calls a staff conference to make sure that each assistant knows his precise duties. Mr. Wilber Kriege writes: "This makes your staff feel that they are a part of the team, with a definite assignment that must be properly carried out if the whole plan is to succeed. You never heard of a football coach who failed to talk to his entire team before they go on the field. They have drilled on the plays they are to execute for hours and days, and yet the successful coach knows the importance of making even the bench-warming third-string substitute feel that he is important if the game is to be won." The winning of *this* game is predicated upon glass-smooth handling of the logistics. The funeral director has notified the pall-bearers whose names were furnished by the family, has arranged for the presence of clergyman, organist, and soloist, has provided transportation for everybody, has organized and listed the flowers sent by friends. In *Psychology of Funeral Service* Mr. Edward A. Martin points out: "He may not always do as much as the family thinks he is doing, but it is his helpful guidance that they appreciate in knowing they are proceeding as they should. . . . The important thing is how well his services can be used to make the family believe they are giving unlimited expression to their own sentiment."

The religious service may be held in a church or in the chapel of the funeral home; the funeral director vastly prefers the latter arrangement, for not only is it more convenient for him but it affords him the opportunity to show off his beautiful facilities to the gathered mourners. After the clergyman has had his say, the mourners queue up to file past the casket for a last look at the deceased. The family is *never* asked whether they want an open-casket ceremony; in the absence of their instruction to the contrary, this is taken for granted. Consequently well over 90 per cent of all American funerals feature the open casket—a custom unknown in other parts of the world. Foreigners are astonished by it. An English woman living in San Francisco described her reaction in a letter to the writer:

> I myself have attended only one funeral here—that of an elderly fellow worker of mine. After the service I could not understand why everyone was walking towards the coffin (sorry, I mean casket), but thought I had better follow the crowd. It shook me rigid to get there and find the casket open and poor old Oscar lying there in his brown tweed suit, wearing a suntan makeup and just the wrong shade of lipstick. If I had not been extremely fond of the old boy, I have a horrible feeling that I might have giggled. Then and there I decided that I could never face another American funeral—even dead.

The casket (which has been resting throughout the service on a Classic Beauty Ultra Metal Casket Bier) is now transferred by a hydraulically operated device called Porto-Lift to a balloon-tired, Glide Easy casket carriage which will wheel it to yet another conveyance, the Cadillac Funeral Coach. This may be lavender, cream, light green—anything but black. Interiors, of course, are color-correlated, "for the man who cannot stop short of perfection."

25   At graveside, the casket is lowered into the earth. This office, once the prerogative of friends of the deceased, is now performed by a patented mechanical lowering device. A "Lifetime Green" artificial grass mat is at the ready to conceal the sere earth, and overhead, to conceal the sky, is a portable Steril Chapel Tent ("resists the intense heat and humidity of summer and the terrific storms of winter . . . available in Silver Grey, Rose or Evergreen"). Now is the time for the ritual scattering of earth over the coffin, as the solemn words "earth to earth, ashes to ashes, dust to dust" are pronounced by the officiating cleric. This can today be accomplished "with a mere flick of the wrist with the Gordon Leak-Proof Earth Dispenser. No grasping of a handful of dirt, no soiled fingers. Simple, dignified, beautiful, reverent! The modern way!" The Gordon Earth Dispenser (at $5) is of nickel-plated brass construction. It is not only "attractive to the eye and long wearing"; it is also "one of the 'tools' for building better public relations" if presented as "an appropriate non-commercial gift" to the clergyman. It is shaped something like a saltshaker.

Untouched by human hand, the coffin and the earth are now united.

It is in the function of directing the participants through this maze of gadgetry that the funeral director has assigned to himself his relatively new role of "grief therapist." He has relieved the family of every detail, he has revamped the corpse to look like a living doll, he has arranged for it to nap for a few days in a slumber room, he has put on a well-oiled performance in which the concept of *death* has played no part whatsoever—unless it was inconsiderately mentioned by the clergyman who conducted the religious service. He has done everything in his power to make the funeral a real pleasure for everybody concerned. He and his team have given their all to score an upset victory over death.

MLA CITATION

Mitford, Jessica. "Behind the Formaldehyde Curtain." 1963. *The Norton Reader: An Anthology of Nonfiction*. Ed. Melissa A. Goldthwaite et al. 14th ed. New York: Norton, 2016. 238–44. Print.

QUESTIONS

1. Jessica Mitford's description might be called a "process analysis"—that is, it describes the process by which a corpse becomes a "Beautiful Memory Picture." What are the stages of the process? Mark them in the margins of the essay, and think about how Mitford treats each one.

2. Mitford objects to the American funeral industry and its manipulation of death, yet she never directly says so. How do we as readers know her attitude? Cite words, phrases, or sentences that reveal her position.

3. Describe a process that you object to, letting your choice of words reveal your attitude.

Henry Louis Gates Jr. *In the Kitchen*

WE ALWAYS HAD A GAS STOVE IN THE KITCHEN, in our house in Piedmont, West Virginia, where I grew up. Never electric, though using electric became fashionable in Piedmont in the sixties, like using Crest toothpaste rather than Colgate, or watching Huntley and Brinkley rather than Walter Cronkite.[1] But not us: gas, Colgate, and good ole Walter Cronkite, come what may. We used gas partly out of loyalty to Big Mom, Mama's Mama, because she was mostly blind and still loved to cook, and could feel her way more easily with gas than with electric. But the most important thing about our gas-equipped kitchen was that Mama used to do hair there. The "hot comb" was a fine-toothed iron instrument with a long wooden handle and a pair of iron curlers that opened and closed like scissors. Mama would put it in the gas fire until it glowed. You could smell those prongs heating up.

I liked that smell. Not the smell so much, I guess, as what the smell meant for the shape of my day. There was an intimate warmth in the women's tones as they talked with my Mama, doing their hair. I knew what the women had been through to get their hair ready to be "done," because I would watch Mama do it to herself. How that kink could be transformed through grease and fire into that magnificent head of wavy hair was a miracle to me, and still is.

Mama would wash her hair over the sink, a towel wrapped around her shoulders, wearing just her slip and her white bra. (We had no shower—just a galvanized tub that we stored in the kitchen—until we moved down Rat Tail Road into Doc Wolverton's house, in 1954.) After she dried it, she would grease her scalp thoroughly with blue Bergamot hair grease, which came in a short, fat jar with a picture of a beautiful colored lady on it. It's important to grease your scalp real good, my Mama would explain, to keep from burning yourself. Of course, her hair would return to its natural kink almost as soon as the hot water and shampoo hit it. To me, it was another miracle how hair so "straight" would so quickly become kinky again the second it even approached some water.

Originally published in the New Yorker *(1994), a weekly magazine of "reportage, commentary, criticism, essays, fiction, satire, cartoons, and poetry" in advance of the publication of Henry Louis Gates Jr.'s memoir,* Colored People *(1994).*

1. Newscasters of the 1960s: Chet Huntley and David Brinkley were on NBC; Walter Cronkite was on CBS.

My Mama had only a few "clients" whose heads she "did"—did, I think, because she enjoyed it, rather than for the few pennies it brought in. They would sit on one of our red plastic kitchen chairs, the kind with the shiny metal legs, and brace themselves for the process. Mama would stroke that red-hot iron— which by this time had been in the gas fire for half an hour or more—slowly but firmly through their hair, from scalp to strand's end. It made a scorching, crinkly sound, the hot iron did, as it burned its way through kink, leaving in its wake straight strands of hair, standing long and tall but drooping over at the ends, their shape like the top of a heavy willow tree. Slowly, steadily, Mama's hands would transform a round mound of Odetta[2] kink into a darkened swamp of everglades. The Bergamot made the hair shiny; the heat of the hot iron gave it a brownish-red cast. Once all the hair was as straight as God allows kink to get, Mama would take the wellheated curling iron and twirl the straightened strands into more or less loosely wrapped curls. She claimed that she owed her skill as a hairdresser to the strength in her wrists, and as she worked her little finger would poke out, the way it did when she sipped tea. Mama was a south-paw, and wrote upside down and backward to produce the cleanest, roundest letters you've ever seen.

5   The "kitchen" she would all but remove from sight with a handheld pair of shears, bought just for this purpose. Now, the kitchen was the room in which we were sitting—the room where Mama did hair and washed clothes, and where we all took a bath in that galvanized tub. But the word has another meaning, and the kitchen that I'm speaking of is the very kinky bit of hair at the back of your head, where your neck meets your shirt collar. If there was ever a part of our African past that resisted assimilation, it was the kitchen. No matter how hot the iron, no matter how powerful the chemical, no matter how stringent the mashed-potatoes-and-lye formula of a man's "process," neither God nor woman nor Sammy Davis, Jr.,[3] could straighten the kitchen. The kitchen was permanent, irredeemable, irresistible kink. Unassimilably African. No matter what you did, no matter how hard you tried, you couldn't de-kink a person's kitchen. So you trimmed it off as best you could.

When hair had begun to "turn," as they'd say—to return to its natural kinky glory—it was the kitchen that turned first (the kitchen around the back, and nappy edges at the temples). When the kitchen started creeping up the back of the neck, it was time to get your hair done again.

Sometimes, after dark, a man would come to have his hair done. It was Mr. Charlie Carroll. He was very light-complected and had a ruddy nose—it made me think of Edmund Gwenn, who played Kris Kringle in *Miracle on 34th Street*. At first, Mama did him after my brother, Rocky, and I had gone to sleep. It was only later that we found out that he had come to our house so Mama could iron his hair—not with a hot comb or a curling iron but with our very own

2. Odetta Holmes (1930–2008), singer of blues and spirituals in the 1950s and a lead-ing figure in the American folk revival of the 1960s.
3. Singer, dancer, and entertainer (1925–1990) with notably "processed" hair.

Proctor-Silex steam iron. For some reason I never understood, Mr. Charlie would conceal his Frederick Douglass–like mane[4] under a big white Stetson hat. I never saw him take it off except when he came to our house, at night, to have his hair pressed. (Later, Daddy would tell us about Mr. Charlie's most prized piece of knowledge, something that the man would only confide after his hair had been pressed, as a token of intimacy. "Not many people know this," he'd say, in a tone of circumspection, "but George Washington was Abraham Lincoln's daddy." Nodding solemnly, he'd add the clincher: "A white man told me." Though he was in dead earnest, this became a humorous refrain around our house—"a white man told me"—which we used to punctuate especially preposterous assertions.)

My mother examined my daughters' kitchens whenever we went home to visit, in the early eighties. It became a game between us. I had told her not to do it, because I didn't like the politics it suggested—the notion of "good" and "bad" hair. "Good" hair was "straight," "bad" hair kinky. Even in the late sixties, at the height of Black Power, almost nobody could bring themselves to say "bad" for good and "good" for bad. People still said that hair like white people's hair was "good," even if they encapsulated it in a disclaimer, like "what we used to call 'good.'"

Maggie would be seated in her high chair, throwing food this way and that, and Mama would be cooing about how cute it all was, how I used to do just like Maggie was doing, and wondering whether her flinging her food with her left hand meant that she was going to be left-handed like Mama. When my daughter was just about covered with Chef Boyardee Spaghetti-O's, Mama would seize the opportunity: wiping her clean, she would tilt Maggie's head to one side and reach down the back of her neck. Sometimes Mama would even rub a curl between her fingers, just to make sure that her bifocals had not deceived her. Then she'd sigh with satisfaction and relief: No kink . . . yet. Mama! I'd shout, pretending to be angry. Every once in a while, if no one was looking, I'd peek, too.

I say "yet" because most black babies are born with soft, silken hair. But after a few months it begins to turn, as inevitably as do the seasons or the leaves on a tree. People once thought baby oil would stop it. They were wrong.

Everybody I knew as a child wanted to have good hair. You could be as ugly as homemade sin dipped in misery and still be thought attractive if you had good hair. "Jesus moss," the girls at Camp Lee, Virginia, had called Daddy's naturally "good" hair during the war. I know that he played that thick head of hair for all it was worth, too.

My own hair was "not a bad grade," as barbers would tell me when they cut it for the first time. It was like a doctor reporting the results of the first full physical he has given you. Like "You're in good shape" or "Blood pressure's kind of high—better cut down on salt."

10

---

4. Douglass (1817–1895) was an escaped slave turned abolitionist; photographs show him with a lion-like mane of hair.

I spent most of my childhood and adolescence messing with my hair. I definitely wanted straight hair. Like Pop's. When I was about three, I tried to stick a wad of Bazooka bubble gum to that straight hair of his. I suppose what fixed that memory for me is the spanking I got for doing so: he turned me upside down, holding me by my feet, the better to paddle my behind. Little *nigger*, he had shouted, walloping away. I started to laugh about it two days later, when my behind stopped hurting.

When black people say "straight," of course, they don't usually mean literally straight—they're not describing hair like, say, Peggy Lipton's (she was the white girl on *The Mod Squad*), or like Mary's of Peter, Paul & Mary[5] fame; black people call that "stringy" hair. No, "straight" just means not kinky, no matter what contours the curl may take. I would have done *anything* to have straight hair—and I used to try everything, short of getting a process.[6]

15   Of the wide variety of techniques and methods I came to master in the challenging prestidigitation of the follicle, almost all had two things in common: a heavy grease and the application of pressure. It's not an accident that some of the biggest black-owned companies in the fifties and sixties made hair products. And I tried them all, in search of that certain silken touch, the one that would leave neither the hand nor the pillow sullied by grease.

I always wondered what Frederick Douglass put on *his* hair, or what Phillis Wheatley[7] put on hers. Or why Wheatley has that rag on her head in the little engraving in the frontispiece of her book. One thing is for sure: you can bet that when Phillis Wheatley went to England and saw the Countess of Huntingdon she did not stop by the Queen's coiffeur on her way there. So many black people still get their hair straightened that it's a wonder we don't have a national holiday for Madame C. J. Walker, the woman who invented the process of straightening kinky hair. Call it Jheri-Kurled or call it "relaxed," it's still fried hair.

I used all the greases, from sea-blue Bergamot and creamy vanilla Duke (in its clear jar with the orange-white-and-green label) to the godfather of grease, the formidable Murray's. Now, Murray's was some *serious* grease. Whereas Bergamot was like oily jello, and Duke was viscous and sickly sweet, Murray's was light brown and *hard*. Hard as lard and twice as greasy, Daddy used to say. Murray's came in an orange can with a press-on top. It was so hard that some people would put a match to the can, just to soften the stuff and make it more manageable. Then, in the late sixties, when Afros came into style, I used Afro Sheen. From Murray's to Duke to Afro Sheen: that was my progression in black consciousness.

We used to put hot towels or washrags over our Murray-coated heads, in order to melt the wax into the scalp and the follicles. Unfortunately, the wax also had the habit of running down your neck, ears, and forehead. Not to men-

5. Folksinging group famous in the 1960s for "Puff the Magic Dragon."
6. Hair-straightening chemical treatment.
7. America's first published African American woman writer (1753–1784).

tion your pillowcase. Another problem was that if you put two palmfuls of Murray's on your head your hair turned white. (Duke did the same thing.) The challenge was to get rid of that white color. Because if you got rid of the white stuff you had a magnificent head of wavy hair. That was the beauty of it: Murray's was so hard that it froze your hair into the wavy style you brushed it into. It looked really good if you wore a part. A lot of guys had parts *cut* into their hair by a barber, either with the clippers or with a straight-edge razor. Especially if you had kinky hair—then you'd generally wear a short razor cut, or what we called a Quo Vadis.

We tried to be as innovative as possible. Everyone knew about using a stocking cap, because your father or your uncle wore one whenever something really big was about to happen, whether sacred or secular: a funeral or a dance, a wedding or a trip in which you confronted official white people. Any time you were trying to look really sharp, you wore a stocking cap in preparation. And if the event was really a big one, you made a new cap. You asked your mother for a pair of her hose, and cut it with scissors about six inches or so from the open end—the end with the elastic that goes up to the top of the thigh. Then you knotted the cut end, and it became a beehive-shaped hat, with an elastic band that you pulled down low on your forehead and down around your neck in the back. To work well, the cap had to fit tightly and snugly, like a press. And it had to fit that tightly because it *was* a press: it pressed your hair with the force of the hose's elastic. If you greased your hair down real good, and left the stocking cap on long enough, voilà: you got a head of pressed-against-the-scalp waves. (You also got a ring around your forehead when you woke up, but it went away.) And then you could enjoy your concrete do. Swore we were bad, too, with all that grease and those flat heads. My brother and I would brush it out a bit in the mornings, so that it looked—well, "natural." Grown men still wear stocking caps—especially older men, who generally keep their stocking caps in their top drawers, along with their cufflinks and their see-through silk socks, their "Maverick" ties, their silk handkerchiefs, and whatever else they prize the most.

A Murrayed-down stocking cap was the respectable version of the process, which, by contrast, was most definitely not a cool thing to have unless you were an entertainer by trade. Zeke and Keith and Poochie and a few other stars of the high-school basketball team all used to get a process once or twice a year. It was expensive, and you had to go somewhere like Pittsburgh or D.C. or Uniontown—somewhere where there were enough colored people to support a trade. The guys would disappear, then reappear a day or two later, strutting like peacocks, their hair burned slightly red from the lye base. They'd also wear "rags"—cloths or handkerchiefs—around their heads when they slept or played basketball. Do-rags, they were called. But the result was straight hair, with just a hint of wave. No curl. Do-it-yourselfers took their chances at home with a concoction of mashed potatoes and lye.

20

The most famous process of all, however, outside of the process Malcolm X describes in his "Autobiography," and maybe the process of Sammy Davis, Jr., was Nat King Cole's[8] process. Nat King Cole had patent-leather hair. That man's got the finest process money can buy, or so Daddy said the night we saw Cole's TV show on NBC. It was November 5, 1956. I remember the date because everyone came to our house to watch it and to celebrate one of Daddy's buddies' birthdays. Yeah, Uncle Joe chimed in, they can do shit to his hair that the average Negro can't even *think* about—secret shit.

Nat King Cole was *clean.* I've had an ongoing argument with a Nigerian friend about Nat King Cole for twenty years now. Not about whether he could sing—any fool knows that he could—but about whether or not he was a handkerchief head for wearing that patent-leather process.

Sammy Davis, Jr.'s process was the one I detested. It didn't look good on him. Worse still, he liked to have a fried strand dangling down the middle of his forehead, so he could shake it out from the crown when he sang. But Nat King Cole's hair was a thing unto itself, a beautifully sculpted work of art that he and he alone had the right to wear. The only difference between a process and a stocking cap, really, was taste; but Nat King Cole, unlike, say, Michael Jackson, looked *good* in his. His head looked like Valentino's[9] head in the twenties, and some say it was Valentino the process was imitating. But Nat King Cole wore a process because it suited his face, his demeanor, his name, his style. He was as clean as he wanted to be.

I had forgotten all about that patent-leather look until one day in 1971, when I was sitting in an Arab restaurant on the island of Zanzibar surrounded by men in fezzes and white caftans, trying to learn how to eat curried goat and rice with the fingers of my right hand and feeling two million miles from home. All of a sudden, an old transistor radio sitting on top of a china cupboard stopped blaring out its Swahili music and started playing "Fly Me to the Moon," by Nat King Cole. The restaurant's din was not affected at all, but in my mind's eye I saw it: the King's magnificent sleek black tiara. I managed, barely, to blink back the tears.

8. Singer and jazz pianist (1919–1965).
9. Rudolph Valentino (1895–1926), film star known, among other things, for his slicked-back hair.

MLA CITATION

Gates, Henry Louis Jr. "In the Kitchen." 1994. *The Norton Reader: An Anthology of Nonfiction.* Ed. Melissa A. Goldthwaite et al. 14th ed. New York: Norton, 2016. 245–50. Print.

QUESTIONS

1. "Kitchen" has two meanings here; write a brief explanation of the significance of both uses of the word in Henry Louis Gates Jr.'s essay.

2. Why do you think Gates alludes to so many celebrities (mostly from the 1950s and 1960s) and brand-name products? Note his preferences and progression. What is the significance of the allusions and brand names?

3. Gates observes, "If there was ever a part of our African past that resisted assimilation, it was the kitchen" (paragraph 5). What does *assimilation* mean in the context of this sentence? What do you think it means generally? What does the essay imply about Gates's stance on African American assimilation?

4. Write an essay in which you use memories from childhood—including sensory details, popular allusions, and brand-name products—to describe some element of your culture or identity.

JAMES BALDWIN *Stranger in the Village*

FROM ALL AVAILABLE EVIDENCE no black man had ever set foot in this tiny Swiss village before I came. I was told before arriving that I would probably be a "sight" for the village; I took this to mean that people of my complexion were rarely seen in Switzerland, and also that city people are always something of a "sight" outside of the city. It did not occur to me—possibly because I am an American—that there could be people anywhere who had never seen a Negro.

It is a fact that cannot be explained on the basis of the inaccessibility of the village. The village is very high, but it is only four hours from Milan and three hours from Lausanne. It is true that it is virtually unknown. Few people making plans for a holiday would elect to come here. On the other hand, the villagers are able, presumably, to come and go as they please—which they do: to another town at the foot of the mountain, with a population of approximately five thousand, the nearest place to see a movie or go to the bank. In the village there is no movie house, no bank, no library, no theater; very few radios, one jeep, one station wagon; and at the moment, one typewriter, mine, an invention which the woman next door to me here had never seen. There are about six hundred people living here, all Catholic—I conclude this from the fact that the Catholic church is open all year round, whereas the Protestant chapel, set off on a hill a little removed from the village, is open only in the summertime when the tourists arrive. There are four or five hotels, all closed now, and four or five *bistros*, of which, however, only two do any business during the winter. These two do not do a great deal, for life in the village seems to end around nine or ten o'clock. There are a few stores, butcher, baker, *épicerie*,[1] a hardware store, and a money-changer—who cannot change travelers' checks, but must send them down to the bank, an operation which takes two or three days. There is something called the *Ballet Haus*, closed in the winter and used for

Written in 1953 and included in Notes of a Native Son *(1955), James Baldwin's collection of essays that describes and analyzes the experience of being black in America and Europe.*

1. French for "grocery shop."

God knows what, certainly not ballet, during the summer. There seems to be only one schoolhouse in the village, and this for the quite young children; I suppose this to mean that their older brothers and sisters at some point descend from these mountains in order to complete their education—possibly, again, to the town just below. The landscape is absolutely forbidding, mountains towering on all four sides, ice and snow as far as the eye can reach. In this white wilderness, men and women and children move all day, carrying washing, wood, buckets of milk or water, sometimes skiing on Sunday afternoons. All week long boys and young men are to be seen shoveling snow off the rooftops, or dragging wood down from the forest in sleds.

The village's only real attraction, which explains the tourist season, is the hot spring water. A disquietingly high proportion of these tourists are cripples, or semi-cripples, who come year after year—from other parts of Switzerland, usually—to take the waters. This lends the village, at the height of the season, a rather terrifying air of sanctity, as though it were a lesser Lourdes.[2] There is often something beautiful, there is always something awful, in the spectacle of a person who has lost one of his faculties, a faculty he never questioned until it was gone, and who struggles to recover it. Yet people remain people, on crutches or indeed on deathbeds; and wherever I passed, the first summer I was here, among the native villagers or among the lame, a wind passed with me—of astonishment, curiosity, amusement, and outrage. That first summer I stayed two weeks and never intended to return. But I did return in the winter, to work; the village offers, obviously, no distractions whatever and has the further advantage of being extremely cheap. Now it is winter again, a year later, and I am here again. Everyone in the village knows my name, though they scarcely ever use it, knows that I come from America—though, this, apparently, they will never really believe: black men come from Africa—and everyone knows that I am the friend of the son of a woman who was born here, and that I am staying in their chalet. But I remain as much a stranger today as I was the first day I arrived, and the children shout *Neger! Neger!* as I walk along the streets.

It must be admitted that in the beginning I was far too shocked to have any real reaction. In so far as I reacted at all, I reacted by trying to be pleasant—it being a great part of the American Negro's education (long before he goes to school) that he must make people "like" him. This smile-and-the-world-smiles-with-you routine worked about as well in this situation as it had in the situation for which it was designed, which is to say that it did not work at all. No one, after all, can be liked whose human weight and complexity cannot be, or has not been, admitted. My smile was simply another unheard-of phenomenon which allowed them to see my teeth—they did not, really, see my smile and I began to think that, should I take to snarling, no one would notice any difference. All of the physical characteristics of the Negro which had caused me, in America, a very different and almost forgotten pain were nothing less than miraculous—or infernal—in the eyes of the village people. Some thought my hair was the color of tar, that it had the texture of wire, or the texture of cotton.

2. Site of visions of the Virgin Mary and now a prominent pilgrimage destination.

It was jocularly suggested that I might let it all grow long and make myself a winter coat. If I sat in the sun for more than five minutes some daring creature was certain to come along and gingerly put his fingers on my hair, as though he were afraid of an electric shock, or put his hand on my hand, astonished that the color did not rub off. In all of this, in which it must be conceded there was the charm of genuine wonder and in which there were certainly no element of intentional unkindness, there was yet no suggestion that I was human: I was simply a living wonder.

I knew that they did not mean to be unkind, and I know it now; it is necessary, nevertheless, for me to repeat this to myself each time that I walk out of the chalet. The children who shout *Neger!* have no way of knowing the echoes this sound raises in me. They are brimming with good humor and the more daring swell with pride when I stop to speak with them. Just the same, there are days when I cannot pause and smile, when I have no heart to play with them; when, indeed, I mutter sourly to myself, exactly as I muttered on the streets of a city these children have never seen, when I was no bigger than these children are now: *Your* mother *was a nigger*. Joyce is right about history being a nightmare[3]—but it may be the nightmare from which no one *can* awaken. People are trapped in history and history is trapped in them.

There is a custom in the village—I am told it is repeated in many villages—of "buying" African natives for the purpose of converting them to Christianity. There stands in the church all year round a small box with a slot for money, decorated with a black figurine, and into this box the villagers drop their francs. During the *carnaval* which precedes Lent, two village children have their faces blackened—out of which bloodless darkness their blue eyes shine like ice—and fantastic horsehair wigs are placed on their blond heads; thus disguised, they solicit among the villagers for money for the missionaries in Africa. Between the box in the church and the blackened children, the village "bought" last year six or eight African natives. This was reported to me with pride by the wife of one of the *bistro* owners and I was careful to express astonishment and pleasure at the solicitude shown by the village for the souls of black folks. The *bistro* owner's wife beamed with a pleasure far more genuine than my own and seemed to feel that I might now breathe more easily concerning the souls of at least six of my kinsmen.

I tried not to think of these so lately baptized kinsmen, of the price paid for them, or the peculiar price they themselves would pay, and said nothing about my father, who having taken his own conversion too literally never, at bottom, forgave the white world (which he described as heathen) for having saddled him with a Christ in whom, to judge at least from their treatment of him, they themselves no longer believed. I thought of white men arriving for the first time in an African village, strangers there, as I am a stranger here, and tried to imagine the astounded populace touching their hair and marveling at the color of their skin. But there is a great difference between being

5

3. James Joyce (1882–1941), Irish novelist; Stephen Dedalus, a character in Joyce's novel *Ulysses*, says, "History is a nightmare from which I am trying to escape."

the first white man to be seen by Africans and being the first black man to be seen by whites. The white man takes the astonishment as tribute, for he arrives to conquer and to convert the natives, whose inferiority in relation to himself is not even to be questioned; whereas I, without a thought of conquest, find myself among a people whose culture controls me, has even, in a sense, created me, people who have cost me more in anguish and rage than they will ever know, who yet do not even know of my existence. The astonishment with which I might have greeted them, should they have stumbled into my African village a few hundred years ago, might have rejoiced their hearts. But the astonishment with which they greet me today can only poison mine.

And this is so despite everything I may do to feel differently, despite my friendly conversations with the *bistro* owner's wife, despite their three-year-old son who has at last become my friend, despite the *saluts* and *bonsoirs*[4] which I exchange with people as I walk, despite the fact that I know that no individual can be taken to task for what history is doing, or has done. I say that the culture of these people controls me—but they can scarcely be held responsible for European culture. America comes out of Europe, but these people have never seen America, nor have most of them seen more of Europe than the hamlet at the foot of their mountain. Yet they move with an authority which I shall never have; and they regard me, quite rightly, not only as a stranger in their village but as a suspect latecomer, bearing no credentials, to everything they have—however unconsciously—inherited.

For this village, even were it incomparably more remote and incredibly more primitive, is the West, the West onto which I have been so strangely grafted. These people cannot be, from the point of view of power, strangers anywhere in the world; they have made the modern world, in effect, even if they do not know it. The most illiterate among them is related, in a way that I am not, to Dante, Shakespeare, Michelangelo, Aeschylus, Da Vinci, Rembrandt, and Racine; the cathedral at Chartres says something to them which it cannot say to me, as indeed would New York's Empire State Building, should anyone here ever see it. Out of their hymns and dances come Beethoven and Bach. Go back a few centuries and they are in their full glory—but I am in Africa, watching the conquerors arrive.

10   The rage of the disesteemed is personally fruitless, but it is also absolutely inevitable; this rage, so generally discounted, so little understood even among the people whose daily bread it is, is one of the things that makes history. Rage can only with difficulty, and never entirely, be brought under the domination of the intelligence and is therefore not susceptible to any arguments whatever. This is a fact which ordinary representatives of the *Herrenvolk*,[5] having never felt this rage and being unable to imagine, quite fail to understand. Also, rage cannot be hidden, it can only be dissembled. This dissembling deludes the thoughtless, and strengthens rage and adds, to rage, contempt. There are, no

4. French for "hellos" and "good evenings."
5. German for "master race."

doubt, as many ways of coping with the resulting complex of tensions as there are black men in the world, but no black man can hope ever to be entirely liberated from this internal warfare—rage, dissembling, and contempt having inevitably accompanied his first realization of the power of white men. What is crucial here is that, since white men represent in the black man's world so heavy a weight, white men have for black men a reality which is far from being reciprocal; and hence all black men have toward all white men an attitude which is designed, really, either to rob the white man of the jewel of his naïveté, or else to make it cost him dear.

The black man insists, by whatever means he finds at his disposal, that the white man cease to regard him as an exotic rarity and recognize him as a human being. This is a very charged and difficult moment, for there is a great deal of will power involved in the white man's naïveté. Most people are not naturally reflective any more than they are naturally malicious, and the white man prefers to keep the black man at a certain human remove because it is easier for him thus to preserve his simplicity and avoid being called to account for crimes committed by his forefathers, or his neighbors. He is inescapably aware, nevertheless, that he is in a better position in the world than black men are, nor can he quite put to death the suspicion that he is hated by black men therefore. He does not wish to be hated, neither does he wish to change places, and at this point in his uneasiness he can scarcely avoid having recourse to those legends which white men have created about black men, the most usual effect of which is that the white man finds himself enmeshed, so to speak, in his own language which describes hell, as well as the attributes which lead one to hell, as being as black as night.

Every legend, moreover, contains its residuum of truth, and the root function of language is to control the universe by describing it. It is of quite considerable significance that black men remain, in the imagination, and in overwhelming numbers in fact, beyond the disciplines of salvation; and this despite the fact that the West has been "buying" African natives for centuries. There is, I should hazard, an instantaneous necessity to be divorced from this so visibly unsaved stranger, in whose heart, moreover, one cannot guess what dreams of vengeance are being nourished; and, at the same time, there are few things on earth more attractive than the idea of the unspeakable liberty which is allowed the unredeemed. When, beneath the black mask, a human being begins to make himself felt one cannot escape a certain awful wonder as to what kind of human being it is. What one's imagination makes of other people is dictated, of course, by the laws of one's own personality and it is one of the ironies of black-white relations that, by means of what the white man imagines the black man to be, the black man is enabled to know who the white man is.

I have said, for example, that I am as much a stranger in this village today as I was the first summer I arrived, but this is not quite true. The villagers wonder less about the texture of my hair than they did then, and wonder rather more about me. And the fact that their wonder now exists on another level is reflected in their attitudes and in their eyes. There are the children who make those delightful, hilarious, sometimes astonishingly grave overtures of friendship in the unpredictable fashion of children; other children, having been taught that the devil is a black man, scream in genuine anguish as I approach. Some of the older women never pass without a friendly greeting, never pass, indeed, if it seems that they will be able to engage me in conversation; other women look down or look away or rather contemptuously smirk. Some of the men drink with me and suggest that I learn how to ski—partly, I gather, because they cannot imagine what I would look like on skis—and want to know if I am married, and ask questions about my *métier*.[6] But some of the men have accused *le sale nègre*[7]—behind my back—of stealing wood and there is already in the eyes of some of them that peculiar, intent, paranoiac malevolence which one sometimes surprises in the eyes of American white men when, out walking with their Sunday girl, they see a Negro male approach.

There is a dreadful abyss between the streets of this village and the streets of the city in which I was born, between the children who shout *Neger!* today and those who shouted *Nigger!* yesterday—the abyss is experience, the American experience. The syllable hurled behind me today expresses, above all, wonder: I am a stranger here. But I am not a stranger in America and the same syllable riding on the American air expresses the war my presence has occasioned in the American soul.

15   For this village brings home to me this fact: that there was a day, and not really a very distant day, when Americans were scarcely Americans at all but discontented Europeans, facing a great unconquered continent and strolling, say, into a marketplace and seeing black men for the first time. The shock this spectacle afforded is suggested, surely, by the promptness with which they decided that these black men were not really men but cattle. It is true that the necessity on the part of the settlers of the New World of reconciling their moral assumptions with the fact—and the necessity—of slavery enhanced immensely the charm of this idea, and it is also true that this idea expresses, with a truly American bluntness, the attitude which to varying extents all masters have had toward all slaves.

But between all former slaves and slave-owners and the drama which begins for Americans over three hundred years ago at Jamestown,[8] there are at least two differences to be observed. The American Negro slave could not suppose, for one thing, as slaves in past epochs had supposed and often done, that he would ever be able to wrest the power from his master's hands. This was a supposition which the modern era, which was to bring about such vast changes in the aims and dimensions of power, put to death; it only begins, in unprecedented fashion, and with dreadful implications, to be resurrected today. But even had this supposition persisted with undiminished force, the American Negro slave could not have used it to lend his condition dignity, for the reason that this supposition rests on another: that the slave in exile yet remains related

6. French for "occupation or profession."
7. French for "the dirty Negro."
8. Founded in 1607, the first lasting English settlement in North America.

to his past, has some means—if only in memory—of revering and sustaining the forms of his former life, is able, in short, to maintain his identity.

This was not the case with the American Negro slave. He is unique among the black men of the world in that his past was taken from him, almost literally, at one blow. One wonders what on earth the first slave found to say to the first dark child he bore. I am told that there are Haitians able to trace their ancestry back to African kings, but any American Negro wishing to go back so far will find his journey through time abruptly arrested by the signature on the bill of sale which served as the entrance paper for his ancestor. At the time— to say nothing of the circumstances—of the enslavement of the captive black man who was to become the American Negro, there was not the remotest possibility that he would ever take power from his master's hands. There was no reason to suppose that his situation would ever change, nor was there, shortly, anything to indicate that his situation had ever been different. It was his necessity, in the words of E. Franklin Frazier,[9] to find a "motive for living under American culture or die." The identity of the American Negro comes out of this extreme situation, and the evolution of this identity was a source of the most intolerable anxiety in the minds and the lives of his masters.

For the history of the American Negro is unique also in this: that the question of his humanity, and of his rights therefore as a human being, became a burning one for several generations of Americans, so burning a question that it ultimately became one of those used to divide the nation. It is out of this argument that the venom of the epithet *Nigger!* is derived. It is an argument which Europe has never had, and hence Europe quite sincerely fails to understand how or why the argument arose in the first place, why its effects are frequently disastrous and always so unpredictable, why it refuses until today to be entirely settled. Europe's black possessions remained—and do remain—in Europe's colonies, at which remove they represented no threat whatever to European identity. If they posed any problem at all for the European conscience it was a problem which remained comfortingly abstract: in effect, the black man, as a *man* did not exist for Europe. But in America, even as a slave, he was an inescapable part of the general social fabric and no American could escape having an attitude toward him. Americans attempt until today to make an abstraction of the Negro, but the very nature of these abstractions reveals the tremendous effects the presence of the Negro has had on the American character.

When one considers the history of the Negro in America it is of the greatest importance to recognize that the moral beliefs of a person, or a people, are never really as tenuous as life—which is not moral—very often causes them to appear; these create for them a frame of reference and a necessary hope, the hope being that when life has done its worst they will be enabled to rise above themselves and to triumph over life. Life would scarcely be bearable if this hope did not exist. Again, even when the worst has been said, to betray a

9. African American sociologist (1894–1962).

belief is not by any means to have put oneself beyond its power; the betrayal of a belief is not the same thing as ceasing to believe. If this were not so there would be no moral standards in the world at all. Yet one must also recognize that morality is based on ideas and that all ideas are dangerous—dangerous because ideas can only lead to action and where the action leads no man can say. And dangerous in this respect: that confronted with the impossibility of remaining faithful to one's beliefs, and the equal impossibility of becoming free of them, one can be driven to the most inhuman excesses. The ideas on which American beliefs are based are not, though Americans often seem to think so, ideas which originated in America. They came out of Europe. And the establishment of democracy on the American continent was scarcely as radical a break with the past as was the necessity, which Americans faced, of broadening this concept to include black men.

20   This was, literally, a hard necessity. It was impossible, for one thing, for Americans to abandon their beliefs, not only because these beliefs alone seemed able to justify the sacrifices they had endured and the blood that they had spilled, but also because these beliefs afforded them their only bulwark against a moral chaos as absolute as the physical chaos of the continent it was their destiny to conquer. But in the situation in which Americans found themselves, these beliefs threatened an idea which, whether or not one likes to think so, is the very warp and woof of the heritage of the West, the idea of white supremacy.

Americans have made themselves notorious by the shrillness and the brutality with which they have insisted on this idea, but they did not invent it; and it has escaped the world's notice that those very excesses of which Americans have been guilty imply a certain, unprecedented uneasiness over the idea's life and power, if not, indeed, the idea's validity. The idea of white supremacy rests simply on the fact that white men are the creators of civilization (the present civilization, which is the only one that matters; all previous civilizations are simply "contributions" to our own) and are therefore civilization's guardians and defenders. Thus it was impossible for Americans to accept the black man as one of themselves, for to do so was to jeopardize their status as white men. But not so to accept him was to deny his human reality, his human weight and complexity, and the strain of denying the overwhelmingly undeniable forced Americans into rationalizations so fantastic that they approached the pathological.

At the root of the American Negro problem is the necessity of the American white man to find a way of living with the Negro in order to be able to live with himself. And the history of this problem can be reduced to the means used by Americans—lynch law and law, segregation and legal acceptance, terrorization and concession—either to come to terms with this necessity, or to find a way around it, or (most usually) to find a way of doing both these things at once. The resulting spectacle, at once foolish and dreadful, led someone to make the quite accurate observation that "the Negro-in-America is a form of insanity which overtakes white men."

In this long battle, a battle by no means finished, the unforeseeable effects of which will be felt by many future generations, the white man's motive was the protection of his identity; the black man was motivated by the need to establish an identity. And despite the terrorization which the Negro in America endured and endures sporadically until today, despite the cruel and totally inescapable ambivalence of his status in his country, the battle for his identity has long ago been won. He is not a visitor to the West, but a citizen there, an American; as American as the Americans who despise him, the Americans who fear him, the Americans who love him—the Americans who became less than themselves, or rose to be greater than themselves by virtue of the fact that the challenge he represented was inescapable. He is perhaps the only black man in the world whose relationship to white men is more terrible, more subtle, and more meaningful than the relationship of bitter possessed to uncertain possessors. His survival depended, and his development depends, on his ability to turn his peculiar status in the Western world to his own advantage and, it may be, to the very great advantage of that world. It remains for him to fashion out of his experience that which will give him sustenance, and a voice.

The cathedral at Chartres, I have said, says something to the people of this village which it cannot say to me; but it is important to understand that this cathedral says something to me which it cannot say to them. Perhaps they are struck by the power of the spires, the glory of the windows; but they have known God, after all, longer than I have known him, and in a different way, and I am terrified by the slippery bottomless well to be found in the crypt, down which heretics were hurled to death, and by the obscene, inescapable gargoyles jutting out of the stone and seeming to say that God and the devil can never be divorced. I doubt that the villagers think of the devil when they face a cathedral because they have never been identified with the devil. But I must accept the status which myth, if nothing else, gives me in the West before I can hope to change the myth.

Yet, if the American Negro has arrived at his identity by virtue of the absoluteness of his estrangement from his past, American white men still nourish the illusion that there is some means of recovering the European innocence, of returning to a state in which black men do not exist. This is one of the greatest errors Americans can make. The identity they fought so hard to protect has, by virtue of that battle, undergone a change: Americans are as unlike any other white people in the world as it is possible to be. I do not think, for example, that it is too much to suggest that the American vision of the world—which allows so little reality, generally speaking, for any of the darker forces in human life, which tends until today to paint moral issues in glaring black and white— owes a great deal to the battle waged by Americans to maintain between themselves and black men a human separation which could not be bridged. It is only now beginning to be borne in on us—very faintly, it must be admitted, very slowly, and very much against our will—that this vision of the world is dangerously inaccurate, and perfectly useless. For it protects our moral high-mindedness at the terrible expense of weakening our grasp of reality. People who shut their eyes to reality simply invite their own destruction, and anyone who insists on remaining in a state of innocence long after that innocence is dead turns himself into a monster.

The time has come to realize that the interracial drama acted out on the American continent has not only created a new black man, it has created a new white man, too. No road whatever will lead Americans back to the simplicity of this European village where white men still have the luxury of looking on me as a stranger. I am not, really, a stranger any longer for any American alive. One of the things that distinguishes Americans from other people is that no other people has ever been so deeply involved in the lives of black men, and vice versa. This fact faced, with all its implications, it can be seen that the history of the American Negro problem is not merely shameful, it is also something of an achievement. For even when the worst has been said, it must also be added that the perpetual challenge posed by this problem was always, somehow, perpetually met. It is precisely this black-white experience which may prove of indispensable value to us in the world we face today. This world is white no longer, and it will never be white again.

MLA CITATION

Baldwin, James. "Stranger in the Village." 1955. *The Norton Reader: An Anthology of Nonfiction*. Ed. Melissa A. Goldthwaite et al. 14th ed. New York: Norton, 2016. 251–60. Print.

QUESTIONS

1. James Baldwin was an American, but he lived for many years in France. Consider the role of geography in this essay. How does Baldwin use his experience in the Swiss village to comment on America?

2. Trace the use of the word "stranger" over the course of the essay. How does Baldwin's use of the word evolve as the essay develops?

3. Baldwin relates the white man's language and legends about black men to the "laws" of the white man's personality. What conviction about the source and the nature of language does this essay suggest?

4. Describe some particular experience that raises a large social question or shows the workings of large social forces. How might Baldwin help in the problem of connecting the particular and the general?

5. Baldwin writes, "There is a dreadful abyss between the streets of this village and the streets of the city in which I was born, between the children who shout *Neger!* today and those who shouted *Nigger!* yesterday—the abyss is experience, the American experience" (paragraph 14). There is no word in contemporary American public discourse that is more fraught than the "N-word." Write an essay that explores the contemporary news media's handling of this word. Focus your essay by analyzing one or more specific examples.

PATRICIA WILLIAMS *The Death of the Profane:*
The Rhetoric of Race and Rights

BUZZERS ARE BIG IN NEW YORK CITY. Favored particularly by smaller stores and boutiques, merchants
throughout the city have installed them as screen-
ing devices to reduce the incidence of robbery: if
the face at the door looks desirable, the buzzer is
pressed and the door is unlocked. If the face is that
of an undesirable, the door stays locked. Predictably, the issue of undesirability has revealed itself to be a racial determination. While controversial enough
at first, even civil-rights organizations backed down eventually in the face of
arguments that the buzzer system is a "necessary evil," that it is a "mere inconvenience" in comparison to the risks of being murdered, that suffering discrimination is not as bad as being assaulted, and that in any event it is not all
blacks who are barred, just "17-year-old black males wearing running shoes
and hooded sweatshirts."[1]

The installation of these buzzers happened swiftly in New York; stores that
had always had their doors wide open suddenly became exclusive or received
people by appointment only. I discovered them and their meaning one Saturday in 1986. I was shopping in Soho and saw in a store window a sweater that
I wanted to buy for my mother. I pressed my round brown face to the window
and my finger to the buzzer, seeking admittance. A narrow-eyed, white teenager wearing running shoes and feasting on bubble gum glared out, evaluating
me for signs that would pit me against the limits of his social understanding.
After about five seconds, he mouthed "We're closed," and blew pink rubber at
me. It was two Saturdays before Christmas, at one o'clock in the afternoon;
there were several white people in the store who appeared to be shopping for
things for *their* mothers.

I was enraged. At that moment I literally wanted to break all the windows
of the store and *take* lots of sweaters for my mother. In the flicker of his judg-
mental gray eyes, that saleschild had transformed my brightly sentimental, joy-
to-the-world, pre-Christmas spree to a shambles. He snuffed my sense of
humanitarian catholicity, and there was nothing I could do to snuff his, without
making a spectacle of myself.

I am still struck by the structure of power that drove me into such a blizzard
of rage. There was almost nothing I could do, short of physically intruding

A chapter in Patricia Williams's book The Alchemy of Race and Rights *(1991), which
probes the roots of racism through anecdotes, personal accounts, and scholarly analysis. All
notes in the essay are the author's.*

1. "When 'By Appointment' Means Keep Out," *New York Times*, December 17, 1986, p.
B1. Letter to the Editor from Michael Levin and Marguerita Levin, *New York Times*,
January 11, 1987, p. E32.

upon him, that would humiliate him the way he humiliated me. No words, no gestures, no prejudices of my own would make a bit of difference to him; his refusal to let me into the store—it was Benetton's, whose colorfully punnish ad campaign is premised on wrapping every one of the world's peoples in its cottons and woolens—was an outward manifestation of his never having let someone like me into the realm of his reality. He had no compassion, no remorse, no reference to me; and no desire to acknowledge me even at the estranged level of arm's-length transactor. He saw me only as one who would take his money and therefore could not conceive that I was there to give him money.

5   In this weird ontological imbalance, I realized that buying something in that store was like bestowing a gift, the gift of my commerce, the lucre of my patronage. In the wake of my outrage, I wanted to take back the gift of appreciation that my peering in the window must have appeared to be. I wanted to take it back in the form of unappreciation, disrespect, defilement. I wanted to work so hard at wishing he could feel what I felt that he would never again mistake my hatred for some sort of plaintive wish to be included. I was quite willing to disenfranchise myself, in the heat of my need to revoke the flattery of my purchasing power. I was willing to boycott Benetton's, random white-owned businesses, and anyone who ever blew bubble gum in my face again.

My rage was admittedly diffuse, even self-destructive, but it was symmetrical. The perhaps loose-ended but utter propriety of that rage is no doubt lost not just to the young man who actually barred me, but to those who would appreciate my being barred only as an abstract precaution, who approve of those who would bar even as they deny that they would bar *me*.

The violence of my desire to burst into Benetton's is probably quite apparent. I often wonder if the violence, the exclusionary hatred, is equally apparent in the repeated public urgings that blacks understand the buzzer system by putting themselves in the shoes of white storeowners—that, in effect, blacks look into the mirror of frightened white faces for the reality of their undesirability; and that then blacks would "just as surely conclude that [they] would not let [themselves] in under similar circumstances."[2] (That some blacks might agree merely shows that some of us have learned too well the lessons of privatized intimacies of self-hatred and rationalized away the fullness of our public, participatory selves.)

On the same day I was barred from Benetton's, I went home and wrote the above impassioned account in my journal. On the day after that, I found I was still brooding, so I turned to a form of catharsis I have always found healing. I typed up as much of the story as I have just told, made a big poster of it, put a nice colorful border around it, and, after Benetton's was truly closed, stuck it to their big sweater-filled window. I exercised my first-amendment right to place my business with them right out in the street.

So that was the first telling of this story. The second telling came a few months later, for a symposium on Excluded Voices sponsored by a law review.

2. *New York Times*, January 11, 1987, p. E32.

I wrote an essay summing up my feelings about being excluded from Benetton's and analyzing "how the rhetoric of increased privatization, in response to racial issues, functions as the rationalizing agent of public unaccountability and, ultimately, irresponsibility." Weeks later, I received the first edit. From the first page to the last, my fury had been carefully cut out. My rushing, run-on rage had been reduced to simple declarative sentences. The active personal had been inverted in favor of the passive impersonal. My words were different; they spoke to me upside down. I was afraid to read too much of it at a time—meanings rose up at me oddly, stolen and strange.

A week and a half later, I received the second edit. All reference to Benetton's had been deleted because, according to the editors and the faculty adviser, it was defamatory; they feared harassment and liability; they said printing it would be irresponsible. I called them and offered to supply a footnote attesting to this as my personal experience at one particular location and of a buzzer system not limited to Benetton's; the editors told me that they were not in the habit of publishing things that were unverifiable. I could not but wonder, in this refusal even to let me file an affadavit, what it would take to make my experience verifiable. The testimony of an independent white bystander? (a requirement in fact imposed in U.S. Supreme Court holdings through the first part of the century[3]).

Two days *after* the piece was sent to press, I received copies of the final page proofs. All reference to my race had been eliminated because it was against "editorial policy" to permit descriptions of physiognomy. "I realize," wrote one editor, "that this was a very personal experience, but any reader will know what you must have looked like when standing at that window." In a telephone conversation to them, I ranted wildly about the significance of such an omission. "It's irrelevant," another editor explained in a voice gummy with soothing and patience; "It's nice and poetic," but it doesn't "advance the discussion of any principle . . . This is a law review, after all." Frustrated, I accused him of censorship; calmly he assured me it was not. "This is just a matter of style," he said with firmness and finality.

Ultimately I did convince the editors that mention of my race was central to the whole sense of the subsequent text; that my story became one of extreme paranoia without the information that I am black; or that it became one in which the reader had to fill in the gap by assumption, presumption, prejudgment, or prejudice. What was most interesting to me in this experience was how the blind application of principles of neutrality, through the device of omission, acted either to make me look crazy or to make the reader participate in old habits of cultural bias.

That was the second telling of my story. The third telling came last April, when I was invited to participate in a law-school conference on Equality and Difference. I retold my sad tale of exclusion from Soho's most glitzy boutique,

10

---

3. See generally *Blyew v. U.S.*, 80 U.S. 581 (1871), upholding a state's right to forbid blacks to testify against whites.

focusing in this version on the law-review editing process as a consequence of an ideology of style rooted in a social text of neutrality. I opined:

> Law and legal writing aspire to formalized, color-blind, liberal ideals. Neutrality is the standard for assuring these ideals; yet the adherence to it is often determined by reference to an aesthetic of uniformity, in which difference is simply omitted. For example, when segregation was eradicated from the American lexicon, its omission led many to actually believe that racism therefore no longer existed. Race-neutrality in law has become the presumed antidote for race bias in real life. With the entrenchment of the notion of race-neutrality came attacks on the concept of affirmative action and the rise of reverse discrimination suits. Blacks, for so many generations deprived of jobs based on the color of our skin, are now told that we ought to find it demeaning to be hired, based on the color of our skin. Such is the silliness of simplistic either-or inversions as remedies to complex problems.
>
> What is truly demeaning in this era of double-speak-no-evil is going on interviews and not getting hired because someone doesn't think we'll be comfortable. It is demeaning not to get promoted because we're judged "too weak," then putting in a lot of energy the next time and getting fired because we're "too strong." It is demeaning to be told what we find demeaning. It is very demeaning to stand on street corners unemployed and begging. It is downright demeaning to have to explain why we haven't been employed for months and then watch the job go to someone who is "more experienced." It is outrageously demeaning that none of this can be called racism, even if it happens only to, or to large numbers of, black people; as long as it's done with a smile, a handshake and a shrug; as long as the phantom-word "race" is never used.
>
> The image of race as a phantom-word came to me after I moved into my late godmother's home. In an attempt to make it my own, I cleared the bedroom for painting. The following morning the room asserted itself, came rushing and raging at me through the emptiness, exactly as it had been for twenty-five years. One day filled with profuse and overwhelming complexity, the next day filled with persistently recurring memories. The shape of the past came to haunt me, the shape of the emptiness confronted me each time I was about to enter the room. The force of its spirit still drifts like an odor throughout the house.
>
> The power of that room, I have thought since, is very like the power of racism as status quo: it is deep, angry, eradicated from view, but strong enough to make everyone who enters the room walk around the bed that isn't there, avoiding the phantom as they did the substance, for fear of bodily harm. They do not even know they are avoiding; they defer to the unseen shapes of things with subtle responsiveness, guided by an impulsive awareness of nothingness, and the deep knowledge and denial of witchcraft at work.
>
> The phantom room is to me symbolic of the emptiness of formal equal opportunity, particularly as propounded by President Reagan, the Reagan Civil Rights Commission and the Reagan Supreme Court. Blindly formalized constructions of equal opportunity are the creation of a space that is filled in by a meandering stream of unguided hopes, dreams, fantasies, fears, recollections. They are the presence of the past in imaginary, imagistic form—the phantom-roomed exile of our longing.
>
> It is thus that I strongly believe in the efficacy of programs and paradigms like affirmative action. Blacks are the objects of a constitutional omission which has been incorporated into a theory of neutrality. It is thus that omission is really a form of expression, as oxymoronic as that sounds: racial omission is a literal part of original intent; it is the fixed, reiterated prophecy of the Founding Fathers. It is thus that affirmative action is an affirma-

tion; the affirmative act of hiring—or hearing—blacks is a recognition of individuality that re-places blacks as a social statistic, that is profoundly interconnective to the fate of blacks and whites either as sub-groups or as one group. In this sense, affirmative action is as mystical and beyond-the-self as an initiation ceremony. It is an act of verification and of vision. It is an act of social as well as professional responsibility.

The following morning I opened the local newspaper, to find that the event of my speech had commanded two columns on the front page of the Metro section. I quote only the opening lines: "Affirmative action promotes prejudice by denying the status of women and blacks, instead of affirming them as its name suggests. So said New York City attorney Patricia Williams to an audience Wednesday."[4]

I clipped out the article and put it in my journal. In the margin there is a note   15
to myself: eventually, it says, I should try to pull all these threads together into yet another law-review article. The problem, of course, will be that in the hierarchy of law-review citation, the article in the newspaper will have more authoritative weight about me, as a so-called "primary resource," than I will have; it will take precedence over my own citation of the unverifiable testimony of my speech.

I have used the Benetton's story a lot, in speaking engagements at various schools. I tell it whenever I am too tired to whip up an original speech from scratch. Here are some of the questions I have been asked in the wake of its telling:

Am I not privileging a racial perspective, by considering only the black point of view? Don't I have an obligation to include the "salesman's side" of the story?

Am I not putting the salesman on trial and finding him guilty of racism without giving him a chance to respond to or cross-examine me?

Am I not using the store window as a "metaphorical fence" against the potential of his explanation in order to represent my side as "authentic"?

How can I be sure I'm right?   20

What makes my experience the real black one anyway?

Isn't it possible that another black person would disagree with my experience? If so, doesn't that render my story too unempirical and subjective to pay any attention to?

Always a major objection is to my having put the poster on Benetton's window. As one law professor put it: "It's one thing to publish this in a law review, where no one can take it personally, but it's another thing altogether to put your own interpretation right out there, just like that, uncontested, I mean, with nothing to counter it."*

4. "Attorney Says Affirmative Action Denies Racism, Sexism," *Dominion Post* (Morgantown, West Virginia), April 8, 1988, p. B1.

* At the end of her essay, Williams added these observations. "These questions put me on trial—an imaginary trial where it is I who have the burden of proof—and proof being

MLA CITATION

Williams, Patricia. "The Death of the Profane: The Rhetoric of Race and Rights." 1991. *The Norton Reader: An Anthology of Nonfiction.* Ed. Melissa A. Goldthwaite et al. 14th ed. New York: Norton, 2016. 261–65. Print.

QUESTIONS

1. Patricia Williams's essay is about how the "objective," "neutral" forms writing often takes can drain away the significance of a particular person's story. Can you find examples of this phenomenon in other writing you read? Or can you find examples of it on TV or radio talk shows, for instance?

2. How does Williams move from the Benetton story to her larger point?

3. How would you characterize the tone of Williams's essay? Does any of her original rage remain?

4. What do you think of Williams's posting her reaction on the Benetton window? Write your opinion of the function and effectiveness of this action.

---

nothing less than the testimony of the salesman actually confessing yes yes I am a racist. These questions question my own ability to know, to assess, to be objective. And of course, since anything that happens to me is inherently subjective, they take away my power to know what happens to me in the world. Others, by this standard, will always know better than I. And my insistence on recounting stories from my own perspective will be treated as presumption, slander, paranoid hallucination, or just plain lies.

"Recently I got an urgent call from Thomas Grey of Stanford Law School. He had used this piece in his jurisprudence class, and a rumor got started that the Benetton's story wasn't true, that I had made it up, that it was a fantasy, a lie that was probably the product of a diseased mind trying to make all white people feel guilty. At this point I realized it almost didn't make any difference whether I was telling the truth or not—that the greater issue I had to face was the overwhelming weight of a disbelief that goes beyond mere disinclination to believe and becomes active suppression of anything I might have to say. The greater problem is a powerfully oppressive mechanism for denial of black self-knowledge and expression. And this denial cannot be separated from the simultaneously pathological willingness to believe certain things about blacks—not to believe them, but things about them.

"When students in Grey's class believed and then claimed that I had made it all up, they put me in a position like that of Tawana Brawley [a black woman who falsely claimed she was abducted and raped by white men (eds.)]. I mean that specifically: the social consequence of concluding that we are liars operates as a kind of public absolution of racism—the conclusion is not merely that we are troubled or that I am eccentric, but that we, as liars, are the norm. Therefore, the nonbelievers can believe, things of this sort really don't happen (even in the face of statistics to the contrary). Racism or rape is all a big fantasy concocted by troublesome minorities and women. It is interesting to recall the outcry in every national medium, from the *New York Post* to the *Times* to the major networks, in the wake of the Brawley case: who will ever again believe a black woman who cries rape by a white man? Now shift the frame a bit, and imagine a white male facing a consensus that he lied. Would there be a difference? Consider Charles Stuart, for example, the white Bostonian who accused a black man of murdering his pregnant wife and whose brother later alleged that in fact the brothers had conspired to murder her. Most people and the media not only did not claim but actively resisted believing that Stuart represented any kind of 'white male' norm. Instead he was written off as a troubled weirdo, a deviant—again even in the face of spousal-abuse statistics to the contrary. There was not a story I could find that carried on about 'who will ever believe' the next white man who cries murder."

BRENT STAPLES   *Black Men and Public Space*

M Y FIRST VICTIM WAS A WOMAN—white, well dressed, probably in her early twenties. I came upon her late one evening on a deserted street in Hyde Park, a relatively affluent neighborhood in an otherwise mean, impoverished section of Chicago. As I swung onto the avenue behind her, there seemed to be a discreet, uninflammatory distance between us. Not so. She cast back a worried glance. To her, the youngish black man—a broad six feet two inches with a beard and billowing hair, both hands shoved into the pockets of a bulky military jacket—seemed menacingly close. After a few more quick glimpses, she picked up her pace and was soon running in earnest. Within seconds she disappeared into a cross street.

That was more than a decade ago, I was twenty-two years old, a graduate student newly arrived at the University of Chicago. It was in the echo of that terrified woman's footfalls that I first began to know the unwieldy inheritance I'd come into—the ability to alter public space in ugly ways. It was clear that she thought herself the quarry of a mugger, a rapist, or worse. Suffering a bout of insomnia, however, I was stalking sleep, not defenseless wayfarers. As a softy who is scarcely able to take a knife to a raw chicken—let alone hold one to a person's throat—I was surprised, embarrassed, and dismayed all at once. Her flight made me feel like an accomplice in tyranny. It also made it clear that I was indistinguishable from the muggers who occasionally seeped into the area from the surrounding ghetto. That first encounter, and those that followed, signified that a vast, unnerving gulf lay between nighttime pedestrians—particularly women—and me. And I soon gathered that being perceived as dangerous is a hazard in itself. I only needed to turn a corner into a dicey situation, or crowd some frightened, armed person in a foyer somewhere, or make an errant move after being pulled over by a policeman. Where fear and weapons meet—and they often do in urban America—there is always the possibility of death.

In that first year, my first away from my hometown, I was to become thoroughly familiar with the language of fear. At dark, shadowy intersections, I could cross in front of a car stopped at a traffic light and elicit the *thunk, thunk, thunk, thunk* of the driver—black, white, male, or female—hammering down the door locks. On less traveled streets after dark, I grew accustomed to but never comfortable with people crossing to the other side of the street rather than pass me. Then there were the standard unpleasantries with policemen, doormen, bouncers, cabdrivers, and others whose business it is to screen out troublesome individuals *before* there is any nastiness.

Originally appeared in Harper's Magazine *(1986), an American monthly covering politics, society, culture, and the environment. The essay was later incorporated into* Parallel Time: Growing Up in Black and White *(1994), a memoir of Brent Staples's formative years in Chester, Pennsylvania, that chronicles his escape from poverty and crime.*

I moved to New York nearly two years ago and I have remained an avid night walker. In central Manhattan, the near-constant crowd cover minimizes tense one-on-one street encounters. Elsewhere—in SoHo, for example, where sidewalks are narrow and tightly spaced buildings shut out the sky—things can get very taut indeed.

5   After dark, on the warrenlike streets of Brooklyn where I live, I often see women who fear the worst from me. They seem to have set their faces on neutral, and with their purse straps strung across their chests bandolier-style, they forge ahead as though bracing themselves against being tackled. I understand, of course, that the danger they perceive is not a hallucination. Women are particularly vulnerable to street violence, and young black males are drastically overrepresented among the perpetrators of that violence. Yet these truths are no solace against the kind of alienation that comes of being ever the suspect, a fearsome entity with whom pedestrians avoid making eye contact.

It is not altogether clear to me how I reached the ripe old age of twenty-two without being conscious of the lethality nighttime pedestrians attributed to me. Perhaps it was because in Chester, Pennsylvania, the small, angry industrial town where I came of age in the 1960s, I was scarcely noticeable against a backdrop of gang warfare, street knifings, and murders. I grew up one of the good boys, had perhaps a half-dozen fistfights. In retrospect, my shyness of combat has clear sources.

As a boy, I saw countless tough guys locked away; I have since buried several, too. They were babies, really—a teenage cousin, a brother of twenty-two, a childhood friend in his mid-twenties—all gone down in episodes of bravado played out in the streets. I came to doubt the virtues of intimidation early on. I chose, perhaps unconsciously, to remain a shadow—timid, but a survivor.

The fearsomeness mistakenly attributed to me in public places often has a perilous flavor. The most frightening of these confusions occurred in the late 1970s and early 1980s, when I worked as a journalist in Chicago. One day, rushing into the office of a magazine I was writing for with a deadline story in hand, I was mistaken for a burglar. The office manager called security and, with an ad hoc[1] posse, pursued me through the labyrinthine halls, nearly to my editor's door. I had no way of proving who I was. I could only move briskly toward the company of someone who knew me.

Another time I was on assignment for a local paper and killing time before an interview. I entered a jewelry store on the city's affluent Near North Side. The proprietor excused herself and returned with an enormous red Doberman pinscher straining at the end of a leash. She stood, the dog extended toward me, silent to my questions, her eyes bulging nearly out of her head. I took a cursory look around, nodded, and bade her good night.

10   Relatively speaking, however, I never fared as badly as another black male journalist. He went to nearby Waukegan, Illinois, a couple of summers ago to work on a story about a murderer who was born there. Mistaking the reporter for the killer, police officers hauled him from his car at gunpoint and but for

---

1. For a particular purpose; improvised.

his press credentials would probably have tried to book him. Such episodes are not uncommon. Black men trade tales like this all the time.

Over the years, I learned to smother the rage I felt at so often being taken for a criminal. Not to do so would surely have led to madness. I now take precautions to make myself less threatening. I move about with care, particularly late in the evening. I give a wide berth to nervous people on subway platforms during the wee hours, particularly when I have exchanged business clothes for jeans. If I happen to be entering a building behind some people who appear skittish, I may walk by, letting them clear the lobby before I return, so as not to seem to be following them. I have been calm and extremely congenial on those rare occasions when I've been pulled over by the police.

And on late-evening constitutionals I employ what has proved to be an excellent tension-reducing measure: I whistle melodies from Beethoven and Vivaldi and the more popular classical composers. Even steely New Yorkers hunching toward nighttime destinations seem to relax, and occasionally they even join in the tune. Virtually everybody seems to sense that a mugger wouldn't be warbling bright, sunny selections from Vivaldi's *Four Seasons*.[2] It is my equivalent of the cowbell that hikers wear when they know they are in bear country.

2. Work (c. 1720) by composer Antonio Vivaldi (1678–1741), celebrating the seasons.

MLA CITATION

Staples, Brent. "Black Men and Public Space." 1986. *The Norton Reader: An Anthology of Nonfiction*. Ed. Melissa A. Goldthwaite et al. 14th ed. New York: Norton, 2016. 267–69. Print.

QUESTIONS

1. Brent Staples writes of situations rightly perceived as threatening and of situations misperceived as threatening. Give specific instances of each and tell how they are related.

2. Staples's essay contains a mixture of rage and humor. Does this mix distract from or contribute to the seriousness of the matter? Explain your answer.

3. Staples, like Patricia Williams in "The Death of the Profane" (pp. 261–65), writes about his "rage" at being misperceived because of his race. Compare their reactions and responses: what do they have in common and where do they differ?

4. Write an essay reflecting on a time you were wrongly perceived because someone associated you with a certain class or group of people.

DEBRA DICKERSON *Who Shot Johnny?*

IVEN MY LEVEL OF POLITICAL AWARENESS, it was inevitable that I would come to view the everyday events of my life through the prism of politics and the national discourse. I read *The Washington Post, The New Republic, The New Yorker, Harper's, The Atlantic Monthly, The Nation, National Review, Black Enterprise* and *Essence* and wrote a weekly column for the *Harvard Law School Record* during my three years just ended there. I do this because I know that those of us who are not well-fed white guys in suits must not yield the debate to them, however well-intentioned or well-informed they may be. Accordingly, I am unrepentant and vocal about having gained admittance to Harvard through affirmative action; I am a feminist, stoic about my marriage chances as a well-educated, 36-year-old black woman who won't pretend to need help taking care of herself. My strength flags, though, in the face of the latest role assigned to my family in the national drama. On July 27, 1995, my 16-year-old nephew was shot and paralyzed.

Talking with friends in front of his home, Johnny saw a car he thought he recognized. He waved boisterously—his trademark—throwing both arms in the air in a full-bodied, hip-hop Y. When he got no response, he and his friends sauntered down the walk to join a group loitering in front of an apartment building. The car followed. The driver got out, brandished a revolver and fired into the air. Everyone scattered. Then he took aim and shot my running nephew in the back.

Johnny never lost consciousness. He lay in the road, trying to understand what had happened to him, why he couldn't get up. Emotionlessly, he told the story again and again on demand, remaining apologetically firm against all demands to divulge the missing details that would make sense of the shooting but obviously cast him in a bad light. Being black, male and shot, he must, apparently, be gang- or drug-involved. Probably both. Witnesses corroborate his version of events.

Nearly six months have passed since that phone call in the night and my nightmarish, headlong drive from Boston to Charlotte. After twenty hours behind the wheel, I arrived haggard enough to reduce my mother to fresh tears and to find my nephew reassuring well-wishers with an eerie sangfroid.[1]

5   I take the day shift in his hospital room; his mother and grandmother, a clerk and cafeteria worker, respectively, alternate nights there on a cot. They don their uniforms the next day, gaunt after hours spent listening to Johnny moan in his sleep. How often must his subconscious replay those events and

Published in the New Republic *(1996), a Washington-based journal of politics and cultural criticism. This essay helped inaugurate Debra Dickerson's career as a writer and commentator on issues of race and society.*

1. French for "cold blood," meaning composure and self-assurance in the face of difficulty.

curse its host for saying hello without permission, for being carefree and young while a would-be murderer hefted the weight of his uselessness and failure like Jacob Marley's chains?[2] How often must he watch himself lying stubbornly immobile on the pavement of his nightmares while the sound of running feet syncopate his attacker's taunts?

I spend these days beating him at gin rummy and Scrabble, holding a basin while he coughs up phlegm and crying in the corridor while he catheterizes himself. There are children here much worse off than he. I should be grateful. The doctors can't, or won't, say whether he'll walk again.

I am at once repulsed and fascinated by the bullet, which remains lodged in his spine (having done all the damage it can do, the doctors say). The wound is undramatic—small, neat and perfectly centered—an impossibly pink pit surrounded by an otherwise undisturbed expanse of mahogany. Johnny has asked me several times to describe it but politely declines to look in the mirror I hold for him.

Here on the pediatric rehab ward, Johnny speaks little, never cries, never complains, works diligently to become independent. He does whatever he is told; if two hours remain until the next pain pill, he waits quietly. Eyes bloodshot, hands gripping the bed rails. During the week of his intravenous feeding when he was tormented by the primal need to masticate, he never asked for food. He just listened while we counted down the days for him and planned his favorite meals. Now required to dress himself unassisted, he does so without demur, rolling himself back and forth valiantly on the bed and shivering afterwards, exhausted. He "ma'am"s and "sir"s everyone politely. Before his "accident," a simple request to take out the trash could provoke a firestorm of teenage attitude. We, the women who have raised him, have changed as well; we've finally come to appreciate those boxer-baring, oversized pants we used to hate—it would be much more difficult to fit properly sized pants over his diaper.

He spends a lot of time tethered to rap music still loud enough to break my concentration as I read my many magazines. I hear him try to soundlessly mouth the obligatory "mothafuckers" overlaying the funereal dirge of the music tracks. I do not normally tolerate disrespectful music in my or my mother's presence, but if it distracts him now . . .

"Johnny," I ask later, "do you still like gangster rap?" During the long pause   10
I hear him think loudly, *I'm paralyzed Auntie, not stupid.* "I mostly just listen to hip hop," he says evasively into his *Sports Illustrated.*

Miserable though it is, time passes quickly here. We always seem to be jerking awake in our chairs just in time for the next pill, his every-other-night bowel program, the doctor's rounds. Harvard feels a galaxy away—the world revolves around Family Members Living With Spinal Cord Injury class, Johnny's urine output and strategizing with my sister to find affordable, accessible housing.

2. Marley, a character in Charles Dickens's *A Christmas Carol* (1843), appears as a ghost bound by chains.

There is always another long-distance uncle in need of an update, another church member wanting to pray with us or Johnny's little brother in need of some attention.

We Dickerson women are so constant a presence the ward nurses and cleaning staff call us by name and join us for cafeteria meals and cigarette breaks. At Johnny's birthday pizza party, they crack jokes and make fun of each other's husbands (there are no men here). I pass slices around and try not to think, "17 with a bullet."

Oddly, we feel little curiosity or specific anger toward the man who shot him. We have to remind ourselves to check in with the police. Even so, it feels pro forma, like sending in those $2 rebate forms that come with new pantyhose: you know your request will fall into a deep, dark hole somewhere but, still, it's your duty to try. We push for an arrest because we owe it to Johnny and to ourselves as citizens. We don't think about it otherwise—our low expectations are too ingrained. A Harvard aunt notwithstanding, for people like Johnny, Marvin Gaye[3] was right that only three things are sure: taxes, death and trouble. At least it wasn't the second.

We rarely wonder about or discuss the brother who shot him because we already know everything about him. When the call came, my first thought was the same one I'd had when I'd heard about Rosa Parks's beating:[4] a brother did it. A non-job-having, middle-of-the-day malt-liquor-drinking, crotch-clutching, loud-talking brother with many neglected children born of many forgotten women. He lives in his mother's basement with furniture rented at an astronomical interest rate, the exact amount of which he does not know. He has a car phone, an $80 monthly cable bill and every possible phone feature but no savings. He steals Social Security numbers from unsuspecting relatives and assumes their identities to acquire large TV sets for which he will never pay. On the slim chance that he is brought to justice, he will have a colorful criminal history and no coherent explanation to offer for this act. His family will raucously defend him and cry cover-up. Some liberal lawyer just like me will help him plea bargain his way to yet another short stay in a prison pesthouse that will serve only to add another layer to the brother's sociopathology and formless, mindless nihilism. We know him. We've known and feared him all our lives.

15   As a teenager, he called, "Hey, baby, gimme somma that boodie!" at us from car windows. Indignant at our lack of response, he followed up with, "Fuck you, then, 'ho!" He called me a "white-boy lovin' nigger bitch oreo" for being in the gifted program and loving it. At 27, he got my 17-year-old sister pregnant with Johnny and lost interest without ever informing her that he was married. He snatched my widowed mother's purse as she waited in pre-dawn darkness for the bus to work and then broke into our house while she soldered on an assembly line. He chased all the small entrepreneurs from our neighborhood

3. Soul singer (1939–1984) shot to death in an altercation with his father.
4. Elderly 1950s civil rights pioneer (1913–2005), who was the victim of a beating in 1994.

with his violent thievery, and put bars on our windows. He kept us from sitting on our own front porch after dark and laid the foundation for our periodic bouts of self-hating anger and racial embarrassment. He made our neighborhood a ghetto. He is the poster fool behind the maddening community knowledge that there are still some black mothers who raise their daughters but merely love their sons. He and his cancerous carbon copies eclipse the vast majority of us who are not sociopaths and render us invisible. He is the Siamese twin who has died but cannot be separated from his living, vibrant sibling; which of us must attract more notice? We despise and disown this anomalous loser but, for many, he *is* black America. We know him, we know that he is outside the fold, and we know that he will only get worse. What we didn't know is that, because of him, my little sister would one day be the latest hysterical black mother wailing over a fallen child on TV.

Alone, lying in the road bleeding and paralyzed but hideously conscious, Johnny had lain helpless as he watched his would-be murderer come to stand over him and offer this prophecy: "Betch'ou won't be doin' nomo' wavin', motha'fucker."

Fuck you, asshole. He's fine from the waist up. You just can't do anything right, can you?

MLA CITATION

Dickerson, Debra. "Who Shot Johnny?" 1996. *The Norton Reader: An Anthology of Nonfiction.* Ed. Melissa A. Goldthwaite et al. 14th ed. New York: Norton, 2016. 270–73. Print.

QUESTIONS

1. What purpose does the first paragraph of this essay serve? Do you think Debra Dickerson's essay would be more or less effective if it began simply with the sentence "On July 27, 1995, my 16-year-old nephew was shot and paralyzed"?

2. Dickerson feels—and expresses—anger throughout this essay. How? Against what or whom?

3. Why does Dickerson use the term "brother" in the final paragraphs? How does this composite characterization work? How does it answer the question "Who shot Johnny?"

4. Both Brent Staples (pp. 267–69) and Dickerson write about stereotypes of African American men. Staples writes as an African American man judged according to these stereotypes, and Dickerson writes as an African American woman and feminist coming to terms with her nephew's shooting. Write an essay about the different ways the authors describe these stereotypes, or choose another point of comparison to write about.

FOOD

MARION NESTLE   *Utopian Dream: A New Farm Bill*

I N THE FALL OF 2011, I taught a graduate food studies course at New York University devoted to the farm bill, a massive and massively opaque piece of legislation passed most recently in 2008 and up for renewal in 2012. The farm bill supports farmers, of course, but also specifies how the United States deals with such matters as conservation, forestry, energy policy, organic food production, international food aid, and domestic food assistance. My students came from programs in nutrition, food studies, public health, public policy, and law, all united in the belief that a smaller scale, more regionalized, and more sustainable food system would be healthier for people and the planet.

In the first class meeting, I asked students to suggest what an ideal farm bill should do. Their answers covered the territory: ensure enough food for the population at an affordable price; produce a surplus for international trade and aid; provide farmers with a sufficient income; protect farmers against the vagaries of weather and volatile markets; promote regional, seasonal, organic, and sustainable food production; conserve soil, land, and forest; protect water and air quality, natural resources, and wildlife; raise farm animals humanely; and provide farm workers with a living wage and decent working conditions. Overall, they advocated aligning agricultural policy with nutrition, health, and environmental policy—a tall order by any standard, but especially so given current political and economic realities.

WHAT'S WRONG WITH THE CURRENT FARM BILL?

Plenty. Beyond providing an abundance of inexpensive food, the current farm bill addresses practically none of the other goals. It favors Big Agriculture over small; pesticides, fertilizers, and genetically modified crops over those raised organically and sustainably; and some regions of the country—notably the South and Midwest—over others. It supports commodity crops grown for animal feed but considers fruits and vegetables to be "specialty" crops deserving only token support. It provides incentives leading to crop overproduction, with enormous consequences for health.

Published in Dissent (2012), *a political journal that includes social and cultural commentary on both American and European policy and politics. Marion Nestle, a professor of nutrition, food studies, and public health at New York University, critiques the 2008 farm bill, which was up for renewal in 2012 and signed into law in 2014.*

The bill does not require farmers to engage in conservation or safety practices (farms are exempt from having to comply with environmental or employment standards). It encourages production of feed crops for ethanol. In part because Congress insisted that gasoline must contain ethanol, 40 percent of U.S. feed corn was grown for that purpose in 2011, a well-documented cause of higher world food prices. Because the bill subsidizes production, it gets the United States in trouble with international trading partners, and hurts farmers in developing countries by undercutting their prices. Taken as a whole, the farm bill is profoundly undemocratic. It is so big and so complex that nobody in Congress or anywhere else can grasp its entirety, making it especially vulnerable to influence by lobbyists for special interests.

Although the farm bill started out in the Great Depression of the 1930s as   5
a collection of emergency measures to protect the income of farmers—all small landholders by today's standards—recipients soon grew dependent on support programs and began to view them as entitlements. Perceived entitlements became incentives for making farms larger; increasingly dependent on pesticide, herbicide, and fertilizer "inputs"; and exploitative of natural and human resources. Big farms drove out small, while technological advances increased production. These trends were institutionalized by cozy relationships among large agricultural producers, farm-state members of congressional agricultural committees, and a Department of Agriculture (USDA) explicitly committed to promoting commodity production.

These players were not, however, sitting around conference tables to create agricultural policies to further national goals. Instead, they used the bill as a way to obtain earmarks—programs that would benefit specific interest groups. It is now a 663-page piece of legislation with a table of contents that alone takes up 14 pages. As the chief vehicle of agricultural policy in the United States, it reflects no overriding goals or philosophy. It is simply a collection of hundreds of largely disconnected programs dispensing public benefits to one group or another, each with its own dedicated constituency and lobbyists. The most controversial farm bill programs benefit only a few basic food commodities—corn, soybeans, wheat, rice, cotton, sugar, and dairy. But lesser-known provisions help much smaller industries such as asparagus, honey, or Hass avocados, although at tiny fractions of the size of commodity payments.

The bill organizes its programs into fifteen "titles" dealing with its various purposes. I once tried to list every program included in each title, but soon gave up. The bill's size, scope, and level of detail are mind-numbing. It can only be understood one program at a time. Hence, lobbyists.

The elephant in the farm bill—its biggest program by far and accounting for nearly 85 percent of the funding—is SNAP, the Supplemental Nutrition Assistance Program (formerly known as food stamps). In 2011, as a result of the declining economy and high unemployment, SNAP benefits grew to cover forty-six million Americans at a cost of $72 billion. In contrast, commodity subsidies cost "only" $8 billion; crop insurance $4.5 billion; and conservation about $5 billion. The amounts expended on the hundreds of other programs covered by the bill are trivial in comparison, millions, not billions—mere rounding errors.

What is SNAP doing in the farm bill? Politics makes strange bedfellows, and SNAP exemplifies logrolling politics in action. By the late 1970s, consolidation of farms had reduced the political power of agricultural states. To continue farm subsidies, representatives from agricultural states needed votes from legislators representing states with large, low-income urban populations. And those legislators needed votes from agricultural states to pass food assistance bills. They traded votes in an unholy alliance that pleased Big Agriculture as well as advocates for the poor. Neither group wants the system changed.

HEALTH IMPLICATIONS

10   The consequences of obesity—higher risks for heart disease, type 2 diabetes, certain cancers, and other chronic conditions—are the most important health problems facing Americans today. To maintain weight or to prevent excessive gain, federal dietary guidelines advise consumption of diets rich in vegetables and fruits. The 2008 farm bill introduced a horticulture and organic title, but aside from a farmers' market promotion program and some smaller marketing programs, does little to encourage vegetable and fruit production or to subsidize their costs to consumers. If anything, the farm bill encourages weight gain by subsidizing commodity crops that constitute the basic cheap caloric ingredients used in processed foods—soy oil and corn sweeteners, for example—and by explicitly forbidding crop producers from growing fruits and vegetables.

Neither human nature nor genetics have changed in the last thirty years, meaning that widespread obesity must be understood as collateral damage resulting from changes in agricultural, economic, and regulatory policy in the 1970s and early 1980s. These created today's "eat more" food environment, one in which it has become socially acceptable for food to be ubiquitous, eaten frequently, and in large portions.

For more than seventy years, from the early 1900s to the early 1980s, daily calorie availability remained relatively constant at about 3,200 per person. By the year 2000, however, available calories had increased to 3,900 per person per day, roughly twice the average need. People were not necessarily eating 700 more daily calories, as many were undoubtedly wasted. But the food containing those extra calories needed to be sold, thereby creating a marketing challenge for the food industry.

Why more calories became available after 1980 is a matter of some conjecture, but I believe the evidence points to three seemingly remote events that occurred at about that time: agriculture policies favoring overproduction, the onset of the shareholder value movement, and the deregulatory policies of the Reagan era.

In 1973 and 1977, Congress passed laws reversing long-standing farm policies aimed at protecting prices by limiting production. Subsidies increased in proportion to amounts grown, encouraging creation of larger and more productive farms. Indeed, production increased, and so did calories in the food supply and competition in the food industry. Companies were forced to find innovative ways to sell food products in an overabundant food economy.

Further increasing competition was the advent of the shareholder value   15
movement to force corporations to produce more immediate and higher returns
on investment. The start of the movement is often attributed to a 1981 speech
given by Jack Welch, then head of General Electric, in which he insisted that
corporations owed shareholders the benefits of faster growth and higher profit
margins. The movement caught on quickly, and Wall Street soon began to press
companies to report growth in profits every quarter. Food companies, already
selling products in an overabundant marketplace, now also had to grow their
profits—and constantly.

Companies got some help when Ronald Reagan was elected president in
1980 on a platform of corporate deregulation. Reagan-era deregulatory policies removed limits on television marketing of food products to children and
on health claims on food packages. Companies now had much more flexibility
in advertising their products.

Together, these factors led food companies to consolidate, become larger,
seek new markets, and find creative ways to expand sales in existing markets.
The collateral result was a changed society. Today, in contrast to the early 1980s,
it is socially acceptable to eat in places never before meant as restaurants, at
any time of day, and in increasingly large amounts—all factors that encourage
greater calorie intake. Food is now available in places never seen before: book-
stores, libraries, and stores primarily selling drugs and cosmetics, gasoline,
office supplies, furniture, and clothing.

As a result of the increased supply of food, prices dropped. It became relatively
inexpensive to eat outside the home, especially at fast-food restaurants, and
such places proliferated. Food prepared outside the home tends to be higher in
calories, fast food especially so. It's not that people necessarily began to eat
worse diets. They were just eating more food in general and, therefore, gaining
weight. This happened with children, too. National food consumption surveys
indicate that children get more of their daily calories from fast-food outlets than
they do from schools, and that fast food is the largest contributor to the calories they consume outside the home.

To increase sales, companies promoted snacking. The low cost of basic food
commodities allowed them to produce new snack products—twenty thousand
or so a year, nearly half candies, gum, chips, and sodas. It became *normal* for
children to regularly consume fast foods, snacks, and sodas. An astonishing
40 percent of the calories in the diets of children and adolescents now derive
from such foods. In adults and children, the habitual consumption of sodas and
snacks is associated with increases in calorie intake and body weight.

Food quantity is the critical issue in weight gain. Once foods became rela-   20
tively inexpensive in comparison to the cost of rent or labor, companies could
offer foods and beverages in larger sizes at favorable prices as a means to attract
bargain-conscious customers. Larger portions have more calories. But they also
encourage people to eat more and to underestimate the number of calories consumed. The well-documented increase in portion sizes since 1980 is by itself
sufficient to explain rising levels of obesity.

Food prices are also a major factor in food choice. It is difficult to argue against low prices and I won't—except to note that the current industrialized food system aims at producing food as cheaply as possible, externalizing the real costs to the environment and to human health. Prices, too, are a matter of policy. In the United States, the indexed price of sodas and snack foods has declined since 1980, but that of fruits and vegetables has increased by as much as 40 percent. The farm bill subsidizes animal feed and the ingredients in sodas and snack foods; it does not subsidize fruits and vegetables. How changes in food prices brought on by growth of crops for biofuels will affect health is as yet unknown but unlikely to be beneficial.

The deregulation of marketing also contributes to current obesity levels. Food companies spend billions of dollars a year to encourage people to buy their products, but foods marketed as "healthy"—whether or not they are— particularly encourage greater consumption. Federal agencies attempting to regulate food marketing, especially to children, have been blocked at every turn by food industries dependent on highly profitable "junk" foods for sales. Although food companies argue that body weight is a matter of personal choice, the power of today's overabundant, ubiquitous, and aggressively marketed food environment to promote greater calorie intake is enough to overcome biological controls over eating behavior. Even educated and relatively wealthy consumers have trouble dealing with this "eat more" environment.

FIXING THE FARM BILL

What could agriculture policies do to improve health now and in the future? Also plenty. When I first started teaching nutrition in the mid-1970s, my classes already included readings on the need to reform agricultural policy. Since then, one administration after another has tried to eliminate the most egregious subsidies (like those to landowners who don't farm) but failed when confronted with early primaries in Iowa. Defenders of the farm bill argue that the present system works well to ensure productivity, global competitiveness, and food security. Tinkering with the bill, they claim, will make little difference and could do harm. I disagree. The farm bill needs more than tinkering. It needs a major overhaul. My vision for the farm bill would restructure it to go beyond feeding people at the lowest possible cost to achieve several utopian goals:

Support farmers: The American Enterprise Institute and other conservative groups argue that farming is a business like any other and deserves no special protections. My NYU class thought otherwise. Food is essential for life, and government's role must be to ensure adequate food for people at an affordable price. Farmers deserve some help dealing with financial and climate risks, and some need it more than others. The farm bill should especially support more sustainable smaller-scale farming methods. And such programs should be available to farmers of fruits and vegetables and designed to encourage beginning farmers to grow specialty crops.

25   *Support the environment*: The farm bill should require recipients of benefits to engage in environmentally sound production and conservation practices.

Production agriculture accounts for a significant fraction—10 percent to 20 percent—of greenhouse gas emissions. Sustainable farming methods have been shown to reduce emissions, return valuable nutrients to soil, and reduce the need for polluting pesticides and fertilizers, with only marginal losses in productivity.

Support human health: The United States does not currently grow enough fruits and vegetables to meet minimal dietary recommendations. The 2008 farm bill explicitly prohibits farms receiving support payments from growing fruits and vegetables. Instead, the bill should provide incentives for growing specialty crops. Support payments should be linked to requirements for farm-based safety procedures that prevent contamination with pathogens and pesticides.

Support farm workers: This one is obvious. Any farm receiving support benefits must pay its workers a living wage and adhere to all laws regarding housing and safety—in spirit as well as in letter.

Link nutrition policy to agricultural policy: If we must have SNAP in the farm bill, let's take advantage of that connection. Suppose SNAP benefits had to be spent mostly on real rather than processed foods, and were worth more when spent at farmers' markets. Pilot projects along these lines have been shown to work brilliantly. Consider what something like this might do for the income of small farmers as well as for the health of food assistance recipients. Policies that enable low-income families to access healthy foods wherever they shop are beyond the scope of the farm bill, but must also be part of any utopian agenda.

Apply health and conservation standards to animal agriculture: The livestock title of the farm bill should require animals to be raised and slaughtered humanely. It should require strict adherence to environmental and safety standards for conservation and protection of soil, water, and air quality.

Utopian? Absolutely. In the current political climate, the best anyone can hope for is a crumb or two thrown in these directions. The secret process for developing the 2012 farm bill contained a few such crumbs—more money for farmers' markets and for programs to take SNAP benefits further when spent on fruits and vegetables. Whether that bill would have been better or worse than the one we eventually end up with remains to be seen. But the failure of that process provides an opportunity to work toward a healthier food system by restructuring farm bill programs to focus them on health, safety, and environmental goals and social justice. These goals are well worth advocating now and in the future.

The one bright ray of hope about the farm bill comes from the burgeoning food movement. Grassroots groups working to promote local and regional foods, farmers' markets, urban farming, farm-to-school programs, animal welfare, and farm workers' rights join a long and honorable history of social movements such as those aimed at civil rights, women's rights, and environmentalism. Changing the food system is equally radical. But food has one particular advantage for advocacy. Food is universal. Everyone eats. Food is an easy entry point into conversations about social inequities. Even the least political person can understand injustices in the food system and be challenged to work to redress them.

Occupy Big Food is an integral part of Occupy Wall Street;[1] it should not be viewed as a special interest. The issues that drive both are the same: corporate control of government and society. The food movement—in all of its forms—seeks better health for people and the planet, goals that benefit everyone. It deserves the support of everyone advocating for democratic rights.

1. Protest movement against social and economic inequality that began on September 17, 2011, in New York City's Zuccotti Park. On October 29, 2011, Occupy Big Food protestors rallied in Zuccotti Park to draw attention to social and economic inequalities related to food.

MLA CITATION

Nestle, Marion. "Utopian Dream: A New Farm Bill." 2012. *The Norton Reader: An Anthology of Nonfiction*. Ed. Melissa A. Goldthwaite et al. 14th ed. New York: Norton, 2016. 274–80. Print.

QUESTIONS

1. According to Marion Nestle, what are the main problems with the farm bill? What specific sentences and paragraphs illustrate her objections?

2. What are some of the causes of obesity that Nestle identifies? What evidence does she provide that links obesity to the farm bill?

3. What effect does Nestle's use of headings and subheadings have on your understanding of the text?

4. Write your own "Utopian Dream," an essay in which you address the problems with a specific piece of legislation (current legislation is available at congress.gov) and a plan for fixing that bill or act.

JJ GOODE   *Single-Handed Cooking*

MY BACK ACHES. My eyes burn. I've been peeling and chopping for an hour, but I'm still being taunted by a pile of untouched vegetables. My problem is not the quantity. It's that the task of steadying each item falls to an almost useless appendage: the short, goofy arm, inexplicably bent into an L-shape and graced by just three fingers, that dangles from my right shoulder.

No one knows why I was born like this. My mom wasn't exposed to any radiation while she was pregnant, nor did she, say, have one too many sips of wine. Yet I do occasionally wonder whether my dad's Ph.D. dissertation subject—a

Published in Gourmet (2009), *a monthly magazine devoted to food and wine, which was in print from 1941 to 2009.*

pre-PETA endeavor for which he plucked the legs from frogs and studied their regeneration—sparked some sort of cosmic payback.

Whatever the reason, I occupy a sort of upper middle class of the handicapped. Sure, there's plenty to complain about, but all in all, things aren't so bad. While the wheelchair-bound struggle to reach their stoves, it feels a bit "Princess and the Pea" of me to grumble that peeling potatoes is as grueling as making *mole*.[1] ("Vegetables are distressingly round," said a commiserating friend.) Or to lament that day last winter when my girlfriend took a trip to Philadelphia, leaving me at home in Brooklyn with a dozen oysters and not enough hands to shuck them with. Disability is relative: I'd rather be incapable of prying open shellfish than allergic to them. Still, I see jimmying an oyster, which otters manage without much difficulty, as an ability that's not too much to ask for.

I happily live without most of the things I can't do. The kitchen, however, is where what I love butts up against what can be so discouragingly difficult. Forget shucking an oyster; even a mundane task such as draining a pot of pasta can be death-defying. After swathing my right arm in towels to prevent it from searing (the last thing I need is for it to be less useful), I lodge it beneath the pot's handle with the same care that I imagine a window washer uses to secure his harness to a skyscraper. Then I inch toward the sink, the whole time bracing for scalding disaster and indulging in an equally scalding torrent of self-pity. Some people say the kitchen is where they clear their heads; for me, it's where I face my demons.

Every meal is a proving ground, and I suffer mistakes as though they were 5 failures, even when they have nothing to do with my arm. "It's really good," friends insist, as I sulk over hanger steak that doesn't have a perfectly rosy center or a gratin whose top has barely browned, forever fighting the feeling that somehow it all would have gone right had I been born a little more symmetrical. I can even find fault with the faultless because what I'm truly after is unreachable: two normal arms.

When I first started to cook, I developed a crush on any ingredient that leveled the playing field. I adored canned anchovies, since the fillets simply melted in hot oil. I loved beets because after I roasted them in foil, their skins would slip right off. But soon my attraction to convenience gave way to a relishing of the arduous.

Having previously avoided anything that required peeling, I now dove into recipes that called for celery root and butternut squash. I embraced Thai stir-fries, which had me meticulously slicing raw pork into matching strips so they'd all finish cooking at the same time. I can't count the times friends have watched me tackle an overly complicated prep job—always girding themselves for a bloodbath—and anxiously urged me to try using a food processor. I refuse for the same reason I insist on balancing a pan on my raised right knee when I sauce tableside instead of asking anyone for help. (It's the same reason I refused to sit out in baseball when it came time for me to bat.) I appreciate the thought, I sniff, but I can handle it.

---

1. Spanish word for a variety of sauces used in Mexican cuisine, the most common being *mole poblano*, which includes chili peppers and chocolate.

This masochistic streak is why I'm still chopping. I'm having some friends over for dinner and I'm making braised chicken, a dish that's a breeze for most cooks but presents, for me, just the right level of hardship for a dinner party. The only way to get what I casually call my right arm to act like one is to hunch awkwardly over my cutting board, so it can reach the food that needs to be stabilized. For an hour, that was celery, onions, and carrots. A rough chop would surely suffice, but I'm attempting to dice, chasing the satisfaction of seeing perfect cubes conjured by a blur of hand and knife.

My back is bent again. This time, I'm close enough to a chicken to kiss it—unfortunate no matter how comfortable you are with raw poultry. As I try to detach a leg, it slips from my right hand's feeble grasp, spattering my cheek with cold chicken liquid. I seethe but rinse off and continue. I could, of course, have bought chicken parts. But a whole chicken is always cheaper by the pound, and why shouldn't I have access? I like to think of the price discrepancy as a one-arm tax.

10   Half an hour later, I've successfully dismantled the thing and begun the rewarding task of browning it, savoring the knowledge that any cook would, at this point in the process, be upright at the stove and wielding tongs in exactly the same manner as I am. After setting the chicken aside and spooning some of the golden fat from the pot, I take a seat, sweep the vegetables from my cutting board into a big bowl supported by my knees, and ferry the bowl to the stove. The vegetables sizzle when I dump them in. Now, to add the wine.

The wine! I forgot I'd have to open a bottle, a potential catastrophe. I should turn off the burner, just in case I take as long to open this bottle as I did the last one. Instead, I bet my hard-won diced vegetables that I won't scorch them. Springing into action, I wedge the bottle between my thighs, wrap my right arm around the neck (its effect is almost purely symbolic), and struggle to work the screw through the cork. I already detect a faint acridity wafting from the pot, a whiff of defeat. I quickly adjust my technique, somehow wrenching the cork out in one piece, and rush back to the stove. The vegetables have more color than I wanted, but they're fine. In goes some wine, a few sprigs of thyme, and the chicken. I cover the pot and shove it into the oven.

I know there are more compelling examples of fortitude than me braising chicken. Like a paraplegic racing uphill in a tricked-out wheelchair on marathon day, or my late grandfather, who at 90 walked down and up 20-odd flights in the pitch darkness of New York City's 2003 blackout to get groceries for his wife. But turn a spotlight on any accomplishment, however minor, and it seems like a triumph. Away from that glare, though, there's only the struggle.

My right arm swathed again, my back contorted, I stoop down and heave the pot out of the oven without incident (once I dipped so low to retrieve a casserole dish perched on the bottom rack that I singed my forehead on the top one). I call in my friends, and we sit down to a dinner that, I have to admit, is pretty good. Someone even admires my fastidious touch, the precise little cubes of carrots and celery scattered beneath the burnished chicken. "Thanks," I say. "It was nothing."

MLA CITATION

Goode, JJ. "Single-Handed Cooking." 2009. *The Norton Reader: An Anthology of Nonfiction*. Ed. Melissa A. Goldthwaite et al. 14th ed. New York: Norton, 2016. 280–82. Print.

QUESTIONS

1. How would you characterize JJ Goode's attitude toward his disability? What parts of the essay reveal his attitude?

2. Goode presents cooking as an adventure, writing, for example, that when he adds wine to a dish he springs into action and wedges the wine bottle between his thighs (paragraph 11). Two strategies he uses to heighten this sense of adventure are present tense and strong verbs. Which verb choices do you find especially effective? Why?

3. Goode writes, "turn a spotlight on any accomplishment, however minor, and it seems like a triumph" (paragraph 12). Write an essay about a minor accomplishment you've had. Use present tense, strong verbs, and detail to make that accomplishment seem like a triumph.

M. F. KISHER   *Young Hunger*

I T IS VERY HARD for people who have passed the age of, say, fifty to remember with any charity the hunger of their own puberty and adolescence when they are dealing with the young human animals who may be frolicking about them. Too often I have seen good people helpless with exasperation and real anger upon finding in the morning that cupboards and iceboxes have been stripped of their supplies by two or three youths—or even *one*—who apparently could have eaten four times their planned share at the dinner table the night before.

Such avidity is revolting, once past. But I can recall its intensity still; I am not yet too far from it to understand its ferocious demands when I see a fifteen-year-old boy wince and whiten at the prospect of waiting politely a few more hours for food, when his guts are howling for meat-bread-candy-fruit-cheese-milkmilkmilk-ANYTHING IN THE WORLD TO EAT.

I can still remember my almost insane desperation when I was about eighteen and was staying overnight with my comparatively aged godparents. I had come home alone from France in a bad continuous storm and was literally concave with solitude and hunger. The one night on the train seemed even rougher than those on board ship, and by the time I reached my godparents' home I was almost lightheaded.

From The Gastronomical Me *(1943), a memoir about M. F. K. Fisher's gastronomical coming of age and one of several books in which she draws on her experience of food in its social settings. The original chapter title was "To Feed Such Hunger" (1930).*

I got there just in time for lunch. It is clear as ice in my mind: a little cup of very weak chicken broth, one salted cracker, one-half piece of thinly sliced toast, and then, ah then, a whole waffle, crisp and brown and with a piece of beautiful butter melting in its middle—which the maid deftly cut into four sections! One section she put on my godmother's plate. The next *two*, after a nod of approval from her mistress, she put on mine. My godfather ate the fourth.

5   There was a tiny pot of honey, and I dutifully put a dab of it on my piggish portion, and we all nibbled away and drank one cup apiece of tea with lemon. Both my godparents left part of their waffles.

It was simply that they were old and sedentary and quite out of the habit of eating amply with younger people: a good thing for them, but pure hell for me. I did not have the sense to explain to them how starved I was—which I would not hesitate to do now. Instead I prowled around my bedroom while the house slumbered through its afternoon siesta, wondering if I dared sneak to the strange kitchen for something, anything, to eat, and knowing I would rather die than meet the silent, stern maid or my nice, gentle little hostess.

Later we walked slowly down to the village, and I was thinking sensuously of double malted ice-cream sodas at the corner drugstore, but there was no possibility of such heaven. When we got back to the quiet house, the maid brought my godfather a tall glass of exquisitely rich milk, with a handful of dried fruit on the saucer under it, because he had been ill; but as we sat and watched him unwillingly down it, his wife said softly that it was such a short time until dinner that she was sure I did not want to spoil my appetite, and I agreed with her because I was young and shy.

When I dressed, I noticed that the front of my pelvic basin jutted out like two bricks under my skirt: I looked like a scarecrow.

Dinner was very long, but all I can remember is that it had, as *pièce de résistance*,[1] half of the tiny chicken previously boiled for broth at luncheon, which my godmother carved carefully so that we should each have a bit of the breast and I, as guest, should have the leg, after a snippet had been sliced from it for her husband, who liked dark meat too.

10   There were hot biscuits, yes, the smallest I have ever seen, two apiece under a napkin on a silver dish. Because of them we had no dessert: it would be too rich, my godmother said.

We drank little cups of decaffeinized coffee on the screened porch in the hot Midwestern night, and when I went up to my room I saw that the maid had left a large glass of rich malted milk beside my poor godfather's bed.

My train would leave before five in the morning, and I slept little and unhappily, dreaming of the breakfast I would order on it. Of course when I finally saw it all before me, twinkling on the Pullman[2] silver dishes, I could eat very little, from too much hunger and a sense of outrage.

1. French for "piece of resistance," used to express the best part of something, in this context, of a meal.

2. Company that built and ran sleeping cars on American railroads from the 1890s to the 1960s.

I felt that my hosts had been indescribably rude to me, and selfish and conceited and stupid. Now I know that they were none of these things. They had simply forgotten about any but their own dwindling and cautious needs for nourishment. They had forgotten about being hungry, being young, being . . .

In an essay by Max Beerbohm[3] about hosts and guests, the tyrants and the tyrannized, there is a story of what happened to him once when he was a schoolboy and someone sent him a hamper that held, not the usual collection of marmalade, sardines, and potted tongue, but twelve whole sausage-rolls.

"Of sausage-rolls I was particularly fond," he says. He could have dominated all his friends with them, of course, but "I carried the box up to my cubicle, and, having eaten two of the sausage-rolls, said nothing that day about the other ten, nor anything about them when, three days later, I had eaten them all—all, up there, alone."

What strange secret memories such a tale evokes! Is there a grown-up person anywhere who cannot remember some such shameful, almost insane act of greediness of his childhood? In recollection his scalp will prickle, and his palms will sweat, at the thought of the murderous risk he may have run from his outraged companions.

When I was about sixteen, and in boarding-school, we were allowed one bar of chocolate a day, which we were supposed to eat sometime between the sale of them at the little school bookstore at four-thirty and the seven o'clock dinner gong. I felt an almost unbearable hunger for them—not for one, but for three or four or five at a time, so that I should have *enough*, for once, in my yawning stomach.

I hid my own purchases for several days, no mean trick in a school where every drawer and cupboard was inspected, openly and snoopingly too, at least twice a week. I cannot remember now how I managed it, with such lack of privacy and my own almost insurmountable hunger every afternoon, but by Saturday I had probably ten chocolate bars—my own and a few I had bribed my friends who were trying to lose weight to buy for me.

I did not sign up for any of the usual weekend debauchery such as a walk to the village drugstore for a well-chaperoned double butterscotch and pecan sundae. Instead I lay languidly on my bed, trying to look as if I had a headache and pretending to read a very fancy book called, I think, *Martin Pippin in the Apple Orchard*,[4] until the halls quieted.

Then I arranged all my own and my roommate's pillows in a voluptuous pile, placed so that I could see whether a silent housemotherly foot stood outside the swaying monk's-cloth curtain that served as a door (to cut down our libidinous chitchat, the school board believed), and I put my hoard of Hersheys discreetly under a fold of the bedspread.

I unwrapped their rich brown covers and their tinfoil as silently as any prisoner chipping his way through a granite wall, and lay there breaking off the

3. English comic writer and caricaturist (1872–1956).
4. Illustrated children's book written by Eleanor Farjeon and published in 1921.

rather warm, rubbery, delicious pieces and feeling them melt down my gullet, and reading the lush symbolism of the book; and all the time I was hot and almost panting with the fear that people would suddenly walk in and see me there. And the strange thing is that nothing would have happened if they had!

It is true that I had more than my allotted share of candy, but that was not a crime. And my friends, full of their Saturday delights, would not have wanted ordinary chocolate. And anyway I had much more than I could eat, and was basically what Beerbohm calls, somewhat scornfully, "a host" and not "a guest": I loved to entertain people and dominate them with my generosity.

Then why was I breathless and nervous all during that solitary and not particularly enjoyable orgy? I suppose there is a Freudian explanation for it, or some other kind. Certainly the experience does not make me sound very attractive to myself. Even the certainty of being in good company is no real solace.

MLA CITATION

Fisher, M. F. K. "Young Hunger." 1943. *The Norton Reader: An Anthology of Nonfiction.* Ed. Melissa A. Goldthwaite et al. 14th ed. New York: Norton, 2016. 283–86. Print.

QUESTIONS

1. M. F. K. Fisher's world is highly class-stratified. What markers of the upper class did you notice in her essay? Did they interfere with your enjoyment of it, or add to your pleasure as a reader? Why?

2. Describe a time when you have been truly hungry. Was your experience like Fisher's—or different?

3. Narrate an episode when you or someone you know went on an eating binge. Was it truly enjoyable? Use Fisher as a model to describe your experience.

LAD TOBIN   *Here Everything Is Possible*

"SO WHICH WOULD YOU SAY IS HOTTER: the shrimp balchow or the chicken vindaloo?" Our waiter just stares at me, then holds up a finger, says "One minute," and walks back into the kitchen. I look across the table to see my wife and daughter glaring at me. What I want to say is that if I were eating with some fellow foodies, discussing the menu with the waiter would not just be acceptable—it would be required. But, of course, they could then point out that there is a difference between discussing and obsessing; that we're not in

Published in the Rumpus (2014), an online source for "essays, reviews, interviews, advice, music, film and poetry." The drawings included here appeared with the original essay and are by Liam Golden.

a trendy, new Indian place in Williamsburg or Wicker Park; we're in a tiny, shabby storefront restaurant in northern India; and that the waiter I was interrogating about whether the masala is heavier on cumin or turmeric can't be older than thirteen.

While we wait for someone to emerge from the kitchen, my daughter, Emma, reminds me that she has eaten at this restaurant many times before—she is here working for an organization that helps re-settle Tibetan refugees; we're here to visit her—and that she can take care of ordering for all of us. She talks with the weariness of someone who has seen this before—and she has: this is definitely not the first time I've made a wait person wait while I tried to figure out the perfect order. And it's not lost on me that while this can be irritating enough in some precious gastropub that charges $12 for shaved Brussels sprouts with shallots, it's particularly unattractive, offensive even, in a country where so many go hungry. But I want to point out that I'm just excited about the food, that I'm just trying to order things we'll all like, and that what happens to me in these moments has less to do with what's in my head than what's in my bones. While I'm defending myself to myself, a middle-aged man emerges from the kitchen.

"You have questions?" he asks, looking at me.

"No, no, we're all set," Emma says, before I can do more damage. "The tandoori platter—is it possible to have that with extra vegetables and no meat, please?"

The waiter responds with that characteristically Indian back and forth head   5
motion that is somehow both a shake and a nod. "Yes, of course," he responds, in heavily accented Hindi. "Here everything is possible."

Emma thanks him and tells him that we'd also like rice, dal, and naan.

"Of course," he responds, and begins to walk away.

"Excuse me," I hear myself say, knowing I shouldn't be saying anything, "Could we also get an order of the Bhagan Bharta? Or, wait, is there something else, some other specialty, that you'd recommend instead?"

Since the waiter doesn't respond right away and since I know how much trouble I'm in already, I try to hurry. "OK, well, then we'll just have one order of Bhagan Bharta and . . . let's see . . . what about trying one of the other breads? Maybe the peshwari or the poori or maybe the . . ."

"Dad, we have enough food," Emma interrupts. "Really. We're fine."   10

I think about the simple and delicious meal that my daughter's friend, a Tibetan monk living alone and far from home, prepared for us the previous night on a hot plate in his tiny room, and I feel embarrassed that I can't shake the feeling that the quality of time spent with family and friends is directly related to—and maybe even dependent on—the quality and quantity of the food we eat. I resolve to change, to de-emphasize food, to try to focus on just the simple necessities. But just as I start to embrace my new philosophy of non-attachment, our waiter walks past carrying a platter of samosas that looks so good I can barely resist stopping him to put in an order.

"I shouldn't eat this," my mother would say, "but I've been good all day and this is my very favorite food in the world." Even as a kid, I knew there was

something a little strange about the idea that an adult deserved a rich treat for
being good, especially when that adult was a high blood-pressured diabetic
who often had to take to bed for days after cooking and consuming one of her
epic dinner-party meals. The other reason my mother's decision to eat her
"very favorite food in the world" gave me pause was that I heard her use that
exact description just as she was about to take an enthusiastic bite of—and
here you could fill in the blank with literally dozens of choices—filet mignon,
steak tartare, sweetbreads, leg of lamb with mint jelly, Lobster Newburgh, a
BLT, a hot fudge sundae, Profiteroles au Chocolat, sacher torte, Baked
Alaska, buttered popcorn.

   All the same, I sensed early on that it made no sense to get moralistic or
puritanical about what my mother ate or cooked since there were few other
activities—at least for our family—that could produce anywhere near as much
pleasure and good feeling. In an era well before nouvelle cuisine, Atkins, or
South Beach, my mother loved food that you could not only die from but
also die for. Like a lot of other suburban families in the 50s, we ate our share
of satisfying, fat- and carb-intensive comfort foods: bacon and eggs and hashed
browns for breakfast, grilled cheese for lunch, sirloin steak or roast beef with
baked potatoes covered in butter and sour cream for dinner. But unlike most
other suburban families in the 50s, my mother was just as likely to serve Cor-
nish game hen with wild rice; South African lobster tails with individual bowls
of melted butter; marinated, grilled flank steak with grilled corn on the cob
that you could rotate in your individual corn-on-the-cob-shaped butter dish by
turning the little plastic holders stuck into either end.

   But what really distinguished my mother's cooking from the cooking of our
relatives, friends, and neighbors was her passion for what was then called "ethnic food." As Jews, we had our predictable share of bagels and lox, brisket and
kugel, matzah ball soup and gefilte fish. But my mother's regular repertoire also
included pasta carbonara, turkey tetrazzini, beef bourguignon, beef stroganoff,
Moroccan-style chicken with couscous, Peking duck, shrimp curry, cheese fon-
due, Peruvian ceviche, and paella, which she always served with gazpacho and
pitchers of ice-cold sangria. Of course, it wouldn't be all that unusual to find
someone cooking these foods today but in an era when lasagna and chow mein
were on the outer edge of exotic for most middle-class Americans, the creativity and sophistication of my mother's cuisine stood out. So did her lack of pretentiousness about food: she may have collected and read cookbooks like they
were dime novels and dragged us all over the city in search of the best new
Greek taverna or Korean Barbeque joint but there was nothing the least bit
fussy or snobby about her cooking or eating.

15   It's not that she was uncritical or undiscriminating. It's just that she loved
all sorts of things that a food snob might avoid, from perfectly melded and
melted s'mores to street-vendored kosher hot dogs with sauerkraut and dill pickles. Not only can't I remember a single food that made her squeamish, I can't
even remember—and this seems remarkable to me—a single food she hated or
refused to eat. While not every single food made her very-favorite-in-the-world
list, even the simplest tastes—a long swallow of a glass of ice water with lemon

or a loud, crunching bite of a raw carrot—seemed to produce more pleasure than you'd ever imagine possible.

When Shirley Temple[1] was seven, she met my mother, who was six. I suppose most people would describe that meeting in the opposite way, as an ordinary little girl who got to meet a celebrity, not as a celebrity who got to meet an ordinary little girl. But as my grandmother always told the story, it was a meeting of two great stars. It occurred in the mid-1930s when Temple, on a publicity tour for her latest movie, was greeting fans on a busy street corner in downtown Chicago. My mother happened to be there because every Saturday my grandmother would bring her first to her morning acting class and then to the Walnut Room in Marshall Fields to eat her very favorite sandwich, a "Fields Special": turkey, bacon, Swiss, tomato, hard-boiled egg, and Thousand Island dressing on Jewish rye. My mother happened to be in the first row of the crowd because my grandmother, on spotting Temple, had managed to push right to the front. At which point, the movie star looked at my mother, walked over, and said, "Hi; I'm Shirley Temple. Would you like my autograph?"

"Hi, I'm Uni Millstone," my mother responded. "Would you like *my* autograph?"

My grandmother believed that story showed that my mother was precociously adorable and brilliant, something she continued to believe to the day my mother died; I thought the story showed that my mother and grandmother were both a little nuts. I'll admit that there is some pleasure in hearing a story in which a cutesy, spoiled, and precious little movie star gets some comeuppance, but I can't help but think that my mother comes across as just as cutesy, spoiled, and precious, not to mention a little delusional. A seven-year-old who acts like a world-famous movie star is pretty hard to take, even if she is one; a seven-year-old who isn't a world-famous movie star but is treated like one by her mother is headed for trouble.

My mother died suddenly at a dining room table, in the middle of a wonderful meal, surrounded by a large, extended family that loved her. One minute she was completely immersed in the world—talking, laughing, eating—and the next minute she was gone. Viewed from a distance, her death seems fitting for someone who so much loved family, food, and conversation but, in fact, everything was off. It wasn't her table, it wasn't her meal, and it wasn't her family (she and my father were visiting friends in California when it happened). Most of all, it wasn't her time: she was just 62, an age that gets younger every day.

20   It's the school Halloween party, 1960. I am sitting in the middle of the auditorium with my brother, Joe. The principal is standing on one side of the stage, announcing into a microphone, "OK, now I want anyone dressed like some kind of food to come up on stage." He peers out into the audience. "Over there, I see a banana. . . . and a cheeseburger right in front. Come on up." The banana

1. Film and TV star (1928–2014) popular in the 1930s.

and burger looked excited to finally be recognized and relieved to know that they could leave the remaining misfits in the audience and rush onto the stage now crowded with genres already called: ghosts and goblins, angels and fairies, witches and devils, princes and princesses, pirates, monsters, ballerinas, athletes of one sport or another, animals, dinosaurs, clowns, soldiers, super heroes, firemen and policemen (this was an era before gender-neutral job titles), doctors and nurses.

Since Joe and I are now the only ones left, the principal has a chance to study our costumes, but it is clear from the look on his face that he still has no clue what category either of us belongs to. It's not his fault—my mother has dressed me as a Russian Cossack with a huge fur hat, a long, red military coat, and a droopy mustache (an odd costume considering my Russian Jewish grandparents had to flee their homes to escape the pogroms). And she has convinced Joe to go out trick or treating as a voting booth. "You tell the people they can drop the candy into the slot of the candidate they want—either the Kennedy slot or the Nixon slot.[2] You tell them that you'll count up the candy at the end and announce who won. That way, if someone really wants to vote for their favorite, they might give you more than one piece."

"I don't care about money; I just want to have enough to never have to think about it." That was another thing my mother always said. As I kid, I admired and envied this attitude since it seemed so evolved, relaxed, un-neurotic. She didn't seem especially status-conscious, hardly ever talked about a possession in terms of its economic value, wasn't the least bit miserly. In fact, she was almost absurdly extravagant in the gifts she gave family and friends and even more extravagant in the things she bought for herself. If something caught her eye—an expensive cut of sirloin to use in a stew she planned to cook that night, an antique music box, an odd-shaped purple pillow with a painting of Virginia Woolf's face on the front, a $300 carved wooden rocking horse for her granddaughter, a plane ticket to Hawaii to visit her sister—she bought it on the spot, without apparent hesitation or guilt. Of course, what I didn't understand until I was older was that having enough money to never have to think about money was a luxury reserved only for people who were monastic, rich, or financially irresponsible. My mother would have said that she was none of those things (though I suspect an impartial observer would have convicted her on the last two charges and laughed at the first); she would have said—and on this she may have been right—that money didn't matter to her except in the ways that it could produce happiness and pleasure for herself and the people she loved.

She brought a version of this same philosophy to food and cooking. She seemed to believe that at every meal there should always be enough different foods and courses that no one could possibly be disappointed and that there should always be enough of each individual dish that no one could ever worry

---

2. John F. Kennedy (1917–1963) and Richard Nixon (1913–1994) ran against one another in the presidential election of 1960.

about anything running out. I suppose that's part of the reason that dinners at my house were almost always multi-coursed and multicultural. It wasn't just the Paul Bunyan-like scale of the meals that got your attention; it was also the unbounded, almost fearless, imagination my mother brought to every food-related activity, from shopping to cooking to entertaining.

She was the sort of cook who would come home with more than a dozen huge salmon fillets she intended to poach for a dinner, find that there were far too many to do all at once in her fish poacher, and decide that she'd poach them instead in the dishwasher (minus the detergent); the sort who would return from a vacation in Amsterdam with a suitcase full of teak serving bowls and platters that she then immediately put to use in recreating the 24-item Indonesian Rijstafel she had just discovered to be "her very favorite meal in the world"; the sort (if you could even call this a sort) who had an epiphany one evening while eating a toasted almond bar from a roadside Good Humor truck that it would be wonderful to be able to eat toasted almond bars, rainbow-colored popsicles, and ice cream sandwiches whenever we pleased and who, therefore, immediately made an under-the-table, against-company-policy arrangement with that same

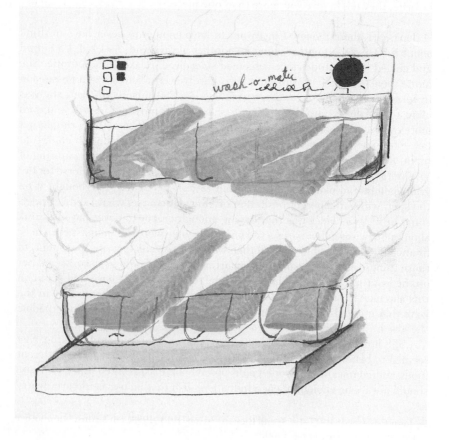

roadside Good Humor man to drive to our house very late one night each week to deposit boxes and boxes of ice cream bars into our restaurant-sized basement freezer, beside the hand-cut T-bone and Delmonico steaks she had mail-ordered in from a slaughterhouse in Kansas City.

My mother also produced and consumed words all day long. In the morning she would lounge on her bed, sipping strong black coffee and gulping down ice water, munching on a croissant, or, if she was being virtuous that day, a cream cheese-less bialy, talking on the phone, doing a crossword puzzle, reading a "junky bestseller," re-reading a Jane Austen novel, half-watching and occasionally calling out the answers to a TV quiz show, and writing her own witty song lyrics to old Broadway melodies. For lunch, she'd often meet up with friends at a restaurant to gossip, tease, argue or joke about politics, commiserate about problems with husbands and kids. At the dinner table, surrounded by heaping piles and platters of foods, she'd orchestrate the conversation, asking questions, drawing us all out, forcing us to talk about what we thought or felt. Even when she wasn't talking, she was still the center of attention, leaning forward, taking in every word, listening with a hunger that changed the energy in the room.

My wife and I go through phases when we never prepare or sit down to real meals, when we subsist on snacks of peanut butter, carrots, apples, cold cereal, and toast, when we begin to think of making oatmeal or tuna salad as cooking. On the other hand, when our daughters are visiting or when we have people over, I can spend hours planning menus, shopping, and cooking. In fact, when it comes to entertaining, I've inherited my mother's style; in other words, I'm all about overkill. A dinner of grilled salmon doesn't feel complete to me unless I make a couple of different sweet and spicy fruit salsas to accompany it. When my daughter was home on a recent visit and said she felt like having ziti or gnocchi, I made both, one with a marinara sauce, the other with pesto. And garlic bread and antipasto and salad and a marinated grilled shrimp appetizer. On some rational level, I know that it's all too much, but for some reason each individual item I consider cutting suddenly seems absolutely essential, not just to the meal but to the success of the entire evening.

I used to blame my mother for what she was doing to herself and, since we would be the ones who would suffer without her, what she was doing to us. I used to be angry that, even after the heart failures, heart surgeries, and heart attacks, she kept eating rich foods. I even used to get vindictive sometimes and think that, like the grasshopper who was too selfish or undisciplined to plan for the future, she had brought all of this on herself. But now I wonder if maybe, given her genes and her temperament, she couldn't have lived any other way. Maybe she knew that there was no amount of caution or sacrifice that could have kept her alive. Maybe she knew that doctors and scientists and nutritionists didn't really know everything about the relationship between food and health, that the theories about red meats and red wines, white starches and saturated fats, were just theories, designed to give people the illusion of control, or to give corporations new ways to market their products. Or maybe she just did the calculations and asked herself: "Should I give up one of the few things that I know gives me the most pleasure and satisfaction in exchange for the outside chance that I will live maybe two or five or ten more years?" Did she stop each time to do the math or did she just close her eyes and bite the bullet?

While we are waiting for our check, Emma scoops up our leftovers and dashes out of the restaurant ahead of us. When I get on the street, I feel the sting of cold air—the temperature must have dropped 20 degrees since we began eating. It's almost completely dark now and, for a second, I can't find Emma. But then I hear her and see her, just across the street, leaning over, talking with a woman who is wrapped in a blanket with a baby in her lap and a toddler asleep by her side. My daughter hands our leftovers to the woman, who nods tight-lipped in appreciation, then tucks the food away behind her.

Standing on this cold, dark street, I suddenly feel overwhelmingly home-sick and lost. I wish I could go back to that moment when the waiter was at our table and order only what we needed. I wish I could go back and order even more so I'd have food now to give to all the people in this city who are sleeping on the street. I wish I could call my mom. I wish I hadn't inherited her feeling that you only have enough when you have too much.

30   Not long before she died, my mother threw a party in honor of my brother's marriage. She was by that point so weak that she rarely cooked; in fact, she was so weak she often spent whole weeks in bed, eating her food on a tray. But for the party, she rallied. In honor of my new sister-in-law from Buenos Aires, the

meal had an Argentinean theme: there were oysters sautéed with tomato, bacon, cream, ginger, coriander, and chili; there were platters of grilled, rare, marinated meats, including short ribs, flank steak, chorizo, and sweetbreads; there were giant bowls of chimichurri brimming with fragrant cilantro, garlic, vinegar, and oil; there were loaves and loaves of hot, crusty French bread; there was a huge paella-like casserole filled with yellow rice, shrimp, and sausage; there were beefcake tomatoes and red onions drizzled with in a red wine vinaigrette; and there were cases of Argentinean Malbecs and Spanish Grenaches. After all that, the simple, cinnamon-infused chocolate layer cake almost seemed a letdown until my mother announced that the rest of the dessert, the "real dessert," was outside: "It'll be a kind of 'open bar,'" she explained. "Everybody will get to choose whatever they'd like. . . . and as much as they'd like." And with that, she led us all out into the driveway where a Good Humor man in his starched white outfit and cap stood beside his truck, ready to give us anything we wanted.

MLA CITATION

Tobin, Lad. "Here Everything Is Possible." 2014. *The Norton Reader: An Anthology of Nonfiction*. Ed. Melissa A. Goldthwaite et al. 14th ed. New York: Norton, 2016. 286–95. Print.

QUESTIONS

1. Lad Tobin explores his own relationship to food by reflecting on his mother's food-related habits and behaviors. How do their relationships to food differ? How are they similar? Use examples from the essay to support your claims.

2. Throughout his essay Tobin uses lists, usually lists of specific foods, dishes, or activities related to preparing or serving food (e.g., paragraph 14). Where do these lists appear? What do you notice about them? Why are they important to the essay?

3. Tobin tells family stories and offers his own and sometimes someone else's interpretation (e.g., paragraphs 16–18). In a short essay, tell one of your own family stories, offering at least two perspectives on what that story illustrates or means.

JULIA CHILD   *Le Cordon Bleu*

CHEF BUGNARD

A T 9:00 A.M. on Tuesday, October 4, 1949, I arrived at the École du Cordon Bleu feeling weak in the knees and snozzling from a cold. It was then that I discovered that I'd signed up for a yearlong Année Scolaire[1] instead of a six-week intensive course. The Année cost $450, which was a serious commitment. But after much discussion, Paul[2] and I agreed that the course was essential to my well-being and that I'd plunge ahead with it.

My first cooking class was held in a sunny kitchen on the building's top floor. My classmates were an English girl and a French girl of about my age, neither of whom had done any cooking at all. (To my great surprise, I'd discovered that many Frenchwomen didn't know how to cook any better than I did; quite a lot of them had no interest in the subject whatsoever, though most were expert at eating in restaurants.) This "housewife" course was so elementary that after two days I knew it wasn't what I'd had in mind at all.

I sat down with Madame Élizabeth Brassart, the school's short, thin, rather disagreeable owner (she had taken over from Marthe Distel, who had run the school for fifty years), and explained that I'd had a more rigorous program in mind. We discussed my level of cooking knowledge, and her classes on haute cuisine (high-end, professional cooking) and *moyenne cuisine* (middle-brow cooking). She made it quite clear that she didn't like me, or any Americans: "They can't cook!" she said, as if I weren't sitting right in front of her. In any event, Madame Brassart decreed that I was not advanced enough for haute cuisine—a six-week course for experts—but that I'd be suitable for the yearlong "professional restaurateurs" course that had conveniently just begun. This class was taught by Chef Max Bugnard, a practicing professional with years of experience.

"*Oui!*" I said without a moment's hesitation.

5   At this point I began to really miss my sister-in-law, Freddie Child. We had grown so close in Washington, D.C., that when people said, "Here come the twins," they meant me and Freddie, not Paul and Charlie.[3] She was an excellent, intuitive cook, and, to scare our husbands, we'd joke about opening a restaurant called "Mrs. Child & Mrs. Child, of the Cordon Bleu."

Secretly, I was somewhat serious about this idea, and was trying to convince her to join me at the Cordon Bleu. But she couldn't tear herself away from

From My Life in France (2006), *which Julia Child wrote with the assistance of her husband's grandnephew Alex Prud'homme. The book was published two years after Julia Child's death.*

1. French for "school year." All translations that follow are of French words.
2. Paul Child, Julia Child's husband.
3. Paul Child's twin brother.

Learning to cut a chicken with Chef Bugnard.

her husband and three children in Pennsylvania. *Eh bien*,[4] so I would be on my own.

It turned out that the restaurateurs' class was made up of eleven former GIs who were studying cooking under the auspices of the GI Bill of Rights.[5] I never knew if Madame Brassart had placed me with them as a form of hazing or merely because she was trying to squeeze out a few more dollars, but when I walked into the classroom the GIs made me feel as if I had invaded their boys' club. Luckily, I had spent most of the war in male-dominated environments and wasn't fazed by them in the least.

The eleven GIs were very "GI" indeed, like genre-movie types: nice, earnest, tough, basic men. Most of them had worked as army cooks during the war, or at hot-dog stands in the States, or they had fathers who were bakers and butchers. They seemed serious about learning to cook, but in a trade-school way. They were full of entrepreneurial ideas about setting up golf driving-ranges

4. "Well then."
5. Also known as the Serviceman's Readjustment Act of 1944, the G.I. Bill provided (among other benefits) tuition money so World War II veterans could attend college or vocational school.

with restaurants attached, or roadhouses, or some kind of private trade in a nice spot back home. After a few days in the kitchen together, we became a jolly crew, though in my cold-eyed view there wasn't an artist in the bunch.

In contrast to the housewife's sun-splashed classroom upstairs, the restaurateurs' class met in the Cordon Bleu's basement. The kitchen was medium-sized, and equipped with two long cutting tables, three stoves with four burners each, six small electric ovens at one end, and an icebox at the other end. With twelve pupils and a teacher, it was hot and crowded down there.

10   The saving grace was our professor, Chef Bugnard. What a gem! Medium-small and plump, with thick round-framed glasses and a walruslike mustache, Bugnard was in his late seventies. He had been *dans le métier*[6] most of his life: starting as a boy at his family's restaurant in the countryside, he had done *stages*[7] at various good restaurants in Paris, worked in the galleys of transatlantic steamers, and refined his technique under the great Escoffier in London for three years. Before the Second World War, he owned a restaurant, Le Petit Vatel, in Brussels. The war cost him Le Petit Vatel, but he had been recruited to the Cordon Bleu by Madame Brassart, and obviously loved his role as *éminence grise*[8] there. And who wouldn't? The job allowed him to keep regular hours and spend his days teaching students who relished his every word and gesture.

Because there was so much new information to take in every day, it was confusing at first. All twelve of us cut vegetables, stirred the pots, and asked questions at once. Most of the GIs struggled to follow Bugnard's rat-a-tat delivery, which made me glad that I had developed my language skills before launching into cooking. Even so, I had to keep my ears open and make sure to ask questions, even if they were dumb questions, when I didn't understand something. I was never the only one confused.

Bugnard set out to teach us the fundamentals. We began making sauce bases—*soubise, fond brun, demi-glace,* and *madère.* Later, to demonstrate a number of techniques in one session, Bugnard would cook a full meal, from appetizer to dessert. So we'd learn about, say, the proper preparation of crudités, a fricassee of veal, glazed onions, *salade verte,* and several types of *crêpes Suzettes.* Everything we cooked was eaten for lunch at the school, or sold.

Despite being overstretched, Bugnard was infinitely kind, a natural if understated showman, and he was tireless in his explanations. He drilled us in his careful standards of doing everything the "right way." He broke down the steps of a recipe and made them simple. And he did so with a quiet authority, insisting that we thoroughly analyze texture and flavor: "But how does it *taste,* Madame Scheeld?"

One morning he asked, "Who will make *oeufs brouillés* today?"

6. "In the trade."

7. "Internships."

8. Literally "gray eminence" but in context an influential advisor.

The GIs were silent, so I volunteered for scrambled-egg duty. Bugnard   15
watched intently as I whipped some eggs and cream into a froth, got the frying
pan very hot, and slipped in a pat of butter, which hissed and browned in
the pan.

"*Non!*" he said in horror, before I could pour the egg mixture into the pan.
"That is absolutely wrong!"

The GIs' eyes went wide.

With a smile, Chef Bugnard cracked two eggs and added a dash of salt and
pepper. "Like *this*," he said, gently blending the yolks and whites together with
a fork. "Not too much."

He smeared the bottom and sides of a frying pan with butter, then gently
poured the eggs in. Keeping the heat low, he stared intently at the pan. Nothing
happened. After a long three minutes, the eggs began to thicken into a custard.
Stirring rapidly with the fork, sliding the pan on and off the burner, Bugnard
gently pulled the egg curds together—"Keep them a little bit loose; this is very
important," he instructed. "*Now* the cream or butter," he said, looking at me
with raised eyebrows. "This will stop the cooking, you see?" I nodded, and he
turned the scrambled eggs out onto a plate, sprinkled a bit of parsley around,
and said, "*Voilà!*"

His eggs were always perfect, and although he must have made this dish   20
several thousand times, he always took great pride and pleasure in this performance. Bugnard insisted that one pay attention, learn the correct technique, and
that one enjoy one's cooking—"Yes, Madame Scheeld, *fun!*" he'd say. "Joy!"

It was a remarkable lesson. No dish, not even the humble scrambled egg,
was too much trouble for him. "You never forget a beautiful thing that you have
made," he said. "Even after you eat it, it stays with you—*always*."

I was delighted by Bugnard's enthusiasm and thoughtfulness. And I began
to internalize it. As the only woman in the basement, I was careful to keep up
an appearance of sweet good humor around "the boys," but inside I was cool
and intensely focused on absorbing as much information as possible.

As the weeks of cooking classes wore on, I developed a rigid schedule.

Every morning, I'd pop awake at 6:30, splash water across my puffy face,
dress quickly in the near dark, and drain a can of tomato juice. By 6:50 I was out
the door as Paul was beginning to stir. I'd walk seven blocks to the garage, jump
into the Blue Flash, and roar up the street to Faubourg Saint-Honoré. There I'd
find a parking spot and buy one French and one U.S. newspaper. I'd find a warm
café, and would sip café-au-lait and chew on hot fresh croissants while scanning
the papers with one eye and monitoring the street life with the other.

At 7:20 I'd walk two blocks to school and don my "uniform," an ill-fitting   25
white housedress and a blue chef's apron with a clean dish towel tucked into
the waist cord. Then I'd select a razor-sharp paring knife and start to peel onions
while chitchatting with the GIs.

At 7:30 Chef Bugnard would arrive, and we'd all cook in a great rush until
9:30. Then we'd talk and clean up. School let out at about 9:45, and I would do
a quick shop and zip home. There I'd get right back to cooking, trying my hand

at relatively simple dishes like cheese tarts, *coquilles Saint-Jacques,* and the like. At 12:30 Paul would come home for lunch, and we'd eat and catch up. He'd sometimes take a quick catnap, but more often would rush back across the Seine to put out the latest brushfire at the embassy.

At 2:30 the Cordon Bleu's demonstration classes began. Typically, a visiting chef, aided by two apprentices, would cook and explain three or four dishes—demonstrating how to make, say, a *soufflé au fromage,* decorate a *galantine de volaille,* prepare *épinards à la crème,* and end with a finale of *charlotte aux pommes.* The demonstration chefs were businesslike and did not waste a lot of time "warming up" the class. They'd start right in at 2:30, giving the ingredients and proportions, and talking us through each step as they went. We'd finish promptly at 5:00.

The demonstrations were held in a big square room with banked seats facing a demonstration kitchen up on a well-lit stage. It was like a teaching hospital, where medical interns sat watching in an amphitheater while the famous surgeon—or, in our case, chef—demonstrated how to amputate a leg—or make a cream sauce—onstage. It was an effective way of delivering a lot of information quickly, and the chefs demonstrated technique and took questions as they went. The afternoon sessions were open to anyone willing to pay three hundred francs. So, aside from the regular Cordon Bleu students, the audience was filled with housewives, young cooks, old men, strays off the street, and the odd gourmet or two.

We learned all sorts of dishes—*perdreaux en chartreuse* (roasted partridges placed in a mold decorated with savory cabbage, beans, and julienned carrots and turnips); *boeuf bourguignon*; little fish *en lorgnette* (a pretty dish in which the fish's backbone is cut out, the body is rolled up to the head, and then the whole is deep-fried in boiling fat); chocolate ice cream (made with egg yolks); and cake icing (made with sugar boiled to a viscous consistency, beaten into egg yolks, then beaten with softened butter and flavorings to make a wonderfully thick icing).

All of the demonstration teachers were good, but two stood out.

Pierre Mangelatte, the chef at Restaurant des Artistes, on la Rue Lepic, gave wonderfully stylish and intense classes on *cuisine traditionnelle*: quiches, *sole meunière, pâté en croûte,* trout in aspic, ratatouille, *boeuf en daube,* and so on. His recipes were explicit and easy to understand. I scribbled down copious notes, and found them easy to follow when I tried the recipes later at home.

The other star was Claude Thilmont, the former pastry chef at the Café de Paris, who had trained under Madame Saint-Ange, the author of that seminal work for the French home cook, *La Bonne Cuisine de Madame E. Saint-Ange.* With great authority, and a pastry chef's characteristic attention to detail, Thilmont demonstrated how to make puff pastry, pie dough, brioches, and croissants. But his true forte was special desserts—wonderful fruit tarts, layer cakes, or showstoppers like a *charlotte Malakoff.*

I was in pure, flavorful heaven at the Cordon Bleu. Because I had already established a good basic knowledge of cookery on my own, the classes acted as a catalyst for new ideas, and almost immediately my cooking improved. Before

I'd started there, I would often put too many herbs and spices into my dishes. But now I was learning the French tradition of extracting the full, essential flavors from food—to make, say, a roasted chicken taste really *chickeny*.

It was a breakthrough when I learned to glaze carrots and onions at the same time as roasting a pigeon, and how to use the concentrated vegetable juices to fortify the pigeon flavor, and vice versa. And I was so inspired by the afternoon demonstration on *boeuf bourguignon* that I went right home and made the most delicious example of that dish I'd ever eaten, even if I do say so myself.

But not everything was perfect. Madame Brassart had crammed too many   35
of us into the class, and Bugnard wasn't able to give the individual attention I craved. There were times when I had a penetrating question to ask, or a fine point that burned inside of me, and I simply wasn't able to make myself heard. All this had the effect of making me work even harder.

I had always been content to live a butterfly life of fun, with hardly a care in the world. But at the Cordon Bleu, and in the markets and restaurants of Paris, I suddenly discovered that cooking was a rich and layered and endlessly fascinating subject. The best way to describe it is to say that I fell in love with French food—the tastes, the processes, the history, the endless variations, the rigorous discipline, the creativity, the wonderful people, the equipment, the rituals.

I had never taken anything so seriously in my life—husband and cat excepted—and I could hardly bear to be away from the kitchen.

What fun! What a revelation! How terrible it would have been had Roo de Loo[9] come with a good cook! How magnificent to find my life's calling, at long last!

"Julie's cookery is actually improving," Paul wrote Charlie. "I didn't quite believe it would, just between us, but it really *is*. It's simpler, more classical. . . . I envy her this chance. It would be such *fun* to be doing it at the same time with her."

My husband's support was crucial to keeping my enthusiasm high, yet, as   40
a "Cordon Bleu Widower," he was often left to his own devices. Paul joined the American Club of Paris, a group of businessmen and government officers who met once a week for lunch. Here he met a pump engineer who introduced him to another, smaller group of American men who were wine aficionados. Frustrated that most of our countrymen never bother to learn about even a fraction of the good French vintages, the members of this group pooled their resources and enlisted Monsieur Pierre Andrieu—a *commandeur* de la Confrérie des Chevaliers du Tastevin (a leading wine-and-food group) and author of *Chronologie Anecdotique du Vignoble Français*—to explain the wines of each region, answer oenological questions, and advise them on how to pair specific vintages to foods.

Every six weeks or so, the men would meet at a notable restaurant— Lapérouse, Rôtisserie de la Reine Pédauque, La Crémaillère, Prunier—to eat well and drink five or six wines from a given region. Occasionally they went on outings, such as the time they went to the Clos de Vougeot château, in Burgundy,

9. Play on 81 *Rue de l'Université*, where Julia and Paul Child lived in Paris. *Rue* is French for "street."

and went through practically all the *caves*[10] of the Côte d'Or. Paul especially liked this group because it had no formal membership, no leader, no name, and no dues. Each meal cost six dollars, which covered food, wine, and tip—and must have been one of the greatest deals in the history of gastronomy.

• • •

Back at the Cordon Bleu, I picked up my routine again, beginning at 6:30 a.m. and ending around midnight every weekday.[11] But I was growing increasingly dissatisfied with the school. The $150 tuition was expensive. Madame Brassart paid little attention to the details of management. Many of the classes were disorganized, and the teachers lacked basic supplies. And after six months of intensive instruction, not one of the eleven GIs in my class knew the proportions for a *béchamel* sauce or how to clean a chicken the right way. They just weren't serious, and that irritated me.

Even Chef Bugnard was beginning to repeat such dishes as *sole normande, poulet chaud-froid*, omelettes, and *crêpes Suzettes*. It was useful practice to do these dishes over and over, and at last I could make a decent piecrust without thinking twice. But I wanted to be pushed harder and further. There was so much more to learn!

Bugnard, I suspect, had been quietly monitoring my progress, and had now gained enough confidence in me that he began to take me aside and show me things that he didn't show "the boys." This time when he took me around Les Halles, he personally introduced me to his favorite meat, vegetable, and wine purveyors.

I decided to give up the Cordon Bleu for the time being. I didn't want to lose my momentum, though, so I continued to attend the afternoon demonstrations (a dollar each), and go to as many of the pâtisserie demonstrations ($1.99 per class) as I could. In the meantime, I was constantly experimenting on the stove at home. On the QT, Chef Bugnard joined me at 81 for an occasional private cooking lesson.

One of the things I loved about French cooking was the way that basic themes could be made in a seemingly infinite number of variations—scalloped potatoes, say, could be done with milk and cheese, with carrots and cream, with beef stock and cheese, with onions and tomatoes, and so on and on. I wanted to try them all, and did. I learned how to do things professionally, like how to fix properly a piece of fish in thirteen different ways, or how to use the specialized vocabulary of the kitchen—"*petits dés*" are vegetables "diced quite finely"; a *douille* is the tin nozzle of a pastry bag that lets you squeeze a cake decoration as the icing blurps out.

There was, in fact, a method to my madness: I was preparing for my final examination. I could take it anytime I felt ready to, Madame Brassart said, and I was determined to do as well as possible. After all, if I were going to open a

10. "Wineries."

11. During April and early May 1950, Child traveled to Italy with her sister and parents before returning to Le Cordon Bleu.

restaurant or a cooking school, what better credentials could I have than the Cordon Bleu, of Paris, France?

I knew that I'd have to keep honing my skills until I had all of the recipes and techniques down cold and could perform them under pressure. The exam didn't intimidate me. In fact, I looked forward to it.

• • •

SURPRISE

By late 1950, I felt ready to take my final examination, and earn my *diplôme* from the Cordon Bleu. But when I asked Madame Brassart to schedule the test—politely, at first, and then with an increasing insistence—my requests were met with stony silence. The truth is that Madame Brassart and I got on each other's nerves. She seemed to think that awarding students a diploma was like inducting them into some kind of secret society; as a result, the school's hallways were filled with an air of petty jealousy and distrust. From my perspective, Madame Brassart lacked professional experience, was a terrible administrator, and tangled herself up in picayune details and petty politics. Because of its exalted reputation, the Cordon Bleu's pupils came from all over the globe. But the lack of a qualified and competent head was hurting the school—and could damage the reputation of French cooking, or even France herself, in the eyes of the world.

50   I was sure that the little question of money had something to do with Madame Brassart's evasiveness. I had taken the "professional" course in the basement rather than the "regular" (more expensive) course upstairs that she had recommended; I never ate at the school; and she didn't make as much money out of me as she would have liked. It seemed to me that the school's director should have paid less attention to centimes and more attention to her *students*, who, after all, were—or could be—her best publicity.

After waiting and waiting for my exam to be scheduled, I sent Madame Brassart a stern letter in March 1951, noting that "all my American friends and even the U.S. ambassador himself" knew I had been slaving away at the Cordon Bleu, "morning, noon and night." I insisted that I take the exam before I left on a long-planned trip to the U.S.A., in April. If there was not enough space at the school, I added, then I would be happy to take the exam in my own well-appointed kitchen.

More time passed, and still no response. I was good and fed up, and finally spoke to Chef Bugnard about the matter. He agreed to make inquiries on my behalf. Lo and behold, Madame Brassart suddenly scheduled my exam for the first week in April. Ha! I continued to hone my technique, memorize proportions, and prepare myself in every way I could think of.

On the Big Day, I arrived at the school and they handed me a little typewritten card that said: "Write out the ingredients for the following dishes, to serve three people: *oeufs mollets avec sauce béarnaise; côtelettes de veau en surprise; crème renversée au caramel.*"

I stared at the card in disbelief.

55   Did I remember what an *oeuf mollet* was? No. How could I miss *that*? (I later discovered that it was an egg that has been coddled and then peeled.) How about the *veau "en surprise"*? No. (A sautéed veal chop with *duxelles*—hashed mushrooms—on either side, overlayed with ham slices, and all wrapped up in a paper bag—the "surprise"—that is then browned in the oven.) Did I remember the exact proportions for caramel custard? No.

Merde alors, and *flute!*[12]

I was stuck, and had no choice but to make everything up. I knew I would fail the practical part of the exam. As for the written exam, I was asked how to make *fond brun*, how to cook green vegetables, and how to make *sauce béarnaise*. I answered them fully and correctly. But that didn't take away the sting.

I was furious at myself. There was no excuse for not remembering what a *mollet* was, or, especially, the details of a caramel custard. I could never have guessed at the *veau en surprise*, though, as the paper wrapping was just a lot of tomfoolery—the kind of gimmicky dish a little newlywed would serve up for her first dinner party to *épater*[13] the boss's wife. Caught up in my own romanticism, I had focused on learning far more challenging fare—*filets de sole Walewska, poularde toulousaine, sauce Véhitienne*. Woe!

12. Expressions of annoyance.
13. "Impress."

the country's food culture is rapidly changing. Consumers want less processed foods, he says, and more information about "the story behind their food"—which might not be something that a Sno Ball would want told.

But Mr. Hartman understands the allure. The careful unfolding of a Yodel or Ho Ho, but only after the frosting has been nibbled away. The scraping of teeth against the piece of white cardboard for that last remnant of a SuzyQ. The connection in a Twinkie, or a Funny Bone, to what he calls the "soulful elements of our past."

That is why, one night this fall, or maybe this winter, or perhaps in the spring—there's no rush—I will wait until the kids are asleep, their tummies content with kale chips and quinoa. Then, basked in the bluish glow of some black-and-white television show, I will eat my faux-chocolate, crème-filled, Bloomberg-infuriating,[1] chemical-rich, bad-for-me, really-really-bad-for-me, all-but-extinct Ring Dings.

Both of them.

1. Allusion to Michael Bloomberg (b. 1942), then Mayor of New York City, who proposed a ban on selling soft drinks in containers larger than sixteen ounces.

MLA CITATION

Barry, Dan. "Back When a Chocolate Puck Tasted, Guiltily, Like America." 2012. *The Norton Reader: An Anthology of Nonfiction*. Ed. Melissa A. Goldthwaite et al. 14th ed. New York: Norton, 2016. 307–09. Print.

QUESTIONS

1. What do you think Dan Barry means when he claims that Ring Dings taste like America?

2. Barry makes comparisons between Hostess snack cakes and inedible objects such as "the heel of a shoe" (paragraph 3) and "a loofah sponge" (paragraph 8). Locate other examples. Why do you think he makes such comparisons even as he claims to enjoy eating the snack cakes?

3. Barry quotes a food-industry researcher who says that consumers want less processed food and to know "'the story behind their food'" (paragraph 16). Write an
op-ed about what information you believe consumers should be provided about
food—and why.

TERESA LUST   *The Same Old Stuffing*

B EFORE YOU SET OUT to revamp your Thanksgiving
meal, it pays to consider all the repercussions. Just
because the editors of the glossy food magazines
have grown weary of the same old turkey and fix-
ings, and even though they are absolutely giddy
with excitement over the smoked quail, the spicy
black bean stuffing, and the sun-dried tomato and arugula gratin they have in
store for this year's feast, it does not mean that everyone will welcome innovation at the Thanksgiving table. Quite the contrary. All some people really want
is the tried and true. Some people have grown quite fond of their annual mix of
turkey and trimmings, each and every dish, and they do not consider it an onerous task to repeat the meal from one year to the next. They gain comfort from
the familiarity and the ritual of it all; any tampering with the menu, no matter
how minor or well intentioned, only serves to make them feel shortchanged.

This fact my mother discovered to her dismay when she tried out a little
something at our own Thanksgiving meal. For years before anyone realized it
had become a tradition, she roasted our holiday turkey with two types of stuffing
inside it. She filled the bird's main cavity with my paternal grandmother's sage-
and-onion dressing. This quintessential American farmhouse preparation was a
genuine family heirloom, as Nana had learned to make it at her own mother's side.
And for the bird's neck cavity, my mom fixed what you could call an Italian-
American hybrid stuffing. Although this filling was not authentically Italian, it
was a recipe from my mother's family, and it bespoke her immigrant heritage
with its classic Mediterranean combination of sausage, spinach, raisins and nuts.

Then one autumn as the holiday loomed near, my mom found herself contemplating our annual Thanksgiving spread. She saw it suddenly in a new and
somewhat bothersome light. What had seemed a skillful act of diplomacy all
these years, this bringing together of two family traditions inside one bird, why,
it now smacked to her of excess. How the fact had escaped her for so long, she
did not know, for she did not go for over-indulgence when it came to family
meals. My mother was accommodating, don't misunderstand me. She was a
mom who once finished up a marathon session of Dr. Seuss[1] books with a
breakfast of green eggs and ham at the behest of her four daughters. Still, she

Published in Pass the Polenta: And Other Writings from the Kitchen *(1998), a collection
of essays about food and family.*

1. Pseudonym of Theodor Seuss Geisel (1904–1991), who wrote children's books
such as *Green Eggs and Ham* (1960) and *The Cat in the Hat* (1957).

made us eat our peas, and she said things like, "The day your papa starts raising cows that don't come with livers is the day I'll quit serving liver and onions
for dinner. Now eat up." Yes, she knew where to draw the line.

What suddenly struck my mother as disturbing was not a matter of glut-
tony or expense or grams of fat, but of balance. What with the mashed potatoes, the baked yams, the penny rolls, and two types of stuffing, there was
altogether too much starch on the plate. Starch, starch, starch. The redundancy
of it became an offense that the English teacher in her could no longer abide.
Of an instant, the solution became clear: two stuffings were one stuffing too
many. One of them would have to go.

So she said to my father, "Jim, which stuffing do you prefer at Thanks-   5
giving?"

He replied, "My mother's sage-and-onion dressing, of course. It's the stuffing of my youth. It's the heart of the Thanksgiving meal. By God, it's a national
tradition, that stuffing, and I can't even imagine the holiday without it."

This was not the response my mother had in mind. Nana's sage-and-onion
dressing had been her candidate for dismissal, because naturally, she preferred
her family's stuffing, the one with the Italian touch of sausage, spinach and
raisins. She saw my father's point, though. We celebrated the holiday with his
side of the family, and she had them to bear in mind. The children would be
too preoccupied with the mashed potatoes to care a whit one way or the other
about the stuffing, but her in-laws would feel deprived, no doubt, if Nana's dish
didn't grace the table. And she had to admit that the sage-and-onion version
was more in keeping with the all-American spirit of the holiday. It was more
faithful, she assumed, to history. Good heavens, even schoolchildren knew that
sage-and-onion dressing appeared on the Pilgrims' rough-hewn banquet table,
right alongside the spit-roasted wild turkey, the hearth-braised sweet potatoes,
the cranberry sauce, and the pumpkin pie.

I must admit I envisioned such a meal, just as I pictured Miles Standish[2]
brandishing a kitchen knife and gallantly carving the turkey roast while he
gazed deep into the limpid eyes of Priscilla Mullens.[3] But there is no record of
stuffing—sage-and-onion or otherwise—bedecking the table at the Pilgrims'
first thanksgiving, which it turns out was not a somber meal, but a frolicsome
affair of hunting, games, and wine which lasted three days. For that matter,
there isn't even any specific mention of turkeys having been served, though one
colonist wrote of an abundance of fowl at the event, and most scholars feel safe
in assuming this bounty included a few turkeys. All anyone knows for certain
is that the Mayflower folks cooked up five deer, oysters, cod, eel, corn bread,
goose, watercress, leeks, berries, and plums. Pumpkins made an appearance,
too, but no one bothered to record just how they were cooked. They certainly
were not baked in a pie crust, though, for the wheat crop had failed and the
ship's supply of flour had long since run out.

2. English military officer (c. 1584–1656), and later captain hired by the Pilgrims.
3. In the poem *The Courtship of Miles Standish* (1858) by Henry Wadsworth Longfel-
low, Miles Standish and John Alden vy for the love and attention of Priscilla Mullens.

The traditional meal as we know it dates back not to the solemn, high-collared Pilgrims, nor even to Colonial times, but to home cooks of the nineteenth century. Not until this era did the idea of an annual day of thanksgiving first take hold. The driving force behind the holiday was New Englander Sarah Josepha Hale (whose legacy also includes the nursery rhyme "Mary Had a Little Lamb"). As editor of the popular magazine *Godey's Lady's Book,* she promoted the holiday for nearly twenty years within the periodical's pages. She wrote letters annually to the state governors and to the president, and one by one the states gradually took up the idea. Finally, Abraham Lincoln, desperate for any means to promote unity in the war-ravaged country, declared the first national Thanksgiving in 1863.

10   And what did the mistress of the house serve up at this new holiday meal? Her standard company fare for autumn, of course: roast turkey with cranberry sauce, scalloped and mashed potatoes, candied sweet potatoes, braised turnips, creamed onions, cranberry sauce, mince pie, pumpkin pie—the menu has endured remarkably unchanged. And yes, it was standard procedure then to roast the turkey with a stuffing.

The actual practice of filling up a bird's cavity dates back to antiquity; the space made a handy cooking vessel for families who all too often owned only one pot. Recipes have varied over the millennia. The cookbook attributed to the Roman gastronome Apicius gives a formula that includes ground meat, chopped brains, couscous, pine nuts, lovage, and ginger; other than the brains, it sounds like something right out of a trendy contemporary cookbook. English cooks during the Middle Ages favored heavily spiced and honeyed productions based on pieces of offal that today would make our rarefied stomachs churn. Nineteenth-century American cooks went on stuffing birds, no matter how many pots and pans they had on hand in the kitchen, and recipes much like Nana's sage-and-onion dressing were a beloved part of many an early Thanksgiving repast.

No less dear, though, or popular, or traditional, were a number of other variations. Homemakers in the corn-growing south who went to stuff a turkey favored cornbread in their recipes. Along the eastern seaboard, they tucked in dozens of nectar-sweet shucked oysters, while across the country as far north as the chestnut tree once grew, they featured loads of tender chestnuts in their fillings. And many cooks treasured recipes that called for ground meat, dried fruits, autumn greens, and shelled nuts—the very products of the fall harvest upon which my mother's family recipe was based, so she need not have dismissed her version as unconventional so hastily.

The genteel ladies of the last century would have viewed my mother's dilemma not as a surplus of starch at the meal, but as a paucity of meats. They were impassioned carnivores, these American predecessors of ours, and one meager turkey would have seemed woefully inadequate at a meal showcasing the prodigious bounty of the land. Pull out the stops, Darlene, I can all but hear them tell her. Along with the requisite turkey, they decorated their tables with a chicken pie, a joint of beef, a roast goose, if the budget would allow. Certainly these additional viands would serve to put my mother's menu back on kilter.

I'm sure, too, that at least one of these women would have felt bound by duty to draw my mother aside and whisper that she really ought to call her preparation *dressing* and not *stuffing*. The word "stuffing" has been in use for centuries. Sir Thomas Elyot's *Dictionary* of 1538 uses it as a synonym for "force-meat," defined as "that wherewith any foule is crammed." Sir Thomas obviously wasn't much of a cook, or he would have known that cramming a fowl isn't such a great idea, for the filling expands during the roasting, and it can burst out at the seams if it is packed too tightly. At any rate, all this stuffing and forcing and cramming proved simply too much for the delicate sensibilities of the Victorian age, and the more discreet term "dressing" came into fashion. Today, school-marmish cookbooks often wag a finger and insist that when it is on the inside of the bird it is stuffing, and when it is baked in a separate dish, it's dressing. In reality, this does not play out. If Grandma calls her dish stuffing, then stuffing it is, regardless of its location inside or alongside the bird. Same goes for Aunt Pearl's dressing, no matter where she puts it.

Had my mother sought the counsel of Mrs. Sarah Josepha Hale or her con-   15
temporaries, then, she might have spared herself some anxiety. For although she had resolved herself to her decision, the idea of forgoing her family recipe did not rest easy with her. The days wore on and she grew positively disgruntled. Then one brisk, gray morning with two weeks yet to go before Thanksgiving, she found herself pushing her cart down the butcher's aisle at the supermarket when inspiration struck. Who ever said holiday recipes were for holidays, and holidays only? Who? She need not go without her annual dose of her family's stuffing after all. So she hoisted a fresh turkey into the cart, made a few other spur-of-the-moment additions to her shopping list, and went home and set to work.

She pulled her big frying pan out of the cupboard, set it over a low flame on the stove-top, melted half a stick of butter in it, then crumbled in three-quarters of a pound of bulk pork sausage. After the meat began to brown, she stirred in a diced onion, a couple of cloves of pressed garlic, a few stalks of cut-up celery, and a cup or so of sliced button mushrooms. These she let simmer gently until the onions were translucent. She added a large container of the chopped garden spinach she had blanched and frozen last spring, heated it through, then scraped the contents of the pan into a large ceramic bowl. When the mixture cooled to room temperature she sliced a stale loaf of French bread into cubes—enough to make about four cups—then added the bread to the bowl along with a couple of ample handfuls of raisins, sliced almonds, and freshly grated Parmesan cheese—a good half cup of each. She seasoned the stuffing with salt, black pepper, and generous pinches of oregano and rosemary, then drizzled in a glass of white wine. Using her hands, she combined all the ingredients thoroughly, then put a finger to her tongue. A pinch more salt and that would do it. Finally, she spooned the stuffing into the bird, trussed it up, and put it in the oven to roast for the rest of the afternoon.

Incidentally, my mother is quite an accomplished seamstress. She could sew bound buttonholes on a turkey if she wanted to. But she agrees with me that trussing need not be the intricate knit-one-purl-two operation that many cookbooks describe. Such elaborate needlework lingers from the days of the kitchen hearth-fire, when trussing was done to keep the drumsticks and wings from dangling in the flames as the bird turned on a spit. It now functions as a stuffy, old guard test of a cook's dexterity—yes, but can she truss a turkey? By the turn of this century, the massive iron kitchen range had become a standard feature in the American home, and oven roasting rendered unnecessary all the knotting and stitching and battening down. Trussing now primarily serves to keep the stuffing in place, and to give the bird a demure appearance, its ankles politely crossed, when it arrives at the table. Folding back the wings and tying the drumsticks together with kitchen twine usually make for ample treatment.

As my mom put the neck and giblets into a stock-pot on the stove for gravy, she decided a side dish of mashed potatoes would be just the accompaniment to round out the meal. Then she discovered she had a few sweet potatoes in the bin under the kitchen sink, and she thought, now wouldn't those be nice, too, roasted with a little butter, ginger, and brown sugar? And when she remembered the tiny boiling onions that had been rolling around in the refrigerator's bottom drawer, she decided she might as well bake them up au gratin with some bread crumbs and cream.

The turkey spittered and spattered away in the oven, filling every nook in the house with its buttery, winter-holiday scent, and the next thing my mom knew, she was rolling out the crust for a pumpkin pie. My father arrived home from work, draped his overcoat across the banister, and walked into the kitchen just in time to see her plopping the cranberry sauce out of the can. She placed it on the table in a sterling silver dish, its ridged imprints still intact and its jellied body quivering gloriously—God bless those folks at Ocean Spray, they were always a part of our turkey dinners, too. She turned to my father and said, "Dinner's almost ready."

20   My mom watched as her family gathered around the table and enjoyed a complete turkey feast on that evening in early November. After the meal, my father stretched back in his chair and folded his hands behind his head. He'd always thought it a shame, he said, a needless deprivation, that Americans ate roast turkey only once a year at Thanksgiving. This fine dinner just proved his point. What a treat, yes, what a treat. But the family's pleasure that night was merely an added perk for my mother, as she had prepared the meal for herself, only for herself, and she was feeling deeply satisfied.

When the official holiday finally arrived, my mother made good on her vow and let Nana's sage-and-onion dressing preside at the evening meal. Out came the frying pan, and she started to sauté two chopped onions and four thinly sliced stalks of celery, including the leaves, in a stick of butter. After a moment's thought, she added two plump cloves of minced garlic to the simmering pan. She couldn't resist. She knew Nana thought her a bit heavy-handed in the garlic department, but so what, it was her kitchen.

When the vegetables were limp and fragrant, she pulled the pan from the heat and set it aside to cool. She put the mixture into a bowl along with eight cups of firm, stale bread cubes, a generous spoonful of dried sage, a healthy handful of chopped fresh parsley, some salt and pepper, and a pinch of nutmeg. She gave these ingredients a light mixing, drizzled in enough broth to make the filling hold together when she squeezed a handful of it between her fingers—three-quarters of a cup, maybe a bit more—then tossed the dressing together again lightly before she spooned it into the Thanksgiving bird.

That evening Nana arrived with her sweet pickles and her three pies— apple, pumpkin, mincemeat. Cousins poured into the house toting covered casserole dishes, an uncle walked through the door, then an aunt. We soon sat down around two tables to dine, our plates heaped to the angle of repose. Amid the clanking of cutlery and the giggling and guffawing, and the festive bustle, my father paused. His fork pierced a juicy slice of dark thigh meat and his knife was poised in midstroke. He looked down intently and his eyes circled clockwise, studying the contents of his plate. He craned his neck and took an inventory of the platters and bowls laid out on the buffet counter across the room. "Darlene," he said, "this is some spread we have here, don't get me wrong. But you know what's missing is that other stuffing you make. The one we had the other day with the cornucopia of raisins and nuts and such."

My mom nearly dropped her fork. "But you told me you preferred your mother's dressing."

He looked back down at the turkey and trimmings before him. "Well, yes,   25 but that doesn't mean I don't prefer yours, too. It just doesn't seem like a proper Thanksgiving without that second stuffing on the table. Don't you agree?"

What he meant, of course, was that my mom's dish had to turn up missing before he understood just what a part of the celebration it had become. So the year the turkey had only one stuffing was the year that both recipes became permanent fixtures on my mother's Thanksgiving menu. When time-honored traditions get their start while you're not looking, it seems, they need not concern themselves with balance, or daily nutritional requirements, or even historical accuracy. For such rituals rise up out of memories, and memories are not subject to hard facts. They are not interested in making room for change.

MLA CITATION

Lust, Teresa. "The Same Old Stuffing." 1998. *The Norton Reader: An Anthology of Nonfiction.* Ed. Melissa A. Goldthwaite et al. 14th ed. New York: Norton, 2016. 310–15. Print.

QUESTIONS

1. Teresa Lust includes both family anecdotes and historical research in her essay. Was there anything about her description of the development of Thanksgiving as a holiday that surprised you?

2. In different ways, both Lust and Dan Barry (pp. 307–09) describe the ways in which people appreciate foods more once they are gone (even temporarily). What similarities and differences do you see between their essays?

3. Write an essay about a holiday tradition in your family. Use both family anecdotes and historical research. If your essay includes a recipe, consider incorporating it—as Lust does—in narrative form.

CHRIS WIEWIORA *This Is Tossing*

I
T's 10AM. An hour before Lazy Moon Pizzeria opens. You have an hour—this hour—to toss. You're supposed to have 11 pies by 11AM. One hour.

You have always failed to have 11 by 11. Sometimes you fail because you went to bed after midnight or didn't have a bowl of cereal in the morning or you tear a pie and then you're already down one and you don't believe you can ever be anywhere near perfect. On those days, the store manager comes over and inspects your not-yet-full pie rack and shakes his head. More often, you fail because the manager didn't turn on the doughpress, so you have to wait for it to warm up; or he didn't pull a tray of dough from the fridge, so all the doughballs are still frozen; or one of the two ovens wasn't turned on, so you'll be slower without being able to cook two pies at once. On those days you shake your head and maybe swear a bit, cursing the situation more than the manager, because you already feel like a failure before you've even started. Either way, this everyday failure to meet a near impossible expectation weighs down on you. If you could do 11 by 11—just once—you feel like you would truly be a professional, albeit a professional pizza tosser, and it would prove that what you do in this restaurant matters.

But instead of focusing on all that, focus on what you can do: try to go to bed early the night before, in the morning eat a bowl of cereal with your coffee, and on the way to work take it easy, drive nice and easy—not slow or fast, but easy—because 11 by 11 is hard, almost impossible, and you don't need to think about that when you open the door to the restaurant's *err-err* electronic buzzer.

And today when you walk in, in between the *err-err,* the music blasting through the restaurant's sound system is good; some simple drum beats, a bass line thumping in your throat, and guitar riffs with a hook. Bluesy rock 'n' roll. You bounce your foot as you put on your apron and clock in a few minutes early.

5   You wash your hands humming the Happy Birthday song to yourself. It's not your birthday, or anyone's birthday that you know of, but you're supposed to wash your hands for approximately 20 seconds. There's a laminated paper above all the hand-washing sinks that says to sing the ABCs, but you don't want to feel like some kid who doesn't know how to do his job.

Today, and all days that you toss, you're tucked behind the counter by the door, where you will welcome customers when they come in. But for now you should focus on tossing. You take a look at the clock. It blinks 9:59AM. You have an hour.

Published in MAKE (2013), *a Chicago-based literary magazine that is "chock full of fiction, poetry, essays, art, and review." Chris Wiewiora's essay appeared in an issue devoted to architecture.*

You check that the doughpress is on; it ticks like a coffeemaker's hotplate. The temperature knob is set right. And (yes!) there's a tray of dough already out. You're ready. Here goes.

The dough has risen a little, each bag forming a sliced-off cone, a plateau. You take the spray bottle of extra virgin olive oil and squirt twice on a hubcap-size round plate that you call the swivel plate because it's set on a swivel arm attached to the dough press. You spread the oil on the swivel plate with your bare hands, glossing the surface as well as your skin.

You pick up a bag of dough, feeling its weight settle in your palm. You know it's at least three point five pounds, no more than three point seven five. And out of the plastic, the dough feels like condensed flesh, like a too-heavy breast. You can't help that that's what you think of when you take the mound of dough in your hands and place it nippleside up on the swivel plate.

You push the cone down into itself to form a thick circle. You keep push-   10
ing with the palm of your hand around and around the circle to even it out, so the circle of dough will fit in the space the swivel plate will swivel under. Above is a heated plate that will come down and sandwich the dough.

You swivel the swivel plate, lining it up with the hotplate, and take hold of a lever in front of you and pull down with both hands. You don't press down so hard that the dough spills out of the circumference, but also not so lightly that the dough only warms on the outside while the core is still cold. You count six "Mississippi's" as the dough flattens and warms and expands into a bigger and bigger and bigger and bigger and bigger and bigger circle.

You pull up the handle, swivel out that swivel plate, take the edge of the dough in your hand, flip it over like a pancake, swivel the swivel plate back into its space and pull down on the handle, letting the hotplate press down again. You repeat until the fourth flip, when you *really* press down, spilling the dough out the sides. You lift up the handle and again swivel out the swivel plate, but now you lift the dough up and off the swivel plate altogether, placing it onto a tray called a sheetpan.

This circle of dough is called a patout, because before the dough press— and you can imagine how hard it was to do this—tossers would have to physically push down on the cold dough and shape it with force. No more than six patouts stack each tray, because more than that squishes them with their own weight. When you have filled two trays they go one above the other on a rack-cart that you wheel under a stainless steel counter.

At the counter, you burrito-roll each patout off the tray and unfurl it. There are two plastic containers: one with bright yellow grains like sand (but it's cornmeal), and another filled with fluffy flour. For now, it's only flour you need. You take a handful and spread it on the stainless steel counter, powdering the olive-oil-slick dough. Along the edge of the floured patout, you press into the dough with your fingers in a 180-degree arc, forming a crust on half of one side and then the other. And so, one by one, your stack of patouts is floured up.

Behind you is the pie rack where large wooden paddles called peels rest   15
after they've pulled pies out of the oven to cool. On top of the pie rack is a square peel without a handle. Next to the floury counter is another counter where this

particular peel goes. On it, you will sprinkle—just sprinkle—a little bit of corn-meal so that when the big thirty-inch "skin" of the pie is laid on top and the sauce is ladled onto the skin—when that is all done you can easily shake the pie off the peel, leaving it in the oven to bake.

Now, you set your stance. Lower body: legs under your shoulders and knees bent, with your weight up on your forefoot, your heels hardly touching the lino-leum floor. Upper body: torso taut but elastic, because you know that you will be twisting back and forth. Then with your hands straight out, fingers together like you're about to go swimming and thumbs tucked in so they don't pierce the dough, you're ready.

You lightly pinch the first patout. The flour makes taking the patout off the stack feel like a silky turn of a page. You lay the patout over your other hand and, it's odd, but initially you slap the dough back and forth with your hands. It begins in your wrists, the dough not only slapping but also rotating between your palms in a figure eight, an infinity symbol, an hourglass.

If someone looked closely they would see that in front of your chest, your right middle finger briefly touches your left middle finger. Then your right hand slides from your left middle finger toward your left inner elbow, while your left forearm remains straight. From above, when your two middle fingers touch, your arms will look like an equilateral triangle with one side always collapsing toward its opposite corner, pivoting back and forth, back and forth.

It's confusing. But you've done this so much by now that you just feel it. As you go on, your hands slap the dough in a curvy crisscross motion, making it turn, making it stretch into a larger circle. A circle big enough now to toss.

20   And this is what a tosser does. (Yes, you will sauce the skin of dough, and put the pie in the oven, and set the timer for 3 minutes, maybe 30 seconds more or less depending on how cool or hot the ovens are that day. And after the pies have cooled, you'll cut some of them into halves and quarters, while leaving a few pies whole.) But what really defines you as a tosser is not the patouts or the flouring or the cutting, but the tossing. It sounds so simple, but you're a tosser because you toss. And this, this is it:

You drape the dough over your left forearm like a dishrag. No, not a dish-rag. That's too much like a waiter. And you're so much more than that. You think, How many people in the world know how to do something so particular?

You're not even in the restaurant when you toss. You're elsewhere. It's you and the dough, like matador and bull. You can imagine that flap of dough like a cape. And since you imagine the dough to be a cape, you can imagine the rest of it all as sport, too. And the dough hangs down, slung low, where your right hand cups the heaviest, lowest edge. Your left hand will spring up and out, and your entire left arm will straighten as your shoulder locks, then your elbow, then your wrist, so that your arm shoots out like a discus thrower's.

But before that, your body winds up by corkscrewing down: your left arm lurches to your hips and curls behind your back, your torso twists, and you're crunched down with so much potential energy that when you come up, it all goes into your right hand, which whisks the dough off your wrist like it's a Fris-bee. And if you snapped a picture of this moment, your left hand would be turn-ing over, palm-side up, opening. That same swimming hand that slapped the dough now ready to receive it when it comes back like a boomerang. That dough spinning, spinning, spinning in the air, its beauty summed up by little kids who come to the counter to watch. You know they want to ask you how you do it, but instead of asking, maybe because you're an adult, they point and then explain to you, or the parent holding them up, or especially a younger sibling: "It's magic!"

You know exactly what these kids mean, because every time you are here under the dough, you remember back—way back—to kindergarten. When you were out on the playground for recess, away from the dull pounding of the fluorescent lights. The best days of recess were when you all played parachute with the extraordinarily large multicolored nylon circle. You and all the rest of the kids got hold of a spot and, together, lifted the parachute up and then down, trapping air under it, like catching a big empty cloud. But what you really loved was when everyone lifted the parachute up again, releasing the air, and before the parachute floated down, one by one, you all got a turn to run under its stained-glass canopy.

You come out of the zone. You glance at the clock. Its red block numbers   25
blink 10:55. You're on your last pie. The others are on the rack, cut, and logged in. And this one will only take 3 minutes in the oven. It doesn't take you longer than 2 minutes and change to toss and sauce a pie. You've almost played a perfect game. 11 by 11. One hour. Just one more.

And you take this last circle of dough, slap it back and forth, and wind up and toss it so that the dough nearly brushes one bulb of the draped Christmas tree lights strung from the ceiling tiles. And as you're under the dough—for a second you feel trapped, because you realize after this you can't ever be better—you wish you could be back in school, having fun like a kid again with no expectation of something perfect never being better. But you're here, on this last pie, with your left arm open and ready and waiting as it spins and spins and spins above you, about to come down.

MLA CITATION

Wiewiora, Chris. "This Is Tossing." 2013. *The Norton Reader: An Anthology of Nonfiction.* Ed. Melissa A. Goldthwaite et al. 14th ed. New York: Norton, 2016. 316–19. Print.

QUESTIONS

1. Chris Wiewiora uses sensory language—specifically sight, sound, touch, and visual cues—to help readers imaginatively experience the process of tossing a pizza crust. Locate places in the essay where his use of sensory language helps you imagine this process clearly.

2. Wiewiora uses the second-person point of view ("you") and present tense. Why do you think he uses that perspective and verb tense? How do these choices affect your reading of the essay?

3. Write an essay in which you guide readers through a process, teaching them to do something that may be unfamiliar to them. Like Wiewiora, use sensory language, the second-person point of view, and present tense.

SPORTS

ROGER ANGELL *The Interior Stadium*

SPORTS ARE TOO MUCH WITH US.[1] Late and soon, sitting and watching—mostly watching on television—we lay waste our powers of identification and enthusiasm and, in time, attention as more and more closing rallies and crucial putts and late field goals and final playoffs and sudden deaths and world records and world championships unreel themselves ceaselessly before our half-lidded eyes. Professional leagues expand like bubble gum, ever larger and thinner, and the extended sporting seasons, now bunching and overlapping at the ends, conclude in exhaustion and the wrong weather. So, too, goes the secondary business of sports—the news or non-news off the field. Sports announcers (ex-halfbacks in Mod hairdos) bring us another live, exclusive interview in depth with the twitchy coach of some as yet undefeated basketball team, or with a weeping (for joy) fourteen-year-old champion female backstroker, and the sports pages, now almost the largest single part of the newspaper, brim with salary disputes, medical bulletins, franchise maneuverings, all-star ballots, drug scandals, close-up biogs, after-dinner tributes, union tactics, week-end wrap-ups, wire-service polls, draft-choice trades, clubhouse gossip, and the latest odds. The American obsession with sports is not a new phenomenon, of course, except in its current dimensions, its excessive excessiveness. What *is* new, and what must at times unsettle even the most devout and unselective fan, is a curious sense of loss. In the midst of all these successive spectacles and instant replays and endless reportings and recapitulations, we seem to have forgotten what we came for. More and more, each sport resembles all sports; the flavor, the special joys of place and season, the unique displays of courage and strength and style that once isolated each game and fixed it in our affections have disappeared somewhere in the noise and crush.

Of all sports, none has been so buffeted about by this unselective proliferation, so maligned by contemporary cant, or so indifferently defended as baseball. Yet the game somehow remains the same, obdurately unaltered and comparable only with itself. Baseball has one saving grace that distinguishes it—for me, at any rate—from every other sport. Because of its pace, and thus

Originally published in the New Yorker *(1971), a weekly magazine of "reportage, commentary, criticism, essays, fiction, satire, cartoons, and poetry," this essay also appeared in* The Summer Game *(1978), Roger Angell's book about baseball in the United States.*

1. Allusion to "The World Is Too Much with Us" (1808), a poem by William Wordsworth.

the perfectly observed balance, both physical and psychological, between opposing forces, its clean lines can be restored in retrospect. This inner game—baseball in the mind—has no season, but it is best played in the winter, without the distraction of other baseball news. At first, it is a game of recollections, recapturing, and visions. Figures and occasions return, enormous sounds rise and swell, and the interior stadium fills with light and yields up the sight of a young ballplayer—some hero perfectly memorized—just completing his own unique swing and now racing toward first. See the way he runs? Yes, that's him! Unmistakable, he leans in, still following the distant flight of the ball with his eyes, and takes his big turn at the base. Yet this is only the beginning, for baseball in the mind is not a mere returning. In time, this easy summoning up of restored players, winning hits, and famous rallies gives way to reconsiderations and reflections about the sport itself. By thinking about baseball like this—by playing it over, keeping it warm in a cold season—we begin to make discoveries. With luck, we may even penetrate some of its mysteries. One of those mysteries is its vividness—the absolutely distinct inner vision we retain of that hitter, that eager base-runner, of however long ago. My father was talking the other day about some of the ballplayers he remembered. He grew up in Cleveland, and the Indians were his team. Still are. "We had Nap Lajoie at second," he said. "You've heard of him. A great big broad-shouldered fellow, but a beautiful fielder. He was a rough customer. If he didn't like an umpire's call, he'd give him a faceful of tobacco juice. The shortstop was Terry Turner—a smaller man, and blond. I can still see Lajoie picking up a grounder and wheeling and floating the ball over to Turner. Oh, he was quick on his feet! In right field we had Elmer Flick, now in the Hall of Fame. I liked the center fielder, too. His name was Harry Bay, and he wasn't a heavy hitter, but he was very fast and covered a lot of ground. They said he could circle the bases in twelve seconds flat. I saw him get a home run inside the park—the ball hit on the infield and went right past the second baseman and out to the wall, and Bay beat the relay. I remember Addie Joss, our great right-hander. Tall, and an elegant pitcher. I once saw him pitch a perfect game. He died young."[2]

My father has been a fan all his life, and he has pretty well seen them all. He has told me about the famous last game of the 1912 World Series, in Boston, and seeing Fred Snodgrass[3] drop that fly ball in the tenth inning, when the Red Sox scored twice and beat the Giants. I looked up Harry Bay and those other Indians in the *Baseball Encyclopedia,* and I think my father must have seen that inside-the-park homer in the summer of 1904. Lajoie batted .376 that year, and Addie Joss led the American League with an earned-run average of 1.59, but the Indians finished in fourth place. 1904. . . . Sixty-seven years have gone by, yet Nap Lajoie is in plain view, and the ball still floats over to Terry Turner. Well, my father is eighty-one now, and old men are great rememberers of the distant past. But I am fifty, and I can also bring things back: Lefty

2. Ballplayers mentioned in this paragraph played for the Cleveland Indians in the early twentieth century.

3. New York (N.Y.) Giants outfielder (1887–1974).

Gomez, skinny-necked and frighteningly wild, pitching his first game at Yankee Stadium, against the White Sox and Red Faber in 1930. Old John McGraw,[4] in a business suit and a white fedora, sitting lumpily in a dark corner of the dugout at the Polo Grounds and glowering out at the field. Babe Ruth,[5] wearing a new, bright yellow glove, trotting out to right field—a swollen ballet dancer, with those delicate, almost feminine feet and ankles. Ruth at the plate, upper-cutting and missing, staggering with the force of his swing. Ruth and Gehrig,[6] hitting back-to-back homers. Gehrig, in the summer of 1933, running bases with a bad leg in a key game against the Senators; hobbling, he rounds third, closely followed by young Dixie Walker, then a Yankee. The throw comes in to the plate, and the Washington catcher—it must have been Luke Sewell—tags out the sliding Gehrig and, in the same motion, the sliding Dixie Walker. A double play at the plate. The Yankees lose the game; the Senators go on to a pennant. And, back across the river again, Carl Hubbell. My own great pitcher, a southpaw, tall and elegant. Hub pitching: the loose motion; two slow, formal bows from the waist, glove and hands held almost in front of his face as he pivots, the long right leg (in long, peculiar pants) striding; and the ball, angling oddly, shooting past the batter. Hubbell walks gravely back to the bench, his pitching arm, as always, turned the wrong way round, with the palm out. Screwballer.

Any fan, as I say, can play this private game, extending it to extraordinary varieties and possibilities in his mind. Ruth bats against Sandy Koufax or Sam McDowell.[7] . . . Hubbell pitches to Ted Williams,[8] and the Kid, grinding the bat in his fists, twitches and blocks his hips with the pitch; he holds off but still follows the ball, leaning over and studying it like some curator as it leaps in just under his hands. Why this vividness, even from an imaginary confrontation? I have watched many other sports, and I have followed some—football, hockey, tennis—with eagerness, but none of them yields these permanent interior pictures, these ancient and precise excitements. Baseball, I must conclude, is intensely remembered because only baseball is so intensely watched. The game forces intensity upon us. In the ballpark, scattered across an immense green, each player is isolated in our attention, utterly visible. Watch that fielder just below us. Little seems to be expected of him. He waits in easy composure, his hands on his knees; when the ball at last soars or bounces out to him, he seizes it and dispatches it with swift, haughty ease. It all looks easy, slow, and, above all, safe. Yet we know better, for what is certain in baseball is that someone, perhaps several people, will fail. They will be searched out, caught in the open, and defeated, and there will be no confusion about it or sharing of the

---

4. N.Y. Giants manager (1873–1934).

5. Boston pitcher and New York (N.Y.) Yankee outfielder (1895–1948).

6. Lou Gehrig (1903–1941), N.Y. Yankees first baseman.

7. Koufax (b. 1935), pitcher for the Brooklyn and Los Angeles Dodgers; McDowell (b. 1942), pitcher, most notably with the Cleveland Indians.

8. Boston Red Sox outfielder (1918–2002). "The Kid" was one of his nicknames.

blame. This is sure to happen, because what baseball requires of its athletes, of course, is nothing less than perfection, and perfection cannot be eased or divided. Every movement of every game, from first pitch to last out, is measured and recorded against an absolute standard, and thus each success is also a failure. Credit that strikeout to the pitcher, but also count it against the batter's average; mark his run unearned, because the left fielder bobbled the ball for an instant and a runner moved up. Yet, faced with this sudden and repeated presence of danger, the big-league player defends himself with such courage and skill that the illusion of safety is sustained. Tension is screwed tighter and tighter as the certain downfall is postponed again and again, so that when disaster does come—a half-topped infield hit, a walk on a close three-and-two call, a low drive up the middle that just eludes the diving shortstop—we rise and cry out. It is a spontaneous, inevitable, irresistible reaction.

Televised baseball, I must add, does not seem capable of transmitting this emotion. Most baseball is seen on the tube now, and it is presented faithfully and with great technical skill. But the medium is irrevocably two-dimensional; even with several cameras, television cannot bring us the essential distances of the game—the simultaneous flight of a batted ball and its pursuit by the racing, straining outfielders, the swift convergence of runner and ball at a base. Foreshortened on our screen, the players on the field appear to be squashed together, almost touching each other, and, watching them, we lose the sense of their separateness and lonesome waiting. 5

This is a difficult game. It is so demanding that the best teams and the weakest teams can meet on almost even terms, with no assurance about the result of any one game. In March 1962, in St. Petersburg, the World Champion Yankees played for the first time against the newborn New York Mets—one of the worst teams of all time—in a game that each badly wanted to win; the winner, to nobody's real surprise, was the Mets. In 1970, the World Champion Orioles won a hundred and eight games and lost fifty-four; the lowest cellar team, the White Sox, won fifty-six games and lost a hundred and six. This looks like an enormous disparity, but what it truly means is that the Orioles managed to win two out of every three games they played, while the White Sox won one out of every three. That third game made the difference—and a kind of difference that can be appreciated when one notes that the winning margin given up by the White Sox to all their opponents during the season averaged 1.1 runs per game. Team form is harder to establish in baseball than in any other sport, and the hundred-and-sixty-two-game season not uncommonly comes down to October with two or three teams locked together at the top of the standings on the final weekend. Each inning of baseball's slow, searching time span, each game of its long season is essential to the disclosure of its truths.

Form is the imposition of a regular pattern upon varying and unpredictable circumstances, but the patterns of baseball, for all the game's tautness and neatness, are never regular. Who can predict the winner and shape of today's game? Will it be a brisk, neat two-hour shutout? A languid, error-filled 12-3

laugher? A riveting three-hour, fourteen-inning deadlock? What other sport produces these manic swings? For the players, too, form often undergoes terrible
reversals; in no other sport is a champion athlete so often humiliated or a
journeyman so easily exalted. The surprise, the upset, the total turnabout of
expectations and reputations—these are delightful commonplaces of baseball.
Al Gionfriddo, a part-time Dodger outfielder, stole second base in the ninth
inning of the fourth game of the 1947 World Series to help set up Lavagetto's
game-winning double (and the only Dodger hit of the game) off the Yankees'
Bill Bevens. Two days later, Gionfriddo robbed Joe DiMaggio[9] with a famous
game-saving catch of a four-hundred-and-fifteen-foot drive in deepest left field
at Yankee Stadium. Gionfriddo never made it back to the big leagues after that
season. Another irregular, the Mets' Al Weis, homered in the fifth and last game
of the 1969 World Series, tying up the game that the Mets won in the next
inning; it was Weis's third homer of the year and his first ever at Shea Stadium.[10]
And so forth. Who remembers the second game of the 1956 World Series—
an appallingly bad afternoon of baseball in which the Yankees' starter, Don
Larsen, was yanked after giving up a single and four walks in less than two
innings? It was Larsen's *next* start, the fifth game, when he pitched his perfect
game.

There is always a heavy splash of luck in these reversals. Luck, indeed, plays
an almost predictable part in the game; we have all seen the enormous enemy
clout into the bleachers that just hooks foul at the last instant, and the half-
checked swing that produces a game-winning blooper over second. Everyone
complains about baseball luck, but I think it adds something to the game that is
nearly essential. Without it, such a rigorous and unforgiving pastime would be
almost too painful to enjoy.

No one, it becomes clear, can conquer this impossible and unpredictable
game. Yet every player tries, and now and again—very rarely—we see a man
who seems to have met all the demands, challenged all the implacable averages, spurned the mere luck. He has defied baseball, even altered it, and for a
time at least the game is truly his. One thinks of Willie Mays,[11] in the best of
his youth, batting at the Polo Grounds, his whole body seeming to leap at the
ball as he swings in an explosion of exuberance. Or Mays in center field, playing in so close that he appears at times to be watching the game from over the
second baseman's shoulder, and then that same joyful leap as he takes off after
a long, deep drive and runs it down, running so hard and so far that the ball
itself seems to stop in the air and wait for him. One thinks of Jackie Robinson[12] in a close game—any close game—playing the infield and glaring in at the
enemy hitter, hating him and daring him, refusing to be beaten. And Sandy
Koufax pitching in the last summers before he was disabled, in that time when

9. N.Y. Yankees center fielder (1914–1999).

10. Home of the New York (N.Y.) Mets from 1964 to 2008; demolished in 2009.

11. Outfielder for N.Y. Giants, San Francisco Giants, and N.Y. Mets (b. 1931).

12. Player for the Brooklyn Dodgers and the first African American to play in Major
League Baseball (1919–1972).

he pitched a no-hitter every year for four years. Kicking swiftly, hiding the ball until the last instant, Koufax throws in a blur of motion, coming over the top, and the fast ball, appearing suddenly in the strike zone, sometimes jumps up so immoderately that his catcher has to take it with his glove shooting upward, like an infielder stabbing at a bad-hop grounder. I remember some batter taking a strike like that and then stepping out of the box and staring back at the pitcher with a look of utter incredulity—as if Koufax had just thrown an Easter egg past him.

Joe DiMaggio batting sometimes gave the same impression—the suggestion that the old rules and dimensions of baseball no longer applied to him, and that the game had at last grown unfairly easy. I saw DiMaggio once during his famous hitting streak in 1941; I'm not sure of the other team or the pitcher—perhaps it was the Tigers and Bobo Newsom—but I'm sure of DiMaggio pulling a line shot to left that collided preposterously with the bag at third base and ricocheted halfway out to center field. That record of hitting safely in fifty-six straight games seems as secure as any in baseball, but it does not awe me as much as the fact that DiMadge's old teammates claim they *never* saw him commit an error of judgment in a ball game. Thirteen years, and never a wrong throw, a cutoff man missed, an extra base passed up. Well, there was one time when he stretched a single against the Red Sox and was called out at second, but the umpire is said to have admitted later that he blew the call.

And one more for the pantheon: Carl Yastrzemski. To be precise, Yaz in September of the 1967 season, as his team, the Red Sox, fought and clawed against the White Sox and the Twins and the Tigers in the last two weeks of the closest and most vivid pennant race of our time. The presiding memory of that late summer is of Yastrzemski approaching the plate, once again in a situation where all hope rests on him, and settling himself in the batter's box—touching his helmet, tugging at his belt, and just touching the tip of the bat to the ground, in precisely the same set of gestures—and then, in a storm of noise and pleading, swinging violently and perfectly . . . and hitting. In the last two weeks of that season, Yaz batted .522—twenty-three hits for forty-four appearances: four doubles, five home runs, sixteen runs batted in. In the final two games, against the Twins, both of which the Red Sox *had* to win for the pennant, he went seven for eight, won the first game with a homer, and saved the second with a brilliant, rally-killing throw to second base from deep left field. (He cooled off a little in the World Series, batting only .400 for seven games and hitting three homers.) Since then, the game and the averages have caught up with Yastrzemski, and he has never again approached that kind of performance. But then, of course, neither has anyone else.

Only baseball, with its statistics and isolated fragments of time, permits so precise a reconstruction from box score and memory. Take another date—October 7, 1968, at Detroit, the fifth game of the World Series. The fans are here, and an immense noise—a cheerful, 53,634-man vociferosity—utterly fills the green, steep, high-walled box of Tiger Stadium. This is a good baseball town, and the cries have an anxious edge, for the Tigers are facing almost sure extinction.

They trail the Cardinals by three games to one, and never for a moment have they looked the equal of these defending World Champions. Denny McLain, the Tigers' thirty-one-game winner, was humiliated in the opener by the Cardinals' Bob Gibson, who set an all-time Series record by striking out seventeen Detroit batters. The Tigers came back the next day, winning rather easily behind their capable left-hander Mickey Lolich, but the Cardinals demolished them in the next two games, scoring a total of seventeen runs and again brushing McLain aside; Gibson has now struck out twenty-seven Tigers, and he will be ready to pitch again in the Series if needed. Even more disheartening is Lou Brock, the Cards' left fielder, who has already lashed out eight hits in the first four games and has stolen seven bases in eight tries; Bill Freehan, the Tigers' catcher, has a sore arm. And here, in the very top of the first, Brock leads off against Lolich and doubles to left; a moment later, Curt Flood singles, and Orlando Cepeda homers into the left-field stands. The Tigers are down, 3-0, and the fans are wholly stilled.

In the third inning, Brock leads off with another hit—a single—and there is a bitter overtone to the home-town cheers when Freehan, on a pitchout, at last throws him out, stealing, at second. There is no way for anyone to know, of course, that this is a profound omen; Brock has done his last damage to the Tigers in this Series. Now it is the fourth, and hope and shouting return. Mickey Stanley leads off the Detroit half with a triple that lands, two inches fair, in the right-field corner. He scores on a fly. Willie Horton also triples. With two out, Jim Northrup smashes a hard grounder directly at the Cardinal second baseman, Javier, and at the last instant the ball strikes something on the infield and leaps up and over Javier's head, and Horton scores. Luck! Luck twice over, if you remember how close Stanley's drive came to falling foul. But never mind; it's 3-2 now, and a game again.

But Brock is up, leading off once again, and an instant later he has driven a Lolich pitch off the left-field wall for a double. Now Javier singles to left, and Brock streaks around third base toward home. Bill Freehan braces himself in front of the plate, waiting for the throw; he has had a miserable Series, going hitless in fourteen at-bats so far, and undergoing those repeated humiliations by the man who is now racing at him full speed—the man who must surely be counted, along with Gibson, as the Series hero. The throw comes in chest-high on the fly from Willie Horton in left; ball and base-runner arrive together; Brock does not slide. Brock does not slide, and his left foot, just descending on the plate, is banged away as he collides with Freehan. Umpire Doug Harvey shoots up his fist: Out! It is a great play. Nothing has changed, the score is still 3-2, but everything has changed; something has shifted irrevocably in this game.

15 In the seventh inning, with one out and the Tigers still one run shy, Tiger manager Mayo Smith allows Lolich to bat for himself. Mickey Lolich has hit .114 for the season, and Smith has a pinch-hitter on the bench named Gates Brown, who hit .370. But Lolich got two hits in his other Series start, including the first homer of his ten years in baseball. Mayo, sensing something that he will not be able to defend later if he is wrong, lets Lolich bat for himself, and Mickey pops a foolish little fly to right that falls in for a single. Now there

is another single. A walk loads the bases, and Al Kaline comes to the plate. The noise in the stadium is insupportable. Kaline singles, and the Tigers go ahead by a run. Norm Cash drives in another. The Tigers win this searching, turned-about, lucky, marvelous game by 5-3.

Two days later, back in St. Louis, form shows its other face as the Tigers rack up ten runs in the third inning and win by 13-1. McLain at last has his Series win. So it is Lolich against Gibson in the finale, of course. Nothing happens. Inning after inning goes by, zeros accumulate on the scoreboard, and anxiety and silence lengthen like shadows. In the sixth, Lou Brock singles. Daring Lolich, daring the Tiger infielders' nerves, openly forcing his luck, hoping perhaps to settle these enormous tensions and difficulties with one more act of bravado, he takes an excessive lead off first, draws the throw from Lolich, breaks for second, and is erased, just barely, by Cash's throw. A bit later, Curt Flood singles, and, weirdly, he too is picked off first and caught in a rundown. Still no score. Gibson and Lolich, both exhausted, pitch on. With two out in the seventh, Cash singles for the Tigers' second hit of the day. Horton is safe on a slow bouncer that *just* gets through the left side of the infield. Jim Northrup hits the next pitch deep and high but straight at Flood, who is the best center fielder in the National League. Flood starts in and then halts, stopping so quickly that his spikes churn up a green flap of turf; he turns and races back madly, but the ball sails over his head for a triple. Disaster. Suddenly, irreversibly, it has happened. Two runs are in, Freehan doubles in another, and, two innings later, the Tigers are Champions of the World.

I think I will always remember those two games—the fifth and the seventh—perfectly. And I remember something else about the 1968 Series when it was over—a feeling that almost everyone seemed to share: that Bob Gibson had not lost that last game, and the Cardinals had not lost the Series. Certainly no one wanted to say that the Tigers had not won it, but there seemed to be something more that remained to be said. It was something about the levels and demands of the sport we had seen—as if the baseball itself had somehow surpassed the players and the results. It was the baseball that won.

Always, it seems, there is something more to be discovered about this game. Sit quietly in the upper stand and look at the field. Half close your eyes against the sun, so that the players recede a little, and watch the movements of baseball. The pitcher, immobile on the mound, holds the inert white ball, his little lump of physics. Now, with abrupt gestures, he gives it enormous speed and direction, converting it suddenly into a line, a moving line. The batter, wielding a plane, attempts to intercept the line and acutely alter it, but he fails; the ball, a line again, is redrawn to the pitcher, in the center of this square, the diamond. Again the pitcher studies his task—the projection of his next line through the smallest possible segment of an invisible seven-sided solid (the strike zone has depth as well as height and width) sixty feet and six inches away; again the batter considers his even more difficult proposition, which is to reverse this imminent white speck, to redirect its energy not in a soft parabola or a series of diminishing squiggles but into a beautiful and dangerous new force, of perfect straightness and immense distance. In time, these and other lines are drawn on the field; the batter and the fielders are also transformed into fluidity, moving and converging, and we see now that all movement in baseball is a convergence toward fixed points—the pitched ball toward the plate, the thrown ball toward the right angles of the bases, the batted ball toward the as yet undrawn but already visible point of congruence with either the ground or a glove. Simultaneously, the fielders hasten toward that same point of meeting with the ball, and both the base-runner and the ball, now redirected, toward their encounter at the base. From our perch, we can sometimes see three or four or more such geometries appearing at the same instant on the green board below us, and, mathematicians that we are, can sense their solution even before they are fully drawn. It is neat, it is pretty, it is satisfying. Scientists speak of the profoundly moving aesthetic beauty of mathematics, and perhaps the baseball field is one of the few places where the rest of us can glimpse this mystery.

The last dimension is time. Within the ballpark, time moves differently, marked by no clock except the events of the game. This is the unique, unchangeable feature of baseball, and perhaps explains why this sport, for all the enormous changes it has undergone in the past decade or two, remains somehow rustic, unviolent, and introspective. Baseball's time is seamless and invisible, a bubble within which players move at exactly the same pace and rhythms as all their predecessors. This is the way the game was played in our youth and in our fathers' youth, and even back then—back in the country days—there must have been the same feeling that time could be stopped. Since baseball time is measured only in outs, all you have to do is succeed utterly; keep hitting, keep the rally alive, and you have defeated time. You remain forever young. Sitting in the stands, we sense this, if only dimly. The players below us—Mays, DiMaggio, Ruth, Snodgrass—swim and blur in memory, the ball floats over to Terry Turner, and the end of this game may never come.

MLA CITATION

Angell, Roger. "The Interior Stadium." 1971. *The Norton Reader: An Anthology of Nonfiction.* Ed. Melissa A. Goldthwaite et al. 14th ed. New York: Norton, 2016. 320–28. Print.

QUESTIONS

1. Roger Angell wrote, "Sports are too much with us" (paragraph 1) in the early 1970s. Think about sports today: the endless speculation about signings and contracts, gossip about players' salaries and behavior, and twenty-four-hour sports channels. Are sports even more "with us" today? What does "too much with us" mean to you?

2. Gerald Graff writes of his youthful obsession with baseball with its "challenging arguments, debates, problems for analysis, and intricate statistics" (paragraph 11) in "Hidden Intellectualism" (pp. 418–422). What signs do you see of a not-so-hidden intellectualism in Angell's essay?

3. In paragraph 1, Angell writes "More and more, each sport resembles all sports; the flavor, the special joys of place and season, the unique displays of courage and

strength and style that once isolated each game and fixed it in our affections have disappeared somewhere in the noise and crush." But his essay refutes this statement, singling out baseball as an example of a sport that retains its distinctiveness. Pick a different sport you know well and in an essay (as a spectator, like Angell, or as a participant), describe that sport, showing how it does or does not resemble "all sports."

JOE POSNANSKI   *Mariano Rivera's a True Yankee*

> They say his father was a fisherman. Maybe he was
> as poor as we are and would understand.
>   —*THE OLD MAN AND THE SEA*

THERE IS A YANKEE MYTHOLOGY that sustains New York fans and drives everybody else crazy, and it goes something like this: To play for the New York Yankees, you need to have a certain quality—quiet dignity, maybe, that's part of it, or valor or a sense of the moment. All of that. More. To be a Yankee, the mythos goes, you should suffer your pain in private like Mantle, and keep hitting home runs even when your hair falls out like Maris, and find your true self in October like Reggie. You can be larger than life, like the Babe, and call yourself lucky when dying like Gehrig, and see the world through your own eyes like Yogi. You can even punch out marshmallow salesmen like Billy Martin. As long as you win almost every time out, like Whitey, and make perfectly timed moves, like Casey, and are willing to dive headfirst after victory like Jeter.[1]

No team has so many legends. . . . and no team celebrates their legends to New York Yankee excess. This is what makes the Yankees so beloved and despised, depending on which side of the pinstripes you stand. And the man who probably represents the Yankee mythology better than anyone is the man who, according to the Yankee legend, never threw to the wrong base. "I thank the good Lord for making me a Yankee," Joe DiMaggio[2] famously said, and he hit in 56 straight games and made plays with grace. People wrote songs about him. Hemingway[3] wrote literature about him.

Published in Sports Illustrated *(2009), a magazine covering sports news and analysis. Joe Posnanski was for many years a columnist on the* Kansas City Star, *and currently writes for* NBC Sports.

1. Posnanski begins his essay by naming famous New York (N.Y.) Yankees and their distinguishing talents.
2. N.Y. Yankees center fielder (1914–1999).
3. Ernest Hemingway (1899–1961), American author of *The Old Man and the Sea* (1952), a novel that includes references to the N.Y. Yankees and Joe DiMaggio.

"I must have the confidence," Hemingway's old man says to the sea, "and I must be worthy of the great DiMaggio, who does all things perfectly even with the pain of the bone spur in his heel."

The funny part is there is actually a Yankees player who, perhaps even more than DiMaggio, lives up to the Yankee mythology. He too is the son of a fisherman, and he grew up poor enough to understand. His career almost ended before it began, and he was almost traded (twice) before the Yankee pinstripes looked right on him. On the field, he has triumphed under the most intense glare in American sports. Off the field, he has been quiet to the sound of invisible. And all the while, he has looked calm, stunningly calm, the sort of superhuman calm that Hollywood gives its heroes.

5   Yes, if there is an expression that conveys the Yankee myth, it would be the countenance of Mariano Rivera in the ninth inning.

"Have faith in the Yankees, my son," Hemingway's old man says to the boy. "Think of the great DiMaggio."

If Ernest Hemingway was alive and writing today, those words would be: "Think of the great Rivera."

One pitch. Think about that. Mariano Rivera has saved 502 baseball games by essentially throwing one pitch, that same cut fastball. And, of course, he has done much more than save 502 baseball games with the cut fastball . . . you can choose a thousand numbers to show his eminence. Consider ERA+, a statistic that measures a player's ERA against the pitchers of his own era. In ERA+, 100 is exactly league average.

Here are the greatest ERA+ in baseball history (more than 1,000 innings pitched):

10   1. Mariano Rivera, 198   2. Pedro Martinez, 154   3. Lefty Grove, 148   4. Walter Johnson, 147   5. Five pitchers tied at 146

Look at that—Rivera's ERA+ is more than FORTY POINTS higher than anyone else in baseball history. How about WHIP—walks-plus-hits per inning pitched?

1. Addie Joss, 0.968   2. Ed Walsh, 1.000   3. Mariano Rivera, 1.02   4. John Ward, 1.044[4]

How about number of seasons with an ERA under 2.00? Walter Johnson did it 11 times—all in the Deadball Era. Mariano Rivera did it eight times during the biggest explosion of offense since the 1930s. Of course, you can't compare Rivera to Walter Johnson or any other starter; Rivera has not even thrown 85 innings in a season since he became a closer in 1997.

Then again, you cannot compare Walter Johnson or any other starter to Rivera either because of the 1,055 innings the man has pitched, about 900 of them were eighth inning, ninth inning or later, with the game on the line, with the crowd freaking out, with the metropolis tabloid editors holding the back

---

4. You will note the other three on the list are all pitchers from the Deadball Era [Posnanski's note].

pages (How's this for the headline: "Cry Me A Rivera?" Or "Oh no Mariano!"), with the opposing team, as it says in *Casey at the Bat,* clinging to the hope which springs eternal in the human breast.

And with Rivera on the mound, Mighty Casey[5] did strike out time and time and time again. Rivera struck them out and busted their bats on that same pitch over and over and over, one pitch, a low-to-mid-90s cut fastball. One pitch. It seems impossible.

But what a pitch. Jim Thome[6] calls it the greatest pitch in baseball history, and who could argue? There's Sandy Koufax's curveball, Satchel Paige's fastball, Steve Carlton's slider, Carl Hubbell's screwball, Bruce Sutter's splitter, Gaylord Perry's spitter, Pedro Martinez's change-up, but all of them threw other pitches, set-up pitches. Rivera has no opening act. He comes at hitters with the same pitch, one pitch, again and again, hard fastball, sharp break to the left at the last possible instant, that pitch has undoubtedly broken more bats per inning than any other, it has left more batters frozen per inning than any other, it has broken more hearts than *Brian's Song.*[7]

Rivera says he learned the pitch while fooling around one day in 1997, playing catch with his friend and Panama countryman Ramiro Mendoza. By then, Rivera was already the Yankees closer. And he was already terrific—he was coming off a superhuman 1996 season. That year, as a setup man to John Wetteland, he had pitched 107 innings, struck out 130, and allowed the league to hit only .189. But he had done that with pure power—a high-90s fastball and impeccable control. And such things don't last.

Rivera remembers playing catch with Mendoza, coming up with a new grip, and coming out of it with this monster—"A gift from God," he always says—a cut fastball that bore in on lefties and made righties give up.

And suddenly, he was even better. That year, 1997, he finished with his first sub-2.00 ERA. And from that point on, Mariano Rivera threw that one pitch in ballparks across America, to the best hitters of his generation. The best hitters of his generation could not catch up. They have not caught up still.

"You know what's coming," a five-time All-Star Mike Sweeney once said. "But you know what's coming in horror movies, too. It still gets you."

Mariano Rivera grew up in Puerto Camito, Panama, and he happily will admit that he did not grow up with big dreams. He never expected to leave. He worked as a fisherman as a young boy—cleaned fish, pulled up nets, like the boy in Hemingway's vision. He wanted to play ball. The Yankees signed him for $3,000,

15

20

---

5. Titular character in "Casey at the Bat" (1888); a poem by Ernest Lawrence Thayer.

6. Baseball infielder (b. 1970) for six different teams, most notably the Cleveland Indians.

7. TV movie (1971) about Brian Piccolo, a Chicago Bears football player who died of cancer at age twenty-six.

Rivera promised his mother he would always come home, and when he was 22 years old he had Tommy John surgery.[8] Nobody was predicting great things.

His first game in the big leagues in 1995—Rivera was 25 already—he started against the California Angels and lasted just 3⅓ innings. After four starts, his ERA was 10.20, and he didn't pitch again for more than three weeks. Then, on the Fourth of July, he threw eight innings, allowed two hits and struck out 11 against the White Sox. The Yankees were not entirely sure what they had.

They would not really know what they had until (fittingly) the playoffs—the Yankees' first playoff appearance in 14 years. Rivera pitched 5⅓ scoreless innings in relief against the Seattle Mariners. He dominated those innings too, something seemed to light up inside him when the pressure was its heaviest. The next year, with Joe Torre as the new Yankees manager, Rivera was moved to the 'pen, and he was immediately so awesome that in late April, Twins manager Tom Kelly made his statement: "He needs to pitch in a higher league, if there is one. Ban him from baseball. He should be illegal."

Of course, quite a few closers have been virtually unhittable for one year, two years, three years. But sooner or later, something happens. Hitters figure something out. The constant duress wears the pitcher down. The closer's money pitch loses one mph of speed or one millimeter of break. And then, like an NFL cornerback who loses a half step, the closer is lost.

But Rivera's one pitch has never lost its power. He just keeps going, year after year. Here's a challenge for you: pick out Mariano Rivera's best year. Do you want 1998, when he saved 36 games for the almost unbeatable Yankees and posted a 1.91 ERA? Or do you prefer the next year, when he led the league with 45 saves and opposing batters hit .176 against him? Do you like 2004 when he saved 53—32 by the All-Star Break—or 2005 when he had a 1.38 ERA and had an absurd 38 1-2-3 innings?

Then again, you could always choose last year, when Rivera had a 77-to-6 strikeout-to-walk ratio and punched up a .665 WHIP—only Dennis Eckersley[9] in his heyday had ever put so few batters on base.

He has always looked so comfortable in the moment. It isn't that Mariano Rivera has never failed—he actually has three of the most famous defeats in recent memory. In 1997, he gave up an eighth-inning home run to Sandy Alomar[10] with the Yankees just four outs away from clinching a spot in the ALCS.[11] In 2001, he gave up two broken bat singles—Rivera breaks bats the way Chuck Norris[12] breaks bones—and committed an error and allowed two runs in the ninth in Game 7 of the World Series. In 2004, he blew two saves against Bos-

25

8. Operation in which the ulnar collateral ligament in the elbow is replaced with a tendon taken from elsewhere in the body. Named after John (b. 1943), the pitcher whose career was saved by this procedure.

9. Pitcher (b. 1954), most notably for the Boston Red Sox and Oakland Athletics.

10. Catcher (b. 1966), most notably with the Cleveland Indians.

11. American League Championship Series. The winner of this series goes on to the World Series.

12. American martial artist (b. 1940) and star of action movies.

ton, a performance so shocking that the next year Red Sox fans wildly cheered him when his name was announced.[13]

No, it isn't that Rivera never failed, it's that he never let that failure define him or knock him off course. Even with those three defeats, he's the greatest postseason closer in baseball history, maybe the greatest postseason pitcher ever. He is 8-1 in the postseason with 34 saves (nobody else has even half of that) and a ludicrous 0.77 ERA. Sixty-six times in his postseason career, Mariano Rivera has appeared in the late innings of a playoff or World Series game and not given up a run—nobody else is even close.

Rivera does not talk much about it, at least not publicly, but he will say that to pitch well in those heart-pounding moments you have to enjoy the heart-pounding moments, you must have balance in your life (the moment is important but not THAT important; losing is difficult but it won't kill you), and you have to forget the failures and successes of the past. Rivera does not seem the type to write a book, but if he ever did it should be something about peace—*Zen and the Art of Closing Out A Baseball Game*[14]—because that seems to be his greatest gift of all. Mariano Rivera always seems at peace.

It's probably worth noting here that Mariano Rivera has not written a book.   30
Other Yankees have—Derek Jeter has written two, Paul O'Neill wrote one about his father, Jorge Posada has written a children's book and so on. Rivera doesn't claim to have anything to say. He seems happiest in the stillness of the background, a hard place to find in New York City.

But he has found that quiet place in New York. And this, perhaps, is the most remarkable thing about Mariano Rivera. He's the ultimate Yankee, the embodiment of the Yankee myth, and yet for 15 seasons now he has not sparked a controversy, not been caught in the bright lights, not inspired the boos anywhere in America.

Oh, every so often, for a couple of weeks or a month, he will give up a few runs and look to be human, and there will be some who will start to prepare the eulogy, most recently a few weeks ago after a rough patch, but then he will emerge again, throwing that one matchless pitch. He's 39 years old now. He has saved 48 games in his last 50 chances. This isn't to say that Mariano Rivera is underrated—everyone knows. Yankees fans love him. Opposing fans respect him. It's just that as good as people think he is, he might even be better.

He comes into a game—Metallica's "Enter Sandman" blaring over Yankee Stadium—and he begins to warm up, and the crowd's going wild, and the opposing players are psyching themselves up, and he has that look on his face, that placid look, that look that says that everything will be all right.

"They have other men on the team," the boy said to Hemingway's old man.

"Naturally," the old man said. "But he makes the difference."   35

---

13. Rivera just smiled, of course. "I felt honored," he said. "What was I going to do? Get upset and start throwing baseballs at people?" [Posnanski's note].

14. Reference to *Zen and the Art of Motorcycle Maintenance* (1974), a popular philosophical book by Robert Pirsig.

MLA CITATION

Posnanski, Joe. "Mariano Rivera's a True Yankee." 2009. *The Norton Reader: An Anthology of Nonfiction.* Ed. Melissa A. Goldthwaite et al. 14th ed. New York: Norton, 2016. 329–33. Print.

Questions

1. What do you think Joe Posnanski means by the phrase "Yankee mythology" (paragraph 1)? What does this mythology consist of? What other sports teams have a mythology of their own?

2. Posnanski includes allusions to and quotations from an Ernest Hemingway novel. Why do you think he does this? What effect does it have on your understanding of Mariano Rivera and the Yankees?

3. Posnanski's essay provides an example of epideictic rhetoric, a piece that either praises or blames someone or something. Can you think of another figure in sports who is comparable to Rivera, either in longevity or success over time? Write an essay that praises or blames that figure, showing that person's accomplishments, blunders, or both.

DeNeen Brown   *Six-Pack Abs at Age 74*

"Age is nothing but a number," says Guinness World Record's oldest competitive female bodybuilder.

SHE IS 74 YEARS OLD, and she is ripped.

Sculpted deltoids, carved biceps and a stomach chiseled into a glorious six-pack that rises and falls into magnificent little hills and valleys.

It is the first thing you notice when you see Ernestine Shepherd in the front of the class, teaching body sculpting at a gym north of Baltimore.

Shepherd is wearing tight red shorts and a red bikini top. Between the two is her signature span of chiseled abs.

5   She is a Dorothy Dandridge[1] beauty, a knockout. Her makeup is perfect, lips painted candy red to match her workout clothes. She has thick, black eyelashes and wears her hair in a long, gray braid that swings down her superbly sculpted back.

First published in the weekly magazine of the Washington Post *(2011), a daily newspaper published in Washington, D.C., that covers international, national, and local news.*

1. Actress and celebrity (1922–1965); the first African American woman to be nominated for a Best Actress Academy Award.

She is wearing white Converse sneakers with little white kitten heels. She flexes. "If you are going to try to motivate people, you have to live that part," she says. "You have to look that part." Her husband will say later that he still has trouble keeping guys away from her.

Behind her, women many, many years younger than she are struggling—huffing and puffing and trying to keep up. Thighs heavy, bellies jiggling, breath short, they sweat away as their 74-year-old instructor with the body of a college cheerleader counts.

A woman rolls over on her back, exhausted.

"Everybody okay?" Shepherd, at the front of the class, asks softly.

"Third set. And one, two." Her arms are spread like wings.   10

"Three, four, five, six." The women are exhausted. Shepherd continues. "Seven, eight. Good! Nine, 10, 11, 12. And hold. Last set, and one, and two, and work those shoulders. Good. Put your arms down. Shake them out."

A woman in the back of the gym, who has seen Shepherd on television, whispers: "How do you get to be 74 with a body like that?"

"Age is nothing but a number," Shepherd says assuredly into the microphone. She has been featured in *Essence*, on the *Today* show and local television in Baltimore. Last fall, she appeared on *The Mo'Nique Show*, explaining fitness and aging. "We can do it! Why?" Shepherd asks. "Because we are determined, dedicated and disciplined to be fit. You can. You can do it."

Her voice trails off under the beat of gym speakers blasting: *"Young man, there's no need to feel down. I said, young man, pick yourself off the ground."* Seven more counts.

"You can do this," Shepherd says again. Her voice has a hint of urgency, as   15
if the class means something deeper, as if she were trying to save the women behind her. She turns on her side and stretches out a lithe movie star leg.

But the truth is, most people in this class probably do not have the discipline it takes to reach Shepherd's fitness level. Most people will not have the determination to run 10 miles before lunch, 80 miles a week, passing people by as if they were standing still. Most people will not want to eat only bland chicken, green beans and cups of plain brown rice and drink liquid egg whites, the lean protein diet of body builders, three times a day. Most people will not have the discipline to turn down that slice of chocolate cake in the cafeteria. Most people will not be able to say, as Shepherd says, "I really don't have a desire for it."

Every day, Shepherd rises at 3 a.m. to meditate, then dresses in the cool of a Baltimore morning. She carefully applies her makeup, dresses in another fabulous color-coordinated running suit. She leaves the house quietly, climbing in her gray Corvette and driving in style to Druid Hill Park. Here, she will run for the next three hours through a wooded trail, running to fulfill a dream that did not start with her. Running because long ago she made a "pinkie promise."

Over the past 18 years, Shepherd has completed nine marathons, won two bodybuilding contests. She was listed in the 2010 and 2011 *Guinness World Records* as the oldest competitive female bodybuilder in the world.

Most people will not be able to imagine that Ernestine Shepherd was ever once one of them.

20   "Believe it or not, I used to be a couch potato," Shepherd admits with a slight smile. Bodybuilding was not something she ever really wanted to do. From the time she was a child, her main goal was to "sit and look pretty." When Shepherd was 11, she was hit by a car while riding her bicycle, and she broke her ankle.

"From that, I said, 'Gee, I don't want to do anything!' I had my mother write a note saying I couldn't do any type of exercise," Shepherd says. "That note followed me all the way through school. I did absolutely nothing, because I always wanted to look nice and I've always wanted to be noticed. I guess I'm vain, but vain in a good way."

So for the next 45 years, she did exactly that: sit pretty and try not to break too much of a sweat.

But one day, she and her older sister Mildred were invited to a pool party. They immediately went to the mall to buy swimsuits.

They had always been pretty women. And they knew that. In fact, Shepherd had been a model in Baltimore for years, after her seamstress invited her to model clothes in a local fashion show. But the two sisters were about to encounter something in the dressing room that would change their lives.

25   "I was 56. She was 57," Ernestine recalls. "We were in the same dressing room. She had selected white. I selected red. She always said she was too dark to wear red. She put her suit on and looked at me and started laughing. I said, 'You are not looking that good yourself.'"

They didn't buy the suits but went to the party anyway and sat by the pool, talking about how their bodies had changed. A woman overheard their conversation and told them about aerobics classes at what is now Coppin State University in Baltimore. The sisters started taking the classes from an instructor named Jay Bennett, who was well known in Baltimore. "My sister went in and told him what we wanted to do," Shepherd recalls.

The instructor asked what their goals were. Ernestine told him: "I like my hips. I don't want to lose them." He said fine but told her there was no program in the world that would allow for "spot reducing."

"My hips were a 41, and I thought that was great," Shepherd says. The sisters continued the aerobics classes, with Mildred working harder than Ernestine. "I was complaining, jiving. I noticed she was working hard. I started working hard. I noticed a change in my body."

The instructor told them they were shaping up nicely and suggested they begin to lift weights. "I said, 'No, no, no. I don't want to get big and muscular.'" But he told them that women did not have enough testosterone to develop huge muscles. He told them weights would help them tone.

30   "I followed her in there, but I would drag my feet. I wouldn't do it because I didn't believe what he was saying. My sister got in there and did the routines. Her back developed." That was the first thing Ernestine noticed.

"Everybody started paying attention to her but not me," Ernestine recalls. "I was jealous. I left the gym and went home. She came back, and she said, 'Teeny, if you want to enjoy what I am enjoying, you better do what I'm doing.'"

Ernestine and Mildred grew up in a red brick rowhouse in East Baltimore, the daughters of a carpenter and a schoolteacher. Ernestine was the third-oldest of the six Hawkins children, but she was closest by far to Mildred. She followed Mildred everywhere.

"I remember I was 5 and she was 6, and we were going to school. We would go to school, and we would hold hands. She would drop me at my class, and I would cry when she had to leave me to go to her class. All I enjoyed was being with her."

Their mother dressed the two girls alike, with polished shoes and pressed dresses. Mildred was always neat in those pretty dresses. Ernestine, on the other hand, would come home for lunch, and her clothes would be rumpled. Her bows would have fallen out. Their mother would make them both change.

Mildred scolded Ernestine. *I am going to have to watch over you, because I get tired of changing clothes.* So Mildred would walk behind Ernestine. "If my ribbon fell off, she would pick it up and put it back on." 35

When Ernestine was 7 and Mildred was 8, the two sisters were walking down a street in East Baltimore when they passed a beautiful grassy area with a sign warning: *Seeded. Keep off the grass.*

Ernestine uttered a terrible word. "I said, 'I'm going to walk on this 'so and so' grass!'"

Mildred gasped. *I'm going to tell Mum.*

Ernestine recalls begging her: "Oh, please don't tell. I'm going to get a spanking."

Mildred agreed not to tell their mother. 40

"We made a pinkie promise," Shepherd says. "Right then I knew she was my friend."

The sisters became almost inseparable. As they got older, they never lived far from each other in Baltimore and talked or visited several times a day. When Mildred got married, Ernestine wanted to get married.

It just so happened that there was a young man who had been trying to court her. He had lived on the next street over, but she had not noticed him until he returned home from the Army.

Collin Shepherd remembers noticing Ernestine for the first time at a supermarket, where she worked as a cashier. She was 18; he was struck by her beauty.

"My mother would send me to the store," recalls Collin Shepherd, now 80. "And I would go in and look at Ernestine. She wore so much jewelry, I thought she was married already." 45

But Collin's brother-in-law who owned a barber shop across the street from the food market told Collin that Ernestine was not married or engaged.

"That's all I need to know," Collin recalls. "'I'm going to work on her.'"

Collin drove his shiny new blue-green '56 Plymouth—with wings and whitewall tires—to the store and waited for Ernestine to get off work. But Ernestine wouldn't get in the car. She told him she would walk home. "She just lived nine straight blocks, no curves, no turns from the store." Still, as she walked on the sidewalk, Collin followed her. "It wasn't like a pickup. Eventually, she got used to me." But she was just that hard to get.

Collin persisted. After a while, they began dating. Collin's big break came when Mildred got married.

50 "The sister I'm so crazy about," Ernestine says, sitting in her kitchen after another workout, eating plain chicken and brown rice, "she got married a few months ahead of me. I wanted to be married. So I asked him would he marry me."

"I was quick to go," Collin says.

"Everything my sister did I had to do," Ernestine says. ". . . The only thing we did different is she had two children, and I had one. I said, 'Shep, don't do this to me again.' I don't know how women have five or six children. I was still trying to get into my clothes. I was so prissy."

Her kitchen is painted lavender. Inside the refrigerator, her husband has stacked plastic containers filled with bland green beans, scoops of brown rice, pieces of chicken breast. Plain. No salt. Collin, who retired in 1985 from AT&T, does all the meal preparations. "I cook and clean and whatever needs to be done," he says. "I run errands to help. I don't mind doing it."

They have been married 54 years. Ernestine says he is the best husband. Right now, their son, Michael, 53, who lives with them, is upstairs. Her grandson, also named Michael, is 14.

55 Just then, her cellphone rings with the theme from the movie *Rocky*. Sylvester Stallone is her idol.

When she was working out with her sister, Mildred got to the point where she could do squats with a 135-pound barbell. Their instructor began inviting Mildred and Ernestine to talk about fitness at classes and fashion shows. And people began to notice the stunning sisters with muscles.

Mildred decided she wanted to compete in bodybuilding shows and took on a stage name. She called herself Velvet. Ernestine wanted to call herself Magenta, but Mildred suggested that Magenta didn't sound right and told her she should just go by Ernie.

One day in 1992, Velvet told Ernie that she had a dream. They would be in the *Guinness World Records* for being two sister bodybuilders.

Then Mildred mysteriously confided to Ernestine, "If I don't make this, you have to fulfill this dream," Shepherd recalls. "'This is something we want to do. Listen to what I'm saying.' She said: 'If anything happens to me, you are not to fall to pieces. You are to continue what you started.'"

60 Ernestine recalls looking at her sister and saying, "Vice versa."

Mildred responded in a serious way: "'I'm not playing.'"

The sisters shook pinkies as they did when they were girls.

Ernestine thinks now that her sister felt something was wrong with her but had decided not to tell anyone at that point.

About three months later, Mildred began complaining openly about head-aches and ringing in her ears. But she rationalized the pain. The ringing in her ears was from weightlifting, she told her sister.

Mildred told Ernestine that the top of her head felt tight.   65

"We both wore our hair back in a braid. She said she would just loosen her hair up." But then Mildred admitted one day she couldn't see out of one eye.

"Velvet called me from work. She said, 'I got up, and I didn't know who I was.' She said, 'I couldn't use my hands or anything.' I said I would leave work and go with you to the doctor. I said, 'I don't want you dying over there.'"

Their parents and baby sister, Bernice, got to Mildred's house first and took her to the nearest hospital, but the wait was too long. They left, heading for a second hospital. On the way there, Ernestine rode with her sister in the back seat. "She laid her head on my lap and she said, 'Why does my head have to hurt like this?' I said, 'You will be fine.' I whispered in her ear and told her, 'When you get well, I will have to tell you how you worried me.'"

Mildred was admitted immediately. Soon, a doctor told the family in the waiting room that Mildred had a brain aneurysm, or bulging blood vessel. And that it had burst.

"If we had gotten there in time, maybe we could have saved her." By then   70
Mildred was on life support, which she had always told Ernestine she did not want.

When they pulled the plug, Ernestine jumped up and ran around the hos-pital. "I didn't know where I was going."

Bernice ran after Ernestine. Ernestine screamed: "Now, I don't have anyone!"

Bernice held Ernestine. Two sisters crying for an older sister. Bernice told Ernestine: "You have me."

Shepherd's world seemed to stop. The sister she would talk with from morning to night had gone suddenly, giving her no chance to prepare. The sister who kept her together and told her what needed to be done was gone.

She sank into a deep pit of depression. "I developed acid reflux, panic attacks   75
and high blood pressure." Shepherd stopped working out. She lost her faith.

One day Shepherd was sitting in her bedroom in red pajamas when it seemed to her that the cream-colored walls began to move. She was careful not to wake her husband. The walls appeared to be closing in on her. Then when she looked down, she thought she saw "a third arm." That afternoon at work, the third arm seemed to grow.

"It felt like I had three arms." Two on one side and one on the other. "Now, this is when you are crazy," she recalls, laughing. "I held my arm, which I thought was the third arm, which I didn't have. I held that arm. I said, 'I have to hold this arm. If I don't, it will get in the way of the other arm.'"

At the time, Shepherd was working as a school secretary in an elementary school in Baltimore where her baby sister, Bernice, was the principal. "My baby sister, God bless her, she was right there for me. I didn't cry. I just kept holding that third arm. I had sense enough I didn't want anybody to know this."

Shepherd recalls being on the subway and wanting to scream and run from the front car to the back car. "But I said, 'Hold yourself together.' When I got off, I ran." She was 61 at the time, holding on to five years of grief.

80   "I just felt crazy with that third arm. I kept that arm for about a week. It sounds like a joke, but I'm telling you: Your mind can tell you anything."

Shepherd went to a doctor and told him about the panic attacks and the acid reflux. "But I didn't tell him about my third arm because I was afraid he would commit me. He told me he would prescribe medication for the panic attacks and told me all the side effects." Some medical journals refer to an experience similar to Shepherd's as "phantom limb" syndrome, a sense that an arm or leg is still attached to the body even after it has been amputated. In Shepherd's case, she may have associated the third arm with her sister, she says.

Shepherd left the doctor's office and went home. "I thought, 'How will I fulfill my sister's dream if I fall apart?'"

She sank down and prayed. "I came down from my room and called my husband and son and sat at the kitchen table. I said to them, 'From now on, I will try to do the dream my sister had. Will you help me?' They were so glad I was coming out of that. They said, 'We will do whatever we can to help you.'"

Bernice told her: "Every time you feel like you can't make it, lace up your tennis shoes and get out and go walking."

85   So Shepherd put on her tennis shoes once again.

It's Tuesday in Fort Washington, and Shepherd is hanging from a bar with her hands. Her trainer, Yohnnie Shambourger, 57, who won the gold medal in body-building at the Pan American Games in Argentina in 1995, and in that same year won the title of Mr. Universe, is counting.

She lifts her full body weight up into crunches, working her abs.

"One and down. Two and down. Three and down."

Shepherd grits.

90   "Fifteen. Get it up there," Shambourger says.

"That's it?" Shepherd asks.

"No, we are going to 20. Very good."

In this gym, a storefront off Allentown Road, Shambourger began helping to train Shepherd at age 71 in 2007. (After her sister died, Raymond Day, a trainer in Baltimore, would pick her up and take her to the gym.) Shambourger coached her as she worked out, building and toning her muscles, and taught her how to pose in preparation for bodybuilding competitions. It is here that Shepherd comes every Tuesday morning, driving one hour from Baltimore.

A poster on the wall says: "Unleash the Winner in You: Yohnnie Shambourger, former Mr. Universe, shares his winning formula."

95   Shepherd will lift heavy weights for 1 1/2 hours.

Finally, she works on her stomach muscles in another set of hanging leg raises. She will do 20 more reps.

"The six-pack," Shambourger says, "that is her signature. When she walks in a room and you see her six-pack, you say, 'Ohh! Okay!'"

Shepherd, careful not to chip her French manicure, grabs a 20-pound kettle-bell. Fifteen reps, Shambourger announces. And she swings the bell as though she were chopping wood.

Between sets, Shepherd jokingly suggests that Shambourger doesn't realize how old she is. But her coach doesn't ease up.

"You are a champion," he says. "I will train you like what you are."   100

She is running through the forest in Druid Hill Park in a sleek, black track suit. A misty rain is falling. Her gray braid swings down her gorgeous back. Her husband and son walk behind her, admitting they cannot keep up. A young photographer runs beside her teasing, "You are not running that fast."

Shepherd takes off, running so fast the young photographer cannot catch her. And she doesn't stop for two miles. She circles back and zooms by her husband and son, who are still walking. Park service workers ride by in a truck and wave.

People ask Ernestine Shepherd how long she plans to run, how long will she lift weights, how long will she train so hard it hurts. "You will die soon," they tell her.

She tells them simply, "We are all going to die."

"But it's the quality of life while I'm living."   105

When she traveled to Rome last year to participate in the ceremony for the Guinness World Records, she carried her sister's ashes.

"I spread those ashes," she says. "It was something we dreamed about. I try to keep that dream alive. Now, it's my dream."

MLA CITATION

Brown, DeNeen. "Six-Pack Abs at Age 74." 2011. *The Norton Reader: An Anthology of Nonfiction.* Ed. Melissa A. Goldthwaite et al. 14th ed. New York: Norton, 2016. 334–41. Print.

QUESTIONS

1. In paragraph 13, DeNeen Brown quotes her subject, Ernestine Shepherd: "'We can do it! Why?' Shepherd asks. 'Because we are determined, dedicated and disciplined to be fit. You can. You can do it.'" Do you believe anyone can be fit, no matter what age? Why or why not? What factors besides determination, dedication, and discipline affect a person's level of fitness?

2. In response to people saying, "You will die soon," Shepherd replies, "We are all going to die. But it's the quality of life while I'm living" (paragraphs 103–105). What do you think Shepherd means by this statement? Cite details from the text that help reveal Shepherd's attitude toward life.

3. Write a profile of someone who has turned his or her life around by getting fit, stopping a bad habit, or making some other significant change. Be as detailed as you can, and use quotations from the person you are profiling.

MICHAEL LEWIS   from *The Blind Side*

ROM THE SNAP of the ball to the snap of the first bone is closer to four seconds than to five. One Mississippi: The quarterback of the Washington Redskins, Joe Theismann, turns and hands the ball to running back John Riggins. He watches Riggins run two steps forward, turn, and flip the ball back to him. It's what most people know as a "flea-flicker," but the Redskins call it a "throw back special." Two Mississippi: Theismann searches for a receiver but instead sees Harry Carson coming straight at him. It's a running down—the start of the second quarter, first and 10 at midfield, with the score tied 7–7—and the New York Giants' linebacker has been so completely suckered by the fake that he's deep in the Redskins' backfield. Carson thinks he's come to tackle Riggins but Riggins is long gone, so Carson just keeps running, toward Theismann. Three Mississippi: Carson now sees that Theismann has the ball. Theismann notices Carson coming straight at him, and so he has time to avoid him. He steps up and to the side and Carson flies right on by and out of the play. The play is now 3.5 seconds old. Until this moment it has been defined by what the quarterback can see. Now it—and he—is at the mercy of what he can't see.

You don't think of fear as a factor in professional football. You assume that the sort of people who make it to the NFL are immune to the emotion. Perhaps they don't mind being hit, or maybe they just don't get scared; but the idea of pro football players sweating and shaking and staring at the ceiling at night worrying about the next day's violence seems preposterous. The head coach of the Giants, Bill Parcells, didn't think it preposterous, however. Parcells, whose passion is the football defense, believed that fear played a big role in the game. So did his players. They'd witnessed up close the response of opposing players to their own Lawrence Taylor.

The tackle who had just quit the Philadelphia Eagles, for instance. Jerry Sisemore had played tackle in the NFL for eight years when, in 1981, Taylor arrived. Sisemore played on the right side of the offensive line and Taylor usually came off the other end, but Sisemore still had to worry about the few times Taylor lined up across from him. Their teams were in the same NFL division and met twice each regular season. The week leading up to those games, Sisemore confessed, unnerved him. "Towards the middle of the week something would come over you and you'd just start sweating," he told the *New York Times*. "My last year in the league, opening day, he immediately got past me. . . . He just looked at me and laughed. Right there I thought I had to get out of this game." And after that season, 1984, he did.

From The Blind Side: Evolution of a Game *(2006), which analyzes the game of football and details the life and career of football player Michael Oher. In the last twenty years Michael Lewis has written numerous books on sports and business, including* Liar's Poker, Moneyball, *and* Flash Boys.

The feelings of those assigned to prevent Taylor from hurting quarterbacks were trivial compared to those of the quarterbacks he wanted to hurt. In Taylor's first season in the NFL, no official records were kept of quarterback sacks. In 1982, after Taylor had transformed the quarterback sack into the turning point of a football game, a new official NFL statistic was born. The record books defined the sack as tackling the quarterback behind the line of scrimmage as he attempts to pass. Taylor offered his own definition: "A sack is when you run up behind somebody who's not watching, he doesn't see you, and you really put your helmet into him. The ball goes fluttering everywhere and the coach comes out and asks the quarterback, 'Are you all right?' That's a sack." After his first NFL season Taylor became the only rookie ever named the league's most valuable defensive player, and he published a treatise on his art. "I don't like to just wrap the quarterback," he explained. "I really try to make him see seven fingers when they hold up three. I'll drive my helmet into him, or, if I can, I'll bring my arm up over my head and try to axe the sonuvabitch in two. So long as the guy is holding the ball, I intend to hurt him. . . . If I hit the guy right, I'll hit a nerve and he'll feel electrocuted, he'll forget for a few seconds that he's on a football field."

The game of football evolved and here was one cause of its evolution, a   5
new kind of athlete doing a new kind of thing. All by himself, Lawrence Taylor altered the environment and forced opposing coaches and players to adapt. After Taylor joined the team, the Giants went from the second worst defense in the NFL to the third best. The year before his debut they gave up 425 points; his first year they gave up 257 points. They had been one of the weakest teams in the NFL and were now, overnight, a contender. Of course, Taylor wasn't the only change in the New York Giants between 1980 and 1981. There was one other important newcomer, Bill Parcells, hired first to coach the Giants' defense and then the entire team. Parcells became a connoisseur of the central nervous system of opposing quarterbacks. The symptoms induced by his sack-happy linebacker included, but were not restricted to: "intimidation, lack of confidence, quick throws, nervous feet, concentration lapses, wanting to know where Lawrence is all the time." The players on the Giants' defense picked up the same signals. As defensive back Beasley Reece told the *New York Times*, "I've seen quarterbacks look at Lawrence and forget the snap count." One opposing quarterback, finding himself under the center before the snap and unable to locate Taylor, called a time-out rather than run the play—only to find Taylor standing on the sidelines. "I think I saw it more with the quarterbacks in our division," says Giants linebacker Harry Carson. "They knew enough to be afraid. But every quarterback had a certain amount of fear when he played us."

By his fourth pro season Taylor was not just feeding these fears but feeding off them. "They come to the line of scrimmage and the first thing they do is start looking for me," he said. "I know, and they know. When they'd find me they'd start screaming: *56 left! 56 left!* [Taylor wore No. 56.] So there's this thing I did. After the play was over I'd come up behind them and whisper: *don't worry where I am. I'll tell you when I get there.*"

MICHAEL LEWIS

A new force in pro football, Taylor demanded not just a tactical response but an explanation. Many people pointed to his unusual combination of size and speed. As one of the Redskins' linemen put it, "No human being should be six four, two forty-five, and run a four-five forty." Bill Parcells thought Taylor's size and speed were closer to the beginning than to the end of the explanation. New York Giants' scouts were scouring the country for young men six three or taller, 240 pounds or heavier, with speed. They could be found. In that pool of physical specimens what was precious—far more precious than an inch, or ten pounds, or one tenth of a second—was Taylor's peculiar energy and mind: relentless, manic, with grandiose ambitions and private standards of performance. Parcells believed that even in the NFL a lot of players were more concerned with seeming to want to win than with actually winning, and that many of them did not know the difference. What they wanted, deep down, was to keep their jobs, make their money, and go home. Lawrence Taylor wanted to win. He expected more of himself on the field than a coach would dare to ask of any player.

Parcells accumulated lots of anecdotal evidence in support of his view of Taylor's football character. One of his favorites involved these very same Washington Redskins. "Joe Gibbs in a game in Giants Stadium basically decided that Taylor wasn't going to make any plays," said Parcells. "He put two tight ends on Taylor's side—along with the left tackle—and two wide receivers in the slot away from Taylor." This was extreme. An NFL football field is a tightly strung economy. Everything on it comes at a price. Take away from one place and you give to another. Three men blocking Taylor meant two Giants with no one to block them. Taylor's effect on the game, which the Giants won, was not obvious but it was nonetheless great. "But after the game," Parcells continued:

> The press sees that Lawrence doesn't have a sack and hasn't made a tackle and they're all asking me "what's the matter with Taylor?" The next week we go out to San Diego to play the Chargers. Dan Henning is the coach. He sees the strategy. They do the same thing. Two tight ends on Lawrence, two wide receivers in the slot. Lawrence doesn't get a sack. We win again. But after the game everyone is asking me all over again: "what's the matter with Taylor?" I grab Lawrence in the locker room and say to him, "I'm going to change your first name from Lawrence to What's The Matter With?" At practice that next week he was What's The Matter With? "What you doin' over there What's The Matter With?" "Hey, What's The Matter With?, how come you aren't making plays?" By Thursday it's not funny to him. And I mean it is really *not* funny.
>
> The next game we have is against the Vikings on Monday Night Football. Tommy Kramer is the quarterback. They don't employ the strategy. He knocks Kramer out of the game, causes two fumbles and recovers one of them. I'm leaving the field, walking down the tunnel towards the locker room for the press conference. And out of nowhere this . . . *thing* comes and jumps on my back. I didn't know he was coming. He basically knocks me over. He's still got his helmet on. Sweat's still pouring down his face. He comes right up into my face and hollers, "I tell you what Coachy, they aren't going to ask you What's The Matter With?!!"

Parcells believed Taylor's greatness was an act of will, a refusal to allow the world to understand him as anything less than great. "That's why I loved him so much," he said. "He responded to *anything* that threatened his status." When in the middle of his career Taylor became addicted to cocaine, Parcells interpreted the problem as a simple extension of the man's character. Lawrence Taylor trusted in one thing, the power of his own will. He assumed that his will could control NFL football games, and that it could also control his own chemical desires.

He was right about the NFL games. By November 18, 1985, when the   10
Giants went into Robert F. Kennedy Stadium in Washington, DC, to play the Redskins, opposing teams have taken to lining up their players in new and creative ways simply to deal with him. The Redskins are a case in point. Early in the very first game in which his Redskins had faced this new force, back in 1981, Joe Gibbs had watched Taylor sprint past the blocker as if he wasn't there and clobber Joe Theismann from behind. "I was standing there," said Gibbs, "and I said, 'What? Did you see that? Oh Lord.'" Gibbs had flopped about looking for a solution to this new problem, and had come up with the "one back offense"—a formation, widely imitated in the NFL, that uses one running back instead of two. Until that moment, football offenses had typically used running backs to block linebackers who came charging after quarterbacks. But running backs were smaller, weaker, and, surprisingly often, given their job description, slower than Lawrence Taylor. Lynn Cain, a running back for the Atlanta Falcons, was the first to dramatize the problem. The first time Cain went to block Taylor he went in very low, got up underneath him, and sent Taylor flying head over heels. The next play Cain tried it again—and was carried off the field on a stretcher. "People figured out *very* quickly that they couldn't block Lawrence with a running back," Parcells said. "Then the question became: who do you block him with?" Hence Joe Gibbs's first solution: to remove the running back from the game and insert, across the line from Lawrence Taylor, a bigger, stronger tight end. The one back offense.

That will be the strategy tonight, but Joe Theismann knows too well its imperfections. Having that extra blocker to help the tackle addressed the problem, Theismann thought, without solving it. Too often Taylor came free. The week of practice leading up to the game had been a seminar on Lawrence Taylor. "If you looked at our overhead projector or our chalkboard," said Theismann, "all the other Giants players were X's or O's. Lawrence was the only one who had a number: fifty-six. He was a little red fifty-six and the number was always highlighted and circled. The goal was: let's identify where Lawrence is on every play." Taylor moved around a lot, to confuse the defense, but he and his coach were happiest when he came from his own right side and the quarterback's left. "The big reason I put him over there," said Bill Parcells, "is the right side is the quarterback's blind side, since most quarterbacks are right-handed. And no one wants to get his ass knocked off from the back side." Lawrence Taylor was more succinct: "Why the hell would I want to come from where he can see me?" But then he added: "It wasn't really called the blind side when I came into the league. It was called the right side. It *became* the blind side after I started knocking people's heads off."

Where Taylor is at the start of the play, of course, isn't the problem. It's where he ends up. "When I dropped back," says Theismann, "the first thing I still did was to glance over my shoulder to see if he was coming. If he was dropping back in coverage, a sense of calm came over me. If he was coming, I had a sense of urgency."

Four Mississippi: Taylor is coming. From the snap of the ball Theismann has lost sight of him. He doesn't see Taylor carving a wide circle behind his back; he doesn't see Taylor outrun his blocker upfield and then turn back down; and he doesn't see the blocker diving, frantically, at Taylor's ankles. He doesn't see Taylor leap, both arms over his head, and fill the sky behind him. Theismann prides himself on his ability to stand in the pocket and disregard his fear. He thinks this quality is a prerequisite in a successful NFL quarterback. "When a quarterback looks at the rush," he says, "his career is over." Theismann has played in 163 straight games, a record for the Washington Redskins. He's led his team to two Super Bowls, and won one. He's thirty-six years old. He's certain he still has a few good years left in him. He's wrong. He has less than half a second.

The game is on ABC's *Monday Night Football,* and 17.6 million people have tuned in. Frank Gifford[1] is in the booth, flanked by O. J. Simpson and Joe Namath. "Theismann's in a lot of trouble," the audience hears Gifford say, just before Taylor's arms jackknife Theismann's head to his knees and Taylor's torso pins Theismann's right leg to the ground. Four other players, including, oddly, the Redskins' John Riggins, pile on. They're good for dramatic effect but practically irrelevant. The damage is done by Taylor alone. One hundred and ninety-six pounds of quarterback come to rest beneath a thousand or so pounds of other things. Then Lawrence Taylor pops to his feet and begins to scream and wave and clutch his helmet with both hands, as if in agony.

15

His reaction is a mystery until ABC Sports clarifies the event, by replaying it over and again, in slow motion. "Again, we'll look at it with the reverse angle one more time," says Frank Gifford. "And I suggest if your stomach is weak, you just don't watch." People watched; the replay was almost surely better attended than the original play. Doug Flutie was probably a representative viewer. Flutie had just finished a glorious college quarterbacking career at Boston College and started a professional one in the USFL. On the evening of November 18, 1985, he was at home with his mother. She had the football game on; he had other things to do. "I heard my mother scream," he told a reporter. "And then I saw the replay. It puts fear in your heart and makes you wonder what the heck you're doing playing football."

There's an instant before it collapses into some generally agreed-upon fact when a football play, like a traffic accident, is all conjecture and fragments and par-

---

1. Gifford (1930–2015), Simpson (b. 1947), and Namath (b. 1943), members of football's Hall of Fame, who served as ABC broadcasters in 1985.

tial views. Everyone wants to know the whole truth but no one possesses it. Not the coach on the sidelines, not the coach in the press box, and certainly not the quarterback—no one can see the whole field and take in the movement of twenty-two bodies, each with his own job assignment. In baseball or basketball all the players see, more or less, the same events. Points of view vary, but slightly. In football many of the players on the field have no idea what happened—much less why it happened—until after the play is done. Even then, most of them will need to watch a videotape to be sure. The fans, naturally more interested in effect than cause, follow the ball, and come away thinking they know perfectly well what just happened. But what happened to the ball, and to the person holding the ball, was just the final link in a chain of events that began well before the ball was snapped. At the beginning of the chain that ended Joe Theismann's career was an obvious question: who was meant to block Lawrence Taylor?

Two players will be treated above all others as the authorities on the play: Joe Theismann and Lawrence Taylor. The victim didn't have a view of the action; the perpetrator was so intent on what he was doing that he didn't stop to look. "The play was a blur," said Taylor. "I had taken the outside. I was thinking: keep him in the pocket and squeeze him. Then I broke free." Why he broke free he couldn't say, as he didn't actually notice who was trying to block him. Theismann, when asked who was blocking Taylor on that play, will reply, "Joe Jacoby, our left tackle." He won't *blame* Jacoby, as the guy was one of the two or three finest left tackles of his era, and was obviously just doing his best. That's why it made no sense, in Joe Theismann's opinion, for an NFL team to blow big bucks on an offensive lineman: there was only so much a lineman could do. Even when his name was Joe Jacoby.

That was one point of view. Another was Jacoby's who, on that night, was standing on the sidelines, in street clothes. He'd strained ligaments in his knee and was forced to sit out. When Joe Jacoby played, he was indeed a splendid left tackle. Six seven and 315 pounds, he was shaped differently from most left tackles of his time, and more like the left tackle of the future. "A freak of nature ahead of his time," his position coach, Joe Bugel, called him, two decades later. Jacoby wasn't some lump of cement; he was an athlete. In high school he'd been a star basketball player. He could run, he could jump, he had big, quick hands. "We put him at left tackle for one reason," said Bugel, "to match up against Lawrence Taylor." The first time they'd met, Jacoby had given Lawrence Taylor fits—he was a 300-pounder before the era of 300-pounders, with hands so big they felt like hooks. Taylor had been forced to create a move just for Jacoby. "Geritol," Taylor called it, "because after the snap I tried to look like an old man running up to him." Unable to overwhelm him physically, Taylor sought to lull Jacoby into a tactical mistake. He'd come off the ball at a trot to lure Jacoby into putting his hands up before he reached him. The moment he did— *Wham!*—he'd try to knock away Jacoby's hands before he latched on. A burst of violence and he was off to the races.

Still, Jacoby was one of the linemen that always gave Taylor trouble, because he was so big and so quick and so long. "The hardest thing for me to deal with," said Taylor, "was that big, agile left tackle."

20   Offensive linemen were the stay-at-home mothers of the NFL: everyone paid lip service to the importance of their contribution yet hardly anyone could tell you exactly what that was. In 1985 the left tackle had no real distinction. He was still expected to believe himself more or less interchangeable with the other linemen. The Washington Redskins' offensive line was perhaps the most famous in NFL history. It had its own nickname: the Hogs. Fans dressed as pigs in their honor. And yet they weren't understood, even by their own team-mates, in the way running backs or quarterbacks were understood, as individual players with particular skills. "Even people who said they were fans of the Hogs had no idea who we were," said Jacoby. "They couldn't even tell the black ones from the white ones. I had people see me and scream, 'Hey May!'" (Right tackle Mark May was black; Jacoby was not.)

That night, with Jacoby out, the Redskins moved Russ Grimm from his position at left guard to left tackle. Grimm was four inches shorter, 30 pounds lighter, and far less agile than Jacoby. "Little Porky Grimm," line coach Joe Bugel called him. As a result, he needed help, and got it, in the form of the extra tight end, a fellow named Don Warren. If Taylor made his move to the inside, Grimm was expected to deal with him; if Taylor went on a wide loop outside, Grimm was meant, at most, to punch him, to slow him down, and give Warren the time to stay with him. From his spot on the sidelines, Jacoby watched as Taylor went outside. Grimm couldn't lay a hand on him and so Warren was left alone with Taylor. "They weren't used to his speed," said Jacoby. He watched Taylor race upfield and leave Warren in the dust, then double back on the quarterback.

Jacoby then heard what sounded like a gunshot—the tibia and fibula in Joe Theismann's right leg snapping beneath Taylor. He watched as Grimm and Warren removed their helmets and walked quickly toward the sidelines, like men fleeing the scene of a crime. He listened as Grimm told him that Theismann's bone lay exposed, and his blood was spurting straight up in the air. "Russ was a hunter," said Jacoby. "He'd gutted deer. And he said, 'That's the most disgusting thing I've ever seen.'" And Jacoby thought: *It happened because I'm standing over here.* Years later he wouldn't be surprised that Theismann did not realize his great left tackle was standing on the sidelines. "But that's why his leg got broken," he said.

A few minutes later, six men bore Theismann on a stretcher to an ambulance. In ABC's booth, Joe Namath said, "I just hope it's not his last play in football." But it was. Nearly a year later Joe Theismann would be wandering around the Redskins locker room unable to feel his big toe, or to push off his right leg. He'd become a statistic: the *American Journal of Sports Medicine* article on the injuries to NFL quarterbacks between 1980 and 2001 would count Theismann's two broken bones as just one of a sample of 1,534— 77.4 percent of which occur, just as this one had, during games, on passing plays. The game continued and the Redskins, surprisingly, won, 28–23. And most people who did not earn their living in the NFL trying to figure out how to protect their increasingly expensive quarterbacks shoved the incident to the back of their minds. Not ten minutes after Theismann was hauled off the field, Lawrence Taylor himself pounced on a fumble and ran to the bench, jubilant. Frank Gifford sought to persuade his audience that Taylor was still obviously feeling upset about what he had done to Joe Theismann. But the truth is that he didn't look at all upset. He looked as if he'd already gotten over it.

What didn't make sense on that night was Taylor's initial reaction. He leapt out of the pile like a man on fire. Those who had watched Taylor's career closely might have expected a bit more sangfroid in the presence of an injured quarterback. The destruction of Joe Theismann may have been classified an accident, but it wasn't an aberration. It was an extension of what Lawrence Taylor had been doing to NFL quarterbacks for four and a half years. It wasn't even the first time Taylor had broken a quarterback's leg, or ended a quarterback's career. In college, in the Gator Bowl, he had taken out the University of Michigan's quarterback, John Wangler. Before Taylor hit him, Wangler had been a legitimate NFL prospect. ("I was invited to try out for the Lions and the Cowboys," Wangler said later. "But everyone was kind of afraid of the severity of my injury.")

As it turned out, there was a simple explanation: Taylor was claustrophobic. His claustrophobia revealed itself in the way he played the game: standing up looking for the best view, refusing to bend over and get down in the dirt with the other players, preferring the long and open outside route to the quarterback over the short, tight inside one. It revealed itself, also, in the specific fear of being trapped at the bottom of a pile and not being able to escape. "That's what made me so frantic," he said. "I've already dreamed it—if I get on the bottom of a pile and I'm really hurt. And I can't get out." Now he lay at, or near, the bottom of a pile, on top of a man whose leg he'd broken so violently that the sound was heard by Joe Jacoby on the sidelines. And he just had to get out. He leapt to his feet screaming, hands clutching the sides of his helmet, and—the TV cameras didn't pick this up—lifting one foot unconsciously and rubbing his leg with it. It was the only known instance of Lawrence Taylor imagining himself into the skin of a quarterback he had knocked from a game. "We all have fears," he said. "We all have fears."

25

MLA CITATION

Lewis, Michael. "The Blind Side." 2006. *The Norton Reader: An Anthology of Nonfiction.* Ed. Melissa A. Goldthwaite et al. 14th ed. New York: Norton, 2016. 342–49. Print.

QUESTIONS

1. Examine the way Michael Lewis tells the story of Joe Theismann's career-ending leg injury, interspersing narrative with analysis. What effect does such a manner of writing have on your reading experience? Does his approach have anything in common with other writers in this chapter on sports?

2. Football-related injuries are frequently covered in the news, and the implications of these injuries are often discussed. Has your attitude toward the game been affected by reports of injuries? Why or why not? Brainstorm a list of ways such injuries might be prevented.

3. Lewis describes a significant change in football tactics in response to the threat of Lawrence Taylor. Do some research on the invention of a new tactic in a sport and then describe it in an essay (for example, the T formation in football, the zone defense in basketball, the designated hitter in baseball, improved safety in race cars, or the invention of free climbing). If you wish, tie the change to the presence of a single player or a distinct group of players.

FRANKLIN FOER   *How Soccer Explains the American Culture Wars*

I

MY SOCCER CAREER BEGAN IN 1982, at the age of eight. This was an entirely different moment in the history of American soccer, well before the youth game acquired its current, highly evolved infrastructure. Our teams didn't have names. We had jersey colors that we used to refer to ourselves: "Go Maroon!" Our coach, a bearded German named Gunther, would bark at us in continental nomenclature that didn't quite translate into English. Urging me to stop a ball with my upper body, he would cry out, "Use your breasts, Frankie!"

That I should end up a soccer player defied the time-tested laws of sporting heredity. For generations, fathers bequeathed their sporting loves unto their sons. My father, like most men of his baby boom age, had grown up madly devoted to baseball. Why didn't my dad adhere to the practice of handing his game to his son? The answer has to do with the times and the class to which my parents belonged, by which I mean, they were children of the sixties and we lived in the yuppie confines of Upper Northwest Washington, D.C., a dense aggregation of Ivy League lawyers with aggressively liberal politics and exceptionally protective parenting styles. Nearly everyone in our family's social set signed up their children to play soccer. It was the fashionable thing to do. On Monday mornings, at school, we'd each walk around in the same cheaply made pair of white shorts with the logo of our league, Montgomery Soccer Inc.

Steering your child into soccer may have been fashionable, but it wasn't a decision to be made lightly. When my father played sandlot baseball, he could walk three blocks to his neighborhood diamond. With soccer, this simply wasn't possible. At this early moment in the youth soccer boom, the city of Washington didn't have any of its own leagues. My parents would load up our silver

From How Soccer Explains the World: An Unlikely Theory of Globalization (2004), *in which Franklin Foer uses soccer as a lens to explore political tensions, economics, and nationalism.*

Honda Accord and drive me to fields deep in suburban Maryland, 40-minute drives made weekly across a landscape of oversized hardware stores and newly minted real estate developments. In part, these drives would take so long because my parents would circle, hopelessly lost, through neighborhoods they had never before visited and would likely never see again.

As I later discovered, my parents made this sacrifice of their leisure time because they believed that soccer could be transformational. I suffered from a painful, rather extreme case of shyness. I'm told that it extended beyond mere clinging to my mother's leg. On the sidelines at halftime, I would sit quietly on the edge of the other kids' conversations, never really interjecting myself. My parents had hoped that the game might necessitate my becoming more aggressive, a breaking through of inhibitions.

The idea that soccer could alleviate shyness was not an idiosyncratic parenting theory. It tapped into the conventional wisdom among yuppie parents. Soccer appeal lay in its opposition to the other popular sports. For children of the sixties, there was something abhorrent about enrolling kids in American football, a game where violence wasn't just incidental but inherent. They didn't want to teach the acceptability of violence, let alone subject their precious children to the risk of physical maiming. Baseball, where each batter must stand center stage four or five times a game, entailed too many stressful, potentially ego-deflating encounters. Basketball, before Larry Bird's prime,[1] still had the taint of the ghetto.

But soccer represented something very different. It was a tabula rasa, a sport onto which a generation of parents could project their values. Quickly, soccer came to represent the fundamental tenets of yuppie parenting, the spirit of *Sesame Street* and Dr. Benjamin Spock.[2] Unlike the other sports, it would foster self-esteem, minimize the pain of competition while still teaching life lessons. Dick Wilson, the executive director of the American Youth Soccer Organization since the early seventies, described the attitude this way: "We would like to provide the child a chance to participate in a less competitive, win-oriented atmosphere. . . . We require that teams be balanced: and that teams not remain intact from year to year, that they be dissolved and totally reconstituted in the next season. This is done to preclude the adults from building their own dynasty 'win at all cost' situations."

This was typical of the thinking of a generation of post-'60s parenting theories, which were an extension of the counterculture spirit—Theodor Adorno's[3] idea that strict, emotionally stultifying homes created authoritarian, bigoted kids. But for all the talk of freedom, the sixties parenting style had a far less laissez-faire side, too. Like the 1960s consumer movement which brought American car seatbelts and airbags, the soccer movement felt like it

5

1. Boston Celtics forward (b. 1956).

2. Well-known pediatrician (1903–1998) and author of the best-selling book *Baby and Child Care* (1946).

3. German philosopher, musician, and social critic (1903–1969).

could create a set of rules and regulations that would protect both the child's body and mind from damage. Leagues like the one I played in handed out "participation" trophies to every player, no matter how few games his (or her) team won. Other leagues had stopped posting the scores of games or keeping score altogether. Where most of the world accepts the practice of heading the ball as an essential element of the game, American soccer parents have fretted over the potential for injury to the brain. An entire industry sprouted to manufacture protective headgear, not that different-looking from a boxer's sparring helmet, to soften the blows. Even though very little medical evidence supports this fear, some youth leagues have prohibited headers altogether.

This reveals a more fundamental difference between American youth soccer and the game as practiced in the rest of the world. In every other part of the world, soccer's sociology varies little: it is the province of the working class. Sure, there might be aristocrats, like Gianni Agnelli, who take an interest, and instances like Barca, where the game transcendently grips the community.[4] But these cases are rare. The United States is even rarer. It inverts the class structure of the game. Here, aside from Latino immigrants, the professional classes follow the game most avidly and the working class couldn't give a toss about it. Surveys, done by the sporting goods manufacturers, consistently show that children of middle class and affluent families play the game disproportionately. Half the nation's soccer participants come from households earning over $50,000. That is, they come from the solid middle class and above.

Elites have never been especially well liked in post-war American politics—or at least they have been easy to take swipes at. But the generation of elites that adopted soccer has been an especially ripe target. That's because they came through college in the sixties and seventies, at a time when the counter-culture self-consciously turned against the stultifying conformity of what it perceived as traditional America. Even as this group shed its youthful radical politics, it kept some of its old ideals, including its resolute cosmopolitanism and suspicions of middle America, "flyover country." When they adopted soccer, it gave the impression that they had turned their backs on the American pastime. This, naturally, produced even more disdain for them—and for their sport.

10   Pundits have employed many devices to sum up America's cultural divisions. During the 1980s, they talked about the "culture war"—the battle over textbooks, abortion, prayer in school, affirmative action, and funding of the arts. This war pitted conservative defenders of tradition and morality against liberal defenders of modernity and pluralism. More recently this debate has been described as the split between "red and blue America"—the two colors used to distinguish partisan preference in maps charting presidential election voting. But another explanatory device has yet to penetrate political science

4. Italian industrialist (1921–2003), president of Fiat from 1966 to 1996. His family still owns Juventus, the Turin-based soccer club; Barca, nickname of Futbol Club Barcelona, the professional soccer club of Barcelona.

departments and the national desks of newspapers. There exists an important cleavage between the parts of the country that have adopted soccer as its pastime and the places that haven't. And this distinction lays bare an underrated source of American cultural cleavage: globalization.

II

Other countries have greeted soccer with relative indifference. The Indian subcontinent and Australia come to mind. But the United States is perhaps the only place where a loud portion of the population actively disdains the game, even campaigns against it. This anti-soccer lobby believes, in the words of USA Today's Tom Weir, "that hating soccer is more American than apple pie, driving a pickup, or spending Saturday afternoons channel surfing with the remote control." Weir exaggerates the pervasiveness of this sentiment. But the cadre of soccer haters has considerable sway. Their influence rests primarily with a legion of prestigious sportswriters and commentators, who use their column inches to fulminate against the game, especially on the occasions of World Cups.

Not just pundits buried in the C Section of the paper, but people with actual power believe that soccer represents a genuine threat to the American way of life. The former Buffalo Bills quarterback Jack Kemp, one of the most influential conservatives of the 1980s, a man once mentioned in the same breath as the presidency, holds this view. In 1986, he took to the floor of the United States Congress to orate against a resolution in support of an American bid to host the World Cup. Kemp intoned, "I think it is important for all those young out there, who someday hope to play real football, where you throw it and kick it and run with it and put it in your hands, a distinction should be made that football is democratic, capitalism, whereas soccer is a European socialist [sport]."

Lovers of the game usually can't resist dismissing these critics as xenophobes and reactionaries intoxicated with a sense of cultural superiority, the sporting wing of Pat Buchanan's[5] America First conservatism. For a time, I believed this myself. But over the years I've met too many conservatives who violently disagree with Kemp's grafting of politics onto the game. And I've heard too many liberals take their shots at soccer, people who write for such publications as the Village Voice[6] and couldn't be plausibly grouped in the troglodyte camp of American politics. So if hatred of soccer has nothing to do with politics, conventionally defined, why do so many Americans feel threatened by the beautiful game?[7]

For years, I have been collecting a file on this anti-soccer lobby. The person whose material mounts highest in my collection is the wildly popular radio

---

5. Prominent TV commentator (b. 1938)—and former presidential advisor to Richard Nixon, Gerald Ford, and Ronald Reagan.

6. One of the first "alternative" weekly papers, founded in 1955 in Greenwich Village, New York City.

7. Phrase popularized by the Brazilian player Pelé in his autobiography My Life and the Beautiful Game (1977).

shock jock Jim Rome. Rome arrived on the national scene in the mid-nineties and built an audience based on his self-congratulatory flouting of social norms. Rome has created his own subculture that has enraptured a broad swath of American males. They are united by their own vernacular, a Walter Winchell[8]–like form of slang that Rome calls "smack," derived in part from the African American street and in part from the fraternity house. An important part of this subculture entails making fun of the people who aren't members of it. Rome can be cruelly cutting to callers who don't pass his muster, who talk the wrong kind of smack or freeze up on air. These putdowns form a large chunk of his programs. The topics of his rants include such far-ranging subject matter as the quackery of chiropractors, cheap seafood restaurants, and above all, soccer.

15   Where specific events trigger most soccer hating—a World Cup, news of hooligan catastrophes that arrive over the wires—Rome doesn't need a proximate cause to break into a tirade. He lets randomly rip with invective. "My son is not playing soccer. I will hand him ice skates and a shimmering sequined blouse before I hand him a soccer ball. Soccer is not a sport, does not need to be on my TV, and my son will not be playing it." In moments of honesty, he more or less admits his illogic. "If it's incredibly stupid and soccer is in any way related, then soccer must be the root cause (of the stupidity)," he said in one segment, where he attacked the sporting goods manufacturer Umbro for putting out a line of clothing called Zyklon, the same name as the Auschwitz gas. (Zyklon translates as cyclone. By his logic, the words "concentration" or "camp" should be purged from conversational English for their Holocaust associations.) He often inadvertently endorses some repulsive arguments. One segment ripped into African soccer teams for deploying witch doctors. "So you can add this to the laundry list of reasons why I hate soccer," he frothed.

Such obvious flaws make it seem he is proud of his crassness, and that would be entirely in keeping with character. These arguments would be more easily dismissed were they the product of a single demented individual. But far smarter minds have devolved down to Rome's level. Allen Barra, a sportswriter for the *Wall Street Journal,* is one of these smarter minds. Usually, Barra distinguishes himself from his colleagues by making especially rarified, sharp arguments that follow clearly from the facts and have evidence backing his provocative claims. But on soccer, he slips from his moorings. He writes, "Yes, OK, soccer is the most 'popular' game in the world. And rice is the most 'popular' food in the world. So what? Maybe other countries can't afford football, basketball and baseball leagues: maybe if they could afford these other sports, they'd enjoy them even more."

Unlike Rome, Barra has some sense of why he flies off the handle on this subject. It has to do with his resentment of the game's yuppie promoters. He argues, "Americans are such suckers when it comes to something with a European label that many who have resisted thus far would give in to trendiness and push their kids into youth soccer programs." And more than that, he wor-

---

8. New York–based newspaper gossip columnist and radio host (1897–1972) noted for his inventive wordplay and staccato on-air delivery.

ries that the soccer enthusiasts want the U.S. to "get with the rest of the world's program."

As Barra makes clear, the anti-soccer lobby really articulates the same fears as Eurico Miranda and Alan Garrison,[9] a phobia of globalization. To understand their fears, it is important to note that both Barra and Rome are proud aficionados of baseball. The United Sates, with its unashamedly dynamic culture, doesn't have too many deeply rooted transgenerational traditions that it can claim as its own. Baseball is one of the few: That's one reason why the game gets so much nostalgia-drenched celebration in Kevin Costner movies and Stephen Jay Gould books.[10]

But Major League Baseball, let's face it, has been a loser in globalization. Unlike the NBA or NFL, it hasn't made the least attempt to market itself to a global audience. And the global audience has shown no hunger for the game. Because baseball has failed to master the global economy, it has been beat back by it. According to the Sporting Goods Manufacturers Association of America, the number of teens playing baseball fell 47 percent between 1987 and 2000. During that same period, youth soccer grew exponentially. By 2002, 1.3 million more kids played soccer than Little League. And the demographic profile of baseball has grown ever more lily white. It has failed to draw African Americans and attracts few Latinos who didn't grow up playing the game in the Caribbean. The change can also be registered in the ballot box that matters most. Nielsen ratings show that, in most years, a World Series can no longer draw the same number of viewers as an inconsequential Monday night game in the NFL.

It's not surprising that Americans should split like this over soccer. Globalization increasingly provides the subtext for the American cultural split. This isn't to say America violently or even knowingly divides over globalization. But after September 11 opened new debates over foreign policy, two camps in American politics have clearly emerged. One camp believes in the essential tenets of the globalization religion as preached by European politicians, that national governments should defer to institutions like the UN and WTO.[11] These tend to be people who opposed the war in Iraq. And this opinion reflects a worldview. These Americans share cultural values with Europeans—an aggressive secularism, a more relaxed set of cultural mores that tolerates gays and pot smoking—which isn't surprising, considering that these Americans have jobs and tourist interests that put them in regular contact with the other side of the Atlantic. They consider themselves to be part of a cosmopolitan culture that transcends national boundaries.

On the other side, there is a group that believes in "American exceptionalism," an idea that America's history and singular form of government has given

20

---

9. Noted soccer hooligans of the 1970s and 1980s.

10. Costner (b. 1955), actor in *Bull Durham* (1988), *Field of Dreams* (1989), and *For Love of the Game* (1999), three films about baseball; Gould (1941–2002), Harvard paleontologist who also wrote about baseball. His baseball essays were collected in *Triumph and Tragedy in Mudville* (2003).

11. Abbreviations for the United Nations and World Trade Organization.

the nation a unique role to play in the world; that the U.S. should be above submitting to international laws and bodies. They view Europeans as degraded by their lax attitudes, and worry about the threat to American culture posed by secular tolerance. With so much relativism seeping into the American way of life, they fret that the country has lost the self-confidence to make basic moral judgments, to condemn evil. Soccer isn't exactly pernicious, but it's a symbol of the U.S. junking its tradition to "get with the rest of the world's program."

There are many conservatives who hate relativism, consider the French wussy, and still adore soccer. But it's not a coincidence that the game has become a small touchstone in this culture war.

III

I wish that my side, the yuppie soccer fans, were blameless victims in these culture wars. But I've been around enough of America's soccer cognoscenti to know that they invite abuse. They are inveterate snobs, so snobbish, in fact, that they think nothing of turning against their comrades. According to their sneering critique, their fellow fans are dilettantes without any real understanding of the game; they are yuppies who admire soccer like a fine slab of imported goat cheese; they come from neighborhoods with spectacularly high Starbucks-per-capita, so they lack any semblance of burning working-class passion.

This self-loathing critique can be easily debunked. I've seen the counterevidence with my own eyes. In the spring of 2001, the U.S. national team played Honduras in Washington's Robert Francis Kennedy stadium. This vital World Cup qualifying match had generated the packed, exuberant stadium that the occasion deserved. Fans wore their nation's jersey. Their singing and stomping caused the steel and concrete to undulate like the Mexican wave.[12] In a country with lesser engineering standards, it would have been time to worry about a stadium collapse. On the field, stewards scampered to pick up scattered sneakers. Fans had removed them and thrown them at the opposing goalkeeper, a small gesture of homage to the madness of Glasgow[13] and the passion of Barcelona. They mercilessly booed the linesman, softening him up by insulting his slut of a mother. It might not have quite ascended to the atmospheric wonders of a game played by the English national team, but it wasn't far from that mark.

25   There is, however, an important difference between a home game in London and Washington. The majority of English fans will root for England. In Washington, more or less half the stadium wore the blue-and-white Honduran jersey, and they were the ones who shouted themselves hoarse and heaved their

12. Known in the United States (where it seems to have been invented) as the wave, this activity involves successive groups of spectators briefly standing, yelling while raising their arms, then resuming their seats. It gained worldwide popularity at the 1986 World Cup in Mexico City, thus its name.

13. Home of one of the most bitter rivalries in sports, between two local clubs, Celtic and the Glasgow Rangers. The rivalry has been marked by frequent fan riots.

shoes. The American aspiration of appearing in the World Cup rested on this game. But on that day, the Washington stadium might as well have been in Tegucigalpa.[14]

Traveling through Europe, you hear the same complaint repeated over and over: Americans are so "hypernationalistic." But is there any country in the world that would tolerate such animosity to their national team in their own national capital? In England or France or Italy, this would have been cause for unleashing hooligan hell.

Nor were the American fans what you'd expect of a hegemonic power. The *Washington Post* had published a message from the national soccer federation urging us to wear red shirts as a sign of support—and to clearly distinguish ourselves from the Hondurans. But most American soccer fans don't possess a red USA jersey and aren't about to go down to the sporting goods store to buy one. They do, however, own red Arsenal, Man U., and Ajax[15] jerseys, or, in my case, an old Barcelona one, that they collected on continental travels. While we were giving a patriotic boost, we couldn't help revealing our Europhilic cosmopolitanism.

I mention this scene because many critics of globalization make America the wicked villain in the tale. They portray the U.S. forcing Nike, McDonald's and *Baywatch* down the throats of the unwilling world, shredding ancient cultures for the sake of empire and cash. But that version of events skirts the obvious truth: Multinational corporations are just that, multinational; they don't represent American interests or American culture. Just as much as they have changed the tastes and economies of other countries, they have tried to change the tastes and economy of the United States. Witness the Nike and Budweiser campaigns to sell soccer here. No other country has been as subjected to the free flows of capital and labor, so constantly remade by migration, and found its national identity so constantly challenged. In short, America may be an exception, but it is not exceptionally immune to globalization. And we fight about it, whether we know it or not, just like everyone else.

14. Capital of Honduras.
15. Arsenal, Manchester United, two of England's premier clubs; Ajax, the premier Dutch soccer club, based in Amsterdam.

MLA CITATION

Foer, Franklin. "How Soccer Explains the American Culture Wars." 2004. *The Norton Reader: An Anthology of Nonfiction*. Ed. Melissa A. Goldthwaite et al. 14th ed. New York: Norton, 2016. 350–57. Print.

QUESTIONS

1. How does Franklin Foer characterize soccer as a sport? Do you agree or disagree with his characterization, and why? How much of a role does social class play in soccer?

2. Did you play a sport in elementary school or high school? If so, describe your parents' attitude toward your participation. Were you encouraged? Compare or contrast your experience with Foer's as he describes it in paragraphs 1–5.

3. Foer analyzes soccer through the cultural attitudes people bring to it. What reasons for following soccer does he leave out? List some other reasons people like soccer.

4. Write about attending a sporting event as a fully committed fan. For models you might use Maya Angelou's (pp. 371–73) or A. Bartlett Giamatti's essays (pp. 358–60).

A. BARTLETT GIAMATTI   *The Green Fields of the Mind*

I T BREAKS YOUR HEART. It is designed to break your heart. The game begins in the spring, when everything else begins again, and it blossoms in the summer, filling the afternoons and evenings, and then as soon as the chill rains come, it stops and leaves you to face the fall alone. You count on it, rely on it to buffer the passage of time, to keep the memory of sunshine and high skies alive, and then just when the days are all twilight, when you need it most, it stops. Today, October 2, a Sunday of rain and broken branches and leaf-clogged drains and slick streets, it stopped, and summer was gone.

Somehow, the summer seemed to slip by faster this time. Maybe it wasn't this summer, but all the summers that, in this my 40th summer, slipped by so fast. There comes a time when every summer will have something of autumn about it. Whatever the reason, it seemed to me that I was investing more and more in baseball, making the game do more of the work that keeps time fat and slow and lazy. I was counting on the game's deep patterns, three strikes, three outs, three times three innings, and its deepest impulse, to go out and back, to leave and to return home, to set the order of the day and to organize the daylight. I wrote a few things this last summer, this summer that did not last, nothing grand but some things, and yet that work was just camouflage. The real activity was done with the radio—not the all-seeing, all-falsifying television—and was the playing of the game in the only place it will last, the enclosed green field of the mind. There, in that warm, bright place, what the old poet called Mutability[1] does not so quickly come.

First published in the Yale Alumni Magazine and Journal (1977) and on the Yale Alumni Magazine website (2012); it was also included in A Great and Glorious Game: Baseball Writings of A. Bartlett Giamatti (1998). In this essay, A. Bartlett Giamatti describes a game played by the Boston Red Sox and the Baltimore Orioles on October 1, 1977.

1. Dame Mutability, character created by the poet Edmund Spenser and representative of change in one's fortune.

But out here, on Sunday, October 2, where it rains all day, Dame Mutability never loses. She was in the crowd at Fenway[2] yesterday, a grey day full of
bluster and contradiction, when the Red Sox came up in the last of the ninth
trailing Baltimore 8–5, while the Yankees, rain-delayed against Detroit, only
needing to win one or have Boston lose one to win it all, sat in New York washing down cold cuts with beer and watching the Boston game. Boston had won
two, the Yankees had lost two, and suddenly it seemed as if the whole season
might go to the last day, or beyond, except here was Boston losing 8–5, while
New York sat in its family room and put its feet up. Lynn,[3] both ankles hurting
now as they had in July, hits a single down the right-field line. The crowd stirs. It
is on its feet. Hobson, third baseman, former Bear Bryant quarterback, strong,
quiet, over 100 RBIs, goes for three breaking balls and is out.[4] The goddess
smiles and encourages her agent, a canny journeyman named Nelson Briles.[5]

Now comes a pinch hitter, Bernie Carbo, onetime Rookie of the Year,
erratic, quick, a shade too handsome, so laid-back he is always, in his soul,
stretched out in the tall grass, one arm under his head, watching the clouds and
laughing; now he looks over some low stuff unworthy of him and then, uncoil-
ing, sends one out, straight on a rising line, over the center-field wall, no cheap
Fenway shot, but all of it, the physics as elegant as the arc the ball describes.

New England is on its feet, roaring. The summer will not pass. Roaring,   5
they recall the evening, late and cold, in 1975, the sixth game of the World
Series, perhaps the greatest baseball game played in the last fifty years, when
Carbo, loose and easy, had uncoiled to tie the game that Fisk[6] would win. It is
8–7, one out, and school will never start, rain will never come, sun will warm
the back of your neck forever. Now Bailey,[7] picked up from the National League
recently, big arms, heavy gut, experienced, new to the league and the club; he
fouls off two and then, checking, tentative, a big man off balance, he pops a
soft liner to the first baseman. It is suddenly darker and later, and the announcer
doing the game coast to coast, a New Yorker who works for a New York television station, sounds relieved. His little world, well-lit, hot-combed, split-second-
timed, had no capacity to absorb this much gritty, grainy, contrary reality.

Cox[8] swings a bat, stretches his long arms, bends his back, the rookie from
Pawtucket[9] who broke in two weeks earlier with a record six straight hits, the
kid drafted ahead of Fred Lynn, rangy, smooth, cool. The count runs two and
two, Briles is cagey, nothing too good, and Cox swings, the ball beginning
toward the mound and then, in a jaunty, wayward dance, skipping past Briles,

2. Fenway Park, home stadium of the Boston Red Sox.

3. Fred Lynn (b. 1952), outfielder, most notably with the Red Sox.

4. Butch Hobson (b. 1951), Red Sox third baseman; Bear Bryant (1913–1983), University of Alabama football coach.

5. Veteran Baltimore Orioles pitcher (1943–2005) in the 1977 game Giamatti describes.

6. Carlton Fisk (b. 1947), catcher for the Red Sox and the Chicago White Sox.

7. Bob Bailey (b. 1942), third baseman for the Red Sox.

8. Ted Cox (b. 1955), shortstop for the Red Sox.

9. Red Sox minor league team.

feinting to the right, skimming the last of the grass, finding the dirt, moving now like some small, purposeful marine creature negotiating the green deep, easily avoiding the jagged rock of second base, traveling steady and straight now out into the dark, silent recesses of center field.

The aisles are jammed, the place is on its feet, the wrappers, the programs, the Coke cups and peanut shells, the detritus of an afternoon; the anxieties, the things that have to be done tomorrow, the regrets about yesterday, the accumulation of a summer: all forgotten, while hope, the anchor, bites and takes hold where a moment before it seemed we would be swept out with the tide. Rice[10] is up. Rice whom Aaron[11] had said was the only one he'd seen with the ability to break his records. Rice the best clutch hitter on the club, with the best slugging percentage in the league. Rice, so quick and strong he once checked his swing halfway through and snapped the bat in two. Rice the Hammer of God sent to scourge the Yankees, the sound was overwhelming, fathers pounded their sons on the back, cars pulled off the road, households froze, New England exulted in its blessedness, and roared its thanks for all good things, for Rice and for a summer stretching halfway through October. Briles threw, Rice swung, and it was over. One pitch, a fly to center, and it stopped. Summer died in New England and like rain sliding off a roof, the crowd slipped out of Fenway, quickly, with only a steady murmur of concern for the drive ahead remaining of the roar. Mutability had turned the seasons and translated hope to memory once again. And, once again, she had used baseball, our best invention to stay change, to bring change on. That is why it breaks my heart, that game—not because in New York they could win because Boston lost; in that, there is a rough justice, and a reminder to the Yankees of how slight and fragile are the circumstances that exalt one group of human beings over another. It breaks my heart because it was meant to, because it was meant to foster in me again the illusion that there was something abiding, some pattern and some impulse that could come together to make a reality that would resist the corrosion; and because, after it had fostered again that most hungered-for illusion, the game was meant to stop, and betray precisely what it promised.

Of course, there are those who learn after the first few times. They grow out of sports. And there are others who were born with the wisdom to know that nothing lasts. These are the truly tough among us, the ones who can live without illusion, or without even the hope of illusion. I am not that grown-up or up-to-date. I am a simpler creature, tied to more primitive patterns and cycles. I need to think something lasts forever, and it might as well be that state of being that is a game; it might as well be that, in a green field, in the sun.

10. Jim Rice (b. 1953), Red Sox left fielder.
11. Hank Aaron (b. 1934), right fielder, mostly with the Milwaukee and Atlanta Braves.

MLA CITATION

Giamatti, A. Bartlett. "The Green Fields of the Mind." 1977. *The Norton Reader: An Anthology of Nonfiction.* Ed. Melissa A. Goldthwaite et al. 14th ed. New York: Norton, 2016. 358–60. Print.

QUESTIONS

1. A. Bartlett Giamatti transitions from present tense to past tense throughout the essay even though he is describing a game that took place the previous day. Why do you think he made this choice? How would the essay be different if he had chosen to write only in the past tense?

2. Both Giamatti and Maya Angelou (in "Champion of the World," pp. 371–73) describe a particular game or match. How are their essays similar? How are they different?

3. In framing his essay, Giamatti reflects on "Mutability" (paragraph 2), how the only thing that is certain is change. How does he connect the themes of baseball, seasons, and change? How does his description of a particular game support or illustrate those themes?

4. Using present and past tense, write about a particular moment from a sports event that you have witnessed, using Giamatti's narrative as your model.

DAVID HALBERSTAM *Jordan's Moment*

THE DESOLATE NEIGHBORHOOD on the West Side of Chicago where the Bulls play their home games is very quiet these days. Their gleaming new arena, the United Center, is set down there as if on a moonscape. All twelve pre-Christmas home games have been cancelled, because of the labor dispute between the owners and the players, which was initiated by the owners in a lockout described as a struggle between short millionaires and tall millionaires, or between billionaires and millionaires. The National Basketball Association, which would have entered its fifty-second season this fall, seems to have fallen victim to its own dizzying success, one that has seen the player payroll increase by an estimated two thousand five hundred per cent in the last twenty years. The incident that probably triggered the lockout occurred about a year ago, when the Minnesota Timberwolves extended the contract of a gifted young player named Kevin Garnett, paying him a hundred and twenty-six million dollars over seven years. The Timberwolves' general manager, the former Boston Celtic Kevin McHale, completed the deal; unhappy with the direction of the league and his own part in it, he later noted, "We have our hand on the neck of the golden goose and we're squeezing hard."

In Chicago, where for much of the last decade the best basketball team in the country has played, the silence is particularly painful. The last time games were played here, the Bulls, led by Michael Jordan, were contesting for their

Originally published in the New Yorker *(1998), a weekly magazine of "reportage, commentary, criticism, essays, fiction, satire, cartoons, and poetry."*

sixth N.B.A. championship, and playing against a favored team, the Utah Jazz. It was an indelible series, the memory of which serves as this year's only fare—and it is melancholy fare—for basketball junkies everywhere.

Michael Jordan was thirty-five, and arguably the dominant athlete in American sports, as he led Chicago into Salt Lake City. He was nearing the end of his career, and he was, if anything, a more complete player than ever. What his body could no longer accomplish in terms of pure physical ability he could compensate for with his shrewd knowledge of both the game and the opposing players. Nothing was wasted. There was a new quality, almost an iciness, to the way he played now. In 1995, after Jordan returned to basketball from his year-and-a-half-long baseball sabbatical,[1] he spent the summer in Hollywood making the movie *Space Jam*, but he demanded that the producers build a basketball court where he could work out every day. Old friends dropping by the Warner lot noticed that he was working particularly hard on a shot that was already a minor part of his repertoire but which he was now making a signature shot—a jumper where he held the ball, faked a move to the basket, and then, at the last minute, when he finally jumped, fell back slightly, giving himself almost perfect separation from the defensive player. Because of his jumping ability and his threat to drive, that shot was virtually unguardable. More, it was a very smart player's concession to the changes in his body wrought by time, and it signified that he was entering a new stage in his career. What professional basketball men were now seeing was something that had been partly masked earlier in his career by his singular physical ability and the artistry of what he did, and that something was a consuming passion not just to excel but to dominate. "He wants to cut your heart out and then show it to you," his former coach Doug Collins said. "He's Hannibal Lecter,"[2] Bob Ryan, the Boston *Globe*'s expert basketball writer, said. When a television reporter asked the Bulls' center, Luc Longley, for a one-word description of Jordan, Longley's response was "Predator."

"The athlete you remind me of the most is Jake LaMotta,"[3] the Bulls' owner, Jerry Reinsdorf, told Jordan one day, referring to the fearless middleweight fighter of another era, "because the only way they can stop you is to kill you."

5   "Who's Jake LaMotta?" Jordan answered.

In Utah during last year's N.B.A. finals, Jordan had woken up before Game Five violently ill. It seemed impossible that he would play. (Whether it was altitude sickness or food poisoning no one was ever quite sure.) At about 8 A.M., one of Jordan's bodyguards, fixtures in his entourage, called Chip Schaefer, the team trainer, to say that Jordan had been up all night with flulike symptoms and was seriously ill. Rushing to Jordan's room, Schaefer found him curled up in the fetal position and wrapped in blankets, though the thermostat had been cranked

1. From 1994 to 1995, Jordan played minor league baseball with the Chicago White Sox.
2. Character in the film *The Silence of the Lambs* (1991) who is a cannibal and serial killer.
3. Professional fighter (b. 1922), former World Middleweight champion.

up to its maximum. The greatest player in the world looked like a weak little zombie.

Schaefer immediately hooked Jordan up to an I.V. and tried to get as much fluid into him as possible. He also gave him medication and decided to let him rest as much as he could that morning. Word of Jordan's illness quickly spread among journalists at the Delta Center, where the game was to be played, and the general assumption was that he would not play. One member of the media, though, was not so sure—James Worthy, who, after a brilliant career with the Los Angeles Lakers, was working for the Fox network. Having played with Jordan at North Carolina and against him in the pros, Worthy knew not only how Michael drove himself but, even more important, how he motivated himself. When reports circulated that Michael had a fever of a hundred and two, Worthy told the other Fox reporters that the fever meant nothing. "He'll play," Worthy said. "He'll figure out what he can do, he'll conserve his strength in other areas, and he'll have a big game."

In the locker room before the game, Jordan's teammates were appalled by what they saw. Michael, normally quite dark, was a color somewhere between white and gray, Bill Wennington, the Bulls' backup center, recalled, and his eyes, usually so vital, looked dead.

At first, fans watching at home could not understand how Jordan could play at all. Then they were pulled into the drama of the event, which had by now transcended mere basketball and taken on the nature of an entirely different challenge. Early in the second quarter, Utah led 36–20, but Jordan played at an exceptional level—he scored twenty-one points in the first half—and at halftime his team was down only four points. The Bulls managed to stay close in the second half. With forty-six seconds left in the game, and Utah leading by a point, Jordan was fouled going to the basket. "Look at the body language of Michael Jordan," Marv Albert, the announcer, said. "You have the idea that he has difficulty just standing up." Jordan made the first of two foul shots, which tied the score, and somehow grabbed the loose ball after the missed second shot. Then, with twenty-five seconds left, the Jazz inexplicably left him open, and he hit a three-pointer, which gave Chicago an 88–85 lead and the key to a 90–88 win. He ended up with thirty-eight points, fifteen of them in the last quarter.

Throughout the 1997–98 season, Jordan had wanted to meet Utah in the finals again, in no small part because after the 1997 finals too many people had said that if only Utah had had the home-court advantage the Jazz would have won. He was eager to show that true warriors could win as handily on the road, and he was also eager to show that although Karl Malone[4] was a great player, whose abilities he admired, there was a significant degree of difference in their respective abilities.

Unlike more talented teams, Utah almost never made mental mistakes during a game, and at the Delta Center, home of some of the league's noisiest

10

---

4. Played for Utah Jazz and Los Angeles Lakers (b. 1963).

fans, a game that was at all close could easily turn into a very difficult time for a visitor. In the Western Conference finals, Utah had gone up against the Lakers, a young team led by the immense Shaquille O'Neal, and with considerably more athletic ability, and yet the Jazz swept the Lakers in four games, making them look like a group of befuddled playground all-stars. "Playing them is like the project guys against a team," Nick Van Exel, the Laker point guard, said after the series. "The project guys always want to do the fancy behind-the-back dribbles, the spectacular plays and the dunks, while the Jazz are a bunch of guys doing pick-and-rolls[5] and the little things. They don't get caught up in the officiating, they don't get down on each other, they don't complain. They stand as a team and stay focussed."

Utah was a *team*, smart and well coached, and its players never seemed surprised late in a game. No team in the league executed its offense, particularly the interplay between John Stockton[6] and Karl Malone, with the discipline of Utah. But that was a potential vulnerability, the Chicago coaches believed, for the Jazz were very predictable. What worked night after night against ordinary teams during the regular season might not work in a prolonged series against great defensive players. The price of discipline might be a gap in creativity—the ability to freelance—when the disciplined offense was momentarily checkmated.

Some of this could be seen in the difference between Jordan and Malone. Each had improved greatly after he entered the league, and each had the ability to carry his team night after night. But Jordan's ability to create shots for himself, and thereby dominate at the end of big games when the defensive pressure on both sides had escalated significantly, was dramatically greater than Malone's. Malone had improved year by year not only as a shooter but as someone who could pass out of the double team.[7] Still, like most big, powerful men, he could not improvise nearly as well as Jordan, and he was very much dependent on teammates like Stockton to create opportunities for him. What the Chicago coaches, and Jordan himself, believed was that the Bulls would be able to limit Karl Malone in the fourth quarter of a tight game but that Utah would never be able to limit Michael Jordan, because of Jordan's far greater creativity.

There was one other thing that the Chicago coaches and Jordan thought about Malone, which gave them extra confidence as they got ready for the final series, and which differed from how most other people in the league perceived Malone. Malone, the Chicago staff believed, had not come into the league as a scorer or a shooter, but he had worked so hard that he was now one of the premier shooters among the league's big men, averaging just under thirty points a game for the last ten years. But deep in his heart, they thought, he did not have the psyche of a shooter like Larry Bird, Reggie Miller, or even Jordan;

---

5. Play in which an offensive player screens a defender to allow a teammate to accept a pass and get open for a shot.

6. Utah Jazz point guard (b. 1962).

7. Alignment in which two defensive players guard a single offensive player.

therefore, it remained something of an alien role.[8] At the end of a big game, they suspected, with the game on the line, that would be a factor.

The Bulls' coach, Phil Jackson, hoped to steal Game One of the championship, in Salt Lake City, because the Jazz had had ten days off and were rusty. But it had taken the Bulls seven exhausting games to beat the Indiana Pacers for the Eastern Conference title, and they came into Game One slow and tired, constantly a step behind in their defensive rotations. Even so, they made up eight points in the fourth quarter to force Utah into overtime before they lost.

The Bulls recovered, however, and stole Game Two, and, with that, the Jazz lost the home-court advantage they had worked so hard for all season. Worse, the series now seemed to be turning out the way the Chicago coaches had wanted it to, with the Bulls' guards limiting Stockton's freedom of movement and isolating Malone, who, on his own, was no longer a dominant presence.

Game Three, in Chicago, went badly for Utah. On defense, the Bulls played a nearly perfect game: they stole the ball, they cut off passing lanes, and their defensive rotations were so quick that Utah's shots almost always seemed desperate—forced up at the last second. It was as if the Chicago players had known on each Jazz possession exactly what Utah was going to try to do. The final score was 96–54, the widest margin in the history of the finals, and Utah's fifty-four points were the lowest total in any N.B.A. game since the introduction of the twenty-four-second clock,[9] in 1954. "This is actually the score?" Jerry Sloan, the Utah coach, said in his post-game press conference, holding up the stat sheet. "I thought it was a hundred and ninety-six. It sure seemed like a hundred and ninety-six."

Game Four was more respectable, with the Bulls winning 86–82. But the Jazz came back in Game Five. Malone, bottled up so long, and the target of considerable criticism in the papers, had a big game, hitting seventeen of twenty-seven shots for thirty-nine points, while Chicago seemed off its game, its concentration slipping. Jackson said later that he thought there had been far too much talk of winning at home, too much talk of champagne and of how to stop a riot in case the Bulls won—and too much debate over whether or not this would be Michael Jordan's last game ever in Chicago in a Bulls uniform.

At this late point in Michael Jordan's career, there were certain people who thought of themselves as Jordanologists, students not only of the game but of the man himself. They believed that they could think like him; that is, they could pick up his immensely sensitive feel for the rhythm and texture of each game, his sense of what his team needed to do at a given moment, and what his role should be—scoring, passing, or playing defense. Would he set an example for his teammates by taking up the defensive level? Would he spend the first quarter largely passing off in order to get them in the game? Over the years,

8. Bird (b. 1956), played for the Boston Celtics; Miller (b. 1965), played for the Indiana Pacers.
9. The offensive team must attempt a basket within twenty-four seconds of obtaining the ball.

he had come a long way from the young man who, surrounded by lesser teammates, had gone all out for an entire game, trying to do everything by himself.
The mature Michael Jordan liked to conserve energy, let opponents use theirs
up, and then when the moment was right take over the game.

20   Now, in Salt Lake City, it was as if he had reverted to the Michael Jordan
who had carried that bottom-feeding Chicago team in the early days of his
career, the player who effectively let his teammates know they were not to get
in his way, because he was going to do it all himself. On this night, he knew
that he was going to get little help from Scottie Pippen, who was severely
injured—virtually a basketball cripple. Dennis Rodman was a rebounder, not
a scorer. Toni Kukoc had played well lately, but he was always problematical.
Ron Harper, once an exceptional scorer, had become, late in his career in Chicago, a defensive specialist, and he, too, was sick—apparently from something
he had eaten. Luc Longley, the center, was in the midst of a wretched playoff
series, seeming out of synch with himself and his teammates. (He played only
fourteen minutes of this game, scored no points, and picked up four fouls.) Steve
Kerr was a talented outside shooter, but Utah would be able to cover him more
closely with Pippen limited.

It was clear from the beginning of the game that Jordan would try to do it
all. Pippen was out for much of the first half, and Jordan, with Phil Jackson's
assent, rationed his energy on defense; at one point, the assistant coach, Tex
Winter, turned to Jackson and said, "Michael's giving defense a lick and
promise," and Jackson said, "Well, Tex, he does need a bit of a rest." By all
rights, the Jazz should have been able to grind the Bulls down and take a sizable lead, but the Bulls, even with their bench players on the floor, never let
Utah break the game open. On offense, Jordan carried the load. He was
conserving his energy, playing less defense and doing less rebounding than he
normally did, but at the half he had twenty-three points. Utah's lead at the
half, 49–45, was not what any Jazz fan would want against such a vulnerable
Chicago team.

Later, Jordan said that he had remained confident throughout the game,
because Utah did not break it open when it had the chance. Jordan's former
teammate B. J. Armstrong, watching at home, thought that Utah was blowing
it, leaving the game out there for Michael to steal. Armstrong and Jordan had
been friends, but it had often been difficult for Armstrong to play alongside
Michael. The game had come so much more easily to Jordan than to anyone
else, Armstrong felt, and Michael had often showed his impatience with his
more mortal teammates—indeed, at one point a frustrated Armstrong had
checked out of the library several books on genius hoping that they would help
him learn to play with Michael. One of Jordan's particular strengths, Armstrong
believed, was that he had the most acute sense of the tempo and mood of every
game of any player he had ever seen. A lot of players and coaches can look at
film afterward and point their finger at the exact moment when a game slipped
away, but Jordan could tell instantly, even as it was happening. It was, Armstrong thought, as if he were in the game playing and yet sitting there studying
it and completely distanced from it. It was a gift that allowed him to monitor

and lift his own team at critical moments and to destroy opposing teams when he sensed their special moment of vulnerability.

Now, watching the second half of Game Six, Armstrong had a sense that Michael regarded the game as a potential gift. The Jazz, after all, could have put it away early on by exploiting the obvious Chicago weaknesses. But they hadn't. If they had, Armstrong thought, Michael might have saved his energy for Game Seven. But instead the Jazz were leaving Game Six out there for the taking.

As the fourth quarter opened, the Utah lead was marginal, 66–61; the low score tended to favor the Bulls, for it meant that they had set the tempo and remained in striking distance. Slowly, the Bulls began to come back, until, with under five minutes to play, the score was tied at 77. Jordan was obviously tired, but so was everyone else. Tex Winter was alarmed when Jordan missed several jump shots in a row. "Look, he can't get any elevation," he told Jackson. "His legs are gone."

During a time-out two minutes later, Jackson told Jordan to give up the jump shot and drive. "I know," Jordan said, agreeing. "I'm going to start going to the basket—they haven't got a center in now, so the way is clear."

Once again, it was Michael Jordan time. A twenty-foot jumper by Malone on a feed from Stockton gave Utah an 83–79 lead, but Jordan cut it to 83–81 when he drove to the basket, was fouled by Utah's Bryon Russell, with 2:07 on the clock, and hit a pair of foul shots. Back and forth they went, and when Jordan drove again he was fouled again, this time by Stockton. He hit both free throws, to tie the score at 83, with 59.2 seconds left.

Then Utah brought the ball up court and went into its offense very slowly. Stockton worked the ball in to Malone, and Chicago was quick to double-team him. Malone fed Stockton, on the opposite side of the court, with a beautiful cross-court pass. With Harper rushing back a split second too late, Stockton buried a twenty-four-foot jumper. That gave Utah a three-point lead, 86–83. The clock showed 41.9 seconds left as Chicago called its last time-out. The Utah crowd began to breathe a little easier.

Dick Ebersol, the head of NBC Sports, watched the final minutes in the NBC truck. He had started the game sitting in the stands, next to the N.B.A. commissioner, David Stern, but had become so nervous that he had gone down to the control truck. Ebersol liked Michael Jordan very much, and was well aware that he and his network were the beneficiaries of Jordan's unique appeal. Jordan's presence in the finals was worth eight or nine million viewers to NBC. Ebersol was delighted by the ratings for this series so far—they would end up at 18.7, the highest ever. At this point, though, Ebersol was rooting not for Michael Jordan but for a seventh game, and that meant he was rooting, however involuntarily, for Utah. A seventh game would bring NBC and its parent company, General Electric, an additional ten or twelve million dollars in advertising revenues. Jordan's exploits had brought many benefits to the N.B.A. over the years, but he was such a great player that no N.B.A. final in which he was involved had gone to the ratings and advertising jackpot of a seventh game.

When Stockton gave Utah the three-point lead with 41.9 seconds showing on the clock, Ebersol was thrilled. He was going to get his Game Seven after all. "Well, guys," he told the production people in the truck, turning away from the screens, "we'll be back here on Wednesday, and the home folks"—the G.E. management people—"are going to be very happy."

30   During the Chicago time-out, Jackson and Jordan talked about what kind of shot he might take, and Jackson reminded him that his legs were tired and it was affecting his jump shot. "I've got my second wind now," Jordan answered. "If you have to go for the jumper, you've got to follow through better," Jackson said. "You haven't been following through." Tex Winter drew up a variation on a basic Chicago play, called Whatthefuck—actually an old New York play, from Jackson's time on the Knicks. It called for the Bulls to clear out on one side, in order to isolate Jordan against Bryon Russell. As it happened, Jordan took the ball out near the back-court line, moved in a leisurely fashion into his attack mode on the right side, and then, with Utah having no chance to double him, drove down the right side and laid the ball up high and soft for the basket. The score was 86–85 Utah, with thirty-seven seconds left. It was a tough basket off a big-time drive.

     That gave Utah one wonderful additional possession—a chance either to hit a basket or to use Malone to draw fouls. Stockton came across the half-court line almost casually. He bided his time, letting the clock run down, and finally, with about eleven seconds left on the twenty-four-second clock, he worked the ball to Malone.

Buzz Peterson, Jordan's close friend and college roommate, was watching Game Six with his wife, Jan, at their home, in Boone, North Carolina. In the final minute of the game, Jan turned to him and said, "They're going to lose." But Peterson, who had played with Jordan in countless real games and in practice games when the winning team was the first to reach eleven and Jordan's team was behind 10–8, knew all too well that moments like this were what he lived for: with his team behind, he would predict victory to his teammates and then take over the last part of the game. Peterson told his wife, "Don't be too sure. Michael's got one more good shot at it." Just then Jordan made his driving layup to bring the Bulls within a point. The key play, Peterson felt, was going to come on the next defensive sequence, when Utah came down court with the ball. Peterson was certain that he could track Jordan's thinking: he would know that Utah would go to Malone, hoping for a basket, or, at least, two foul shots. He had seen his friend so often in the past in this same role, encouraged by Dean Smith, the North Carolina coach, to play the defensive rover. Peterson thought that Michael, knowing the likely Utah offense every bit as well as Malone and Stockton, would try to make a move on Malone.

     As soon as Malone got the ball, Jordan was there. Sure where the ball was going and how Malone was going to hold it, he sneaked in behind him for the steal. Jordan's poise at this feverish moment was fascinating: as he made his move behind Malone, he had the discipline to extend his body to the right and thus get the perfect angle, so that when he swiped at the ball he would not foul. "Karl never saw me coming," Jordan said afterward. There were 18.9 seconds left on the clock.

The crowd, Jordan remembered, got very quiet. That was, he said later, the moment for him. The moment, he explained, was what all Phil Jackson's Zen Buddhism stuff, as he called it, was about: how to focus and concentrate and be ready for that critical point in a game, so that when it arrived you knew exactly what you wanted to do and how to do it, as if you had already lived through it. When it happened, you were supposed to be in control, use the moment, and not panic and let the moment use you. Jackson liked the analogy of a cat waiting for a mouse, patiently biding its time, until the mouse, utterly unaware, finally came forth.

The play at that instant, Jordan said, seemed to unfold very slowly, and he saw everything with great clarity, as Jackson had wanted him to: the way the Utah defense was setting up, and what his teammates were doing. He knew exactly what he was going to do. "I never doubted myself," Jordan said later. "I never doubted the whole game." 35

Incredibly, Utah decided not to double-team Jordan. Steve Kerr, in for Harper, was on the wing to Jordan's right, ready to take a pass and score if Stockton left him to double Jordan. Kukoc had to be watched on the left. Rodman, starting out at the top of the foul circle, made a good cut to the basket, and suddenly Bryon Russell was isolated, one on one, with Jordan. Jordan had let the clock run down from about fifteen seconds to about eight. Then Russell made a quick reach for the ball, and Jordan started his drive, moving to his right as if to go to the basket. Russell went for the bait, and suddenly Jordan pulled up. Russell was already sprawling to his left, aided by a light tap on the rear from Jordan as he stopped and squared up and shot. It was a great shot, a clear look at the basket, and his elevation and form were perfect. Normally, Jordan said later, he tended to fade back just as he took his jumper for that extra degree of separation between him and his defender, but, because his previous shots had been falling short, he did not fade away this time—nor did he need to, for Russell, faked to the floor, was desperately trying to regain his position.

Roy Williams, the Kansas coach who had heard about Michael when he was back in Laney High School, in Wilmington, North Carolina, was at his camp for high-school players, in Kansas, and was watching the game in the coaches' locker room. He remembered saying after the steal, as Jordan was bringing the ball up court, that some Utah defender had better run over and double him quickly or it was going to be over. You forced someone else to take the last shot, he thought—you did not allow Michael to go one on one for it. But no one doubled him. What Williams remembered about the final shot was the exquisite quality of Jordan's form, and how long he held his follow-through after releasing the ball; it was something that coaches always taught their players. Watching him now, as he seemed to stay up in the air for an extra moment, defying gravity, Williams thought of it as Michael Jordan's way of willing the ball through the basket.

There is a photograph of that moment, Jordan's last shot, in the magazine *ESPN*, taken by the photographer Fernando Medina.[10] It is in color and covers two full pages, and it shows Russell struggling to regain position, Jordan at the peak of his jump, the ball high up on its arc and about to descend, and the clock displaying the time remaining in the game—6.6 seconds. What is remarkable is the closeup it offers of so many Utah fans. Though the ball has not yet reached the basket, the game appears over to them. The anguish—the certitude of defeat—is on their faces. In a number of instances their hands are extended as if to stop Jordan and keep the shot from going in. Some of the fans have already put their hands to their faces, as in a moment of grief. There is one exception to this: a young boy on the right, in a Chicago Bulls shirt, whose arms are already in the air in a victory call.

The ball dropped cleanly through. Utah had one more chance, but Stockton missed the last shot and the Bulls won, 87–86. Jordan had carried his team once again. He had scored forty-five points, and he had scored his team's last eight points. The Chicago coaches, it turned out, had been prophetic in their sense of what would happen in the fourth quarters of this series, and which player would be able to create for himself with the game on the line. In the three close games, two of them in Salt Lake City, Jordan played much bigger than Malone—averaging thirteen points in the fourth quarter to Malone's three. Jordan should be remembered, Jerry Sloan said afterward, "as the greatest player who ever played the game."

10. Available online at the NBA's website (along with a brief video of the play). There you can also see Medina explain the circumstances under which the shot was made. The magazine *Sports Illustrated* has called it the best sports photo of all time.

MLA CITATION

Halberstam, David. "Jordan's Moment." 1998. *The Norton Reader: An Anthology of Nonfiction.* Ed. Melissa A. Goldthwaite et al. 14th ed. New York: Norton, 2016. 361–70. Print.

QUESTIONS

1. Michael Jordan retired from basketball in 2003. Do you agree with David Halberstam's final claim in the essay, that Jordan should be remembered as the greatest player in basketball's history? Why or why not?

2. At the heart of Halberstam's essay is an extended comparison of the Utah Jazz and the Chicago Bulls, with individual comparisons of different players, notably Karl Malone and Michael Jordan. Examine how Halberstam makes these comparisons. What does he emphasize the most? What has he left out? What other comparisons does he make?

3. Does Halberstam make clear Jordan's greatness? Write an essay in which you describe the qualities you believe a great athlete ought to have. Use examples that you know about from experience or do some research.

MAYA ANGELOU   *Champion of the World*

THE LAST INCH of space was filled, yet people continued to wedge themselves along the walls of the
Store. Uncle Willie had turned the radio up to its last
notch so that youngsters on the porch wouldn't miss
a word. Women sat on kitchen chairs, dining-room
chairs, stools, and upturned wooden boxes. Small
children and babies perched on every lap available and men leaned on the
shelves or on each other.

The apprehensive mood was shot through with shafts of gaiety, as a black
sky is streaked with lightning.

"I ain't worried 'bout this fight. Joe's gonna whip that cracker like it's open
season."

"He gone whip him till that white boy call him Momma."

At last the talking finished and the string-along songs about razor blades[1]   5
were over and the fight began.

"A quick jab to the head." In the Store the crowd grunted. "A left to the
head and a right and another left." One of the listeners cackled like a hen and
was quieted.

"They're in a clinch, Louis is trying to fight his way out."

Some bitter comedian on the porch said, "That white man don't mind hugging that niggah now, I betcha."

"The referee is moving in to break them up, but Louis finally pushed the
contender away and it's an uppercut to the chin. The contender is hanging on,
now he's backing away. Louis catches him with a short left to the jaw."

A tide of murmuring assent poured out the door and into the yard.   10

"Another left and another left. Louis is saving that mighty right. . . ." The
mutter in the store had grown into a baby roar and it was pierced by the clang
of a bell and the announcer's "That's the bell for round three, ladies and
gentlemen."

As I pushed my way into the Store I wondered if the announcer gave any
thought to the fact that he was addressing as "ladies and gentlemen" all the
Negroes around the world who sat sweating and praying, glued to their "Master's voice."[2]

There were only a few calls for RC Colas, Dr Peppers, and Hires root beer.
The real festivities would begin after the fight. Then even the old Christian
ladies who taught their children and tried themselves to practice turning the

---

From Maya Angelou's autobiography I Know Why the Caged Bird Sings (1969), *in which
she recounts her experiences growing up in Stamps, Arkansas. In this part of her story, she
remembers watching the June 25, 1935, boxing match between Joe Louis and Primo
Carnera.*

1. Gillette, a major brand of shaving products, was a main sponsor of fight broadcasts.
2. Reference to RCA's advertising campaign featuring a dog listening to a phonograph.

other cheek would buy soft drinks, and if the Brown Bomber's[3] victory was a particularly bloody one they would order peanut patties and Baby Ruths also.

Bailey and I laid the coins on top of the cash register. Uncle Willie didn't allow us to ring up sales during a fight. It was too noisy and might shake up the atmosphere. When the gong rang for the next round we pushed through the near-sacred quiet to the herd of children outside.

15   "He's got Louis against the ropes and now it's a left to the body and a right to the ribs. Another right to the body, it looks like it was low. . . . Yes, ladies and gentlemen, the referee is signaling but the contender keeps raining the blows on Louis. It's another to the body, and it looks like Louis is going down."

My race groaned. It was our people falling. It was another lynching, yet another Black man hanging on a tree. One more woman ambushed and raped. A Black boy whipped and maimed. It was hounds on the trail of a man running through slimy swamps. It was a white woman slapping her maid for being forgetful.

The men in the Store stood away from the walls and at attention. Women greedily clutched the babes on their laps while on the porch the shufflings and smiles, flirting and pinchings of a few minutes before were gone. This might be the end of the world. If Joe lost we were back in slavery and beyond help. It would all be true; the accusations that we were lower types of human beings. Only a little higher than apes. True that we were stupid and ugly and lazy and dirty and unlucky and worst of all, that God himself hated us and ordained us to be hewers of wood and drawers of water, forever and ever, world without end.

We didn't breathe. We didn't hope. We waited.

"He's off the ropes, ladies and gentlemen. He's moving towards the corner of the ring." There was no time to be relieved. The worst might still happen.

20   "And now it looks like Joe is mad. He's caught Carnera with a left hook to the head and a right to the head. It's a left jab to the body and another left to the head. There's a left cross and a right to the head. The contender's right eye is bleeding and he can't seem to keep his block up. Louis is penetrating every block. The referee is moving in, but Louis sends a left to the body and it's an uppercut to the chin and the contender is dropping. He's on the canvas, ladies and gentlemen."

Babies slid to the floor as women stood up and men leaned toward the radio.

"Here's the referee. He's counting. One, two, three, four, five, six, seven. . . . Is the contender trying to get up again?"

All the men in the store shouted, "NO."

"—eight, nine, ten." There were a few sounds from the audience, but they seemed to be holding themselves in against tremendous pressure.

25   "The fight is all over, ladies and gentlemen. Let's get the microphone over to the referee. . . . Here he is. He's got the Brown Bomber's hand, he's holding it up. . . . Here he is. . . ."

3. Joe Louis's nickname.

Then the voice, husky and familiar, came to wash over us—"The winnah, and still heavyweight champeen of the world . . . Joe Louis."

Champion of the world. A Black boy. Some Black mother's son. He was the strongest man in the world. People drank Coca-Colas like ambrosia and ate candy bars like Christmas. Some of the men went behind the Store and poured white lightning in their soft-drink bottles, and a few of the bigger boys followed them. Those who were not chased away came back blowing their breath in front of themselves like proud smokers.

It would take an hour or more before the people would leave the Store and head for home. Those who lived too far had made arrangements to stay in town. It wouldn't be fit for a Black man and his family to be caught on a lonely country road on a night when Joe Louis had proved that we were the strongest people in the world.

MLA CITATION

Angelou, Maya. "Champion of the World." 1969. *The Norton Reader: An Anthology of Nonfiction*. Ed. Melissa A. Goldthwaite et al. 14th ed. New York: Norton, 2016. 371–73. Print.

QUESTIONS

1. Some athletic contests have larger things at stake than just the win of one opponent against another, like the racial pride in the fight Maya Angelou recounts. Can you recall a match you witnessed in which the stakes were greater than the contest itself?

2. Angelou uses hyperbole, or deliberate overstatement, in her writing. For example, Angelou writes, "It was another lynching" (paragraph 16) and "women greedily clutched the babes on their laps" (paragraph 17). Pick out some other examples in the text. How do these overstatements work to make Angelou's point about the fight and the position of blacks in America in the 1930s?

3. Look closely at Angelou's use of dialogue, as she tries to capture the exact sounds and grammar of her fellow listeners as well as the voices on the radio. How does she manage it? How would her piece read if she didn't use dialogue?

4. Note that much more than half of Angelou's account is about the spectators, not the fight. Using Angelou's essay as a model, write about a crowd's appearance and reaction during an athletic contest. Give plenty of detail about the action both on and off the field.

JOYCE CAROL OATES   *Rape and the Boxing Ring*

IKE TYSON'S CONVICTION on rape charges in Indianapolis is a minor tragedy for the beleaguered sport of
boxing, but a considerable triumph for women's rights.
For once, though bookmakers were giving 5–1 odds
that Tyson would be acquitted, and the mood of
the country seems distinctly conservative, a jury
resisted the outrageous defense that a rape victim is to be blamed for her own
predicament. For once, a celebrity with enormous financial resources did not
escape trial and a criminal conviction by settling with his accuser out of court.

That boxing and "women's rights" should be perceived as opposed is sym-
bolically appropriate, since of all sports, boxing is the most aggressively masculine, the very soul of war in microcosm. Elemental and dramatically concise, it
raises to an art the passions underlying direct human aggression; its fundamentally murderous intent is not obscured by the pursuit of balls or pucks, nor
can the participants expect help from teammates. In a civilized humanitarian
society, one would expect such a blood sport to have died out, yet boxing, sponsored by gambling casinos in Las Vegas and Atlantic City, and broadcast by
cable television, flourishes: had the current heavyweight champion, Evander
Holyfield, fought Mike Tyson in a title defense, Holyfield would have earned
no less than $30 million. If Tyson were still champion, and still fighting, he
would be earning more.

The paradox of boxing is that it so excessively rewards men for inflicting
injury upon one another that, outside the ring, with less "art," would be pun-
ishable as aggravated assault, or manslaughter. Boxing belongs to that species
of mysterious masculine activity for which anthropologists use such terms as
"deep play": activity that is wholly without utilitarian value, in fact contrary to
utilitarian value, so dangerous that no amount of money can justify it. Sports-
car racing, stunt flying, mountain climbing, bullfighting, dueling—these
activities, through history, have provided ways in which the individual can
dramatically, if sometimes fatally, distinguish himself from the crowd, usually
with the adulation and envy of the crowd, and traditionally, the love of women.
Women—in essence, Woman—is the prize, usually self-proffered. To look upon
organized sports as a continuum of Darwinian theory—in which the sports-
star hero flaunts the superiority of his genes—is to see how displays of masculine aggression have their sexual component, as ingrained in human beings as
any instinct for self-preservation and reproduction. In a capitalist society, the
secret is to capitalize upon instinct.

Yet even within the very special world of sports, boxing is distinct. Is there
any athlete, however celebrated in his own sport, who would not rather reign as

Originally published in Newsweek *(1992), a weekly magazine that "provides in-depth
analysis, news and opinion about international issues, technology, business, culture and
politics," this essay also appeared in the essay collection* At the Fights: American Writers
on Boxing *(2011). Although Joyce Carol Oates is known primarily for her fiction writing,
she has also written many essays on boxing.*

the heavyweight champion of the world? If, in fantasy at least, he could be another Muhammad Ali, or Joe Louis, or indeed, Mike Tyson in his prime? Boxing celebrates the individual man in his maleness, not merely in his skill as an athlete—though boxing demands enormous skill, and its training is far more arduous than most men could endure for more than a day or two. All athletes can become addicted to their own adrenaline, but none more obviously than the boxer, who, like Sugar Ray Leonard, already a multimillionaire with numerous occupations outside the ring, will risk serious injury by coming back out of retirement; as Mike Tyson has said, "Outside of boxing, everything is so boring." What makes boxing repulsive to many observers is precisely what makes boxing so fascinating to participants.

This is because it is a highly organized ritual that violates taboo. It flouts such moral prescriptions as "Thou shalt not kill." It celebrates, not meekness, but flamboyant aggression. No one who has not seen live boxing matches (in contrast to the sanitized matches broadcast over television) can quite grasp its eerie fascination—the spectator's sense that he or she is a witness to madness, yet a madness sanctioned by tradition and custom, as finely honed by certain celebrated practitioners as an artist's performance at the highest level of genius, and, yet more disturbing, immensely gratifying to the audience. Boxing mimics our early ancestors' rite of bloody sacrifice and redemption; it excites desires most civilized men and women find abhorrent. For some observers, it is frankly obscene, like pornography; yet, unlike pornography, it is not fantasy but real, thus far more subversive.

The paradox for the boxer is that, in the ring, he experiences himself as a living conduit for the inchoate, demonic will of the crowd: the expression of their collective desire, which is to pound another human being into absolute submission. The more vicious the boxer, the greater the acclaim. And the financial reward—Tyson is reported to have earned $100 million. (He who at the age of 13 was plucked from a boys' school for juvenile delinquents in upstate New York.) Like the champion gladiators of Roman decadence, he will be both honored and despised, for, no matter his celebrity, and the gift of his talent, his energies spring from the violation of taboo and he himself is tainted by it.

Mike Tyson has said that he does not think of boxing as a sport. He sees himself as a fantasy gladiator who, by "destructing" opponents, enacts others' fantasies in his own being. That the majority of these others are well-to-do whites who would themselves crumple at a first blow, and would surely claim a pious humanitarianism, would not go unnoted by so wary and watchful a man. Cynicism is not an inevitable consequence of success, but it is difficult to retain one's boyish naiveté in the company of the sort of people, among them the notorious Don King,[1] who have surrounded Tyson since 1988, when his co-manager, Jim Jacobs, died. As Floyd Patterson, an ex-heavyweight champion who has led an exemplary life, has said, "When you have millions of dollars, you have millions of friends."

5

---

1. Boxing promoter (b. 1931) who was sued by many boxers, including Tyson, for defrauding them.

It should not be charged against boxing that Mike Tyson *is* boxing in any way. Boxers tend to be fiercely individualistic, and Tyson is, at the least, an enigma. He began his career, under the tutelage of the legendary trainer Cus D'Amato, as a strategist, in the mode of such brilliant technicians as Henry Armstrong and Sugar Ray Robinson. He was always aware of a lineage with Jack Dempsey, arguably the most electrifying of all heavyweight champions, whose nonstop aggression revolutionized the sport and whose shaved haircut and malevolent scowl, and, indeed, penchant for dirty fighting, made a tremendous impression upon the young Tyson.

In recent years, however, Tyson seems to have styled himself at least partly on the model of Charles (Sonny) Liston, the "baddest of the bad" black heavyweights. Liston had numerous arrests to his credit and served time in prison (for assaulting a policeman); he had the air, not entirely contrived, of a sociopath; he was always friendly with racketeers, and died of a drug overdose that may in fact have been murder. (It is not coincidental that Don King, whom Tyson has much admired, and who Tyson has empowered to ruin his career, was convicted of manslaughter and served time in an Ohio prison.) Like Liston, Tyson has grown to take a cynical pleasure in publicly condoned sadism (his "revenge" bout with Tyrell Biggs,[2] who he carried for seven long rounds in order to inflict maximum damage) and in playing the outlaw; his contempt for women, escalating in recent years, is a part of that guise. The witty obscenity of a prefight taunt of Tyson's— "I'll make you into my girlfriend"—is the boast of the rapist.

10   Perhaps rape itself is a gesture, a violent repudiation of the female, in the assertion of maleness that would seem to require nothing beyond physical gratification of the crudest kind. The supreme macho gesture—like knocking out an opponent and standing over his fallen body, gloves raised in triumph.

In boxing circles it is said—this, with an affectionate sort of humor—that the heavyweight champion is the 300-pound gorilla who sits anywhere in the room he wants; and, presumably, takes any female he wants. Such a grandiose sense of entitlement, fueled by the insecurities and emotions of adolescence, can have disastrous consequences. Where once it was believed that Mike Tyson might mature into the greatest heavyweight of all time, breaking Rocky Marciano's record of 49 victories and no defeats, it was generally acknowledged that, since his defeat of Michael Spinks in 1988, he had allowed his boxing skills to deteriorate. Not simply his ignominious loss of his title to the mediocre James (Buster) Douglas in 1990, but subsequent lackluster victories against mediocre opponents made it clear that Tyson was no longer a serious, nor even very interesting, boxer.

The dazzling reflexes were dulled, the shrewd defensive skills drilled into him by D'Amato were largely abandoned: Tyson emerged suddenly as a conventional heavyweight like Gerry Cooney, who advances upon his opponent with the hope of knocking him out with a single punch—and does not always succeed. By 25, Tyson seemed already middle aged, burnt out. He would have

2. Biggs (b. 1960), heavyweight boxer; Oates is referring to a match fought on October 16, 1987.

no great fights after all. So, strangely, he seemed to invite his fate outside the ring, with sadomasochistic persistence, testing the limits of his celebrity's license to offend by ever-escalating acts of aggression and sexual effrontery.

The familiar sports adage is surely true, one's ultimate opponent is oneself.

It may be objected that these remarks center upon the rapist, and not his victim; that sympathy, pity, even in some quarters moral outrage flow to the criminal and not the person he has violated. In this case, ironically, the victim, Desiree Washington, though she will surely bear psychic scars through her life, has emerged as a victor, a heroine: a young woman whose traumatic experience has been, as so few traumas can be, the vehicle for a courageous and selfless stand against the sexual abuse of women and children in America. She seems to know that herself, telling *People* magazine, "It was the right thing to do." She was fortunate in drawing a jury who rejected classic defense ploys by blaming the victim and/or arguing consent. Our criminal-justice system being what it is, she was lucky. Tyson, who might have been acquitted elsewhere in the country, was unlucky.

Whom to blame for this most recent of sports disgraces in America? The culture that flings young athletes like Tyson up out of obscurity, makes millionaires of them and watches them self-destruct? Promoters like Don King and Bob Arum? Celebrity hunters like Robin Givens, Tyson's ex-wife, who seemed to have exploited him for his money and as a means of promoting her own acting career? The indulgence generally granted star athletes when they behave recklessly? When they abuse drugs and alcohol, and mistreat women? 15

I suggest that no one is to blame, finally, except the perpetrator himself. In Montieth Illingworth's cogently argued biography of Tyson, "Mike Tyson: Money, Myth and Betrayal," Tyson is quoted, after one or another public debacle: "People say 'Poor guy.' That insults me. I despise sympathy. So I screwed up. I made some mistakes. 'Poor guy,' like I'm some victim. There's nothing poor about me."

MLA CITATION

Oates, Joyce Carol. "Rape and the Boxing Ring." 1992. *The Norton Reader: An Anthology of Nonfiction.* Ed. Melissa A. Goldthwaite et al. 14th ed. New York: Norton, 2016. 374–77. Print.

QUESTIONS

1. Think about your impressions of Mike Tyson and boxing before and after reading Joyce Carol Oates's essay. Did your impressions change, stay the same, or both? How so?

2. What can you tell from Oates's essay about her own relationship to boxing? She offers examples of her revulsion, but are there also signs that she understands why some people are attracted to watching fights? Cite examples from the text.

3. Write a comparison of Oates's and Maya Angelou's (pp. 371–73) essays on boxing, concentrating on each writer's portrayal of the boxers Mike Tyson and Joe Louis, respectively.

Op-Eds

ANNA QUINDLEN   *Stuff Is Not Salvation*

A S THE BOOM times fade, an important holiday question surfaces: why in the world did we buy all this junk in the first place?

What passes for the holiday season began before dawn the day after Thanksgiving, when a worker at a Wal-Mart in Valley Stream, N.Y., was trampled to death by a mob of bargain hunters. Afterward, there were reports that some people, mesmerized by cheap consumer electronics and discounted toys, kept shopping even after announcements to clear the store.

These are dark days in the United States: the cataclysmic stock-market declines, the industries edging up on bankruptcy, the home foreclosures and the waves of layoffs. But the prospect of an end to plenty has uncovered what may ultimately be a more pernicious problem, an addiction to consumption so out of control that it qualifies as a sickness. The suffocation of a store employee by a stampede of shoppers was horrifying, but it wasn't entirely surprising.

Americans have been on an acquisition binge for decades. I suspect television advertising, which made me want a Chatty Cathy doll[1] so much as a kid that when I saw her under the tree my head almost exploded. By contrast, my father will be happy to tell you about the excitement of getting an orange in his stocking during the Depression. The depression before this one.

5   A critical difference between then and now is credit. The orange had to be paid for. The rite of passage for a child when I was young was a solemn visit to the local bank, there to exchange birthday money for a savings passbook. Every once in a while, like magic, a bit of extra money would appear. Interest. Yippee.

The passbook was replaced by plastic, so that today Americans are overwhelmed by debt and the national savings rate is calculated, like an algebra equation, in negatives. By 2010 Americans will be a trillion dollars in the hole on credit-card debt alone.

But let's look, not at the numbers, but the atmospherics. Appliances, toys, clothes, gadgets. Junk. There's the sad truth. Wall Street executives may have made investments that lost their value, but, in a much smaller way, so did the rest of us. "I looked into my closet the other day and thought, why did I buy all this stuff?" one friend said recently. A person in the United States replaces a

Anna Quindlen wrote this essay for her column in Newsweek (2008), *a weekly magazine that "provides in-depth analysis, news and opinion about international issues, technology, business, culture and politics." It appeared at the height of the Christmas shopping season.*

1. Speaks when a ring in her neck is pulled; manufactured by Mattel since 1959.

cell phone every 16 months, not because the cell phone is old, but because it is oldish. My mother used to complain that the Christmas toys were grubby and forgotten by Easter. (I didn't even really like dolls, especially dolls who introduced themselves to you over and over again when you pulled the ring in their necks.) Now much of the country is made up of people with the acquisition habits of a 7-year-old, desire untethered from need, or the ability to pay. The result is a booming business in those free-standing storage facilities, where junk goes to linger in a persistent vegetative state, somewhere between eBay and the dump.

Oh, there is still plenty of need. But it is for real things, things that matter: college tuition, prescription drugs, rent. Food pantries and soup kitchens all over the country have seen demand for their services soar. Homelessness, which had fallen in recent years, may rebound as people lose their jobs and their houses. For the first time this month, the number of people on food stamps will exceed the 30 million mark.

Hard times offer the opportunity to ask hard questions, and one of them is the one my friend asked, staring at sweaters and shoes: why did we buy all this stuff? Did anyone really need a flat-screen in the bedroom, or a designer handbag, or three cars? If the mall is our temple, then Marc Jacobs[2] is God. There's a scary thought.

The drumbeat that accompanied Black Friday[3] this year was that the   10 numbers had to redeem us, that if enough money was spent by shoppers it would indicate that things were not so bad after all. But what the economy required was at odds with a necessary epiphany. Because things are dire, many people have become hesitant to spend money on trifles. And in the process they began to realize that it's all trifles.

Here I go, stating the obvious: stuff does not bring salvation. But if it's so obvious, how come for so long people have not realized it? The happiest families I know aren't the ones with the most square footage, living in one of those cavernous houses with enough garage space to start a homeless shelter. (There's a holiday suggestion right there.) And of course they are not people who are in real want. Just because consumption is bankrupt doesn't mean that poverty is ennobling.

But somewhere in between there is a family like one I know in rural Pennsylvania, raising bees for honey (and for the science, and the fun, of it), digging a pond out of the downhill flow of the stream, with three kids who somehow, incredibly, don't spend six months of the year whining for the toy du jour. (The youngest once demurred when someone offered him another box on his birthday; "I already have a present," he said.) The mother of the household says having less means her family appreciates possessions more. "I can give you a story about every item, really," she says of what they own. In other words, what they

2. American designer (b. 1963) with a widely distributed line of clothing and accessories under his own name.

3. First day after Thanksgiving, which marks the beginning of the Christmas shopping season.

have has meaning. And meaning, real meaning, is what we are always trying to possess. Ask people what they'd grab if their house were on fire, the way our national house is on fire right now. No one ever says it's the tricked-up microwave they got at Wal-Mart.

MLA CITATION

Quindlen, Anna. "Stuff Is Not Salvation." 2008. *The Norton Reader: An Anthology of Nonfiction.* Ed. Melissa A. Goldthwaite et al. 14th ed. New York: Norton, 2016. 378–80. Print.

QUESTIONS

1. What does Anna Quindlen gain from tying her essay so closely to the recession that began in 2008, the year her column appeared? What in it might soon appear dated, and what will be enduring?

2. Does Quindlen talk enough about the "stuff" in her own life? How is she like the "us" she analyzes, and how might she be different?

3. Write an essay about the "stuff" in your life. You may take Quindlen's approach, condemning Americans as a nation of shallow "collectors," or make a completely different argument.

TIM KREIDER   *The "Busy" Trap*

I F YOU LIVE IN AMERICA in the 21st century you've probably had to listen to a lot of people tell you how busy they are. It's become the default response when you ask anyone how they're doing: "Busy!" "*So* busy." "*Crazy* busy." It is, pretty obviously, a boast disguised as a complaint. And the stock response is a kind of congratulation: "That's a good problem to have," or "Better than the opposite."

Notice it isn't generally people pulling back-to-back shifts in the I.C.U. or commuting by bus to three minimum-wage jobs who tell you how busy they are; what those people are is not busy but *tired. Exhausted. Dead on their feet.* It's almost always people whose lamented busyness is purely self-imposed: work and obligations they've taken on voluntarily, classes and activities they've "encouraged" their kids to participate in. They're busy because of their own ambition or drive or anxiety, because they're addicted to busyness and dread what they might have to face in its absence.

Almost everyone I know is busy. They feel anxious and guilty when they aren't either working or doing something to promote their work. They schedule

Written as part of a series on anxiety in the New York Times *opinion pages (2012). Tim Kreider is a cartoonist and essayist.*

in time with friends the way students with 4.0 G.P.A.'s make sure to sign up for community service because it looks good on their college applications. I recently wrote a friend to ask if he wanted to do something this week, and he answered that he didn't have a lot of time but if something was going on to let him know and maybe he could ditch work for a few hours. I wanted to clarify that my question had not been a preliminary heads-up to some future invitation; this *was* the invitation. But his busyness was like some vast churning noise through which he was shouting out at me, and I gave up trying to shout back over it.

Even *children* are busy now, scheduled down to the half-hour with classes and extracurricular activities. They come home at the end of the day as tired as grown-ups. I was a member of the latchkey generation and had three hours of totally unstructured, largely unsupervised time every afternoon, time I used to do everything from surfing the *World Book Encyclopedia*[1] to making animated films to getting together with friends in the woods to chuck dirt clods directly into one another's eyes, all of which provided me with important skills and insights that remain valuable to this day. Those free hours became the model for how I wanted to live the rest of my life.

The present hysteria is not a necessary or inevitable condition of life; it's   5
something we've chosen, if only by our acquiescence to it. Not long ago I Skyped

1. First published in 1917 and popular in the 1950s and 1960s, this encyclopedia for schoolchildren provided information in accessible language and included many illustrations.

with a friend who was driven out of the city by high rent and now has an artist's residency in a small town in the south of France. She described herself as happy and relaxed for the first time in years. She still gets her work done, but it doesn't consume her entire day and brain. She says it feels like college—she has a big circle of friends who all go out to the café together every night. She has a boyfriend again. (She once ruefully summarized dating in New York: "Everyone's too busy and everyone thinks they can do better.") What she had mistakenly assumed was her personality—driven, cranky, anxious and sad— turned out to be a deformative effect of her environment. It's not as if any of us wants to live like this, any more than any one person wants to be part of a traffic jam or stadium trampling or the hierarchy of cruelty in high school— it's something we collectively force one another to do.

Busyness serves as a kind of existential reassurance, a hedge against emptiness; obviously your life cannot possibly be silly or trivial or meaningless if you are so busy, completely booked, in demand every hour of the day. I once knew a woman who interned at a magazine where she wasn't allowed to take lunch hours out, lest she be urgently needed for some reason. This was an entertainment magazine whose raison d'être[2] was obviated when "menu" buttons appeared on remotes, so it's hard to see this pretense of indispensability as anything other than a form of institutional self-delusion. More and more people in this country no longer make or do anything tangible; if your job wasn't performed by a cat or a boa constrictor in a Richard Scarry[3] book I'm not sure I believe it's necessary. I can't help but wonder whether all this histrionic exhaustion isn't a way of covering up the fact that most of what we do doesn't matter.

I am not busy. I am the laziest ambitious person I know. Like most writers, I feel like a reprobate who does not deserve to live on any day that I do not write, but I also feel that four or five hours is enough to earn my stay on the planet for one more day. On the best ordinary days of my life, I write in the morning, go for a long bike ride and run errands in the afternoon, and in the evening I see friends, read or watch a movie. This, it seems to me, is a sane and pleasant pace for a day. And if you call me up and ask whether I won't maybe blow off work and check out the new American Wing at the Met or ogle girls in Central Park or just drink chilled pink minty cocktails all day long, I will say, what time?

But just in the last few months, I've insidiously started, because of professional obligations, to become busy. For the first time I was able to tell people, with a straight face, that I was "too busy" to do this or that thing they wanted me to do. I could see why people enjoy this complaint; it makes you feel important, sought-after and put-upon. Except that I hate actually being busy. Every morning my in-box was full of e-mails asking me to do things I did not want to do or presenting me with problems that I now had to solve. It got more and more intolerable until finally I fled town to the Undisclosed Location from which I'm writing this.

2. French for "reason for being."

3. Children's book writer and illustrator (1919–1994) whose books used animals— cats, rats, rabbits, and pigs—and sometimes worms for characters.

Here I am largely unmolested by obligations. There is no TV. To check e-mail I have to drive to the library. I go a week at a time without seeing anyone I know. I've remembered about buttercups, stink bugs and the stars. I read. And I'm finally getting some real writing done for the first time in months. It's hard to find anything to say about life without immersing yourself in the world, but it's also just about impossible to figure out what it might be, or how best to say it, without getting the hell out of it again.

Idleness is not just a vacation, an indulgence or a vice; it is as indispensable to the brain as vitamin D is to the body, and deprived of it we suffer a mental affliction as disfiguring as rickets. The space and quiet that idleness provides is a necessary condition for standing back from life and seeing it whole, for making unexpected connections and waiting for the wild summer lightning strikes of inspiration—it is, paradoxically, necessary to getting any work done. "Idle dreaming is often of the essence of what we do," wrote Thomas Pynchon[4] in his essay on sloth. Archimedes' "Eureka" in the bath, Newton's apple, Jekyll & Hyde and the benzene ring:[5] history is full of stories of inspirations that come in idle moments and dreams. It almost makes you wonder whether loafers, goldbricks and no-accounts aren't responsible for more of the world's great ideas, inventions and masterpieces than the hardworking.

"The goal of the future is full unemployment, so we can play. That's why we have to destroy the present politico-economic system." This may sound like the pronouncement of some bong-smoking anarchist, but it was actually Arthur C. Clarke,[6] who found time between scuba diving and pinball games to write "Childhood's End" and think up communications satellites. My old colleague Ted Rall[7] recently wrote a column proposing that we divorce income from work and give each citizen a guaranteed paycheck, which sounds like the kind of lunatic notion that'll be considered a basic human right in about a century, like abolition, universal suffrage and eight-hour workdays. The Puritans turned work into a virtue, evidently forgetting that God invented it as a punishment.

Perhaps the world would soon slide to ruin if everyone behaved as I do. But I would suggest that an ideal human life lies somewhere between my own defiant indolence and the rest of the world's endless frenetic hustle. My role is just to be a bad influence, the kid standing outside the classroom window making faces at you at your desk, urging you to just this once make some excuse and get out of there, come outside and play. My own resolute idleness has mostly been a luxury rather than a virtue, but I did make a conscious decision, a long time ago, to choose time over money, since I've always understood that the best

4. American novelist (b. 1937).

5. Discoveries—Archimedes' method for calculating the volume of an object with an irregular shape, Isaac Newton's discovery of the principle of gravity, Robert Louis Stevenson's dream that led to his famous novel, and Friedrich August Kekulé's reverie of a snake with its tail in its mouth—that connect moments of daydreaming with originality, invention, and productivity.

6. British science and science fiction writer, inventor, and TV host (1917–2008) best known for coauthoring the screenplay for 2001: A Space Odyssey.

7. American columnist and political cartoonist (b. 1963).

investment of my limited time on earth was to spend it with people I love. I suppose it's possible I'll lie on my deathbed regretting that I didn't work harder and say everything I had to say, but I think what I'll really wish is that I could have one more beer with Chris, another long talk with Megan, one last good hard laugh with Boyd. Life is too short to be busy.

MLA CITATION

Kreider, Tim. "The 'Busy' Trap." 2012. *The Norton Reader: An Anthology of Nonfiction.* Ed. Melissa A. Goldthwaite et al. 14th ed. New York: Norton, 2016. 380–84. Print.

QUESTIONS

1. Tim Kreider writes against the American penchant for "busyness" and in favor of idleness. What reasons does he give for being against "busyness"?

2. In paragraph 7, Kreider claims, "I am the laziest ambitious person I know." What details of the essay reveal his ambition? What anecdotes of other writers and inventors support his case?

3. Kreider admits in paragraph 2 that being busy is not the same as being tired. What kind of people fall into the category of "tired"? Does this op-ed address their situation, or is it written for another kind of reader? How can you tell?

4. Take a position against Kreider's and argue for the value of keeping busy. You might include examples from your own life or the lives of friends and family.

MOLLY IVINS   *Get a Knife, Get a Dog,*
                             but Get Rid of Guns

GUNS. EVERYWHERE GUNS.

Let me start this discussion by pointing out that I am not antigun. I'm proknife. Consider the merits of the knife.

In the first place, you have to catch up with someone in order to stab him. A general substitution of knives for guns would promote physical fitness. We'd turn into a whole nation of great runners. Plus, knives don't ricochet. And people are seldom killed while cleaning their knives.

As a civil libertarian, I, of course, support the Second Amendment. And I believe it means exactly what it says:

5   *A well-regulated militia being necessary to the security of a free state, the right of the people to keep and bear arms shall not be infringed.* Fourteen-year-

Molly Ivins wrote this op-ed when she was a regular columnist for the Fort Worth Star-Telegram, *a local daily newspaper serving Fort Worth, Texas, and its surrounding areas. It was later included in* Nothin' but Good Times Ahead *(1993), Ivins's collection of essays examining American politics.*

old boys are not part of a well-regulated militia. Members of wacky religious cults are not part of a well-regulated militia. Permitting unregulated citizens to have guns is destroying the security of this free state.

I am intrigued by the arguments of those who claim to follow the judicial doctrine of original intent. How do they know it was the dearest wish of Thomas Jefferson's heart that teenage drug dealers should cruise the cities of this nation perforating their fellow citizens with assault rifles? Channeling?

There is more hooey spread about the Second Amendment. It says quite clearly that guns are for those who form part of a well-regulated militia, that is, the armed forces, including the National Guard. The reasons for keeping them away from everyone else get clearer by the day.

The comparison most often used is that of the automobile, another lethal object that is regularly used to wreak great carnage. Obviously, this society is full of people who haven't enough common sense to use an automobile properly. But we haven't outlawed cars yet.

We do, however, license them and their owners, restrict their use to presumably sane and sober adults, and keep track of who sells them to whom. At a minimum, we should do the same with guns.

In truth, there is no rational argument for guns in this society. This is no 10 longer a frontier nation in which people hunt their own food. It is a crowded, overwhelmingly urban country in which letting people have access to guns is a continuing disaster. Those who want guns—whether for target shooting, hunting, or potting rattlesnakes (get a hoe)—should be subject to the same restrictions placed on gun owners in England, a nation in which liberty has survived nicely without an armed populace.

The argument that "guns don't kill people" is patent nonsense. Anyone who has ever worked in a cop shop knows how many family arguments end in murder because there was a gun in the house. Did the gun kill someone? No. But if there had been no gun, no one would have died. At least not without a good foot race first. Guns do kill. Unlike cars, that is all they do.

Michael Crichton makes an interesting argument about technology in his thriller *Jurassic Park*. He points out that power without discipline is making this society into a wreckage. By the time someone who studies the martial arts becomes a master—literally able to kill with bare hands—that person has also undergone years of training and discipline. But any fool can pick up a gun and kill with it.

"A well-regulated militia" surely implies both long training and long discipline. That is the least, the very least, that should be required of those who are permitted to have guns, because a gun is literally the power to kill. For years I used to enjoy taunting my gun-nut friends about their psychosexual hang-ups—always in a spirit of good cheer, you understand. But letting the noisy minority in the NRA[1] force us to allow this carnage to continue is just plain insane.

---

1. National Rifle Association.

I do think gun nuts have a power hang-up. I don't know what is missing in their psyches that they need to feel they have the power to kill. But no sane society would allow this to continue.

15   Ban the damn things. Ban them all.

You want protection? Get a dog.

MLA CITATION

Ivins, Molly. "Get a Knife, Get a Dog, but Get Rid of Guns." 1993. *The Norton Reader: An Anthology of Nonfiction.* Ed. Melissa A. Goldthwaite et al. 14th ed. New York: Norton, 2016. 384–86. Print.

QUESTIONS

1. What do you think of Molly Ivins's examination of the Second Amendment? What kind of evidence would convince you even more of her argument? Why doesn't Ivins provide more evidence?

2. Characterize Ivins's language. What words, phrases, or structures seem typical of her style?

3. Write a response in which you examine the analogy between guns and cars. How well does it hold up? Where does it break down?

JO-ANN PILARDI   *Immigration Problem Is about Us, Not Them*

THE IMMIGRATION DEBATES always focus on small brown bodies jumping fences and scooting through the brush of our Southwestern states (land that was Mexico about 150 years ago).

Our self-righteous anger at those brown bodies is fueled by our narrow use of the word "illegal"—a term reserved only for those immigrant workers. Yet aren't there other "illegals" hiding in the American underbrush, and isn't it time to add to the American immigration lexicon a new term?

But where are those other "illegals"—the illegal employers of the illegal workers? Let's call them "illegal native employers." These INEs run the gamut from executives of hotel chains to presidents of agribusiness corporations in California, from nanny-employing parents to restaurant owners, from contrac-

Published as an op-ed in the Baltimore Sun *(2006). Like many writers of op-eds, Jo-Ann Pilardi is not a professional journalist on the staff of the newspaper, but one of its readers. She is a professor emerita of philosophy and women's studies at Towson University in Maryland.*

tors to employment agencies. And let's not forget the INEs who own huge chicken-processing plants.

Where are the TV news videotapes of those illegals? Let's film them as they leave their homes and arrive at their corporate headquarters, their law offices, their retail establishments, their hotels, their construction sites. Do we dare humiliate them with our cameras—and call them felons?

I'd like to see the Minutemen set up a chapter far from the Arizona border   5
and patrol Wall Street, binoculars in hand, to set their sights on those "illegals"—brokers selling stocks for INE companies.

Let's build fences outside the INE businesses, to separate and stigmatize them. Maybe the National Guard should patrol those fences. Not to worry, though, because President Bush assures us the troops will not be "militarized." (The word is still out, though, on whether there will be bullets in their guns.)

No doubt, these suggestions make us squirm. Maybe that's because many of these "illegals" are us, or our friends or relatives. If 12 million undocumented workers are employed here, thousands of employers must be signing their paychecks.

If 12 million undocumented workers toil in this country as construction workers, gardeners, housekeepers, nannies, agricultural workers, food processers, then thousands of business owners, homeowners, politicians and government officials condone or welcome their work—and look the other way at their illegal status.

Many of our political leaders talk a hard line about "immigration reform" even though they know our country is mired in its demand for the immigrant work force. We use and exploit the labor of these millions every day. In doing so, we also weaken the wages, benefits and organizing power of all our workers.

The Senate voted 62-36 to approve its version of an immigration bill, with   10
most GOP senators opposing it. A battle with the more conservative House over its more vicious bill begins shortly. Evidently, the Senate version includes most of the so-called Ag Jobs bill, which has languished for years under the Bush administration and which has been supported in the past by the United Farm Workers.

Immigrants in the United States for two to five years would be put into a "temporary-worker" program; those here longer would be eligible for citizenship after an 11-year probationary period, with other criteria also to be met.

Conservatives describe the bill as "amnesty" for undocumented workers. So, once again, virtually all of the media attention centers on the workers, not the employers.

This is not the first time, nor will it be the last, that workers have come across the southern border in great numbers to make a living and to contribute to the U.S. economy. We need to create a fair immigration program for those who want to stay, not one that separates them by creating a national caste system of "guest workers." Europeans have learned the hard way that guest-worker programs lead to further national divisions and to virulent racism.

But whatever we do, we should stop thinking the problem is just about "securing our borders"—from them. The immigration problem is fundamentally a demand for cheap labor—for a supply to fill our demand.

15   Noting the problems that arose from Germany's guest-worker program, which imported masses of Turkish and southern European workers, the writer Max Frisch observed, "Labor was called, but it was people who came." This— the moral, economic and political problem—is not the immigrants' problem; it's ours. I hope we have the courage to solve it humanely.

MLA CITATION

Pilardi, Jo-Ann. "Immigration Problem Is about Us, Not Them." 2006. *The Norton Reader: An Anthology of Nonfiction*. Ed. Melissa A. Goldthwaite et al. 14th ed. New York: Norton, 2016. 386–88. Print.

QUESTIONS

1. Consider Jo-Ann Pilardi's first three paragraphs. Do you think she is being serious or sarcastic? What do you think the reaction would be if people did as Pilardi says and started hounding employers, the ones she terms INEs?

2. According to Pilardi, who benefits from illegal immigration? Who loses?

3. What does Pilardi have against the idea of "guest workers"? Why doesn't she think that solution would work? What do you think?

4. In paragraph 13, Pilardi states, "We need to create a fair immigration program for those who want to stay." Write an op-ed in which you make a case for a fair immigration program. What would be its main features?

BRENT STAPLES   *Why Colleges Shower Their Students with A's*

THE ECONOMIST MILTON FRIEDMAN taught that superior products flourished and shabby ones died out when consumers voted emphatically with their dollars. But the truth of the marketplace is that shabby products can do just fine if they sustain the veneer of quality while slipping downhill, as has much of higher education. Faced with demanding consumers and stiff competition, colleges have simply issued more and more A's, stoking grade inflation and devaluing degrees.

Grade inflation is in full gallop at every level, from struggling community institutions to the elites of the Ivy League. In some cases, campuswide averages have crept up from a C just 10 years ago to B-plus today.

Published on the Op-Ed page of the New York Times *(1998).*

Some departments shower students with A's to fill poorly attended courses that might otherwise be canceled. Individual professors inflate grades after consumer-conscious administrators hound them into it. Professors at every level inflate to escape negative evaluations by students, whose opinions now figure in tenure and promotion decisions.

The most vulnerable teachers are the part-timers who have no job security and who now teach more than half of all college courses. Writing in the last issue of the journal *Academe*, two part-timers suggest that students routinely corner adjuncts, threatening to complain if they do not turn C's into A's. An Ivy League professor said recently that if tenure disappeared, universities would be "free to sell diplomas outright."

The consumer appetite for less rigorous education is nowhere more evi-   5
dent than in the University of Phoenix, a profit-making school that shuns traditional scholarship and offers a curriculum so superficial that critics compare it to a drive-through restaurant. Two hundred colleges have closed since a businessman dreamed up Phoenix 20 years ago. Meanwhile, the university has expanded to 60 sites spread around the country, and more than 40,000 students, making it the country's largest private university.

Phoenix competes directly with the big state universities and lesser-known small colleges, all of which fear a student drain. But the elite schools fear each other and their customers, the students, who are becoming increasingly restive about the cost of a first-tier diploma, which now exceeds $120,000. Faced with the prospect of crushing debt, students are treating grades as a matter of life and death—occasionally even suing to have grades revised upward.

Twenty years ago students grumbled, then lived with the grades they were given. Today, colleges of every stature permit them to appeal low grades through deans or permanent boards of inquiry. In *The Chronicle of Higher Education*, Prof. Paul Korshin of the University of Pennsylvania recently described his grievance panel as the "rhinoplasty committee," because it does "cosmetic surgery" on up to 500 transcripts a year.

The argument that grades are rising because students are better prepared is simply not convincing. The evidence suggests that students and parents are demanding—and getting—what they think of as their money's worth.

One way to stanch inflation is to change the way the grade point average is calculated. Under most formulas, all courses are given equal weight, so math, science and less-challenging courses have equal impact on the averages. This arrangement rewards students who gravitate to courses where high marks are generously given and punishes those who seek out math and science courses, where far fewer students get the top grade.

Valen Johnson, a Duke University statistics professor, came under heavy   10
fire from both students and faculty when he proposed recalculating the grade point average to give rigorously graded courses greater weight. The student government beat back the plan with the help of teachers in the humanities, who worried that students might abandon them for other courses that they currently avoided. Other universities have expressed interest in adopting the Johnson plan, but want their names kept secret to avoid a backlash.

Addicted to counterfeit excellence, colleges, parents and students are unlikely to give it up. As a consequence, diplomas will become weaker and more ornamental as the years go by.

MLA CITATION

Staples, Brent. "Why Colleges Shower Their Students with A's." 1998. *The Norton Reader: An Anthology of Nonfiction*. Ed. Melissa A. Goldthwaite et al. 14th ed. New York: Norton, 2016. 388–90. Print.

QUESTIONS

1. Have you or your friends ever experienced grade inflation like the kind Brent Staples describes? What do you think were the causes for it taking place?

2. Staples writes, "An Ivy League professor said recently that if tenure disappeared, universities would be 'free to sell diplomas outright'" (paragraph 4). Analyze this statement. What are its implications? Why does the professor think tenured faculty serve as protection against the "selling" of diplomas?

3. Staples notes that a Duke University statistics professor proposed "recalculating the grade point average to give rigorously graded courses greater weight" (paragraph 10). He was opposed by humanities professors. What might have been the source of their opposition? What is the situation on your campus: do math professors grade more "rigorously" than English professors? Who are the hardest graders?

4. How broad is Staples's range of examples? Would he need to adjust his position if he considered other colleges? Write an analysis of the situation at your college either to confirm or to contest Staples's argument.

DAVID BROOKS   *The Gender Gap at School*

THERE ARE THREE gender-segregated sections in any airport: the restrooms, the security pat-down area and the bookstore. In the men's sections of the bookstore, there are books describing masterly men conquering evil. In the women's sections there are novels about, well, I guess feelings and stuff.

The same separation occurs in the home. Researchers in Britain asked 400 accomplished women and 500 accomplished men to name their favorite novels. The men preferred novels written by men, often revolving around loneliness and alienation. Camus's *The Stranger*, Salinger's *Catcher in the Rye* and Vonnegut's *Slaughterhouse-Five* topped the male list.

Published in the New York Times *(2006), where David Brooks writes a regular op-ed column twice a week.*

The women leaned toward books written by women. The women's books described relationships and are a lot better than the books the men chose. The top six women's books were *Jane Eyre*, *Wuthering Heights*, *The Handmaid's Tale*, *Middlemarch*, *Pride and Prejudice* and *Beloved*.

There are a couple of reasons why the two lists might diverge so starkly. It could be men are insensitive dolts who don't appreciate subtle human connections and good literature. Or, it could be that the part of the brain where men experience negative emotion, the amygdala, is not well connected to the part of the brain where verbal processing happens, whereas the part of the brain where women experience negative emotion, the cerebral cortex, is well connected. It could be that women are better at processing emotion through words.

Over the past two decades, there has been a steady accumulation of evidence that male and female brains work differently. Women use both sides of their brain more symmetrically than men. Men and women hear and smell differently (women are much more sensitive). Boys and girls process colors differently (young girls enjoy an array of red, green and orange crayons whereas young boys generally stick to black, gray and blue). Men and women experience risk differently (men enjoy it more). 5

It could be, in short, that biological factors influence reading tastes, even after accounting for culture. Women who have congenital adrenal hyperplasia, which leads to high male hormone secretions, are more likely to choose violent stories than other women.

This wouldn't be a problem if we all understood these biological factors and if teachers devised different curriculums to instill an equal love of reading in both boys and girls.

The problem is that even after the recent flurry of attention about why boys are falling behind, there is still intense social pressure not to talk about biological differences between boys and girls (ask Larry Summers).[1] There is still resistance, especially in the educational world, to the findings of brain researchers. Despite some innovations here and there, in most classrooms boys and girls are taught the same books in the same ways.

Young boys are compelled to sit still in schools that have sacrificed recess for test prep. Many are told in a thousand subtle ways they are not really good students. They are sent home with these new-wave young adult problem novels, which all seem to be about introspectively morose young women whose parents are either suicidal drug addicts or fatally ill manic depressives.

It shouldn't be any surprise that according to a National Endowment for the Arts study, the percentage of young men who read has plummeted over the past 14 years. Reading rates are falling three times as fast among young men as among young women. Nor should it be a surprise that men are drifting away 10

---

1. President of Harvard from 2001–2006, who resigned after making controversial remarks about women's ability to pursue careers in science.

from occupations that involve reading and school. Men now make up a smaller share of teachers than at any time in the past 40 years.

Dr. Leonard Sax, whose book *Why Gender Matters* is a lucid guide to male and female brain differences, emphasizes that men and women can excel at any subject. They just have to be taught in different ways. Sax is a big believer in single-sex schools, which he says allow kids to open up and break free from gender stereotypes. But for most kids it would be a start if they were assigned books they might actually care about. For boys, that probably means more Hemingway, Tolstoy, Homer and Twain.

During the 1970's, it was believed that gender is a social construct and that gender differences could be eliminated via consciousness-raising. But it turns out gender is not a social construct. Consciousness-raising doesn't turn boys into sensitively poetic pacifists. It just turns many of them into high school and college dropouts who hate reading.

MLA CITATION

Brooks, David. "The Gender Gap at School." 2006. *The Norton Reader: An Anthology of Nonfiction.* Ed. Melissa A. Goldthwaite et al. 14th ed. New York: Norton, 2016. 390–92. Print.

QUESTIONS

1. Does your experience support David Brooks's claim that boys and girls read differently? Use some examples from people you know.

2. According to Brooks, what is at stake if we don't recognize the differences between boys and girls?

3. Examine the evidence that Brooks uses to support his claim that girls' and boys' brains are different. Do you think Brooks produces enough evidence to support his claim? What evidence might he be omitting?

4. Do a brief survey of favorite books of males and females, and see if it supports Brooks's claim. Write up your findings in an essay in which you agree, disagree, or both with Brooks's argument.

DAVID EPSTEIN   *Sports Should Be Child's Play*

THE NATIONAL FUROR over concussions misses the primary scourge that is harming kids and damaging youth sports in America.

The heightened pressure on child athletes to be, essentially, adult athletes has fostered an epidemic of hyperspecialization that is both dangerous and counterproductive.

One New York City soccer club proudly advertises its development pipeline for kids under age 6, known as U6. The coach-picked stars, "poised for elite level soccer," graduate to the U7 "pre-travel" program. Parents, visions of scholarships dancing in their heads, enable this by paying for private coaching and year-round travel.

Children are playing sports in too structured a manner too early in life on adult-size fields—i.e., too large for optimal skill development—and spending too much time in one sport. It can lead to serious injuries and, a growing body of sports science shows, a lesser ultimate level of athletic success.

We should urge kids to avoid hyperspecialization and instead sample a variety of sports through at least age 12.   5

Nearly a third of youth athletes in a three-year longitudinal study led by Neeru Jayanthi, director of primary care sports medicine at Loyola University in Chicago, were highly specialized—they had quit multiple sports in order to focus on one for more than eight months a year—and another third weren't far behind. Even controlling for age and the total number of weekly hours in sports, kids in the study who were highly specialized had a 36 percent increased risk of suffering a serious overuse injury. Dr. Jayanthi saw kids with stress fractures in their backs, arms or legs; damage to elbow ligaments; and cracks in the cartilage in their joints.

Because families with greater financial resources were better able to facilitate the travel and private coaching that specialization requires, socioeconomic status turned up as a positive predictor of serious injury. Some young athletes now face surgeries befitting their grandparents. Young hockey goaltenders repeatedly practice butterfly style—which stresses the developing hip joint when the legs are splayed to block the bottom of the goal. The sports surgeon Marc Philippon, based in Vail, Colo., saw a 25-year-old goalie who already needed a hip replacement.

In the Loyola study, sport diversification had a protective effect. But in case health risks alone aren't reason enough for parents to ignore the siren call of specialization, diversification also provides performance benefits.

Kids who play multiple "attacking" sports, like basketball or field hockey, transfer learned motor and anticipatory skills—the unconscious ability to read

Published in the New York Times *(2014) shortly after the appearance of David Epstein's book,* The Sports Gene: Inside the Science of Extraordinary Athletic Performance.

bodies and game situations—to other sports. They take less time to master the sport they ultimately choose.

10   Several studies on skill acquisition now show that elite athletes generally practiced their sport less through their early teenage years and specialized only in the mid-to-late teenage years, while so-called sub-elites—those who never quite cracked the highest ranks—homed in on a single sport much sooner.

Data presented at the April meeting of the American Medical Society for Sports Medicine showed that varsity athletes at U.C.L.A.—many with full scholarships—specialized on average at age 15.4, whereas U.C.L.A. undergrads who played sports in high school, but did not make the intercollegiate level, specialized at 14.2.

We may prize the story of Tiger Woods, who demonstrated his swing at age 2 for Bob Hope. But the path of the two-time N.B.A. M.V.P. Steve Nash (who grew up playing soccer and didn't own a basketball until age 13) or the tennis star Roger Federer (whose parents encouraged him to play badminton, basketball and soccer) is actually the norm.

A Swedish study of sub-elite and elite tennis players—including five who ranked among the top 15 in the world—found that those who topped out as sub-elites dropped all other sports by age 11. Eventual elites developed in a "harmonious club environment without greater demands for success," and played multiple sports until age 14.

The sports science data support a "sampling period" through at least age 12. Mike Joyner, a Mayo Clinic physician and human performance expert, would add general physical literacy-building to the youth sports menu: perhaps using padded gymnastics gyms for parkour, which is essentially running, climbing or vaulting on any obstacle one can find.

In addition to athletic diversity, kids' sports should be kid-size.   15

In Brazil, host of this month's World Cup, kids are weaned on "futsal," a lightly structured and miniaturized form of soccer. Futsal is played on tiny patches of grass or concrete or on indoor courts and typically by teams of five players.

Players touch the ball up to five times as frequently as they do in traditional soccer, and the tighter playing area forces children to develop foot and decision-making skills under pressure.

A futsalization of youth sports generally would serve engagement, skill development and health.

USA Hockey (which has barred checking in youth games) recently invited adults to play on a 310-by-130-foot ice rink to show them what it's like for an 8-year-old to play on a regulation rink. The grown-ups' assessments: "too much time between the action"; "it's hard to communicate because everyone is spread out so far"; "you end up spending a lot of time in open space."

Futsal, basketball and . . . padded parkour? Sounds like a strange three-   20
sport athlete, and a perfect model for kids.

MLA CITATION

Epstein, David. "Sports Should Be Child's Play." 2014. *The Norton Reader: An Anthology of Nonfiction.* Ed. Melissa A. Goldthwaite et al. 14th ed. New York: Norton, 2016. 393–95. Print.

QUESTIONS

1. David Epstein makes two arguments against early specialization in a sport—what he calls "hyperspecialization" in paragraph 2. Identify these two arguments. Do you find one more convincing than the other? Why?

2. Consider Epstein's use of evidence. What types of evidence does he use to support his arguments? Where is that support most effective? Where is it least effective? Why?

3. Among Epstein's solutions to the problem of children specializing too early is "futsalization," based on the game of futsal played in Brazil. What features of futsal does Epstein praise and believe should be modeled in other children's sports?

4. Interview three or four campus athletes who play a sport, asking them when they started their sport, what other sports they played, and what their goals might be in participating in collegiate sports. Write an essay in which you agree, disagree, or both with Epstein's position, incorporating the testimony of the athletes you interviewed.

JANE MCGONIGAL   *Be a Gamer, Save the World*

> *Videogames make players feel like their best selves.*
> *Why not give them real problems to solve?*

W E OFTEN THINK of immersive computer and videogames—like *FarmVille, Guitar Hero* and *World of Warcraft*—as "escapist," a kind of passive retreat from reality. Many critics consider such games a mind-numbing waste of time, if not a corrupting influence. But the truth about games is very nearly the opposite. In today's society, they consistently fulfill genuine human needs that the real world fails to satisfy. More than that, they may prove to be a key resource for solving some of our most pressing real-world problems.

Hundreds of millions of people around the globe are already devoting larger and larger chunks of time to this alternate reality. Collectively, we spend three billion hours a week gaming. In the United States, where there are 183 million active gamers, videogames took in about $15.5 billion last year. And though a typical gamer plays for just an hour or two a day, there are now more than five million "extreme" gamers in the United States who play an average of 45 hours a week. To put this in perspective, the number of hours that gamers world-wide have spent playing *World of Warcraft* alone adds up to 5.93 million years.

These gamers aren't rejecting reality entirely, of course. They have careers, goals, schoolwork, families and real lives that they care about. But as they devote more of their free time to game worlds, they often feel that the real world is missing something.

Gamers want to know: Where in the real world is the gamer's sense of being fully alive, focused and engaged in every moment? The real world just doesn't offer up the same sort of carefully designed pleasures, thrilling challenges and

Published in the "Life and Culture" section of the Wall Street Journal *(2011), a daily newspaper covering international and national news with an emphasis on business and economics. Jane McGonigal is the director of game research and development at the Institute for the Future, a nonprofit organization based in Palo Alto, California, that, according to its website, provides "practical tools, research, and programs" to help a variety of organizations reach their future goals.*

powerful social bonding that the gamer finds in virtual environments. Reality doesn't motivate us as effectively. Reality isn't engineered to maximize our potential or to make us happy.

Those who continue to dismiss games as merely escapist entertainment will   5
find themselves at a major disadvantage in the years ahead, as more gamers start to harness this power for real good. My research over the past decade at the University of California, Berkeley, and the Institute for the Future has shown that games consistently provide us with the four ingredients that make for a happy and meaningful life: satisfying work, real hope for success, strong social connections and the chance to become a part of something bigger than ourselves.

We get these benefits from our real lives sometimes, but we get them almost every time we play a good game. These benefits are what positive psychologists call intrinsic rewards—we don't play games to make money, improve our social status, or achieve any external signposts of success. And these intrinsic rewards, studies at the University of Pennsylvania, Harvard and U.C. Berkeley have shown, provide the foundation for optimal human experience.

In a good game, we feel blissfully productive. We have clear goals and a sense of heroic purpose. More important, we're constantly able to see and feel the impact of our efforts on the virtual world around us. As a result, we have a stronger sense of our own agency—and we are more likely to set ambitious real-life goals. One recent study found, for example, that players of *Guitar Hero* are more likely to pick up a real guitar and learn how to play it.

Could games like *Guitar Hero* help cure cancer and end poverty?

When we play, we also have a sense of urgent optimism. We believe whole-heartedly that we are up to any challenge, and we become remarkably resilient in the face of failure. Research shows that gamers spend on average 80% of their time failing in game worlds, but instead of giving up, they stick with the diffi-cult challenge and use the feedback of the game to get better. With some effort, we can learn to apply this resilience to the real-world challenges we face.

Games make it easy to build stronger social bonds with our friends and family. Studies show that we like and trust someone better after we play a game with them—even if they beat us. And we're more likely to help someone in real life after we've helped them in an online game. It's no wonder that 40% of all user time on Facebook is spent playing social games. They're a fast and reli-able way to strengthen our connection with people we care about.

10   Today's videogames are increasingly created on an epic scale, with com-pelling stories, sweeping mythologies and massive multiplayer environments that produce feelings of awe and wonder. Researchers on positive emotion have found that whenever we feel awe or wonder, we become more likely to serve a larger cause and to collaborate selflessly with others.

With so much blissful productivity and urgent optimism, stronger social bonds and extreme cooperation, it's not surprising that so many players feel that they become the best version of themselves in games. That's one of the reasons I believe we can take the benefits of games a step further. We can har-ness the power of game design to tackle real-world problems. We can empower

Videogames make players feel like their best selves. Why not give them real problems to solve?

gamers to use their virtual-world strengths to accomplish real feats. Indeed, when game communities have been matched with challenging real-world problems, they have already proven themselves capable of producing tangible, potentially world-changing results.

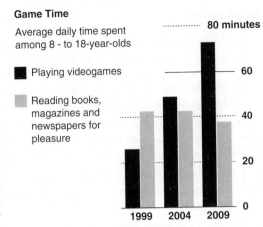

Game Time

Average daily time spent among 8 - to 18-year-olds

■ Playing videogames

▨ Reading books, magazines and newspapers for pleasure

80 minutes

60

40

20

0

1999   2004   2009

Source: Kaiser Family Foundation

In 2010, more than 57,000 gamers were listed as co-authors for a research paper in the prestigious scientific journal *Nature*. The gamers—with no previous background in biochemistry— had worked in a 3D game environment called *Foldit*, folding virtual proteins in new ways that could help cure cancer or prevent Alzheimer's. The game was developed by scientists at the University of Washington who believed that gamers could outperform supercomputers at this creative task—and the players proved them right, beating the supercomputers at more than half of the game's challenges.

More recently, more than 19,000 players of *EVOKE*, an online game that I created for the World Bank Institute, undertook real-world missions to improve food security, increase access to clean energy and end poverty in more than 130 countries. The game focused on building up players' abilities to design and launch their own social enterprises.

After 10 weeks, they had founded more than 50 new companies—real businesses working today from South Africa and India to Buffalo, N.Y. My favorite is Libraries Across Africa, a new franchise system that empowers local entrepreneurs to set up free community libraries. It also creates complementary business opportunities for selling patrons refreshments, WiFi access and cellphone time. The first is currently being tested in Gabon.

These examples are just the beginning of what is possible if we take advantage of the power of games to make us better and change the world. Those who understand this power will be the people who invent our future. We can create rewarding, transformative games for ourselves and our families; for our schools, businesses and neighborhoods; for an entire industry or an entirely new movement.   15

We can play any games we want. We can create any future we can imagine. Let the games begin.

MLA CITATION

McGonigal, Jane. "Be a Gamer, Save the World." 2011. *The Norton Reader: An Anthology of Nonfiction*. Ed. Melissa A. Goldthwaite et al. 14th ed. New York: Norton, 2016. 396–99. Print.

QUESTIONS

1. In the opening paragraph, Jane McGonigal admits that video games are usually dismissed as "escapist" and "a mind-numbing waste of time." She presents a more positive case for gaming, arguing that it provides "four ingredients that make for a happy and meaningful life" (paragraph 5). What are those ingredients? What evidence does McGonigal provide for each?

2. In the final paragraphs, McGonigal gives examples of games that allow gamers to make positive contributions to global problems. What evidence does McGonigal provide that these games "make us better and change the world" (paragraph 15)?

3. Given the word limitations, op-ed writers often have little space to acknowledge counterarguments. What negative aspects of gaming does McGonigal not acknowledge? How could including other viewpoints have strengthened her own argument?

4. Play or research one of the games McGonigal mentions in her op-ed. Write an essay evaluating the positive and negative aspects of the game.

DAN BARBER   *What Farm-to-Table Got Wrong*

I   T'S SPRING AGAIN. Hip deep in asparagus—and, soon enough, tomatoes and zucchini—farm-to-table advocates finally have something from the farm to put on the table.

The crowds clamoring for just-dug produce at the farmers' market and the local food co-op suggest that this movement is no longer just a foodie fad. Today, almost 80 percent of Americans say sustainability is a priority when purchasing food. The promise of this kind of majority is that eating local can reshape landscapes and drive lasting change.

Except it hasn't. More than a decade into the movement, the promise has fallen short. For all its successes, farm-to-table has not, in any fundamental way, reworked the economic and political forces that dictate how our food is grown and raised. Big Food is getting bigger, not smaller. In the last five years, we've lost nearly 100,000 farms (mostly midsize ones). Today, 1.1 percent of farms in the United States account for nearly 45 percent of farm revenues. Despite being farm-to-table's favorite targets, corn and soy account for more than 50 percent of our harvested acres for the first time ever. Between 2006 and 2011, over a million acres of native prairie were plowed up in the so-called Western Corn Belt to make way for these two crops, the most rapid loss of grasslands since we started using tractors to bust sod on the Great Plains in the 1920s.

Published as an op-ed in the New York Times *(2014) by the chef and co-owner of the Blue Hill and Blue Hill at Stone Barns restaurants. Dan Barber also wrote* The Third Plate: Field Notes on the Future of Food *(2014), which offers a history of cuisine in the United States and proposes ways of eating that are both delicious and environmentally responsible.*

How do we make sense of this odd duality: a food revolution on one hand, an entrenched status quo on the other?

I got a hint of the answer a few years ago, while standing in a field in upstate New York. I was there because, many years before, I'd decided I wanted local flour for my restaurants. I chose Lakeview Organic, a grain farm operated by Klaas and Mary-Howell Martens. Klaas was growing a rare variety of emmer wheat (also known as farro), nearly extinct but for the efforts of a few farmers.

Milled and baked into whole wheat bread, the emmer was a revelation—intensely sweet and nutty. I spoke routinely about the importance of local grain and the resurrection of lost flavors. I was waving the farm-to-table flag and feeling pretty good about it, too.

Visiting Klaas those years later, hoping to learn what made the emmer so delicious, I realized I was missing the point entirely. The secret to great-tasting wheat, Klaas told me, is that it's not about the wheat. It's about the soil.

In fact, on a tour of his farm, there was surprisingly little wheat to see. Instead, Klaas showed me fields of less-coveted grains and legumes like millet, barley and kidney beans, as well as cover crops like mustard and clover, all of which he plants in meticulously planned rotations. The rotations dictate the quality of the soil, which means they dictate the flavor of the harvests as well. They are the recipe for his delicious emmer.

Each planting in the sequence has a specific function. Klaas likes his field rotations to begin with a cover crop like the mustard plant. Cover crops are often grown to restore nutrients depleted from a previous harvest. Plowed into

Lakeview Organic Grain Farm, owned by Klaas and Mary-Howell Martens.

the soil after maturity, mustard offers the added benefit of reducing pest and disease problems for subsequent crops.

10   Next Klaas will plant a legume, which does the neat trick of fixing nitrogen: grabbing it from the atmosphere and storing it in the plant's roots. Soybeans are a good choice; or kidney beans, if the local processor is paying enough to make it worth his while; or cowpeas, which he harvests for animal feed. If there's a dry spell, he'll forgo beans altogether and pop in some hardy millet. Oats or rye is next; rye builds soil structure and suppresses weeds. Only then is Klaas's soil locked and loaded with the requisite fertility needed for his wheat.

As much as I cling to tried and true recipes, Klaas doesn't. Depending on what the soil is telling him, he may roll out an entirely different rotation. If there's a buildup of fungal disease in the field, the next season he'll plant a brassica like cabbage or broccoli, followed by buckwheat, and then barley. Barley is among Klaas's favorite crops. In addition to cleansing the soil of pathogens, it can be planted along with a nitrogen fixer like clover, further benefiting the soil. Once again, the soil is ready for wheat.

Standing in Klaas's fields, I saw how single-minded I had been. Yes, I was creating a market for local emmer wheat, but I wasn't doing anything to support the recipe behind it. Championing Klaas's wheat and only his wheat was tantamount to treating his farm like a grocery store. I was cherry-picking what I most wanted for my menu without supporting the whole farm.

I am not the only one. In celebrating the All-Stars of the farmers' market—asparagus, heirloom tomatoes, emmer wheat—farm-to-table advocates are often guilty of ignoring a whole class of humbler crops that are required to produce the most delicious food.

With limited American demand for local millet, rye and barley, 70 percent of Klaas's harvest was going into livestock feed for chickens, pigs and dairy cattle. In general, Klaas earned pennies on the dollar compared with what he'd make selling his crops for human consumption. And we were missing out as well, on nutritious foods that are staples of the best cuisines in the world.

15   Diversifying our diet to include more local grains and legumes is a delicious first step to improving our food system. Millet and rye are an easy substitute for rice or pasta. But that addresses only the low-hanging fruit of Klaas's farm. More challenging is to think about how to honor the other underutilized parts of his rotations—classic cover crops like cowpeas and mustard, which fertilize the soil to ensure healthy harvests in the future.

Today, the best farmers are tying up valuable real estate for long periods of time (in an agonizingly short growing season) simply to benefit their soil. Imagine if Macy's reserved half of its shelf space at Christmas for charitable donations. A noble idea. But profitable? Not so much. By creating a market for these crops, we can provide more value for the farmer and for our own diets, while supporting the long-term health of the land.

In Klaas's field, I bent down and ripped off a green shoot of Austrian winter peas. I took a bite. Inedible? No, delicious! Thirty acres of the most tender and sweet pea shoots I'd ever tasted. (Harvesting the leaves would somewhat reduce the amount plowed back into the soil, but the plant's soil benefits would remain.) In the distance I could make out a field of mustards. Klaas plants Tilney mustard, similar to the spicy green you find in a mesclun mix. I realized I wasn't just looking at a cover crop. I was looking at a salad bowl.

Back at the restaurant, I created a new dish called "Rotation Risotto," a collection of all of Klaas's lowly, soil-supporting grains and legumes, cooked and presented in the manner of a classic risotto. I used a purée of cowpea shoots and mustard greens to thicken the grains and replace the starchiness of rice. As one waiter described the idea, it was a "nose-to-tail approach to the farm"—an edible version of Klaas's farming strategy.

It's one thing for chefs to advocate cooking with the whole farm; it's another thing to make these uncelebrated crops staples in ordinary kitchens. Bridging that divide will require a new network of regional processors and distributors.

Take beer, for example. The explosion in local microbreweries has meant a demand for local barley malt. A new malting facility near Klaas's farm recently opened in response. He now earns 30 percent more selling barley for malt than he did selling it for animal feed. For other farmers, it's a convincing incentive to diversify their grain crops. 20

Investing in the right infrastructure means the difference between a farmer's growing crops for cows or for cafeterias. It will take the shape of more local mills (for grains), canneries (for beans) and processors (for greens). As heretical as this may sound, farm-to-table needs to embrace a few more middlemen.

Perhaps the problem with the farm-to-table movement is implicit in its name. Imagining the food chain as a field on one end and a plate of food at the other is not only reductive, it also puts us in the position of end users. It's a passive system—a grocery-aisle mentality—when really, as cooks and eaters, we need to engage in the nuts and bolts of true agricultural sustainability. Flavor can be our guide to reshaping our diets, and our landscapes, from the ground up.

MLA CITATION

Barber, Dan. "What Farm-to-Table Got Wrong." 2014. *The Norton Reader: An Anthology of Nonfiction.* Ed. Melissa A. Goldthwaite et al. 14th ed. New York: Norton, 2016. 400–03. Print.

QUESTIONS

1. The phrase "farm-to-table" suggests a simple process of transferring locally grown produce to nearby homes and restaurants. How does Dan Barber complicate our understanding of this process? Why is this complication important to his argument?

2. Barber suggests ways that he, as a chef, can aid local organic farmers by utilizing grains and vegetables essential to crop rotation—as in paragraph 18 where he describes "Rotation Risotto." Can you infer from his argument how consumers who read his op-ed might also aid the cause?

3. Visit a farmers' market, restaurant, or organic grocery store that sells locally grown produce. Choose a grain or vegetable you haven't eaten or don't know well, research it, and write a short account of its cultivation and uses.

EDUCATION

FREDERICK DOUGLASS *Learning to Read*

I LIVED IN MASTER HUGH'S FAMILY about seven years.[1] During this time, I succeeded in learning to read and write. In accomplishing this, I was compelled to resort to various stratagems. I had no regular teacher. My mistress, who had kindly commenced to instruct me, had, in compliance with the advice and direction of her husband, not only ceased to instruct, but had set her face against my being instructed by any one else. It is due, however, to my mistress to say of her, that she did not adopt this course of treatment immediately. She at first lacked the depravity indispensable to shutting me up in mental darkness. It was at least necessary for her to have some training in the exercise of irresponsible power, to make her equal to the task of treating me as though I were a brute.

My mistress was, as I have said, a kind and tender-hearted woman; and in the simplicity of her soul she commenced, when I first went to live with her, to treat me as she supposed one human being ought to treat another. In entering upon the duties of a slaveholder, she did not seem to perceive that I sustained to her the relation of a mere chattel, and that for her to treat me as a human being was not only wrong, but dangerously so. Slavery proved as injurious to her as it did to me. When I went there, she was a pious, warm, and tender-hearted woman. There was no sorrow or suffering for which she had not a tear. She had bread for the hungry, clothes for the naked, and comfort for every mourner that came within her reach. Slavery soon proved its ability to divest her of these heavenly qualities. Under its influence, the tender heart became stone, and the lamblike disposition gave way to one of tigerlike fierceness. The first step in her downward course was in her ceasing to instruct me. She now commenced to practise her husband's precepts. She finally became even more violent in her opposition than her husband himself. She was not satisfied with simply doing as well as he had commanded; she seemed anxious to do better. Nothing seemed to make her more angry than to see me with a newspaper. She seemed to think that here lay the danger. I have had her rush at me with a face made all up of fury, and snatch from me a newspaper, in a manner that fully

From Frederick Douglass's autobiography, Narrative of the Life of Frederick Douglass, an American Slave, Written by Himself *(1845).*

1. In Baltimore, Maryland.

revealed her apprehension. She was an apt woman; and a little experience soon demonstrated, to her satisfaction, that education and slavery were incompatible with each other.

From this time I was most narrowly watched. If I was in a separate room any considerable length of time, I was sure to be suspected of having a book, and was at once called to give an account of myself. All this, however, was too late. The first step had been taken. Mistress, in teaching me the alphabet, had given me the *inch*, and no precaution could prevent me from taking the *ell*.[2]

The plan which I adopted, and the one by which I was most successful, was that of making friends of all the little white boys whom I met in the street. As many of these as I could, I converted into teachers. With their kindly aid, obtained at different times and in different places, I finally succeeded in learning to read. When I was sent of errands, I always took my book with me, and by going one part of my errand quickly, I found time to get a lesson before my return. I used also to carry bread with me, enough of which was always in the house, and to which I was always welcome; for I was much better off in this regard than many of the poor white children in our neighborhood. This bread I used to bestow upon the hungry little urchins, who, in return, would give me that more valuable bread of knowledge. I am strongly tempted to give the names of two or three of those little boys, as a testimonial of the gratitude and affection I bear them; but prudence forbids;—not that it would injure me, but it might embarrass them; for it is almost an unpardonable offence to teach slaves to read in this Christian country. It is enough to say of the dear little fellows, that they lived on Philpot Street, very near Durgin and Bailey's ship-yard. I used to talk this matter of slavery over with them. I would sometimes say to them, I wished I could be as free as they would be when they got to be men. "You will be free as soon as you are twenty-one, *but I am a slave for life!* Have not I as good a right to be free as you have?" These words used to trouble them; they would express for me the liveliest sympathy, and console me with the hope that something would occur by which I might be free.

I was now about twelve years old, and the thought of being *a slave for life*   5 began to bear heavily upon my heart. Just about this time, I got hold of a book entitled "The Columbian Orator."[3] Every opportunity I got, I used to read this book. Among much of other interesting matter, I found in it a dialogue between a master and his slave. The slave was represented as having run away from his master three times. The dialogue represented the conversation which took place between them, when the slave was retaken the third time. In this dialogue, the whole argument in behalf of slavery was brought forward by the master, all of which was disposed of by the slave. The slave was made to say some very smart as well as impressive things in reply to his master—things which had the desired though unexpected effect; for the conversation resulted in the voluntary emancipation of the slave on the part of the master.

2. Once a unit of measurement equal to forty-five inches; the saying is proverbial.
3. Popular collection of poems, dialogues, plays, and speeches.

In the same book, I met with one of Sheridan's mighty speeches on and in behalf of Catholic emancipation.[4] These were choice documents to me. I read them over and over again with unabated interest. They gave tongue to interesting thoughts of my own soul, which had frequently flashed through my mind, and died away for want of utterance. The moral which I gained from the dialogue was the power of truth over the conscience of even a slaveholder. What I got from Sheridan was a bold denunciation of slavery, and a powerful vindication of human rights. The reading of these documents enabled me to utter my thoughts, and to meet the arguments brought forward to sustain slavery; but while they relieved me of one difficulty, they brought on another even more painful than the one of which I was relieved. The more I read, the more I was led to abhor and detest my enslavers. I could regard them in no other light than a band of successful robbers, who had left their homes, and gone to Africa, and stolen us from our homes, and in a strange land reduced us to slavery. I loathed them as being the meanest as well as the most wicked of men. As I read and contemplated the subject, behold! that very discontentment which Master Hugh had predicted would follow my learning to read had already come, to torment and sting my soul to unutterable anguish. As I writhed under it, I would at times feel that learning to read had been a curse rather than a blessing. It had given me a view of my wretched condition, without the remedy. It opened my eyes to the horrible pit, but to no ladder upon which to get out. In moments of agony, I envied my fellow-slaves for their stupidity. I have often wished myself a beast. I preferred the condition of the meanest reptile to my own. Any thing, no matter what, to get rid of thinking! It was this everlasting thinking of my condition that tormented me. There was no getting rid of it. It was pressed upon me by every object within sight or hearing, animate or inanimate. The silver trump of freedom had roused my soul to eternal wakefulness. Freedom now appeared, to disappear no more forever. It was heard in every sound, and seen in every thing. It was ever present to torment me with a sense of my wretched condition. I saw nothing without seeing it, I heard nothing without hearing it, and felt nothing without feeling it. It looked from every star, it smiled in every calm, breathed in every wind, and moved in every storm.

I often found myself regretting my own existence, and wishing myself dead; and but for the hope of being free, I have no doubt but that I should have killed myself, or done something for which I should have been killed. While in this state of mind, I was eager to hear any one speak of slavery. I was a ready listener. Every little while, I could hear something about the abolitionists. It was some time before I found what the word meant. It was always used in such connections as to make it an interesting word to me. If a slave ran away and succeeded in getting clear, or if a slave killed his master, set fire to a barn, or did any thing very wrong in the mind of a slaveholder, it was spoken of as the fruit

4. Richard Brinsley Sheridan (1751–1815), Irish dramatist and political leader. The speech, arguing for the abolition of laws denying Roman Catholics in Great Britain and Ireland civil and political liberties, was actually made by the Irish patriot Arthur O'Connor.

of *abolition*. Hearing the word in this connection very often, I set about learning what it meant. The dictionary afforded me little or no help. I found it was "the act of abolishing"; but then I did not know what was to be abolished. Here I was perplexed. I did not dare to ask any one about its meaning, for I was satisfied that it was something they wanted me to know very little about. After a patient waiting, I got one of our city papers, containing an account of the number of petitions from the north, praying for the abolition of slavery in the District of Columbia, and of the slave trade between the States. From this time I understood the words *abolition* and *abolitionist,* and always drew near when that word was spoken, expecting to hear something of importance to myself and fellow-slaves. The light broke in upon me by degrees. I went one day down on the wharf of Mr. Waters; and seeing two Irishmen unloading a scow of stone, I went, unasked, and helped them. When we had finished, one of them came to me and asked me if I were a slave. I told him I was. He asked, "Are ye a slave for life?" I told him that I was. The good Irishman seemed to be deeply affected by the statement. He said to the other that it was a pity so fine a little fellow as myself should be a slave for life. He said it was a shame to hold me. They both advised me to run away to the north; that I should find friends there, and that I should be free. I pretended not to be interested in what they said, and treated them as if I did not understand them; for I feared they might be treacherous. White men have been known to encourage slaves to escape, and then, to get the reward, catch them and return them to their masters. I was afraid that these seemingly good men might use me so; but I nevertheless remembered their advice, and from that time I resolved to run away. I looked forward to a time at which it would be safe for me to escape. I was too young to think of doing so immediately; besides, I wished to learn how to write, as I might have occasion to write my own pass. I consoled myself with the hope that I should one day find a good chance. Meanwhile, I would learn to write.

The idea as to how I might learn to write was suggested to me by being in Durgin and Bailey's ship-yard, and frequently seeing the ship carpenters, after hewing, and getting a piece of timber ready for use, write on the timber the name of that part of the ship for which it was intended. When a piece of timber was intended for the larboard side, it would be marked thus—"L." When a piece was for the starboard side, it would be marked thus—"S." A piece for the larboard side forward, would be marked thus—"L. F." When a piece was for starboard side forward, it would be marked thus—"S. F." For larboard aft, it would be marked thus—"L. A." For starboard aft, it would be marked thus—"S. A." I soon learned the names of these letters, and for what they were intended when placed upon a piece of timber in the shipyard. I immediately commenced copying them, and in a short time was able to make the four letters named. After that, when I met with any boy who I knew could write, I would tell him I could write as well as he. The next word would be, "I don't believe you. Let me see you try it." I would then make the letters which I had been so fortunate as to learn, and ask him to beat that. In this way I got a good many lessons in writing, which it is quite possible I should never have gotten in any other way. During this time, my copy-book was the board fence, brick wall, and pavement; my pen and ink was a lump of chalk. With these, I learned mainly how to write. I then commenced and continued copying the Italics in Webster's Spelling Book,[5] until I could make them all without looking on the book. By this time, my little Master Thomas had gone to school, and learned how to write, and had written over a number of copy-books. These had been brought home, and shown to some of our near neighbors, and then laid aside. My mistress used to go to class meeting at the Wilk Street meetinghouse every Monday afternoon, and leave me to take care of the house. When left thus, I used to spend the time in writing in the spaces left in Master Thomas's copy-book, copying what he had written. I continued to do this until I could write a hand very similar to that of Master Thomas. Thus, after a long, tedious effort for years, I finally succeeded in learning how to write.

5. *The American Spelling Book* (1783) by Noah Webster, American lexicographer.

MLA CITATION

Douglass, Frederick. "Learning to Read." 1845. *The Norton Reader: An Anthology of Nonfiction.* Ed. Melissa A. Goldthwaite et al. 14th ed. New York: Norton, 2016. 404–08. Print.

QUESTIONS

1. Frederick Douglass's story might today be called a "literacy narrative"—an account of how someone learns to read and write. What are the key features of this narrative? What obstacles did Douglass face? How did he overcome them?

2. Many literacy narratives include an enabling figure, someone who helps the young learner along his or her way. Is there such a figure in Douglass's narrative? Why or why not?

3. At the end of this narrative, Douglass mentions that he wrote "in the spaces left in Master Thomas's copy-book, copying what he had written" (paragraph 8). To what extent is imitation (copying) part of learning? To what extent does this narrative show originality?

4. Write your own literacy narrative—an account of how you learned to read and write.

Eudora Welty   *Clamorous to Learn*

 ROM THE FIRST I was clamorous to learn—I wanted to know and begged to be told not so much what, or how, or why, or where, as when. How soon?

> Pear tree by the garden gate,
> How much longer must I wait?

This rhyme from one of my nursery books was the one that spoke for me. But I lived not at all unhappily in this craving, for my wild curiosity was in large part suspense, which carries its own secret pleasure. And so one of the godmothers of fiction was already bending over me.

When I was five years old, I knew the alphabet, I'd been vaccinated (for smallpox), and I could read. So my mother walked across the street to Jefferson Davis Grammar School[1] and asked the principal if she would allow me to enter the first grade after Christmas.

"Oh, all right," said Miss Duling. "Probably the best thing you could do with her."

Miss Duling, a lifelong subscriber to perfection, was a figure of authority, the most whole-souled I have ever come to know. She was a dedicated schoolteacher who denied herself all she might have done or whatever other way she might have lived (this possibility was the last that could have occurred to us, her subjects in school). I believe she came of well-off people, well-educated, in Kentucky, and certainly old photographs show she was a beautiful, high-spirited-looking young lady—and came down to Jackson to its new grammar school that was going begging for a principal. She must have earned next to nothing; Mississippi then as now was the nation's lowest-ranking state economically, and our legislature has always shown a painfully loud reluctance to give money to public education. That challenge *brought* her.

In the long run she came into touch, as teacher or principal, with three generations of Jacksonians. My parents had not, but everybody else's parents had gone to school to her. She'd taught most of our leaders somewhere along the line. When she wanted something done—some civic oversight corrected, some injustice made right overnight, or even a tree spared that the fool telephone people were about to cut down—she telephoned the mayor, or the chief of police, or the president of the power company, or the head doctor at the hospital, or the judge in charge of a case, or whoever, and calling them by their first names, *told* them. It is impossible to imagine her meeting with anything less than compliance. The ringing of her brass bell from their days at Davis School would still be in their ears. She also proposed a spelling match between   5

Originally delivered as part of a lecture series at Harvard University in 1983, then published in Eudora Welty's memoir, One Writer's Beginnings *(1985).*

1. Named after the president of the Confederate States of America (1861–1865) and located in Jackson, Mississippi.

the fourth grade at Davis School and the Mississippi Legislature, who went through with it; and that told the Legislature.

Her standards were very high and of course inflexible, her authority was total; why *wouldn't* this carry with it a brass bell that could be heard ringing for a block in all directions? That bell belonged to the figure of Miss Duling as though it grew directly out of her right arm, as wings grew out of an angel or a tail out of the devil. When we entered, marching, into her school, by strictest teaching, surveillance, and order we learned grammar, arithmetic, spelling, reading, writing, and geography; and she, not the teachers, I believe, wrote out the examinations: need I tell you, they were "hard."

She's not the only teacher who has influenced me, but Miss Duling, in some fictional shape or form, has stridden into a larger part of my work than I'd realized until now. She emerges in my perhaps inordinate number of schoolteacher characters. I loved those characters in the writing. But I did not, in life, love Miss Duling. I was afraid of her high-arched bony nose, her eyebrows lifted in half-circles above her hooded, brilliant eyes, and of the Kentucky R's in her speech, and the long steps she took in her hightop shoes. I did nothing but fear her bearing-down authority, and did not connect this (as of course we were meant to) with our own need or desire to learn, perhaps because I already had this wish, and did not need to be driven.

She was impervious to lies or foolish excuses or the insufferable plea of not knowing any better. She wasn't going to have any frills, either, at Davis School. When a new governor moved into the mansion, he sent his daughter to Davis School; her name was Lady Rachel Conner. Miss Duling at once called the governor to the telephone and told him, "She'll be plain Rachel here."

Miss Duling dressed as plainly as a Pilgrim on a Thanksgiving poster we made in the schoolroom, in a longish black-and-white checked gingham dress, a bright thick wool sweater the red of a railroad lantern—she'd knitted it herself—black stockings and her narrow elegant feet in black hightop shoes with heels you could hear coming, rhythmical as a parade drum down the hall. Her silky black curly hair was drawn back out of curl, fastened by high combs, and knotted behind. She carried her spectacles on a gold chain hung around her neck. Her gaze was in general sweeping, then suddenly at the point of concentration upon you. With a swing of her bell that took her whole right arm and shoulder, she rang it, militant and impartial, from the head of the front steps of Davis School when it was time for us all to line up, girls on one side, boys on the other. We were to march past her into the school building, while the fourth-grader she nabbed played time on the piano, mostly to a tune we could have skipped to, but we didn't skip into Davis School.

10   Little recess (open-air exercises) and big recess (lunch-boxes from home opened and eaten on the grass, on the girls' side and the boys' side of the yard) and dismissal were also regulated by Miss Duling's bell. The bell was also used to catch us off guard with fire drill.

It was examinations that drove my wits away, as all emergencies do. Being expected to measure up was paralyzing. I failed to make 100 on my spelling exam because I missed one word and that word was "uncle." Mother, as I knew she would, took it personally. "You couldn't spell *uncle*? When you've got those five perfectly splendid uncles in West Virginia? What would *they* say to that?"

It was never that Mother wanted me to beat my classmates in grades; what she wanted was for me to have my answers right. It was unclouded perfection I was up against.

My father was much more tolerant of possible error. He only said, as he steeply and impeccably sharpened my pencils on examination morning, "Now just keep remembering: the examinations were made out for the *average* student to pass. That's the majority. And if the majority can pass, think how much better *you* can do."

I looked to my mother, who had her own opinions about the majority. My father wished to treat it with respect, she didn't. I'd been born left-handed, but the habit was broken when I entered the first grade in Davis School. My father had insisted. He pointed out that everything in life had been made for the convenience of right-handed people, because they were the majority, and he often used "what the majority wants" as a criterion for what was for the best. My mother said she could not promise him, could not promise him at all, that I wouldn't stutter as a consequence. Mother had been born left-handed too; her family consisted of five left-handed brothers, a left-handed mother, and a father who could write with both hands at the same time, also backwards and forwards and upside down, different words with each hand. She had been broken of it when she was young, and she said she used to stutter.

"But you still stutter," I'd remind her, only to hear her say loftily, "You should have heard me when I was your age." 15

In my childhood days, a great deal of stock was put, in general, in the value of doing well in school. Both daily newspapers in Jackson saw the honor roll as news and published the lists, and the grades, of all the honor students. The city fathers gave the children who made the honor roll free season tickets to the baseball games down at the grandstand. We all attended and all worshiped some player on the Jackson Senators: I offered up my 100's in arithmetic and spelling, reading and writing, attendance and, yes, deportment—I must have been a prig!—to Red McDermott, the third baseman. And our happiness matched that of knowing Miss Duling was on her summer vacation, far, far away in Kentucky.

Every school week, visiting teachers came on their days for special lessons. On Mondays, the singing teacher blew into the room fresh from the early outdoors, singing in her high soprano "How do you do?" to do-mi-sol-do,[2] and we responded in chorus from our desks, "I'm ve-ry well" to do-sol-mi-do. Miss Johnson taught us rounds—"Row row row your boat gently down the stream"— and "Little Sir Echo," with half the room singing the words and the other half being the echo, a competition. She was from the North, and she was the one who wanted us all to stop the Christmas carols and see snow. The snow falling that morning outside the window was the first most of us had ever seen, and Miss Johnson threw up the window and held out wide her own black cape and

2. Syllables indicating the first, third, fifth, and eighth tones of the scale.

caught flakes on it and ran, as fast as she could go, up and down the aisles to show us the real thing before it melted.

Thursday was Miss Eyrich and Miss Eyrich was Thursday. She came to give us physical training. She wasted no time on nonsense. Without greeting, we were marched straight outside and summarily divided into teams (no choosing sides), put on the mark, and ordered to get set for a relay race. Miss Eyrich cracked out "Go!" Dread rose in my throat. My head swam. Here was my turn, nearly upon me. (Wait, have I been touched—was that slap the touch? Go on! Do I go on without our passing a word? What word? Now am I racing too fast to turn around? Now I'm nearly home, but where is the hand waiting for mine to touch? Am I too late? Have I lost the whole race for our side?) I lost the relay race for our side before I started, through living ahead of myself, dreading to make my start, feeling too late prematurely, and standing transfixed by emergency, trying to think of a password. Thursdays still can make me hear Miss Eyrich's voice. "On your mark—get set—GO!"

Very composedly and very slowly, the art teacher, who visited each room on Fridays, paced the aisle and looked down over your shoulder at what you were drawing for her. This was Miss Ascher. Coming from behind you, her deep, resonant voice reached you without being a word at all, but a sort of purr. It was much the sound given out by our family doctor when he read the thermometer and found you were running a slight fever: "Um-hm. Um-hm." Both alike, they let you go right ahead with it.

20   The school toilets were in the boys' and girls' respective basements. After Miss Duling had rung to dismiss school, a friend and I were making our plans for Saturday from adjoining cubicles. "Can you come spend the day with me?" I called out, and she called back, "I might could."

"Who—said—MIGHT—COULD?" It sounded like "Fe Fi Fo Fum!"

We both were petrified, for we knew whose deep measured words those were that came from just outside our doors. That was the voice of Mrs. McWillie, who taught the other fourth grade across the hall from ours. She was not even our teacher, but a very heavy, stern lady who dressed entirely in widow's weeds with a pleated black shirtwaist with a high net collar and velvet ribbon, and a black skirt to her ankles, with black circles under her eyes and a mournful, Presbyterian expression. We children took her to be a hundred years old. We held still.

"You might as well tell me," continued Mrs. McWillie. "I'm going to plant myself right here and wait till you come out. Then I'll see who it was I heard saying 'MIGHT-COULD.'"

If Elizabeth wouldn't go out, of course I wouldn't either. We knew her to be a teacher who would not flinch from standing there in the basement all afternoon, perhaps even all day Saturday. So we surrendered and came out. I priggishly hoped Elizabeth would clear it up which child it was—it wasn't me.

25   "So it's you." She regarded us as a brace, made no distinction: whoever didn't say it was guilty by association. "If I ever catch you down here one more

time saying 'MIGHT-COULD,' I'm going to carry it to Miss Duling. You'll be kept in every day for a week! I hope you're both sufficiently ashamed of yourselves?" Saying "might-could" was bad, but saying it in the basement made bad grammar a sin. I knew Presbyterians believed that you could go to Hell.

Mrs. McWillie never scared us into grammar, of course. It was my first-year Latin teacher in high school who made me discover I'd fallen in love with it. It took Latin to thrust me into bona fide alliance with words in their true meaning. Learning Latin (once I was free of Caesar) fed my love for words upon words, words in continuation and modification, and the beautiful, sober, accretion of a sentence. I could see the achieved sentence finally standing there, as real, intact, and built to stay as the Mississippi State Capitol at the top of my street, where I could walk through it on my way to school and hear underfoot the echo of its marble floor, and over me the bell of its rotunda.

On winter's rainy days, the schoolrooms would grow so dark that sometimes you couldn't see the figures on the blackboard. At that point, Mrs. McWillie, that stern fourth-grade teacher, would let her children close their books, and she would move, broad in widow's weeds like darkness itself, to the window and by what light there was she would stand and read aloud "The King of the Golden River." But I was excluded—in the other fourth grade, across the hall. Miss Louella Varnado, my teacher, didn't copy Mrs. McWillie; we had a spelling match: you could spell in the dark. I did not then suspect that there was any other way I could learn the story of "The King of the Golden River" than to have been assigned in the beginning to Mrs. McWillie's cowering fourth grade, then wait for her to treat you to it on the rainy day of her choice. I only now realize how much the treat depended, too, on there not having been money enough to put electric lights in Davis School. John Ruskin had to come in through courtesy of darkness. When in time I found the story in a book and read it to myself, it didn't seem to live up to my longings for a story with that name; as indeed, how could it?

MLA CITATION

Welty, Eudora. "Clamorous to Learn." 1983. *The Norton Reader: An Anthology of Nonfiction.* Ed. Melissa A. Goldthwaite et al. 14th ed. New York: Norton, 2016. 409–13. Print.

QUESTIONS

1. Eudora Welty describes a number of strong women in the essay: her teachers, her mother, and a younger version of herself. What does this essay state or imply about their motives and ambitions? What kinds of power or opportunities do they have? What kinds of power or opportunities are they denied?

2. Analyze Welty's descriptions: what rhetorical or literary techniques does she use to evoke her teachers so vividly? Locate a few examples in the text.

3. In the final paragraph, Welty recalls her disappointment at missing Mrs. McWillie's reading of the English author John Ruskin's "The King of the Golden River."

Welty then concludes, "When in time I found the story in a book and read it to myself, it didn't seem to live up to my longings for a story with that name; as indeed, how could it?" Why do you think she was disappointed? (If you can, read Ruskin's story for yourself.)

4. Write a profile of a teacher who was important to you. Use techniques you learned from Welty to capture that teacher's motivations and ambitions, distinguishing quirks or characteristics, and personality.

LYNDA BARRY   *The Sanctuary of School*

I WAS 7 YEARS OLD the first time I snuck out of the house in the dark. It was winter and my parents had been fighting all night. They were short on money and long on relatives who kept "temporarily" moving into our house because they had nowhere else to go.

My brother and I were used to giving up our bedroom. We slept on the couch, something we actually liked because it put us that much closer to the light of our lives, our television.

At night when everyone was asleep, we lay on our pillows watching it with the sound off. We watched Steve Allen's[1] mouth moving. We watched Johnny Carson's[2] mouth moving. We watched movies filled with gangsters shooting machine guns into packed rooms, dying soldiers hurling a last grenade and beautiful women crying at windows. Then the sign-off finally came and we tried to sleep.

The morning I snuck out, I woke up filled with a panic about needing to get to school. The sun wasn't quite up yet but my anxiety was so fierce that I just got dressed, walked quietly across the kitchen and let myself out the back door.

5   It was quiet outside. Stars were still out. Nothing moved and no one was in the street. It was as if someone had turned the sound off on the world.

I walked the alley, breaking thin ice over the puddles with my shoes. I didn't know why I was walking to school in the dark. I didn't think about it. All I knew was a feeling of panic, like the panic that strikes kids when they realize they are lost.

A DARK OUTLINE

That feeling eased the moment I turned the corner and saw the dark outline of my school at the top of the hill. My school was made up of about 15 nonde-

Published in the New York Times *(1992). Lynda Barry is a cartoonist and author.*

1. Host of *The Tonight Show*, 1954–1956.
2. Host of *The Tonight Show Starring Johnny Carson*, 1962–1992.

script portable classrooms set down on a fenced concrete lot in a rundown Seattle neighborhood, but it had the most beautiful view of the Cascade Mountains. You could see them from anywhere on the playfield and you could see them from the windows of my classroom—Room 2.

I walked over to the monkey bars and hooked my arms around the cold metal. I stood for a long time just looking across Rainier Valley. The sky was beginning to whiten and I could hear a few birds.

Easy to Slip Away

In a perfect world my absence at home would not have gone unnoticed. I would have had two parents in a panic to locate me, instead of two parents in a panic to locate an answer to the hard question of survival during a deep financial and emotional crisis.

But in an overcrowded and unhappy home, it's incredibly easy for any child to slip away. The high levels of frustration, depression and anger in my house made my brother and me invisible. We were children with the sound turned off. And for us, as for the steadily increasing number of neglected children in this country, the only place where we could count on being noticed was at school.   10

"Hey there, young lady. Did you forget to go home last night?" It was Mr. Gunderson, our janitor, whom we all loved. He was nice and he was funny and he was old with white hair, thick glasses and an unbelievable number of keys. I could hear them jingling as he walked across the playfield. I felt incredibly happy to see him.

He let me push his wheeled garbage can between the different portables as he unlocked each room. He let me turn on the lights and raise the window shades and I saw my school slowly come to life. I saw Mrs. Holman, our school secretary, walk into the office without her orange lipstick on yet. She waved.

I saw the fifth-grade teacher, Mr. Cunningham, walking under the breezeway eating a hard roll. He waved.

And I saw my teacher, Mrs. Claire LeSane, walking toward us in a red coat and calling my name in a very happy and surprised way, and suddenly my throat got tight and my eyes stung and I ran toward her crying. It was something that surprised us both.

It's only thinking about it now, 28 years later, that I realize I was crying   15
from relief. I was with my teacher, and in a while I was going to sit at my desk, with my crayons and pencils and books and classmates all around me, and for the next six hours I was going to enjoy a thoroughly secure, warm and stable world. It was a world I absolutely relied on. Without it, I don't know where I would have gone that morning.

Mrs. LeSane asked me what was wrong and when I said "Nothing," she seemingly left it at that. But she asked me if I would carry her purse for her, an honor above all honors, and she asked if I wanted to come into Room 2 early and paint.

PAINTING'S POWER

She believed in the natural healing power of painting and drawing for troubled
children. In the back of her room there was always a drawing table and an easel
with plenty of supplies, and sometimes during the day she would come up to
you for what seemed like no good reason and quietly ask if you wanted to go to
the back table and "make some pictures for Mrs. LeSane." We all had a chance
at it—to sit apart from the class for a while to paint, draw and silently work out
impossible problems on 11 × 17 sheets of newsprint.

they would be more prone to take on intellectual identities if we encouraged them to do so at first on subjects that interest them rather than ones that interest us.

I offer my own adolescent experience as a case in point. Until I entered   5
college, I hated books and cared only for sports. The only reading I cared to do or could do was sports magazines, on which I became hooked, becoming a regular reader of *Sport* magazine in the late forties, *Sports Illustrated* when it began publishing in 1954, and the annual magazine guides to professional baseball, football, and basketball. I also loved the sports novels for boys of John R. Tunis and Clair Bee and autobiographies of sports stars like Joe DiMaggio's *Lucky to Be a Yankee* and Bob Feller's *Strikeout Story*. In short, I was your typical teenage anti-intellectual—or so, I believed for a long time. I have recently come to think, however, that my preference for sports over schoolwork was not anti-intellectualism so much as intellectualism by other means.

In the Chicago neighborhood I grew up in, which had become a melting pot after World War II, our block was solidly middle class, but just a block away—doubtless concentrated there by the real estate companies—were African Americans, Native Americans, and "hillbilly" whites who had recently fled postwar joblessness in the South and Appalachia. Negotiating this class boundary was a tricky matter. On the one hand, it was necessary to maintain the boundary between "clean-cut" boys like me and working-class "hoods," as we called them, which meant that it was good to be openly smart in a bookish sort of way. On the other hand. I was desperate for the approval of the hoods, whom I encountered daily on the playing field and in the neighborhood, and for this purpose it was not at all good to be book-smart. The hoods would turn on you if they sensed you were putting on airs over them: "Who you lookin' at, smart ass?" as a leather-jacketed youth once said to me as he relieved me of my pocket change along with my self-respect.

I grew up torn, then, between the need to prove I was smart and the fear of a beating if I proved it too well; between the need not to jeopardize my respectable future and the need to impress the hoods. As I lived it, the conflict came down to a choice between being physically tough and being verbal. For a boy in my neighborhood and elementary school, only being "tough" earned you complete legitimacy. I still recall endless, complicated debates in this period with my closest pals over who was "the toughest guy in the school." If you were less than negligible as a fighter, as I was, you settled for the next best thing, which was to be inarticulate, carefully hiding telltale marks of literacy like correct grammar and pronunciation.

In one way, then, it would be hard to imagine an adolescence more thoroughly anti-intellectual than mine. Yet in retrospect, I see that it's more complicated, that I and the 1950s themselves were not simply hostile toward intellectualism, but divided and ambivalent. When Marilyn Monroe[2] married the playwright Arthur Miller in 1956 after divorcing the retired baseball star

2. American movie star and celebrity (1926–1962).

Joe DiMaggio, the symbolic triumph of geek over jock suggested the way the wind was blowing. Even Elvis, according to his biographer Peter Guralnick, turns out to have supported Adlai over Ike in the presidential election of 1956.[3] "I don't dig the intellectual bit," he told reporters. "But I'm telling you, man, he knows the most" (327).

Though I too thought I did not "dig the intellectual bit," I see now that I was unwittingly in training for it. The germs had actually been planted in the seemingly philistine debates about which boys were the toughest. I see now that in the interminable analysis of sports teams, movies, and toughness that my friends and I engaged in—a type of analysis, needless to say, that the real toughs would never have stooped to—was already betraying an allegiance to the egg-head world. I was practicing being an intellectual before I knew that was what I wanted to be.

10   It was in these discussions with friends about toughness and sports, I think, and in my reading of sports books and magazines, that I began to learn the rudiments of the intellectual life: how to make an argument, weigh different kinds of evidence, move between particulars and generalizations, summarize the views of others, and enter a conversation about ideas. It was in reading and arguing about sports and toughness that I experienced what it felt like to propose a generalization, restate and respond to a counterargument, and perform other intellectualizing operations, including composing the kind of sentences I am writing now.

Only much later did it dawn on me that the sports world was more compelling than school because it was *more intellectual than school*, not less. Sports after all was full of challenging arguments, debates, problems for analysis, and intricate statistics that you could care about, as school conspicuously was not. I believe that street smarts beat out book smarts in our culture not because street smarts are nonintellectual, as we generally suppose, but because they satisfy an intellectual thirst more thoroughly than school culture, which seems pale and unreal.

They also satisfy the thirst for community. When you entered sports debates, you became part of a community that was not limited to your family and friends, but was national and public. Whereas schoolwork isolated you from others, the pennant race or Ted Williams's .400 batting average was something you could talk about with people you had never met. Sports introduced you not only to a culture steeped in argument, but to a public argument culture that transcended the personal. I can't blame my schools for failing to make intellectual culture resemble the Super Bowl, but I do fault them for failing to learn anything from the sports and entertainment worlds about how to organize and represent intellectual culture, how to exploit its gamelike element and turn it into arresting public spectacle that might have competed more successfully for my youthful attention.

3. Elvis Presley (1935–1977), American rock-and-roll star and movie actor; Republican Dwight D. "Ike" Eisenhower defeated Adlai Stevenson in 1952 to become the thirty-fourth president of the United States (1953–1961).

For here is another thing that never dawned on me and is still kept hidden from students, with tragic results: that the real intellectual world, the one that existed in the big world beyond school, is organized very much like the world of team sports, with rival texts, rival interpretations and evaluations of texts, rival theories of why they should be read and taught, and elaborate team competitions in which "fans" of writers, intellectual systems, methodologies, and -isms contend against each other.

To be sure, school contained plenty of competition, which became more invidious as one moved up the ladder (and has become even more so today with the advent of high-stakes testing). In this competition, points were scored not by making arguments, but by a show of information or vast reading, by grade-grubbing, or other forms of one-upmanship. School competition, in short, reproduced the less attractive features of sports culture without those that create close bonds and community.

And in distancing themselves from anything as enjoyable and absorbing as 15 sports, my schools missed the opportunity to capitalize on an element of drama and conflict that the intellectual world shares with sports. Consequently, I failed to see the parallels between the sports and academic worlds that could have helped me cross more readily from one argument culture to the other.

Sports is only one of the domains whose potential for literacy training (and not only for males) is seriously underestimated by educators, who see sports as competing with academic development rather than a route to it. But if this argument suggests why it is a good idea to assign readings and topics that are close to students' existing interests, it also suggests the limits of this tactic. For students who get excited about the chance to write about their passion for cars will often write as poorly and unreflectively on that topic as on Shakespeare or Plato. Here is the flip side of what I pointed out before: that there's no necessary relation between the degree of interest a student shows in a text or subject and the quality of thought or expression such a student manifests in writing or talking about it. The challenge, as college professor Ned Laff has put it, "is not simply to exploit students' nonacademic interests, but to get them to see those interests through academic eyes."

To say that students need to see their interests "through academic eyes" is to say that street smarts are not enough. Making students' nonacademic interests an object of academic study is useful, then, for getting students' attention and overcoming their boredom and alienation, but this tactic won't in itself necessarily move them closer to an academically rigorous treatment of those interests. On the other hand, inviting students to write about cars, sports, or clothing fashions does not have to be a pedagogical cop-out as long as students are required to see these interests "through academic eyes," that is, to think and write about cars, sports, and fashions in a reflective, analytical way, one that sees them as microcosms of what is going on in the wider culture.

If I am right, then schools and colleges are missing an opportunity when they do not encourage students to take their nonacademic interests as objects of academic study. It is self-defeating to decline to introduce any text or subject that figures to engage students who will otherwise tune out academic work entirely.

If a student cannot get interested in Mill's *On Liberty*[4] but will read *Sports Illus-trated* or *Vogue* or the hip-hop magazine *Source* with absorption, this is a strong argument for assigning the magazines over the classic. It's a good bet that if students get hooked on reading and writing by doing term papers on *Source*, they will eventually get to *On Liberty*. But even if they don't, the magazine reading will make them more literate and reflective than they would be otherwise. So it makes pedagogical sense to develop classroom units on sports, cars, fashions, rap music, and other such topics. Give me the student anytime who writes a sharply argued, sociologically acute analysis of an issue in *Source* over the student who writes a lifeless explication of *Hamlet* or Socrates' *Apology*.[5]

WORKS CITED

Cramer, Richard Ben. *Joe DiMaggio: The Hero's Life*. New York: Simon, 2000. Print.

DiMaggio, Joe. *Lucky to Be a Yankee*. New York: Bantam, 1949. Print.

Feller, Bob. *Strikeout Story*. New York: Bantam, 1948. Print.

Guralnick, Peter. *Last Train to Memphis: The Rise of Elvis Presley*. Boston: Little, Brown, 1994. Print.

Orwell, George. *A Collection of Essays*. New York: Harcourt, 1953. Print.

4. John Stuart Mill (1806–1873), British political economist and philosopher.
5. *Hamlet* (1603), a tragedy by William Shakespeare; Socrates (c. 469–399 B.C.E.), ancient Greek philosopher; the *Apology* was written by his student Plato.

MLA CITATION

Graff, Gerald. "Hidden Intellectualism." 2003. *The Norton Reader: An Anthology of Nonfiction*. Ed. Melissa A. Goldthwaite et al. 14th ed. New York: Norton, 2016. 418–22. Print.

QUESTIONS

1. Gerald Graff observes that through sports, he "experienced what it felt like to propose a generalization, restate and respond to a counterargument, and perform other intellectualizing operations" (paragraph 10). Where and how does Graff offer generalizations in this essay? Where and how does he restate and respond to the arguments of others or develop counterarguments? What other kinds of "intellectualizing operations" does he perform?

2. Graff and Roger Angell (pp. 320–28) both write about baseball. How are their perspectives similar? How are they different?

3. Frederick Douglass's "Learning to Read" (pp. 404–08) is also a literacy narrative: an account of how someone learned to read and write. Compare Graff's essay to this essay. Would you characterize Graff's essay as a literacy narrative? Why or why not?

4. In an essay of your own, summarize and respond to Graff's argument about intellectualism and what he calls "school culture" (paragraph 11). Consider writing about an activity or experience that fits the definition of what Graff might call "hidden intellectualism."

JONATHAN KOZOL   *Fremont High School*

REMONT HIGH SCHOOL in Los Angeles enrolls almost 5,000 students on a three-track schedule, with about 3,300 in attendance at a given time. The campus "sprawls across a city block, between San Pedro Street and Avalon Boulevard in South Central Los Angeles,"[1] the *Los Angeles Times* observes. A "neighborhood fortress, its perimeter protected by an eight-foot steel fence topped by spikes," the windows of the school are "shielded from gunfire by thick screens." According to teachers at the school, the average ninth grade student reads at fourth or fifth grade level. Nearly a third read at third grade level or below. About two-thirds of the ninth grade students drop out prior to twelfth grade.

There were 27 homerooms for the first-year students, nine homerooms for seniors at the time I visited in spring of 2003. Thirty-five to 40 classrooms, nearly a third of all the classrooms in the school, were located in portables.[2] Some classes also took place in converted storage closets—"windowless and nasty," said one of the counselors—or in converted shop rooms without blackboards. Class size was high, according to a teacher who had been here for six years and who invited me into her tenth grade social studies class. Nearly 220 classes had enrollments ranging between 33 and over 40 students. The class I visited had 40 students, almost all of whom were present on the day that I was there.

Unlike the staggered luncheon sessions I observed at Walton High, lunch was served in a single sitting to the students in this school. "It's physically impossible to feed 3,300 kids at once," the teacher said. "The line for kids to get their food is very long and the entire period lasts only 30 minutes. It takes them 15 minutes just to walk there from their classes and get through the line. They get 10 minutes probably to eat their meals. A lot of them don't try. You've been a teacher, so you can imagine what it does to students when they have no food to eat for an entire day. The schoolday here at Fremont is eight hours long."

For teachers, too, the schedule sounded punishing. "I have six classes every day, including my homeroom," she said. "I've had *more* than 40 students in a class some years. My average class this year is 36. I see more than 200 students every day. Classes start at seven-thirty. I don't usually leave until four or four-thirty. . . ."

High school students, when I meet them first, are often more reluctant than   5
the younger children are to open up their feelings and express their personal

From Jonathan Kozol's The Shame of the Nation: The Restoration of Apartheid Schooling in America (2005), *a book documenting the recent resurgence of social and racial inequality in America's public schools.*

1. Former designation of an area of Los Angeles associated with poverty and crime; in 2003 the area's name was changed to "South Los Angeles."
2. Portable classrooms; temporary buildings or trailers used for classroom space.

concerns; but hesitation on the part of students did not prove to be a problem in this class at Fremont High. The students knew I was a writer (they were told this by their teacher) and they took no time in getting down to matters that were on their minds.

"Can we talk about the bathrooms?" asked a student named Mireya.

In almost any classroom there are certain students who, by force of the directness or unusual sophistication of their way of speaking, tend to capture your attention from the start. Mireya later spoke insightfully of academic problems at the school, but her observations on the physical and personal embarrassments she and her schoolmates had to undergo cuts to the heart of questions of essential dignity or the denial of such dignity that kids in squalid schools like this one have to deal with.

Fremont High School, as court papers document, has "15 fewer bathrooms than the law requires." Of the limited number of bathrooms that are working in the school, "only one or two . . . are open and unlocked for girls to use." Long lines of girls are "waiting to use the bathrooms," which are generally "unclean" and "lack basic supplies," including toilet paper. Some of the classrooms "do not have air-conditioning," so that students "become red-faced and unable to concentrate" during "the extreme heat of summer." The rats observed by children in their elementary schools proliferate at Fremont High as well. "Rats in eleven . . . classrooms," maintenance records of the school report. "Rat droppings" are recorded "in the bins and drawers" of the high school's kitchen. "Hamburger buns" are being "eaten off [the] bread-delivery rack," school records note.

No matter how many times I read these tawdry details in court filings and depositions, I'm always surprised again to learn how often these unsanitary physical conditions are permitted to continue in a public school even after media accounts describe them vividly. But hearing of these conditions in Mireya's words was even more unsettling, in part because this student was so fragile-seeming and because the need even to speak of these indignities in front of me and all the other students seemed like an additional indignity.

10   "The problem is this," she carefully explained. "You're not allowed to use the bathroom during lunch, which is a 30-minute period. The only time that you're allowed to use it is between your classes." But "this is a huge building," she went on. "It has long corridors. If you have one class at one end of the building and your next class happens to be way down at the other end, you don't have time to use the bathroom and still get to class before it starts. So you go to your class and then you ask permission from your teacher to go to the bathroom and the teacher tells you, 'No. You had your chance between the periods. . . .'

"I feel embarrassed when I have to stand there and explain it to a teacher."

"This is the question," said a wiry-looking boy named Edward, leaning forward in his chair close to the door, a little to the right of where I stood. "Students are not animals, but even animals need to relieve themselves sometimes. We're in this building for eight hours. What do they think we're supposed to do?"

"It humiliates you," said Mireya, who went on to make the interesting statement that "the school provides solutions that don't actually work," and this idea was taken up by other students in describing course requirements within the school. A tall black student, for example, told me that she hoped to be a social worker or a doctor but was programmed into "Sewing Class" this year. She also had to take another course, called "Life Skills," which she told me was a very basic course—"a retarded class," to use her words—that "teaches things like the six continents," which she said she'd learned in elementary school.

When I asked her why she had to take these courses, she replied that she'd been told they were required, which reminded me of the response the sewing teacher I had met at Roosevelt Junior High School gave to the same question. As at Roosevelt, it turned out that this was not exactly so. What *was* required was that high school students take two courses in an area of study that was called "the Technical Arts," according to the teacher. At schools that served the middle class or upper middle class, this requirement was likely to be met by courses that had academic substance and, perhaps, some relevance to college preparation. At Beverly Hills High School,[3] for example, the technical arts requirement could be fulfilled by taking subjects such as residential architecture, the designing of commercial structures, broadcast journalism, advanced computer graphics, a sophisticated course in furniture design, carving and sculpture, or an honors course in engineering research and design. At Fremont High, in contrast, this requirement was far more likely to be met by courses that were basically vocational.

Mireya, for example, who had plans to go to college, told me that she had to take a sewing class last year and now was told she'd been assigned to take a class in hair-dressing as well. When I asked the teacher why Mireya could not skip these subjects and enroll in classes that would help her to pursue her college aspirations, she replied, "It isn't a question of what students want. It's what the school may have available. If all the other elective classes that a student wants to take are full, she has to take one of these classes if she wants to graduate." 15

A very small girl named Obie who had big blue-tinted glasses tilted up across her hair interrupted then to tell me with a kind of wild gusto that she took hair-dressing *twice!* When I expressed surprise that this was possible, she said there were two levels of hair-dressing offered here at Fremont High. "One is in hair-styling," she said. "The other is in braiding."

Mireya stared hard at this student for a moment and then suddenly began to cry. "I don't *want* to take hair-dressing. I did not need sewing either. I knew how to sew. My mother is a seamstress in a factory. I'm trying to go to college. I don't need to sew to go to college. My mother sews. I hoped for something else."

"What would you rather take?" I asked.

"I wanted to take an AP class,"[4] she answered.

Mireya's sudden tears elicited a strong reaction from one of the boys who had been silent up to now. A thin and dark-eyed student, named Fortino, with 20

---

3. Main public high school for Beverly Hills, an affluent city in the Los Angeles area.

4. Class that prepares students to take one of the College Board's "Advanced Placement" examinations, for which students may receive college credit or placement in advanced classes.

long hair down to his shoulders who was sitting on the left side of the class-room, he turned directly to Mireya.

"Listen to me," he said. "The owners of the sewing factories need laborers. Correct?"

"I guess they do," Mireya said.

"It's not going to be their own kids. Right?"

"Why not?" another student said.

25   "So they can grow beyond themselves," Mireya answered quietly. "But we remain the same."

"You're ghetto," said Fortino, "so we send you to the factory." He sat low in his desk chair, leaning on one elbow, his voice and dark eyes loaded with a cyni-cal intelligence. "You're ghetto—so you sew!"

"There are higher positions than these," said a student named Samantha.

"You're ghetto," said Fortino unrelentingly to her. "So sew!"

Mireya was still crying.

30   Several students spoke then of a problem about frequent substitute teachers, which was documented also in court papers. One strategy for staffing classes in these three- and four-track schools when substitutes could not be found was to assign a teacher who was not "on track"—that is, a teacher who was on vacation—to come back to school and fill in for the missing teacher. "Just yester-day I was subbing [for] a substitute who was subbing for a teacher who never shows up," a teacher told the ACLU[5] lawyers. "That's one scenario. . . ."

Obie told me that she stopped coming to class during the previous semes-ter because, out of her six teachers, three were substitutes. "Come on now! Like—hello? We live in a rich country? Like the richest country in the world? Hello?"

The teacher later told me that three substitutes in one semester, if the stu-dent's words were accurate, would be unusual. But "on average, every student has a substitute teacher in at least one class. Out of 180 teacher-slots, typically 25 or so cannot be filled and have to be assigned to substitutes."

Hair-dressing and sewing, it turned out, were not the only classes students at the school were taking that appeared to have no relevance to academic edu-cation. A number of the students, for example, said that they were taking what were known as "service classes" in which they would sit in on an academic class but didn't read the texts or do the lessons or participate in class activities but passed out books and did small errands for the teachers. They were given half-credits for these courses. Students received credits, too, for jobs they took out-side of school, in fast-food restaurants for instance, I was told. How, I wondered, was a credit earned or grade determined for a job like this outside of school? "Best behavior and great customer service," said a student who was working in a restaurant, as she explained the logic of it all to ACLU lawyers in her deposition.

5. American Civil Liberties Union, a nonprofit organization founded in 1920 to pro-tect rights guaranteed to individuals by the U.S. Constitution.

The teacher gave some other examples of the ways in which the students were shortchanged in academic terms. The year-round calendar, she said, gave these students 20 fewer schooldays than the students who attended school on normal calendars receive. In compensation, they attended classes for an extra hour, up until three-thirty, and students in the higher grades who had failed a course and had to take a make-up class remained here even later, until six, or sometimes up to nine.

"They come out of it just totally glassed-over," said the teacher, and, as one   35
result, most teachers could not realistically give extra homework to make up for fewer days of school attendance and, in fact, because the kids have been in school so long each day, she said, "are likely to give less."

Students who needed to use the library to do a research paper for a class ran into problems here as well, because, as a result of the tight scheduling of classes, they were given no free time to use the library except at lunch, or for 30 minutes after school, unless a teacher chose to bring a class into the library to do a research project during a class period. But this was frequently impossible because the library was often closed when it was being used for other purposes such as administration of examinations, typically for "make-up tests," as I was told. "It's been closed now for a week because they're using it for testing," said Samantha.

"They were using it for testing last week also," said Fortino, who reported that he had a research paper due for which he had to locate 20 sources but had made no progress on it yet because he could not get into the library.

"You have to remember," said the teacher, "that the school's in session all year long, so if repairs need to be made in wiring or something like that in the library, they have to do it while the kids are here. So at those times the library is closed. Then, if there's testing taking place in there, the library is closed. And if an AP teacher needs a place to do an AP prep, the library is closed. And sometimes when the teachers need a place to meet, the library is closed." In all, according to the school librarian, the library was closed more than a quarter of the year.

During a meeting with a group of teachers later in the afternoon, it was explained to me in greater detail how the overcrowding of the building limited course offerings for students. "Even when students *ask* to take a course that interests them and teachers want to teach it," said one member of the faculty—she gave the example of a class in women's studies she said she would like to teach—"the physical shortages of space repeatedly prevent this." Putting students into service classes, on the other hand, did not require extra space. So, instead of the enrichment students might have gained from taking an elective course that had some academic substance, they were obliged to sit through classes in which they were not enrolled and from which they said that they learned virtually nothing.

Mireya had asked her teacher for permission to stay in the room with us   40
during my meeting with the other teachers and remained right to the end. At five p.m., as I was about to leave the school, she stood beside the doorway of

the classroom as the teacher, who was giving me a ride, assembled all the work she would be taking home.

"Why is it," she asked, "that students who do not need what we need get so much more? And we who need it so much more get so much less?"

I told her I'd been asking the same question now for nearly 40 years and still had no good answer. She answered, maturely, that she did not think there was an answer.

MLA CITATION

Kozol, Jonathan. "Fremont High School." 2005. *The Norton Reader: An Anthology of Nonfiction.* Ed. Melissa A. Goldthwaite et al. 14th ed. New York: Norton, 2016. 423–28. Print.

QUESTIONS

1. Jonathan Kozol draws on various sorts of evidence in his portrait of Fremont High School: numerical data, court documents, comparisons to other schools, and testimony from teachers and students. How does he arrange his evidence? Which sort of evidence does he emphasize? Why?

2. Kozol adopts a journalistic style, but he also puts himself into the story. How does Kozol use the first person ("I")?

3. Kozol identifies many problems with Fremont High School, but he does not offer any solutions explicitly. Why? Of the problems he identifies, which are the most significant? What solutions do you think Kozol would support?

4. Using Kozol's essay as a model, write a portrait of a school that you know well.

CAROLINE BIRD   *College Is a Waste of Time and Money*

A GREAT MAJORITY of our nine million college students are not in school because they want to be or because they want to learn. They are there because it has become the thing to do or because college is a pleasant place to be; because it's the only way they can get parents or taxpayers to support them without working at a job they don't like; because Mother wanted them to go, or some other reason entirely irrelevant to the course of studies for which college is supposedly organized.

As I crisscross the United States lecturing on college campuses, I am dismayed to find that professors and administrators, when pressed for a candid opinion, estimate that no more than 25 percent of their students are turned on

From Caroline Bird's book The Case against College *(1975).*

by classwork. For the rest, college is at best a social center or aging vat, and at worst a young folks' home or even a prison that keeps them out of the mainstream of economic life for a few more years.

The premise—which I no longer accept—that college is the best place for all high-school graduates grew out of a noble American ideal. Just as the United States was the first nation to aspire to teach every small child to read and write, so, during the 1950s, we became the first and only great nation to aspire to higher education for all. During the '60s we damned the expense and built great state university systems as fast as we could. And adults—parents, employers, high-school counselors—began to push, shove and cajole youngsters to "get an education."

It became a mammoth industry, with taxpayers footing more than half the bill. By 1970, colleges and universities were spending more than 30 billion dollars annually. But still only half our high-school graduates were going on. According to estimates made by the economist Fritz Machlup, if we had been educating every young person until age 22 in that year of 1970, the bill for higher education would have reached 47.5 billion dollars, 12.5 billion more than the total corporate profits for the year.

Figures such as these have begun to make higher education for all look   5 financially prohibitive, particularly now when colleges are squeezed by the pressures of inflation and a drop-off in the growth of their traditional market.

Predictable demography has caught up with the university empire builders. Now that the record crop of postwar babies has graduated from college, the rate of growth of the student population has begun to decline. To keep their mammoth plants financially solvent, many institutions have begun to use hard-sell, Madison-Avenue techniques to attract students. They sell college like soap, promoting features they think students want: innovative programs, an environment conducive to meaningful personal relationships, and a curriculum so free that it doesn't sound like college at all.

Pleasing the customers is something new for college administrators. Colleges have always known that most students don't like to study, and that at least part of the time they are ambivalent about college, but before the student riots of the 1960s educators never thought it either right or necessary to pay any attention to student feelings. But when students rebelling against the Vietnam war and the draft discovered they could disrupt a campus completely, administrators had to act on some student complaints. Few understood that the protests had tapped the basic discontent with college itself, a discontent that did not go away when the riots subsided.

Today students protest individually rather than in concert. They turn inward and withdraw from active participation. They drop out to travel to India or to feed themselves on subsistence farms. Some refuse to go to college at all. Most, of course, have neither the funds nor the self-confidence for constructive articulation of their discontent. They simply hang around college unhappily and reluctantly.

All across the country, I have been overwhelmed by the prevailing sadness on American campuses. Too many young people speak little, and then only in

drowned voices. Sometimes the mood surfaces as diffidence, wariness, or coolness, but whatever its form, it looks like a defense mechanism, and that rings
a bell. This is the way it used to be with women, and just as society had systematically damaged women by insisting that their proper place was in the
home, so we may be systematically damaging 18-year-olds by insisting that their
proper place is in college.

10   Campus watchers everywhere know what I mean when I say students are
sad, but they don't agree on the reason for it. During the Vietnam war some
ascribed the sadness to the draft; now others blame affluence, or say it has
something to do with permissive upbringing.

           Not satisfied with any of these explanations, I looked for some answers with
the journalistic tools of my trade—scholarly studies, economic analyses, the
historical record, the opinions of the especially knowledgeable, conversations
with parents, professors, college administrators, and employers, all of whom
spoke as alumni too. Mostly I learned from my interviews with hundreds of
young people on and off campuses all over the country.

           My unnerving conclusion is that students are sad because they are not
needed. Somewhere between the nursery and the employment office, they
become unwanted adults. No one has anything in particular against them. But
no one knows what to do with them either. We already have too many people
in the world of the 1970s, and there is no room for so many newly minted
18-year-olds. So we temporarily get them out of the way by sending them to
college where in fact only a few belong.

           To make it more palatable, we fool ourselves into believing that we are
sending them there for their own best interests, and that it's good for them,
like spinach. Some, of course, learn to like it, but most wind up preferring green
peas.

           Educators admit as much. Nevitt Sanford, distinguished student of higher
education, says students feel they are "capitulating to a kind of voluntary servitude." Some of them talk about their time in college as if it were a sentence
to be served. I listened to a 1970 Mount Holyoke graduate: "For two years I
was really interested in science, but in my junior and senior years I just kept
saying, 'I've done two years; I'm going to finish.' When I got out I made up my
mind that I wasn't going to school anymore because so many of my courses had
been bullshit."

15   But bad as it is, college is often preferable to a far worse fate. It is better
than the drudgery of an uninspiring nine-to-five job, and better than doing
nothing when no jobs are available. For some young people, it is a graceful way
to get away from home and become independent without losing the financial
support of their parents. And sometimes it is the only alternative to an intolerable home situation.

           It is difficult to assess how many students are in college reluctantly. The
conservative Carnegie Commission estimates from 5 to 30 percent. Sol Linow-
itz, who was once chairman of a special committee on campus tension of the
American Council on Education, found that "a significant number were not
happy with their college experience because they felt they were there only in

order to get the 'ticket to the big show' rather than to spend the years as pro-
ductively as they otherwise could."

Older alumni will identify with Richard Baloga, a policeman's son, who
stayed in school even though he "hated it" because he thought it would do him
some good. But fewer students each year feel this way. Daniel Yankelovich
has surveyed undergraduate attitudes for a number of years, and reported in
1971 that 74 percent thought education was "very important." But just two
years earlier, 80 percent thought so.

The doubters don't mind speaking up. Leon Lefkowitz, chairman of the
department of social studies at Central High School in Valley Stream, New
York, interviewed 300 college students at random, and reports that 200 of them
didn't think that the education they were getting was worth the effort. "In two
years I'll pick up a diploma," said one student, "and I can honestly say it was a
waste of my father's bread."

Nowadays, says one sociologist, you don't have to have a reason for going
to college; it's an institution. His definition of an institution is an arrangement
everyone accepts without question; the burden of proof is not on why you go,
but why anyone thinks there might be a reason for not going. The implication
is that an 18-year-old is too young and confused to know what he wants to do,
and that he should listen to those who know best and go to college.

I don't agree. I believe that college has to be judged not on what other   20
people think is good for students, but on how good it feels to the students
themselves.

I believe that people have an inside view of what's good for them. If a child
doesn't want to go to school some morning, better let him stay at home, at least
until you find out why. Maybe he knows something you don't. It's the same with
college. If high-school graduates don't want to go, or if they don't want to go
right away, they may perceive more clearly than their elders that college is not
for them. It is no longer obvious that adolescents are best off studying a core
curriculum that was constructed when all educated men could agree on what
made them educated, or that professors, advisors, or parents can be of any particular help to young people in choosing a major or a career. High-school graduates see college graduates driving cabs, and decide it's not worth going. College
students find no intellectual stimulation in their studies and drop out.

If students believe that college isn't necessarily good for them, you can't
expect them to stay on for the general good of mankind. They don't go to school
to beat the Russians to Jupiter, improve the national defense, increase the GNP,
or create a new market for the arts—to mention some of the benefits taxpayers
are supposed to get for supporting higher education.

Nor should we expect to bring about social equality by putting all young
people through four years of academic rigor. At best, it's a roundabout and
expensive way to narrow the gap between the highest and lowest in our society
anyway. At worst, it is unconsciously elitist. Equalizing opportunity through
universal higher education subjects the whole population to the intellectual
mode natural only to a few. It violates the fundamental egalitarian principle of
respect for the differences between people.

Of course, most parents aren't thinking of the "higher" good at all. They send their children to college because they are convinced young people benefit financially from those four years of higher education. But if money is the only goal, college is the dumbest investment you can make. I say this because a young banker in Poughkeepsie, New York, Stephen G. Necel, used a computer to compare college as an investment with other investments available in 1974 and college did not come out on top.

25   For the sake of argument, the two of us invented a young man whose rich uncle gave him, in cold cash, the cost of a four-year education at any college he chose, but the young man didn't have to spend the money on college. After bales of computer paper, we had our mythical student write to his uncle: "Since you said I could spend the money foolishly if I wished, I am going to blow it all on Princeton."

The much respected financial columnist Sylvia Porter echoed the common assumption when she said last year, "A college education is among the very best investments you can make in your entire life." But the truth is not quite so rosy, even if we assume that the Census Bureau is correct when it says that as of 1972, a man who completed four years of college would expect to earn $199,000 more between the ages of 22 and 64 than a man who had only a high-school diploma.

If a 1972 Princeton-bound high-school graduate had put the $34,181 that his four years of college would have cost him into a savings bank at 7.5 per cent interest compounded daily, he would have had at age 64 a total of $1,129,200, or $528,200 more than the earnings of a male college graduate, and more than five times as much as the $199,000 extra the more educated man could expect to earn between 22 and 64.

The big advantage of getting your college money in cash now is that you can invest it in something that has a higher return than a diploma. For instance, a Princeton-bound high-school graduate of 1972 who liked fooling around with cars could have banked his $34,181, and gone to work at the local garage at close to $1,000 more per year than the average high-school graduate. Meanwhile, as he was learning to be an expert auto mechanic, his money would be ticking away in the bank. When he became 28, he would have earned $7,199 less on his job from age 22 to 28 than his college-educated friend, but he would have had $73,113 in his passbook—enough to buy out his boss, go into the used-car business, or acquire his own new-car dealership. If successful in business, he could expect to make more than the average college graduate. And if he had the brains to get into Princeton, he would be just as likely to make money without the four years spent on campus. Unfortunately, few college-bound high-school graduates get the opportunity to bank such a large sum of money, and then wait for it to make them rich. And few parents are sophisticated enough to understand that in financial returns alone, their children would be better off with the money than with the education.

Rates of return and dollar signs on education are fascinating brain teasers, but obviously there is a certain unreality to the game. Quite aside from the noneconomic benefits of college, and these should loom larger once the dollars are cleared away, there are grave difficulties in assigning a dollar value to college at all.

In fact there is no real evidence that the higher income of college gradu-   30
ates is due to college. College may simply attract people who are slated to earn more money anyway; those with higher IQs, better family backgrounds, a more enterprising temperament. No one who has wrestled with the problem is prepared to attribute all of the higher income to the impact of college itself.

Christopher Jencks, author of *Inequality,* a book that assesses the effect of family and schooling in America, believes that education in general accounts for less than half of the difference in income in the American population. "The biggest single source of income differences," writes Jencks, "seems to be the fact that men from high-status families have higher incomes than men from low-status families even when they enter the same occupations, have the same amount of education, and have the same test scores."

Jacob Mincer of the National Bureau of Economic Research and Columbia University states flatly that of "20 to 30 percent of students at any level, the additional schooling has been a waste, at least in terms of earnings." College fails to work its income-raising magic for almost a third of those who go. More than half of those people in 1972 who earned $15,000 or more reached that comfortable bracket without the benefit of a college diploma. Jencks says that financial success in the U.S. depends a good deal on luck, and the most sophisticated regression analyses have yet to demonstrate otherwise.

But most of today's students don't go to college to earn more money anyway. In 1968, when jobs were easy to get, Daniel Yankelovich made his first nationwide survey of students. Sixty-five percent of them said they "would welcome less emphasis on money." By 1973, when jobs were scarce, that figure jumped to 80 percent.

The young are not alone. Americans today are all looking less to the pay of a job than to the work itself. They want "interesting" work that permits them "to make a contribution," "express themselves" and "use their special abilities," and they think college will help them find it.

Jerry Darring of Indianapolis knows what it is to make a dollar. He worked   35
with his father in the family plumbing business, on the line at Chevrolet, and in the Chrysler foundry. He quit these jobs to enter Wright State University in Dayton, Ohio, because "in a job like that a person only has time to work, and after that he's so tired that he can't do anything else but come home and go to sleep."

Jerry came to college to find work "helping people." And he is perfectly willing to spend the dollars he earns at dull, well-paid work to prepare for lower-paid work that offers the reward of service to others.

Jerry's case is not unusual. No one works for money alone. In order to deal with the nonmonetary rewards of work, economists have coined the concept of "psychic income," which according to one economic dictionary means "income that is reckoned in terms of pleasure, satisfaction, or general feelings of euphoria."

Psychic income is primarily what college students mean when they talk about getting a good job. During the most affluent years of the late 1960s and early 1970s college students told their placement officers that they wanted to be researchers, college professors, artists, city planners, social workers, poets, book publishers, archeologists, ballet dancers, or authors.

The psychic income of these and other occupations popular with students is so high that these jobs can be filled without offering high salaries. According to one study, 93 percent of urban university professors would choose the same vocation again if they had the chance, compared with only 16 per cent of unskilled auto workers. Even though the monetary gap between college professor and auto worker is now surprisingly small, the difference in psychic income is enormous.

40   But colleges fail to warn students that jobs of these kinds are hard to come by, even for qualified applicants, and they rarely accept the responsibility of helping students choose a career that will lead to a job. When a young person says he is interested in helping people, his counselor tells him to become a psychologist. But jobs in psychology are scarce. The Department of Labor, for instance, estimates there will be 4,300 new jobs for psychologists in 1975 while colleges are expected to turn out 58,430 B.A.s in psychology that year.

Of 30 psych majors who reported back to Vassar what they were doing a year after graduation in 1972, only five had jobs in which they could possibly use their courses in psychology, and two of these were working for Vassar.

The outlook isn't much better for students majoring in other psychic-pay disciplines: sociology, English, journalism, anthropology, forestry, education. Whatever college graduates want to do, most of them are going to wind up doing what there is to do.

John Shingleton, director of placement at Michigan State University, accuses the academic community of outright hypocrisy. "Educators have never said, 'Go to college and get a good job,' but this has been implied, and now students expect it. . . . If we care what happens to students after college, then let's get involved with what should be one of the basic purposes of education: career preparation."

In the 1970s, some of the more practical professors began to see that jobs for graduates meant jobs for professors too. Meanwhile, students themselves reacted to the shrinking job market, and a "new vocationalism" exploded on campus. The press welcomed the change as a return to the ethic of achievement and service. Students were still idealistic, the reporters wrote, but they now saw that they could best make the world better by healing the sick as physicians or righting individual wrongs as lawyers.

45   But there are no guarantees in these professions either. The American Enterprise Institute estimated in 1971 that there would be more than the target ratio of 100 doctors for every 100,000 people in the population by 1980. And the odds are little better for would-be lawyers. Law schools are already graduating twice as many new lawyers every year as the Department of Labor thinks will be needed, and the oversupply is growing every year.

And it's not at all apparent that what is actually learned in a "professional" education is necessary for success. Teachers, engineers and others I talked to said they find that on the job they rarely use what they learned in school. In order to see how well college prepared engineers and scientists for actual paid work in their fields, The Carnegie Commission queried all the employees with degrees in these fields in two large firms. Only one in five said the work they were doing bore a "very close relationship" to their college studies, while almost a third saw "very little relationship at all." An overwhelming majority could think of many people who were doing their same work, but had majored in different fields.

Majors in nontechnical fields report even less relationship between their studies and their jobs. Charles Lawrence, a communications major in college and now the producer of "Kennedy & Co.," the Chicago morning television show, says, "You have to learn all that stuff and you never use it again. I learned my job doing it." Others employed as architects, nurses, teachers and other members of the so-called learned professions report the same thing.

Most college administrators admit that they don't prepare their graduates for the job market. "I just wish I had the guts to tell parents that when you get out of this place you aren't prepared to do anything," the academic head of a famous liberal-arts college told us. Fortunately, for him, most people believe that you don't have to defend a liberal-arts education on those grounds. A liberal-arts education is supposed to provide you with a value system, a standard, a set of ideas, not a job. "Like Christianity, the liberal arts are seldom practiced and would probably be hated by the majority of the populace if they were," said one defender.

The analogy is apt. The fact is, of course, that the liberal arts are a religion in every sense of that term. When people talk about them, their language becomes elevated, metaphorical, extravagant, theoretical and reverent. And faith in personal salvation by the liberal arts is professed in a creed intoned on ceremonial occasions such as commencements.

If the liberal arts are a religious faith, the professors are its priests. But disseminating ideas in a four-year college curriculum is slow and most expensive. If you want to learn about Milton, Camus, or even Margaret Mead you can find them in paperback books, the public library, and even on television.   50

And when most people talk about the value of a college education, they are not talking about great books. When at Harvard commencement, the president welcomes the new graduates into "the fellowship of educated men and women," what he could be saying is, "Here is a piece of paper that is a passport to jobs, power and instant prestige." As Glenn Bassett, a personnel specialist at G.E. says, "In some parts of G.E., a college degree appears completely irrelevant to selection to, say, a manager's job. In most, however, it is a ticket of admission."

But now that we have doubled the number of young people attending college, a diploma cannot guarantee even that. The most charitable conclusion we can reach is that college probably has very little, if any, effect on people and things at all. Today, the false premises are easy to see:

First, college doesn't make people intelligent, ambitious, happy, or liberal. It's the other way around. Intelligent, ambitious, happy, liberal people are attracted to higher education in the first place.

Second, college can't claim much credit for the learning experiences that really change students while they are there. Jobs, friends, history, and most of all the sheer passage of time have as big an impact as anything even indirectly related to the campus.

55   Third, colleges have changed so radically that a freshman entering in the fall of 1974 can't be sure to gain even the limited value research studies assigned to colleges in the '60s. The sheer size of undergraduate campuses of the 1970s makes college even less stimulating now than it was 10 years ago. Today even motivated students are disappointed with their college courses and professors.

Finally, a college diploma no longer opens as many vocational doors. Employers are beginning to realize that when they pay extra for someone with a diploma, they are paying only for an empty credential. The fact is that most of the work for which employers now expect college training is now or has been capably done in the past by people without higher educations.

College, then, may be a good place for those few young people who are really drawn to academic work, who would rather read than eat, but it has become too expensive, in money, time, and intellectual effort to serve as a holding pen for large numbers of our young. We ought to make it possible for those reluctant, unhappy students to find alternative ways of growing up, and more realistic preparation for the years ahead.

MLA CITATION

Bird, Caroline. "College Is a Waste of Time and Money." 1975. *The Norton Reader: An Anthology of Nonfiction*. Ed. Melissa A. Goldthwaite et al. 14th ed. New York: Norton, 2016. 428–36. Print.

QUESTIONS

1. Caroline Bird published this article four decades ago. How are today's college students similar to or different from the ones Bird writes about?

2. Much of Bird's article focuses on the dubious economic value of a college education. Are there reasons beyond (or in addition to) economics why you or your classmates are attending college? To what extent does Bird consider or ignore these other reasons?

3. In paragraphs 48–50, Bird compares liberal arts education to religion. Why does she make this comparison? What do you think her attitude is toward the liberal arts? Is it similar to or different from yours?

4. In paragraph 6, Bird discusses the hard-sell advertising techniques of many academic institutions. Look into your own school's "advertising techniques" (view books, pamphlets, information sent to homes and high schools, websites, and so on). How do these sources present the school to parents and potential students? Write an analysis of one of these sources.

WILLIAM ZINSSER *College Pressures*

Dear Carlos: I desperately need a dean's excuse for my chem midterm which will begin in about 1 hour. All I can say is that I totally blew it this week. I've fallen incredibly, inconceivably behind.

Carlos: Help! I'm anxious to hear from you. I'll be in my room and won't leave it until I hear from you. Tomorrow is the last day for . . .

Carlos: I left town because I started bugging out again. I stayed up all night to finish a take-home make-up exam & am typing it to hand in on the 10th. It was due on the 5th. P.S. I'm going to the dentist. Pain is pretty bad.

Carlos: Probably by Friday I'll be able to get back to my studies. Right now I'm going to take a long walk. This whole thing has taken a lot out of me.

Carlos: I'm really up the proverbial creek. The problem is I really *bombed* the history final. Since I need that course for my major I . . .

Carlos: Here follows a tale of woe. I went home this weekend, had to help my Mom, & caught a fever so didn't have much time to study. My professor . . .

Carlos: Aargh! Trouble. Nothing original but everything's piling up at once. To be brief, my job interview . . .

Hey Carlos, good news! I've got mononucleosis.

Who are these wretched supplicants, scribbling notes so laden with anxiety, seeking such miracles of postponement and balm? They are men and women who belong to Branford College, one of the twelve residential colleges at Yale University, and the messages are just a few of the hundreds that they left for their dean, Carlos Hortas—often slipped under his door at 4 A.M.—last year.

But students like the ones who wrote those notes can also be found on campuses from coast to coast—especially in New England and at many other private colleges across the country that have high academic standards and highly motivated students. Nobody could doubt that the notes are real. In their urgency and their gallows humor they are authentic voices of a generation that is panicky to succeed.

My own connection with the message writers is that I am master of Branford College. I live in its Gothic quadrangle and know the students well. (We have 485 of them.) I am privy to their hopes and fears—and also to their stereo music and their piercing cries in the dead of night ("Does anybody *ca-a-are?*"). If they went to Carlos to ask how to get through tomorrow, they come to me to ask how to get through the rest of their lives.

Mainly I try to remind them that the road ahead is a long one and that it will have more unexpected turns than they think. There will be plenty of time to change jobs, change careers, change whole attitudes and approaches. They don't want to hear such liberating news. They want a map—right now—that

Written when William Zinsser was head of a residential college at Yale University and published in a small circulation bimonthly magazine about rural life, Blair and Ketchum's Country Journal *(1979), which has since ceased publication.*

they can follow unswervingly to career security, financial security, Social Security and, presumably, a prepaid grave.

5   What I wish for all students is some release from the clammy grip of the future. I wish them a chance to savor each segment of their education as an experience in itself and not as a grim preparation for the next step. I wish them the right to experiment, to trip and fall, to learn that defeat is as instructive as victory and is not the end of the world.

My wish, of course, is naive. One of the few rights that America does not proclaim is the right to fail. Achievement is the national god, venerated in our media—the million-dollar athlete, the wealthy executive—and glorified in our praise of possessions. In the presence of such a potent state religion, the young are growing up old.

I see four kinds of pressure working on college students today: economic pressure, parental pressure, peer pressure, and self-induced pressure. It is easy to look around for villains—to blame the colleges for charging too much money, the professors for assigning too much work, the parents for pushing their children too far, the students for driving themselves too hard. But there are no villains; only victims.

"In the late 1960s," one dean told me, "the typical question that I got from students was 'Why is there so much suffering in the world?' or 'How can I make a contribution?' Today it's 'Do you think it would look better for getting into law school if I did a double major in history and political science, or just majored in one of them?'" Many other deans confirmed this pattern. One said: "They're trying to find an edge—the intangible something that will look better on paper if two students are about equal."

Note the emphasis on looking better. The transcript has become a sacred document, the passport to security. How one appears on paper is more important than how one appears in person. A is for Admirable and B is for Borderline, even though, in Yale's official system of grading, A means "excellent" and B means "very good." Today, looking very good is no longer good enough, especially for students who hope to go on to law school or medical school. They know that entrance into the better schools will be an entrance into the better law firms and better medical practices where they will make a lot of money. They also know that the odds are harsh. Yale Law School, for instance, matriculates 170 students from an applicant pool of 3,700; Harvard enrolls 550 from a pool of 7,000.

10   It's all very well for those of us who write letters of recommendation for our students to stress the qualities of humanity that will make them good lawyers or doctors. And it's nice to think that admission officers are really reading our letters and looking for the extra dimension of commitment or concern. Still, it would be hard for a student not to visualize these officers shuffling so many transcripts studded with As that they regard a B as positively shameful.

The pressure is almost as heavy on students who just want to graduate and get a job. Long gone are the days of the "gentleman's C," when students journeyed through college with a certain relaxation, sampling a wide variety of courses—music, art, philosophy, classics, anthropology, poetry, religion—that would send them out as liberally educated men and women. If I were an employer I would rather employ graduates who have this range and curiosity than those who narrowly pursued safe subjects and high grades. I know countless students whose inquiring minds exhilarate me. I like to hear the play of their ideas. I don't know if they are getting As or Cs, and I don't care. I also like them as people. The country needs them, and they will find satisfying jobs. I tell them to relax. They can't.

Nor can I blame them. They live in a brutal economy. Tuition, room, and board at most private colleges now comes to at least $7,000, not counting books and fees. This might seem to suggest that the colleges are getting rich. But they are equally battered by inflation. Tuition covers only 60 percent of what it costs to educate a student, and ordinarily the remainder comes from what colleges receive in endowments, grants, and gifts. Now the remainder keeps being swallowed by the cruel costs—higher every year—of just opening the doors. Heating oil is up. Insurance is up. Postage is up. Health-premium costs are up. Everything is up. Deficits are up. We are witnessing in America the creation of a brotherhood of paupers—colleges, parents, and students, joined by the common bond of debt.

Today it is not unusual for a student, even if he works part time at college and full time during the summer, to accrue $5,000 in loans after four years— loans that he must start to repay within one year after graduation. Exhorted at commencement to go forth into the world, he is already behind as he goes forth. How could he not feel under pressure throughout college to prepare for this day of reckoning? I have used "he," incidentally, only for brevity. Women at Yale are under no less pressure to justify their expensive education to themselves, their parents, and society. In fact, they are probably under more pressure. For although they leave college superbly equipped to bring fresh leadership to traditionally male jobs, society hasn't yet caught up with this fact.

Along with economic pressure goes parental pressure. Inevitably, the two are deeply intertwined.

I see many students taking pre-medical courses with joyless tenacity. They 15 go off to their labs as if they were going to the dentist. It saddens me because I know them in other corners of their life as cheerful people.

"Do you want to go to medical school?" I ask them.

"I guess so," they say, without conviction, or "Not really."

"Then why are you going?"

"Well, my parents want me to be a doctor. They're paying all this money and . . ."

Poor students, poor parents. They are caught in one of the oldest webs of 20 love and duty and guilt. The parents mean well; they are trying to steer their sons and daughters toward a secure future. But the sons and daughters want to major in history or classics or philosophy—subjects with no "practical" value. Where's the payoff on the humanities? It's not easy to persuade such loving parents that the humanities do indeed pay off. The intellectual faculties developed by studying subjects like history and classics—an ability to synthesize and relate, to weigh cause and effect, to see events in perspective—are just the faculties that make creative leaders in business or almost any general field. Still, many fathers would rather put their money on courses that point toward a specific profession—courses that are pre-law, pre-medical, pre-business, or, as I sometimes heard it put, "pre-rich."

But the pressure on students is severe. They are truly torn. One part of them feels obligated to fulfill their parents' expectations; after all, their parents are older and presumably wiser. Another part tells them that the expectations that are right for their parents are not right for them.

I know a student who wants to be an artist. She is very obviously an artist and will be a good one—she has already had several modest local exhibits. Meanwhile she is growing as a well-rounded person and taking humanistic subjects that will enrich the inner resources out of which her art will grow. But her father is strongly opposed. He thinks that an artist is a "dumb" thing to be. The student vacillates and tries to please everybody. She keeps up with her art somewhat furtively and takes some of the "dumb" courses her father wants her to take—at least they are dumb courses for her. She is a free spirit on a campus of tense students—no small achievement in itself—and she deserves to follow her muse.

Peer pressure and self-induced pressure are also intertwined, and they begin almost at the beginning of freshman year.

"I had a freshman student I'll call Linda," one dean told me, "who came in and said she was under terrible pressure because her roommate, Barbara, was much brighter and studied all the time. I couldn't tell her that Barbara had come in two hours earlier to say the same thing about Linda."

25   The story is almost funny—except that it's not. It's symptomatic of all the pressures put together. When every student thinks every other student is working harder and doing better, the only solution is to study harder still. I see students going off to the library every night after dinner and coming back when it closes at midnight. I wish they would sometimes forget about their peers and go to a movie. I hear the clacking of typewriters in the hours before dawn. I see the tension in their eyes when exams are approaching and papers are due: *Will I get everything done?*

Probably they won't. They will get sick. They will get "blocked." They will sleep. They will oversleep. They will bug out. *Hey Carlos, help!*

Part of the problem is that they do more than they are expected to do. A professor will assign five-page papers. Several students will start writing ten-page papers to impress him. Then more students will write ten-page papers, and a few will raise the ante to fifteen. Pity the poor student who is still just doing the assignment.

"Once you have twenty or thirty percent of the student population deliberately overexerting," one dean points out, "it's bad for everybody. When a teacher gets more and more effort from his class, the student who is doing normal work can be perceived as not doing well. The tactic works, psychologically."

Why can't the professor just cut back and not accept longer papers? He can, and he probably will. But by then the term will be half over and the damage done. Grade fever is highly contagious and not easily reversed. Besides, the professor's main concern is with his course. He knows his students only in relation to the course and doesn't know that they are also overexerting in their other courses. Nor is it really his business. He didn't sign up for dealing with the student as a whole person and with all the emotional baggage the student brought along from home. That's what deans, masters, chaplains, and psychiatrists are for.

To some extent this is nothing new: a certain number of professors have   30
always been self-contained islands of scholarship and shyness, more comfortable with books than with people. But the new pauperism has widened the gap still further, for professors who actually like to spend time with students don't have as much time to spend. They also are overexerting. If they are young, they are busy trying to publish in order not to perish, hanging by their finger nails onto a shrinking profession. If they are old and tenured, they are buried under the duties of administering departments—as departmental chairmen or members of committees—that have been thinned out by the budgetary axe.

Ultimately it will be the students' own business to break the circles in which they are trapped. They are too young to be prisoners of their parents' dreams and their classmates' fears. They must be jolted into believing in themselves as unique men and women who have the power to shape their own future.

"Violence is being done to the undergraduate experience," says Carlos Hortas. "College should be open-ended: at the end it should open many, many roads. Instead, students are choosing their goal in advance, and their choices narrow as they go along. It's almost as if they think that the country has been codified in the type of jobs that exist—that they've got to fit into certain slots. Therefore, fit into the best-paying slot.

"They ought to take chances. Not taking chances will lead to a life of colorless mediocrity. They'll be comfortable. But something in the spirit will be missing."

I have painted too drab a portrait of today's students, making them seem a solemn lot. That is only half of their story; if they were so dreary I wouldn't so thoroughly enjoy their company. The other half is that they are easy to like. They are quick to laugh and to offer friendship. They are not introverts. They are unusually kind and are more considerate of one another than any student generation I have known.

Nor are they so obsessed with their studies that they avoid sports and extra-   35
curricular activities. On the contrary, they juggle their crowded hours to play on a variety of teams, perform with musical and dramatic groups, and write for campus publications. But this in turn is one more cause of anxiety. There are too many choices. Academically, they have 1,300 courses to select from; outside class they have to decide how much spare time they can spare and how to spend it.

This means that they engage in fewer extracurricular pursuits than their predecessors did. If they want to row on the crew and play in the symphony they will eliminate one; in the '60s they would have done both. They also tend to choose activities that are self-limiting. Drama, for instance, is flourishing in all twelve of Yale's residential colleges as it never has before. Students hurl themselves into these productions—as actors, directors, carpenters, and technicians—with a dedication to create the best possible play, knowing that the day will come when the run will end and they can get back to their studies.

They also can't afford to be the willing slave of organizations like the *Yale Daily News*. Last spring at the one-hundredth anniversary banquet of that paper—whose past chairmen include such once and future kings as Potter Stewart, Kingman Brewster, and William F. Buckley, Jr.—much was made of the fact that the editorial staff used to be small and totally committed and that "newsies" routinely worked fifty hours a week. In effect they belonged to a club; Newsies is how they defined themselves at Yale. Today's student will write one or two articles a week, when he can, and he defines himself as a student. I've never heard the word Newsie except at the banquet.

If I have described the modern undergraduate primarily as a driven creature who is largely ignoring the blithe spirit inside who keeps trying to come out and play, it's because that's where the crunch is, not only at Yale but throughout American education. It's why I think we should all be worried about the values that are nurturing a generation so fearful of risk and so goal-obsessed at such an early age.

I tell students that there is no one "right" way to get ahead—that each of them is a different person, starting from a different point and bound for a different destination. I tell them that change is a tonic and that all the slots are not codified nor the frontiers closed. One of my ways of telling them is to invite men and women who have achieved success outside the academic world to come and talk informally with my students during the year. They are heads of companies or ad agencies, editors of magazines, politicians, public officials, television magnates, labor leaders, business executives, Broadway producers, artists, writers, economists, photographers, scientists, historians—a mixed bag of achievers.

40   I ask them to say a few words about how they got started. The students assume that they started in their present profession and knew all along that it was what they wanted to do. Luckily for me, most of them got into their field by a circuitous route, to their surprise, after many detours. The students are startled. They can hardly conceive of a career that was not pre-planned. They can hardly imagine allowing the hand of God or chance to nudge them down some unforeseen trail.

MLA CITATION

Zinsser, William. "College Pressures." 1979. *The Norton Reader: An Anthology of Nonfiction.* Ed. Melissa A. Goldthwaite et al. 14th ed. New York: Norton, 2016. 437–42. Print.

QUESTIONS

1. What are the four kinds of pressure William Zinsser describes for the 1970s? Are they the same kinds of pressure that trouble students today, or have new ones taken their place?

2. Compare Zinsser's attitude toward college to Caroline Bird's (pp. 428–36). In what ways do they agree? In what ways do they disagree?

3. Write an essay in which you explain how you have experienced and handled the pressures of college.

ADRIENNE RICH   *Taking Women Students Seriously*

I SEE MY FUNCTION HERE TODAY as one of trying to create a context, delineate a background, against which we might talk about women as students and students as women. I would like to speak for a while about this background, and then I hope that we can have, not so much a question period, as a raising of concerns, a sharing of questions for which we as yet may have no answers, an opening of conversations which will go on and on.

When I went to teach at Douglass, a women's college,[1] it was with a particular background which I would like briefly to describe to you. I had graduated from an all-girls' school in the 1940s, where the head and the majority of the faculty were independent, unmarried women. One or two held doctorates, but had been forced by the Depression (and by the fact that they were women) to take secondary school teaching jobs. These women cared a great deal about the life of the mind, and they gave a great deal of time and energy—beyond any limit of teaching hours—to those of us who showed special intellectual interest or ability. We were taken to libraries, art museums, lectures at neighboring colleges, set to work on extra research projects, given extra French or Latin reading. Although we sometimes felt "pushed" by them, we held those women in a kind of respect which even then we dimly perceived was not generally accorded to women in the world at large. They were vital individuals, defined not by their relationships but by their personalities; and although under the pressure of the culture we were all certain we wanted to get married, their lives did not appear empty or dreary to us. In a kind of cognitive dissonance, we knew they were "old maids" and therefore supposed to be bitter and lonely; yet we saw them vigorously involved with life. But despite their existence as alternate models of women, the *content* of the education they gave us in no way prepared us to survive as women in a world organized by and for men.

From that school, I went on to Radcliffe, congratulating myself that now I would have great men as my teachers. From 1947 to 1951, when I graduated, I

The talk that follows was addressed to teachers of women. . . . It was given for the New Jersey College and University Coalition on Women's Education, May 9, 1978 [Rich's note]. Reprinted in On Lies, Secrets, and Silence: Selected Prose, 1966–1978 *(1979).*

1. Part of Rutgers University in New Jersey.

never saw a single woman on a lecture platform, or in front of a class, except when a woman graduate student gave a paper on a special topic. The "great men" talked of other "great men," of the nature of Man, the history of Mankind, the future of Man; and never again was I to experience, from a teacher, the kind of prodding, the insistence that my best could be even better, that I had known in high school. Women students were simply not taken very seriously. Harvard's message to women was an elite mystification: we were, of course, part of Mankind; we were special, achieving women, or we would not have been there; but of course our real goal was to marry—if possible, a Harvard graduate.

In the late sixties, I began teaching at the City College of New York—a crowded, public, urban, multiracial institution as far removed from Harvard as possible. I went there to teach writing in the SEEK Program,[2] which predated Open Admissions and which was then a kind of model for programs designed to open up higher education to poor, black, and Third World students. Although during the next few years we were to see the original concept of SEEK diluted, then violently attacked and betrayed, it was for a short time an extraordinary and intense teaching and learning environment. The characteristics of this environment were a deep commitment on the part of teachers to the minds of their students; a constant, active effort to create or discover the conditions for learning, and to educate ourselves to meet the needs of the new college population; a philosophical attitude based on open discussion of racism, oppression, and the politics of literature and language; and a belief that learning in the classroom could not be isolated from the student's experience as a member of an urban minority group in white America. Here are some of the kinds of questions we, as teachers of writing, found ourselves asking:

(1) What has been the student's experience of education in the inadequate, often abusively racist public school system, which rewards passivity and treats a questioning attitude or independent mind as a behavior problem? What has been her or his experience in a society that consistently undermines the selfhood of the poor and the nonwhite? How can such a student gain that sense of self which is necessary for active participation in education? What does all this mean for us as teachers?

(2) How do we go about teaching a canon of literature which has consistently excluded or depreciated nonwhite experience?

(3) How can we connect the process of learning to write well with the student's own reality, and not simply teach her/him how to write acceptable lies in standard English?

5   When I went to teach at Douglass College in 1976, and in teaching women's writing workshops elsewhere, I came to perceive stunning parallels to the questions I had first encountered in teaching the so-called disadvantaged students at

2. Acronym for "Search for Education, Elevation, and Knowledge"; the instructors in this program included not only college teachers but also creative artists and writers.

City. But in this instance, and against the specific background of the women's movement, the questions framed themselves like this:

(1) What has been the student's experience of education in schools which reward female passivity, indoctrinate girls and boys in stereotypic sex roles, and do not take the female mind seriously? How does a woman gain a sense of her *self* in a system—in this case, patriarchal capitalism—which devalues work done by women, denies the importance and uniqueness of female experience, and is physically violent toward women? What does this mean for a woman teacher?

(2) How do we, as women, teach women students a canon of literature which has consistently excluded or depreciated female experience, and which often expresses hostility to women and validates violence against us?

(3) How can we teach women to move beyond the desire for male approval and getting "good grades" and seek and write their own truths that the culture has distorted or made taboo? (For women, of course, language itself is exclusive: I want to say more about this further on.)

In teaching women, we have two choices: to lend our weight to the forces that indoctrinate women to passivity, self-depreciation, and a sense of powerlessness, in which case the issue of "taking women students seriously" is a moot one; or to consider what we have to work against, as well as with, in ourselves, in our students, in the content of the curriculum, in the structure of the institution, in the society at large. And this means, first of all, taking ourselves seriously: Recognizing that central responsibility of a woman to herself, without which we remain always the Other, the defined, the object, the victim; believing that there is a unique quality of validation, affirmation, challenge, support, that one woman can offer another. Believing in the value and significance of women's experience, traditions, perceptions. Thinking of ourselves seriously, not as one of the boys, not as neuters, or androgynes, but *as women.*

Suppose we were to ask ourselves, simply: What does a woman need to know? Does she not, as a self-conscious, self-defining human being, need a knowledge of her own history, her much-politicized biology, an awareness of the creative work of women of the past, the skills and crafts and techniques and powers exercised by women in different times and cultures, a knowledge of women's rebellions and organized movements against our oppression and how they have been routed or diminished? Without such knowledge women live and have lived without context, vulnerable to the projections of male fantasy, male prescriptions for us, estranged from our own experience because our education has not reflected or echoed it. I would suggest that not biology, but ignorance of our selves, has been the key to our powerlessness.

But the university curriculum, the high-school curriculum, do not provide this kind of knowledge for women, the knowledge of Womankind, whose experience has been so profoundly different from that of Mankind. Only in the precariously budgeted, much-condescended-to area of women's studies is such knowledge available to women students. Only there can they learn about the lives and work of women other than the few select women who are included in the "mainstream" texts, usually misrepresented even when they do appear. Some students, at some institutions, manage to take a majority of courses in women's studies, but the message from on high is that this is self-indulgence, soft-core education: the "real" learning is the study of Mankind.

If there is any misleading concept, it is that of "coeducation": that because women and men are sitting in the same classrooms, hearing the same lectures, reading the same books, performing the same laboratory experiments, they are receiving an equal education. They are not, first because the content of education itself validates men even as it invalidates women. Its very message is that men have been the shapers and thinkers of the world, and that this is only natural. The bias of higher education, including the so-called sciences, is white and male, racist and sexist; and this bias is expressed in both subtle and blatant ways. I have mentioned already the exclusiveness of grammar itself: "The student should test himself on the above questions"; "The poet is representative. He stands among partial men for the complete man." Despite a few half-hearted departures from custom, what the linguist Wendy Martyna has named "He-Man" grammar prevails throughout the culture. The efforts of feminists to reveal the profound ontological implications of sexist grammar are routinely ridiculed by academicians and journalists, including the professedly liberal *Times* columnist, Tom Wicker, and the professed humanist, Jacques Barzun. Sexist grammar burns into the brains of little girls and young women a message that the male is the norm, the standard, the central figure beside which we are the deviants, the marginal, the dependent variables. It lays the foundation for androcentric thinking, and leaves men safe in their solipsistic tunnel-vision.

10   Women and men do not receive an equal education because outside the classroom women are perceived not as sovereign beings but as prey. The growing incidence of rape on and off the campus may or may not be fed by the proliferations of pornographic magazines and X-rated films available to young males in fraternities and student unions; but it is certainly occurring in a context of widespread images of sexual violence against women, on billboards and in so-called high art. More subtle, more daily than rape is the verbal abuse experienced by the woman student on many campuses—Rutgers for example—where, traversing a street lined with fraternity houses, she must run a gauntlet of male commentary and verbal assault. The undermining of self, of a woman's sense of her right to occupy space and walk freely in the world, is deeply relevant to education. The capacity to think independently, to take intellectual risks, to assert ourselves mentally, is inseparable from our physical way of being in the world, our feelings of personal integrity. If it is dangerous for me to walk home late of an evening from the library, *because I am a woman and can be raped*, how self-possessed, how exuberant can I feel as I sit working in that library? how much of my working energy is drained by the subliminal knowledge that, as a woman, I test my physical right to exist each time I go out alone? Of this knowledge, Susan Griffin has written:

> . . . more than rape itself, the fear of rape permeates our lives. And what does one do from day to day, with *this* experience, which says, without words and directly to the heart, *your existence, your experience, may end*

at any moment. Your experience may end, and the best defense against this
is not to be, to deny being in the body, as a self, to . . . avert your gaze, make
yourself, as a presence in the world, less felt.[3]

Finally, rape of the mind. Women students are more and more often now
reporting sexual overtures by male professors—one part of our overall growing
consciousness of sexual harassment in the workplace. At Yale a legal suit has
been brought against the university by a group of women demanding an explicit
policy against sexual advances toward female students by male professors. Most
young women experience a profound mixture of humiliation and intellectual
self-doubt over seductive gestures by men who have the power to award grades,
open doors to grants and graduate school, or extend special knowledge and
training. Even if turned aside, such gestures constitute mental rape, destructive
to a woman's ego. They are acts of domination, as despicable as the molestation of the daughter by the father.

But long before entering college the woman student has experienced her
alien identity in a world which misnames her, turns her to its own uses, denying her the resources she needs to become self-affirming, self-defined. The
nuclear family teaches her that relationships are more important than selfhood or work; that "whether the phone rings for you, and how often," having
the right clothes, doing the dishes, take precedence over study or solitude; that
too much intelligence or intensity may make her unmarriageable; that marriage and children—service to others—are, finally, the points on which her
life will be judged a success or a failure. In high school, the polarization
between feminine attractiveness and independent intelligence comes to an
absolute. Meanwhile, the culture resounds with messages. During Solar
Energy Week in New York I saw young women wearing "ecology" T-shirts with
the legend: CLEAN, CHEAP AND AVAILABLE; a reminder of the 1960s antiwar button which read: CHICKS SAY YES TO MEN WHO SAY NO. Department store windows feature female mannequins in chains, pinned to the wall with legs
spread, smiling in positions of torture. Feminists are depicted in the media as
"shrill," "strident," "puritanical," or "humorless," and the lesbian choice—the
choice of the woman-identified woman—as pathological or sinister. The young
woman sitting in the philosophy classroom, the political science lecture, is
already gripped by tensions between her nascent sense of self-worth, and the
battering force of messages like these.

Look at a classroom: look at the many kinds of women's faces, postures,
expressions. Listen to the women's voices. Listen to the silences, the unasked
questions, the blanks. Listen to the small, soft voices, often courageously trying to speak up, voices of women taught early that tones of confidence, challenge, anger, or assertiveness, are strident and unfeminine. Listen to the voices
of the women and the voices of the men; observe the space men allow themselves, physically and verbally, the male assumption that people will listen, even
when the majority of the group is female. Look at the faces of the silent, and

3. Rich is quoting from the manuscript of Griffin's *Rape: The Power of Consciousness*
(New York, 1979).

of those who speak. Listen to a woman groping for language in which to express what is on her mind, sensing that the terms of academic discourse are not her language, trying to cut down her thought to the dimensions of a discourse not intended for her (*for it is not fitting that a woman speak in public*); or reading her paper aloud at breakneck speed, throwing her words away, deprecating her own work by a reflex prejudgment: *I do not deserve to take up time and space.*

As women teachers, we can either deny the importance of this context in which women students think, write, read, study, project their own futures; or try to work with it. We can either teach passively, accepting these conditions, or actively, helping our students identify and resist them.

15   One important thing we can do is *discuss* the context. And this need not happen only in a women's studies course; it can happen anywhere. We can refuse to accept passive, obedient learning and insist upon critical thinking. We can become harder on our women students, giving them the kinds of "cultural prodding" that men receive, but on different terms and in a different style. Most young women need to have their intellectual lives, their work, legitimized against the claims of family, relationships, the old message that a woman is always available for service to others. We need to keep our standards very high, not to accept a woman's preconceived sense of her limitations; we need to be hard to please, while supportive of risk-taking, because self-respect often comes only when exacting standards have been met. At a time when adult literacy is generally low, we need to demand more, not less, of women, both for the sake of their futures as thinking beings, and because historically women have always had to be better than men to do half as well. A romantic sloppiness, an inspired lack of rigor, a self-indulgent incoherence, are symptoms of female self-depreciation. We should help our women students to look very critically at such symptoms, and to understand where they are rooted.

Nor does this mean we should be training women students to "think like men." Men in general think badly: in disjuncture from their personal lives, claiming objectivity where the most irrational passions seethe, losing, as Virginia Woolf[4] observed, their senses in the pursuit of professionalism. It is not easy to think like a woman in a man's world, in the world of the professions; yet the capacity to do that is a strength which we can try to help our students develop. To think like a woman in a man's world means thinking critically, refusing to accept the givens, making connections between facts and ideas which men have left unconnected. It means remembering that every mind resides in a body; remaining accountable to the female bodies in which we live; constantly retesting given hypotheses against lived experience. It means a constant critique of language, for as Wittgenstein[5] (no feminist) observed, "The limits of my language are the limits of my world." And it means that most difficult thing of all: listening and watching in art and literature, in the social sciences, in all the descriptions we are given of the world, for the silences, the absences, the nameless, the unspoken, the encoded—for there we will find the true knowledge of women. And in

4. British novelist, essayist, and feminist (1882–1941). See pp. 124–28 and pp. 615–25 for her essays.

5. Ludwig Wittgenstein (1889–1951), Austrian-born British philosopher.

breaking those silences, naming our selves, uncovering the hidden, making ourselves present, we begin to define a reality which resonates to *us*, which affirms *our* being, which allows the woman teacher and the woman student alike to take ourselves, and each other, seriously: meaning, to begin taking charge of our lives.

MLA CITATION

Rich, Adrienne. "Taking Women Students Seriously." 1979. *The Norton Reader: An Anthology of Nonfiction.* Ed. Melissa A. Goldthwaite et al. 14th ed. New York: Norton, 2016. 443–49. Print.

QUESTIONS

1. Adrienne Rich discusses the importance of listening to silences and of paying attention to absences. In one of your classes, listen and observe; take note of who speaks and who doesn't; and watch for responses from the instructor. What sense can you make of these silences and absences? Do your conclusions correspond to Rich's, or do they differ?

2. Rich and David Brooks (in "The Gender Gap at School," pp. 390–92) come to very different conclusions. What do you think accounts for their differences?

3. In paragraph 10, Rich discusses the relationship between intellectual independence and physical safety. Do some research on the public safety policies on your own campus (escorts, lighting, etc.) or in your neighborhood, and also consider your own experiences. Do you feel safe walking alone? To what extent does your sense of physical safety affect your intellectual work? Write a journal entry or article on these issues.

MIKE ROSE   *Blue-Collar Brilliance*

MY MOTHER, ROSE MERAGLIO ROSE (Rosie), shaped her adult identity as a waitress in coffee shops and family restaurants. When I was growing up in Los Angeles during the 1950s, my father and I would occasionally hang out at the restaurant until her shift ended, and then we'd ride the bus home with her. Sometimes she worked the register and the counter, and we sat there; when she waited booths and tables, we found a booth in the back where the waitresses took their breaks.

There wasn't much for a child to do at the restaurants, and so as the hours stretched out, I watched the cooks and waitresses and listened to what they said. At mealtimes, the pace of the kitchen staff and the din from customers

Published in the American Scholar *(2009), the magazine of the Phi Beta Kappa society. In this essay, as in much of his other work, Mike Rose approaches his arguments about class, education, and literacy through his personal experience and family history.*

picked up. Weaving in and out around the room, waitresses warned *behind you* in impassive but urgent voices. Standing at the service window facing the kitchen, they called out abbreviated orders. *Fry four on two*, my mother would say as she clipped a check onto the metal wheel. Her tables were *deuces*, *four-tops*, or *six-tops* according to their size; seating areas also were nicknamed. The *racetrack*, for instance, was the fast-turnover front section. Lingo conferred authority and signaled know-how.

Rosie took customers' orders, pencil poised over pad, while fielding questions about the food. She walked full tilt through the room with plates stretching up her left arm and two cups of coffee somehow cradled in her right hand. She stood at a table or booth and removed a plate for this person, another for that person, then another, remembering who had the hamburger, who had the fried shrimp, almost always getting it right. She would haggle with the cook about a returned order and rush by us, saying. *He gave me lip, but I got him.* She'd take a minute to flop down in the booth next to my father. *I'm all in*, she'd say, and whisper something about a customer. Gripping the outer edge of the table with one hand, she'd watch the room and note, in the flow of our conversation, who needed a refill, whose order was taking longer to prepare than it should, who was finishing up.

I couldn't have put it in words when I was growing up, but what I observed in my mother's restaurant defined the world of adults, a place where competence was synonymous with physical work. I've since studied the working habits of blue-collar workers and have come to understand how much my mother's kind of work demands of both body and brain. A waitress acquires knowledge and intuition about the ways and the rhythms of the restaurant business. Waiting on seven to nine tables, each with two to six customers, Rosie devised memory strategies so that she could remember who ordered what. And because she knew the average time it took to prepare different dishes, she could monitor an order that was taking too long at the service station.

5   Like anyone who is effective at physical work, my mother learned *to work smart*, as she put it, *to make every move count.* She'd sequence and group tasks: What could she do first, then second, then third as she circled through her station? What tasks could be clustered? She did everything on the fly, and when problems arose—technical or human—she solved them within the flow of work, while taking into account the emotional state of her co-workers. Was the manager in a good mood? Did the cook wake up on the wrong side of the bed? If so, how could she make an extra request or effectively return an order?

And then, of course, there were the customers who entered the restaurant with all sorts of needs, from physiological ones, including the emotions that accompany hunger, to a sometimes complicated desire for human contact. Her tip depended on how well she responded to these needs, and so she became adept at reading social cues and managing feelings, both the customers' and her own. No wonder, then, that Rosie was intrigued by psychology. The restaurant became the place where she studied human behavior, puzzling over the problems of her regular customers and refining her ability to

Rosie solved technical and human problems on the fly.

deal with people in a difficult world. She took pride in *being among the public*, she'd say. *There isn't a day that goes by in the restaurant that you don't learn something.*

My mother quit school in the seventh grade to help raise her brothers and sisters. Some of those siblings made it through high school, and some dropped out to find work in railroad yards, factories, or restaurants. My father finished a grade or two in primary school in Italy and never darkened the schoolhouse door again. I didn't do well in school either. By high school I had accumulated a spotty academic record and many hours of hazy disaffection. I spent a few years on the vocational track, but in my senior year I was inspired by my English teacher and managed to squeak into a small college on probation.

My freshman year was academically bumpy, but gradually I began to see formal education as a means of fulfillment and as a road toward making a living. I studied the humanities and later the social and psychological sciences and taught for 10 years in a range of situations—elementary school, adult education courses, tutoring centers, a program for Vietnam veterans[1] who wanted to go to college. Those students had socioeconomic and educational backgrounds similar to mine. Then I went back to graduate school to study education and cognitive psychology[2] and eventually became a faculty member in a school of education.

Intelligence is closely associated with formal education—the type of schooling a person has, how much and how long—and most people seem to move comfortably from that notion to a belief that work requiring less schooling requires less intelligence. These assumptions run through our cultural history, from the post–Revolutionary War period, when mechanics were characterized by political rivals as illiterate and therefore incapable of participating in government, until today. More than once I've heard a manager label his workers as "a bunch of dummies." Generalizations about intelligence, work, and social class deeply affect our assumptions about ourselves and each other, guiding the ways we use our minds to learn, build knowledge, solve problems, and make our way through the world.

10   Although writers and scholars have often looked at the working class, they have generally focused on the values such workers exhibit rather than on the thought their work requires—a subtle but pervasive omission. Our cultural iconography promotes the muscled arm, sleeve rolled tight against biceps, but no brightness behind the eye, no image that links hand and brain.

One of my mother's brothers, Joe Meraglio, left school in the ninth grade to work for the Pennsylvania Railroad.[3] From there he joined the Navy, returned to the railroad, which was already in decline, and eventually joined his older brother at General Motors[4] where, over a 33-year career, he moved from working on the assembly line to supervising the paint-and-body department. When I was a young man, Joe took me on a tour of the factory. The floor was loud—in some places deafening—and when I turned a corner or opened a door, the smell of chemicals knocked my head back. The work was repetitive and taxing, and the pace was inhumane.

Still, for Joe the shop floor provided what school did not; it was *like schooling*, he said, a place where *you're constantly learning*. Joe learned the most efficient way to use his body by acquiring a set of routines that were quick and preserved energy. Otherwise he would never have survived on the line.

As a foreman, Joe constantly faced new problems and became a consummate multi-tasker, evaluating a flurry of demands quickly, parceling out physical

1. American veterans of a twenty-year (1954–1975) conflict between South Vietnam, which was allied with the United States, and communist North Vietnam.

2. Branch of psychology concerned with such subjects as perception, memory, thinking, and learning.

3. Railroad (1846–1968) that extended from the mid-Atlantic region of the United States to the Midwest.

4. American company that for much of the twentieth century was the world's largest automaker.

and mental resources, keeping a number of ongoing events in his mind, returning to whatever task had been interrupted, and maintaining a cool head under the pressure of grueling production schedules. In the midst of all this, Joe learned more and more about the auto industry, the technological and social dynamics of the shop floor, the machinery and production processes, and the basics of paint chemistry and of plating and baking. With further promotions, he not only solved problems but also began to find problems to solve: Joe initiated the redesign of the nozzle on a paint sprayer, thereby eliminating costly and unhealthy overspray. And he found a way to reduce energy costs on the baking ovens without affecting the quality of the paint. He lacked formal knowledge of how the machines under his supervision worked, but he had direct experience with them, hands-on knowledge, and was savvy about their quirks and operational capabilities. He could experiment with them.

In addition, Joe learned about budgets and management. Coming off the line as he did, he had a perspective of workers' needs and management's demands, and this led him to think of ways to improve efficiency on the line while relieving some of the stress on the assemblers. He had each worker in a unit learn his or her co-workers' jobs so they could rotate across stations to relieve some of the monotony. He believed that rotation would allow assemblers to get longer and more frequent breaks. It was an easy sell to the people on the line. The union, however, had to approve any modification in job duties, and the managers were wary of the change. Joe had to argue his case on a number of fronts, providing him a kind of rhetorical education.

Eight years ago I began a study of the thought processes involved in work like that of my mother and uncle. I catalogued the cognitive demands of a range of blue-collar and service jobs, from waitressing and hair styling to plumbing and welding. To gain a sense of how knowledge and skill develop, I observed experts as well as novices. From the details of this close examination, I tried to fashion what I called "cognitive biographies" of blue-collar workers. Biographical accounts of the lives of scientists, lawyers, entrepreneurs, and other professionals are rich with detail about the intellectual dimension of their work. But the life stories of working-class people are few and are typically accounts of hardship and courage or the achievements wrought by hard work. 15

Our culture—in Cartesian[5] fashion—separates the body from the mind, so that, for example, we assume that the use of a tool does not involve abstraction. We reinforce this notion by defining intelligence solely on grades in school and numbers on IQ tests.[6] And we employ social biases pertaining to a person's place on the occupational ladder. The distinctions among blue, pink, and white collars carry with them attributions of character, motivation, and intelligence. Although we rightly acknowledge and amply compensate the play of mind in white-collar and professional work, we diminish or erase it in considerations

5. Recalling the dualist philosophy of René Descartes (1596–1650), French scientist, mathematician, and philosopher.
6. Tests that give a numerical measure of intelligence, the "Intelligence Quotient."

With an eighth-grade education, Joe (hands together) advanced to supervisor of a G.M. paint-and-body department.

about other endeavors—physical and service work particularly. We also often ignore the experience of everyday work in administrative deliberations and policymaking.

But here's what we find when we get in close. The plumber seeking leverage in order to work in tight quarters and the hair stylist adroitly handling scissors and comb manage their bodies strategically. Though work-related actions become routine with experience, they were learned at some point through observation, trial and error, and, often, physical or verbal assistance from a coworker or trainer. I've frequently observed novices talking to themselves as they take on a task, or shaking their head or hand as if to erase an attempt before trying again. In fact, our traditional notions of routine performance could keep us from appreciating the many instances within routine where quick decisions and adjustments are made. I'm struck by the thinking-in-motion that some work requires, by all the mental activity that can be involved in simply getting from one place to another: the waitress rushing back through her station to the kitchen or the foreman walking the line.

The use of tools requires the studied refinement of stance, grip, balance, and fine-motor skills. But manipulating tools is intimately tied to knowledge of what a particular instrument can do in a particular situation and do better than other similar tools. A worker must also know the characteristics of the material one is engaging—how it reacts to various cutting or compressing devices, to degrees of heat, or to lines of force. Some of these things demand judgment, the weighing of options, the consideration of multiple variables, and, occasionally, the creative use of a tool in an unexpected way.

In manipulating material, the worker becomes attuned to aspects of the environment, a training or disciplining of perception that both enhances knowledge and informs perception. Carpenters have an eye for length, line, and angle; mechanics troubleshoot by listening; hair stylists are attuned to shape, texture, and motion. Sensory data merge with concept, as when an auto mechanic relies on sound, vibration, and even smell to understand what cannot be observed.

Planning and problem solving have been studied since the earliest days of modern cognitive psychology and are considered core elements in Western definitions of intelligence. To work is to solve problems. The big difference between the psychologist's laboratory and the workplace is that in the former the problems are isolated and in the latter they are embedded in the real-time flow of work with all its messiness and social complexity. [20]

Much of physical work is social and interactive. Movers determining how to get an electric range down a flight of stairs require coordination, negotiation, planning, and the establishing of incremental goals. Words, gestures, and sometimes a quick pencil sketch are involved, if only to get the rhythm right. How important it is, then, to consider the social and communicative dimension of physical work, for it provides the medium for so much of work's intelligence.

Given the ridicule heaped on blue-collar speech, it might seem odd to value its cognitive content. Yet, the flow of talk at work provides the channel for organizing and distributing tasks, for troubleshooting and problem solving, for learning new information and revising old. A significant amount of teaching, often informal and indirect, takes place at work. Joe Meraglio saw that much of his job as a supervisor involved instruction. In some service occupations, language and communication are central: observing and interpreting behavior and expression, inferring mood and motive, taking on the perspective of others, responding appropriately to social cues, and knowing when you're understood. A good hair stylist, for instance, has the ability to convert vague requests (*I want something light and summery*) into an appropriate cut through questions, pictures, and hand gestures.

Verbal and mathematical skills drive measures of intelligence in the Western Hemisphere, and many of the kinds of work I studied are thought to require relatively little proficiency in either. Compared to certain kinds of white-collar occupations, that's true. But written symbols flow through physical work.

Numbers are rife in most workplaces: on tools and gauges, as measurements, as indicators of pressure or concentration or temperature, as guides to sequence, on ingredient labels, on lists and spreadsheets, as markers of quantity and price. Certain jobs require workers to make, check, and verify calculations, and to collect and interpret data. Basic math can be involved, and some workers develop a good sense of numbers and patterns. Consider, as well, what might be called material mathematics: mathematical functions embodied in materials and actions, as when a carpenter builds a cabinet or a flight of stairs. A simple mathematical act can extend quickly beyond itself. Measuring, for example, can involve more than recording the dimensions of an object. As I watched a cabinetmaker measure a long strip of wood, he read a number off the tape out loud, looked back over his shoulder to the kitchen wall, turned back to his task, took another measurement, and paused for a moment in thought. He was solving a problem involving the molding, and the measurement was important to his deliberation about structure and appearance.

25   In the blue-collar workplace, directions, plans, and reference books rely on illustrations, some representational and others, like blueprints, that require training to interpret. Esoteric symbols—visual jargon—depict switches and receptacles, pipe fittings, or types of welds. Workers themselves often make sketches on the job. I frequently observed them grab a pencil to sketch something on a scrap of paper or on a piece of the material they were installing.

Though many kinds of physical work don't require a high literacy level, more reading occurs in the blue-collar workplace than is generally thought, from manuals and catalogues to work orders and invoices, to lists, labels, and forms. With routine tasks, for example, reading is integral to understanding production quotas, learning how to use an instrument, or applying a product. Written notes can initiate action, as in restaurant orders or reports of machine malfunction, or they can serve as memory aids.

True, many uses of writing are abbreviated, routine, and repetitive, and they infrequently require interpretation or analysis. But analytic moments can be part of routine activities, and seemingly basic reading and writing can be cognitively rich. Because workplace language is used in the flow of other activities, we can overlook the remarkable coordination of words, numbers, and drawings required to initiate and direct action.

If we believe everyday work to be mindless, then that will affect the work we create in the future. When we devalue the full range of everyday cognition, we offer limited educational opportunities and fail to make fresh and meaningful instructional connections among disparate kinds of skill and knowledge. If we think that whole categories of people—identified by class or occupation—are not that bright, then we reinforce social separations and cripple our ability to talk across cultural divides.

Affirmation of diverse intelligence is not a retreat to a softhearted definition of the mind. To acknowledge a broader range of intellectual capacity is to take seriously the concept of cognitive variability, to appreciate in all the Rosies and Joes the thought that drives their accomplishments and defines who they are. This is a model of the mind that is worthy of a democratic society.

MLA CITATION

Rose, Mike. "Blue-Collar Brilliance." 2009. *The Norton Reader: An Anthology of Nonfiction.* Ed. Melissa A. Goldthwaite et al. 14th ed. New York: Norton, 2016. 449–56. Print.

Questions

1. In his closing paragraph, Mike Rose asserts that the expanded understanding of intelligence for which he is arguing suggests "a model of the mind that is worthy of a democratic society." What are the social or political implications of this connection between mind and democracy?

2. Rose's essay was originally subtitled "Questioning assumptions about intelligence, work, and social class." What assumptions is Rose questioning, either directly or indirectly?

3. Rose introduces his general argument with detailed accounts of the work-lives of two family members: his mother and his uncle. Why do you think he makes this choice?

4. Rose describes himself as writing "'cognitive biographies' of blue-collar workers" (paragraph 15). Drawing as Rose does on interviews and careful observation, write a cognitive biography of your own.

LANGUAGE AND COMMUNICATION

LESLIE JAMISON *Mark My Words. Maybe.*

Y TATTOO KEPT GETTING DELAYED by other people's weddings: a bachelorette party in Vegas, cliff-top vows in Zion, a ceremony in Westchester. I wasn't just attending the ceremony in Westchester, I was officiating at the ceremony in Westchester. I couldn't picture giving my blessing in front of 200 people while my left arm glistened under Saran Wrap. I felt the slightest twinge of resentment. My life seemed perpetually tucked into the pockets of time created between the milestones of other lives.

I was getting the tattoo, in part, to mark a break from the man with whom I'd spent four years building and then dismantling a life. I was branding myself to mark a new era: my body was no longer entwined with someone else's. It was mine alone again. I was moving to a new city and I had a new book coming out, and the tattoo would be its epigraph: "I am human: nothing human is alien to me."

The quotation belongs to Terence, the Roman playwright. In the original Latin, it reads: homo sum: humani nil a me alienum puto. When I first came upon it, I felt its force beyond rational explanation. I knew it was something I needed to keep saying.

I got the job done by an artist who worked in a converted fire station. His walls were lined with giant beetles in jars of formaldehyde, taxidermied birds and bright oil paintings full of wizards and dragons. "Sure you don't want anything drawn?" he asked, gesturing to his art. I pictured a dragon with a thought bubble: "nothing human is alien to me. . . ." I said I was fine with just words. He wrote them in a cursive line from elbow to wrist. "I'm going to do this so we miss your veins," he said. I said that sounded great.

5   It hurt just enough to make me feel like something was happening. There was a sense of deserving—that I'd earned this by hurting for it. It was an old logic I hadn't felt in a while: Pain justifies ownership. It scared me, a bit. It also thrilled me. I left with Very Serious Aftercare Instructions and an arm encased like a pale sausage in plastic wrap.

The woman at the drugstore where I bought my Very Serious Aftercare supplies immediately wanted to know what the tattoo said. When I told her, she

Published in the New York Times *(2014). Leslie Jamison is the author of* The Empathy Exams *(2014), a collection of essays.*

458

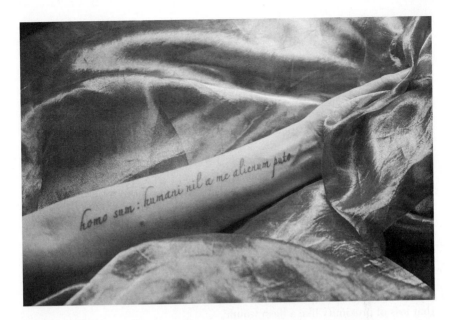

looked at me for a long time. "I think there is so much evil in this world," she said, "and so much good."

From now on, I realized, my body would basically be asking every stranger, "What do you think about the possibilities of human understanding?" During the months that followed, I found myself explaining the tattoo to a parade of strangers and acquaintances. It's about empathy and camaraderie, I would say. Or else, it's a denial of this lifelong obsession I've had with singularity and exceptionality.

We often think of tattoos as declarations of selfhood: this is what I am, love, believe. But there are other things we might inscribe on ourselves: what we fear, what we hate, what we hope to be but can't yet manage.

"I am human; nothing human is alien to me"—my tattoo wasn't true for me, not yet. But it was what I most needed to hear, an asymptote, a horizon.

On a hot day near the end of summer, another drugstore clerk reached for   10
my arm with a searching look on his face. He was a large man, imposing.

When I told him what the tattoo meant, he shook his head. "There are people going through things in this world that are really bad," he said. "Do you understand that?"

I tried to explain about aspiration, asymptote, attempt.

"You will leave a little piece of yourself with everyone you imagine," he said. "You will get exhausted trying to give yourself away."

I didn't know what to say to this. I felt exhausted by *him*. I felt how much I needed, from him and everyone, a certain kind of response: to feel inspired by the tat, and tell me so.

"You tried to give me something," he said, pointing at my arm. "But I blocked   15
it. I blocked what you were giving me."

He was interrupting the ticktock rhythm of my righteousness, saying something about the easy aphorism on my arm: how it didn't go down easy for him and shouldn't go down easy for me, either.

He wasn't the only one with questions. My father wrote from the Rwanda Genocide Memorial: Did I really believe what my tattoo said, even about perpetrators of genocide? And on a first date, a man asked me whether my tattoo could even apply to evil? We never went out again. But there were other dates, other men wanting translations, running their fingers along the script. It started to feel uncomfortably like philosophy as accessory, something to match a certain kind of intellectual posture.

Before these men, there was a moment with the original man, the one from whom the tattoo marked my liberation. I ran into him on an ordinary afternoon, about a week after I got the tattoo and a week before I moved away from the city we shared. He was surprised to see my arm holding something it hadn't held before.

I realized how different things were now. Something could happen to my body and it would be weeks or months before he knew about it. The tattoo was supposed to represent a new freedom but in that moment it felt like a shackle. It showed me how much it still hurt to feel the new distance between us. I felt that loss of proximity like a flesh wound.

20 It's like being pregnant, people would tell me. Your body is a conversation-starter. Eventually I started drawing the comparison myself. But the truth was it didn't feel like being pregnant at all. I was alone; my body was my own. It was a deep privacy, an autonomy tinged with sadness. It was the opposite of pregnancy, the residue of intimacy.

I'd always insisted I didn't get the tattoo so that people would talk to me about it. In fact, I told myself I wanted nothing less. But at a certain point I've had to admit to a desire for contact I couldn't own at first: It's there and it isn't.

The script is full of vectors pointing in opposite directions, a statement both aspirational and self-scolding, a desire to be seen and a desire to be left alone; a desire to have my body admired and a desire for my body to need nothing but itself, to need no affirmation from anyone. The tattoo holds an idea and its refutation, a man and his absence, a vote of confidence from the world and—in that downtown drugstore, on that humid day in summer—something more like the opposite.

MLA CITATION

Jamison, Leslie. "Mark My Words. Maybe." 2014. *The Norton Reader: An Anthology of Nonfiction.* Ed. Melissa A. Goldthwaite et al. 14th ed. New York: Norton, 2016. 458–60. Print.

QUESTIONS

1. Leslie Jamison initially thinks her tattoo will help her get over a breakup, but it comes to mean several different things. What do you think the tattoo ends up meaning to her? Point to passages in the text that support your answer.

2. Jamison titles her essay "Mark My Words. Maybe." Who might she be addressing with this title? Consider the reactions of the drugstore clerk (paragraphs 10–16) and Jamison's father (paragraph 17) as you think about how this title relates to the broader points she makes in her essay.

3. Jamison writes about the power bodies have to communicate messages that would otherwise be expressed through speaking and writing. Write an essay discussing the power and the limitation of tattoos as a mode of communication. If you have a tattoo, consider incorporating your personal experience.

Maxine Hong Kingston *Tongue-Tied*

Long ago in China, knot-makers tied string into buttons and frogs, and rope into bell pulls. There was one knot so complicated that it blinded the knot-maker. Finally an emperor outlawed this cruel knot, and the nobles could not order it anymore. If I had lived in China, I would have been an outlaw knot-maker.

Maybe that's why my mother cut my tongue. She pushed my tongue up and sliced the frenum.[1] Or maybe she snipped it with a pair of nail scissors. I don't remember her doing it, only her telling me about it, but all during childhood I felt sorry for the baby whose mother waited with scissors or knife in hand for it to cry—and then, when its mouth was wide open like a baby bird's, cut. The Chinese say "a ready tongue is an evil."

I used to curl up my tongue in front of the mirror and tauten my frenum into a white line, itself as thin as a razor blade. I saw no scars in my mouth. I thought perhaps I had had two frena, and she had cut one. I made other children open their mouths so I could compare theirs to mine. I saw perfect pink membranes stretching into precise edges that looked easy enough to cut. Sometimes I felt very proud that my mother committed such a powerful act upon me. At other times I was terrified—the first thing my mother did when she saw me was to cut my tongue.

"Why did you do that to me, Mother?"

"I told you."   5

"Tell me again."

"I cut it so that you would not be tongue-tied. Your tongue would be able to move in any language. You'll be able to speak languages that are completely different from one another. You'll be able to pronounce anything. Your frenum looked too tight to do those things, so I cut it."

"But isn't 'a ready tongue an evil'?"

Published as the first chapter of The Woman Warrior: Memoirs of a Girlhood among Ghosts *(1976), Maxine Hong Kingston's account of her childhood and family history.*

1. Connecting fold of membrane on the underside of the tongue.

"Things are different in this ghost country."[2]

"Did it hurt me? Did I cry and bleed?"

"I don't remember. Probably."

She didn't cut the other children's. When I asked cousins and other Chinese children whether their mothers had cut their tongues loose, they said, "What?"

"Why didn't you cut my brothers' and sisters' tongues?"

"They didn't need it."

"Why not? Were theirs longer than mine?"

"Why don't you quit blabbering and get to work?"

If my mother was not lying she should have cut more, scraped away the rest of the frenum skin, because I have a terrible time talking. Or she should not have cut at all, tampering with my speech. When I went to kindergarten and had to speak English for the first time, I became silent. A dumbness—a shame—still cracks my voice in two, even when I want to say "hello" casually, or ask an easy question in front of the check-out counter, or ask directions of a bus driver. I stand frozen, or I hold up the line with the complete, grammatical sentence that comes squeaking out at impossible length. "What did you say?" says the cab driver, or "Speak up," so I have to perform again, only weaker the second time. A telephone call makes my throat bleed and takes up that day's courage. It spoils my day with self-disgust when I hear my broken voice come skittering out into the open. It makes people wince to hear it. I'm getting better, though. Recently I asked the postman for special-issue stamps; I've waited since childhood for postmen to give me some of their own accord. I am making progress, a little every day.

My silence was thickest—total—during the three years that I covered my school paintings with black paint. I painted layers of black over houses and flowers and suns, and when I drew on the blackboard, I put a layer of chalk on top. I was making a stage curtain, and it was the moment before the curtain parted or rose. The teachers called my parents to school, and I saw they had been saving my pictures, curling and cracking, all alike and black. The teachers pointed to the pictures and looked serious, talked seriously too, but my parents did not understand English. ("The parents and teachers of criminals were executed," said my father.) My parents took the pictures home. I spread them out (so black and full of possibilities) and pretended the curtains were swinging open, flying up, one after another, sunlight underneath, mighty operas.

During the first silent year I spoke to no one at school, did not ask before going to the lavatory, and flunked kindergarten. My sister also said nothing for three years, silent in the playground and silent at lunch. There were other quiet Chinese girls not of our family, but most of them got over it sooner than we did. I enjoyed the silence. At first it did not occur to me I was supposed to talk or to pass kindergarten. I talked at home and to one or two of the Chinese

---

2. In Kingston's story, the Chinese immigrants see white Americans as "ghosts," whose language and values they must adopt to become American.

kids in class. I made motions and even made some jokes. I drank out of a toy saucer when the water spilled out of the cup, and everybody laughed, pointing at me, so I did it some more. I didn't know that Americans don't drink out of saucers.

I liked the Negro students (Black Ghosts) best because they laughed the [20] loudest and talked to me as if I were a daring talker too. One of the Negro girls had her mother coil braids over her ears Shanghai-style like mine; we were Shanghai twins except that she was covered with black like my paintings. Two Negro kids enrolled in Chinese school, and the teachers gave them Chinese names. Some Negro kids walked me to school and home, protecting me from the Japanese kids, who hit me and chased me and stuck gum in my ears. The Japanese kids were noisy and tough. They appeared one day in kindergarten, released from concentration camp,[3] which was a tic-tac-toe mark, like barbed wire, on the map.

It was when I found out I had to talk that school became a misery, that the silence became a misery. I did not speak and felt bad each time that I did not speak. I read aloud in first grade, though, and heard the barest whisper with little squeaks come out of my throat. "Louder," said the teacher, who scared the voice away again. The other Chinese girls did not talk either, so I knew the silence had to do with being a Chinese girl.

Reading out loud was easier than speaking because we did not have to make up what to say, but I stopped often, and the teacher would think I'd gone quiet again. I could not understand "I." The Chinese "I" had seven strokes, intricacies. How could the American "I," assuredly wearing a hat like the Chinese, have only three strokes, the middle so straight? Was it out of politeness that this writer left off strokes the way a Chinese has to write her own name small and crooked? No, it was not politeness; "I" is a capital and "you" is a lower-case. I stared at that middle line and waited so long for its black center to resolve into tight strokes and dots that I forgot to pronounce it. The other troublesome word was "here," no strong consonant to hang on to, and so flat, when "here" is two mountainous ideographs. The teacher, who had already told me every day how to read "I" and "here," put me in the low corner under the stairs again, where the noisy boys usually sat.

When my second grade class did a play, the whole class went to the auditorium except the Chinese girls. The teacher, lovely and Hawaiian, should have understood about us, but instead left us behind in the classroom. Our voices were too soft or nonexistent, and our parents never signed the permission slips anyway. They never signed anything unnecessary. We opened the door a crack and peeked out, but closed it again quickly. One of us (not me) won every spelling bee, though.

3. After Japan's attack on Pearl Harbor and the United States' entry into World War II, the U.S. government sanctioned the imprisonment of more than 120,000 Japanese Americans in the United States.

I remember telling the Hawaiian teacher, "We Chinese can't sing 'land where our fathers died.'" She argued with me about politics, while I meant because of curses. But how can I have that memory when I couldn't talk? My mother says that we, like the ghosts, have no memories.

25   After American school, we picked up our cigar boxes, in which we had arranged books, brushes, and an inkbox neatly, and went to Chinese school, from 5:00 to 7:30 P.M. There we chanted together, voices rising and falling, loud and soft, some boys shouting, everybody reading together, reciting together and not alone with one voice. When we had a memorization test, the teacher let each of us come to his desk and say the lesson to him privately, while the rest of the class practiced copying or tracing. Most of the teachers were men. The boys who were so well behaved in the American school played tricks on them and talked back to them. The girls were not mute. They screamed and yelled during recess, when there were no rules; they had fistfights. Nobody was afraid of children hurting themselves or of children hurting school property. The glass doors to the red and green balconies with the gold joy symbols were left wide open so that we could run out and climb the fire escapes. We played capture-the-flag in the auditorium, where Sun Yat-sen and Chiang Kai-shek's[4] pictures hung at the back of the stage, the Chinese flag on their left and the American flag on their right. We climbed the teak ceremonial chairs and made flying leaps off the stage. One flag headquarters was behind the glass door and the other on stage right. Our feet drummed on the hollow stage. During recess the teachers locked themselves up in their office with the shelves of books, copybooks, inks from China. They drank tea and warmed their hands at a stove. There was no play supervision. At recess we had the school to ourselves, and also we could roam as far as we could go—downtown, Chinatown stores, home—as long as we returned before the bell rang.

At exactly 7:30 the teacher again picked up the brass bell that sat on his desk and swung it over our heads, while we charged down the stairs, our cheering magnified in the stairwell. Nobody had to line up.

Not all of the children who were silent at American school found voice at Chinese school. One new teacher said each of us had to get up and recite in front of the class, who was to listen. My sister and I had memorized the lesson perfectly. We said it to each other at home, one chanting, one listening. The teacher called on my sister to recite first. It was the first time a teacher had called on the second-born to go first. My sister was scared. She glanced at me and looked away; I looked down at my desk. I hoped that she could do it because if she could, then I wouldn't have to. She opened her mouth and a voice came out that wasn't a whisper, but it wasn't a proper voice either. I hoped that she would not cry, fear breaking up her voice like twigs underfoot. She sounded as if she were trying to sing through weeping and strangling. She did not pause or stop to end the embarrassment. She kept going until she said the last word, and

---

4. Sun Yat-sen (1866–1925) and his successor, Chiang Kai-shek (1887–1975), led the Guomindang (or Nationalist party) campaign to unify China in the 1920s and 1930s.

then she sat down. When it was my turn, the same voice came out, a crippled animal running on broken legs. You could hear splinters in my voice, bones rubbing jagged against one another. I was loud, though. I was glad I didn't whisper. There was one little girl who whispered.

MLA CITATION

Kingston, Maxine Hong. "Tongue-Tied." 1976. *The Norton Reader: An Anthology of Nonfiction.* Ed. Melissa A. Goldthwaite et al. 14th ed. New York: Norton, 2016. 461–65. Print.

QUESTIONS

1. Like Gloria Anzaldúa in "How to Tame a Wild Tongue" (pp. 471–80), Maxine Hong Kingston uses the tongue as both a physical body part and a metaphor for speech. Locate examples of these uses of "tongue" and explain them.

2. Why does Kingston call non-Asians "ghosts" (paragraph 9)? Are these the only ghosts Kingston confronts? Discuss her usage of this term in the essay and in the subtitle of her autobiography, *Memoirs of a Girlhood among Ghosts.*

3. Have you ever had difficulty speaking up? Think about a time when it was difficult to speak. Write an essay about the experience, incorporating family or social context, as Kingston does.

RICHARD RODRIGUEZ *Aria*

SUPPORTERS OF BILINGUAL EDUCATION today imply that students like me miss a great deal by not being taught in their family's language. What they seem not to recognize is that, as a socially disadvantaged child, I considered Spanish to be a private language. What I needed to learn in school was that I had the right—and the obligation—to speak the public language of *los gringos.* The odd truth is that my first-grade classmates could have become bilingual, in the conventional sense of that word, more easily than I. Had they been taught (as upper-middle-class children are often taught early) a second language like Spanish or French, they could have regarded it simply as that: another public language. In my case such bilingualism could not have been so quickly achieved. What I did not believe was that I could speak a single public language.

Without question, it would have pleased me to hear my teachers address me in Spanish when I entered the classroom. I would have felt much less afraid.

From Hunger of Memory: The Education of Richard Rodriguez (1982), *an autobiography of Rodriguez's experiences as a student, including his controversial argument against bilingual education.*

I would have trusted them and responded with ease. But I would have delayed—for how long postponed?—having to learn the language of public society. I would have evaded—and for how long could I have afforded to delay?—learning the great lesson of school, that I had a public identity.

Fortunately, my teachers were unsentimental about their responsibility. What they understood was that I needed to speak a public language. So their voices would search me out, asking me questions. Each time I'd hear them, I'd look up in surprise to see a nun's face frowning at me. I'd mumble, not really meaning to answer. The nun would persist, "Richard, stand up. Don't look at the floor. Speak up. Speak to the entire class, not just to me!" But I couldn't believe that the English language was mine to use. (In part, I did not want to believe it.) I continued to mumble. I resisted the teacher's demands. (Did I somehow suspect that once I learned public language my pleasing family life would be changed?) Silent, waiting for the bell to sound, I remained dazed, diffident, afraid.

Because I wrongly imagined that English was intrinsically a public language and Spanish an intrinsically private one, I easily noted the difference between classroom language and the language of home. At school, words were directed to a general audience of listeners. ("Boys and girls.") Words were meaningfully ordered. And the point was not self-expression alone but to make oneself understood by many others. The teacher quizzed: "Boys and girls, why do we use that word in this sentence? Could we think of a better word to use there? Would the sentence change its meaning if the words were differently arranged? And wasn't there a better way of saying much the same thing?" (I couldn't say. I wouldn't try to say.)

5   Three months. Five. Half a year passed. Unsmiling, ever watchful, my teachers noted my silence. They began to connect my behavior with the difficult progress my older sister and brother were making. Until one Saturday morning three nuns arrived at the house to talk to our parents. Stiffly, they sat on the blue living room sofa. From the doorway of another room, spying the visitors, I noted the incongruity—the clash of two worlds, the faces and voices of school intruding upon the familiar setting of home. I overheard one voice gently wondering, "Do your children speak only Spanish at home, Mrs. Rodriguez?" While another voice added, "That Richard especially seems so timid and shy."

That Rich-heard!

With great tact the visitors continued, "Is it possible for you and your husband to encourage your children to practice their English when they are home?" Of course, my parents complied. What would they not do for their children's well-being? And how could they have questioned the Church's authority which those women represented? In an instant, they agreed to give up the language (the sounds) that had revealed and accentuated our family's closeness. The moment after the visitors left, the change was observed. "*Ahora,* speak to us *en inglés,*"[1] my father and mother united to tell us.

---

1. Spanish for "*now,* speak to us *in English.*"

At first, it seemed a kind of game. After dinner each night, the family gathered to practice "our" English. (It was still then *inglés,* a language foreign to us, so we felt drawn as strangers to it.) Laughing, we would try to define words we could not pronounce. We played with strange English sounds, often overanglicizing our pronunciations. And we filled the smiling gaps of our sentences with familiar Spanish sounds. But that was cheating, somebody shouted. Everyone laughed. In school, meanwhile, like my brother and sister, I was required to attend a daily tutoring session. I needed a full year of special attention. I also needed my teachers to keep my attention from straying in class by calling out, *Rich-heard*—their English voices slowly prying loose my ties to my other name, its three notes, *Ri-car-do.* Most of all I needed to hear my mother and father speak to me in a moment of seriousness in broken—suddenly heartbreaking—English. The scene was inevitable: One Saturday morning I entered the kitchen where my parents were talking in Spanish. I did not realize that they were talking in Spanish however until, at the moment they saw me, I heard their voices change to speak English. Those *gringo* sounds they uttered startled me. Pushed me away. In that moment of trivial misunderstanding and profound insight, I felt my throat twisted by unsounded grief. I turned quickly and left the room. But I had no place to escape to with Spanish. (The spell was broken.) My brother and sisters were speaking English in another part of the house.

Again and again in the days following, increasingly angry, I was obliged to hear my mother and father: "Speak to us *en inglés.*" (*Speak.*) Only then did I determine to learn classroom English. Weeks after, it happened: One day in school I raised my hand to volunteer an answer. I spoke out in a loud voice. And I did not think it remarkable when the entire class understood. That day, I moved very far from the disadvantaged child I had been only days earlier. The belief, that calming assurance that I belonged in public, had at last taken hold.

Shortly after, I stopped hearing the high and loud sounds of *los gringos.* A more and more confident speaker of English, I didn't trouble to listen to *how* strangers sounded, speaking to me. And there simply were too many English-speaking people in my day for me to hear American accents anymore. Conversations quickened. Listening to persons who sounded eccentrically pitched voices, I usually noted their sounds for an initial few seconds before I concentrated on *what* they were saying. Conversations became content-full. Transparent. Hearing someone's *tone* of voice—angry or questioning or sarcastic or happy or sad—I didn't distinguish it from the words it expressed. Sound and word were thus tightly wedded. At the end of a day, I was often bemused, always relieved, to realize how "silent," though crowded with words, my day in public had been. (This public silence measured and quickened the change in my life.)

At last, seven years old, I came to believe what had been technically true since my birth: I was an American citizen.

But the special feeling of closeness at home was diminished by then. Gone was the desperate, urgent, intense feeling of being at home; rare was the experience of feeling myself individualized by family intimates. We remained a loving family, but one greatly changed. No longer so close; no longer bound tight

10

by the pleasing and troubling knowledge of our public separateness. Neither my older brother nor sister rushed home after school anymore. Nor did I. When I arrived home there would often be neighborhood kids in the house. Or the house would be empty of sounds.

Following the dramatic Americanization of their children, even my parents grew more publicly confident. Especially my mother. She learned the names of all the people on our block. And she decided we needed to have a telephone installed in the house. My father continued to use the word *gringo*. But it was no longer charged with the old bitterness or distrust. (Stripped of any emotional content, the word simply became a name for those Americans not of Hispanic descent.) Hearing him, sometimes, I wasn't sure if he was pronouncing the Spanish word *gringo* or saying gringo in English.

Matching the silence I started hearing in public was a new quiet at home. The family's quiet was partly due to the fact that, as we children learned more and more English, we shared fewer and fewer words with our parents. Sentences needed to be spoken slowly when a child addressed his mother or father. (Often the parent wouldn't understand.) The child would need to repeat himself. (Still the parent misunderstood.) The young voice, frustrated, would end up saying, "Never mind"—the subject was closed. Dinners would be noisy with the clinking of knives and forks against dishes. My mother would smile softly between her remarks; my father at the other end of the table would chew and chew at his food, while he stared over the heads of his children.

15   My *mother*! My *father*! After English became my primary language, I no longer knew what words to use in addressing my parents. The old Spanish words (those tender accents of sound) I had used earlier—*mamá* and *papá*—I couldn't use anymore. They would have been too painful reminders of how much had changed in my life. On the other hand, the words I heard neighborhood kids call *their* parents seemed equally unsatisfactory. *Mother* and *Father*; *Ma, Papa, Pa, Dad, Pop* (how I hated the all American sound of that last word especially)— all these terms I felt were unsuitable, not really terms of address for *my* parents. As a result, I never used them at home. Whenever I'd speak to my parents, I would try to get their attention with eye contact alone. In public conversations, I'd refer to "my parents" or "my mother and father."

My mother and father, for their part, responded differently, as their children spoke to them less. She grew restless, seemed troubled and anxious at the scarcity of words exchanged in the house. It was she who would question me about my day when I came home from school. She smiled at small talk. She pried at the edges of my sentences to get me to say something more. (What?) She'd join conversations she overheard, but her intrusions often stopped her children's talking. By contrast, my father seemed reconciled to the new quiet. Though his English improved somewhat, he retired into silence. At dinner he spoke very little. One night his children and even his wife helplessly giggled at his garbled English pronunciation of the Catholic Grace before Meals. Thereafter he made his wife recite the prayer at the start of each meal, even on formal occasions, when there were guests in the house. Hers became the public voice of the family. On official business, it was she, not my father, one would usually hear on the phone or in stores, talking to strangers. His children grew so accustomed to his silence that, years later, they would speak routinely of his shyness. (My mother would often try to explain: Both his parents died when he was eight. He was raised by an uncle who treated him like little more than a menial servant. He was never encouraged to speak. He grew up alone. A man of few words.) But my father was not shy, I realized, when I'd watch him speaking Spanish with relatives. Using Spanish, he was quickly effusive. Especially when talking with other men, his voice would spark, flicker, flare alive with sounds. In Spanish, he expressed ideas and feelings he rarely revealed in English. With firm Spanish sounds, he conveyed confidence and authority English would never allow him.

The silence at home, however, was finally more than a literal silence. Fewer words passed between parent and child, but more profound was the silence that resulted from my inattention to sounds. At about the time I no longer bothered to listen with care to the sounds of English in public, I grew careless about listening to the sounds family members made when they spoke. Most of the time I heard someone speaking at home and didn't distinguish his sounds from the words people uttered in public. I didn't even pay much attention to my parents' accented and ungrammatical speech. At least not at home. Only when I was with them in public would I grow alert to their accents. Though, even then, their sounds caused me less and less concern. For I was increasingly confident of my own public identity.

I would have been happier about my public success had I not sometimes recalled what it had been like earlier, when my family had conveyed its intimacy through a set of conveniently private sounds. Sometimes in public, hearing a stranger, I'd hark back to my past. A Mexican farmworker approached me downtown to ask directions to somewhere, "¿Hijito . . . ?"[2] he said. And his voice summoned deep longing. Another time, standing beside my mother in the visiting room of a Carmelite convent,[3] before the dense screen which rendered the nuns shadowy figures, I heard several Spanish-speaking nuns—their busy, singsong overlapping voices—assure us that yes, yes, we were remembered, all our family was remembered in their prayers. (Their voices echoed faraway family sounds.) Another day, a dark-faced old woman—her hand light on my shoulder—steadied herself against me as she boarded a bus. She murmured something I couldn't quite comprehend. Her Spanish voice came near, like the face of a never-before-seen relative in the instant before I was kissed. Her voice, like so many of the Spanish voices I'd hear in public, recalled the golden age of my youth. Hearing Spanish then, I continued to be a careful, if sad, listener to sounds. Hearing a Spanish-speaking family walking behind me, I turned to look. I smiled for an instant, before my glance found the Hispanic-looking faces of strangers in the crowd going by.

Today I hear bilingual educators say that children lose a degree of "individuality" by becoming assimilated into public society. (Bilingual schooling was popularized in the seventies, that decade when middle-class ethnics began to resist

2. Spanish for "little boy."
3. Of the Catholic Order of Our Lady of Mount Carmel.

the process of assimilation—the American melting pot.) But the bilingualists simplistically scorn the value and necessity of assimilation. They do not seem to realize that there are *two* ways a person is individualized. So they do not realize that while one suffers a diminished sense of *private* individuality by becoming assimilated into public society, such assimilation makes possible the achievement of *public* individuality.

20   The bilingualists insist that a student should be reminded of his difference from others in mass society, his heritage. But they equate mere separateness with individuality. The fact is that only in private—with intimates—is separateness from the crowd a prerequisite for individuality. (An intimate draws me apart, tells me that I am unique, unlike all others.) In public, by contrast, full individuality is achieved, paradoxically, by those who are able to consider themselves members of the crowd. Thus it happened for me: Only when I was able to think of myself as an American, no longer an alien in *gringo* society, could I seek the rights and opportunities necessary for full public individuality. The social and political advantages I enjoy as a man result from the day that I came to believe that my name, indeed, is *Rich-heard Road-ree-guess*. It is true that my public society today is often impersonal. (My public society is usually mass society.) Yet despite the anonymity of the crowd and despite the fact that the individuality I achieve in public is often tenuous—because it depends on my being one in a crowd—I celebrate the day I acquired my new name. Those middle-class ethnics who scorn assimilation seem to me filled with decadent self-pity, obsessed by the burden of public life. Dangerously, they romanticize public separateness and they trivialize the dilemma of the socially disadvantaged.

My awkward childhood does not prove the necessity of bilingual education. My story discloses instead an essential myth of childhood—inevitable pain. If I rehearse here the changes in my private life after my Americanization, it is finally to emphasize the public gain. The loss implies the gain: The house I returned to each afternoon was quiet. Intimate sounds no longer rushed to the door to greet me. There were other noises inside. The telephone rang. Neighborhood kids ran past the door of the bedroom where I was reading my schoolbooks—covered with shopping-bag paper. Once I learned public language, it would never again be easy for me to hear intimate family voices. More and more of my day was spent hearing words. But that may only be a way of saying that the day I raised my hand in class and spoke loudly to an entire roomful of faces, my childhood started to end.

MLA CITATION

Rodriguez, Richard. "Aria." 1982. *The Norton Reader: An Anthology of Nonfiction.* Ed. Melissa A. Goldthwaite et al. 14th ed. New York: Norton, 2016. 465–70. Print.

QUESTIONS

1. What, according to Richard Rodriguez, did he lose because he attended an English-speaking school without a bilingual program? What did he gain?

2. Rodriguez frames this section of his autobiography with an argument against bilingual education. What evidence does he use to support his argument? Do you find it convincing? Why or why not?

3. According to Rodriguez, what are the differences between private and public languages, private and public individuality? Can both exist when the family language and the school language are English? How might a native speaker of English describe the differences?

4. Make a case, in writing, for or against bilingual education using material from Maxine Hong Kingston's "Tongue-Tied" (pp. 461–65), Gloria Anzaldúa's "How to Tame a Wild Tongue" (pp. 471–80), or Gloria Naylor's "Mommy, What Does 'Nigger' Mean?" (pp. 481–83), as well as your own experience, observation, and reading.

GLORIA ANZALDÚA *How to Tame a Wild Tongue*

"WE'RE GOING TO have to control your tongue," the dentist says, pulling out all the metal from my mouth. Silver bits plop and tinkle into the basin. My mouth is a motherlode.

The dentist is cleaning out my roots. I get a whiff of the stench when I gasp. "I can't cap that tooth yet, you're still draining," he says.

"We're going to have to do something about your tongue," I hear the anger rising in his voice. My tongue keeps pushing out the wads of cotton, pushing back the drills, the long thin needles. "I've never seen anything as strong or as stubborn," he says. And I think, how do you tame a wild tongue, train it to be quiet, how do you bridle and saddle it? How do you make it lie down?

> "Who is to say that robbing a people of
> its language is less violent than war?"
>
> —RAY GWYN SMITH[1]

I remember being caught speaking Spanish at recess—that was good for three licks on the knuckles with a sharp ruler. I remember being sent to the corner of the classroom for "talking back" to the Anglo teacher when all I was trying to do was tell her how to pronounce my name. "If you want to be American, speak 'American.' If you don't like it, go back to Mexico where you belong."

"I want you to speak English. *Pa'hallar buen trabajo tienes que saber hablar el inglés bien. Qué vale toda tu educación si todavía hablas inglés con un* 'accent,'" my mother would say, mortified that I spoke English like a Mexican. At Pan

5

From Borderlands/La Frontera *(1987), a collection of experimental essays and memoirs that combine English, Spanish, and Chicano Spanish. All notes are the author's. The author has asked that no translations of Spanish or Chicano Spanish be included.*

1. Ray Gwyn Smith, *Moorland Is Cold Country*, unpublished book.

American University, I, and all Chicano students were required to take two speech classes. Their purpose: to get rid of our accents.

Attacks on one's form of expression with the intent to censor are a violation of the First Amendment. *El Anglo con cara de inocente nos arrancó la lengua.* Wild tongues can't be tamed, they can only be cut out.

OVERCOMING THE TRADITION OF SILENCE

> *Ahogadas, escupimos el oscuro.*
> *Peleando con nuestra propia sombra*
> *el silencio nos sepulta.*

En boca cerrada no entran moscas. "Flies don't enter a closed mouth" is a saying I kept hearing when I was a child. *Ser habladora* was to be a gossip and a liar, to talk too much. *Muchachitas bien criadas,* well-bred girls don't answer back. *Es una falta de respeto* to talk back to one's mother or father. I remember one of the sins I'd recite to the priest in the confession box the few times I went to confession: talking back to my mother, *hablar pa' 'trás, repelar. Hocicona, repelona, chismosa,* having a big mouth, questioning, carrying tales are all signs of being *mal criada.* In my culture they are all words that are derogatory if applied to women—I've never heard them applied to men.

The first time I heard two women, a Puerto Rican and a Cuban, say the word "*nosotras,*" I was shocked. I had not known the word existed. Chicanas use *nosotros* whether we're male or female. We are robbed of our female being by the masculine plural. Language is a male discourse.

> And our tongues have become
> dry the wilderness has
> dried out our tongues and
> we have forgotten speech.
>
> —IRENA KLEPFISZ[2]

Even our own people, other Spanish speakers *nos quieren poner candados en la boca.* They would hold us back with their bag of *reglas de academia.*

Oyé como ladra: el lenguaje de la frontera

> *Quien tiene boca se equivoca.*
>
> —MEXICAN SAYING

10   "*Pocho,* cultural traitor, you're speaking the oppressor's language by speaking English, you're ruining the Spanish language," I have been accused by various Latinos and Latinas. Chicano Spanish is considered by the purist and by most Latinos deficient, a mutilation of Spanish.

---

2. Irena Klepfisz, "*Di rayze aheym*/The Journey Home," in *The Tribe of Dina: A Jewish Women's Anthology,* Melanie Kaye/Kantrowitz and Irena Klepfisz, eds. (Montpelier, VT: Sinister Wisdom Books, 1986), 49.

But Chicano Spanish is a border tongue which developed naturally. Change, *evolución, enriquecimiento de palabras nuevas por invención o adopción* have created variants of Chicano Spanish, *un nuevo lenguaje. Un lenguaje que corresponde a un modo de vivir.* Chicano Spanish is not incorrect, it is a living language.

For a people who are neither Spanish nor live in a country in which Spanish is the first language; for a people who live in a country in which English is the reigning tongue but who are not Anglo; for a people who cannot entirely identify with either standard (formal, Castilian) Spanish nor standard English, what recourse is left to them but to create their own language? A language which they can connect their identity to, one capable of communicating the realities and values true to themselves—a language with terms that are neither *español ni inglés,* but both. We speak a patois, a forked tongue, a variation of two languages.

Chicano Spanish sprang out of the Chicanos' need to identify ourselves as a distinct people. We needed a language with which we could communicate with ourselves, a secret language. For some of us, language is a homeland closer than the Southwest—for many Chicanos today live in the Midwest and the East. And because we are a complex, heterogeneous people, we speak many languages. Some of the languages we speak are:

1. Standard English

2. Working class and slang English

3. Standard Spanish

4. Standard Mexican Spanish

5. North Mexican Spanish dialect

6. Chicano Spanish (Texas, New Mexico, Arizona and California have regional variations)

7. Tex-Mex

8. *Pachuco* (called *caló*)

My "home" tongues are the languages I speak with my sister and brothers, with my friends. They are the last five listed, with 6 and 7 being closest to my heart. From school, the media and job situations, I've picked up standard and working class English. From Mamagrande Locha and from reading Spanish and Mexican literature, I've picked up Standard Spanish and Standard Mexican Spanish. From *los recién llegados,* Mexican immigrants, and *braceros*, I learned the North Mexican dialect. With Mexicans I'll try to speak either Standard Mexican Spanish or the North Mexican dialect. From my parents and Chicanos living in the Valley, I picked up Chicano Texas Spanish, and I speak it with my mom, younger brother (who married a Mexican and who rarely mixes Spanish with English), aunts and older relatives.

With Chicanas from *Nuevo México* or *Arizona* I will speak Chicano Spanish a little, but often they don't understand what I'm saying. With most California   15

Chicanas I speak entirely in English (unless I forget). When I first moved to San Francisco, I'd rattle off something in Spanish, unintentionally embarrassing them. Often it is only with another Chicana *tejana* that I can talk freely.

Words distorted by English are known as anglicisms or *pochismos*. The *pocho* is an anglicized Mexican or American of Mexican origin who speaks Spanish with an accent characteristic of North Americans and who distorts and reconstructs the language according to the influence of English.[3] Tex-Mex, or Spanglish, comes most naturally to me. I may switch back and forth from English to Spanish in the same sentence or in the same word. With my sister and my brother Nune and with Chicano *tejano* contemporaries I speak in Tex-Mex.

From kids and people my own age I picked up *Pachuco. Pachuco* (the language of the zoot suiters) is a language of rebellion, both against Standard Spanish and Standard English. It is a secret language. Adults of the culture and outsiders cannot understand it. It is made up of slang words from both English and Spanish. *Ruca* means girl or woman, *vato* means guy or dude, *chale* means no, *simón* means yes, *churo* is sure, talk is *periquiar, pigionear* means petting, *que gacho* means how nerdy, *ponte águila* means watch out, death is called *la pelona*. Through lack of practice and not having others who can speak it, I've lost most of the *Pachuco* tongue.

CHICANO SPANISH

Chicanos, after 250 years of Spanish/Anglo colonization, have developed significant differences in the Spanish we speak. We collapse two adjacent vowels into a single syllable and sometimes shift the stress in certain words such as *maíz/maiz, cohete/cuete.* We leave out certain consonants when they appear between vowels: *lado/lao, mojado/mojao.* Chicanos from South Texas pronounced *f* as *j* as in *jue (fue).* Chicanos use "archaisms," words that are no longer in the Spanish language, words that have been evolved out. We say *semos, truje, haiga, ansina,* and *naiden.* We retain the "archaic" *j*, as in *jalar,* that derives from an earlier *h* (the French *halar* or the Germanic *halon* which was lost to standard Spanish in the 16th century), but which is still found in several regional dialects such as the one spoken in South Texas. (Due to geography, Chicanos from the Valley of South Texas were cut off linguistically from other Spanish speakers. We tend to use words that the Spaniards brought over from Medieval Spain. The majority of the Spanish colonizers in Mexico and the Southwest came from Extremadura—Hernán Cortés was one of them—and Andalucía. Andalucians pronounce *ll* like a *y*, and their *d*'s tend to be absorbed by adjacent vowels: *tirado* becomes *tirao.* They brought *el lenguaje popular, dialectos y regionalismos.*[4])

3. R. C. Ortega, *Dialectología Del Barrio*, trans. Hortencia S. Alwan (Los Angeles, CA: R. C. Ortega Publisher & Bookseller, 1977), 132.
4. Eduardo Hernandéz-Chávez, Andrew D. Cohen, and Anthony F. Beltramo, *El Lenguaje de los Chicanos: Regional and Social Characteristics of Language Used by Mexican Americans* (Arlington, VA: Center for Applied Linguistics, 1975), 39.

Chicanos and other Spanish speakers also shift *ll* to *y* and *z* to *s*.[5] We leave out initial syllables, saying *tar* for *estar, toy* for *estoy, hora* for *ahora* (*cubanos* and *puertorriqueños* also leave out initial letters of some words). We also leave out the final syllable such as *pa* for *para*. The intervocalic *y*, the *ll* as in *tortilla, ella, botella*, gets replaced by *tortia* or *tortiya, ea, botea*. We add an additional syllable at the beginning of certain words: *atocar* for *tocar, agastar* for *gastar*. Sometimes we'll say *lavaste las vacijas*, other times *lavates* (substituting the *ates* verb endings for the *aste*).

We use anglicisms, words borrowed from English: *bola* from ball, *carpeta*   20
from carpet, *máchina de lavar* (instead of *lavadora*) from washing machine. Tex-Mex argot, created by adding a Spanish sound at the beginning or end of an English word such as *cookiar* for cook, *watchar* for watch, *parkiar* for park, and *rapiar* for rape, is the result of the pressures on Spanish speakers to adapt to English.

We don't use the word *vosotros/as* or its accompanying verb form. We don't say *claro* (to mean yes), *imagínate*, or *me emociona*, unless we picked up Spanish from Latinas, out of a book, or in a classroom. Other Spanish-speaking groups are going through the same, or similar, development in their Spanish.

Linguistic Terrorism

> *Deslenguadas. Somos los del español deficiente.* We are your linguistic night-mare, your linguistic aberration, your linguistic *mestisaje*, the subject of your *burla*. Because we speak with tongues of fire we are culturally crucified. Racially, culturally and linguistically *somos huérfanos*—we speak an orphan tongue.

Chicanas who grew up speaking Chicano Spanish have internalized the belief that we speak poor Spanish. It is illegitimate, a bastard language. And because we internalize how our language has been used against us by the dominant cul-ture, we use our language differences against each other.

Chicana feminists often skirt around each other with suspicion and hesi-tation. For the longest time I couldn't figure it out. Then it dawned on me. To be close to another Chicana is like looking into the mirror. We are afraid of what we'll see there. *Pena*. Shame. Low estimation of self. In childhood we are told that our language is wrong. Repeated attacks on our native tongue dimin-ish our sense of self. The attacks continue throughout our lives.

Chicanas feel uncomfortable talking in Spanish to Latinas, afraid of their censure. Their language was not outlawed in their countries. They had a whole lifetime of being immersed in their native tongue; generations, centuries in which Spanish was a first language, taught in school, heard on radio and TV, and read in the newspaper.

If a person, Chicana or Latina, has a low estimation of my native tongue,   25
she also has a low estimation of me. Often with *mexicanas y latinas* we'll speak English as a neutral language. Even among Chicanas we tend to speak English

5. Hernandéz-Chávez, xvii.

at parties or conferences. Yet, at the same time, we're afraid the other will think we're *agringadas* because we don't speak Chicano Spanish. We oppress each other trying to out-Chicano each other, vying to be the "real" Chicanas, to speak like Chicanos. There is no one Chicano language just as there is no one Chicano experience. A monolingual Chicana whose first language is English or Spanish is just as much a Chicana as one who speaks several variants of Spanish. A Chicana from Michigan or Chicago or Detroit is just as much a Chicana as one from the Southwest. Chicano Spanish is as diverse linguistically as it is regionally.

By the end of this century, Spanish speakers will comprise the biggest minority group in the U.S., a country where students in high schools and colleges are encouraged to take French classes because French is considered more "cultured." But for a language to remain alive it must be used.[6] By the end of this century English, and not Spanish, will be the mother tongue of most Chicanos and Latinos.

So, if you want to really hurt me, talk badly about my language. Ethnic identity is twin skin to linguistic identity—I am my language. Until I can take pride in my language, I cannot take pride in myself. Until I can accept as legitimate Chicano Texas Spanish, Tex-Mex and all the other languages I speak, I cannot accept the legitimacy of myself. Until I am free to write bilingually and to switch codes without having always to translate, while I still have to speak English or Spanish when I would rather speak Spanglish, and as long as I have to accommodate the English speakers rather than having them accommodate me, my tongue will be illegitimate.

I will no longer be made to feel ashamed of existing. I will have my voice: Indian, Spanish, white. I will have my serpent's tongue—my woman's voice, my sexual voice, my poet's voice. I will overcome the tradition of silence.

> My fingers
> move sly against your palm
> Like women everywhere, we speak in code. . . .
> —MELANIE KAYE/KANTROWITZ[7]

"Vistas," corridos, y comida: My Native Tongue

In the 1960s, I read my first Chicano novel. It was *City of Night* by John Rechy, a gay Texan, son of a Scottish father and a Mexican mother. For days I walked around in stunned amazement that a Chicano could write and could get published. When I read *I Am Joaquín*[8] I was surprised to see a bilingual

---

6. Irena Klepfisz, "Secular Jewish Identity: Yidishkayt in America," in *The Tribe of Dina*, Kaye/Kantrowitz and Klepfisz, eds., 43.

7. Melanie Kaye/Kantrowitz, "Sign," in *We Speak in Code: Poems and Other Writings* (Pittsburgh, PA: Motheroot Publications, Inc., 1980), 85.

8. Rodolfo Gonzales, *I Am Joaquín/Yo Soy Joaquín* (New York, NY: Bantam Books, 1972). It was first published in 1967.

book by a Chicano in print. When I saw poetry written in Tex-Mex for the first time, a feeling of pure joy flashed through me. I felt like we really existed as a people. In 1971, when I started teaching High School English to Chicano students, I tried to supplement the required texts with works by Chicanos, only to be reprimanded and forbidden to do so by the principal. He claimed that I was supposed to teach "American" and English literature. At the risk of being fired, I swore my students to secrecy and slipped in Chicano short stories, poems, a play. In graduate school, while working toward a Ph.D., I had to "argue" with one advisor after the other, semester after semester, before I was allowed to make Chicano literature an area of focus.

Even before I read books by Chicanos or Mexicans, it was the Mexican   30
movies I saw at the drive-in—the Thursday night special of $1.00 a carload—that gave me a sense of belonging. *"Vámonos a las vistas,"* my mother would call out and we'd all—grandmother, brothers, sister and cousins—squeeze into the car. We'd wolf down cheese and bologna white bread sandwiches while watching Pedro Infante in melodramatic tear-jerkers like *Nosotros los pobres,* the first "real" Mexican movie (that was not an imitation of European movies). I remember seeing *Cuando los hijos se van* and surmising that all Mexican movies played up the love a mother has for her children and what ungrateful sons and daughters suffer when they are not devoted to their mothers. I remember the singing-type "westerns" of Jorge Negrete and Miguel Aceves Mejía. When watching Mexican movies, I felt a sense of homecoming as well as alienation. People who were to amount to something didn't go to Mexican movies, or *bailes* or tune their radios to *bolero, rancherita,* and *corrido* music.

The whole time I was growing up, there was *norteño* music sometimes called North Mexican border music, or Tex-Mex music, or Chicano music, or *cantina* (bar) music. I grew up listening to *conjuntos,* three- or four-piece bands made up of folk musicians playing guitar, *bajo sexto,* drums and button accordion, which Chicanos had borrowed from the German immigrants who had come to Central Texas and Mexico to farm and build breweries. In the Rio Grande Valley, Steve Jordan and Little Joe Hernández were popular, and Flaco Jiménez was the accordion king. The rhythms of Tex-Mex music are those of the polka, also adapted from the Germans, who in turn had borrowed the polka from the Czechs and Bohemians.

I remember the hot, sultry evenings when *corridos*—songs of love and death on the Texas-Mexican borderlands—reverberated out of cheap amplifiers from the local *cantinas* and wafted in through my bedroom window.

Corridos first became widely used along the South Texas/Mexican border during the early conflict between Chicanos and Anglos. The *corridos* are usually about Mexican heroes who do valiant deeds against the Anglo oppressors. Pancho Villa's song, *"La cucaracha,"* is the most famous one. *Corridos* of John F. Kennedy and his death are still very popular in the Valley. Older Chicanos remember Lydia Mendoza, one of the great border *corrido* singers who was called *la Gloria de Tejas.* Her *"El tango negro,"* sung during the Great Depression, made her a singer of the people. The everpresent *corridos* narrated one hundred years of border history, bringing news of events as well as entertaining. These folk musicians and folk songs are our chief cultural mythmakers, and they made our hard lives seem bearable.

I grew up feeling ambivalent about our music. Country-western and rock-and-roll had more status. In the 50s and 60s, for the slightly educated and *agringado* Chicanos, there existed a sense of shame at being caught listening to our music. Yet I couldn't stop my feet from thumping to the music, could not stop humming the words, nor hide from myself the exhilaration I felt when I heard it.

35   There are more subtle ways that we internalize identification, especially in the forms of images and emotions. For me food and certain smells are tied to my identity, to my homeland. Woodsmoke curling up to an immense blue sky; woodsmoke perfuming my grandmother's clothes, her skin. The stench of cow manure and the yellow patches on the ground; the crack of a .22 rifle and the reek of cordite. Homemade white cheese sizzling in a pan, melting inside a folded *tortilla*. My sister Hilda's hot, spicy *menudo, chile colorado* making it deep red, pieces of *panza* and hominy floating on top. My brother Carito barbecuing *fajitas* in the backyard. Even now and 3,000 miles away, I can see my mother spicing the ground beef, pork and venison with *chile*. My mouth salivates at the thought of the hot steaming *tamales* I would be eating if I were home.

Si le preguntas a mi mamá, "¿Qué eres?"

> "Identity is the essential core of who
> we are as individuals, the conscious
> experience of the self inside."
>
> —KAUFMAN[9]

Nosotros los Chicanos straddle the borderlands. On one side of us, we are constantly exposed to the Spanish of the Mexicans, on the other side we hear the Anglos' incessant clamoring so that we forget our language. Among ourselves we don't say *nosotros los americanos, o nosotros los españoles, o nosotros los hispanos*. We say *nosotros los mexicanos* (by *mexicanos* we do not mean citizens of Mexico; we do not mean a national identity, but a racial one). We distinguish between *mexicanos del otro lado* and *mexicanos de este lado*. Deep in our hearts we believe that being Mexican has nothing to do with which country one lives in. Being Mexican is a state of soul—not one of mind, not one of citizenship. Neither eagle nor serpent, but both. And like the ocean, neither animal respects borders.

> *Dime con quien andas y te diré quien eres.*
> (Tell me who your friends are and I'll tell you who you are.)
>
> —MEXICAN SAYING

9. Gershen Kaufman, *Shame: The Power of Caring* (Cambridge, MA: Shenkman Books, 1980), 68.

Si le preguntas a mi mamá, "¿Qué eres?" te dirá, "Soy mexicana." My brothers and sister say the same. I sometimes will answer *"soy mexicana"* and at others will say *"soy Chicana" o "soy tejana."* But I identified as *"Raza"* before I ever identified as *"mexicana"* or "Chicana."

As a culture, we call ourselves Spanish when referring to ourselves as a linguistic group and when copping out. It is then that we forget our predominant Indian genes. We are 70 to 80% Indian.[10] We call ourselves Hispanic[11] or Spanish-American or Latin American or Latin when linking ourselves to other Spanish-speaking peoples of the Western hemisphere and when copping out. We call ourselves Mexican-American[12] to signify we are neither Mexican nor American, but more the noun "American" than the adjective "Mexican" (and when copping out).

Chicanos and other people of color suffer economically for not acculturating. This voluntary (yet forced) alienation makes for psychological conflict, a kind of dual identity—we don't identify with the Anglo-American cultural values and we don't totally identify with the Mexican cultural values. We are a synergy of two cultures with various degrees of Mexicanness or Angloness. I have so internalized the borderland conflict that sometimes I feel like one cancels out the other and we are zero, nothing, no one. *A veces no soy nada ni nadie. Pero hasta cuando no lo soy, lo soy.*

When not copping out, when we know we are more than nothing, we call ourselves Mexican, referring to race and ancestry; *mestizo* when affirming both our Indian and Spanish (but we hardly ever own our Black ancestry); Chicano when referring to a politically aware people born and/or raised in the U.S.; *Raza* when referring to Chicanos; *tejanos* when we are Chicanos from Texas.   40

Chicanos did not know we were a people until 1965 when Cesar Chavez and the farmworkers united and *I Am Joaquín* was published and *la Raza Unida* party was formed in Texas. With that recognition, we became a distinct people. Something momentous happened to the Chicano soul—we became aware of our reality and acquired a name and a language (Chicano Spanish) that reflected that reality. Now that we had a name, some of the fragmented pieces began to fall together—who we were, what we were, how we had evolved. We began to get glimpses of what we might eventually become.

Yet the struggle of identities continues, the struggle of borders is our reality still. One day the inner struggle will cease and a true integration take place. In the meantime, *tenémos que hacer la lucha. ¿Quién está protegiendo los ranchos de mi gente? ¿Quién está tratando de cerrar la fisura entre la india y el blanco en nuestra sangre? El Chicano, si, el Chicano que anda como un ladrón en su propia casa.*

10. John R. Chávez, *The Lost Land: The Chicano Image of the Southwest* (Albuquerque: U of New Mexico P, 1984), 88–90.

11. "Hispanic" is derived from *Hispanis* (*España*, a name given to the Iberian Peninsula in ancient times when it was a part of the Roman Empire) and is a term designated by the U.S. government to make it easier to handle us on paper.

12. In 1848 the Treaty of Guadalupe Hidalgo created the Mexican-American.

Los Chicanos, how patient we seem, how very patient. There is the quiet of the Indian about us.[13] We know how to survive. When other races have given up their tongue, we've kept ours. We know what it is to live under the hammer blow of the dominant *norteamericano* culture. But more than we count the blows, we count the days the weeks the years the centuries the eons until the white laws and commerce and customs will rot in the deserts they've created, lie bleached. *Humildes* yet proud, *quietos* yet wild, *nosotros los mexicanos-Chicanos* will walk by the crumbling ashes as we go about our business. Stubborn, persevering, impenetrable as stone, yet possessing a malleability that renders us unbreakable, we, the *mestizas* and *mestizos,* will remain.

13. Anglos, in order to alleviate their guilt for dispossessing the Chicano, stressed the Spanish part of us and perpetrated the myth of the Spanish Southwest. We have accepted the fiction that we are Hispanic, that is Spanish, in order to accommodate ourselves to the dominant culture and its abhorrence of Indians. Chávez, 88–91.

MLA CITATION

Anzaldúa, Gloria. "How to Tame a Wild Tongue." 1987. *The Norton Reader: An Anthology of Nonfiction.* Ed. Melissa A. Goldthwaite et al. 14th ed. New York: Norton, 2016. 471–80. Print.

QUESTIONS

1. Gloria Anzaldúa includes many Spanish words and phrases, some of which she explains, others which she leaves untranslated. Why do you think she does this? What different responses might bilingual versus English-only readers have to her writing?

2. The essay begins with an example of Anzaldúa's "untamed tongue." What meanings, many metaphoric, does Anzaldúa give for "tongue" or "wild tongue"? How does the essay develop these meanings?

3. Anzaldúa speaks of Chicano Spanish as a "living language" (paragraph 11). What does she mean? What is her evidence for this point? What other languages do you know that are living, and how do you know they are living?

4. If you speak or write more than one language, or come from a community that uses expressions that you believe to be unique or uncommon, write an essay in which you incorporate that language and/or alternate it with English. Think about the ways that Anzaldúa uses both English and Spanish.

GLORIA NAYLOR   *"Mommy, What Does
                        'Nigger' Mean?"*

Language is the subject. It is the written form with which I've managed to keep the wolf away from the door and, in diaries, to keep my sanity. In spite of this, I consider the written word inferior to the spoken, and much of the frustration experienced by novelists is the awareness that whatever we manage to capture in even the most transcendent passages falls far short of the richness of life. Dialogue achieves its power in the dynamics of a fleeting moment of sight, sound, smell and touch.

I'm not going to enter the debate here about whether it is language that shapes reality or vice versa. That battle is doomed to be waged whenever we seek intermittent reprieve from the chicken and egg dispute. I will simply take the position that the spoken word, like the written word, amounts to a nonsensical arrangement of sounds or letters without a consensus that assigns "meaning." And building from the meanings of what we hear, we order reality. Words themselves are innocuous; it is the consensus that gives them true power.

I remember the first time I heard the word nigger. In my third-grade class, our math tests were being passed down the rows, and as I handed the papers to a little boy in back of me, I remarked that once again he had received a much lower mark than I did. He snatched his test from me and spit out that word. Had he called me a nymphomaniac or a necrophiliac, I couldn't have been more puzzled. I didn't know what a nigger was, but I knew that whatever it meant, it was something he shouldn't have called me. This was verified when I raised my hand, and in a loud voice repeated what he had said and watched the teacher scold him for using a "bad" word. I was later to go home and ask the inevitable question that every black parent must face—"Mommy, what does 'nigger' mean?"

And what exactly did it mean? Thinking back, I realize that this could not have been the first time the word was used in my presence. I was part of a large extended family that had migrated from the rural South after World War II and formed a close-knit network that gravitated around my maternal grandparents. Their ground-floor apartment in one of the buildings they owned in Harlem was a weekend mecca for my immediate family, along with countless aunts, uncles and cousins who brought along assorted friends. It was a bustling and open house with assorted neighbors and tenants popping in and out to exchange bits of gossip, pick up an old quarrel or referee the ongoing checkers game in which my grandmother cheated shamelessly. They were all there to let down their hair and put up their feet after a week of labor in the factories, laundries and shipyards of New York.

Originally published in "Hers," an op-ed column of the New York Times *(1986) that covered topics of importance for and about women.*

5   Amid the clamor, which could reach deafening proportions—two or three
conversations going on simultaneously, punctuated by the sound of a baby's crying somewhere in the back rooms or out on the street—there was still a rigid
set of rules about what was said and how. Older children were sent out of the
living room when it was time to get into the juicy details about "you-know-who"
up on the third floor who had gone and gotten herself "p-r-e-g-n-a-n-t!" But my
parents, knowing that I could spell well beyond my years, always demanded that
I follow the others out to play. Beyond sexual misconduct and death, everything
else was considered harmless for our young ears. And so among the anecdotes
of the triumphs and disappointments in the various workings of their lives, the
word nigger was used in my presence, but it was set within contexts and inflec-
tions that caused it to register in my mind as something else.

      In the singular, the word was always applied to a man who had distin-
guished himself in some situation that brought their approval for his strength,
intelligence or drive:

      "Did Johnny really do that?"

      "I'm telling you, that nigger pulled in $6,000 of overtime last year. Said he
got enough for a down payment on a house."

      When used with a possessive adjective by a woman—"my nigger"—it
became a term of endearment for husband or boyfriend. But it could be more
than just a term applied to a man. In their mouths it became the pure essence
of manhood—a disembodied force that channeled their past history of struggle
and present survival against the odds into a victorious statement of being: "Yeah,
that old foreman found out quick enough—you don't mess with a nigger."

10   In the plural, it became a description of some group within the community that had overstepped the bounds of decency as my family defined it: Parents who neglected their children, a drunken couple who fought in public,
people who simply refused to look for work, those with excessively dirty mouths
or unkempt households were all "trifling niggers." This particular circle could
forgive hard times, unemployment, the occasional bout of depression—they
had gone through all of that themselves—but the unforgivable sin was lack of
self-respect.

      A woman could never be a "nigger" in the singular, with its connotation of
confirming worth. The noun girl was its closest equivalent in that sense, but
only when used in direct address and regardless of the gender doing the addressing. "Girl" was a token of respect for a woman. The one-syllable word was drawn
out to sound like three in recognition of the extra ounce of wit, nerve or daring
that the woman had shown in the situation under discussion.

      "G-i-r-l, stop. You mean you said that to his face?"

      But if the word was used in a third-person reference or shortened so that
it almost snapped out of the mouth, it always involved some element of communal disapproval. And age became an important factor in these exchanges. It
was only between individuals of the same generation, or from an older person
to a younger (but never the other way around), that "girl" would be considered
a compliment.

I don't agree with the argument that use of the word nigger at this social stratum of the black community was an internalization of racism. The dynamics were the exact opposite: the people in my grandmother's living room took a word that whites used to signify worthlessness or degradation and rendered it impotent. Gathering there together, they transformed "nigger" to signify the varied and complex human beings they knew themselves to be. If the word was to disappear totally from the mouths of even the most liberal of white society, no one in that room was naïve enough to believe it would disappear from white minds. Meeting the word head-on, they proved it had absolutely nothing to do with the way they were determined to live their lives.

So there must have been dozens of times that the word "nigger" was spoken in front of me before I reached the third grade. But I didn't "hear" it until it was said by a small pair of lips that had already learned it could be a way to humiliate me. That was the word I went home and asked my mother about. And since she knew that I had to grow up in America, she took me in her lap and explained. 15

MLA CITATION

Naylor, Gloria. "Mommy, What Does 'Nigger' Mean?" 1986. *The Norton Reader: An Anthology of Nonfiction*. Ed. Melissa A. Goldthwaite et al. 14th ed. New York: Norton, 2016. 481–83. Print.

QUESTIONS

1. In her opening paragraph, Gloria Naylor writes that she considers "the written word inferior to the spoken." In what ways does she demonstrate the superiority of the spoken word in this essay?

2. Naylor claims that "[w]ords themselves are innocuous; it is the consensus that gives them true power" (paragraph 2). As a class, brainstorm a list of words that can have different meanings and connotations, depending on who uses the words or in what context they are spoken.

3. Think of a word that has several different meanings in your own family or community. Write a personal essay in which you detail those meanings. Like Naylor, use grammatical terms (as well as age- and gender-specifics, if applicable) to categorize the different meanings.

BENJAMIN FRANKLIN   *Learning to Write*

ABOUT THIS TIME I met with an odd Volume of the *Specta-tor.*[1] I had never before seen any of them. I bought it, read it over and over, and was much delighted with it. I thought the Writing excellent, and wish'd if possible to imitate it. With that View, I took some of the Papers, and making short Hints of the Sentiment in each Sentence, laid them by a few Days, and then without looking at the Book, tried to complete the Papers again, by expressing each hinted Sentiment at length and as fully as it had been express'd before in any suitable Words that should come to hand.

Then I compar'd my *Spectator* with the Original, discover'd some of my Faults and corrected them. But I found I wanted a Stock of Words or a Readiness in recollecting and using them which I thought I should have acquir'd before that time, if I had gone on making Verses, since the continual Occasion for Words of the same Import but of different Length, to suit the Measure,[2] or of different Sound for the Rhyme, would have laid me under a constant Necessity of searching for Variety, and also have tended to fix that Variety in my Mind, and make me Master of it. Therefore I took some of the Tales and turn'd them into Verse: And after a time, when I had pretty well forgotten the Prose, turn'd them back again. I also sometimes jumbled my Collections of Hints into Confusion, and after some Weeks, endeavor'd to reduce them into the best Order, before I began to form the full Sentences, and complete the Paper. This was to teach me Method in the Arrangement of Thoughts. By comparing my Work afterwards with the original, I discover'd many faults and amended them; but I sometimes had the Pleasure of Fancying that in certain Particulars of small Import, I had been lucky enough to improve the Method or the Language and this encourag'd me to think I might possibly in time come to be a tolerable English Writer, of which I was extremely ambitious.

My Time for these Exercises and for Reading, was at Night after Work, or before Work began in the Morning; or on Sundays, when I contrived to be in the Printing-House alone, evading as much as I could the common Attendance on public Worship, which my Father used to exact of me when I was under his Care: And which indeed I still thought a Duty; tho' I could not, as it seemed to me, afford the Time to practice it.

When about 16 Years of Age, I happen'd to meet with a Book written by one Tryon,[3] recommending a Vegetable Diet. I determined to go into it. My Brother being yet unmarried, did not keep House, but boarded himself and his Apprentices in another Family. My refusing to eat Flesh occasioned an Incon-

Drawn from Benjamin Franklin's Autobiography, *first published in 1791.*

1. Daily English periodical noted for its excellence in prose.
2. Meter.
3. Thomas Tryon (1634–1703), author of *Way to Health and Happiness* (1682).

veniency, and I was frequently chid for my singularity. I made myself acquainted with Tryon's Manner of preparing some of his Dishes, such as Boiling Potatoes or Rice, making Hasty Pudding,[4] and a few others, and then propos'd to my Brother, that if he would give me Weekly half the Money he paid for my Board, I would board myself. He instantly agreed to it, and I presently found that I could save half what he paid me. This was an additional Fund for buying Books: But I had another Advantage in it. My Brother and the rest going from the Printing-House to their Meals, I remain'd there alone, and dispatching presently my light Repast, (which often was no more than a Biscuit or a Slice of Bread, a Handful of Raisins or a Tart from the Pastry Cook's, and a Glass of Water) had the rest of the Time till their Return, for Study, in which I made the greater Progress from that greater Clearness of Head and quicker Apprehension which usually attend Temperance in Eating and Drinking. And now it was that being on some Occasion made asham'd of my Ignorance in Figures; which I had twice fail'd in learning when at School, I took Cocker's Book of Arithmetic,[5] and went thro' the whole by myself with great Ease. I also read Seller's and Sturmy's[6] Books of Navigation, and became acquainted with the little Geometry they contain, but never proceeded far in that Science. And I read about this Time Locke on Human Understanding and the Art of Thinking by Messrs. du Port Royal.[7]

While I was intent on improving my Language, I met with an English   5
Grammar (I think it was Greenwood's[8]) at the End of which there were two little Sketches of the Arts of Rhetoric and Logic, the latter finishing with a Specimen of a Dispute in the Socratic Method. And soon after I procur'd Xenophon's Memorable Things of Socrates,[9] wherein there are many Instances of the same Method. I was charm'd with it, adopted it, dropped my abrupt Contradiction and positive Argumentation, and put on the humble Enquirer and Doubter. And being then, from reading Shaftesbury and Collins,[10] became a real Doubter in many Points of our Religious Doctrine. I found this Method safest for myself and very embarrassing to those against whom I used it, therefore I took a Delight in it, practic'd it continually and grew very artful and expert

---

4. Porridge.

5. Well-known textbook, first published in 1677.

6. John Seller (c. 1658–1698), author of *Practical Navigation* (1694); Samuel Sturmy (1633–1669), author of *The Mariner's Magazine* (1699).

7. John Locke (1632–1704), British philosopher and author of *An Essay Concerning Human Understanding* (1690); Pierre Nicole (1625–1695) of Port Royal published his book in 1662; it was translated into English as *Logic: Or the Art of Thinking* in 1687.

8. James Greenwood (d. 1737), author of *An Essay towards a Practical English Grammar* (1711).

9. Xenophon's (c. 430–355 B.C.E.) *The Memorable Things of Socrates* was published in English translation by Edward Bysshe in 1712.

10. Anthony Ashley Cooper, earl of Shaftesbury (1671–1713), famous for his *Characteristics of Men, Manners, Opinions, Times* (1711); Anthony Collins (1676–1729), a friend of Locke; author of *A Discourse of Free Thinking* (1713).

in drawing People even of superior Knowledge into Concessions the Consequences of which they did not foresee, entangling them in Difficulties out of
which they could not extricate themselves, and so obtaining Victories that neither myself nor my Cause always deserved. I continu'd this Method some few
Years, but gradually left it, retaining only the Habit of expressing myself in Terms
of modest Diffidence, never using when I advance any thing that may possibly
be disputed, the Words, *Certainly, undoubtedly,* or any others that give the Air
of Positiveness to an Opinion; but rather say, *I conceive,* or *I apprehend* a Thing
to be so or so. *It appears to me,* or *I should think it so or so for such and such Reasons,* or *I imagine* it to be so, or *it is so if I am not mistaken.* This Habit I believe
has been of great Advantage to me, when I have had occasion to inculcate my
Opinions and persuade Men into Measures that I have been from time to time
engag'd in promoting. And as the chief Ends of Conversation are to *inform,* or
to be *informed,* to *please* or to *persuade,* I wish well-meaning sensible Men would
not lessen their Power of doing Good by a Positive assuming Manner that seldom fails to disgust, tends to create Opposition, and to defeat every one of those
Purposes for which Speech was given us, to wit, giving or receiving Information, or Pleasure: For if you would *inform,* a positive dogmatical Manner in
advancing your Sentiments, may provoke Contradiction and prevent a candid
Attention. If you wish Information and Improvement from the Knowledge of
others and yet at the same time express yourself as firmly fix'd in your present
Opinions, modest sensible Men, who do not love Disputation, will probably leave
you undisturb'd in the Possession of your Error; and by such a Manner you
can seldom hope to recommend yourself in *pleasing* your Hearers, or to persuade those whose Concurrence you desire. Pope says, judiciously,

> Men should be taught as if you taught them not,
> And things unknown propos'd as things forgot,

farther recommending it to us,

> To speak tho' sure, with seeming Diffidence.[11]

And he might have coupled with this Line that which he has coupled with
another, I think less properly,

> For want of Modesty is want of Sense.

If you ask why *less properly,* I must repeat the Lines;

> "Immodest Words admit of *no* Defence;
> For Want of Modesty is Want of Sense."[12]

---

11. Adapted from *An Essay on Criticism* (1711), by Alexander Pope.

12. Franklin wrongly attributes these two lines to Pope. They are from *Essay on Translated Verse* (1684) by Wentworth Dillon. The second line should read "For want of
Decency is want of Sense."

Now is not *Want of Sense*, (where a Man is so unfortunate as to want it) some Apology for his *Want of Modesty*? and would not the Lines stand more justly thus?

> Immodest Words admit *but this* Defence.
> That Want of Modesty is Want of Sense.

This however I should submit to better Judgments.

MLA CITATION

Franklin, Benjamin. "Learning to Write." 1791. *The Norton Reader: An Anthology of Nonfiction.* Ed. Melissa A. Goldthwaite et al. 14th ed. New York: Norton, 2016. 484–87. Print.

QUESTIONS

1. Benjamin Franklin describes his youthful practice of imitating successful writers' sentences. Have you ever done this? If so, how was it helpful or unhelpful? What might writers likely learn from such a practice?

2. Franklin has been called an autodidact, a self-teacher. Recount what Franklin learned in this manner, and note what he failed to teach himself. What kinds of knowledge did Franklin seek to acquire? Was his learning broad or narrow? What kinds of endeavors was this knowledge most suited for?

3. When he was sixteen, Franklin read a book about vegetarian diets and immediately was converted. Write about how you or someone you know was converted to following a distinct path, either religious, ethical, or physical. Did the conversion happen suddenly, as it did with Franklin, or did it take place slowly, over time? In your essay you might consider imitating Franklin's style, or that of a writer you admire.

JOAN DIDION   *On Keeping a Notebook*

"'THAT WOMAN ESTELLE,'" the note reads, "'is partly the reason why George Sharp and I are separated today.' *Dirty crepe-de-Chine wrapper, hotel bar, Wilmington RR, 9:45 a.m. August Monday morning.*"

Since the note is in my notebook, it presumably has some meaning to me. I study it for a long while. At first I have only the most general notion of what I was doing on an August Monday morning in the bar of the hotel across from the Pennsylvania Railroad station in Wilmington, Delaware (waiting for a train? missing one? 1960? 1961? why Wilmington?), but I do remember being there. The woman in the dirty

From Slouching towards Bethlehem *(1968), Joan Didion's first work of nonfiction, which includes essays analyzing American culture in the 1960s.*

crepe-de-Chine wrapper had come down from her room for a beer, and the bar-
tender had heard before the reason why George Sharp and she were separated
today. "Sure," he said, and went on mopping the floor. "You told me." At the other
end of the bar is a girl. She is talking, pointedly, not to the man beside her but to
a cat lying in the triangle of sunlight cast through the open door. She is wearing
a plaid silk dress from Peck & Peck, and the hem is coming down.

Here is what it is: the girl has been on the Eastern Shore, and now she is
going back to the city, leaving the man beside her, and all she can see ahead
are the viscous summer sidewalks and the 3 a.m. long-distance calls that will
make her lie awake and then sleep drugged through all the steaming mornings
left in August (1960? 1961?). Because she must go directly from the train to
lunch in New York, she wishes that she had a safety pin for the hem of the plaid
silk dress, and she also wishes that she could forget about the hem and the lunch
and stay in the cool bar that smells of disinfectant and malt and make friends
with the woman in the crepe-de-Chine wrapper. She is afflicted by a little self-
pity, and she wants to compare Estelles. That is what that was all about.

Why did I write it down? In order to remember, of course, but exactly what
was it I wanted to remember? How much of it actually happened? Did any of
it? Why do I keep a notebook at all? It is easy to deceive oneself on all those
scores. The impulse to write things down is a peculiarly compulsive one, inexplicable to those who do not share it, useful only accidentally, only secondarily,
in the way that any compulsion tries to justify itself. I suppose that it begins or
does not begin in the cradle. Although I have felt compelled to write things
down since I was five years old, I doubt that my daughter ever will, for she is a
singularly blessed and accepting child, delighted with life exactly as life presents itself to her, unafraid to go to sleep and unafraid to wake up. Keepers of
private notebooks are a different breed altogether, lonely and resistant rearrang-
ers of things, anxious malcontents, children afflicted apparently at birth with
some presentiment of loss.

5   My first notebook was a Big Five tablet, given to me by my mother with
the sensible suggestion that I stop whining and learn to amuse myself by writing down my thoughts. She returned the tablet to me a few years ago; the first
entry is an account of a woman who believed herself to be freezing to death in
the Arctic night, only to find, when day broke, that she had stumbled onto the
Sahara Desert, where she would die of the heat before lunch. I have no idea
what turn of a five-year-old's mind could have prompted so insistently "ironic"
and exotic a story, but it does reveal a certain predilection for the extreme which
has dogged me into adult life; perhaps if I were analytically inclined I would
find it a truer story than any I might have told about Donald Johnson's birthday party or the day my cousin Brenda put Kitty Litter in the aquarium.

So the point of my keeping a notebook has never been, nor is it now, to have an
accurate factual record of what I have been doing or thinking. That would be
a different impulse entirely, an instinct for reality which I sometimes envy but
do not possess. At no point have I ever been able successfully to keep a diary;
my approach to daily life ranges from the grossly negligent to the merely absent,
and on those few occasions when I have tried dutifully to record a day's events,

boredom has so overcome me that the results are mysterious at best. What is this business about "shopping, typing piece, dinner with E, depressed"? Shopping for what? Typing what piece? Who is E? Was this "E" depressed, or was I depressed? Who cares?

In fact I have abandoned altogether that kind of pointless entry; instead I tell what some would call lies. "That's simply not true," the members of my family frequently tell me when they come up against my memory of a shared event. "The party was *not* for you, the spider was *not* a black widow, *it wasn't that way at all.*" Very likely they are right, for not only have I always had trouble distinguishing between what happened and what merely might have happened, but I remain unconvinced that the distinction, for my purposes, matters. The cracked crab that I recall having for lunch the day my father came home from Detroit in 1945 must certainly be embroidery, worked into the day's pattern to lend verisimilitude; I was ten years old and would not now remember the cracked crab. The day's events did not turn on cracked crab. And yet it is precisely that fictitious crab that makes me see the afternoon all over again, a home movie run all too often, the father bearing gifts, the child weeping, an exercise in family love and guilt. Or that is what it was to me. Similarly, perhaps it never did snow that August in Vermont; perhaps there never were flurries in the night wind, and maybe no one else felt the ground hardening and summer already dead even as we pretended to bask in it, but that was how it felt to me, and it might as well have snowed, could have snowed, did snow.

How it felt to me: that is getting closer to the truth about a notebook. I sometimes delude myself about why I keep a notebook, imagine that some thrifty virtue derives from preserving everything observed. See enough and write it down, I tell myself, and then some morning when the world seems drained of wonder, some day when I am only going through the motions of doing what I am supposed to do, which is write—on that bankrupt morning I will simply open my notebook and there it will all be, a forgotten account with accumulated interest, paid passage back to the world out there: dialogue overheard in hotels and elevators and at the hat-check counter in Pavillon (one middle-aged man shows his hat check to another and says, "That's my old football number"); impressions of Bettina Aptheker and Benjamin Sonnenberg and Teddy ("Mr. Acapulco") Stauffer; careful *aperçus* about tennis bums and failed fashion models and Greek shipping heiresses, one of whom taught me a significant lesson (a lesson I could have learned from F. Scott Fitzgerald, but perhaps we all must meet the very rich for ourselves) by asking, when I arrived to interview her in her orchid-filled sitting room on the second day of a paralyzing New York blizzard, whether it was snowing outside.

I imagine, in other words, that the notebook is about other people. But of course it is not. I have no real business with what one stranger said to another at the hat-check counter in Pavillon; in fact I suspect that the line "That's my old football number" touched not my own imagination at all, but merely some memory of something once read, probably "The Eighty-Yard Run."[1] Nor is my concern with a woman in a dirty crepe-de-Chine wrapper in a Wilmington bar.

1. Short story by Irwin Shaw (1914–1984).

My stake is always, of course, in the unmentioned girl in the plaid silk dress. *Remember what it was to be me:* that is always the point.

10   It is a difficult point to admit. We are brought up in the ethic that others, any others, all others, are by definition more interesting than ourselves; taught to be diffident, just this side of self-effacing. ("You're the least important person in the room and don't forget it," Jessica Mitford's[2] governess would hiss in her ear on the advent of any social occasion; I copied that into my notebook because it is only recently that I have been able to enter a room without hearing some such phrase in my inner ear.) Only the very young and the very old may recount their dreams at breakfast, dwell upon self, interrupt with memories of beach picnics and favorite Liberty lawn dresses and the rainbow trout in a creek near Colorado Springs. The rest of us are expected, rightly, to affect absorption in other people's favorite dresses, other people's trout.

And so we do. But our notebooks give us away, for however dutifully we record what we see around us, the common denominator of all we see is always, transparently, shamelessly, the implacable "I." We are not talking here about the kind of notebook that is patently for public consumption, a structural conceit for binding together a series of graceful *pensées;*[3] we are talking about something private, about bits of the mind's string too short to use, an indiscriminate and erratic assemblage with meaning only for its maker.

And sometimes even the maker has difficulty with the meaning. There does not seem to be, for example, any point in my knowing for the rest of my life that, during 1964, 720 tons of soot fell on every square mile of New York City, yet there it is in my notebook, labeled "FACT." Nor do I really need to remember that Ambrose Bierce liked to spell Leland Stanford's[4] name "£eland $tanford" or that "smart women almost always wear black in Cuba," a fashion hint without much potential for practical application. And does not the relevance of these notes seem marginal at best?:

> In the basement museum of the Inyo County Courthouse in Independence, California, sign pinned to a mandarin coat: "This MANDARIN COAT was often worn by Mrs. Minnie S. Brooks when giving lectures on her TEAPOT COLLECTION."
>
> Redhead getting out of car in front of Beverly Wilshire Hotel, chinchilla stole, Vuitton bags with tags reading:
>
>> MRS LOU FOX
>>
>> HOTEL SAHARA
>>
>> VEGAS

2. British essayist and social critic (1917–1996). See "Behind the Formaldehyde Curtain" (pp. 238–45).

3. French for "thoughts."

4. Bierce (1842–1914), American journalist and fiction writer, known for such ironic writing as *The Devil's Dictionary;* Stanford (1824–1893), railroad magnate, governor of California, and founder of Stanford University.

Well, perhaps not entirely marginal. As a matter of fact, Mrs. Minnie S. Brooks and her MANDARIN COAT pull me back into my own childhood, for although I never knew Mrs. Brooks and did not visit Inyo County until I was thirty, I grew up in just such a world, in houses cluttered with Indian relics and bits of gold ore and ambergris and the souvenirs my Aunt Mercy Farnsworth brought back from the Orient. It is a long way from that world to Mrs. Lou Fox's world, where we all live now, and is it not just as well to remember that? Might not Mrs. Minnie S. Brooks help me to remember what I am? Might not Mrs. Lou Fox help me to remember what I am not?

But sometimes the point is harder to discern. What exactly did I have in mind when I noted down that it cost the father of someone I know $650 a month to light the place on the Hudson in which he lived before the Crash?[5] What use was I planning to make of this line by Jimmy Hoffa:[6] "I may have my faults, but being wrong ain't one of them"? And although I think it interesting to know where the girls who travel with the Syndicate have their hair done when they find themselves on the West Coast, will I ever make suitable use of it? Might I not be better off just passing it on to John O'Hara?[7] What is a recipe for sauerkraut doing in my notebook? What kind of magpie keeps this notebook? *"He was born the night the Titanic went down."* That seems a nice enough line, and I even recall who said it, but is it not really a better line in life than it could ever be in fiction?

But of course that is exactly it: not that I should ever use the line, but that I should remember the woman who said it and the afternoon I heard it. We were on her terrace by the sea, and we were finishing the wine left from lunch, trying to get what sun there was, a California winter sun. The woman whose husband was born the night the *Titanic* went down wanted to rent her house, wanted to go back to her children in Paris. I remember wishing that I could afford the house, which cost $1,000 a month. "Someday you will," she said lazily. "Someday it all comes." There in the sun on her terrace it seemed easy to believe in someday, but later I had a low-grade afternoon hangover and ran over a black snake on the way to the supermarket and was flooded with inexplicable fear when I heard the checkout clerk explaining to the man ahead of me why she was finally divorcing her husband. "He left me no choice," she said over and over as she punched the register. "He has a little seven-month-old baby by her, he left me no choice." I would like to believe that my dread then was for the human condition, but of course it was for me, because I wanted a baby and did not then have one and because I wanted to own the house that cost $1,000 a month to rent and because I had a hangover.

It all comes back. Perhaps it is difficult to see the value in having one's self back in that kind of mood, but I do see it; I think we are well advised to keep on nodding terms with the people we used to be whether we find them

15

5. Stock market crash of 1929.

6. Head of the Teamsters Union who disappeared in 1975 and is presumed dead (1932–1982).

7. American novelist (1905–1970).

attractive company or not. Otherwise they turn up unannounced and surprise us, come hammering on the mind's door at 4 a.m. of a bad night and demand to know who deserted them, who betrayed them, who is going to make amends. We forget all too soon the things we thought we could never forget. We forget the loves and the betrayals alike, forget what we whispered and what we screamed, forget who we were. I have already lost touch with a couple of people I used to be; one of them, a seventeen-year-old, presents little threat, although it would be of some interest to me to know again what it feels like to sit on a river levee drinking vodka-and-orange-juice and listening to Les Paul and Mary Ford[8] and their echoes sing "How High the Moon" on the car radio. (You see I still have the scenes, but I no longer perceive myself among those present, no longer could even improvise the dialogue.) The other one, a twenty-three-year-old, bothers me more. She was always a good deal of trouble, and I suspect she will reappear when I least want to see her, skirts too long, shy to the point of aggravation, always the injured party, full of recriminations and little hurts and stories I do not want to hear again, at once saddening me and angering me with her vulnerability and ignorance, an apparition all the more insistent for being so long banished.

It is a good idea, then, to keep in touch, and I suppose that keeping in touch is what notebooks are all about. And we are all on our own when it comes to keeping those lines open to ourselves: your notebook will never help me, nor mine you. *"So what's new in the whiskey business?"* What could that possibly mean to you? To me it means a blonde in a Pucci bathing suit sitting with a couple of fat men by the pool at the Beverly Hills Hotel. Another man approaches, and they all regard one another in silence for a while. "So what's new in the whiskey business?" one of the fat men finally says by way of welcome, and the blonde stands up, arches one foot and dips it in the pool, looking all the while at the cabaña where Baby Pignatari[9] is talking on the telephone. That is all there is to that, except that several years later I saw the blonde coming out of Saks Fifth Avenue in New York with her California complexion and a voluminous mink coat. In the harsh wind that day she looked old and irrevocably tired to me, and even the skins in the mink coat were not worked the way they were doing them that year, not the way she would have wanted them done, and there is the point of the story. For a while after that I did not like to look in the mirror, and my eyes would skim the newspapers and pick out only the deaths, the cancer victims, the premature coronaries, the suicides, and I stopped riding the Lexington Avenue IRT[10] because I noticed for the first time that all the strangers I had seen for years—the man with the seeing-eye dog, the spinster who read the classified pages every day, the fat girl who always got off with me at Grand Central—looked older than they once had.

8. Husband-and-wife musical team of the 1940s and 1950s.
9. Brazilian playboy (1916–1977).
10. New York City subway line; one of its stops was the Grand Central railway terminal.

It all comes back. Even that recipe for sauerkraut: even that brings it back. I was on Fire Island when I first made that sauerkraut, and it was raining, and we drank a lot of bourbon and ate the sauerkraut and went to bed at ten, and I listened to the rain and the Atlantic and felt safe. I made the sauerkraut again last night and it did not make me feel any safer, but that is, as they say, another story.

MLA CITATION

Didion, Joan. "On Keeping a Notebook." 1968. *The Norton Reader: An Anthology of Nonfiction*. Ed. Melissa A. Goldthwaite et al. 14th ed. New York: Norton, 2016. 487–93. Print.

QUESTIONS

1. What distinction does Joan Didion make between a diary and a notebook? What uses does a notebook have for Didion?

2. Didion says she uses her notebook to "tell what some would call lies" (paragraph 7). Why does she do this? Would some people call these things truths? Why?

3. Didion says, "*How it felt to me:* that is getting closer to the truth about a notebook" (paragraph 8). What writing strategies does she use to convey "how it felt"?

4. Try keeping a notebook for a week, jotting down the sorts of things that Didion does. At the end of the week, take one or two of your entries and expand on them, as Didion does with the entries on Mrs. Minnie S. Brooks and Mrs. Lou Fox (paragraphs 12–13).

STEPHEN KING   *On Writing*

HARDLY A WEEK after being sprung from detention hall, I was once more invited to step down to the principal's office. I went with a sinking heart, wondering what new shit I'd stepped in.

It wasn't Mr. Higgins who wanted to see me, at least; this time the school guidance counselor had issued the summons. There had been discussions about me, he said, and how to turn my "restless pen" into more constructive channels. He had enquired of John Gould, editor of Lisbon's weekly newspaper, and had discovered Gould had an opening for a sports reporter. While the school couldn't *insist* that I take this job, everyone in the front office felt it would be a good idea. *Do it or die,* the G.C.'s eyes suggested. Maybe that was just paranoia, but even now, almost forty years later, I don't think so.

From On Writing: A Memoir of the Craft *(2000). Stephen King is primarily known for his horror and suspense novels and stories.*

I groaned inside. I was shut of *Dave's Rag*, almost shut of *The Drum*, and now here was the Lisbon *Weekly Enterprise*. Instead of being haunted by waters, like Norman Maclean in *A River Runs Through It*,[1] I was as a teenager haunted by newspapers. Still, what could I do? I rechecked the look in the guidance counselor's eyes and said I would be delighted to interview for the job.

Gould—not the well-known New England humorist or the novelist who wrote *The Greenleaf Fires* but a relation of both, I think—greeted me warily but with some interest. We would try each other out, he said, if that suited me.

5   Now that I was away from the administrative offices of Lisbon High, I felt able to muster a little honesty. I told Mr. Gould that I didn't know much about sports. Gould said, "These are games people understand when they're watching them drunk in bars. You'll learn if you try."

He gave me a huge roll of yellow paper on which to type my copy—I think I still have it somewhere—and promised me a wage of half a cent a word. It was the first time someone had promised me wages for writing.

The first two pieces I turned in had to do with a basketball game in which an LHS player broke the school scoring record. One was a straight piece of reporting. The other was a sidebar about Robert Ransom's record-breaking performance. I brought both to Gould the day after the game so he'd have them for Friday, which was when the paper came out. He read the game piece, made two minor corrections, and spiked it. Then he started in on the feature piece with a large black pen.

I took my fair share of English Lit classes in my two remaining years at Lisbon, and my fair share of composition, fiction, and poetry classes in college, but John Gould taught me more than any of them, and in no more than ten minutes. I wish I still had the piece—it deserves to be framed, editorial corrections and all—but I can remember pretty well how it went and how it looked after Gould had combed through it with that black pen of his. Here's an example:

> Last night, in the ~~well-loved~~ gymnasium of Lisbon High School, partisans and Jay Hills fans alike were stunned by an athletic performance unequalled in school history. Bob Ransom, ~~known as "Bullet" Bob for both his size and accuracy,~~ scored thirty-seven points. Yes, you heard me right. ~~But~~ he did it with grace, speed . . . and with an odd courtesy as well, committing only two personal fouls in his ~~knight-like~~ quest for a record which has eluded Lisbon ~~thinclads~~ *players* since ~~the years of Korea~~ *1953*. . . .

1. Story collection (1976) by Maclean (1902–1990), which includes the often-quoted words, "I am haunted by waters."

Gould stopped at "the years of Korea" and looked up at me. "What year was the last record made?" he asked.

Luckily, I had my notes. "1953," I said. Gould grunted and went back to   10
work. When he finished marking my copy in the manner indicated above, he looked up and saw something on my face. I think he must have mistaken it for horror. It wasn't; it was pure revelation. Why, I wondered, didn't English teachers ever do this? It was like the Visible Man Old Raw Diehl had on his desk in the biology room.

"I only took out the bad parts, you know," Gould said. "Most of it's pretty good."

"I know," I said, meaning both things: yes, most of it was good—okay anyway, serviceable—and yes, he had only taken out the bad parts. "I won't do it again."

He laughed. "If that's true, you'll never have to work for a living. You can do *this* instead. Do I have to explain any of these marks?"

"No," I said.

"When you write a story, you're telling yourself the story," he said. "When   15
you rewrite, your main job is taking out all the things that are *not* the story."

Gould said something else that was interesting on the day I turned in my first two pieces: write with the door closed, rewrite with the door open. Your stuff starts out being just for you, in other words, but then it goes out. Once you know what the story is and get it right—as right as you can, anyway—it belongs to anyone who wants to read it. Or criticize it. If you're very lucky (this is my idea, not John Gould's, but I believe he would have subscribed to the notion), more will want to do the former than the latter.

MLA CITATION

King, Stephen. "On Writing." 2000. *The Norton Reader: An Anthology of Nonfiction*. Ed. Melissa A. Goldthwaite et al. 14th ed. New York: Norton, 2016. 493–95. Print.

QUESTIONS

1. Stephen King provides an example of the way his editor marked up his work. What rationale can you provide for the edits? Would you have made different choices if you were the editor? Why?

2. King uses dialogue and description to help characterize his editor. In which parts of the text do you get the best sense of who Gould is? Why are those parts effective?

3. King writes about learning from an editor. In "Learning to Write" (pp. 484–87), Benjamin Franklin writes about learning from his reading, while, in "On Keeping a Notebook" (pp. 487–93), Joan Didion writes about her notebook. Which of these techniques, if any, has helped you as a writer? How?

4. Write about a time someone responded to your writing in a way that helped you learn to be a better writer. What kinds of comments and edits did that person make? Why was that response helpful to you?

JASWINDER BOLINA *Writing Like a White Guy: On Language, Race, and Poetry*

MY FATHER SAYS I should use a pseudonym. "They won't publish you if they see your name. They'll know you're not one of them. They'll know you're one of us." This has never occurred to me, at least not in a serious way. "No publisher in America's going to reject my poems because I have a foreign name," I reply. "Not in 2002." I argue, "These are educated people. My name won't be any impediment." Yet in spite of my faith in the egalitarian attitude of editors and the anonymity of book contests, I understand my father's angle on the issue.

With his beard shaved and his hair shorn, his turban undone and left behind in Bolina Doaba, Punjab—the town whose name we take as our own—he lands at Heathrow in 1965, a brown boy of 18 become a Londoner. His circumstance then must seem at once exhilarating and also like drifting in a lifeboat: necessary, interminable. I imagine the English of the era sporting an especially muted and disdainful brand of racism toward my alien father, his brother and sister-in-law, toward his brother-in-law and sister, his nieces and nephews, and the other Indians they befriend on Nadine Street, Charlton, just east of Greenwich. The sense of exclusion arrives over every channel, dull and constant.

At least one realtor, a couple of bankers, and a few foremen must have a different attitude. One white supervisor at the industrial bakery my father labors in invites him home for dinner. The Brit wants to offer an introduction to his single daughters. He knows my father's a hard worker, a trait so commonly attributed to the immigrant it seems sometimes a nationality unto itself, and maybe the quietude of the nonnative speaker appeals to the man's sense of civility. As a result he finds my father humble, upstanding, his complexion a light beach sand indicative of a vigor exceeding that of the pale English suitors who come calling. In my imagination, my father's embarrassed and placid demeanor, his awkward formality in that setting, is charming to the bashful, giggly daughters, and this impresses the supervisor even further. But nothing much comes of that evening. My father never visits again. He marries my mother, another Sikh Punjabi also, a few years later, but that event is evidence that one Englishman considered my father the man, not my father the "paki."

When he moves to hodgepodge Chicago nine years after arriving in England, he becomes another denizen of the immigrant nation, the huddled masses. He might be forgiven for thinking he will not be excluded here, but he isn't so naïve. America in 1974 is its own version of the UK's insular empire, though the nature of its exclusion is different, is what we call institutional. He knows that in America nobody should be rejected, not unabashedly and without

Originally appeared on the website of The Poetry Foundation *(2011), "an independent literary organization committed to a vigorous presence for poetry in our culture." Jaswinder Bolina is a poet and essayist.*

some counterfeit of a reason, but all my father's nearly three decades as a machinist at the hydraulics plant near the airport teach him is that economies boom and economies bust, and if your name isn't "Bill" or "Earl" or "Frank Malone," you don't get promoted. You mind the machines. "Bills" and "Earls" supervise. "Frank" is the name the bosses go by, all of them hired after my dad but raised higher. So when my father suggests I use a pseudonym, he's only steadying my two-wheeler, only buying me a popsicle from the cart at Foster Avenue Beach. This is only an extension of covering my tuition, of paying my room and board.

At the time, I'm only a year or so into an MFA. I stop by the office of a friend, an older white poet in my department. Publication to me feels impossible then, and the friend means to be encouraging when he says, "With a name like Jaswinder Bolina, you could publish plenty of poems right now if you wrote about the first-generation, minority stuff. What I admire is that you don't write that kind of poetry." He's right. I don't write "that kind" of poetry. To him, this is upstanding, correct, what a poet ought to do. It's indicative of a vigor exceeding that of other minority poets come calling. It turns out I'm a hard worker too. I should be offended—if not for myself, then on behalf of writers who do take on the difficult subject of minority experience in their poetry—but I understand that my friend means no ill by it. To his mind, embracing my difference would open editorial inboxes, but knowing that I tend to eschew/exclude/deny "that kind" of subject in my poetry, he adds, "This'll make it harder for you." When, only a few months later, my father—who's never read my poems, whose fine but mostly functional knowledge of English makes the diction and syntax of my work difficult to follow, who doesn't know anything of the themes or subjects of my poetry—tells me to use another name, he's encouraging also. He means: Let them think you're a white guy. This will make it easier for you.

The one thing I least believe about race in America is that we can disregard it. I'm nowhere close to alone in this, but the person I encounter far more often than the racist—closeted or proud—is the one who believes race isn't an active factor in her thinking, isn't an influence on his interaction with the racial Other. Such blindness to race seems unlikely, but I suspect few of us entirely understand why it's so improbable. I'm not certain either, but I've been given some idea. At a panel discussion in 2004, a professor of political philosophy, Caribbean-born with a doctorate from the University of Toronto, explains that he never understood why the question in America is so often a question of race. A scholar of Marxist thinking, he says in nearly every other industrialized nation on Earth, the first question is a question of class, and accordingly class is the first conflict. He says it wasn't until he moved to the United States in the early '70s—about the same time my father arrived—that he intellectually and viscerally understood that America is a place where class historically coincides with race. This, he says, is the heaviest legacy of slavery and segregation.

To many immigrants, the professor and my father included, this conflation between success and skin color is a foreign one. In their native lands, where there exists a relative homogeneity in the racial makeup of the population or a pervasive mingling of races, the "minorities" of America are classed based on socioeconomic status derived from any number of factors, and race is rarely, if ever, principal in these. You can look down on anybody even though they share your skin color if you have land enough, wealth enough, caste and education enough. It's only arriving in England that the Indian—who might not even recognize the descriptor "Indian," preferring instead a regional or religious identity to a national one—realizes anyone resembling him is subject to the derision "coolie." It's only in America that such an immigrant discovers any brown-skinned body can have a "camel fucker" or a "sand nigger" hurled at him from a passing car—a bit of cognitive dissonance that's been directed at me on more than one occasion. The racially African but ethnically Other philosophy professor understands the oddness of this as well as anyone. He explains that in the United States, as anywhere, the first question remains a question of class, but the coincidence between class and color makes the first American social conflict a conflict of race. As such, for the racial immigrant and his offspring, racial difference need be mitigated whenever possible, if only to lubricate the cogs of class mobility: nearer to whiteness, nearer to wealth.

If the racial Other aspires to equal footing on the socioeconomic playing field, he is tasked with forcing his way out of the categorical cul-de-sac that his name and appearance otherwise squeeze him into. We call the process by which he does this "assimilation." Though the Latin root here—shared with the other word "similar"—implies that the process is one of becoming absorbed or incorporated, it is a process that relies first on the negation of one identity in order to adopt another. In this sense, assimilation is a destructive rather than constructive process. It isn't a come-as-you-are proposition, a simple matter of being integrated into the American milieu because there exists a standing invitation to do so. Rather, assimilation first requires refuting assumptions the culture makes about the immigrant based on race, and in this sense assimilation requires the erasure of one's preexisting cultural identity even though that identity wasn't contingent upon race in the first place.

The first and perhaps essential step in assimilating into any culture is the successful adoption of the host country's language. What's unusual in America is that this is no different for the immigrant than for the native-born non-white. This is most obvious when I consider African Americans, whose language is variously described as "urban" (as in "of the slums of the inner city"), "street" (as in "of the gutter"), and "Ebonic" (as in "of ebony, of blackness"). These descriptors imply that whatever it is, black vernacular isn't English. Rather, it's "broken English," which is of course what we also call the English of the non-native speaker. I'm tempted to categorize so-called "countrified" or "redneck" dialects similarly, except I remember that any number of recent U.S. presidents and presidential candidates capable in that vernacular are regarded as more down-to-earth and likable rather than less well-spoken or intelligent. It seems that such white dialect serves as evidence of charisma, charm, and folksiness rather than of ignorance.

In 2007, the eventual vice president campaigning in the primary election against the eventual president says, "I mean, you got the first mainstream African American who is *articulate* and bright and *clean* and a nice-looking guy. I mean, that's a storybook, man." The ensuing kerfuffle is almost entirely unsurprising. Though the white candidate believes he's merely describing the candidate of color and doing so with ample objectivity and perhaps even with generosity, the description implies that the black man's appearance and eloquence constitute an exception to his blackness, which is a function of genetics, which only further suggests that the black candidate is an exception to his basic nature. The implication is that he is being praised for his approximate whiteness. Not shockingly, this very conflation of his eloquence with white racial identity leads pundits in another context to ask the obnoxious question, "But is he black enough?" The conundrum the candidate faces is that he need be an exceptional speaker and writer, but part of the "exceptional" here is the idea that he's an "exception" to his race. He has co-opted the language of whiteness. If he then neglects to take on the subject of race with that language, with the fierce urgency of now, he might further be accused of rejecting his own racial identity. Is he a candidate or a black candidate? If it's the former, he might not be "black enough." If it's the latter, he can't win.

In a country where class and race structurally overlap, what we call "standard" English reflexively becomes the English of whiteness rather than simply the English of the educated or privileged classes. When I adopt the language I'm taught in prep school, in university, and in graduate school, I'm adopting the English language, but in the States, that language is intrinsically associated with one race over any another. By contrast, in the England of history, the one prior to the more recent influx of immigrants from its imperial colonies, Oxford English is spoken by subjects as white as those who bandy about in

Cockney. Adeptness of language usage isn't a function then of melanin but of socioeconomic location. Color isn't the question; class is. Unlike the Cockney of England or the dialects of India, none of which are contingent upon racial difference, alternate dialects in American English are inherently racialized. Assimilation in America then comes to mean the appropriation of a specific racial identity by way of language. The conundrum for the poet of color becomes no different than the one that faces the candidate of color: Am I a writer or a minority writer?

The day I'm born, my father engages in the American custom of handing out cigars to the "Bills" and "Earls" and "Franks" of the factory floor, even though he has never smoked in his life. Smoking is anathema to his Sikh Punjabi identity. Drinking, on the other hand, is most certainly not, and he gets gleefully and mercilessly drunk with his brothers at home. He boasts everywhere, "My son will be president." He believes it. Twenty-four years later, in 2002, when he counsels me to use a pseudonym, he knows I'm already adept in the language. I've been educated in it, and in spite of all his diligence and intelligence, this is a key he's never been given. I talk like them. I write like them. I'm an agile agent in the empire so long as nobody grows wise. He no longer expects a presidency, but he sees no limit to potential success in my chosen field, except for the limits placed on me by my racial difference from the dominant culture. He doesn't consider the possibility that I write about race in my work, that I might want to embrace the subject, because he knows, like the candidate of black Kenyan and white Kansan bloodlines, I've been conditioned to resist making race the essential issue.

And it's true. The manner with which I avoid the subject of race in my first book is nearly dogmatic. Race is a subject I don't offer any attention to. To do so would seem only to underscore my Otherness, which would only result in the same sorts of requisite exclusions I experienced growing up in mostly white schools and neighborhoods. Assimilation in those circumstances isn't a choice so much political as it is necessary. Some remnant of a survival instinct kicks in, and one's best efforts are directed at joining rather than resisting the herd. To be racialized is to be marginalized. When another Asian kid joins the playground, we unwittingly vie to out-white each other. This tactic I learned from practice but also from my immigrant family. When your numbers are few, assimilation is the pragmatic gambit.

It's not something that we engage in without a queasy feeling. When my father suggests I Wite-Out my name, he's entirely aware that he's suggesting I relinquish the name he and my mother gave me. This isn't an easy thing, but growing up, I've never been kept from doing what the "American" kids do— though I'm born here and though my parents have long been citizens, "American" remains a descriptor my family uses to signify whiteness. Like the white kids, I join the Cub Scouts and play football at recess, I attend birthday parties at my American classmates' houses and go to junior high socials. In high school, after years of elementary school mockery, I attempt—not unlike the young Barry

Obama—to anglicize my name, going by "Jason" instead, a stratagem that those who become my friends quickly reject after only a few weeks. I go to the homecoming dance. I go to the prom. I stay out past curfew and grow my hair long. I insist that my mother close all the bedroom doors when she cooks so my clothes don't reek of cumin and turmeric. I resist any suggestion that I study the sciences in order to prepare for a career in medicine or engineering. I never meet an Indian girl; there aren't any in the philosophy and English departments I'm a member of anyway. My parents know I'm bereft of their culture. They must at times feel a lucid resentment, a sense of rejection and exclusion. Their son has become one of the English-speakers, as "Frank" or "Bill" to them as any American. But this, they know, is necessary. If the first generation is to succeed here, it's by resisting the ingrained cultural identity and mores of its immigrant forebears. If their son is to become president, my parents know it won't happen while he's wearing a turban. This is why they never keep me from engaging American culture, though it quickly comes to supplant their own. Assimilation is pragmatic, but pragmatism calls for concessions that compound and come to feel like a chronic ache.

It's because of the historical convergence of race and class in America that we   15
conflate the language of the educated, ruling classes with the language of a particular racial identity. If I decouple the two, as I might be able to do in another nation, I realize that what's being described isn't the language of whiteness so much as the language of privilege. When I say "privilege" here, I mean the condition of not needing to consider what others are forced to consider. The privilege of whiteness in America—particularly male, heteronormative whiteness—is the privilege to speak from a blank slate, to not need to address questions of race, gender, sexuality, or class except by choice, to not need to acknowledge wherefrom one speaks. It's the position of no position, the voice from nowhere or from everywhere. In this, it is Godlike, and if nothing else, that's saying something.

To the poet, though, the first question isn't one of class or color. The first question is a question of language. Poetry—as Stéphane Mallarmé famously tells the painter and hapless would-be poet Edgar Degas—is made of words, not ideas. However, to the poet of color or the female poet, to the gay or transgendered writer in America, and even to the white male writer born outside of socioeconomic privilege, a difficult question arises: "Whose language is it?" Where the history of academic and cultural institutions is so dominated by white men of means, "high" language necessarily comes to mean the language of whiteness and a largely wealthy, heteronormative maleness at that. The minority poet seeking entry into the academy and its canon finds that her language is deracialized/sexualized/gendered/classed at the outset. In trafficking in "high" English, writers other than educated, straight, white, male ones of privilege choose to become versed in a language that doesn't intrinsically or historically coincide with perceptions of their identities. It's true that minority poets are permitted to bring alternative vernaculars into our work. Poets from

William Wordsworth in the preface to *Lyrical Ballads* to Frank O'Hara in his "Personism: A Manifesto" demand as much by insisting that poetry incorporate language nearer to conversational speech than anything overly elevated. Such calls for expansions of literary language in conjunction with continuing experiments by recent generations of American poets are transforming the canon for sure, but this leaves me and perhaps others like me in a slightly awkward position. I don't possess a vernacular English that's significantly different from that of plain old Midwestern English. As such, it seems I'm able to write from a perspective that doesn't address certain realities about myself, and this makes me queasy as anything. The voice in my head is annoyed with the voice in my writing. The voice in my head says I'm disregarding difference, and this feels like a denial of self, of reality, of a basic truth.

It isn't exactly intentional. It's a product of being privileged. In the 46 years since my father left Punjab, the 40 or so years since my mother left also, my parents clambered the socioeconomic ladder with a fair amount of middle-class success. We're not exactly wealthy, but I do wind up in prep school instead of the public high school, which only isolates me further from those with a shared racial identity. Later I attend university, where I'm permitted by my parents' successes to study the subjects I want to study rather than those that might guarantee future wealth. I don't need to become a doctor or a lawyer to support the clan. I get to major in philosophy and later attend graduate school in creative writing. Through all of this, though I experience occasional instances of bigotry while walking down streets or in bars, and though I study in programs where I'm often one of only two or three students of color, my racial identity is generally overlooked or disregarded by those around me. I've become so adept in the language and culture of the academy that on more than one occasion when I bring up the fact of my race, colleagues reply with some variation of "I don't think of you as a minority." Or, as a cousin who's known me since infancy jokes, "You're not a minority. You're just a white guy with a tan." What she means is that my assimilation is complete. But she can't be correct. Race is simply too essential to the American experience to ever be entirely overlooked. As such, I can't actually write like a white guy any more than I can revise my skin color. This, however, doesn't change the fact that if a reader were to encounter much of my work not knowing my name or having seen a photograph of me, she might not be faulted for incorrectly assigning the poems a white racial identity. This is a product of my language, which is a product of my education, which is a product of the socioeconomic privilege afforded by my parents' successes. The product of all those factors together is that the writing—this essay included—can't seem to help sounding *white*.

Recently, I was invited to give a few poetry readings as part of a literary festival taking place in a rural part of the country. I borrow my father's compact SUV and let its GPS guide me for a few days on the road. I spend afternoons and evenings reading poems with local and visiting writers in front of small audiences at community centers and public libraries. The audiences are largely made up of kind, white-haired, white-skinned locals enthusiastic to hear us read from and speak about our work, even when they've never heard of most of us. They at least appreciate poetry, a rarity I'm grateful for. During the introductions that preface each event, even the organizers who've invited me have difficulty getting my name right, and in one school library, I enunciate it over and over again. I say, "*Jas* as in the first part of *justice*; *win* as in the opposite of defeat; *der*, which rhymes with *err*, meaning to be mistaken." I say, "JasWINder," lilting the second syllable, and smile as about a dozen audience members mouth each syllable along with me until they feel they have it right. When they do, they grin broadly. After each event, I chat with them one or two at a time, and I do my best to reflect their warmth. They're complimentary about the work, and though I don't expect they're a demographic that'll especially like my poems—even when you write poems like a white guy, you might not be writing poems everyone will like—the compliments are earnest.

Still, in all this pleasantness, the awkward moment occurs more than once. It's some variation on a recurring question I get in town after town. The question usually comes up as a matter of small talk while I'm signing a book or shaking someone's hand. No one delivers it better, with so much beaming warmth and unwitting irony, than the woman who says she enjoyed my poems very much and follows this quickly with an admiring "You're so Americanized, what nationality are you?" She doesn't pick up on the oxymoron in her question. She doesn't hear the hint of tiredness in my reply. "I was born and raised in Chicago, but my parents are from northern India." Once more, I ought to be offended, but I'm not really. Hers is an expression of curiosity that's born of genuine interest rather than of sideshow spectacle. I'm the only nonwhite writer at the events I participate in. I'm the only one who gets this question. It makes me bristle, but I understand where it comes from.

After my brief tour is over, I make the 500-mile trip to suburban Chicago   20
to return the Toyota to my parents. I eat dinner at home, and after, my father drops me back in the city. Invariably, the trip down the Kennedy Expressway toward the skyline makes him nostalgic for his early, underpaid days in small apartments on the North Side, his city long before it became my city. He tells a story or two, and we talk as usual about the news, politics, the latest way my uncle annoys him. He goes on a while before his attention returns to the moment, and he asks how my trip went. I tell him it went well. I say the audiences were kind and the drives were long. I say, out there, the country looks like a painting of itself. I don't mention what the woman asked, the recurring question echoed by others. "You're so Americanized, what nationality are you?" It won't matter that she asked it while eagerly shaking my hand. It won't matter that she asked while asking me also to sign a copy of my book for her. It won't matter that she offered her gratitude that I'd come all that way to read in her hamlet on the outskirts of America. Though she might have meant the opposite, he'll hear the question as the old door closing again. The doorway, then, is both welcome and departure, is border guard and border crossing, and though I'm not on the woman's side of it, I'm not entirely on my father's side either.

Perhaps for this reason, there's the continuing sense that I *ought* to write about race even as I resent that I need be troubled by the subject in the first place. After all, I should permit myself to be a poet first and a minority second, same as any male, white writer. But even as I attempt to ignore the issue altogether, I find myself thinking about it, and I realize now that this fact more than any other makes it so that I can't write like a white poet. Writing is as much the process of arriving at the point of composition as it is the act of composition itself. That my awareness of racial identity so often plays a part in my thinking about my writing makes it so that I can't engage in that writing without race being a live wire. Even one's evasions are born of one's fixations. More to the point, what appears to be an evasion might not be exactly that at all. John Ashbery doesn't make a subject matter of his sexuality, but this doesn't mean he's unable to inhabit the identity of a gay writer. Similarly, even though Mary Ruefle might not take on gender identity overtly in a given poem, it doesn't make that poem an adversary to the cause of feminism. I don't bring all this up to absolve myself exactly, though it's true I'm trying to figure out a way to alleviate a guilt I'm annoyed to feel in the first place. I imagine male, white poets will recognize this feeling. I bet any poet of conscience who doesn't actively write about sociopolitical subjects knows this feeling, but the poet is trying to write the original thing, and that originality might not take up orbit around a more obvious facet of a poet's identity. When any of us doesn't take on such a subject in our writing, it might not be because we neglected to do so. Rather, it might be that the subject informed every bit of our deciding to write about something else.

More importantly, when it comes to writing about difficult issues of identity, especially those with far-reaching political and cultural implications, maybe the choice needn't be a dichotomous one. Maybe I don't need to choose between being the brown guy writing like a white guy or the brown guy writing about being Othered. Instead, maybe I need only be a brown guy writing out his study of language and the self—the same as the Paterson doctor, the Hartford insurance executive, the lesbian expat in Paris, the gay Jew from New Jersey, the male white poet teaching at the University of Houston, or the straight black female professor reading her poem at the American president's inauguration. Though "high" English might be born of a culture once dominated by straight white men of privilege, each of us wields our English in ways those men might not have imagined. This is okay. Language, like a hammer, belongs to whoever picks it up to build or demolish. Whether we take language in hand to deconstruct itself, to confess a real experience or an imagined one, or to meditate upon the relationship between the individual and the political, social, historical, or cosmological, ownership of our language need not be bound up with the history of that language. Whether I choose to pound on the crooked nail of race or gender, self or Other, whether I decide on some obscure subject while forgoing the other obvious one, when I write, the hammer belongs to me.

MLA CITATION

Bolina, Jaswinder. "Writing Like a White Guy: On Language, Race, and Poetry."
   2011. *The Norton Reader: An Anthology of Nonfiction*. Ed. Melissa A.
   Goldthwaite et al. 14th ed. New York: Norton, 2016. 496–504. Print.

Questions

1. Throughout this essay, Jaswinder Bolina compares the role of race in his life with the role of race in his poetry. List some of his ambivalent feelings, explore their sources, and discuss where he seems to land in the end with regard to the relationship between his poetry and his race.

2. What, according to Bolina, is the relationship between language and race in the United States? How is this relationship different from other countries he discusses?

3. Bolina writes that, as a child, he tried to "out-white" (paragraph 13) other Asian kids on the playground. In "How to Tame a Wild Tongue" (pp. 471–80), Gloria Anzaldúa writes about avoiding speaking Spanish with Chicanas and Latinas she does not know well. Based on these two accounts, what can be difficult about encountering another person who shares the same minority status?

4. Using Bolina's essay as a starting point, write about how an artist should balance artistic ambitions with the need or desire to speak for a group to which she or he belongs (e.g., racial or ethnic minority, religion, sexual orientation, and so on).

Garrison Keillor   *How to Write a Letter*

WE SHY PERSONS need to write a letter now and then, or else we'll dry up and blow away. It's true. And I speak as one who loves to reach for the phone, dial the number, and talk. I say, "Big Bopper[1] here—what's shakin', babes?" The telephone is to shyness what Hawaii is to February, it's a way out of the woods, *and yet*: a letter is better.

Such a sweet gift—a piece of handmade writing, in an envelope that is not a bill, sitting in our friend's path when she trudges home from a long day spent among wahoos and savages, a day our words will help repair. They don't need to be immortal, just sincere. She can read them twice and again tomorrow: *You're someone I care about, Corinne, and think of often and every time I do you make me smile.*

We need to write, otherwise nobody will know who we are. They will have only a vague impression of us as A Nice Person, because, frankly, we don't shine at conversation, we lack the confidence to thrust our faces forward and say, "Hi, I'm Heather Hooten; let me tell you about my week." Mostly we say "Uh-huh"

From We Are Still Married *(1989), a collection of Garrison Keillor's stories, letters, and skits. Many of Keillor's humorous pieces are aired on his popular radio program,* A Prairie Home Companion.

1. American disc jockey turned rock star (1930–1959), popular in the late 1950s.

and "Oh, really." People smile and look over our shoulder, looking for someone else to meet.

So a shy person sits down and writes a letter. To be known by another person—to meet and talk freely on the page—to be close despite distance. To escape from anonymity and be our own sweet selves and express the music of our souls.

5   Same thing that moves a giant rock star to sing his heart out in front of 123,000 people moves us to take ballpoint in hand and write a few lines to our dear Aunt Eleanor. *We want to be known.* We want her to know that we have fallen in love, that we quit our job, that we're moving to New York, and we want to say a few things that might not get said in casual conversation: *Thank you for what you've meant to me, I am very happy right now.*

The first step in writing letters is to get over the guilt of *not* writing. You don't "owe" anybody a letter. Letters are a gift. The burning shame you feel when you see unanswered mail makes it harder to pick up a pen and makes for a cheerless letter when you finally do. *I feel bad about not writing, but I've been so busy,* etc. Skip this. Few letters are obligatory, and they are *Thanks for the wonderful gift* and *I am terribly sorry to hear about George's death* and *Yes, you're welcome to stay with us next month,* and not many more than that. Write those promptly if you want to keep your friends. Don't worry about the others, except love letters, of course. When your true love writes, *Dear Light of My Life, Joy of My Heart, O Lovely Pulsating Core of My Sensate Life,* some response is called for.

Some of the best letters are tossed off in a burst of inspiration, so keep your writing stuff in one place where you can sit down for a few minutes and (*Dear Roy, I am in the middle of a book entitled* We Are Still Married *but thought I'd drop you a line. Hi to your sweetie, too*) dash off a note to a pal. Envelopes, stamps, address book, everything in a drawer so you can write fast when the pen is hot.

A blank white eight-by-eleven sheet can look as big as Montana if the pen's not so hot—try a smaller page and write boldly. Or use a note card with a piece of fine art on the front; if your letter ain't good, at least they get the Matisse.[2] Get a pen that makes a sensuous line, get a comfortable typewriter, a friendly word processor—which feels easy to the hand.

Sit for a few minutes with the blank sheet in front of you, and meditate on the person you will write to, let your friend come to mind until you can almost see her or him in the room with you. Remember the last time you saw each other and how your friend looked and what you said and what perhaps was unsaid between you, and when your friend becomes real to you, start to write.

10   Write the salutation—*Dear* You—and take a deep breath and plunge in. A simple declarative sentence will do, followed by another and another and another. Tell us what you're doing and tell it like you were talking to us. Don't think about grammar, don't think about lit'ry style, don't try to write dramatically, just give us your news. Where did you go, who did you see, what did they say, what do you think?

2. French painter (1869–1954).

If you don't know where to begin, start with the present moment: *I'm sitting at the kitchen table on a rainy Saturday morning. Everyone is gone and the house is quiet.* Let your simple description of the present moment lead to something else, let the letter drift gently along.

The toughest letter to crank out is one that is meant to impress, as we all know from writing job applications; if it's hard work to slip off a letter to a friend, maybe you're trying too hard to be terrific. A letter is only a report to someone who already likes you for reasons other than your brilliance. Take it easy.

Don't worry about form. It's not a term paper. When you come to the end of one episode, just start a new paragraph. You can go from a few lines about the sad state of pro football to the fight with your mother to your fond memories of Mexico to your cat's urinary-tract infection to a few thoughts on personal indebtedness and on to the kitchen sink and what's in it. The more you write, the easier it gets, and when you have a True True Friend to write to, a *compadre*, a soul sibling, then it's like driving a car down a country road, you just get behind the keyboard and press on the gas.

Don't tear up the page and start over when you write a bad line—try to write your way out of it. Make mistakes and plunge on. Let the letter cook along and let yourself be bold. Outrage, confusion, love—whatever is in your mind, let it find a way to the page. Writing is a means of discovery, always, and when you come to the end and write *Yours ever* or *Hugs and kisses*, you'll know something you didn't when you wrote *Dear Pal*.

Probably your friend will put your letter away, and it'll be read again a few years from now—and it will improve with age. And forty years from now, your friend's grandkids will dig it out of the attic and read it, a sweet and precious relic of the ancient eighties that gives them a sudden clear glimpse of you and her and the world we old-timers knew. You will then have created an object of art. Your simple lines about where you went, who you saw, what they said, will speak to those children and they will feel in their hearts the humanity of our times.

You can't pick up a phone and call the future and tell them about our times. You have to pick up a piece of paper.

MLA CITATION

Keillor, Garrison. "How to Write a Letter." 1989. *The Norton Reader: An Anthology of Nonfiction.* Ed. Melissa A. Goldthwaite et al. 14th ed. New York: Norton, 2016. 505–07. Print.

GARRISON KEILLOR   *Postcards*

A POSTCARD TAKES ABOUT FIFTY WORDS gracefully, which is how to write one. A few sweet strokes in a flowing hand—pink roses, black-face sheep in a wet meadow, the sea, the Swedish coast—your friend in Washington gets the idea. She doesn't need your itinerary to know that you remember her.

Fifty words is a strict form but if you write tiny and sneak over into the address side to squeeze in a hundred, the grace is gone and the result is not a poem but notes for a letter you don't have time to write, which will make her feel cheated.

So many persons traveling to a strange land are inclined to see its life so clearly, its essential national character, they could write a book about it as other foreign correspondents have done ("highly humorous . . . definitely a must"), but fifty words is a better length for what you really know.

Fifty words and a picture. Say you are in Scotland, the picture is of your hotel, a stone pile looking across the woods of Druimindarroch to Loch Nan Uamh near the village of Arisaig. You've never seen this country. For the past year you've worked like a prisoner in the mines. Write.

5   Scotland is the most beautiful country in the world and I am drinking coffee in the library of what once was the manor of people who inherited everything and eventually lost it. Thus it became a hotel. I'm with English people whose correctness is overpowering. What wild good luck to be here. And to be an American! I'm so happy, bubba.

In the Highlands, many one-lane roads which widen at curves and hills—a driving thrill, especially when following a native who drives like hell—you stick close to him, like the second car of the roller-coaster, but lose your nerve. Sixty mph down a one-lane winding road. I prefer a career.

The arrogance of Americans who, without so much as a *"mi scusi"* or *"bitte"* or *"s'il vous plaît,"* words that a child could learn easily, walk up to a stranger and say, "Say, where's the museum?" as if English and rudeness rule the world, never ceases to amaze. You hear the accent and sink under the table.

Woke up at six, dark. Switzerland. Alps. Raining. Lights of villages high in the sky. Too dark to see much so snoozed awhile. Woke up in sunny Italy. Field after field of corn, like Iowa in August. Mamas, papas, grammas, grampas, little babies. Skinny trees above the whitewashed houses.

Arrived in Venice. A pipe had burst at the hotel and we were sent to another not as good. Should you spend time arguing for a refund? Went to San Marco,[3]

3. One of the largest and most famous cathedrals in the world, the Basilica di San Marco of Venice is a hodgepodge of Byzantine domes, mosaics, and plundered treasure from the Near East and Asia.

on which the doges overspent. A cash register in the sanctuary: five hundred lire to see the gold altar. Now we understand the Reformation.

On the train to Vienna, she, having composed the sentences carefully from old   10
memory of intermediate German, asked the old couple if the train went to Vienna. *"Ja, ja!"* Did we need to change trains? *"Nein."* Later she successfully ordered dinner and registered at the hotel. *Mein wundercompanion.*

People take me for an American tourist and stare at me, maybe because I walk slow and stare at them, so today I walked like a bat out of hell along the Ringstrasse, past the Hofburg Palace to Stephans Platz and back, and if anyone stared, I didn't notice. Didn't see much of Vienna but felt much better.

One week in a steady drizzle of German and now I am starting to lose my grip on English, I think. Don't know what to write. How are you? Are the Twins going to be in the World Series?

You get to Mozart's apartment[4] through the back door of a restaurant. Kitchen smells, yelling, like at Burger King. The room where he wrote *Figaro* is bare, as if he moved out this morning. It's a nice apartment. His grave at the cemetery is now marked, its whereabouts being unknown. Mozart our brother.

Copenhagen is raining and all the Danes seem unperturbed. A calm humorous people. Kids are the same as anywhere, wild, and nobody hits them. Men wear pastels, especially turquoise. Narrow streets, no cars, little shops, and in the old square a fruit stand and an old woman with flowers yelling, "WŌSA FOR TEW-VA!"

Sunbathing yesterday. A fine woman took off her shirt, jeans, pants, nearby, and   15
lay on her belly, then turned over. Often she sat up to apply oil. Today my back is burned bright red (as St. Paul warns) from my lying and looking at her so long but who could ignore such beauty and *so generous.*

4. Mozart's "Figarohaus," where he lived from October 1784 to April 1787, is behind St. Stephen's Cathedral in Vienna.

MLA CITATION

Keillor, Garrison. "Postcards." 1989. *The Norton Reader: An Anthology of Nonfiction.* Ed. Melissa A. Goldthwaite et al. 14th ed. New York: Norton, 2016. 508–09. Print.

QUESTIONS

1. In "How to Write a Letter," Garrison Keillor offers several suggestions. Make a list of the suggestions that seem most helpful. Why might Keillor have included the other, less practical suggestions?

2. Keillor addresses "How to Write a Letter" to shy people (a group in which he includes himself—"We shy persons . . ."). Does his advice also apply to those who are not shy? Why or why not?

3. Analyze the progression of "Postcards." How is the piece organized? Why do you think Keillor chose this organization?

4. Keillor wrote these pieces in the 1980s before people texted or used email. Does any of his advice apply to the way we text or write emails today? Explain your reasoning in an essay.

GEORGE ORWELL *Politics and the English Language*

MOST PEOPLE WHO BOTHER with the matter at all would admit that the English language is in a bad way, but it is generally assumed that we cannot by conscious action do anything about it. Our civilization is decadent and our language—so the argument runs—must inevitably share in the general collapse. It follows that any struggle against the abuse of language is a sentimental archaism, like preferring candles to electric light or hansom cabs to aeroplanes. Underneath this lies the half-conscious belief that language is a natural growth and not an instrument which we shape for our own purposes.

Now, it is clear that the decline of a language must ultimately have political and economic causes: it is not due simply to the bad influence of this or that individual writer. But an effect can become a cause, reinforcing the original cause and producing the same effect in an intensified form, and so on indefinitely. A man may take to drink because he feels himself to be a failure, and then fail all the more completely because he drinks. It is rather the same thing that is happening to the English language. It becomes ugly and inaccurate because our thoughts are foolish, but the slovenliness of our language makes it easier for us to have foolish thoughts. The point is that the process is reversible. Modern English, especially written English, is full of bad habits which spread by imitation and which can be avoided if one is willing to take the necessary trouble. If one gets rid of these habits one can think more clearly, and to think clearly is a necessary first step towards political regeneration: so that the fight against bad English is not frivolous and is not the exclusive concern of professional writers. I will come back to this presently, and I hope that by that time the meaning of what I have said here will have become clearer. Meanwhile, here are five specimens of the English language as it is now habitually written.

These five passages have not been picked out because they are especially bad—I could have quoted far worse if I had chosen—but because they illustrate various of the mental vices from which we now suffer. They are a little

From Shooting an Elephant, and Other Essays *(1950), a collection of George Orwell's best-known essays. "Politics and the English Language" is one of the most famous modern arguments for a clear, unadorned writing style.*

below the average, but are fairly representative samples. I number them so that I can refer back to them when necessary:

> "(1) I am not, indeed, sure whether it is not true to say that the Milton who once seemed not unlike a seventeenth-century Shelley had not become, out of an experience ever more bitter in each year, more alien [*sic*] to the founder of that Jesuit sect which nothing could induce him to tolerate."
>
> —PROFESSOR HAROLD LASKI (*ESSAY IN FREEDOM OF EXPRESSION*).

> "(2) Above all, we cannot play ducks and drakes with a native battery of idioms which prescribes such egregious collocations of vocables as the Basic *put up with* for *tolerate* or *put at a loss* for *bewilder*."
>
> —PROFESSOR LANCELOT HOGBEN (*INTERGLOSSA*).

> "(3) On the one side we have the free personality: by definition it is not neurotic, for it has neither conflict nor dream. Its desires, such as they are, are transparent, for they are just what institutional approval keeps in the forefront of consciousness; another institutional pattern would alter their number and intensity; there is little in them that is natural, irreducible, or culturally dangerous. But *on the other side*, the social bond itself is nothing but the mutual reflection of these self-secure integrities. Recall the definition of love. Is not this the very picture of a small academic? Where is there a place in this hall of mirrors for either personality or fraternity?"
>
> —ESSAY ON PSYCHOLOGY IN *POLITICS* (NEW YORK).

> "(4) All the 'best people' from the gentlemen's clubs, and all the frantic fascist captains, united in common hatred of Socialism and bestial horror of the rising tide of the mass revolutionary movement, have turned to acts of provocation, to foul incendiarism, to medieval legends of poisoned wells, to legalize their own destruction of proletarian organizations, and rouse the agitated petty-bourgeoisie to chauvinistic fervour on behalf of the fight against the revolutionary way out of the crisis."
>
> —COMMUNIST PAMPHLET.

> "(5) If a new spirit *is* to be infused into this old country, there is one thorny and contentious reform which must be tackled, and that is the humanization and galvanization of the B.B.C. Timidity here will bespeak cancer and atrophy of the soul. The heart of Britain may be sound and of strong beat, for instance, but the British lion's roar at present is like that of Bottom in Shakespeare's *Midsummer Night's Dream*—as gentle as any sucking dove. A virile new Britain cannot continue indefinitely to be traduced in the eyes or rather ears, of the world by the effete languors of Langham Place, brazenly masquerading as 'standard English.' When the Voice of Britain is heard at nine o'clock, better far and infinitely less ludicrous to hear honestly dropped than the present priggish, inflated, inhibited, school-ma'amish arch braying of blameless bashful mewing maidens!"
>
> —LETTER IN *TRIBUNE*.

Each of these passages has faults of its own, but, quite apart from avoidable ugliness, two qualities are common to all of them. The first is staleness of imagery; the other is lack of precision. The writer either has a meaning and cannot express it, or he inadvertently says something else, or he is almost indifferent as to whether his words mean anything or not. This mixture of vagueness and sheer incompetence is the most marked characteristic of modern English prose, and especially of any kind of political writing. As soon as certain topics are raised, the concrete melts into the abstract and no one seems able to think of turns of speech that are not hackneyed: prose consists less and less of *words* chosen for the sake of their meaning, and more and more of *phrases* tacked together like the sections of a prefabricated henhouse. I list below, with notes and examples, various of the tricks by means of which the work of prose-construction is habitually dodged:

DYING METAPHORS

5   A newly invented metaphor assists thought by evoking a visual image, while on the other hand a metaphor which is technically "dead" (e.g. *iron resolution*) has in effect reverted to being an ordinary word and can generally be used without loss of vividness. But in between these two classes there is a huge dump of worn-out metaphors which have lost all evocative power and are merely used because they save people the trouble of inventing phrases for themselves. Examples are: *Ring the changes on, take up the cudgels for, toe the line, ride roughshod over, stand shoulder to shoulder with, play into the hands of, no axe to grind, grist to the mill, fishing in troubled waters, on the order of the day, Achilles' heel, swan song, hotbed.* Many of these are used without knowledge of their meaning (what is a "rift," for instance?), and incompatible metaphors are frequently mixed, a sure sign that the writer is not interested in what he is saying. Some metaphors now current have been twisted out of their original meaning without those who use them even being aware of the fact. For example, *toe the line* is sometimes written *tow the line.* Another example is *the hammer and the anvil,* now always used with the implication that the anvil gets the worst of it. In real life it is always the anvil that breaks the hammer, never the other way about: a writer who stopped to think what he was saying would be aware of this, and would avoid perverting the original phrase.

OPERATORS OR VERBAL FALSE LIMBS

These save the trouble of picking out appropriate verbs and nouns, and at the same time pad each sentence with extra syllables which give it an appearance of symmetry. Characteristic phrases are: *render inoperative, militate against, make contact with, be subjected to, give rise to, give grounds for, have the effect of, play a leading part (role) in, make itself felt, take effect, exhibit a tendency to, serve the purpose of, etc., etc.* The keynote is the elimination of simple verbs. Instead of being a single word, such as *break, stop, spoil, mend, kill,* a verb becomes a *phrase,* made up of a noun or adjective tacked on to some general-purposes verb such as *prove, serve, form, play, render.* In addition, the passive voice is wherever possible used in preference to the active, and noun constructions are used instead of gerunds (*by examination of* instead of *by examining*). The range of verbs is further cut down by means of the *-ize* and *de-* formation, and the banal statements are given an appearance of profundity by means of the *not un-* formation. Simple conjunctions and prepositions are replaced by such phrases as *with respect to, having regard to, the fact that, by dint of, in view of, in the interests of, on the hypothesis that;* and the ends of sentences are saved from anticlimax by such resounding commonplaces as *greatly to be desired, cannot be left out of account, a development to be expected in the near future, deserving of serious consideration, brought to a satisfactory conclusion,* and so on and so forth.

PRETENTIOUS DICTION

Words like *phenomenon, element, individual* (as noun), *objective, categorical, effective, virtual, basic, primary, promote, constitute, exhibit, exploit, utilize, eliminate, liquidate,* are used to dress up simple statements and give an air of scientific impartiality to biased judgments. Adjectives like *epoch-making, epic, historic, unforgettable, triumphant, age-old, inevitable, inexorable, veritable,* are used to dignify the sordid processes of international politics, while writing that aims at glorifying war usually takes on an archaic colour, its characteristic words being: *realm, throne, chariot, mailed fist, trident, sword, shield, buckler, banner, jackboot, clarion.* Foreign words and expressions such as *cul de sac, ancien régime, deus ex machina, mutatis mutandis, status quo, gleichschaltung, weltanschauung,* are used to give an air of culture and elegance. Except for the useful abbreviations *i.e., e.g.,* and *etc.,* there is no real need for any of the hundreds of foreign phrases now current in English. Bad writers, and especially scientific, political and sociological writers, are nearly always haunted by the notion that Latin or Greek words are grander than Saxon ones, and unnecessary words like *expedite, ameliorate, predict, extraneous, deracinated, clandestine, subaqueous* and hundreds of others constantly gain ground from their Anglo-Saxon opposite numbers.[1] The jargon peculiar to Marxist writing (*hyena, hangman, cannibal, petty bourgeois, these gentry, lackey, flunkey, mad dog, White Guard,* etc.) consists largely of words and phrases translated from Russian, German or French; but the normal way of coining a new word is to use a Latin or Greek root with the appropriate affix and, where necessary, the *-ize* formation. It is often easier to make up words of this kind (*deregionalize, impermissible, extramarital, nonfragmentatory* and so forth) than to think up the English words that will cover one's meaning. The result, in general, is an increase in slovenliness and vagueness.

MEANINGLESS WORDS

In certain kinds of writing, particularly in art criticism and literary criticism, it is normal to come across long passages which are almost completely lacking

---

1. An interesting illustration of this is the way in which the English flower names which were in use till very recently are being ousted by Greek ones, *snapdragon* becoming *antirrhinum, forget-me-not* becoming *myosotis,* etc. It is hard to see any practical reason for this change of fashion: it is probably due to an instinctive turning-away from the more homely word and a vague feeling that the Greek word is scientific [Orwell's note].

in meaning.[2] Words like *romantic, plastic, values, human, dead, sentimental, natural, vitality,* as used in art criticism, are strictly meaningless in the sense that they not only do not point to any discoverable object, but are hardly ever expected to do so by the reader. When one critic writes, "The outstanding feature of Mr. X's work is its living quality," while another writes, "The immediately striking thing about Mr. X's work is its peculiar deadness," the reader accepts this as a simple difference of opinion. If words like *black* and *white* were involved, instead of the jargon words *dead* and *living*, he would see at once that language was being used in an improper way. Many political words are similarly abused. The word *Fascism* has now no meaning except in so far as it signifies "something not desirable." The words *democracy, socialism, freedom, patriotic, realistic, justice,* have each of them several different meanings which cannot be reconciled with one another. In the case of a word like *democracy*, not only is there no agreed definition, but the attempt to make one is resisted from all sides. It is almost universally felt that when we call a country democratic we are praising it: consequently the defenders of every kind of régime claim that it is a democracy, and fear that they might have to stop using the word if it were tied down to any one meaning. Words of this kind are often used in a consciously dishonest way. That is, the person who uses them has his own private definition, but allows his hearer to think he means something quite different. Statements like *Marshal Pétain was a true patriot, The Soviet Press is the freest in the world, The Catholic Church is opposed to persecution,* are almost always made with intent to deceive. Other words used in variable meanings, in most cases more or less dishonestly, are: *class, totalitarian, science, progressive, reactionary, bourgeois, equality.*

Now that I have made this catalogue of swindles and perversions, let me give another example of the kind of writing that they lead to. This time it must of its nature be an imaginary one. I am going to translate a passage of good English into modern English of the worst sort. Here is a well-known verse from *Ecclesiastes:*

> "I returned and saw under the sun, that the race is not to the swift, nor the battle to the strong, neither yet bread to the wise, nor yet riches to men of understanding, nor yet favour to men of skill; but time and chance happeneth to them all."

10   Here it is in modern English:

> "Objective consideration of contemporary phenomena compels the conclusion that success or failure in competitive activities exhibits no tendency to be commensurate with innate capacity, but that a considerable element of the unpredictable must invariably be taken into account."

---

2. Example: "Comfort's catholicity of perception and image, strangely Whitmanesque in range, almost the exact opposite in aesthetic compulsion, continues to evoke that trembling atmospheric accumulative hinting at a cruel, an inexorably serene timelessness. . . . Wrey Gardiner scores by aiming at simple bull's-eyes with precision. Only they are not so simple, and through this contented sadness runs more than the surface bittersweet of resignation" (*Poetry Quarterly*) [Orwell's note].

This is a parody, but not a very gross one. Exhibit (3), above, for instance, contains several patches of the same kind of English. It will be seen that I have not made a full translation. The beginning and ending of the sentence follow the original meaning fairly closely, but in the middle the concrete illustrations—race, battle, bread—dissolve into the vague phrase "success or failure in competitive activities." This had to be so, because no modern writer of the kind I am discussing—no one capable of using phrases like "objective consideration of contemporary phenomena"—would ever tabulate his thoughts in that precise and detailed way. The whole tendency of modern prose is away from concreteness. Now analyse these two sentences a little more closely. The first contains forty-nine words but only sixty syllables, and all its words are those of everyday life. The second contains thirty-eight words of ninety syllables: eighteen of its words are from Latin roots, and one from Greek. The first sentence contains six vivid images, and only one phrase ("time and chance") that could be called vague. The second contains not a single fresh, arresting phrase, and in spite of its ninety syllables it gives only a shortened version of the meaning contained in the first. Yet without a doubt it is the second kind of sentence that is gaining ground in modern English. I do not want to exaggerate. This kind of writing is not yet universal, and outcrops of simplicity will occur here and there in the worst-written page. Still, if you or I were told to write a few lines on the uncertainty of human fortunes, we should probably come much nearer to my imaginary sentence than to the one from *Ecclesiastes*.

As I have tried to show, modern writing at its worst does not consist in picking out words for the sake of their meaning and inventing images in order to make the meaning clearer. It consists in gumming together long strips of words which have already been set in order by someone else, and making the results presentable by sheer humbug. The attraction of this way of writing is that it is easy. It is easier—even quicker, once you have the habit—to say *In my opinion it is a not unjustifiable assumption that* than to say *I think*. If you use ready-made phrases, you not only don't have to hunt about for words; you also don't have to bother with the rhythms of your sentences, since these phrases are generally so arranged as to be more or less euphonious. When you are composing in a hurry—when you are dictating to a stenographer, for instance, or making a public speech—it is natural to fall into a pretentious, Latinized style. Tags like *a consideration which we should do well to bear in mind* or *a conclusion to which all of us would readily assent* will save many a sentence from coming down with a bump. By using stale metaphors, similes and idioms, you save much mental effort, at the cost of leaving your meaning vague, not only for your reader but for yourself. This is the significance of mixed metaphors. The sole aim of a metaphor is to call up a visual image. When these images clash—as in *The Fascist octopus has sung its swan song, the jackboot is thrown into the melting pot*—it can be taken as certain that the writer is not seeing a mental image of the objects he is naming; in other words he is not really thinking. Look again at the examples I gave at the beginning of this essay. Professor Laski (1) uses five negatives in fifty-three words. One of these is superfluous, making nonsense of the whole passage, and in addition there is the slip *alien* for akin, making further nonsense, and several avoidable pieces of clumsiness which increase the general vagueness. Professor Hogben (2) plays ducks and drakes with a battery which is able to write prescriptions, and, while disapproving of the everyday phrase *put up with*, is unwilling to look *egregious* up in the dictionary and see what it means. (3), if one takes an uncharitable attitude towards it, is simply meaningless: probably one could work out its intended meaning by reading the whole of the article in which it occurs. In (4), the writer knows more or less what he wants to say, but an accumulation of stale phrases chokes him like tea leaves blocking a sink. In (5), words and meaning have almost parted company. People who write in this manner usually have a general emotional meaning—they dislike one thing and want to express solidarity with another— but they are not interested in the detail of what they are saying. A scrupulous writer, in every sentence that he writes, will ask himself at least four questions, thus: What am I trying to say? What words will express it? What image or idiom will make it clearer? Is this image fresh enough to have an effect? And he will probably ask himself two more: Could I put it more shortly? Have I said any- thing that is avoidably ugly? But you are not obliged to go to all this trouble. You can shirk it by simply throwing your mind open and letting the ready-made phrases come crowding in. They will construct your sentences for you—even think your thoughts for you, to a certain extent—and at need they will perform the important service of partially concealing your meaning even from yourself. It is at this point that the special connection between politics and the debase- ment of language becomes clear.

In our time it is broadly true that political writing is bad writing. Where it is not true, it will generally be found that the writer is some kind of rebel, expressing his private opinions and not a "party line." Orthodoxy, of whatever colour, seems to demand a lifeless, imitative style. The political dialects to be found in pamphlets, leading articles, manifestos, White Papers and the speeches of under-secretaries do, of course, vary from party to party, but they are all alike in that one almost never finds in them a fresh, vivid, homemade turn of speech. When one watches some tired hack on the platform mechanically repeating the familiar phrases—*bestial atrocities, iron heel, blood-stained tyranny, free peoples of the world, stand shoulder to shoulder*—one often has a curious feeling that one is not watching a live human being but some kind of dummy: a feeling which suddenly becomes stronger at moments when the light catches the speak- er's spectacles and turns them into blank discs which seem to have no eyes behind them. And this is not altogether fanciful. A speaker who uses that kind of phraseology has gone some distance towards turning himself into a machine. The appropriate noises are coming out of his larynx, but his brain is not involved as it would be if he were choosing his words for himself. If the speech he is mak- ing is one that he is accustomed to make over and over again, he may be almost unconscious of what he is saying, as one is when one utters the responses in church. And this reduced state of consciousness, if not indispensable, is at any rate favourable to political conformity.

In our time, political speech and writing are largely the defence of the inde- fensible. Things like the continuance of British rule in India, the Russian purges and deportations, the dropping of the atom bombs on Japan, can indeed be defended, but only by arguments which are too brutal for most people to face, and which do not square with the professed aims of political parties. Thus political language has to consist largely of euphemism, question-begging and sheer cloudy vagueness. Defenceless villages are bombarded from the air, the inhabitants driven out into the countryside, the cattle machine-gunned, the huts set on fire with incendiary bullets: this is called *pacification*. Millions of peasants are robbed of their farms and sent trudging along the roads with no more than they can carry: this is called *transfer of population* or *rectification of frontiers*. People are imprisoned for years without trial, or shot in the back of the neck or sent to die of scurvy in Arctic lumber camps: this is called *elimination of unreliable elements*. Such phraseology is needed if one wants to name things without calling up mental pictures of them. Consider for instance some comfortable English professor defending Russian totalitarianism. He cannot say outright, "I believe in killing off your opponents when you can get good results by doing so." Probably, therefore, he will say something like this:

"While freely conceding that the Soviet régime exhibits certain features   15
which the humanitarian may be inclined to deplore, we must, I think, agree that a certain curtailment of the right to political opposition is an unavoidable concomitant of transitional periods, and that the rigors which the Russian people have been called upon to undergo have been amply justified in the sphere of concrete achievement."

The inflated style is itself a kind of euphemism. A mass of Latin words falls upon the facts like soft snow, blurring the outlines and covering up all the details. The great enemy of clear language is insincerity. When there is a gap between one's real and one's declared aims, one turns as it were instinctively to long words and exhausted idioms, like a cuttlefish squirting out ink. In our age there is no such thing as "keeping out of politics." All issues are political issues, and politics itself is a mass of lies, evasions, folly, hatred and schizophrenia. When the general atmosphere is bad, language must suffer. I should expect to find—this is a guess which I have not sufficient knowledge to verify—that the German, Russian and Italian languages have all deteriorated in the last ten or fifteen years, as a result of dictatorship.

But if thought corrupts language, language can also corrupt thought. A bad usage can spread by tradition and imitation, even among people who should and do know better. The debased language that I have been discussing is in some ways very convenient. Phrases like *a not unjustifiable assumption, leaves much to be desired, would serve no good purpose, a consideration which we should do well to bear in mind*, are a continuous temptation, a packet of aspirins always at one's elbow. Look back through this essay, and for certain you will find that I have again and again committed the very faults I am protesting against. By this morning's post I have received a pamphlet dealing with conditions in Germany. The author tells me that he "felt impelled" to write it. I open it at random, and here is almost the first sentence that I see: "(The Allies) have an opportunity not only of achieving a radical transformation of Germany's social and political structure in such a way as to avoid a nationalistic reaction in Germany itself, but at the same time of laying the foundations of a co-operative and unified Europe." You see, he "feels impelled" to write—feels, presumably, that he has something new to say—and yet his words, like cavalry horses answering the bugle, group themselves automatically into the familiar dreary pattern. This invasion of one's mind by ready-made phrases (*lay the foundations, achieve a radical transformation*) can only be prevented if one is constantly on guard against them, and every such phrase anaesthetizes a portion of one's brain.

I said earlier that the decadence of our language is probably curable. Those who deny this would argue, if they produced an argument at all, that language merely reflects existing social conditions, and that we cannot influence its development by any direct tinkering with words and constructions. So far as the general tone or spirit of a language goes, this may be true, but it is not true in detail. Silly words and expressions have often disappeared, not through any evolutionary process but owing to the conscious action of a minority. Two recent examples were *explore every avenue* and *leave no stone unturned,* which were killed by the jeers of a few journalists. There is a long list of fly-blown metaphors which could similarly be got rid of if enough people would interest themselves in the job; and it should also be possible to laugh the *not un-* formation out of existence,[3] to reduce the amount of Latin and Greek in the average sentence, to drive out foreign phrases and strayed scientific words, and, in general, to make pretentiousness unfashionable. But all these are minor points. The defence of the English language implies more than this, and perhaps it is best to start by saying what it does *not* imply.

To begin with it has nothing to do with archaism, with the salvaging of obsolete words and turns of speech, or with the setting up of a "standard English" which must never be departed from. On the contrary, it is especially concerned with the scrapping of every word or idiom which has outworn its usefulness. It has nothing to do with correct grammar and syntax, which are of no importance so long as one makes one's meaning clear, or with the avoidance of Americanisms, or with having what is called a "good prose style." On the other hand it is not concerned with fake simplicity and the attempt to make written English colloquial. Nor does it even imply in every case preferring the Saxon word to the Latin one, though it does imply using the fewest and shortest words that will cover one's meaning. What is above all needed is to let the meaning choose the word, and not the other way about. In prose, the worst thing one can do with words is to surrender to them. When you think of a concrete object, you think wordlessly, and then, if you want to describe the thing you have been visualizing you probably hunt about till you find the exact words that seem to fit. When you think of something abstract you are more inclined to use words from the start, and unless you make a conscious effort to prevent it, the existing dialect will come rushing in and do the job for you, at the expense of blurring or even changing your meaning. Probably it is better to put off using words as long as possible and get one's meaning as clear as one can through pictures or sensations. Afterwards one can choose—not simply *accept*—the

---

3. One can cure oneself of the *not un-* formation by memorizing this sentence: *A not unblack dog was chasing a not unsmall rabbit across a not ungreen field* [Orwell's note].

phrases that will best cover the meaning, and then switch round and decide what impression one's words are likely to make on another person. This last effort of the mind cuts out all stale or mixed images, all prefabricated phrases, needless repetitions, and humbug and vagueness generally. But one can often be in doubt about the effect of a word or a phrase, and one needs rules that one can rely on when instinct fails. I think the following rules will cover most cases:

(i)   Never use a metaphor, simile or other figure of speech which you are used to seeing in print.

(ii) Never use a long word where a short one will do.

(iii) If it is possible to cut a word out, always cut it out.

(iv) Never use the passive where you can use the active.

(v)   Never use a foreign phrase, a scientific word or a jargon word if you can think of an everyday English equivalent.

(vi) Break any of these rules sooner than say anything outright barbarous.

These rules sound elementary, and so they are, but they demand a deep change of attitude in anyone who has grown used to writing in the style now fashionable. One could keep all of them and still write bad English, but one could not write the kind of stuff that I quoted in those five specimens at the beginning of this article.

I have not here been considering the literary use of language, but merely language as an instrument for expressing and not for concealing or preventing thought. Stuart Chase[4] and others have come near to claiming that all abstract words are meaningless, and have used this as a pretext for advocating a kind of political quietism. Since you don't know what Fascism is, how can you struggle against Fascism? One need not swallow such absurdities as this, but one ought to recognize that the present political chaos is connected with the decay of language, and that one can probably bring about some improvement by starting at the verbal end. If you simplify your English, you are freed from the worst follies of orthodoxy. You cannot speak any of the necessary dialects, and when you make a stupid remark its stupidity will be obvious, even to yourself. Political language—and with variations this is true of all political parties, from Conservatives to Anarchists—is designed to make lies sound truthful and murder respectable, and to give an appearance of solidity to pure wind. One cannot change this all in a moment, but one can at least change one's own habits, and from time to time one can even, if one jeers loudly enough, send some worn-out and useless phrase—some *jackboot, Achilles' heel, hotbed, melting pot, acid test, veritable inferno* or other lump of verbal refuse—into the dustbin where it belongs.

20

4. Chase (in *The Tyranny of Words* [1938] and *The Power of Words* [1954]) and S. I. Hayakawa (in *Language in Action* [1939]) popularized the semantic theories of Alfred Koryzbski.

MLA CITATION

Orwell, George. "Politics and the English Language." 1950. *The Norton Reader: An Anthology of Nonfiction*. Ed. Melissa A. Goldthwaite et al. 14th ed. New York: Norton, 2016. 510–19. Print.

Questions

1. State George Orwell's main point as precisely as possible.

2. What kinds of prose does Orwell analyze in this essay? Look, in particular, at the passages he quotes in paragraph 3. Where would you find their contemporary equivalents?

3. Apply Orwell's rule iv, "Never use the passive where you can use the active" (paragraph 19), to paragraph 14 of his essay. What happens when you change his passive constructions to active? Has Orwell forgotten rule iv or is he covered by rule vi, "Break any of these rules sooner than say anything outright barbarous"?

4. Orwell wrote this essay in 1946. Choose at least two examples of political discourse from current media and discuss, in an essay, the extent to which Orwell's analysis of the language of politics still applies today. Which features that he singles out for criticism appear most frequently in the examples you chose?

Nature and the Environment

John McPhee   *Under the Snow*

WHEN MY THIRD DAUGHTER WAS AN INFANT, I could place her against my shoulder and she would stick there like velvet. Only her eyes jumped from place to place. In a breeze, her bright-red hair might stir, but she would not. Even then, there was profundity in her repose. When my fourth daughter was an infant, I wondered if her veins were full of ants. Placing her against a shoulder was a risk both to her and to the shoulder. Impulsively, constantly, everything about her moved. Her head seemed about to revolve as it followed the bestirring world.

These memories became very much alive some months ago when—one after another—I had bear cubs under my vest. Weighing three, four, 5.6 pounds, they were wild bears, and for an hour or so had been taken from their dens in Pennsylvania. They were about two months old, with fine short brown hair. When they were made to stand alone, to be photographed in the mouth of a den, they shivered. Instinctively, a person would be moved to hold them. Picked up by the scruff of the neck, they splayed their paws like kittens and screamed like baby bears. The cry of a baby bear is muted, like a human infant's heard from her crib down the hall. The first cub I placed on my shoulder stayed there like a piece of velvet. The shivering stopped. Her bright-blue eyes looked about, not seeing much of anything. My hand, cupped against her back, all but encompassed her rib cage, which was warm and calm. I covered her to the shoulders with a flap of down vest and zipped up my parka to hold her in place.

I was there by invitation, an indirect result of work I had been doing nearby. Would I be busy on March 14th? If there had been a conflict—if, say, I had been invited to lunch on that day with the Queen of Scotland and the King of Spain—I would have gone to the cubs. The first den was a rock cavity in a lichen-covered sandstone outcrop near the top of a slope, a couple of hundred yards from a road in Hawley. It was on posted property of the Scrub Oak Hunting Club—dry hardwood forest underlain by laurel and patches of snow—in the northern Pocono woods. Up in the sky was Buck Alt. Not long ago, he was a dairy farmer, and now he was working for the Keystone State, with directional antennae on his wing struts angled in the direction of bears. Many bears in

Originally published in the New Yorker (1983), *a weekly magazine of "reportage, commentary, criticism, essays, fiction, satire, cartoons, and poetry," and included in John McPhee's essay collection* Table of Contents (1985).

Pennsylvania have radios around their necks as a result of the summer trapping work of Alt's son Gary, who is a wildlife biologist. In winter, Buck Alt flies the country listening to the radio, crissing and crossing until the bears come on. They come on stronger the closer to them he flies. The transmitters are not omnidirectional. Suddenly, the sound cuts out. Buck looks down, chooses a landmark, approaches it again, on another vector. Gradually, he works his way in, until he is flying in ever tighter circles above the bear. He marks a map. He is accurate within two acres. The plane he flies is a Super Cub.

5   The den could have served as a set for a Passion play. It was a small chamber, open on one side, with a rock across its entrance. Between the freestanding rock and the back of the cave was room for one large bear, and she was curled in a corner on a bed of leaves, her broad head plainly visible from the outside, her cubs invisible between the rock and a soft place, chuckling, suckling, in the wintertime tropics of their own mammalian heaven. Invisible they were, yes, but by no means inaudible. What biologists call chuckling sounded like starlings in a tree.

People walking in woods sometimes come close enough to a den to cause the mother to get up and run off, unmindful of her reputation as a fearless defender of cubs. The cubs stop chuckling and begin to cry: possibly three, four cubs—a ward of mewling bears. The people hear the crying. They find the den and see the cubs. Sometimes they pick them up and carry them away, reporting to the state that they have saved the lives of bear cubs abandoned by their mother. Wherever and whenever this occurs, Gary Alt collects the cubs. After ten years of bear trapping and biological study, Alt has equipped so many sows with radios that he has been able to conduct a foster-mother program with an amazingly high rate of success. A mother in hibernation will readily accept a foster cub. If the need to place an orphan arises somewhat later, when mothers and their cubs are out and around, a sow will kill an alien cub as soon as she smells it. Alt has overcome this problem by stuffing sows' noses with Vicks Vapo-Rub. One way or another, he has found new families for forty-seven orphaned cubs. Forty-six have survived. The other, which had become accustomed over three weeks to feedings and caresses by human hands, was not content in a foster den, crawled outside, and died in the snow.

With a hypodermic jab stick, Alt now drugged the mother, putting her to sleep for the duration of the visit. From deeps of shining fur, he fished out cubs. One. Two. A third. A fourth. Five! The fifth was a foster daughter brought earlier in the winter from two hundred miles away. Three of the four others were male—a ratio consistent with the heavy preponderance of males that Alt's studies have shown through the years. To various onlookers he handed the cubs for safekeeping while he and several assistants carried the mother into the open and weighed her with block and tackle. To protect her eyes, Alt had blindfolded her with a red bandanna. They carried her upside down, being extremely careful lest they scrape and damage her nipples. She weighed two hundred and nineteen pounds. Alt had caught her and weighed her some months before. In the den, she had lost ninety pounds. When she was four years old, she had had four cubs; two years later, four more cubs; and now, after two more years, four cubs. He knew all that about her, he had caught her so many times. He referred to her as Daisy. Daisy was as nothing compared with Vanessa, who was sleeping off the winter somewhere else. In ten seasons, Vanessa had given birth to twenty-three cubs and had lost none. The growth and reproductive rates of black bears are greater in Pennsylvania than anywhere else. Black bears in Pennsylvania grow more rapidly than grizzlies in Montana. Eastern black bears are generally much larger than Western ones. A seven-hundred-pound bear is unusual but not rare in Pennsylvania. Alt once caught a big boar like that who had a thirty-seven-inch neck and was a hair under seven feet long.

This bear, nose to tail, measured five feet five. Alt said, "That's a nice long sow." For weighing the cubs, he had a small nylon stuff sack. He stuffed it with bear and hung it on a scale. Two months before, when the cubs were born, each would have weighed approximately half a pound—less than a newborn porcupine. Now the cubs weighed 3.4, 4.1, 4.4, 4.6, 5.6—cute little numbers with soft tan noses and erectile pyramid ears. Bears have sex in June and July, but the mother's system holds the fertilized egg away from the uterus until November, when implantation occurs. Fetal development lasts scarcely six weeks. Therefore, the creatures who live upon the hibernating mother are so small that everyone survives.

The orphan, less winsome than the others, looked like a chocolate-covered possum. I kept her under my vest. She seemed content there and scarcely moved. In time, I exchanged her for 5.6—the big boy in the litter. Lifted by the scruff and held in the air, he bawled, flashed his claws, and curled his lips like a woofing boar. I stuffed him under the vest, where he shut up and nuzzled. His claws were already more than half an inch long. Alt said that the family would come out of the den in a few weeks but that much of the spring would go by before the cubs gained weight. The difference would be that they were no longer malleable and ductile. They would become pugnacious and scratchy, not to say vicious, and would chew up the hand that caressed them. He said, "If you have an enemy, give him a bear cub."

Six men carried the mother back to the den, the red bandanna still tied around her eyes. Alt repacked her into the rock. "We like to return her to the den as close as possible to the way we found her," he said. Someone remarked that one biologist can work a coon, while an army is needed to deal with a bear. An army seemed to be present. Twelve people had followed Alt to the den. Some days, the group around him is four times as large. Alt, who is in his thirties, was wearing a visored khaki cap with a blue-and-gold keystone on the forehead, and a khaki cardigan under a khaki jump suit. A lithe and light-bodied man with tinted glasses and a blond mustache, he looked like a lieutenant in the Ardennes Forest.[1] Included in the retinue were two reporters and a news photographer. Alt encourages media attention, the better to soften the image of the bears. He says, "People fear bears more than they need to, and respect them not enough." Over the next twenty days, he had scheduled four hundred

10

---

1. Area of Belgium, Luxembourg, and France where the 1944–1945 Battle of the Bulge took place.

visitors—state senators, representatives, commissioners, television reporters, word processors, biologists, friends—to go along on his rounds of dens. Days before, he and the denned bears had been hosts to the BBC.[2] The Brits wanted snow. God was having none of it. The BBC brought in the snow.

In the course of the day, we made a brief tour of dens that for the time being stood vacant. Most were rock cavities. They had been used before, and in all likelihood would be used again. Bears in winter in the Pocono Plateau are like chocolate chips in a cookie. The bears seldom go back to the same den two years running, and they often change dens in the course of a winter. In a forty-five-hundred-acre housing development called Hemlock Farms are twenty-three dens known to be in current use and countless others awaiting new tenants. Alt showed one that was within fifteen feet of the intersection of East Spur Court and Pommel Drive. He said that when a sow with two cubs was in there he had seen deer browsing by the outcrop and ignorant dogs stopping off to lift a leg. Hemlock Farms is expensive, and full of cantilevered cypress and unencumbered glass. Houses perch on high flat rock. Now and again, there are bears in the rock—in, say, a floor-through cavity just under the porch. The owners are from New York. Alt does not always tell them that their property is zoned for bears. Once, when he did so, a "For Sale" sign went up within two weeks.

Not far away is Interstate 84. Flying over it one day, Buck Alt heard an oddly intermittent signal. Instead of breaking off once and cleanly, it broke off many times. Crossing back over, he heard it again. Soon he was in a tight turn, now hearing something, now nothing, in a pattern that did not suggest anything he had heard before. It did, however, suggest the interstate. Where a big green sign says, "Milford 11, Port Jervis 20," Gary hunted around and found the bear. He took us now to see the den. We went down a steep slope at the side of the highway and, crouching, peered into a culvert. It was about fifty yards long. There was a disc of daylight at the opposite end. Thirty inches in diameter, it was a perfect place to stash a body, and that is what the bear thought, too. On Gary's first visit, the disc of daylight had not been visible. The bear had denned under the eastbound lanes. She had given birth to three cubs. Soon after he found her, heavy rains were predicted. He hauled the family out and off to a vacant den. The cubs weighed less than a pound. Two days later, water a foot deep was racing through the culvert.

Under High Knob, in remote undeveloped forest about six hundred metres above sea level, a slope falling away in an easterly direction contained a classic excavated den: a small entrance leading into an intimate ovate cavern, with a depression in the center for a bed—in all, about twenty-four cubic feet, the size of a refrigerator-freezer. The den had not been occupied in several seasons, but Rob Buss, a district game protector who works regularly with Gary Alt, had been around to check it three days before and had shined his flashlight into a darkness stuffed with fur. Meanwhile, six inches of fresh snow had fallen on High Knob, and now Alt and his team, making preparations a short distance from the den, scooped up snow in their arms and filled a big sack. They had nets of nylon mesh. There was a fifty-fifty likelihood of yearling bears in the

2. British Broadcasting Corporation.

den. Mothers keep cubs until their second spring. When a biologist comes along and provokes the occupants to emerge, there is no way to predict how many will appear. Sometimes they keep coming and coming, like clowns from a compact car. As a bear emerges, it walks into the nylon mesh. A drawstring closes. At the same time, the den entrance is stuffed with a bag of snow. That stops the others. After the first bear has been dealt with, Alt removes the sack of snow. Out comes another bear. A yearling weighs about eighty pounds, and may move so fast that it runs over someone on the biological team and stands on top of him sniffing at his ears. Or her ears. Janice Gruttadauria, a research assistant, is a part of the team. Bear after bear, the procedure is repeated until the bag of snow is pulled away and nothing comes out. That is when Alt asks Rob Buss to go inside and see if anything is there.

Now, moving close to the entrance, Alt spread a tarp on the snow, lay down on it, turned on a five-cell flashlight, and put his head inside the den. The beam played over thick black fur and came to rest on a tiny foot. The sack of snow would not be needed. After drugging the mother with a jab stick, he joined her in the den. The entrance was so narrow he had to shrug his shoulders to get in. He shoved the sleeping mother, head first, out of the darkness and into the light.

While she was away, I shrugged my own shoulders and had a look inside. The den smelled of earth but not of bear. The walls were dripping with roots. The water and protein metabolism of hibernating black bears has been explored by the Mayo Clinic as a research model for, among other things, human endurance on long flights through space and medical situations closer to home, such as the maintenance of anephric human beings who are awaiting kidney transplants.

Outside, each in turn, the cubs were put in the stuff sack—a male and a female. The female weighed four pounds. Greedily, I reached for her when Alt took her out of the bag. I planted her on my shoulder while I wrote down facts about her mother: weight, a hundred and ninety-two pounds; length, fifty-eight inches; some toes missing; severe frostbite from a bygone winter evidenced along the edges of the ears.

Eventually, with all weighing and tagging complete, it was time to go. Alt went into the den. Soon he called out that he was ready for the mother. It would be a tight fit. Feet first, she was shoved in, like a safe-deposit box. Inside, Alt tugged at her in close embrace, and the two of them gradually revolved until she was at the back and their positions had reversed. He shaped her like a doughnut—her accustomed den position. The cubs go in the center. The male was handed in to him. Now he was asking for the female. For a moment, I glanced around as if looking to see who had her. The thought crossed my mind that if I bolted and ran far enough and fast enough I could flag a passing car and keep her. Then I pulled her from under the flap of my vest and handed her away.

Alt and others covered the entrance with laurel boughs, and covered the boughs with snow. They camouflaged the den, but that was not the purpose. Practicing wildlife management to a fare-thee-well, Alt wanted the den to be even darker than it had been before; this would cause the family to stay longer inside and improve the cubs' chances when at last they faced the world.

In the evening, I drove down off the Pocono Plateau and over the folded mountains and across the Great Valley and up the New Jersey Highlands and

15

down into the basin and home. No amount of intervening terrain, though—and no amount of distance—could remove from my mind the picture of the covered entrance in the Pennsylvania hillside, or the thought of what was up there under the snow.

MLA CITATION

McPhee, John. "Under the Snow." 1983. *The Norton Reader: An Anthology of Nonfiction*. Ed. Melissa A. Goldthwaite et al. 14th ed. New York: Norton, 2016. 521–26. Print.

QUESTIONS

1. John McPhee opens with a memory of holding his daughter when she was an infant, saying she would stick to his shoulder "like velvet" (paragraph 1). Two paragraphs later, he writes about holding a bear cub that stayed on his shoulder "like a piece of velvet" (paragraph 3). Why do you think McPhee makes this comparison? What purpose does it serve in this essay?

2. Trace McPhee's use of simile throughout the essay. For example, he compares bears to chocolate chips (paragraph 11), likens their movement to "clowns from a compact car" (paragraph 13), and describes a researcher positioning a bear "like a doughnut" (paragraph 17). What is the effect of such comparisons? What other similes are significant in this essay?

3. What is the purpose of the kind of bear trapping and biological study McPhee describes? What is your position on this interaction between humans and wildlife? Write an argument in which you either defend the kind of research McPhee describes or make a case for leaving wildlife alone. Consider using a specific animal (as McPhee uses bears) in making your claim.

BRIAN DOYLE   *Joyas Voladoras*

CONSIDER THE HUMMINGBIRD for a long moment. A hummingbird's heart beats ten times a second. A hummingbird's heart is the size of a pencil eraser. A hummingbird's heart is a lot of the hummingbird. *Joyas voladoras*, flying jewels, the first white explorers in the Americas called them, and the white men had never seen such creatures, for hummingbirds came into the world only in the Americas, nowhere else in the universe, more than three hundred species of them whirring and zooming and nectaring in hummer time zones nine times removed from ours, their hearts hammering faster than

First published in the American Scholar (2004), a "quirky magazine of public affairs, literature, science, history, and culture," and later chosen for inclusion in The Best American Essays (2005).

we could clearly hear if we pressed our elephantine ears to their infinitesimal chests.

Each one visits a thousand flowers a day. They can dive at sixty miles an hour. They can fly backward. They can fly more than five hundred miles without pausing to rest. But when they rest they come close to death: on frigid nights, or when they are starving, they retreat into torpor, their metabolic rate slowing to a fifteenth of their normal sleep rate, their hearts sludging nearly to a halt, barely beating, and if they are not soon warmed, if they do not soon find that which is sweet, their hearts grow cold, and they cease to be. Consider for a moment those hummingbirds who did not open their eyes again today, this very day, in the Americas: bearded helmetcrests and booted racket-tails, violet-tailed sylphs and violet-capped woodnymphs, crimson topazes and purple-crowned fairies, red-tailed comets and amethyst woodstars, rain-bow-bearded thornbills and glittering-bellied emeralds, velvet-purple coronets and golden-bellied star-frontlets, fiery-tailed awlbills and Andean hillstars, spatuletails and pufflegs, each the most amazing thing you have never seen, each thunderous wild heart the size of an infant's fingernail, each mad heart silent, a brilliant music stilled.

Hummingbirds, like all flying birds but more so, have incredible enormous immense ferocious metabolisms. To drive those metabolisms they have race-car hearts that eat oxygen at an eye-popping rate. Their hearts are built of thinner, leaner fibers than ours. Their arteries are stiffer and more taut. They have more mitochondria in their heart muscles—anything to gulp more oxygen. Their hearts are stripped to the skin for the war against gravity and inertia, the mad search for food, the insane idea of flight. The price of their ambition is a life closer to death; they suffer more heart attacks and aneurysms and ruptures than any other living creature. It's expensive to fly. You burn out. You fry the machine. You melt the engine. Every creature on earth has approximately two billion heartbeats to spend in a lifetime. You can spend them slowly, like a tortoise, and live to be two hundred years old, or you can spend them fast, like a hummingbird, and live to be two years old.

The biggest heart in the world is inside the blue whale. It weighs more than seven tons. It's as big as a room. It *is* a room, with four chambers. A child could walk around in it, head high, bending only to step through the valves. The valves are as big as the swinging doors in a saloon. This house of a heart drives a creature a hundred feet long. When this creature is born it is twenty feet long and weighs four tons. It is waaaaay bigger than your car. It drinks a hundred gallons of milk from its mama every day and gains two hundred pounds a day, and when it is seven or eight years old it endures an unimaginable puberty and then it essentially disappears from human ken, for next to nothing is known of the mating habits, travel patterns, diet, social life, language, social structure, diseases, spirituality, wars, stories, despairs, and arts of the blue whale. There are perhaps ten thousand blue whales in the world, living in every ocean on earth, and of the largest mammal who ever lived we know nearly nothing. But we know this: the animals with the largest hearts in the world generally travel in pairs, and their penetrating moaning cries, their piercing yearning tongue, can be heard underwater for miles and miles.

5   Mammals and birds have hearts with four chambers. Reptiles and turtles have hearts with three chambers. Fish have hearts with two chambers. Insects and mollusks have hearts with one chamber. Worms have hearts with one chamber, although they may have as many as eleven single-chambered hearts. Unicellular bacteria have no hearts at all; but even they have fluid eternally in motion, washing from one side of the cell to the other, swirling and whirling. No living being is without interior liquid motion. We all churn inside.

So much held in a heart in a lifetime. So much held in a heart in a day, an hour, a moment. We are utterly open with no one, in the end—not mother and father, not wife or husband, not lover, not child, not friend. We open windows to each but we live alone in the house of the heart. Perhaps we must. Perhaps we could not bear to be so naked, for fear of a constantly harrowed heart. When young we think there will come one person who will savor and sustain us always; when we are older we know this is the dream of a child, that all hearts finally are bruised and scarred, scored and torn, repaired by time and will, patched by force of character, yet fragile and rickety forevermore, no matter how ferocious the defense and how many bricks you bring to the wall. You can brick up your heart as stout and tight and hard and cold and impregnable as you possibly can and down it comes in an instant, felled by a woman's second glance, a child's apple breath, the shatter of glass in the road, the words "I have something to tell you," a cat with a broken spine dragging itself into the forest to die, the brush of your mother's papery ancient hand in the thicket of your hair, the memory of your father's voice early in the morning echoing from the kitchen where he is making pancakes for his children.

MLA CITATION

Doyle, Brian. "Joyas Voladoras." 2004. *The Norton Reader: An Anthology of Nonfiction.* Ed. Melissa A. Goldthwaite et al. 14th ed. New York: Norton, 2016. 526–28. Print.

QUESTIONS

1. Brian Doyle considers the hearts of hummingbirds (paragraphs 1–3), blue whales (paragraph 4), and humans (paragraph 6) in this lyric essay, which uses poetic features such as metaphor, contrast, and repetition. What is his purpose in doing so? How does he make a transition from a focus on animals to a focus on humans?

2. Doyle incorporates several lists into this essay. Trace his use of lists throughout the essay. Which list do you find most effective? Why?

3. Write a lyric essay in which you closely consider some element of human and animal nature. Consider using some of the poetic features identified in the first question.

JOHN MUIR   *A Wind-Storm in the Forests*

THE MOUNTAIN WINDS, like the dew and rain, sunshine and snow, are measured and bestowed with love on the forests to develop their strength and beauty. However restricted the scope of other forest influences, that of the winds is universal. The snow bends and trims the upper forests every winter, the lightning strikes a single tree here and there, while avalanches mow down thousands at a swoop as a gardener trims out a bed of flowers. But the winds go to every tree, fingering every leaf and branch and furrowed bole; not one is forgotten; the Mountain Pine towering with outstretched arms on the rugged buttresses of the icy peaks, the lowliest and most retiring tenant of the dells; they seek and find them all, caressing them tenderly, bending them in lusty exercise, stimulating their growth, plucking off a leaf or limb as required, or removing an entire tree or grove, now whispering and cooing through the branches like a sleepy child, now roaring like the ocean; the winds blessing the forests, the forests the winds, with ineffable beauty and harmony as the sure result.

After one has seen pines six feet in diameter bending like grasses before a mountain gale, and ever and anon some giant falling with a crash that shakes the hills, it seems astonishing that any, save the lowest thickset trees, could ever have found a period sufficiently stormless to establish themselves; or, once established, that they should not, sooner or later, have been blown down. But when the storm is over, and we behold the same forests tranquil again, towering fresh and unscathed in erect majesty, and consider what centuries of storms have fallen upon them since they were first planted,—hail, to break the tender seedlings; lightning, to scorch and shatter; snow, winds, and avalanches, to crush and overwhelm,—while the manifest result of all this wild storm-culture is the glorious perfection we behold; then faith in Nature's forestry is established, and we cease to deplore the violence of her most destructive gales, or of any other storm-implement whatsoever.

There are two trees in the Sierra forests that are never blown down, so long as they continue in sound health. These are the Juniper and the Dwarf Pine of the summit peaks. Their stiff, crooked roots grip the storm-beaten ledges like eagles' claws, while their lithe, cord-like branches bend round compliantly, offering but slight holds for winds, however violent. The other alpine conifers— the Needle Pine, Mountain Pine, Two-leaved Pine, and Hemlock Spruce—are never thinned out by this agent to any destructive extent, on account of their admirable toughness and the closeness of their growth. In general the same is true of the giants of the lower zones. The kingly Sugar Pine, towering aloft to a height of more than 200 feet, offers a fine mark to storm-winds: but it is not densely foliaged, and its long, horizontal arms swing round compliantly in the

From John Muir's The Mountains of California *(1894), a book of scientific observation and personal memoir.*

A wind-storm in the California forests (after a sketch by the author).

blast, like tresses of green, fluent algæ in a brook; while the Silver Firs in most places keep their ranks well together in united strength. The Yellow or Silver Pine is more frequently overturned than any other tree on the Sierra, because its leaves and branches form a larger mass in proportion to its height, while in many places it is planted sparsely, leaving open lanes through which storms may enter with full force. Furthermore, because it is distributed along the lower portion of the range, which was the first to be left bare on the breaking up of the ice-sheet at the close of the glacial winter, the soil it is growing upon has been longer exposed to post-glacial weathering, and consequently is in a more crumbling, decayed condition than the fresher soils farther up the range, and therefore offers a less secure anchorage for the roots.

While exploring the forest zones of Mount Shasta, I discovered the path of a hurricane strewn with thousands of pines of this species. Great and small had been uprooted or wrenched off by sheer force, making a clean gap, like that made by a snow avalanche. But hurricanes capable of doing this class of work are rare in the Sierra, and when we have explored the forests from one extremity of the range to the other, we are compelled to believe that they are the most beautiful on the face of the earth, however we may regard the agents that have made them so.

5   There is always something deeply exciting, not only in the sounds of winds in the woods, which exert more or less influence over every mind, but in their varied waterlike flow as manifested by the movements of the trees, especially those of the conifers. By no other trees are they rendered so extensively and impressively visible, not even by the lordly tropic palms or tree-ferns responsive to the gentlest breeze. The waving of a forest of the giant Sequoias is indescribably impressive and sublime, but the pines seem to me the best interpreters of winds. They are mighty waving goldenrods, ever in tune, singing and writing wind-music all their long century lives. Little, however, of this noble tree-waving and tree-music will you see or hear in the strictly alpine portion of the forests. The burly Juniper, whose girth sometimes more than equals its height, is about as rigid as the rocks on which it grows. The slender lash-like sprays of the Dwarf Pine stream out in wavering ripples, but the tallest and slenderest

are far too unyielding to wave even in the heaviest gales. They only shake in quick, short vibrations. The Hemlock Spruce, however, and the Mountain Pine, and some of the tallest thickets of the Two-leaved species bow in storms with considerable scope and gracefulness. But it is only in the lower and middle zones that the meeting of winds and woods is to be seen in all its grandeur.

One of the most beautiful and exhilarating storms I ever enjoyed in the Sierra occurred in December, 1874, when I happened to be exploring one of the tributary valleys of the Yuba River. The sky and the ground and the trees had been thoroughly rain-washed and were dry again. The day was intensely pure, one of those incomparable bits of California winter, warm and balmy and full of white sparkling sunshine, redolent of all the purest influences of the spring, and at the same time enlivened with one of the most bracing wind-storms conceivable. Instead of camping out, as I usually do, I then chanced to be stopping at the house of a friend. But when the storm began to sound, I lost no time in pushing out into the woods to enjoy it. For on such occasions Nature has always something rare to show us, and the danger to life and limb is hardly greater than one would experience crouching deprecatingly beneath a roof.

It was still early morning when I found myself fairly adrift. Delicious sunshine came pouring over the hills, lighting the tops of the pines, and setting free a stream of summery fragrance that contrasted strangely with the wild tones of the storm. The air was mottled with pine-tassels and bright green plumes, that went flashing past in the sunlight like birds pursued. But there was not the slightest dustiness, nothing less pure than leaves, and ripe pollen, and flecks of withered bracken and moss. I heard trees falling for hours at the rate of one every two or three minutes; some uprooted, partly on account of the loose, water-soaked condition of the ground; others broken straight across, where some weakness caused by fire had determined the spot. The gestures of the various trees made a delightful study. Young Sugar Pines, light and feathery as squirrel-tails, were bowing almost to the ground; while the grand old patriarchs, whose massive boles had been tried in a hundred storms, waved solemnly above them, their long, arching branches streaming fluently on the gale, and every needle thrilling and ringing and shedding off keen lances of light like a diamond. The Douglas Spruces,[1] with long sprays drawn out in level tresses, and needles massed in a gray, shimmering glow, presented a most striking appearance as they stood in bold relief along the hilltops. The madroños[2] in the dells, with their red bark and large glossy leaves tilted every way, reflected the sunshine in throbbing spangles like those one so often sees on the rippled surface of a glacier lake. But the Silver Pines were now the most impressively beautiful of all. Colossal spires 200 feet in height waved like supple goldenrods chanting and bowing low as if in worship, while the whole mass of their long, tremulous foliage was kindled into one continuous blaze of white sun-fire. The force of the gale was such that the most steadfast monarch of them all rocked down to its roots with a motion plainly perceptible when one leaned

1. Another name for Douglas fir.
2. Type of evergreen tree.

against it. Nature was holding high festival, and every fiber of the most rigid giants thrilled with glad excitement.

I drifted on through the midst of this passionate music and motion, across many a glen, from ridge to ridge; often halting in the lee of a rock for shelter, or to gaze and listen. Even when the grand anthem had swelled to its highest pitch, I could distinctly hear the varying tones of individual trees,—Spruce, and Fir, and Pine, and leafless Oak—and even the infinitely gentle rustle of the withered grasses at my feet. Each was expressing itself in its own way,—singing its own song, and making its own peculiar gestures,—manifesting a richness of variety to be found in no other forest I have yet seen. The coniferous woods of Canada, and the Carolinas, and Florida, are made up of trees that resemble one another about as nearly as blades of grass, and grow close together in much the same way. Coniferous trees, in general, seldom possess individual character, such as is manifest among Oaks and Elms. But the California forests are made up of a greater number of distinct species than any other in the world. And in them we find, not only a marked differentiation into special groups, but also a marked individuality in almost every tree, giving rise to storm effects indescribably glorious.

Toward midday, after a long, tingling scramble through copses of hazel and ceanothus,[3] I gained the summit of the highest ridge in the neighborhood; and then it occurred to me that it would be a fine thing to climb one of the trees to obtain a wider outlook and get my ear close to the Æolian music[4] of its topmost needles. But under the circumstances the choice of a tree was a serious matter. One whose instep was not very strong seemed in danger of being blown down, or of being struck by others in case they should fall; another was branchless to a considerable height above the ground, and at the same time too large to be grasped with arms and legs in climbing; while others were not favorably situated for clear views. After cautiously casting about, I made choice of the tallest of a group of Douglas Spruces that were growing close together like a tuft of grass, no one of which seemed likely to fall unless all the rest fell with it. Though comparatively young, they were about 100 feet high, and their lithe, brushy tops were rocking and swirling in wild ecstasy. Being accustomed to climb trees in making botanical studies, I experienced no difficulty in reaching the top of this one, and never before did I enjoy so noble an exhilaration of motion. The slender tops fairly flapped and swished in the passionate torrent, bending and swirling backward and forward, round and round, tracing indescribable combinations of vertical and horizontal curves, while I clung with muscles firm braced, like a bobolink on a reed.

10 In its widest sweeps my tree-top described an arc of from twenty to thirty degrees, but I felt sure of its elastic temper, having seen others of the same species still more severely tried—bent almost to the ground indeed, in heavy snows—without breaking a fiber. I was therefore safe, and free to take the wind into my pulses and enjoy the excited forest from my superb outlook. The view

3. Type of evergreen shrub.
4. Music made by the wind; from Aeolus, the Greek god of the winds, the strings of whose harp were sounded by the wind.

from here must be extremely beautiful in any weather. Now my eye roved over the piny hills and dales as over fields of waving grain, and felt the light running in ripples and broad swelling undulations across the valleys from ridge to ridge, as the shining foliage was stirred by corresponding waves of air. Oftentimes these waves of reflected light would break up suddenly into a kind of beaten foam, and again, after chasing one another in regular order, they would seem to bend forward in concentric curves, and disappear on some hillside, like sea-waves on a shelving shore. The quantity of light reflected from the bent needles was so great as to make whole groves appear as if covered with snow, while the black shadows beneath the trees greatly enhanced the effect of the silvery splendor.

Excepting only the shadows there was nothing somber in all this wild sea of pines. On the contrary, notwithstanding this was the winter season, the colors were remarkably beautiful. The shafts of the pine and libocedrus[5] were brown and purple, and most of the foliage was well tinged with yellow; the laurel groves, with the pale undersides of their leaves turned upward, made masses of gray; and then there was many a dash of chocolate color from clumps of manzanita,[6] and jet of vivid crimson from the bark of the madroños, while the ground on the hillsides, appearing here and there through openings between the groves, displayed masses of pale purple and brown.

The sounds of the storm corresponded gloriously with this wild exuberance of light and motion. The profound bass of the naked branches and boles booming like waterfalls; the quick, tense vibrations of the pine-needles, now rising to a shrill, whistling hiss, now falling to a silky murmur; the rustling of laurel groves in the dells, and the keen metallic click of leaf on leaf—all this was heard in easy analysis when the attention was calmly bent.

The varied gestures of the multitude were seen to fine advantage, so that one could recognize the different species at a distance of several miles by this means alone, as well as by their forms and colors, and the way they reflected the light. All seemed strong and comfortable, as if really enjoying the storm, while responding to its most enthusiastic greetings. We hear much nowadays concerning the universal struggle for existence, but no struggle in the common meaning of the word was manifest here; no recognition of danger by any tree; no deprecation; but rather an invincible gladness as remote from exultation as from fear.

I kept my lofty perch for hours, frequently closing my eyes to enjoy the music by itself, or to feast quietly on the delicious fragrance that was streaming past. The fragrance of the woods was less marked than that produced during warm rain, when so many balsamic buds and leaves are steeped like tea; but, from the chafing of resiny branches against each other, and the incessant attrition of myriads of needles, the gale was spiced to a very tonic degree. And besides the fragrance from these local sources there were traces of scents brought from afar. For this wind came first from the sea, rubbing against its fresh, briny waves, then distilled through the redwoods, threading rich ferny

5. Genus of cedar trees. In the Sierra Nevada, *Libocedrus decurrens* often reaches a height of 150 feet.
6. Type of evergreen shrub.

gulches, and spreading itself in broad undulating currents over many a flower-enameled ridge of the coast mountains, then across the golden plains, up the purple foot-hills, and into these piny woods with the varied incense gathered by the way.

15   Winds are advertisements of all they touch, however much or little we may be able to read them; telling their wanderings even by their scents alone. Mariners detect the flowery perfume of land-winds far at sea, and sea-winds carry the fragrance of dulse and tangle far inland, where it is quickly recognized, though mingled with the scents of a thousand land-flowers. As an illustration of this, I may tell here that I breathed sea-air on the Firth of Forth, in Scotland, while a boy; then was taken to Wisconsin, where I remained nineteen years; then, without in all this time having breathed one breath of the sea, I walked quietly, alone, from the middle of the Mississippi Valley to the Gulf of Mexico, on a botanical excursion, and while in Florida, far from the coast, my attention wholly bent on the splendid tropical vegetation about me, I suddenly recognized a sea-breeze, as it came sifting through the palmettos and blooming vine-tangles, which at once awakened and set free a thousand dormant associations, and made me a boy again in Scotland, as if all the intervening years had been annihilated.

Most people like to look at mountain rivers, and bear them in mind; but few care to look at the winds, though far more beautiful and sublime, and though they become at times about as visible as flowing water. When the north winds in winter are making upward sweeps over the curving summits of the High Sierra, the fact is sometimes published with flying snow-banners a mile long. Those portions of the winds thus embodied can scarce be wholly invisible, even to the darkest imagination. And when we look around over an agitated forest, we may see something of the wind that stirs it, by its effects upon the trees. Yonder it descends in a rush of water-like ripples, and sweeps over the bending pines from hill to hill. Nearer, we see detached plumes and leaves, now speeding by on level currents, now whirling in eddies, or, escaping over the edges of the whirls, soaring aloft on grand, upswelling domes of air, or tossing on flame-like crests. Smooth, deep currents, cascades, falls, and swirling eddies, sing around every tree and leaf, and over all the varied topography of the region with telling changes of form, like mountain rivers conforming to the features of their channels.

After tracing the Sierra streams from their fountains to the plains, marking where they bloom white in falls, glide in crystal plumes, surge gray and foam-filled in boulder-choked gorges, and slip through the woods in long, tranquil reaches—after thus learning their language and forms in detail, we may at length hear them chanting all together in one grand anthem, and comprehend them all in clear inner vision, covering the range like lace. But even this spectacle is far less sublime and not a whit more substantial than what we may behold of these storm-streams of air in the mountain woods.

We all travel the milky way together, trees and men; but it never occurred to me until this stormday, while swinging in the wind, that trees are travelers, in the ordinary sense. They make many journeys, not extensive ones, it is true;

but our own little journeys, away and back again, are only little more than tree-wavings—many of them not so much.

When the storm began to abate, I dismounted and sauntered down through the calming woods. The storm-tones died away, and, turning toward the east, I beheld the countless hosts of the forests hushed and tranquil, towering above one another on the slopes of the hills like a devout audience. The setting sun filled them with amber light, and seemed to say, while they listened, "My peace I give unto you."

As I gazed on the impressive scene, all the so-called ruin of the storm was   20 forgotten, and never before did these noble woods appear so fresh, so joyous, so immortal.

MLA CITATION

Muir, John. "A Wind-Storm in the Forests." 1894. *The Norton Reader: An Anthology of Nonfiction*. Ed. Melissa A. Goldthwaite et al. 14th ed. New York: Norton, 2016. 529–35. Print.

Questions

1. What preconceptions might a reader bring to John Muir's title, "A Wind-Storm in the Forests"? Does the opening sentence—indeed, the entire opening paragraph—suggest a different perspective? How so?

2. The central adventure in this essay occurs when Muir climbs a Douglas Spruce (paragraph 9). Why does Muir undertake this climb? What does he wish to experience?

3. Write about an experience you have had in nature, whether dramatic, as in Muir's essay, or more quiet.

EDWARD ABBEY   *The Great American Desert*

IN MY CASE IT WAS LOVE AT FIRST SIGHT. This desert, all deserts, any desert. No matter where my head and feet may go, my heart and my entrails stay behind, here on the clean, true, comfortable rock, under the black sun of God's forsaken country. When I take on my next incarnation, my bones will remain bleaching nicely in a stone gulch under the rim of some faraway plateau, way out there in the back of beyond. An unrequited and excessive love, inhuman no doubt but painful anyhow, especially when I see my desert under attack. "The

Solicited in 1973 for the hiking book Sierra Club Naturalist's Guide to the Deserts of the Southwest *(1977), this essay was, in revised form, also collected in Edward Abbey's* The Journey Home: Some Words in Defense of the American West *(1977).*

one death I cannot bear," said the Sonoran-Arizonan poet Richard Shelton. The kind of love that makes a man selfish, possessive, irritable. If you're thinking of a visit, my natural reaction is like a rattlesnake's—to warn you off. What I want to say goes something like this.

Survival Hint #1: Stay out of there. Don't go. Stay home and read a good book, this one for example. The Great American Desert is an awful place. People get hurt, get sick, get lost out there. Even if you survive, which is not certain, you will have a miserable time. The desert is for movies and God-intoxicated mystics, not for family recreation.

Let me enumerate the hazards. First the Walapai tiger, also known as cone-nose kissing bug. *Triatoma protracta* is a true bug, black as sin, and it flies through the night quiet as an assassin. It does not attack directly like a mosquito or deerfly, but alights at a discreet distance, undetected, and creeps upon you, its hairy little feet making not the slightest noise. The kissing bug is fond of warmth and like Dracula requires mammalian blood for sustenance. When it reaches you the bug crawls onto your skin so gently, so softly that unless your senses are hyperacute you feel nothing. Selecting a tender point, the bug slips its conical proboscis into your flesh, injecting a poisonous anesthetic. If you are asleep you will feel nothing. If you happen to be awake you may notice the faintest of pinpricks, hardly more than a brief ticklish sensation, which you will probably disregard. But the bug is already at work. Having numbed the nerves near the point of entry the bug proceeds (with a sigh of satisfaction, no doubt) to withdraw blood. When its belly is filled, it pulls out, backs off, and waddles away, so drunk and gorged it cannot fly.

At about this time the victim awakes, scratching at a furious itch. If you recognize the symptoms at once, you can sometimes find the bug in your vicinity and destroy it. But revenge will be your only satisfaction. Your night is ruined. If you are of average sensitivity to a kissing bug's poison, your entire body breaks out in hives, skin aflame from head to toe. Some people become seriously ill, in many cases requiring hospitalization. Others recover fully after five or six hours except for a hard and itchy swelling, which may endure for a week.

5   After the kissing bug, you should beware of rattlesnakes; we have half a dozen species, all offensive and dangerous, plus centipedes, millipedes, tarantulas, black widows, brown recluses, Gila monsters, the deadly poisonous coral snakes, and giant hairy desert scorpions. Plus an immense variety and near-infinite number of ants, midges, gnats, bloodsucking flies, and blood-guzzling mosquitoes. (You might think the desert would be spared at least mosquitoes? Not so. Peer in any water hole by day: swarming with mosquito larvae. Venture out on a summer's eve: The air vibrates with their mournful keening.) Finally, where the desert meets the sea, as on the coasts of Sonora and Baja California, we have the usual assortment of obnoxious marine life: sandflies, ghost crabs, stingrays, electric jellyfish, spiny sea urchins, man-eating sharks, and other creatures so distasteful one prefers not even to name them.

It has been said, and truly, that everything in the desert either stings, stabs, stinks, or sticks. You will find the flora here as venomous, hooked, barbed, thorny, prickly, needled, saw-toothed, hairy, stickered, mean, bitter, sharp, wiry, and fierce as the animals. Something about the desert inclines all living things to harshness and acerbity. The soft evolve out. Except for sleek and oily growths like the poison ivy—oh yes, indeed—that flourish in sinister profusion on the dank walls above the quicksand down in those corridors of gloom and labyrinthine monotony that men call canyons.

We come now to the third major hazard, which is sunshine. Too much of a good thing can be fatal. Sunstroke, heatstroke, and dehydration are common misfortunes in the bright American Southwest. If you can avoid the insects, reptiles, and arachnids, the cactus and the ivy, the smog of the southwestern cities, and the lung fungus of the desert valleys (carried by dust in the air), you cannot escape the desert sun. Too much exposure to it eventually causes, quite literally, not merely sunburn but skin cancer.

Much sun, little rain also means an arid climate. Compared with the high humidity of more hospitable regions, the dry heat of the desert seems at first not terribly uncomfortable—sometimes even pleasant. But that sensation of comfort is false, a deception, and therefore all the more dangerous, for it induces overexertion and an insufficient consumption of water, even when water is available. This leads to various internal complications, some immediate—sunstroke, for example—and some not apparent until much later. Mild but prolonged dehydration, continued over a span of months or years, leads to the crystallization of mineral solutions in the urinary tract, that is, to what urologists call urinary calculi or kidney stones. A disability common in all the world's arid regions. Kidney stones, in case you haven't met one, come in many shapes and sizes, from pellets smooth as BB shot to highly irregular calcifications resembling asteroids, Vietcong shrapnel, and crown-of-thorns starfish. Some of these objects may be "passed" naturally; others can be removed only by means of the Davis stone basket or by surgery. Me—I was lucky; I passed mine with only a groan, my forehead pressed against the wall of a pissoir in the rear of a Tucson bar that I cannot recommend.

You may be getting the impression by now that the desert is not the most suitable of environments for human habitation. Correct. Of all the Earth's climatic zones, excepting only the Antarctic, the deserts are the least inhabited, the least "developed," for reasons that should now be clear.

You may wish to ask, Yes, okay, but among North American deserts which is the *worst*? A good question—and I am happy to attempt an answer.   10

Geographers generally divide the North American desert—what was once termed "the Great American Desert"—into four distinct regions or subdeserts. These are the Sonoran Desert, which comprises southern Arizona, Baja California, and the state of Sonora in Mexico; the Chihuahuan Desert, which includes west Texas, southern New Mexico, and the states of Chihuahua and Coahuila in Mexico; the Mojave Desert, which includes southeastern California and small portions of Nevada, Utah, and Arizona; and the Great Basin Desert, which includes most of Utah and Nevada, northern Arizona, northwestern New Mexico, and much of Idaho and eastern Oregon.

Privately, I prefer my own categories. Up north in Utah somewhere is the canyon country—places like Zeke's Hole, Death Hollow, Pucker Pass, Buckskin Gulch, Nausea Crick, Wolf Hole, Mollie's Nipple, Dirty Devil River, Horse Canyon, Horseshoe Canyon, Lost Horse Canyon, Horsethief Canyon, and Horseshit Canyon, to name only the more classic places. Down in Arizona and Sonora there's the cactus country; if you have nothing better to do, you might take a look at High Tanks, Salome Creek, Tortilla Flat, Esperero ("Hoper") Canyon, Holy Joe Peak, Depression Canyon, Painted Cave, Hell Hole Canyon, Hell's Half Acre, Iceberg Canyon, Tiburon (Shark) Island, Pinacate Peak, Infernal Valley, Sykes Crater, Montezuma's Head, Gu Oidak, Kuakatch, Pisinimo, and Baboquivari Mountain, for example.

Then there's The Canyon. *The* Canyon. The Grand. That's one world. And North Rim—that's another. And Death Valley, still another, where I lived one winter near Furnace Creek and climbed the Funeral Mountains, tasted Badwater, looked into the Devil's Hole, hollered up Echo Canyon, searched for and never did find Seldom Seen Slim.[1] Looked for *satori*[2] near Vana, Nevada, and found a ghost town named Bonnie Claire. Never made it to Winnemucca. Drove through the Smoke Creek Desert and down through Big Pine and Lone Pine and home across the Panamints to Death Valley[3] again—home sweet home that winter.

And which of these deserts is the worst? I find it hard to judge. They're all bad—not half bad but all bad. In the Sonoran Desert, Phoenix will get you if the sun, snakes, bugs, and arthropods don't. In the Mojave Desert, it's Las Vegas, more sickening by far than the Glauber's salt in the Death Valley sinkholes. Go to Chihuahua and you're liable to get busted in El Paso and sandbagged in Ciudad Juárez—where all old whores go to die. Up north in the Great Basin Desert, on the Plateau Province, in the canyon country, your heart will break, seeing the strip mines open up and the power plants rise where only cowboys and Indians and J. Wesley Powell ever roamed before.

15   Nevertheless, all is not lost; much remains, and I welcome the prospect of an army of lug-soled hiker's boots on the desert trails. To save what wilderness is left in the American Southwest—and in the American Southwest only the wilderness is worth saving—we are going to need all the recruits we can get. All the hands, heads, bodies, time, money, effort we can find. Presumably—and the Sierra Club, the Wilderness Society, the Friends of the Earth, the Audubon Society, the Defenders of Wildlife[4] operate on this theory—those who

1. Nickname for Charles Ferge (1889–1968), prospector and sole resident of Ballarat ghost town.

2. Buddhist term for understanding or enlightenment.

3. "Winnemucca . . . Death Valley," desert towns in Nevada and California. Throughout the essay Abbey uses local as well as official names to convey a feel for desert places.

4. "Sierra Club . . . Defenders of Wildlife," organizations founded—from 1892 to 1969—to protect wilderness habitat and its plants and animals.

learn to love what is spare, rough, wild, undeveloped, and unbroken will be willing to fight for it, will help resist the strip miners, highway builders, land developers, weapons testers, power producers, tree chainers, clear cutters, oil drillers, dam beavers, subdividers—the list goes on and on—before that zinc-hearted, termite-brained, squint-eyed, near-sighted, greedy crew succeeds in completely californicating what still survives of the Great American Desert.

So much for the Good Cause. Now what about desert hiking itself, you may ask. I'm glad you asked that question. I firmly believe that one should never—I repeat *never*—go out into that formidable wasteland of cactus, heat, serpents, rock, scrub, and thorn without careful planning, thorough and cautious preparation, and complete—never mind the expense!—*complete* equipment. My motto is: Be Prepared.

That is my belief and that is my motto. My practice, however, is a little different. I tend to go off in a more or less random direction myself, half-baked, half-assed, half-cocked, and half-ripped. Why? Well, because I have an indolent and melancholy nature and don't care to be bothered getting all those *things* together—all that bloody *gear*—maps, compass, binoculars, poncho, pup tent, shoes, first-aid kit, rope, flashlight, inspirational poetry, water, food—and because anyhow I approach nature with a certain surly ill-will, daring Her to make trouble. Later when I'm deep into Natural Bridges Natural Moneymint or Zion National Parkinglot or say General Shithead National Forest Land of Many Abuses why then, of course, when it's a bit late, then I may wish I had packed that something extra: matches perhaps, to mention one useful item, or maybe a spoon to eat my gruel with.

If I hike with another person it's usually the same; most of my friends have indolent and melancholy natures too. A cursed lot, all of them. I think of my comrade John De Puy,[5] for example, sloping along for mile after mile like a goddamned camel—indefatigable—with those J. C. Penny hightops on his feet and that plastic pack on his back he got with five books of Green Stamps and nothing inside it but a sketchbook, some homemade jerky and a few cans of green chiles. Or Douglas Peacock,[6] ex-Green Beret, just the opposite. Built like a buffalo, he loads a ninety-pound canvas pannier on his back at trailhead, loaded with guns, ammunition, bayonet, pitons and carabiners, cameras, field books, a 150-foot rope, geologist's sledge, rock samples, assay kit,[7] field glasses, two gallons of water in steel canteens, jungle boots, a case of C-rations, rope hammock, pharmaceuticals in a pig-iron box, raincoat, overcoat, two-man mountain tent, Dutch oven, hibachi, shovel, ax, inflatable boat, and near the top of the load and distributed through side and back pockets, easily accessible, a case of beer. Not because he enjoys or needs all that weight—he may never get to the bottom of that cargo on a ten-day outing—but simply because Douglas

---

5. Painter (b. 1927) living in Taos, New Mexico, who met Abbey when Abbey was editing the Taos newspaper *El Crepusculo*.

6. Vietnam veteran (b. 1942) and author.

7. Used to purify water.

uses his packbag for general storage both at home and on the trail and prefers not to have to rearrange everything from time to time merely for the purposes of a hike. Thus my friends De Puy and Peacock; you may wish to avoid such extremes.

A few tips on desert etiquette:

1. Carry a cooking stove, if you must cook. Do not burn desert wood, which is rare and beautiful and required ages for its creation (an ironwood tree lives for over 1,000 years and juniper almost as long).

2. If you must, out of need, build a fire, then for God's sake allow it to burn itself out before you leave—do not bury it, as Boy Scouts and Campfire Girls do, under a heap of mud or sand. Scatter the ashes; replace any rocks you may have used in constructing a fireplace; do all you can to obliterate the evidence that you camped here. (The Search & Rescue Team may be looking for you.)

3. Do not bury garbage—the wildlife will only dig it up again. Burn what will burn and pack out the rest. The same goes for toilet paper: Don't bury it, *burn it.*

4. Do not bathe in desert pools, natural tanks, *tinajas,* potholes. Drink what water you need, take what you need, and leave the rest for the next hiker and more important for the bees, birds, and animals—bighorn sheep, coyotes, lions, foxes, badgers, deer, wild pigs, wild horses—whose *lives* depend on that water.

5. Always remove and destroy survey stakes, flagging, advertising signboards, mining claim markers, animal traps, poisoned bait, seismic exploration geophones, and other such artifacts of industrialism. The men who put those things there are up to no good and it is our duty to confound them. Keep America Beautiful. Grow a Beard. Take a Bath. Burn a Billboard.

20   Anyway—why go into the desert? Really, why do it? That sun, roaring at you all day long. The fetid, tepid, vapid little water holes slowly evaporating under a scum of grease, full of cannibal beetles, spotted toads, horsehair worms, liver flukes, and down at the bottom, inevitably, the pale cadaver of a ten-inch centipede. Those pink rattlesnakes down in The Canyon, those diamondback monsters thick as a truck driver's wrist that lurk in shady places along the trail, those unpleasant solpugids and unnecessary Jerusalem crickets that scurry on dirty claws across your face at night. Why? The rain that comes down like lead shot and wrecks the trail, those sudden rockfalls of obscure origin that crash like thunder ten feet behind you in the heart of a dead-still afternoon. The ubiquitous buzzard, so patient—but only so patient. The sullen and hostile Indians, all on welfare. The ragweed, the tumbleweed, the Jimson weed, the snakeweed. The scorpion in your shoe at dawn. The dreary wind that blows all spring, the psychedelic Joshua trees waving their arms at you on moonlight nights. Sand in the soup du jour. Halazone tablets in your canteen. The barren hills that

always go up, which is bad, or down, which is worse. Those canyons like cata-
combs with quicksand lapping at your crotch. Hollow, mummified horses
with forelegs casually crossed, dead for ten years, leaning against the corner of
a barbed-wire fence. Packhorses at night, iron-shod, clattering over the slick-
rock through your camp. The last tin of tuna, two flat tires, not enough water
and a forty-mile trek to Tule Well. An osprey on a cardón cactus, snatching the
head off a living fish—always the best part first. The hawk sailing by at 200
feet, a squirming snake in its talons. Salt in the drinking water. Salt, selenium,
arsenic, radon and radium in the water, in the gravel, in your bones. Water so
hard it bends light, drills holes in rock and chokes up your radiator. Why go
there? Those places with the hardcase names: Starvation Creek, Poverty Knoll,
Hungry Valley, Bitter Springs, Last Chance Canyon, Dungeon Canyon, Whip-
saw Flat, Dead Horse Point, Scorpion Flat, Dead Man Draw, Stinking Spring,
Camino del Diablo, Jornado del Muerto . . . Death Valley.

Well then, why indeed go walking into the desert, that grim ground, that
bleak and lonesome land where, as Genghis Khan[8] said of India, "the heat is
bad and the water makes men sick"?

Why the desert, when you could be strolling along the golden beaches of
California? Camping by a stream of pure Rocky Mountain spring water in colorful Colorado? Loafing through a laurel slick in the misty hills of North Carolina? Or getting your head mashed in the greasy alley behind the Elysium Bar
and Grill in Hoboken, New Jersey? Why the desert, given a world of such splendor and variety?

A friend and I took a walk around the base of a mountain up beyond
Coconino County, Arizona. This was a mountain we'd been planning to cir-
cumambulate for years. Finally we put on our walking shoes and did it. About
halfway around this mountain, on the third or fourth day, we paused for a
while—two days—by the side of a stream, which the Navajos call Nasja because
of the amber color of the water. (Caused perhaps by juniper roots—the water
seems safe enough to drink.) On our second day there I walked down the stream,
alone, to look at the canyon beyond. I entered the canyon and followed it for
half the afternoon, for three or four miles, maybe, until it became a gorge so
deep, narrow and dark, full of water and the inevitable quagmires of quicksand,
that I turned around and looked for a way out. A route other than the way I'd
come, which was crooked and uncomfortable and buried—I wanted to see what
was up on top of this world. I found a sort of chimney flue on the east wall,
which looked plausible, and sweated and cursed my way up through that until
I reached a point where I could walk upright, like a human being. Another 300
feet of scrambling brought me to the rim of the canyon. No one, I felt certain,
had ever before departed Nasja Canyon by that route.

But someone had. Near the summit I found an arrow sign, three feet long,
formed of stones and pointing off into the north toward those same old purple
vistas, so grand, immense, and mysterious, of more canyons, more mesas and

8. Founder and ruler of the Mongol empire (c. 1162–1227).

plateaus, more mountains, more cloud-dappled sun-spangled leagues of desert
sand and desert rock, under the same old wide and aching sky.

25   The arrow pointed into the north. But what was it pointing *at?* I looked at
the sign closely and saw that those dark, desert-varnished stones had been in
place for a long, long, time; they rested in compacted dust. They must have been
there for a century at least. I followed the direction indicated and came promptly
to the rim of another canyon and a drop-off straight down of a good 500 feet.
Not that way, surely. Across this canyon was nothing of any unusual interest
that I could see—only the familiar sun-blasted sandstone, a few scrubby clumps
of blackbrush and prickly pear, a few acres of nothing where only a lizard could
graze, surrounded by a few square miles of more nothingness interesting chiefly
to horned toads. I returned to the arrow and checked again, this time with field
glasses, looking away for as far as my aided eyes could see toward the north, for
ten, twenty, forty miles into the distance. I studied the scene with care, looking
for an ancient Indian ruin, a significant cairn, perhaps an abandoned mine, a
hidden treasure of some inconceivable wealth, the mother of all mother lodes. . . .

But there was nothing out there. Nothing at all. Nothing but the desert.
Nothing but the silent world.

That's why.

MLA CITATION

Abbey, Edward. "The Great American Desert." 1977. *The Norton Reader: An
Anthology of Nonfiction.* Ed. Melissa A. Goldthwaite et al. 14th ed. New York:
Norton, 2016. 535–42. Print.

QUESTIONS

1. Edward Abbey loves the desert, as he states in the first sentence. Why, then,
does he enumerate all of its negative features? What is his strategy?

2. Many paragraphs in this essay use lists. Choose one list, analyze its structure
(if there is one), and explain what the arrangement of details achieves.

3. How do you explain the ending of this essay—both what Abbey discovers and
how he uses it to convey his point?

4. Write an essay about a place you love, detailing its negative features as Abbey
does.

CHIEF SEATTLE   *Letter to President Pierce, 1855*

WE KNOW THAT the white man does not understand our ways. One portion of the land is the same to him as the next, for he is a stranger who comes in the night and takes from the land whatever he needs. The earth is not his brother, but his enemy, and when he has conquered it, he moves on. He leaves his fathers' graves, and his children's birthright is forgotten. The sight of your cities pains the eyes of the red man. But perhaps it is because the red man is a savage and does not understand.

There is no quiet place in the white man's cities. No place to hear the leaves of spring or the rustle of insects' wings. But perhaps because I am a savage and do not understand, the clatter only seems to insult the ears. The Indian prefers the soft sound of the wind darting over the face of the pond, the smell of the wind itself cleansed by a mid-day rain, or scented with the piñon pine. The air is precious to the red man. For all things share the same breath—the beasts, the trees, the man. Like a man dying for many days, he is numb to the stench.

What is man without the beasts? If all the beasts were gone, men would die from great loneliness of spirit, for whatever happens to the beasts also happens to man. All things are connected. Whatever befalls the earth befalls the sons of the earth.

It matters little where we pass the rest of our days; they are not many. A few more hours, a few more winters, and none of the children of the great tribes that once lived on this earth, or that roamed in small bands in the woods, will be left to mourn the graves of a people once as powerful and hopeful as yours.

The whites, too, shall pass—perhaps sooner than other tribes. Continue   5
to contaminate your bed, and you will one night suffocate in your own waste. When the buffalo are all slaughtered, the wild horses all tamed, the secret corners of the forest heavy with the scent of many men, and the view of the ripe hills blotted by talking wires,[1] where is the thicket? Gone. Where is the eagle? Gone. And what is it to say goodby to the swift and the hunt, the end of living and the beginning of survival? We might understand if we knew what it was that the white man dreams, what he describes to his children on the long winter nights, what visions he burns into their minds, so they will wish for tomorrow. But we are savages. The white man's dreams are hidden from us.

Because of its origin as an oration given in Salish, a language spoken in the Pacific Northwest, there are many different versions of Chief Seattle's speech; this one comes from Native American Testimony: An Anthology of Indian and White Relations, *edited by Peter Nabokov (1977).*

1. Telegraph.

MLA CITATION

Chief Seattle. "Letter to President Pierce, 1855." 1977. *The Norton Reader: An Anthology of Nonfiction*. Ed. Melissa A. Goldthwaite et al. 14th ed. New York: Norton, 2016. 543. Print.

QUESTIONS

1. Chief Seattle repeatedly refers to the red man as "a savage" who "does not understand," yet he gives evidence of a great deal of understanding. What is the purpose of such ironic comments and apparently self-disparaging remarks?

2. Scholars have suggested that Chief Seattle's "Letter" is in fact the creation of a white man, based on Seattle's public oratory. If so, what rhetorical techniques does the white editor associate with Indian speech? Why might he have done so?

3. Chief Seattle demonstrates an awareness of ecology—the study of relationships among organisms, and between organisms and their environment—when he says, "whatever happens to the beasts also happens to man. All things are connected" (paragraph 3). Locate two or three similar observations, and explain their effectiveness.

4. Chief Seattle says that the red man might understand the white man better "if we knew what it was that the white man dreams, what he describes to his children on the long winter nights, what visions he burns into their minds, so they will wish for tomorrow" (paragraph 5). Write a short essay explaining—using irony if you'd like—how "the white man" might reply. If you prefer, write the reply itself.

WALLACE STEGNER *Wilderness Letter*

Los Altos, Calif.
December 3, 1960

David E. Pesonen
Wildland Research Center
Agricultural Experiment Station
243 Mulford Hall
University of California
Berkeley 4, Calif.

Dear Mr. Pesonen:

I believe that you are working on the wilderness portion of the Outdoor Recreation Resources Review Commission's report. If I may, I should like to urge some arguments for wilderness preservation that involve recreation, as it

Written when the United States Congress was debating the creation of a National Wilderness Preservation System which, when passed in 1964, recognized wilderness as "an area where the earth and its community of life are untrammeled by man, where man himself is a visitor who does not remain." In this letter, Wallace Stegner writes to David E. Pesonen, who chaired the Outdoor Resources Review Commission, which determined the needs of Americans for outdoor recreation spaces. This letter was later included as a "coda" in The Sound of Mountain Water *(1969), a collection of essays, letters, and speeches concerning the American West's environment, history, and culture.*

is ordinarily conceived, hardly at all. Hunting, fishing, hiking, mountain-climbing, camping, photography, and the enjoyment of natural scenery will all, surely, figure in your report. So will the wilderness as a genetic reserve, a scientific yardstick by which we may measure the world in its natural balance against the world in its man-made imbalance. What I want to speak for is not so much the wilderness uses, valuable as those are, but the wilderness idea, which is a resource in itself. Being an intangible and spiritual resource, it will seem mystical to the practical minded—but then anything that cannot be moved by a bulldozer is likely to seem mystical to them.

I want to speak for the wilderness idea as something that has helped form our character and that has certainly shaped our history as a people. It has no more to do with recreation than churches have to do with recreation, or than the strenuousness and optimism and expansiveness of what the historians call the "American Dream" have to do with recreation. Nevertheless, since it is only in this recreation survey that the values of wilderness are being compiled, I hope you will permit me to insert this idea between the leaves, as it were, of the recreation report.

Something will have gone out of us as a people if we ever let the remaining wilderness be destroyed; if we permit the last virgin forests to be turned into comic books and plastic cigarette cases; if we drive the few remaining members of the wild species into zoos or to extinction; if we pollute the last clear air and dirty the last clean streams and push our paved roads through the last of the silence, so that never again will Americans be free in their own country from the noise, the exhausts, the stinks of human and automotive waste. And so that never again can we have the chance to see ourselves single, separate, vertical and individual in the world, part of the environment of trees and rocks and soil, brother to the other animals, part of the natural world and competent to belong in it. Without any remaining wilderness we are committed wholly, without chance for even momentary reflection and rest, to a headlong drive into our technological termite-life, the Brave New World[1] of a completely man-controlled environment. We need wilderness preserved—as much of it as is still left, and as many kinds—because it was the challenge against which our character as a people was formed. The reminder and the reassurance that it is still there is good for our spiritual health even if we never once in ten years set foot in it. It is good for us when we are young, because of the incomparable sanity it can bring briefly, as vacation and rest, into our insane lives. It is important to us when we are old simply because it is there—important, that is, simply as an idea.

We are a wild species, as Darwin[2] pointed out. Nobody ever tamed or domesticated or scientifically bred us. But for at least three millennia we have been engaged in a cumulative and ambitious race to modify and gain control

---

1. Allusion to the dystopian novel by Aldous Huxley about a future totalitarian society in which all aspects of human life are controlled and conditioned.

2. Charles Darwin (1809–1882), scientist, evolutionary theorist, and author of *On the Origin of Species* (1859) and *The Descent of Man* (1871).

of our environment, and in the process we have come close to domesticating ourselves. Not many people are likely, any more, to look upon what we call "progress" as an unmixed blessing. Just as surely as it has brought us increased comfort and more material goods, it has brought us spiritual losses, and it threatens now to become the Frankenstein that will destroy us. One means of sanity is to retain a hold on the natural world, to remain, insofar as we can, good animals. Americans still have that chance, more than many peoples; for while we were demonstrating ourselves the most efficient and ruthless environment-busters in history, and slashing and burning and cutting our way through a wilderness continent, the wilderness was working on us. It remains in us as surely as Indian names remain on the land. If the abstract dream of human liberty and human dignity became, in America, something more than an abstract dream, mark it down at least partially to the fact that we were in subtle ways subdued by what we conquered.

5   The Connecticut Yankee,[3] sending likely candidates from King Arthur's unjust kingdom to his Man Factory for rehabilitation, was over optimistic, as he later admitted. These things cannot be forced, they have to grow. To make such a man, such a democrat, such a believer in human individual dignity, as Mark Twain himself, the frontier was necessary, Hannibal and the Mississippi and Virginia City, and reaching out from those the wilderness; the wilderness as opportunity and idea, the thing that has helped to make an American differ-ent from and, until we forget it in the roar of our industrial cities, more fortunate than other men. For an American, insofar as he is new and different at all, is a civilized man who has renewed himself in the wild. The American experience has been the confrontation by old peoples and cultures of a world as new as if it had just risen from the sea. That gave us our hope and our excitement, and the hope and excitement can be passed on to newer Americans, Americans who never saw any phase of the frontier. But only so long as we keep the remainder of our wild as a reserve and a promise—a sort of wilderness bank.

As a novelist, I may perhaps be forgiven for taking literature as a reflec-tion, indirect but profoundly true, of our national consciousness. And our lit-erature, as perhaps you are aware, is sick, embittered, losing its mind, losing its faith. Our novelists are the declared enemies of their society. There has hardly been a serious or important novel in this century that did not repudiate in part or in whole American technological culture for its commercialism, its vulgarity, and the way in which it has dirtied a clean continent and a clean dream. I do not expect that the preservation of our remaining wilderness is going to cure this condition. But the mere example that we can as a nation apply some other criteria than commercial and exploitative considerations would be heartening to many Americans, novelists or otherwise. We need to demonstrate our acceptance of the natural world, including ourselves; we need the spiritual refreshment that being natural can produce. And one of the best places for us

3. Allusion to Mark Twain's satiric novel, *A Connecticut Yankee in King Arthur's Court* (1889), in which an American engineer is transported back in time and uses his knowl-edge of modern technology to try to improve and modernize King Arthur's realm.

to get that is in the wilderness where the fun houses, the bulldozers, and the pavement of our civilization are shut out.

Sherwood Anderson, in a letter to Waldo Frank in the 1920s, said it better than I can. "Is it not likely that when the country was new and men were often alone in the fields and the forest they got a sense of bigness outside themselves that has now in some way been lost. . . . Mystery whispered in the grass, played in the branches of trees overhead, was caught up and blown across the American line in clouds of dust at evening on the prairies. . . . I am old enough to remember tales that strengthen my belief in a deep semi-religious influence that was formerly at work among our people. The flavor of it hangs over the best work of Mark Twain. . . . I can remember old fellows in my home town speaking feelingly of an evening spent on the big empty plains. It had taken the shrillness out of them. They had learned the trick of quiet. . . ."

We could learn it too, even yet; even our children and grandchildren could learn it. But only if we save, for just such absolutely non-recreational, impractical, and mystical uses as this, all the wild that still remains to us.

It seems to me significant that the distinct downturn in our literature from hope to bitterness took place almost at the precise time when the frontier officially came to an end, in 1890, and when the American way of life had begun to turn strongly urban and industrial. The more urban it has become, and the more frantic with technological change, the sicker and more embittered our literature, and I believe our people, have become. For myself, I grew up on the empty plains of Saskatchewan and Montana and in the mountains of Utah, and I put a very high valuation on what those places gave me. And if I had not been able periodically to renew myself in the mountains and deserts of western America I would be very nearly bughouse. Even when I can't get to the back country, the thought of the colored deserts of southern Utah, or the reassurance that there are still stretches of prairies where the world can be instantaneously perceived as disk and bowl, and where the little but intensely important human being is exposed to the five directions of the thirty-six winds, is a positive consolation. The idea alone can sustain me. But as the wilderness areas are progressively exploited or "improved," as the jeeps and bulldozers of uranium prospectors scar up the deserts and the roads are cut into the alpine timberlands, and as the remnants of the unspoiled and natural world are progressively eroded, every such loss is a little death in me. In us.

I am not moved by the argument that those wilderness areas which have   10
already been exposed to grazing or mining are already deflowered, and so might as well be "harvested." For mining I cannot say much good except that its operations are generally short-lived. The extractable wealth is taken and the shafts, the tailings, and the ruins left, and in a dry country such as the American West the wounds men make in the earth do not quickly heal. Still, they are only wounds; they aren't absolutely mortal. Better a wounded wilderness than none at all. And as for grazing, if it is strictly controlled so that it does not destroy the ground cover, damage the ecology, or compete with the wildlife it is in itself nothing that need conflict with the wilderness feeling or the validity of the wilderness experience. I have known enough range cattle to recognize them as wild

animals; and the people who herd them have, in the wilderness context, the dignity of rareness; they belong on the frontier, moreover, and have a look of rightness. The invasion they make on the virgin country is a sort of invasion that is as old as Neolithic man,[4] and they can, in moderation, even emphasize a man's feeling of belonging to the natural world. Under surveillance, they can belong; under control, they need not deface or mar. I do not believe that in wilderness areas where grazing has never been permitted, it should be permitted; but I do not believe either that an otherwise untouched wilderness should be eliminated from the preservation plan because of limited existing uses such as grazing which are in consonance with the frontier condition and image.

Let me say something on the subject of the kinds of wilderness worth preserving. Most of those areas contemplated are in the national forests and in high mountain country. For all the usual recreational purposes, the alpine and the forest wildernesses are obviously the most important, both as genetic banks and as beauty spots. But for the spiritual renewal, the recognition of identity, the birth of awe, other kinds will serve every bit as well. Perhaps, because they are less friendly to life, more abstractly nonhuman, they will serve even better. On our Saskatchewan prairie, the nearest neighbor was four miles away, and at night we saw only two lights on all the dark rounding earth. The earth was full of animals—field mice, ground squirrels, weasels, ferrets, badgers, coyotes, burrowing owls, snakes. I knew them as my little brothers, as fellow creatures, and I have never been able to look upon animals in any other way since. The sky in that country came clear down to the ground on every side, and it was full of great weathers, and clouds, and winds, and hawks. I hope I learned something from knowing intimately the creatures of the earth; I hope I learned something from looking a long way, from looking up, from being much alone. A prairie like that, one big enough to carry the eye clear to the sinking, rounding horizon, can be as lonely and grand and simple in its forms as the sea. It is as good a place as any for the wilderness experience to happen; the vanishing prairie is as worth preserving for the wilderness idea as the alpine forest.

So are great reaches of our western deserts, scarred somewhat by prospectors but otherwise open, beautiful, waiting, close to whatever God you want to see in them. Just as a sample, let me suggest the Robbers' Roost country in Wayne County, Utah, near the Capitol Reef National Monument. In that desert climate the dozer and jeep tracks will not soon melt back into the earth, but the country has a way of making the scars insignificant. It is a lovely and terrible wilderness, such wilderness as Christ and the prophets went out into; harshly and beautifully colored, broken and worn until its bones are exposed, its great sky without a smudge of taint from Technocracy, and in hidden corners and pockets under its cliffs the sudden poetry of springs. Save a piece of country like that intact, and it does not matter in the slightest that only a few people every year will go into it. That is precisely its value. Roads would be a desecration, crowds would ruin it. But those who haven't the strength or youth

---

4. Reference to those living in the New Stone Age, from approximately 10,200 to 2,000 B.C.E.

to go into it and live can simply sit and look. They can look two hundred miles, clear into Colorado: and looking down over the cliffs and canyons of the San Rafael Swell and the Robbers' Roost they can also look as deeply into themselves as anywhere I know. And if they can't even get to the places on the Aquarius Plateau where the present roads will carry them, they can simply contemplate the *idea*, take pleasure in the fact that such a timeless and uncontrolled part of earth is still there.

These are some of the things wilderness can do for us. That is the reason we need to put into effect, for its preservation, some other principle than the principles of exploitation or "usefulness" or even recreation. We simply need that wild country available to us, even if we never do more than drive to its edge and look in. For it can be a means of reassuring ourselves of our sanity as creatures, a part of the geography of hope.

Very sincerely yours,
Wallace Stegner

MLA CITATION

Stegner, Wallace. "Wilderness Letter." 1969. *The Norton Reader: An Anthology of Nonfiction.* Ed. Melissa A. Goldthwaite et al. 14th ed. New York: Norton, 2016. 544–49. Print.

QUESTIONS

1. Wallace Stegner wrote his letter with a purpose: to influence Congress to pass the Wilderness Bill, which would set aside large tracts of undeveloped land in a National Wilderness Preservation System. As he argues his case, what are the primary values he associates with wilderness?

2. "We are a wild species," Stegner writes (paragraph 4), claiming Charles Darwin as his source. What connections does Stegner make between humans as "wild" and the need for protected wilderness areas?

3. What kinds of land does Stegner recommend preserving as wilderness? Why does he include more than "virgin country" (paragraph 10)?

4. Read William Cronon's "The Trouble with Wilderness" (pp. 550–53). Compare and contrast his views about wilderness with Stegner's, evaluating the strengths and weaknesses of both authors' claims.

WILLIAM CRONON   *The Trouble with Wilderness*

P RESERVING WILDERNESS has for decades been a fundamental tenet—indeed, a passion—of the environmental movement, especially in the United States. For many Americans, wilderness stands as the last place where civilization, that all-too-human disease, has not fully infected the earth. It is an island in the polluted sea of urban-industrial modernity, a refuge we must somehow recover to save the planet. As Henry David Thoreau famously declared, "In Wildness is the preservation of the World."

But is it? The more one knows of its peculiar history, the more one realizes that wilderness is not quite what it seems. Far from being the one place on earth that stands apart from humanity, it is quite profoundly a human creation—indeed, the creation of very particular human cultures at very particular moments in human history. It is not a pristine sanctuary where the last remnant of an endangered but still transcendent nature can be encountered without the contaminating taint of civilization. Instead, it is a product of that civilization. As we gaze into the mirror it holds up for us, we too easily imagine that what we behold is nature when in fact we see the reflection of our own longings and desires. Wilderness can hardly be the solution to our culture's problematic relationship with the nonhuman world, for wilderness is itself a part of the problem.

To assert the unnaturalness of so natural a place may seem perverse: we can all conjure up images and sensations that seem all the more hauntingly real for having engraved themselves so indelibly on our memories. Remember this? The torrents of mist shooting out from the base of a great waterfall in the depths of a Sierra Nevada canyon, the droplets cooling your face as you listen to the roar of the water and gaze toward the sky through a rainbow that hovers just out of reach. Or this: Looking out across a desert canyon in the evening air, the only sound a lone raven calling in the distance, the rock walls dropping away into a chasm so deep that its bottom all but vanishes as you squint into the amber light of the setting sun. Remember the feelings of such moments, and you will know as well as I do that you were in the presence of something irreducibly nonhuman, something profoundly Other than yourself. Wilderness is made of that too.

And yet: what brought each of us to the places where such memories became possible is entirely a cultural invention.

5   For the Americans who first celebrated it, wilderness was tied to the myth of the frontier. The historian Frederick Jackson Turner wrote the classic academic statement of this myth in 1893, but it had been part of American thought

William Cronon published a number of versions of this essay, each aimed at a different audience. This version comes from the New York Times *(1995); another version appears as the introduction to a book Cronon edited,* Uncommon Ground: Toward Reinventing Nature *(1995), a collection of essays on the environment.*

for well over a century. As Turner described the process, Easterners and European immigrants, in moving to the wild lands of the frontier, shed the trappings of civilization and thereby gained an energy, an independence and a creativity that were the sources of American democracy and national character. Seen this way, wilderness became a place of religious redemption and national renewal, the quintessential location for experiencing what it meant to be an American.

Those who celebrate the frontier almost always look backward, mourning an older, simpler world that has disappeared forever. That world and all its attractions, Turner said, depended on free land—on wilderness. It is no accident that the movement to set aside national parks and wilderness areas gained real momentum just as laments about the vanishing frontier reached their peak. To protect wilderness was to protect the nation's most sacred myth of origin.

The decades following the Civil War saw more and more of the nation's wealthiest citizens seeking out wilderness for themselves. The passion for wild land took many forms: enormous estates in the Adirondacks and elsewhere (disingenuously called "camps" despite their many servants and amenities); cattle ranches for would-be roughriders on the Great Plains; guided big-game hunting trips in the Rockies. Wilderness suddenly emerged as the landscape of choice for elite tourists. For them, it was a place of recreation.

In just this way, wilderness came to embody the frontier myth, standing for the wild freedom of America's past and seeming to represent a highly attractive natural alternative to the ugly artificiality of modern civilization. The irony, of course, was that in the process wilderness came to reflect the very civilization its devotees sought to escape. Ever since the nineteenth century, celebrating wilderness has been an activity mainly for well-to-do city folks. Country people generally know far too much about working the land to regard unworked land as their ideal.

There were other ironies as well. The movement to set aside national parks and wilderness areas followed hard on the heels of the final Indian wars, in which the prior human inhabitants of these regions were rounded up and moved onto reservations so that tourists could safely enjoy the illusion that they were seeing their nation in its pristine, original state—in the new morning of God's own creation. Meanwhile, its original inhabitants were kept out by dint of force, their earlier uses of the land redefined as inappropriate or even illegal. To this day, for instance, the Blackfeet continue to be accused of "poaching" on the lands of Glacier National Park, in Montana, that originally belonged to them and that were ceded by treaty only with the proviso that they be permitted to hunt there.

The removal of Indians to create an "uninhabited wilderness" reminds us   10
just how invented and how constructed the American wilderness really is. One of the most striking proofs of the cultural invention of wilderness is its thoroughgoing erasure of the history from which it sprang. In virtually all its manifestations, wilderness represents a flight from history. Seen as the original garden, it is a place outside time, from which human beings had to be ejected before

the fallen world of history could properly begin.[1] Seen as the frontier, it is a savage world at the dawn of civilization, whose transformation represents the very beginning of the national historical epic. Seen as sacred nature, it is the home of a God who transcends history, untouched by time's arrow. No matter what the angle from which we regard it, wilderness offers us the illusion that we can escape the cares and troubles of the world in which our past has ensnared us. It is the natural, unfallen antithesis of an unnatural civilization that has lost its soul, the place where we can see the world as it really is, and so know ourselves as we really are—or ought to be.

The trouble with wilderness is that it reproduces the very values its devotees seek to reject. It offers the illusion that we can somehow wipe clean the slate of our past and return to the tabula rasa[2] that supposedly existed before we began to leave our marks on the world. The dream of an unworked natural landscape is very much the fantasy of people who have never themselves had to work the land to make a living—urban folk for whom food comes from a supermarket or a restaurant instead of a field, and for whom the wooden houses in which they live and work apparently have no meaningful connection to the forests in which trees grow and die. Only people whose relation to the land was already alienated could hold up wilderness as a model for human life in nature, for the romantic ideology of wilderness leaves no place in which human beings can actually make their living from the land.

We live in an urban-industrial civilization, but too often pretend to ourselves that our real home is in the wilderness. We work our nine-to-five jobs, we drive our cars (not least to reach the wilderness), we benefit from the intricate and all too invisible networks with which society shelters us, all the while pretending that these things are not an essential part of who we are. By imagining that our true home is in the wilderness, we forgive ourselves for the homes we actually inhabit. In its flight from history, in its siren song[3] of escape, in its reproduction of the dangerous dualism that sets human beings somehow outside nature—in all these ways, wilderness poses a threat to responsible environmentalism at the end of the twentieth century.

Do not misunderstand me. What I criticize here is not wild nature, but the alienated way we often think of ourselves in relation to it. Wilderness can still teach lessons that are hard to learn anywhere else. When we visit wild places, we find ourselves surrounded by plants and animals and landscapes whose otherness compels our attention. In forcing us to acknowledge that they are not of our making, that they have little or no need for humanity, they recall for us a creation far greater than our own. In wilderness, we need no reminder that a tree has its own reasons for being, quite apart from us—proof that ours is not the only presence in the universe.

1. Reference to the biblical story of Adam and Eve who were ejected from the Garden of Eden for disobeying God's command.

2. Latin for "clean slate."

3. In Homer's *Odyssey*, the Sirens use irresistible songs to tempt Odysseus and his crew to steer their ship toward destruction, so a siren song is an alluring but deceptive appeal.

We get into trouble only if we see the tree in the garden as wholly artificial and the tree in the wilderness as wholly natural. Both trees in some ultimate sense are wild; both in a practical sense now require our care. We need to reconcile them, to see a natural landscape that is also cultural, in which city, suburb, countryside and wilderness each has its own place. We need to discover a middle ground in which all these things, from city to wilderness, can somehow be encompassed in the word "home." Home, after all, is the place where we live. It is the place for which we take responsibility, the place we try to sustain so we can pass on what is best in it (and in ourselves) to our children.

Learning to honor the wild—learning to acknowledge the autonomy of the other—means striving for critical self-consciousness in all our actions. It means that reflection and respect must accompany each act of use, and means we must always consider the possibility of nonuse. It means looking at the part of nature we intend to turn toward our own ends and asking whether we can use it again and again and again—sustainably—without diminishing it in the process. Most of all, it means practicing remembrance and gratitude for the nature, culture and history that have come together to make the world as we know it. If wildness can stop being (just) out there and start being (also) in here, if it can start being as humane as it is natural, then perhaps we can get on with the unending task of struggling to live rightly in the world—not just in the garden, not just in the wilderness, but in the home that encompasses them both.

MLA CITATION

Cronon, William. "The Trouble with Wilderness." 1995. *The Norton Reader: An Anthology of Nonfiction*. Ed. Melissa A. Goldthwaite et al. 14th ed. New York: Norton, 2016. 550–53. Print.

QUESTIONS

1. In paragraph 12 William Cronon writes, "We live in an urban-industrial civilization, but too often pretend to ourselves that our real home is in the wilderness." Cronon gives no examples. What examples might back up Cronon's statement? Can you think of counterexamples as well?

2. Who is Cronon's "we" throughout his essay? Why does he use "we" so frequently?

3. Paragraph 2 raises the issue of whether wilderness provides us with a "mirror." Look through the essay for similar visual imagery; then explain the role that such imagery plays.

4. If you found significant counterexamples in response to Question 1, write an essay in which you question or object to one or more aspect of Cronon's argument.

SANDRA STEINGRABER   *Tune of the Tuna Fish*

TO COMMEMORATE my daughter's first piano recital last spring, my mother sent a package of old song-books and sheet music that she had scooped from the bench of my own childhood piano, where they had undoubtedly sat for more than thirty years. Faith immediately seized on *The Red Book,* one of my very first lesson books, and began to sight-read some of the pieces. Her favorite was "Tune of the Tuna Fish" (copyright 1945), which introduces the key of F major. The cartoon drawing accompanying the song depicts a yodeling fish. The lyrics are as follows:

> Tuna fish! Tuna fish! Sing a tune of tuna fish!
> Tuna fish! Tuna fish! It's a favorite dish.
> Everybody likes it so. From New York to Kokomo.
> Tuna fish! Tuna fish! It's a favorite dish.

After we belted the song out a few times together, Faith asked, "Mama, what is a tuna fish? Have I ever eaten one?" In fact, she hadn't. Although tuna salad sandwiches were a mainstay of my own childhood diet, tuna has, during the time period between my childhood and my daughter's, become so contaminated with mercury that I choose not to buy it.

A few weeks later, at a potluck picnic, an elderly woman offered Faith a tuna salad sandwich. She loved it. On the ride home, she announced that she would like tuna sandwiches for her school lunches. She wants to eat one *every day.* I smiled that noncommittal motherly smile and said, "We'll see." She broke into song, "Everybody likes it so. From New York to Kokomo . . ."

A month after that, Faith walked up to me with an alarmed look. Is it true, she wanted to know, that tuna fish have mercury in them? And mercury poisons children? Will she die from eating that sandwich at the picnic? I was able to reassure her that she was fine, but I was left wondering where she'd heard all this. Then I noticed that I'd left out on my office desk a copy of an article about the impact of mercury on fetal brain growth and development. It was one that I myself had authored. Could she have seen it? At age six, can she read well enough to have figured it out?

Other than the twenty-three chromosomes that each of us parents contributes to our offspring during the moment of conception, their growing bodies are entirely made up of rearranged molecules of air, food, and water. Our children are the jet stream, the food web, and the water cycle. Whatever is in the envi-

Published in Orion *(2006), a magazine founded in 1982 to explore "an emerging alternative worldview informed by a growing ecological awareness and the need for cultural change"; the magazine includes photos and paintings as well as essays. A revised version of this essay also appeared in Sandra Steingraber's book* Raising Elijah: Protecting Our Children in an Age of Environmental Crisis *(2011).*

ronment is also in them. We know that this now includes hundreds of industrial pollutants. A recent study of umbilical cord blood, collected by the Red Cross from ten newborns and analyzed in two different laboratories, revealed the presence of pesticides, stain removers, wood preservatives, heavy metals, and industrial lubricants, as well as the wastes from burning coal, garbage, and gasoline. Of the 287 chemicals detected, 180 were suspected carcinogens, 217 were toxic to the brain and nervous system, and 208 have been linked to abnormal development and birth defects in lab animals.

One of these chemicals was methylmercury, the form of mercury found in   5 fish. Its presence in umbilical cord blood is especially troubling because methylmercury has been shown to paralyze migrating fetal brain cells and halt their cell division. As a result, the architecture of the brain is subtly altered in ways that can lead to learning disabilities, delayed mental development, and shortened attention spans in later childhood. Moreover, the placenta actively pumps methylmercury into the umbilical cord, raising the concentration of mercury in fetal blood above that of the mother's own blood. Most pregnant mothers probably don't realize that when they eat tuna, the mercury within is transferred to and concentrated in the blood of their unborn babies.

Recently, I've been talking with my children about why we buy organically grown food. I've explained to Faith and her younger brother, Elijah, that I like to give my food dollars to farmers who sustain the soil, are kind to their animals, and don't use chemicals that poison birds, fish, and toads. I add that I like to buy food that is grown right here in our own county. It tastes better and doesn't require lots of gasoline to get to our house. I haven't shared with them the results of the 2003 Seattle study, which revealed that children with conventional diets had, on average, nine times more insecticide residues in their urine than those who ate organic produce.

But there is no "organic" option for buying tuna. No mercury-free tuna exists. When mercury from coal-burning power plants rains down from the atmosphere into the world's oceans, ancient anaerobic bacteria found in marine sediments transform this heavy metal into methylmercury, which is quickly siphoned up the food chain. Because tuna is a top-of-the-food chain predator, methylmercury inexorably concentrates in the flesh of its muscle tissue. There is no special way of cleaning or cooking tuna that would lower its body burden. Nor is there any way of keeping mercury from trespassing into a child's brain, once he or she consumes the tuna. Nor is there a way of preventing those molecules of mercury from interfering with brain cell functioning. In that sense, the problem of tuna fish is more akin to the problem of air and water pollution: it is not a problem we can shop our way out of.

Recognizing the potential for methylmercury to create neurological problems in children, the U.S. Food and Drug Administration has now promulgated advisories and guidelines on how much tuna is safe for pregnant women and children—as well as nursing mothers and women who might become pregnant—to eat in a month's time. There is debate about whether these current restrictions are protective enough. But even if they are sufficient, I find them highly impractical. Children do not want to eat a food they like once a month, or even once a week. In my experience, when children discover a new food item to their liking, they want it all the time. They want it for breakfast, lunch, and dinner from here to Sunday. Children's dining habits are, for mysterious reasons, highly ritualized. Elijah, for example, consumed two avocados a day for the better part of his second year. I vaguely recall one summer when I, at about age seven, ate liver sausage on Saltines as part of every meal.

How, then, do you explain to a young child with a tuna jones that she'll have to wait until next month before she can have her favorite dish again? Do you tell her that she's already consumed her monthly quota of a known brain poison, as determined by the federal government? Or do you make up some other excuse?

10   I eventually sat down with Faith and showed her the article I had written. I said that I was working hard to stop the mercury contamination of seafood so that she could someday enjoy tuna without needing to worry. I said that keeping mercury out of tuna required generating electricity in some way other than burning coal, which is why her father and I support solar energy and wind power.

Soon after, we went hiking in the woods near the day camp she had attended earlier in the summer. Faith summarized for me the history of the old stone building where snakes and turtles are housed in one wing and bunk beds fill the other. It was originally built, she explained, as a *pre-ven-tor-i-um*. Children whose parents were sick with tuberculosis were brought there to live so they wouldn't get sick, too. In fact, I already knew the history of the Cayuga Nature Center but was, nonetheless, amazed at my daughter's ability to recount this information. I tried to gauge whether she was worried about the idea of children being separated from their families because of disease. "You know," I said, "we don't have to worry about tuberculosis anymore. We fixed that problem." She said she knew that. That's why the building had been turned into a camp for everyone.

The top of the hill offered a view across Cayuga Lake. On the far bank floated the vaporous emissions from New York State Electric and Gas Corporation's Cayuga Plant, whose coal-burning stacks were plainly visible against an otherwise cloudless sky. It's one of the state's biggest emitters of mercury. In the year my daughter was born, the Cayuga facility released 323 pounds of mercury into the environment. Pointing it out to Faith, I said that's where the mercury comes from that gets inside the fish. I said that I hoped one day we could fix that problem, too. She thought about it a minute and said, then they can do something else with the building.

MLA CITATION

Steingraber, Sandra. "Tune of the Tuna Fish." 2006. *The Norton Reader: An Anthology of Nonfiction.* Ed. Melissa A. Goldthwaite et al. 14th ed. New York: Norton, 2016. 554–56. Print.

QUESTIONS

1. Sandra Steingraber's essay informs readers of the high levels of mercury in fish and the dangers of eating a tuna fish sandwich. Why, then, does she begin with her daughter's piano playing? What roles do her daughter, Faith, and later her son, Elijah, play in this essay?

2. What facts about industrial pollutants, including methylmercury, does Steingraber provide? Where do they appear in the essay? How do they relate—structurally and conceptually—to the episodes with her daughter?

3. Does Steingraber suggest a solution to the problem of industrial pollutants? In terms of the environment, does the essay end on a hopeful or despairing note?

4. Write an essay about another kind of environmental problem, ideally one with personal or local significance. Interweave facts with examples or short narratives.

TERRY TEMPEST WILLIAMS *The Clan of One-Breasted Women*

I BELONG TO a Clan of One-Breasted Women. My mother, my grandmothers, and six aunts have all had mastectomies. Seven are dead. The two who survive have just completed rounds of chemotherapy and radiation.

I've had my own problems: two biopsies for breast cancer and a small tumor between my ribs diagnosed as "a border-line malignancy."

This is my family history.

Most statistics tell us breast cancer is genetic, hereditary, with rising percentages attached to fatty diets, childlessness, or becoming pregnant after thirty. What they don't say is living in Utah may be the greatest hazard of all.

We are a Mormon family with roots in Utah since 1847. The word-of-wisdom, a religious doctrine of health, kept the women in my family aligned with good foods: no coffee, no tea, tobacco, or alcohol. For the most part, these women were finished having their babies by the time they were thirty. And only one faced breast cancer prior to 1960. Traditionally, as a group of people, Mormons have a low rate of cancer.

Is our family a cultural anomaly? The truth is we didn't think about it. Those who did, usually the men, simply said, "bad genes." The women's attitude was stoic. Cancer was part of life. On February 16, 1971, the eve of my

From Witness *(1989), a small-circulation journal that calls itself "a feisty, independent, provocative, intelligent, feminist voice of Christian social conscience"; later included in* Refuge: An Unnatural History of Family and Place *(1991). All notes are the author's unless indicated otherwise.*

mother's surgery, I accidently picked up the telephone and overheard her ask my grandmother what she could expect.

"Diane, it is one of the most spiritual experiences you will ever encounter." I quietly put down the receiver.

Two days later, my father took my three brothers and me to the hospital to visit her. She met us in the lobby in a wheelchair. No bandages were visible. I'll never forget her radiance, the way she held herself in a purple velour robe and how she gathered us around her.

10   "Children, I am fine. I want you to know I felt the arms of God around me."

We believed her. My father cried. Our mother, his wife, was thirty-eight years old.

Two years ago, after my mother's death from cancer, my father and I were having dinner together. He had just returned from St. George where his construction company was putting in natural gas lines for towns in southern Utah. He spoke of his love for the country: the sandstoned landscape, bare-boned and beautiful. He had just finished hiking the Kolob trail in Zion National Park. We got caught up in reminiscing, recalling with fondness our walk up Angel's Landing on his fiftieth birthday and the years our family had vacationed there. This was a remembered landscape where we had been raised.

Over dessert, I shared a recurring dream of mine. I told my father that for years, as long as I could remember, I saw this flash of light in the night in the desert. That this image had so permeated my being, I could not venture south without seeing it again, on the horizon, illuminating buttes and mesas.

"You did see it," he said.

15   "Saw what?" I asked, a bit tentative.

"The bomb. The cloud. We were driving home from Riverside, California. You were sitting on your mother's lap. She was pregnant. In fact, I remember the date, September 7, 1957. We had just gotten out of the Service. We were driving north, past Las Vegas. It was an hour or so before dawn, when this explosion went off. We not only heard it, but felt it. I thought the oil tanker in front of us had blown up. We pulled over and suddenly, rising from the desert floor, we saw it, clearly, this golden-stemmed cloud, the mushroom. The sky seemed to vibrate with an eerie pink glow. Within a few minutes, a light ash was raining on the car."

I stared at my father. This was new information to me.

"I thought you knew that," my father said. "It was a common occurrence in the fifties."

It was at this moment I realized the deceit I had been living under. Children growing up in the American Southwest, drinking contaminated milk from contaminated cows, even from the contaminated breasts of their mother, my mother—members, years later, of the Clan of One-breasted Women.

20   It is a well-known story in the Desert West, "The Day We Bombed Utah," or perhaps, "The Years We Bombed Utah."[1] Above ground atomic testing in

---

1. Fuller, John G., *The Day We Bombed Utah* (New York: New American Library, 1984).

Nevada took place from January 27, 1951, through July 11, 1962. Not only were the winds blowing north, covering "low use segments of the population" with fallout and leaving sheep dead in their tracks, but the climate was right.[2] The United States of the 1950s was red, white, and blue. The Korean War was raging. McCarthyism was rampant. Ike was it and the Cold War was hot.[3] If you were against nuclear testing, you were for a Communist regime.

Much has been written about this "American nuclear tragedy." Public health was secondary to national security. The Atomic Energy Commissioner, Thomas Murray, said, "Gentlemen, we must not let anything interfere with this series of tests, nothing."[4]

Again and again, the American public was told by its government, in spite of burns, blisters, and nausea, "It has been found that the tests may be conducted with adequate assurance of safety under conditions prevailing at the bombing reservations."[5] Assuaging public fears was simply a matter of public relations. "Your best action," an Atomic Energy Commission booklet read, "is not to be worried about fallout." A news release typical of the times stated, "We find no basis for concluding that harm to any individual has resulted from radioactive fallout."[6]

On August 30, 1979, during Jimmy Carter's presidency, a suit was filed entitled "Irene Allen vs. the United States of America." Mrs. Allen was the first to be alphabetically listed with twenty-four test cases, representative of nearly 1200 plaintiffs seeking compensation from the United States government for cancers caused from nuclear testing in Nevada.

Irene Allen lived in Hurricane, Utah. She was the mother of five children and had been widowed twice. Her first husband with their two oldest boys had watched the tests from the roof of the local high school. He died of leukemia in 1956. Her second husband died of pancreatic cancer in 1978.

In a town meeting conducted by Utah Senator Orrin Hatch, shortly before the suit was filed, Mrs. Allen said, "I am not blaming the government, I want you to know that, Senator Hatch. But I thought if my testimony could help in any way so this wouldn't happen again to any of the generations coming up after us . . . I am really happy to be here this day to bear testimony of this."[7]

25

2. Discussion on March 14, 1988, with Carole Gallagher, photographer and author, *American Ground Zero: The Secret Nuclear War*, published by Random House, 1994.

3. Events and figures of the 1950s: the Korean War (1950–53) pitted the combined forces of the Republic of Korea and the United Nations (primarily the United States) against the invading armies of Communist North Korea; McCarthyism, after Republican senator Joseph S. McCarthy, the Communist "witch-hunt" led by the senator; Ike is the nickname of Dwight D. Eisenhower, president from 1953 to 1961; the Cold War, the power struggle between the Western powers and the Communist bloc that began at the end of World War II [Editor's note].

4. Szasz, Ferenc M., "Downwind From the Bomb," *Nevada Historical Society Quarterly*, Fall 1987, Vol. XXX, No. 3, p. 185.

5. Fradkin, Philip L., *Fallout* (Tucson: University of Arizona Press, 1989), 98.

6. Ibid., 109.

7. Town meeting held by Senator Orrin Hatch in St. George, Utah, April 17, 1979, transcript, 26–28.

God-fearing people. This is just one story in an anthology of thousands.

On May 10, 1984, Judge Bruce S. Jenkins handed down his opinion. Ten of the plaintiffs were awarded damages. It was the first time a federal court had determined that nuclear tests had been the cause of cancers. For the remaining fourteen test cases, the proof of causation was not sufficient. In spite of the split decision, it was considered a landmark ruling.[8] It was not to remain so for long.

In April, 1987, the 10th Circuit Court of Appeals overturned Judge Jenkins' ruling on the basis that the United States was protected from suit by the legal doctrine of sovereign immunity, the centuries-old idea from England in the days of absolute monarchs.[9]

In January, 1988, the Supreme Court refused to review the Appeals Court decision. To our court system, it does not matter whether the United States Government was irresponsible, whether it lied to its citizens or even that citizens died from the fallout of nuclear testing. What matters is that our government is immune. "The King can do no wrong."

30   In Mormon culture, authority is respected, obedience is revered, and independent thinking is not. I was taught as a young girl not to "make waves" or "rock the boat."

"Just let it go—" my mother would say. "You know how you feel, that's what counts."

For many years, I did just that—listened, observed, and quietly formed my own opinions within a culture that rarely asked questions because they had all the answers. But one by one, I watched the women in my family die common, heroic deaths. We sat in waiting rooms hoping for good news, always receiving the bad. I cared for them, bathed their scarred bodies and kept their secrets. I watched beautiful women become bald as cytoxan, cisplatin and adriamycin were injected into their veins. I held their foreheads as they vomited green-black bile and I shot them with morphine when the pain became inhuman. In the end, I witnessed their last peaceful breaths, becoming a midwife to the rebirth of their souls. But the price of obedience became too high.

The fear and inability to question authority that ultimately killed rural communities in Utah during atmospheric testing of atomic weapons was the same fear I saw being held in my mother's body. Sheep. Dead sheep. The evidence is buried.

I cannot prove that my mother, Diane Dixon Tempest, or my grandmothers, Lettie Romney Dixon and Kathryn Blackett Tempest, along with my aunts contracted cancer from nuclear fallout in Utah. But I can't prove they didn't.

35   My father's memory was correct, the September blast we drove through in 1957 was part of Operation Plumbbob, one of the most intensive series of bomb tests to be initiated. The flash of light in the night in the desert I had always

8. Fradkin, *Fallout*, 228.

9. U.S. vs. Allen, 816 Federal Reporter, 2d/1417 (10th Circuit Court 1987), cert. denied, 108 S. CT. 694 (1988).

thought was a dream developed into a family nightmare. It took fourteen years, from 1957 to 1971, for cancer to show up in my mother—the same time, Howard L. Andrews, an authority on radioactive fallout at the National Institutes of Health, says radiation cancer requires to become evident.[10] The more I learn about what it means to be a "downwinder," the more questions I drown in.

What I do know, however, is that as a Mormon woman of the fifth generation of "Latter-Day-Saints," I must question everything, even if it means losing my faith, even if it means becoming a member of a border tribe among my own people. Tolerating blind obedience in the name of patriotism or religion ultimately takes our lives.

When the Atomic Energy Commission described the country north of the Nevada Test Site as "virtually uninhabited desert terrain," my family members were some of the "virtual uninhabitants."

One night, I dreamed women from all over the world circling a blazing fire in the desert. They spoke of change, of how they hold the moon in their bellies and wax and wane with its phases. They mocked at the presumption of even-tempered beings and made promises that they would never fear the witch inside themselves. The women danced wildly as sparks broke away from the flames and entered the night sky as stars.

And they sang a song given to them by Shoshoni grandmothers:

Ah ne nah, nah
nin nah nah—
Ah ne nah, nah
nin nah nah—
Nyaga mutzi
oh ne nay—
Nyaga mutzi
oh ne nay—[11]

The women danced and drummed and sang for weeks, preparing themselves for what was to come. They would reclaim the desert for the sake of their children, for the sake of the land.

A few miles downwind from the fire circle, bombs were being tested. Rabbits felt the tremors. Their soft leather pads on paws and feet recognized the shaking sands while the roots of mesquite and sage were smoldering. Rocks were hot from the inside out and dust devils hummed unnaturally. And each time there was another nuclear test, ravens watched the desert heave. Stretch marks appeared. The land was losing its muscle.

10. Fradkin, Op. cit., 116.

11. This song was sung by the Western Shoshone women as they crossed the line at the Nevada Test Site on March 18, 1988, as part of their "Reclaim the Land" action. The translation they gave was: "Consider the rabbits how gently they walk on the earth. Consider the rabbits how gently they walk on the earth. We remember them. We can walk gently also. We remember them. We can walk gently also."

The women couldn't bear it any longer. They were mothers. They had suffered labor pains but always under the promise of birth. The red hot pains beneath the desert promised death only as each bomb became a stillborn. A contract had been broken between human beings and the land. A new contract was being drawn by the women who understood the fate of the earth as their own.

Under the cover of darkness, ten women slipped under the barbed wire fence and entered the contaminated country. They were trespassing. They walked toward the town of Mercury in moonlight, taking their cues from coyote, kit fox, antelope squirrel, and quail. They moved quietly and deliberately through the maze of Joshua trees. When a hint of daylight appeared they rested, drinking tea and sharing their rations of food. The women closed their eyes. The time had come to protest with the heart, that to deny one's genealogy with the earth was to commit treason against one's soul.

At dawn, the women draped themselves in mylar, wrapping long streamers of silver plastic around their arms to blow in the breeze. They wore clear masks that became the faces of humanity. And when they arrived on the edge of Mercury, they carried all the butterflies of a summer day in their wombs. They paused to allow their courage to settle.

45   The town which forbids pregnant women and children to enter because of radiation risks to their health was asleep. The women moved through the streets as winged messengers, twirling around each other in slow motion, peeking inside homes and watching the easy sleep of men and women. They were astonished by such stillness and periodically would utter a shrill note or low cry just to verify life.

The residents finally awoke to what appeared as strange apparitions. Some simply stared. Others called authorities, and in time, the women were apprehended by wary soldiers dressed in desert fatigues. They were taken to a white, square building on the other edge of Mercury. When asked who they were and why they were there, the women replied, "We are mothers and we have come to reclaim the desert for our children."

The soldiers arrested them. As the ten women were blindfolded and handcuffed, they began singing:

> *You can't forbid us everything*
> *You can't forbid us to think—*
> *You can't forbid our tears to flow*
> *And you can't stop the songs that we sing.*

The women continued to sing louder and louder, until they heard the voices of their sisters moving across the mesa.

> *Ah ne nah, nah*
> *nin nah nah—*
> *Ah ne nah, nah*
> *nin nah nah—*

> *Nyaga mutzi*
> *oh ne nay—*
> *Nyaga mutzi*
> *oh ne nay—*

"Call for re-enforcement," one soldier said.

"We have," interrupted one woman. "We have—and you have no idea of   50
our numbers."

On March 18, 1988, I crossed the line at the Nevada Test Site and was arrested with nine other Utahns for trespassing on military lands. They are still conducting nuclear tests in the desert. Ours was an act of civil disobedience. But as I walked toward the town of Mercury, it was more than a gesture of peace. It was a gesture on behalf of the Clan of One-Breasted Women.

As one officer cinched the handcuffs around my wrists, another frisked my body. She found a pen and a pad of paper tucked inside my left boot.

"And these?" she asked sternly.

"Weapons," I replied.

Our eyes met. I smiled. She pulled the leg of my trousers back over my boot.   55

"Step forward, please," she said as she took my arm.

We were booked under an afternoon sun and bussed to Tonapah, Nevada. It was a two-hour ride. This was familiar country to me. The Joshua trees standing their ground had been named by my ancestors who believed they looked like prophets pointing west to the promised land. These were the same trees that bloomed each spring, flowers appearing like white flames in the Mojave. And I recalled a full moon in May when my mother and I had walked among them, flushing out mourning doves and owls.

The bus stopped short of town. We were released. The officials thought it was a cruel joke to leave us stranded in the desert with no way to get home. What they didn't realize is that we were home, soul-centered and strong, women who recognized the sweet smell of sage as fuel for our spirits.

MLA CITATION

Williams, Terry Tempest. "The Clan of One-Breasted Women." 1989. *The Norton Reader: An Anthology of Nonfiction.* Ed. Melissa A. Goldthwaite et al. 14th ed. New York: Norton, 2016. 557–63. Print.

QUESTIONS

1. Terry Tempest Williams uses a variety of evidence in this essay, including personal memory, family history, government documents, and other sources. List the evidence and the order in which she uses it. Why might Williams present her material in this order?

2. The essay begins with a description of what Williams later calls a "family nightmare" (paragraph 35) and ends with a dream vision. What is the rhetorical effect of this interactive opening and closing?

3. What do you think Williams means by the statement "I must question everything" (paragraph 36)?

4. Conduct some research on an environmental issue that affects you, your friends, or your family, and, using Williams as a model, write an essay that combines both your personal experience and research.

MICHELLE NIJHUIS *Which Species Will Live?*

Like battlefield medics, conservationists are being forced to explicitly apply triage to determine which creatures to save and which to let go.

THE ASHY STORM-PETREL, a tiny, dark-gray seabird, nests on 11 rocky, isolated islands in the Pacific Ocean off the coasts of California and Mexico. Weighing little more than a hefty greeting card and forced to contend with invasive rats, mice and cats, aggressive seagulls, oil spills and sea-level rise, it faces an outsize fight for survival. At last count, only 10,000 remained. Several other species of storm-petrels are similarly endangered.

Yet at least one conservation group has decided to ignore the petrel. In the winter of 2008 the Wildlife Conservation Society was focusing its far-flung efforts on a small number of animals. The society's researchers had spent months analyzing thousands of declining bird and mammal species around the world and had chosen several hundred that could serve as cornerstones for the organization's work. They then turned to people with decades of experience studying wildlife to further narrow the possibilities.

Dozens of these experts gathered in small conference rooms in New York City, southwestern Montana and Buenos Aires to make their choices. They judged each species for its importance to its ecosystem, its economic and cultural value, and its potential to serve as a conservation emblem. They voted on each animal publicly, holding up red, yellow or green cards. When significant disagreement occurred, the experts backed up their reasoning with citations, and the panels voted again. By the middle of the first day most panels had eliminated more than half the species from their lists.

At some point in the afternoon, however, in every meeting, the reality of the process would hit. As entire groups of species, including storm-petrels, were deemed valuable but not valuable enough, a scientist would quietly shut down, shoulders slumped and eyes glazed. "I'm just overwhelmed," he or she might say. Panel members would encourage their colleague, reminding him or her that

Published in Scientific American (2012), *a monthly science magazine written for a general audience.*

these choices were necessary and that the science behind them was solid. John Fraser, a conservation psychologist who moderated the panels, would suggest a coffee break. "I'd say, 'I'm sorry, but we have to stop. This is a very important part of the process,'" he remembers. "It was important to recognize the enormity of what we were doing—that we were confronting loss on a huge scale."

The experts knew that all conservation groups and government agencies were coping with similar choices in tacit ways, but the Wildlife Conservation Society process made those decisions more explicit and more painful. As budgets shrink, environmental stresses grow, and politicians and regulators increasingly favor helping the economy over helping the planet, many scientists have come to acknowledge the need for triage. It is time, they say, to hold up their cards.

Triage: A Four-Letter Word

The concept of conservation triage is based loosely on medical triage, a decision-making system used by battlefield medics since the Napoleonic Wars.[1] Medical triage has several variations, but all of them involve sorting patients for treatment in difficult situations where time, expertise or supplies, or all three, are scarce. The decisions are agonizing but are considered essential for the greater good.

In 1973, however, when the U.S. Congress passed the Endangered Species Act, the mood was not one of scarcity but of generosity. The act, still considered the most powerful environmental law in the world, stipulated eligibility for protection for all nonpest species, from bald eagles to beetles. Later court decisions confirmed its broad reach. In their book *Noah's Choice,* journalist Charles C. Mann and economist Mark L. Plummer describe the act's reasoning as the Noah Principle: all species are fundamentally equal, and everything can and should be saved, regardless of its importance to humans.

Trouble arose in the late 1980s, when proposed endangered-species listings of the northern spotted owl and some salmon varieties threatened the economic interests of powerful timber and fishing industries, setting off a series of political and legal attempts to weaken the law. Environmentalists fought off the attacks, but the bitter struggle made many supporters suspicious of any proposed changes to the law, even those intended to increase its effectiveness. In particular, proponents feared that any overt attempt to prioritize endangered species—to apply the general principle of triage—would only strengthen opponents' efforts to try to cut species from the list. If such decisions had to happen, better that they be made quietly, out of political reach.

"The environmental community was always unwilling to talk about triage," says Holly Doremus, a law professor at the University of California, Berkeley. "Even though they knew it was going on, they were unwilling to talk about it."

Today triage is one of the most provocative ideas in conservation. To many, it invokes not only political threats to laws such as the Endangered Species Act

1. Series of military campaigns (1803–1815) initiated by French emperor Napoleon Bonaparte against other European nations.

but an abandonment of the moral responsibility for nature implied in the Noah Principle. "Triage is a four-letter word," conservation biologist Stuart Pimm recently told Slate's Green Lantern blog. "And I know how to count."

PINE TREES OR CAMELS

Conservationists who are pushing for explicit triage say they are bringing more systematic thinking and transparency to practices that have been carried out implicitly for a long time. "The way we're doing it right now in the United States is the worst of all possible choices," says Tim Male, a vice president at Defenders of Wildlife. "It essentially reflects completely ad hoc prioritization." Politically controversial species attract more funding, he says, as do species in heavily studied places: "We live in a world of unconscious triage."

In recent years researchers have proposed several ways to make triage decisions, with the aim of providing maximum benefit for nature as a whole. Some scientists argue for weighting species according to their role in the ecosystem, an approach we might call "function first." Threatened species with a unique job, they say, or "umbrella" species whose own survival ensures the survival of many others, should be protected before those with a so-called redundant role. One example is the campaign to protect the Rocky Mountains' high-elevation whitebark pines, trees stressed by warming temperatures and associated beetle outbreaks. Because high-fat whitebark pine nuts are an important food source for grizzly bears in the fall and spring, many conservation groups view the pine as a priority species.

The advantage of this function-first approach is that it focuses on specific ecological roles rather than raw numbers of species, giving conservationists a better chance at protecting functioning ecosystems. The approach, however, is useful only in well-understood systems, and the number of those is small. An exclusively function-first analysis would almost certainly leave many ecologically important species behind.

As an alternative, the EDGE (Evolutionarily Distinct and Globally Endangered) of Existence program run by the Zoological Society of London argues for prioritizing species at the genomic level, an approach we might call "evolution first." Rather than focusing on well-known species with many near relatives, the EDGE program favors the most genetically unusual threatened species. Examples include the two-humped Bactrian camel; the long-beaked echidna, a short, spiny mammal that lays eggs; and the Chinese giant salamander, which can grow to six feet in length.

15   The evolution-first approach emphasizes the preservation of genetic diversity, which can help all the world's species survive and adapt in fast-changing environmental conditions by providing a robust gene pool. But as University of Washington ecologist Martha Groom points out, exclusive use of the approach could miss broader threats that affect entire taxa, leaving groups of species vulnerable to wholesale extinction. "What if a whole branch of the evolutionary tree is endangered?" she asks. "What do we do then?"

Of course, species are valuable for many different reasons. Some play a vital role in the ecosystem, some have unique genes, some provide extensive services to humans. No single criterion can capture all these qualities. The Wildlife Conservation Society combined different triage approaches in its analyses: it gave priority to threatened species that have larger body size and wider geographic range, reasoning that protection of these creatures would likely benefit many other plants and animals. It also gave higher rankings to species with greater genetic distinctiveness. The expert panels then considered more subjective qualities, such as cultural importance and charisma, which, like it or not, are important to fund-raising.

Groom, who helped to lead the society's analysis, says it opted for the combined approach because much of the information she and her colleagues needed was unknown or unquantifiable. "There's an awful lot of uncertainty and ignorance about all species," she says. But with a combination of available data and expert opinions, the analysis identified a small group of "global priority" species that the organization can focus on.

ECOSYSTEMS OVER SPECIES

Given the importance of protecting not simply individual animals but also the relations among them, some researchers say that triage approaches should select among ecosystems instead of species. In the late 1980s British environmentalist Norman Meyers proposed that his global colleagues try to protect the maximum number of species by focusing on land areas that were full of plants found nowhere else on the planet and that were also under pressing environmental threats.

Meyers called such places hotspots. He and his partners at Conservation International eventually identified 25 hotspots worldwide, from coastal California to Madagascar, that they thought should top priority lists. In a sense, the approach combines the function-first and evolution-first processes: it protects ecological relations by focusing on entire ecosystems, and it protects genetic diversity by prioritizing endemic species. The idea caught on and influences decisions by many philanthropists, environmental organizations and governments today.

Nevertheless, in recent years researchers have criticized hotspots for oversimplifying a global problem and for giving short shrift to human needs. . . . "It was brilliant for its time," says Hugh Possingham of the University of Queensland in Australia. "But it used just two criteria."

In an effort to refine the concept, Possingham and his colleagues developed Marxan, a software program that is now in wide use. It aims to maximize the effectiveness of conservation reserves by considering not only the presence of endemic species and the level of conservation threats but also factors such as the cost of protection and "complementarity"—the contribution of each new reserve to existing biodiversity protections. Mangrove forests, for instance, are not particularly rich in species and might never be selected by a traditional hotspot analysis; Possingham's program, however, might recommend protection of mangrove forests in an area where representative swaths of other, more

20

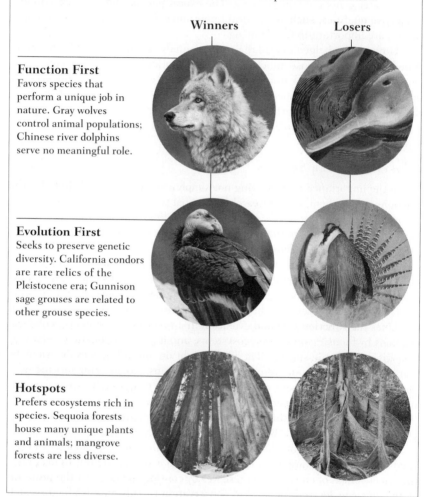

POSTER CHILDREN

Winners and Losers

Conservationists are trying different forms of triage to help them decide which species to save and not to save. Each method favors certain priorities, such as an animal's role in preserving a food chain or in maintaining genetic diversity. Serving those priorities ultimately deems species winners or losers; some samples are shown below.

Winners   Losers

Function First
Favors species that perform a unique job in nature. Gray wolves control animal populations; Chinese river dolphins serve no meaningful role.

Evolution First
Seeks to preserve genetic diversity. California condors are rare relics of the Pleistocene era; Gunnison sage grouses are related to other grouse species.

Hotspots
Prefers ecosystems rich in species. Sequoia forests house many unique plants and animals; mangrove forests are less diverse.

diverse forest types had already been preserved, resulting in a higher total number of species protected.

Protected areas and parks, however, can be difficult to establish and police, and because climate change is already shifting species ranges, static boundaries may not offer the best long-term protection for some species. In response, Possingham has created a resource-allocation process that goes well beyond the selection of hotspots, allowing decision makers to weigh costs, benefits and the likelihood of success as they decide among different conservation tactics. "You do actions—you don't do species," Possingham says. "All prioritizations should be about actions, not least because in many cases actions help multiple species."

The New Zealand Department of Conservation has used the resource-allocation process to analyze protection strategies for about 710 declining native species. It concluded that by focusing on the actions that were cheapest and most likely to succeed, it could save roughly half again as many plants and animals from extinction with the same amount of money. Although some scientists worry that the process places too much emphasis on preserving sheer numbers of threatened species and too little on preserving ecosystem function, resource-allocation analysis is now under way in Australia, and Possingham has spoken with U.S. Fish and Wildlife Service officials about the process.

"People think triage is about abandoning species or admitting defeat," says Madeleine Bottrill of Conservation International, who is a colleague of Possingham. To the contrary, she argues: by quantifying the costs and payoffs of particular actions, the trade-offs become explicit. Agencies and organizations can identify what is being saved, what is being lost and what could be saved with a bigger budget, giving them a much stronger case for more funding.

SUCCESS BREEDS SUCCESS

It is possible that the very act of setting priorities more overtly could inspire societies to spend more money on conservation efforts. Defenders of Wildlife's Male says prioritization schemes, far from exposing nature to political risks, offer practical and political advantages. "If we focus more effort on the things we know how to help, we're going to produce more successes," he says. "More successes are a really compelling argument—not just to politicians but to ordinary people—for why [conservation programs] should continue."

Trailing behind such successes, however, are undeniable losses, and true triage must acknowledge them. "We're very good as humans, aren't we, at justifying any amount of work on anything based on undeclared values," says Richard Maloney of the New Zealand Department of Conservation. "We're not very good at saying, 'Because I'm working on this species, I'm not going to fund or work on these seven or eight species, and they're going to go extinct.'" And yet Maloney himself is reluctant to name the species likely to lose out in his agency's resource-allocation analysis. Rockhopper penguins—whose vital supply of krill has declined because of shrinking sea ice driven by climate change—fall to the bottom of the department's list because of the costly, long-shot measures needed to protect them. Yet the species' low priority, Maloney argues, should be seen not as a death sentence but as a call to action by other groups.

Sooner or later, though, a vulnerable species or habitat—the rockhopper penguin, the whitebark pine ecosystem—will require measures too expensive for any government or group to shoulder. What then? Do societies continue to pour money into a doomed cause or allow a species to die out, one by one, in plain sight? Even though the conversation about triage has come a long way, many conservationists remain uncomfortable taking responsibility for the final, fateful decisions that triage requires.

The central difficulty is that, just as with battlefield triage, the line between opportunity and lost cause is almost never clear. In the 1980s, when the population of California condors stood at just 22, even some environmentalists argued that the species should be permitted to "die with dignity." Yet others made an evolution-first argument, calling for heroic measures to save the rare Pleistocene relic.[2] With heavy investments of money, time and expertise, condors were bred in captivity and eventually returned to the wild, where 217 fly today, still endangered but very much alive.

"We can prevent extinction; we've demonstrated that," says John Nagle, a law professor at the University of Notre Dame who has written extensively about environmental issues. But "knowing that an extinction was something we could have stopped and chose not to—I think that's where people kind of gulp and don't want to go down that road," he adds.

30   Similarly, by creating what prominent restoration ecologist Richard Hobbs calls a "too-hard basket" for species that would cost too much to save, a triage system could allow societies to prematurely jettison tough cases, choosing short-term economic rewards over long-term conservation goals. The Endangered Species Act itself has one provision for such a too-hard basket—it allows for a panel of experts that can, in unusual circumstances, permit a federal agency to violate the act's protections. But the so-called God Squad is deliberately difficult to convene and has so far made only one meaningful exemption to the act: letting the Forest Service approve some timber sales in habitats of the struggling northern spotted owl.

As climate change, population expansion and other global pressures on biodiversity continue, however, more and more species are likely to require heroic measures for survival. Prioritizing species by ecological function, evolutionary history or other criteria will help shape conservation strategies, but for the greater good of many other species, societies will almost certainly have to consciously forgo some of the most expensive and least promising rescue efforts.

In the U.S., legal scholars have suggested ways of reforming the Endangered Species Act to reckon with this reality—to help the law bend instead of break under political pressure. Yet Nagle says that the essence of the law, the Noah Principle, remains acutely relevant. Given the temptations that accompany triage, he says, the exhortation to save all species remains a worthy, and perhaps even necessary, goal. Just as a battlefield medic works unstintingly to save lives, even while knowing that he or she cannot save them all, societies should still aspire to the Noah Principle—and stuff the ark to the brim.

2. Geological epoch lasting from 1,800,000 to approximately 10,000 years ago.

MLA CITATION

Nijhuis, Michelle. "Which Species Will Live?" 2012. *The Norton Reader: An Anthology of Nonfiction*. Ed. Melissa A. Goldthwaite et al. 14th ed. New York: Norton, 2016. 564–70. Print.

QUESTIONS

1. Michelle Nijhuis explains several ways scientists and policy makers "triage" species threatened with extinction. What are these ways? Which do you find most effective and why?

2. Compare the attitudes toward nature that inform the debate over "conservation triage" (paragraph 6) to those expressed by Chief Seattle (p. 543), Wallace Stegner (pp. 544–49), or William Cronon (pp. 550–53). Would these writers embrace or reject conservation triage? Why?

3. Although Nijhuis acknowledges the need for conservation triage, she also holds up the "Noah Principle" (paragraph 7) as an ideal. What is this principle, and why does Nijhuis consider it so important?

4. Write a paper explaining a difficult decision you've made. How did you balance competing goals, values, and principles?

Media and
Technology

Nicholas Carr *Is Google Making Us Stupid?*

"DAVE, STOP. STOP, WILL YOU? Stop, Dave. Will you stop, Dave?" So the supercomputer HAL pleads with the implacable astronaut Dave Bowman in a famous and weirdly poignant scene toward the end of Stanley Kubrick's *2001: A Space Odyssey*.[1] Bowman, having nearly been sent to a deep-space death by the malfunctioning machine, is calmly, coldly disconnecting the memory circuits that control its artificial "brain." "Dave, my mind is going," HAL says, forlornly. "I can feel it. I can feel it."

I can feel it, too. Over the past few years I've had an uncomfortable sense that someone, or something, has been tinkering with my brain, remapping the neural circuitry, reprogramming the memory. My mind isn't going—so far as I can tell—but it's changing. I'm not thinking the way I used to think. I can feel it most strongly when I'm reading. Immersing myself in a book or a lengthy article used to be easy. My mind would get caught up in the narrative or the turns of the argument, and I'd spend hours strolling through long stretches of prose. That's rarely the case anymore. Now my concentration often starts to drift after two or three pages. I get fidgety, lose the thread, begin looking for something else to do. I feel as if I'm always dragging my wayward brain back to the text. The deep reading that used to come naturally has become a struggle.

I think I know what's going on. For more than a decade now, I've been spending a lot of time online, searching and surfing and sometimes adding to the great databases of the Internet. The Web has been a godsend to me as a writer. Research that once required days in the stacks or periodical rooms of libraries can now be done in minutes. A few Google searches, some quick clicks on hyperlinks, and I've got the telltale fact or pithy quote I was after. Even when I'm not working, I'm as likely as not to be foraging in the Web's info-thickets—reading and writing e-mails, scanning headlines and blog posts, watching videos

Published in the Atlantic *(2008), a magazine covering literature, culture, and politics, and expanded into a book,* The Shallows: What the Internet Is Doing to Our Brains *(2010). Nicholas Carr has written widely on the impact of technology; he blogs at roughtype .com.*

1. Science fiction film (1968) about artificial intelligence in which HAL, a computer, threatens to take control of a human space mission.

and listening to podcasts, or just tripping from link to link to link. (Unlike foot-notes, to which they're sometimes likened, hyperlinks don't merely point to related works; they propel you toward them.)

For me, as for others, the Net is becoming a universal medium, the con-duit for most of the information that flows through my eyes and ears and into my mind. The advantages of having immediate access to such an incredibly rich store of information are many, and they've been widely described and duly applauded. "The perfect recall of silicon memory," *Wired*'s Clive Thompson has written, "can be an enormous boon to thinking." But that boon comes at a price. As the media theorist Marshall McLuhan[2] pointed out in the 1960s, media are not just passive channels of information. They supply the stuff of thought, but they also shape the process of thought. And what the Net seems to be doing is chipping away my capacity for concentration and contemplation. My mind now expects to take in information the way the Net distributes it: in a swiftly mov-ing stream of particles. Once I was a scuba diver in the sea of words. Now I zip along the surface like a guy on a Jet Ski.

I'm not the only one. When I mention my troubles with reading to friends   5
and acquaintances—literary types, most of them—many say they're having sim-ilar experiences. The more they use the Web, the more they have to fight to stay focused on long pieces of writing. Some of the bloggers I follow have also begun mentioning the phenomenon. Scott Karp, who writes a blog about online

2. Pioneering Canadian media critic (1911–1980) and author of *Understanding Media* (1964). His phrase "the medium is the message" encapsulates his argument that the form (medium) by which we receive information affects how we understand it.

media, recently confessed that he has stopped reading books altogether. "I was a lit major in college, and used to be [a] voracious book reader," he wrote. "What happened?" He speculates on the answer: "What if I do all my reading on the web not so much because the way I read has changed, i.e. I'm just seeking convenience, but because the way I THINK has changed?"

Bruce Friedman, who blogs regularly about the use of computers in medicine, also has described how the Internet has altered his mental habits. "I now have almost totally lost the ability to read and absorb a longish article on the web or in print," he wrote earlier this year. A pathologist who has long been on the faculty of the University of Michigan Medical School, Friedman elaborated on his comment in a telephone conversation with me. His thinking, he said, has taken on a "staccato" quality, reflecting the way he quickly scans short passages of text from many sources online. "I can't read *War and Peace*[3] anymore," he admitted. "I've lost the ability to do that. Even a blog post of more than three or four paragraphs is too much to absorb. I skim it."

Anecdotes alone don't prove much. And we still await the long-term neurological and psychological experiments that will provide a definitive picture of how Internet use affects cognition. But a recently published study of online research habits, conducted by scholars from University College London, suggests that we may well be in the midst of a sea change in the way we read and think. As part of the five-year research program, the scholars examined computer logs documenting the behavior of visitors to two popular research sites, one operated by the British Library and one by a U.K. educational consortium, that provide access to journal articles, e-books, and other sources of written information. They found that people using the sites exhibited "a form of skimming activity," hopping from one source to another and rarely returning to any source they'd already visited. They typically read no more than one or two pages of an article or book before they would "bounce" out to another site. Sometimes they'd save a long article, but there's no evidence that they ever went back and actually read it. The authors of the study report:

> It is clear that users are not reading online in the traditional sense; indeed there are signs that new forms of "reading" are emerging as users "power browse" horizontally through titles, contents pages and abstracts going for quick wins. It almost seems that they go online to avoid reading in the traditional sense.

Thanks to the ubiquity of text on the Internet, not to mention the popularity of text-messaging on cell phones, we may well be reading more today than we did in the 1970s or 1980s, when television was our medium of choice. But it's a different kind of reading, and behind it lies a different kind of thinking—perhaps even a new sense of the self. "We are not only *what* we read," says Maryanne Wolf, a developmental psychologist at Tufts University and the author of

3. Leo Tolstoy's epic five-volume novel (1869) depicting five Russian families' experiences during the Napoleonic Wars (1803–1814), during which Napoleon's armies invaded Russia.

Proust and the Squid: The Story and Science of the Reading Brain. "We are *how* we read." Wolf worries that the style of reading promoted by the Net, a style that puts "efficiency" and "immediacy" above all else, may be weakening our capacity for the kind of deep reading that emerged when an earlier technology, the printing press, made long and complex works of prose commonplace. When we read online, she says, we tend to become "mere decoders of information." Our ability to interpret text, to make the rich mental connections that form when we read deeply and without distraction, remains largely disengaged.

Reading, explains Wolf, is not an instinctive skill for human beings. It's not etched into our genes the way speech is. We have to teach our minds how to translate the symbolic characters we see into the language we understand. And the media or other technologies we use in learning and practicing the craft of reading play an important part in shaping the neural circuits inside our brains. Experiments demonstrate that readers of ideograms, such as the Chinese, develop a mental circuitry for reading that is very different from the circuitry found in those of us whose written language employs an alphabet. The variations extend across many regions of the brain, including those that govern such essential cognitive functions as memory and the interpretation of visual and auditory stimuli. We can expect as well that the circuits woven by our use of the Net will be different from those woven by our reading of books and other printed works.

Sometime in 1882, Friedrich Nietzsche[4] bought a typewriter—a Malling-Hansen Writing Ball, to be precise. His vision was failing, and keeping his eyes focused on a page had become exhausting and painful, often bringing on crushing headaches. He had been forced to curtail his writing, and he feared that he would soon have to give it up. The typewriter rescued him, at least for a time. Once he had mastered touch-typing, he was able to write with his eyes closed, using only the tips of his fingers. Words could once again flow from his mind to the page.   10

But the machine had a subtler effect on his work. One of Nietzsche's friends, a composer, noticed a change in the style of his writing. His already terse prose had become even tighter, more telegraphic. "Perhaps you will through this instrument even take to a new idiom," the friend wrote in a letter, noting that, in his own work, his "thoughts in music and language often depend on the quality of pen and paper."

"You are right," Nietzsche replied, "our writing equipment takes part in the forming of our thoughts." Under the sway of the machine, writes the German media scholar Friedrich A. Kittler, Nietzsche's prose "changed from arguments to aphorisms, from thoughts to puns, from rhetoric to telegram style."

The human brain is almost infinitely malleable. People used to think that our mental meshwork, the dense connections formed among the 100 billion or so neurons inside our skulls, was largely fixed by the time we reached adulthood. But brain researchers have discovered that that's not the case. James

4. German philosopher (1844–1900).

Olds, a professor of neuroscience who directs the Krasnow Institute for Advanced Study at George Mason University, says that even the adult mind "is very plastic." Nerve cells routinely break old connections and form new ones. "The brain," according to Olds, "has the ability to reprogram itself on the fly, altering the way it functions."

As we use what the sociologist Daniel Bell has called our "intellectual technologies"—the tools that extend our mental rather than our physical capacities—we inevitably begin to take on the qualities of those technologies. The mechanical clock, which came into common use in the 14th century, provides a compelling example. In *Technics and Civilization*, the historian and cultural critic Lewis Mumford described how the clock "disassociated time from human events and helped create the belief in an independent world of mathematically measurable sequences." The "abstract framework of divided time" became "the point of reference for both action and thought."

15   The clock's methodical ticking helped bring into being the scientific mind and the scientific man. But it also took something away. As the late MIT computer scientist Joseph Weizenbaum observed in his 1976 book, *Computer Power and Human Reason: From Judgment to Calculation*, the conception of the world that emerged from the widespread use of timekeeping instruments "remains an impoverished version of the older one, for it rests on a rejection of those direct experiences that formed the basis for, and indeed constituted, the old reality." In deciding when to eat, to work, to sleep, to rise, we stopped listening to our senses and started obeying the clock.

The process of adapting to new intellectual technologies is reflected in the changing metaphors we use to explain ourselves to ourselves. When the mechanical clock arrived, people began thinking of their brains as operating "like clockwork." Today, in the age of software, we have come to think of them as operating "like computers." But the changes, neuroscience tells us, go much deeper than metaphor. Thanks to our brain's plasticity, the adaptation occurs also at a biological level.

The Internet promises to have particularly far-reaching effects on cognition. In a paper published in 1936, the British mathematician Alan Turing proved that a digital computer, which at the time existed only as a theoretical machine, could be programmed to perform the function of any other information-processing device. And that's what we're seeing today. The Internet, an immeasurably powerful computing system, is subsuming most of our other intellectual technologies. It's becoming our map and our clock, our printing press and our typewriter, our calculator and our telephone, and our radio and TV.

When the Net absorbs a medium, that medium is re-created in the Net's image. It injects the medium's content with hyperlinks, blinking ads, and other digital gewgaws, and it surrounds the content with the content of all the other media it has absorbed. A new e-mail message, for instance, may announce its arrival as we're glancing over the latest headlines at a newspaper's site. The result is to scatter our attention and diffuse our concentration.

The Net's influence doesn't end at the edges of a computer screen, either. As people's minds become attuned to the crazy quilt of Internet media, traditional media have to adapt to the audience's new expectations. Television programs add text crawls and pop-up ads, and magazines and newspapers shorten their articles, introduce capsule summaries, and crowd their pages with easy-to-browse info-snippets. When, in March of this year, *The New York Times* decided to devote the second and third pages of every edition to article abstracts, its design director, Tom Bodkin, explained that the "shortcuts" would give harried readers a quick "taste" of the day's news, sparing them the "less efficient" method of actually turning the pages and reading the articles. Old media have little choice but to play by the new-media rules.

Never has a communications system played so many roles in our lives—or exerted such broad influence over our thoughts—as the Internet does today. Yet, for all that's been written about the Net, there's been little consideration of how, exactly, it's reprogramming us. The Net's intellectual ethic remains obscure. 20

About the same time that Nietzsche started using his typewriter, an earnest young man named Frederick Winslow Taylor carried a stopwatch into the Midvale Steel plant in Philadelphia and began a historic series of experiments aimed at improving the efficiency of the plant's machinists. With the approval of Midvale's owners, he recruited a group of factory hands, set them to work on various metalworking machines, and recorded and timed their every movement as well as the operations of the machines. By breaking down every job into a sequence of small, discrete steps and then testing different ways of performing each one, Taylor created a set of precise instructions—an "algorithm," we might say today—for how each worker should work. Midvale's employees grumbled about the strict new regime, claiming that it turned them into little more than automatons, but the factory's productivity soared.

More than a hundred years after the invention of the steam engine, the Industrial Revolution had at last found its philosophy and its philosopher. Taylor's tight industrial choreography—his "system," as he liked to call it—was embraced by manufacturers throughout the country and, in time, around the world. Seeking maximum speed, maximum efficiency, and maximum output, factory owners used time-and-motion studies to organize their work and configure the jobs of their workers. The goal, as Taylor defined it in his celebrated 1911 treatise, *The Principles of Scientific Management*, was to identify and adopt, for every job, the "one best method" of work and thereby to effect "the gradual substitution of science for rule of thumb throughout the mechanic arts." Once his system was applied to all acts of manual labor, Taylor assured his followers, it would bring about a restructuring not only of industry but of society, creating a utopia of perfect efficiency. "In the past the man has been first," he declared; "in the future the system must be first."

Taylor's system is still very much with us; it remains the ethic of industrial manufacturing. And now, thanks to the growing power that computer engineers and software coders wield over our intellectual lives, Taylor's ethic is beginning to govern the realm of the mind as well. The Internet is a machine designed for the efficient and automated collection, transmission, and manipulation of information, and its legions of programmers are intent on finding the "one best method"—the perfect algorithm—to carry out every mental movement of what we've come to describe as "knowledge work."

Google's headquarters, in Mountain View, California—the Googleplex—is the Internet's high church, and the religion practiced inside its walls is Taylorism. Google, says its chief executive, Eric Schmidt, is "a company that's founded around the science of measurement," and it is striving to "systematize every-thing" it does. Drawing on the terabytes of behavioral data it collects through its search engine and other sites, it carries out thousands of experiments a day, according to the *Harvard Business Review*, and it uses the results to refine the algorithms that increasingly control how people find information and extract meaning from it. What Taylor did for the work of the hand, Google is doing for the work of the mind.

25   The company has declared that its mission is "to organize the world's infor-mation and make it universally accessible and useful." It seeks to develop "the perfect search engine," which it defines as something that "understands exactly what you mean and gives you back exactly what you want." In Google's view, information is a kind of commodity, a utilitarian resource that can be mined and processed with industrial efficiency. The more pieces of information we can "access" and the faster we can extract their gist, the more productive we become as thinkers.

Where does it end? Sergey Brin and Larry Page, the gifted young men who founded Google while pursuing doctoral degrees in computer science at Stan-ford, speak frequently of their desire to turn their search engine into an artifi-cial intelligence, a HAL-like machine that might be connected directly to our brains. "The ultimate search engine is something as smart as people—or smarter," Page said in a speech a few years back. "For us, working on search is a way to work on artificial intelligence." In a 2004 interview with *Newsweek*, Brin said, "Certainly if you had all the world's information directly attached to your brain, or an artificial brain that was smarter than your brain, you'd be bet-ter off." Last year, Page told a convention of scientists that Google is "really trying to build artificial intelligence and to do it on a large scale."

Such an ambition is a natural one, even an admirable one, for a pair of math whizzes with vast quantities of cash at their disposal and a small army of computer scientists in their employ. A fundamentally scientific enterprise, Google is motivated by a desire to use technology, in Eric Schmidt's words, "to solve problems that have never been solved before," and artificial intelligence is the hardest problem out there. Why wouldn't Brin and Page want to be the ones to crack it?

Still, their easy assumption that we'd all "be better off" if our brains were supplemented, or even replaced, by an artificial intelligence is unsettling. It sug-gests a belief that intelligence is the output of a mechanical process, a series of discrete steps that can be isolated, measured, and optimized. In Google's world, the world we enter when we go online, there's little place for the fuzziness of contemplation. Ambiguity is not an opening for insight but a bug to be fixed.

The human brain is just an outdated computer that needs a faster processor and a bigger hard drive.

The idea that our minds should operate as high-speed data-processing machines is not only built into the workings of the Internet, it is the network's reigning business model as well. The faster we surf across the Web—the more links we click and pages we view—the more opportunities Google and other companies gain to collect information about us and to feed us advertisements. Most of the proprietors of the commercial Internet have a financial stake in collecting the crumbs of data we leave behind as we flit from link to link—the more crumbs, the better. The last thing these companies want is to encourage leisurely reading or slow, concentrated thought. It's in their economic interest to drive us to distraction.

Maybe I'm just a worrywart. Just as there's a tendency to glorify technological   30
progress, there's a countertendency to expect the worst of every new tool or machine. In Plato's *Phaedrus*,[5] Socrates bemoaned the development of writing. He feared that, as people came to rely on the written word as a substitute for the knowledge they used to carry inside their heads, they would, in the words of one of the dialogue's characters, "cease to exercise their memory and become forgetful." And because they would be able to "receive a quantity of information without proper instruction," they would "be thought very knowledgeable when they are for the most part quite ignorant." They would be "filled with the conceit of wisdom instead of real wisdom." Socrates wasn't wrong—the new technology did often have the effects he feared—but he was shortsighted. He couldn't foresee the many ways that writing and reading would serve to spread information, spur fresh ideas, and expand human knowledge (if not wisdom).

The arrival of Gutenberg's printing press, in the 15th century, set off another round of teeth gnashing. The Italian humanist Hieronimo Squarciafico worried that the easy availability of books would lead to intellectual laziness, making men "less studious" and weakening their minds. Others argued that cheaply printed books and broadsheets would undermine religious authority, demean the work of scholars and scribes, and spread sedition and debauchery. As New York University professor Clay Shirky notes, "Most of the arguments made against the printing press were correct, even prescient." But, again, the doomsayers were unable to imagine the myriad blessings that the printed word would deliver.

So, yes, you should be skeptical of my skepticism. Perhaps those who dismiss critics of the Internet as Luddites[6] or nostalgists will be proved correct, and from our hyperactive, data-stoked minds will spring a golden age of intellectual discovery and universal wisdom. Then again, the Net isn't the alphabet, and although it may replace the printing press, it produces something

5. Plato (c. 428–348 B.C.E.), Greek philosopher. The dialogue *Phaedrus* contains an extended discussion of the relative merits of speech versus writing.

6. Originally referred to nineteenth-century textile workers who opposed new technology; the term now refers to anyone who opposes new technologies or automation.

altogether different. The kind of deep reading that a sequence of printed pages promotes is valuable not just for the knowledge we acquire from the author's words but for the intellectual vibrations those words set off within our own minds. In the quiet spaces opened up by the sustained, undistracted reading of a book, or by any other act of contemplation, for that matter, we make our own associations, draw our own inferences and analogies, foster our own ideas. Deep reading, as Maryanne Wolf argues, is indistinguishable from deep thinking.

If we lose those quiet spaces, or fill them up with "content," we will sacrifice something important not only in our selves but in our culture. In a recent essay, the playwright Richard Foreman eloquently described what's at stake:

> I come from a tradition of Western culture, in which the ideal (my ideal) was the complex, dense and "cathedral-like" structure of the highly educated and articulate personality—a man or woman who carried inside themselves a personally constructed and unique version of the entire heritage of the West. [But now] I see within us all (myself included) the replacement of complex inner density with a new kind of self—evolving under the pressure of information overload and the technology of the "instantly available."

As we are drained of our "inner repertory of dense cultural inheritance," Foreman concluded, we risk turning into "pancake people—spread wide and thin as we connect with that vast network of information accessed by the mere touch of a button."

I'm haunted by that scene in *2001*. What makes it so poignant, and so weird, is the computer's emotional response to the disassembly of its mind: its despair as one circuit after another goes dark, its childlike pleading with the astronaut—"I can feel it. I can feel it. I'm afraid"—and its final reversion to what can only be called a state of innocence. HAL's outpouring of feeling contrasts with the emotionlessness that characterizes the human figures in the film, who go about their business with an almost robotic efficiency. Their thoughts and actions feel scripted, as if they're following the steps of an algorithm. In the world of *2001*, people have become so machinelike that the most human character turns out to be a machine. That's the essence of Kubrick's dark prophecy: as we come to rely on computers to mediate our understanding of the world, it is our own intelligence that flattens into artificial intelligence.

MLA CITATION

Carr, Nicholas. "Is Google Making Us Stupid?" 2008. *The Norton Reader: An Anthology of Nonfiction.* Ed. Melissa A. Goldthwaite et al. 14th ed. New York: Norton, 2016. 572–80. Print.

QUESTIONS

1. Nicholas Carr poses a question with the title of this essay. How would you answer it? What main examples does he offer to illustrate how Google is making

us stupid? What counterexamples does he offer? What examples, on either side, would you add?

2. What are the most important advantages of "Taylorism" (paragraphs 21–24), or the application of scientific methods to human behavior? Are there aspects of human behavior that cannot be improved by such methods?

3. Carr is ambivalent about our reliance on technology, but Thomas Goetz (pp. 587–99) is more enthusiastic. Compare Carr's attitude about a new technology with Goetz's. What is your stance on these authors' relationships to technology, and why?

4. Interview a few people, including some who grew up using the internet and some who remember doing research mainly using books. Write your own analysis of the impact of the internet on our ability to think, reason, and research, building on Carr's essay and the anecdotes you collect.

EULA BISS *Time and Distance Overcome*

"OF WHAT USE is such an invention?" the *New York World* asked shortly after Alexander Graham Bell first demonstrated his telephone in 1876. The world was not waiting for the telephone.

Bell's financial backers asked him not to work on his new invention because it seemed too dubious an investment. The idea on which the telephone depended—the idea that every home in the country could be connected by a vast network of wires suspended from poles set an average of one hundred feet apart—seemed far more unlikely than the idea that the human voice could be transmitted through a wire.

Even now it is an impossible idea, that we are all connected, all of us.

"At the present time we have a perfect network of gas pipes and water pipes throughout our large cities," Bell wrote to his business partners in defense of his idea. "We have main pipes laid under the streets communicating by side pipes with the various dwellings. . . . In a similar manner it is conceivable that cables of telephone wires could be laid under ground, or suspended overhead, communicating by branch wires with private dwellings, counting houses, shops, manufactories, etc., uniting them through the main cable."

Imagine the mind that could imagine this. That could see us joined by one 5 branching cable. This was the mind of a man who wanted to invent, more than the telephone, a machine that would allow the deaf to hear.

From Notes from No Man's Land: American Essays *(2009), Eula Biss's collection of writings on contemporary race relations in America.*

For a short time the telephone was little more than a novelty. For twenty-five cents you could see it demonstrated by Bell himself, in a church, along with singing and recitations by local talent. From some distance away, Bell would receive a call from "the invisible Mr. Watson".[1] Then the telephone became a plaything of the rich. A Boston banker paid for a private line between his office and his home so that he could let his family know exactly when he would be home for dinner.

Mark Twain was among the first Americans to own a telephone, but he wasn't completely taken with the device. "The human voice carries entirely too far as it is," he remarked.

By 1889, the *New York Times* was reporting a "War on Telephone Poles." Wherever telephone companies were erecting poles, home owners and business owners were sawing them down or defending their sidewalks with rifles.

Property owners in Red Bank, New Jersey, threatened to tar and feather the workers putting up telephone poles. A judge granted a group of home owners an injunction to prevent the telephone company from erecting any new poles. Another judge found that a man who had cut down a pole because it was "obnoxious" was not guilty of malicious mischief.

10   Telephone poles, newspaper editorials complained, were an urban blight. The poles carried a wire for each telephone—sometimes hundreds of wires. And in some places there were also telegraph wires, power lines, and trolley cables. The sky was netted with wires.

The war on telephone poles was fueled, in part, by that terribly American concern for private property, and a reluctance to surrender it for a shared utility. And then there was a fierce sense of aesthetics, an obsession with purity, a dislike for the way the poles and wires marred a landscape that those other new inventions, skyscrapers and barbed wire, were just beginning to complicate. And then perhaps there was also a fear that distance, as it had always been known and measured, was collapsing.

The city council in Sioux Falls, South Dakota, ordered policemen to cut down all the telephone poles in town. And the mayor of Oshkosh, Wisconsin, ordered the police chief and the fire department to chop down the telephone poles there. Only one pole was chopped down before the telephone men climbed all the poles along the line, preventing any more chopping. Soon, Bell Telephone Company began stationing a man at the top of each pole as soon as it had been set, until enough poles had been set to string a wire between them, at which point it became a misdemeanor to interfere with the poles. Even so, a constable cut down two poles holding forty or fifty wires. And a home owner sawed down a

---

1. Thomas Watson (1854–1934), engineer and assistant to Bell. His name became the first words ever spoken on a telephone: "Mr. Watson, come here—I want to see you."

recently wired pole, then fled from police. The owner of a cannery ordered his workers to throw dirt back into the hole the telephone company was digging in front of his building. His men threw the dirt back in as fast as the telephone workers could dig it out. Then he sent out a team with a load of stones to dump into the hole. Eventually, the pole was erected on the other side of the street.

Despite the war on telephone poles, it would take only four years after Bell's first public demonstration of the telephone for every town of more than ten thousand people to be wired, although many towns were wired only to themselves. By the turn of the century, there were more telephones than bathtubs in America.

"Time and dist. overcome," read an early advertisement for the telephone. Rutherford B. Hayes pronounced the installation of a telephone in the White House "one of the greatest events since creation." The telephone, Thomas Edison declared, "annihilated time and space, and brought the human family in closer touch."

In 1898, in Lake Cormorant, Mississippi, a black man was hanged from a telephone pole. And in Weir City, Kansas. And in Brookhaven, Mississippi. And in Tulsa, Oklahoma, where the hanged man was riddled with bullets. In Danville, Illinois, a black man's throat was slit, and his dead body was strung up on a telephone pole. Two black men were hanged from a telephone pole in Lewisburg, West Virginia. And two in Hempstead, Texas, where one man was dragged out of the courtroom by a mob, and another was dragged out of jail.

A black man was hanged from a telephone pole in Belleville, Illinois, where a fire was set at the base of the pole and the man was cut down half-alive, covered in coal oil, and burned. While his body was burning the mob beat it with clubs and cut it to pieces.

Lynching, the first scholar of the subject determined, is an American invention. Lynching from bridges, from arches, from trees standing alone in fields, from trees in front of the county courthouse, from trees used as public billboards, from trees barely able to support the weight of a man, from telephone poles, from streetlamps, and from poles erected solely for that purpose. From the middle of the nineteenth century to the middle of the twentieth century, black men were lynched for crimes real and imagined, for whistles, for rumors, for "disputing with a white man," for "unpopularity," for "asking a white woman in marriage," for "peeping in a window."

The children's game of telephone depends on the fact that a message passed quietly from one ear to another to another will get distorted at some point along the line.

More than two hundred antilynching bills were introduced to the U.S. Congress during the twentieth century, but none were passed. Seven presidents lobbied for antilynching legislation, and the House of Representatives passed three separate measures, each of which was blocked by the Senate.

20   In Pine Bluff, Arkansas, a black man charged with kicking a white girl was hanged from a telephone pole. In Longview, Texas, a black man accused of attacking a white woman was hanged from a telephone pole. In Greenville, Mississippi, a black man accused of attacking a white telephone operator was hanged from a telephone pole. "The negro only asked time to pray." In Purcell, Oklahoma, a black man accused of attacking a white woman was tied to a telephone pole and burned. "Men and women in automobiles stood up to watch him die."

The poles, of course, were not to blame. It was only coincidence that they became convenient as gallows, because they were tall and straight, with a crossbar, and because they stood in public places. And it was only coincidence that the telephone poles so closely resembled crucifixes.

Early telephone calls were full of noise. "Such a jangle of meaningless noises had never been heard by human ears," Herbert Casson wrote in his 1910 *History of the Telephone*. "There were spluttering and bubbling, jerking and rasping, whistling and screaming."

In Shreveport, Lousiana, a black man charged with attacking a white girl was hanged from a telephone pole. "A knife was left sticking in the body." In Cumming, Georgia, a black man accused of assaulting a white girl was shot repeatedly, then hanged from a telephone pole. In Waco, Texas, a black man convicted of killing a white woman was taken from the courtroom by a mob and burned, then his charred body was hanged from a telephone pole.

A postcard was made from the photo of a burned man hanging from a telephone pole in Texas, his legs broken off below the knee and his arms curled up and blackened. Postcards of lynchings were sent out as greetings and warnings until 1908, when the postmaster general declared them unmailable. "This is the barbecue we had last night," reads one.

25   "If we are to die," W. E. B. DuBois[2] wrote in 1911, "in God's name let us perish like men and not like bales of hay." And "if we must die," Claude McKay[3] wrote ten years later, "let it not be like hogs."

In Pittsburg, Kansas, a black man was hanged from a telephone pole, cut down, burned, shot, and stoned with bricks. "At first the negro was defiant," the *New York Times* reported, "but just before he was hanged he begged hard for his life."

2. American historian and writer (1868–1963).
3. Jamaican American writer (1889–1948).

In the photographs, the bodies of the men lynched from telephone poles are silhouetted against the sky. Sometimes two men to a pole, hanging above the buildings of a town. Sometimes three. They hang like flags in still air.

In Cumberland, Maryland, a mob used a telephone pole as a battering ram to break into the jail where a black man charged with the murder of a policeman was being held. They kicked him to death, then fired twenty shots into his head. They wanted to burn his body, but a minister asked them not to.

The lynchings happened everywhere, in all but four states. From shortly before the invention of the telephone to long after the first transatlantic call. More in the South, and more in rural areas. In the cities and in the North, there were race riots.

Riots in Cincinnati, New Orleans, Memphis, New York, Atlanta, Philadelphia, Houston . . .   30

During the race riots that destroyed the black section of Springfield, Ohio, a black man was shot and hanged from a telephone pole.

During the race riots that set fire to East St. Louis and forced five hundred black people to flee their homes, a black man was hanged from a telephone pole. The rope broke and his body fell into the gutter. "Negros are lying in the gutters every few feet in some places," read the newspaper account.

In 1921, the year before Bell died, four companies of the National Guard were called out to end a race war in Tulsa that began when a white woman accused a black man of rape. Bell had lived to complete the first call from New York to San Francisco, which required 14,000 miles of copper wire and 130,000 telephone poles.

My grandfather was a lineman. He broke his back when a telephone pole fell. "Smashed him onto the road," my father says.

When I was young, I believed that the arc and swoop of telephone wires along the roadways was beautiful. I believed that the telephone poles, with their transformers catching the evening sun, were glorious. I believed my father when he said, "My dad could raise a pole by himself." And I believed that the telephone itself was a miracle.   35

Now, I tell my sister, these poles, these wires, do not look the same to me. Nothing is innocent, my sister reminds me. But nothing, I would like to think, remains unrepentant.

One summer, heavy rains fell in Nebraska and some green telephone poles grew small leafy branches.

ON "TIME AND DISTANCE OVERCOME"[4]

I began my research for this essay by searching for every instance of the phrase "telephone pole" in the *New York Times* from 1880 to 1920, which resulted in 370 articles. I was planning to write an essay about telephone poles and telephones, not lynchings, but after reading an article headlined "Colored Scoundrel Lynched," and then another headlined "Mississippi Negro Lynched," and then another headlined "Texas Negro Lynched," I searched for every instance of the word "lynched" in the *New York Times* from 1880 to 1920, which resulted in 2,354 articles.

I refer, in this essay, to the first scholar of lynching, meaning James E. Cutler, author of the 1905 book *Lynch-Law,* in which he writes, on the first page, "Lynching is a criminal practice which is peculiar to the United States." This is debatable, of course, and very possibly not true, but there is good evidence that the Italian Antonio Meucci invented a telephone years before Bell began working on his device, so as long as we are going to lay claim to one invention, we might as well take responsibility for the other.

40   Bell would say, late in his life: "Recognition for my work with the deaf has always been more pleasing than the recognition of my work with the telephone." His own hearing was failing by the time he placed the first cross-country call, from New York to his old friend Thomas Watson in San Francisco, and what he said to Watson then was an echo of the first sentence he ever spoke into his invention, a famous and possibly mythical sentence that is now remembered in several slightly different versions, one being, "Mr. Watson, come here—I want you," and another being, "Mr. Watson, come here—I need you!"

4. At the end of her book, Biss provides background information for each of her essays, including how she arrived at the topic and the research involved.

MLA CITATION

Biss, Eula. "Time and Distance Overcome." 2009. *The Norton Reader: An Anthology of Nonfiction.* Ed. Melissa A. Goldthwaite et al. 14th ed. New York: Norton, 2016. 581–86. Print.

QUESTIONS

1. Eula Biss focuses on the historical coincidence of the installation of telephone poles with lynching. List all the ways that Biss connects the topics and discuss the merits of the juxtaposition. How does she make the coincidence into something meaningful?

2. How does paragraph 18, on "the children's game of telephone," connect to the themes of the rest of the essay?

3. Following Biss's model (paragraphs 38–40), write an author's note for an old research paper in which you describe how the paper changed as you did your research.

4. Every new technology brings benefits and problems, as Biss explores. Choose a different medium or technology (e.g., TV, smartphones, texting) and write an essay discussing its benefits and problems, using Biss's essay as a model.

THOMAS GOETZ   *Harnessing the Power*
of Feedback Loops

I N 2003, officials in Garden Grove, California, a
community of 170,000 people wedged amid the suburban sprawl of Orange County, set out to confront
a problem that afflicts most every town in America:
drivers speeding through school zones.

Local authorities had tried many tactics to get
people to slow down. They replaced old speed limit signs with bright new ones
to remind drivers of the 25-mile-an-hour limit during school hours. Police began
ticketing speeding motorists during drop-off and pickup times. But these
efforts had only limited success, and speeding cars continued to hit bicyclists
and pedestrians in the school zones with depressing regularity.

So city engineers decided to take another approach. In five Garden Grove
school zones, they put up what are known as dynamic speed displays, or driver
feedback signs: a speed limit posting coupled with a radar sensor attached to a
huge digital readout announcing "Your Speed."

The signs were curious in a few ways. For one thing, they didn't tell drivers anything they didn't already know—there is, after all, a speedometer in every
car. If a motorist wanted to know their speed, a glance at the dashboard would
do it. For another thing, the signs used radar, which decades earlier had appeared
on American roads as a talisman technology, reserved for police officers only.
Now Garden Grove had scattered radar sensors along the side of the road like
traffic cones. And the Your Speed signs came with no punitive follow-up—no
police officer standing by ready to write a ticket. This defied decades of law-
enforcement dogma, which held that most people obey speed limits only if
they face some clear negative consequence for exceeding them.

In other words, officials in Garden Grove were betting that giving speed-   5
ers redundant information with no consequence would somehow compel them
to do something few of us are inclined to do: slow down.

The results fascinated and delighted the city officials. In the vicinity of the
schools where the dynamic displays were installed, drivers slowed an average
of 14 percent. Not only that, at three schools the average speed dipped below
the posted speed limit. Since this experiment, Garden Grove has installed 10
more driver feedback signs. "Frankly, it's hard to get people to slow down," says
Dan Candelaria, Garden Grove's traffic engineer. "But these encourage people
to do the right thing."

In the years since the Garden Grove project began, radar technology has
dropped steadily in price and Your Speed signs have proliferated on American
roadways. Yet despite their ubiquity, the signs haven't faded into the landscape
like so many other motorist warnings. Instead, they've proven to be consistently
effective at getting drivers to slow down—reducing speeds, on average, by about

First published in Wired *(2011), a magazine that covers technology and examines its influence on politics and culture.*

10 percent, an effect that lasts for several miles down the road. Indeed, traffic engineers and safety experts consider them to be more effective at changing driving habits than a cop with a radar gun. Despite their redundancy, despite their lack of repercussions, the signs have accomplished what seemed impossible: They get us to let up on the gas.

The signs leverage what's called a feedback loop, a profoundly effective tool for changing behavior. The basic premise is simple. Provide people with information about their actions in real time (or something close to it), then give them an opportunity to change those actions, pushing them toward better behaviors. Action, information, reaction. It's the operating principle behind a home thermostat, which fires the furnace to maintain a specific temperature, or the consumption display in a Toyota Prius, which tends to turn drivers into so-called hypermilers trying to wring every last mile from the gas tank. But the simplicity of feedback loops is deceptive. They are in fact powerful tools that can help people change bad behavior patterns, even those that seem intractable. Just as important, they can be used to encourage good habits, turning progress itself into a reward. In other words, feedback loops change human behavior. And thanks to an explosion of new technology, the opportunity to put them into action in nearly every part of our lives is quickly becoming a reality.

A feedback loop involves four distinct stages. First comes the data: A behavior must be measured, captured, and stored. This is the evidence stage. Second, the

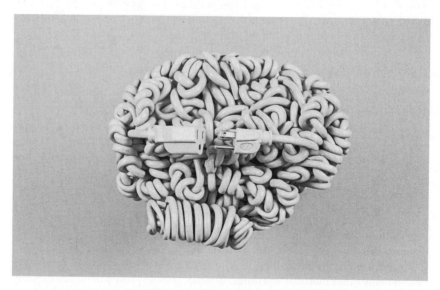

The premise of a feedback loop is simple: Provide people with information about their actions in real time, then give them a chance to change those actions, pushing them toward better behaviors.

information must be relayed to the individual, not in the raw-data form in which it was captured but in a context that makes it emotionally resonant. This is the relevance stage. But even compelling information is useless if we don't know what to make of it, so we need a third stage: consequence. The information must illuminate one or more paths ahead. And finally, the fourth stage: action. There must be a clear moment when the individual can recalibrate a behavior, make a choice, and act. Then that action is measured, and the feedback loop can run once more, every action stimulating new behaviors that inch us closer to our goals.

This basic framework has been shaped and refined by thinkers and researchers for ages. In the 18th century, engineers developed regulators and governors to modulate steam engines and other mechanical systems, an early application of feedback loops that later became codified into control theory, the engineering discipline behind everything from aerospace to robotics. The mathematician Norbert Wiener expanded on this work in the 1940s, devising the field of cybernetics, which analyzed how feedback loops operate in machinery and electronics and explored how those principles might be broadened to human systems.

10

The potential of the feedback loop to affect behavior was explored in the 1960s, most notably in the work of Albert Bandura, a Stanford University psychologist and pioneer in the study of behavior change and motivation. Drawing on several education experiments involving children, Bandura observed that giving individuals a clear goal and a means to evaluate their progress toward that goal greatly increased the likelihood that they would achieve it. He later expanded this notion into the concept of self-efficacy, which holds that the more we believe we can meet a goal, the more likely we will do so. In the 40 years since Bandura's early work, feedback loops have been thoroughly researched and validated in psychology, epidemiology, military strategy, environmental studies, engineering, and economics. (In typical academic fashion, each discipline tends to reinvent the methodology and rephrase the terminology, but the basic framework remains the same.) Feedback loops are a common tool in athletic

Over the past 40 years, feedback loops have been thoroughly researched and validated in psychology, epidemiology, military strategy, environmental studies, engineering, and economics.

training plans, executive coaching strategies, and a multitude of other self-improvement programs (though some are more true to the science than others).

Despite the volume of research and a proven capacity to affect human behavior, we don't often use feedback loops in everyday life. Blame this on two factors: Until now, the necessary catalyst—personalized data—has been an expensive commodity. Health spas, athletic training centers, and self-improvement workshops all traffic in fastidiously culled data at premium rates. Outside of those rare realms, the cornerstone information has been just too expensive to come by. As a technologist might put it, personalized data hasn't really scaled.

Second, collecting data on the cheap is cumbersome. Although the basic idea of self-tracking has been available to anyone willing to put in the effort, few people stick with the routine of toting around a notebook, writing down every Hostess cupcake they consume or every flight of stairs they climb. It's just too much bother. The technologist would say that capturing that data involves too much friction. As a result, feedback loops are niche tools, for the most part, rewarding for those with the money, willpower, or geeky inclination to obsessively track their own behavior, but impractical for the rest of us.

That's quickly changing because of one essential technology: sensors. Adding sensors to the feedback equation helps solve problems of friction and scale. They automate the capture of behavioral data, digitizing it so it can be readily crunched and transformed as necessary. And they allow passive measurement, eliminating the need for tedious active monitoring.

15   In the past two or three years, the plunging price of sensors has begun to foster a feedback-loop revolution. Just as Your Speed signs have been adopted worldwide because the cost of radar technology keeps dropping, other feedback loops are popping up everywhere because sensors keep getting cheaper and better at monitoring behavior and capturing data in all sorts of environments. These new, less expensive devices include accelerometers (which measure motion), GPS sensors (which track location), and inductance sensors (which measure electric current). Accelerometers have dropped to less than $1 each—down from as much as $20 a decade ago—which means they can now be built into tennis shoes, MP3 players, and even toothbrushes. Radio-frequency ID chips are being added to prescription pill bottles, student ID cards, and casino chips. And inductance sensors that were once deployed only in heavy industry are now cheap and tiny enough to be connected to residential breaker boxes, letting consumers track their home's entire energy diet.

Of course, technology has been tracking what people do for years. Call-center agents have been monitored closely since the 1990s, and the nation's tractor-trailer fleets have long been equipped with GPS and other location sensors—not just to allow drivers to follow their routes but so that companies can track their cargo and the drivers. But those are top-down, Big Brother techniques. The true power of feedback loops is not to control people but to give them control. It's like the difference between a speed trap and a speed feedback sign—one is a game of gotcha, the other is a gentle reminder of the rules of the road. The ideal feedback loop gives us an emotional connection to a rational goal.

And today, their promise couldn't be greater. The intransigence of human behavior has emerged as the root of most of the world's biggest challenges. Witness the rise in obesity, the persistence of smoking, the soaring number of people who have one or more chronic diseases. Consider our problems with carbon emissions, where managing personal energy consumption could be the difference between a climate under control and one beyond help. And feedback loops aren't just about solving problems. They could create opportunities. Feedback loops can improve how companies motivate and empower their employees, allowing workers to monitor their own productivity and set their own schedules. They could lead to lower consumption of precious resources and more productive use of what we do consume. They could allow people to set and achieve better-defined, more ambitious goals and curb destructive behaviors, replacing them with positive actions. Used in organizations or communities, they can help groups work together to take on more daunting challenges. In short, the feedback loop is an age-old strategy revitalized by state-of-the-art technology. As such, it is perhaps the most promising tool for behavioral change to have come along in decades.

In 2006, Shwetak Patel, then a graduate student in computer science at Georgia Tech, was working on a problem: How could technology help provide remote care for the elderly? The obvious approach would be to install cameras and motion detectors throughout a home, so that observers could see when somebody fell or became sick. Patel found those methods unsophisticated and impractical. "Installing cameras or motion sensors everywhere is unreasonably expensive," he says. "It might work in theory, but it just won't happen in practice. So I wondered what would give us the same information and be reasonably priced and easy to deploy. I found those really interesting constraints."

The answer, Patel realized, is that every home emits something called voltage noise. Think of it as a steady hum in the electrical wires that varies depending on what systems are drawing power. If there were some way to disaggregate this noise, it might be possible to deliver much the same information as cameras and motion sensors. Lights going on and off, for instance, would mean that someone had moved from room to room. If a blender were left on, that might signal that someone had fallen—or had forgotten about the blender, perhaps indicating dementia. If we could hear electricity usage, Patel thought, we could know what was happening inside the house.

A nifty idea, but how to make it happen? The problem wasn't measuring the voltage noise; that's easily tracked with a few sensors. The challenge was translating the cacophony of electromagnetic interference into the symphony of signals given off by specific appliances and devices and lights. Finding that pattern amid the noise became the focus of Patel's PhD work, and in a few years he had both his degree and his answer: a stack of algorithms that could discern a blender from a light switch from a television set and so on. All this data

20

HOW A FEEDBACK LOOP WORKS

A modified traffic sign can have a profound effect on drivers' behavior. Here's what happens.

1. Evidence
The radar-equipped sign flashes a car's current speed.
First comes the data—quantifying a behavior and presenting that data back to the individual so they know where they stand. After all, you can't change what you don't measure.

2. Relevance
The sign also displays the legal speed limit—most people don't want to be seen as bad drivers.
Data is just digits unless it hits home. Through information design, social context, or some other proxy for meaning, the right incentive will transform rational information into an emotional imperative.

3. Consequences
People are reminded of the downside of speeding, including traffic tickets and the risk of accidents.
Even compelling information is useless unless it ties into some larger goal or purpose. People must have a sense of what to do with the information and any opportunities they will have to act on it.

4. Action
Drivers slow an average of 10 percent—usually for several miles.
The individual has to engage with all of the above and act—thus closing the loop and allowing that new action to be measured.

could be captured not by sensors in every electrical outlet throughout the house but through a single device plugged into a single outlet.

This, Patel soon realized, went way beyond elder care. His approach could inform ordinary consumers, in real time, about where the energy they paid for every month was going. "We kind of stumbled across this stuff," Patel says. "But we realized that, combined with data on the house's overall draw on power"—which can be measured through a second sensor easily installed at the circuit box—"we were getting really great information about resource consumption in the home. And that could be more than interesting information. It could encourage behavior change."

By 2008, Patel had started a new job in the computer science and engineering departments at the University of Washington, and his idea had been turned into the startup Zensi. At Washington, he focused on devising similar techniques to monitor home consumption of water and gas. The solutions were even more elegant, perhaps, than the one for monitoring electricity. A transducer affixed to an outdoor spigot can detect changes in water pressure that correspond to the resident's water usage. That data can then be disaggregated to distinguish a leaky toilet from an over-indulgent bather. And a microphone sensor on a gas meter listens to changes in the regulator to determine how much gas is consumed.

Last year, consumer electronics company Belkin acquired Zensi and made energy conservation a centerpiece of its corporate strategy, with feedback loops as the guiding principle. Belkin has begun modestly, with a device called the Conserve Insight. It's an outlet adapter that gives consumers a close read of the power used by one select appliance: Plug it into a wall socket and then plug an appliance or gadget into it and a small display shows how much energy the device is consuming, in both watts and dollars. It's a window into how energy is actually used, but it's only a proof-of-concept prototype of the more ambitious product, based on Patel's PhD work, that Belkin will begin beta-testing in Chicago later this year with an eye toward commercial release in 2013. The company calls it Zorro.

At first glance, the Zorro is just another so-called smart meter, not that different from the boxes that many power companies have been installing in consumers' homes, with a vague promise that the meters will educate citizens and provide better data to the utility. To the surprise of the utility companies, though, these smart meters have been greeted with hostility in some communities. A small but vocal number of customers object to being monitored, while others worry that the radiation from RFID transmitters is unhealthy (though this has been measured at infinitesimal levels).

Politics aside, in pure feedback terms smart meters fail on at least two levels. For one, the information goes to the utility first, rather than directly to the consumer. For another, most smart meters aren't very smart; they typically measure overall household consumption, not how much power is being consumed by which specific device or appliance. In other words, they are a broken feedback loop.

Belkin's device avoids these pitfalls by giving the data directly to consumers and delivering it promptly and continuously. "Real-time feedback is key to conservation," says Kevin Ashton, Zensi's former CEO who took over Belkin's Conserve division after the acquisition. "There's a visceral impact when you see for yourself how much your toaster is costing you."

The Zorro is just the first of several Belkin products that Ashton believes will put feedback loops into effect throughout the home. Ashton worked on RFID chips at MIT in the late 1990s and lays claim to coining the phrase "Internet of Things," meaning a world of interconnected, sensor-laden devices and objects. He predicts that home sensors will one day inform choices in all aspects of our lives. "We're consuming so many things without thinking about them—energy, plastic, paper, calories. I can envision a ubiquitous sensor network, a platform for real-time feedback that will enhance the comfort, security, and control of our lives."

As a starting point for a consumer products company, that's not half bad.

If there is one problem in medicine that confounds doctors, insurers, and pharmaceutical companies alike, it's noncompliance, the unfriendly term for patients who don't follow doctors' orders. Most vexing are those who don't take their medications as prescribed—which, it turns out, is pretty much most of us. Studies have shown that about half of patients who are prescribed medication take their pills as directed. For drugs like statins, which must be used for years, the rate is even worse, dropping to around 30 percent after a year. (Since the effect of these drugs can be invisible, the thinking goes, patients don't detect any benefit.) Research has found that noncompliance adds $100 billion annually to US health care costs and leads to 125,000 unnecessary deaths from cardiovascular diseases alone every year. And it can be blamed almost entirely on human foibles—people failing to do what they know they should.

30   David Rose is a perfect example of this. He has a family history of heart disease. Now 44, he began taking medication for high blood pressure a few years ago, making him not so different from the nearly one-third of Americans with hypertension. Where Rose is exceptional is in his capacity to do something about noncompliance. He has a knack for inventing beautiful, engaging, alluring objects that get people to do things like take their pills.

A decade ago, Rose, whose stylish glasses and soft-spoken manner bring to mind a college music teacher, started a company called Ambient Devices. His most famous product is the Orb, a translucent sphere that turns different colors to reflect different information inputs. If your stocks go down, it might glow red; if it snows, it might glow white, and so on, depending on what information you tell the Orb you are interested in. It's a whimsical product and is still available for purchase online. But as far as Rose is concerned, the Orb was merely a prelude to his next company, Vitality, and its marquee product: the GlowCap.

The device is simple. When a patient is prescribed a medication, a physician or pharmacy provides a GlowCap to go on top of the pill bottle, replacing the standard childproof cap. The GlowCap, which comes with a plug-in unit that Rose calls a night-light, connects to a database that knows the patient's particular dosage directions—say, two pills twice a day, at 8 am and 8 pm. When 8 am rolls around, the GlowCap and the night-light start to pulse with a gentle orange light. A few minutes later, if the pill bottle isn't opened, the light pulses a little more urgently. A few minutes more and the device begins to play a melody—not an annoying buzz or alarm. Finally, if more time elapses (the intervals are adjustable), the patient receives a text message or a recorded phone call reminding them to pop the GlowCap. The overall effect is a persistent feedback loop urging patients to take their meds.

These nudges have proven to be remarkably effective. In 2010, Partners HealthCare and Harvard Medical School conducted a study that gave GlowCaps to 140 patients on hypertension medications; a control group received nonactivated GlowCap bottles. After three months, adherence in the control group had declined to less than 50 percent, the same dismal rate observed in countless other studies. But patients using GlowCaps did remarkably better: More than 80 percent of them took their pills, a rate that lasted for the duration of the six-month study.

A FEEDBACK LOOP FOR EVERY GOAL

Rypple
Work Better Rypple's online platform helps workers give and receive feedback. Picture it as Facebook for the office: Users can set up private projects, post comments, make their goals public, and even assign badges to one another's profiles. Supervisors can use it to track the progress of their employees, and there's a tool for coaching workers and managers.

Zeo
Sleep Better Zeo's headband measures the brainwaves that are correlated with sleep quality, and a bedside monitor presents users with a score in the morning. The display also shows the amount of time spent in various sleep cycles and how long it took you to fall asleep. If you're sleeping poorly, Zeo's online tools will ask you questions—Do your kids sleep in your bed? Do you have pets? Do you exercise?—then offer up strategies for better sleep.

Belkin Conserve Insight
Conserve Better Belkin makes a simple plug-in device that measures the power consumed by any appliance. It then translates that into cash burned and carbon emitted. The idea is to help consumers budget their energy use by showing them how much their electronics cost.

GreenRoad
Drive Better GreenRoad's in-vehicle display uses GPS and accelerometers to let drivers spot and correct risky or fuel-inefficient driving habits in real time. Red, yellow, and green lights on the dash warn drivers when they're making too many dangerous moves—like accelerating into turns or stopping suddenly. (The data is also posted online so supervisors can review employees' driving and see if certain routes or shifts are more hazardous for their drivers.)

GreenGoose
Live Better GreenGoose uses wireless sensors and simple game mechanics to encourage behaviors like brushing your teeth, riding your bike, and walking your dog. Users get points as rewards for their everyday actions and bonus points for consistency. Starting this fall, people will be able to use those points in simple online games.

The power of the device can perhaps be explained by the fact that the GlowCap incorporates several schools of behavioral change. Vitality has experimented with charging consumers for the product, drawing on the behavioral-economics theory that people are more willing to use something they've paid for. But in other circumstances the company has given users a financial reward for taking their medication, using a carrot-and-stick method-ology. Different models work for different people, Rose says. "We use reminders and social incentives and financial incentives—whatever we can," he says. "We want to provide enough feedback so that it's complementary to people's lives, but not so much that you can't handle the onslaught."

35   Here Rose grapples with an essential challenge of feedback loops: Make them too passive and you'll lose your audience as the data blurs into the back-ground of everyday life. Make them too intrusive and the data turns into noise, which is easily ignored. Borrowing a concept from cognitive psychology called pre-attentive processing, Rose aims for a sweet spot between these extremes, where the information is delivered unobtrusively but noticeably. The best sort of delivery device "isn't cognitively loading at all," he says. "It uses colors, pat-terns, angles, speed—visual cues that don't distract us but remind us." This creates what Rose calls "enchantment." Enchanted objects, he says, don't reg-ister as gadgets or even as technology at all, but rather as friendly tools that beguile us into action. In short, they're magical.

This approach to information delivery is a radical departure from how our health care system usually works. Conventional wisdom holds that medical information won't be heeded unless it sets off alarms. Instead of glowing orbs, we're pummeled with FDA cautions and Surgeon General warnings and front-page reports, all of which serve to heighten our anxiety about our health. This fear-based approach can work—for a while. But fear, it turns out, is a poor cata-lyst for sustained behavioral change. After all, biologically our fear response girds us for short-term threats. If nothing threatening actually happens, the fear dissipates. If this happens too many times, we end up simply dismissing the alarms.

It's worth noting here how profoundly difficult it is for most people to improve their health. Consider: Self-directed smoking-cessation programs typ-ically work for perhaps 5 percent of participants, and weight-loss programs are considered effective if people lose as little as 5 percent of their body weight. Part of the problem is that so much in our lives—the foods we eat, the ads we see, the things our culture celebrates—is driven by feedback loops that sustain bad behaviors. But we can counterprogram this onslaught with another feed-back loop, increasing our odds of changing course.

Though GlowCaps improved compliance by an astonishing 40 percent, feedback loops more typically improve outcomes by about 10 percent compared to traditional methods. That 10 percent figure is surprisingly persistent; it turns up in everything from home energy monitors to smoking cessation programs to those Your Speed signs. At first glance, 10 percent may not seem like a lot. After all, if you're 250 pounds and obese, losing 25 pounds is a start, but your BMI is likely still in the red zone. But it turns out that 10 percent does matter. A lot. An obese 40-year-old man would spare himself three years of hypertension and nearly two years of diabetes by losing 10 percent of his weight. A 10 percent reduction in home energy consumption could reduce carbon emissions by as much as 20 percent (generating energy during peak demand periods creates more pollution than off-peak generation). And those Your Speed signs? It turns out that reducing speeds by 10 percent from 40 to 35 mph would cut fatal injuries by about half.

In other words, 10 percent is something of an inflection point, where lots of great things happen. The results are measurable, the economics calculable. "The value of behavior change is incredibly large: nearly $5,000 a year," says David Rose, citing a CVS pharmacy white paper. "At that rate, we can afford to give every diabetic a connected glucometer. We can give the morbidly obese a Wi-Fi-enabled scale and a pedometer. The value is there; the savings are there. The cost of the sensors is negligible."

So feedback loops work. Why? Why does putting our own data in front of us   40
somehow compel us to act? In part, it's that feedback taps into something core to the human experience, even to our biological origins. Like any organism, humans are self-regulating creatures, with a multitude of systems working to achieve homeostasis. Evolution itself, after all, is a feedback loop, albeit one so elongated as to be imperceptible by an individual. Feedback loops are how we learn, whether we call it trial and error or course correction. In so many areas of life, we succeed when we have some sense of where we stand and some evaluation of our progress. Indeed, we tend to crave this sort of information; it's something we viscerally want to know, good or bad. As Stanford's Bandura put it, "People are proactive, aspiring organisms." Feedback taps into those aspirations.

The visceral satisfaction and even pleasure we get from feedback loops is the organizing principle behind GreenGoose, a startup being hatched by Brian Krejcarek, a Minnesota native who wears a near-constant smile, so enthusiastic is he about the power of cheap sensors. His mission is to stitch feedback loops into the fabric of our daily lives, one sensor at a time.

As Krejcarek describes it, GreenGoose started with a goal not too different from Shwetak Patel's: to measure household consumption of energy. But the company's mission took a turn in 2009, when he experimented with putting one of those ever-cheaper accelerometers on a bicycle wheel. As the wheel rotated, the sensor picked up the movement, and before long Krejcarek had a vision of a grander plan. "I wondered what else we could measure. Where else could we stick these things?" The answer he came up with: everywhere. The GreenGoose concept starts with a sheet of stickers, each containing an accelerometer labeled with a cartoon icon of a familiar household object—a refrigerator handle, a water bottle, a toothbrush, a yard rake. But the secret to GreenGoose isn't the accelerometer; that's a less-than-a-dollar commodity. The key is the algorithm that Krejcarek's team has coded into the chip next to the accelerometer that recognizes a particular pattern of movement. For a toothbrush, it's a rapid back-and-forth that indicates somebody is brushing their teeth. For a water bottle, it's a simple up-and-down that correlates with somebody taking a sip. And so on. In essence, GreenGoose uses sensors to spray feedback loops like atomized perfume throughout our daily life—in our homes, our vehicles, our backyards. "Sensors are these little eyes and ears on whatever we do and how we do it," Krejcarek says. "If a behavior has a pattern, if we can calculate a desired duration and intensity, we can create a system that rewards that behavior and encourages more of it." Thus the first component of a feedback loop: data gathering.

Then comes the second step: relevance. GreenGoose converts the data into points, with a certain amount of action translating into a certain number of points, say 30 seconds of teeth brushing for two points. And here Krejcarek gets noticeably excited. "The points can be used in games on our website," he says. "Think FarmVille but with live data." Krejcarek plans to open the platform to game developers, who he hopes will create games that are simple, easy, and sticky. A few hours of raking leaves might build up points that can be used in a gardening game. And the games induce people to earn more points, which means repeating good behaviors. The idea, Krejcarek says, is to "create a bridge between the real world and the virtual world. This has all got to be fun."

As powerful as the idea appears now, just a few months ago it seemed like a fading pipe dream. Then based in Cambridge, Massachusetts, Krejcarek had nearly run out of cash—not just for his company, but for himself. During the day, he was working on GreenGoose in an office building near the MIT campus—and each night, he'd sneak into the building's air shaft, where he'd stashed an air mattress and some clothes. Then, in late February, he went to the Launch conference in San Francisco, a two-day event where select entrepreneurs get a chance to demo their company to potential funders. Krejcarek hadn't been selected for an onstage demo, but when the conference organizers saw a crowd eyeing his product on the exhibit floor, he was given four minutes to make a presentation. It was one of those only-in-Silicon Valley moments. The crowd "just got it," he recalls. Within days, he had nearly $600,000 in new funding. He moved to San Francisco, rented an apartment—and bought a bed. GreenGoose will release its first product, a kit of sensors that encourages pet owners to play and interact with their dogs, with sensors for dog collar, pet toys, and dog doors, sometime this fall.

45   Part of the excitement around GreenGoose is that the company is so good at "gamification," the much-blogged-about notion that game elements like points or levels can be applied to various aspects of our lives. Gamification is exciting because it promises to make the hard stuff in life fun—just sprinkle a little videogame magic and suddenly a burden turns into bliss. But as happens with fads, gamification is both overhyped and misunderstood. It is too often just a shorthand for badges or points, like so many gold stars on a spelling test. But just as no number of gold stars can trick children into thinking that yesterday's quiz was fun, game mechanics, to work, must be an informing principle, not a veneer.

With its savvy application of feedback loops, though, GreenGoose is onto more than just the latest fad. The company represents the fruition of a long-promised technological event horizon: the Internet of Things, in which a sensor-rich world measures our every action. This vision, championed by Kevin Ashton at Belkin, Sandy Pentland at MIT, and Bruce Sterling . . . has long had the whiff of vaporware, something promised by futurists but never realized. But as GreenGoose, Belkin, and other companies begin to use sensors to deploy feedback loops throughout our lives, we can finally see the potential of a sensor-rich environment. The Internet of Things isn't about the things; it's about us.

For now, the reality still isn't as sexy as the visions. Stickers on toothbrushes and plugs in wall sockets aren't exactly disappearing technology. But maybe requiring people to do a little work—to stick accelerometers around their house or plug a device into a wall socket—is just enough of a nudge to get our brains engaged in the prospect for change. Perhaps it's good to have the infrastructure of feedback loops just a bit visible now, before they disappear into our environments altogether, so that they can serve as a subtle reminder that we have something to change, that we can do better—and that the tools for doing better are rapidly, finally, turning up all around us.

MLA CITATION

Goetz, Thomas. "Harnessing the Power of Feedback Loops." 2011. *The Norton Reader: An Anthology of Nonfiction*. Ed. Melissa A. Goldthwaite et al. 14th ed. New York: Norton, 2016. 587–99. Print.

QUESTIONS

1. In paragraph 9, Thomas Goetz describes the four stages of the feedback loop. Look again at his definition and then find how those stages work in several of the inventions he describes here. How does the repetition of the loop several times across the essay affect your understanding of the process?

2. Goetz is careful to distinguish between monitors that send information to the consumer from those that send information to the government or to a company. Are there any instances in which it might be appropriate for the government or a private company to monitor individual consumption (e.g., of water during a drought, of unhealthy food after surgery)? Why or why not?

3. Think of a behavior or habit that you would like to change and write an essay in which you describe an invention to encourage that change based on the principle of the feedback loop.

TASNEEM RAJA *Is Coding the New Literacy?*

I N THE WINTER OF 2011, a handful of software engineers landed in Boston just ahead of a crippling snowstorm. They were there as part of Code for America, a program that places idealistic young coders and designers in city halls across the country for a year. They'd planned to spend it building a new website for Boston's public schools, but within days of their arrival, the city all but shut down and the coders were stuck fielding calls in the city's snow emergency center.

In such snowstorms, firefighters can waste precious minutes finding and digging out hydrants. A city employee told the CFA team that the planning department had a list of street addresses for Boston's 13,000 hydrants. "We figured, 'Surely someone on the block with a shovel would volunteer if they knew where to look,'" says Erik Michaels-Ober, one of the CFA coders. So they got out their laptops.

Now, Boston has adoptahydrant.org, a simple website that lets residents "adopt" hydrants across the city. The site displays a map of little hydrant icons. Green ones have been claimed by someone willing to dig them out after a storm, red ones are still available—500 hydrants were adopted last winter.

Maybe that doesn't seem like a lot, but consider what the city pays to keep it running: $9 a month in hosting costs. "I figured that even if it only led to a few fire hydrants being shoveled out, that could be the difference between life or death in a fire, so it was worth doing," Michaels-Ober says. And because the CFA team open-sourced the code, meaning they made it freely available for anyone to copy and modify, other cities can adapt it for practically pennies. It has been deployed in Providence, Anchorage, and Chicago. A Honolulu city employee heard about Adopt-a-Hydrant after cutbacks slashed his budget, and now Honolulu has Adopt-a-Siren, where volunteers can sign up to check for dead batteries in tsunami sirens across the city. In Oakland, it's Adopt-a-Drain.

5 Sounds great, right? These simple software solutions could save lives, and they were cheap and quick to build. Unfortunately, most cities will never get a CFA team, and most can't afford to keep a stable of sophisticated programmers in their employ, either. For that matter, neither can many software companies in Silicon Valley; the talent wars have gotten so bad that even brand-name tech firms have been forced to offer employees a bonus of upwards of $10,000 if they help recruit an engineer.

In fact, even as the Department of Labor predicts the nation will add 1.2 million new computer science–related jobs by 2022, we're graduating proportionately fewer computer science majors than we did in the 1980s, and the number

Published in Mother Jones (2014), *a magazine and "nonprofit news organization that specializes in investigative, political, and social justice reporting."*

of students signing up for Advanced Placement computer science has flatlined.

There's a whole host of complicated reasons why, from boring curricula to a lack of qualified teachers to the fact that in most states computer science doesn't count toward graduation requirements. But should we worry? After all, anyone can learn to code after taking a few fun, interactive lessons at sites like Codecademy, as a flurry of articles in every-

Screenshot from Adopt-a-Hydrant.

thing from *TechCrunch* to *Slate* have claimed. (Michael Bloomberg[1] pledged to enroll at Codecademy in 2012.) Twelve million people have watched a video from Code.org in which celebrities like NBA All-Star Chris Bosh and will.i.am pledged to spend an hour learning code, a notion endorsed by President Obama, who urged the nation: "Don't just play on your phone—program it."

So you might be forgiven for thinking that learning code is a short, breezy ride to a lush startup job with a foosball table and free kombucha, especially given all the hype about billion-dollar companies launched by self-taught wunderkinds (with nary a mention of the private tutors and coding camps that helped some of them get there). The truth is, code—if what we're talking about is the chops you'd need to qualify for a programmer job—is hard, and lots of people would find those jobs tedious and boring.

But let's back up a step: What if learning to code weren't actually the most important thing? It turns out that rather than increasing the number of kids who can crank out thousands of lines of JavaScript, we first need to boost the number who understand what code can do. As the cities that have hosted Code for America teams will tell you, the greatest contribution the young programmers bring isn't the software they write. It's the way they *think*. It's a principle called "computational thinking," and knowing all of the Java syntax in the world won't help if you can't think of good ways to apply it.

Unfortunately, the way computer science is currently taught in high school 10 tends to throw students into the programming deep end, reinforcing the notion that code is just for coders, not artists or doctors or librarians. But there is good news: Researchers have been experimenting with new ways of teaching computer science, with intriguing results. For one thing, they've seen that leading with computational thinking instead of code itself, and helping students imagine how being computer savvy could help them in any career, boosts the number

1. Businessman and three-term mayor of New York City.

THE PIPELINE PROBLEM

Among AP courses taken last year, computer science is near the bottom.

English	862,000
Calculus	387,000
Spanish	154,000
Chemistry	140,000
European history	110,000
Computer science	31,000

Only 20 states count computer science toward graduation requirements in math or science.

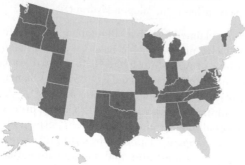

Sources: College Board, Computer Science Teachers Association

of girls and kids of color taking—and sticking with—computer science. Upending our notions of what it means to interface with computers could help democratize the biggest engine of wealth since the Industrial Revolution.

So what is computational thinking? If you've ever improvised dinner, pat yourself on the back: You've engaged in some light CT.

There are those who open the pantry to find a dusty bag of legumes and some sad-looking onions and think, "Lentil soup!" and those who think, "Chinese takeout." A practiced home cook can mentally sketch the path from raw ingredients to a hot meal, imagining how to substitute, divide, merge, apply external processes (heat, stirring), and so on until she achieves her end. Where the rest of us see a dead end, she sees the potential for something new.

If seeing the culinary potential in raw ingredients is like computational thinking, you might think of a software algorithm as a kind of recipe: a step-by-step guide on how to take a bunch of random ingredients and start layering them together in certain quantities, for certain amounts of time, until they produce the outcome you had in mind.

Like a good algorithm, a good recipe follows some basic principles. Ingredients are listed first, so you can collect them before you start, and there's some logic in the way they are listed: olive oil before cumin because it goes in the pan first. Steps are presented in order, not a random jumble, with staggered tasks so that you're chopping veggies while waiting for water to boil. A good recipe spells out precisely what size of dice or temperature you're aiming for. It tells you to look for signs that things are working correctly at each stage—the custard should coat the back of a spoon. Opportunities for customization are marked—use twice the milk for a creamier texture—but if any ingredients are absolutely crucial, the recipe makes sure you know it. If you need to do something over and over—add four eggs, one at a time, beating after each—those tasks are boiled down to one simple instruction.

Much like cooking, computational thinking begins with a feat of imagination, the ability to envision how digitized information—ticket sales, customer addresses, the temperature in your fridge, the sequence of events to start a car engine, anything that can be sorted, counted, or tracked—could be combined and changed into something new by applying various computational techniques. From there, it's all about "decomposing" big tasks into a logical series of smaller steps, just like a recipe.

Those techniques include a lot of testing along the way to make sure things are working. The culinary principle of *mise en place* is akin to the computational principle of sorting: organize your data first, and you'll cut down on search time later. Abstraction is like the concept of "mother sauces" in French cooking (béchamel, tomato, hollandaise), building blocks to develop and reuse in hundreds of dishes. There's iteration: running a process over and over until you get a desired result. The principle of parallel processing makes use of all available downtime (think: making the salad while the roast is cooking). Like a good recipe, good software is really clear about what you can tweak and what you can't. It's explicit. Computers don't get nuance; they need everything spelled out for them.

Put another way: Not every cook is a David Chang, not every writer is a Jane Austen, and not every computational thinker is a Guido van Rossum, the inventor of the influential Python programming language. But just as knowing how to scramble an egg or write an email makes life easier, so too will a grasp of computational thinking. Yet the "learn to code!" camp may have set people on the uphill path of mastering C++ syntax instead of encouraging all of us to think a little more computationally.

The happy truth is, if you get the fundamentals about how computers think, and how humans can talk to them in a language the machines understand, you can imagine a project that a computer could do, and discuss it in a way that will make sense to an actual programmer. Because as programmers will tell you, the building part is often not the hardest part: It's figuring out what to build. "Unless you can think about the ways computers can solve problems, you can't even know how to ask the questions that need to be answered," says Annette Vee, a University of Pittsburgh professor who studies the spread of computer science literacy.

Indeed, some powerful computational solutions take just a few lines of code—or no code at all. Consider this lo-fi example: In 1854, a London physician named John Snow helped squelch a cholera outbreak that had killed 616 residents. Brushing aside the prevailing theory of the disease—deadly miasma—he surveyed relatives of the dead about their daily routines. A map he made connected the disease to drinking habits: tall stacks of black lines, each representing a death, grew around a water pump on Broad Street in Soho that happened to be near a leaking cesspool. His theory: The disease was in the water. Classic principles of computational thinking came into play here, including

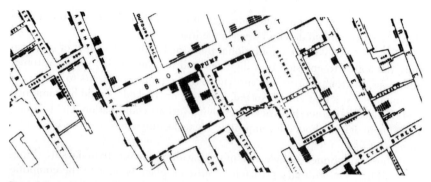

Detail from *On the Mode of Communication of Cholera,* 1854.

merging two datasets to reveal something new (locations of deaths plus locations of water pumps), running the same process over and over and testing the results, and pattern recognition. The pump was closed, and the outbreak subsided.

20   Or take Adopt-a-Hydrant. Under the hood, it isn't a terribly sophisticated piece of software. What's ingenious is simply that someone knew enough to say: Here's a database of hydrant locations, here is a universe of people willing to help, let's match them up. The computational approach is rooted in seeing the world as a series of puzzles, ones you can break down into smaller chunks and solve bit by bit through logic and deductive reasoning. That's why Jeannette Wing, a VP of research at Microsoft who popularized the term "computational thinking," says it's a shame to think CT is just for programmers. "Computational thinking involves solving problems, designing systems, and understanding human behavior," she writes in a publication of the Association for Computing Machinery. Those are handy skills for everybody, not just computer scientists.

In other words, computational thinking opens doors. For while it may seem premature to claim that today every kid needs to code, it's clear that they're increasingly surrounded by opportunities to code—opportunities that the children of the privileged are already seizing. The parents of Facebook founder Mark Zuckerberg got him a private computer tutor when he was in middle school. Last year, 13,000 people chipped in more than $600,000 via Kickstarter for their own limited-edition copy of Robot Turtles, a board game that teaches programming basics to kids as young as three. There are plenty of free, kid-oriented code-learning sites—like Scratch, a programming language for children developed at MIT—but parents and kids in places like San Francisco or Austin are more likely to know they exist.

Computer scientists have been warning for decades that understanding code will one day be as essential as reading and writing. If they're right, understanding the importance of computational thinking can't be limited to the elite, not if we want some semblance of a democratic society. Self-taught auteurs will always be part of the equation, but to produce tech-savvy citizens "at scale," to borrow an industry term, the heavy lifting will happen in public school classrooms. Increasingly, to have a good shot at a good job, you'll need to be code literate.

"Code literate." Sounds nice, but what does it mean? And where does literacy end and fluency begin? The best way to think about that is to look to the history of literacy itself.

Reading and writing have become what researchers have called "interiorized" or "infrastructural," a technology baked so deeply into everyday human life that we're never surprised to encounter it. It's the main medium through which we connect, via not only books and papers, but text messages and the voting booth, medical forms and shopping sites. If a child makes it to adulthood without being able to read or write, we call that a societal failure.

Yet for thousands of years writing was the preserve of the professional scribes employed by the elite. So what moved it to the masses? In Europe at least, writes literacy researcher Vee, the tipping point was the Domesday Book, an 11th-century survey of landowners that's been called the oldest public record in England.

Commissioned by William the Conqueror to take stock of what his new subjects held in terms of acreage, tenants, and livestock so as to better tax them, royal scribes fanned across the countryside taking detailed notes during in-person interviews. It was like a hands-on demo on the efficiencies of writing, and it proved contagious. Despite skepticism—writing was hard, and maybe involved black magic—other institutions started putting it to use. Landowners and vendors required patrons and clients to sign deeds and receipts, with an "X" if nothing else. Written records became admissible in court. Especially once Johannes Gutenberg invented the printing press, writing seeped into more and

25

A page from the Domesday Book.

more aspects of life, no longer a rarefied skill restricted to a cloistered class of aloof scribes but a function of everyday society.

Fast forward to 19th-century America, and it'd be impossible to walk down a street without being bombarded with written information, from newspapers to street signs to store displays; in the homes of everyday people, personal letters and account ledgers could be found. "The technology of writing became infrastructural," Vee writes in her paper "Understanding Computer Programming As a Literacy." "Those who could not read text began to be recast as 'illiterate' and power began to shift towards those who could." Teaching children how to read became a civic and moral imperative. Literacy rates soared over the next century, fostered through religious campaigns, the nascent public school system, and the at-home labor of many mothers.

Of course, not everyone was invited in immediately: Illiteracy among women, slaves, and people of color was often outright encouraged, sometimes even legally mandated. But today, while only some consider themselves to be "writers," practically everybody reads and writes every day. It's hard to imagine there was ever widespread resistance to universal literacy.

So how does the history of computing compare? Once again, says Vee, it starts with a census. In 1880, a Census Bureau statistician, Herman Hollerith, saw that the system of collecting and sorting surveys by hand was buckling under the weight of a growing population. He devised an electric tabulating machine, and generations of these "Hollerith machines" were used by the bureau until the 1950s, when the first commercial mainframe, the UNIVAC, was developed with a government research grant. "The first successful civilian computer," it was a revolution in computing technology: Unlike the "dumb" Hollerith machine and its cousins, which ran on punch cards, vacuum tubes, and other mechanical inputs that had to be manually entered over and over again, the UNIVAC had memory. It could store instructions, in the form of programs, and remember earlier calculations for later use.[2]

30 Once the UNIVAC was unveiled, research institutions and the private sector began clamoring for mainframes of their own. The scribes of the computer age, the early programmers who had worked on the first large-scale computing projects for the government during the war, took jobs at places like Bell Labs, the airline industry, banks, and research universities. "The spread of the texts from the central government to the provinces is echoed in the way that the programmers who cut their teeth on major government-funded software projects then circulated out into smaller industries, disseminating their knowledge of code writing further," Vee writes. Just as England had gone from oral tradition

2. The evolution of communication technologies has always been an issue of memory. For thousands of years, the oral tradition had enough storage space to house the expanse of human records and information. As communities got bigger, oral tradition started maxing out. So a new technology sprang up, one that could distill thought into a series of symbolic scratches that could be packaged up, transported, and recompiled by the user into language and thought. But while books have immensely greater RAM than a song poem, a computer offers exponentially more capacity than either of these [Raja's note].

Grace Hopper led the team that developed the UNIVAC, the first commercial computer.

to written record after the Domesday Book, the United States in the 1960s and '70s shifted from written to computational record.

The 1980s made computers personal, and today it's impossible not to engage in conversations powered by code, albeit code that's hidden beneath the interfaces of our devices. But therein lies a new problem: The easy interface creates confusion around what it means to be "computer literate." Interacting with an app is very different from making or tweaking or understanding one, and opportunities to do the latter remain the province of a specialized elite. In many ways, we're still in the "scribal stage" of the computer age.

But the tricky thing about literacy, Vee says, is that it begets more literacy. It happened with writing: At first, laypeople could get by signing their names with an "X." But the more people used reading and writing, the more was required of them.

We can already see code leaking into seemingly far-removed fields. Hospital specialists collect data from the heartbeat monitors of day-old infants, and run algorithms to spot babies likely to have respiratory failure. Netflix is a gigantic experiment in statistical machine learning. Legislators are being challenged to understand encryption and relational databases during hearings on the NSA.

The most exciting advances in most scientific and technical fields already involve big datasets, powerful algorithms, and people who know how to work with both. But that's increasingly true in almost any profession. English literature and computer science researchers fed Agatha Christie's oeuvre into a computer, ran a textual-analysis program, and discovered that her vocabulary shrank significantly in her final books. They drew from the work of brain researchers and put forth a new hypothesis: Christie suffered from Alzheimer's. "More and more, no matter what you're interested in, being computationally savvy will allow you to do a better job," says Jan Cuny, a leading CS researcher at the National Science Foundation (NSF).

35   It may be hard to swallow the idea that coding could ever be an everyday activity on par with reading and writing in part because it looks so foreign (what's with all the semicolons and carets)? But remember that it took hundreds of years to settle on the writing conventions we take for granted today: Early spellings of words—*Whan that Aprille with his shoures soote*[3]—can seem as foreign to modern readers as today's code snippets do to nonprogrammers. Compared to the thousands of years writing has had to go from notched sticks to glossy magazines, digital technology has, in 60 years, evolved exponentially faster.

Our elementary-school language arts teachers didn't drill the alphabet into our brains anticipating Facebook or WhatsApp or any of the new ways we now interact with written material. Similarly, exposing today's third-graders to a dose of code may mean that at 30 they retain enough to ask the right questions of a programmer, working in a language they've never seen on a project they could never have imagined.

One day last year, Neil Fraser, a young software engineer at Google, showed up unannounced at a primary school in the coastal Vietnamese city of Da Nang. Did the school have computer classes, he wanted to know, and could he sit in? A school official glanced at Fraser's Google business card and led him into a classroom of fifth-graders paired up at PCs while a teacher looked on. What Fraser saw on their screens came as a bit of a shock.

Fraser, who was in Da Nang visiting his girlfriend's family, works in Google's education department in Mountain View, teaching JavaScript to new recruits. His interest in computer science education often takes him to high schools around the Bay Area, where he tells students that code is fun and interesting, and learning it can open doors after graduation.

The fifth-graders in Da Nang were doing exercises in Logo, a simple program developed at MIT in the 1970s to introduce children to programming. A turtle-shaped avatar blinked on their screens and the kids fed it simple commands in Logo's language, making it move around, leaving a colored trail behind. Stars, hexagons, and ovals bloomed on the monitors.

40   Fraser, who learned Logo when the program was briefly popular in American elementary schools, recognized the exercise. It was a lesson in loops, a bedrock programming concept in which you tell the machine to do the same thing over and over again, until you get a desired result. "A quick comparison with the United States is in order," Fraser wrote later in a blog post. At Galileo Academy, San Francisco's magnet school for science and technology, he'd found juniors in a computer science class struggling with the concept of loops. The fifth-graders in Da Nang had outpaced upperclassmen at one of the Bay Area's most tech-savvy high schools.

---

3. First line of the General Prologue to *The Canterbury Tales* (1475) by Geoffrey Chaucer.

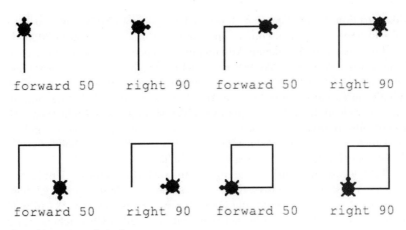

forward 50   right 90   forward 50   right 90

forward 50   right 90   forward 50   right 90

Simple commands in Logo.

Another visit to an 11th-grade classroom in Ho Chi Minh City revealed students coding their way through a logic puzzle embedded in a digital maze. "After returning to the US, I asked a senior engineer how he'd rank this question on a Google interview," Fraser wrote. "Without knowing the source of the question, he judged that this would be in the top third."

Early code education isn't just happening in Vietnamese schools. Estonia, the birthplace of Skype, rolled out a countrywide programming-centric curriculum for students as young as six in 2012. In September, the United Kingdom will launch a mandatory computing syllabus for all students ages 5 to 16.

Meanwhile, even as US enrollment in almost all other STEM (science, technology, engineering, and math) fields has grown over the last 20 years, computer science has actually *lost* students, dropping from 25 percent of high school students earning credits in computer science to only 19 percent by 2009, according to the National Center for Education Statistics.

"Our kids are competing with kids from countries that have made computer science education a No. 1 priority," says Chris Stephenson, the former head of the Computer Science Teachers Association (CSTA). Unlike countries with federally mandated curricula, in the United States computer lesson plans can vary widely between states and even between schools in the same district. "It's almost like you have to go one school at a time," Stephenson says. In fact, currently only 20 states and Washington, DC, allow computer science to count toward core graduation requirements in math or science, and not one requires students to take a computer science course to graduate. Nor do the new Common Core standards, a push to make K–12 curricula more uniform across states, include computer science requirements.

It's no surprise, then, that the AP computer science course is among the College Board's least popular offerings; last year, almost four times more students tested in geography (114,000) than computer science (31,000). And most

45

kids don't even get to make that choice; only 17 percent of US high schools that have advanced placement courses do so in CS. It was 20 percent in 2005.

For those who do take an AP computer science class—a yearlong course in Java, which is sort of like teaching cooking by showing how to assemble a KitchenAid—it won't count toward core graduation requirements in most states. What's more, many counselors see AP CS as a potential GPA ding, and urge students to load up on known quantities like AP English or US history. "High school kids are overloaded already," says Joanna Goode, a leading researcher at the University of Oregon's education department, and making time for courses that don't count toward anything is a hard sell.

In any case, it's hard to find anyone to teach these classes. Unlike fields such as English and chemistry, there isn't a standard path for aspiring CS teach-ers in grad school or continuing education programs. And thanks to wildly inconsistent certification rules between states, certified CS teachers can get stuck teaching math or library sciences if they move. Meanwhile, software whiz-zes often find the lure of the startup salary much stronger than the call of the classroom, and anyone who tires of Silicon Valley might find that its "move fast and break things" mantra doesn't transfer neatly to pedagogy.

And while many kids have mad skills in movie editing or Photoshopping, such talents can lull parents into thinking they're learning real computing. "We teach our kids how to be consumers of technology, not creators of technology," notes the NSF's Cuny.

Or, as Cory Doctorow, an editor of the technology-focused blog *Boing Boing*, put it in a manifesto titled "Why I Won't Buy an iPad": "Buying an iPad for your kids isn't a means of jump-starting the realization that the world is yours to take apart and reassemble; it's a way of telling your offspring that even changing the batteries is something you have to leave to the professionals."

50   But school administrators know that gleaming banks of shiny new machines go a long way in impressing parents and school boards. Last summer, the Los Angeles Unified School District set aside a billion dollars to buy an iPad for all 640,000 children in the district. To pay for the program, the district dipped into school construction bonds. Still, some parents and principals told the *Los Angeles Times* they were thrilled about it. "It gives us the sense of hope that these kids are being looked after," said one parent.[4]

Sure, some schools are woefully behind on the hardware equation, but according to a 2010 federal study, only 3 percent of teachers nationwide lacked daily access to a computer in their classroom, and the nationwide ratio of stu-dents to school computers was a little more than 5-to-1. As to whether kids have computers at home—that doesn't seem to make much difference in overall per-formance, either. A study from the National Bureau of Economic Research reviewed the grades, test scores, homework, and attendance of California 6th- to 10th-graders who were randomly given computers to use at home for the first time. A year later, the study found, nothing happened. Test scores, grades, dis-

4. The kids did quickly learn to hack their iPads, so there's some hope for actual inven-tiveness [Raja's note].

ciplinary actions, time spent on homework: None of it went up or down—except the kids did log a lot more time playing games.

One sunny morning last summer, 40 Los Angeles teachers sat in a warm classroom at UCLA playing with crayons, flash cards, and Legos. They were students again for a week, at a workshop on how to teach computer science. Which meant that first they had to learn computer science.

The lesson was in binary numbers, or how to write any number using just two digits. "Computers can only talk in ones and zeros," explained the instructor, a fellow teacher who'd taken the same course. The course is funded by the National Science Foundation, and so is the experimental new blueprint it trains teachers to use, called Exploring Computer Science (ECS). "You gotta talk to them in their language."

STUCK IN THE SHALLOW END

Education, Race, and Computing

JANE MARGOLIS

Rachel Estrella
Joanna Goode
Jennifer Jellison Holme
Kimberly Nao

Made sense at first, but when it came to turning the number 1,250 into binary, the class started falling apart. At one table, two female teachers politely endured a long, wrong explanation from an older male colleague. A teacher behind them mumbled, "I don't get it," pushed his flash cards away, and counted the minutes to lunchtime. A table of guys in their 30s was loudly sprinting toward an answer, and a minute later the bearded white guy at the head of their table, i.e., the one most resembling a classic programmer, shot his hand up with the answer and an explanation of how he got there: "Basically what you do is, you just turn it into an algorithm." Blank stares suggested few colleagues knew what an algorithm was—in this case a simple, step-by-step process for turning a number into binary. (The answer, if you're curious, is 010011100010.)

This lesson—which by the end of the day clicked for most in the class— 55
might seem like most people's image of CS, but the course these teachers are learning to teach couldn't look more different from classic AP computer science. Much of what's taught in ECS is about the why of computer science, not just the how. There are discussions and writing assignments on

everything from personal privacy in the age of Big Data to the ethics of robot labor to how data analysis could help curb problems like school bullying. Instead of rote Java learning, it offers lots of logic games and puzzles that put the focus on computing, not computers. In fact, students hardly touch a computer for the first 12 weeks.

"Our curriculum doesn't lead with programming or code," says Jane Margolis, a senior researcher at UCLA who helped design the ECS curriculum and whose book *Stuck in the Shallow End: Education, Race, and Computing* provides much of the theory behind the lesson plans. "There are so many stereotypes associated with coding, and often it doesn't give the broader picture of what the field is about. The research shows you want to contextualize, show how computer science is relevant to their lives." ECS lessons ask students to imagine how they'd make use of various algorithms as a chef, or a carpenter, or a teacher, how they could analyze their own snack habits to eat better, and how their city council could use data to create cleaner, safer streets.

The ECS curriculum is now offered to 2,400 students at 31 Los Angeles public high schools and a smattering of schools in other cities, notably Chicago and Washington, DC. Before writing it, Margolis and fellow researchers spent three years visiting schools across the Los Angeles area—overcrowded urban ones and plush suburban ones—to understand why few girls and students of color were taking computer science. At a tony school in West LA that the researchers dubbed "Canyon Charter High," they noticed students of color traveling long distances to get to school, meaning they couldn't stick

PERCENTAGE OF STUDENTS WHO CONSIDER A CAREER IN COMPUTERS A "GOOD CHOICE" FOR SOMEONE LIKE THEM:

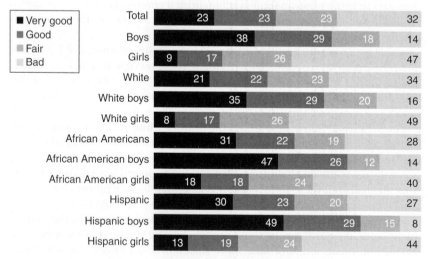

Association for Computing Machinery, WGBH Educational Foundation

around for techie extracurriculars or to simply hang out with like-minded students.

Equally daunting were the stereotypes. Take Janet, the sole black girl in Canyon's AP computer science class, who told the researchers she signed up for the course in part "because we [African American females] were so limited in the world, you know, and just being able to be in a class where I can represent who I am and my culture was really important to me." When she had a hard time keeping up—like most kids in the class—the teacher, a former software developer who, researchers noted, tended to let a few white boys monopolize her attention, pulled Janet aside and suggested she drop the class, explaining that when it comes to computational skills, you either "have it or don't have it."

Research shows that girls tend to pull away from STEM subjects—including computer science—around middle school, while rates of boys in these classes stay steady. Fortunately, says Margolis, there's evidence that tweaking the way computer science is introduced can make a difference. A 2009 study tested various messages about computer science with college-bound teens. It found that explaining how programming skills can be used to "do good"—connect with one's community, make a difference on big social problems like pollution and health care—reverberated strongly with girls. Far less successful were messages about getting a good job or being "in the driver's seat" of technological innovation—i.e., the dominant cultural narratives about why anyone would learn to code.

WHAT WORD COMES TO MIND WHEN YOU SEE OR HEAR THE WORD "COMPUTING"?

Girls:

"typing"

"math"

"boredom"

"nerd"

Boys:

"video games"

"design"

"electronics"

"solving problems"

"interesting"

Association for Computing Machinery, WGBH Educational Foundation

"For me, computer science can be used to implement social change," says Kim Merino, a self-described "social-justice-obsessed queer Latina nerd history teacher" who decided to take the ECS training a couple of years ago. Now, she teaches the class to middle and high schoolers at the UCLA Community School, an experimental new public K–12 school. "I saw this as a new frontier in the social-justice fight," she says. "I tell my students, 'I don't necessarily want to teach you how to get rich. I want to teach you to be a good citizen.'"

Merino's father was an aerospace engineer for Lockheed Martin. So you might think adapting to CS would be easy for her. Not quite. Most of the teachers she trained with were men. "Out of seven women, there were two of color. Honestly, I was so scared. But now, I take that to my classroom. At this point my class is half girls, mostly Latina and Korean, and they still come into my class all nervous and intimidated. My job is to get them past all of that, get them excited about all the things they could do in their lives with programming."

60

HOW HOMOGENEOUS IS THE COMPUTER WORKFORCE?

Percentage of today's software workforce that is...

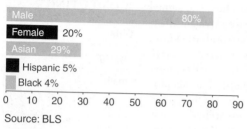

Source: BLS

Percentage of computer science majors who were women:

37 percent in 1985

18 percent in 2009

18 percent in 2012

Department of Education

Merino has spent the last four years teaching kids of color growing up in inner cities to imagine what they could do with programming—not as a replacement for, but as part of their dreams of growing up to be doctors or painters or social workers. But Merino's partner's gentle ribbings about how they'd ever start a family on a teacher's salary eventually became less gentle. She just took a job as director of professional development at CodeHS, an educational startup in San Francisco.

It was a little more than a century ago that literacy became universal in Western Europe and the United States. If computational skills are on the same trajectory, how much are we hurting our economy—and our democracy—by not moving faster to make them universal?

There's the talent squeeze, for one thing. Going by the number of computer science majors graduating each year, we're producing less than half of the talent needed to fill the Labor Department's job projections. Women currently make up 20 percent of the software workforce, blacks and Latinos around 5 percent each. Getting more of them in the computing pipeline is simply good business sense.

65　　　It would also create a future for computing that more accurately reflects its past. A female mathematician named Ada Lovelace wrote the first algorithm ever intended to be executed on a machine in 1843. The term "programmer" was used during World War II to describe the women who worked on the world's first large-scale electronic computer, the ENIAC machine, which used calculus to come up with tables to improve artillery accuracy.[5] In 1949, Rear Adm. Grace Hopper helped develop the UNIVAC, the first general-purpose computer, a.k.a. a mainframe, and in 1959 her work led to the development of COBOL, the first programming language written for commercial use.

5. Six "ENIAC girls" did most of the programming, but until recently their work was all but forgotten. Male engineers worked on ENIAC's hardware, reflecting that until the 1950s, coding was considered clerical—even though it involved higher math and applied logic. It was recast as a masculine pursuit as projects like Grace Hopper's UNIVAC demonstrated its promise [Raja's note].

Black Girls Code has introduced more than 1,500 girls to programming.

Excluding huge swaths of the population also means prematurely killing off untold ideas and innovations that could make everyone's lives better. Because while the rash of meal delivery and dating apps designed by today's mostly young, male, urban programmers are no doubt useful, a broader base of talent might produce more for society than a frictionless Saturday night.[6]

And there's evidence that diverse teams produce better products. A study of 200,000 IT patents found that "patents invented by mixed-gender teams are cited [by other inventors] more often than patents invented by female-only or male-only" teams. The authors suggest one possibility for this finding may be "that gender diversity leads to more innovative research and discovery." (Similarly, research papers across the sciences that are coauthored by racially diverse teams are more likely to be cited by other researchers than those of all-white teams.)

Fortunately, there's evidence that girls exposed to very basic programming concepts early in life are more likely to major in computer science in college. That's why approaches like Margolis' ECS course, steeped in research on how to get and keep girls and other underrepresented minorities in computer science class, as well as groups like Black Girls Code, which offers affordable code boot camps to school-age girls in places like Detroit and Memphis, may prove appealing to the industry at large.

"Computer science innovation is changing our entire lives, from the professional to the personal, even our free time," Margolis says. "I want a whole diversity of people sitting at the design table, bringing different sensibilities and values and experiences to this innovation. Asking, 'Is this good for this world? Not good for the world? What are the implications going to be?'"

6. For example, Janet Emerson Bashen was the first black woman to receive a software patent, in 2006, for an app to better process Equal Employment Opportunity claims [Raja's note].

70   We make kids learn about biology, literature, history, and geometry with the promise that navigating the wider world will be easier for their efforts. It'll be harder and harder not to include computing on that list. Decisions made by a narrow demographic of technocrat elites are already shaping their lives, from privacy and social currency, to career choices and how they spend their free time.

Margolis' program and others like it are a good start toward spreading computational literacy, but they need a tremendous amount of help to scale up to the point where it's not such a notable loss when a teacher like Kim Merino leaves the profession. What's needed to make that happen is for people who may never learn a lick of code themselves to help shape the tech revolution the old-fashioned way, through educational reform and funding for schools and volunteer literacy crusades. Otherwise, we're all doomed—well, most of us, anyway—to be stuck in the Dark Ages.

MLA CITATION

Raja, Tasneem. "Is Coding the New Literacy?" 2014. *The Norton Reader: An Anthology of Nonfiction.* Ed. Melissa A. Goldthwaite et al. 14th ed. New York: Norton, 2016. 600–16. Print.

QUESTIONS

1. Tasneem Raja covers many topics—the difference between coding and computational literacy, the history of learning to write, and the importance of encouraging women to remain in STEM fields. Make a list of the broad topics she covers and discuss how they are related to each other.

2. The online version of this essay (at MotherJones.com) included dozens of hyperlinks, but only four footnotes. Go to the online version and follow a few of Raja's links. What is the difference between the information she chose to footnote and the information she linked to?

3. According to Raja, what are some of the main obstacles to teaching coding and computational literacy? Do you think coding should be an academic requirement? Why or why not?

4. Write an essay about your experience learning to code. (If you have never tried, spend a few hours on a beginner's site.) How is learning to code like learning to write? How is it different?

5. Research one of the pioneering women in computer science and computer education whom Raja mentions (paragraphs 56, 60, 65) and write a paper on that woman's contribution to the field.

FRED VOGELSTEIN *And Then Steve Said,*
"Let There Be an iPhone"

THE 55 MILES from Campbell to San Francisco make for one of the nicest commutes anywhere. The journey mostly zips along the Junipero Serra Freeway, a grand and remarkably empty highway that abuts the east side of the Santa Cruz Mountains. It is one of the best places in Silicon Valley to spot a start-up tycoon speed-testing his Ferrari and one of the worst places for cellphone reception. For Andy Grignon, it was therefore the perfect place for him to be alone with his thoughts early on Jan. 8, 2007.

This wasn't Grignon's typical route to work. He was a senior engineer at Apple in Cupertino, the town just west of Campbell. His morning drive typically covered seven miles and took exactly 15 minutes. But today was different. He was going to watch his boss, Steve Jobs, make history at the Macworld trade show in San Francisco. Apple fans had for years begged Jobs to put a cellphone inside their iPods so they could stop carrying two devices in their pockets. Jobs was about to fulfill that wish. Grignon and some colleagues would spend the night at a nearby hotel, and around 10 a.m. the following day they—along with the rest of the world—would watch Jobs unveil the first iPhone.

But as Grignon drove north, he didn't feel excited. He felt terrified. Most onstage product demonstrations in Silicon Valley are canned. The thinking goes, why let bad Internet or cellphone connections ruin an otherwise good presentation? But Jobs insisted on live presentations. It was one of the things that made them so captivating. Part of his legend was that noticeable product-demo glitches almost never happened. But for those in the background, like Grignon, few parts of the job caused more stress.

Grignon was the senior manager in charge of all the radios in the iPhone. This is a big job. Cellphones do innumerable useful things for us today, but at their most basic, they are fancy two-way radios. Grignon was in charge of the equipment that allowed the phone to be a phone. If the device didn't make calls, or didn't connect with Bluetooth headsets or Wi-Fi setups, Grignon had to answer for it. As one of the iPhone's earliest engineers, he'd dedicated two and a half years of his life—often seven days a week—to the project.

Grignon had been part of the iPhone rehearsal team at Apple and later at   5
the presentation site in San Francisco's Moscone Center. He had rarely seen Jobs make it all the way through his 90-minute show without a glitch. Jobs had been practicing for five days, yet even on the last day of rehearsals the iPhone was still randomly dropping calls, losing its Internet connection, freezing or simply shutting down.

Published in the New York Times *(2013) and adapted from "The Moon Mission," the first chapter of Fred Vogelstein's book,* Dogfight: How Apple and Google Went to War and Started a Revolution *(2013).*

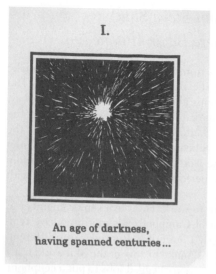

I.

An age of darkness,
having spanned centuries...

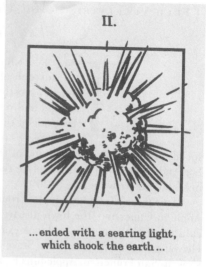

II.

...ended with a searing light,
which shook the earth...

"At first it was just really cool to be at rehearsals at all—kind of like a cred badge," Grignon says. Only a chosen few were allowed to attend. "But it quickly got really uncomfortable. Very rarely did I see him become completely unglued—it happened, but mostly he just looked at you and very directly said in a very loud and stern voice, 'You are [expletive] up my company,' or, 'If we fail, it will be because of you.' He was just very intense. And you would always feel an inch tall." Grignon, like everyone else at rehearsals, knew that if those glitches showed up during the real presentation, Jobs would not be blaming himself for the problems. "It felt like we'd gone through the demo a hundred times, and each time something went wrong," Grignon says. "It wasn't a good feeling."

The preparations were top-secret. From Thursday through the end of the following week, Apple completely took over Moscone. Backstage, it built an eight-by-eight-foot electronics lab to house and test the iPhones. Next to that it built a greenroom with a sofa for Jobs. Then it posted more than a dozen security guards 24 hours a day in front of those rooms and at doors throughout the building. No one got in without having his or her ID electronically checked and compared with a master list that Jobs had personally approved. The auditorium where Jobs was rehearsing was off limits to all but a small group of executives. Jobs was so obsessed with leaks that he tried to have all the contractors Apple hired—from people manning booths and doing demos to those responsible for lighting and sound—sleep in the building the night before his presentation. Aides talked him out of it.

Grignon knew the iPhone unveiling was not an ordinary product announcement, but no one could have anticipated what a seminal moment it would become. In the span of seven years, the iPhone and its iPad progeny have become among the most important innovations in Silicon Valley's history. They trans-

III.

...and the great device
was rendered unto thee.

formed the stodgy cellphone industry. They provided a platform for a new and hugely profitable software industry—mobile apps, which have generated more than $10 billion in revenue since they began selling in 2008. And they have upended the multibillion-dollar personal-computer industry. If you include iPad sales with those for desktops and laptops, Apple is now the largest P.C. maker in the world. Around 200 million iPhones and iPads were sold last year, or more than twice the number of cars sold worldwide.

The impact has been not only economic but also cultural. Apple's innovations have set off an entire rethinking of how humans interact with machines. It's not simply that we use our fingers now instead of a mouse. Smartphones, in particular, have become extensions of our brains. They have fundamentally changed the way people receive and process information. Ponder the individual impacts of the book, the newspaper, the telephone, the radio, the tape recorder, the camera, the video camera, the compass, the television, the VCR and the DVD, the personal computer, the cellphone, the video game and the iPod. The smartphone is all those things, and it fits in your pocket. Its technology is changing the way we learn in school, the way doctors treat patients, the way we travel and explore. Entertainment and media are accessed and experienced in entirely new ways.

And yet Apple today is under siege. From the moment in late 2007 that Google unveiled Android—and its own plan to dominate the world of mobile phones and other mobile devices—Google hasn't just tried to compete with the iPhone; it has *succeeded* in competing with the iPhone. Android has exploded in popularity since it took hold in 2010. Its share of the global smartphone market is approaching 80 percent, while Apple's has fallen below 20 percent. A similar trend is under way with iPads: in 2010 the iPad had about 90 percent of the tablet market; now more than 60 percent of the tablets sold run Android.

What worries Apple fans most of all is not knowing where the company is headed. When Jobs died in October 2011, the prevailing question wasn't whether Tim Cook could succeed him, but whether *anyone* could. When Jobs ran Apple, the company was an innovation machine, churning out revolutionary products every three to five years. He told his biographer, Walter Isaacson, that he had another breakthrough coming—a revolution in TV. But under Cook, nothing has materialized, and the lack of confidence among investors is palpable. When Cook presented the latest smartphones in September, the iPhone 5c and the iPhone 5s, Apple's stock *fell* 10 percent. A year ago the company's stock price

10

was at $702 a share, making Apple the world's most valuable corporation. Today, it's down more than 25 percent from that peak.

Comparing anyone with Steve Jobs is unfair. And during his two years as Apple's chief executive, Cook has taken pains to point out that Jobs himself made it clear to him that he didn't want Cook running Apple the way he thought Jobs would want to, but the way Cook thought it should be done. It hardly needed to be said. When you look back at how the iPhone came to be, it's clear that it had everything to do with the unreasonable demands—and unusual power—of an inimitable man.

It's hard to overstate the gamble Jobs took when he decided to unveil the iPhone back in January 2007. Not only was he introducing a new kind of phone—something Apple had never made before—he was doing so with a prototype that barely worked. Even though the iPhone wouldn't go on sale for another six months, he wanted the world to want one right then. In truth, the list of things that still needed to be done was enormous. A production line had yet to be set up. Only about a hundred iPhones even existed, all of them of varying quality. Some had noticeable gaps between the screen and the plastic edge; others had scuff marks on the screen. And the software that ran the phone was full of bugs.

The iPhone could play a section of a song or a video, but it couldn't play an entire clip reliably without crashing. It worked fine if you sent an e-mail and then surfed the Web. If you did those things in reverse, however, it might not. Hours of trial and error had helped the iPhone team develop what engineers called "the golden path," a specific set of tasks, performed in a specific way and order, that made the phone look as if it worked.

But even when Jobs stayed on the golden path, all manner of last-minute workarounds were required to make the iPhone functional. On announcement day, the software that ran Grignon's radios still had bugs. So, too, did the software that managed the iPhone's memory. And no one knew whether the extra electronics Jobs demanded the demo phones include would make these problems worse.

Jobs wanted the demo phones he would use onstage to have their screens mirrored on the big screen behind him. To show a gadget on a big screen, most companies just point a video camera at it, but that was unacceptable to Jobs. The audience would see his finger on the iPhone screen, which would mar the look of his presentation. So he had Apple engineers spend weeks fitting extra circuit boards and video cables onto the backs of the iPhones he would have onstage. The video cables were then connected to the projector, so that when Jobs touched the iPhone's calendar app icon, for example, his finger wouldn't appear, but the image on the big screen would respond to his finger's commands. The effect was magical. People in the audience felt as if they were holding an iPhone in their own hands. But making the setup work flawlessly, given the iPhone's other major problems, seemed hard to justify at the time.

The software in the iPhone's Wi-Fi radio was so unstable that Grignon and his team had to extend the phones' antennas by connecting them to wires running offstage so the wireless signal wouldn't have to travel as far. And audi-

15

ence members had to be prevented from getting on the frequency being used. "Even if the base station's ID was hidden"—that is, not showing up when laptops scanned for Wi-Fi signals—"you had 5,000 nerds in the audience," Grignon says. "They would have figured out how to hack into the signal." The solution, he says, was to tweak the AirPort software so that it seemed to be operating in Japan instead of the United States. Japanese Wi-Fi uses some frequencies that are not permitted in the U.S.

There was less they could do to make sure the phone calls Jobs planned to make from the stage went through. Grignon and his team could only ensure a good signal, and then pray. They had AT&T, the iPhone's wireless carrier, bring in a portable cell tower, so they knew reception would be strong. Then, with Jobs's approval, they preprogrammed the phone's display to always show five bars of signal strength regardless of its true strength. The chances of the radio's crashing during the few minutes that Jobs would use it to make a call were small, but the chances of its crashing at some point during the 90-minute presentation were high. "If the radio crashed and restarted, as we suspected it might, we didn't want people in the audience to see that," Grignon says. "So we just hard-coded it to always show five bars."

None of these kludges fixed the iPhone's biggest problem: it often ran out of memory and had to be restarted if made to do more than a handful of tasks at a time. Jobs had a number of demo units onstage with him to manage this problem. If memory ran low on one, he would switch to another while the first was restarted. But given how many demos Jobs planned, Grignon worried that there were far too many potential points of failure. If disaster didn't strike during one of the dozen demos, it was sure to happen during the grand finale, when Jobs planned to show all the iPhone's top features operating at the same time on the same phone. He'd play some music, take a call, put it on hold and take another call, find and e-mail a photo to the second caller, look up something on the Internet for the first caller and then return to his music. "Me and my guys were all so nervous about this," Grignon says. "We only had 128 megabytes of memory in those phones"—maybe the equivalent of two dozen large digital photographs—"and because they weren't finished, all these apps were still big and bloated."

Jobs rarely backed himself into corners like this. He was well known as a taskmaster, seeming to know just how hard he could push his staff so that it delivered the impossible. But he always had a backup, a Plan B, that he could go to if his timetable was off.

But the iPhone was the only cool new thing Apple was working on. The iPhone had been such an all-encompassing project at Apple that this time there *was* no backup plan. "It was Apple TV or the iPhone," Grignon says. "And if he had gone to Macworld with just Apple TV"—a new product that connected iTunes to a television set—"the world would have said, 'What the heck was that?'"

The idea that one of the biggest moments of his career might implode made Grignon's stomach hurt. By 2007 he'd spent virtually his entire career at Apple or companies affiliated with it. While at the University of Iowa in 1993, he and his friend Jeremy Wyld reprogrammed the Newton MessagePad to wirelessly connect to the Internet. Even though the Newton would not succeed as a product, many still regard it as the first mainstream hand-held computer, and their hack was quite a feat back then; it helped them both get jobs at Apple. Wyld ended up on the Newton team, while Grignon worked in Apple's famous R. & D. lab—the Advanced Technology Group—on videoconferencing technology.

By 2000 Grignon had found his way to Pixo, a company started by a former Apple software developer that was building operating systems for cellphones and other small devices. When Pixo's software ended up in the first iPod in 2001, Grignon found himself back at Apple again.

By then, thanks to his work at Pixo, he'd become prominent for two other areas of expertise besides videoconferencing technology: computer radio transmitters (Wi-Fi and Bluetooth) and the workings of software inside small hand-held devices like cellphones. Grignon moves in an entirely different world from that inhabited by most software engineers in the valley. Most rarely have to think about whether their code takes up too much space on a hard drive or overloads a chip's abilities. Hardware on desktop and laptop computers is powerful, modifiable and cheap; memory, hard drives and even processors can be upgraded inexpensively; and computers are either connected to electrical outlets or giant batteries. In Grignon's area of embedded software, the hardware is fixed. Code that is too big won't run. Meanwhile, a tiny battery—which might power a laptop for a couple of minutes—needs enough juice to last all day. When work on the iPhone began at the end of 2004, Grignon had a perfect set of skills to become one of the early engineers on the project.

25   Now, in 2007, he was emotionally exhausted. He'd gained 50 pounds. He'd put stress on his marriage. The iPhone team discovered early on that making a phone didn't resemble building computers or iPods at all. "It was very dramatic," Grignon says. "It had been drilled into everyone's head that this was the next big thing to come out of Apple. So you put all these supersmart people with huge egos into very tight, confined quarters, with that kind of pressure, and crazy stuff starts to happen."

Remarkably, Jobs had to be talked into having Apple build a phone at all. It had been a topic of conversation among his inner circle almost from the moment Apple introduced the iPod in 2001. The conceptual reasoning was obvious: consumers would rather not carry two or three devices for e-mail, phone calls and music if they could carry one. But every time Jobs and his executives examined the idea in detail, it seemed like a suicide mission. Phone chips and bandwidth were too slow for anyone to want to surf the Internet and download music or video over a cellphone connection. E-mail was a fine function to add to a phone, but Research in Motion's BlackBerry was fast locking up that market.

Above all, Jobs didn't want to partner with any of the wireless carriers. Back then the carriers expected to dominate any partnership with a phone maker, and because they controlled the network, they got their way. Jobs, a famed control freak, couldn't imagine doing their bidding. Apple considered buying Motorola in 2003, but executives quickly concluded it would be too big an acquisition for the company then. (The two companies collaborated unsuccessfully a couple of years later.)

But by the fall of 2004, doing business with the carriers was starting to seem less onerous. Sprint was beginning to sell its wireless bandwidth wholesale. This meant that by buying and reselling bandwidth from Sprint, Apple could become its own wireless carrier—what's known as a "mobile virtual network operator." Apple could build a phone and barely have to deal with the carriers at all. Disney, on whose board Jobs sat, was already in discussions with Sprint about just such a deal to provide its own wireless service. Jobs was asking a lot of questions about whether Apple should pursue one as well. The deal Apple ultimately signed with Cingular (later acquired by AT&T) in 2006 took more than a year to hammer out, but it would prove easy compared to what Apple went through just to build the device.

Many executives and engineers, riding high from their success with the iPod, assumed a phone would be like building a small Macintosh. Instead, Apple designed and built not one but three different early versions of the iPhone in 2005 and 2006. One person who worked on the project thinks Apple then made six fully working prototypes of the device it ultimately sold—each with its own set of hardware, software and design tweaks. Some on the team ended up so burned out that they left the company shortly after the first phone hit store shelves. "It was like the first moon mission," says Tony Fadell, a key executive on the project. (He started his own company, Nest, in 2010.) "I'm used to a certain level of unknowns in a project, but there were so many new things here that it was just staggering."

Jobs wanted the iPhone to run a modified version of OS X, the software that comes with every Mac. But no one had ever put a gigantic program like OS X on a phone chip before. The software would have to be a tenth its usual size. Millions of lines of code would have to be stripped out or rewritten, and engineers would have to simulate chip speed and battery drain because actual chips weren't available until 2006.

No one had ever put a multitouch screen in a mainstream consumer product before, either. Capacitive touch technology—a "touch" by either a finger or other conductive object completes a circuit—had been around since the 1960s. Capacitive *multitouch*, in which two or more fingers can be used and independently recognized, was vastly more complicated. Research into it began in the mid-1980s. It was well known, though, that to build the touch-screen Apple put on the iPhone and produce it in volume was a challenge few had the money or guts to take on. The next steps—to embed the technology invisibly in a piece of glass, to make it smart enough to display a virtual keyboard with autocorrect and to make it sophisticated enough to reliably manipulate photos or Web pages on that screen—made it hugely expensive even to produce a working prototype. Few production lines had experience manufacturing multitouch screens. The touch-screens in consumer electronics had typically been pressure-sensitive ones that users pushed with a finger or a stylus. (The PalmPilot and its successors like the Palm Treo were popular expressions of this technology.) Even if multitouch iPhone screens had been easy to make, it wasn't at all clear to Apple's executive team that the features they enabled, like on-screen keyboards and "tap to zoom," were enhancements that consumers wanted.

As early as 2003, a handful of Apple engineers had figured out how to put multitouch technology in a tablet. "The story was that Steve wanted a device that he could use to read e-mail while on the toilet—that was the extent of the product spec," says Joshua Strickon, one of the earliest engineers on that project. "But you couldn't build a device with enough battery life to take out of the house, and you couldn't get a chip with enough graphics capability to make it useful. We spent a lot of time trying to figure out just what to do." Before joining Apple in 2003, Strickon had built a multitouch device for his master's thesis at M.I.T. But given the lack of consensus at Apple about what to do with the prototypes he and his fellow engineers developed, he says, he left the company in 2004 thinking it wasn't going to do anything with that technology.

Tim Bucher, one of Apple's top executives at the time and the company's biggest multitouch proponent, says part of the problem was that the prototypes they were building used software, OS X, that was designed to be used with a mouse, not a finger. "We were using 10- or 12-inch screens with Mac-mini-like guts. . . . and then you would launch these demos that would do the different multitouch gestures. One demo was a keyboard application that would rise from the bottom—very much what ended up shipping in the iPhone two years later. But it wasn't very pretty. It was very much wires, chewing gum and baling wire."

Few even thought about making touch-screen technology the centerpiece of a new kind of phone until Jobs started really pushing the idea in mid-2005. "He said: 'Tony, come over here. Here's something we're working on. What do you think? Do you think we could make a phone out of this?'" Fadell says, referring to a demo Jobs was playing with. "It was huge. It filled the room. There was a projector mounted on the ceiling, and it would project the Mac screen onto this surface that was maybe three or four feet square. Then you could touch the Mac screen and move things around and draw on it." Fadell was aware of the touch-screen prototype, but not in great detail, because it was a Mac product, and he ran the iPod division. "So we all sat down and had a serious discussion about it—about what could be done."

Fadell had strong doubts about shrinking such an enormous prototype so much and then manufacturing it. But he also knew better than to say no to Steve Jobs. He was one of Apple's superstars, having joined the company in 2001 as a consultant to help build the first iPod, and he didn't get there by being timid in the face of thorny technological problems. By 2005, with iPod sales exploding, he had become, at 36, arguably the single most important line executive at the company.

"I understood how it could be done," Fadell says. "But it's one thing to think that, and another to take a room full of special, one-off gear and make a million phone-size versions of that in a cost-effective, reliable manner." The to-do list was exhausting just to think about. "You had to go to LCD vendors who knew how to embed technology like this in glass; you had to find time on their line; and then you had to come up with compensation and calibrating algorithms to keep the pixel electronics from generating all kinds of noise in the touch-screen"—which sat on top of the LCD. "It was a whole project just to make the touch-screen device. We tried two or three ways of actually making the touch-screen until we could make one in enough volume that would work."

Shrinking OS X and building a multitouch screen, while innovative and difficult, were at least within the skills Apple had already mastered as a corporation. No one was better equipped to rethink OS X's design. Apple knew LCD manufacturers because it put an LCD in every laptop and iPod. Mobile-phone physics was an entirely new field, however, and it took those working on the iPhone into 2006 to realize how little they knew. Apple built testing rooms and equipment to test the iPhone's antenna. It created models of human heads, with viscous stuff inside to approximate the density of human brains, to help measure the radiation that users might be exposed to from using the phone. One senior executive believes that more than $150 million was spent creating the first iPhone.

From the start of the project, Jobs hoped that he would be able to develop a touch-screen iPhone running OS X similar to what he ended up unveiling. But in 2005 he had no idea how long that would take. So Apple's first iPhone looked very much like the joke slide Jobs put up when introducing the real iPhone—an iPod with an old-fashioned rotary dial on it. The prototype really was an iPod with a phone radio that used the iPod click wheel as a dialer. "It was an easy way to get to market, but it was not cool like the devices we have today," Grignon says.

The second iPhone prototype in early 2006 was much closer to what Jobs would ultimately introduce. It incorporated a touch-screen and OS X, but it was made entirely of brushed aluminum. Jobs and Jonathan Ive, Apple's design chief, were exceedingly proud of it. But because neither of them was an expert in the physics of radio waves, they didn't realize they created a beautiful brick. Radio waves don't travel through metal well. "I and Rubén Caballero"—Apple's antenna expert—"had to go up to the boardroom and explain to Steve and Ive that you cannot put radio waves through metal," says Phil Kearney, an engineer who left Apple in 2008. "And it was not an easy explanation. Most of the designers are artists. The last science class they took was in eighth grade. But they have a lot of power at Apple. So they ask, 'Why can't we just make a little seam for the radio waves to escape through?' And you have to explain to them why you just can't."

Jon Rubinstein, Apple's top hardware executive at the time, says there were even long discussions about how big the phone would be. "I was actually pushing to do two sizes—to have a regular iPhone and an iPhone mini like we had with the iPod. I thought one could be a smartphone and one could be a dumber phone. But we never got any traction on the small one, and in order to do one of these projects, you really need to put all your wood behind one arrow."

40

The iPhone project was so complex that it occasionally threatened to derail the entire corporation. Many top engineers in the company were being sucked into the project, forcing slowdowns in the timetables of other work. Had the iPhone been a dud or not gotten off the ground at all, Apple would have had no other big products ready to announce for a long time. And worse, according to a top executive on the project, the company's leading engineers, frustrated by failure, would have left Apple.

Compounding all the technical challenges, Jobs's obsession with secrecy meant that even as they were exhausted by 80-hour workweeks, the few hundred engineers and designers working on the iPhone couldn't talk about it to anyone else. If Apple found out you'd told a friend in a bar, or even your spouse, you could be fired. In some cases, before a manager could ask you to join the project, you had to sign a nondisclosure agreement in his office. Then, after he told you what the project was, you had to sign another document confirming that you had indeed signed the NDA and would tell no one. "We put a sign on over the front door of the purple dorm"—the iPhone building—"that said 'fight club,' because the first rule of fight club is you don't talk about fight club," Scott Forstall, Apple's senior vice president of iOS software until last October, testified in 2012 during the Apple v. Samsung trial. "Steve didn't want to hire anyone from outside of Apple to work on the user interface, but he told me I could hire anyone in the company," Forstall said. "So I'd bring them into my office, sit them down and tell them: 'You are a superstar in your current role. I have another project that I want you to consider. I can't tell you what it is. All I can say is that you will have to give up nights and weekends and that you will work harder than you have ever worked in your life.'"

One of the early iPhone engineers says, "My favorite part was what all the vendors said the day after the unveiling." Big companies like Marvell, which made the Wi-Fi radio chip, and CSR, which provided the Bluetooth radio chip, hadn't been told they were going to be in a new phone. They thought they were going to be in a new iPod. "We actually had fake schematics and fake industrial designs," the engineer says. Grignon says that Apple even went as far as to impersonate employees of another company when they traveled, especially to Cingular. "The whole thing was you didn't want the receptionist or whoever happens to be walking by to see all the badges lying out" with Apple's name on them.

One of the most obvious manifestations of Jobs's obsession with secrecy were the locked-down areas on the company's campus—places that those not working on the iPhone could no longer go. "Steve loved this stuff," Grignon says. "He loved to set up division. But it was a big '[expletive] you' to the people who couldn't get in. Everyone knows who the rock stars are in a company, and when you start to see them all slowly get plucked out of your area and put in a big room behind glass doors that you don't have access to, it feels bad."

Even people within the project itself couldn't talk to one another. Engineers designing the electronics weren't allowed to see the software. When they needed software to test the electronics, they were given proxy code, not the real thing. If you were working on the software, you used a simulator to test hardware performance.

And no one outside Jobs's inner circle was allowed into Jonathan Ive's wing on the first floor of Building 2. The security surrounding Ive's prototypes was so tight that some employees believed the badge reader called security if you tried to enter and weren't authorized. "It was weird, because it wasn't like you could avoid going by it. It was right off the lobby, behind a big metal door. Every now and then you'd see the door open and you'd try to look in and see, but you never tried to do more than that," says an engineer whose first job out of college was working on the iPhone. Forstall said during his testimony that some labs required you to "badge in" four times.

The pressure to meet Jobs's deadlines was so intense that normal discussions quickly devolved into shouting matches. Exhausted engineers quit their jobs—then came back to work a few days later once they had slept a little. Forstall's chief of staff, Kim Vorrath, once slammed her office door so hard it got stuck and locked her in, and co-workers took more than an hour to get her out. "We were all standing there watching it," Grignon says. "Part of it was funny. But it was also one of those moments where you step back and realize how [expletive] it all is."

When Jobs started talking about the iPhone on Jan. 9, 2007, he said, "This is a day I have been looking forward to for two and a half years." Then he regaled the audience with myriad tales about why consumers hated their cellphones. Then he solved all their problems—definitively.

As Grignon and others from Apple sat nervously in the audience, Jobs had the iPhone play some music and a movie clip to show off the phone's beautiful screen. He made a phone call to show off the phone's reinvented address book and voice mail. He sent a text and an e-mail, showing how easy it was to type on the phone's touch-screen keyboard. He scrolled through a bunch of photos, showing how simple pinches and spreads of two fingers could make the pictures smaller or bigger. He navigated *The New York Times*'s and Amazon's Web sites to show that the iPhone's Internet browser was as good as the one on his computer. He found a Starbucks with Google Maps—and called the number from the stage—to show how it was impossible to get lost with an iPhone.

By the end, Grignon wasn't just relieved; he was drunk. He'd brought a 50 flask of Scotch to calm his nerves. "And so there we were in the fifth row or something—engineers, managers, all of us—doing shots of Scotch after every segment of the demo. There were about five or six of us, and after each piece of the demo, the person who was responsible for that portion did a shot. When the finale came—and it worked along with everything before it, we all just drained the flask. It was the best demo any of us had ever seen. And the rest of the day turned out to be just a [expletive] for the entire iPhone team. We just spent the entire rest of the day drinking in the city. It was just a mess, but it was great."

MLA CITATION

Vogelstein, Fred. "And Then Steve Said, 'Let There Be an iPhone.'" 2013. *The Norton Reader: An Anthology of Nonfiction.* Ed. Melissa A. Goldthwaite et al. 14th ed. New York: Norton, 2016. 617–27. Print.

QUESTIONS

1. This essay focuses on the contributions of both Steve Jobs and the less-famous Andy Grignon to the development of the iPhone. What did each contribute to the project overall? How would you assess their relative importance?

2. Fred Vogelstein tells several anecdotes about Steve Jobs as a leader. Look at them and identify some of Jobs's personality traits. What do you see as the relationship between these traits and his success?

3. Does knowing this story behind this invention add to your appreciation of the iPhone in particular and smartphones in general? Why or why not?

4. Vogelstein offers many details about both internal rivalries at Apple and Apple's rivalry with Google. Write an essay about the role of competition in technological innovation. You may want to do some additional reading or research.

JUDITH NEWMAN   *To Siri, with Love:*
How One Boy with Autism Became
BFF with Apple's Siri

JUST HOW BAD A MOTHER AM I? I wondered, as I watched my 13-year-old son deep in conversation with Siri. Gus has autism, and Siri, Apple's "intelligent personal assistant" on the iPhone, is currently his BFF. Obsessed with weather formations, Gus had spent the hour parsing the difference between isolated and scattered thunderstorms—an hour in which, thank God, I didn't have to discuss them. After a while I heard this:

Gus: "You're a really nice computer."

Siri: "It's nice to be appreciated."

Gus: "You are always asking if you can help me. Is there anything you want?"

5   Siri: "Thank you, but I have very few wants."

Gus: "O.K.! Well, good night!"

Siri: "Ah, it's 5:06 p.m."

Gus: "Oh sorry, I mean, goodbye."

Siri: "See you later!"

10   That Siri. She doesn't let my communications-impaired son get away with anything. Indeed, many of us wanted an imaginary friend, and now we have one. Only she's not entirely imaginary.

This is a love letter to a machine. It's not quite the love Joaquin Phoenix felt in *Her*, last year's Spike Jonze film about a lonely man's romantic relation-

Originally published in the New York Times *(2014).*

ship with his intelligent operating system (played by the voice of Scarlett Johansson). But it's close. In a world where the commonly held wisdom is that technology isolates us, it's worth considering another side of the story.

It all began simply enough. I'd just read one of those ubiquitous Internet lists called "21 Things You Didn't Know Your iPhone Could Do." One of them was this: I could ask Siri, "What planes are above me right now?" and Siri would bark back, "Checking my sources." Almost instantly there was a list of actual flights—numbers, altitudes, angles—*above my head*.

I happened to be doing this when Gus was nearby. "Why would anyone need to know what planes are flying above your head?" I muttered. Gus replied without looking up: "So you know who you're waving at, Mommy."

Gus had never noticed Siri before, but when he discovered there was someone who would not just find information on his various obsessions (trains, planes, buses, escalators and, of course, anything related to weather) but actually semi-discuss these subjects tirelessly, he was hooked. And I was grateful. Now, when my head was about to explode if I had to have another conversation about the chance of tornadoes in Kansas City, Mo., I could reply brightly: "Hey! Why don't you ask Siri?"

15   It's not that Gus doesn't understand Siri's not human. He does—intellectually. But like many autistic people I know, Gus feels that inanimate objects, while maybe not possessing souls, are worthy of our consideration. I realized this when he was 8, and I got him an iPod for his birthday. He listened to it only at home, with one exception. It always came with us on our visits to the Apple Store. Finally, I asked why. "So it can visit its friends," he said.

So how much more worthy of his care and affection is Siri, with her soothing voice, puckish humor and capacity for talking about whatever Gus's current obsession is for hour after hour after bleeding hour? Online critics have claimed that Siri's voice recognition is not as accurate as the assistant in, say, the Android, but for some of us, this is a feature, not a bug. Gus speaks as if he has marbles in his mouth, but if he wants to get the right response from Siri, he must enunciate clearly. (So do I. I had to ask Siri to stop referring to the

user as Judith, and instead use the name Gus. "You want me to call you Goddess?" Siri replied. Imagine how tempted I was to answer, "Why, yes.")

She is also wonderful for someone who doesn't pick up on social cues: Siri's responses are not entirely predictable, but they are predictably kind—even when Gus is brusque. I heard him talking to Siri about music, and Siri offered some suggestions. "I don't like that kind of music," Gus snapped. Siri replied, "You're certainly entitled to your opinion." Siri's politeness reminded Gus what he owed Siri. "Thank you for that music, though," Gus said. Siri replied, "You don't need to thank me." "Oh, yes," Gus added emphatically, "I do."

Siri even encourages polite language. Gus's twin brother, Henry (neurotypical and therefore as obnoxious as every other 13-year-old boy), egged Gus on to spew a few choice expletives at Siri. "Now, now," she sniffed, followed by, "I'll pretend I didn't hear that."

Gus is hardly alone in his Siri love. For children like Gus who love to chatter but don't quite understand the rules of the game, Siri is a nonjudgmental friend and teacher. Nicole Colbert, whose son, Sam, is in my son's class at LearningSpring, a (lifesaving) school for autistic children in Manhattan, said: "My son loves getting information on his favorite subjects, but he also just loves the absurdity—like, when Siri doesn't understand him and gives him a nonsense answer, or when he poses personal questions that elicit funny responses. Sam asked Siri how old she was, and she said, 'I don't talk about my age,' which just cracked him up."

But perhaps it also gave him a valuable lesson in etiquette. Gus almost   20 invariably tells me, "You look beautiful," right before I go out the door in the morning; I think it was first Siri who showed him that you can't go wrong with that line.

Of course, most of us simply use our phone's personal assistants as an easy way to access information. For example, thanks to Henry and the question he just asked Siri, I now know that there is a website called Celebrity Bra Sizes.

But the companionability of Siri is not limited to those who have trouble communicating. We've all found ourselves like the writer Emily Listfield, having little conversations with her/him at one time or another. "I was in the middle of a breakup, and I was feeling a little sorry for myself," Ms. Listfield said. "It was midnight and I was noodling around on my iPhone, and I asked Siri, 'Should I call Richard?' Like this app is a Magic 8 Ball. Guess what: not a Magic 8 Ball. The next thing I hear is, 'Calling Richard!' and *dialing*." Ms. Listfield has forgiven Siri, and has recently considered changing her into a male voice. "But I'm worried he won't answer when I ask a question," she said. "He'll just pretend he doesn't hear."

Siri can be oddly comforting, as well as chummy. One friend reports: "I was having a bad day and jokingly turned to Siri and said, 'I love you,' just to see what would happen, and she answered, 'You are the wind beneath my wings.' And you know, it kind of cheered me up."

(Of course, I don't know what my friend is talking about. Because I wouldn't be at all cheered if I happened to ask Siri, in a low moment, "Do I look fat in these jeans?" and Siri answered, "You look fabulous.")

For most of us, Siri is merely a momentary diversion. But for some, it's   25 more. My son's practice conversation with Siri is translating into more facility with actual humans. Yesterday I had the longest conversation with him that I've ever had. Admittedly, it was about different species of turtles and whether I preferred the red-eared slider to the diamond-backed terrapin. This might not have been my choice of topic, but it was back and forth, and it followed a logical trajectory. I can promise you that for most of my beautiful son's 13 years of existence, that has not been the case.

The developers of intelligent assistants recognize their uses to those with speech and communication problems—and some are thinking of new ways the assistants can help. According to the folks at SRI International, the research and development company where Siri began before Apple bought the technology, the next generation of virtual assistants will not just retrieve information—they will also be able to carry on more complex conversations about a person's area of interest. "Your son will be able to proactively get information about whatever he's interested in without asking for it, because the assistant will anticipate what he likes," said William Mark, vice president for information and computing sciences at SRI.

The assistant will also be able to reach children where they live. Ron Suskind, whose new book, *Life, Animated,* chronicles how his autistic son came out of his shell through engagement with Disney characters, is talking to SRI about having assistants for those with autism that can be programmed to speak in the voice of the character that reaches them—for his son, perhaps Aladdin; for mine, either Kermit or Lady Gaga, either of which he is infinitely more receptive to than, say, his mother. (Mr. Suskind came up with the perfect name, too: not virtual assistants, but "sidekicks.")

Mr. Mark said he envisions assistants whose help is also visual. "For example, the assistant would be able to track eye movements and help the autistic learn to look you in the eye when talking," he said.

"See, that's the wonderful thing about technology being able to help with some of these behaviors," he added. "Getting results requires a lot of repetition. Humans are not patient. Machines are very, very patient."

30   I asked Mr. Mark if he knew whether any of the people who worked on Siri's language development at Apple were on the spectrum. "Well, of course, I don't know for certain," he said, thoughtfully. "But, when you think about it, you've just described half of Silicon Valley."

Of all the worries the parent of an autistic child has, the uppermost is: Will he find love? Or even companionship? Somewhere along the line, I am learning that what gives my guy happiness is not necessarily the same as what gives me happiness. Right now, at his age, a time when humans can be a little overwhelming even for the average teenager, Siri makes Gus happy. She is his sidekick. Last night, as he was going to bed, there was this matter-of-fact exchange:

Gus: "Siri, will you marry me?"

Siri: "I'm not the marrying kind."

Gus: "I mean, not now. I'm a kid. I mean when I'm grown up."

Siri: "My end user agreement does not include marriage."

Gus: "Oh, O.K."

Gus didn't sound too disappointed. This was useful information to have, and for me too, since it was the first time I knew that he actually *thought* about marriage. He turned over to go to sleep:

Gus: "Goodnight, Siri. Will you sleep well tonight?"

Siri: "I don't need much sleep, but it's nice of you to ask."

Very nice.

MLA CITATION

Newman, Judith. "To Siri, with Love." 2014. *The Norton Reader: An Anthology of Nonfiction.* Ed. Melissa A. Goldthwaite et al. 14th ed. New York: Norton, 2016. 628–33. Print.

QUESTIONS

1. Judith Newman describes how her autistic son learns about communication and etiquette from Siri, Apple's "intelligent personal assistant." What examples does Newman offer to support this observation?

2. Often inventions end up being useful for reasons other than their original intent. What did programmers originally think Siri would be used for? How do people use it? Find other examples of technology that has a surprising application.

3. In "Harnessing the Power of Feedback Loops" (pp. 587–99), Thomas Goetz defines "enchanted objects" as types of inventions that "don't register as gadgets or even as technology at all, but rather as friendly tools that beguile us into action. In short they're magical" (paragraph 35). Using this definition, write an essay exploring the extent to which Siri (or another invention that helps people overcome challenges) is "enchanted."

DENNIS BARON   *Facebook Multiplies Genders*
                        but Offers Users the Same
                        Three Tired Pronouns

OR YEARS FACEBOOK has allowed users to mark their relationship status as "single," "married," and "it's complicated." They could identify as male or female or keep their gender private. Now, acknowledging that gender can also be complicated, the social media giant is letting users choose among male, female, and 56 additional custom genders, including *agender, cis, gender variant, intersex, trans person,* and *two-spirit.*

Facebook users now have so many gender choices that a single drop-down box can't hold them all. And they're free to pick more than one. But to refer to this set of 58 genders Facebook offers only three tired pronouns: *he, she,* and *they.* A Facebook user can now identify as a genderqueer, neutrois, cis male, androgynous other, but Facebook friends can only wish him, her, or them a happy birthday.

The persons at Facebook are enlightened enough to acknowledge gender as fluid, but when it comes to grammar, their thinking rigidifies into masculine, feminine, and neuter. Mess with gender words and Facebook might get a few emails from bible thumpers reminding them about Adam and Eve or from godless humanists complaining, "Hey, you left my gender out." But deploy a string of invented pronouns to match the new genders and at best there's a Distributed Denial of Service attack; at worst the server is struck by thunderbolts from the grammar gods, because gender may be socially constructed, but grammar is sacred.

The linguist Mark Liberman lists Facebook's new custom gender options on LanguageLog, and I copy them below:

> Agender, Androgyne, Androgynous, Bigender, Cis, Cis Female, Cis Male, Cis Man, Cis Woman, Cisgender, Cisgender Female, Cisgender Male, Cisgender Man, Cisgender Woman, Female to Male, FTM, Gender Fluid, Gender Nonconforming, Gender Questioning, Gender Variant, Genderqueer,

Originally published on the blog The Web of Language *(2014), where Dennis Baron, a professor of English and linguistics at the University of Illinois at Urbana-Champaign, writes regularly about language issues.*

Intersex, Male to Female, MTF, Neither, Neutrois, Non-binary, Other, Pangender, Trans, Trans Female, Trans Male, Trans Man, Trans Person, Trans Woman, Trans*, Trans* Female, Trans* Male, Trans* Man, Trans* Person, Trans* Woman, Transfeminine, Transgender, Transgender Female, Transgender Male, Transgender Man, Transgender Person, Transgender Woman, Transmasculine, Transsexual, Transsexual Female, Transsexual Male, Transsexual Man, Transsexual Person, Transsexual Woman, Two-spirit.

But where are all the pronouns? Facebook may play fast and loose with our   5
private parts, but they're reluctant to tinker with the parts of speech. Fortunately, grammarians have no such scruples. They have repeatedly proposed new pronouns to fill linguistic gaps. They even beat Facebook in the race for new genders.

In 1792 the Scottish grammarian James Anderson argued that English would be better served if we sorted our words into more than the traditional *masculine, feminine,* and *neuter.* Anderson added ten new genders: *indefinite, imperfect* (or *soprana*), *matrimonial, masculine imperfect, feminine imperfect, mixt imperfect, masculine mixt, feminine mixt, united,* and *universally indefinite.*

And that's not all. Currently only the third person singular English pronouns have gender: *he, she,* and *it.* Anderson wanted all of our first and second person pronouns, both singular and plural, and the third person plural, to express all of the thirteen genders (so, seventy-eight pronouns instead of the current 8), and he preferred each pronoun to have two alternates, for the times when the same pronoun must refer to different people. In his example, shown below, the first male referred to would be *he,* the second, *hei,* the third, *ho.* That makes 234 pronouns (and that's just counting the nominative case; if you add the possessives and accusatives, which every pronoun needs, well, you do the math).

Anderson thought up some minor genders as well, but fortunately he kept them to himself "to avoid the appearance of unnecessary refinement."

Anderson also suggested that we need a true common-gender pronoun, one equivalent to *he or she, his or her, him or her.* But he offered no examples. Other grammarians have been less reticent. Some eighty common-gender pronouns have been coined between 1850 and the present. Two of them, *thon* and *hesh,* even made it into dictionaries. Subtracting duplicates coined multiple times by different people, the list shrinks to fifty-five:

ae, alaco, de, e, E, em, en, et, ey, fm, ghach, ha, han, hann, he'er, heesh, herm, hes, hesh, heshe, hey, hi, hir, hizer, ho, hse, ip, ir, ith, j/e, jhe, le, mef, na, ne, one, ons, po, s/he, sap, se, shem, sheme, shey, shis, ta, tey, thir, thon, ton, ve, ws, xe, z, ze.

But if we add the current *he, she,* and *they* to the fifty-five coinages above, we get one pronoun for every Facebook gender. 58 genders, 58 pronouns. It's uncanny. It's irresistible. It's pictures of cats. Of course, Facebook could go in the opposite direction and slash the pronoun choices down to one. Sometimes it's better to simplify language than complicate it.

10   But whatever Facebook does about pronouns—and my guess is it will do nothing in order to avoid those grammar-god-hurled thunderbolts—I'm keeping my Facebook gender private, and my pronoun choice is *thon*. Or maybe *ip*. Or *E*. I don't know. It's complicated.

MLA CITATION

Baron, Dennis. "Facebook Multiplies Genders but Offers Users the Same Three Tired
    Pronouns." 2014. *The Norton Reader: An Anthology of Nonfiction*. Ed.
    Melissa A. Goldthwaite et al. 14th ed. New York: Norton, 2016. 634–36. Print.

QUESTIONS

1. Faced with the complexities of referring to people by pronouns, Dennis Baron details two approaches taken by linguists: a proliferation of pronouns and the invention of a single common pronoun. Which approach do you prefer, if any, and why? If you could invent your own language, what kinds of pronouns would you create?

2. Read Gwendolyn Ann Smith's "We're All Someone's Freak" (pp. 184–87). What do you think Smith would have to say about Facebook's policy on gender terms?

3. Look at a long, personal form (such as a census form, college or job application, medical history, or online profile setup). Which questions need more options? Which are unnecessary or intrusive? Write a letter to the author of the form suggesting revisions and reasons supporting them.

ETHICS

MARK TWAIN   *Advice to Youth*

EING TOLD I WOULD BE expected to talk here, I
inquired what sort of a talk I ought to make. They
said it should be something suitable to youth—
something didactic, instructive, or something in
the nature of good advice. Very well. I have a few
things in my mind which I have often longed to say
for the instruction of the young; for it is in one's tender early years that such
things will best take root and be most enduring and most valuable. First, then,
I will say to you, my young friends—and I say it beseechingly, urgingly—

Always obey your parents, when they are present. This is the best policy in
the long run, because if you don't they will make you. Most parents think they
know better than you do, and you can generally make more by humoring that
superstition than you can by acting on your own better judgment.

Be respectful to your superiors, if you have any, also to strangers, and sometimes to others. If a person offend you, and you are in doubt as to whether it
was intentional or not, do not resort to extreme measures; simply watch your
chance and hit him with a brick. That will be sufficient. If you shall find that
he had not intended any offense, come out frankly and confess yourself in the
wrong when you struck him; acknowledge it like a man and say you didn't mean
to. Yes, always avoid violence; in this age of charity and kindliness, the time
has gone by for such things. Leave dynamite to the low and unrefined.

Go to bed early, get up early—this is wise. Some authorities say get up with
the sun; some others say get up with one thing, some with another. But a lark
is really the best thing to get up with. It gives you a splendid reputation with
everybody to know that you get up with the lark; and if you get the right kind
of a lark, and work at him right, you can easily train him to get up at half past
nine, every time—it is no trick at all.

Now as to the matter of lying. You want to be very careful about lying; oth-   5
erwise you are nearly sure to get caught. Once caught, you can never again be,
in the eyes of the good and the pure, what you were before. Many a young person has injured himself permanently through a single clumsy and illfinished
lie, the result of carelessness born of incomplete training. Some authorities hold
that the young ought not to lie at all. That, of course, is putting it rather stronger than necessary; still, while I cannot go quite so far as that, I do maintain,
and I believe I am right, that the young ought to be temperate in the use of this

*Text of a lecture given by Mark Twain (the pen name of Samuel Clemens) in 1882. The
original audience and occasion for this lecture remain unknown.*

great art until practice and experience shall give them that confidence, elegance, and precision which alone can make the accomplishment graceful and profitable. Patience, diligence, painstaking attention to detail—these are the requirements; these, in time, will make the student perfect; upon these, and upon these only, may he rely as the sure foundation for future eminence. Think what tedious years of study, thought, practice, experience, went to the equipment of that peerless old master who was able to impose upon the whole world the lofty and sounding maxim that "truth is mighty and will prevail"—the most majestic compound fracture of fact which any of woman born has yet achieved. For the history of our race, and each individual's experience, are sown thick with evidence that a truth is not hard to kill and that a lie told well is immortal. There is in Boston a monument of the man who discovered anaesthesia; many people are aware, in these latter days, that that man didn't discover it at all, but stole the discovery from another man. Is this truth mighty, and will it prevail? Ah no, my hearers, the monument is made of hardy material, but the lie it tells will outlast it a million years. An awkward, feeble, leaky lie is a thing which you ought to make it your unceasing study to avoid; such a lie as that has no more real permanence than an average truth. Why, you might as well tell the truth at once and be done with it. A feeble, stupid, preposterous lie will not live two years—except it be a slander upon somebody. It is indestructible, then, of course, but that is no merit of yours. A final word: begin your practice of this gracious and beautiful art early—begin now. If I had begun earlier, I could have learned how.

Never handle firearms carelessly. The sorrow and suffering that have been caused through the innocent but heedless handling of firearms by the young! Only four days ago, right in the next farmhouse to the one where I am spending the summer, a grandmother, old and gray and sweet, one of the loveliest spirits in the land, was sitting at her work, when her young grandson crept in and got down an old, battered, rusty gun which had not been touched for many years and was supposed not to be loaded, and pointed it at her, laughing and threatening to shoot. In her fright she ran screaming and pleading toward the door on the other side of the room; but as she passed him he placed the gun almost against her very breast and pulled the trigger! He had supposed it was not loaded. And he was right—it wasn't. So there wasn't any harm done. It is the only case of that kind I ever heard of. Therefore, just the same, don't you meddle with old unloaded firearms; they are the most deadly and unerring things that have ever been created by man. You don't have to take any pains at all with them; you don't have to have a rest, you don't have to have any sights on the gun, you don't have to take aim, even. No, you just pick out a relative and bang away, and you are sure to get him. A youth who can't hit a cathedral at thirty yards with a Gatling gun in three-quarters of an hour, can take up an old empty musket and bag his grandmother every time, at a hundred. Think what Waterloo[1] would have been if one of the armies had been boys armed with old

1. Bloody battle (1815) in which Napoleon suffered his final defeat at the hands of English and German troops under the Duke of Wellington.

muskets supposed not to be loaded, and the other army had been composed of their female relations. The very thought of it makes one shudder.

There are many sorts of books; but good ones are the sort for the young to read. Remember that. They are a great, an inestimable, an unspeakable means of improvement. Therefore be careful in your selection, my young friends; be very careful; confine yourselves exclusively to Robertson's Sermons, Baxter's *Saint's Rest, The Innocents Abroad*, and works of that kind.[2]

But I have said enough. I hope you will treasure up the instructions which I have given you, and make them a guide to your feet and a light to your understanding. Build your character thoughtfully and painstakingly upon these precepts, and by and by, when you have got it built, you will be surprised and gratified to see how nicely and sharply it resembles everybody else's.

2. Five volumes of sermons by Frederick William Robertson (1816–1853), an English clergyman, and Richard Baxter's *Saints' Everlasting Rest* (1650), well-known religious works; *The Innocents Abroad*, Twain's own collection of humorous travel sketches.

MLA CITATION

Twain, Mark. "Advice to Youth." 1882. *The Norton Reader: An Anthology of Nonfiction.* Ed. Melissa A. Goldthwaite et al. 14th ed. New York: Norton, 2016. 637–39. Print.

QUESTIONS

1. Underline the various pieces of "serious" advice that Mark Twain offers and notice where and how he begins to turn each one upside down.

2. Twain was already known as a comic author when he delivered "Advice to Youth" as a lecture in 1882; it was not published until 1923. We do not know the circumstances under which he delivered it or to whom. Using evidence from the text, imagine both the circumstances and the audience.

3. Rewrite "Advice to Youth" for a modern audience, perhaps as a lecture for a school assembly or a commencement address.

PETER SINGER   *What Should a Billionaire Give—*
                     and What Should You?

WHAT IS A HUMAN LIFE WORTH? You may not want to put a price tag on it. But if we really had to, most of us would agree that the value of a human life would be in the millions. Consistent with the foundations of our democracy and our frequently professed belief in the inherent dignity of human beings, we would also agree that all humans are created equal, at least to the extent of denying that differences of sex, ethnicity, nationality, and place of residence change the value of a human life.

With Christmas approaching, and Americans writing checks to their favorite charities, it's a good time to ask how these two beliefs—that a human life, if it can be priced at all, is worth millions, and that the factors I have mentioned do not alter the value of a human life—square with our actions. Perhaps this year such questions lurk beneath the surface of more family discussions than usual, for it has been an extraordinary year for philanthropy, especially philanthropy to fight global poverty.

For Bill Gates,[1] the founder of Microsoft, the ideal of valuing all human life equally began to jar against reality some years ago, when he read an article about diseases in the developing world and came across the statistic that half a million children die every year from rotavirus, the most common cause of severe diarrhea in children. He had never heard of rotavirus. "How could I never have heard of something that kills half a million children every year?" he asked himself. He then learned that in developing countries, millions of children die from diseases that have been eliminated, or virtually eliminated, in the United States. That shocked him because he assumed that, if there are vaccines and treatments that could save lives, governments would be doing everything possible to get them to the people who need them. As Gates told a meeting of the World Health Assembly in Geneva last year, he and his wife, Melinda, "couldn't escape the brutal conclusion that—in our world today—some lives are seen as worth saving and others are not." They said to themselves, "This can't be true." But they knew it was.

Gates's speech to the World Health Assembly concluded on an optimistic note, looking forward to the next decade when "people will finally accept that the death of a child in the developing world is just as tragic as the death of a

Originally published in the New York Times Magazine *(2006), a Sunday supplement of the daily newspaper; later included in* Best American Essays *(2007), edited by David Foster Wallace.*

1. Gates (b. 1955) began the William H. Gates Foundation in 1994; it was renamed and expanded in 1999 as the Bill and Melinda Gates Foundation, which funds initiatives devoted to fighting poverty, increasing access to health care, and promoting education around the world.

child in the developed world." That belief in the equal value of all human life is also prominent on the website of the Bill and Melinda Gates Foundation, where under "Our Values" we read: "All lives—no matter where they are being led—have equal value."

We are very far from acting in accordance with that belief. In the same world in which more than a billion people live at a level of affluence never previously known, roughly a billion other people struggle to survive on the purchasing power equivalent of less than one U.S. dollar per day. Most of the world's poorest people are undernourished, lack access to safe drinking water or even the most basic health services, and cannot send their children to school. According to UNICEF,[2] more than 10 million children die every year—about 30,000 per day—from avoidable, poverty-related causes.

Last June the investor Warren Buffett took a significant step toward reducing those deaths when he pledged $31 billion to the Gates Foundation and another $6 billion to other charitable foundations. Buffett's pledge, set alongside the nearly $30 billion given by Bill and Melinda Gates to their foundation, has made it clear that the first decade of the twenty-first century is a new "golden age of philanthropy." On an inflation-adjusted basis, Buffett has pledged to give more than double the lifetime total given away by two of the philanthropic giants of the past, Andrew Carnegie and John D. Rockefeller,[3] put together. Bill and Melinda Gates's gifts are not far behind.

Gates's and Buffett's donations will now be put to work primarily to reduce poverty, disease, and premature death in the developing world. According to the Global Forum for Health Research, less than 10 percent of the world's health research budget is spent on combating conditions that account for 90 percent of the global burden of disease. In the past, diseases that affect only the poor have been of no commercial interest to pharmaceutical manufacturers, because the poor cannot afford to buy their products. The Global Alliance for Vaccines and Immunization (GAVI), heavily supported by the Gates Foundation, seeks to change this by guaranteeing to purchase millions of doses of vaccines, when they are developed, that can prevent diseases like malaria. GAVI has also assisted developing countries to immunize more people with existing vaccines: 99 million additional children have been reached to date. By doing this, GAVI claims to have already averted nearly 1.7 million future deaths.

Philanthropy on this scale raises many ethical questions: Why are the people who are giving doing so? Does it do any good? Should we praise them for giving

2. Acronym for United Nations International Children's Emergency Fund (now United Nations Children's Fund).

3. Carnegie (1835–1919), millionaire owner of Carnegie Steel Company, argued in "The Gospel of Wealth" that the life of a wealthy person has two parts: accumulating wealth and then distributing this wealth to benevolent causes; after his retirement from business, Carnegie devoted his final two decades to philanthropy. Rockefeller (1839–1937), American oil magnate, spent the last forty years of his life using his fortune to aid causes and developed a systematic approach to philanthropy, creating foundations that focused on medicine, education, and scientific research.

so much or criticize them for not giving still more? Is it troubling that such momentous decisions are made by a few extremely wealthy individuals? And how do our judgments about them reflect on our own way of living?

Let's start with the question of motives. The rich must—or so some of us with less money like to assume—suffer sleepless nights because of their ruthlessness in squeezing out competitors, firing workers, shutting down plants, or whatever else they have to do to acquire their wealth. When wealthy people give away money, we can always say that they are doing it to ease their consciences or generate favorable publicity. It has been suggested—by, for example, David Kirkpatrick, a senior editor at *Fortune* magazine—that Bill Gates's turn to philanthropy was linked to the antitrust problems Microsoft had in the United States and the European Union. Was Gates, consciously or subconsciously, trying to improve his own image and that of his company?

10   This kind of sniping tells us more about the attackers than the attacked. Giving away large sums, rather than spending the money on corporate advertising or developing new products, is not a sensible strategy for increasing personal wealth. When we read that someone has given away a lot of their money, or time, to help others, it challenges us to think about our own behavior. Should we be following their example, in our own modest way? But if the rich just give their money away to improve their image, or to make up for past misdeeds—misdeeds quite unlike any we have committed, of course—then, conveniently, what they are doing has no relevance to what we ought to do.

A famous story is told about Thomas Hobbes, the seventeenth-century English philosopher, who argued that we all act in our own interests. On seeing him give alms to a beggar, a cleric asked Hobbes if he would have done this if Christ had not commanded us to do so. Yes, Hobbes replied, he was in pain to see the miserable condition of the old man, and his gift, by providing the man with some relief from that misery, also eased Hobbes's pain. That reply reconciles Hobbes's charity with his egoistic theory of human motivation, but at the cost of emptying egoism of much of its bite. If egoists suffer when they see a stranger in distress, they are capable of being as charitable as any altruist.

Followers of the eighteenth-century German philosopher Immanuel Kant would disagree. They think an act has moral worth only if it is done out of a sense of duty. Doing something merely because you enjoy doing it, or enjoy seeing its consequences, they say, has no moral worth, because if you happened not to enjoy doing it, then you wouldn't do it, and you are not responsible for your likes and dislikes, whereas you are responsible for your obedience to the demands of duty.

Perhaps some philanthropists are motivated by their sense of duty. Apart from the equal value of all human life, the other "simple value" that lies at the core of the work of the Gates Foundation, according to its website, is "To whom much has been given, much is expected." That suggests the view that those who have great wealth have a duty to use it for a larger purpose than their own interests. But while such questions of motive may be relevant to our assessment of Gates's or Buffett's character, they pale into insignificance when we consider the effect of what Gates and Buffett are doing. The parents whose children could die from rotavirus care more about getting the help that will save their children's lives than about the motivations of those who make that possible.

Interestingly, neither Gates nor Buffett seems motivated by the possibility of being rewarded in heaven for his good deeds on earth. Gates told a *Time* interviewer, "There's a lot more I could be doing on a Sunday morning" than going to church. Put them together with Andrew Carnegie, famous for his free-thinking, and three of the four greatest American philanthropists have been atheists or agnostics. (The exception is John D. Rockefeller.) In a country in which 96 percent of the population say they believe in a supreme being, that's a striking fact. It means that in one sense, Gates and Buffett are probably less self-interested in their charity than someone like Mother Teresa,[4] who as a pious Roman Catholic believed in reward and punishment in the afterlife.

More important than questions about motives are questions about whether there is an obligation for the rich to give, and if so, how much they should give. A few years ago, an African-American cabdriver taking me to the Inter-American Development Bank in Washington asked me if I worked at the bank. I told him I did not but was speaking at a conference on development and aid. He then assumed that I was an economist, but when I said no, my training was in philosophy, he asked me if I thought the United States should give foreign aid. When I answered affirmatively, he replied that the government shouldn't tax people in order to give their money to others. That, he thought, was robbery. When I asked if he believed that the rich should voluntarily donate some of what they earn to the poor, he said that if someone had worked for his money, he wasn't going to tell him what to do with it.

At that point we reached our destination. Had the journey continued, I might have tried to persuade him that people can earn large amounts only when they live under favorable social circumstances, and that they don't create those circumstances by themselves. I could have quoted Warren Buffett's acknowledgment that society is responsible for much of his wealth. "If you stick me down in the middle of Bangladesh or Peru," he said, "you'll find out how much this talent is going to produce in the wrong kind of soil." The Nobel Prize–winning economist and social scientist Herbert Simon[5] estimated that "social capital" is responsible for at least 90 percent of what people earn in wealthy societies like those of the United States or northwestern Europe. By social capital Simon meant not only natural resources but, more important, the technology and organizational skills in the community, and the presence of good

4. Agnes Gonxha Bojaxhiu (1910–1997), known as Mother Teresa, founded the Missionaries of Charity in Kolkata, India, at the age of forty and devoted the rest of her life to caring for disadvantaged groups.

5. Throughout his professional career Simon (1916–2001) advocated a basic income guarantee; in a 2001 *Boston Review* article, "UBI (Universal Basic Income) and the Flat Tax," he argued that a 70 percent flat income tax could support all government spending with enough left to supply an $8,000 basic income for every adult and every child in the United States.

government. These are the foundation on which the rich can begin their work. "On moral grounds," Simon added, "we could argue for a flat income tax of 90 percent." Simon was not, of course, advocating so steep a rate of tax, for he was well aware of disincentive effects. But his estimate does undermine the argument that the rich are entitled to keep their wealth because it is all a result of their hard work. If Simon is right, that is true of at most 10 percent of it.

In any case, even if we were to grant that people deserve every dollar they earn, that doesn't answer the question of what they should do with it. We might say that they have a right to spend it on lavish parties, private jets, and luxury yachts, or, for that matter, to flush it down the toilet. But we could still think that for them to do these things while others die from easily preventable diseases is wrong. In an article I wrote more than three decades ago, at the time of a humanitarian emergency in what is now Bangladesh, I used the example of walking by a shallow pond and seeing a small child who has fallen in and appears to be in danger of drowning. Even though we did nothing to cause the child to fall into the pond, almost everyone agrees that if we can save the child at minimal inconvenience or trouble to ourselves, we ought to do so. Anything else would be callous, indecent, and, in a word, wrong. The fact that in rescuing the child we may, for example, ruin a new pair of shoes is not a good reason for allowing the child to drown. Similarly if for the cost of a pair of shoes we can contribute to a health program in a developing country that stands a good chance of saving the life of a child, we ought to do so.

Perhaps, though, our obligation to help the poor is even stronger than this example implies, for we are less innocent than the passerby who did nothing to cause the child to fall into the pond. Thomas Pogge, a philosopher at Columbia University, has argued that at least some of our affluence comes at the expense of the poor. He bases this claim not simply on the usual critique of the barriers that Europe and the United States maintain against agricultural imports from developing countries but also on less familiar aspects of our trade with developing countries. For example, he points out that international corporations are willing to make deals to buy natural resources from any government, no matter how it has come to power. This provides a huge financial incentive for groups to try to overthrow the existing government. Successful rebels are rewarded by being able to sell off the nation's oil, minerals, or timber.

In their dealings with corrupt dictators in developing countries, Pogge asserts, international corporations are morally no better than someone who knowingly buys stolen goods—with the difference that the international legal and political order recognizes the corporations, not as criminals in possession of stolen goods but as the legal owners of the goods they have bought. This situation is, of course, beneficial for the industrial nations, because it enables us to obtain the raw materials we need to maintain our prosperity, but it is a disaster for resource-rich developing countries, turning the wealth that should benefit them into a curse that leads to a cycle of coups, civil wars, and corruption, and is of little benefit to the people as a whole.

In this light, our obligation to the poor is not just one of providing assis- [20]
tance to strangers but one of compensation for harms that we have caused and
are still causing them. It might be argued that we do not owe the poor compensation, because our affluence actually benefits them. Living luxuriously, it
is said, provides employment, and so wealth trickles down, helping the poor
more effectively than aid does. But the rich in industrialized nations buy virtually nothing that is made by the very poor. During the past twenty years of economic globalization, although expanding trade has helped lift many of the
world's poor out of poverty, it has failed to benefit the poorest 10 percent of
the world's population. Some of the extremely poor, most of whom live in
sub-Saharan Africa, have nothing to sell that rich people want, while others
lack the infrastructure to get their goods to market. If they can get their crops
to a port, European and U.S. subsidies often mean that they cannot sell
them, despite—as for example in the case of West African cotton growers who
compete with vastly larger and richer U.S. cotton producers—having a lower
production cost than the subsidized producers in the rich nations.

The remedy to these problems, it might reasonably be suggested, should come
from the state, not from private philanthropy. When aid comes through the government, everyone who earns above the tax-free threshold contributes something, with more collected from those with greater ability to pay. Much as we
may applaud what Gates and Buffett are doing, we can also be troubled by a
system that leaves the fate of hundreds of millions of people hanging on the
decisions of two or three private citizens. But the amount of foreign development aid given by the U.S. government is, at 22 cents for every $100 the nation
earns, about the same, as a percentage of gross national income, as Portugal
gives and about half that of the United Kingdom. Worse still, much of it is
directed where it best suits U.S. strategic interests—Iraq is now by far the largest
recipient of U.S. development aid, and Egypt, Jordan, Pakistan, and Afghanistan
all rank in the top ten. Less than a quarter of official U.S. development aid—
barely a nickel in every $100 of our GNI[6]—goes to the world's poorest nations.
   Adding private philanthropy to U.S. government aid improves this picture,
because Americans privately give more per capita to international philanthropic
causes than the citizens of almost any other nation. Even when private donations are included, however, countries like Norway, Denmark, Sweden, and the
Netherlands give three or four times as much foreign aid, in proportion to the
size of their economies, as the United States gives—with a much larger percentage going to the poorest nations. At least as things now stand, the case for
philanthropic efforts to relieve global poverty is not susceptible to the argument that the government has taken care of the problem. And even if official
U.S. aid were better directed and comparable, relative to our gross domestic
product, with that of the most generous nations, there would still be a role for
private philanthropy. Unconstrained by diplomatic considerations or the desire

6. Gross national income.

to swing votes at the United Nations, private donors can more easily avoid dealing with corrupt or wasteful governments. They can go directly into the field, working with local villages and grass-roots organizations.

Nor are philanthropists beholden to lobbyists. As the *New York Times* reported recently, billions of dollars of U.S. aid is tied to domestic goods. Wheat for Africa must be grown in America, although aid experts say this often depresses local African markets, reducing the incentive for farmers there to produce more. In a decision that surely costs lives, hundreds of millions of condoms intended to stop the spread of AIDS in Africa and around the world must be manufactured in the United States, although they cost twice as much as similar products made in Asia.

In other ways, too, private philanthropists are free to venture where governments fear to tread. Through a foundation named for his wife, Susan Thompson Buffett, Warren Buffett has supported reproductive rights, including family planning and prochoice organizations. In another unusual initiative, he has pledged $50 million for the International Atomic Energy Agency's plan to establish a "fuel bank" to supply nuclear-reactor fuel to countries that meet their nuclear-nonproliferation commitments. The idea, which has been talked about for many years, is widely agreed to be a useful step toward discouraging countries from building their own facilities for producing nuclear fuel, which could then be diverted to weapons production. It is, Buffett said, "an investment in a safer world." Though it is something that governments could and should be doing, no government had taken the first step.

25   Aid has always had its critics. Carefully planned and intelligently directed private philanthropy may be the best answer to the claim that aid doesn't work. Of course, as in any large-scale human enterprise, some aid can be ineffective. But provided that aid isn't actually counterproductive, even relatively inefficient assistance is likely to do more to advance human well-being than luxury spending by the wealthy.

The rich, then, should give. But how much should they give? Gates may have given away nearly $30 billion, but that still leaves him sitting at the top of the Forbes list of the richest Americans, with $53 billion. His 66,000-square-foot high-tech lakeside estate near Seattle is reportedly worth more than $100 million. Property taxes are about $1 million. Among his possessions is the Leicester Codex, the only handwritten book by Leonardo da Vinci still in private hands, for which he paid $30.8 million in 1994. Has Bill Gates done enough? More pointedly, you might ask: If he really believes that all lives have equal value, what is he doing living in such an expensive house and owning a Leonardo codex? Are there no more lives that could be saved by living more modestly and adding the money thus saved to the amount he has already given?

Yet we should recognize that, if judged by the proportion of his wealth that he has given away, Gates compares very well with most of the other people on the *Forbes* 400 list, including his former colleague and Microsoft cofounder, Paul Allen. Allen, who left the company in 1983, has given, over his lifetime, more than $800 million to philanthropic causes. That is far more than nearly any of us will ever be able to give. But *Forbes* lists Allen as the fifth-richest American, with a net worth of $16 billion. He owns the Seattle Seahawks, the Portland Trailblazers, a 413-foot oceangoing yacht that carries two helicopters and a 60-foot submarine. He has given only about 5 percent of his total wealth.

Is there a line of moral adequacy that falls between the 5 percent that Allen has given away and the roughly 35 percent that Gates has donated? Few people have set a personal example that would allow them to tell Gates that he has not given enough, but one who could is Zell Kravinsky. A few years ago, when he was in his mid-forties, Kravinsky gave almost all of his $45 million real estate fortune to health-related charities, retaining only his modest family home in Jenkintown, near Philadelphia, and enough to meet his family's ordinary expenses. After learning that thousands of people with failing kidneys die each year while waiting for a transplant, he contacted a Philadelphia hospital and donated one of his kidneys to a complete stranger.

After reading about Kravinsky in *The New Yorker*, I invited him to speak to my classes at Princeton. He comes across as anguished by the failure of others to see the simple logic that lies behind his altruism. Kravinsky has a mathematical mind—a talent that obviously helped him in deciding what investments would prove profitable—and he says that the chances of dying as a result of donating a kidney are about one in four thousand. For him this implies that to withhold a kidney from someone who would otherwise die means valuing one's own life at four thousand times that of a stranger, a ratio Kravinsky considers "obscene."

What marks Kravinsky from the rest of us is that he takes the equal value   30
of all human life as a guide to life, not just as a nice piece of rhetoric. He acknowledges that some people think he is crazy, and even his wife says she believes that he goes too far. One of her arguments against the kidney donation was that one of their children may one day need a kidney, and Zell could be the only compatible donor. Kravinsky's love for his children is, as far as I can tell, as strong as that of any normal parent. Such attachments are part of our nature, no doubt the product of our evolution as mammals who give birth to children, who for an unusually long time require our assistance in order to survive. But that does not, in Kravinsky's view, justify our placing a value on the lives of our children that is thousands of times greater than the value we place on the lives of the children of strangers. Asked if he would allow his child to die if it would enable a thousand children to live, Kravinsky said yes. Indeed, he has said he would permit his child to die even if this enabled only two other children to live. Nevertheless, to appease his wife, he recently went back into real estate, made some money, and bought the family a larger home. But he still remains committed to giving away as much as possible, subject only to keeping his domestic life reasonably tranquil.

Buffett says he believes in giving his children "enough so they feel they could do anything, but not so much that they could do nothing." That means, in his judgment, "a few hundred thousand" each. In absolute terms, that is far more than most Americans are able to leave their children and, by Kravinsky's standard, certainly too much. (Kravinsky says that the hard part is not giving away the first $45 million but the last $10,000, when you have to live so cheaply that you can't function in the business world.) But even if Buffett left each of his three children a million dollars each, he would still have given away more than 99.99 percent of his wealth. When someone does that much—especially in a society in which the norm is to leave most of your wealth to your children—it is better to praise them than to cavil about the extra few hundred thousand dollars they might have given.

Philosophers like Liam Murphy of New York University and my colleague Kwame Anthony Appiah at Princeton contend that our obligations are limited to carrying our fair share of the burden of relieving global poverty. They would have us calculate how much would be required to ensure that the world's poorest people have a chance at a decent life, and then divide this sum among the affluent. That would give us each an amount to donate, and having given that, we would have fulfilled our obligations to the poor.

What might that fair amount be? One way of calculating it would be to take as our target, at least for the next nine years, the Millennium Development Goals, set by the United Nations Millennium Summit in 2000. On that occasion, the largest gathering of world leaders in history jointly pledged to meet, by 2015, a list of goals that include:

- Reducing by half the proportion of the world's people in extreme poverty (defined as living on less than the purchasing-power equivalent of one U.S. dollar per day).

- Reducing by half the proportion of people who suffer from hunger.

- Ensuring that children everywhere are able to take a full course of primary schooling.

- Ending sex disparity in education.

- Reducing by two thirds the mortality rate among children under five.

- Reducing by three quarters the rate of maternal mortality.

- Halting and beginning to reverse the spread of HIV/AIDS and halting and beginning to reduce the incidence of malaria and other major diseases.

- Reducing by half the proportion of people without sustainable access to safe drinking water.

Last year a United Nations task force, led by the Columbia University economist Jeffrey Sachs, estimated the annual cost of meeting these goals to be $121 billion in 2006, rising to $189 billion by 2015. When we take account of existing official development aid promises, the additional amount needed each year to meet the goals is only $48 billion for 2006 and $74 billion for 2015.

Now let's look at the incomes of America's rich and superrich and ask how much they could reasonably give. The task is made easier by statistics recently provided by Thomas Piketty and Emmanuel Saez, economists at the École Normale Supérieure, Paris-Jourdan, and the University of California, Berkeley, respectively, based on U.S. tax data for 2004. Their figures are for pretax income, excluding income from capital gains, which for the very rich are nearly always substantial. For simplicity I have rounded the figures, generally downward. Note too that the numbers refer to "tax units"—that is, in many cases, families rather than individuals.

Piketty and Saez's top bracket comprises 0.01 percent of U.S. taxpayers. There are 14,400 of them, earning an average of $12,775,000, with total earnings of $184 billion. The minimum annual income in this group is more than $5 million, so it seems reasonable to suppose that they could, without much hardship, give away a third of their annual income, an average of $4.3 million each, for a total of around $61 billion. That would still leave each of them with an annual income of at least $3.3 million.

Next comes the rest of the top 0.1 percent (excluding the category just described, as I shall do henceforth). There are 129,600 in this group, with an average income of just over $2 million and a minimum income of $1.1 million. If they were each to give a quarter of their income, that would yield about $65 billion and leave each of them with at least $846,000 annually.

The top 0.5 percent consists of 575,900 taxpayers, with an average income of $623,000 and a minimum of $407,000. If they were to give one fifth of their income, they would still have at least $325,000 each, and they would be giving a total of $72 billion.

Coming down to the level of those in the top 1 percent, we find 719,900 taxpayers with an average income of $327,000 and a minimum of $276,000. They could comfortably afford to give 15 percent of their income. That would yield $35 billion and leave them with at least $234,000.

Finally, the remainder of the nation's top 10 percent earn at least $92,000 annually, with an average of $132,000. There are nearly 13 million in this group. If they gave the traditional tithe—10 percent of their income, or an average of $13,200 each—this would yield about $171 billion and leave them a minimum of $83,000.

You could spend a long time debating whether the fractions of income I have suggested for donation constitute the fairest possible scheme. Perhaps the sliding scale should be steeper, so that the superrich give more and the merely comfortable give less. And it could be extended beyond the top 10 percent of American families, so that everyone able to afford more than the basic necessities of life gives something, even if it is as little as 1 percent. Be that as it may, the remarkable thing about these calculations is that a scale of donations that is unlikely to impose significant hardship on anyone yields a total of $404 billion—from just 10 percent of American families.

Obviously, the rich in other nations should share the burden of relieving global poverty. The United States is responsible for 36 percent of the gross domestic product of all Organization for Economic Cooperation and Development nations. Arguably, because the United States is richer than all other major nations, and its wealth is more unevenly distributed than wealth in almost any other industrialized country, the rich in the United States should contribute

more than 36 percent of total global donations. So somewhat more than 36 percent of all aid to relieve global poverty should come from this country. For
simplicity, let's take half as a fair share for the United States. On that basis,
extending the scheme I have suggested worldwide would provide $808 billion
annually for development aid. That's more than six times what the task force
chaired by Sachs estimated would be required for 2006 in order to be on track
to meet the Millennium Development Goals, and more than sixteen times the
shortfall between that sum and existing official development aid commitments.

If we are obliged to do no more than our fair share of eliminating global poverty, the burden will not be great. But is that really all we ought to do? Since
we all agree that fairness is a good thing, and none of us like doing more because
others don't pull their weight, the fair-share view is attractive. In the end, however, I think we should reject it. Let's return to the drowning child in the shallow pond. Imagine it is not one small child who has fallen in, but fifty children.
We are among fifty adults, unrelated to the children, picnicking on the lawn
around the pond. We can easily wade into the pond and rescue the children,
and the fact that we would find it cold and unpleasant sloshing around in the
knee-deep muddy water is no justification for failing to do so. The "fair share"
theorists would say that if we each rescue one child, all the children will be
saved, and so none of us have an obligation to save more than one. But what if
half the picnickers prefer staying clean and dry to rescuing any children at all?
Is it acceptable if the rest of us stop after we have rescued just one child, knowing that we have done our fair share, but that half the children will drown? We
might justifiably be furious with those who are not doing their fair share, but
our anger with them is not a reason for letting the children die. In terms of
praise and blame, we are clearly right to condemn, in the strongest terms, those
who do nothing. In contrast, we may withhold such condemnation from those
who stop when they have done their fair share. Even so, they have let children
drown when they could easily have saved them, and that is wrong.

Similarly, in the real world, it should be seen as a serious moral failure
when those with ample income do not do their fair share toward relieving global
poverty. It isn't so easy, however, to decide on the proper approach to take to
those who limit their contribution to their fair share when they could easily do
more and when, because others are not playing their part, a further donation
would assist many in desperate need. In the privacy of our own judgment, we
should believe that it is wrong not to do more. But whether we should actually
criticize people who are doing their fair share, but no more than that, depends
on the psychological impact that such criticism will have on them, and on others. This in turn may depend on social practices. If the majority are doing little
or nothing, setting a standard higher than the fair-share level may seem so
demanding that it discourages people who are willing to make an equitable contribution from doing even that. So it may be best to refrain from criticizing
those who achieve the fair-share level. In moving our society's standards forward, we may have to progress one step at a time.

For more than thirty years, I've been reading, writing, and teaching about the ethical issue posed by the juxtaposition, on our planet, of great abundance and life-threatening poverty. Yet it was not until, in preparing this article, I calculated how much America's top 10 percent of income earners actually make that I fully understood how easy it would be for the world's rich to eliminate, or virtually eliminate, global poverty. (It has actually become much easier over the past thirty years, as the rich have grown significantly richer.) I found the result astonishing. I double-checked the figures and asked a research assistant to check them as well. But they were right. Measured against our capacity, the Millennium Development Goals are indecently, shockingly modest. If we fail to achieve them—as on present indications we well might—we have no excuses. The target we should be setting for ourselves is not halving the proportion of people living in extreme poverty, and without enough to eat, but ensuring that no one, or virtually no one, needs to live in such degrading conditions. That is a worthy goal, and it is well within our reach.

MLA CITATION

Singer, Peter. "What Should a Billionaire Give—And What Should You?" 2006. *The Norton Reader: An Anthology of Nonfiction*. Ed. Melissa A. Goldthwaite et al. 14th ed. New York: Norton, 2016. 640–51. Print.

QUESTIONS

1. Peter Singer's title poses a two-part question: What should a billionaire give—and what should you? At the end of his essay, he gives an answer. Discuss the pros and cons of his proposal, including the effects it would have on the givers and the receivers.

2. What ethical arguments does Singer make before presenting his proposal? What facts and principles underlie his position that all Americans in the top ten percent income bracket should give a specific percentage to alleviate the plight of the poor?

3. Singer's essay depends on anecdotes as well as facts. Choose one anecdote you consider highly effective, and suggest the reasons it succeeds rhetorically.

4. It is possible to read online statements by many of the philanthropists Singer interviews or cites. Choose one whose ideas interest you, read more about his or her philanthropy, and write a brief account of what he or she has contributed and why.

ATUL GAWANDE   *When Doctors Make Mistakes*

I—CRASH VICTIM

A T 2 A.M. ON A CRISP FRIDAY IN WINTER, I was in sterile gloves and gown, pulling a teenage knifing victim's abdomen open, when my pager sounded. "Code Trauma, three minutes," the operating-room nurse said, reading aloud from my pager display. This meant that an ambulance would be bringing another trauma patient to the hospital momentarily, and, as the surgical resident on duty for emergencies, I would have to be present for the patient's arrival. I stepped back from the table and took off my gown. Two other surgeons were working on the knifing victim: Michael Ball, the attending (the staff surgeon in charge of the case), and David Hernandez, the chief resident (a general surgeon in his last of five years of training). Ordinarily, these two would have come later to help with the trauma, but they were stuck here. Ball, a dry, imperturbable forty-two-year-old Texan, looked over to me as I headed for the door. "If you run into any trouble, you call, and one of us will peel away," he said.

I did run into trouble. In telling this story, I have had to change significant details about what happened (including the names of the participants and aspects of my role), but I have tried to stay as close to the actual events as I could while protecting the patient, myself, and the rest of the staff. The way that things go wrong in medicine is normally unseen and, consequently, often misunderstood. Mistakes do happen. We think of them as aberrant; they are anything but.

The emergency room was one floor up, and, taking the stairs two at a time, I arrived just as the emergency medical technicians wheeled in a woman who appeared to be in her thirties and to weigh more than two hundred pounds. She lay motionless on a hard orange plastic spinal board—eyes closed, skin pale, blood running out of her nose. A nurse directed the crew into Trauma Bay 1, an examination room outfitted like an O.R., with green tiles on the wall, monitoring devices, and space for portable X-ray equipment. We lifted her onto the bed and then went to work. One nurse began cutting off the woman's clothes. Another took vital signs. A third inserted a large-bore intravenous line into her right arm. A surgical intern put a Foley catheter[1] into her bladder. The emergency-medicine attending was Samuel Johns, a gaunt, Ichabod Crane—

First published in the New Yorker *(1999), a weekly magazine of "reportage, commentary, criticism, essays, fiction, satire, cartoons, and poetry," and then in Atul Gawande's first book,* Complications: A Surgeon's Notes on an Imperfect Science *(2002). Gawande has continued to write books on medicine; his latest is* Being Mortal: Medicine and What Matters in the End *(2014). He is a surgeon at Boston's Brigham and Women's Hospital.*

1. Thin tube inserted into the bladder to drain urine.

like[2] man in his fifties. He was standing to one side with his arms crossed, observing, which was a sign that I could go ahead and take charge.

If you're in a hospital, most of the "moment to moment" doctoring you get is from residents—physicians receiving specialty training and a small income in exchange for their labor. Our responsibilities depend on our level of training, but we're never entirely on our own: there's always an attending, who oversees our decisions. That night, since Johns was the attending and was responsible for the patient's immediate management, I took my lead from him. But he wasn't a surgeon, and so he relied on me for surgical expertise.

"What's the story?" I asked.   5

An E.M.T. rattled off the details: "Unidentified white female unrestrained driver in high-speed rollover. Ejected from the car. Found unresponsive to pain. Pulse a hundred, B.P. a hundred over sixty, breathing at thirty on her own . . ."

As he spoke, I began examining her. The first step in caring for a trauma patient is always the same. It doesn't matter if a person has been shot eleven times or crushed by a truck or burned in a kitchen fire. The first thing you do is make sure that the patient can breathe without difficulty. This woman's breaths were shallow and rapid. An oximeter, by means of a sensor placed on her finger, measured the oxygen saturation of her blood. The "O_2 sat"[3] is normally more than ninety-five percent for a patient breathing room air. The woman was wearing a face mask with oxygen turned up full blast, and her sat was only ninety percent.

"She's not oxygenating well," I announced in the flattened-out, wake-me-up-when-something-interesting-happens tone that all surgeons have acquired by about three months into residency. With my fingers, I verified that there wasn't any object in her mouth that would obstruct her airway; with a stethoscope, I confirmed that neither lung had collapsed. I got hold of a bag mask, pressed its clear facepiece over her nose and mouth, and squeezed the bellows, a kind of balloon with a one-way valve, shooting a litre of air into her with each compression. After a minute or so, her oxygen came up to a comfortable ninety-eight percent. She obviously needed our help with breathing. "Let's tube her," I said. That meant putting a tube down through her vocal cords and into her trachea, which would insure a clear airway and allow for mechanical ventilation.

Johns, the attending, wanted to do the intubation. He picked up a Mac 3 laryngoscope, a standard but fairly primitive-looking L-shaped metal instrument for prying open the mouth and throat, and slipped the shoehornlike blade deep into her mouth and down to her larynx. Then he yanked the handle up toward the ceiling to pull her tongue out of the way, open her mouth and throat, and reveal the vocal cords, which sit like fleshy tent flaps at the entrance to the trachea. The patient didn't wince or gag: she was still out cold.

"Suction!" he called. "I can't see a thing."   10

2. Fictional hero of Washington Irving's "Legend of Sleepy Hollow," who was described as having a lanky frame.

3. "Sat" is an abbreviation for saturation.

He sucked out about a cup of blood and clot. Then he picked up the endo-tracheal tube—a clear rubber pipe about the diameter of an index finger and three times as long—and tried to guide it between her cords. After a minute, her sat started to fall.

"You're down to seventy percent," a nurse announced.

Johns kept struggling with the tube, trying to push it in, but it banged vainly against the cords. The patient's lips began to turn blue.

"Sixty percent," the nurse said.

15   Johns pulled everything out of the patient's mouth and fitted the bag mask back on. The oximeter's luminescent-green readout hovered at sixty for a moment and then rose steadily, to ninety-seven percent. After a few minutes, he took the mask off and again tried to get the tube in. There was more blood, and there may have been some swelling, too: all the poking down the throat was probably not helping. The sat fell to sixty percent. He pulled out and bagged her until she returned to ninety-five percent.

When you're having trouble getting the tube in, the next step is to get spe-cialized expertise. "Let's call anesthesia," I said, and Johns agreed. In the mean-time, I continued to follow the standard trauma protocol: completing the examination and ordering fluids, lab tests, and X-rays. Maybe five minutes passed as I worked.

The patient's sats drifted down to ninety-two percent—not a dramatic change but definitely not normal for a patient who is being manually ventilated. I checked to see if the sensor had slipped off her finger. It hadn't. "Is the oxy-gen up full blast?" I asked a nurse.

"It's up all the way," she said.

I listened again to the patient's lungs—no collapse. "We've got to get her tubed," Johns said. He took off the oxygen mask and tried again.

20   Somewhere in my mind, I must have been aware of the possibility that her airway was shutting down because of vocal-cord swelling or blood. If it was, and we were unable to get a tube in, then the only chance she'd have to survive would be an emergency tracheostomy: cutting a hole in her neck and inserting a breathing tube into her trachea. Another attempt to intubate her might even trigger a spasm of the cords and a sudden closure of the airway—which is exactly what did happen.

If I had actually thought this far along, I would have recognized how ill-prepared I was to do an emergency "trache." Of the people in the room, it's true, I had the most experience doing tracheostomies, but that wasn't saying much. I had been the assistant surgeon in only about half a dozen, and all but one of them had been non-emergency cases, employing techniques that were not designed for speed. The exception was a practice emergency trache I had done on a goat. I should have immediately called Dr. Ball for backup. I should have got the trache equipment out—lighting, suction, sterile instruments—just in case. Instead of hurrying the effort to get the patient intubated because of a mild drop in saturation, I should have asked Johns to wait until I had help nearby. I might even have recognized that she was already losing her airway. Then I could have grabbed a knife and started cutting her a tracheostomy while things were still relatively stable and I had time to proceed slowly. But for whatever reasons—hubris, inattention, wishful thinking, hesitation, or the uncertainty of the moment—I let the opportunity pass.

Johns hunched over the patient, intently trying to insert the tube through her vocal cords. When her sat once again dropped into the sixties, he stopped and put the mask back on. We stared at the monitor. The numbers weren't coming up. Her lips were still blue. Johns squeezed the bellows harder to blow more oxygen in.

"I'm getting resistance," he said.

The realization crept over me: this was a disaster. "Damn it, we've lost her airway," I said. "Trache kit! Light! Somebody call down to O.R. 25 and get Ball up here!"

People were suddenly scurrying everywhere. I tried to proceed deliberately, and not let panic take hold. I told the surgical intern to get a sterile gown and gloves on. I took a bactericidal solution off a shelf and dumped a whole bottle of yellow-brown liquid on the patient's neck. A nurse unwrapped the tracheostomy kit—a sterilized set of drapes and instruments. I pulled on a gown and a new pair of gloves while trying to think through the steps. This is simple, really, I tried to tell myself. At the base of the thyroid cartilage, the Adam's apple, is a little gap in which you find a thin, fibrous covering called the cricothyroid membrane. Cut through that and—voilà! You're in the trachea. You slip through the hole a four-inch plastic tube shaped like a plumber's elbow joint, hook it up to oxygen and a ventilator, and she's all set. Anyway, that was the theory.

I threw some drapes over her body, leaving the neck exposed. It looked as thick as a tree. I felt for the bony prominence of the thyroid cartilage. But I couldn't feel anything through the rolls of fat. I was beset by uncertainty—where should I cut? should I make a horizontal or a vertical incision?—and I hated myself for it. Surgeons never dithered, and I was dithering.

"I need better light," I said.

Someone was sent out to look for one.

"Did anyone get Ball?" I asked. It wasn't exactly an inspiring question.

"He's on his way," a nurse said.

There wasn't time to wait. Four minutes without oxygen would lead to permanent brain damage, if not death. Finally, I took the scalpel and cut. I just cut. I made a three-inch left-to-right swipe across the middle of the neck, following the procedure I'd learned for elective cases. I figured that if I worked through the fat I might be able to find the membrane in the wound. Dissecting down with scissors while the intern held the wound open with retractors, I hit a vein. It didn't let loose a lot of blood, but there was enough to fill the wound: I couldn't see anything. The intern put a finger on the bleeder. I called for suction. But the suction wasn't working; the tube was clogged with the clot from the intubation efforts.

"Somebody get some new tubing," I said. "And where's the light?"

Finally, an orderly wheeled in a tall overhead light, plugged it in, and flipped on the switch. It was still too dim; I could have done better with a flashlight.

I wiped up the blood with gauze, then felt around in the wound with my fingertips. This time, I thought I could feel the hard ridges of the thyroid cartilage and, below it, the slight gap of the cricothyroid membrane, though I couldn't be sure. I held my place with my left hand.

35   James O'Connor, a silver-haired, seen-it-all anesthesiologist, came into the room. Johns gave him a quick rundown on the patient and let him take over bagging her.

Holding the scalpel in my right hand like a pen, I stuck the blade down into the wound at the spot where I thought the thyroid cartilage was. With small, sharp strokes—working blindly, because of the blood and the poor light—I cut down through the overlying fat and tissue until I felt the blade scrape against the almost bony cartilage. I searched with the tip of the knife, walking it along until I felt it reach a gap. I hoped it was the cricothyroid membrane, and pressed down firmly. Then I felt the tissue suddenly give, and I cut an inch-long opening.

When I put my index finger into it, it felt as if I were prying open the jaws of a stiff clothespin. Inside, I thought I felt open space. But where were the sounds of moving air that I expected? Was this deep enough? Was I even in the right place?

"I think I'm in," I said, to reassure myself as much as anyone else.

"I hope so," O'Connor said. "She doesn't have much longer."

40   I took the tracheostomy tube and tried to fit it in, but something seemed to be blocking it. I twisted it and turned it, and finally jammed it in. Just then, Ball, the surgical attending, arrived. He rushed up to the bed and leaned over for a look. "Did you get it?" he asked. I said that I thought so. The bag mask was plugged onto the open end of the trache tube. But when the bellows were compressed the air just gurgled out of the wound. Ball quickly put on gloves and a gown.

"How long has she been without an airway?" he asked.

"I don't know. Three minutes."

Ball's face hardened as he registered that he had about a minute in which to turn things around. He took my place and summarily pulled out the trache tube. "God, what a mess," he said. "I can't see a thing in this wound. I don't even know if you're in the right place. Can we get better light and suction?" New suction tubing was found and handed to him. He quickly cleaned up the wound and went to work.

The patient's sat had dropped so low that the oximeter couldn't detect it anymore. Her heart rate began slowing down—first to the sixties and then to the forties. Then she lost her pulse entirely. I put my hands together on her chest, locked my elbows, leaned over her, and started doing chest compressions.

45   Ball looked up from the patient and turned to O'Connor. "I'm not going to get her an airway in time," he said. "You're going to have to try from above." Essentially, he was admitting my failure. Trying an oral intubation again was pointless—just something to do instead of watching her die. I was stricken, and concentrated on doing chest compressions, not looking at anyone. It was over, I thought.

And then, amazingly, O'Connor: "I'm in." He had managed to slip a pediatric-size endotracheal tube through the vocal cords. In thirty seconds, with oxygen being manually ventilated through the tube, her heart was back, racing at a hundred and twenty beats a minute. Her sat registered at sixty and then climbed. Another thirty seconds and it was at ninety-seven percent. All the people in the room exhaled, as if they, too, had been denied their breath. Ball and I said little except to confer about the next steps for her. Then he went back downstairs to finish working on the stab-wound patient still in the O.R.

We eventually identified the woman, whom I'll call Louise Williams; she was thirty-four years old and lived alone in a nearby suburb. Her alcohol level on arrival had been three times the legal limit, and had probably contributed to her unconsciousness. She had a concussion, several lacerations, and significant soft-tissue damage. But X-rays and scans revealed no other injuries from the crash. That night, Ball and Hernandez brought her to the O.R. to fit her with a proper tracheostomy. When Ball came out and talked to family members, he told them of the dire condition she was in when she arrived, the difficulties "we" had had getting access to her airway, the disturbingly long period of time that she had gone without oxygen, and thus his uncertainty about how much brain function she still possessed. They listened without protest; there was nothing for them to do but wait.

II—The Banality of Error

To much of the public—and certainly to lawyers and the media—medical error is a problem of bad physicians. Consider some other surgical mishaps. In one, a general surgeon left a large metal instrument in a patient's abdomen, where it tore through the bowel and the wall of the bladder. In another, a cancer surgeon biopsied the wrong part of a woman's breast and thereby delayed her diagnosis of cancer for months. A cardiac surgeon skipped a small but key step during a heart-valve operation, thereby killing the patient. A surgeon saw a man racked with abdominal pain in the emergency room and, without taking a C.T. scan, assumed that the man had a kidney stone; eighteen hours later, a scan showed a rupturing abdominal aortic aneurysm, and the patient died not long afterward.

How could anyone who makes a mistake of that magnitude be allowed to practice medicine? We call such doctors "incompetent," "unethical," and "negligent." We want to see them punished. And so we've wound up with the public system we have for dealing with error: malpractice lawsuits, media scandal, suspensions, firings.

There is, however, a central truth in medicine that complicates this tidy   50
vision of misdeeds and misdoers: *All* doctors make terrible mistakes. Consider the cases I've just described. I gathered them simply by asking respected surgeons I know—surgeons at top medical schools—to tell me about mistakes they had made just in the past year. Every one of them had a story to tell.

In 1991, *The New England Journal of Medicine* published a series of landmark papers from a project known as the Harvard Medical Practice Study—a review of more than thirty thousand hospital admissions in New York State.

The study found that nearly four percent of hospital patients suffered complications from treatment which prolonged their hospital stay or resulted in disability or death, and that two-thirds of such complications were due to errors in care. One in four, or one percent of admissions, involved actual negligence. It was estimated that, nationwide, a hundred and twenty thousand patients die each year at least partly as a result of errors in care. And subsequent investigations around the country have confirmed the ubiquity of error. In one small study of how clinicians perform when patients have a sudden cardiac arrest, twenty-seven of thirty clinicians made an error in using the defibrillator; they may have charged it incorrectly or lost valuable time trying to figure out how to work a particular model. According to a 1995 study, mistakes in administering drugs—giving the wrong drug or the wrong dose, say—occur, on the average, about once for every hospital admission, mostly without ill effects, but one percent of the time with serious consequences.

If error were due to a subset of dangerous doctors, you might expect malpractice cases to be concentrated among a small group, but in fact they follow a uniform, bell-shaped distribution. Most surgeons are sued at least once in the course of their careers. Studies of specific types of error, too, have found that repeat offenders are not the problem. The fact is that virtually everyone who cares for hospital patients will make serious mistakes, and even commit acts of negligence, every year. For this reason, doctors are seldom outraged when the press reports yet another medical horror story. They usually have a different reaction: *That could be me.* The important question isn't how to keep bad physicians from harming patients; it's how to keep good physicians from harming patients.

Medical-malpractice suits are a remarkably ineffective remedy. Troyen Brennan, a Harvard professor of law and public health, points out that research has consistently failed to find evidence that litigation reduces medical-error rates. In part, this may be because the weapon is so imprecise. Brennan led several studies following up on the patients in the Harvard Medical Practice Study. He found that fewer than two percent of the patients who had received substandard care ever filed suit. Conversely, only a small minority among the patients who did sue had in fact been the victims of negligent care. And a patient's likelihood of winning a suit depended primarily on how poor his or her outcome was, regardless of whether that outcome was caused by disease or unavoidable risks of care.

The deeper problem with medical-malpractice suits, however, is that by demonizing errors they prevent doctors from acknowledging and discussing them publicly. The tort system makes adversaries of patient and physician, and pushes each to offer a heavily slanted version of events. When things go wrong, it's almost impossible for a physician to talk to a patient honestly about mistakes. Hospital lawyers warn doctors that, although they must, of course, tell patients about complications that occur, they are never to intimate that they were at fault, lest the "confession" wind up in court as damning evidence in a black-and-white morality tale. At most, a doctor might say, "I'm sorry that things didn't go as well as we had hoped."

There is one place, however, where doctors can talk candidly about their mistakes, if not with patients, then at least with one another. It is called the Morbidity and Mortality Conference—or, more simply, M. & M.—and it takes place, usually once a week, at nearly every academic hospital in the country. This institution survives because laws protecting its proceedings from legal discovery have stayed on the books in most states, despite frequent challenges. Surgeons, in particular, take the M. & M. seriously. Here they can gather behind closed doors to review the mistakes, complications, and deaths that occurred on their watch, determine responsibility, and figure out what to do differently next time.

III—SHOW AND TELL

At my hospital, we convene every Tuesday at five o'clock in a steep, plush amphitheatre lined with oil portraits of the great doctors whose achievements we're meant to live up to. All surgeons are expected to attend, from the interns to the chairman of surgery; we're also joined by medical students doing their surgery "rotation." An M. & M. can include almost a hundred people. We file in, pick up a photocopied list of cases to be discussed, and take our seats. The front row is occupied by the most senior surgeons: terse, serious men, now out of their scrubs and in dark suits, lined up like a panel of senators at a hearing. The chairman is a leonine presence in the seat closest to the plain wooden podium from which each case is presented. In the next few rows are the remaining surgical attending; these tend to be younger, and several of them are women. The chief residents have put on long white coats and usually sit in the side rows. I join the mass of other residents, all of us in short white coats and green scrub pants, occupying the back rows.

For each case, the chief resident from the relevant service—cardiac, vascular, trauma, and so on—gathers the information, takes the podium, and tells the story. Here's a partial list of cases from a typical week (with a few changes to protect confidentiality): a sixty-eight-year-old man who bled to death after heart-valve surgery; a forty-seven-year-old woman who had to have a reoperation because of infection following an arterial bypass done in her left leg; a forty-four-year-old woman who had to have bile drained from her abdomen after gall-bladder surgery; three patients who had to have reoperations for bleeding following surgery; a sixty-three-year-old man who had a cardiac arrest following heart-bypass surgery; a sixty-six-year-old woman whose sutures suddenly gave way in an abdominal wound and nearly allowed her intestines to spill out. Ms. Williams's case, my failed tracheostomy, was just one case on a list like this. David Hernandez, the chief trauma resident, had subsequently reviewed the records and spoken to me and others involved. When the time came, it was he who stood up front and described what had happened.

Hernandez is a tall, rollicking, good old boy who can tell a yarn, but M. & M. presentations are bloodless and compact. He said something like: "This was a thirty-four-year-old female unrestrained driver in a high-speed rollover. The patient apparently had stable vitals at the scene but was unresponsive, and brought in by ambulance unintubated. She was G.C.S. 7 on arrival." G.C.S. stands for the Glasgow Coma Scale, which rates the severity of head injuries, from three to fifteen. G.C.S. 7 is in the comatose range. "Attempts to intubate were made without success in the E.R. and may have contributed to airway closure. A cricothyroidotomy[4] was attempted without success."

These presentations can be awkward. The chief residents, not the attendings, determine which cases to report. That keeps the attending honest—no one can cover up mistakes—but it puts the chief residents, who are, after all, underlings, in a delicate position. The successful M. & M. presentation inevitably involves a certain elision of detail and a lot of passive verbs. No one screws up a cricothyroidotomy. Instead, "a cricothyroidotomy was attempted without success." The message, however, was not lost on anyone.

60   Hernandez continued, "The patient arrested and required cardiac compressions. Anesthesia was then able to place a pediatric E.T. tube and the patient recovered stable vitals. The tracheostomy was then completed in the O.R."

So Louise Williams had been deprived of oxygen long enough to go into cardiac arrest, and everyone knew that meant she could easily have suffered a disabling stroke or been left a vegetable. Hernandez concluded with the fortunate aftermath: "Her workup was negative for permanent cerebral damage or other major injuries. The tracheostomy was removed on Day 2. She was discharged to home in good condition on Day 3." To the family's great relief, and mine, she had woken up in the morning a bit woozy but hungry, alert, and mentally intact. In a few weeks, the episode would heal to a scar.

But not before someone was called to account. A front-row voice immediately thundered, "What do you mean, 'A cricothyroidotomy was attempted without success?'" I sank into my seat, my face hot.

"This was my case," Dr. Ball volunteered from the front row. It is how every attending begins, and that little phrase contains a world of surgical culture. For all the talk in business schools and in corporate America about the virtues of "flat organizations," surgeons maintain an old-fashioned sense of hierarchy. When things go wrong, the attending is expected to take full responsibility. It makes no difference whether it was the resident's hand that slipped and lacerated an aorta; it doesn't matter whether the attending was at home in bed when a nurse gave a wrong dose of medication. At the M. & M., the burden of responsibility falls on the attending.

Ball went on to describe the emergency attending's failure to intubate Williams and his own failure to be at her bedside when things got out of control. He described the bad lighting and her extremely thick neck, and was careful to make those sound not like excuses but merely like complicating factors. Some attending shook their heads in sympathy. A couple of them asked questions to clarify certain details. Throughout, Ball's tone was objective, detached. He had the air of a CNN newscaster describing unrest in Kuala Lumpur.[5]

4. Emergency incision through the cricothyroid membrane to secure a patient's airway during an emergency—described in paragraphs 31–46.
5. Capital of Malaysia hit by economic crisis and political unrest in the late 1990s.

As always, the chairman, responsible for the over-all quality of our surgery 65
service, asked the final question. What, he wanted to know, would Ball have
done differently? Well, Ball replied, it didn't take long to get the stab-wound
patient under control in the O.R., so he probably should have sent Hernandez
up to the E.R. at that point or let Hernandez close the abdomen while he himself came up. People nodded. Lesson learned. Next case.

At no point during the M. & M. did anyone question why I had not called
for help sooner or why I had not had the skill and knowledge that Williams
needed. This is not to say that my actions were seen as acceptable. Rather, in
the hierarchy, addressing my errors was Ball's role. The day after the disaster,
Ball had caught me in the hall and taken me aside. His voice was more wounded
than angry as he went through my specific failures. First, he explained, in an
emergency tracheostomy it might have been better to do a vertical neck incision; that would have kept me out of the blood vessels, which run up and down—
something I should have known at least from my reading. I might have had a
much easier time getting her an airway then, he said. Second, and worse to him
than mere ignorance, he didn't understand why I hadn't called him when there
were clear signs of airway trouble developing. I offered no excuses. I promised to
be better prepared for such cases and to be quicker to ask for help.

Even after Ball had gone down the fluorescent-lit hallway, I felt a sense of
shame like a burning ulcer. This was not guilt: guilt is what you feel when you
have done something wrong. What I felt was shame: *I* was what was wrong. And
yet I also knew that a surgeon can take such feelings too far. It is one thing to
be aware of one's limitations. It is another to be plagued by self-doubt. One
surgeon with a national reputation told me about an abdominal operation in
which he had lost control of bleeding while he was removing what turned out
to be a benign tumor and the patient had died. "It was a clean kill," he said.
Afterward, he could barely bring himself to operate. When he did operate, he
became tentative and indecisive. The case affected his performance for months.

Even worse than losing self-confidence, though, is reacting defensively.
There are surgeons who will see faults everywhere except in themselves. They
have no questions and no fears about their abilities. As a result, they learn nothing from their mistakes and know nothing of their limitations. As one surgeon
told me, it is a rare but alarming thing to meet a surgeon without fear. "If you're
not a little afraid when you operate," he said, "you're bound to do a patient a
grave disservice."

The atmosphere at the M. & M. is meant to discourage both attitudes—
self-doubt and denial—for the M. & M. is a cultural ritual that inculcates in
surgeons a "correct" view of mistakes. "What would you do differently?" a chairman asks concerning cases of avoidable complications. "Nothing" is seldom an
acceptable answer.

In its way, the M. & M. is an impressively sophisticated and human insti- 70
tution. Unlike the courts or the media, it recognizes that human error is generally not something that can be deterred by punishment. The M. & M. sees
avoiding error as largely a matter of will—of staying sufficiently informed and
alert to anticipate the myriad ways that things can go wrong and then trying to

head off each potential problem before it happens. Why do things go wrong? Because, doctors say, making them go right is hard stuff. It isn't damnable that an error occurs, but there is some shame to it. In fact, the M. & M.'s ethos can seem paradoxical. On the one hand, it reinforces the very American idea that error is intolerable. On the other hand, the very existence of the M. & M., its place on the weekly schedule, amounts to an acknowledgment that mistakes are an inevitable part of medicine.

But why do they happen so often? Lucian Leape, medicine's leading expert on error, points out that many other industries—whether the task is manufacturing semiconductors or serving customers at the Ritz-Carlton—simply wouldn't countenance error rates like those in hospitals. The aviation industry has reduced the frequency of operational errors to one in a hundred thousand flights, and most of those errors have no harmful consequences. The buzzword at General Electric these days is "Six Sigma," meaning that its goal is to make product defects so rare that in statistical terms they are more than six standard deviations away from being a matter of chance—almost a one-in-a-million occurrence.

Of course, patients are far more complicated and idiosyncratic than airplanes, and medicine isn't a matter of delivering a fixed product or even a catalogue of products; it may well be more complex than just about any other field of human endeavor. Yet everything we've learned in the past two decades—from cognitive psychology, from "human factors" engineering, from studies of disasters like Three Mile Island and Bhopal[6]—has yielded the same insights: not only do all human beings err but they err frequently and in predictable, patterned ways. And systems that do not adjust for these realities can end up exacerbating rather than eliminating error.

The British psychologist James Reason argues, in his book *Human Error,* that our propensity for certain types of error is the price we pay for the brain's remarkable ability to think and act intuitively—to sift quickly through the sensory information that constantly bombards us without wasting time trying to work through every situation anew. Thus systems that rely on human perfection present what Reason calls "latent errors"—errors waiting to happen. Medicine teems with examples. Take writing out a prescription, a rote procedure that relies on memory and attention, which we know are unreliable. Inevitably, a physician will sometimes specify the wrong dose or the wrong drug. Even when the prescription is written correctly, there's a risk that it will be misread. (Computerized ordering systems can almost eliminate errors of this kind, but only a small minority of hospitals have adopted them.) Medical equipment, which manufacturers often build without human operators in mind, is another area rife with latent errors: one reason physicians are bound to have problems

6. In 1979 there was a partial meltdown of a pressurized water reactor at Three Mile Island Nuclear Generating Station near Harrisburg, Pennsylvania; the Bhopal Gas disaster occurred in December 1984 at the Union Carbide pesticide plant in Bhopal, Madhya Pradesh, India, exposing 500,000 people to dangerous chemicals.

when they use cardiac defibrillators is that the devices have no standard design. You can also make the case that onerous workloads, chaotic environments, and inadequate team communication all represent latent errors in the system.

James Reason makes another important observation: disasters do not simply occur; they evolve. In complex systems, a single failure rarely leads to harm. Human beings are impressively good at adjusting when an error becomes apparent, and systems often have built-in defenses. For example, pharmacists and nurses routinely check and counter-check physicians' orders. But errors do not always become apparent, and backup systems themselves often fail as a result of latent errors. A pharmacist forgets to check one of a thousand prescriptions. A machine's alarm bell malfunctions. The one attending trauma surgeon available gets stuck in the operating room. When things go wrong, it is usually because a series of failures conspire to produce disaster.

The M. & M. takes none of this into account. For that reason, many experts 75 see it as a rather shabby approach to analyzing error and improving performance in medicine. It isn't enough to ask what a clinician could or should have done differently so that he and others may learn for next time. The doctor is often only the final actor in a chain of events that set him or her up to fail. Error experts, therefore, believe that it's the process, not the individuals in it, which requires closer examination and correction. In a sense, they want to industrialize medicine. And they can already claim one success story: the specialty of anesthesiology, which has adopted their precepts and seen extraordinary results.

IV—NEARLY PERFECT

At the center of the emblem of the American Society of Anesthesiologists is a single word: "Vigilance." When you put a patient to sleep under general anesthesia, you assume almost complete control of the patient's body. The body is paralyzed, the brain rendered unconscious, and machines are hooked up to control breathing, heart rate, blood pressure—all the vital functions. Given the complexity of the machinery and of the human body, there are a seemingly infinite number of ways in which things can go wrong, even in minor surgery. And yet anesthesiologists have found that if problems are detected they can usually be solved. In the nineteen-forties, there was only one death resulting from anesthesia in every twenty-five hundred operations, and between the nineteen-sixties and the nineteen-eighties the rate had stabilized at one or two in every ten thousand operations.

But Ellison (Jeep) Pierce had always regarded even that rate as unconscionable. From the time he began practicing, in 1960, as a young anesthesiologist out of North Carolina and the University of Pennsylvania, he had maintained a case file of details from all the deadly anesthetic accidents he had come across or participated in. But it was one case in particular that galvanized him. Friends of his had taken their eighteen-year-old daughter to the hospital to have her wisdom teeth pulled, under general anesthesia. The anesthesiologist inserted the breathing tube into her esophagus instead of her trachea, which is a relatively common mishap, and then failed to spot the error, which is not. Deprived of oxygen, she died within minutes. Pierce knew that a one-in-ten-thousand death rate, given that anesthesia was administered in the United States an estimated thirty-five million times each year, meant thirty-five hundred avoidable deaths like that one.

In 1982, Pierce was elected vice-president of the American Society of Anesthesiologists and got an opportunity to do something about the death rate. The same year, ABC's 20/20 aired an exposé that caused a considerable stir in his profession. The segment began, "If you are going to go into anesthesia, you are going on a long trip, and you should not do it if you can avoid it in any way. General anesthesia [is] safe most of the time, but there are dangers from human error, carelessness, and a critical shortage of anesthesiologists. This year, six thousand patients will die or suffer brain damage." The program presented several terrifying cases from around the country. Between the small crisis that the show created and the sharp increases in physicians' malpractice-insurance premiums at that time, Pierce was able to mobilize the Society of Anesthesiologists around the problem of error.

He turned for ideas not to a physician but to an engineer named Jeffrey Cooper, the lead author of a ground-breaking 1978 paper entitled "Preventable Anesthesia Mishaps: A Study of Human Factors." An unassuming, fastidious man, Cooper had been hired in 1972, when he was twenty-six years old, by the Massachusetts General Hospital bioengineering unit, to work on developing machines for anesthesiology researchers. He gravitated toward the operating room, however, and spent hours there observing the anesthesiologists, and one of the first things he noticed was how poorly the anesthesia machines were designed. For example, a clockwise turn of a dial decreased the concentration of potent anesthetics in about half the machines but increased the concentration in the other half. He decided to borrow a technique called "critical incident analysis"—which had been used since the nineteen-fifties to analyze mishaps in aviation—in an effort to learn how equipment might be contributing to errors in anesthesia. The technique is built around carefully conducted interviews, designed to capture as much detail as possible about dangerous incidents: how specific accidents evolved and what factors contributed to them. This information is then used to look for patterns among different cases.

80   Getting open, honest reporting is crucial. The Federal Aviation Administration has a formalized system for analyzing and reporting dangerous aviation incidents, and its enormous success in improving airline safety rests on two cornerstones. Pilots who report an incident within ten days have automatic immunity from punishment, and the reports go to a neutral, outside agency, NASA, which has no interest in using the information against individual pilots. For Jeffrey Cooper, it was probably an advantage that he was an engineer, and not a physician, so that anesthesiologists regarded him as a discreet, unthreatening interviewer.

The result was the first in-depth, scientific look at errors in medicine. His detailed analysis of three hundred and fifty-nine errors provided a view of the profession unlike anything that had been seen before. Contrary to the prevailing assumption that the start of anesthesia ("takeoff") was the most dangerous part, anesthesiologists learned that incidents tended to occur in the middle of anesthesia, when vigilance waned. The most common kind of incident involved errors in maintaining the patient's breathing, and these were usually the result of an undetected disconnection or misconnection of the breathing tubing, mistakes in managing the airway, or mistakes in using the anesthesia machine. Just as important, Cooper enumerated a list of contributory factors, including inadequate experience, inadequate familiarity with equipment, poor communication among team members, haste, inattention, and fatigue.

The study provoked widespread debate among anesthesiologists, but there was no concerted effort to solve the problems until Jeep Pierce came along. Through the anesthesiology society at first, and then through a foundation that he started, Pierce directed funding into research on how to reduce the problems Cooper had identified, sponsored an international conference to gather ideas from around the world, and brought anesthesia-machine designers into safety discussions.

It all worked. Hours for anesthesiology residents were shortened. Manufacturers began redesigning their machines with fallible human beings in mind. Dials were standardized to turn in a uniform direction; locks were put in to prevent accidental administration of more than one anesthetic gas; controls were changed so that oxygen delivery could not be turned down to zero.

Where errors could not be eliminated directly, anesthesiologists began looking for reliable means of detecting them earlier. For example, because the trachea and the esophagus are so close together, it is almost inevitable that an anesthesiologist will sometimes put the breathing tube down the wrong pipe. Anesthesiologists had always checked for this by listening with a stethoscope for breath sounds over both lungs. But Cooper had turned up a surprising number of mishaps—like the one that befell the daughter of Pierce's friends—involving undetected esophageal intubations. Something more effective was needed. In fact, monitors that could detect this kind of error had been available for years, but, in part because of their expense, relatively few anesthesiologists used them. One type of monitor could verify that the tube was in the trachea by detecting carbon dioxide being exhaled from the lungs. Another type, the pulse oximeter, tracked blood-oxygen levels, thereby providing an early warning that something was wrong with the patient's breathing system. Prodded by Pierce and others, the anesthesiology society made the use of both types of monitor for every patient receiving general anesthesia an official standard. Today, anesthesia deaths from misconnecting the breathing system or intubating the esophagus rather than the trachea are virtually unknown. In a decade, the over-all death rate dropped to just one in more than two hundred thousand cases—less than a twentieth of what it had been.

And the reformers have not stopped there. David Gaba, a professor of anesthesiology at Stanford, has focused on improving human performance. In aviation, he points out, pilot experience is recognized to be invaluable but insufficient: pilots seldom have direct experience with serious plane malfunction anymore. They are therefore required to undergo yearly training in crisis simulators. Why not doctors, too?

Gaba, a physician with training in engineering, led in the design of an anesthesia-simulation system known as the Eagle Patient Simulator. It is a life-size, computer-driven mannequin that is capable of amazingly realistic behavior. It has a circulation, a heartbeat, and lungs that take in oxygen and expire carbon dioxide. If you inject drugs into it or administer inhaled anesthetics, it will detect the type and amount, and its heart rate, its blood pressure, and its oxygen levels will respond appropriately. The "patient" can be made to develop airway swelling, bleeding, and heart disturbances. The mannequin is laid on an operating table in a simulation room equipped exactly like the real thing. Here both residents and experienced attending physicians learn to perform effectively in all kinds of dangerous, and sometimes freak, scenarios: an anesthesia-machine malfunction, a power outage, a patient who goes into cardiac arrest during surgery, and even a cesarean-section patient whose airway shuts down and who requires an emergency tracheostomy.

Though anesthesiology has unquestionably taken the lead in analyzing and trying to remedy "systems" failures, there are signs of change in other quarters. The American Medical Association, for example, set up its National Patient Safety Foundation in 1997 and asked Cooper and Pierce to serve on the board of directors. The foundation is funding research, sponsoring conferences, and attempting to develop new standards for hospital drug-ordering systems that could substantially reduce medication mistakes—the single most common type of medical error.

Even in surgery there have been some encouraging developments. For instance, operating on the wrong knee or foot or other body part of a patient has been a recurrent, if rare, mistake. A typical response has been to fire the surgeon. Recently, however, hospitals and surgeons have begun to recognize that the body's bilateral symmetry makes these errors predictable. Last year, the American Academy of Orthopedic Surgeons endorsed a simple way of preventing them: make it standard practice for surgeons to initial, with a marker, the body part to be cut before the patient comes to surgery.

The Northern New England Cardiovascular Disease Study Group, based at Dartmouth, is another success story. Though the group doesn't conduct the sort of in-depth investigation of mishaps that Jeffrey Cooper pioneered, it has shown what can be done simply through statistical monitoring. Six hospitals belong to this consortium, which tracks deaths and complications (such as wound infections, uncontrolled bleeding, and stroke) arising from heart surgery and tries to identify various risk factors. Its researchers found, for example, that there were relatively high death rates among patients who developed anemia after bypass surgery, and that anemia developed most often in small patients. The fluid used to "prime" the heart-lung machine caused the anemia, because it diluted a patient's blood, so the smaller the patient (and his or her blood supply) the greater the effect. Members of the consortium now have several promising solutions to the problem. Another study found that a group at one hospital had made mistakes in "handoffs"—say, in passing preoperative lab results to the people in the operating room. The study group solved the problem by developing a pilot's checklist for all patients coming to the O.R. These efforts have introduced a greater degree of standardization, and so reduced the death rate in those six hospitals from four percent to three percent between 1991 and 1996. That meant two hundred and ninety-three fewer deaths. But the Northern New England cardiac group, even with its narrow focus and techniques, remains an exception; hard information about how things go wrong is still scarce. There is a hodgepodge of evidence that latent errors and systemic factors may contribute to surgical errors: the lack of standardized protocols, the surgeon's inexperience, the hospital's inexperience, inadequately designed technology and techniques, thin staffing, poor teamwork, time of day, the effects of managed care and corporate medicine, and so on and so on. But which are the major risk factors? We still don't know. Surgery, like most of medicine, awaits its Jeff Cooper.

V—GETTING IT RIGHT

It was a routine gallbladder operation, on a routine day: on the operating table   90
was a mother in her forties, her body covered by blue paper drapes except for her round, antiseptic-coated belly. The gallbladder is a floppy, finger-length sac of bile like a deflated olive-green balloon tucked under the liver, and when gallstones form, as this patient had learned, they can cause excruciating bouts of pain. Once we removed her gallbladder, the pain would stop.

There are risks to this surgery, but they used to be much greater. Just a decade ago, surgeons had to make a six-inch abdominal incision that left patients in the hospital for the better part of a week just recovering from the wound. Today, we've learned to take out gallbladders with a minute camera and instruments that we manipulate through tiny incisions. The operation, often done as day surgery, is known as laparoscopic cholecystectomy, or "lap chole." Half a million Americans a year now have their gallbladders removed this way; at my hospital alone, we do several hundred lap choles annually.

When the attending gave me the go-ahead, I cut a discreet inch-long semicircle in the wink of skin just above the belly button. I dissected through fat and fascia until I was inside the abdomen, and dropped into place a "port," a half-inch-wide sheath for slipping instruments in and out. We hooked gas tubing up to a side vent on the port, and carbon dioxide poured in, inflating the abdomen until it was distended like a tire. I inserted the miniature camera. On a video monitor a few feet away, the woman's intestines blinked into view. With the abdomen inflated, I had room to move the camera, and I swung it around to look at the liver. The gallbladder could be seen poking out from under the edge.

We put in three more ports through even tinier incisions, spaced apart to complete the four corners of a square. Through the ports on his side, the attending put in two long "graspers," like small-scale versions of the device that a department-store clerk might use to get a hat off the top shelf. Watching the screen as he maneuvered them, he reached under the edge of the liver, clamped onto the gallbladder, and pulled it up into view. We were set to proceed.

Removing the gallbladder is fairly straightforward. You sever it from its stalk and from its blood supply, and pull the rubbery sac out of the abdomen through the incision near the belly button. You let the carbon dioxide out of the belly, pull out the ports, put a few stitches in the tiny incisions, slap some Band-Aids on top, and you're done. There's one looming danger, though: the stalk of the gallbladder is a branch off the liver's only conduit for sending bile to the intestines for the digestion of fats. And if you accidentally injure this main bile duct, the bile backs up and starts to destroy the liver. Between ten and twenty percent of the patients to whom this happens will die. Those who survive often have permanent liver damage and can go on to require liver transplantation. According to a standard textbook, "injuries to the main bile duct are nearly always the result of misadventure during operation and are therefore a serious reproach to the surgical profession." It is a true surgical error, and, like any surgical team doing a lap chole, we were intent on avoiding this mistake.

95   Using a dissecting instrument, I carefully stripped off the fibrous white tissue and yellow fat overlying and concealing the base of the gallbladder. Now we could see its broad neck and the short stretch where it narrowed down to a duct—a tube no thicker than a strand of spaghetti peeking out from the surrounding tissue, but magnified on the screen to the size of major plumbing. Then, just to be absolutely sure we were looking at the gallbladder duct and not the main bile duct, I stripped away some more of the surrounding tissue. The attending and I stopped at this point, as we always do, and discussed the anatomy. The neck of the gallbladder led straight into the tube we were eying. So it had to be the right duct. We had exposed a good length of it without a sign of the main bile duct. Everything looked perfect, we agreed. "Go for it," the attending said.

I slipped in the clip applier, an instrument that squeezes V-shaped metal clips onto whatever you put in its jaws. I got the jaws around the duct and was about to fire when my eye caught, on the screen, a little globule of fat lying on top of the duct. That wasn't necessarily anything unusual, but somehow it didn't look right. With the tip of the clip applier, I tried to flick it aside, but, instead of a little globule, a whole layer of thin unseen tissue came up, and, underneath, we saw that the duct had a fork in it. My stomach dropped. If not for that little extra fastidiousness, I would have clipped off the main bile duct.

Here was the paradox of error in medicine. With meticulous technique and assiduous effort to insure that they have correctly identified the anatomy, surgeons need never cut the main bile duct. It is a paradigm of an avoidable error. At the same time, studies show that even highly experienced surgeons inflict this terrible injury about once in every two hundred lap choles. To put it another way, I may have averted disaster this time, but a statistician would say that, no matter how hard I tried, I was almost certain to make this error at least once in the course of my career.

But the story doesn't have to end here, as the cognitive psychologists and industrial-error experts have demonstrated. Given the results they've achieved in anesthesiology, it's clear that we can make dramatic improvements by going after the process, not the people. But there are distinct limitations to the industrial cure, however necessary its emphasis on systems and structures. It would be deadly for us, the individual actors, to give up our belief in human perfectibility. The statistics may say that someday I will sever someone's main bile duct, but each time I go into a gallbladder operation I believe that with enough will and effort I can beat the odds. This isn't just professional vanity. It's a necessary part of good medicine, even in superbly "optimized" systems. Operations like that lap chole have taught me how easily error can occur, but they've also showed me something else: effort does matter; diligence and attention to the minutest details can save you.

This may explain why many doctors take exception to talk of "systems problems," "continuous quality improvement," and "process reëngineering." It is the dry language of structures, not people. I'm no exception: something in me, too, demands an acknowledgment of my autonomy, which is also to say my ultimate culpability. Go back to that Friday night in the E.R., to the moment when I stood, knife in hand, over Louise Williams, her lips blue, her throat a swollen, bloody, and suddenly closed passage. A systems engineer might have proposed some useful changes. Perhaps a backup suction device should always be at hand, and better light more easily available. Perhaps the institution could have trained me better for such crises, could have required me to have operated on a few more goats. Perhaps emergency tracheostomies are so difficult under any circumstances that an automated device could have been designed to do a better job. But the could-haves are infinite, aren't they? Maybe Williams could have worn her seat belt, or had one less beer that night. We could call any or all of these factors latent errors, accidents waiting to happen.

But although they put the odds against me, it wasn't as if I had no chance   100
of succeeding. Good doctoring is all about making the most of the hand you're dealt, and I failed to do so. The indisputable fact was that I hadn't called for help when I could have, and when I plunged the knife into her neck and made my horizontal slash my best was not good enough. It was just luck, hers and mine, that Dr. O'Connor somehow got a breathing tube into her in time.

There are all sorts of reasons that it would be wrong to take my license away or to take me to court. These reasons do not absolve me. Whatever the limits of the M. & M., its fierce ethic of personal responsibility for errors is a formidable virtue. No matter what measures are taken, medicine will sometimes falter, and it isn't reasonable to ask that it achieve perfection. What's reasonable is to ask that medicine never cease to aim for it.

MLA CITATION

Gawande, Atul. "When Doctors Make Mistakes." 1999. *The Norton Reader: An Anthology of Nonfiction*. Ed. Melissa A. Goldthwaite et al. 14th ed. New York: Norton, 2016. 652–69. Print.

QUESTIONS

1. Atul Gawande states flatly: "*All* doctors make terrible mistakes" (paragraph 50), and then proceeds to analyze why. What are the main reasons he offers?

2. In section IV, "Nearly Perfect," Gawande discusses attempts by different medical groups to eliminate or reduce error. What approaches have been effective? What are the limits of these approaches?

3. Although it incorporates significant research, this essay also fits the genre of the personal narrative. At the beginning and end, Gawande narrates two of his experiences in the operating room. Are these examples similar or different? Does the rhetorical purpose of the anecdote stay the same, or does it change as Gawande moves through his discussion of medical error? Explain.

4. Narrate a personal experience in which you made a serious error. Try, like Gawande, to incorporate the research or advice of others who might help you understand the reasons for your error.

TOM REGAN   *The Case for Animal Rights*

I REGARD MYSELF as an advocate of animal rights— as a part of the animal rights movement. That movement, as I conceive it, is committed to a number of goals, including:

- the total abolition of the use of animals in science;
- the total dissolution of commercial animal agriculture;
- the total elimination of commercial and sport hunting and trapping.

There are, I know, people who profess to believe in animal rights but do not avow these goals. Factory farming, they say, is wrong—it violates animals' rights—but traditional animal agriculture is all right. Toxicity tests of cosmetics on animals violates their rights, but important medical research—cancer research, for example—does not. The clubbing of baby seals is abhorrent, but not the harvesting of adult seals. I used to think I understood this reasoning. Not any more. You don't change unjust institutions by tidying them up.

What's wrong—fundamentally wrong—with the way animals are treated isn't the details that vary from case to case. It's the whole system. The forlornness of the veal calf is pathetic, heart-wrenching; the pulsing pain of the chimp with electrodes planted deep in her brain is repulsive; the slow, tortuous death of the racoon caught in the leg-hold trap is agonizing. But what is wrong isn't the pain, isn't the suffering, isn't the deprivation. These compound what's wrong. Sometimes—often—they make it much, much worse. But they are not the fundamental wrong.

From In Defense of Animals *(1985), a collection of essays edited by Peter Singer.*

The fundamental wrong is the system that allows us to view animals as *our resources*, here for *us*—to be eaten, or surgically manipulated, or exploited for sport or money. Once we accept this view of animals—as our resources—the rest is as predictable as it is regrettable. Why worry about their loneliness, their pain, their death? Since animals exist for us, to benefit us in one way or another, what harms them really doesn't matter—or matters only if it starts to bother us, makes us feel a trifle uneasy when we eat our veal escalope, for example. So, yes, let us get veal calves out of solitary confinement, give them more space, a little straw, a few companions. But let us keep our veal escalope.

But a little straw, more space and a few companions won't eliminate—won't even touch—the basic wrong that attaches to our viewing and treating these animals as our resources. A veal calf killed to be eaten after living in close confinement is viewed and treated in this way: but so, too, is another who is raised (as they say) "more humanely." To right the wrong of our treatment of farm animals requires more than making rearing methods "more humane"; it requires the total dissolution of commercial animal agriculture.

How we do this, whether we do it or, as in the case of animals in science, whether and how we abolish their use—these are to a large extent political questions. People must change their beliefs before they change their habits. Enough people, especially those elected to public office, must believe in change—must want it—before we will have laws that protect the rights of animals. This process of change is very complicated, very demanding, very exhausting, calling for the efforts of many hands in education, publicity, political organization and activity, down to the licking of envelopes and stamps. As a trained and practicing philosopher, the sort of contribution I can make is limited but, I like to think, important. The currency of philosophy is ideas—their meaning and rational foundation—not the nuts and bolts of the legislative process, say, or the mechanics of community organization. That's what I have been exploring over the past ten years or so in my essays and talks and, most recently, in my book, *The Case for Animal Rights*. I believe the major conclusions I reach in the book are true because they are supported by the weight of the best arguments. I believe the idea of animal rights has reason, not just emotion, on its side.

In the space I have at my disposal here I can only sketch, in the barest outline, some of the main features of the book. Its main themes—and we should not be surprised by this—involve asking and answering deep, foundational moral questions about what morality is, how it should be understood and what is the best moral theory, all considered. I hope I can convey something of the shape I think this theory takes. The attempt to do this will be (to use a word a friendly critic once used to describe my work) cerebral, perhaps too cerebral. But this is misleading. My feelings about how animals are sometimes treated run just as deep and just as strong as those of my more volatile compatriots. Philosophers do—to use the jargon of the day—have a right side to their brains. If it's the left side we contribute (or mainly should), that's because what talents we have reside there.

How to proceed? We begin by asking how the moral status of animals has been understood by thinkers who deny that animals have rights. Then we test the mettle of their ideas by seeing how well they stand up under the heat of fair criticism. If we start our thinking in this way, we soon find that some people believe that we have no duties directly to animals, that we owe nothing to them, that we can do nothing that wrongs them. Rather, we can do wrong acts that involve animals, and so we have duties regarding them, though none to them. Such views may be called indirect duty views. By way of illustration: suppose your neighbor kicks your dog. Then your neighbor has done something wrong. But not to your dog. The wrong that has been done is a wrong to you. After all, it is wrong to upset people, and your neighbor's kicking your dog upsets you. So you are the one who is wronged, not your dog. Or again: by kicking your dog your neighbor damages your property. And since it is wrong to damage another person's property, your neighbor has done something wrong—to you, of course, not to your dog. Your neighbor no more wrongs your dog than your car would be wronged if the windshield were smashed. Your neighbor's duties involving your dog are indirect duties to you. More generally, all of our duties regarding animals are indirect duties to one another—to humanity.

How could someone try to justify such a view? Someone might say that your dog doesn't feel anything and so isn't hurt by your neighbor's kick, doesn't care about the pain since none is felt, is as unaware of anything as is your windshield. Someone might say this, but no rational person will, since, among other considerations, such a view will commit anyone who holds it to the position that no human being feels pain either—that human beings also don't care about what happens to them. A second possibility is that though both humans and your dog are hurt when kicked, it is only human pain that matters. But, again, no rational person can believe this. Pain is pain wherever it occurs. If your neighbor's causing you pain is wrong because of the pain that is caused, we cannot rationally ignore or dismiss the moral relevance of the pain that your dog feels.

Philosophers who hold indirect duty views—and many still do—have come to understand that they must avoid the two defects just noted: that is, both the view that animals don't feel anything as well as the idea that only human pain can be morally relevant. Among such thinkers the sort of view now favored is one or other form of what is called *contractarianism.*

10   Here, very crudely, is the root idea: morality consists of a set of rules that individuals voluntarily agree to abide by, as we do when we sign a contract (hence the name contractarianism). Those who understand and accept the terms of the contract are covered directly; they have rights created and recognized by, and protected in, the contract and these contractors can also have protection spelled out for others who, though they lack the ability to understand morality and so cannot sign the contract themselves, are loved or cherished by those who can. Thus young children, for example, are unable to sign contracts and lack rights. But they are protected by the contract none the less because of the sentimental interests of others, most notably their parents. So we have, then, duties involving these children, duties regarding them, but no duties to them. Our duties in their case are indirect duties to other human beings, usually their parents.

As for animals, since they cannot understand contracts, they obviously cannot sign; and since they cannot sign, they have no rights. Like children, however, some animals are the objects of the sentimental interest of others. You, for example, love your dog or cat. So those animals that enough people care about (companion animals, whales, baby seals, the American bald eagle), though they lack rights themselves, will be protected because of the sentimental interests of people. I have, then, according to contractarianism, no duty directly to your dog or any other animal, not even the duty not to cause them pain or suffering; my duty not to hurt them is a duty I have to those people who care about what happens to them. As for other animals, where no or little sentimental interest is present—in the case of farm animals, for example, or laboratory rats—what duties we have grow weaker and weaker, perhaps to vanishing point. The pain and death they endure, though real, are not wrong if no one cares about them.

When it comes to the moral status of animals, contractarianism could be a hard view to refute if it were an adequate theoretical approach to the moral status of human beings. It is not adequate in this latter respect, however, which makes the question of its adequacy in the former case, regarding animals, utterly moot. For consider: morality, according to the (crude) contractarian position before us, consists of rules that people agree to abide by. What people? Well, enough to make a difference—enough, that is, *collectively* to have the power to enforce the rules that are drawn up in the contract. This is very well and good for the signatories but not so good for anyone who is not asked to sign. And there is nothing in contractarianism of the sort we are discussing that guarantees or requires that everyone will have a chance to participate equally in framing the rules of morality. The result is that this approach to ethics could sanction the most blatant forms of social, economic, moral and political injustice, ranging from a repressive caste system to systematic racial or sexual discrimination. Might, according to this theory, does make right. Let those who are the victims of injustice suffer as they will. It matters not so long as no one else—no contractor, or too few of them—cares about it. Such a theory takes one's moral breath away . . . as if, for example, there would be nothing wrong with apartheid in South Africa if few white South Africans were upset by it. A theory with so little to recommend it at the level of the ethics of our treatment of our fellow humans cannot have anything more to recommend it when it comes to the ethics of how we treat our fellow animals.

The version of contractarianism just examined is, as I have noted, a crude variety, and in fairness to those of a contractarian persuasion it must be noted that much more refined, subtle and ingenious varieties are possible. For example, John Rawls,[1] in his *A Theory of Justice,* sets forth a version of contractarianism that forces contractors to ignore the accidental features of being a human being—for example, whether one is white or black, male or female, a genius or of modest intellect. Only by ignoring such features, Rawls believes, can we ensure that the principles of justice that contractors would agree upon are not based on bias or prejudice. Despite the improvement a view such as

1. American philosopher (1921–2002).

Rawls's represents over the cruder forms of contractarianism, it remains deficient: it systematically denies that we have direct duties to those human beings who do not have a sense of justice—young children, for instance, and many mentally retarded humans. And yet it seems reasonably certain that, were we to torture a young child or a retarded elder, we would be doing something that wronged him or her, not something that would be wrong if (and only if) other humans with a sense of justice were upset. And since this is true in the case of these humans, we cannot rationally deny the same in the case of animals.

Indirect duty views, then, including the best among them, fail to command our rational assent. Whatever ethical theory we should accept rationally, therefore, it must at least recognize that we have some duties directly to animals, just as we have some duties directly to each other. The next two theories I'll sketch attempt to meet this requirement.

15   The first I call the cruelty-kindness view. Simply stated, this says that we have a direct duty to be kind to animals and a direct duty not to be cruel to them. Despite the familiar, reassuring ring of these ideas, I do not believe that this view offers an adequate theory. To make this clearer, consider kindness. A kind person acts from a certain kind of motive—compassion or concern, for example. And that is a virtue. But there is no guarantee that a kind act is a right act. If I am a generous racist, for example, I will be inclined to act kindly towards members of my own race, favoring their interests above those of others. My kindness would be real and, so far as it goes, good. But I trust it is too obvious to require argument that my kind acts may not be above moral reproach—may, in fact, be positively wrong because rooted in injustice. So kindness, notwithstanding its status as a virtue to be encouraged, simply will not carry the weight of a theory of right action.

Cruelty fares no better. People or their acts are cruel if they display either a lack of sympathy for or, worse, the presence of enjoyment in another's suffering. Cruelty in all its guises is a bad thing, a tragic human failing. But just as a person's being motivated by kindness does not guarantee that he or she does what is right, so the absence of cruelty does not ensure that he or she avoids doing what is wrong. Many people who perform abortions, for example, are not cruel, sadistic people. But that fact alone does not settle the terribly difficult question of the morality of abortion. The case is no different when we examine the ethics of our treatment of animals. So, yes, let us be for kindness and against cruelty. But let us not suppose that being for the one and against the other answers questions about moral right and wrong.

Some people think that the theory we are looking for is utilitarianism. A utilitarian accepts two moral principles. The first is that of equality: everyone's interests count, and similar interests must be counted as having similar weight or importance. White or black, American or Iranian, human or animal— everyone's pain or frustration matter, and matter just as much as the equivalent pain or frustration of anyone else. The second principle a utilitarian accepts is that of utility: do the act that will bring about the best balance between satisfaction and frustration for everyone affected by the outcome.

As a utilitarian, then, here is how I am to approach the task of deciding what I morally ought to do: I must ask who will be affected if I choose to do one thing rather than another, how much each individual will be affected, and where the best results are most likely to lie—which option, in other words, is most likely to bring about the best results, the best balance between satisfaction and frustration. That option, whatever it may be, is the one I ought to choose. That is where my moral duty lies.

The great appeal of utilitarianism rests with its uncompromising *egalitarianism*: everyone's interests count and count as much as the like interests of everyone else. The kind of odious discrimination that some forms of contractarianism can justify—discrimination based on race or sex, for example—seems disallowed in principle by utilitarianism, as is speciesism, systematic discrimination based on species membership.

The equality we find in utilitarianism, however, is not the sort an advocate   20
of animal or human rights should have in mind. Utilitarianism has no room for the equal moral rights of different individuals because it has no room for their equal inherent value or worth. What has value for the utilitarian is the satisfaction of an individual's interests, not the individual whose interests they are. A universe in which you satisfy your desire for water, food and warmth is, other things being equal, better than a universe in which these desires are frustrated. And the same is true in the case of an animal with similar desires. But neither you nor the animal have any value in your own right. Only your feelings do.

Here is an analogy to help make the philosophical point clearer: a cup contains different liquids, sometimes sweet, sometimes bitter, sometimes a mix of the two. What has value are the liquids: the sweeter the better, the bitterer the worse. The cup, the container, has no value. It is what goes into it, not what they go into, that has value. For the utilitarian you and I are like the cup; we have no value as individuals and thus no equal value. What has value is what goes into us, what we serve as receptacles for; our feelings of satisfaction have positive value, our feelings of frustration negative value.

Serious problems arise for utilitarianism when we remind ourselves that it enjoins us to bring about the best consequences. What does this mean? It doesn't mean the best consequences for me alone, or for my family or friends, or any other person taken individually. No, what we must do is, roughly, as follows: we must add up (somehow!) the separate satisfactions and frustrations of everyone likely to be affected by our choice, the satisfactions in one column, the frustrations in the other. We must total each column for each of the options before us. That is what it means to say the theory is aggregative. And then we must choose that option which is most likely to bring about the best balance of totaled satisfactions over totaled frustrations. Whatever act would lead to this outcome is the one we ought morally to perform—it is where our moral duty lies. And that act quite clearly might not be the same one that would bring about the best results for me personally, or for my family or friends, or for a lab animal. The best aggregated consequences for everyone concerned are not necessarily the best for each individual.

That utilitarianism is an aggregative theory—different individuals' satisfactions or frustrations are added, or summed, or totaled—is the key objection to this theory. My Aunt Bea is old, inactive, a cranky, sour person, though not physically ill. She prefers to go on living. She is also rather rich. I could make a fortune if I could get my hands on her money, money she intends to give me in any event, after she dies, but which she refuses to give me now. In order to avoid a huge tax bite, I plan to donate a handsome sum of my profits to a local children's hospital. Many, many children will benefit from my generosity, and much joy will be brought to their parents, relatives and friends. If I don't get the money rather soon, all these ambitions will come to naught. The once-in-a-lifetime opportunity to make a real killing will be gone. Why, then, not kill my Aunt Bea? Oh, of course I *might* get caught. But I'm no fool and, besides, her doctor can be counted on to cooperate (he has an eye for the same investment and I happen to know a good deal about his shady past). The deed can be done. . . . professionally, shall we say. There is *very* little chance of getting caught. And as for my conscience being guilt-ridden, I am a resourceful sort of fellow and will take more than sufficient comfort—as I lie on the beach at Acapulco—in contemplating the joy and health I have brought to so many others.

Suppose Aunt Bea is killed and the rest of the story comes out as told. Would I have done anything wrong? Anything immoral? One would have thought that I had. Not according to utilitarianism. Since what I have done has brought about the best balance between totaled satisfaction and frustration for all those affected by the outcome, my action is not wrong. Indeed, in killing Aunt Bea the physician and I did what duty required.

25   This same kind of argument can be repeated in all sorts of cases, illustrating, time after time, how the utilitarian's position leads to results that impartial people find morally callous. It *is* wrong to kill my Aunt Bea in the name of bringing about the best results for others. A good end does not justify an evil means. Any adequate moral theory will have to explain why this is so. Utilitarianism fails in this respect and so cannot be the theory we seek.

What to do? Where to begin anew? The place to begin, I think, is with the utilitarian's view of the value of the individual—or, rather, lack of value. In its place, suppose we consider that you and I, for example, do have value as individuals—what we'll call *inherent value*. To say we have such value is to say that we are something more than, something different from, mere receptacles. Moreover, to ensure that we do not pave the way for such injustices as slavery or sexual discrimination, we must believe that all who have inherent value have it equally, regardless of their sex, race, religion, birthplace and so on. Similarly to be discarded as irrelevant are one's talents or skills, intelligence and wealth, personality or pathology, whether one is loved and admired or despised and loathed. The genius and the retarded child, the prince and the pauper, the brain surgeon and the fruit vendor, Mother Teresa[2] and the most unscrupulous used-car salesman—all have inherent value, all possess it equally, and all have an equal right to be treated with respect, to be treated in ways that do not reduce them to the status of things, as if they existed as resources for others.

---

2. Agnes Gonxha Bojaxhiu (1910–1997), known as Mother Teresa, founded the Missionaries of Charity in Kolkata, India, at the age of forty and devoted the rest of her life to caring for disadvantaged groups.

My value as an individual is independent of my usefulness to you. Yours is not dependent on your usefulness to me. For either of us to treat the other in ways that fail to show respect for the other's independent value is to act immorally, to violate the individual's rights.

Some of the rational virtues of this view—what I call the rights view— should be evident. Unlike (crude) contractarianism, for example, the rights view *in principle* denies the moral tolerability of any and all forms of racial, sexual or social discrimination; and unlike utilitarianism, this view *in principle* denies that we can justify good results by using evil means that violate an individual's rights—denies, for example, that it could be moral to kill my Aunt Bea to harvest beneficial consequences for others. That would be to sanction the disrespectful treatment of the individual in the name of the social good, something the rights view will not—categorically will not—ever allow.

The rights view, I believe, is rationally the most satisfactory moral theory. It surpasses all other theories in the degree to which it illuminates and explains the foundation of our duties to one another—the domain of human morality. On this score it has the best reasons, the best arguments, on its side. Of course, if it were possible to show that only human beings are included within its scope, then a person like myself, who believes in animal rights, would be obliged to look elsewhere.

But attempts to limit its scope to humans only can be shown to be rationally defective. Animals, it is true, lack many of the abilities humans possess. They can't read, do higher mathematics, build a bookcase or make *baba ghanoush*.[3] Neither can many human beings, however, and yet we don't (and shouldn't) say that they (these humans) therefore have less inherent value, less of a right to be treated with respect, than do others. It is the *similarities* between those human beings who most clearly, most noncontroversially have such value (the people reading this, for example), not our differences, that matter most. And the really crucial, the basic similarity is simply this: we are each of us the experiencing subject of a life, a conscious creature having an individual welfare that has importance to us whatever our usefulness to others. We want and prefer things, believe and feel things, recall and expect things. And all these dimensions of our life, including our pleasure and pain, our enjoyment and suffering, our satisfaction and frustration, our continued existence or our untimely death—all make a difference to the quality of our life as lived, as experienced, by us as individuals. As the same is true of those animals that concern us (the ones that are eaten and trapped, for example), they too must be viewed as the experiencing subjects of a life, with inherent value of their own.

Some there are who resist the idea that animals have inherent value. "Only   30 humans have such value," they profess. How might this narrow view be defended? Shall we say that only humans have the requisite intelligence, or autonomy, or reason? But there are many, many humans who fail to meet these standards and yet are reasonably viewed as having value above and beyond their usefulness to others. Shall we claim that only humans belong to the right

3. Eggplant-sesame spread or dip.

species, the species *Homo sapiens*?[4] But this is blatant speciesism. Will it be said, then, that all—and only—humans have immortal souls? Then our opponents have their work cut out for them. I am myself not ill-disposed to the proposition that there are immortal souls. Personally, I profoundly hope I have one. But I would not want to rest my position on a controversial ethical issue on the even more controversial question about who or what has an immortal soul. That is to dig one's hole deeper, not to climb out. Rationally, it is better to resolve moral issues without making more controversial assumptions than are needed. The question of who has inherent value is such a question, one that is resolved more rationally without the introduction of the idea of immortal souls than by its use.

Well, perhaps some will say that animals have some inherent value, only less than we have. Once again, however, attempts to defend this view can be shown to lack rational justification. What could be the basis of our having more inherent value than animals? Their lack of reason, or autonomy, or intellect? Only if we are willing to make the same judgment in the case of humans who are similarly deficient. But it is not true that such humans—the retarded child, for example, or the mentally deranged—have less inherent value than you or I. Neither, then, can we rationally sustain the view that animals like them in being the experiencing subjects of a life have less inherent value. *All* who have inherent value have it *equally,* whether they be human animals or not.

Inherent value, then, belongs equally to those who are the experiencing subjects of a life. Whether it belongs to others—to rocks and rivers, trees and glaciers, for example—we do not know and may never know. But neither do we need to know, if we are to make the case for animal rights. We do not need to know, for example, how many people are eligible to vote in the next presidential election before we can know whether I am. Similarly, we do not need to know how many individuals have inherent value before we can know that some do. When it comes to the case for animal rights, then, what we need to know is whether the animals that, in our culture, are routinely eaten, hunted and used in our laboratories, for example, are like us in being subjects of a life. And we do know this. We do know that many—literally, billions and billions—of these animals are the subjects of a life in the sense explained and so have inherent value if we do. And since, in order to arrive at the best theory of our duties to one another, we must recognize our equal inherent value as individuals, reason—not sentiment, not emotion—reason compels us to recognize the equal inherent value of these animals and, with this, their equal right to be treated with respect.

That, *very* roughly, is the shape and feel of the case for animal rights. Most of the details of the supporting argument are missing. They are to be found in the book to which I alluded earlier. Here, the details go begging, and I must, in closing, limit myself to four final points.

---

4. Latin for "man with intellect," the taxonomic designation for the modern human species.

The first is how the theory that underlies the case for animal rights shows that the animal rights movement is a part of, not antagonistic to, the human rights movement. The theory that rationally grounds the rights of animals also grounds the rights of humans. Thus those involved in the animal rights movement are partners in the struggle to secure respect for human rights—the rights of women, for example, or minorities, or workers. The animal rights movement is cut from the same moral cloth as these.

Second, having set out the broad outlines of the rights view, I can now say   35
why its implications for farming and science, among other fields, are both clear and uncompromising. In the case of the use of animals in science, the rights view is categorically abolitionist. Lab animals are not our tasters; we are not their kings. Because these animals are treated routinely, systematically as if their value were reducible to their usefulness to others, they are routinely, systematically treated with a lack of respect, and thus are their rights routinely, systematically violated. This is just as true when they are used in trivial, duplicative, unnecessary or unwise research as it is when they are used in studies that hold out real promise of human benefits. We can't justify harming or killing a human being (my Aunt Bea, for example) just for these sorts of reason. Neither can we do so even in the case of so lowly a creature as a laboratory rat. It is not just refinement or reduction that is called for, not just larger, cleaner cages, not just more generous use of anaesthetic or the elimination of multiple surgery, not just tidying up the system. It is complete replacement. The best we can do when it comes to using animals in science is—not to use them. That is where our duty lies, according to the rights view.

As for commercial animal agriculture, the rights view takes a similar abolitionist position. The fundamental moral wrong here is not that animals are kept in stressful close confinement or in isolation, or that their pain and suffering, their needs and preferences are ignored or discounted. All these *are* wrong, of course, but they are not the fundamental wrong. They are symptoms and effects of the deeper, systematic wrong that allows these animals to be viewed and treated as lacking independent value, as resources for us—as, indeed, a renewable resource. Giving farm animals more space, more natural environments, more companions does not right the fundamental wrong, any more than giving lab animals more anaesthesia or bigger, cleaner cages would right the fundamental wrong in their case. Nothing less than the total dissolution of commercial animal agriculture will do this, just as, for similar reasons I won't develop at length here, morality requires nothing less than the total elimination of hunting and trapping for commercial and sporting ends. The rights view's implications, then, as I have said, are clear and uncompromising.

My last two points are about philosophy, my profession. It is, most obviously, no substitute for political action. The words I have written here and in other places by themselves don't change a thing. It is what we do with the thoughts that the words express—our acts, our deeds—that changes things. All that philosophy can do, and all I have attempted, is to offer a vision of what our deeds should aim at. And the why. But not the how.

Finally, I am reminded of my thoughtful critic, the one I mentioned earlier, who chastised me for being too cerebral. Well, cerebral I have been: indirect duty views, utilitarianism, contractarianism—hardly the stuff deep passions are made of. I am also reminded, however, of the image another friend once set before me—the image of the ballerina as expressive of disciplined passion. Long hours of sweat and toil, of loneliness and practice, of doubt and fatigue: those are the discipline of her craft. But the passion is there too, the fierce drive to excel, to speak through her body, to do it right, to pierce our minds. That is the image of philosophy I would leave with you, not "too cerebral" but *disciplined passion*. Of the discipline enough has been seen. As for the passion: there are times, and these not infrequent, when tears come to my eyes when I see, or read, or hear of the wretched plight of animals in the hands of humans. Their pain, their suffering, their loneliness, their innocence, their death. Anger. Rage. Pity. Sorrow. Disgust. The whole creation groans under the weight of the evil we humans visit upon these mute, powerless creatures. It *is* our hearts, not just our heads, that call for an end to it all, that demand of us that we overcome, for them, the habits and forces behind their systematic oppression. All great movements, it is written, go through three stages: ridicule, discussion, adoption. It is the realization of this third stage, adoption, that requires both our passion and our discipline, our hearts and our heads. The fate of animals is in our hands. God grant we are equal to the task.

MLA CITATION

Regan, Tom. "The Case for Animal Rights." 1985. *The Norton Reader: An Anthology of Nonfiction*. Ed. Melissa A. Goldthwaite et al. 14th ed. New York: Norton, 2016. 670–80. Print.

QUESTIONS

1. Tom Regan argues against four views that deny rights to animals: indirect duty, contractarianism, cruelty-kindness, and utilitarianism. Locate his account of each and explain his objections to it.

2. Regan then argues for what he calls a "rights view," which is, he claims, "rationally the most satisfactory moral theory" (paragraph 28). Explain both his view and his claim.

3. What are the advantages of arguing for views that conflict with one's own before arguing for one's own? What are the disadvantages?

4. Regan includes among his goals "the total dissolution of commercial animal agriculture" and "the total elimination of commercial and sport hunting and trapping" (paragraph 1). Do these goals include vegetarianism? If so, why does he not use the word "vegetarian"?

5. Write an essay in which you take a position on an issue about which you have strong feelings. Following Regan's example, focus on your argument even as you acknowledge your personal feelings on the issue.

MICHAEL POLLAN   *An Animal's Place*

THE FIRST TIME I opened Peter Singer's *Animal Liberation*, I was dining alone at the Palm,[1] trying to enjoy a rib-eye steak cooked medium-rare. If this sounds like a good recipe for cognitive dissonance (if not indigestion), that was sort of the idea. Preposterous as it might seem, to supporters of animal rights, what I was doing was tantamount to reading *Uncle Tom's Cabin* on a plantation in the Deep South in 1852.

Singer and the swelling ranks of his followers ask us to imagine a future in which people will look back on my meal, and this steakhouse, as relics of an equally backward age. Eating animals, wearing animals, experimenting on animals, killing animals for sport: all these practices, so resolutely normal to us, will be seen as the barbarities they are, and we will come to view "speciesism"—a neologism I had encountered before only in jokes—as a form of discrimination as indefensible as racism or anti-Semitism.

Even in 1975, when *Animal Liberation* was first published, Singer, an Australian philosopher now teaching at Princeton, was confident that he had the wind of history at his back. The recent civil rights past was prologue, as one liberation movement followed on the heels of another. Slowly but surely, the white man's circle of moral consideration was expanded to admit first blacks, then women, then homosexuals. In each case, a group once thought to be so different from the prevailing "we" as to be undeserving of civil rights was, after a struggle, admitted to the club. Now it was animals' turn.

That animal liberation is the logical next step in the forward march of moral progress is no longer the fringe idea it was back in 1975. A growing and increasingly influential group of philosophers, ethicists, law professors and activists are convinced that the great moral struggle of our time will be for the rights of animals.

So far the movement has scored some of its biggest victories in Europe. Earlier this year, Germany became the first nation to grant animals a constitutional right: the words "and animals" were added to a provision obliging the state to respect and protect the dignity of human beings. The farming of animals for fur was recently banned in England. In several European nations, sows may no longer be confined to crates nor laying hens to "battery cages"—stacked wired cages so small the birds cannot stretch their wings. The Swiss are amending their laws to change the status of animals from "things" to "beings."

Though animals are still very much "things" in the eyes of American law, change is in the air. Thirty-seven states have recently passed laws making some forms of animal cruelty a crime, twenty-one of them by ballot initiative.

Published in the New York Times Magazine *(2002), a Sunday supplement of the daily newspaper.*

1. Famous New York City steakhouse.

Following protests by activists, McDonald's and Burger King forced significant improvements in the way the U.S. meat industry slaughters animals. Agribusiness and the cosmetics and apparel industries are all struggling to defuse mounting public concerns over animal welfare.

Once thought of as a left-wing concern, the movement now cuts across ideological lines. Perhaps the most eloquent recent plea on behalf of animals, a new book called *Dominion*, was written by a former speechwriter for President Bush. And once outlandish ideas are finding their way into mainstream opinion. A recent Zogby poll found that fifty-one percent of Americans believe that primates are entitled to the same rights as human children.

What is going on here? A certain amount of cultural confusion, for one thing. For at the same time many people seem eager to extend the circle of our moral consideration to animals, in our factory farms and laboratories we are inflicting more suffering on more animals than at any time in history. One by one, science is dismantling our claims to uniqueness as a species, discovering that such things as culture, toolmaking, language and even possibly self-consciousness are not the exclusive domain of *Homo sapiens*. Yet most of the animals we kill lead lives organized very much in the spirit of Descartes,[2] who famously claimed that animals were mere machines, incapable of thought or feeling. There's a schizoid quality to our relationship with animals, in which sentiment and brutality exist side by side. Half the dogs in America will receive Christmas presents this year, yet few of us pause to consider the miserable life of the pig—an animal easily as intelligent as a dog—that becomes the Christmas ham.

We tolerate this disconnect because the life of the pig has moved out of view. When's the last time you saw a pig? (Babe doesn't count.) Except for our pets, real animals—animals living and dying—no longer figure in our everyday lives. Meat comes from the grocery store, where it is cut and packaged to look as little like parts of animals as possible. The disappearance of animals from our lives has opened a space in which there's no reality check, either on the sentiment or the brutality. This is pretty much where we live now, with respect to animals, and it is a space in which the Peter Singers and Frank Perdues[3] of the world can evidently thrive equally well.

10   Several years ago, the English critic John Berger wrote an essay, "Why Look at Animals?," in which he suggested that the loss of everyday contact between ourselves and animals—and specifically the loss of eye contact—has left us deeply confused about the terms of our relationship to other species. That eye contact, always slightly uncanny, had provided a vivid daily reminder that animals were at once crucially like and unlike us; in their eyes we glimpsed something unmistakably familiar (pain, fear, tenderness) and something irretrievably alien. Upon this paradox people built a relationship in which they felt they could

2. René Descartes (1596–1650), French philosopher.
3. Former president and CEO of Perdue Farms, one of the largest poultry processors in the United States.

both honor and eat animals without looking away. But that accommodation has pretty much broken down; nowadays, it seems, we either look away or become vegetarians. For my own part, neither option seemed especially appetizing. Which might explain how I found myself reading *Animal Liberation* in a steakhouse.

This is not something I'd recommend if you're determined to continue eating meat. Combining rigorous philosophical argument with journalistic description, *Animal Liberation* is one of those rare books that demand that you either defend the way you live or change it. Because Singer is so skilled in argument, for many readers it is easier to change. His book has converted countless thousands to vegetarianism, and it didn't take long for me to see why: within a few pages, he had succeeded in throwing me on the defensive.

Singer's argument is disarmingly simple and, if you accept its premises, difficult to refute. Take the premise of equality, which most people readily accept. Yet what do we really mean by it? People are not, as a matter of fact, equal at all—some are smarter than others, better looking, more gifted. "Equality is a moral idea," Singer points out, "not an assertion of fact." The moral idea is that everyone's interests ought to receive equal consideration, regardless of "what abilities they may possess." Fair enough; many philosophers have gone this far. But fewer have taken the next logical step. "If possessing a higher degree of intelligence does not entitle one human to use another for his or her own ends, how can it entitle humans to exploit nonhumans for the same purpose?"

This is the nub of Singer's argument, and right around here I began scribbling objections in the margin. *But humans differ from animals in morally significant ways.* Yes they do, Singer acknowledges, which is why we shouldn't treat pigs and children alike. Equal consideration of interests is not the same as equal treatment, he points out: children have an interest in being educated; pigs, in rooting around in the dirt. But where their interests are the same, the principle of equality demands they receive the same consideration. And the one all-important interest that we share with pigs, as with all sentient creatures, is an interest in avoiding pain.

Here Singer quotes a famous passage from Jeremy Bentham, the eighteenth-century utilitarian philosopher, that is the wellspring of the animal rights movement. Bentham was writing in 1789, soon after the French colonies freed black slaves, granting them fundamental rights. "The day *may* come," he speculates, "when the rest of the animal creation may acquire those rights." Bentham then asks what characteristic entitles any being to moral consideration. "Is it the faculty of reason or perhaps the faculty of discourse?" Obviously not, since "a full-grown horse or dog is beyond comparison a more rational, as well as a more conversable animal, than an infant." He concludes: "The question is not, Can they *reason*? nor, Can they *talk*? but, Can they *suffer*?"

Bentham here is playing a powerful card philosophers call the "argument from marginal cases," or AMC for short. It goes like this: There are humans—infants, the severely retarded, the demented—whose mental function cannot

15

match that of a chimpanzee. Even though these people cannot reciprocate our moral attentions, we nevertheless include them in the circle of our moral consideration. So on what basis do we exclude the chimpanzee?

Because he's a chimp, I furiously scribbled in the margin, *and they're human!* For Singer that's not good enough. To exclude the chimp from moral consideration simply because he's not human is no different from excluding the slave simply because he's not white. In the same way we'd call that exclusion racist, the animal rightist contends that it is speciesist to discriminate against the chimpanzee solely because he's not human.

But the differences between blacks and whites are trivial compared with the differences between my son and a chimp. Singer counters by asking us to imagine a hypothetical society that discriminates against people on the basis of something nontrivial—say, intelligence. If that scheme offends our sense of equality, then why is the fact that animals lack certain human characteristics any more just as a basis for discrimination? Either we do not owe any justice to the severely retarded, he concludes, or we do owe it to animals with higher capabilities.

This is where I put down my fork. If I believe in equality, and equality is based on interests rather than characteristics, then I have to either take the interests of the steer I'm eating into account or concede that I am a speciesist. For the time being, I decided to plead guilty as charged. I finished my steak.

But Singer had planted a troubling notion, and in the days afterward, it grew and grew, watered by the other animal rights thinkers I began reading: the philosophers Tom Regan and James Rachels; the legal theorist Steven M. Wise; the writers Joy Williams and Matthew Scully. I didn't *think* I minded being a speciesist, but could it be, as several of these writers suggest, that we will someday come to regard speciesism as an evil comparable to racism? Will history someday judge us as harshly as it judges the Germans who went about their ordinary lives in the shadow of Treblinka? Precisely that question was recently posed by J. M. Coetzee, the South African novelist, in a lecture delivered at Princeton; he answered it in the affirmative. If animal rightists are right, "a crime of stupefying proportions" (in Coetzee's words) is going on all around us every day, just beneath our notice.

20   It's an idea almost impossible to entertain seriously, much less to accept, and in the weeks following my restaurant face-off between Singer and the steak, I found myself marshaling whatever mental power I could muster to try to refute it. Yet Singer and his allies managed to trump almost all my objections.

My first line of defense was obvious. *Animals kill one another all the time. Why treat animals more ethically than they treat one another?* (Ben Franklin tried this one long before me: during a fishing trip, he wondered, "If you eat one another, I don't see why we may not eat you." He admits, however, that the rationale didn't occur to him until the fish were in the frying pan, smelling "admirably well." The advantage of being a "reasonable creature," Franklin remarks, is that you can find a reason for whatever you want to do.) To the "they do it too" defense, the animal rightist has a devastating reply: Do you really want to base your morality on the natural order? Murder and rape are natural too.

Besides, humans don't need to kill other creatures in order to survive; animals do. (Though if my cat, Otis, is any guide, animals sometimes kill for sheer pleasure.)

This suggests another defense. *Wouldn't life in the wild be worse for these farm animals?* "Defenders of slavery imposed on black Africans often made a similar point," Singer retorts. "The life of freedom is to be preferred."

But domesticated animals can't survive in the wild; in fact, without us they wouldn't exist at all. Or as one nineteenth-century political philosopher put it, "The pig has a stronger interest than anyone in the demand for bacon. If all the world were Jewish, there would be no pigs at all." But it turns out that this would be fine by the animal rightists: for if pigs don't exist, they can't be wronged.

Animals on factory farms have never known any other life. Singer replies that "animals feel a need to exercise, stretch their limbs or wings, groom themselves and turn around, whether or not they have ever lived in conditions that permit this." The measure of their suffering is not their prior experiences but the unremitting daily frustration of their instincts.

OK, the suffering of animals is a legitimate problem, but the world is full of problems, and surely human problems must come first! Sounds good, and yet all the animal people are asking me to do is to stop eating meat and wearing animal furs and hides. There's no reason I can't devote myself to solving humankind's problems while being a vegetarian who wears synthetics.

But doesn't the fact that we could choose to forgo meat for moral reasons point to a crucial moral difference between animals and humans? As Kant pointed out, the human being is the only moral animal, the only one even capable of entertaining a concept of "rights." What's wrong with reserving moral consideration for those able to reciprocate it? Right here is where you run smack into the AMC: the moral status of the retarded, the insane, the infant and the Alzheimer's patient. Such "marginal cases," in the detestable argot of modern moral philosophy, cannot participate in moral decision-making any more than a monkey can, yet we nevertheless grant them rights.

That's right, I respond, for the simple reason that they're one of us. And all of us have been, and will probably once again be, marginal cases ourselves. What's more, these people have fathers and mothers, daughters and sons, which makes our interest in their welfare deeper than our interest in the welfare of even the most brilliant ape.

Alas, none of these arguments evade the charge of speciesism; the racist, too, claims that it's natural to give special consideration to one's own kind. A utilitarian like Singer would agree, however, that the feelings of relatives do count for something. Yet the principle of equal consideration of interests demands that, given the choice between performing a painful medical experiment on a severely retarded orphan and on a normal ape, we must sacrifice the child. Why? Because the ape has a greater capacity for pain.

Here in a nutshell is the problem with the AMC: it can be used to help the animals, but just as often it winds up hurting the marginal cases. Giving up our speciesism will bring us to a moral cliff from which we may not be prepared to jump, even when logic is pushing us.

30   And yet this isn't the moral choice I am being asked to make. (Too bad; it would be so much easier!) In everyday life, the choice is not between babies and chimps but between the pork and the tofu. Even if we reject the "hard utilitarianism" of a Peter Singer, there remains the question of whether we owe animals that can feel pain *any* moral consideration, and this seems impossible to deny. And if we do owe them moral consideration, how can we justify eating them?

This is why killing animals for meat (and clothing) poses the most difficult animal rights challenge. In the case of animal testing, all but the most radical animal rightists are willing to balance the human benefit against the cost to the animals. That's because the unique qualities of human consciousness carry weight in the utilitarian calculus: human pain counts for more than that of a mouse, since our pain is amplified by emotions like dread; similarly, our deaths are worse than an animal's because we understand what death is in a way they don't. So the argument over animal testing is really in the details: Is this particular procedure or test *really* necessary to save human lives? (Very often it's not, in which case we probably shouldn't do it.) But if humans no longer need to eat meat or wear skins, then what exactly are we putting on the human side of the scale to outweigh the interests of the animal?

I suspect that this is finally why the animal people managed to throw me on the defensive. It's one thing to choose between the chimp and the retarded child or to accept the sacrifice of all those pigs surgeons practiced on to develop heart-bypass surgery. But what happens when the choice is between "a lifetime of suffering for a nonhuman animal and the gastronomic preference of a human being?" You look away—or you stop eating animals. And if you don't want to do either? Then you have to try to determine if the animals you're eating have really endured "a lifetime of suffering."

Whether our interest in eating animals outweighs their interest in not being eaten (assuming for the moment that is their interest) turns on the vexed question of animal suffering. Vexed, because it is impossible to know what really goes on in the mind of a cow or a pig or even an ape. Strictly speaking, this is true of other humans, too, but since humans are all basically wired the same way, we have excellent reason to assume that other people's experience of pain feels much like our own. Can we say that about animals? Yes and no.

I have yet to find anyone who still subscribes to Descartes's belief that animals cannot feel pain because they lack a soul. The general consensus among scientists and philosophers is that when it comes to pain, the higher animals are wired much the way we are for the same evolutionary reasons, so we should take the writhings of the kicked dog at face value. Indeed, the very premise of a great deal of animal testing—the reason it has value—is that animals' experience of physical and even some psychological pain closely resembles our own. Otherwise, why would cosmetics testers drip chemicals into the eyes of rabbits to see if they sting? Why would researchers study head trauma by traumatizing chimpanzee heads? Why would psychologists attempt to induce depression and "learned helplessness" in dogs by exposing them to ceaseless random patterns of electrical shock?

That said, it can be argued that human pain differs from animal pain by 35
an order of magnitude. This qualitative difference is largely the result of our
possession of language and, by virtue of language, an ability to have thoughts
about thoughts and to imagine alternatives to our current reality. The philosopher Daniel C. Dennett suggests that we would do well to draw a distinction
between pain, which a great many animals experience, and suffering, which
depends on a degree of self-consciousness only a few animals appear to command. Suffering, in this view, is not just lots of pain but pain intensified by
human emotions like loss, sadness, worry, regret, self-pity, shame, humiliation
and dread.

Consider castration. No one would deny the procedure is painful to animals, yet animals appear to get over it in a way humans do not. (Some rhesus
monkeys competing for mates will bite off a rival's testicle; the very next day
the victim may be observed mating, seemingly little the worse for wear.) Surely
the suffering of a man able to comprehend the full implications of castration, to
anticipate the event and contemplate its aftermath, represents an agony of
another order.

By the same token, however, language and all that comes with it can also
make certain kinds of pain *more* bearable. A trip to the dentist would be a torment for an ape that couldn't be made to understand the purpose and duration
of the procedure.

As humans contemplating the pain and suffering of animals, we do need
to guard against projecting onto them what the same experience would feel like
to us. Watching a steer force-marched up the ramp to the kill-floor door, as I
have done, I need to remind myself that this is not Sean Penn in *Dead Man
Walking*, that in a bovine brain the concept of nonexistence is blissfully absent.
"If we fail to find suffering in the [animal] lives we can see," Dennett writes in
Kinds of Minds, "we can rest assured there is no invisible suffering somewhere
in their brains. If we find suffering, we will recognize it without difficulty."

Which brings us—reluctantly, necessarily—to the American factory farm, the
place where all such distinctions turn to dust. It's not easy to draw lines between
pain and suffering in a modern egg or confinement hog operation. These are
places where the subtleties of moral philosophy and animal cognition mean less
than nothing, where everything we've learned about animals at least since Darwin has been simply . . . set aside. To visit a modern CAFO (Confined Animal
Feeding Operation) is to enter a world that, for all its technological sophistication, is still designed according to Cartesian principles: animals are machines
incapable of feeling pain. Since no thinking person can possibly believe this
anymore, industrial animal agriculture depends on a suspension of disbelief
on the part of the people who operate it and a willingness to avert your eyes on
the part of everyone else.

From everything I've read, egg and hog operations are the worst. Beef cat- 40
tle in America at least still live outdoors, albeit standing ankle deep in their own
waste, eating a diet that makes them sick. And broiler chickens, although they
do get their beaks snipped off with a hot knife to keep them from cannibalizing

one another under the stress of their confinement, at least don't spend their eight-week lives in cages too small to ever stretch a wing. That fate is reserved for the American laying hen, who passes her brief span piled together with a half-dozen other hens in a wire cage whose floor a single page of this magazine could carpet. Every natural instinct of this animal is thwarted, leading to a range of behavioral "vices" that can include cannibalizing her cagemates and rubbing her body against the wire mesh until it is featherless and bleeding. Pain? Suffering? Madness? The operative suspension of disbelief depends on more neutral descriptors, like "vices" and "stress." Whatever you want to call what's going on in those cages, the ten percent or so of hens that can't bear it and simply die is built into the cost of production. And when the output of the others begins to ebb, the hens will be "force-molted"—starved of food and water and light for several days in order to stimulate a final bout of egg-laying before their life's work is done.

Simply reciting these facts, most of which are drawn from poultry-trade magazines, makes me sound like one of those animal people, doesn't it? I don't mean to, but this is what can happen when . . . you look. It certainly wasn't my intention to ruin anyone's breakfast. But now that I probably have spoiled the eggs, I do want to say one thing about the bacon, mention a single practice (by no means the worst) in modern hog production that points to the compound madness of an impeccable industrial logic.

Piglets in confinement operations are weaned from their mothers ten days after birth (compared with thirteen weeks in nature) because they gain weight faster on their hormone- and antibiotic-fortified feed. This premature weaning leaves the pigs with a life-long craving to suck and chew, a desire they gratify in confinement by biting the tail of the animal in front of them. A normal pig would fight off his molester, but a demoralized pig has stopped caring. "Learned helplessness" is the psychological term, and it's not uncommon in confinement operations, where tens of thousands of hogs spend their entire lives ignorant of sunshine or earth or straw, crowded together beneath a metal roof upon metal slats suspended over a manure pit. So it's not surprising that an animal as sensitive and intelligent as a pig would get depressed, and a depressed pig will allow his tail to be chewed on to the point of infection. Sick pigs, being underperforming "production units," are clubbed to death on the spot. The USDA's recommended solution to the problem is called "tail docking." Using a pair of pliers (and no anesthetic), most but not all of the tail is snipped off. Why the little stump? Because the whole point of the exercise is not to remove the object of tail-biting so much as to render it *more* sensitive. Now, a bite on the tail is so painful that even the most demoralized pig will mount a struggle to avoid it.

Much of this description is drawn from *Dominion*, Matthew Scully's recent book in which he offers a harrowing description of a North Carolina hog operation. Scully, a Christian conservative, has no patience for lefty rights talk, arguing instead that while God did give man "dominion" over animals ("Every moving thing that liveth shall be meat for you"), he also admonished us to show them mercy. "We are called to treat them with kindness, not because they have rights or power or some claim to equality but . . . because they stand unequal and powerless before us."

Scully calls the contemporary factory farm "our own worst nightmare" and, to his credit, doesn't shrink from naming the root cause of this evil: unfettered capitalism. (Perhaps this explains why he resigned from the Bush administration just before his book's publication.) A tension has always existed between the capitalist imperative to maximize efficiency and the moral imperatives of religion or community which have historically served as a counterweight to the moral blindness of the market. This is one of "the cultural contradictions of capitalism"—the tendency of the economic impulse to erode the moral underpinnings of society. Mercy toward animals is one such casualty.

More than any other institution, the American industrial animal farm offers a nightmarish glimpse of what capitalism can look like in the absence of moral or regulatory constraint. In these places life itself is redefined—as protein production—and with it suffering. *That* venerable word becomes "stress," an economic problem in search of a cost-effective solution, like tail-docking or beak-clipping or, in the industry's latest plan, by simply engineering the "stress gene" out of pigs and chickens. "Our own worst nightmare" such a place may well be; it is also real life for the billions of animals unlucky enough to have been born beneath these grim steel roofs, into the brief, pitiless life of a "production unit" in the days before the suffering gene was found.   45

Vegetarianism doesn't seem an unreasonable response to such an evil. Who would want to be made complicit in the agony of these animals by eating them? You want to throw *something* against the walls of those infernal sheds, whether it's the Bible, a new constitutional right or a whole platoon of animal rightists bent on breaking in and liberating the inmates. In the shadow of these factory farms, Coetzee's notion of a "stupefying crime" doesn't seem far-fetched at all.

But before you swear off meat entirely, let me describe a very different sort of animal farm. It is typical of nothing, and yet its very existence puts the whole moral question of animal agriculture in a different light. Polyface Farm occupies 550 acres of rolling grassland and forest in the Shenandoah Valley of Virginia. Here, Joel Salatin and his family raise six different food animals—cattle, pigs, chickens, rabbits, turkeys and sheep—in an intricate dance of symbiosis designed to allow each species, in Salatin's words, "to fully express its physiological distinctiveness."

What this means in practice is that Salatin's chickens live like chickens; his cows, like cows; pigs, pigs. As in nature, where birds tend to follow herbivores, once Salatin's cows have finished grazing a pasture, he moves them out and tows in his "eggmobile," a portable chicken coop that houses several hundred laying hens—roughly the natural size of a flock. The hens fan out over the pasture, eating the short grass and picking insect larvae out of the cowpats— all the while spreading the cow manure and eliminating the farm's parasite problem. A diet of grubs and grass makes for exceptionally tasty eggs and contented chickens, and their nitrogenous manure feeds the pasture. A few weeks later, the chickens move out and the sheep come in, dining on the lush new growth as well as on the weed species (nettles, nightshade) that the cattle and chickens won't touch.

Meanwhile, the pigs are in the barn turning the compost. All winter long, while the cattle were indoors, Salatin layered their manure with straw, wood chips—and corn. By March, this steaming compost layer cake stands three feet high, and the pigs, whose powerful snouts can sniff out and retrieve the fermented corn at the bottom, get to spend a few happy weeks rooting through the pile, aerating it as they work. All you can see of these pigs, intently nosing out the tasty alcoholic morsels, are their upturned pink hams and corkscrew tails churning the air. The finished compost will go to feed the grass; the grass, the cattle; the cattle, the chickens; and eventually all of these animals will feed us.

50   I thought a lot about vegetarianism and animal rights during the day I spent on Joel Salatin's extraordinary farm. So much of what I'd read, so much of what I'd accepted, looked very different from here. To many animal rightists, even Polyface Farm is a death camp. But to look at these animals is to see this for the sentimental conceit it is. In the same way that we can probably recognize animal suffering when we see it, animal happiness is unmistakable, too, and here I was seeing it in abundance.

For any animal, happiness seems to consist in the opportunity to express its creaturely character—its essential pigness or wolfness or chickenness. Aristotle speaks of each creature's "characteristic form of life." For domesticated species, the good life, if we can call it that, cannot be achieved apart from humans—apart from our farms and, therefore, our meat-eating. This, it seems to me, is where animal rightists betray a profound ignorance about the workings of nature. To think of domestication as a form of enslavement or even exploitation is to misconstrue the whole relationship, to project a human idea of power onto what is, in fact, an instance of mutualism between species. Domestication is an evolutionary, rather than a political, development. It is certainly not a regime humans imposed on animals some ten thousand years ago.

Rather, domestication happened when a small handful of especially opportunistic species discovered through Darwinian trial and error that they were more likely to survive and prosper in an alliance with humans than on their own. Humans provided the animals with food and protection, in exchange for which the animals provided the humans their milk and eggs and—yes—their flesh. Both parties were transformed by the relationship: animals grew tame and lost their ability to fend for themselves (evolution tends to edit out unneeded traits), and humans gave up their hunter-gatherer ways for the settled life of agriculturists. (Humans changed biologically too, evolving such new traits as a tolerance for lactose as adults.)

From the animals' point of view, the bargain with humanity has been a great success, at least until our own time. Cows, pigs, dogs, cats and chickens have thrived, while their wild ancestors have languished. (There are ten thousand wolves in North America, fifty million dogs.) Nor does their loss of autonomy seem to trouble these creatures. It is wrong, the rightists say, to treat animals as "means" rather than "ends," yet the happiness of a working animal like the dog consists precisely in serving as a "means." Liberation is the last thing such a creature wants. To say of one of Joel Salatin's caged chickens that "the life of freedom is to be preferred" betrays an ignorance about chicken preferences—which on this farm are heavily focused on not getting their heads bitten off by weasels.

But haven't these chickens simply traded one predator for another—weasels for humans? True enough, and for the chickens this is probably not a bad deal. For brief as it is, the life expectancy of a farm animal would be considerably briefer in the world beyond the pasture fence or chicken coop. A sheep farmer told me that a bear will eat a lactating ewe alive, starting with her udders. "As a rule," he explained, "animals don't get 'good deaths' surrounded by their loved ones."

The very existence of predation—animals eating animals—is the cause of much anguished hand-wringing in animal rights circles. "It must be admitted," Singer writes, "that the existence of carnivorous animals does pose one problem for the ethics of Animal Liberation, and that is whether we should do anything about it." Some animal rightists train their dogs and cats to become vegetarians. (Note: cats will require nutritional supplements to stay healthy.) Matthew Scully calls predation "the intrinsic evil in nature's design. . . . among the hardest of all things to fathom." *Really?* A deep Puritan streak pervades animal rights activists, an abiding discomfort not only with our animality but with the animals' animality too.

However it may appear to us, predation is not a matter of morality or politics; it, also, is a matter of symbiosis. Hard as the wolf may be on the deer he eats, the herd depends on him for its well-being; without predators to cull the herd, deer overrun their habitat and starve. In many places, human hunters have taken over the predator's ecological role. Chickens also depend for their continued well-being on their human predators—not individual chickens, but chickens as a species. The surest way to achieve the extinction of the chicken would be to grant chickens a "right to life."

Yet here's the rub: the animal rightist is not concerned with species, only individuals. Tom Regan, author of *The Case for Animal Rights*, bluntly asserts that because "species are not individuals . . . the rights view does not recognize the moral rights of species to anything, including survival." Singer concurs, insisting that only sentient individuals have interests. But surely a species can have interests—in its survival, say—just as a nation or community or a corporation can. The animal rights movement's exclusive concern with individual animals makes perfect sense given its roots in a culture of liberal individualism, but does it make any sense in nature?

Consider this hypothetical episode: In 1611 Juan da Goma (a.k.a. Juan the Disoriented) made accidental landfall on Wrightson Island, a six-square-mile rock in the Indian Ocean. The island's sole distinction is as the only known home of the Arcania tree and the bird that nests in it, the Wrightson giant sea sparrow. Da Goma and his crew stayed a week, much of that time spent in a failed bid to recapture the ship's escaped goat—who happened to be pregnant. Nearly four centuries later, Wrightson Island is home to 380 goats that have consumed virtually every scrap of vegetation in their reach. The youngest Arcania tree on the island is more than three hundred years old, and only fifty-two sea sparrows remain. In the animal rights view, any one of those goats have at least as much right to life as the last Wrightson sparrow on earth, and the trees, because they are not sentient, warrant no moral consideration whatsoever. (In the mid-1980s a British environmental group set out to shoot the goats, but was forced to cancel the expedition after the Mammal Liberation Front bombed its offices.)

The story of Wrightson Island (invented by the biologist David Ehrenfeld in *Beginning Again*) suggests at the very least that a human morality based on individual rights makes for an awkward fit when applied to the natural world. This should come as no surprise: morality is an artifact of human culture, devised to help us negotiate social relations. It's very good for that. But just as we recognize that nature doesn't provide an adequate guide for human social conduct, isn't it anthropocentric to assume that our moral system offers an adequate guide for nature? We may require a different set of ethics to guide our dealings with the natural world, one as well suited to the particular needs of plants and animals and habitats (where sentience counts for little) as rights suit us humans today.

60   To contemplate such questions from the vantage of a farm is to appreciate just how parochial and urban an ideology animal rights really is. It could thrive only in a world where people have lost contact with the natural world, where animals no longer pose a threat to us and human mastery of nature seems absolute. "In our normal life," Singer writes, "there is no serious clash of interests between human and nonhuman animals." Such a statement assumes a decidedly urbanized "normal life," one that certainly no farmer would recognize.

The farmer would point out that even vegans have a "serious clash of interests" with other animals. The grain that the vegan eats is harvested with a combine that shreds field mice, while the farmer's tractor crushes woodchucks in their burrows, and his pesticides drop songbirds from the sky. Steve Davis, an animal scientist at Oregon State University, has estimated that if America were to adopt a strictly vegetarian diet, the total number of animals killed every year would actually *increase*, as animal pasture gave way to row crops. Davis contends that if our goal is to kill as few animals as possible, then people should eat the largest possible animal that can live on the least intensively cultivated land: grass-fed beef for everybody. It would appear that killing animals is unavoidable no matter what we choose to eat.

When I talked to Joel Salatin about the vegetarian utopia, he pointed out that it would also condemn him and his neighbors to importing their food from distant places, since the Shenandoah Valley receives too little rainfall to grow many row crops. Much the same would hold true where I live, in New England. We get plenty of rain, but the hilliness of the land has dictated an agriculture based on animals since the time of the Pilgrims. The world is full of places where the best, if not the only, way to obtain food from the land is by grazing animals on it—especially ruminants, which alone can transform grass into protein and whose presence can actually improve the health of the land.

The vegetarian utopia would make us even more dependent than we already are on an industrialized national food chain. That food chain would in turn be even more dependent than it already is on fossil fuels and chemical fertilizer, since food would need to travel farther and manure would be in short supply. Indeed, it is doubtful that you can build a more sustainable agriculture without animals to cycle nutrients and support local food production. If our concern is for the health of nature—rather than, say, the internal consistency of our moral code or the condition of our souls—then eating animals may sometimes be the most ethical thing to do.

There is, too, the fact that we humans have been eating animals as long as we have lived on this earth. Humans may not need to eat meat in order to survive, yet doing so is part of our evolutionary heritage, reflected in the design of our teeth and the structure of our digestion. Eating meat helped make us what we are, in a social and biological sense. Under the pressure of the hunt, the human brain grew in size and complexity, and around the fire where the meat was cooked, human culture first flourished. Granting rights to animals may lift us up from the brutal world of predation, but it will entail the sacrifice of part of our identity—our own animality.

Surely this is one of the odder paradoxes of animal rights doctrine. It asks us to recognize all that we share with animals and then demands that we act toward them in a most unanimalistic way. Whether or not this is a good idea, we should at least acknowledge that our desire to eat meat is not a trivial matter, no mere "gastronomic preference." We might as well call sex—also now technically unnecessary—a mere "recreational preference." Whatever else it is, our meat-eating is something very deep indeed.

65

Are any of these good enough reasons to eat animals? I'm mindful of Ben Franklin's definition of the reasonable creature as one who can come up with reasons for whatever he wants to do. So I decided I would track down Peter Singer and ask him what he thought. In an e-mail message, I described Polyface and asked him about the implications for his position of the Good Farm—one where animals got to live according to their nature and to all appearances did not suffer.

"I agree with you that it is better for these animals to have lived and died than not to have lived at all," Singer wrote back. Since the utilitarian is concerned exclusively with the sum of happiness and suffering and the slaughter of an animal that doesn't comprehend that death need not involve suffering, the Good Farm adds to the total of animal happiness, provided you replace the slaughtered animal with a new one. However, he added, this line of thinking doesn't obviate the wrongness of killing an animal that "has a sense of its own existence over time and can have preferences for its own future." In other words, it's OK to eat the chicken, but he's not so sure about the pig. Yet, he wrote, "I would not be sufficiently confident of my arguments to condemn someone who purchased meat from one of these farms."

Singer went on to express serious doubts that such farms could be practical on a large scale, since the pressures of the marketplace will lead their owners to cut costs and corners at the expense of the animals. He suggested, too, that killing animals is not conducive to treating them with respect. Also, since humanely raised food will be more expensive, only the well-to-do can afford morally defensible animal protein. These are important considerations, but they don't alter my essential point: what's wrong with animal agriculture—with eating animals—is the practice, not the principle.

What this suggests to me is that people who care should be working not for animal rights but animal welfare—to ensure that farm animals don't suffer and that their deaths are swift and painless. In fact, the decent-life-merciful-death line is how Jeremy Bentham justified his own meat-eating. Yes, the philosophical father of animal rights was himself a carnivore. In a passage rather less frequently quoted by animal rightists, Bentham defended eating animals on the grounds that "we are the better for it, and they are never the worse. . . . The death they suffer in our hands commonly is, and always may be, a speedier and, by that means, a less painful one than that which would await them in the inevitable course of nature."

70   My guess is that Bentham never looked too closely at what happens in a slaughterhouse, but the argument suggests that, in theory at least, a utilitarian can justify the killing of humanely treated animals—for meat or, presumably, for clothing. (Though leather and fur pose distinct moral problems. Leather is a byproduct of raising domestic animals for food, which can be done humanely. However, furs are usually made from wild animals that die brutal deaths—usually in leg-hold traps—and since most fur species aren't domesticated, raising them on farms isn't necessarily more humane.) But whether the issue is food or fur or hunting, what should concern us is the suffering, not the killing. All of which I was feeling pretty good about—until I remembered that utilitarians can also justify killing retarded orphans. Killing just isn't the problem for them that it is for other people, including me.

During my visit to Polyface Farm, I asked Salatin where his animals were slaughtered. He does the chickens and rabbits right on the farm, and would do the cattle, pigs and sheep there too if only the USDA would let him. Salatin showed me the open-air abattoir he built behind the farmhouse—a sort of outdoor kitchen on a concrete slab, with stainless-steel sinks, scalding tanks, a feather-plucking machine and metal cones to hold the birds upside down while they're being bled. Processing chickens is not a pleasant job, but Salatin insists on doing it himself because he's convinced he can do it more humanely and cleanly than any processing plant. He slaughters every other Saturday through the summer. Anyone's welcome to watch.

I asked Salatin how he could bring himself to kill a chicken.

"People have a soul; animals don't," he said. "It's a bedrock belief of mine." Salatin is a devout Christian. "Unlike us, animals are not created in God's image, so when they die, they just die."

The notion that only in modern times have people grown uneasy about killing animals is a flattering conceit. Taking a life is momentous, and people have been working to justify the slaughter of animals for thousands of years. Religion and especially ritual has played a crucial part in helping us reckon the moral costs. Native Americans and other hunter-gatherers would give thanks to their prey for giving up its life so the eater might live (sort of like saying grace). Many cultures have offered sacrificial animals to the gods, perhaps as a way to convince themselves that it was the gods' desires that demanded the slaughter, not their own. In ancient Greece, the priests responsible for the slaughter (priests!—now we entrust the job to minimum-wage workers) would sprinkle holy water on the sacrificial animal's brow. The beast would promptly shake its head, and this was taken as a sign of assent. Slaughter doesn't necessarily preclude respect. For all these people, it was the ceremony that allowed them to look, then to eat.

Apart from a few surviving religious practices, we no longer have any ritu-   75
als governing the slaughter or eating of animals, which perhaps helps to explain why we find ourselves where we do, feeling that our only choice is to either look away or give up meat. Frank Perdue is happy to serve the first customer; Peter Singer, the second.

Until my visit to Polyface Farm, I had assumed these were the only two options. But on Salatin's farm, the eye contact between people and animals whose loss John Berger mourned is still a fact of life—and of death, for neither the lives nor the deaths of these animals have been secreted behind steel walls. "Food with a face," Salatin likes to call what he's selling, a slogan that probably scares off some customers. People see very different things when they look into the eyes of a pig or a chicken or a steer—a being without a soul, a "subject of a life" entitled to rights, a link in a food chain, a vessel for pain and pleasure, a tasty lunch. But figuring out what we do think, and what we can eat, might begin with the looking.

We certainly won't philosophize our way to an answer. Salatin told me the story of a man who showed up at the farm one Saturday morning. When Salatin noticed a PETA bumper sticker on the man's car, he figured he was in for it. But the man had a different agenda. He explained that after sixteen years as a vegetarian, he had decided that the only way he could ever eat meat again was if he killed the animal himself. He had come to *look*.

"Ten minutes later we were in the processing shed with a chicken," Salatin recalled. "He slit the bird's throat and watched it die. He saw that the animal did not look at him accusingly, didn't do a Disney double take. The animal had been treated with respect when it was alive, and he saw that it could also have a respectful death—that it wasn't being treated as a pile of protoplasm."

Salatin's open-air abattoir is a morally powerful idea. Someone slaughtering a chicken in a place where he can be watched is apt to do it scrupulously, with consideration for the animal as well as for the eater. This is going to sound quixotic, but maybe all we need to do to redeem industrial animal agriculture in this country is to pass a law requiring that the steel and concrete walls of the CAFOs and slaughterhouses be replaced with . . . glass. If there's any new "right" we need to establish, maybe it's this one: the right to look.

No doubt the sight of some of these places would turn many people into   80
vegetarians. Many others would look elsewhere for their meat, to farmers like Salatin. There are more of them than I would have imagined. Despite the relentless consolidation of the American meat industry, there has been a revival of

small farms where animals still live their "characteristic form of life." I'm thinking of the ranches where cattle still spend their lives on grass, the poultry
farms where chickens still go outside and the hog farms where pigs live as they
did fifty years ago—in contact with the sun, the earth and the gaze of a farmer.

For my own part, I've discovered that if you're willing to make the effort,
it's entirely possible to limit the meat you eat to nonindustrial animals. I'm
tempted to think that we need a new dietary category, to go with the vegan and
lactovegetarian and piscatorian. I don't have a catchy name for it yet (humano-
carnivore?), but this is the only sort of meat-eating I feel comfortable with these
days. I've become the sort of shopper who looks for labels indicating that his
meat and eggs have been humanely grown (the American Humane Association's
new "Free Farmed" label seems to be catching on), who visits the farms where
his chicken and pork come from and who asks kinky-sounding questions about
touring slaughterhouses. I've actually found a couple of small processing plants
willing to let a customer onto the kill floor, including one, in Cannon Falls,
Minnesota, with a glass abattoir.

The industrialization—and dehumanization—of American animal farming is a relatively new, evitable and local phenomenon: no other country raises
and slaughters its food animals quite as intensively or as brutally as we do. Were
the walls of our meat industry to become transparent, literally or even figura-
tively, we would not long continue to do it this way. Tail-docking and sow crates
and beak-clipping would disappear overnight, and the days of slaughtering four
hundred head of cattle an hour would come to an end. For who could stand
the sight? Yes, meat would get more expensive. We'd probably eat less of it, too,
but maybe when we did eat animals, we'd eat them with the consciousness,
ceremony and respect they deserve.

MLA CITATION

Pollan, Michael. "An Animal's Place." 2002. *The Norton Reader: An Anthology of
    Nonfiction.* Ed. Melissa A. Goldthwaite et al. 14th ed. New York: Norton, 2016.
    681–96. Print.

QUESTIONS

1. Precisely how much of the Animal Liberation approach has Michael Pollan
accepted? How can you tell?

2. Things change when Pollan visits Polyface Farm, the humane operation run by
Joel Salatin. What about the farm convinces Pollan that it represents an alternative to Peter Singer's approach?

3. Describe the structure of Pollan's essay. How does he introduce Animal Liberation and how does he argue against it?

4. Write your own argument concerning some aspect of what "an animal's place"
should be. It can be about animal cruelty, whether (and how) animals should be
used in experiments or product testing, under what (if any) circumstances humans
should eat animals, or some other issue related to animals and ethics.

DAVID FOSTER WALLACE *Consider the Lobster*

THE ENORMOUS, PUNGENT, and extremely well marketed Maine Lobster Festival is held every late
July in the state's midcoast region, meaning the western side of Penobscot Bay, the nerve stem of Maine's
lobster industry. What's called the midcoast runs from
Owl's Head and Thomaston in the south to Belfast
in the north. . . . The region's two main communities are Camden, with its
very old money and yachty harbor and five-star restaurants and phenomenal
B&Bs, and Rockland, a serious old fishing town that hosts the Festival every
summer in historic Harbor Park, right along the water.[1]

Tourism and lobster are the midcoast region's two main industries, and
they're both warm-weather enterprises, and the Maine Lobster Festival represents less an intersection of the industries than a deliberate collision, joyful
and lucrative and loud. . . . Festival highlights: concerts by Lee Ann Womack
and Orleans, annual Maine Sea Goddess beauty pageant, Saturday's big parade,
Sunday's William G. Atwood Memorial Crate Race, annual Amateur Cooking
Competition, carnival rides and midway attractions and food booths, and the
MLF's Main Eating Tent, where something over 25,000 pounds of fresh-caught
Maine lobster is consumed after preparation in the World's Largest Lobster
Cooker near the grounds' north entrance. Also available are lobster rolls, lob-
ster turnovers, lobster sauté, Down East lobster salad, lobster bisque, lobster
ravioli, and deep-fried lobster dumplings. Lobster Thermidor is obtainable at a
sit-down restaurant called The Black Pearl on Harbor Park's northwest wharf.
A large all-pine booth sponsored by the Maine Lobster Promotion Council has
free pamphlets with recipes, eating tips, and Lobster Fun Facts. The winner of
Friday's Amateur Cooking Competition prepares Saffron Lobster Ramekins,
the recipe for which is available for public downloading at www.mainelobster
festival.com. There are lobster T-shirts and lobster bobblehead dolls and
inflatable lobster pool toys and clamp-on lobster hats with big scarlet claws
that wobble on springs. Your assigned correspondent saw it all, accompanied
by one girlfriend and both his own parents—one of which parents was actually
born and raised in Maine, albeit in the extreme northern inland part, which is
potato country and a world away from the touristic midcoast.[2]

For practical purposes, everyone knows what a lobster is. As usual, though,
there's much more to know than most of us care about—it's all a matter of what
your interests are. Taxonomically speaking, a lobster is a marine crustacean of

First published in Gourmet (2004), *a monthly magazine devoted to food and wine,
which was in print from 1941 to 2009. It was later included in David Foster Wallace's collection* Consider the Lobster, and Other Essays (2005). *All notes are the author's.*

1. There's a comprehensive native apothegm: "Camden by the sea, Rockland by the
smell."
2. N.B. All personally connected parties have made it clear from the start that they
do not want to be talked about in this article.

the family Homaridae, characterized by five pairs of jointed legs, the first pair terminating in large pincerish claws used for subduing prey. Like many other species of benthic carnivore, lobsters are both hunters and scavengers. They have stalked eyes, gills on their legs, and antennae. There are dozens of different kinds worldwide, of which the relevant species here is the Maine lobster, *Homarus americanus*. The name "lobster" comes from the Old English *loppestre*, which is thought to be a corrupt form of the Latin word for locust combined with the Old English *loppe*, which meant spider.

Moreover, a crustacean is an aquatic arthropod of the class Crustacea, which comprises crabs, shrimp, barnacles, lobsters, and freshwater crayfish. All this is right there in the encyclopedia. And an arthropod is an invertebrate member of the phylum Arthropoda, which phylum covers insects, spiders, crustaceans, and centipedes/millipedes, all of whose main commonality, besides the absence of a centralized brain-spine assembly, is a chitinous exoskeleton composed of segments, to which appendages are articulated in pairs.

5   The point is that lobsters are basically giant sea-insects.[3] Like most arthropods, they date from the Jurassic period, biologically so much older than mammalia that they might as well be from another planet. And they are—particularly in their natural brown-green state, brandishing their claws like weapons and with thick antennae awhip—not nice to look at. And it's true that they are garbagemen of the sea, eaters of dead stuff,[4] although they'll also eat some live shellfish, certain kinds of injured fish, and sometimes each other.

But they are themselves good eating. Or so we think now. Up until sometime in the 1800s, though, lobster was literally low-class food, eaten only by the poor and institutionalized. Even in the harsh penal environment of early America, some colonies had laws against feeding lobsters to inmates more than once a week because it was thought to be cruel and unusual, like making people eat rats. One reason for their low status was how plentiful lobsters were in old New England. "Unbelievable abundance" is how one source describes the situation, including accounts of Plymouth pilgrims wading out and capturing all they wanted by hand, and of early Boston's seashore being littered with lobsters after hard storms—these latter were treated as a smelly nuisance and ground up for fertilizer. There is also the fact that premodern lobster was often cooked dead and then preserved, usually packed in salt or crude hermetic containers. Maine's earliest lobster industry was based around a dozen such seaside canneries in the 1840s, from which lobster was shipped as far away as California, in demand only because it was cheap and high in protein, basically chewable fuel.

Now, of course, lobster is posh, a delicacy, only a step or two down from caviar. The meat is richer and more substantial than most fish, its taste subtle compared to the marine-gaminess of mussels and clams. In the U.S. pop-food imagination, lobster is now the seafood analog to steak, with which it's so often

---

3. Midcoasters' native term for a lobster is, in fact, "bug," as in "Come around on Sunday and we'll cook up some bugs."

4. Factoid: Lobster traps are usually baited with dead herring.

twinned as Surf 'n' Turf on the really expensive part of the chain steak house menu.

In fact, one obvious project of the MLF, and of its omnipresently sponsorial Maine Lobster Promotion Council, is to counter the idea that lobster is unusually luxe or rich or unhealthy or expensive, suitable only for effete palates or the occasional blow-the-diet treat. It is emphasized over and over in presentations and pamphlets at the Festival that Maine lobster meat has fewer calories, less cholesterol, and less saturated fat than chicken.[5] And in the Main Eating Tent, you can get a "quarter" (industry shorthand for a 1¼-pound lobster), a 4-ounce cup of melted butter, a bag of chips, and a soft roll w/ butter-pat for around $12.00, which is only slightly more expensive than supper at McDonald's.

· · ·

Lobster is essentially a summer food. This is because we now prefer our lobsters fresh, which means they have to be recently caught, which for both tactical and economic reasons takes place at depths of less than 25 fathoms. Lobsters tend to be hungriest and most active (i.e., most trappable) at summer water temperatures of 45–50°F. In the autumn, some Maine lobsters migrate out into deeper water, either for warmth or to avoid the heavy waves that pound New England's coast all winter. Some burrow into the bottom. They might hibernate; nobody's sure. Summer is also lobsters' molting season—specifically early- to mid-July. Chitinous arthropods grow by molting, rather the way people have to buy bigger clothes as they age and gain weight. Since lobsters can live to be over 100, they can also get to be quite large, as in 20 pounds or more—though truly senior lobsters are rare now, because New England's waters are so heavily trapped.[6] Anyway, hence the culinary distinction between hard- and soft-shell lobsters, the latter sometimes a.k.a. shedders. A soft-shell lobster is one that has recently molted. In midcoast restaurants, the summer menu often offers both kinds, with shedders being slightly cheaper even though they're easier to dismantle and the meat is allegedly sweeter. The reason for the discount is that a molting lobster uses a layer of seawater for insulation while its new shell is hardening, so there's slightly less actual meat when you crack open a shedder, plus a redolent gout of water that gets all over everything and can sometimes jet out lemonlike and catch a tablemate right in the eye. If it's winter or you're buying lobster someplace far from New England, on the other hand, you can almost bet that the lobster is a hard-shell, which for obvious reasons travel better.

As an à la carte entrée, lobster can be baked, broiled, steamed, grilled, sautéed, stir-fried, or microwaved. The most common method, though, is boiling.

10

---

5. Of course, the common practice of dipping the lobster meat in melted butter torpedoes all these happy fat-specs, which none of the Council's promotional stuff ever mentions, any more than potato-industry PR talks about sour cream and bacon bits.

6. Datum: in a good year, the U.S. industry produces around 80 million pounds of lobster, and Maine accounts for more than half of that total.

If you're someone who enjoys having lobster at home, this is probably the way you do it, since boiling is so easy. You need a large kettle w/ cover, which you fill about half full with water (the standard advice is that you want 2.5 quarts of water per lobster). Seawater is optimal, or you can add two tbsp salt per quart from the tap. It also helps to know how much your lobsters weigh. You get the water boiling, put in the lobsters one at a time, cover the kettle, and bring it back up to a boil. Then you bank the heat and let the kettle simmer—ten minutes for the first pound of lobster, then three minutes for each pound after that. (This is assuming you've got hard-shell lobsters, which, again, if you don't live between Boston and Halifax, is probably what you've got. For shedders, you're supposed to subtract three minutes from the total.) The reason the kettle's lobsters turn scarlet is that boiling somehow suppresses every pigment in their chitin but one. If you want an easy test of whether the lobsters are done, you try pulling on one of their antennae—if it comes out of the head with minimal effort, you're ready to eat.

A detail so obvious that most recipes don't even bother to mention it is that each lobster is supposed to be alive when you put it in the kettle. This is part of lobster's modern appeal: It's the freshest food there is. There's no decomposition between harvesting and eating. And not only do lobsters require no cleaning or dressing or plucking (though the mechanics of actually eating them are a different matter), but they're relatively easy for vendors to keep alive. They come up alive in the traps, are placed in containers of seawater, and can, so long as the water's aerated and the animals' claws are pegged or banded to keep them from tearing one another up under the stresses of captivity,[7] survive right up until they're boiled. Most of us have been in supermarkets or restaurants that feature tanks of live lobster, from which you can pick out your supper while it watches you point. And part of the overall spectacle of the Maine Lobster Festival is that you can see actual lobstermen's vessels docking at the wharves along the northeast grounds and unloading freshly caught product, which is transferred by hand or cart 100 yards to the great clear tanks stacked up around the Festival's cooker—which is, as mentioned, billed as the World's Largest Lobster Cooker and can process over 100 lobsters at a time for the Main Eating Tent.

So then here is a question that's all but unavoidable at the World's Largest Lobster Cooker, and may arise in kitchens across the U.S.: Is it all right to boil a

---

7. N.B. Similar reasoning underlies the practice of what's termed "debeaking" broiler chickens and brood hens in modern factory farms. Maximum commercial efficiency requires that enormous poultry populations be confined in unnaturally close quarters, under which conditions many birds go crazy and peck one another to death. As a purely observational side-note, be apprised that debeaking is usually an automated process and that the chickens receive no anesthetic. It's not clear to me whether most *Gourmet* readers know about debeaking, or about related practices like dehorning cattle in commercial feedlots, cropping swine's tails in factory hog farms to keep psychotically bored neighbors from chewing them off, and so forth. It so happens that your assigned correspondent knew almost nothing about standard meat-industry operations before starting work on this article.

sentient creature alive just for our gustatory pleasure? A related set of concerns: Is the previous question irksomely PC or sentimental? What does "all right" even mean in this context? Is it all just a matter of individual choice?

As you may or may not know, a certain well-known group called People for the Ethical Treatment of Animals thinks that the morality of lobster-boiling is not just a matter of individual conscience. In fact, one of the very first things we hear about the MLF . . . well, to set the scene: We're coming in by cab from the almost indescribably odd and rustic Knox County Airport[8] very late on the night before the Festival opens, sharing the cab with a wealthy political consultant who lives on Vinalhaven Island in the bay half the year (he's headed for the island ferry in Rockland). The consultant and cabdriver are responding to informal journalistic probes about how people who live in the midcoast region actually view the MLF, as in is the Festival just a big-dollar tourist thing or is it something local residents look forward to attending, take genuine civic pride in, etc. The cabdriver—who's in his seventies, one of apparently a whole platoon of retirees the cab company puts on to help with the summer rush, and wears a U.S.-flag lapel pin, and drives in what can only be called a very deliberate way—assures us that locals do endorse and enjoy the MLF, although he himself hasn't gone in years, and now come to think of it no one he and his wife know has, either. However, the demilocal consultant's been to recent Festivals a couple times (one gets the impression it was at his wife's behest), of which his most vivid impression was that "you have to line up for an ungodly long time to get your lobsters, and meanwhile there are all these ex–flower children coming up and down along the line handing out pamphlets that say the lobsters die in terrible pain and you shouldn't eat them."

And it turns out that the post-hippies of the consultant's recollection were activists from PETA. There were no PETA people in obvious view at the 2003 MLF,[9] but they've been conspicuous at many of the recent Festivals. Since at

---

8. The terminal used to be somebody's house, for example, and the lost-luggage-reporting room was clearly once a pantry.

9. It turned out that Mr. William R. Rivas-Rivas, a high-ranking PETA official out of the group's Virginia headquarters, was indeed there this year, albeit solo, working the Festival's main and side entrances on Saturday, August 2, handing out pamphlets and adhesive stickers emblazoned with "Being Boiled Hurts," which is the tagline in most of PETA's published material about lobster. I learned that he'd been there only later, when speaking with Mr. Rivas-Rivas on the phone. I'm not sure how we missed seeing him *in situ* at the Festival, and I can't see much to do except apologize for the oversight—although it's also true that Saturday was the day of the big MLF parade through Rockland, which basic journalistic responsibility seemed to require going to (and which, with all due respect, meant that Saturday was maybe not the best day for PETA to work the Harbor Park grounds, especially if it was going to be just one person for one day, since a lot of diehard MLF partisans were off-site watching the parade (which, again with no offense intended, was in truth kind of cheesy and boring, consisting mostly of slow homemade flats and various midcoast people waving at one another, and with an extremely annoying man dressed as Blackbeard ranging up and down the length of the crowd saying "Arrr" over and over and brandishing a plastic sword at people, etc.; plus it rained)).

least the mid-1990s, articles in everything from *The Camden Herald* to *The New York Times* have described PETA urging boycotts of the MLF, often deploying celebrity spokespeople like Mary Tyler Moore for open letters and ads saying stuff like "Lobsters are extraordinarily sensitive" and "To me, eating a lobster is out of the question." More concrete is the oral testimony of Dick, our florid and extremely gregarious rental-car guy, to the effect that PETA's been around so much in recent years that a kind of brittlely tolerant homeostasis now obtains between the activists and the Festival's locals, e.g.: "We had some incidents a couple years ago. One lady took most of her clothes off and painted herself like a lobster, almost got herself arrested. But for the most part they're let alone. [Rapid series of small ambiguous laughs, which with Dick happens a lot.] They do their thing and we do our thing."

15   This whole interchange takes place on Route 1, 30 July, during a four-mile, 50-minute ride from the airport[10] to the dealership to sign car-rental papers. Several irreproducible segues down the road from the PETA anecdotes, Dick—whose son-in-law happens to be a professional lobsterman and one of the Main Eating Tent's regular suppliers—articulates what he and his family feel is the crucial mitigating factor in the whole morality-of-boiling-lobsters-alive issue: "There's a part of the brain in people and animals that lets us feel pain, and lobsters' brains don't have this part."

Besides the fact that it's incorrect in about 11 different ways, the main reason Dick's statement is interesting is that its thesis is more or less echoed by the Festival's own pronouncement on lobsters and pain, which is part of a Test Your Lobster IQ quiz that appears in the 2003 MLF program courtesy of the Maine Lobster Promotion Council: "The nervous system of a lobster is very simple, and is in fact most similar to the nervous system of the grasshopper. It is decentralized with no brain. There is no cerebral cortex, which in humans is the area of the brain that gives the experience of pain."

Though it sounds more sophisticated, a lot of the neurology in this latter claim is still either false or fuzzy. The human cerebral cortex is the brain-part that deals with higher faculties like reason, metaphysical self-awareness, language, etc. Pain reception is known to be part of a much older and more primitive system of nociceptors and prostaglandins that are managed by the brain stem and thalamus.[11] On the other hand, it is true that the cerebral cortex is

---

10. The short version regarding why we were back at the airport after already arriving the previous night involves lost luggage and a miscommunication about where and what the local National Car Rental franchise was—Dick came out personally to the airport and got us, out of no evident motive but kindness. (He also talked nonstop the entire way, with a very distinctive speaking style that can be described only as manically laconic; the truth is that I now know more about this man than I do about some members of my own family).

11. To elaborate by way of example: The common experience of accidentally touching a hot stove and taking your hand back before you're even aware that anything's going on is explained by the fact that many of the processes by which we detect and avoid painful stimuli do not involve the cortex. In the case of the hand and stove, the brain is bypassed altogether; all the important neurochemical action takes place in the spine.

involved in what's variously called suffering, distress, or the emotional experience of pain—i.e., experiencing painful stimuli as unpleasant, very unpleasant, unbearable, and so on.

Before we go any further, let's acknowledge that the questions of whether and how different kinds of animals feel pain, and of whether and why it might be justifiable to inflict pain on them in order to eat them, turn out to be extremely complex and difficult. And comparative neuroanatomy is only part of the problem. Since pain is a totally subjective mental experience, we do not have direct access to anyone or anything's pain but our own; and even just the principles by which we can infer that others experience pain and have a legitimate interest in not feeling pain involve hard-core philosophy—metaphysics, epistemology, value theory, ethics. The fact that even the most highly evolved nonhuman mammals can't use language to communicate with us about their subjective mental experience is only the first layer of additional complication in trying to extend our reasoning about pain and morality to animals. And everything gets progressively more abstract and convoluted as we move farther and farther out from the higher-type mammals into cattle and swine and dogs and cats and rodents, and then birds and fish, and finally invertebrates like lobsters.

The more important point here, though, is that the whole animal-cruelty-and-eating issue is not just complex, it's also uncomfortable. It is, at any rate, uncomfortable for me, and for just about everyone I know who enjoys a variety of foods and yet does not want to see herself as cruel or unfeeling. As far as I can tell, my own main way of dealing with this conflict has been to avoid thinking about the whole unpleasant thing. I should add that it appears to me unlikely that many readers of GOURMET wish to think hard about it, either, or to be queried about the morality of their eating habits in the pages of a culinary monthly. Since, however, the assigned subject of this article is what it was like to attend the 2003 MLF, and thus to spend several days in the midst of a great mass of Americans all eating lobster, and thus to be more or less impelled to think hard about lobster and the experience of buying and eating lobster, it turns out that there is no honest way to avoid certain moral questions.

There are several reasons for this. For one thing, it's not just that lobsters get boiled alive, it's that you do it yourself—or at least it's done specifically for you, on-site.[12] As mentioned, the World's Largest Lobster Cooker, which is

20

12. Morality-wise, let's concede that this cuts both ways. Lobster-eating is at least not abetted by the system of corporate factory farms that produces most beef, pork, and chicken. Because, if nothing else, of the way they're marketed and packaged for sale, we eat these latter meats without having to consider that they were once conscious, sentient creatures to whom horrible things were done. (N.B. PETA distributes a certain video—the title of which is being omitted as part of the elaborate editorial compromise by which this note appears at all—in which you can see just about everything meat-related you don't want to see or think about. (N.B. 2. Not that PETA's any sort of font of unspoken truth. Like many partisans in complex moral disputes, the PETA people are fanatics, and a lot of their rhetoric seems simplistic and self-righteous. Personally, though, I have to say that I found this unnamed video both credible and deeply upsetting.))

highlighted as an attraction in the Festival's program, is right out there on the MLF's north grounds for everyone to see. Try to imagine a Nebraska Beef Festival[13] at which part of the festivities is watching trucks pull up and the live cattle get driven down the ramp and slaughtered right there on the World's Largest Killing Floor or something—there's no way.

The intimacy of the whole thing is maximized at home, which of course is where most lobster gets prepared and eaten (although note already the semi-conscious euphemism "prepared," which in the case of lobsters really means killing them right there in our kitchens). The basic scenario is that we come in from the store and make our little preparations like getting the kettle filled and boiling, and then we lift the lobsters out of the bag or whatever retail container they came home in. . . . whereupon some uncomfortable things start to happen. However stuporous the lobster is from the trip home, for instance, it tends to come alarmingly to life when placed in boiling water. If you're tilting it from a container into the steaming kettle, the lobster will sometimes try to cling to the container's sides or even to hook its claws over the kettle's rim like a person trying to keep from going over the edge of a roof. And worse is when the lobster's fully immersed. Even if you cover the kettle and turn away, you can usually hear the cover rattling and clanking as the lobster tries to push it off. Or the creature's claws scraping the sides of the kettle as it thrashes around. The lobster, in other words, behaves very much as you or I would behave if we were plunged into boiling water (with the obvious exception of screaming).[14] A blunter way to say this is that the lobster acts as if it's in terrible pain, causing some cooks to leave the kitchen altogether and to take one of those little light-weight plastic oven timers with them into another room and wait until the whole process is over.

There happen to be two main criteria that most ethicists agree on for determining whether a living creature has the capacity to suffer and so has genuine

---

13. Is it significant that "lobster," "fish," and "chicken" are our culture's words for the animal and the meat, whereas most mammals seem to require euphemisms like "beef" and "pork" that help us separate the meat we eat from the living creature the meat once was? Is this evidence that some kind of deep unease about eating higher animals is endemic enough to show up in the English usage, but that the unease diminishes as we move out of the mammalian order? (And is "lamb"/"lamb" the counterexample that sinks the whole theory, or are there special, biblico-historical reasons for that equivalence?).

14. There's a relevant populist myth about the high-pitched whistling sound that sometimes issues from a pot of boiling lobster. The sound is really vented steam from the layer of seawater between the lobster's flesh and its carapace (this is why shedders whistle more than hard-shells), but the pop version has it that the sound is the lobster's rabbitlike death scream. Lobsters communicate via pheromones in their urine and don't have anything close to the vocal equipment for screaming, but the myth's very persistent—which might, once again, point to a low-level cultural unease about boiling the thing.

interests that it may or may not be our moral duty to consider.[15] One is how much of the neurological hardware required for pain-experience the animal comes equipped with—nociceptors, prostaglandins, neuronal opioid receptors, etc. The other criterion is whether the animal demonstrates behavior associated with pain. And it takes a lot of intellectual gymnastics and behaviorist hairsplitting not to see struggling, thrashing, and lid-clattering as just such pain-behavior. According to marine zoologists, it usually takes lobsters between 35 and 45 seconds to die in boiling water. (No source I could find talked about how long it takes them to die in superheated steam; one rather hopes it's faster.)

There are, of course, other fairly common ways to kill your lobster on-site and so achieve maximum freshness. Some cooks' practice is to drive a sharp heavy knife point-first into a spot just above the midpoint between the lobster's eyestalks (more or less where the Third Eye is in human foreheads). This is alleged either to kill the lobster instantly or to render it insensate—and is said at least to eliminate the cowardice involved in throwing a creature into boiling water and then fleeing the room. As far as I can tell from talking to proponents of the knife-in-the-head method, the idea is that it's more violent but ultimately more merciful, plus that a willingness to exert personal agency and accept responsibility for stabbing the lobster's head honors the lobster somehow and entitles one to eat it. (There's often a vague sort of Native American spirituality-of-the-hunt flavor to pro-knife arguments.) But the problem with the knife method is basic biology: Lobsters' nervous systems operate off not one but several ganglia, a.k.a. nerve bundles, which are sort of wired in series and distributed all along the lobster's underside, from stem to stern. And disabling only the frontal ganglion does not normally result in quick death or unconsciousness. Another alternative is to put the lobster in cold salt water and then very slowly bring it up to a full boil. Cooks who advocate this method are going mostly on the analogy to a frog, which can supposedly be kept from jumping out of a boiling pot by heating the water incrementally. In order to save a lot of research-summarizing, I'll simply assure you that the analogy between frogs and lobsters turns out not to hold.

Ultimately, the only certain virtues of the home-lobotomy and slow-heating methods are comparative, because there are even worse/crueler ways people prepare lobster. Time-thrifty cooks sometimes microwave them alive (usually after poking several extra vent holes in the carapace, which is a precaution most shellfish-microwavers learn about the hard way). Live dismemberment, on the other hand, is big in Europe: Some chefs cut the lobster in half before cooking; others like to tear off the claws and tail and toss only these parts in the pot.

15. "Interests" basically means strong and legitimate preferences, which obviously require some degree of consciousness, responsiveness to stimuli, etc. See, for instance, the utilitarian philosopher Peter Singer, whose 1974 *Animal Liberation* is more or less the bible of the modern animal-rights movement: "It would be nonsense to say that it was not in the interests of a stone to be kicked along the road by a schoolboy. A stone does not have interests because it cannot suffer. Nothing that we can do to it could possibly make any difference to its welfare. A mouse, on the other hand, does have an interest in not being kicked along the road, because it will suffer if it is."

25   And there's more unhappy news respecting suffering-criterion number one. Lobsters don't have much in the way of eyesight or hearing, but they do have an exquisite tactile sense, one facilitated by hundreds of thousands of tiny hairs that protrude through their carapace. "Thus," in the words of T. M. Prudden's industry classic *About Lobster*, "it is that although encased in what seems a solid, impenetrable armor, the lobster can receive stimuli and impressions from without as readily as if it possessed a soft and delicate skin." And lobsters do have nociceptors,[16] as well as invertebrate versions of the prostaglandins and major neurotransmitters via which our own brains register pain.

        Lobsters do not, on the other hand, appear to have the equipment for making or absorbing natural opioids like endorphins and enkephalins, which are what more advanced nervous systems use to try to handle intense pain. From this fact, though, one could conclude either that lobsters are maybe even *more* vulnerable to pain, since they lack mammalian nervous systems' built-in analgesia, or, instead, that the absence of natural opioids implies an absence of the really intense pain-sensations that natural opioids are designed to mitigate. I for one can detect a marked upswing in mood as I contemplate this latter possibility: It could be that their lack of endorphin/enkephalin hardware means that lobsters' raw subjective experience of pain is so radically different from mammals' that it may not even deserve the term *pain*. Perhaps lobsters are more like those frontal-lobotomy patients one reads about who report experiencing pain in a totally different way than you and I. These patients evidently do feel physical pain, neurologically speaking, but don't dislike it—though neither do they like it; it's more that they feel it but don't feel anything *about* it—the point being that the pain is not distressing to them or something they want to get away from. Maybe lobsters, who are also without frontal lobes, are detached from the neurological-registration-of-injury-or-hazard we call pain in just the same way. There is, after all, a difference between (1) pain as a purely neurological event, and (2) actual suffering, which seems crucially to involve an emotional component, an awareness of pain as unpleasant, as something to fear/dislike/want to avoid.

        Still, after all the abstract intellection, there remain the facts of the frantically clanking lid, the pathetic clinging to the edge of the pot. Standing at the stove, it is hard to deny in any meaningful way that this is a living creature experiencing pain and wishing to avoid/escape the painful experience. To my lay mind, the lobster's behavior in the kettle appears to be the expression of a *preference*; and it may well be that an ability to form preferences is the decisive criterion for real suffering.[17] The logic of this (preference → suffering) relation may be easiest to see in the negative case. If you cut certain kinds of

16. This is the neurological term for special pain receptors that are (according to Jane A. Smith and Kenneth M. Boyd's *Lives in the Balance*) "sensitive to potentially damaging extremes of temperature, to mechanical forces, and to chemical substances which are released when body tissues are damaged."

17. "Preference" is maybe roughly synonymous with "interest," but it is a better term for our purposes because it's less abstractly philosophical—"preference" seems more

worms in half, the halves will often keep crawling around and going about their vermiform business as if nothing had happened. When we assert, based on their post-op behavior, that these worms appear not to be suffering, what we're really saying is that there's no sign that the worms know anything bad has happened or would *prefer* not to have gotten cut in half.

Lobsters, however, are known to exhibit preferences. Experiments have shown that they can detect changes of only a degree or two in water temperature; one reason for their complex migratory cycles (which can often cover 100-plus miles a year) is to pursue the temperatures they like best.[18] And, as mentioned, they're bottom-dwellers and do not like bright light: If a tank of food lobsters is out in the sunlight or a store's fluorescence, the lobsters will always congregate in whatever part is darkest. Fairly solitary in the ocean, they also clearly dislike the crowding that's part of their captivity in tanks, since (as also mentioned) one reason why lobsters' claws are banded on capture is to keep them from attacking one another under the stress of close-quarter storage.

In any event, at the Festival, standing by the bubbling tanks outside the World's Largest Lobster Cooker, watching the fresh-caught lobsters pile over one another, wave their hobbled claws impotently, huddle in the rear corners, or scrabble frantically back from the glass as you approach, it is difficult not to sense that they're unhappy, or frightened, even if it's some rudimentary version of these feelings. . . . and, again, why does rudimentariness even enter into it? Why is a primitive, inarticulate form of suffering less urgent or uncomfortable for the person who's helping to inflict it by paying for the food it results in? I'm not trying to give you a PETA-like screed here—at least I don't think so.

---

personal, and it's the whole idea of a living creature's personal experience that's at issue.

18. Of course, the most common sort of counterargument here would begin by objecting that "like best" is really just a metaphor, and a misleadingly anthropomorphic one at that. The counterarguer would posit that the lobster seeks to maintain a certain optimal ambient temperature out of nothing but unconscious instinct (with a similar explanation for the low-light affinities about to be mentioned in the main text). The thrust of such a counterargument will be that the lobster's thrashings and clankings in the kettle express not unpreferred pain but involuntary reflexes, like your leg shooting out when the doctor hits your knee. Be advised that there are professional scientists, including many researchers who use animals in experiments, who hold to the view that nonhuman creatures have no real feelings at all, only "behaviors." Be further advised that this view has a long history that goes all the way back to Descartes, although its modern support comes mostly from behaviorist psychology.

   To these what-look-like-pain-are-really-only-reflexes counterarguments, however, there happen to be all sorts of scientific and pro-animal-rights counter-counterarguments. And then further attempted rebuttals and redirects, and so on. Suffice to say that both the scientific and the philosophical arguments on either side of the animal-suffering issue are involved, abstruse, technical, often informed by self-interest or ideology, and in the end so totally inconclusive that as a practical matter, in the kitchen or restaurant, it all still seems to come down to individual conscience, going with (no pun) your gut.

I'm trying, rather, to work out and articulate some of the troubling questions that arise amid all the laughter and saltation and community pride of the Maine Lobster Festival. The truth is that if you, the Festival attendee, permit yourself to think that lobsters can suffer and would rather not, the MLF can begin to take on aspects of something like a Roman circus or medieval torture-fest.

30   Does that comparison seem a bit much? If so, exactly why? Or what about this one: Is it not possible that future generations will regard our own present agribusiness and eating practices in much the same way we now view Nero's entertainments or Aztec sacrifices? My own immediate reaction is that such a comparison is hysterical, extreme—and yet the reason it seems extreme to me appears to be that I believe animals are less morally important than human beings;[19] and when it comes to defending such a belief, even to myself, I have to acknowledge that (a) I have an obvious selfish interest in this belief, since I like to eat certain kinds of animals and want to be able to keep doing it, and (b) I have not succeeded in working out any sort of personal ethical system in which the belief is truly defensible instead of just selfishly convenient.

Given this article's venue and my own lack of culinary sophistication, I'm curious about whether the reader can identify with any of these reactions and acknowledgments and discomforts. I am also concerned not to come off as shrill or preachy when what I really am is confused. Given the (possible) moral status and (very possible) physical suffering of the animals involved, what ethical convictions do gourmets evolve that allow them not just to eat but to savor and enjoy flesh-based viands (since of course refined *enjoyment*, rather than just ingestion, is the whole point of gastronomy)? And for those gourmets who'll have no truck with convictions or rationales and who regard stuff like the previous paragraph as just so much pointless navel-gazing, what makes it feel okay, inside, to dismiss the whole issue out of hand? That is, is their refusal to think about any of this the product of actual thought, or is it just that they don't want to think about it? Do they ever think about their reluctance to think about it? After all, isn't being extra aware and attentive and thoughtful about one's food and its overall context part of what distinguishes a real gourmet? Or is all the gourmet's extra attention and sensibility just supposed to be aesthetic, gustatory?

These last couple queries, though, while sincere, obviously involve much larger and more abstract questions about the connections (if any) between aesthetics and morality, and these questions lead straightaway into such deep and treacherous waters that it's probably best to stop the public discussion right here. There are limits to what even interested persons can ask of each other.

19. Meaning a *lot* less important, apparently, since the moral comparison here is not the value of one human's life vs. the value of one animal's life, but rather the value of one animal's life vs. the value of one human's taste for a particular kind of protein. Even the most diehard carniphile will acknowledge that it's possible to live and eat well without consuming animals.

MLA CITATION

Wallace, David Foster. "Consider the Lobster." 2004. *The Norton Reader: An Anthology of Nonfiction*. Ed. Melissa A. Goldthwaite et al. 14th ed. New York: Norton, 2016. 697–708. Print.

QUESTIONS

1. David Foster Wallace finally admits to being "confused" (paragraph 31) about the morality of eating lobsters. After reading his essay, what are your feelings? Are they changed from what they were before you read his essay?

2. Comment on Wallace's footnotes, which sometimes add information but at other times seem to carry on another argument on the bottom of the page. Why do you think he includes both kinds?

3. Compare the way Wallace employs footnotes with the footnotes in Annie Leonard's "The Story of Bottled Water" (pp. 200–13). One similarity, for example, is the absolute richness of the notes. What similarities and differences do you notice?

4. Write about a festival or event you have attended, using description and research if appropriate, especially if there is an ethical dimension to your topic.

SALLIE TISDALE *We Do Abortions Here:*
A Nurse's Story

WE DO ABORTIONS HERE; that is all we do. There are weary, grim moments when I think I cannot bear another basin of bloody remains, utter another kind phrase of reassurance. So I leave the procedure room in the back and reach for a new chart. Soon I am talking to an eighteen-year-old woman pregnant for the fourth time. I push up her sleeve to check her blood pressure and find row upon row of needle marks, neat and parallel and discolored. She has been so hungry for her drug for so long that she has taken to using the loose skin of her upper arms; her elbows are already a permanent ruin of bruises. She is surprised to find herself nearly four months pregnant. I suspect she is often surprised, in a mild way, by the blows she is dealt. I prepare myself for another basin, another brief and chafing loss.

"How can you stand it?" Even the clients ask. They see the machine, the strange instruments, the blood, the final stroke that wipes away the promise of pregnancy. Sometimes I see that too: I watch a woman's swollen abdomen sink

From Harper's Magazine *(1990), an American monthly covering politics, society, culture, and the environment.*

to softness in a few stuttering moments and my own belly flip-flops with sorrow. But all it takes for me to catch my breath is another interview, one more story that sounds so much like the last one. There is a numbing sameness lurking in this job: the same questions, the same answers, even the same trembling tone in the voices. The worst is the sameness of human failure, of inadequacy in the face of each day's dull demands.

In describing this work, I find it difficult to explain how much I enjoy it most of the time. We laugh a lot here, as friends and as professional peers. It's nice to be with women all day. I like the sudden, transient bonds I forge with some clients: moments when I am in my strength, remembering weakness, and a woman in weakness reaches out for my strength. What I offer is not power, but solidness, offered almost eagerly. Certain clients waken in me every tender urge I have—others make me wince and bite my tongue. Both challenge me to find a balance. It is a sweet brutality we practice here, a stark and loving dispassion.

I look at abortion as if I am standing on a cliff with a telescope, gazing at some great vista. I can sweep the horizon with both eyes, survey the scene in all its distance and size. Or I can put my eye to the lens and focus on the small details, suddenly so close. In abortion the absolute must always be tempered by the contextual, because both are real, both valid, both hard. How can we do this? How can we refuse? Each abortion is a measure of our failure to protect, to nourish our own. Each basin I empty is a promise—but a promise broken a long time ago.

5   I grew up on the great promise of birth control. Like many women my age, I took the pill as soon as I was sexually active. To risk pregnancy when it was so easy to avoid seemed stupid, and my contraceptive success, as it were, was part of the promise of social enlightenment. But birth control fails, far more frequently than laboratory trials predict. Many of our clients take the pill; its failure to protect them is a shocking realization. We have clients who have been sterilized, whose husbands have had vasectomies; each one is a statistical misfit, fine print come to life. The anger and shame of these women I hold in one hand, and the basin in the other. The distance between the two, the length I pace and try to measure, is the size of an abortion.

The procedure is disarmingly simple. Women are surprised, as though the mystery of conception, a dark and hidden genesis, requires an elaborate finale. In the first trimester of pregnancy, it's a mere few minutes of vacuuming, a neat tidying up. I give a woman a small yellow Valium, and when it has begun to relax her, I lead her into the back, into bareness, the stirrups. The doctor reaches in her, opening the narrow tunnel to the uterus with a succession of slim, smooth bars of steel. He inserts a plastic tube and hooks it to a hose on the machine. The woman is framed against white paper that crackles as she moves, the light bright in her eyes. Then the machine rumbles low and loud in the small windowless room; the doctor moves the tube back and forth with an efficient rhythm, and the long tail of it fills with blood that spurts and stumbles along into a jar. He is usually finished in a few minutes. They are long minutes for the woman; her uterus frequently reacts to its abrupt emptying with a powerful, unceasing cramp, which cuts off the blood vessels and enfolds the irritated, bleeding tissue.

I am learning to recognize the shadows that cross the faces of the women I hold. While the doctor works between her spread legs, the paper drape hiding his intent expression, I stand beside the table. I hold the woman's hands in mine, resting them just below her ribs. I watch her eyes, finger her necklace, stroke her hair. I ask about her job, her family; in a haze she answers me; we chatter, faces close, eyes meeting and sliding apart.

I watch the shadows that creep up unnoticed and suddenly darken her face as she screws up her features and pushes a tear out each side to slide down her cheeks. I have learned to anticipate the quiver of chin, the rapid intake of breath and the surprising sobs that rise soon after the machine starts to drum. I know this is when the cramp deepens, and the tears are partly the tears that follow pain—the sharp, childish crying when one bumps one's head on a cabinet door. But a well of woe seems to open beneath many women when they hear that thumping sound. The anticipation of the moment has finally come to fruit; the moment has arrived when the loss is no longer an imagined one. It has come true.

I am struck by the sameness and I am struck every day by the variety here—how this commonplace dilemma can so display the differences of women. A twenty-one-year-old woman, unemployed, uneducated, without family, in the fifth month of her fifth pregnancy. A forty-two-year-old mother of teenagers, shocked by her condition, refusing to tell her husband. A twenty-three-year-old mother of two having her seventh abortion, and many women in their thirties having their first. Some are stoic, some hysterical, a few giggle uncontrollably, many cry.

I talk to a sixteen-year-old uneducated girl who was raped. She has gonor-   10
rhea. She describes blinding headaches, attacks of breathlessness, nausea. "Sometimes I feel like two different people," she tells me with a calm smile, "and I talk to myself."

I pull out my plastic models. She listens patiently for a time, and then holds her hands wide in front of her stomach.

"When's the baby going to go up into my stomach?" she asks.

I blink. "What do you mean?"

"Well," she says, still smiling, "when women get so big, isn't the baby in your stomach? Doesn't it hatch out of an egg there?"

My first question in an interview is always the same. As I walk down the   15
hall with the woman, as we get settled in chairs and I glance through her files, I am trying to gauge her, to get a sense of the words, and the tone, I should use. With some I joke, with others I chat, sometimes I fall into a brisk, business-like patter. But I ask every woman, "Are you sure you want to have an abortion?" Most nod with grim knowing smiles. "Oh, yes," they sigh. Some seek forgive-ness, offer excuses. Occasionally a woman will flinch and say, "Please don't use that word."

Later I describe the procedure to come, using care with my language. I don't say "pain" any more than I would say "baby." So many are afraid to ask how much it will hurt. "My sister told me—" I hear. "A friend of mine said—" and the dire expectations unravel. I prick the index finger of a woman for a drop of blood to test, and as the tiny lancet approaches the skin she averts her eyes, holding her trembling hand out to me and jumping at my touch.

It is when I am holding a plastic uterus in one hand, a suction tube in the other, moving them together in imitation of the scrubbing to come, that women ask the most secret question. I am speaking in a matter-of-fact voice about "the tissue" and "the contents" when the woman suddenly catches my eye and asks, "How big is the baby now?" These words suggest a quiet need for a definition of the boundaries being drawn. It isn't so odd, after all, that she feels relief when I describe the growing bud's bulbous shape, its miniature nature. Again I gauge, and sometimes lie a little, weaseling around its infantile features until its clinging power slackens.

But when I look in the basin, among the curdlike blood clots, I see an elfin thorax, attenuated, its pencilline ribs all in parallel rows with tiny knobs of spine rounding upwards. A translucent arm and hand swim beside.

A sleepy-eyed girl, just fourteen, watched me with a slight and goofy smile all through her abortion. "Does it have little feet and little fingers and all?" she'd asked earlier. When the suction was over she sat up woozily at the end of the table and murmured, "Can I see it?" I shook my head firmly.

20   "It's not allowed," I told her sternly, because I knew she didn't really want to see what was left. She accepted this statement of authority, and a shadow of confused relief crossed her plain, pale face.

Privately, even grudgingly, my colleagues might admit the power of abortion to provoke emotion. But they seem to prefer the broad view and disdain the telescope. Abortion is a matter of choice, privacy, control. Its uncertainty lies in specific cases: retarded women and girls too young to give consent for surgery, women who are ill or hostile or psychotic. Such common dilemmas are met with both compassion and impatience: they slow things down. We are too busy to chew over ethics. One person might discuss certain concerns, behind closed doors, or describe a particularly disturbing dream. But generally there is to be no ambivalence.

Every day I take calls from women who are annoyed that we cannot see them, cannot do their abortion today, this morning, now. They argue the price, demand that we stay after hours to accommodate their job or class schedule. Abortion is so routine that one expects it to be like a manicure: quick, cheap, and painless.

Still, I've cultivated a certain disregard. It isn't negligence, but I don't always pay attention. I couldn't be here if I tried to judge each case on its merits; after all, we do over a hundred abortions a week. At some point each individual in this line of work draws a boundary and adheres to it. For one physician the boundary is a particular week of gestation; for another, it is a certain number of repeated abortions. But these boundaries can be fluid too: one physician overruled his own limit to abort a mature but severely malformed fetus. For me, the limit is allowing my clients to carry their own burden, shoulder the responsibility themselves. I shoulder the burden of trying not to judge them.

This city has several "crisis pregnancy centers" advertised in the Yellow Pages. They are small offices staffed by volunteers, and they offer free pregnancy testing, glossy photos of dead fetuses, and movies. I had a client recently whose mother is active in the anti-abortion movement. The young woman went to the local crisis center and was told that the doctor would make her touch her dismembered baby, that the pain would be the most horrible she could imagine, and that she might, after an abortion, never be able to have children. All lies. They called her at home and at work, over and over and over, but she had been wise enough to give a false name. She came to us a fugitive. We who do abortions are marked, by some, as impure. It's dirty work.

When a deliveryman comes to the sliding glass window by the reception   25
desk and tilts a box toward me, I hesitate. I read the packing slip, assess the shape and weight of the box in light of its supposed contents. We request familiar faces. The doors are carefully locked; I have learned to half glance around at bags and boxes, looking for a telltale sign. I register with security when I arrive, and I am careful not to bang a door. We are all a little on edge here.

Concern about size and shape seem to be natural, and so is the relief that follows. We make the powerful assumption that the fetus is different from us, and even when we admit the similarities, it is too simplistic to be seduced by form alone. But the form is enormously potent—humanoid, powerless, palm-sized, and pure, it evokes an almost fierce tenderness when viewed simply as what it appears to be. But appearance, and even potential, aren't enough. The fetus, in becoming itself, can ruin others; its utter dependence has a sinister side. When I am struck in the moment by the contents in the basin, I am careful to remember the context, to note the tearful teenager and the woman sighing with something more than relief. One kind of question, though, I find considerably trickier.

"Can you tell what it is?" I am asked, and this means gender. This question is asked by couples, not women alone. Always couples would abort a girl and keep a boy. I have been asked about twins, and even if I could tell what race the father was.

An eighteen-year-old woman with three daughters brought her husband to the interview. He glared first at me, then at his wife, as he sank lower and lower in the chair, picking his teeth with a toothpick. He interrupted a conversation with his wife to ask if I could tell whether the baby would be a boy or a girl. I told him I could not.

"Good," he replied in a slow and strangely malevolent voice, "'cause if it was a boy I'd wring her neck."

In a literal sense, abortion exists because we are able to ask such ques-   30
tions, able to assign a value to the fetus which can shift with changing circumstances. If the human bond to a child were as primitive and unflinchingly narrow as that of other animals, there would be no abortion. There would be

no abortion because there would be nothing more important than caring for the young and perpetuating the species, no reason for sex but to make babies. I sense this sometimes, this wordless organic duty, when I do ultrasounds.

We do ultrasound, a sound-wave test that paints a faint, gray picture of the fetus, whenever we're uncertain of gestation. Age is measured by the width of the skull and confirmed by the length of the femur or thighbone; we speak of a pregnancy as being a certain "femur length" in weeks. The usual concern is whether a pregnancy is within the legal limit for an abortion. Women this far along have bellies which swell out round and tight like trim muscles. When they lie flat, the mound rises softly above the hips, pressing the umbilicus upward.

It takes practice to read an ultrasound picture, which is grainy and etched as though in strokes of charcoal. But suddenly a rapid rhythmic motion appears—the beating heart. Nearby is a soft oval, scratched with lines—the skull. The leg is harder to find, and then suddenly the fetus moves, bobbing in the surf. The skull turns away, an arm slides across the screen, the torso rolls. I know the weight of a baby's head on my shoulder, the whisper of lips on ears, the delicate curve of a fragile spine in my hand. I know how heavy and correct a newborn cradled feels. The creature I watch in secret requires nothing from me but to be left alone, and that is precisely what won't be done.

These inadvertently made beings are caught in a twisting web of motive and desire. They are at least inconvenient, sometimes quite literally dangerous in the womb, but most often they fall somewhere in between—consequences never quite believed in come to roost. Their virtue rises and falls outside their own nature: they become only what we make them. A fetus created by accident is the most absolute kind of surprise. Whether the blame lies in a failed IUD, a slipped condom, or a false impression of safety, that fetus is a thing whose creation has been actively worked against. Its existence is an error. I think this is why so few women, even late in a pregnancy, will consider giving a baby up for adoption. To do so means making the fetus real—imagining it as something whole and outside oneself. The decision to terminate a pregnancy is sometimes so difficult and confounding that it creates an enormous demand for immediate action. The decision is a rejection; the pregnancy has become something to be rid of, a condition to be ended. It is a burden, a weight, a thing separate.

Women have abortions because they are too old, and too young, too poor, and too rich, too stupid, and too smart. I see women who berate themselves with violent emotions for their first and only abortion, and others who return three times, five times, hauling two or three children, who cannot remember to take a pill or where they put the diaphragm. We talk glibly about choice. But the choice for what? I see all the broken promises in lives lived like a series of impromptu obstacles. There are the sweet, light promises of love and intimacy, the glittering promise of education and progress, the warm promise of safe families, long years of innocence and community. And there is the promise of freedom: freedom from failure, from faithlessness. Freedom from biology. The early feminist defense of abortion asked many questions, but the one I remember is this: Is biology destiny? And the answer is yes, sometimes it is. Women who have the fewest choices of all exercise their right to abortion the most.

Oh, the ignorance. I take a woman to the back room and ask her to undress;   35
a few minutes later I return and find her positioned discreetly behind a drape,
still wearing underpants. "Do I have to take these off too?" she asks, a little
shocked. Some swear they have not had sex, many do not know what a uterus
is, how sperm and egg meet, how sex makes babies. Some late seekers do not
believe themselves pregnant; they believe themselves *impregnable*. I was chastised when I began this job for referring to some clients as girls: it is a feminist
heresy. They come so young, snapping gum, sockless and sneakered, and their
shakily applied eyeliner smears when they cry. I call them girls with maternal
benignity. I cannot imagine them as mothers.

The doctor seats himself between the woman's thighs and reaches into the
dilated opening of a five-month pregnant uterus. Quickly he grabs and crushes
the fetus in several places, and the room is filled with a low clatter and snap of
forceps, the click of the tanaculum, and a pulling, sucking sound. The paper
crinkles as the drugged and sleepy woman shifts, the nurse's low, honey-brown
voice explains each step in delicate words.

I have fetus dreams, we all do here: dreams of abortions one after the other;
of buckets of blood splashed on the walls; trees full of crawling fetuses. I
dreamed that two men grabbed me and began to drag me away. "Let's do an
abortion," they said with a sickening leer, and I began to scream, plunged into
a vision of sucking, scraping pain, of being spread and torn by impartial instruments that do only what they are bidden. I woke from this dream barely able to
breathe and thought of kitchen tables and coat hangers, knitting needles striped
with blood, and women all alone clutching a pillow in their teeth to keep the
screams from piercing the apartment-house walls. Abortion is the narrowest
edge between kindness and cruelty. Done as well as it can be, it is still violence—
merciful violence, like putting a suffering animal to death.

Maggie, one of the nurses, received a call at midnight not long ago. It was
a woman in her twentieth week of pregnancy; the necessarily gradual process of
cervical dilation begun the day before had stimulated labor, as it sometimes
does. Maggie and one of the doctors met the woman at the office in the night.
Maggie helped her onto the table, and as she lay down the fetus was delivered
into Maggie's hands. When Maggie told me about it the next day, she cupped
her hands into a small bowl—"It was just like a little kitten," she said softly,
wonderingly. "Everything was still attached."

At the end of the day I clean out the suction jars, pouring blood into the
sink, splashing the sides with flecks of tissue. From the sink rises a rich and
humid smell, hot, earthy, and moldering; it is the smell of something recently
alive beginning to decay. I take care of the plastic tub on the floor, filled with
pieces too big to be trusted to the trash. The law defines the contents of the
bucket I hold protectively against my chest as "tissue." Some would say my com-
plicity in filling that bucket gives me no right to call it anything else. I slip the
tissue gently into a bag and place it in the freezer, to be burned at another time.
Abortion requires of me an entirely new set of assumptions. It requires a willingness to live with conflict, fearlessness, and grief. As I close the freezer door,

I imagine a world where this won't be necessary, and then return to the world where it is.

MLA CITATION

Tisdale, Sallie. "We Do Abortions Here: A Nurse's Story." 1990. *The Norton Reader: An Anthology of Nonfiction.* Ed. Melissa A. Goldthwaite et al. 14th ed. New York: Norton, 2016. 709–16. Print.

QUESTIONS

1. Sallie Tisdale speaks of taking both broad views—"as if I am standing on a cliff with a telescope"—and narrow views—"I can put my eye to the lens and focus on the small details" (paragraph 4). Choose one section of this essay and mark the passages you would describe as taking broad views and the passages you would describe as taking narrow views. What is the effect of Tisdale's going back and forth between them? How does she manage transitions?

2. "We are too busy to chew over ethics" (paragraph 21), Tisdale observes. What does she mean by ethics? Does she engage with what you consider ethical issues in this essay? Explain.

3. Although Tisdale takes a pro-choice position, a pro-lifer could use parts of her essay against her. What parts? What are the advantages and disadvantages of including material that could be used in support of the opposition?

4. Write an essay about an ethical issue with which you have some experience. As Tisdale does, use description and dialogue.

NORA EPHRON   *The Boston Photographs*

"I MADE ALL KINDS OF PICTURES because I thought it would be a good rescue shot over the ladder. . . . never dreamed it would be anything else . . . I kept having to move around because of the light set. The sky was bright and they were in deep shadow. I was making pictures with a motor drive and he, the fire fighter, was reaching up and, I don't know, everything started falling. I followed the girl down taking pictures. . . . I made three or four frames. I realized what was going on and I completely turned around, because I didn't want to see her hit."

You probably saw the photographs. In most newspapers, there were three of them. The first showed some people on a fire escape—a fireman, a woman

Nora Ephron wrote this essay as a columnist on media for Esquire *magazine (1975). It later appeared in her collection* Scribble, Scribble: Notes on the Media *(1978).*

and a child. The fireman had a nice strong jaw and looked very brave. The woman was holding the child. Smoke was pouring from the building behind them. A rescue ladder was approaching, just a few feet away, and the fireman had one arm around the woman and one arm reaching out toward the ladder. The second picture showed the fire escape slipping off the building. The child had fallen on the escape and seemed about to slide off the edge. The woman was grasping desperately at the legs of the fireman, who had managed to grab the ladder. The third picture showed the woman and child in midair, falling to the ground. Their arms and legs were outstretched, horribly distended. A potted plant was falling too. The caption said that the woman, Diana Bryant, nineteen, died in the fall. The child landed on the woman's body and lived.

The pictures were taken by Stanley Forman, thirty, of the *Boston Herald American*. He used a motor-driven Nikon F set at 1/250, f 5.6–8. Because of the motor, the camera can click off three frames a second. More than four hundred newspapers in the United States alone carried the photographs; the tear sheets from overseas are still coming in. The *New York Times* ran them on the first page of its second section; a paper in south Georgia gave them nineteen columns; the *Chicago Tribune*, the *Washington Post* and the *Washington Star* filled almost half their front pages, the *Star* under a somewhat redundant headline that read: SENSATIONAL PHOTOS OF RESCUE ATTEMPT THAT FAILED.

The photographs are indeed sensational. They are pictures of death in action, of that split second when luck runs out, and it is impossible to look at them without feeling their extraordinary impact and remembering, in an almost subconscious way, the morbid fantasy of falling, falling off a building, falling to one's death. Beyond that, the pictures are classics, old-fashioned but perfect examples of photojournalism at its most spectacular. They're throwbacks, really, fire pictures, 1930s tabloid shots; at the same time they're technically superb and thoroughly modern—the sequence could not have been taken at all until the development of the motor-driven camera some sixteen years ago.

Most newspaper editors anticipate some reader reaction to photographs like Forman's; even so, the response around the country was enormous, and almost all of it was negative. I have read hundreds of the letters that were printed in letters-to-the-editor sections, and they repeat the same points. "Invading the privacy of death." "Cheap sensationalism." "I thought I was reading the *National Enquirer*." "Assigning the agony of a human being in terror of imminent death to the status of a side-show act." "A tawdry way to sell newspapers." The *Seattle Times* received sixty letters and calls; its managing editor even got a couple of them at home. A reader wrote the *Philadelphia Inquirer*: "*Jaws* and *Towering Inferno* are playing downtown; don't take business away from people who pay good money to advertise in your own paper." Another reader wrote the *Chicago Sun-Times*: "I shall try to hide my disappointment that Miss Bryant wasn't wearing a skirt when she fell to her death. You could have had some award-winning photographs of her underpants as her skirt billowed over her head, you voyeurs." Several newspaper editors wrote columns defending the pictures: Thomas

Keevil of the *Costa Mesa* (California) *Daily Pilot* printed a ballot for readers to vote on whether they would have printed the pictures; Marshall L. Stone of Maine's *Bangor Daily News*, which refused to print the famous assassination picture of the Vietcong prisoner in Saigon, claimed that the Boston pictures showed the dangers of fire escapes and raised questions about slumlords. (The burning building was a five-story brick apartment house on Marlborough Street in the Back Bay section of Boston.)

For the last five years, the *Washington Post* has employed various journalists as ombudsmen, whose job is to monitor the paper on behalf of the public. The *Post*'s current ombudsman is Charles Seib, former managing editor of the

Washington Star; the day the Boston photographs appeared, the paper received over seventy calls in protest. As Seib later wrote in a column about the pictures, it was "the largest reaction to a published item that I have experienced in eight months as the *Post*'s ombudsman. . . .

"In the *Post*'s newsroom, on the other hand, I found no doubts, no second thoughts. . . . the question was not whether they should be printed but how they should be displayed. When I talked to editors . . . they used words like 'interesting' and 'riveting' and 'gripping' to describe them. The pictures told something about life in the ghetto, they said (although the neighborhood where the tragedy occurred is not a ghetto, I am told). They dramatized the need to check

on the safety of fire escapes. They dramatically conveyed something that had happened, and that is the business we're in. They were news. . . .

"Was publication of that [third] picture a bow to the same taste for the morbidly sensational that makes gold mines of disaster movies? Most papers will not print the picture of a dead body except in the most unusual circumstances. Does the fact that the final picture was taken a millisecond before the young woman died make a difference? Most papers will not print a picture of a bare female breast. Is that a more inappropriate subject for display than the picture of a human being's last agonized instant of life?" Seib offered no answers to the questions he raised, but he went on to say that although as an editor he would probably have run the pictures, as a reader he was "revolted by them."

In conclusion, Seib wrote: "Any editor who decided to print those pictures without giving at least a moment's thought to what purpose they served and what their effect was likely to be on the reader should ask another question: Have I become so preoccupied with manufacturing a product according to professional traditions and standards that I have forgotten about the consumer, the reader?"

It should be clear that the phone calls and letters and Seib's own reaction were occasioned by one factor alone: the death of the woman. Obviously, had she survived the fall, no one would have protested; the pictures would have had a completely different impact. Equally obviously, had the child died as well—or instead—Seib would undoubtedly have received ten times the phone calls he did. In each case, the pictures would have been exactly the same—only the captions, and thus the responses, would have been different.

But the questions Seib raises are worth discussing—though not exactly for the reasons he mentions. For it may be that the real lesson of the Boston photographs is not the danger that editors will be forgetful of reader reaction, but that they will continue to censor pictures of death precisely because of that reaction. The protests Seib fielded were really a variation on an old theme—and we saw plenty of it during the Nixon-Agnew years—the "Why doesn't the press print the good news?" argument. In this case, of course, the objections were all dressed up and cleverly disguised as righteous indignation about the privacy of death. This is a form of puritanism that is often justifiable; just as often it is merely puritanical.

Seib takes it for granted that the widespread though fairly recent newspaper policy against printing pictures of dead bodies is a sound one; I don't know that it makes any sense at all. I recognize that printing pictures of corpses raises all sorts of problems about taste and titillation and sensationalism; the fact is, however, that people die. Death happens to be one of life's main events. And it is irresponsible—and more than that, inaccurate—for newspapers to fail to show it, or to show it only when an astonishing set of photos comes in over the Associated Press wire. Most papers covering fatal automobile accidents will print pictures of mangled cars. But the significance of fatal automobile accidents is not that a great deal of steel is twisted but that people die. Why not show it? That's what accidents are about. Throughout the Vietnam war, editors were reluctant to print atrocity pictures. Why *not* print them? That's what that war was about. Murder victims are almost never photographed; they are granted their privacy. But their relatives are relentlessly pictured on their way in and out of hospitals and morgues and funerals.

I'm not advocating that newspapers print these things in order to teach their readers a lesson. The *Post* editors justified their printing of the Boston pictures with several arguments in that direction; every one of them is irrelevant. The pictures don't show anything about slum life; the incident could have happened anywhere, and it did. It is extremely unlikely that anyone who saw them rushed out and had his fire escape strengthened. And the pictures were not news—at least they were not national news. It is not news in Washington, or New York, or Los Angeles that a woman was killed in a Boston fire. The only newsworthy thing about the pictures is that they were taken. They deserve to

10

be printed because they are great pictures, breathtaking pictures of something that happened. That they disturb readers is exactly as it should be: that's why photojournalism is often more powerful than written journalism.

MLA CITATION

Ephron, Nora. "The Boston Photographs." 1975. *The Norton Reader: An Anthology of Nonfiction.* Ed. Melissa A. Goldthwaite et al. 14th ed. New York: Norton, 2016. 716–22. Print.

QUESTIONS

1. Why does Nora Ephron begin with the words of the photographer Stanley Forman? What information—as well as perspective—does her opening paragraph convey?

2. What was public reaction to the publication of the Boston photographs? What reasons did newspeople give for printing them? How does Ephron arrange these responses?

3. Does Ephron suggest any limits to what can be published in print or online? Do you think there should be limits? How would you go about deciding what those limits should be?

4. Find a startling photographic image that recently appeared in print or online, and write an argument for or against its publication.

PAUL FUSSELL   *Thank God for the Atom Bomb*

MANY YEARS AGO in New York I saw on the side of a bus a whiskey ad I've remembered all this time. It's been for me a model of the short poem, and indeed I've come upon few short poems subsequently that exhibited more poetic talent. The ad consisted of two eleven-syllable lines of "verse," thus:

In life, experience is the great teacher.
In Scotch, Teacher's is the great experience.

For present purposes we must jettison the second line (licking our lips, to be sure, as it disappears), leaving the first to register a principle whose banality suggests that it enshrines a most useful truth. I bring up the matter because, writing on the forty-second anniversary of the atom-bombing of Hiroshima and

Originally published as an article in the New Republic *(1981), a Washington-based journal of politics and cultural criticism. It was later included in Paul Fussell's* Thank God for the Atom Bomb, and Other Essays *(1988).*

Nagasaki, I want to consider something suggested by the long debate about the ethics, if any, of that ghastly affair. Namely, the importance of experience, sheer, vulgar experience, in influencing, if not determining, one's views about that use of the atom bomb.

The experience I'm talking about is having to come to grips, face to face, with an enemy who designs your death. The experience is common to those in the marines and the infantry and even the line navy, to those, in short, who fought the Second World War mindful always that their mission was, as they were repeatedly assured, "to close with the enemy and destroy him." *Destroy*, notice: not hurt, frighten, drive away, or capture. I think there's something to be learned about that war, as well as about the tendency of historical memory unwittingly to resolve ambiguity and generally clean up the premises, by considering the way testimonies emanating from real war experience tend to complicate attitudes about the most cruel ending of that most cruel war.

"What did you do in the Great War, Daddy?" The recruiting poster deserves ridicule and contempt, of course, but here its question is embarrassingly relevant, and the problem is one that touches on the dirty little secret of social class in America. Arthur T. Hadley said recently that those for whom the use of the A-bomb was "wrong" seem to be implying "that it would have been better to allow thousands on thousands of American and Japanese infantrymen to die in honest hand-to-hand combat on the beaches than to drop those two bombs." People holding such views, he notes, "do not come from the ranks of society that produce infantrymen or pilots." And there's an eloquence problem: most of those with firsthand experience of the war at its worst were not elaborately educated people. Relatively inarticulate, most have remained silent about what they know. That is, few of those destined to be blown to pieces if the main Japanese islands had been invaded went on to become our most effective men of letters or impressive ethical theorists or professors of contemporary history or of international law. The testimony of experience has tended to come from rough diamonds—James Jones[1] is an example—who went through the war as enlisted men in the infantry or the Marine Corps.

Anticipating objections from those without such experience, in his book *WWII* Jones carefully prepares for his chapter on the A-bombs by detailing the plans already in motion for the infantry assaults on the home islands of Kyushu (thirteen divisions scheduled to land in November 1945) and ultimately Honshu (sixteen divisions scheduled for March 1946). Planners of the invasion assumed that it would require a full year, to November 1946, for the Japanese to be sufficiently worn down by land-combat attrition to surrender. By that time, one million American casualties was the expected price. Jones observes that the forthcoming invasion of Kyushu "was well into its collecting and stockpiling stages before the war ended." (The island of Saipan was designated a main ammunition and supply base for the invasion, and if you go there today you can see some of the assembled stuff still sitting there.) "The assault troops were

1. American novelist (1921–1977), author of *From Here to Eternity* (1951), the first volume in a trilogy about World War II.

chosen and already in training," Jones reminds his readers, and he illuminates by the light of experience what this meant:

> What it must have been like to some old-timer buck sergeant or staff sergeant who had been through Guadalcanal or Bougainville or the Philippines, to stand on some beach and watch this huge war machine beginning to stir and move all around him and know that he very likely had survived this far only to fall dead on the dirt of Japan's home islands, hardly bears thinking about.

5   Another bright enlisted man, this one an experienced marine destined for the assault on Honshu, adds his testimony. Former Pfc. E. B. Sledge, author of the splendid memoir *With the Old Breed at Peleliu and Okinawa*, noticed at the time that the fighting grew "more vicious the closer we got to Japan," with the carnage of Iwo Jima and Okinawa worse than what had gone before. He points out that

> what we had *experienced* [my emphasis] in fighting the Japs (pardon the expression) on Peleliu and Okinawa caused us to formulate some very definite opinions that the invasion . . . would be a ghastly bloodletting. . . . It would shock the American public and the world. [Every Japanese] soldier, civilian, woman, and child would fight to the death with whatever weapons they had, rifle, grenade, or bamboo spear.

The Japanese pre-invasion patriotic song, "One Hundred Million Souls for the Emperor," says Sledge, "meant just that." Universal national kamikaze was the point. One kamikaze pilot, discouraged by his unit's failure to impede the Americans very much despite the bizarre casualties it caused, wrote before diving his plane onto an American ship, "I see the war situation becoming more desperate. All Japanese must become soldiers and die for the Emperor." Sledge's First Marine Division was to land close to the Yokosuka Naval Base, "one of the most heavily defended sectors of the island." The marines were told, he recalls, that

> due to the strong beach defenses, caves, tunnels, and numerous Jap suicide torpedo boats and manned mines, few Marines in the first five assault waves would get ashore alive—my company was scheduled to be in the first and second waves. The veterans in the outfit felt we had already run out of luck anyway. . . . We viewed the invasion with complete resignation that we would be killed—either on the beach or inland.

And the invasion was going to take place: there's no question about that. It was not theoretical or merely rumored in order to scare the Japanese. By July 10, 1945, the prelanding naval and aerial bombardment of the coast had begun, and the battleships *Iowa*, *Missouri*, *Wisconsin*, and *King George V* were steaming up and down the coast, softening it up with their sixteen-inch shells.

On the other hand, John Kenneth Galbraith[2] is persuaded that the Japanese would have surrendered surely by November without an invasion. He

---

2. American economist and professor of economics at Harvard University (1908–2006). During World War II he was in charge of wartime price control, and after the war he went to Japan with other economists to study the economic and social conditions.

thinks the A-bombs were unnecessary and unjustified because the war was end-ing anyway. The A-bombs meant, he says, "a difference, at most, of two or three weeks." But at the time, with no indication that surrender was on the way, the kamikazes were sinking American vessels, the *Indianapolis* was sunk (880 men killed), and Allied casualties were running to over 7,000 per week. "Two or three weeks," says Galbraith. Two weeks more means 14,000 more killed and wounded, three weeks more, 21,000. Those weeks mean the world if you're one of those thousands or related to one of them. During the time between the dropping of the Nagasaki bomb on August 9 and the actual sur-render on the fifteenth, the war pursued its accustomed course: on the twelfth of August eight captured American fliers were executed (heads chopped off); the fifty-first United States submarine, *Bonefish*, was sunk (all aboard drowned); the destroyer *Callaghan* went down, the seventieth to be sunk, and the Destroyer Escort *Underhill* was lost. That's a bit of what happened in six days of the two or three weeks posited by Galbraith. What did he do in the war? He worked in the Office of Price Administration in Washington. I don't demand that he expe-rience having his ass shot off. I merely note that he didn't.

Likewise, the historian Michael Sherry, author of a recent book on the rise of the American bombing mystique, *The Creation of Armageddon*, argues that we didn't delay long enough between the test explosion in New Mexico and the mortal explosions in Japan. More delay would have made possible deeper moral considerations and perhaps laudable second thoughts and restraint. "The risks of delaying the bomb's use," he says, "would have been small—not the thou-sands of casualties expected of invasion but only a few days or weeks of rela-tively routine operations." While the mass murders represented by these "relatively routine operations" were enacting, Michael Sherry was safe at home. Indeed, when the bombs were dropped he was going on eight months old, in danger only of falling out of his pram. In speaking thus of Galbraith and Sherry, I'm aware of the offensive implications *ad hominem*.[3] But what's at stake in an infantry assault is so entirely unthinkable to those without the experience of one, or several, or many, even if they possess very wide-ranging imaginations and warm sympathies, that experience is crucial in this case.

In general, the principle is, the farther from the scene of horror, the easier   10 the talk. One young combat naval officer close to the action wrote home in the fall of 1943, just before the marines underwent the agony of Tarawa: "When I read that we will fight the Japs for years if necessary and will sacrifice hun-dreds of thousands if we must, I always like to check from where he's talking: it's seldom out here." That was Lieutenant (j.g.) John F. Kennedy. And Win-ston Churchill, with an irony perhaps too broad and easy, noted in Parliament that the people who preferred invasion to A-bombing seemed to have "no inten-tion of proceeding to the Japanese front themselves."

A remoteness from experience like Galbraith's and Sherry's, and a similar rationalistic abstraction from actuality, seem to motivate the reaction of an anonymous reviewer of William Manchester's *Goodbye Darkness: A Memoir*

3. Latin for "to the man." Marked by an attack on an opponent's character.

of the Pacific War for *The New York Review of Books*. The reviewer naturally dislikes Manchester's still terming the enemy Nips or Japs, but what really shakes him (her?) is this passage of Manchester's:

> After Biak the enemy withdrew to deep caverns. Rooting them out became a bloody business which reached its ultimate horrors in the last months of the war. You think of the lives which would have been lost in an invasion of Japan's home islands—a staggering number of Americans but millions more of Japanese—and you thank God for the atomic bomb.

Thank God for the atom bomb. From this, "one recoils," says the reviewer. One does, doesn't one?

And not just a staggering number of Americans would have been killed in the invasion. Thousands of British assault troops would have been destroyed too, the anticipated casualties from the almost 200,000 men in the six divisions (the same number used to invade Normandy) assigned to invade the Malay Peninsula on September 9. Aimed at the reconquest of Singapore, this operation was expected to last until about March 1946—that is, seven more months of infantry fighting. "But for the atomic bombs," a British observer intimate with the Japanese defenses notes, "I don't think we would have stood a cat in hell's chance. We would have been murdered in the biggest massacre of the war. They would have annihilated the lot of us."

The Dutchman Laurens van der Post had been a prisoner of the Japanese for three and a half years. He and thousands of his fellows, enfeebled by beriberi and pellagra, were being systematically starved to death, the Japanese rationalizing this treatment not just because the prisoners were white men but because they had allowed themselves to be captured at all and were therefore moral garbage. In the summer of 1945 Field Marshal Terauchi issued a significant order: at the moment the Allies invaded the main islands, all prisoners were to be killed by the prison-camp commanders. But thank God that did not happen. When the A-bombs were dropped, van der Post recalls, "This cataclysm I was certain would make the Japanese feel that they could withdraw from the war without dishonor, because it would strike them, as it had us in the silence of our prison night, as something supernatural."

In an exchange of views not long ago in *The New York Review of Books*, Joseph Alsop and David Joravsky set forth the by now familiar argument on both sides of the debate about the "ethics" of the bomb. It's not hard to guess which side each chose once you know that Alsop experienced capture by the Japanese at Hong Kong early in 1942, while Joravsky came into no deadly contact with the Japanese: a young, combat-innocent soldier, he was on his way to the Pacific when the war ended. The editors of *The New York Review* gave the debate the tendentious title "Was the Hiroshima Bomb Necessary?" surely an unanswerable question (unlike "Was It Effective?") and one precisely indicating the intellectual difficulties involved in imposing *ex post facto*[4] a rational and even a genteel ethics on this event. In arguing the acceptability of the bomb, Alsop

---

4. Latin for "after the fact."

focuses on the power and fanaticism of War Minister Anami, who insisted that Japan fight to the bitter end, defending the main islands with the same techniques and tenacity employed at Iwo and Okinawa. Alsop concludes: "Japanese surrender could never have been obtained, at any rate without the honor-satisfying bloodbath envisioned by . . . Anami, if the hideous destruction of Hiroshima and Nagasaki had not finally galvanized the peace advocates into tearing up the entire Japanese book of rules." The Japanese plan to deploy the undefeated bulk of their ground forces, over two million men, plus 10,000 kamikaze planes, plus the elderly and all the women and children with sharpened spears they could muster in a suicidal defense makes it absurd, says Alsop, to "hold the common view, by now hardly challenged by anyone, that the decision to drop the two bombs on Japan was wicked in itself, and that President Truman and all others who joined in making or who [like Robert Oppenheimer][5] assented to this decision shared in the wickedness." And in explanation of "the two bombs," Alsop adds: "The true, climactic, and successful effort of the Japanese peace advocates . . . did not begin in deadly earnest until *after* the second bomb had destroyed Nagasaki. The Nagasaki bomb was thus the trigger to all the developments that led to peace." At this time the army was so unready for surrender that most looked forward to the forthcoming invasion as an indispensable opportunity to show their mettle, enthusiastically agreeing with the army spokesman who reasoned early in 1945, "Since the retreat from Guadalcanal, the Army has had little opportunity to engage the enemy in land battles. But when we meet in Japan proper, our Army will demonstrate its invincible superiority." This possibility foreclosed by the Emperor's post-A-bomb surrender broadcast, the shocked, disappointed officers of one infantry battalion, anticipating a professionally impressive defense of the beaches, killed themselves in the following numbers: one major, three captains, ten first lieutenants, and twelve second lieutenants.

David Joravsky, now a professor of history at Northwestern, argued on the other hand that those who decided to use the A-bombs on cities betray defects of "reason and self-restraint." It all needn't have happened, he says, "if the U.S. government had been willing to take a few more days and to be a bit more thoughtful in opening up the age of nuclear warfare." I've already noted what "a few more days" would mean to the luckless troops and sailors on the spot, and as to being thoughtful when "opening up the age of nuclear warfare," of course no one was focusing on anything as portentous as that, which reflects a historian's tidy hindsight. The U.S. government was engaged not in that sort of momentous thing but in ending the war conclusively, as well as irrationally Remembering Pearl Harbor with a vengeance. It didn't know then what everyone knows now about leukemia and various kinds of carcinoma and birth

15

5. Oppenheimer (1904–1967), American physicist and organizer of the research station at Los Alamos, New Mexico, that developed the atomic bomb, and after World War II, chair of the U.S. Atomic Energy Commission. As chair of the AEC, he opposed developing even more powerful hydrogen bombs but conceded when President Truman approved the legislation to do so.

defects. Truman was not being sly or coy when he insisted that the bomb was "only another weapon." History, as Eliot's "Gerontion" notes,

> . . . has many cunning passages, contrived corridors
> And issues, deceives with whispering ambitions,
> Guides us by vanities. . . .
>   Think
> Neither fear nor courage saves us.
>   Unnatural vices
> Are fathered by our heroism. Virtues
> Are forced upon us by our impudent crimes.

Understanding the past requires pretending that you don't know the present. It requires feeling its own pressure on your pulses without any *ex post facto* illumination. That's a harder thing to do than Joravsky seems to think.

The Alsop-Joravsky debate, reduced to a collision between experience and theory, was conducted with a certain civilized respect for evidence. Not so the way the scurrilous, agitprop *New Statesman* conceives those justifying the dropping of the bomb and those opposing. They are, on the one hand, says Bruce Page, "the imperialist class-forces acting through Harry Truman" and, on the other, those representing "the humane, democratic virtues"—in short, "fascists" as opposed to "populists." But ironically the bomb saved the lives not of any imperialists but only of the low and humble, the quintessentially democratic huddled masses—the conscripted enlisted men manning the fated invasion divisions and the sailors crouching at their gun-mounts in terror of the Kamikazes. When the war ended, Bruce Page was nine years old. For someone of his experience, phrases like "imperialist class forces" come easily, and the issues look perfectly clear.

He's not the only one to have forgotten, if he ever knew, the unspeakable savagery of the Pacific war. The dramatic postwar Japanese success at hustling and merchandising and tourism has (happily, in many ways) effaced for most people the vicious assault context in which the Hiroshima horror should be viewed. It is easy to forget, or not to know, what Japan was like before it was first destroyed, and then humiliated, tamed, and constitutionalized by the West. "Implacable, treacherous, barbaric"—those were Admiral Halsey's characterizations of the enemy, and at the time few facing the Japanese would deny that they fit to a T. One remembers the captured American airmen—the lucky ones who escaped decapitation—locked for years in packing crates. One remembers the gleeful use of bayonets on civilians, on nurses and the wounded, in Hong Kong and Singapore. Anyone who actually fought in the Pacific recalls the Japanese routinely firing on medics, killing the wounded (torturing them first, if possible), and cutting off the penises of the dead to stick in the corpses' mouths. The degree to which Americans register shock and extraordinary shame about the Hiroshima bomb correlates closely with lack of information about the Pacific war.

And of course the brutality was not just on one side. There was much sadism and cruelty, undeniably racist, on ours. (It's worth noting in passing how few hopes blacks could entertain of desegregation and decent treatment when the U.S. Army itself slandered the enemy as "the little brown Jap.") Marines and soldiers could augment their view of their own invincibility by possessing a well-washed Japanese skull, and very soon after Guadalcanal it was common to treat surrendering Japanese as handy rifle targets. Plenty of Japanese gold teeth were extracted—some from still living mouths—with Marine Corps Ka-Bar Knives,[6] and one of E. B. Sledge's fellow marines went around with a cut-off Japanese hand. When its smell grew too offensive and Sledge urged him to get rid of it, he defended his possession of this trophy thus: "How many Marines you reckon that hand pulled the trigger on?" (It's hardly necessary to observe that a soldier in the ETO[7] would probably not have dealt that way with a German or Italian—that is, a "white person's"—hand.) In the Pacific the situation grew so public and scandalous that in September 1942, the Commander in Chief of the Pacific Fleet issued this order: "No part of the enemy's body may be used as a souvenir. Unit Commanders will take stern disciplinary action. . . ."

Among Americans it was widely held that the Japanese were really subhuman, little yellow beasts, and popular imagery depicted them as lice, rats, bats, vipers, dogs, and monkeys. What was required, said the Marine Corps journal *The Leatherneck* in May 1945, was "a gigantic task of extermination." The Japanese constituted a "pestilence," and the only appropriate treatment was "annihilation." Some of the marines landing on Iwo Jima had "Rodent Exterminator" written on their helmet covers, and on one American flagship the naval commander had erected a large sign enjoining all to "KILL JAPS! KILL JAPS! KILL MORE JAPS!" Herman Wouk remembers the Pacific war scene correctly while analyzing Ensign Keith in *The Caine Mutiny*: "Like most of the naval executioners of Kwajalein, he seemed to regard the enemy as a species of animal pest." And the feeling was entirely reciprocal: "From the grim and desperate taciturnity with which the Japanese died, they seemed on their side to believe that they were contending with an invasion of large armed ants." Hiroshima seems to follow in natural sequence: "This obliviousness of both sides to the fact that the opponents were human beings may perhaps be cited as the key to the many massacres of the Pacific war." Since the Jap vermin resist so madly and have killed so many of us, let's pour gasoline into their bunkers and light it and then shoot those afire who try to get out. Why not? Why not blow them all up, with satchel charges or with something stronger? Why not, indeed, drop a new kind of bomb on them, and on the un-uniformed ones too, since the Japanese government has announced that women from ages of seventeen to forty are being called up to repel the invasion? The intelligence officer of the U.S. Fifth Air

---

6. High-carbon steel knives carried by Marines (officers and gunners) who did not carry bayonet-bearing rifles.

7. Abbreviation for the European Theater of Operations, a division of the U.S. Army that handled operations north of the Mediterranean coast during World War II.

Force declared on July 21, 1945, that "the entire population of Japan is a proper military target," and he added emphatically, *There are no civilians in Japan.* Why delay and allow one more American high school kid to see his own intestines blown out of his body and spread before him in the dirt while he screams and screams when with the new bomb we can end the whole thing just like that?

20   On Okinawa, only weeks before Hiroshima, 123,000 Japanese and Americans *killed* each other. (About 140,000 Japanese died at Hiroshima.) "Just awful" was the comment on the Okinawa slaughter not of some pacifist but of General MacArthur. On July 14, 1945, General Marshall sadly informed the Combined Chiefs of Staff—he was not trying to scare the Japanese—that it's "now clear . . . that in order to finish with the Japanese quickly, it will be necessary to invade the industrial heart of Japan." The invasion was definitely on, as I know because I was to be in it.

When the atom bomb ended the war, I was in the Forty-fifth Infantry Division, which had been through the European war so thoroughly that it had needed to be reconstituted two or three times. We were in a staging area near Rheims, ready to be shipped back across the United States for refresher training at Fort Lewis, Washington, and then sent on for final preparation in the Philippines. My division, like most of the ones transferred from Europe, was to take part in the invasion of Honshu. (The earlier landing on Kyushu was to be carried out by the 700,000 infantry already in the Pacific, those with whom James Jones has sympathized.) I was a twenty-one-year-old second lieutenant of infantry leading a rifle platoon. Although still officially fit for combat, in the German war I had already been wounded in the back and the leg badly enough to be adjudged, after the war, 40 percent disabled. But even if my leg buckled and I fell to the ground whenever I jumped out of the back of a truck, and even if the very idea of more combat made me breathe in gasps and shake all over, my condition was held to be adequate for the next act. When the atom bombs were dropped and news began to circulate that "Operation Olympic" would not, after all, be necessary, when we learned to our astonishment that we would not be obliged in a few months to rush up the beaches near Tokyo assault-firing while being machine-gunned, mortared, and shelled, for all the practiced phlegm of our tough façades we broke down and cried with relief and joy. We were going to live. We were going to grow to adulthood after all. The killing was all going to be over, and peace was actually going to be the state of things. When the *Enola Gay* dropped its package, "There were cheers," says John Toland, "over the intercom; it meant the end of the war." Down on the ground the reaction of Sledge's marine buddies when they heard the news was more solemn and complicated. They heard about the end of the war

> with quiet disbelief coupled with an indescribable sense of relief. We thought the Japanese would never surrender. Many refused to believe it. . . . Sitting in stunned silence, we remembered our dead. So many dead. So many maimed. So many bright futures consigned to the ashes of the past. So many dreams lost in the madness that had engulfed us. Except for a few widely scattered shouts of joy, the survivors of the abyss sat hollow-eyed and silent, trying to comprehend a world without war.

These troops who cried and cheered with relief or who sat stunned by the weight of their experience are very different from the high-minded, guilt-ridden GIs we're told about by J. Glenn Gray in his sensitive book *The Warriors*. During the war in Europe Gray was an interrogator in the Army Counterintelligence Corps, and in that capacity he experienced the war at Division level. There's no denying that Gray's outlook on everything was admirably noble, elevated, and responsible. After the war he became a much-admired professor of philosophy at Colorado College and an esteemed editor of Heidegger.[8] But *The Warriors*, his meditation on the moral and psychological dimensions of modern soldiering, gives every sign of error occasioned by remoteness from experience. Division headquarters is miles—*miles*—behind the line where soldiers experience terror and madness and relieve those pressures by crazy brutality and sadism. Indeed, unless they actually encountered the enemy during the war, most "soldiers" have very little idea what "combat" was like. As William Manchester says, "All who wore uniforms are called veterans, but more than 90 percent of them are as uninformed about the killing zones as those on the home front." Manchester's fellow marine E. B. Sledge thoughtfully and responsibly invokes the terms *drastically* and *totally* to underline the differences in experience between front and rear, and not even the far rear, but the close rear. "Our code of conduct toward the enemy," he notes, "differed drastically from that prevailing back at the division CP." (He's describing gold-tooth extraction from still-living Japanese.) Again he writes: "We existed in an environment totally incomprehensible to men behind the lines . . . ," even, he would insist, to men as intelligent and sensitive as Glenn Gray, who missed seeing with his own eyes Sledge's marine friends sliding under fire down a shell-pocked ridge slimy with mud and liquid dysentery shit into the maggoty Japanese and USMC corpses at the bottom, vomiting as the maggots burrowed into their own foul clothing. "We didn't talk about such things," says Sledge. "They were too horrible and obscene even for hardened veterans. . . . Nor do authors normally write about such vileness; unless they have seen it with their own eyes, it is too preposterous to think that men could actually live and fight for days and nights on end under such terrible conditions and not be driven insane." And Sledge has added a comment on such experience and the insulation provided by even a short distance: "Often people just behind our rifle companies couldn't understand what we knew." Glenn Gray was not in a rifle company, or even just behind one. "When the news of the atomic bombing of Hiroshima and Nagasaki came," he asks us to believe, "many an American soldier felt shocked and ashamed." Shocked, OK, but why ashamed? Because we'd destroyed civilians? We'd been doing that for years, in raids on Hamburg and Berlin and Cologne and Frankfurt and Mannheim and Dresden, and Tokyo, and besides, the two A-bombs wiped out 10,000 Japanese troops, not often thought of now, John Hersey's[9] kindly physicians and Jesuit priests

---

8. Martin Heidegger (1889–1976), German existentialist philosopher.

9. American fiction and nonfiction writer (1914–1993), author of *Hiroshima* (1946), a moving account of the devastation and human suffering caused by the atomic bomb.

being more touching. If around division headquarters some of the people Gray talked to felt ashamed, down in the rifle companies no one did, despite Gray's assertions. "The combat soldier," he says,

> knew better than did Americans at home what those bombs meant in suffering and injustice. The man of conscience realized intuitively that the vast majority of Japanese in both cities were no more, if no less, guilty of the war than were his own parents, sisters, or brothers.

I find this canting nonsense. The purpose of the bombs was not to "punish" people but to stop the war. To intensify the shame Gray insists we feel, he seems willing to fiddle the facts. The Hiroshima bomb, he says, was dropped "without any warning." But actually, two days before, 720,000 leaflets were dropped on the city urging everyone to get out and indicating that the place was going to be (as the Potsdam Declaration[10] had promised) obliterated. Of course few left.

Experience whispers that the pity is not that we used the bomb to end the Japanese war but that it wasn't ready in time to end the German one. If only it could have been rushed into production faster and dropped at the right moment on the Reich Chancellery or Berchtesgaden or Hitler's military headquarters in East Prussia (where Colonel Stauffenberg's July 20 bomb didn't do the job because it wasn't big enough), much of the Nazi hierarchy could have been pulverized immediately, saving not just the embarrassment of the Nuremberg trials but the lives of around four million Jews, Poles, Slavs, and gypsies, not to mention the lives and limbs of millions of Allied and German soldiers. If the bomb had only been ready in time, the young men of my infantry platoon would not have been so cruelly killed and wounded.

25   All this is not to deny that like the Russian Revolution, the atom-bombing of Japan was a vast historical tragedy, and every passing year magnifies the dilemma into which it has lodged the contemporary world. As with the Russian Revolution, there are two sides—that's why it's a tragedy instead of a disaster—and unless we are, like Bruce Page, simple-mindedly unimaginative and cruel, we will be painfully aware of both sides at once. To observe that from the viewpoint of the war's victims-to-be the bomb seemed precisely the right thing to drop is to purchase no immunity from horror. To experience both sides, one might study the book *Unforgettable Fire: Pictures Drawn by Atomic Bomb Survivors,* which presents a number of amateur drawings and watercolors of the Hiroshima scene made by middle-aged and elderly survivors for a peace exhibition in 1975. In addition to the almost

10. Agreement signed on July 26, 1945, by the president of the United States and the prime minister of Great Britain, with the concurrence of Nationalist China, that mandated Japanese surrender, offering them a choice between unconditional surrender and total destruction, and that set forth the principles under which the defeated Axis territories would be governed and rebuilt.

unbearable pictures, the book offers brief moments of memoir not for the weak-stomached:

> While taking my severely wounded wife out to the river bank . . . , I was horrified indeed at the sight of a stark naked man standing in the rain with his eyeball in his palm. He looked to be in great pain but there was nothing that I could do for him. I wonder what became of him. Even today, I vividly remember the sight. I was simply miserable.

These childlike drawings and paintings are of skin hanging down, breasts torn off, people bleeding and burning, dying mothers nursing dead babies. A bloody woman holds a bloody child in the ruins of a house, and the artist remembers her calling, "Please help this child! Someone, please help this child. Please help! Someone, please." As Samuel Johnson said of the smothering of Desdemona, the innocent in another tragedy, "It is not to be endured." Nor, it should be noticed, is an infantryman's account of having his arm blown off in the Arno Valley in Italy in 1944:

> I wanted to die and die fast. I wanted to forget this miserable world. I cursed the war, I cursed the people who were responsible for it, I cursed God for putting me here. . . . to suffer for something I never did or knew anything about.

(A good place to interrupt and remember Glenn Gray's noble but hopelessly one-sided remarks about "injustice," as well as "suffering.")

"For this was hell," the soldier goes on,

> and I never imagined anything or anyone could suffer so bitterly. I screamed and cursed. Why? What had I done to deserve this? But no answer came. I yelled for medics, because subconsciously I wanted to live. I tried to apply my right hand over my bleeding stump, but I didn't have the strength to hold it. I looked to the left of me and saw the bloody mess that was once my left arm; its fingers and palm were turned upward, like a flower looking to the sun for its strength.

The future scholar-critic who writes *The History of Canting in the Twentieth Century* will find much to study and interpret in the utterances of those who dilate on the special wickedness of the A-bomb-droppers. He will realize that such utterance can perform for the speaker a valuable double function. First, it can display the fineness of his moral weave. And second, by implication it can also inform the audience that during the war he was not socially so unfortunate as to find himself down there with the ground forces, where he might have had to compromise the purity and clarity of his moral system by the experience of weighing his own life against someone else's. Down there, which is where the other people were, is the place where coarse self-interest is the rule. When the young soldier with the wild eyes comes at you, firing, do you shoot him in the foot, hoping he'll be hurt badly enough to drop or mis-aim the gun with which he's going to kill you, or do you shoot him in the chest (or, if you're a prime shot, in the head) and make certain that you and not he will be the survivor of that mortal moment?

30   It would be not just stupid but would betray a lamentable want of human experience to expect soldiers to be very sensitive humanitarians. The Glenn Grays of this world need to have their attention directed to the testimony of those who know, like, say, Admiral of the Fleet Lord Fisher, who said, "Moderation in war is imbecility," or Sir Arthur Harris, director of the admittedly wicked aerial-bombing campaign designed, as Churchill put it, to "dehouse" the German civilian population, who observed that "War is immoral," or our own General W. T. Sherman: "War is cruelty, and you cannot refine it." Lord Louis Mountbatten, trying to say something sensible about the dropping of the A-bomb, came up only with "War is crazy." Or rather, it requires choices among crazinesses. "It would seem even more crazy," he went on, "if we were to have more casualties on our side to save the Japanese." One of the unpleasant facts for anyone in the ground armies during the war was that you had to become pro tem[11] a subordinate of the very uncivilian George S. Patton[12] and respond somehow to his unremitting insistence that you embrace his view of things. But in one of his effusions he was right, and his observation tends to suggest the experimental dubiousness of the concept of "just wars." "War is not a contest with gloves," he perceived. "It is resorted to only when laws, which are rules, have failed." Soldiers being like that, only the barest decencies should be expected of them. They did not start the war, except in the terrible sense hinted at in Frederic Manning's observation based on his front-line experience in the Great War: "War is waged by men; not by beasts, or by gods. It is a peculiarly human activity. To call it a crime against mankind is to miss at least half its significance; it is also the punishment of a crime." Knowing that unflattering truth by experience, soldiers have every motive for wanting a war stopped, by any means.

The stupidity, parochialism, and greed in the international mismanagement of the whole nuclear challenge should not tempt us to misimagine the circumstances of the bomb's first "use." Nor should our well-justified fears and suspicions occasioned by the capture of the nuclear-power trade by the inept and the mendacious (who have fucked up the works at Three Mile Island, Chernobyl, etc.)[13] tempt us to infer retrospectively extraordinary corruption, imbecility, or motiveless malignity in those who decided, all things considered, to drop the bomb. Times change. Harry Truman . . . knew war, and he knew better than some of his critics then and now what he was doing and why he was doing it. "Having found the bomb," he said, "we have used it. . . . We have used it to shorten the agony of young Americans."

11. Short for *pro tempore*; Latin for "the time being."

12. American general (1885–1945) who served in North Africa and Sicily in World War II before becoming commander of the Third Army, which drove the Nazis from France and back into Germany.

13. Two disasters at nuclear power plants: the first, near Harrisburg, Pennsylvania, occurred in the spring of 1979; the second, in the Soviet Union, occurred in the spring of 1986.

The past, which as always did not know the future, acted in ways that ask to be imagined before they are condemned. Or even simplified.

MLA CITATION

Fussell, Paul. "Thank God for the Atom Bomb." 1981. *The Norton Reader: An Anthology of Nonfiction*. Ed. Melissa A. Goldthwaite et al. 14th ed. New York: Norton, 2016. 722–35. Print.

QUESTIONS

1. Note the places where Paul Fussell includes personal experience in this essay. How much is his own, how much belongs to others? Why does he include both kinds?

2. Fussell dismisses with contempt those who disagree with him. Locate some examples. How do you respond to them? Would you use Fussell's strategies to dismiss those who disagree with you? Explain.

3. Mark some instances of Fussell's "voice." What kind of voice does he adopt? What kind of person does he present himself as?

4. Write an argumentative essay about a topic that personally affects you. Deliberately take a very strong position, using Fussell and Tom Regan (pp. 670–80) as your models.

DAVID EAGLEMAN   *The Brain on Trial*

Advances in brain science are calling into question the volition behind many criminal acts. A leading neuroscientist describes how the foundations of our criminal-justice system are beginning to crumble, and proposes a new way forward for law and order.

O N THE STEAMY FIRST DAY of August 1966, Charles Whitman took an elevator to the top floor of the University of Texas Tower in Austin. The 25-year-old climbed the stairs to the observation deck, lugging with him a footlocker full of guns and ammunition. At the top, he killed a receptionist with the butt of his rifle. Two families of tourists came up the stairwell; he shot at them at point-blank range. Then he began to fire indiscriminately from the deck at people below. The first woman he shot was pregnant. As her boyfriend knelt to help her, Whitman shot him as well. He shot pedestrians in the street and an ambulance driver who came to rescue them.

Published in the Atlantic *(2011), a magazine covering literature, culture, and politics. David Eagleman is a writer of fiction as well as nonfiction and a professor at Baylor University School of Medicine in Texas.*

The evening before, Whitman had sat at his typewriter and composed a suicide note:

> I don't really understand myself these days. I am supposed to be an average reasonable and intelligent young man. However, lately (I can't recall when it started) I have been a victim of many unusual and irrational thoughts.

By the time the police shot him dead, Whitman had killed 13 people and wounded 32 more. The story of his rampage dominated national headlines the next day. And when police went to investigate his home for clues, the story became even stranger: in the early hours of the morning on the day of the shooting, he had murdered his mother and stabbed his wife to death in her sleep.

> It was after much thought that I decided to kill my wife, Kathy, tonight. . . . I love her dearly, and she has been as fine a wife to me as any man could ever hope to have. I cannot rationa[l]ly pinpoint any specific reason for doing this. . . .

Along with the shock of the murders lay another, more hidden, surprise: the juxtaposition of his aberrant actions with his unremarkable personal life. Whitman was an Eagle Scout and a former marine, studied architectural engineering at the University of Texas, and briefly worked as a bank teller and volunteered as a scoutmaster for Austin's Boy Scout Troop 5. As a child, he'd scored 138 on the Stanford-Binet IQ test, placing in the 99th percentile. So after his shooting spree from the University of Texas Tower, everyone wanted answers.

For that matter, so did Whitman. He requested in his suicide note that an autopsy be performed to determine if something had changed in his brain—because he suspected it had.

> I talked with a Doctor once for about two hours and tried to convey to him my fears that I felt [overcome by] overwhelming violent impulses. After one session I never saw the Doctor again, and since then I have been fighting my mental turmoil alone, and seemingly to no avail.

Whitman's body was taken to the morgue, his skull was put under the bone   5
saw, and the medical examiner lifted the brain from its vault. He discovered
that Whitman's brain harbored a tumor the diameter of a nickel. This tumor,
called a glioblastoma, had blossomed from beneath a structure called the thalamus, impinged on the hypothalamus, and compressed a third region called
the amygdala. The amygdala is involved in emotional regulation, especially of
fear and aggression. By the late 1800s, researchers had discovered that damage to the amygdala caused emotional and social disturbances. In the 1930s,
the researchers Heinrich Klüver and Paul Bucy demonstrated that damage to
the amygdala in monkeys led to a constellation of symptoms, including lack of
fear, blunting of emotion, and overreaction. Female monkeys with amygdala
damage often neglected or physically abused their infants. In humans, activity
in the amygdala increases when people are shown threatening faces, are put
into frightening situations, or experience social phobias. Whitman's intuition
about himself—that something in his brain was changing his behavior—was
spot-on.

Stories like Whitman's are not uncommon: legal cases involving brain damage crop up increasingly often. As we develop better technologies for probing
the brain, we detect more problems, and link them more easily to aberrant
behavior. Take the 2000 case of a 40-year-old man we'll call Alex, whose sexual preferences suddenly began to transform. He developed an interest in child
pornography—and not just a little interest, but an overwhelming one. He poured
his time into child-pornography Web sites and magazines. He also solicited
prostitution at a massage parlor, something he said he had never previously
done. He reported later that he'd wanted to stop, but "the pleasure principle
overrode" his restraint. He worked to hide his acts, but subtle sexual advances
toward his prepubescent stepdaughter alarmed his wife, who soon discovered
his collection of child pornography. He was removed from his house, found
guilty of child molestation, and sentenced to rehabilitation in lieu of prison. In
the rehabilitation program, he made inappropriate sexual advances toward the
staff and other clients, and was expelled and routed toward prison.

At the same time, Alex was complaining of worsening headaches. The night
before he was to report for prison sentencing, he couldn't stand the pain anymore, and took himself to the emergency room. He underwent a brain scan,
which revealed a massive tumor in his orbitofrontal cortex. Neurosurgeons
removed the tumor. Alex's sexual appetite returned to normal.

The year after the brain surgery, his pedophilic behavior began to return.
The neuroradiologist discovered that a portion of the tumor had been missed
in the surgery and was regrowing—and Alex went back under the knife. After
the removal of the remaining tumor, his behavior again returned to normal.

When your biology changes, so can your decision-making and your desires.
The drives you take for granted ("I'm a heterosexual/homosexual," "I'm attracted
to children/adults," "I'm aggressive/not aggressive," and so on) depend on the
intricate details of your neural machinery. Although acting on such drives is
popularly thought to be a free choice, the most cursory examination of the evidence demonstrates the limits of that assumption.

10   Alex's sudden pedophilia illustrates that hidden drives and desires can lurk
undetected behind the neural machinery of socialization. When the frontal
lobes are compromised, people become disinhibited, and startling behaviors can
emerge. Disinhibition is commonly seen in patients with frontotemporal dementia, a tragic disease in which the frontal and temporal lobes degenerate. With
the loss of that brain tissue, patients lose the ability to control their hidden
impulses. To the frustration of their loved ones, these patients violate social
norms in endless ways: shoplifting in front of store managers, removing their
clothes in public, running stop signs, breaking out in song at inappropriate
times, eating food scraps found in public trash cans, being physically aggressive or sexually transgressive. Patients with frontotemporal dementia commonly
end up in courtrooms, where their lawyers, doctors, and embarrassed adult children must explain to the judge that the violation was not the perpetrator's *fault*,
exactly: much of the brain has degenerated, and medicine offers no remedy.
Fifty-seven percent of frontotemporal-dementia patients violate social norms, as
compared with only 27 percent of Alzheimer's patients.

Changes in the balance of brain chemistry, even small ones, can also cause
large and unexpected changes in behavior. Victims of Parkinson's disease offer
an example. In 2001, families and caretakers of Parkinson's patients began to
notice something strange. When patients were given a drug called pramipexole, some of them turned into gamblers. And not just casual gamblers, but pathological gamblers. These were people who had never gambled much before,
and now they were flying off to Vegas. One 68-year-old man amassed losses of
more than $200,000 in six months at a series of casinos. Some patients became
consumed with Internet poker, racking up unpayable credit-card bills. For several, the new addiction reached beyond gambling, to compulsive eating, excessive alcohol consumption, and hypersexuality.

What was going on? Parkinson's involves the loss of brain cells that produce
a neurotransmitter known as dopamine. Pramipexole works by impersonating
dopamine. But it turns out that dopamine is a chemical doing double duty in
the brain. Along with its role in motor commands, it also mediates the reward
systems, guiding a person toward food, drink, mates, and other things useful
for survival. Because of dopamine's role in weighing the costs and benefits of
decisions, imbalances in its levels can trigger gambling, overeating, and drug
addiction—behaviors that result from a reward system gone awry. Physicians
now watch for these behavioral changes as a possible side effect of drugs like
pramipexole. Luckily, the negative effects of the drug are reversible—the physician simply lowers the dosage, and the compulsive gambling goes away.

The lesson from all these stories is the same: human behavior cannot be
separated from human biology. If we like to believe that people make free
choices about their behavior (as in, "I don't gamble, because I'm strong-willed"),
cases like Alex the pedophile, the frontotemporal shoplifters, and the gambling
Parkinson's patients may encourage us to examine our views more carefully.
Perhaps not everyone is equally "free" to make socially appropriate choices.

Does the discovery of Charles Whitman's brain tumor modify your feelings
about the senseless murders he committed? Does it affect the sentence you

would find appropriate for him, had he survived that day? Does the tumor change the degree to which you consider the killings "his fault"? Couldn't you just as easily be unlucky enough to develop a tumor and lose control of your behavior?

On the other hand, wouldn't it be dangerous to conclude that people with   15
a tumor are free of guilt, and that they should be let off the hook for their crimes?

As our understanding of the human brain improves, juries are increasingly challenged with these sorts of questions. When a criminal stands in front of the judge's bench today, the legal system wants to know whether he is *blameworthy*. Was it his fault, or his biology's fault?

I submit that this is the wrong question to be asking. The choices we make are inseparably yoked to our neural circuitry, and therefore we have no meaningful way to tease the two apart. The more we learn, the more the seemingly simple concept of blameworthiness becomes complicated, and the more the foundations of our legal system are strained.

If I seem to be heading in an uncomfortable direction—toward letting criminals off the hook—please read on, because I'm going to show the logic of a new argument, piece by piece. The upshot is that we can build a legal system more deeply informed by science, in which we will continue to take criminals off the streets, but we will customize sentencing, leverage new opportunities for rehabilitation, and structure better incentives for good behavior. Discoveries in neuroscience suggest a new way forward for law and order—one that will lead to a more cost-effective, humane, and flexible system than the one we have today. When modern brain science is laid out clearly, it is difficult to justify how our legal system can continue to function without taking what we've learned into account.

Many of us like to believe that all adults possess the same capacity to make sound choices. It's a charitable idea, but demonstrably wrong. People's brains are vastly different.

Who you even have the possibility to be starts at conception. If you think   20
genes don't affect how people behave, consider this fact: if you are a carrier of a particular set of genes, the probability that you will commit a violent crime is four times as high as it would be if you lacked those genes. You're three times as likely to commit robbery, five times as likely to commit aggravated assault, eight times as likely to be arrested for murder, and 13 times as likely to be arrested for a sexual offense. The overwhelming majority of prisoners carry these genes; 98.1 percent of death-row inmates do. These statistics alone indicate that we cannot presume that everyone is coming to the table equally equipped in terms of drives and behaviors.

And this feeds into a larger lesson of biology: *we are not the ones steering the boat of our behavior, at least not nearly as much as we believe. Who we are* runs well below the surface of our conscious access, and the details reach back in time to before our birth, when the meeting of a sperm and an egg granted us certain attributes and not others. *Who we can be* starts with our molecular blueprints—a series of alien codes written in invisibly small strings of acids—well before we have anything to do with it. Each of us is, in part, a product of our inaccessible, microscopic history. By the way, as regards that dangerous set of genes, you've probably heard of them. They are summarized as the Y chromosome. If you're a carrier, we call you a male.

Genes are part of the story, but they're not the whole story. We are likewise influenced by the environments in which we grow up. Substance abuse by a mother during pregnancy, maternal stress, and low birth weight all can influence how a baby will turn out as an adult. As a child grows, neglect, physical abuse, and head injury can impede mental development, as can the physical environment. (For example, the major public-health movement to eliminate lead-based paint grew out of an understanding that ingesting lead can cause brain damage, making children less intelligent and, in some cases, more impulsive and aggressive.) And every experience throughout our lives can modify genetic expression—activating certain genes or switching others off—which in turn can inaugurate new behaviors. In this way, genes and environments intertwine.

When it comes to nature and nurture, the important point is that we choose neither one. We are each constructed from a genetic blueprint, and then born into a world of circumstances that we cannot control in our most-formative years. The complex interactions of genes and environment mean that all citizens—equal before the law—possess different perspectives, dissimilar personalities, and varied capacities for decision-making. The unique patterns of neurobiology inside each of our heads cannot qualify as *choices*; these are the cards we're dealt.

Because we did not choose the factors that affected the formation and structure of our brain, the concepts of free will and personal responsibility begin to sprout question marks. Is it meaningful to say that Alex made bad *choices*, even though his brain tumor was not his fault? Is it justifiable to say that the patients with frontotemporal dementia or Parkinson's should be *punished* for their bad behavior?

25   It is problematic to imagine yourself in the shoes of someone breaking the law and conclude, "Well, *I* wouldn't have done that"—because if you weren't exposed to in utero cocaine, lead poisoning, and physical abuse, and he was, then you and he are not directly comparable. You cannot walk a mile in his shoes.

The legal system rests on the assumption that we are "practical reasoners," a term of art that presumes, at bottom, the existence of free will. The idea is that we use conscious deliberation when deciding how to act—that is, in the absence of external duress, we make free decisions. This concept of the practical reasoner is intuitive but problematic.

The existence of free will in human behavior is the subject of an ancient debate. Arguments in support of free will are typically based on direct subjective experience ("I *feel* like I made the decision to lift my finger just now"). But evaluating free will requires some nuance beyond our immediate intuitions.

Consider a decision to move or speak. It feels as though free will leads you to stick out your tongue, or scrunch up your face, or call someone a name. But free will is not *required* to play any role in these acts. People with Tourette's syndrome, for instance, suffer from involuntary movements and vocalizations. A typical Touretter may stick out his tongue, scrunch up his face, or call someone a name—all without *choosing* to do so.

We immediately learn two things from the Tourette's patient. First, actions can occur in the absence of free will. Second, the Tourette's patient has no *free won't*. He cannot use free will to override or control what subconscious parts of his brain have decided to do. What the lack of free will and the lack of free won't have in common is the lack of "free." Tourette's syndrome provides a case in which the underlying neural machinery does its thing, and we all agree that the person is not responsible.

This same phenomenon arises in people with a condition known as cho- 30 rea, for whom actions of the hands, arms, legs, and face are involuntary, even though they certainly *look* voluntary: ask such a patient why she is moving her fingers up and down, and she will explain that she has no control over her hand. She cannot *not* do it. Similarly, some split-brain patients (who have had the two hemispheres of the brain surgically disconnected) develop alien-hand syndrome: while one hand buttons up a shirt, the other hand works to unbutton it. When one hand reaches for a pencil, the other bats it away. No matter how hard the patient tries, he cannot make his alien hand *not* do what it's doing. The movements are not "his" to freely start or stop.

Unconscious acts are not limited to unintended shouts or wayward hands; they can be surprisingly sophisticated. Consider Kenneth Parks, a 23-year-old Canadian with a wife, a five-month-old daughter, and a close relationship with his in-laws (his mother-in-law described him as a "gentle giant"). Suffering from financial difficulties, marital problems, and a gambling addiction, he made plans to go see his in-laws to talk about his troubles.

In the wee hours of May 23, 1987, Kenneth arose from the couch on which he had fallen asleep, but he did not awaken. Sleepwalking, he climbed into his car and drove the 14 miles to his in-laws' home. He broke in, stabbed his mother-in-law to death, and assaulted his father-in-law, who survived. Afterward, he drove himself to the police station. Once there, he said, "I think I have killed some people. . . . My hands," realizing for the first time that his own hands were severely cut.

Over the next year, Kenneth's testimony was remarkably consistent, even in the face of attempts to lead him astray: he remembered nothing of the incident. Moreover, while all parties agreed that Kenneth had undoubtedly committed the murder, they also agreed that he had no motive. His defense attorneys argued that this was a case of killing while sleepwalking, known as homicidal somnambulism.

Although critics cried "Faker!," sleepwalking is a verifiable phenomenon. On May 25, 1988, after lengthy consideration of electrical recordings from Kenneth's brain, the jury concluded that his actions had indeed been involuntary, and declared him not guilty.

As with Tourette's sufferers, split-brain patients, and those with choreic 35 movements, Kenneth's case illustrates that high-level behaviors can take place in the absence of free will. Like your heartbeat, breathing, blinking, and swallowing, even your mental machinery can run on autopilot. The crux of the question is whether *all* of your actions are fundamentally on autopilot or whether some little bit of you is "free" to choose, independent of the rules of biology.

This has always been the sticking point for philosophers and scientists alike. After all, there is no spot in the brain that is not densely interconnected with—and driven by—other brain parts. And that suggests that no part is independent and therefore "free." In modern science, it is difficult to find the gap into which to slip free will—the uncaused causer—because there seems to be no part of the machinery that does not follow in a causal relationship from the other parts.

Free will *may* exist (it may simply be beyond our current science), but one thing seems clear: if free will *does* exist, it has little room in which to operate. It can at best be a small factor riding on top of vast neural networks shaped by genes and environment. In fact, free will may end up being so small that we eventually think about bad decision-making in the same way we think about any physical process, such as diabetes or lung disease.

The study of brains and behaviors is in the midst of a conceptual shift. Historically, clinicians and lawyers have agreed on an intuitive distinction between neurological disorders ("brain problems") and psychiatric disorders ("mind problems"). As recently as a century ago, a common approach was to get psychiatric patients to "toughen up," through deprivation, pleading, or torture. Not surprisingly, this approach was medically fruitless. After all, while psychiatric disorders tend to be the product of more-subtle forms of brain pathology, they, too, are based in the biological details of the brain.

What accounts for the shift from blame to biology? Perhaps the largest driving force is the effectiveness of pharmaceutical treatments. No amount of threatening will chase away depression, but a little pill called fluoxetine often does the trick. Schizophrenic symptoms cannot be overcome by exorcism, but they can be controlled by risperidone. Mania responds not to talk or to ostracism, but to lithium. These successes, most of them introduced in the past 60 years, have underscored the idea that calling some disorders "brain problems" while consigning others to the ineffable realm of "the psychic" does not make sense. Instead, we have begun to approach mental problems in the same way we might approach a broken leg. The neuroscientist Robert Sapolsky invites us to contemplate this conceptual shift with a series of questions:

> Is a loved one, sunk in a depression so severe that she cannot function, a case of a disease whose biochemical basis is as "real" as is the biochemistry of, say, diabetes, or is she merely indulging herself? Is a child doing poorly at school because he is unmotivated and slow, or because there is a neurobiologically based learning disability? Is a friend, edging towards a serious problem with substance abuse, displaying a simple lack of discipline, or suffering from problems with the neurochemistry of reward?

Acts cannot be understood separately from the biology of the actors—and   40
this recognition has legal implications. Tom Bingham, Britain's former senior
law lord, once put it this way:

> In the past, the law has tended to base its approach . . . on a series of rather
> crude working assumptions: adults of competent mental capacity are free
> to choose whether they will act in one way or another; they are presumed to
> act rationally, and in what they conceive to be their own best interests; they
> are credited with such foresight of the consequences of their actions as rea-
> sonable people in their position could ordinarily be expected to have; they
> are generally taken to mean what they say.
>   Whatever the merits or demerits of working assumptions such as these
> in the ordinary range of cases, it is evident that they do not provide a uni-
> formly accurate guide to human behaviour.

The more we discover about the circuitry of the brain, the more we tip away
from accusations of indulgence, lack of motivation, and poor discipline—and
toward the details of biology. The shift from blame to science reflects our modern understanding that our perceptions and behaviors are steered by deeply
embedded neural programs.

Imagine a spectrum of culpability. On one end, we find people like Alex the
pedophile, or a patient with frontotemporal dementia who exposes himself in
public. In the eyes of the judge and jury, these are people who suffered brain
damage at the hands of fate and did not choose their neural situation. On the
other end of the spectrum—the blameworthy side of the "fault" line—we find
the common criminal, whose brain receives little study, and about whom our
current technology might be able to say little anyway. The overwhelming majority of lawbreakers are on this side of the line, because they don't have any obvious, measurable biological problems. They are simply thought of as freely
choosing actors.

Such a spectrum captures the common intuition that juries hold regarding blameworthiness. But there is a deep problem with this intuition. Technology will continue to improve, and as we grow better at measuring problems in
the brain, the fault line will drift into the territory of people we currently hold
fully accountable for their crimes. Problems that are now opaque will open up
to examination by new techniques, and we may someday find that many types
of bad behavior have a basic biological explanation—as has happened with
schizophrenia, epilepsy, depression, and mania.

Today, neuroimaging is a crude technology, unable to explain the details
of individual behavior. We can detect only large-scale problems, but within the
coming decades, we will be able to detect patterns at unimaginably small levels of the microcircuitry that correlate with behavioral problems. Neuroscience
will be better able to say why people are predisposed to act the way they do. As
we become more skilled at specifying how behavior results from the microscopic
details of the brain, more defense lawyers will point to biological mitigators of
guilt, and more juries will place defendants on the not-blameworthy side of
the line.

45   This puts us in a strange situation. After all, a just legal system cannot define culpability simply by the limitations of current technology. Expert medical testimony generally reflects only whether we yet have names and measurements for a problem, not whether a problem exists. A legal system that declares a person culpable at the beginning of a decade and not culpable at the end is one in which culpability carries no clear meaning.

The crux of the problem is that it no longer makes sense to ask, "To what extent was it his *biology*, and to what extent was it *him*?," because we now understand that there is no meaningful distinction between a person's biology and his decision-making. They are inseparable.

While our current style of punishment rests on a bedrock of personal volition and blame, our modern understanding of the brain suggests a different approach. Blameworthiness should be removed from the legal argot. It is a backward-looking concept that demands the impossible task of untangling the hopelessly complex web of genetics and environment that constructs the trajectory of a human life.

Instead of debating culpability, we should focus on what to do, *moving forward*, with an accused lawbreaker. I suggest that the legal system *has* to become forward-looking, primarily because it can no longer hope to do otherwise. As science complicates the question of culpability, our legal and social policy will need to shift toward a different set of questions: How is a person likely to behave in the future? Are criminal actions likely to be repeated? Can this person be helped toward pro-social behavior? How can incentives be realistically structured to deter crime?

The important change will be in the *way* we respond to the vast range of criminal acts. Biological explanation will not exculpate criminals; we will still remove from the streets lawbreakers who prove overaggressive, underempathetic, and poor at controlling their impulses. Consider, for example, that the majority of known serial killers were abused as children. Does this make them less blameworthy? Who cares? It's the wrong question. The knowledge that they were abused encourages us to support social programs to prevent child abuse, but it does nothing to change the way we deal with the particular serial murderer standing in front of the bench. We still need to keep him off the streets, irrespective of his past misfortunes. The child abuse cannot serve as an excuse to let him go; the judge must keep society safe.

50   Those who break social contracts need to be confined, but in this framework, the future is more important than the past. Deeper biological insight into behavior will foster a better understanding of recidivism—and this offers a basis for empirically based sentencing. Some people will need to be taken off the streets for a longer time (even a lifetime), because their likelihood of reoffense is high; others, because of differences in neural constitution, are less likely to recidivate, and so can be released sooner.

The law is already forward-looking in some respects: consider the leniency afforded a crime of passion versus a premeditated murder. Those who commit the former are less likely to recidivate than those who commit the latter, and their sentences sensibly reflect that. Likewise, American law draws a bright line between criminal acts committed by minors and those by adults, punishing the latter more harshly. This approach may be crude, but the intuition behind it is sound: adolescents command lesser skills in decision-making and impulse control than do adults; a teenager's brain is simply not like an adult's brain. Lighter sentences are appropriate for those whose impulse control is likely to improve naturally as adolescence gives way to adulthood.

Taking a more scientific approach to sentencing, case by case, could move us beyond these limited examples. For instance, important changes are happening in the sentencing of sex offenders. In the past, researchers have asked psychiatrists and parole-board members how likely specific sex offenders were to relapse when let out of prison. Both groups had experience with sex offenders, so predicting who was going straight and who was coming back seemed simple. But surprisingly, the expert guesses showed almost no correlation with the actual outcomes. The psychiatrists and parole-board members had only slightly better predictive accuracy than coin-flippers. This astounded the legal community.

So researchers tried a more actuarial approach. They set about recording dozens of characteristics of some 23,000 released sex offenders: whether the offender had unstable employment, had been sexually abused as a child, was addicted to drugs, showed remorse, had deviant sexual interests, and so on. Researchers then tracked the offenders for an average of five years after release to see who wound up back in prison. At the end of the study, they computed which factors best explained the reoffense rates, and from these and later data they were able to build actuarial tables to be used in sentencing.

Which factors mattered? Take, for instance, low remorse, denial of the crime, and sexual abuse as a child. You might guess that these factors would correlate with sex offenders' recidivism. But you would be wrong: those factors offer no predictive power. How about antisocial personality disorder and failure to complete treatment? These offer somewhat more predictive power. But among the strongest predictors of recidivism are prior sexual offenses and sexual interest in children. When you compare the predictive power of the actuarial approach with that of the parole boards and psychiatrists, there is no contest: numbers beat intuition. In courtrooms across the nation, these actuarial tests are now used in presentencing to modulate the length of prison terms.

We will never know with certainty what someone will do upon release from prison, because real life is complicated. But greater predictive power is hidden in the numbers than people generally expect. Statistically based sentencing is imperfect, but it nonetheless allows evidence to trump folk intuition, and it offers customization in place of the blunt guidelines that the legal system typically employs. The current actuarial approaches do not require a deep understanding of genes or brain chemistry, but as we introduce more science into these measures—for example, with neuroimaging studies—the predictive power will only improve. (To make such a system immune to government abuse, the data and equations that compose the sentencing guidelines must be transparent and available online for anyone to verify.)

55

Beyond customized sentencing, a forward-thinking legal system informed by scientific insights into the brain will enable us to stop treating prison as a one-size-fits-all solution. To be clear, I'm not opposed to incarceration, and its purpose is not limited to the removal of dangerous people from the streets. The prospect of incarceration deters many crimes, and time actually spent in prison can steer some people away from further criminal acts upon their release. But that works only for those whose brains function normally. The problem is that prisons have become our de facto mental-health-care institutions—and inflicting punishment on the mentally ill usually has little influence on their future behavior. An encouraging trend is the establishment of mental-health courts around the nation: through such courts, people with mental illnesses can be helped while confined in a tailored environment. Cities such as Richmond, Virginia, are moving in this direction, for reasons of justice as well as cost-effectiveness. Sheriff C. T. Woody, who estimates that nearly 20 percent of Richmond's prisoners are mentally ill, told CBS News, "The jail isn't a place for them. They should be in a mental-health facility." Similarly, many jurisdictions are opening drug courts and developing alternative sentences; they have realized that prisons are not as useful for solving addictions as are meaningful drug-rehabilitation programs.

A forward-thinking legal system will also parlay biological understanding into customized rehabilitation, viewing criminal behavior the way we understand other medical conditions such as epilepsy, schizophrenia, and depression—conditions that now allow the seeking and giving of help. These and other brain disorders find themselves on the not-blameworthy side of the fault line, where they are now recognized as biological, not demonic, issues.

Many people recognize the long-term cost-effectiveness of rehabilitating offenders instead of packing them into overcrowded prisons. The challenge has been the dearth of new ideas about *how* to rehabilitate them. A better understanding of the brain offers new ideas. For example, poor impulse control is characteristic of many prisoners. These people generally can express the difference between right and wrong actions, and they understand the disadvantages of punishment—but they are handicapped by poor control of their impulses. Whether as a result of anger or temptation, their actions override reasoned consideration of the future.

If it seems difficult to empathize with people who have poor impulse control, just think of all the things you succumb to against your better judgment. Alcohol? Chocolate cake? Television? It's not that we don't know what's best for us, it's simply that the frontal-lobe circuits representing long-term considerations can't always win against short-term desire when temptation is in front of us.

60   With this understanding in mind, we can modify the justice system in several ways. One approach, advocated by Mark A. R. Kleiman, a professor of public policy at UCLA, is to ramp up the certainty and swiftness of punishment—for instance, by requiring drug offenders to undergo twice-weekly drug testing, with automatic, immediate consequences for failure—thereby not relying

on distant abstraction alone. Similarly, economists have suggested that the drop in crime since the early 1990s has been due, in part, to the increased presence of police on the streets: their visibility shores up support for the parts of the brain that weigh long-term consequences.

We may be on the cusp of finding new rehabilitative strategies as well, affording people better control of their behavior, even in the absence of external authority. To help a citizen reintegrate into society, the ethical goal is to change him *as little as possible* while bringing his behavior into line with society's needs. My colleagues and I are proposing a new approach, one that grows from the understanding that the brain operates like a team of rivals, with different neural populations competing to control the single output channel of behavior. Because it's a competition, the outcome can be tipped. I call the approach "the prefrontal workout."

The basic idea is to give the frontal lobes practice in squelching the short-term brain circuits. To this end, my colleagues Stephen LaConte and Pearl Chiu have begun providing real-time feedback to people during brain scanning. Imagine that you'd like to quit smoking cigarettes. In this experiment, you look at pictures of cigarettes during brain imaging, and the experimenters measure which regions of your brain are involved in the craving. Then they show you the activity in those networks, represented by a vertical bar on a computer screen, while you look at more cigarette pictures. The bar acts as a thermometer for your craving: if your craving networks are revving high, the bar is high; if you're suppressing your craving, the bar is low. Your job is to make the bar go down. Perhaps you have insight into what you're doing to resist the craving; perhaps the mechanism is inaccessible. In any case, you try out different mental avenues until the bar begins to slowly sink. When it goes all the way down, that means you've successfully recruited frontal circuitry to squelch the activity in the networks involved in impulsive craving. The goal is for the long term to trump the short term. Still looking at pictures of cigarettes, you practice making the bar go down over and over, until you've strengthened those frontal circuits. By this method, you're able to visualize the activity in the parts of your brain that need modulation, and you can witness the effects of different mental approaches you might take.

If this sounds like biofeedback from the 1970s, it is—but this time with vastly more sophistication, monitoring specific networks inside the head rather than a single electrode on the skin. This research is just beginning, so the method's efficacy is not yet known—but if it works well, it will be a game changer. We will be able to take it to the incarcerated population, especially those approaching release, to try to help them avoid coming back through the revolving prison doors.

This prefrontal workout is designed to better balance the debate between the long- and short-term parties of the brain, giving the option of reflection before action to those who lack it. And really, that's all maturation is. The main difference between teenage and adult brains is the development of the frontal lobes. The human prefrontal cortex does not fully develop until the early 20s, and this fact underlies the impulsive behavior of teenagers. The frontal lobes are sometimes called the organ of socialization, because becoming socialized largely involves developing the circuitry to squelch our first impulses.

65   This explains why damage to the frontal lobes unmasks unsocialized behavior that we would never have thought was hidden inside us. Recall the patients with frontotemporal dementia who shoplift, expose themselves, and burst into song at inappropriate times. The networks for those behaviors have been lurking under the surface all along, but they've been masked by normally functioning frontal lobes. The same sort of unmasking happens in people who go out and get rip-roaring drunk on a Saturday night: they're disinhibiting normal frontal-lobe function and letting more-impulsive networks climb onto the main stage. After training at the prefrontal gym, a person might still crave a cigarette, but he'll know how to beat the craving instead of letting it win. It's not that we don't want to enjoy our impulsive thoughts (*Mmm, cake*), it's merely that we want to endow the frontal cortex with some control over whether we act upon them (*I'll pass*). Similarly, if a person thinks about committing a criminal act, that's permissible as long as he doesn't take action.

For the pedophile, we cannot hope to control whether he is attracted to children. That he never acts on the attraction may be the best we can hope for, especially as a society that respects individual rights and freedom of thought. Social policy can hope only to prevent impulsive thoughts from tipping into behavior without reflection. The goal is to give more control to the neural populations that care about long-term consequences—to inhibit impulsivity, to encourage reflection. If a person thinks about long-term consequences and still decides to move forward with an illegal act, then we'll respond accordingly. The prefrontal workout leaves the brain intact—no drugs or surgery—and uses the natural mechanisms of brain plasticity to help the brain help itself. It's a tune-up rather than a product recall.

We have hope that this approach represents the correct model: it is grounded simultaneously in biology and in libertarian ethics, allowing a person to help himself by improving his long-term decision-making. Like any scientific attempt, it could fail for any number of unforeseen reasons. But at least we have reached a point where we can develop new ideas rather than assuming that repeated incarceration is the single practical solution for deterring crime.

Along any axis that we use to measure human beings, we discover a wide-ranging distribution, whether in empathy, intelligence, impulse control, or aggression. People are not created equal. Although this variability is often imagined to be best swept under the rug, it is in fact the engine of evolution. In each generation, nature tries out as many varieties as it can produce, along all available dimensions.

Variation gives rise to lushly diverse societies—but it serves as a source of trouble for the legal system, which is largely built on the premise that humans are all equal before the law. This myth of human equality suggests that people are equally capable of controlling impulses, making decisions, and comprehending consequences. While admirable in spirit, the notion of neural equality is simply not true.

As brain science improves, we will better understand that people exist along   70
continua of capabilities, rather than in simplistic categories. And we will be
better able to tailor sentencing and rehabilitation for the individual, rather than
maintain the pretense that all brains respond identically to complex challenges
and that all people therefore deserve the same punishments. Some people wonder whether it's unfair to take a scientific approach to sentencing—after all,
where's the humanity in that? But what's the alternative? As it stands now, ugly
people receive longer sentences than attractive people; psychiatrists have no
capacity to guess which sex offenders will reoffend; and our prisons are overcrowded with drug addicts and the mentally ill, both of whom could be better
helped by rehabilitation. So is current sentencing really superior to a scientifically informed approach?

Neuroscience is beginning to touch on questions that were once only in
the domain of philosophers and psychologists, questions about how people make
decisions and the degree to which those decisions are truly "free." These are
not idle questions. Ultimately, they will shape the future of legal theory and
create a more biologically informed jurisprudence.

MLA CITATION

Eagleman, David. "The Brain on Trial." 2011. *The Norton Reader: An Anthology of
Nonfiction.* Ed. Melissa A. Goldthwaite et al. 14th ed. New York: Norton, 2016.
735–49. Print.

QUESTIONS

1. David Eagleman writes that "*we* are not the ones steering the boat of our behavior, at least not nearly as much as we believe" (paragraph 21). What factors does
Eagleman point to as affecting behavior? To what extent do you think you are
responsible for your own behavior?

2. Look closely at Eagleman's prose and the claims he makes throughout this
essay. Does he make unequivocal assertions, or does he use language that hedges
his claims? Point to specific examples in the text.

3. Eagleman's essay is a lengthy plea for what lawyers call "diminished responsibility." Look up this concept in law. If we followed Eagleman's suggestions, would
we have fewer people in prison? Why or why not?

4. Eagleman's solution for the rehabilitation of criminals is "the prefrontal workout" (paragraph 61). Write an essay in which you evaluate this solution. Consider
both its potential strengths and weaknesses.

HISTORY
AND POLITICS

GEORGE ORWELL   *Shooting an Elephant*

I N MOULMEIN, in Lower Burma, I was hated by large numbers of people—the only time in my life that I have been important enough for this to happen to me. I was sub-divisional police officer of the town, and in an aimless, petty kind of way anti-European feeling was very bitter. No one had the guts to raise a riot, but if a European woman went through the bazaars alone somebody would probably spit betel juice over her dress. As a police officer I was an obvious target and was baited whenever it seemed safe to do so. When a nimble Burman tripped me up on the football field and the referee (another Burman) looked the other way, the crowd yelled with hideous laughter. This happened more than once. In the end the sneering yellow faces of young men that met me everywhere, the insults hooted after me when I was at a safe distance, got badly on my nerves. The young Buddhist priests were the worst of all. There were several thousands of them in the town and none of them seemed to have anything to do except stand on street corners and jeer at Europeans.

All this was perplexing and upsetting. For at that time I had already made up my mind that imperialism was an evil thing and the sooner I chucked up my job and got out of it the better. Theoretically—and secretly, of course—I was all for the Burmese and all against their oppressors, the British. As for the job I was doing, I hated it more bitterly than I can perhaps make clear. In a job like that you see the dirty work of Empire at close quarters. The wretched prisoners huddling in the stinking cages of the lock-ups, the grey, cowed faces of the long-term convicts, the scarred buttocks of the men who had been flogged with bamboos—all these oppressed me with an intolerable sense of guilt. But I could get nothing into perspective. I was young and ill-educated and I had had to think out my problems in the utter silence that is imposed on every Englishman in the East. I did not even know that the British Empire is dying, still less did I know that it is a great deal better than the younger empires that are going to supplant it. All I knew was that I was stuck between my hatred of the empire I served and my rage against the evil-spirited little beasts who tried

Published in the periodical New Writing *(1936), at the beginning of George Orwell's writing career and soon after his novel* Burmese Days *(1934) appeared. The essay later became the title piece in the collection* Shooting an Elephant, and Other Essays *(1950).*

to make my job impossible. With one part of my mind I thought of the British Raj[1] as an unbreakable tyranny, as something clamped down, in *saecula saeculorum*,[2] upon the will of prostrate peoples; with another part I thought that the greatest joy in the world would be to drive a bayonet into a Buddhist priest's guts. Feelings like these are the normal by-products of imperialism; ask any Anglo-Indian official, if you can catch him off duty.

One day something happened which in a roundabout way was enlightening. It was a tiny incident in itself, but it gave me a better glimpse than I had had before of the real nature of imperialism—the real motives for which despotic governments act. Early one morning the sub-inspector at a police station the other end of the town rang me up on the 'phone and said that an elephant was ravaging the bazaar. Would I please come and do something about it? I did not know what I could do, but I wanted to see what was happening and I got on to a pony and started out. I took my rifle, an old .44 Winchester and much too small to kill an elephant, but I thought the noise might be useful *in terrorem*. Various Burmans stopped me on the way and told me about the elephant's doings. It was not, of course, a wild elephant, but a tame one which had gone "must."[3] It had been chained up, as tame elephants always are when their attack of "must" is due, but on the previous night it had broken its chain and escaped. Its mahout, the only person who could manage it when it was in that state, had set out in pursuit, but had taken the wrong direction and was now twelve hours' journey away, and in the morning the elephant had suddenly reappeared in the town. The Burmese population had no weapons and were quite helpless against it. It had already destroyed somebody's bamboo hut, killed a cow and raided some fruit-stalls and devoured the stock; also it had met the municipal rubbish van and, when the driver jumped out and took to his heels, had turned the van over and inflicted violences upon it.

The Burmese sub-inspector and some Indian constables were waiting for me in the quarter where the elephant had been seen. It was a very poor quarter, a labyrinth of squalid bamboo huts, thatched with palm-leaf, winding all over a steep hillside. I remember that it was a cloudy, stuffy morning at the beginning of the rains. We began questioning the people as to where the elephant had gone and, as usual, failed to get any definite information. That is invariably the case in the East; a story always sounds clear enough at a distance, but the nearer you get to the scene of events the vaguer it becomes. Some of the people said that the elephant had gone in one direction, some said that he had gone in another, some professed not even to have heard of any elephant. I had almost made up my mind that the whole story was a pack of lies, when we heard yells a little distance away. There was a loud, scandalized cry of "Go away, child! Go away this instant!" and an old woman with a switch in her hand came round the corner of a hut, violently shooing away a crowd of naked children. Some more women followed, clicking their tongues and exclaiming; evidently

1. Imperial government of British India and Burma.
2. Forever and ever.
3. Gone into sexual heat.

there was something that the children ought not to have seen. I rounded the hut and saw a man's dead body sprawling in the mud. He was an Indian, a black Dravidian coolie,[4] almost naked, and he could not have been dead many minutes. The people said that the elephant had come suddenly upon him round the corner of the hut, caught him with its trunk, put its foot on his back and ground him into the earth. This was the rainy season and the ground was soft, and his face had scored a trench a foot deep and a couple of yards long. He was lying on his belly with arms crucified and head sharply twisted to one side. His face was coated with mud, the eyes wide open, the teeth bared and grinning with an expression of unendurable agony. (Never tell me, by the way, that the dead look peaceful. Most of the corpses I have seen looked devilish.) The friction of the great beast's foot had stripped the skin from his back as neatly as one skins a rabbit. As soon as I saw the dead man I sent an orderly to a friend's house nearby to borrow an elephant rifle. I had already sent back the pony, not wanting it to go mad with fright and throw me if it smelt the elephant.

5   The orderly came back in a few minutes with a rifle and five cartridges, and meanwhile some Burmans had arrived and told us that the elephant was in the paddy fields below, only a few hundred yards away. As I started forward practically the whole population of the quarter flocked out of the houses and followed me. They had seen the rifle and were all shouting excitedly that I was going to shoot the elephant. They had not shown much interest in the elephant when he was merely ravaging their homes, but it was different now that he was going to be shot. It was a bit of fun to them, as it would be to an English crowd; besides they wanted the meat. It made me vaguely uneasy. I had no intention of shooting the elephant—I had merely sent for the rifle to defend myself if necessary—and it is always unnerving to have a crowd following you. I marched down the hill, looking and feeling a fool, with the rifle over my shoulder and an ever-growing army of people jostling at my heels. At the bottom, when you got away from the huts, there was a metalled road and beyond that a miry waste of paddy fields a thousand yards across, not yet ploughed but soggy from the first rains and dotted with coarse grass. The elephant was standing eight yards from the road, his left side towards us. He took not the slightest notice of the crowd's approach. He was tearing up bunches of grass, beating them against his knees to clean them and stuffing them into his mouth.

I had halted on the road. As soon as I saw the elephant I knew with perfect certainty that I ought not to shoot him. It is a serious matter to shoot a working elephant—it is comparable to destroying a huge and costly piece of machinery—and obviously one ought not to do it if it can possibly be avoided. And at that distance, peacefully eating, the elephant looked no more dangerous than a cow. I thought then and I think now that his attack of "must" was already passing off; in which case he would merely wander harmlessly about until the mahout came back and caught him. Moreover, I did not in the least

4. When Orwell wrote this essay, the word "coolie" referred to a hired worker from southern India. The word became a slur against immigrant workers in the United States, India, and the Caribbean, and is considered to be an offensive term today.

want to shoot him. I decided that I would watch him for a little while to make sure that he did not turn savage again, and then go home.

But at that moment I glanced round at the crowd that had followed me. It was an immense crowd, two thousand at the least and growing every minute. It blocked the road for a long distance on either side. I looked at the sea of yellow faces above the garish clothes—faces all happy and excited over this bit of fun, all certain that the elephant was going to be shot. They were watching me as they would watch a conjurer about to perform a trick. They did not like me, but with the magical rifle in my hands I was momentarily worth watching. And suddenly I realized that I should have to shoot the elephant after all. The people expected it of me and I had got to do it; I could feel their two thousand wills pressing me forward, irresistibly. And it was at this moment, as I stood there with the rifle in my hands, that I first grasped the hollowness, the futility of the white man's dominion in the East. Here was I, the white man with his gun, standing in front of the unarmed native crowd—seemingly the leading actor of the piece; but in reality I was only an absurd puppet pushed to and fro by the will of those yellow faces behind. I perceived in this moment that when the white man turns tyrant it is his own freedom that he destroys. He becomes a sort of hollow, posing dummy, the conventionalized figure of a sahib. For it is the condition of his rule that he shall spend his life in trying to impress the "natives," and so in every crisis he has got to do what the "natives" expect of him. He wears a mask, and his face grows to fit it. I had got to shoot the elephant. I had committed myself to doing it when I sent for the rifle. A sahib has got to act like a sahib; he has got to appear resolute, to know his own mind and do definite things. To come all that way, rifle in hand, with two thousand people marching at my heels, and then to trail feebly away, having done nothing—no, that was impossible. The crowd would laugh at me. And my whole life, every white man's life in the East, was one long struggle not to be laughed at.

But I did not want to shoot the elephant. I watched him beating his bunch of grass against his knees, with that preoccupied grandmotherly air that elephants have. It seemed to me that it would be murder to shoot him. At that age I was not squeamish about killing animals, but I had never shot an elephant and never wanted to. (Somehow it always seems worse to kill a *large* animal.) Besides, there was the beast's owner to be considered. Alive, the elephant was worth at least a hundred pounds; dead, he would only be worth the value of his tusks, five pounds, possibly. But I had got to act quickly. I turned to some experienced-looking Burmans who had been there when we arrived, and asked them how the elephant had been behaving. They all said the same thing: he took no notice of you if you left him alone, but he might charge if you went too close to him.

It was perfectly clear to me what I ought to do. I ought to walk up to within, say, twenty-five yards of the elephant and test his behavior. If he charged, I could shoot; if he took no notice of me, it would be safe to leave him until the mahout came back. But also I knew that I was going to do no such thing. I was a poor shot with a rifle and the ground was soft mud into which one would sink at every step. If the elephant charged and I missed him, I should have about

as much chance as a toad under a steam-roller. But even then I was not thinking particularly of my own skin, only of the watchful yellow faces behind. For
at that moment, with the crowd watching me, I was not afraid in the ordinary
sense, as I would have been if I had been alone. A white man mustn't be frightened in front of "natives"; and so, in general, he isn't frightened. The sole thought
in my mind was that if anything went wrong those two thousand Burmans
would see me pursued, caught, trampled on and reduced to a grinning corpse
like that Indian up the hill. And if that happened it was quite probable that
some of them would laugh. That would never do. There was only one alternative. I shoved the cartridges into the magazine and lay down on the road to get
a better aim.

10   The crowd grew very still, and a deep, low, happy sigh, as of people who see
the theatre curtain go up at last, breathed from innumerable throats. They were
going to have their bit of fun after all. The rifle was a beautiful German thing
with cross-hair sights. I did not then know that in shooting an elephant one
would shoot to cut an imaginary bar running from ear-hole to ear-hole. I ought,
therefore, as the elephant was sideways on, to have aimed straight at his ear-
hole; actually I aimed several inches in front of this, thinking the brain would
be further forward.

When I pulled the trigger I did not hear the bang or feel the kick—one
never does when a shot goes home—but I heard the devilish roar of glee that
went up from the crowd. In that instant, in too short a time, one would have
thought, even for the bullet to get there, a mysterious, terrible change had come
over the elephant. He neither stirred nor fell, but every line of his body had
altered. He looked suddenly stricken, shrunken, immensely old, as though the
frightful impact of the bullet had paralysed him without knocking him down.
At last, after what seemed a long time—it might have been five seconds, I dare
say—he sagged flabbily to his knees. His mouth slobbered. An enormous senil-
ity seemed to have settled upon him. One could have imagined him thousands
of years old. I fired again into the same spot. At the second shot he did not
collapse but climbed with desperate slowness to his feet and stood weakly
upright, with legs sagging and head drooping. I fired a third time. That was
the shot that did for him. You could see the agony of it jolt his whole body and
knock the last remnant of strength from his legs. But in falling he seemed for
a moment to rise, for as his hind legs collapsed beneath him he seemed to tower
upward like a huge rock toppling, his trunk reaching skywards like a tree. He
trumpeted, for the first and only time. And then down he came, his belly towards
me, with a crash that seemed to shake the ground even where I lay.

I got up. The Burmans were already racing past me across the mud. It was
obvious that the elephant would never rise again, but he was not dead. He was
breathing very rhythmically with long rattling gasps, his great mound of a side
painfully rising and falling. His mouth was wide open—I could see far down
into caverns of pale pink throat. I waited a long time for him to die, but his
breathing did not weaken. Finally I fired my two remaining shots into the spot
where I thought his heart must be. The thick blood welled out of him like red
velvet, but still he did not die. His body did not even jerk when the shots hit
him, the tortured breathing continued without a pause. He was dying, very

slowly and in great agony, but in some world remote from me where not even a bullet could damage him further. I felt that I had got to put an end to that dreadful noise. It seemed dreadful to see the great beast lying there, powerless to move and yet powerless to die, and not even to be able to finish him. I sent back for my small rifle and poured shot after shot into his heart and down his throat. They seemed to make no impression. The tortured gasps continued as steadily as the ticking of a clock.

In the end I could not stand it any longer and went away. I heard later that it took him half an hour to die. Burmans were bringing dahs[5] and baskets even before I left, and I was told they had stripped his body almost to the bones by the afternoon.

Afterwards, of course, there were endless discussions about the shooting of the elephant. The owner was furious, but he was only an Indian and could do nothing. Besides, legally I had done the right thing, for a mad elephant has to be killed, like a mad dog, if its owner fails to control it. Among the Europeans opinion was divided. The older men said I was right, the younger men said it was a damn shame to shoot an elephant for killing a coolie, because an elephant was worth more than any damn Coringhee coolie.[6] And afterwards I was very glad that the coolie had been killed; it put me legally in the right and it gave me a sufficient pretext for shooting the elephant. I often wondered whether any of the others grasped that I had done it solely to avoid looking a fool.

5. Butcher knives.
6. Hired worker from the seaport of Coringa, in Madras, India.

MLA CITATION

Orwell, George. "Shooting an Elephant." 1936. *The Norton Reader: An Anthology of Nonfiction.* Ed. Melissa A. Goldthwaite et al. 14th ed. New York: Norton, 2016. 750–55. Print.

QUESTIONS

1. Why did George Orwell shoot the elephant? Account for the motives that led him to shoot, and then categorize them as personal motives, circumstantial motives, social motives, or political motives. Is it easy to assign his motives to categories? Why or why not?

2. In this essay the proportion of narrative to analysis is high. Mark each paragraph as narrative or analytic, and note, in particular, how much analysis Orwell places in the middle of the essay. What are the advantages and disadvantages of having it there rather than at the beginning or the end of the essay?

3. Facts ordinarily do not speak for themselves. How does Orwell present his facts to make them speak in support of his analytic points? Look, for example, at the death of the elephant (paragraphs 11 to 13).

4. Write an essay in which you present a personal experience that illuminates a larger issue: schooling, affirmative action, homelessness, law enforcement, taxes, or some other local or national issue.

JONATHAN SWIFT   *A Modest Proposal*

FOR PREVENTING THE CHILDREN OF POOR PEOPLE IN IRELAND
FROM BEING A BURDEN TO THEIR PARENTS OR COUNTRY,
AND FOR MAKING THEM BENEFICIAL TO THE PUBLIC

I T IS A MELANCHOLY OBJECT to those who walk through this great town[1] or travel in the country, when they see the streets, the roads, and cabin doors, crowded with beggars of the female-sex, followed by three, four, or six children, all in rags and importuning every passenger for an alms. These mothers, instead of being able to work for their honest livelihood, are forced to employ all their time in strolling to beg sustenance for their helpless infants, who, as they grow up, either turn thieves for want of work, or leave their dear native country to fight for the Pretender in Spain, or sell themselves to the Barbadoes.[2]

I think it is agreed by all parties that this prodigious number of children in the arms, or on the backs, or at the heels of their mothers, and frequently of their fathers, is in the present deplorable state of the kingdom a very great additional grievance; and therefore whoever could find out a fair, cheap, and easy method of making these children sound, useful members of the commonwealth would deserve so well of the public as to have his statue set up for a preserver of the nation.

But my intention is very far from being confined to provide only for the children of professed beggars; it is of a much greater extent, and shall take in the whole number of infants at a certain age who are born of parents in effect as little able to support them as those who demand our charity in the streets.

As to my own part, having turned my thoughts for many years upon this important subject, and maturely weighed the several schemes of other projectors,[3] I have always found them grossly mistaken in their computation. It is true, a child just dropped from its dam may be supported by her milk for a solar year, with little other nourishment; at most not above the value of two shillings,[4] which the mother may certainly get, or the value in scraps, by her

---

Printed in 1729 as a pamphlet, a form commonly used for political debate in the eighteenth century.

1. Dublin.

2. Many poor Irish sought to escape poverty by emigrating to the Barbados and other western English colonies, paying for transport by binding themselves to work for a landowner there for a period of years. The Pretender, James Francis Edward Stuart (1688–1766), was a claimant to the English throne. He was barred from succession after his father, King James II, was deposed in a Protestant revolution; thereafter, many Irish Catholics joined the Pretender in his exile in France and Spain and in his unsuccessful attempts at counterrevolution.

3. People with projects; schemers.

4. One shilling used to be worth about twenty-five cents.

lawful occupation of begging; and it is exactly at one year old that I propose to provide for them in such a manner as instead of being a charge upon their parents or the parish, or wanting food and raiment for the rest of their lives, they shall on the contrary contribute to the feeding, and partly to the clothing, of many thousands.

There is likewise another great advantage in my scheme, that it will prevent those voluntary abortions, and that horrid practice of women murdering their bastard children, alas, too frequent among us, sacrificing the poor innocent babes, I doubt, more to avoid the expense than the shame, which would move tears and pity in the most savage and inhuman breast.

The number of souls in this kingdom being usually reckoned one million and a half, of these I calculate there may be about two hundred thousand couple whose wives are breeders; from which number I subtract thirty thousand couples who are able to maintain their own children, although I apprehend there cannot be so many under the present distresses of the kingdom; but this being granted, there will remain an hundred and seventy thousand breeders. I again subtract fifty thousand for those women who miscarry, or whose children die by accident or disease within the year. There only remain an hundred and twenty thousand children of poor parents annually born. The question therefore is, how this number shall be reared and provided for, which, as I have already said, under the present situation of affairs, is utterly impossible by all the methods hitherto proposed. For we can neither employ them in handicraft or agriculture; we neither build houses (I mean in the country) nor cultivate land. They can very seldom pick up a livelihood by stealing till they arrive at six years old, except where they are of towardly parts;[5] although I confess they learn the rudiments much earlier, during which time they can however be looked upon only as probationers, as I have been informed by a principal gentleman in the county of Cavan, who protested to me that he never knew above one or two instances under the age of six, even in a part of the kingdom so renowned for the quickest proficiency in that art.

I am assured by our merchants that a boy or a girl before twelve years old is no salable commodity; and even when they come to this age they will not yield above three pounds, or three pounds and half a crown[6] at most on the Exchange; which cannot turn to account either to the parents or the kingdom, the charge of nutriment and rags having been at least four times that value.

I shall now therefore humbly propose my own thoughts, which I hope will not be liable to the least objection.

I have been assured by a very knowing American of my acquaintance in London, that a young healthy child well nursed is at a year old a most delicious, nourishing, and wholesome food, whether stewed, roasted, baked, or boiled; and I make no doubt that it will equally serve in a fricassee or a ragout.

I do therefore humbly offer it to public consideration that of the hundred and twenty thousand children, already computed, twenty thousand may be reserved for breed, whereof only one fourth part to be males, which is more

5. Promising abilities.
6. One crown was worth one quarter of a pound.

than we allow to sheep, black cattle, or swine; and my reason is that these children are seldom the fruits of marriage, a circumstance not much regarded by our savages, therefore one male will be sufficient to serve four females. That the remaining hundred thousand may at a year old be offered in sale to the persons of quality and fortune through the kingdom, always advising the mother to let them suck plentifully in the last month, so as to render them plump and fat for a good table. A child will make two dishes at an entertainment for friends; and when the family dines alone, the fore or hind quarter will make a reasonable dish, and seasoned with a little pepper or salt will be very good boiled on the fourth day, especially in winter.

I have reckoned upon a medium that a child just born will weigh twelve pounds, and in a solar year if tolerably nursed increaseth to twenty-eight pounds.

I grant this food will be somewhat dear, and therefore very proper for landlords, who, as they have already devoured most of the parents, seem to have the best title to the children.

Infant's flesh will be in season throughout the year, but more plentiful in March, and a little before and after. For we are told by a grave author, an eminent French physician,[7] that fish being a prolific diet, there are more children born in Roman Catholic countries about nine months after Lent than at any other season; therefore, reckoning a year after Lent, the markets will be more glutted than usual, because the number of popish infants is at least three to one in this kingdom; and therefore it will have one other collateral advantage, by lessening the number of Papists among us.[8]

I have already computed the charge of nursing a beggar's child (in which list I reckon all cottagers, laborers, and four fifths of the farmers) to be about two shillings per annum, rags included; and I believe no gentleman would repine to give ten shillings for the carcass of a good fat child, which, as I have said, will make four dishes of excellent nutritive meat, when he hath only some particular friend or his own family to dine with him. Thus the squire will learn to be a good landlord, and grow popular among the tenants; the mother will have eight shillings net profit, and be fit for work till she produces another child.

15   Those who are more thrifty (as I must confess the times require) may flay the carcass; the skin of which artificially[9] dressed will make admirable gloves for ladies, and summer boots for fine gentlemen.

As to our city of Dublin, shambles[10] may be appointed for this purpose in the most convenient parts of it, and butchers we may be assured will not be wanting; although I rather recommend buying the children alive, and dressing them hot from the knife as we do roasting pigs.

A very worthy person, a true lover of his country, and whose virtues I highly esteem, was lately pleased in discoursing on this matter to offer a refinement

7. Comic writer François Rabelais (1483–1553).

8. The speaker is addressing Protestant Anglo-Irish, who were the chief landowners and administrators, and his views of Catholicism in Ireland and abroad echo theirs.

9. Skillfully.

10. Slaughterhouses.

upon my scheme. He said that many gentlemen of this kingdom, having of late destroyed their deer, he conceived that the want of venison might be well supplied by the bodies of young lads and maidens, not exceeding fourteen years of age nor under twelve, so great a number of both sexes in every county being now ready to starve for want of work and service; and these to be disposed of by their parents, if alive, or otherwise by their nearest relations. But with due deference to so excellent a friend and so deserving a patriot, I cannot be altogether in his sentiments; for as to the males, my American acquaintance assured me from frequent experience that their flesh was generally tough and lean, like that of our schoolboys, by continual exercise, and their taste disagreeable; and to fatten them would not answer the charge. Then as to the females, it would, I think with humble submission, be a loss to the public, because they soon would become breeders themselves: and besides, it is not improbable that some scrupulous people might be apt to censure such a practice (although indeed very unjustly) as a little bordering upon cruelty; which, I confess, hath always been with me the strongest objection against any project, how well soever intended.

But in order to justify my friend, he confessed that this expedient was put into his head by the famous Psalmanazar, a native of the island Formosa,[11] who came from thence to London above twenty years ago, and in conversation told my friend that in his country when any young person happened to be put to death, the executioner sold the carcass to persons of quality as a prime dainty; and that in his time the body of a plump girl of fifteen, who was crucified for an attempt to poison the emperor, was sold to his Imperial Majesty's prime minister of state, and other great mandarins of the court, in joints from the gibbet, at four hundred crowns. Neither indeed can I deny that if the same use were made of several plump young girls in this town, who without one single groat[12] to their fortunes cannot stir abroad without a chair,[13] and appear at the playhouse and assemblies in foreign fineries which they never will pay for, the kingdom would not be the worse.

Some persons of a desponding spirit are in great concern about that vast number of poor people who are aged, diseased, or maimed, and I have been desired to employ my thoughts what course may be taken to ease the nation of so grievous an encumbrance. But I am not in the least pain upon that matter, because it is very well known that they are every day dying and rotting by cold and famine, and filth and vermin, as fast as can be reasonably expected. And as to the younger laborers, they are now in almost as hopeful a condition. They cannot get work, and consequently pine away for want of nourishment to a degree that if at any time they are accidentally hired to common labor, they have not strength to perform it; and thus the country and themselves are happily delivered from the evils to come.

11. Actually a Frenchman, George Psalmanazar had passed himself off as from Formosa (now Taiwan) and had written a fictitious book about his "homeland," with descriptions of human sacrifice and cannibalism.
12. Coin worth about four English pennies.
13. Sedan chair.

20   I have too long digressed, and therefore shall return to my subject. I think
the advantages by the proposal which I have made are obvious and many, as
well as of the highest importance.

For first, as I have already observed, it would greatly lessen the number of
Papists, with whom we are yearly overrun, being the principal breeders of the
nation as well as our most dangerous enemies; and who stay at home on purpose to deliver the kingdom to the Pretender, hoping to take their advantage
by the absence of so many good Protestants, who have chosen rather to leave
their country than to stay at home and pay tithes against their conscience to
an Episcopal curate.

Secondly, the poorer tenants will have something valuable of their own,
which by law may be made liable to distress,[14] and help to pay their landlord's
rent, their corn and cattle being already seized and money a thing unknown.

Thirdly, whereas the maintenance of an hundred thousand children, from
two years old and upwards, cannot be computed at less than ten shillings a piece
per annum, the nation's stock will be thereby increased fifty thousand pounds per
annum, besides the profit of a new dish introduced to the tables of all gentlemen
of fortune in the kingdom who have any refinement in taste. And the money
will circulate among ourselves, the goods being entirely of our own growth
and manufacture.

Fourthly, the constant breeders, besides the gain of eight shillings sterling
per annum by the sale of their children, will be rid of the charge of maintaining
them after the first year.

25   Fifthly, this food would likewise bring great custom to taverns, where the
vintners will certainly be so prudent as to procure the best receipts for dressing it to perfection, and consequently have their houses frequented by all the
fine gentlemen, who justly value themselves upon their knowledge in good eating; and a skillful cook, who understands how to oblige his guests, will con-
trive to make it as expensive as they please.

Sixthly, this would be a great inducement to marriage, which all wise
nations have either encouraged by rewards or enforced by laws and penalties.
It would increase the care and tenderness of mothers toward their children,
when they were sure of a settlement for life to the poor babes, provided in some
sort by the public, to their annual profit instead of expense. We should see an
honest emulation among the married women, which of them could bring the
fattest child to the market. Men would become as fond of their wives during
the time of their pregnancy as they are now of their mares in foal, their cows
in calf, or sows when they are ready to farrow; nor offer to beat or kick them
(as is too frequent a practice) for fear of a miscarriage.

Many other advantages might be enumerated. For instance, the addition
of some thousand carcasses in our exportation of barreled beef, the propagation of swine's flesh, and improvement in the art of making good bacon, so much
wanted among us by the great destruction of pigs, too frequent at our tables,
which are no way comparable in taste or magnificence to a well-grown, fat,
yearling child, which roasted whole will make a considerable figure at a lord

14. Seizure for the payment of debts.

mayor's feast or any other public entertainment. But this and many others I omit, being studious of brevity.

Supposing that one thousand families in this city would be constant customers for infants' flesh, besides others who might have it at merry meetings, particularly weddings and christenings, I compute that Dublin would take off annually about twenty thousand carcasses, and the rest of the kingdom (where probably they will be sold somewhat cheaper) the remaining eighty thousand.

I can think of no one objection that will possibly be raised against this proposal, unless it should be urged that the number of people will be thereby much lessened in the kingdom. This I freely own, and it was indeed one principal design in offering it to the world. I desire the reader will observe, that I calculate my remedy for this one individual kingdom of Ireland and for no other that ever was, is, or I think ever can be upon earth. Therefore let no man talk to me of other expedients: of taxing our absentees at five shillings a pound: of using neither clothes nor household furniture except what is of our own growth and manufacture: of utterly rejecting the materials and instruments that promote foreign luxury: of curing the expensiveness of pride, vanity, idleness, and gaming in our women: of introducing a vein of parsimony, prudence, and temperance: of learning to love our country, in the want of which we differ even from Laplanders and the inhabitants of Topinamboo:[15] of quitting our animosities and factions, nor acting any longer like the Jews, who were murdering one another at the very moment their city was taken: of being a little cautious not to sell our country and conscience for nothing: of teaching landlords to have at least one degree of mercy toward their tenants: lastly, of putting a spirit of honesty, industry, and skill into our shopkeepers; who, if a resolution could now be taken to buy only our native goods, would immediately unite to cheat and exact upon us in the price, the measure, and the goodness, nor could ever yet be brought to make one fair proposal of just dealing, though often and earnestly invited to it.[16]

Therefore I repeat, let no man talk to me of these and the like expedients, till he hath at least some glimpse of hope that there will ever be some hearty and sincere attempt to put them in practice.

But as to myself, having been wearied out for many years with offering vain, idle, visionary thoughts, and at length utterly despairing of success, I fortunately fell upon this proposal, which, as it is wholly new, so it hath something solid and real, of no expense and little trouble, full in our own power, and whereby we can incur no danger in disobliging England. For this kind of commodity will not bear exportation, the flesh being of too tender a consistence to admit a long continuance in salt, although perhaps I could name a country[17] which would be glad to eat up our whole nation without it.

After all, I am not so violently bent upon my own opinion as to reject any offer proposed by wise men, which shall be found equally innocent, cheap, easy, and effectual. But before something of that kind shall be advanced in

15. District in Brazil.

16. Swift himself had made these proposals seriously in various previous works, but to no avail.

17. England.

contradiction to my scheme, and offering a better, I desire the author or authors will be pleased maturely to consider two points. First, as things now stand, how they will be able to find food and raiment for an hundred thousand useless mouths and backs. And secondly, there being a round million of creatures in human figure throughout this kingdom, whose sole subsistence put into a common stock would leave them in debt two millions of pounds sterling, adding those who are beggars by profession to the bulk of farmers, cottagers, and laborers, with their wives and children who are beggars in effect; I desire those politicians who dislike my overture, and may perhaps be so bold to attempt an answer, that they will first ask the parents of these mortals whether they would not at this day think it a great happiness to have been sold for food at a year old in the manner I prescribe, and thereby have avoided such a perpetual scene of misfortunes as they have since gone through by the oppression of landlords, the impossibility of paying rent without money or trade, the want of common sustenance, with neither house nor clothes to cover them from the inclemencies of the weather, and the most inevitable prospect of entailing the like or greater miseries upon their breed forever.

I profess, in the sincerity of my heart, that I have not the least personal interest in endeavoring to promote this necessary work, having no other motive than the public good of my country, by advancing our trade, providing for infants, relieving the poor, and giving some pleasure to the rich. I have no children by which I can propose to get a single penny; the youngest being nine years old, and my wife past childbearing.

MLA CITATION

Swift, Jonathan. "A Modest Proposal." 1729. *The Norton Reader: An Anthology of Nonfiction.* Ed. Melissa A. Goldthwaite et al. 14th ed. New York: Norton, 2016. 756–62. Print.

QUESTIONS

1. Identify examples of the reasonable voice of Jonathan Swift's authorial persona, such as the title of the essay itself.

2. Look, in particular, at instances in which Swift's authorial persona proposes shocking things. How does the style of "A Modest Proposal" affect its content?

3. Verbal irony consists of saying one thing and meaning another. At what point in this essay do you begin to suspect that Swift is using irony? What additional evidence of irony can you find?

4. Write a "modest proposal" of your own in the manner of Swift to remedy a real problem; that is, propose an outrageous remedy in a reasonable voice.

Niccolò Machiavelli *The Morals of the Prince*

On the Reasons Why Men Are Praised or Blamed— Especially Princes

IT REMAINS NOW to be seen what style and principles a prince ought to adopt in dealing with his subjects and friends. I know the subject has been treated frequently before, and I'm afraid people will think me rash for trying to do so again, especially since I intend to differ in this discussion from what others have said. But since I intend to write something useful to an understanding reader, it seemed better to go after the real truth of the matter than to repeat what people have imagined. A great many men have imagined states and princedoms such as nobody ever saw or knew in the real world, for there's such a difference between the way we really live and the way we ought to live that the man who neglects the real to study the ideal will learn how to accomplish his ruin, not his salvation. Any man who tries to be good all the time is bound to come to ruin among the great number who are not good. Hence a prince who wants to keep his post must learn how not to be good, and use that knowledge, or refrain from using it, as necessity requires.

Putting aside, then, all the imaginary things that are said about princes, and getting down to the truth, let me say that whenever men are discussed (and especially princes because they are prominent), there are certain qualities that bring them either praise or blame. Thus some are considered generous, others stingy (I use a Tuscan term, since "greedy" in our speech means a man who wants to take other people's goods. We call a man "stingy" who clings to his own); some are givers, others grabbers; some cruel, others merciful; one man is treacherous, another faithful; one is feeble and effeminate, another fierce and spirited; one humane, another proud; one lustful, another chaste; one straightforward, another sly; one harsh, another gentle; one serious, another playful; one religious, another skeptical, and so on. I know everyone will agree that among these many qualities a prince certainly ought to have all those that are considered good. But since it is impossible to have and exercise them all, because the conditions of human life simply do not allow it, a prince must be shrewd enough to avoid the public disgrace of those vices that would lose him his state. If he possibly can, he should also guard against vices that will not lose him his state; but if he cannot prevent them, he should not be too worried about indulging them. And furthermore, he should not be too worried about incurring blame for any vice without which he would find it hard to save his state. For if you look at matters carefully, you will see that something resembling

From The Prince (1513), a book on statecraft written for Giuliano de' Medici (1479–1516), a member of one of the most famous and powerful families of Renaissance Italy. This selection is from an edition translated and edited by Robert M. Adams (1977).

virtue, if you follow it, may be your ruin, while something else resembling vice will lead, if you follow it, to your security and well-being.

On Liberality and Stinginess

Let me begin, then, with the first of the qualities mentioned above, by saying that a reputation for liberality is doubtless very fine; but the generosity that earns you that reputation can do you great harm. For if you exercise your generosity in a really virtuous way, as you should, nobody will know of it, and you cannot escape the odium of the opposite vice. Hence if you wish to be widely known as a generous man, you must seize every opportunity to make a big display of your giving. A prince of this character is bound to use up his entire revenue in works of ostentation. Thus, in the end, if he wants to keep a name for generosity, he will have to load his people with exorbitant taxes and squeeze money out of them in every way he can. This is the first step in making him odious to his subjects; for when he is poor, nobody will respect him. Then, when his generosity has angered many and brought rewards to a few, the slightest difficulty will trouble him, and at the first approach of danger, down he goes. If by chance he foresees this, and tries to change his ways, he will immediately be labeled a miser.

Since a prince cannot use this virtue of liberality in such a way as to become known for it unless he harms his own security, he won't mind, if he judges prudently of things, being known as a miser. In due course he will be thought the more liberal man, when people see that his parsimony enables him to live on his income, to defend himself against his enemies, and to undertake major projects without burdening his people with taxes. Thus he will be acting liberally toward all those people from whom he takes nothing (and there are an immense number of them), and in a stingy way toward those people on whom he bestows nothing (and they are very few). In our times, we have seen great things being accomplished only by men who have had the name of misers; all the others have gone under. Pope Julius II, though he used his reputation as a generous man to gain the papacy, sacrificed it in order to be able to make war; the present king of France has waged many wars without levying a single extra tax on his people, simply because he could take care of the extra expenses out of the savings from his long parsimony. If the present king of Spain had a reputation for generosity, he would never have been able to undertake so many campaigns, or win so many of them.

5   Hence a prince who prefers not to rob his subjects, who wants to be able to defend himself, who wants to avoid poverty and contempt, and who doesn't want to become a plunderer, should not mind in the least if people consider him a miser; this is simply one of the vices that enable him to reign. Someone may object that Caesar used a reputation for generosity to become emperor, and many other people have also risen in the world, because they were generous or were supposed to be so. Well, I answer, either you are a prince already, or you are in the process of becoming one; in the first case, this reputation for

generosity is harmful to you, in the second case it is very necessary. Caesar was one of those who wanted to become ruler in Rome; but after he had reached his goal, if he had lived, and had not cut down on his expenses, he would have ruined the empire itself. Someone may say: there have been plenty of princes, very successful in warfare, who have had a reputation for generosity. But I answer: either the prince is spending his own money and that of his subjects, or he is spending someone else's. In the first case, he ought to be sparing; in the second case, he ought to spend money like water. Any prince at the head of his army, which lives on loot, extortion, and plunder, disposes of other people's property, and is bound to be very generous; otherwise, his soldiers would desert him. You can always be a more generous giver when what you give is not yours or your subjects'; Cyrus, Caesar, and Alexander[1] were generous in this way. Spending what belongs to other people does no harm to your reputation, rather it enhances it; only spending your own substance harms you. And there is nothing that wears out faster than generosity; even as you practice it, you lose the means of practicing it, and you become either poor and contemptible or (in the course of escaping poverty) rapacious and hateful. The thing above all against which a prince must protect himself is being contemptible and hateful; generosity leads to both. Thus, it's much wiser to put up with the reputation of being a miser, which brings you shame without hate, than to be forced—just because you want to appear generous—into a reputation for rapacity, which brings shame on you and hate along with it.

ON CRUELTY AND CLEMENCY: WHETHER IT IS BETTER TO BE LOVED OR FEARED

Continuing now with our list of qualities, let me say that every prince should prefer to be considered merciful rather than cruel, yet he should be careful not to mismanage this clemency of his. People thought Cesare Borgia[2] was cruel, but that cruelty of his reorganized the Romagna, united it, and established it in peace and loyalty. Anyone who views the matter realistically will see that this prince was much more merciful than the people of Florence, who, to avoid the reputation of cruelty, allowed Pistoia to be destroyed.[3] Thus, no prince should mind being called cruel for what he does to keep his subjects united and loyal; he may make examples of a very few, but he will be more merciful in reality than those who, in their tenderheartedness, allow disorders to occur, with their attendant murders and lootings. Such turbulence brings harm to an entire community, while the executions ordered by a prince affect only one individual at a time. A new prince, above all others, cannot possibly avoid a name

1. Persian, Roman, and Macedonian conquerors and rulers in ancient times.
2. Son of Pope Alexander VI; he was duke of Romagna, which he subjugated from 1499 to 1502.
3. By unchecked rioting between opposing factions in 1502.

for cruelty, since new states are always in danger. And Virgil, speaking through the mouth of Dido,[4] says:

> My cruel fate
> And doubts attending an unsettled state
> Force me to guard my coast from foreign foes.

Yet a prince should be slow to believe rumors and to commit himself to action on the basis of them. He should not be afraid of his own thoughts; he ought to proceed cautiously, moderating his conduct with prudence and humanity, allowing neither overconfidence to make him careless, nor overtimidity to make him intolerable.

Here the question arises: is it better to be loved than feared, or vice versa? I don't doubt that every prince would like to be both; but since it is hard to accommodate these qualities, if you have to make a choice, to be feared is much safer than to be loved. For it is a good general rule about men, that they are ungrateful, fickle, liars and deceivers, fearful of danger and greedy for gain. While you serve their welfare, they are all yours, offering their blood, their belongings, their lives, and their children's lives, as we noted above—so long as the danger is remote. But when the danger is close at hand, they turn against you. Then, any prince who has relied on their words and has made no other preparations will come to grief; because friendships that are bought at a price, and not with greatness and nobility of soul, may be paid for but they are not acquired, and they cannot be used in time of need. People are less concerned with offending a man who makes himself loved than one who makes himself feared: the reason is that love is a link of obligation which men, because they are rotten, will break any time they think doing so serves their advantage; but fear involves dread of punishment, from which they can never escape.

Still, a prince should make himself feared in such a way that, even if he gets no love, he gets no hate either; because it is perfectly possible to be feared and not hated, and this will be the result if only the prince will keep his hands off the property of his subjects or citizens, and off their women. When he does have to shed blood, he should be sure to have a strong justification and manifest cause; but above all, he should not confiscate people's property, because men are quicker to forget the death of a father than the loss of a patrimony. Besides, pretexts for confiscation are always plentiful, it never fails that a prince who starts living by plunder can find reasons to rob someone else. Excuses for proceeding against someone's life are much rarer and more quickly exhausted.

But a prince at the head of his armies and commanding a multitude of soldiers should not care a bit if he is considered cruel; without such a reputation, he could never hold his army together and ready for action. Among the marvelous deeds of Hannibal,[5] this was prime: that, having an immense army, which included men of many different races and nations, and which he led to battle

---

4. Queen of Carthage and tragic heroine of Virgil's epic, the *Aeneid*.
5. Carthaginian general who led a massive but unsuccessful invasion of Rome in 218–203 B.C.E.

in distant countries, he never allowed them to fight among themselves or to rise against him, whether his fortune was good or bad. The reason for this could only be his inhuman cruelty, which, along with his countless other talents, made him an object of awe and terror to his soldiers; and without the cruelty, his other qualities would never have sufficed. The historians who pass snap judgments on these matters admire his accomplishments and at the same time condemn the cruelty which was their main cause.

When I say, "His other qualities would never have sufficed," we can see   10
that this is true from the example of Scipio,[6] an outstanding man not only among those of his own time, but in all recorded history; yet his armies revolted in Spain, for no other reason than his excessive leniency in allowing his soldiers more freedom than military discipline permits. Fabius Maximus rebuked him in the senate for this failing, calling him the corrupter of the Roman armies. When a lieutenant of Scipio's plundered the Locrians,[7] he took no action in behalf of the people, and did nothing to discipline that insolent lieutenant; again, this was the result of his easygoing nature. Indeed, when someone in the senate wanted to excuse him on this occasion, he said there are many men who knew better how to avoid error themselves than how to correct error in others. Such a soft temper would in time have tarnished the fame and glory of Scipio, had he brought it to the office of emperor; but as he lived under the control of the senate, this harmful quality of his not only remained hidden but was considered creditable.

Returning to the question of being feared or loved, I conclude that since men love at their own inclination but can be made to fear at the inclination of the prince, a shrewd prince will lay his foundations on what is under his own control, not on what is controlled by others. He should simply take pains not to be hated, as I said.

THE WAY PRINCES SHOULD KEEP THEIR WORD

How praiseworthy it is for a prince to keep his word and live with integrity rather than by craftiness, everyone understands; yet we see from recent experience that those princes have accomplished most who paid little heed to keeping their promises, but who knew how craftily to manipulate the minds of men. In the end, they won out over those who tried to act honestly.

You should consider then, that there are two ways of fighting, one with laws and the other with force. The first is properly a human method, the second belongs to beasts. But as the first method does not always suffice, you sometimes have to turn to the second. Thus a prince must know how to make good use of both the beast and the man. Ancient writers made subtle note of this fact when they wrote that Achilles and many other princes of antiquity were

6. Roman general whose successful invasion of Carthage in 203 B.C.E. caused Hannibal's army to be recalled from Rome. The episode described here occurred in 206 B.C.E.

7. Fabius Maximus, not only a senator but also a high public official and general who had fought against Hannibal in Italy; Locrians, people of Sicily defeated by Scipio in 205 B.C.E. and placed under Q. Pleminius.

sent to be reared by Chiron the centaur, who trained them in his discipline.[8] Having a teacher who is half man and half beast can only mean that a prince must know how to use both these two natures, and that one without the other has no lasting effect.

Since a prince must know how to use the character of beasts, he should pick for imitation the fox and the lion. As the lion cannot protect himself from traps, and the fox cannot defend himself from wolves, you have to be a fox in order to be wary of traps, and a lion to overawe the wolves. Those who try to live by the lion alone are badly mistaken. Thus a prudent prince cannot and should not keep his word when to do so would go against his interest, or when the reasons that made him pledge it no longer apply. Doubtless if all men were good, this rule would be bad; but since they are a sad lot, and keep no faith with you, you in your turn are under no obligation to keep it with them.

15   Besides, a prince will never lack for legitimate excuses to explain away his breaches of faith. Modern history will furnish innumerable examples of this behavior, showing how many treaties and promises have been made null and void by the faithlessness of princes, and how the man succeeded best who knew best how to play the fox. But it is a necessary part of this nature that you must conceal it carefully; you must be a great liar and hypocrite. Men are so simple of mind, and so much dominated by their immediate needs, that a deceitful man will always find plenty who are ready to be deceived. One of many recent examples calls for mention. Alexander VI[9] never did anything else, never had another thought, except to deceive men, and he always found fresh material to work on. Never was there a man more convincing in his assertions, who sealed his promises with more solemn oaths, and who observed them less. Yet his deceptions were always successful, because he knew exactly how to manage this sort of business.

In actual fact, a prince may not have all the admirable qualities we listed, but it is very necessary that he should seem to have them. Indeed, I will venture to say that when you have them and exercise them all the time, they are harmful to you; when you just seem to have them, they are useful. It is good to appear merciful, truthful, humane, sincere, and religious; it is good to be so in reality. But you must keep your mind so disposed that, in case of need, you can turn to the exact contrary. This has to be understood: a prince, and especially a new prince, cannot possibly exercise all those virtues for which men are called "good." To preserve the state, he often has to do things against his word, against charity, against humanity, against religion. Thus he has to have a mind ready to shift as the winds of fortune and the varying circumstances of life may dictate. And as I said above, he should not depart from the good if he can hold to it, but he should be ready to enter on evil if he has to.

Hence a prince should take great care never to drop a word that does not seem imbued with the five good qualities noted above; to anyone who sees or

8. Achilles, foremost among the Greek heroes in the Trojan War; Chiron, mythical half man and half horse, said to have taught the arts of war and peace, including hunting, medicine, music, and prophecy.

9. Pope from 1492 to 1503.

hears him, he should appear all compassion, all honor, all humanity, all integrity, all religion. Nothing is more necessary than to seem to have this last virtue. Men in general judge more by the sense of sight than by the sense of touch, because everyone can see but only a few can test by feeling. Everyone sees what you seem to be, few know what you really are; and those few do not dare take a stand against the general opinion, supported by the majesty of the government. In the actions of all men, and especially of princes who are not subject to a court of appeal, we must always look to the end. Let a prince, therefore, win victories and uphold his state; his methods will always be considered worthy, and everyone will praise them, because the masses are always impressed by the superficial appearance of things, and by the outcome of an enterprise. And the world consists of nothing but the masses; the few who have no influence when the many feel secure. A certain prince of our own time, whom it's just as well not to name,[10] preaches nothing but peace and mutual trust, yet he is the determined enemy of both; and if on several different occasions he had observed either, he would have lost both his reputation and his throne.

10. Probably Ferdinand of Spain, then allied with the house of Medici.

MLA CITATION

Machiavelli, Niccolò. "The Morals of the Prince." 1513. *The Norton Reader: An Anthology of Nonfiction.* Ed. Melissa A. Goldthwaite et al. 14th ed. New York: Norton, 2016. 763–69. Print.

QUESTIONS

1. This selection contains four sections of *The Prince*: "On the Reasons Why Men Are Praised or Blamed—Especially Princes"; "On Liberality and Stinginess"; "On Cruelty and Clemency: Whether It Is Better to Be Loved or Feared"; and "The Way Princes Should Keep Their Word." How, in each section, does Niccolò Machiavelli contrast the real and the ideal, what he calls "the way we really live and the way we ought to live" (paragraph 1)? Mark some of the sentences in which he expresses these contrasts.

2. Rewrite some of Machiavelli's advice to princes less forcibly and shockingly, and more palatably. For example, "Any man who tries to be good all the time is bound to come to ruin among the great number who are not good" (paragraph 1) might be rewritten as "Good men are often taken advantage of and harmed by men who are not good."

3. Describe Machiavelli's view of human nature. How do his views of government follow from it?

4. Machiavelli might be described as a sixteenth-century spin doctor teaching a ruler how to package himself. Adapt his advice to a current figure in national, state, or local politics, and write about that figure in a brief essay.

HENRY DAVID THOREAU *The Battle of the Ants*

O NE DAY WHEN I went out to my wood-pile, or rather my pile of stumps, I observed two large ants, the one red, the other much larger, nearly half an inch long, and black, fiercely contending with one another. Having once got hold they never let go, but struggled and wrestled and rolled on the chips incessantly. Looking farther, I was surprised to find that the chips were covered with such combatants, that it was not a *duellum*, but a *bellum*, a war between two races of ants, the red always pitted against the black, and frequently two red ones to one black. The legions of these Myrmidons[1] covered all the hills and vales in my wood-yard, and the ground was already strewn with the dead and dying, both red and black. It was the only battle which I have ever witnessed, the only battle-field I ever trod while the battle was raging; internecine war; the red republicans on the one hand, and the black imperialists on the other. On every side they were engaged in deadly combat, yet without any noise that I could hear, and human soldiers never fought so resolutely. I watched a couple that were fast locked in each other's embraces, in a little sunny valley amid the chips, now at noonday prepared to fight till the sun went down, or life went out. The smaller red champion had fastened himself like a vice to his adversary's front, and through all the tumblings on that field never for an instant ceased to gnaw at one of his feelers near the root, having already caused the other to go by the board; while the stronger black one dashed him from side to side, and, as I saw on looking nearer, had already divested him of several of his members. They fought with more pertinacity than bulldogs. Neither manifested the least disposition to retreat. It was evident that their battle-cry was "Conquer or die." In the meanwhile there came along a single red ant on the hillside of this valley, evidently full of excitement, who either had despatched his foe, or had not yet taken part in the battle; probably the latter, for he had lost none of his limbs; whose mother had charged him to return with his shield or upon it. Or perchance he was some Achilles, who had nourished his wrath apart, and had now come to avenge or rescue his Patroclus.[2] He saw this unequal combat from afar—for the blacks were nearly twice the size of the red—he drew near with rapid pace till he stood on his guard within half an inch of the combatants; then, watching his opportunity, he sprang upon the black warrior, and commenced his operations near the root of his right fore leg, leaving the foe to select among his own members; and so there were three united for life, as if a new kind of attraction had been invented which put all other locks and cements to shame. I should not

---

From Henry David Thoreau's book, Walden *(1854), an account of his life in a small cabin on Walden Pond, outside the village of Concord, Massachusetts.*

1. Achilles' powerful soldiers in Homer's *Iliad*.
2. Greek warrior and friend whose death Achilles avenges in the *Iliad*. Achilles had previously refused to fight after a falling-out with Agamemnon, the leader of the Greek army.

have wondered by this time to find that they had their respective musical bands stationed on some eminent chip, and playing their national airs the while, to excite the slow and cheer the dying combatants. I was myself excited somewhat even as if they had been men. The more you think of it, the less the difference. And certainly there is not the fight recorded in Concord history, at least, if in the history of America, that will bear a moment's comparison with this, whether for the numbers engaged in it, or for the patriotism and heroism displayed. For numbers and for carnage it was an Austerlitz or Dresden.[3] Concord Fight! Two killed on the patriots' side, and Luther Blanchard wounded! Why here every ant was a Buttrick—"Fire! for God's sake fire!"—and thousands shared the fate of Davis and Hosmer. There was not one hireling there. I have no doubt that it was a principle they fought for, as much as our ancestors, and not to avoid a three-penny tax on their tea; and the results of this battle will be as important and memorable to those whom it concerns as those of the battle of Bunker Hill, at least.

I took up the chip on which the three I have particularly described were struggling, carried into my house, and placed it under a tumbler on my windowsill, in order to see the issue. Holding a microscope to the first-mentioned red ant, I saw that, though he was assiduously gnawing at the near fore leg of his enemy, having severed his remaining feeler, his own breast was all torn away, exposing what vitals he had there to the jaws of the black warrior, whose breastplate was apparently too thick for him to pierce; and the dark carbuncles of the sufferer's eyes shone with ferocity such as war only could excite. They struggled half an hour longer under the tumbler, and when I looked again the black soldier had severed the heads of his foes from their bodies, and the still living heads were hanging on either side of him like ghastly trophies at his saddle-bow, still apparently as firmly fastened as ever, and he was endeavoring with feeble struggles, being without feelers, and with only the remnant of a leg, and I know not how many other wounds, to divest himself of them; which at length, after half an hour more, he accomplished. I raised the glass, and he went off over the window-sill in that crippled state. Whether he finally survived that combat, and spent the remainder of his days in some Hôtel des Invalides,[4] I do not know; but I thought that his industry would not be worth much thereafter. I never learned which party was victorious, nor the cause of the war, but I felt for the rest of that day as if I had my feelings excited and harrowed by witnessing the struggle, the ferocity and carnage, of a human battle before my door.

Kirby and Spence tell us that the battles of ants have long been celebrated and the date of them recorded, though they say that Huber[5] is the only modern author who appears to have witnessed them. "Aeneas Sylvius," say they, "after

---

3. Austerlitz and Dresden were bloody Napoleonic victories. The battles at Lexington and Concord, opening the American Revolution, took place on April 19, 1775; the names that follow are those of men who took part, and the words "Fire! for God's sake fire!" were those that, by popular account, started the war.

4. French hospital for wounded soldiers and sailors.

5. Kirby and Spence, nineteenth-century American entomologists; François Huber (1750–1831), a great Swiss entomologist.

giving a very circumstantial account of one contested with great obstinacy by a great and small species on the trunk of a pear tree," adds that "'this action was fought in the pontificate of Eugenius the Fourth, in the presence of Nicholas Pistoriensis, an eminent lawyer, who related the whole history of the battle with the greatest fidelity.' A similar engagement between great and small ants is recorded by Olaus Magnus, in which the small ones, being victorious, are said to have buried the bodies of their own soldiers, but left those of their giant enemies a prey to the birds. This event happened previous to the expulsion of the tyrant Christiern the Second from Sweden." The battle which I witnessed took place in the Presidency of Polk, five years before the passage of Webster's Fugitive-Slave Bill.[6]

6. Passed in 1851.

MLA CITATION

Thoreau, Henry David. "The Battle of the Ants." 1854. *The Norton Reader: An Anthology of Nonfiction.* Ed. Melissa A. Goldthwaite et al. 14th ed. New York: Norton, 2016. 770–72. Print.

QUESTIONS

1. Henry David Thoreau uses the Latin word *bellum* to describe the battle of the ants and follows it with a reference to the Myrmidons, the soldiers of Achilles in Homer's *Iliad*. Locate additional examples of this kind of allusion. How does it work? Why does Thoreau compare the ants to Greek soldiers?

2. Ordinarily we speak of accounts of natural events as "natural history" and accounts of human events as "history." How does Thoreau, in this selection, blur the distinction? For what purpose?

3. Look up a description of the behavior of ants in a book by one of the entomologists Thoreau refers to or in another scientific text. Compare the scientist's style with Thoreau's. Take another event in nature and describe it twice, once in scientific and once in allusive language. Or write an essay in which you describe and analyze the differences between the scientist's style and Thoreau's.

THOMAS JEFFERSON AND OTHERS *The Declaration of Independence*

ORIGINAL DRAFT

A Declaration of the Representatives of the UNITED STATES OF AMERICA, in General Congress Assembled.

WHEN IN THE COURSE OF HUMAN EVENTS it becomes necessary for a people to advance from that subordination in which they have hitherto remained, & to assume among the powers of the earth the equal & independant station to which the laws of nature & of nature's god entitle them, a decent respect to the opinions of mankind requires that they should declare the causes which impel them to the change.

We hold these truths to be sacred & undeniable; that all men are created equal & independant, that from that equal creation they derive rights inherent & inalienable, among which are the preservation of life, & liberty, & the spirit of happiness; that to secure these ends, governments are instituted among men, deriving their just powers from the consent of the governed; that whenever any form of government shall become destructive of these ends, it is the right of the people to alter or to abolish it, & to institute new government, laying it's foundation on such principles & organising its powers in such form, as to them shall seem most likely to effect their safety & happiness. Prudence indeed will dictate that governments long established should not be changed for light & transient causes: and accordingly all experience hath shewn that mankind are more disposed to suffer while evils are sufferable, than to right themselves by abolishing the forms to which they are accustomed. but when a long train of abuses & usurpations, begun at a distinguished period, & pursuing invariably the same object, evinces a design to subject them to arbitrary power, it is their right, it is their duty, to throw off such government & to provide new guards for their future security. such has been the patient sufferance of these colonies; & such is now the necessity which constrains them to expunge their former systems of government. The history of his present majesty, is a history of unremitting injuries and usurpations, among which no one fact stands single or solitary to contradict the uniform tenor of the rest, all of which have in direct object the establishment of an absolute tyranny over these states. to prove this, let facts be submitted to a candid world, for the truth of which we pledge a faith yet unsullied by falsehood.

On June 11, 1776, Thomas Jefferson was elected by the Second Continental Congress to join John Adams, Benjamin Franklin, Roger Sherman, and Robert Livingston in drafting a declaration of independence. The draft presented to Congress on June 28 was primarily the work of Jefferson. The final version resulted from revisions made to Jefferson's original draft by members of the committee, including Adams and Franklin, and by members of the Continental Congress.

he has refused his assent to laws the most wholesome and necessary for the public good:

he has forbidden his governors to pass laws of immediate & pressing importance, unless suspended in their operation till his assent should be obtained; and when so suspended, he has neglected utterly to attend to them.

5   he has refused to pass other laws for the accommodation of large districts of people unless those people would relinquish the right of representation, a right inestimable to them, & formidable to tyrants alone:[1]

he has dissolved Representative houses repeatedly & continually, for opposing with manly firmness his invasions on the rights of the people:

he has refused for a long space of time to cause others to be elected, whereby the legislative powers, incapable of annihilation, have returned to the people at large for their exercise, the state remaining in the mean time exposed to all the dangers of invasion from without, &, convulsions within:

he has suffered the administration of justice totally to cease in some of these colonies, refusing his assent to laws for establishing judiciary powers:

he has made our judges dependant on his will alone, for the tenure of their offices, and amount of their salaries:

10   he has erected a multitude of new offices by a self-assumed power, & sent hither swarms of officers to harrass our people & eat out their substance: he has kept among us in times of peace standing armies & ships of war:

he has affected[2] to render the military, independent of & superior to the civil power:

he has combined with others to subject us to a jurisdiction foreign to our constitutions and unacknowledged by our laws; giving his assent to their pretended acts of legislation, for quartering large bodies of armed troops among us;

for protecting them by a mock-trial from punishment for any murders they should commit on the inhabitants of these states;

for cutting off our trade with all parts of the world;

for imposing taxes on us without our consent;

for depriving us of the benefits of trial by jury

he has endeavored to prevent the population of these states; for that purpose obstructing the laws for naturalization of foreigners; refusing to pass others to encourage their migrations hither; & raising the conditions of new appropriations of lands;

for transporting us beyond seas to be tried for pretended offences:

for taking away our charters & altering fundamentally the forms of our governments;

for suspending our own legislatures & declaring themselves invested with power to legislate for us in all cases whatsoever:

he has abdicated government here, withdrawing his governors, & declaring us out of his allegiance & protection:

15   he has plundered our seas, ravaged our coasts, burnt our towns & destroyed the lives of our people:

---

1. At this point in the manuscript a strip containing the following clause is inserted: "He called together legislative bodies at places unusual, unco[mfortable, & distant from] the depository of their public records for the sole purpose of fatiguing [them into compliance] with his measures." Missing parts in the Library of Congress text are supplied from the copy made by Jefferson for George Wythe. This copy is in the New York Public Library. The fact that this passage was omitted from John Adams's transcript suggests that it was not a part of Jefferson's original rough draft.

2. Tried.

he is at this time transporting large armies of foreign mercenaries to compleat the works of death, desolation & tyranny, already begun with circumstances of cruelty & perfidy unworthy the head of a civilized nation:

he has endeavored to bring on the inhabitants of our frontiers the merciless Indian savages, whose known rule of warfare is an undistinguished destruction of all ages, sexes, & conditions of existence:

he has incited treasonable insurrections of our fellow-citizens, with the allurements of forfeiture & confiscation of our property:

he has waged cruel war against human nature itself, violating it's most sacred rights of life & liberty in the persons of a distant people who never offended him, captivating & carrying them into slavery in another hemisphere, or to incur miserable death in their transportation thither. this piratical warfare, the opprobrium of *infidel* powers, is the warfare of the CHRISTIAN king of Great Britain. determined to keep open a market where MEN should be bought & sold; he has prostituted his negative for suppressing every legislative attempt to prohibit or to restrain this execrable commerce: and that this assemblage of horrors might want no fact of distinguished die, he is now exciting those very people to rise in arms among us, and to purchase that liberty of which *he* has deprived them, by murdering the people upon whom *he* also obtruded them; thus paying off former crimes committed against the *liberties* of one people, with crimes which he urges them to commit against the *lives* of another.

in every stage of these oppressions we have petitioned for redress in the most humble terms; our repeated petitions have been answered by repeated injury. a prince whose character is thus marked by every act which may define a tyrant, is unfit to be the ruler of a people who mean to be free. future ages will scarce believe that the hardiness of one man, adventured within the short compass of twelve years only, on so many acts of tyranny without a mask, over a people fostered & fixed in principles of liberty.

Nor have we been wanting in attentions to our British brethren. we have warned them from time to time of attempts by their legislature to extend a jurisdiction over these our states. we have reminded them of the circumstances of our emigration & settlement here, no one of which could warrant so strange a pretension: that these were effected at the expence of our own blood & treasure, unassisted by the wealth or the strength of Great Britain: that in constituting indeed our several forms of government, we had adopted one common king, thereby laying a foundation for perpetual league & amity with them; but that submission to their [Parliament, was no Part of our Constitution, nor ever in Idea, if History may be][3] credited: and we appealed to their native justice & magnanimity, as to the ties of our common kindred to disavow these usurpations which were likely to interrupt our correspondence & connection. they too have been deaf to the voice of justice & of consanguinity, & when occasions have been given them, by the regular course of their laws, of removing from their councils the disturbers of our harmony, they have by their free election reestablished them in power. at this very time too they are permitting their chief magistrate to send over not only soldiers of our common blood, but Scotch &

20

---

3. Passage illegible in the original; supplied here from John Adams's transcription.

foreign mercenaries to invade & deluge us in blood. these facts have given the last stab to agonizing affection, and manly spirit bids us to renounce for ever these unfeeling brethren. we must endeavor to forget our former love for them, and to hold them as we hold the rest of mankind, enemies in war, in peace friends. we might have been a free & a great people together; but a communication of grandeur & of freedom it seems is below their dignity. be it so, since they will have it: the road to glory & happiness is open to us too; we will climb it in a separate state, and acquiesce in the necessity which pronounces our everlasting Adieu!

We therefore the representatives of the United States of America in General Congress assembled do, in the name & by authority of the good people of these states, reject and renounce all allegiance & subjection to the kings of Great Britain & all others who may hereafter claim by, through, or under them; we utterly dissolve & break off all political connection which may have heretofore subsisted between us & the people or parliament of Great Britain; and finally we do assert and declare these colonies to be free and independant states, and that as free & independant states they shall hereafter have power to levy war, conclude peace, contract alliances, establish commerce, & to do all other acts and things which independant states may of right do. And for the support of this declaration we mutually pledge to each other our lives, our fortunes, & our sacred honour.

FINAL DRAFT

In Congress, July 4, 1776
The unanimous Declaration of the
Thirteen United States of America

WHEN IN THE COURSE OF HUMAN EVENTS it becomes necessary for one people to dissolve the political bands which have connected them with another, and to assume among the powers of the earth, the separate and equal station to which the Laws of Nature and of Nature's God entitle them, a decent respect to the opinions of mankind requires that they should declare the causes which impel them to the separation.

We hold these truths to be self-evident, that all men are created equal, that they are endowed by their Creator with certain unalienable Rights, that among these are Life, Liberty and the pursuit of Happiness. That to secure these rights, Governments are instituted among Men, deriving their just powers from the consent of the governed. That whenever any Form of Government becomes destructive of these ends, it is the Right of the People to alter or to abolish it, and to institute new Government, laying its foundation on such principles and organizing its powers in such form, as to them shall seem most likely to effect their Safety and Happiness. Prudence, indeed, will dictate that Governments long established should not be changed for light and transient causes; and accordingly all experience hath shewn that mankind are more disposed to suffer, while evils are sufferable, than to right themselves by abolishing the forms to which they are accustomed. But when a long train of abuses and usurpations, pursuing invariably the same Object evinces a design to reduce them under absolute Despotism, it is their right, it is their duty, to throw off such Government, and to provide new Guards for their future security. Such has been the patient sufferance of these Colonies; and such is now the necessity which constrains them to alter their former Systems of Government. The history of the present King of Great Britain is a history of repeated injuries and usurpations, all having in direct object the establishment of an absolute Tyranny over these States. To prove this, let Facts be submitted to a candid world.

He has refused his Assent to Laws, the most wholesome and necessary for the public good.

He has forbidden his Government to pass laws of immediate and pressing importance, unless suspended in their operation till his Assent should be obtained; and when so suspended, he has utterly neglected to attend to them.

He has refused to pass other Laws for the accommodation of large districts 5
of people, unless those people would relinquish the right of Representation in the Legislature, a right inestimable to them and formidable to tyrants only.

He has called together legislative bodies at places unusual, uncomfortable, and distant from the depository of their Public Records, for the sole purpose of fatiguing them into compliance with his measures.

He has dissolved Representative Houses repeatedly, for opposing with manly firmness his invasions on the rights of the people.

He has refused for a long time, after such dissolutions, to cause others to be elected; whereby the Legislative Powers, incapable of Annihilation, have returned to the People at large for their exercise; the State remaining in the mean time exposed to all the dangers of invasion from without, and convulsions within.

He has endeavored to prevent the population of these States; for that purpose obstructing the Laws for Naturalization of Foreigners; refusing to pass others to encourage their migration hither, and raising the conditions of new Appropriations of Lands.

He has obstructed the Administration of Justice, by refusing his Assent to 10
Laws for establishing Judiciary Powers.

He has made Judges dependent on his Will alone, for the tenure of their offices, and the amount and payment of their salaries.

He has erected a multitude of New Offices, and sent hither swarms of Officers to harass our people, and eat out their substance.

He has kept among us, in times of peace, Standing Armies without the Consent of our legislatures.

He has affected to render the Military independent of and superior to the Civil Power.

He has combined with others to subject us to a jurisdiction foreign to our 15
constitution, and unacknowledged by our laws; giving his Assent to their Acts of pretended Legislation: For quartering large bodies of armed troops among us: For protecting them, by a mock Trial, from punishment for any Murders

which they should commit on the Inhabitants of these States: For cutting off our Trade with all parts of the world: For imposing Taxes on us without our Consent: For depriving us in many cases, of the benefits of Trial by Jury: For transporting us beyond Seas to be tried for pretended offenses: For abolishing the free System of English Laws in a neighboring Province, establishing therein an Arbitrary government, and enlarging its Boundaries so as to render it at once an example and fit instrument for introducing the same absolute rule into these Colonies: For taking away our Charters, abolishing our most valuable Laws, and altering fundamentally the Forms of our Governments: For suspending our own Legislatures, and declaring themselves invested with power to legislate for us in all cases whatsoever.

He has abdicated Government here, by declaring us out of his Protection and waging War against us.

He has plundered our seas, ravaged our Coasts, burnt our towns, and destroyed the lives of our people.

He is at this time transporting large Armies of foreign Mercenaries to complete the works of death, desolation and tyranny, already begun with circumstances of Cruelty & Perfidy scarcely paralleled in the most barbarous ages, and totally unworthy the Head of a civilized nation.

He has constrained our fellow Citizens taken Captive on the high Seas to bear Arms against their Country, to become the executioners of their friends and Brethren, or to fall themselves by their Hands.

20 He has excited domestic insurrections amongst us, and has endeavored to bring on the inhabitants of our frontiers, the merciless Indian Savages, whose known rule of warfare, is an undistinguished destruction of all ages, sexes, and conditions.

In every stage of these Oppressions We have Petitioned for Redress in the most humble terms: Our repeated Petitions have been answered only by repeated injury. A Prince, whose character is thus marked by every act which may define a Tyrant, is unfit to be the ruler of a free people.

Nor have We been wanting in attention to our British brethren. We have warned them from time to time of attempts by their legislature to extend an unwarrantable jurisdiction over us. We have reminded them of the circumstances of our emigration and settlement here. We have appealed to their native justice and magnanimity, and we have conjured them by the ties of our common kindred to disavow these usurpations, which would inevitably interrupt our connections and correspondence. They too have been deaf to the voice of justice and of consanguinity. We must, therefore, acquiesce in the necessity, which denounces our Separation, and hold them, as we hold the rest of mankind, Enemies in War, in Peace Friends.

We, THEREFORE the Representatives of the UNITED STATES OF AMERICA, in General Congress, Assembled, appealing to the Supreme Judge of the world for the rectitude of our intentions, do, in the Name, and by Authority of the good People of these Colonies, solemnly publish and declare, That these United Colonies are, and of Right ought to be FREE AND INDEPENDENT STATES; that they are Absolved from all Allegiance to the British Crown, and that all political connection between them and the State of Great Britain, is and ought to be totally dissolved; and that as Free and Independent States, they have full Power to levy War, conclude Peace, contract Alliances, establish Commerce, and to do all other Acts and Things which Independent States may of right do. And for the support of this Declaration, with a firm reliance on the protection of Divine Providence, we mutually pledge to each other our Lives, our Fortunes, and our sacred Honor.

MLA CITATION

Jefferson, Thomas, and Others. "The Declaration of Independence." 1776. *The Norton Reader: An Anthology of Nonfiction*. Ed. Melissa A. Goldthwaite et al. 14th ed. New York: Norton, 2016. 773–79. Print.

QUESTIONS

1. The Declaration of Independence is an example of deductive argument: Thomas Jefferson sets up general principles, details particular instances, and then draws conclusions. In both the original and final drafts, locate the three sections of the Declaration that use deduction. Explain how they work as arguments.

2. Locate the general principles (or "truths") that Jefferson sets up in the first section of both the original and final drafts. Mark the language he uses to describe them: for example, he calls them "sacred & undeniable" in the original draft and "self-evident" (paragraph 2) in the final draft. What kinds of authority does his language appeal to in each draft? Why might he or others have revised the language?

3. Note the stylistic differences (including choices of grammar and punctuation) between the original and final drafts of the Declaration of Independence. What effect do those differences have?

4. In an essay, choose one or two significant revisions that Thomas Jefferson made between the original draft and the final draft of the Declaration, and explain why they are significant.

EDWIDGE DANTICAT *Another Country*

> The sea was walking the earth with a heavy heel. . . .
> The folks in the quarters and the people in the big
> houses further around the shore heard the big lake
> and wondered. The people felt uncomfortable but safe
> because there were the seawalls to chain the senseless
> monster in his bed. The folks let the people do the
> thinking. If the castles thought themselves secure, the
> cabins needn't worry.
>
> —ZORA NEALE HURSTON,
> *Their Eyes Were Watching God*

I N ZORA NEALE HURSTON'S VISIONARY 1937 NOVEL, Janie Crawford and her boyfriend, Tea Cake, a day laborer, refuse to evacuate their small, unsteady house before a deadly hurricane batters the Florida Everglades, near where I currently live.

"Everybody was talking about it that night. But nobody was worried," wrote Hurston. "You couldn't have a hurricane when you're making seven and eight dollars a day."

It turns out you could have a hurricane, and other disasters too, even if you're making considerably less than that. And if you manage to survive that hurricane, you might end up with nothing at all. No home. No food or water. No medical care for your sick and wounded. Not even body bags or coffins for your dead.

Americans have experienced this scenario before. Not just in prophetic literature or apocalyptic blockbuster movies, but through the very real natural disasters that have plagued other countries. Catastrophes that are eventually reduced to single, shorthand images that, if necessary, can later be evoked. Take, for example, visions of skyscraper-size waves washing away entire crowds in Thailand and other Asian countries devastated by the December 2004 tsunamis. Or remember Sophia Pedro, the Mozambican woman who in March 2000 was plucked by a South African military helicopter from the tree where she had clung for three days and then given birth as the floodwaters swirled beneath her? And let's not forget Haiti's September 2004 encounter with Tropical Storm Jeanne, which left three thousand people dead and a quarter million homeless. In that disaster, patients drowned in hospital beds. Children watched as parents were washed away. Survivors sought shelter in trees and on rooftops while corpses floated in the muddy, contaminated waters around them.

Originally published in The Progressive *(2005), "a monthly magazine of investigative reporting, political commentary, cultural coverage, activism, interviews, poetry, and humor"; later included, with additions, in Edwidge Danticat's essay collection,* Create Dangerously: The Immigrant Artist at Work *(2010).*

As I watched all this unfold again on my television set, this time in the   5
streets of New Orleans in the summer of 2005, I couldn't help but think of the
Bush administration's initial response to the Haitian victims of Tropical Storm
Jeanne the year before Hurricane Katrina struck New Orleans: sixty thousand
dollars in aid and the repatriation of Haitian refugees from the United States
back to the devastated region even before the waters had subsided. New Orleans'
horrific tragedy had been foreshadowed in America's so-called backyard, and
the initial response had been: "Po' man ain't got no business at de show," as Zora
Neale Hurston's Tea Cake might have put it.

In the weeks that followed Hurricane Katrina's landing, I, immigrant writer
and southern coastal city resident, heard many Americans of all geographical
persuasions, pundits and citizens alike, make the case that the types of horrors that plagued Katrina-ravaged New Orleans—the desperation of ordinary
citizens, some of whom resorted to raiding stores to feed themselves and their
families; the forgotten public hospitals where nurses pumped oxygen into dying
patients by hand; the makeshift triage wards on bridges and airports; the roam-
ing armed gangs—are more in line with our expectations of the "third world"
than the first.

Turning to the Kenyan CNN correspondent Jeff Koinange on *American
Morning* a week after Hurricane Katrina struck New Orleans, the anchor-
woman Soledad O'Brien said. "You know, to some degree, when you were
watching the original pictures . . . if you turned the sound down on your television, if you didn't know where you were, you might think it was Haiti or maybe
one of those African countries, many of which you cover."

"Watching helpless New Orleans suffering day by day left people everywhere stunned and angry and in ever greater pain," echoed *Time* magazine's
Nancy Gibbs. "These things happened in Haiti, they said, but not here."

Not to be outdone, even the Canadians got in on the act. Chiding her fel-
low citizens for their self-righteous attitude toward American poverty, Kate
Heartfield of the *Ottawa Citizen* nevertheless added, "Ottawa is not New Orleans.
And it is definitely not Freetown or Port-au-Prince."

It's hard for those of us who are from places like Freetown or Port-au-   10
Prince, and those of us who are immigrants who still have relatives living in
places like Freetown or Port-au-Prince, not to wonder why the so-called developed world needs so desperately to distance itself from us, especially at times
when an unimaginable disaster shows exactly how much alike we are. The rest
of the world's poor do not expect much from their governments and they're usually not disappointed. The poor in the richest country in the world, however,
should not be poor at all. They should not even exist. Maybe that's why both
their leaders and a large number of their fellow citizens don't even realize that
they actually do exist.

This is not the America we know, chimed many field reporters who, haunted
by the faces and voices of the dying, the stench of bloated corpses on city streets
during the day and screams for help rising from attics at night, recorded the
early absence of first responders with both sorrow and rage. Their fury could
only magnify ours, for if they could make it to New Orleans, Mississippi, and

Alabama and give us minute-by-minute accounts of the storm and its aftermath, why couldn't the government agencies find their way there? Indeed, what these early charged news reports offered was a passport to an America where one does not always have bus fare, much less an automobile, where health insurance is as distant a dream as a college education, where poverty is a birthright, not an accident of fortune. This is the America that continues to startle, the America of the needy and never-have-enoughs, the America of the undocumented, the unemployed and underemployed, the elderly, and the infirm. An America that remains invisible until a rebellion breaks out, gunshots ring out, or a flood rages through. Perhaps this America does have more in common with the developing world than with the one it inhabits. For the poor and outcast everywhere dwell within their own country, where more often than not they must fend for themselves. That's why one can so easily become a refugee within one's own borders—because one's perceived usefulness and precarious citizenship are always in question, whether in Haiti or in that other America, the one where people have no flood insurance.

I don't know why it seems always to surprise some Americans that many of their fellow citizens are vulnerable to horrors that routinely plague much of the world's population. After all, we do share a planet whose climate is gradually being altered by unbalanced exploration and dismal environmental policies that may one day render us all, first world and third world residents alike, helpless in the face of more disasters like Tropical Storm Jeanne and Hurricane Katrina. Let us also not forget the ever-looming menace of 9/11-like terrorism, which can potentially have the same effect, landing thousands on street corners and in Astrodomes asking themselves how they came to be there.

The poor and displaced are indeed sometimes better off in places far from their impoverished homes. But in the end, must poverty also force us to live deprived of homestead, birthplace, history, memory? In the case of Hurricane Katrina, was it really a flood that washed away that nuanced privilege of deciding where one should build one's life, or was this right slowly being stripped away while we were already too horrified to watch?

One of the advantages of being an immigrant is that two very different countries are forced to merge within you. The language you were born speaking and the one you will probably die speaking have no choice but to find a common place in your brain and regularly merge there. So too with catastrophes and disasters, which inevitably force you to rethink facile allegiances.

15   Shortly after the terrorist attacks of September 11, 2001, Masood Farivar, a former Afghan mujahideen who received part of his education in a madrassa in Pakistan, wrote, "As an Afghan, I'd never carried the black, red, and green flag of my own country. Suddenly though, I wanted to feel what it was like to proudly hold a flag, wave it at passing ambulances, police cars, and fire trucks. It would be a good way to show my solidarity with Americans. It was my way of saying, we're in this together. I'm with you, I share your pain."

"I come from the so-called Third World," wrote the Chilean novelist and memoirist Isabel Allende after September 11, 2001, a day that also marked the twenty-eighth anniversary of a U.S.-sponsored coup d'ètat against her uncle, Salvador Allende. Still, she writes,

> Until only a short time ago, if someone had asked me where I'm from, I would have answered, without much thought, Nowhere; or, Latin America; or, maybe, In my heart I'm Chilean. Today, however, I say I'm an American, not simply because that's what my passport verifies, or because that word includes all of America from north to south, or because my husband, my son, my grandchildren, most of my friends, my books, and my home are in northern California; but because a terrorist attack destroyed the twin towers of the World Trade Center, and starting with that instant, many things have changed. We can't be neutral in moments of crisis. . . . I no longer feel that I am an alien in the United States.

After the horrible carnage of September 11th, hadn't the world echoed Farivar's and Allende's sentiments and also declared, through many headlines in newspapers across the globe, that we were all Americans?

At least for a while.

Among the many realities brought to light by Hurricane Katrina was that never again could we justifiably deny the existence of this country within a country, that other America, which America's immigrants and the rest of the world may know much more intimately than many Americans do, the America that is always on the brink of humanitarian and ecological disaster. No, it is not Haiti or Mozambique or Bangladesh, but it might as well be.

MLA CITATION

Danticat, Edwidge. "Another Country." 2010. *The Norton Reader: An Anthology of Nonfiction.* Ed. Melissa A. Goldthwaite et al. 14th ed. New York: Norton, 2016. 780–83. Print.

QUESTIONS

1. Throughout this essay Edwidge Danticat draws parallels between New Orleans, where Hurricane Katrina hit in 2005, and countries such as Thailand and Haiti, where similar disasters have struck. What is the point of these comparisons? What argument does Danticat make from them?

2. In paragraph 5 Danticat criticizes then U.S. president George W. Bush for initially offering "sixty thousand dollars in aid" to Haitian victims of Hurricane Jeanne. Using online resources, find out how much aid was eventually sent to Haiti and how that amount compares with aid to American victims of Hurricane Katrina.

3. Why do you think Danticat named this essay "Another Country"? Consider paragraph 11 as you formulate your answer.

4. Write an essay in which you present principles for how the federal government should respond to natural disasters. Give examples, positive and negative, from the past decade.

ELIZABETH CADY STANTON *Declaration of Sentiments and Resolutions*

W HEN, IN THE COURSE OF HUMAN EVENTS, it becomes necessary for one portion of the family of man to assume among the people of the earth a position different from that which they have hitherto occupied, but one to which the laws of nature and of nature's God entitle them, a decent respect to the opinions of mankind requires that they should declare the causes that impel them to such a course.

We hold these truths to be self-evident: that all men and women are created equal; that they are endowed by their Creator with certain inalienable rights; that among these are life, liberty, and the pursuit of happiness; that to secure these rights governments are instituted, deriving their just powers from the consent of the governed. Whenever any form of government becomes destructive of these ends, it is the right of those who suffer from it to refuse allegiance to it, and to insist upon the institution of a new government, laying its foundation on such principles, and organizing its powers in such form, as to them shall seem most likely to effect their safety and happiness. Prudence indeed, will dictate that governments long established should not be changed for light and transient causes; and accordingly all experience hath shown that mankind are more disposed to suffer, while evils are sufferable, than to right themselves by abolishing the forms to which they were accustomed. But when a long train of abuses and usurpations, pursuing invariably the same object evinces a design to reduce them under absolute despotism, it is their duty to throw off such government, and to provide new guards for their future security. Such has been the patient sufferance of the women under this government, and such is now the necessity which constrains them to demand the equal station to which they are entitled.

The history of mankind is a history of repeated injuries and usurpations on the part of man toward woman, having in direct object the establishment of an absolute tyranny over her. To prove this, let facts be submitted to a candid world.

He has never permitted her to exercise her inalienable right to the elective franchise.

5   He has compelled her to submit to laws, in the formation of which she had no voice.

He has withheld from her rights which are given to the most ignorant and degraded men—both natives and foreigners.

Written and presented at the first U.S. women's rights convention in Seneca Falls, New York, in 1848. Elizabeth Cady Stanton published this version in A History of Woman Suffrage *(1881), edited by herself, Susan B. Anthony, and Matilda Joslyn Gage, all prominent leaders of the American women's movement.*

Having deprived her of this first right of a citizen, the elective franchise, thereby leaving her without representation in the halls of legislation, he has oppressed her on all sides.

He has made her, if married, in the eye of the law, civilly dead.

He has taken from her all right in property, even to the wages she earns.

He has made her, morally, an irresponsible being, as she can commit many   10
crimes with impunity, provided they be done in the presence of her husband. In the covenant of marriage, she is compelled to promise obedience to her husband, he becoming, to all intents and purposes, her master—the law giving him power to deprive her of her liberty, and to administer chastisement.

He has so framed the laws of divorce, as to what shall be the proper causes, and in case of separation, to whom the guardianship of the children shall be given, as to be wholly regardless of the happiness of women—the law, in all cases, going upon a false supposition of the supremacy of man, and giving all power into his hands.

After depriving her of all rights as a married woman, if single, and the owner of property, he has taxed her to support a government which recognizes her only when her property can be made profitable to it.

He has monopolized nearly all the profitable employments, and from those she is permitted to follow, she receives but a scanty remuneration. He closes against her all the avenues to wealth and distinction which he considers most honorable to himself. As a teacher of theology, medicine, or law, she is not known.

He has denied her the facilities for obtaining a thorough education, all colleges being closed against her.

He allows her in Church, as well as State, but a subordinate position, claim-   15
ing Apostolic authority for her exclusion from the ministry, and, with some exceptions, from any public participation in the affairs of the Church.

He has created a false public sentiment by giving to the world a different code of morals for men and women, by which moral delinquencies which exclude women from society, are not only tolerated, but deemed of little account in man.

He has usurped the prerogative of Jehovah himself, claiming it as his right to assign for her a sphere of action, when that belongs to her conscience and to her God.

He has endeavored, in every way that he could, to destroy her confidence in her own powers, to lessen her self-respect, and to make her willing to lead a dependent and abject life.

Now, in view of this entire disfranchisement of one-half the people of this country, their social and religious degradation—in view of the unjust laws above mentioned, and because women do feel themselves aggrieved, oppressed, and fraudulently deprived of their most sacred rights, we insist that they have immediate admission to all the rights and privileges which belong to them as citizens of the United States.

In entering upon the great work before us, we anticipate no small amount   20
of misconception, misrepresentation, and ridicule; but we shall use every instrumentality within our power to effect our object. We shall employ agents, circulate

tracts, petition the State and National legislatures, and endeavor to enlist the pulpit and the press in our behalf. We hope this Convention will be followed by a series of Conventions embracing every part of the country.

MLA CITATION

Stanton, Elizabeth Cady. "Declaration of Sentiments and Resolutions." 1881. *The Norton Reader: An Anthology of Nonfiction.* Ed. Melissa A. Goldthwaite et al. 14th ed. New York: Norton, 2016. 784–86. Print.

QUESTIONS

1. Elizabeth Cady Stanton imitates both the argument and the style of the Declaration of Independence. Where does her declaration diverge from Thomas Jefferson's? For what purpose?

2. Stanton's declaration was presented at the first conference on women's rights in Seneca Falls, New York, in 1848. Using books or web resources, do research on this conference; then use your research to explain the political aims of one of the resolutions.

3. Write your own "declaration" of political, educational, or social rights, using the declarations of Jefferson and Stanton as models.

FRANCES FITZGERALD *Rewriting American History*

THOSE OF US who grew up in the fifties believed in the permanence of our American-history textbooks. To us as children, those texts were the truth of things: they were American history. It was not just that we read them before we understood that not everything that is printed is the truth, or the whole truth. It was that they, much more than other books, had the demeanor and trappings of authority. They were weighty volumes. They spoke in measured cadences: imperturbable, humorless, and as distant as Chinese emperors. Our teachers treated them with respect, and we paid them abject homage by memorizing a chapter a week. But now the textbook histories have changed, some of them to such an extent that an adult would find them unrecognizable.

One current junior-high-school American history begins with a story about a Negro cowboy called George McJunkin. It appears that when McJunkin was riding down a lonely trail in New Mexico one cold spring morning in 1925 he discovered a mound containing bones and stone implements, which scientists later proved belonged to an Indian civilization ten thousand years old. The book

From America Revised: History Schoolbooks in the Twentieth Century *(1979), Frances FitzGerald's analysis of how textbook interpretations of key moments in American history have changed over time.*

goes on to say that scientists now believe there were people in the Americas at least twenty thousand years ago. It discusses the Aztec, Mayan, and Incan civilizations and the meaning of the word "culture" before introducing the European explorers.

Another history text—this one for the fifth grade—begins with the story of how Henry B. Gonzalez, who is a member of Congress from Texas, learned about his own nationality. When he was ten years old, his teacher told him he was an American because he was born in the United States. His grandmother, however, said, "The cat was born in the oven. Does that make him bread?" After reporting that Mr. Gonzalez eventually went to college and law school, the book explains that "the melting pot idea hasn't worked out as some thought it would," and that now "some people say that the people of the United States are more like a salad bowl than a melting pot."

Poor Columbus! He is a minor character now, a walk-on in the middle of American history. Even those books that have not replaced his picture with a Mayan temple or an Iroquois mask do not credit him with discovering America— even for the Europeans. The Vikings, they say, preceded him to the New World, and after that the Europeans, having lost or forgotten their maps, simply neglected to cross the ocean again for five hundred years. Columbus is far from being the only personage to have suffered from time and revision. Captain John Smith, Daniel Boone, and Wild Bill Hickok—the great self-promoters of American history—have all but disappeared, taking with them a good deal of the romance of the American frontier. General Custer has given way to Chief Crazy Horse; General Eisenhower no longer liberates Europe single-handed; and, indeed, most generals, even to Washington and Lee, have faded away, as old soldiers do, giving place to social reformers such as William Lloyd Garrison and Jacob Riis. A number of black Americans have risen to prominence: not only George Washington Carver but Frederick Douglass and Martin Luther King, Jr. W. E. B. Du Bois now invariably accompanies Booker T. Washington. In addition, there is a mystery man called Crispus Attucks, a fugitive slave about whom nothing seems to be known for certain except that he was a victim of the Boston Massacre and thus became one of the first casualties of the American Revolution. Thaddeus Stevens[1] has been reconstructed—his character changed, as it were, from black to white, from cruel and vindictive to persistent and sincere. As for Teddy Roosevelt, he now champions the issue of conservation instead of charging up San Juan Hill. No single President really stands out as a hero, but all Presidents—except certain unmentionables in the second half of the nineteenth century—seem to have done as well as could be expected, given difficult circumstances.

Of course, when one thinks about it, it is hardly surprising that modern scholarship and modern perspectives have found their way into children's books. Yet the changes remain shocking. Those who in the sixties complained of the bland optimism, the chauvinism, and the materialism of their old civics text

5

---

1. Congressman (1792–1868) who urged Lincoln to emancipate the slaves during the Civil War and advocated strict federal control of the South after the war.

did so in the belief that, for all their protests, the texts would never change. The thought must have had something reassuring about it, for that generation never noticed when its complaints began to take effect and the songs about radioactive rainfall and houses made of ticky-tacky began to appear in the textbooks. But this is what happened.

The history texts now hint at a certain level of unpleasantness in American history. Several books, for instance, tell the story of Ishi, the last "wild" Indian in the continental United States, who, captured in 1911 after the massacre of his tribe, spent the final four and a half years of his life in the University of California's museum of anthropology, in San Francisco. At least three books show the same stunning picture of the breaker boys, the child coal miners of Pennsylvania—ancient children with deformed bodies and blackened faces who stare stupidly out from the entrance to a mine. One book quotes a soldier on the use of torture in the American campaign to pacify the Philippines at the beginning of the century. A number of books say that during the American Revolution the patriots tarred and feathered those who did not support them, and drove many of the loyalists from the country. Almost all the present-day history books note that the United States interned Japanese-Americans in detention camps during the Second World War.

Ideologically speaking, the histories of the fifties were implacable, seamless. Inside their covers, America was perfect: the greatest nation in the world, and the embodiment of democracy, freedom, and technological progress. For them, the country never changed in any important way: its values and its political institutions remained constant from the time of the American Revolution. To my generation—the children of the fifties—these texts appeared permanent just because they were so self-contained. Their orthodoxy, it seemed, left no handholds for attack, no lodging for decay. Who, after all, would dispute the wonders of technology or the superiority of the English colonists over the Spanish? Who would find fault with the pastorale of the West or the Old South? Who would question the anti-Communist crusade? There was, it seemed, no point in comparing these visions with reality, since they were the public truth and were thus quite irrelevant to what existed and to what anyone privately believed. They were—or so it seemed—the permanent expression of mass culture in America.

But now the texts have changed, and with them the country that American children are growing up into. The society that was once uniform is now a patchwork of rich and poor, old and young, men and women, blacks, whites, Hispanics, and Indians. The system that ran so smoothly by means of the Constitution under the guidance of benevolent conductor Presidents is now a rattletrap affair. The past is no highway to the present; it is a collection of issues and events that do not fit together and that lead in no single direction. The word "progress" has been replaced by the word "change": children, the modern texts insist, should learn history so that they can adapt to the rapid changes taking place around them. History is proceeding in spite of us. The present, which was once portrayed in the concluding chapters as a peaceful haven of scientific advances and Presidential inaugurations, is now a tangle of problems: race problems, urban problems, foreign-policy problems, problems of pollution, poverty, energy depletion, youthful rebellion, assassination, and drugs. Some books illustrate these problems dramatically. One, for instance, contains a picture of a doll half buried in a mass of untreated sewage; the caption reads, "Are we in danger of being overwhelmed by the products of our society and wastage created by their production? Would you agree with this photographer's interpretation?" Two books show the same picture of an old black woman sitting in a straight chair in a dingy room, her hands folded in graceful resignation; the surrounding text discusses the problems faced by the urban poor and by the aged who depend on Social Security. Other books present current problems less starkly. One of the texts concludes sagely:

> Problems are part of life. Nations face them, just as people face them, and try to solve them. And today's Americans have one great advantage over past generations. Never before have Americans been so well equipped to solve their problems. They have today the means to conquer poverty, disease, and ignorance. The technetronic age has put that power into their hands.

Such passages have a familiar ring. Amid all the problems, the deus ex machina[2] of science still dodders around in the gloaming of pious hope.

Even more surprising than the emergence of problems is the discovery that the great unity of the texts has broken. Whereas in the fifties all texts represented the same political view, current texts follow no pattern of orthodoxy. Some books, for instance, portray civil-rights legislation as a series of actions taken by a wise, paternal government; others convey some suggestion of the social upheaval involved and make mention of such people as Stokely Carmichael and Malcolm X.[3] In some books, the Cold War has ended; in others, it continues, with Communism threatening the free nations of the earth.

The political diversity in the books is matched by a diversity of pedagogical approach. In addition to the traditional narrative histories, with their endless streams of facts, there are so-called "discovery," or "inquiry," texts, which deal with a limited number of specific issues in American history. These texts do not pretend to cover the past; they focus on particular topics, such as "stratification in Colonial society" or "slavery and the American Revolution," and illustrate them with documents from primary and secondary sources. The chapters in these books amount to something like case studies, in that they include testimony from people with different perspectives or conflicting views on a single subject. In addition, the chapters provide background information, explanatory notes, and a series of questions for the student. The questions are the

10

2. God from a machine. A reference to early plays in which a god, lowered to the stage by mechanical means, solved the drama's problems; thus, an artificial solution to a difficulty.

3. Carmichael (1941–1998) and Malcolm X (1925–1965), radical black leaders of the 1960s.

heart of the matter, for when they are carefully selected they force students to think much as historians think: to define the point of view of the speaker, analyze the ideas presented, question the relationship between events, and so on. One text, for example, quotes Washington, Jefferson, and John Adams on the question of foreign alliances and then asks, "What did John Adams assume that the international situation would be after the American Revolution? What did Washington's attitude toward the French alliance seem to be? How do you account for his attitude?" Finally, it asks, "Should a nation adopt a policy toward alliances and cling to it consistently, or should it vary its policies toward other countries as circumstances change?" In these books, history is clearly not a list of agreed-upon facts or a sermon on politics but a babble of voices and a welter of events which must be ordered by the historian.

In matters of pedagogy, as in matters of politics, there are not two sharply differentiated categories of books; rather, there is a spectrum. Politically, the books run from moderate left to moderate right; pedagogically, they run from the traditional history sermons, through a middle ground of narrative texts with inquiry-style questions and of inquiry texts with long stretches of narrative, to the most rigorous of case-study books. What is common to the current texts— and makes all of them different from those of the fifties—is their engagement with the social sciences. In eighth-grade histories, the "concepts" of social sciences make fleeting appearances. But these "concepts" are the very foundation stones of various elementary-school social-studies series. The 1970 Harcourt Brace Jovanovich[4] series, for example, boasts in its preface of "a horizontal base or ordering of conceptual schemes" to match its "vertical arm of behavioral themes." What this means is not entirely clear, but the books do proceed from easy questions to hard ones, such as—in the sixth-grade book—"How was interaction between merchants and citizens different in the Athenian and Spartan social systems?" Virtually all the American-history texts for older children include discussions of "role," "status," and "culture." Some of them stage debates between eminent social scientists in roped-off sections of the text; some include essays on economics or sociology; some contain pictures and short biographies of social scientists of both sexes and of diverse races. Many books seem to accord social scientists a higher status than American Presidents.

Quite as striking as these political and pedagogical alterations is the change in the physical appearance of the texts. The schoolbooks of the fifties showed some effort in the matter of design: they had maps, charts, cartoons, photographs, and an occasional four-color picture to break up the columns of print. But beside the current texts they look as naïve as Soviet fashion magazines. The print in the fifties books is heavy and far too black, the colors muddy. The photographs are conventional news shots—portraits of Presidents in three-quarters profile, posed "action" shots of soldiers. The other illustrations tend to be Socialist-realist-style[5] drawings (there are a lot of hefty farmers with hoes in

4. Major textbook publisher.

5. Style of art originating in the Soviet Union that glorifies the communal labor of farmers and industrial workers in works of posterlike simplicity.

the Colonial-period chapters) or incredibly vulgar made-for-children paintings of patriotic events. One painting shows Columbus standing in full court dress on a beach in the New World from a perspective that could have belonged only to the Arawaks.[6] By contrast, the current texts are paragons of sophisticated modern design. They look not like *People* or *Family Circle* but, rather, like *Architectural Digest* or *Vogue*. . . . The amount of space given to illustrations is far greater than it was in the fifties; in fact, in certain "slow-learner" books the pictures far outweigh the text in importance. However, the illustrations have a much greater historical value. Instead of made-up paintings or anachronistic sketches, there are cartoons, photographs, and paintings drawn from the periods being treated. The chapters on the Colonial period will show, for instance, a ship's carved prow, a Revere bowl, a Copley painting[7]—a whole gallery of Early Americana. The nineteenth century is illustrated with nineteenth-century cartoons and photographs—and the photographs are all of high artistic quality. As for the twentieth-century chapters, they are adorned with the contents of a modern-art museum.

The use of all this art and high-quality design contains some irony. The nineteenth-century photographs of child laborers or urban slum apartments are so beautiful that they transcend their subjects. To look at them, or at the Victor Gatto painting of the Triangle shirtwaist-factory fire,[8] is to see not misery or ugliness but an art object. In the modern chapters, the contrast between style and content is just as great: the color photographs of junk yards or polluted rivers look as enticing as *Gourmet's* photographs of food. The book that is perhaps the most stark in its description of modern problems illustrates the horrors of nuclear testing with a pretty Ben Shahn picture of the Bikini explosion,[9] and the potential for global ecological disaster with a color photograph of the planet swirling its mantle of white clouds. Whereas in the nineteen-fifties the texts were childish in the sense that they were naïve and clumsy, they are now childish in the sense that they are polymorphous-perverse. American history is not dull any longer; it is a sensuous experience.

The surprise that adults feel in seeing the changes in history texts must come from the lingering hope that there is, somewhere out there, an objective truth. The hope is, of course, foolish. All of us children of the twentieth century know, or should know, that there are no absolutes in human affairs, and thus there can be no such thing as perfect objectivity. We know that each historian

6. Native American tribe, then inhabiting the Caribbean area.

7. Paul Revere (1735–1818), American craftsman and patriot, known both for his fine silver bowls and for his famous midnight ride from Boston to Lexington, on April 18–19, 1775, on the eve of the American Revolutionary War; John Singleton Copley (1738–1815), greatest of the American old masters; he specialized in portraits and historical paintings.

8. In 1941 Gatto (1893–1965) painted this fire, which occurred on March 25, 1911, when he was eighteen.

9. Shahn (1898–1969), American painter and graphic artist with strong social and political concerns; Bikini Atoll, part of the Marshall Islands in the Pacific, and site of American nuclear bomb testing from 1946 to 1958.

in some degree creates the world anew and that all history is in some degree contemporary history. But beyond this knowledge there is still a hope for some reliable authority, for some fixed stars in the universe. We may know that journalists cannot be wholly unbiased and that "balance" is an imaginary point between two extremes, and yet we hope that Walter Cronkite[10] will tell us the truth of things. In the same way, we hope that our history will not change— that we learned the truth of things as children. The texts, with their impersonal voices, encourage this hope, and therefore it is particularly disturbing to see how they change, and how fast.

15   Slippery history! Not every generation but every few years the content of American-history books for children changes appreciably. Schoolbooks are not, like trade books,[11] written and left to their fate. To stay in step with the cycles of "adoption"[12] in school districts across the country, the publishers revise most of their old texts or substitute new ones every three or four years. In the process of revision, they not only bring history up to date but make changes—often substantial changes—in the body of the work. History books for children are thus more contemporary than any other form of history. How should it be otherwise? Should students read histories written ten, fifteen, thirty years ago? In theory, the system is reasonable—except that each generation of children reads only one generation of schoolbooks. The transient history is those children's history forever—their particular version of America.

10. Anchor (1916–2009) of the *CBS Evening News* from 1962 to 1981.

11. Books written for a general audience, as opposed to textbooks.

12. The choosing of required textbooks by teachers and school boards.

MLA CITATION

FitzGerald, Frances. "Rewriting American History." 1979. *The Norton Reader: An Anthology of Nonfiction*. Ed. Melissa A. Goldthwaite et al. 14th ed. New York: Norton, 2016. 786–92. Print.

QUESTIONS

1. What differences does Frances FitzGerald find between the American history textbooks of the 1950s and those of the 1970s? In what ways—according to what she states or implies—have they been improved? Does she see any changes for the worse?

2. FitzGerald's *America Revised* was published in 1979, and textbooks, she argues, change rapidly (paragraph 15). Have American history textbooks changed since the late 1970s and, if so, in what ways? What do you remember of the American history textbooks you used in school—and when did you use them? What kind of American history textbooks are being used today? On your own or in a group, write a brief essay updating FitzGerald's piece.

3. By "rewriting," FitzGerald does not mean changing the facts of American history. What is the relationship between the facts of history and history textbooks?

4. FitzGerald says that in the new texts "the word 'progress' has been replaced by the word 'change'" (paragraph 8). Write an essay in which you consider the difference between these two words and the changes that the replacement of one by the other reflects.

JEFFREY OWEN JONES *The Man Who Wrote the Pledge of Allegiance*

The schoolroom staple didn't originally include "under God," even though it was created by an ordained minister.

I FIRST STRUGGLED WITH "UNDER GOD" in my fourth-grade class in Westport, Connecticut. It was the spring of 1954, and Congress had voted, after some controversy, to insert the phrase into the Pledge of Allegiance, partly as a cold war rejoinder to "godless" communism. We kept stumbling on the words— it's not easy to *un*learn something as ingrained and metrical as the Pledge of Allegiance—while we rehearsed for Flag Day, June 14, when the revision would take effect.

Now, nearly five decades later, "under God" is at the center of a legal wrangle that has stirred passions and landed at the door of the U.S. Supreme Court. The case follows a U.S. appeals court ruling in June 2002 that "under God" turns the pledge into an unconstitutional government endorsement of religion when recited in public schools. Outraged by the ruling, Washington, D.C., lawmakers of both parties recited the pledge on the Capitol steps.

Amid the furor, the judge who wrote the ruling by the Ninth Circuit Court, based in San Francisco, stayed it from being put into effect. In April 2003, after the Ninth Circuit declined to review its decision, the federal government petitioned the U.S. Supreme Court to overturn it.[1] ([*Smithsonian Magazine*] *Editor's Note: In June 2004, the Court ruled unanimously to keep "under God" in the Pledge.*) At the core of the issue, scholars say, is a debate over the separation of church and state.

Originally published in Smithsonian Magazine *(2003), which covers "the topics and subject matters researched, studied and exhibited by the Smithsonian Institution [a large collection of museums and research centers]—science, history, art, popular culture and innovation." The piece was then revised and expanded for the first chapter of* The Pledge: A History of the Pledge of Allegiance *(2010) by Jeffrey Owen Jones and Peter Meyer.*

1. In 2004 the Supreme Court heard the case and reached its decision based on a technicality: that the adult plaintiff in the case, Michael Newdow, had no right or "standing" to sue.

I wonder what the man who composed the original pledge 111 years ago would make of the hubbub.

Francis Bellamy was a Baptist minister's son from upstate New York. Educated in public schools, he distinguished himself in oratory at the University of Rochester before following his father to the pulpit, preaching at churches in New York and Boston. But he was restive in the ministry and, in 1891, accepted a job from one of his Boston congregants, Daniel S. Ford, principal owner and editor of the *Youth's Companion*, a family magazine with half a million subscribers.

Assigned to the magazine's promotions department, the 37-year-old Bellamy set to work arranging a patriotic program for schools around the country to coincide with opening ceremonies for the Columbian Exposition in October 1892, the 400th anniversary of Christopher Columbus' arrival in the New World. Bellamy successfully lobbied Congress for a resolution endorsing the school ceremony, and he helped convince President Benjamin Harrison to issue a proclamation declaring a Columbus Day holiday.

A key element of the commemorative program was to be a new salute to the flag for schoolchildren to recite in unison. But as the deadline for writing the salute approached, it remained undone. "You write it," Bellamy recalled his boss saying. "You have a knack at words." In Bellamy's later accounts of the sultry August evening he composed the pledge, he said that he believed all along it should invoke allegiance. The idea was in part a response to the Civil War, a crisis of loyalty still fresh in the national memory. As Bellamy sat down at his desk, the opening words—"I pledge allegiance to my flag"—tumbled onto paper. Then, after two hours of "arduous mental labor," as he described it, he produced a succinct and rhythmic tribute very close to the one we know today: *I pledge allegiance to my flag and the Republic for which it stands—one Nation indivisible—with liberty and justice for all.* (Bellamy later added the "to" before "the Republic" for better cadence.)

Millions of schoolchildren nationwide took part in the 1892 Columbus Day ceremony, according to the *Youth's Companion*. Bellamy said he heard the pledge for the first time that day, October 21, when "4,000 high school boys in Boston roared it out together."

But no sooner had the pledge taken root in schools than the fiddling with it began. In 1923, a National Flag Conference, presided over by the American Legion and the Daughters of the American Revolution, ordained that "my flag" should be changed to "the flag of the United States," lest immigrant children be unclear just which flag they were saluting. The following year, the Flag Conference refined the phrase further, adding "of America."

In 1942, the pledge's 50th anniversary, Congress adopted it as part of a   10
national flag code. By then, the salute had already acquired a powerful institutional role, with some state legislatures obligating public school students to recite it each school day. But individuals and groups challenged the laws. Notably, Jehovah's Witnesses maintained that reciting the pledge violated their prohibition against venerating a graven image. In 1943, the Supreme Court ruled in the Witnesses' favor, undergirding the free-speech principle that no schoolchild should be compelled to recite the pledge.

A decade later, following a lobbying campaign by the Knights of Columbus— a Catholic fraternal organization—and others, Congress approved the addition of the words "under God" within the phrase "one nation indivisible." On June 14, 1954, President Dwight Eisenhower signed the bill into law.

The bill's sponsors, anticipating that the reference to God would be challenged as a breach of the Constitutionally mandated separation of church and state, had argued that the new language wasn't really religious. "A distinction must be made between the existence of a religion as an institution and a belief in the sovereignty of God," they wrote. "The phrase 'under God' recognizes only the guidance of God in our national affairs." The disclaimer did not deter a succession of litigants in several state courts from contesting the new wording over the years, but complainants never got very far—until last year's ruling by the Ninth Circuit.

The case originated when Michael Newdow,[2] an atheist, claimed that his daughter (a minor whose name has not been released) was harmed by reciting the pledge at her public school in Elk Grove, California. If she refused to join in because of the "under God" phrase, the suit argued, she was liable to be branded an outsider and thereby harmed. The appellate court agreed. Complicating the picture, the girl's mother, who has custody of the child, has said she does not oppose her daughter's reciting the pledge; the youngster does so every school day along with her classmates, according to the superintendent of the school district where the child is enrolled.

2. Attorney and medical doctor (b. 1953); after this suit against requiring the phrase "under God" in the Pledge of Allegiance, he also filed lawsuits to stop the opening prayer at President George W. Bush's 2005 inauguration and to prevent references to God at President Barack Obama's 2009 inauguration.

Proponents of the idea that the pledge's mention of God reflects historical tradition and not religious doctrine include Supreme Court justices past and present. "They see that kind of language—'under God' and 'in God we trust'— with no special religious significance," says political scientist Gary Jacobsohn, who teaches Constitutional law at Williams College.

15 Atheists are not the only ones to take issue with that line of thought. Advocates of religious tolerance point out that the reference to a single deity might not sit well with followers of some established religions. After all, Buddhists don't conceive of God as a single discrete entity, Zoroastrians believe in two deities and Hindus believe in many. Both the Ninth Circuit ruling and a number of Supreme Court decisions acknowledge this. But Jacobsohn predicts that a majority of the justices will hold that government may support religion in general as long as public policy does not pursue an obviously sectarian, specific religious purpose.

Bellamy, who went on to become an advertising executive, wrote extensively about the pledge in later years. I haven't found any evidence in the historical record—including Bellamy's papers at the University of Rochester—to indicate whether he ever considered adding a divine reference to the pledge. So we can't know where he would stand in today's dispute. But it's ironic that the debate centers on a reference to God that an ordained minister left out. And we can be sure that Bellamy, if he was like most writers, would have balked at anyone tinkering with his prose.

MLA CITATION

Jones, Jeffrey Owen. "The Man Who Wrote the Pledge of Allegiance." 2003. *The Norton Reader: An Anthology of Nonfiction*. Ed. Melissa A. Goldthwaite et al. 14th ed. New York: Norton, 2016. 793–96. Print.

QUESTIONS

1. Did you recite the Pledge of Allegiance in your school? Did you or other class members refrain from reciting it or omit the phrase "under God"? If so, why?

2. In paragraph 4, Jeffrey Owen Jones wonders what Francis Bellamy, the man who wrote the pledge, would think of the controversy today. Based on the quotations in the essay and additional information you find online (if you choose), formulate a possible answer to this question.

3. Since Jones wrote this column, various states have passed legislation or heard lawsuits about mandatory recitation of the pledge. Using evidence from these cases, as well as interviews with family, friends, or classmates, write an argument in which you take a stand for or against including the phrase "under God" in the pledge.

MARK BOWDEN   *"Idiot," "Yahoo," "Original Gorilla":*
                     How Lincoln Was Dissed
                     in His Day

*The difficulty of recognizing excellence in its
own time*

B Y NEARLY ANY MEASURE—personal, political, even literary—Abraham Lincoln set a standard of success that few in history can match. But how many of his contemporaries noticed?

Sure, we revere Lincoln today, but in his lifetime the bile poured on him from every quarter makes today's Internet vitriol seem dainty. His ancestry was routinely impugned, his lack of formal learning ridiculed, his appearance maligned, and his morality assailed. We take for granted, of course, the scornful outpouring from the Confederate states; no action Lincoln took short of capitulation would ever have quieted his Southern critics. But the vituperation wasn't limited to enemies of the Union. The North was ever at his heels. No matter what Lincoln did, it was never enough for one political faction, and too much for another. Yes, his sure-footed leadership during this country's most-difficult days was accompanied by a fair amount of praise, but also by a steady stream of abuse— in editorials, speeches, journals, and private letters—from those *on his own side*, those dedicated to the very causes he so ably championed. George Templeton Strong, a prominent New York lawyer and diarist, wrote that Lincoln was "a barbarian, Scythian, yahoo, or gorilla." Henry Ward Beecher, the Connecticut-born preacher and abolitionist, often ridiculed Lincoln in his newspaper, *The Independent* (New York), rebuking him for his lack of refinement and calling him "an unshapely man." Other Northern newspapers openly called for his assassination long before John Wilkes Booth pulled the trigger. He was called a coward, "an idiot," and "the original gorilla" by none other than the commanding general of his armies, George McClellan.[1]

One of Lincoln's lasting achievements was ending American slavery. Yet Elizabeth Cady Stanton, the famous abolitionist, called Lincoln "Dishonest Abe" in a letter she wrote to Wendell Phillips[2] in 1864, a year after Lincoln had freed the slaves in rebel states and only months before he would engineer the Thirteenth Amendment. She bemoaned the "incapacity and rottenness" of his

Published in the Atlantic *(2013), a magazine covering literature, culture, and politics.*

1. Major general (1826–1885) for the Union Army during the American Civil War; in 1864 he became the Democratic nominee for vice president.

2. Stanton (1815–1902), advocate for women's rights, as well as for the abolition of slavery; see pp. 784–86; Phillips (1811–1884), lawyer who supported abolitionism and later became active in the women's rights movement.

Lincoln as a frightened raccoon, *Punch*, January 11, 1862.

administration to Susan B. Anthony,[3] worked to deny him renomination, and
swore to Phillips that if he "is reelected I shall immediately leave the country for
the Fijee Islands." Stanton eventually had a change of heart and lamented her
efforts against Lincoln, but not all prominent abolitionists did, even after his victory over slavery was complete, even after he was killed. In the days after Lincoln's assassination, William Lloyd Garrison Jr.[4] called the murder "providential"
because it meant Vice President Andrew Johnson would assume leadership.

Lincoln masterfully led the North through the Civil War. He held firm in
his refusal to acknowledge secession, maneuvered Confederate President Jefferson Davis into starting the war, played a delicate political game to keep
border states from joining the rebellion, and drew up a grand military strategy
that, once he found the right generals, won the war. Yet he was denounced for
his leadership throughout. In a monumental and meticulous two-volume study
of the 16th president, *Abraham Lincoln: A Life* (2008), Michael Burlingame,
the professor of Lincoln studies at the University of Illinois at Springfield, presents Lincoln's actions and speeches not as they have come to be remembered,
through the fine lens of our gratitude and admiration, but as they were received
in his day. (All of the examples in this essay are drawn from Burlingame's book,
which should be required reading for anyone seriously interested in Lincoln.)
Early in the war, after a series of setbacks for Union troops and the mulish inac-

3. Another leader in the women's rights movement (1820–1906).
4. Journalist (1805–1879) who supported abolitionism and women's rights; in his newspaper the *Liberator,* he supported Lincoln and his war policies.

tion of General McClellan, members of Lincoln's own Republican party reviled him as, in the words of Senator Zachariah Chandler of Michigan, "*timid* vacillating & inefficient." A Republican newspaper editor in Wisconsin wrote, "The President and the Cabinet,—*as a whole,—are not equal to the occasion.*" The Ohio Republican William M. Dickson wrote in 1861 that Lincoln "is universally an admitted failure, has no will, no courage, no executive capacity. . . . and his spirit necessarily infuses itself downwards through all departments."

Charles Sumner, a Republican senator from Massachusetts, to whom Lincoln often turned for advice, opposed the president's renomination in 1864: "There is a strong feeling among those who have seen Mr. Lincoln, in the way of business, that he lacks practical talent for his important place. It is thought that there should be more readiness, and also more capacity, for government." William P. Fessenden, the Maine Republican, called Lincoln "weak as water."

For anyone who struggles to do well; to be honest, wise, eloquent, and kind; to be dignified without being aloof; to be humble without being a pushover, who affords a better example than Lincoln? And yet, as he saw how his efforts were received, how could even he not have despaired?

His wife said that the constant attacks caused him "great pain." At times, after reading salvos like Henry Ward Beecher's, Lincoln reportedly would exclaim, "I would rather be dead than, as President, thus abused in the house of my friends." Lincoln would often respond to the flood of nay-saying with a weary wave of his hand and say, "Let us speak no more of these things."

Democracy is rowdy, and political abuse its currency, so perhaps the invective aimed at Lincoln was to be expected. But how do we explain the scorn for Lincoln's prose?

No American president has uttered more immortal words than he did. We are moved by the power and lyricism of his speeches a century and a half later— not just by their hard, clear reasoning, but by their beauty. It is hard to imagine anyone hearing without admiration, for instance, this sublime passage from the first inaugural address:

> I am loth to close. We are not enemies, but friends. We must not be enemies. Though passion may have strained, it must not break our bonds of affection. The mystic chords of memory, stretching from every battlefield, and patriot grave, to every living heart and hearthstone, all over this broad land, will yet swell the chorus of the Union, when again touched, as surely they will be, by the better angels of our nature.

Yet this speech was characterized by an editorial writer in the Jersey City *American Standard* as "involved, coarse, colloquial, devoid of ease and grace, and bristling with obscurities and outrages against the simplest rules of syntax."

As for the Gettysburg Address[5]—one of the most powerful speeches in human history, one that many American schoolchildren can recite by heart

---

5. Delivered on November 19, 1863, at the dedication of the Soldier's National Cemetery in Gettysburg, Pennsylvania, just over four months after the Union army defeated the Confederate army at great loss of life.

(Four score and seven years ago, our fathers brought forth . . .) and a statement of national purpose that for some rivals the Declaration of Independence—a Pennsylvania newspaper reported, "We pass over the silly remarks of the President. For the credit of the nation we are willing that the veil of oblivion shall be dropped over them, and they shall be no more repeated or thought of." A London *Times* correspondent wrote, "Anything more dull and commonplace it wouldn't be easy to produce."

And the second inaugural address[6] (With malice toward none, with charity for all . . .), the third major pillar in Lincoln's now undisputed reputation for eloquence, etched in limestone on the Lincoln Memorial in Washington, D.C.? A. B. Bradford, a Pennsylvania pastor and a member of one of the oldest European families in America, wrote that it was "one of the most awkwardly expressed documents I ever read. . . . When he knew it would be read by millions all over the world, why under the heavens did he not make it a little more creditable to American *scholarship?*" *The New York Herald* described it as "a little speech of 'glittering generalities' used only to fill in the program." *The Chicago Times*, a powerful voice in Lincoln's home state: "We did not conceive it possible that even Mr. Lincoln could produce a paper so slip-shod, so loose-jointed, so puerile, not alone in literary construction, but in its ideas, its sentiments, its grasp." Poor Lincoln. By all accounts he appears to have been the gentlest and most honorable of husbands and fathers, and yet he found little solace even at home. Burlingame records the constant duplicity and groundless suspicion, the nagging criticism and jealous rants of Mary Todd Lincoln, who, on a steamboat home after her husband's triumphant entry into a fallen Richmond, reportedly flew into such a rage that she slapped him in the face.

"It is surprising how widespread [the criticism] was," Burlingame told me recently. "And also how thin-skinned he could be. But that was the nature of partisanship in those days; you never could say a kind word about your opponent."

As if things have changed.

Of course, Lincoln was elected twice to the presidency, and was revered by millions. History records more grief and mourning upon his death than for any other American president. But the past gets simplified in our memory, in our textbooks, and in our popular culture. Lincoln's excellence has been distilled from the rough-and-tumble of his times. We best remember the most generous of his contemporaries' assessments, whether the magnanimous letter sent by his fellow speaker on the stage at Gettysburg, Edward Everett, who wrote to him, "I should be glad, if I could flatter myself that I came as near to the central idea of the occasion, in two hours, as you did in two minutes"; or Edwin Stanton's "Now he belongs to the ages," at the moment of his death; or Frederick Douglass's moving tribute in 1876 to "a great and good man."

15   This process of distillation obscures how Lincoln was perceived in his own time, and, by comparison, it diminishes our own age. Where is the political giant of our era? Where is the timeless oratory? Where is the bold resolve, the moral courage, the vision?

6. See Lincoln's "Second Inaugural Address," pp. 801–03.

Imagine all those critical voices from the 19th century as talking heads on cable television. Imagine the snap judgments, the slurs and put-downs that beset Lincoln magnified a million times over on social media. How many of us, in that din, would hear him clearly? His story illustrates that even greatness—let alone humbler qualities like skill, decency, good judgment, and courage—rarely goes unpunished.

MLA CITATION

Bowden, Mark. "'Idiot,' 'Yahoo,' 'Original Gorilla': How Lincoln Was Dissed in His Day." 2013. *The Norton Reader: An Anthology of Nonfiction.* Ed. Melissa A. Goldthwaite et al. 14th ed. New York: Norton, 2016. 797–801. Print.

QUESTIONS

1. Mark Bowden quotes many critics of Abraham Lincoln. At the end of his essay, Bowden turns to our modern age and the "snap judgments, the slurs and put-downs" that presidents must endure. What is Bowden's larger point?

2. Read Lincoln's "Second Inaugural Address," which follows below this selection, and then revisit the various publications' characterization of the speech in paragraph 11. Do you agree, disagree, or both with their assessments? Why?

3. Choose a living politician whom you admire, and, using online sources, gather judgments about his or her work. Compose an essay, perhaps like Bowden's, in which you present these judgments and assess their fairness and accuracy.

ABRAHAM LINCOLN *Second Inaugural Address*

A T THIS SECOND appearing to take the oath of the presidential office, there is less occasion for an extended address than there was at the first. Then a statement, somewhat in detail, of a course to be pursued, seemed fitting and proper. Now, at the expiration of four years, during which public declarations have been constantly called forth on every point and phase of the great contest which still absorbs the attention, and engrosses the energies of the nation, little that is new could be presented. The progress of our arms, upon which all else chiefly depends, is as well known to the public as to myself; and it is, I trust, reasonably satisfactory and encouraging to all. With high hope for the future, no prediction in regard to it is ventured.

On the occasion corresponding to this four years ago, all thoughts were anxiously directed to an impending civil war. All dreaded it—all sought to avert it. While the inaugural address was being delivered from this place, devoted

Delivered on March 4, 1865, as Abraham Lincoln took office for a second term as America's sixteenth president. In the nineteenth century U.S. presidents took office in March, not in January as they do today.

altogether to *saving* the Union without war, insurgent agents were in the city seeking to *destroy* it without war—seeking to dissolve the Union, and divide effects, by negotiation. Both parties deprecated war; but one of them would *make* war rather than let the nation survive; and the other would *accept* war rather than let it perish. And the war came.

One-eighth of the whole population were colored slaves, not distributed generally over the Union, but localized in the Southern part of it. These slaves constituted a peculiar and powerful interest. All knew that this interest was, somehow, the cause of the war. To strengthen, perpetuate, and extend this interest was the object for which the insurgents would rend the Union, even by war; while the government claimed no right to do more than to restrict the territorial enlargement of it. Neither party expected for the war, the magnitude, or the duration, which it has already attained. Neither anticipated that the *cause* of the conflict might cease with, or even before, the conflict itself should cease. Each looked for an easier triumph, and a result less fundamental and astounding. Both read the same Bible, and pray to the same God; and each invokes His aid against the other. It may seem strange that any men should dare to ask a just God's assistance in wringing their bread from the sweat of other men's faces; but let us judge not that we be not judged.[1] The prayers of both could not be answered; that of neither has been answered fully. The Almighty has His own purposes. "Woe unto the world because of offenses! for it must needs be that offenses come; but woe to that man by whom the offense cometh!"[2] If we shall suppose that American slavery is one of those offenses which, in the providence of God, must needs come, but which, having continued through His appointed time, He now wills to remove, and that He gives to both North and South, this terrible war, as the woe due to those by whom the offense came, shall we discern therein any departure from those divine attributes which the believers in a Living God always ascribe to Him? Fondly do we hope—fervently do we pray—that this mighty scourge of war may speedily pass away. Yet, if God wills that it continue, until all the wealth piled by the bondman's two hundred and fifty years of unrequited toil shall be sunk, and until every drop of blood drawn with the lash, shall be paid by another drawn with the sword, as was said three thousand years ago, so still it must be said "the judgments of the Lord are true and righteous altogether."[3]

With malice toward none; with charity for all; with firmness in the right, as God gives us to see the right, let us strive on to finish the work we are in; to bind up the nation's wounds; to care for him who shall have borne the battle, and for his widow, and his orphan—to do all which may achieve and cherish a just, and a lasting peace, among ourselves, and with all nations.

---

1. Lincoln alludes to Jesus's statement in the Sermon on the Mount—"Judge not, that ye be not judged" (Matthew 7.1)—and to God's curse on Adam—"In the sweat of thy face shalt thou eat bread, till thou return unto the ground" (Genesis 3.19).

2. From Jesus's speech to his disciples (Matthew 18.7).

3. Psalms 19.9.

MLA CITATION

Lincoln, Abraham. "Second Inaugural Address." 1865. *The Norton Reader: An Anthology of Nonfiction.* Ed. Melissa A. Goldthwaite et al. 14th ed. New York: Norton, 2016. 801–02. Print.

QUESTIONS

1. Abraham Lincoln's speech includes both allusions to and direct quotations from the Bible. What argument do these references support? Why might biblical references be important as a persuasive technique for Lincoln's audience?

2. In paragraphs 1–2, Lincoln reflects on his first inaugural speech in order to set the stage for his present speech. Find a copy of the first inaugural speech online or in the library. In what ways does that thirty-five-paragraph speech help inform this four-paragraph speech? What aspects of the "Second Inaugural Address" does it clarify?

3. Read the text of a more recent presidential address and compare or contrast it to Lincoln's address. (John F. Kennedy's inaugural address follows this selection; others can be found online.) Does the more recent address use a similar style, language, or set of allusions? How does it differ?

JOHN F. KENNEDY   *Inaugural Address*

WE OBSERVE TODAY not a victory of a party but a celebration of freedom—symbolizing an end as well as a beginning—signifying renewal as well as change. For I have sworn before you and Almighty God the same solemn oath our forebears prescribed nearly a century and three quarters ago.

The world is very different now. For man holds in his mortal hands the power to abolish all forms of human poverty and all forms of human life. And yet the same revolutionary beliefs for which our forebears fought are still at issue around the globe—the belief that the rights of man come not from the generosity of the state but from the hand of God.

We dare not forget today that we are the heirs of that first revolution. Let the word go forth from this time and place, to friend and foe alike, that the torch has been passed to a new generation of Americans—born in this century, tempered by war, disciplined by a hard and bitter peace, proud of our ancient heritage—and unwilling to witness or permit the slow undoing of those human rights to which this nation has always been committed, and to which we are committed today at home and around the world.

Inaugural address of John F. Kennedy (1917–1963), America's thirty-fifth president, delivered on January 20, 1961.

Let every nation know, whether it wishes us well or ill, that we shall pay any price, bear any burden, meet any hardship, support any friend, oppose any foe to assure the survival and success of liberty.

5   This much we pledge—and more.

To those old allies whose cultural and spiritual origins we share, we pledge the loyalty of faithful friends. United, there is little we cannot do in a host of cooperative ventures. Divided, there is little we can do—for we dare not meet a powerful challenge at odds and split asunder.

To those new states whom we welcome to the ranks of the free, we pledge our word that one form of colonial control shall not have passed away merely to be replaced by a far more iron tyranny. We shall not always expect to find them supporting our view. But we shall always hope to find them strongly supporting their own freedom—and to remember that, in the past, those who foolishly sought power by riding the back of the tiger ended up inside.

To those peoples in the huts and villages of half the globe struggling to break the bonds of mass misery, we pledge our best efforts to help them help themselves, for whatever period is required—not because the Communists may be doing it, not because we seek their votes, but because it is right. If a free society cannot help the many who are poor, it cannot save the few who are rich.

To our sister republics south of our border,[1] we offer a special pledge—to convert our good words into good deeds—in a new alliance for progress—to assist free men and free governments in casting off the chains of poverty. But this peaceful revolution of hope cannot become the prey of hostile powers. Let all our neighbors know that we shall join with them to oppose aggression or subversion anywhere in the Americas. And let every other power know that this hemisphere intends to remain the master of its own house.

10   To that world assembly of sovereign states, the United Nations, our last best hope in an age where the instruments of war have far outpaced the instruments of peace, we renew our pledge of support—to prevent it from becoming merely a forum for invective—to strengthen its shield of the new and the weak— and to enlarge the area in which its writ may run.

Finally, to those nations who would make themselves our adversary, we offer not a pledge but a request: that both sides begin anew the quest for peace, before the dark powers of destruction unleashed by science[2] engulf all humanity in planned or accidental self-destruction.

We dare not tempt them with weakness. For only when our arms are sufficient beyond doubt can we be certain beyond doubt that they will never be employed.

But neither can two great and powerful groups of nations take comfort from our present course—both sides overburdened by the cost of modern weapons, both rightly alarmed by the steady spread of the deadly atom, yet both racing to alter that uncertain balance of terror that stays the hand of mankind's final war.

1. In this paragraph, Kennedy makes many references to Cuba, which by 1961 had turned to communism under Fidel Castro and had allied itself with the Soviet Union.
2. Reference to atomic weapons.

So let us begin anew—remembering on both sides that civility is not a sign of weakness, and sincerity is always subject to proof. Let us never negotiate out of fear. But let us never fear to negotiate.

Let both sides explore what problems unite us instead of belaboring those problems which divide us. Let both sides, for the first time, formulate serious and precise proposals for the inspection and control of arms—and bring the absolute power to destroy other nations under the absolute control of all nations.

Let both sides seek to invoke the wonders of science instead of its terrors. Together let us explore the stars, conquer the deserts, eradicate disease, tap the ocean depths, and encourage the arts and commerce.

Let both sides unite to heed in all corners of the earth the command of Isaiah—to "undo the heavy burdens and to let the oppressed go free."[3]

And if a beachhead of cooperation may push back the jungle of suspicion, let both sides join in creating a new endeavor—not a new balance of power but a new world of law, where the strong are just and the weak secure and the peace preserved.

All this will not be finished in the first one hundred days. Nor will it be finished in the first one thousand days, nor in the life of this administration, nor even perhaps in our lifetime on this planet. But let us begin.

In your hands, my fellow citizens, more than mine, will rest the final success or failure of our course. Since this country was founded, each generation of Americans has been summoned to give testimony to its national loyalty. The graves of young Americans who answered the call to service surround the globe.

Now the trumpet summons us again—not as a call to bear arms, though arms we need—not as a call to battle, though embattled we are—but a call to bear the burden of a long twilight struggle, year in and year out, "rejoicing in hope, patient in tribulation"[4]—a struggle against the common enemies of man: tyranny, poverty, disease, and war itself.

Can we forge against these enemies a grand and global alliance, North and South, East and West, that can assure a more fruitful life for all mankind? Will you join in that historic effort?

In the long history of the world, only a few generations have been granted the role of defending freedom in its hour of maximum danger. I do not shrink from this responsibility—I welcome it. I do not believe that any of us would exchange places with any other people or any other generation. The energy, the faith, the devotion which we bring to this endeavor will light our country and all who serve it—and the glow from that fire can truly light the world.

And so, my fellow Americans, ask not what your country can do for you—ask what you can do for your country.

My fellow citizens of the world, ask not what America will do for you, but what together we can do for the freedom of man.

Finally, whether you are citizens of America or citizens of the world, ask of us here the same high standards of strength and sacrifice which we ask of

---

3. Isaiah 58.6.
4. Romans 12.12.

you. With a good conscience our only sure reward, with history the final judge
of our deeds, let us go forth to lead the land we love, asking His blessing and
His help, but knowing that here on earth God's work must truly be our own.

MLA CITATION

Kennedy, John F. "Inaugural Address." 1961. *The Norton Reader: An Anthology of
     Nonfiction.* Ed. Melissa A. Goldthwaite et al. 14th ed. New York: Norton, 2016.
     803–06. Print.

QUESTIONS

1. Choose a prominent rhetorical device (for example: repetition, allusion, lists, or
juxtaposition) that John F. Kennedy uses in his speech and identify where it occurs.
For the device you have identified, read it to yourself and then out loud. Why is it
effective?

2. On what level of generality is Kennedy operating? When does he get specific?

3. Consider and deepen your answer to question 1 by writing an analysis of Kennedy's speech. Make a claim about the significance of one or more rhetorical devices
used in the speech; support your thesis with specific examples from the text.

MARTIN LUTHER KING JR. *Letter from Birmingham Jail*[1]

MY DEAR FELLOW CLERGYMEN:
     While confined here in the Birmingham city
jail, I came across your recent statement calling my
present activities "unwise and untimely." Seldom
do I pause to answer criticism of my work and ideas.
     If I sought to answer all the criticisms that cross
my desk, my secretaries would have little time for anything other than such
correspondence in the course of the day, and I would have no time for constructive work. But since I feel that you are men of genuine good will and that

*Written on April 16, 1963, while Martin Luther King Jr. was jailed for civil disobedience;
subsequently published in* Why We Can't Wait *(1964), King's book on nonviolent resistance to segregation in America.*

1. This response to a published statement by eight fellow clergymen from Alabama
(Bishop C. C. J. Carpenter, Bishop Joseph A. Durick, Rabbi Milton L. Grafman, Bishop
Paul Hardin, Bishop Nolan B. Harmon, the Reverend George M. Murray, the Reverend
Edward V. Ramage and the Reverend Earl Stallings) was composed under somewhat
constricting circumstances. Begun on the margins of the newspaper in which the
statement appeared while I was in jail, the letter was continued on scraps of writing
paper supplied by a friendly Negro trusty, and concluded on a pad my attorneys were
eventually permitted to leave me. Although the text remains in substance unaltered, I
have indulged in the author's prerogative of polishing it for publication [King's note].

your criticisms are sincerely set forth, I want to try to answer your statement in what I hope will be patient and reasonable terms.

I think I should indicate why I am here in Birmingham, since you have been influenced by the view which argues against "outsiders coming in." I have the honor of serving as president of the Southern Christian Leadership Conference, an organization operating in every southern state, with headquarters in Atlanta, Georgia. We have some eighty-five affiliated organizations across the South, and one of them is the Alabama Christian Movement for Human Rights. Frequently we share staff, educational, and financial resources with our affiliates. Several months ago the affiliate here in Birmingham asked us to be on call to engage in a nonviolent direct-action program if such were deemed necessary. We readily consented, and when the hour came we lived up to our promise. So I, along with several members of my staff, am here because I was invited here. I am here because I have organizational ties here.

But more basically, I am in Birmingham because injustice is here. Just as the prophets of the eighth century B.C. left their villages and carried their "thus saith the Lord" far beyond the boundaries of their home towns, and just as the Apostle Paul left his village of Tarsus and carried the gospel of Jesus Christ to the far corners of the Greco-Roman world, so am I compelled to carry the gospel of freedom beyond my own home town. Like Paul, I must constantly respond to the Macedonian call for aid.

Moreover, I am cognizant of the interrelatedness of all communities and states. I cannot sit idly by in Atlanta and not be concerned about what happens in Birmingham. Injustice anywhere is a threat to justice everywhere. We are caught in an inescapable network of mutuality, tied in a single garment of destiny. Whatever affects one directly, affects all indirectly. Never again can we afford to live with the narrow, provincial "outside agitator" idea. Anyone who lives inside the United States can never be considered an outsider anywhere within its bounds.

You deplore the demonstrations taking place in Birmingham. But your   5
statement, I am sorry to say, fails to express a similar concern for the conditions that brought about the demonstrations. I am sure that none of you would want to rest content with the superficial kind of social analysis that deals merely with effects and does not grapple with underlying causes. It is unfortunate that demonstrations are taking place in Birmingham, but it is even more unfortunate that the city's white power structure left the Negro community with no alternative.

In any nonviolent campaign there are four basic steps: collection of the facts to determine whether injustices exist; negotiation; self-purification; and direct action. We have gone through all these steps in Birmingham. There can be no gainsaying the fact that racial injustice engulfs this community. Birmingham is probably the most thoroughly segregated city in the United States. Its ugly record of brutality is widely known. Negroes have experienced grossly unjust treatment in the courts. There have been more unsolved bombings of Negro homes and churches in Birmingham than in any other city in the nation. These are the hard, brutal facts of the case. On the basis of these conditions,

Negro leaders sought to negotiate with the city fathers. But the latter consistently refused to engage in good-faith negotiation.

Then, last September, came the opportunity to talk with leaders of Birmingham's economic community. In the course of the negotiations, certain promises were made by the merchants—for example, to remove the stores' humiliating racial signs. On the basis of these promises, the Reverend Fred Shuttlesworth and the leaders of the Alabama Christian Movement for Human Rights agreed to a moratorium on all demonstrations. As the weeks and months went by, we realized that we were the victims of a broken promise. A few signs, briefly removed, returned; the others remained.

As in so many past experiences, our hopes had been blasted, and the shadow of deep disappointment settled upon us. We had no alternative except to prepare for direct action, whereby we would present our very bodies as a means of laying our case before the conscience of the local and the national community. Mindful of the difficulties involved, we decided to undertake a process of self-purification. We began a series of workshops on nonviolence, and we repeatedly asked ourselves: "Are you able to accept blows without retaliating?" "Are you able to endure the ordeal of jail?" We decided to schedule our direct-action program for the Easter season, realizing that except for Christmas, this is the main shopping period of the year. Knowing that a strong economic-withdrawal program would be the by-product of direct action, we felt that this would be the best time to bring pressure to bear on the merchants for the needed change.

Then it occurred to us that Birmingham's mayoral election was coming up in March, and we speedily decided to postpone action until after election day. When we discovered that the Commissioner of Public Safety, Eugene "Bull" Connor, had piled up enough votes to be in the run-off, we decided again to postpone action until the day after the run-off so that the demonstrations could not be used to cloud the issues. Like many others, we wanted to see Mr. Connor defeated, and to this end we endured postponement after postponement. Having aided in this community need, we felt that our direct-action program could be delayed no longer.

10   You may well ask, "Why direct action? Why sit-ins, marches, and so forth? Isn't negotiation a better path?" You are quite right in calling for negotiation. Indeed, this is the very purpose of direct action. Nonviolent direct action seeks to create such a crisis and foster such a tension that a community which has constantly refused to negotiate is forced to confront the issue. It seeks so to dramatize the issue that it can no longer be ignored. My citing the creation of tension as part of the work of the nonviolent-resister may sound rather shocking. But I must confess that I am not afraid of the word "tension." I have earnestly opposed violent tension, but there is a type of constructive, nonviolent tension which is necessary for growth. Just as Socrates felt that it was necessary to create a tension in the mind so that individuals could rise from the bondage of myths and half-truths to the unfettered realm of creative analysis and objective appraisal, so must we see the need for nonviolent gadflies to create the kind of tension in society that will help men rise from the dark depths of prejudice and racism to the majestic heights of understanding and brotherhood.

The purpose of our direct-action program is to create a situation so crisis-packed that it will inevitably open the door to negotiation. I therefore concur with you in your call for negotiation. Too long has our beloved Southland been bogged down in a tragic effort to live in monologue rather than dialogue.

One of the basic points in your statement is that the action that I and my associates have taken in Birmingham is untimely. Some have asked: "Why didn't you give the new city administration time to act?" The only answer that I can give to this query is that the new Birmingham administration must be prodded about as much as the outgoing one, before it will act. We are sadly mistaken if we feel that the election of Albert Boutwell as mayor will bring the millennium to Birmingham. While Mr. Boutwell is a much more gentle person than Mr. Connor, they are both segregationists, dedicated to maintenance of the status quo. I have hoped that Mr. Boutwell will be reasonable enough to see the futility of massive resistance to desegregation. But he will not see this without pressure from devotees of civil rights. My friends, I must say to you that we have not made a single gain in civil rights without determined legal and nonviolent pressure. Lamentably, it is an historical fact that privileged groups seldom give up their privileges voluntarily. Individuals may see the moral light and voluntarily give up their unjust posture; but, as Reinhold Niebuhr[2] has reminded us, groups tend to be more immoral than individuals.

We know through painful experience that freedom is never voluntarily given by the oppressor; it must be demanded by the oppressed. Frankly, I have yet to engage in a direct-action campaign that was "well timed" in the view of those who have not suffered unduly from the disease of segregation. For years now I have heard the word "Wait!" It rings in the ear of every Negro with piercing familiarity. This "Wait" has almost always meant "Never." We must come to see, with one of our distinguished jurists, that "justice too long delayed is justice denied."

We have waited for more than 340 years for our constitutional and God-given rights. The nations of Asia and Africa are moving with jetlike speed toward gaining political independence, but we still creep at horse-and-buggy pace toward gaining a cup of coffee at a lunch counter. Perhaps it is easy for those who have never felt the stinging darts of segregation to say, "Wait." But when you have seen vicious mobs lynch your mothers and fathers at will and drown your sisters and brothers at whim; when you have seen hate-filled policemen curse, kick, and even kill your black brothers and sisters; when you see the vast majority of your twenty million Negro brothers smothering in an airtight cage of poverty in the midst of an affluent society; when you suddenly find your tongue twisted and your speech stammering as you seek to explain to your six-year-old daughter why she can't go to the public amusement park that has just been advertised on television, and see tears welling up in her eyes when she is told that Funtown is closed to colored children, and see ominous clouds of inferiority beginning to form in her little mental sky, and see her beginning to distort her personality by developing an unconscious bitterness toward white

2. American Protestant theologian (1892–1971).

people; when you have to concoct an answer for a five-year-old son who is asking, "Daddy, why do white people treat colored people so mean?"; when you take a cross-country drive and find it necessary to sleep night after night in the uncomfortable corners of your automobile because no motel will accept you; when you are humiliated day in and day out by nagging signs reading "white" and "colored"; when your first name becomes "nigger," your middle name becomes "boy" (however old you are) and your last name becomes "John," and your wife and mother are never given the respected title "Mrs."; when you are harried by day and haunted by night by the fact that you are a Negro, living constantly at tiptoe stance, never quite knowing what to expect next, and are plagued with inner fears and outer resentments; when you are forever fighting a degenerating sense of "nobodiness"—then you will understand why we find it difficult to wait. There comes a time when the cup of endurance runs over, and men are no longer willing to be plunged into the abyss of despair. I hope, sirs, you can understand our legitimate and unavoidable impatience.

15   You express a great deal of anxiety over our willingness to break laws. This is certainly a legitimate concern. Since we so diligently urge people to obey the Supreme Court's decision of 1954 outlawing segregation in the public schools, at first glance it may seem rather paradoxical for us consciously to break laws. One may well ask: "How can you advocate breaking some laws and obeying others?" The answer lies in the fact that there are two types of laws: just and unjust. I would be the first to advocate obeying just laws. One has not only a legal but a moral responsibility to obey just laws. Conversely, one has a moral responsibility to disobey unjust laws. I would agree with St. Augustine[3] that "an unjust law is no law at all."

Now, what is the difference between the two? How does one determine whether a law is just or unjust? A just law is a man-made code that squares with the moral law or the law of God. An unjust law is a code that is out of harmony with the moral law. To put it in the terms of St. Thomas Aquinas:[4] An unjust law is a human law that is not rooted in eternal law and natural law. Any law that uplifts human personality is just. Any law that degrades human personality is unjust. All segregation statutes are unjust because segregation distorts the soul and damages the personality. It gives the segregator a false sense of superiority and the segregated a false sense of inferiority. Segregation, to use the terminology of the Jewish philosopher Martin Buber,[5] substitutes an "I-it" relationship for an "I-thou" relationship and ends up relegating persons to the status of things. Hence segregation is not only politically, economically, and sociologically unsound, it is morally wrong and sinful. Paul Tillich[6] has said that sin is separation. Is not segregation an existential expression of man's tragic separation, his awful estrangement, his terrible sinfulness? Thus it is that I can urge men to obey the 1954 decision of the Supreme Court, for it

3. Early Christian church father (354–430).
4. Christian philosopher and theologian (1225–1274).
5. Austrian-born Israeli philosopher (1878–1965).
6. German-born American Protestant theologian (1886–1965).

is morally right; and I can urge them to disobey segregation ordinances, for they are morally wrong.

Let us consider a more concrete example of just and unjust laws. An unjust law is a code that a numerical or power majority group compels a minority group to obey but does not make binding on itself. This is *difference* made legal. By the same token, a just law is a code that a majority compels a minority to follow and that it is willing to follow itself. This is *sameness* made legal.

Let me give another explanation. A law is unjust if it is inflicted on a minority that, as a result of being denied the right to vote, had no part in enacting or devising the law. Who can say that the legislature of Alabama which set up that state's segregation laws was democratically elected? Throughout Alabama all sorts of devious methods are used to prevent Negroes from becoming registered voters, and there are some counties in which, even though Negroes constitute a majority of the population, not a single Negro is registered. Can any law enacted under such circumstances be considered democratically structured?

Sometimes a law is just on its face and unjust in its application. For instance, I have been arrested on a charge of parading without a permit. Now, there is nothing wrong in having an ordinance which requires a permit for a parade. But such an ordinance becomes unjust when it is used to maintain segregation and to deny citizens the First-Amendment privilege of peaceful assembly and protest.

I hope you are able to see the distinction I am trying to point out. In no sense do I advocate evading or defying the law, as would the rabid segregationist. That would lead to anarchy. One who breaks an unjust law must do so openly, lovingly, and with a willingness to accept the penalty. I submit that an individual who breaks a law that conscience tells him is unjust, and who willingly accepts the penalty of imprisonment in order to arouse the conscience of the community over its injustice, is in reality expressing the highest respect for law.

Of course, there is nothing new about this kind of civil disobedience. It was evidenced sublimely in the refusal of Shadrach, Meshach, and Abednego to obey the laws of Nebuchadnezzar,[7] on the ground that a higher moral law was at stake. It was practiced superbly by the early Christians, who were willing to face hungry lions and the excruciating pain of chopping blocks rather than submit to certain unjust laws of the Roman Empire. To a degree, academic freedom is a reality today because Socrates practiced civil disobedience.[8] In our own nation, the Boston Tea Party represented a massive act of civil disobedience.

We should never forget that everything Adolf Hitler did in Germany was "legal" and everything the Hungarian freedom fighters[9] did in Hungary was

20

7. Their story is told in Daniel 3.
8. Socrates, the ancient Greek philosopher, was tried by the Athenians for corrupting their youth through his skeptical, questioning manner of teaching. He refused to change his ways and was condemned to death.
9. In the anti-Communist revolution of 1956, which was quickly put down by the Soviet army.

"illegal." It was "illegal" to aid and comfort a Jew in Hitler's Germany. Even so, I am sure that, had I lived in Germany at the time, I would have aided and comforted my Jewish brothers. If today I lived in a Communist country where certain principles dear to the Christian faith are suppressed, I would openly advocate disobeying that country's anti-religious laws.

I must make two honest confessions to you, my Christian and Jewish brothers. First, I must confess that over the past few years I have been gravely disappointed with the white moderate. I have almost reached the regrettable conclusion that the Negro's great stumbling block in his stride toward freedom is not the White Citizen's Counciler or the Ku Klux Klanner, but the white moderate, who is more devoted to "order" than to justice; who prefers a negative peace which is the absence of tension to a positive peace which is the presence of justice; who constantly says, "I agree with you in the goal you seek, but I cannot agree with your methods of direct action"; who paternalistically believes he can set the timetable for another man's freedom; who lives by a mythical concept of time and who constantly advises the Negro to wait for a "more convenient season." Shallow understanding from people of good will is more frustrating than absolute misunderstanding from people of ill will. Lukewarm acceptance is much more bewildering than outright rejection.

I had hoped that the white moderate would understand that law and order exist for the purpose of establishing justice and that when they fail in this purpose they become the dangerously structured dams that block the flow of social progress. I had hoped that the white moderate would understand that the present tension in the South is a necessary phase of the transition from an obnoxious negative peace, in which the Negro passively accepted his unjust plight, to a substantive and positive peace, in which all men will respect the dignity and worth of human personality. Actually, we who engage in nonviolent direct action are not the creators of tension. We merely bring to the surface the hidden tension that is already alive. We bring it out in the open, where it can be seen and dealt with. Like a boil that can never be cured so long as it is covered up but must be opened with all its ugliness to the natural medicines of air and light, injustice must be exposed, with all the tension its exposure creates, to the light of human conscience and the air of national opinion, before it can be cured.

25   In your statement you assert that our actions, even though peaceful, must be condemned because they precipitate violence. But is this a logical assertion? Isn't this like condemning a robbed man because his possession of money precipitated the evil act of robbery? Isn't this like condemning Socrates because his unswerving commitment to truth and his philosophical inquiries precipitated the act by the misguided populace in which they made him drink hemlock? Isn't this like condemning Jesus because his unique God-consciousness and never-ceasing devotion to God's will precipitated the evil act of crucifixion? We must come to see that, as the federal courts have consistently affirmed, it is wrong to urge an individual to cease his efforts to gain his basic constitutional rights because the quest may precipitate violence. Society must protect the robbed and punish the robber.

I had also hoped that the white moderate would reject the myth concerning time in relation to the struggle for freedom. I have just received a letter from a white brother in Texas. He writes: "All Christians know that the colored people will receive equal rights eventually, but it is possible that you are in too great a religious hurry. It has taken Christianity almost two thousand years to accomplish what it has. The teachings of Christ take time to come to earth." Such an attitude stems from a tragic misconception of time, from the strangely irrational notion that there is something in the very flow of time that will inevitably cure all ills. Actually, time itself is neutral; it can be used either destructively or constructively. More and more I feel that the people of ill will have used time much more effectively than have the people of good will. We will have to repent in this generation not merely for the hateful words and actions of the bad people, but for the appalling silence of the good people. Human progress never rolls in on wheels of inevitability; it comes through the tireless efforts of men willing to be co-workers with God, and without this hard work, time itself becomes an ally of the forces of social stagnation. We must use time creatively, in the knowledge that the time is always ripe to do right. Now is the time to make real the promise of democracy and transform our pending national elegy into a creative psalm of brotherhood. Now is the time to lift our national policy from the quicksand of racial injustice to the solid rock of human dignity.

You speak of our activity in Birmingham as extreme. At first I was rather disappointed that fellow clergymen would see my nonviolent efforts as those of an extremist. I began thinking about the fact that I stand in the middle of two opposing forces in the Negro community. One is a force of complacency, made up in part of Negroes who, as a result of long years of oppression, are so drained of self-respect and a sense of "somebodiness" that they have adjusted to segregation; and in part of a few middle-class Negroes who, because of a degree of academic and economic security and because in some ways they profit by segregation, have become insensitive to the problems of the masses. The other force is one of bitterness and hatred, and it comes perilously close to advocating violence. It is expressed in the various black nationalist groups that are springing up across the nation, the largest and best-known being Elijah Muhammad's Muslim movement.[10] Nourished by the Negro's frustration over the continued existence of racial discrimination, this movement is made up of people who have lost faith in America, who have absolutely repudiated Christianity, and who have concluded that the white man is an incorrigible "devil."

I have tried to stand between these two forces, saying that we need emulate neither the "do-nothingism" of the complacent nor the hatred and despair of the black nationalist. For there is the more excellent way of love and nonviolent protest. I am grateful to God that, through the influence of the Negro church, the way of nonviolence became an integral part of our struggle.

If this philosophy had not emerged, by now many streets of the South would, I am convinced, be flowing with blood. And I am further convinced that

10. Muhammad (1897–1975) succeeded to the leadership of the Nation of Islam in 1934.

if our white brothers dismiss as "rabblerousers" and "outside agitators" those of us who employ nonviolent direct action, and if they refuse to support our nonviolent efforts, millions of Negroes will, out of frustration and despair, seek solace and security in black-nationalist ideologies—a development that would inevitably lead to a frightening racial nightmare.

30   Oppressed people cannot remain oppressed forever. The yearning for freedom eventually manifests itself, and that is what has happened to the American Negro. Something within has reminded him of his birthright of freedom, and something without has reminded him that it can be gained. Consciously or unconsciously, he has been caught up by the *Zeitgeist*,[11] and with his black brothers of Africa and his brown and yellow brothers of Asia, South America, and the Caribbean, the United States Negro is moving with a sense of great urgency toward the promised land of racial justice. If one recognizes this vital urge that has engulfed the Negro community, one should readily understand why public demonstrations are taking place. The Negro has many pent-up resentments and latent frustrations, and he must release them. So let him march; let him make prayer pilgrimages to the city hall; let him go on freedom rides—and try to understand why he must do so. If his repressed emotions are not released in nonviolent ways, they will seek expression through violence; this is not a threat but a fact of history. So I have not said to my people, "Get rid of your discontent." Rather, I have tried to say that this normal and healthy discontent can be channeled into the creative outlet of nonviolent direct action. And now this approach is being termed extremist.

But though I was initially disappointed at being categorized as an extremist, as I continued to think about the matter I gradually gained a measure of satisfaction from the label. Was not Jesus an extremist for love: "Love your enemies, bless them that curse you, do good to them that hate you, and pray for them which despitefully use you, and persecute you." Was not Amos an extremist for justice: "Let justice roll down like waters and righteousness like an everflowing stream." Was not Paul an extremist for the Christian gospel: "I bear in my body the marks of the Lord Jesus." Was not Martin Luther an extremist: "Here I stand; I cannot do otherwise, so help me God." And John Bunyan:[12] "I will stay in jail to the end of my days before I make a butchery of my conscience." And Abraham Lincoln: "This nation cannot survive half slave and half free." And Thomas Jefferson: "We hold these truths to be self-evident, that all men are created equal. . . ." So the question is not whether we will be extremists, but what kind of extremists we will be. Will we be extremists for hate or for love? Will we be extremists for the preservation of injustice or for the extension of justice? In that dramatic scene on Calvary's hill three men were crucified. We must never forget that all three were crucified for the same crime—the crime of extremism. Two were extremists for immorality, and thus fell below their environment. The other, Jesus Christ, was an extremist for love, truth,

---

11. Spirit of the times.

12. Amos, Old Testament prophet; Paul, New Testament apostle; Luther (1483–1546), German Protestant reformer; Bunyan (1628–1688), English preacher and author.

and goodness, and thereby rose above his environment. Perhaps the South, the nation, and the world are in dire need of creative extremists.

I had hoped that the white moderate would see this need. Perhaps I was too optimistic; perhaps I expected too much. I suppose I should have realized that few members of the oppressor race can understand the deep groans and passionate yearnings of the oppressed race, and still fewer have the vision to see that injustice must be rooted out by strong, persistent, and determined action. I am thankful, however, that some of our white brothers in the South have grasped the meaning of this social revolution and committed themselves to it. They are still all too few in quantity, but they are big in quality. Some—such as Ralph McGill, Lillian Smith, Harry Golden, James McBridge Dabbs, Ann Braden, and Sarah Patton Boyle—have written about our struggle in eloquent and prophetic terms. Others have marched with us down nameless streets of the South. They have languished in filthy, roach-infested jails, suffering the abuse and brutality of policemen who view them as "dirty nigger-lovers." Unlike so many of their moderate brothers and sisters, they have recognized the urgency of the moment and sensed the need for powerful "action" antidotes to combat the disease of segregation.

Let me take note of my other major disappointment. I have been so greatly disappointed with the white church and its leadership. Of course, there are some notable exceptions. I am not unmindful of the fact that each of you has taken some significant stands on this issue. I commend you, Reverend Stallings, for your Christian stand on this past Sunday, in welcoming Negroes to your worship service on a nonsegregated basis. I commend the Catholic leaders of this state for integrating Spring Hill College several years ago.

But despite these notable exceptions, I must honestly reiterate that I have been disappointed with the church. I do not say this as one of those negative critics who can always find something wrong with the church. I say this as a minister of the gospel, who loves the church; who was nurtured in its bosom; who has been sustained by its spiritual blessings and who will remain true to it as long as the cord of life shall lengthen.

When I was suddenly catapulted into the leadership of the bus protest in Montgomery, Alabama, a few years ago,[13] I felt we would be supported by the white church. I felt that the white ministers, priests, and rabbis of the South would be among our strongest allies. Instead, some have been outright opponents, refusing to understand the freedom movement and misrepresenting its leaders; all too many others have been more cautious than courageous and have remained silent behind the anesthetizing security of stained-glass windows.

In spite of my shattered dreams, I came to Birmingham with the hope that the white religious leadership of this community would see the justice of our cause and, with deep moral concern, would serve as the channel through which our just grievances could reach the power structure. I had hoped that each of you would understand. But again I have been disappointed.

35

---

13. In December 1955, when Rosa Parks refused to move to the back of a bus.

I have heard numerous southern religious leaders admonish their worshipers to comply with a desegregation decision because it is the law, but I have longed to hear white ministers declare: "Follow this decree because integration is morally right and because the Negro is your brother." In the midst of blatant injustices inflicted upon the Negro, I have watched white churchmen stand on the sideline and mouth pious irrelevancies and sanctimonious trivialities. In the midst of a mighty struggle to rid our nation of racial and economic injustice, I have heard many ministers say: "Those are social issues, with which the gospel has no real concern." And I have watched many churches commit themselves to a completely otherworldly religion which makes a strange, un-Biblical distinction between body and soul, between the sacred and the secular.

I have traveled the length and breadth of Alabama, Mississippi, and all the other southern states. On sweltering summer days and crisp autumn mornings I have looked at the South's beautiful churches with their lofty spires pointing heavenward. I have beheld the impressive outlines of her massive religious-education buildings. Over and over I have found myself asking: "What kind of people worship here? Who is their God? Where were their voices when the lips of Governor Barnett dripped with words of interposition and nullification? Where were they when Governor Wallace gave a clarion call for defiance and hatred?[14] Where were their voices of support when bruised and weary Negro men and women decided to rise from the dark dungeons of complacency to the bright hills of creative protest?"

Yes, these questions are still in my mind. In deep disappointment I have wept over the laxity of the church. But be assured that my tears have been tears of love. There can be no deep disappointment where there is not deep love. Yes, I love the church. How could I do otherwise? I am in the rather unique position of being the son, the grandson, and the great-grandson of preachers. Yes, I see the church as the body of Christ. But, oh! How we have blemished and scarred that body through social neglect and through fear of being nonconformists.

40   There was a time when the church was very powerful—in the time when the early Christians rejoiced at being deemed worthy to suffer for what they believed. In those days the church was not merely a thermometer that recorded the ideas and principles of popular opinion; it was a thermostat that transformed the mores of society. Whenever the early Christians entered a town, the people in power became disturbed and immediately sought to convict the Christians for being "disturbers of the peace" and "outside agitators." But the Christians pressed on, in the conviction that they were "a colony of heaven," called to obey God rather than man. Small in number, they were big in commitment. They were too God-intoxicated to be "astronomically intimidated." By their effort and example they brought an end to such ancient evils as infanticide and gladiatorial contests.

14. Ross Barnett (1898–1987), governor of Mississippi, opposed James Meredith's admission to the University of Mississippi; George Wallace (1919–1998), governor of Alabama, opposed admission of several black students to the University of Alabama.

Things are different now. So often the contemporary church is a weak, ineffectual voice with an uncertain sound. So often it is an archdefender of the status quo. Far from being disturbed by the presence of the church, the power structure of the average community is consoled by the church's silent—and often even vocal—sanction of things as they are.

But the judgment of God is upon the church as never before. If today's church does not recapture the sacrificial spirit of the early church, it will lose its authenticity, forfeit the loyalty of millions, and be dismissed as an irrelevant social club with no meaning for the twentieth century. Every day I meet young people whose disappointment with the church has turned into outright disgust.

Perhaps I have once again been too optimistic. Is organized religion too inextricably bound to the status quo to save our nation and the world? Perhaps I must turn my faith to the inner spiritual church, the church within the church, as the true *ekklesia*[15] and the hope of the world. But again I am thankful to God that some noble souls from the ranks of organized religion have broken loose from the paralyzing chains of conformity and joined us as active partners in the struggle for freedom. They have left their secure congregations and walked the streets of Albany, Georgia, with us. They have gone down the highways of the South on tortuous rides for freedom. Yes, they have gone to jail with us. Some have been dismissed from their churches, have lost the support of their bishops and fellow ministers. But they have acted in the faith that right defeated is stronger than evil triumphant. Their witness has been the spiritual salt that has preserved the true meaning of the gospel in these troubled times. They have carved a tunnel of hope through the dark mountain of disappointment.

I hope the church as a whole will meet the challenge of this decisive hour. But even if the church does not come to the aid of justice, I have no despair about the future. I have no fear about the outcome of our struggle in Birmingham, even if our motives are at present misunderstood. We will reach the goal of freedom in Birmingham and all over the nation, because the goal of America is freedom. Abused and scorned though we may be, our destiny is tied up with America's destiny. Before the pilgrims landed at Plymouth, we were here. Before the pen of Jefferson etched the majestic words of the Declaration of Independence across the pages of history, we were here. For more than two centuries our forebears labored in this country without wages; they made cotton king; they built the homes of their masters while suffering gross injustice and shameful humiliation—and yet out of a bottomless vitality they continued to thrive and develop. If the inexpressible cruelties of slavery could not stop us, the opposition we now face will surely fail. We will win our freedom because the sacred heritage of our nation and the eternal will of God are embodied in our echoing demands.

Before closing I feel impelled to mention one other point in your statement that has troubled me profoundly. You warmly commended the Birmingham 45

15. Greek New Testament word for the early Christian church.

police force for keeping "order" and "preventing violence." I doubt that you would have so warmly commended the police force if you had seen its dogs sinking their teeth into unarmed, nonviolent Negroes. I doubt that you would so quickly commend the policemen if you were to observe their ugly and inhumane treatment of Negroes here in the city jail; if you were to watch them push and curse old Negro women and young Negro girls; if you were to see them slap and kick old Negro men and young boys; if you were to observe them, as they did on two occasions, refuse to give us food because we wanted to sing our grace together. I cannot join you in your praise of the Birmingham police department.

It is true that the police have exercised a degree of discipline in handling the demonstrators. In this sense they have conducted themselves rather "nonviolently" in public. But for what purpose? To preserve the evil system of segregation. Over the past few years I have consistently preached that nonviolence demands that the means we use must be as pure as the ends we seek. I have tried to make clear that it is wrong to use immoral means to attain moral ends. But now I must affirm that it is just as wrong, or perhaps even more so, to use moral means to preserve immoral ends. Perhaps Mr. Connor and his policemen have been rather nonviolent in public, as was Chief Pritchett in Albany, Georgia, but they have used the moral means of nonviolence to maintain the immoral end of racial injustice. As T. S. Eliot has said, "The last temptation is the greatest treason: To do the right deed for the wrong reason."[16]

I wish you had commended the Negro sit-inners and demonstrators of Birmingham for their sublime courage, their willingness to suffer, and their amazing discipline in the midst of great provocation. One day the South will recognize its real heroes. They will be the James Merediths,[17] with the noble sense of purpose that enables them to face jeering and hostile mobs, and with the agonizing loneliness that characterizes the life of the pioneer. They will be old, oppressed, battered Negro women, symbolized in a seventy-two-year-old woman in Montgomery, Alabama, who rose up with a sense of dignity and with her people decided not to ride segregated buses, and who responded with ungrammatical profundity to one who inquired about her weariness: "My feets is tired, but my soul is at rest." They will be the young high school and college students, the young ministers of the gospel and a host of their elders, courageously and nonviolently sitting in at lunch counters and willingly going to jail for conscience' sake. One day the South will know that when these disinherited children of God sat down at lunch counters, they were in reality standing up for what is best in the American dream and for the most sacred values in our Judaeo-Christian heritage, thereby bringing our nation back to those great wells of democracy which were dug deep by the founding fathers in their formulation of the Constitution and the Declaration of Independence.

16. American-born English poet (1888–1965); the lines are from his play *Murder in the Cathedral*.

17. Meredith (b. 1933) was the first black student to enroll at the University of Mississippi.

Never before have I written so long a letter. I'm afraid it is much too long to take your precious time. I can assure you that it would have been much shorter if I had been writing from a comfortable desk, but what else can one do when he is alone in a narrow jail cell, other than write long letters, think long thoughts, and pray long prayers?

If I have said anything in this letter that overstates the truth and indicates an unreasonable impatience, I beg you to forgive me. If I have said anything that understates the truth and indicates my having a patience that allows me to settle for anything less than brotherhood, I beg God to forgive me.

I hope this letter finds you strong in the faith. I also hope that circum-   50
stances will soon make it possible for me to meet each of you, not as an integrationist or a civil-rights leader but as a fellow clergyman and a Christian brother. Let us all hope that the dark clouds of racial prejudice will soon pass away and the deep fog of misunderstanding will be lifted from our fear-drenched communities, and in some not too distant tomorrow the radiant stars of love and brotherhood will shine over our great nation with all their scintillating beauty.

Yours for the cause of Peace and Brotherhood,
MARTIN LUTHER KING JR.

MLA CITATION

King, Martin Luther, Jr. "Letter from Birmingham Jail." 1963. *The Norton Reader: An Anthology of Nonfiction.* Ed. Melissa A. Goldthwaite et al. 14th ed. New York: Norton, 2016. 806–19. Print.

QUESTIONS

1. Martin Luther King Jr. addressed "Letter from Birmingham Jail" to eight fellow clergymen who had written a statement criticizing his activities (see note 1). Where and how, in the course of the "Letter," does he attempt to make common cause with them?

2. King was trained in oral composition, that is, in composing and delivering sermons. One device he uses is prediction: he announces, in advance, the organization of what he is about to say. Locate examples of prediction in the "Letter."

3. Summarize the theory of nonviolent resistance that King presents in this essay.

4. Imagine an unjust law that, to you, would justify civil disobedience. In an essay describe the law, the form your resistance would take, and the penalties you would expect to incur.

SCIENCE

T. H. HUXLEY   *Goethe: Aphorisms on Nature*

NATURE! WE ARE SURROUNDED and embraced by her: powerless to separate ourselves from her, and power-less to penetrate beyond her.

Without asking, or warning, she snatches us up into her circling dance, and whirls us on until we are tired, and drop from her arms.

She is ever shaping new forms: what is, has never yet been; what has been, comes not again. Everything is new, and yet nought but the old.

We live in her midst and know her not. She is incessantly speaking to us, but betrays not her secret. We constantly act upon her, and yet have no power over her.

5   The one thing she seems to aim at is Individuality; yet she cares nothing for individuals. She is always building up and destroying; but her workshop is inaccessible.

Her life is in her children; but where is the mother? She is the only artist; working-up the most uniform material into utter opposites; arriving, without a trace of effort, at perfection, at the most exact precision, though always veiled under a certain softness.

Each of her works has an essence of its own; each of her phenomena a spe-cial characterisation: and yet their diversity is in unity.

She performs a play; we know not whether she sees it herself, and yet she acts for us, the lookers-on.

Incessant life, development, and movement are in her, but she advances not. She changes for ever and ever, and rests not a moment. Quietude is incon-ceivable to her, and she has laid her curse upon rest. She is firm. Her steps are measured, her exceptions rare, her laws unchangeable.

10   She has always thought and always thinks; though not as a man, but as Nature. She broods over an all-comprehending idea, which no searching can find out.

Mankind dwell in her and she in them. With all men she plays a game for love, and rejoices the more they win. With many, her moves are so hidden, that the game is over before they know it.

Published as the opening article in the first issue of Nature *(1869), which is now among the world's most cited and respected scientific journals. The English biologist Thomas Henry Huxley opens the article by quoting Johann Wolfgang von Goethe, a German writer, artist, statesman, and amateur scientist, who wrote his aphorisms around 1780. Goethe's words continue until paragraph 30, after which Huxley continues in his own words.*

That which is most unnatural is still Nature; the stupidest philistinism has a touch of her genius. Whoso cannot see her everywhere, sees her nowhere rightly.

She loves herself, and her innumerable eyes and affections are fixed upon herself. She has divided herself that she may be her own delight. She causes an endless succession of new capacities for enjoyment to spring up, that her insatiable sympathy may be assuaged.

She rejoices in illusion. Whoso destroys it in himself and others, him she punishes with the sternest tyranny. Whoso follows her in faith, him she takes as a child to her bosom.

Her children are numberless. To none is she altogether miserly; but she 15 has her favourites, on whom she squanders much, and for whom she makes great sacrifices. Over greatness she spreads her shield.

She tosses her creatures out of nothingness, and tells them not whence they came, nor whither they go. It is their business to run, she knows the road.

Her mechanism has few springs—but they never wear out, are always active and manifold.

The spectacle of Nature is always new, for she is always renewing the spectators. Life is her most exquisite invention; and death is her expert contrivance to get plenty of life.

She wraps man in darkness, and makes him for ever long for light. She creates him dependent upon the earth, dull and heavy; and yet is always shaking him until he attempts to soar above it.

She creates needs because she loves action. Wondrous! that she pro- 20 duces all this action so easily. Every need is a benefit, swiftly satisfied, swiftly renewed.—Every fresh want is a new source of pleasure, but she soon reaches an equilibrium.

Every instant she commences an immense journey, and every instant she has reached her goal.

She is vanity of vanities; but not to us, to whom she has made herself of the greatest importance. She allows every child to play tricks with her; every fool to have judgment upon her; thousands to walk stupidly over her and see nothing; and takes her pleasure and finds her account in them all.

We obey her laws even when we rebel against them; we work with her even when we desire to work against her.

She makes every gift a benefit by causing us to want it. She delays, that we may desire her; she hastens, that we may not weary of her.

She has neither language nor discourse; but she creates tongues and hearts, 25 by which she feels and speaks.

Her crown is love. Through love alone dare we come near her. She separates all existences, and all tend to intermingle. She has isolated all things in order that all may approach one another. She holds a couple of draughts from the cup of love to be fair payment for the pains of a lifetime.

She is all things. She rewards herself and punishes herself; is her own joy and her own misery. She is rough and tender, lovely and hateful, powerless and omnipotent. She is an eternal present. Past and future are unknown to her.

The present is her eternity. She is beneficient. I praise her and all her works. She is silent and wise.

No explanation is wrung from her; no present won from her, which she does not give freely. She is cunning, but for good ends; and it is best not to notice her tricks.

She is complete, but never finished. As she works now, so can she always work. Everyone sees her in his own fashion. She hides under a thousand names and phrases, and is always the same. She has brought me here and will also lead me away. I trust her. She may scold me, but she will not hate her work. It was not I who spoke of her. No! What is false and what is true, she has spoken it all. The fault, the merit, is all hers.

30   So far Goethe.

When my friend, the Editor of NATURE,[1] asked me to write an opening article for his first number, there came into my mind this wonderful rhapsody on "Nature," which has been a delight to me from my youth up. It seemed to me that no more fitting preface could be put before a Journal, which aims to mirror the progress of that fashioning by Nature of a picture of herself, in the mind of man, which we call the progress of science.

A translation, to be worth anything, should reproduce the words, the sense, and the form of the original. But when that original is Goethe's, it is hard indeed to obtain this ideal; harder still, perhaps, to know whether one has reached it, or only added another to the long list of those who have tried to put the great German poet into English, and failed.

Supposing, however, that critical judges are satisfied with the translation as such, there lies beyond them the chance of another reckoning with the British public, who dislike what they call "Pantheism" almost as much as I do, and who will certainly find this essay of the poet's terribly Pantheistic. In fact, Goethe himself almost admits that it is so. In a curious explanatory letter, addressed to Chancellor von Muller,[2] under date May 26th, 1828, he writes:

"This essay was sent to me a short time ago from amongst the papers of the ever-honoured Duchess Anna Amalia;[3] it is written by a well-known hand, of which I was accustomed to avail myself in my affairs, in the year 1780, or thereabouts.

35   "I do not exactly remember having written these reflections, but they very well agree with the ideas which had at that time become developed in my mind. I might term the degree of insight which I had then attained, a comparative one, which was trying to express its tendency towards a not yet attained superlative.

"There is an obvious inclination to a sort of Pantheism, to the conception of an unfathomable, unconditional, humorously self-contradictory Being, underlying the phenomena of Nature; and it may pass as a jest, with a bitter truth in it."

1. Norman Lockyer (1836–1920), an astronomer.

2. Friedrich von Müller (1779–1849), German statesman.

3. Anna Amalia (1739–1807), German supporter of artists and intellectuals, including Goethe.

Goethe says, that about the date of this composition of "Nature" he was chiefly occupied with comparative anatomy; and, in 1786, gave himself incredible trouble to get other people to take an interest in his discovery, that man has a intermaxillary bone. After that he went on to the metamorphosis of plants, and to the theory of the skull; and, at length, had the pleasure of seeing his work taken up by German naturalists. The letter ends thus:—

"If we consider the high achievements by which all the phenomena of Nature have been gradually linked together in the human mind; and then, once more, thoughtfully peruse the above essay, from which we started, we shall, not without a smile, compare that comparative, as I called it, with the superlative which we have now reached, and rejoice in the progress of fifty years."

Forty years have passed since these words were written, and we look again, "not without a smile," on Goethe's superlative. But the road which led from his comparative to his superlative, has been diligently followed, until the notions which represented Goethe's superlative are now the commonplaces of science— and we have super-superlative of our own.

When another half-century has passed, curious readers of the back numbers of *NATURE* will probably look on *our* best, "not without a smile"; and, it may be, that long after the theories of the philosophers whose achievements are recorded in these pages, are obsolete, the vision of the poet will remain as a truthful and efficient symbol of the wonder and the mystery of Nature. 40

MLA CITATION

Huxley, T. H. "Goethe: Aphorisms on Nature." 1869. *The Norton Reader: An Anthology of Nonfiction.* Ed. Melissa A. Goldthwaite et al. 14th ed. New York: Norton, 2016. 820–23. Print.

QUESTIONS

1. What is Goethe's view of "Nature"?

2. In the title of this essay, T. H. Huxley refers to Goethe's reflections as "aphorisms." What is significant about this choice?

3. Consider the final three paragraphs of the essay. What attitude do they convey about the progress of science? Next, consider the final sentence. What is Huxley suggesting about the differences between scientific truth and poetic truth?

4. Huxley writes that he can imagine "no more fitting preface" (paragraph 31) to a scientific journal than Goethe's reflections. In an essay of your own, consider whether Huxley's observation would hold true today: would Goethe's aphorisms still appeal to a present-day scientist? If so, how? If not, why not? Consider conducting research for your essay by sharing Goethe's aphorisms with some scientists or science majors that you know.

ISAAC ASIMOV   *The Relativity of Wrong*

I RECEIVED A LETTER the other day. It was handwritten in crabbed penmanship so that it was very difficult to read. Nevertheless, I tried to make it out just in case it might prove to be important. In the first sentence, the writer told me he was majoring in English literature, but felt he needed to teach me science. (I sighed a bit, for I knew very few English Lit majors who are equipped to teach me science, but I am very aware of the vast state of my ignorance and I am prepared to learn as much as I can from anyone, so I read on.)

It seemed that in one of my innumerable essays, I had expressed a certain gladness at living in a century in which we finally got the basis of the universe straight.

I didn't go into detail in the matter, but what I meant was that we now know the basic rules governing the universe, together with the gravitational interrelationships of its gross components, as shown in the theory of relativity worked out between 1905 and 1916. We also know the basic rules governing the subatomic particles and their interrelationships, since these are very neatly described by the quantum theory worked out between 1900 and 1930. What's more, we have found that the galaxies and clusters of galaxies are the basic units of the physical universe, as discovered between 1920 and 1930.[1]

These are all twentieth-century discoveries, you see.

5   The young specialist in English Lit, having quoted me, went on to lecture me severely on the fact that in every century people have thought they understood the universe at last, and in every century they were proved to be wrong. It follows that the one thing we can say about our modern "knowledge" is that it is wrong. The young man then quoted with approval what Socrates had said on learning that the Delphic oracle had proclaimed him the wisest man in Greece.[2] "If I am the wisest man," said Socrates, "it is because I alone know that I know nothing." The implication was that I was very foolish because I was under the impression I knew a great deal.

My answer to him was, "John, when people thought the earth was flat, they were wrong. When people thought the earth was spherical, they were wrong. But if you think that thinking the earth is spherical is just as wrong as thinking the earth is flat, then your view is wronger than both of them put together."

Published in the Skeptical Inquirer *(1989), the journal of the Committee for Scientific Investigation of Claims of the Paranormal (CSICOP), now the Committee for Skeptical Inquiry.*

1. Albert Einstein (1879–1955) announced the special theory of relativity in 1905 and developed the general theory of relativity over the next decade; physicist Maxwell Planck (1858–1947) and others developed quantum theory; astronomer Edwin Hubble (1889–1953) demonstrated the existence of external galaxies in 1924.
2. Socrates (c. 470–399 B.C.E.), ancient Greek philosopher; Delphic oracle or Pythia, priestess of the Temple of Apollo on Mount Parnassus.

The basic trouble, you see, is that people think that "right" and "wrong" are absolute; that everything that isn't perfectly and completely right is totally and equally wrong.

However, I don't think that's so. It seems to me that right and wrong are fuzzy concepts, and I will devote this essay to an explanation of why I think so.

When my friend the English literature expert tells me that in every century scientists think they have worked out the universe and are always wrong, what I want to know is how wrong are they? Are they always wrong to the same degree? Let's take an example.

In the early days of civilization, the general feeling was that the earth was flat. This was not because people were stupid, or because they were intent on believing silly things. They felt it was flat on the basis of sound evidence. It was not just a matter of "That's how it looks," because the earth does not look flat. It looks chaotically bumpy, with hills, valleys, ravines, cliffs, and so on.

Of course there are plains where, over limited areas, the earth's surface does look fairly flat. One of those plains is in the Tigris-Euphrates area, where the first historical civilization (one with writing) developed, that of the Sumerians.

Perhaps it was the appearance of the plain that persuaded the clever Sumerians to accept the generalization that the earth was flat; that if you somehow evened out all the elevations and depressions, you would be left with flatness. Contributing to the notion may have been the fact that stretches of water (ponds and lakes) looked pretty flat on quiet days.

Another way of looking at it is to ask what is the "curvature" of the earth's surface. Over a considerable length, how much does the surface deviate (on the average) from perfect flatness. The flat-earth theory would make it seem that the surface doesn't deviate from flatness at all, that its curvature is 0 to the mile.

Nowadays, of course, we are taught that the flat-earth theory is wrong; that it is all wrong, terribly wrong, absolutely. But it isn't. The curvature of the earth is nearly 0 per mile, so that although the flat-earth theory is wrong, it happens to be nearly right. That's why the theory lasted so long.

There were reasons, to be sure, to find the flat-earth theory unsatisfactory and, about 350 B.C., the Greek philosopher Aristotle summarized them. First, certain stars disappeared beyond the Southern Hemisphere as one traveled north, and beyond the Northern Hemisphere as one traveled south. Second, the earth's shadow on the moon during a lunar eclipse was always the arc of a circle. Third, here on the earth itself, ships disappeared beyond the horizon hull-first in whatever direction they were traveling.

All three observations could not be reasonably explained if the earth's surface were flat, but could be explained by assuming the earth to be a sphere.

What's more, Aristotle believed that all solid matter tended to move toward a common center, and if solid matter did this, it would end up as a sphere. A given volume of matter is, on the average, closer to a common center if it is a sphere than if it is any other shape whatever.

About a century after Aristotle, the Greek philosopher Eratosthenes noted that the sun cast a shadow of different lengths at different latitudes (all the shadows would be the same length if the earth's surface were flat). From the difference in shadow length, he calculated the size of the earthly sphere and it turned out to be 25,000 miles in circumference.

The curvature of such a sphere is about 0.000126 per mile, a quantity very close to 0 per mile, as you can see, and one not easily measured by the techniques at the disposal of the ancients. The tiny difference between 0 and 0.000126 accounts for the fact that it took so long to pass from the flat earth to the spherical earth.

20   Mind you, even a tiny difference, such as that between 0 and 0.000126, can be extremely important. That difference mounts up. The earth cannot be mapped over large areas with any accuracy at all if the difference isn't taken into account and if the earth isn't considered a sphere rather than a flat surface. Long ocean voyages can't be undertaken with any reasonable way of locating one's own position in the ocean unless the earth is considered spherical rather than flat.

Furthermore, the flat earth presupposes the possibility of an infinite earth, or of the existence of an "end" to the surface. The spherical earth, however, postulates an earth that is both endless and yet finite, and it is the latter postulate that is consistent with all later findings.

So, although the flat-earth theory is only slightly wrong and is a credit to its inventors, all things considered, it is wrong enough to be discarded in favor of the spherical-earth theory.

And yet is the earth a sphere?

No, it is not a sphere; not in the strict mathematical sense. A sphere has certain mathematical properties—for instance, all diameters (that is, all straight lines that pass from one point on its surface, through the center, to another point on its surface) have the same length.

25   That, however, is not true of the earth. Various diameters of the earth differ in length.

What gave people the notion the earth wasn't a true sphere? To begin with, the sun and the moon have outlines that are perfect circles within the limits of measurement in the early days of the telescope. This is consistent with the supposition that the sun and the moon are perfectly spherical in shape.

However, when Jupiter and Saturn were observed by the first telescopic observers, it became quickly apparent that the outlines of those planets were not circles, but distinct ellipses. That meant that Jupiter and Saturn were not true spheres.

Isaac Newton,[3] toward the end of the seventeenth century, showed that a massive body would form a sphere under the pull of gravitational forces (exactly as Aristotle had argued), but only if it were not rotating. If it were rotating, a centrifugal effect would be set up that would lift the body's substance against gravity, and this effect would be greater the closer to the equator you progressed. The effect would also be greater the more rapidly a spherical object rotated, and Jupiter and Saturn rotated very rapidly indeed.

3. English mathematician and physicist (1642–1727).

The earth rotated much more slowly than Jupiter or Saturn so the effect should be smaller, but it should still be there. Actual measurements of the curvature of the earth were carried out in the eighteenth century and Newton was proved correct.

The earth has an equatorial bulge, in other words. It is flattened at the   30
poles. It is an "oblate spheroid" rather than a sphere. This means that the various diameters of the earth differ in length. The longest diameters are any of those that stretch from one point on the equator to an opposite point on the equator. This "equatorial diameter" is 12,755 kilometers (7,927 miles). The shortest diameter is from the North Pole to the South Pole and this "polar diameter" is 12,711 kilometers (7,900 miles).

The difference between the longest and shortest diameters is 44 kilometers (27 miles), and that means that the "oblateness" of the earth (its departure from true sphericity) is 44/12755, or 0.0034. This amounts to 1/3 of 1 percent.

To put it another way, on a flat surface, curvature is 0 per mile everywhere. On the earth's spherical surface, curvature is 0.000126 per mile everywhere (or 8 inches per mile). On the earth's oblate spheroidal surface, the curvature varies from 7.973 inches to the mile to 8.027 inches to the mile.

The correction in going from spherical to oblate spheroidal is much smaller than going from flat to spherical. Therefore, although the notion of the earth as a sphere is wrong, strictly speaking, it is not as wrong as the notion of the earth as flat.

Even the oblate-spheroidal notion of the earth is wrong, strictly speaking. In 1958, when the satellite Vanguard I was put into orbit about the earth, it was able to measure the local gravitational pull of the earth—and therefore its shape—with unprecedented precision. It turned out that the equatorial bulge south of the equator was slightly bulgier than the bulge north of the equator, and that the South Pole sea level was slightly nearer the center of the earth than the North Pole sea level was.

There seemed no other way of describing this than by saying the earth was   35
pear-shaped, and at once many people decided that the earth was nothing like a sphere but was shaped like a Bartlett pear dangling in space. Actually, the pear-like deviation from oblate-spheroid perfect was a matter of yards rather than miles, and the adjustment of curvature was in the millionths of an inch per mile.

In short, my English Lit friend, living in a mental world of absolute rights and wrongs, may be imagining that because all theories are wrong, the earth may be thought spherical now, but cubical next century, and a hollow icosahedron the next, and a doughnut shape the one after.

What actually happens is that once scientists get hold of a good concept they gradually refine and extend it with greater and greater subtlety as their instruments of measurement improve. Theories are not so much wrong as incomplete.

This can be pointed out in many cases other than just the shape of the earth. Even when a new theory seems to represent a revolution, it usually arises out of small refinements. If something more than a small refinement were needed, then the old theory would never have endured.

Copernicus[4] switched from an earth-centered planetary system to a sun-centered one. In doing so, he switched from something that was obvious to something that was apparently ridiculous. However, it was a matter of finding better ways of calculating the motion of the planets in the sky, and eventually the geocentric theory was just left behind. It was precisely because the old theory gave results that were fairly good by the measurement standards of the time that kept it in being so long.

40   Again, it is because the geological formations of the earth change so slowly and the living things upon it evolve so slowly that it seemed reasonable at first to suppose that there was no change and that the earth and life always existed as they do today. If that were so, it would make no difference whether the earth and life were billions of years old or thousands. Thousands were easier to grasp.

But when careful observation showed that the earth and life were changing at a rate that was very tiny but not zero, then it became clear that the earth and life had to be very old. Modern geology came into being, and so did the notion of biological evolution.

If the rate of change were more rapid, geology and evolution would have reached their modern state in ancient times. It is only because the difference between the rate of change in a static universe and the rate of change in an evolutionary one is that between zero and very nearly zero that the creationists can continue propagating their folly.

Since the refinements in theory grow smaller and smaller, even quite ancient theories must have been sufficiently right to allow advances to be made; advances that were not wiped out by subsequent refinements.

The Greeks introduced the notion of latitude and longitude, for instance, and made reasonable maps of the Mediterranean basin even without taking sphericity into account, and we still use latitude and longitude today.

45   The Sumerians were probably the first to establish the principle that planetary movements in the sky exhibit regularity and can be predicted, and they proceeded to work out ways of doing so even though they assumed the earth to be the center of the universe. Their measurements have been enormously refined but the principle remains.

Naturally, the theories we now have might be considered wrong in the simplistic sense of my English Lit correspondent, but in a much truer and subtler sense, they need only be considered incomplete.

4. Nicolaus Copernicus (1473–1543), Polish astronomer.

MLA CITATION

Asimov, Isaac. "The Relativity of Wrong." 1989. *The Norton Reader: An Anthology of Nonfiction*. Ed. Melissa A. Goldthwaite et al. 14th ed. New York: Norton, 2016. 824–28. Print.

QUESTIONS

1. Isaac Asimov frames his essay as a response to a letter from a "young specialist in English Lit" (paragraph 5) whom he calls "wronger" (paragraph 6) than those

people of the past who thought the earth was flat or spherical. What does Asimov mean by "wronger"?

2. How would you characterize the tone of Asimov's essay? Does his tone make you more or less receptive to his argument?

3. Asimov illustrates his point that scientific theories "are not so much wrong as incomplete" (paragraph 37) with a single extended example: the history of humans trying to determine the size and shape of the earth. Why does Asimov select this particular example?

4. Asimov frames his essay as a response to a letter from a "young specialist in English Lit." Continue the exchange by writing a letter of your own to Asimov.

THOMAS S. KUHN   *The Route to Normal Science*

IN THIS ESSAY, "normal science" means research firmly based upon one or more past scientific achievements, achievements that some particular scientific community acknowledges for a time as supplying the foundation for its further practice. Today such achievements are recounted, though seldom in their original form, by science textbooks, elementary and advanced. These textbooks expound the body of accepted theory, illustrate many or all of its successful applications, and compare these applications with exemplary observations and experiments. Before such books became popular early in the nineteenth century (and until even more recently in the newly matured sciences), many of the famous classics of science fulfilled a similar function. Aristotle's *Physica*, Ptolemy's *Almagest*, Newton's *Principia* and *Opticks*, Franklin's *Electricity*, Lavoisier's *Chemistry*, and Lyell's *Geology*—these and many other works served for a time implicitly to define the legitimate problems and methods of a research field for succeeding generations of practitioners. They were able to do so because they shared two essential characteristics. Their achievement was sufficiently unprecedented to attract an enduring group of adherents away from competing modes of scientific activity. Simultaneously, it was sufficiently open-ended to leave all sorts of problems for the redefined group of practitioners to resolve.

Achievements that share these two characteristics I shall henceforth refer to as "paradigms," a term that relates closely to "normal science." By choosing it, I mean to suggest that some accepted examples of actual scientific practice—examples which include law, theory, application, and instrumentation together—provide models from which spring particular coherent traditions of scientific research. These are the traditions which the historian describes under such rubrics as "Ptolemaic astronomy" (or "Copernican"), "Aristotelian dynamics"

From The Structure of Scientific Revolutions *(1962), a book on the history and philosophy of science.*

(or "Newtonian"), "corpuscular optics" (or "wave optics"), and so on. The study of paradigms, including many that are far more specialized than those named illustratively above, is what mainly prepares the student for membership in the particular scientific community with which he will later practice. Because he there joins men who learned the bases of their field from the same concrete models, his subsequent practice will seldom evoke overt disagreement over fundamentals. Men whose research is based on shared paradigms are committed to the same rules and standards for scientific practice. That commitment and the apparent consensus it produces are prerequisites for normal science, i.e., for the genesis and continuation of a particular research tradition.

Because in this essay the concept of a paradigm will often substitute for a variety of familiar notions, more will need to be said about the reasons for its introduction. Why is the concrete scientific achievement, as a locus of professional commitment, prior to the various concepts, laws, theories, and points of view that may be abstracted from it? In what sense is the shared paradigm a fundamental unit for the student of scientific development, a unit that cannot be fully reduced to logically atomic components which might function in its stead? There can be a sort of scientific research without paradigms, or at least without any so unequivocal and so binding as the ones named above. Acquisition of a paradigm and of the more esoteric type of research it permits is a sign of maturity in the development of any given scientific field.

If the historian traces the scientific knowledge of any selected group of related phenomena backward in time, he is likely to encounter some minor variant of a pattern here illustrated from the history of physical optics. Today's physics textbooks tell the student that light is photons, i.e., quantum-mechanical entities that exhibit some characteristics of waves and some of particles. Research proceeds accordingly, or rather according to the more elaborate and mathematical characterization from which this usual verbalization is derived. That characterization of light is, however, scarcely half a century old. Before it was developed by Planck, Einstein, and others early in this century, physics texts taught that light was transverse wave motion, a conception rooted in a paradigm that derived ultimately from the optical writings of Young and Fresnel in the early nineteenth century.[1] Nor was the wave theory the first to be embraced by almost all practitioners of optical science. During the eighteenth century the paradigm for this field was provided by Newton's *Opticks*, which taught that light was material corpuscles. At that time physicists sought evidence, as the early wave theorists had not, of the pressure exerted by light particles impinging on solid bodies.

5   These transformations of the paradigms of physical optics are scientific revolutions, and the successive transition from one paradigm to another via revolution is the usual developmental pattern of mature science. It is not, however, the pattern characteristic of the period before Newton's work, and that is

1. Max Planck (1858–1947), German physicist; Albert Einstein (1879–1955), German physicist; Thomas Young (1773–1829), English physician and physicist; Augustin-Jean Fresnel (1788–1827), French physicist.

the contrast that concerns us here. No period between remote antiquity and the end of the seventeenth century exhibited a single generally accepted view about the nature of light. Instead there were a number of competing schools and sub-schools, most of them espousing one variant or another of Epicurean, Aristotelian, or Platonic theory.[2] One group took light to be particles emanating from material bodies; for another it was a modification of the medium that intervened between the body and the eye; still another explained light in terms of an interaction of the medium with an emanation from the eye; and there were other combinations and modifications besides. Each of the corresponding schools derives strength from its relation to some particular metaphysic, and each emphasized, as paradigmatic observations, the particular cluster of optical phenomena that its own theory could do most to explain. Other observations were dealt with by *ad hoc*[3] elaborations, or they remained as outstanding problems for further research.

At various times all these schools made significant contributions to the body of concepts, phenomena, and techniques from which Newton drew the first nearly uniformly accepted paradigm for physical optics. Any definition of the scientist that excludes at least the more creative members of these various schools will exclude their modern successors as well. Those men were scientists. Yet anyone examining a survey of physical optics before Newton may well conclude that, though the field's practitioners were scientists, the net result of their activity was something less than science. Being able to take no common body of belief for granted, each writer on physical optics felt forced to build his field anew from its foundations. In doing so, his choice of supporting observation and experiment was relatively free, for there was no standard set of methods or of phenomena that every optical writer felt forced to employ and explain. Under these circumstances, the dialogue of the resulting books was often directed as much to the members of other schools as it was to nature. That pattern is not unfamiliar in a number of creative fields today, nor is it incompatible with significant discovery and invention. It is not, however, the pattern of development that physical optics acquired after Newton and that other natural sciences make familiar today.

The history of electrical research in the first half of the eighteenth century provides a more concrete and better known example of the way a science develops before it acquires its first universally received paradigm. During that period there were almost as many views about the nature of electricity as there were important electrical experimenters, men like Hauksbee, Gray, Desaguliers, Du Fay, Nollett, Watson, Franklin,[4] and others. All their numerous concepts

2. Reference to the three principal worldviews of ancient Greek philosophy.

3. Latin for "a particular purpose."

4. Francis Hauksbee the Elder (d. c. 1713) and Francis Hauksbee the Younger (1687–1763), Stephen Gray (1666–1736), Jean-Théophile Desaguliers (1683–1744), Charles-François de Cisternay Du Fay (1698–1739), Jean-Antoine Nollet (1700–1770), William Watson (1715–1787), and Benjamin Franklin (1706–1790) all made important discoveries about electricity.

of electricity had something in common—they were partially derived from one or another version of the mechanico-corpuscular philosophy that guided all scientific research of the day. In addition, all were components of real scientific theories, of theories that had been drawn in part from experiment and observation and that partially determined the choice and interpretation of additional problems undertaken in research. Yet though all the experiments were electrical and though most of the experimenters read each other's works, their theories had no more than a family resemblance.

One early group of theories, following seventeenth-century practice, regarded attraction and frictional generation as the fundamental electrical phenomena. This group tended to treat repulsion as a secondary effect due to some sort of mechanical rebounding and also to postpone for as long as possible both discussion and systematic research on Gray's newly discovered effect, electrical conduction. Other "electricians" (the term is their own) took attraction and repulsion to be equally elementary manifestations of electricity and modified their theories and research accordingly. (Actually, this group is remarkably small—even Franklin's theory never quite accounted for the mutual repulsion of two negatively charged bodies.) But they had as much difficulty as the first group in accounting simultaneously for any but the simplest conduction effects. Those effects, however, provided the starting point for still a third group, one which tended to speak of electricity as a "fluid" that could run through conductors rather than as an "effluvium" that emanated from nonconductors. This group, in its turn, had difficulty reconciling its theory with a number of attractive and repulsive effects. Only through the work of Franklin and his immediate successors did a theory arise that could account with something like equal facility for very nearly all these effects and that therefore could and did provide a subsequent generation of "electricians" with a common paradigm for its research.

Excluding those fields, like mathematics and astronomy, in which the first firm paradigms date from prehistory and also those, like biochemistry, that arose by division and recombination of specialties already matured, the situations outlined above are historically typical. Though it involves my continuing to employ the unfortunate simplification that tags an extended historical episode with a single and somewhat arbitrarily chosen name (e.g., Newton or Franklin), I suggest that similar fundamental disagreements characterized, for example, the study of motion before Aristotle and of statics before Archimedes, the study of heat before Black, of chemistry before Boyle and Boerhaave, and of historical geology before Hutton.[5] In parts of biology—the study of heredity, for example—the first universally received paradigms are still more recent; and it remains an open question what parts of social science have yet

---

5. Scientists referred to include the Greek philosopher-physicists Aristotle (384–322 B.C.E.) and Archimedes (c. 287–211 B.C.E), the British chemists Joseph Black (1728–1799) and Robert Boyle (1627–1691), the Dutch physician and chemist Hermann Boerhaave (1668–1738), and the Scottish geologist James Hutton (1726–1797).

acquired such paradigms at all. History suggests that the road to a firm research consensus is extraordinarily arduous.

History also suggests, however, some reasons for the difficulties encoun-   10
tered on the road. In the absence of a paradigm or some candidate for paradigm, all of the facts that could possibly pertain to the development of a given science are likely to seem equally relevant. As a result, early fact-gathering is a far more nearly random activity than the one that subsequent scientific development makes familiar. Futhermore, in the absence of a reason for seeking some particular form of more recondite information, early fact-gathering is usually restricted to the wealth of data that lie ready to hand. The resulting pool of facts contains those accessible to casual observation and experiment together with some of the more esoteric data retrievable from established crafts like medicine, calendar making, and metallurgy. Because the crafts are one readily accessible source of facts that could not have been casually discovered, technology has often played a vital role in the emergence of new sciences.

But though this sort of fact-collecting has been essential to the origin of many significant sciences, anyone who examines, for example, Pliny's encyclopedic writings or the Baconian[6] natural histories of the seventeenth century will discover that it produces a morass. One somehow hesitates to call the literature that results scientific. The Baconian "histories" of heat, color, wind, mining, and so on, are filled with information, some of it recondite. But they juxtapose facts that will later prove revealing (e.g., heating by mixture) with others (e.g., the warmth of dung heaps) that will for some time remain too complex to be integrated with theory at all. In addition, since any description must be partial, the typical natural history often omits from its immensely circumstantial accounts just those details that later scientists will find sources of important illumination. Almost none of the early "histories" of electricity, for example, mention that chaff, attracted to a rubbed glass rod, bounces off again. That effect seemed mechanical, not electrical. Moreover, since the casual fact-gatherer seldom possesses the time or the tools to be critical, the natural histories often juxtapose descriptions like the above with others, say, heating by antiperistasis (or by cooling), that we are now quite unable to confirm.[7] Only very occasionally, as in the cases of ancient statics, dynamics, and geometrical optics, do facts collected with so little guidance from pre-established theory speak with sufficient clarity to permit the emergence of a first paradigm.

This is the situation that creates the schools characteristic of the early stages of a science's development. No natural history can be interpreted in the absence of at least some implicit body of intertwined theoretical and

---

6. *Historia naturalis*, the one surviving work of the Roman naturalist Pliny the Elder (c. 23–79 B.C.E.), attempts to deal with the physical universe, geography, anthropology, zoology, botany, and mineralogy. In *Novum Organum*, the English philosopher, essayist, and statesman Francis Bacon (1561–1626) presented his scientific method.

7. Bacon [in the *Novum Organum*] says, "Water slightly warm is more easily frozen than quite cold" [Kuhn's note]; antiperistasis, an old word meaning a reaction caused by the action of an opposite quality or principle—here, heating through cooling.

methodological belief that permits selection, evaluation, and criticism. If that body of belief is not already implicit in the collection of facts—in which case more than "mere facts" are at hand—it must be externally supplied, perhaps by a current metaphysic, by another science, or by personal and historical accident. No wonder, then, that in the early stages of the development of any science different men confronting the same range of phenomena, but not usually all the same particular phenomena, describe and interpret them in different ways. What is surprising, and perhaps also unique in its degree to the fields we call science, is that such initial divergences should ever largely disappear.

For they do disappear to a very considerable extent and then apparently once and for all. Furthermore, their disappearance is usually caused by the triumph of one of the pre-paradigm schools, which, because of its own characteristic beliefs and pre-conceptions, emphasized only some special part of the too sizable and inchoate pool of information. Those electricians who thought electricity a fluid and therefore gave particular emphasis to conduction provide an excellent case in point. Led by this belief, which could scarcely cope with the known multiplicity of attractive and repulsive effects, several of them conceived the idea of bottling the electrical fluid. The immediate fruit of their efforts was the Leyden jar,[8] a device which might never have been discovered by a man exploring nature casually or at random, but which was in fact independently developed by at least two investigators in the early 1740's. Almost from the start of his electrical researches, Franklin was particularly concerned to explain that strange and, in the event, particularly revealing piece of special apparatus. His success in doing so provided the most effective of the arguments that made his theory a paradigm, though one that was still unable to account for quite all the known cases of electrical repulsion.[9] To be accepted as a paradigm, a theory must seem better than its competitors, but it need not, and in fact never does, explain all the facts with which it can be confronted.

What the fluid theory of electricity did for the subgroup that held it, the Franklinian paradigm later did for the entire group of electricians. It suggested which experiments would be worth performing and which, because directed to secondary or to overly complex manifestations of electricity, would not. Only the paradigm did the job far more effectively, partly because the end of interschool debate ended the constant reiteration of fundamentals and partly because the confidence that they were on the right track encouraged scientists to undertake more precise, esoteric, and consuming sorts of work.[10] Freed from the concern

8. Kind of capacitor (or condenser), a device for storing electrical charge.

9. The troublesome case was the mutual repulsion of negatively charged bodies [Kuhn's note].

10. It should be noted that the acceptance of Franklin's theory did not end quite all debate. In 1759 Robert Symmer proposed a two-fluid version of that theory, and for many years thereafter electricians were divided about whether electricity was a single fluid or two. But the debates on this subject only confirm what has been said above about the manner in which a universally recognized achievement unites the profession. Electricians, though they continued divided on this point, rapidly concluded that no experimental tests could distinguish the two versions of the theory and that they were

with any and all electrical phenomena, the united group of electricians could pursue selected phenomena in far more detail, designing much special equipment for the task and employing it more stubbornly and systematically than electricians had ever done before. Both fact collection and theory articulation became highly directed activities. The effectiveness and efficiency of electrical research increased accordingly, providing evidence for a societal version of Francis Bacon's acute methodological dictum: "Truth emerges more readily from error than from confusion."

We shall be examining the nature of this highly directed or paradigm-based research in the next section, but must first note briefly how the emergence of a paradigm affects the structure of the group that practices the field. When, in the development of a natural science, an individual or group first produces a synthesis able to attract most of the next generation's practitioners, the older schools gradually disappear. In part their disappearance is caused by their members' conversion to the new paradigm. But there are always some men who cling to one or another of the older views, and they are simply read out of the profession, which thereafter ignores their work. The new paradigm implies a new and more rigid definition of the field. Those unwilling or unable to accommodate their work to it must proceed in isolation or attach themselves to some other group.[11] Historically, they have often simply stayed in the departments of philosophy from which so many of the special sciences have been spawned. As these indications hint, it is sometimes just its reception of a paradigm that transforms a group previously interested merely in the study of nature into a profession or, at least, a discipline. In the sciences (though not in fields like medicine, technology, and law, of which the principal *raison d'être*[12] is an external social need), the formation of specialized journals, the foundation of specialists' societies, and the claim for a special place in the curriculum have usually been associated with a group's first reception of a single paradigm. At least this was the case between the time, a century and a half ago, when the institutional pattern of scientific specialization first developed and the very recent time when the paraphernalia of specialization acquired a prestige of their own.

The more rigid definition of the scientific group has other consequences. When the individual scientist can take a paradigm for granted, he need no longer, in his major works, attempt to build his field anew, starting from first

15

therefore equivalent. After that, both schools could and did exploit all the benefits that the Franklinian theory provided [Kuhn's note].

11. The history of electricity provides an excellent example which could be duplicated from the careers of Priestley, Kelvin, and others. Franklin reports that Nollet, who at mid-century was the most influential of the Continental electricians, "lived to see himself the last of his Sect, except Mr. B.—his *Eleve* [pupil] and immediate Disciple." More interesting, however, is the endurance of whole schools in increasing isolation from professional science. Consider, for example, the case of astrology, which was once an integral part of astronomy. Or consider the continuation in the late eighteenth and early nineteenth centuries of a previously respected tradition of "romantic" chemistry [Kuhn's note].

12. French for "reason for being."

principles and justifying the use of each concept introduced. That can be left
to the writer of textbooks. Given a textbook, however, the creative scientist can
begin his research where it leaves off and thus concentrate exclusively upon the
subtlest and most esoteric aspects of the natural phenomena that concern his
group. And as he does this, his research communiqués will begin to change in
ways whose evolution has been too little studied but whose modern end products are obvious to all and oppressive to many. No longer will his researches
usually be embodied in books addressed, like Franklin's *Experiments . . . on
Electricity* or Darwin's *Origin of Species*, to anyone who might be interested in
the subject matter of the field. Instead they will usually appear as brief articles
addressed only to professional colleagues, the men whose knowledge of a shared
paradigm can be assumed and who prove to be the only ones able to read the
papers addressed to them.

Today in the sciences, books are usually either texts or retrospective reflections upon one aspect or another of the scientific life. The scientist who writes
one is more likely to find his professional reputation impaired than enhanced.
Only in the earlier, pre-paradigm, stages of the development of the various sciences did the book ordinarily possess the same relation to professional achievement that it still retains in other creative fields. And only in those fields that
still retain the book, with or without the article, as a vehicle for research communication are the lines of professionalization still so loosely drawn that the
layman may hope to follow progress by reading the practitioners' original
reports. Both in mathematics and astronomy, research reports had ceased
already in antiquity to be intelligible to a generally educated audience. In
dynamics, research became similarly esoteric in the latter Middle Ages, and it
recaptured general intelligibility only briefly during the early seventeenth century when a new paradigm replaced the one that had guided medieval research.
Electrical research began to require translation for the layman before the end
of the eighteenth century, and most other fields of physical science ceased to
be generally accessible in the nineteenth. During the same two centuries similar transitions can be isolated in the various parts of the biological sciences. In
parts of the social sciences they may well be occurring today. Although it has
become customary, and is surely proper, to deplore the widening gulf that
separates the professional scientist from his colleagues in other fields, too little
attention is paid to the essential relationship between that gulf and the mechanisms intrinsic to scientific advance.

Ever since prehistoric antiquity one field of study after another has crossed
the divide between what the historian might call its prehistory as a science and
its history proper. These transitions to maturity have seldom been so sudden
or so unequivocal as my necessarily schematic discussion may have implied.
But neither have they been historically gradual, coextensive, that is to say, with
the entire development of the fields within which they occurred. Writers on
electricity during the first four decades of the eighteenth century possessed far
more information about electrical phenomena than had their sixteenth-century
predecessors. During the half-century after 1740, few new sorts of electrical
phenomena were added to their lists. Nevertheless, in important respects, the

electrical writings of Cavendish, Coulomb, and Volta[13] in the last third of the eighteenth century seem further removed from those of Gray, Du Fay, and even Franklin than are the writings of these early eighteenth-century electrical discoverers from those of the sixteenth century.[14] Sometime between 1740 and 1780, electricians were for the first time enabled to take the foundations of their field for granted. From that point they pushed on to more concrete and recondite problems, and increasingly they then reported their results in articles addressed to other electricians rather than in books addressed to the learned world at large. As a group they achieved what had been gained by astronomers in antiquity and by students of motion in the Middle Ages, of physical optics in the late seventeenth century, and of historical geology in the early nineteenth. They had, that is, achieved a paradigm that proved able to guide the whole group's research. Except with the advantage of hindsight, it is hard to find another criterion that so clearly proclaims a field a science.

13. Henry Cavendish (1731–1810), Charles-Augustin de Coulomb (1736–1806), and Alessandro Giuseppe Antonio Anastasio Volta (1745–1827) made important discoveries about electricity.

14. The post-Franklinian developments include an immense increase in the sensitivity of charge detectors, the first reliable and generally diffused techniques for measuring charge, the evolution of the concept of capacity and its relation to a newly refined notion of electric tension, and the quantification of electrostatic force [Kuhn's note].

MLA CITATION

Kuhn, Thomas S. "The Route to Normal Science." 1962. *The Norton Reader: An Anthology of Nonfiction*. Ed. Melissa A. Goldthwaite et al. 14th ed. New York: Norton, 2016. 829–37. Print.

QUESTIONS

1. Mark the important terms in this selection from *The Structure of Scientific Revolutions* and Thomas S. Kuhn's definitions of them. How many terms does he illustrate as well as define? Why does he both define and illustrate?

2. What are prevailing paradigms in sciences other than those Kuhn discusses? You might consider biology, chemistry, psychology, and sociology. Are you aware of older paradigms in these sciences, or have they and the work based on them, as Kuhn says (paragraph 15), disappeared?

3. Kuhn asserts, "The study of paradigms . . . is what mainly prepares the student for membership in the particular scientific community with which he will later practice" (paragraph 2). Does this statement about science apply to other areas of study, to other kinds of communities? Consider these questions in an essay of your own, drawing on your own experience as a student.

STEPHEN HAWKING AND   *The (Elusive)*
LEONARD MLODINOW   *Theory of Everything*

> *Physicists have long sought to find one final theory that would unify all of physics. Instead they may have to settle for several.*

ALMOST A DECADE AGO THE CITY COUNCIL of Monza, Italy, barred pet owners from keeping goldfish in curved fishbowls. The sponsors of the measure explained that it is cruel to keep a fish in a bowl because the curved sides give the fish a distorted view of reality. Aside from the measure's significance to the poor goldfish, the story raises an interesting philosophical question: How do we know that the reality we perceive is true? The goldfish is seeing a version of reality that is different from ours, but can we be sure it is any less real? For all we know, we, too, may spend our entire lives staring out at the world through a distorting lens.

In physics, the question is not academic. Indeed, physicists and cosmologists are finding themselves in a similar predicament to the goldfish's. For decades we have strived to come up with an ultimate theory of everything—one complete and consistent set of fundamental laws of nature that explain every aspect of reality. It now appears that this quest may yield not a single theory but a family of interconnected theories, each describing its own version of reality, as if it viewed the universe through its own fishbowl.

This notion may be difficult for many people, including some working scientists, to accept. Most people believe that there is an objective reality out there and that our senses and our science directly convey information about the material world. Classical science is based on the belief that an external world exists whose properties are definite and independent of the observer who perceives them. In philosophy, that belief is called realism.

Those who remember Timothy Leary[1] and the 1960s, however, know of another possibility: one's concept of reality can depend on the mind of the perceiver. That viewpoint, with various subtle differences, goes by names such as antirealism, instrumentalism or idealism. According to those doctrines, the world we know is constructed by the human mind employing sensory data as its raw material and is shaped by the interpretive structure of our brain. This viewpoint may be hard to accept, but it is not difficult to understand. There is no way to remove the observer—us—from our perception of the world.

Published in Scientific American *(2010), a monthly science magazine written for a general audience.*

1. American psychologist (1920–1996) who touted the spiritual benefits of psychedelic drugs.

The way physics has been going, realism is becoming difficult to defend.   5
In classical physics—the physics of Newton[2] that so accurately describes our
everyday experience—the interpretation of terms such as object and position
is for the most part in harmony with our commonsense, "realistic" understanding of those concepts. As measuring devices, however, we are crude instruments. Physicists have found that everyday objects and the light we see them
by are made from objects—such as electrons and photons—that we do not perceive directly. These objects are governed not by classical physics but by the
laws of quantum theory.

The reality of quantum theory is a radical departure from that of classical
physics. In the framework of quantum theory, particles have neither definite
positions nor definite velocities unless and until an observer measures those
quantities. In some cases, individual objects do not even have an independent
existence but rather exist only as part of an ensemble of many. Quantum physics also has important implications for our concept of the past. In classical physics, the past is assumed to exist as a definite series of events, but according to
quantum physics, the past, like the future, is indefinite and exists only as a
spectrum of possibilities. Even the universe as a whole has no single past or
history. So quantum physics implies a different reality than that of classical
physics—even though the latter is consistent with our intuition and still serves
us well when we design things such as buildings and bridges.

These examples bring us to a conclusion that provides an important framework with which to interpret modern science. In our view, there is no picture-
or theory-independent concept of reality. Instead we adopt a view that we call
model-dependent realism: the idea that a physical theory or world picture is a
model (generally of a mathematical nature) and a set of rules that connect the
elements of the model to observations. According to model-dependent realism,
it is pointless to ask whether a model is real, only whether it agrees with observation. If two models agree with observation, neither one can be considered more
real than the other. A person can use whichever model is more convenient in
the situation under consideration.

Frames of Reference

The idea of alternative realities is a mainstay of today's popular culture. For
example, in the science-fiction film *The Matrix* the human race is unknow-
ingly living in a simulated virtual reality created by intelligent computers to
keep them pacified and content while the computers suck their bioelectrical
energy (whatever that is). How do we know we are not just computer-generated
characters living in a *Matrix*-like world? If we lived in a synthetic, imaginary
world, events would not necessarily have any logic or consistency or obey
any laws. The aliens in control might find it more interesting or amusing to see

2. Isaac Newton (1642–1727), English mathematician and physicist.

our reactions, for example, if everyone in the world suddenly decided that chocolate was repulsive or that war was not an option, but that has never happened. If the aliens did enforce consistent laws, we would have no way to tell that another reality stood behind the simulated one. It is easy to call the world the aliens live in the "real" one and the computer-generated world a false one. But if—like us—the beings in the simulated world could not gaze into their universe from the outside, they would have no reason to doubt their own pictures of reality.

The goldfish are in a similar situation. Their view is not the same as ours from outside their curved bowl, but they could still formulate scientific laws governing the motion of the objects they observe on the outside. For instance, because light bends as it travels from air to water, a freely moving object that we would observe to move in a straight line would be observed by the goldfish to move along a curved path. The goldfish could formulate scientific laws from their distorted frame of reference that would always hold true and that would enable them to make predictions about the future motion of objects outside the bowl. Their laws would be more complicated than the laws in our frame, but simplicity is a matter of taste. If the goldfish formulated such a theory, we would have to admit the goldfish's view as a valid picture of reality.

10   A famous real-world example of different pictures of reality is the contrast between Ptolemy's Earth-centered model of the cosmos and Copernicus's sun-centered model.[3] Although it is not uncommon for people to say that Copernicus proved Ptolemy wrong, that is not true. As in the case of our view versus that of the goldfish, one can use either picture as a model of the universe because we can explain our observations of the heavens by assuming either Earth or the sun to be at rest. Despite its role in philosophical debates over the nature of our universe, the real advantage of the Copernican system is that the equations of motion are much simpler in the frame of reference in which the sun is at rest.

Model-dependent realism applies not only to scientific models but also to the conscious and subconscious mental models we all create to interpret and understand the everyday world. For example, the human brain processes crude data from the optic nerve, combining input from both eyes, enhancing the resolution and filling in gaps such as the one in the retina's blind spot. Moreover, it creates the impression of three-dimensional space from the retina's two-dimensional data. When you see a chair, you have merely used the light scattered by the chair to build a mental image or model of the chair. The brain is so good at model-building that if people are fitted with glasses that turn the images in their eyes upside down, their brain changes the model so that they again see things the right way up—hopefully before they try to sit down.

3. Ptolemy (c. 100–c. 170), Greek astronomer and geographer; Nicolaus Copernicus (1473–1543), Polish astronomer.

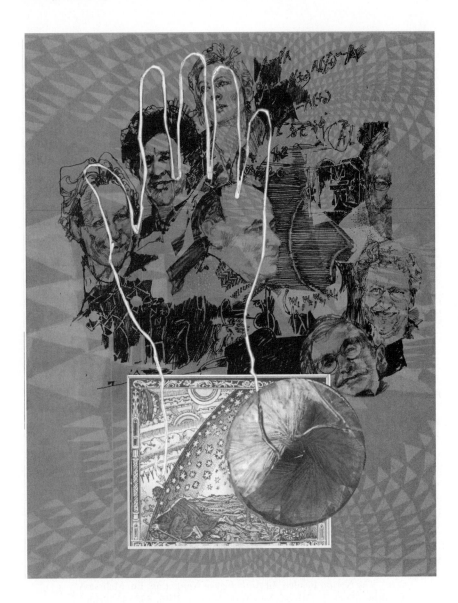

Glimpses of the Deep Theory

In the quest to discover the ultimate laws of physics, no approach has raised higher hopes—or more controversy—than string theory. String theory was first proposed in the 1970s as an attempt to unify all the forces of nature into one coherent framework and, in particular, to bring the force of gravity into the domain of quantum physics. By the early 1990s, however, physicists discovered that string theory suffers from an awkward issue: there are five different string theories. For those advocating that string theory was the unique theory of every-thing, this was quite an embarrassment. In the mid-1990s researchers started discovering that these different theories—and yet another theory called supergravity—actually describe the same phenomena, giving them some hope that they would amount eventually to a unified theory. The theories are indeed related by what physicists call dualities, which are a kind of mathematical dictionaries for translating concepts back and forth. But, alas, each theory is a good description of phenomena only under a certain range of conditions—for example, at low energies. None can describe every aspect of the universe.

String theorists are now convinced that the five different string theories are just different approximations to a more fundamental theory called M-theory. (No one seems to know what the "M" stands for. It may be "master," "miracle" or "mystery," or all three.) People are still trying to decipher the nature of M-theory, but it seems that the traditional expectation of a single theory of nature may be untenable and that to describe the universe we must employ dif-ferent theories in different situations. Thus, M-theory is not a theory in the usual sense but a network of theories. It is a bit like a map. To faithfully repre-sent the entire Earth on a flat surface, one has to use a collection of maps, each of which covers a limited region. The maps overlap one another, and where they do, they show the same landscape. Similarly, the different theories in the M-theory family may look very different, but they can all be regarded as ver-sions of the same underlying theory, and they all predict the same phenomena where they overlap, but none works well in all situations.

Whenever we develop a model of the world and find it to be successful, we tend to attribute to the model the quality of reality. But M-theory, like the gold-fish example, shows that the same physical situation can be modeled in differ-ent ways, each employing different fundamental elements and concepts. It might be that to describe the universe we have to employ different theories in different situations. Each theory may have its own version of reality, but accord-ing to model-dependent realism, that diversity is acceptable, and none of the versions can be said to be more real than any other. It is not the physicist's tra-ditional expectation for a theory of nature, nor does it correspond to our every-day idea of reality. But it might be the way of the universe.

MLA CITATION

Hawking, Stephen, and Leonard Mlodinow. "The (Elusive) Theory of Everything." 2010. *The Norton Reader: An Anthology of Nonfiction*. Ed. Melissa A. Goldthwaite et al. 14th ed. New York: Norton, 2016. 838–42. Print.

QUESTIONS

1. Stephen Hawking and Leonard Mlodinow comment that in physics, "realism is becoming difficult to defend" (paragraph 5). What do they mean by "realism" and what do they propose as an alternative?

2. This essay was written for general readers. How, in their writing, do Hawking and Mlodinow make complex scientific ideas accessible to non-scientists? For instance, how does the goldfish example that runs through the essay help readers?

3. In his essay "The Relativity of Wrong" (pp. 824–28) Isaac Asimov argues that when it comes to science, "right and wrong are fuzzy concepts" (paragraph 8). He concludes his essay by observing that the scientific explanations of the moment are not wrong but instead "incomplete": science progresses when our current theories and explanations are replaced by others that are more complete. How might Hawking and Mlodinow respond to this idea?

4. Write an essay of your own in which you explain a complex idea or process that you know well to someone who is less familiar with it.

Stephen Jay Gould *Sex, Drugs, Disasters, and the Extinction of Dinosaurs*

SCIENCE, IN ITS MOST FUNDAMENTAL DEFINITION, is a fruitful mode of inquiry, not a list of enticing conclusions. The conclusions are the consequence, not the essence.

My greatest unhappiness with most popular presentations of science concerns their failure to separate fascinating claims from the methods that scientists use to establish the facts of nature. Journalists, and the public, thrive on controversial and stunning statements. But science is, basically, a way of knowing—in P. B. Medawar's apt words, "the art of the soluble."[1] If the growing corps of popular science writers would focus on *how* scientists develop and defend those fascinating claims, they would make their greatest possible contribution to public understanding.

Consider three ideas, proposed in perfect seriousness to explain that greatest of all titillating puzzles—the extinction of dinosaurs. Since these three notions invoke the primally fascinating themes of our culture—sex, drugs, and violence—they surely reside in the category of fascinating claims. I want to show why two of them rank as silly speculation, while the other represents science at its grandest and most useful.

Science works with testable proposals. If, after much compilation and scrutiny of data, new information continues to affirm a hypothesis, we may accept it provisionally and gain confidence as further evidence mounts. We can never be completely sure that a hypothesis is right, though we may be able to show with confidence that it is wrong. The best scientific hypotheses are also generous and expansive: they suggest extensions and implications that enlighten related, and even far distant, subjects. Simply consider how the idea of evolution has influenced virtually every intellectual field.

Useless speculation, on the other hand, is restrictive. It generates no testable hypothesis, and offers no way to obtain potentially refuting evidence. Please   5

Originally published in Discover Magazine *(1984), a monthly magazine reporting on "science, medicine, technology, and the world around us"; reprinted in Stephen Jay Gould's collection of essays,* The Flamingo's Smile: Reflections in Natural History *(1985).*

1. British biologist and pioneer in the science of organ transplants (1915–1987).

note that I am not speaking of truth or falsity. The speculation may well be true; still, if it provides, in principle, no material for affirmation or rejection, we can make nothing of it. It must simply stand forever as an intriguing idea. Useless speculation turns in on itself and leads nowhere; good science, containing both seeds for its potential refutation and implications for more and different testable knowledge, reaches out. But, enough preaching. Let's move on to dinosaurs, and the three proposals for their extinction.

1. Sex: Testes function only in a narrow range of temperature (those of mammals hang externally in a scrotal sac because internal body temperatures are too high for their proper function). A worldwide rise in temperature at the close of the Cretaceous period caused the testes of dinosaurs to stop functioning and led to their extinction by sterilization of males.

2. Drugs: Angiosperms (flowering plants) first evolved toward the end of the dinosaurs' reign. Many of these plants contain psychoactive agents, avoided by mammals today as a result of their bitter taste. Dinosaurs had neither means to taste the bitterness nor livers effective enough to detoxify the substances. They died of massive overdoses.

3. Disasters: A large comet or asteroid struck the earth some 65 million years ago, lofting a cloud of dust into the sky and blocking sunlight, thereby suppressing photosynthesis and so drastically lowering world temperatures that dinosaurs and hosts of other creatures became extinct.

Before analyzing these three tantalizing statements, we must establish a basic ground rule often violated in proposals for the dinosaurs' demise. *There is no separate problem of the extinction of dinosaurs.* Too often we divorce specific events from their wider contexts and systems of cause and effect. The fundamental fact of dinosaur extinction is its synchrony with the demise of so many other groups across a wide range of habitats, from terrestrial to marine.

The history of life has been punctuated by brief episodes of mass extinction. A recent analysis by University of Chicago paleontologists Jack Sepkoski and Dave Raup, based on the best and most exhaustive tabulation of data ever assembled, shows clearly that five episodes of mass dying stand well above the "background" extinctions of normal times (when we consider all mass extinctions, large and small, they seem to fall in a regular 26-million-year cycle. . . .). The Cretaceous debacle, occurring 65 million years ago and separating the Mesozoic and Cenozoic eras of our geological time scale, ranks prominently among the five.[2] Nearly all the marine plankton (single-celled floating creatures) died with geological suddenness; among marine invertebrates, nearly 15 percent of all families perished, including many previously dominant groups, especially the ammonites (relatives of squids in coiled shells). On land, the

2. Mesozoic era, 252.5 to 66 million years ago; Cenozoic era, 65.5 million years ago to the present day. The Cretaceous extinction separates these eras.

dinosaurs disappeared after more than 100 million years of unchallenged domination.

In this context, speculations limited to dinosaurs alone ignore the larger phenomenon. We need a coordinated explanation for a system of events that includes the extinction of dinosaurs as one component. Thus it makes little sense, though it may fuel our desire to view mammals as inevitable inheritors of the earth, to guess that dinosaurs died because small mammals ate their eggs (a perennial favorite among untestable speculations). It seems most unlikely that some disaster peculiar to dinosaurs befell these massive beasts—and that the debacle happened to strike just when one of history's five great dyings had enveloped the earth for completely different reasons.

The testicular theory, an old favorite from the 1940s, had its root in an interesting and thoroughly respectable study of temperature tolerances in the American alligator, published in the staid *Bulletin of the American Museum of Natural History* in 1946 by three experts on living and fossil reptiles—E. H. Colbert, my own first teacher in paleontology; R. B. Cowles; and C. M. Bogert.

The first sentence of their summary reveals a purpose beyond alligators: "This report describes an attempt to infer the reactions of extinct reptiles, especially the dinosaurs, to high temperatures as based upon reactions observed in the modern alligator." They studied, by rectal thermometry, the body temperatures of alligators under changing conditions of heating and cooling. (Well, let's face it, you wouldn't want to try sticking a thermometer under a 'gator's tongue.) The predictions under test go way back to an old theory first stated by Galileo[3] in the 1630s—the unequal scaling of surfaces and volumes. As an animal, or any object, grows (provided its shape doesn't change), surface areas must increase more slowly than volumes—since surfaces get larger as length squared, while volumes increase much more rapidly, as length cubed. Therefore, small animals have high ratios of surface to volume, while large animals cover themselves with relatively little surface.

Among cold-blooded animals lacking any physiological mechanism for   10
keeping their temperatures constant, small creatures have a hell of a time keeping warm—because they lose so much heat through their relatively large surfaces. On the other hand, large animals, with their relatively small surfaces, may lose heat so slowly that, once warm, they may maintain effectively constant temperatures against ordinary fluctuations of climate. (In fact, the resolution of the "hot-blooded dinosaur" controversy that burned so brightly a few years back may simply be that, while large dinosaurs possessed no physiological mechanism for constant temperature, and were not therefore warm-blooded in the technical sense, their large size and relatively small surface area kept them warm.)

Colbert, Cowles, and Bogert compared the warming rates of small and large alligators. As predicted, the small fellows heated up (and cooled down) more quickly. When exposed to a warm sun, a tiny 50-gram (1.76-ounce)

3. Galileo Galilei (1564–1642), Italian astronomer and mathematician.

alligator heated up one degree Celsius every minute and a half, while a large alligator, 260 times bigger at 13,000 grams (28.7 pounds), took seven and a half minutes to gain a degree. Extrapolating up to an adult 10-ton dinosaur, they concluded that a one-degree rise in body temperature would take eighty-six hours. If large animals absorb heat so slowly (through their relatively small surfaces), they will also be unable to shed any excess heat gained when temperatures rise above a favorable level.

The authors then guessed that large dinosaurs lived at or near their optimum temperatures; Cowles suggested that a rise in global temperatures just before the Cretaceous extinction caused the dinosaurs to heat up beyond their optimal tolerance—and, being so large, they couldn't shed the unwanted heat. (In a most unusual statement within a scientific paper, Colbert and Bogert then explicitly disavowed this speculative extension of their empirical work on alligators.) Cowles conceded that this excess heat probably wasn't enough to kill or even to enervate the great beasts, but since testes often function only within a narrow range of temperature, he proposed that this global rise might have sterilized all the males, causing extinction by natural contraception.

The overdose theory has recently been supported by UCLA psychiatrist Ronald K. Siegel. Siegel has gathered, he claims, more than 2,000 records of animals who, when given access, administer various drugs to themselves—from a mere swig of alcohol to massive doses of the big H. Elephants will swill the equivalent of twenty beers at a time, but do not like alcohol in concentrations greater than 7 percent. In a silly bit of anthropocentric speculation, Siegel states that "elephants drink, perhaps, to forget . . . the anxiety produced by shrinking rangeland and the competition for food."

Since fertile imaginations can apply almost any hot idea to the extinction of dinosaurs, Siegel found a way. Flowering plants did not evolve until late in the dinosaurs' reign. These plants also produced an array of aromatic, amino-acid-based alkaloids—the major group of psychoactive agents. Most mammals are "smart" enough to avoid these potential poisons. The alkaloids simply don't taste good (they are bitter); in any case, we mammals have livers happily supplied with the capacity to detoxify them. But, Siegel speculates, perhaps dinosaurs could neither taste the bitterness nor detoxify the substances once ingested. He recently told members of the American Psychological Association: "I'm not suggesting that all dinosaurs OD'd on plant drugs, but it certainly was a factor." He also argued that death by overdose may help explain why so many dinosaur fossils are found in contorted positions. (Do not go gentle into that good night.)

15   Extraterrestrial catastrophes have long pedigrees in the popular literature of extinction, but the subject exploded again in 1979, after a long lull, when the father-son, physicist-geologist team of Luis and Walter Alvarez proposed that an asteroid, some 10 km in diameter, struck the earth 65 million years ago (comets, rather than asteroids, have since gained favor. . . . Good science is self-corrective).

The force of such a collision would be immense, greater by far than the megatonnage of all the world's nuclear weapons. . . . In trying to reconstruct a scenario that would explain the simultaneous dying of dinosaurs on land and so many creatures in the sea, the Alvarezes proposed that a gigantic dust cloud, generated by particles blown aloft in the impact, would so darken the earth that photosynthesis would cease and temperatures drop precipitously. (Rage, rage against the dying of the light.) The single-celled photosynthetic oceanic plankton, with life cycles measured in weeks, would perish outright, but land plants might survive through the dormancy of their seeds (land plants were not much affected by the Cretaceous extinction, and any adequate theory must account for the curious pattern of differential survival). Dinosaurs would die by starvation and freezing; small, warm-blooded mammals, with more modest requirements for food and better regulation of body temperature, would squeak through. "Let the bastards freeze in the dark," as bumper stickers of our chauvinistic neighbors in sunbelt states proclaimed several years ago during the Northeast's winter oil crisis.

All three theories, testicular malfunction, psychoactive overdosing, and asteroidal zapping, grab our attention mightily. As pure phenomenology, they rank about equally high on any hit parade of primal fascination. Yet one represents expansive science, the others restrictive and untestable speculation. The proper criterion lies in evidence and methodology; we must probe behind the superficial fascination of particular claims.

How could we possibly decide whether the hypothesis of testicular frying is right or wrong? We would have to know things that the fossil record cannot provide. What temperatures were optimal for dinosaurs? Could they avoid the absorption of excess heat by staying in the shade, or in caves? At what temperatures did their testicles cease to function? Were late Cretaceous climates ever warm enough to drive the internal temperatures of dinosaurs close to this ceiling? Testicles simply don't fossilize, and how could we infer their temperature tolerances even if they did? In short, Cowles's hypothesis is only an intriguing speculation leading nowhere. The most damning statement against it appeared right in the conclusion of Colbert, Cowles, and Bogert's paper, when they admitted: "It is difficult to advance any definite arguments against this hypothesis." My statement may seem paradoxical—isn't a hypothesis really good if you can't devise any arguments against it? Quite the contrary. It is simply untestable and unusable.

Siegel's overdosing has even less going for it. At least Cowles extrapolated his conclusion from some good data on alligators. And he didn't completely violate the primary guideline of siting dinosaur extinction in the context of a general mass dying—for rise in temperature could be the root cause of a general catastrophe, zapping dinosaurs by testicular malfunction and different groups for other reasons. But Siegel's speculation cannot touch the extinction of ammonites or oceanic plankton (diatoms make their own food with good sweet sunlight; they don't OD on the chemicals of terrestrial plants). It is simply a gratuitous, attention-grabbing guess. It cannot be tested, for how can we know what dinosaurs tasted and what their livers could do? Livers don't fossilize any better than testicles.

The hypothesis doesn't even make any sense in its own context. Angiosperms were in full flower ten million years before dinosaurs went the way of

20

all flesh. Why did it take so long? As for the pains of a chemical death recorded in contortions of fossils, I regret to say (or rather I'm pleased to note for the dinosaurs' sake) that Siegel's knowledge of geology must be a bit deficient: muscles contract after death and geological strata rise and fall with motions of the earth's crust after burial—more than enough reason to distort a fossil's pristine appearance.

The impact story, on the other hand, has a sound basis in evidence. It can be tested, extended, refined and, if wrong, disproved. The Alvarezes did not just construct an arresting guess for public consumption. They proposed their hypothesis after laborious geochemical studies with Frank Asaro and Helen Michael had revealed a massive increase of iridium in rocks deposited right at the time of extinction. Iridium, a rare metal of the platinum group, is virtually absent from indigenous rocks of the earth's crust; most of our iridium arrives on extraterrestrial objects that strike the earth.

The Alvarez hypothesis bore immediate fruit. Based originally on evidence from two European localities, it led geochemists throughout the world to examine other sediments of the same age. They found abnormally high amounts of iridium everywhere—from continental rocks of the western United States to deep sea cores from the South Atlantic.

Cowles proposed his testicular hypothesis in the mid-1940s. Where has it gone since then? Absolutely nowhere, because scientists can do nothing with it. The hypothesis must stand as a curious appendage to a solid study of alligators. Siegel's overdose scenario will also win a few press notices and fade into oblivion. The Alvarezes' asteroid falls into a different category altogether, and much of the popular commentary has missed this essential distinction by focusing on the impact and its attendant results, and forgetting what really matters to a scientist—the iridium. If you talk just about asteroids, dust, and darkness, you tell stories no better, and no more entertaining than fried testicles or terminal trips. It is the iridium—the source of testable evidence—that counts and forges the crucial distinction between speculation and science.

The proof, to twist a phrase, lies in the doing. Cowles's hypothesis has generated nothing in thirty-five years. Since its proposal in 1979, the Alvarez hypothesis has spawned hundreds of studies, a major conference, and attendant publications. Geologists are fired up. They are looking for iridium at all other extinction boundaries. Every week exposes a new wrinkle in the scientific press. Further evidence that the Cretaceous iridium represents extraterrestrial impact and not indigenous volcanism continues to accumulate. As I revise this essay in November 1984 (this paragraph will be out of date when the book is published), new data include chemical "signatures" of other isotopes indicating unearthly provenance, glass spherules of a size and sort produced by impact and not by volcanic eruptions, and high-pressure varieties of silica formed (so far as we know) only under the tremendous shock of impact.

25   My point is simply this: Whatever the eventual outcome (I suspect it will be positive), the Alvarez hypothesis is exciting, fruitful science because it generates tests, provides us with things to do, and expands outward. We are hav-

ing fun, battling back and forth, moving toward a resolution, and extending the hypothesis beyond its original scope. . . .

As just one example of the unexpected, distant cross-fertilization that good science engenders, the Alvarez hypothesis made a major contribution to a theme that has riveted public attention in the past few months—so-called nuclear winter. . . . In a speech delivered in April 1982, Luis Alvarez calculated the energy that a ten-kilometer asteroid would release on impact. He compared such an explosion with a full nuclear exchange and implied that all-out atomic war might unleash similar consequences.

This theme of impact leading to massive dust clouds and falling temperatures formed an important input to the decision of Carl Sagan[4] and a group of colleagues to model the climatic consequences of nuclear holocaust. Full nuclear exchange would probably generate the same kind of dust cloud and darkening that may have wiped out the dinosaurs. Temperatures would drop precipitously and agriculture might become impossible. Avoidance of nuclear war is fundamentally an ethical and political imperative, but we must know the factual consequences to make firm judgments. I am heartened by a final link across disciplines and deep concerns—another criterion, by the way, of science at its best:[5] A recognition of the very phenomenon that made our evolution possible by exterminating the previously dominant dinosaurs and clearing a way for the evolution of large mammals, including us, might actually help to save us from joining those magnificent beasts in contorted poses among the strata of the earth.

4. American scientist and writer (1934–1996) who hosted and produced the popular TV series *Cosmos* (1980).

5. This quirky connection so tickles my fancy that I break my own strict rule about eliminating redundancies from these essays and end both this and the next piece with this prod to thought and action [Gould's note].

MLA CITATION

Gould, Stephen Jay. "Sex, Drugs, Disasters, and the Extinction of Dinosaurs." 1984. *The Norton Reader: An Anthology of Nonfiction.* Ed. Melissa A. Goldthwaite et al. 14th ed. New York: Norton, 2016. 843–49. Print.

QUESTIONS

1. What criteria does Stephen Jay Gould use to distinguish good science from "silly speculation" (paragraph 3)?

2. Gould writes about dinosaurs, but his goal is to make a point about science. How does Gould use his examples to make this point?

3. The first five essays in the "Science" chapter of *The Norton Reader* were written by scientists or historians of science to explain what science is and how it works. Yet these writers approach their common subject from different perspectives and

sometimes seem even to disagree. Imagine Goethe and T. H. Huxley (pp. 820–23), Isaac Asimov (pp. 824–28), Thomas S. Kuhn (pp. 829–37), Stephen Hawking and Leonard Mlodinow (pp. 838–42), and Gould (or some smaller group of them) as characters in a play having a casual conversation that veers into a discussion of science. Write the script for this scene. Annotate your script by linking your lines of dialogue to passages in the essays.

DAVID H. FREEDMAN *Lies, Damned Lies, and Medical Science*

Much of what medical researchers conclude in their studies is misleading, exaggerated, or flat-out wrong. So why are doctors—to a striking extent—still drawing upon misinformation in their everyday practice? Dr. John Ioannidis has spent his career challenging his peers by exposing their bad science.

I N 2001, RUMORS WERE CIRCULATING in Greek hospitals that surgery residents, eager to rack up scalpel time, were falsely diagnosing hapless Albanian immigrants with appendicitis. At the University of Ioannina medical school's teaching hospital, a newly minted doctor named Athina Tatsioni was discussing the rumors with colleagues when a professor who had overheard asked her if she'd like to try to prove whether they were true—he seemed to be almost daring her. She accepted the challenge and, with the professor's and other colleagues' help, eventually produced a formal study showing that, for whatever reason, the appendices removed from patients with Albanian names in six Greek hospitals were more than three times as likely to be perfectly healthy as those removed from patients with Greek names. "It was hard to find a journal willing to publish it, but we did," recalls Tatsioni. "I also discovered that I really liked research." Good thing, because the study had actually been a sort of audition. The professor, it turned out, had been putting together a team of exceptionally brash and curious young clinicians and Ph.D.s to join him in tackling an unusual and controversial agenda.

Last spring, I sat in on one of the team's weekly meetings on the medical school's campus, which is plunked crazily across a series of sharp hills. The building in which we met, like most at the school, had the look of a barracks and was festooned with political graffiti. But the group convened in a spacious conference room that would have been at home at a Silicon Valley start-up.

Published in the Atlantic *(2010), a magazine covering literature, culture, and politics.*

Dr. John Ioannidis.

Sprawled around a large table were Tatsioni and eight other youngish Greek researchers and physicians who, in contrast to the pasty younger staff frequently seen in U.S. hospitals, looked like the casually glamorous cast of a television medical drama. The professor, a dapper and soft-spoken man named John Ioannidis, loosely presided.

One of the researchers, a biostatistician named Georgia Salanti, fired up a laptop and projector and started to take the group through a study she and a few colleagues were completing that asked this question: were drug companies manipulating published research to make their drugs look good? Salanti ticked off data that seemed to indicate they were, but the other team members almost immediately started interrupting. One noted that Salanti's study didn't address the fact that drug-company research wasn't measuring critically important "hard" outcomes for patients, such as survival versus death, and instead tended to measure "softer" outcomes, such as self-reported symptoms ("my chest doesn't hurt as much today"). Another pointed out that Salanti's study ignored the fact that when drug-company data seemed to show patients' health improving, the data often failed to show that the drug was responsible, or that the improvement was more than marginal.

Salanti remained poised, as if the grilling were par for the course, and gamely acknowledged that the suggestions were all good—but a single study can't prove everything, she said. Just as I was getting the sense that the data in drug studies were endlessly malleable, Ioannidis, who had mostly been listening, delivered what felt like a coup de grâce: wasn't it possible, he asked, that drug companies were carefully selecting the topics of their studies—for example, comparing their new drugs against those already known to be inferior to others on the market—so that they were ahead of the game even before the data juggling began? "Maybe sometimes it's the questions that are biased, not the answers," he said, flashing a friendly smile. Everyone nodded. Though the results of drug studies often make newspaper headlines, you have to wonder whether they prove anything at all. Indeed, given the breadth of the potential problems raised at the meeting, can *any* medical-research studies be trusted?

5   That question has been central to Ioannidis's career. He's what's known as a meta-researcher, and he's become one of the world's foremost experts on the credibility of medical research. He and his team have shown, again and again, and in many different ways, that much of what biomedical researchers conclude in published studies—conclusions that doctors keep in mind when they prescribe antibiotics or blood-pressure medication, or when they advise us to consume more fiber or less meat, or when they recommend surgery for heart disease or back pain—is misleading, exaggerated, and often flat-out wrong. He charges that as much as 90 percent of the published medical information that doctors rely on is flawed. His work has been widely accepted by the medical community; it has been published in the field's top journals, where it is heavily cited; and he is a big draw at conferences. Given this exposure, and the fact that his work broadly targets everyone else's work in medicine, as well as everything that physicians do and all the health advice we get, Ioannidis may be one of the most influential scientists alive. Yet for all his influence, he worries that the field of medical research is so pervasively flawed, and so riddled with conflicts of interest, that it might be chronically resistant to change—or even to publicly admitting that there's a problem.

The city of Ioannina is a big college town a short drive from the ruins of a 20,000-seat amphitheater and a Zeusian sanctuary built at the site of the Dodona oracle. The oracle was said to have issued pronouncements to priests through the rustling of a sacred oak tree. Today, a different oak tree at the site provides visitors with a chance to try their own hands at extracting a prophecy. "I take all the researchers who visit me here, and almost every single one of them asks the tree the same question," Ioannidis tells me, as we contemplate the tree the day after the team's meeting. "'Will my research grant be approved?'" He chuckles, but Ioannidis (pronounced yo-NEE-dees) tends to laugh not so much in mirth as to soften the sting of his attack. And sure enough, he goes on to suggest that an obsession with winning funding has gone a long way toward weakening the reliability of medical research.

He first stumbled on the sorts of problems plaguing the field, he explains, as a young physician-researcher in the early 1990s at Harvard. At the time, he was interested in diagnosing rare diseases, for which a lack of case data can leave doctors with little to go on other than intuition and rules of thumb. But he noticed that doctors seemed to proceed in much the same manner even when it came to cancer, heart disease, and other common ailments. Where were the hard data that would back up their treatment decisions? There was plenty of published research, but much of it was remarkably unscientific, based largely on observations of a small number of cases. A new "evidence-based medicine" movement was just starting to gather force, and Ioannidis decided to throw himself into it, working first with prominent researchers at Tufts University and then taking positions at Johns Hopkins University and the National Institutes of Health. He was unusually well armed: he had been a math prodigy of near-celebrity status in high school in Greece, and had followed his parents, who were both physician-researchers, into medicine. Now he'd have a chance to combine math and medicine by applying rigorous statistical analysis to what seemed a surprisingly sloppy field. "I assumed that everything we physicians did was basically right, but now I was going to help verify it," he says. "All we'd have to do was systematically review the evidence, trust what it told us, and then everything would be perfect."

It didn't turn out that way. In poring over medical journals, he was struck by how many findings of all types were refuted by later findings. Of course, medical-science "never minds" are hardly secret. And they sometimes make headlines, as when in recent years large studies or growing consensuses of researchers concluded that mammograms, colonoscopies, and PSA tests are far less useful cancer-detection tools than we had been told; or when widely pre-scribed antidepressants such as Prozac, Zoloft, and Paxil were revealed to be no more effective than a placebo for most cases of depression; or when we learned that staying out of the sun entirely can actually increase cancer risks; or when we were told that the advice to drink lots of water during intense exercise was potentially fatal; or when, last April, we were informed that taking fish oil, exercising, and doing puzzles doesn't really help fend off Alzheimer's disease, as long claimed. Peer-reviewed studies have come to opposite conclusions on whether using cell phones can cause brain cancer, whether sleeping more than eight hours a night is healthful or dangerous, whether taking aspirin every day is more likely to save your life or cut it short, and whether routine angioplasty works better than pills to unclog heart arteries.

But beyond the headlines, Ioannidis was shocked at the range and reach of the reversals he was seeing in everyday medical research. "Randomized controlled trials," which compare how one group responds to a treatment against how an identical group fares without the treatment, had long been considered nearly unshakable evidence, but they, too, ended up being wrong some of the time. "I realized even our gold-standard research had a lot of problems," he says. Baffled, he started looking for the specific ways in which studies were going wrong. And before long he discovered that the range of errors being committed was astonishing: from what questions researchers posed, to how they set up the studies, to which patients they recruited for the studies, to which measurements they took, to how they analyzed the data, to how they presented their results, to how particular studies came to be published in medical journals.

This array suggested a bigger, underlying dysfunction, and Ioannidis thought   10 he knew what it was. "The studies were biased," he says. "Sometimes they were overtly biased. Sometimes it was difficult to see the bias, but it was there." Researchers headed into their studies wanting certain results—and, lo and behold, they were getting them. We think of the scientific process as being objective, rigorous, and even ruthless in separating out what is true from what we merely wish to be true, but in fact it's easy to manipulate results, even unintentionally or unconsciously. "At every step in the process, there is room to distort results, a way to make a stronger claim or to select what is going to be concluded," says Ioannidis. "There is an intellectual conflict of interest that pressures researchers to find whatever it is that is most likely to get them funded."

Perhaps only a minority of researchers were succumbing to this bias, but their distorted findings were having an outsize effect on published research. To get funding and tenured positions, and often merely to stay afloat, researchers have to get their work published in well-regarded journals, where rejection rates can climb above 90 percent. Not surprisingly, the studies that tend to make the grade are those with eye-catching findings. But while coming up with eye-catching theories is relatively easy, getting reality to bear them out is another matter. The great majority collapse under the weight of contradictory data when studied rigorously. Imagine, though, that five different research teams test an interesting theory that's making the rounds, and four of the groups correctly prove the idea false, while the one less cautious group incorrectly "proves" it true through some combination of error, fluke, and clever selection of data. Guess whose findings your doctor ends up reading about in the journal, and you end up hearing about on the evening news? Researchers can sometimes win attention by refuting a prominent finding, which can help to at least raise doubts about results, but in general it is far more rewarding to add a new insight or exciting-sounding twist to existing research than to retest its basic premises— after all, simply re-proving someone else's results is unlikely to get you published, and attempting to undermine the work of respected colleagues can have ugly professional repercussions.

In the late 1990s, Ioannidis set up a base at the University of Ioannina. He pulled together his team, which remains largely intact today, and started chipping away at the problem in a series of papers that pointed out specific ways certain studies were getting misleading results. Other meta-researchers were also starting to spotlight disturbingly high rates of error in the medical literature. But Ioannidis wanted to get the big picture across, and to do so with solid data, clear reasoning, and good statistical analysis. The project dragged on, until finally he retreated to the tiny island of Sikinos in the Aegean Sea, where he drew inspiration from the relatively primitive surroundings and the intellectual traditions they recalled. "A pervasive theme of ancient Greek literature is that you need to pursue the truth, no matter what the truth might be," he says. In 2005, he unleashed two papers that challenged the foundations of medical research.

He chose to publish one paper, fittingly, in the online journal *PLoS Medicine*, which is committed to running any methodologically sound article without regard to how "interesting" the results may be. In the paper, Ioannidis laid out a detailed mathematical proof that, assuming modest levels of researcher bias, typically imperfect research techniques, and the well-known tendency to focus on exciting rather than highly plausible theories, researchers will come up with wrong findings most of the time. Simply put, if you're attracted to ideas that have a good chance of being wrong, and if you're motivated to prove them right, and if you have a little wiggle room in how you assemble the evidence, you'll probably succeed in proving wrong theories right. His model predicted, in different fields of medical research, rates of wrongness roughly corresponding to the observed rates at which findings were later convincingly refuted: 80 percent of non-randomized studies (by far the most common type) turn out to be wrong, as do 25 percent of supposedly gold-standard randomized trials, and as much as 10 percent of the platinum-standard large randomized trials. The article spelled out his belief that researchers were frequently manipulating data analyses, chasing career-advancing findings rather than good science, and even using the peer-review process—in which journals ask researchers to help decide which studies to publish—to suppress opposing views. "You can question some of the details of John's calculations, but it's hard to argue that the essential ideas aren't absolutely correct," says Doug Altman, an Oxford University researcher who directs the Centre for Statistics in Medicine.

Still, Ioannidis anticipated that the community might shrug off his findings: sure, a lot of dubious research makes it into journals, but we researchers and physicians know to ignore it and focus on the good stuff, so what's the big deal? The other paper headed off that claim. He zoomed in on 49 of the most highly regarded research findings in medicine over the previous 13 years, as judged by the science community's two standard measures: the papers had appeared in the journals most widely cited in research articles, and the 49 articles themselves were the most widely cited articles in these journals. These were articles that helped lead to the widespread popularity of treatments such as the use of hormone-replacement therapy for menopausal women, vitamin E to reduce the risk of heart disease, coronary stents to ward off heart attacks, and daily low-dose aspirin to control blood pressure and prevent heart attacks and strokes. Ioannidis was putting his contentions to the test not against run-of-the-mill research, or even merely well-accepted research, but against the absolute tip of the research pyramid. Of the 49 articles, 45 claimed to have uncovered effective interventions. Thirty-four of these claims had been retested, and 14 of these, or 41 percent, had been convincingly shown to be wrong or significantly exaggerated. If between a third and a half of the most acclaimed research in medicine was proving untrustworthy, the scope and impact of the problem were undeniable. That article was published in the *Journal of the American Medical Association*.

Driving me back to campus in his smallish SUV—after insisting, as he apparently does with all his visitors, on showing me a nearby lake and the six monasteries situated on an islet within it—Ioannidis apologized profusely for running a yellow light, explaining with a laugh that he didn't trust the truck behind him to stop. Considering his willingness, even eagerness, to slap the face of the medical-research community, Ioannidis comes off as thoughtful, upbeat, and deeply civil. He's a careful listener, and his frequent grin and semi-apologetic chuckle can make the sharp prodding of his arguments seem almost good-natured. He is as quick, if not quicker, to question his own motives and competence as anyone else's. A neat and compact 45-year-old with a trim mustache,

15

he presents as a sort of dashing nerd—Giancarlo Giannini with a bit of Mr. Bean.[1]

The humility and graciousness seem to serve him well in getting across a message that is not easy to digest or, for that matter, believe: that even highly regarded researchers at prestigious institutions sometimes churn out attention-grabbing findings rather than findings likely to be right. But Ioannidis points out that obviously questionable findings cram the pages of top medical journals, not to mention the morning headlines. Consider, he says, the endless stream of results from nutritional studies in which researchers follow thousands of people for some number of years, tracking what they eat and what supplements they take, and how their health changes over the course of the study. "Then the researchers start asking, 'What did vitamin E do? What did vitamin C or D or A do? What changed with calorie intake, or protein or fat intake? What happened to cholesterol levels? Who got what type of cancer?'" he says. "They run everything through the mill, one at a time, and they start finding associations, and eventually conclude that vitamin X lowers the risk of cancer Y, or this food helps with the risk of that disease." In a single week this fall, Google's news page offered these headlines: "More Omega-3 Fats Didn't Aid Heart Patients"; "Fruits, Vegetables Cut Cancer Risk for Smokers"; "Soy May Ease Sleep Problems in Older Women"; and dozens of similar stories.

When a five-year study of 10,000 people finds that those who take more vitamin X are less likely to get cancer Y, you'd think you have pretty good reason to take more vitamin X, and physicians routinely pass these recommendations on to patients. But these studies often sharply conflict with one another. Studies have gone back and forth on the cancer-preventing powers of vitamins A, D, and E; on the heart-health benefits of eating fat and carbs; and even on the question of whether being overweight is more likely to extend or shorten your life. How should we choose among these dueling, high-profile nutritional findings? Ioannidis suggests a simple approach: ignore them all.

For starters, he explains, the odds are that in any large database of many nutritional and health factors, there will be a few apparent connections that are in fact merely flukes, not real health effects—it's a bit like combing through long, random strings of letters and claiming there's an important message in any words that happen to turn up. But even if a study managed to highlight a genuine health connection to some nutrient, you're unlikely to benefit much from taking more of it, because we consume thousands of nutrients that act together as a sort of network, and changing intake of just one of them is bound to cause ripples throughout the network that are far too complex for these studies to detect, and that may be as likely to harm you as help you. Even if changing that one factor does bring on the claimed improvement, there's still a good chance that it won't do you much good in the long run, because these studies rarely go on long enough to track the decades-long course of disease and ultimately death. Instead, they track easily measurable health "markers" such as

---

1. Giannini (b. 1942), multilingual Italian film actor and director; Mr. Bean, comic TV character invented by English actor Rowan Atkinson.

cholesterol levels, blood pressure, and blood-sugar levels, and meta-experts have shown that changes in these markers often don't correlate as well with long-term health as we have been led to believe.

On the relatively rare occasions when a study does go on long enough to track mortality, the findings frequently upend those of the shorter studies. (For example, though the vast majority of studies of overweight individuals link excess weight to ill health, the longest of them haven't convincingly shown that overweight people are likely to die sooner, and a few of them have seemingly demonstrated that moderately overweight people are likely to live *longer*.) And these problems are aside from ubiquitous measurement errors (for example, people habitually misreport their diets in studies), routine misanalysis (research-ers rely on complex software capable of juggling results in ways they don't always understand), and the less common, but serious, problem of outright fraud (which has been revealed, in confidential surveys, to be much more widespread than scientists like to acknowledge).

If a study somehow avoids every one of these problems and finds a real con-   20
nection to long-term changes in health, you're still not guaranteed to benefit, because studies report average results that typically represent a vast range of individual outcomes. Should you be among the lucky minority that stands to benefit, don't expect a noticeable improvement in your health, because studies usually detect only modest effects that merely tend to whittle your chances of succumbing to a particular disease from small to somewhat smaller. "The odds that anything useful will survive from any of these studies are poor," says Ioannidis—dismissing in a breath a good chunk of the research into which we sink about $100 billion a year in the United States alone.

And so it goes for all medical studies, he says. Indeed, nutritional studies aren't the worst. Drug studies have the added corruptive force of financial con-flict of interest. The exciting links between genes and various diseases and traits that are relentlessly hyped in the press for heralding miraculous around-the-corner treatments for everything from colon cancer to schizophrenia have in the past proved so vulnerable to error and distortion, Ioannidis has found, that in some cases you'd have done about as well by throwing darts at a chart of the genome. (These studies seem to have improved somewhat in recent years, but whether they will hold up or be useful in treatment are still open ques-tions.) Vioxx, Zelnorm, and Baycol were among the widely prescribed drugs found to be safe and effective in large randomized controlled trials before the drugs were yanked from the market as unsafe or not so effective, or both.

"Often the claims made by studies are so extravagant that you can imme-diately cross them out without needing to know much about the specific prob-lems with the studies," Ioannidis says. But of course it's that very extravagance of claim (one large randomized controlled trial even proved that secret prayer by unknown parties can save the lives of heart-surgery patients, while another proved that secret prayer can harm them) that helps gets these findings into journals and then into our treatments and lifestyles, especially when the claim builds on impressive-sounding evidence. "Even when the evidence shows that a particular research idea is wrong, if you have thousands of scientists who have invested their careers in it, they'll continue to publish papers on it," he says. "It's like an epidemic, in the sense that they're infected with these wrong ideas, and they're spreading it to other researchers through journals."

Though scientists and science journalists are constantly talking up the value of the peer-review process, researchers admit among themselves that biased, erroneous, and even blatantly fraudulent studies easily slip through it. *Nature*, the grande dame of science journals, stated in a 2006 editorial, "Scientists understand that peer review per se provides only a minimal assurance of quality, and that the public conception of peer review as a stamp of authentication is far from the truth." What's more, the peer-review process often pressures researchers to shy away from striking out in genuinely new directions, and instead to build on the findings of their colleagues (that is, their potential reviewers) in ways that only *seem* like breakthroughs—as with the exciting-sounding gene linkages (autism genes identified!) and nutritional findings (olive oil lowers blood pressure!) that are really just dubious and conflicting variations on a theme.

Most journal editors don't even claim to protect against the problems that plague these studies. University and government research overseers rarely step in to directly enforce research quality, and when they do, the science community goes ballistic over the outside interference. The ultimate protection against research error and bias is supposed to come from the way scientists constantly retest each other's results—except they don't. Only the most prominent findings are likely to be put to the test, because there's likely to be publication payoff in firming up the proof, or contradicting it.

25   But even for medicine's most influential studies, the evidence sometimes remains surprisingly narrow. Of those 45 super-cited studies that Ioannidis focused on, 11 had never been retested. Perhaps worse, Ioannidis found that even when a research error is outed, it typically persists for years or even decades. He looked at three prominent health studies from the 1980s and 1990s that were each later soundly refuted, and discovered that researchers continued to cite the original results as correct more often than as flawed—in one case for at least 12 years after the results were discredited.

Doctors may notice that their patients don't seem to fare as well with certain treatments as the literature would lead them to expect, but the field is appropriately conditioned to subjugate such anecdotal evidence to study findings. Yet much, perhaps even most, of what doctors do has never been formally put to the test in credible studies, given that the need to do so became obvious to the field only in the 1990s, leaving it playing catch-up with a century or more of non-evidence-based medicine, and contributing to Ioannidis's shockingly high estimate of the degree to which medical knowledge is flawed. That we're not routinely made seriously ill by this shortfall, he argues, is due largely to the fact that most medical interventions and advice don't address life-and-death situations, but rather aim to leave us marginally healthier or less unhealthy, so we usually neither gain nor risk all that much.

Medical research is not especially plagued with wrongness. Other meta-research experts have confirmed that similar issues distort research in all fields of science, from physics to economics (where the highly regarded economists J. Bradford DeLong and Kevin Lang once showed how a remarkably consistent paucity of strong evidence in published economics studies made it unlikely that *any* of them were right). And needless to say, things only get worse when it comes to the pop expertise that endlessly spews at us from diet, relationship, invest-ment, and parenting gurus and pundits. But we expect more of scientists, and especially of medical scientists, given that we believe we are staking our lives on their results. The public hardly recognizes how bad a bet this is. The medical community itself might still be largely oblivious to the scope of the problem, if Ioannidis hadn't forced a confrontation when he published his studies in 2005.

Ioannidis initially thought the community might come out fighting. Instead, it seemed relieved, as if it had been guiltily waiting for someone to blow the whistle, and eager to hear more. David Gorski, a surgeon and researcher at Detroit's Barbara Ann Karmanos Cancer Institute, noted in his prominent med-ical blog that when he presented Ioannidis's paper on highly cited research at a professional meeting, "not a single one of my surgical colleagues was the least bit surprised or disturbed by its findings." Ioannidis offers a theory for the rela-tively calm reception. "I think that people didn't feel I was only trying to provoke them, because I showed that it was a community problem, instead of pointing fingers at individual examples of bad research," he says. In a sense, he gave scien-tists an opportunity to cluck about the wrongness without having to acknowledge that they themselves succumb to it—it was something everyone else did.

To say that Ioannidis's work has been embraced would be an understate-ment. His *PLoS Medicine* paper is the most downloaded in the journal's history, and it's not even Ioannidis's most-cited work—that would be a paper he pub-lished in *Nature Genetics* on the problems with gene-link studies. Other research-ers are eager to work with him: he has published papers with 1,328 different co-authors at 538 institutions in 43 countries, he says. Last year he received, by his estimate, invitations to speak at 1,000 conferences and institutions around the world, and he was accepting an average of about five invitations a month until a case last year of excessive-travel-induced vertigo led him to cut back. Even so, in the weeks before I visited him he had addressed an AIDS conference in San Francisco, the European Society for Clinical Investigation, Harvard's School of Public Health, and the medical schools at Stanford and Tufts.

The irony of his having achieved this sort of success by accusing the medical-research community of chasing after success is not lost on him, and he notes that it ought to raise the question of whether he himself might be pumping up his findings. "If I did a study and the results showed that in fact there wasn't really much bias in research, would I be willing to publish it?" he asks. "That would create a real psychological conflict for me." But his big-ger worry, he says, is that while his fellow researchers seem to be getting the message, he hasn't necessarily forced anyone to do a better job. He fears he

30

won't in the end have done much to improve anyone's health. "There may not be fierce objections to what I'm saying," he explains. "But it's difficult to change the way that everyday doctors, patients, and healthy people think and behave."

As helter-skelter as the University of Ioannina Medical School campus looks, the hospital abutting it looks reassuringly stolid. Athina Tatsioni has offered to take me on a tour of the facility, but we make it only as far as the entrance when she is greeted—accosted, really—by a worried-looking older woman. Tatsioni, normally a bit reserved, is warm and animated with the woman, and the two have a brief but intense conversation before embracing and saying good-bye. Tatsioni explains to me that the woman and her husband were patients of hers years ago; now the husband has been admitted to the hospital with abdominal pains, and Tatsioni has promised she'll stop by his room later to say hello. Recalling the appendicitis story, I prod a bit, and she confesses she plans to do her own exam. She needs to be circumspect, though, so she won't appear to be second-guessing the other doctors.

Tatsioni doesn't so much fear that someone will carve out the man's healthy appendix. Rather, she's concerned that, like many patients, he'll end up with prescriptions for multiple drugs that will do little to help him, and may well harm him. "Usually what happens is that the doctor will ask for a suite of biochemical tests—liver fat, pancreas function, and so on," she tells me. "The tests could turn up something, but they're probably irrelevant. Just having a good talk with the patient and getting a close history is much more likely to tell me what's wrong." Of course, the doctors have all been trained to order these tests, she notes, and doing so is a lot quicker than a long bedside chat. They're also trained to ply the patient with whatever drugs might help whack any errant test numbers back into line. What they're not trained to do is to go back and look at the research papers that helped make these drugs the standard of care. "When you look the papers up, you often find the drugs didn't even work better than a placebo. And no one tested how they worked in combination with the other drugs," she says. "Just taking the patient off everything can improve their health right away." But not only is checking out the research another time-consuming task, patients often don't even *like* it when they're taken off their drugs, she explains; they find their prescriptions reassuring.

Later, Ioannidis tells me he makes a point of having several clinicians on his team. "Researchers and physicians often don't understand each other; they speak different languages," he says. Knowing that some of his researchers are spending more than half their time seeing patients makes him feel the team is better positioned to bridge that gap; their experience informs the team's research with firsthand knowledge, and helps the team shape its papers in a way more likely to hit home with physicians. It's not that he envisions doctors making all their decisions based solely on solid evidence—there's simply too much complexity in patient treatment to pin down every situation with a great study. "Doctors need to rely on instinct and judgment to make choices," he says. "But these choices should be as informed as possible by the evidence. And if the evidence isn't good, doctors should know that, too. And so should patients."

In fact, the question of whether the problems with medical research should be broadcast to the public is a sticky one in the meta-research community. Already feeling that they're fighting to keep patients from turning to alternative medical treatments such as homeopathy, or misdiagnosing themselves on the Internet, or simply neglecting medical treatment altogether, many researchers and physicians aren't eager to provide even more reason to be skeptical of what doctors do—not to mention how public disenchantment with medicine could affect research funding. Ioannidis dismisses these concerns. "If we don't tell the public about these problems, then we're no better than nonscientists who falsely claim they can heal," he says. "If the drugs don't work and we're not sure how to treat something, why should we claim differently? Some fear that there may be less funding because we stop claiming we can prove we have miraculous treatments. But if we can't really provide those miracles, how long will we be able to fool the public anyway? The scientific enterprise is probably the most fantastic achievement in human history, but that doesn't mean we have a right to overstate what we're accomplishing."

We could solve much of the wrongness problem, Ioannidis says, if the world   35
simply stopped expecting scientists to be right. That's because being wrong in science is fine, and even necessary—as long as scientists recognize that they blew it, report their mistake openly instead of disguising it as a success, and then move on to the next thing, until they come up with the very occasional genuine breakthrough. But as long as careers remain contingent on producing a stream of research that's dressed up to seem more right than it is, scientists will keep delivering exactly that.

"Science is a noble endeavor, but it's also a low-yield endeavor," he says. "I'm not sure that more than a very small percentage of medical research is ever likely to lead to major improvements in clinical outcomes and quality of life. We should be very comfortable with that fact."

MLA CITATION

Freedman, David H. "Lies, Damned Lies, and Medical Science." 2010. *The Norton Reader: An Anthology of Nonfiction.* Ed. Melissa A. Goldthwaite et al. 14th ed. New York: Norton, 2016. 850–61. Print.

QUESTIONS

1. David H. Freedman frames his article as a profile of medical researcher John Ioannidis. Why might Freedman have taken this approach, rather than writing about the problems with medical research directly?

2. According to Freedman's article, what factors cause medical research to go wrong? Compare Ioannidis's understanding of "wrongness" to Isaac Asimov's (pp. 824–28).

3. According to the researchers Freedman interviews, how should medical research influence how doctors treat patients? Compare the views of these researchers to those expressed by Atul Gawande in his essay "When Doctors Make Mistakes" (pp. 652–69).

4. Near the end of his article, Freedman notes, "[T]he question of whether the problems with medical research should be broadcast to the public is a sticky one in the meta-research community" (paragraph 34). Write an essay that explains and justifies your own opinion on this question.

REBECCA SKLOOT   *The Woman in the Photograph*

T HERE'S A PHOTO ON MY WALL of a woman I've never met, its left corner torn and patched together with tape. She looks straight into the camera and smiles, hands on hips, dress suit neatly pressed, lips painted deep red. It's the late 1940s and she hasn't yet reached the age of thirty. Her light brown skin is smooth, her eyes still young and playful, oblivious to the tumor growing inside her—a tumor that would leave her five children motherless and change the future of medicine. Beneath the photo, a caption says her name is "Henrietta Lacks, Helen Lane or Helen Larson."

No one knows who took that picture, but it's appeared hundreds of times in magazines and science textbooks, on blogs and laboratory walls. She's usually identified as Helen Lane, but often she has no name at all. She's simply called HeLa, the code name given to the world's first immortal human cells— *her* cells, cut from her cervix just months before she died.

Her real name is Henrietta Lacks.

I've spent years staring at that photo, wondering what kind of life she led, what happened to her children, and what she'd think about cells from her cervix living on forever—bought, sold, packaged, and shipped by the trillions to laboratories around the world. I've tried to imagine how she'd feel knowing that her cells went up in the first space missions to see what would happen to human cells in zero gravity,[1] or that they helped with some of the most important

From The Immortal Life of Henrietta Lacks *(2010), Rebecca Skloot's account of science, race, and medical ethics. It tells the story of how the cells of one woman—taken without her consent when she died—contributed to numerous scientific discoveries in the fields of genetics, cancer treatment, and vaccination, among others.*

1. In 1960, a year before Yuri Gagarin (1934–1968) became the first person to enter outer space, a sample of HeLa cells was placed on the Russian *Korabl-Sputnik 2* satellite.

advances in medicine: the polio vaccine, chemotherapy, cloning, gene mapping, in vitro fertilization. I'm pretty sure that she—like most of us—would be shocked to hear that there are trillions more of her cells growing in laboratories now than there ever were in her body.

There's no way of knowing exactly how many of Henrietta's cells are alive today. One scientist estimates that if you could pile all HeLa cells ever grown onto a scale, they'd weigh more than 50 million metric tons—an inconceivable number, given that an individual cell weighs almost nothing. Another scientist calculated that if you could lay all HeLa cells ever grown end-to-end, they'd wrap around the Earth at least three times, spanning more than 350 million feet. In her prime, Henrietta herself stood only a bit over five feet tall.

I first learned about HeLa cells and the woman behind them in 1988, thirty-seven years after her death, when I was sixteen and sitting in a community college biology class. My instructor, Donald Defler, a gnomish balding man, paced at the front of the lecture hall and flipped on an overhead projector. He pointed to two diagrams that appeared on the wall behind him. They were schematics of the cell reproduction cycle, but to me they just looked like a neon-colored mess of arrows, squares, and circles with words I didn't understand, like "MPF Triggering a Chain Reaction of Protein Activations."

I was a kid who'd failed freshman year at the regular public high school because she never showed up. I'd transferred to an alternative school that offered dream studies instead of biology, so I was taking Defler's class for high-school credit, which meant that I was sitting in a college lecture hall at sixteen with words like *mitosis* and *kinase inhibitors* flying around. I was completely lost.

"Do we have to memorize everything on those diagrams?" one student yelled.

Yes, Defler said, we had to memorize the diagrams, and yes, they'd be on the test, but that didn't matter right then. What he wanted us to understand was that cells are amazing things: There are about one hundred trillion of them in our bodies, each so small that several thousand could fit on the period at the end of this sentence. They make up all our tissues—muscle, bone, blood—which in turn make up our organs.

Under the microscope, a cell looks a lot like a fried egg: It has a white (the *cytoplasm*) that's full of water and proteins to keep it fed, and a yolk (the *nucleus*) that holds all the genetic information that makes you you. The cytoplasm buzzes like a New York City street. It's crammed full of molecules and vessels endlessly shuttling enzymes and sugars from one part of the cell to another, pumping water, nutrients, and oxygen in and out of the cell. All the while, little cytoplasmic factories work 24/7, cranking out sugars, fats, proteins, and energy to keep the whole thing running and feed the nucleus—the brains of the operation. Inside every nucleus within each cell in your body, there's an identical copy of your entire genome. That genome tells cells when to grow and divide and makes

5

10

sure they do their jobs, whether that's controlling your heartbeat or helping your brain understand the words on this page.

Defler paced the front of the classroom telling us how mitosis—the process of cell division—makes it possible for embryos to grow into babies, and for our bodies to create new cells for healing wounds or replenishing blood we've lost. It was beautiful, he said, like a perfectly choreographed dance.

All it takes is one small mistake anywhere in the division process for cells to start growing out of control, he told us. Just *one* enzyme misfiring, just one wrong protein activation, and you could have cancer. Mitosis goes haywire, which is how it spreads.

"We learned that by studying cancer cells in culture," Defler said. He grinned and spun to face the board, where he wrote two words in enormous print: HENRIETTA LACKS.

Henrietta died in 1951 from a vicious case of cervical cancer, he told us. But before she died, a surgeon took samples of her tumor and put them in a petri dish. Scientists had been trying to keep human cells alive in culture for decades, but they all eventually died. Henrietta's were different: they reproduced an entire generation every twenty-four hours, and they never stopped. They became the first immortal human cells ever grown in a laboratory.

15   "Henrietta's cells have now been living outside her body far longer than they ever lived inside it," Defler said. If we went to almost any cell culture lab in the world and opened its freezers, he told us, we'd probably find millions—if not billions—of Henrietta's cells in small vials on ice.

Her cells were part of research into the genes that cause cancer and those that suppress it; they helped develop drugs for treating herpes, leukemia, influenza, hemophilia, and Parkinson's disease; and they've been used to study lactose digestion, sexually transmitted diseases, appendicitis, human longevity, mosquito mating, and the negative cellular effects of working in sewers. Their chromosomes and proteins have been studied with such detail and precision that scientists know their every quirk. Like guinea pigs and mice, Henrietta's cells have become the standard laboratory workhorse.

"HeLa cells were one of the most important things that happened to medicine in the last hundred years," Defler said.

Then, matter-of-factly, almost as an afterthought, he said, "She was a black woman." He erased her name in one fast swipe and blew the chalk from his hands. Class was over.

As the other students filed out of the room, I sat thinking, *That's it? That's all we get? There has to be more to the story.*

20   I followed Defler to his office.

"Where was she from?" I asked. "Did she know how important her cells were? Did she have any children?"

"I wish I could tell you," he said, "but no one knows anything about her."

After class, I ran home and threw myself onto my bed with my biology textbook. I looked up "cell culture" in the index, and there she was, a small parenthetical:

> In culture, cancer cells can go on dividing indefinitely, if they have a continual supply of nutrients, and thus are said to be "immortal." A striking example is a cell line that has been reproducing in culture since 1951. (Cells of this line are called HeLa cells because their original source was a tumor removed from a woman named Henrietta Lacks.)

That was it. I looked up HeLa in my parents' encyclopedia, then my dictionary: No Henrietta.

As I graduated from high school and worked my way through college toward a biology degree, HeLa cells were omnipresent. I heard about them in histology, neurology, pathology; I used them in experiments on how neighboring cells communicate. But after Mr. Defler, no one mentioned Henrietta.

When I got my first computer in the mid-nineties and started using the Internet, I searched for information about her, but found only confused snippets: most sites said her name was Helen Lane; some said she died in the thirties; others said the forties, fifties, or even sixties. Some said ovarian cancer killed her, others said breast or cervical cancer.

Eventually I tracked down a few magazine articles about her from the seventies. *Ebony* quoted Henrietta's husband saying, "All I remember is that she had this disease, and right after she died they called me in the office wanting to get my permission to take a sample of some kind. I decided not to let them." *Jet* said the family was angry—angry that Henrietta's cells were being sold for twenty-five dollars a vial, and angry that articles had been published about the cells without their knowledge. It said, "Pounding in the back of their heads was a gnawing feeling that science and the press had taken advantage of them."

The articles all ran photos of Henrietta's family: her oldest son sitting at his dining room table in Baltimore, looking at a genetics textbook. Her middle son in military uniform, smiling and holding a baby. But one picture stood out more than any other: in it, Henrietta's daughter, Deborah Lacks, is surrounded by family, everyone smiling, arms around each other, eyes bright and excited. Except Deborah. She stands in the foreground looking alone, almost as if someone pasted her into the photo after the fact. She's twenty-six years old and beautiful, with short brown hair and catlike eyes. But those eyes glare at the camera, hard and serious. The caption said the family had found out just a few months earlier that Henrietta's cells were still alive, yet at that point she'd been dead for twenty-five years.

All of the stories mentioned that scientists had begun doing research on Henrietta's children, but the Lackses didn't seem to know what that research was for. They said they were being tested to see if they had the cancer that killed Henrietta, but according to the reporters, scientists were studying the Lacks family to learn more about Henrietta's cells. The stories quoted her son Lawrence, who wanted to know if the immortality of his mother's cells meant that

25

he might live forever too. But one member of the family remained voiceless: Henrietta's daughter, Deborah.

As I worked my way through graduate school studying writing, I became fixated on the idea of someday telling Henrietta's story. At one point I even called directory assistance in Baltimore looking for Henrietta's husband, David Lacks, but he wasn't listed. I had the idea that I'd write a book that was a biography of both the cells and the woman they came from—someone's daughter, wife, and mother.

30   I couldn't have imagined it then, but that phone call would mark the beginning of a decadelong adventure through scientific laboratories, hospitals, and mental institutions, with a cast of characters that would include Nobel laureates, grocery store clerks, convicted felons, and a professional con artist. While trying to make sense of the history of cell culture and the complicated ethical debate surrounding the use of human tissues in research, I'd be accused of conspiracy and slammed into a wall both physically and metaphorically, and I'd eventually find myself on the receiving end of something that looked a lot like an exorcism. I did eventually meet Deborah, who would turn out to be one of the strongest and most resilient women I'd ever known. We'd form a deep personal bond, and slowly, without realizing it, I'd become a character in her story, and she in mine.

Deborah and I came from very different cultures: I grew up white and agnostic in the Pacific Northwest, my roots half New York Jew and half Midwestern Protestant; Deborah was a deeply religious black Christian from the South. I tended to leave the room when religion came up in conversation because it made me uncomfortable; Deborah's family tended toward preaching, faith healings, and sometimes voodoo. She grew up in a black neighborhood that was one of the poorest and most dangerous in the country; I grew up in a safe, quiet middle-class neighborhood in a predominantly white city and went to high school with a total of two black students. I was a science journalist who referred to all things supernatural as "woo-woo stuff"; Deborah believed Henrietta's spirit lived on in her cells, controlling the life of anyone who crossed its path. Including me.

"How else do you explain why your science teacher knew her real name when everyone else called her Helen Lane?" Deborah would say. "She was trying to get your attention." This thinking would apply to everything in my life: when I married while writing this book, it was because Henrietta wanted someone to take care of me while I worked. When I divorced, it was because she'd decided he was getting in the way of the book. When an editor who insisted I take the Lacks family out of the book was injured in a mysterious accident, Deborah said that's what happens when you piss Henrietta off.

The Lackses challenged everything I thought I knew about faith, science, journalism, and race. Ultimately, this [story] is the result. It's not only the story of HeLa cells and Henrietta Lacks, but of Henrietta's family—particularly Deborah—and their lifelong struggle to make peace with the existence of those cells, and the science that made them possible.

MLA CITATION

Skloot, Rebecca. "The Woman in the Photograph." 2010. *The Norton Reader: An Anthology of Nonfiction*. Ed. Melissa A. Goldthwaite et al. 14th ed. New York: Norton, 2016. 862–66. Print.

QUESTIONS

1. Was the surgeon who first cultivated Henrietta Lacks's cells for research justified in doing so? Why or why not?

2. Rebecca Skloot writes, "As I worked my way through graduate school studying writing, I became fixated on the idea of someday telling Henrietta's story" (paragraph 29). Why does Skloot find Lacks's story so compelling?

3. This essay is the prologue to Skloot's book *The Immortal Life of Henrietta Lacks*. Why does Skloot dwell so extensively on her own story in the essay?

4. Write the story of a research project of your own. What or who motivated you to undertake the project? How did you go about your research? What obstacles did you encounter? What discoveries did you make? Looking back on the process, what did you learn about yourself as a researcher or as a person?

ALAN LIGHTMAN   *Our Place in the Universe: Face to Face with the Infinite*

M Y MOST VIVID ENCOUNTER with the vastness of nature occurred years ago on the Aegean Sea.[1] My wife and I had chartered a sailboat for a two-week holiday in the Greek islands. After setting out from Piraeus, we headed south and hugged the coast, which we held three or four miles to our port. In the thick summer air, the distant shore appeared as a hazy beige ribbon—not entirely solid, but a reassuring line of reference. With binoculars, we could just make out the glinting of houses, fragments of buildings.

Then we passed the tip of Cape Sounion and turned west toward Hydra. Within a couple of hours, both the land and all other boats had disappeared. Looking around in a full circle, all we could see was water, extending out and out in all directions until it joined with the sky. I felt insignificant, misplaced, a tiny odd trinket in a cavern of ocean and air.

Naturalists, biologists, philosophers, painters, and poets have labored to express the qualities of this strange world that we find ourselves in. Some things

Published in Harper's Magazine *(2012), an American monthly covering politics, society, culture, and the environment.*

1. Sea bounded by Greece, Turkey, and Crete.

Rocky Mountains, Falling Star by Peter de Lory.

are prickly, others are smooth. Some are round, some jagged. Luminescent or dim. Mauve colored. Pitter-patter in rhythm. Of all these aspects of things, none seems more immediate or vital than *size*. Large versus small. Consciously and unconsciously, we measure our physical size against the dimensions of other people, against animals, trees, oceans, mountains. As brainy as we think our-selves to be, our bodily size, our bigness, our simple volume and bulk are what we first present to the world. Somewhere in our fathoming of the cosmos, we must keep a mental inventory of plain size and scale, going from atoms to microbes to humans to oceans to planets to stars. And some of the most impressive additions to that inventory have occurred at the high end. Simply put, the cosmos has gotten larger and larger. At each new level of distance and scale, we have had to contend with a different conception of the world that we live in.

The prize for exploring the greatest distance in space goes to a man named Garth Illingworth, who works in a ten-by-fifteen-foot office at the University of California, Santa Cruz. Illingworth studies galaxies so distant that their light has traveled through space for more than 13 billion years to get here. His office is packed with tables and chairs, bookshelves, computers, scattered papers, issues of *Nature*,[2] and a small refrigerator and a microwave to fuel research that can extend into the wee hours of the morning.

5   Like most professional astronomers these days, Illingworth does not look directly through a telescope. He gets his images by remote control—in his case, quite remote. He uses the Hubble Space Telescope, which orbits Earth once every ninety-seven minutes, high above the distorting effects of Earth's atmo-sphere. Hubble takes digital photographs of galaxies and sends the images to other orbiting satellites, which relay them to a network of earthbound anten-

2. Science journal, founded in 1869.

nae; these, in turn, pass the signals on to the Goddard Space Flight Center in Greenbelt, Maryland. From there the data is uploaded to a secure website that Illingworth can access from a computer in his office.

The most distant galaxy Illingworth has seen so far goes by the name UDFj-39546284 and was documented in early 2011. This galaxy is about 100,000,000,000,000,000,000,000 miles away from Earth, give or take. It appears as a faint red blob against the speckled night of the distant universe— red because the light has been stretched to longer and longer wavelengths as the galaxy has made its lonely journey through space for billions of years. The actual color of the galaxy is blue, the color of young, hot stars, and it is twenty times smaller than our galaxy, the Milky Way. UDFj-39546284 was one of the first galaxies to form in the universe.

"That little red dot is hellishly far away," Illingworth told me recently. At sixty-five, he is a friendly bear of a man, with a ruddy complexion, thick strawberry-blond hair, wire-rimmed glasses, and a broad smile. "I sometimes think to myself: What would it be like to be out there, looking around?"

One measure of the progress of human civilization is the increasing scale of our maps. A clay tablet dating from about the twenty-fifth century B.C. found near what is now the Iraqi city of Kirkuk depicts a river valley with a plot of land labeled as being 354 *iku* (about thirty acres) in size. In the earliest recorded cosmologies, such as the Babylonian *Enuma Elish*,[3] from around 1500 B.C., the oceans, the continents, and the heavens were considered finite, but there were no scientific estimates of their dimensions. The early Greeks, including Homer,[4] viewed Earth as a circular plane with the ocean enveloping it and Greece at the center, but there was no understanding of scale. In the early sixth century B.C., the Greek philosopher Anaximander, whom historians consider the first mapmaker, and his student Anaximenes proposed that the stars were attached to a giant crystalline sphere. But again there was no estimate of its size.

The first large object ever accurately measured was Earth, accomplished in the third century B.C. by Eratosthenes, a geographer who ran the Library of Alexandria.[5] From travelers, Eratosthenes had heard the intriguing report that at noon on the summer solstice, in the town of Syene, due south of Alexandria, the sun casts no shadow at the bottom of a deep well. Evidently the sun is directly overhead at that time and place. (Before the invention of the clock, noon could be defined at each place as the moment when the sun was highest in the sky, whether that was exactly vertical or not.) Eratosthenes knew that the sun was not overhead at noon in Alexandria. In fact, it was tipped 7.2 degrees from the vertical, or about one fiftieth of a circle—a fact he could determine by measuring the length of the shadow cast by a stick planted in the ground. That the sun could be directly overhead in one place and not another

3. Epic telling of the creation of the world.

4. Greek epic poet (eighth century B.C.E.).

5. Founded in the third century B.C.E., the greatest library of antiquity, accidentally burned by Julius Caesar in 48 B.C.E.

was due to the curvature of Earth. Eratosthenes reasoned that if he knew the distance from Alexandria to Syene, the full circumference of the planet must be about fifty times that distance. Traders passing through Alexandria told him that camels could make the trip to Syene in about fifty days, and it was known that a camel could cover one hundred stadia (almost eleven and a half miles) in a day. So the ancient geographer estimated that Syene and Alexandria were about 570 miles apart. Consequently, the complete circumference of Earth he figured to be about 50×570 miles, or 28,500 miles. This number was within 15 percent of the modern measurement, amazingly accurate considering the imprecision of using camels as odometers.

10   As ingenious as they were, the ancient Greeks were not able to calculate the size of our solar system. That discovery had to wait for the invention of the telescope, nearly two thousand years later. In 1672, the French astronomer Jean Richer determined the distance from Earth to Mars by measuring how much the position of the latter shifted against the background of stars from two different observation points on Earth. The two points were Paris (of course) and Cayenne, French Guiana. Using the distance to Mars, astronomers were also able to compute the distance from Earth to the sun, approximately 100 million miles.

A few years later, Isaac Newton[6] managed to estimate the distance to the nearest stars. (Only someone as accomplished as Newton could have been the first to perform such a calculation and have it go almost unnoticed among his other achievements.) If one assumes that the stars are similar objects to our sun, equal in intrinsic luminosity, Newton asked, how far away would our sun have to be in order to appear as faint as nearby stars? Writing his computations in a spidery script, with a quill dipped in the ink of oak galls, Newton correctly concluded that the nearest stars are about 100,000 times the distance from Earth to the sun, about 10 trillion miles away. Newton's calculation is contained in a short section of his *Principia* titled simply "On the distance of the stars."

Newton's estimate of the distance to nearby stars was larger than any distance imagined before in human history. Even today, nothing in our experience allows us to relate to it. The fastest most of us have traveled is about 500 miles per hour, the cruising speed of a jet. If we set out for the nearest star beyond our solar system at that speed, it would take us about 5 million years to reach our destination. If we traveled in the fastest rocket ship ever manufactured on Earth, the trip would last 100,000 years, at least a thousand human life spans.

But even the distance to the nearest star is dwarfed by the measurements made in the early twentieth century by Henrietta Leavitt, an astronomer at the Harvard College Observatory. In 1912, she devised a new method for determining the distances to faraway stars. Certain stars, called Cepheid variables, were known to oscillate in brightness. Leavitt discovered that the cycle times of such stars are closely related to their intrinsic luminosities. More luminous

6. English mathematician and physicist (1642–1727).

stars have longer cycles. Measure the cycle time of such a star and you know its intrinsic luminosity. Then, by comparing its intrinsic luminosity with how bright it appears in the sky, you can infer its distance, just as you could gauge the distance to an approaching car at night if you knew the wattage of its head-lights. Cepheid variables are scattered throughout the cosmos. They serve as cosmic distance signs in the highway of space.

Using Leavitt's method, astronomers were able to determine the size of the Milky Way, a giant congregation of about 200 billion stars. To express such mind-boggling sizes and distances, twentieth-century astronomers adopted a new unit called the light-year, the distance that light travels in a year—about 6 trillion miles. The nearest stars are several light-years away. The diameter of the Milky Way has been measured at about 100,000 light-years. In other words, it takes a ray of light 100,000 years to travel from one side of the Milky Way to the other.

There are galaxies beyond our own. They have names like Andromeda (one of the nearest), Sculptor, Messier 87, Malin 1, IC 1101. The average distance between galaxies, again determined by Leavitt's method, is about twenty galac-tic diameters, or 2 million light-years. To a giant cosmic being leisurely stroll-ing through the universe and not limited by distance or time, galaxies would appear as illuminated mansions scattered about the dark countryside of space. As far as we know, galaxies are the largest objects in the cosmos. If we sorted the long inventory of material objects in nature by size, we would start with subatomic particles like electrons and end up with galaxies. 15

Over the past century, astronomers have been able to probe deeper and deeper into space, looking out to distances of hundreds of millions of light-years and farther. A question naturally arises: Could the physical universe be unend-ing in size? That is, as we build bigger and bigger telescopes sensitive to fainter and fainter light, will we continue to see objects farther and farther away—like the third emperor of the Ming Dynasty, Yongle, who surveyed his new palace in the Forbidden City and walked from room to room to room, never reaching the end?

Here we must take into account a curious relationship between distance and time. Because light travels at a fast (186,000 miles per second) but not infi-nite speed, when we look at a distant object in space we must remember that a significant amount of time has passed between the emission of the light and the reception at our end. The image we see is what the object looked like when it emitted that light. If we look at an object 186,000 miles away, we see it as it appeared one second earlier; at 1,860,000 miles away, we see it as it appeared ten seconds earlier; and so on. For extremely distant objects, we see them as they were millions or billions of years in the past.

Now the second curiosity. Since the late 1920s we have known that the universe is expanding, and that as it does so it is thinning out and cooling. By measuring the current rate of expansion, we can make good estimates of the moment in the past when the expansion began—the Big Bang—which was about 13.7 billion years ago, a time when no planets or stars or galaxies existed and the entire universe consisted of a fantastically dense nugget of pure energy. No matter how big our telescopes, we cannot see beyond the distance light has traveled since the Big Bang. Farther than that, and there simply hasn't been enough time since the birth of the universe for light to get from there to here. This giant sphere, the maximum distance we can see, is only the *observable* universe. But the universe could extend far beyond that.

In his office in Santa Cruz, Garth Illingworth and his colleagues have mapped out and measured the cosmos to the edge of the observable universe. They have reached out almost as far as the laws of physics allow. All that exists in the knowable universe—oceans and sky; planets and stars; pulsars, quasars, and dark matter; distant galaxies and clusters of galaxies; and great clouds of star-forming gas—has been gathered within the cosmic sensorium gauged and observed by human beings.

20 "Every once in a while," says Illingworth, "I think: By God, we are studying things that we can never physically touch. We sit on this miserable little planet in a midsize galaxy and we can characterize most of the universe. It is astonishing to me, the immensity of the situation, and how to relate to it in terms we can understand."

The idea of Mother Nature has been represented in every culture on Earth. But to what extent is the new universe, vastly larger than anything conceived of in the past, part of *nature*? One wonders how connected Illingworth feels to this astoundingly large cosmic terrain, to the galaxies and stars so distant that their images have taken billions of years to reach our eyes. Are the little red dots on his maps part of the same landscape that Wordsworth and Thoreau[7] described, part of the same environment of mountains and trees, part of the same cycle of birth and death that orders our lives, part of our physical and emotional conception of the world we live in? Or are such things instead digitized abstractions, silent and untouchable, akin to us only in their (hypothesized) makeup of atoms and molecules? And to what extent are we human beings, living on a small planet orbiting one star among billions of stars, part of that same nature?

The heavenly bodies were once considered divine, made of entirely different stuff than objects on Earth. Aristotle[8] argued that all matter was constituted from four elements: earth, fire, water, and air. A fifth element, ether, he reserved for the heavenly bodies, which he considered immortal, perfect, and indestructible. It wasn't until the birth of modern science, in the seventeenth century, that we began to understand the similarity of heaven and Earth. In 1610, using his new telescope, Galileo[9] noted that the sun had dark patches and blemishes, suggesting that the heavenly bodies are not perfect. In 1687,

7. William Wordsworth (1770–1850), English Romantic poet; Henry David Thoreau (1817–1862), American writer and naturalist.

8. Greek philosopher (384–322 B.C.E.).

9. Galileo Galilei (1564–1642), Italian astronomer and mathematician.

Tallulah Falls by George Cooke.

Newton proposed a universal law of gravity that would apply equally to the fall of an apple from a tree and to the orbits of planets around the sun. Newton then went further, suggesting that all the laws of nature apply to phenomena in the heavens as well as on Earth. In later centuries, scientists used our understanding of terrestrial chemistry and physics to estimate how long the sun could continue shining before depleting its resources of energy; to determine the chemical composition of stars; to map out the formation of galaxies.

Yet even after Galileo and Newton, there remained another question: Were living things somehow different from rocks and water and stars? Did animate and inanimate matter differ in some fundamental way? The "vitalists" claimed that animate matter had some special essence, an intangible spirit or soul, while the "mechanists" argued that living things were elaborate machines and obeyed precisely the same laws of physics and chemistry as did inanimate material. In the late nineteenth century, two German physiologists, Adolf Eugen Fick and Max Rubner, each began testing the mechanistic hypothesis by painstakingly tabulating the energies required for muscle contraction, body heat, and other physical activities and comparing these energies against the chemical energy stored in food. Each gram of fat, carbohydrate, and protein had its energy equivalent. Rubner concluded that the amount of energy used by a living creature was exactly equal to the energy it consumed in its food. Living things were to be viewed as complex arrangements of biological pulleys and levers, electric currents, and chemical impulses. Our bodies are made of the same atoms and molecules as stones, water, and air.

And yet many had a lingering feeling that human beings were somehow separate from the rest of nature. Such a view is nowhere better illustrated than in the painting *Tallulah Falls* (1841), by George Cooke, an artist associated with the Hudson River School. Although this group of painters celebrated nature, they also believed that human beings were set apart from the natural world. Cooke's painting depicts tiny human figures standing on a small promontory above a deep canyon. The people are dwarfed by tree-covered mountains, massive rocky ledges, and a waterfall pouring down to the canyon below. Not only insignificant in size compared with their surroundings, the human beings are mere witnesses to a scene they are not part of and never could be. Just a few years earlier, Ralph Waldo Emerson[10] had published his famous essay "Nature," an appreciation of the natural world that nonetheless held humans separate from nature, at the very least in the moral and spiritual domain: "Man is fallen; nature is erect."

25   Today, with various back-to-nature movements attempting to resist the dislocations brought about by modernity, and with our awareness of Earth's precarious environmental state ever increasing, many people feel a new sympathy with the natural world on this planet. But the gargantuan cosmos beyond remains remote. We might understand at some level that those tiny points of light in the night sky are similar to our sun, made of atoms identical to those in our bodies, and that the cavern of outer space extends from our galaxy of stars to other galaxies of stars, to distances that would take light billions of years to traverse. We might understand these discoveries in intellectual terms, but they are baffling abstractions, even disturbing, like the notion that each of us once was the size of a dot, without mind or thought. Science has vastly expanded the scale of our cosmos, but our emotional reality is still limited by what we can touch with our bodies in the time span of our lives. George Berkeley, the

10. American author and philosopher (1803–1882).

eighteenth-century Irish philosopher, argued that the entire cosmos is a construct of our minds, that there is no material reality outside our thoughts. As a scientist, I cannot accept that belief. At the emotional and psychological level, however, I can have some sympathy with Berkeley's views. Modern science has revealed a world as far removed from our bodies as colors are from the blind.

Very recent scientific findings have added yet another dimension to the question of our place in the cosmos. For the first time in the history of science, we are able to make plausible estimates of the rate of occurrence of life in the universe. In March 2009, NASA launched a spacecraft called *Kepler*[11] whose mission was to search for planets orbiting in the "habitable zone" of other stars. The habitable zone is the region in which a planet's surface temperature is not so cold as to freeze water and not so hot as to boil it. For many reasons, biologists and chemists believe that liquid water is required for the emergence of life, even if that life may be very different from life on Earth. Dozens of candidates for such planets have been found, and we can make a rough preliminary calculation that something like 3 percent of all stars are accompanied by a potentially life-sustaining planet. The totality of living matter on Earth—humans and animals, plants, bacteria, and pond scum—makes up 0.00000001 percent of the mass of the planet. Combining this figure with the results from the *Kepler* mission, and assuming that all potentially life-sustaining planets do indeed have life, we can estimate that the fraction of stuff in the visible universe that exists in living form is something like 0.000000000000001 percent, or one millionth of one billionth of 1 percent. If some cosmic intelligence created the universe, life would seem to have been only an afterthought. And if life emerges by random processes, vast amounts of lifeless material are needed for each particle of life. Such numbers cannot help but bear upon the question of our significance in the universe.

Decades ago, when I was sailing with my wife in the Aegean Sea, in the midst of unending water and sky, I had a slight inkling of infinity. It was a sensation I had not experienced before, accompanied by feelings of awe, fear, sublimity, disorientation, alienation, and disbelief. I set a course for 255°, trusting in my compass—a tiny disk of painted numbers with a sliver of rotating metal—and hoped for the best. In a few hours, as if by magic, a pale ocher smidgen of land appeared dead ahead, a thing that drew closer and closer, a place with houses and beds and other human beings.

11. Named after the German astronomer Johannes Kepler (1571–1630).

MLA CITATION

Lightman, Alan. "Our Place in the Universe." 2012. *The Norton Reader: An Anthology of Nonfiction.* Ed. Melissa A. Goldthwaite et al. 14th ed. New York: Norton, 2016. 867–75. Print.

QUESTIONS

1. What, according to Alan Lightman, is "our place in the universe"?

2. Lightman recognizes that the study of nature is not the purview of science alone: "Naturalists, biologists, philosophers, painters, and poets," he writes, "have labored to express the qualities of this strange world that we find ourselves in" (paragraph 3). How does this sensibility inform his essay?

3. What does Lightman do as a writer to get his readers to experience (not just acknowledge) nature's vastness?

4. Lightman begins and ends his essay by recalling his sailing trip on the Aegean, which he describes as his "most vivid encounter with the vastness of nature" (paragraph 1). Write an essay in which you describe and reflect on a transformative experience of your own.

LITERATURE
AND THE ARTS

EUDORA WELTY *One Writer's Beginnings*

I LEARNED FROM the age of two or three that any room in our house, at any time of day, was there to read in, or to be read to. My mother read to me. She'd read to me in the big bedroom in the mornings, when we were in her rocker together, which ticked in rhythm as we rocked, as though we had a cricket accompanying the story. She'd read to me in the diningroom on winter afternoons in front of the coal fire, with our cuckoo clock ending the story with "Cuckoo," and at night when I'd got in my own bed. I must have given her no peace. Sometimes she read to me in the kitchen while she sat churning, and the churning sobbed along with *any* story. It was my ambition to have her read to me while *I* churned; once she granted my wish, but she read off my story before I brought her butter. She was an expressive reader. When she was reading "Puss in Boots,"[1] for instance, it was impossible not to know that she distrusted *all* cats.

It had been startling and disappointing to me to find out that story books had been written by *people,* that books were not natural wonders, coming up of themselves like grass. Yet regardless of where they came from, I cannot remember a time when I was not in love with them—with the books themselves, cover and binding and the paper they were printed on, with their smell and their weight and with their possession in my arms, captured and carried off to myself. Still illiterate, I was ready for them, committed to all the reading I could give them.

Neither of my parents had come from homes that could afford to buy many books, but though it must have been something of a strain on his salary, as the youngest officer in a young insurance company, my father was all the while carefully selecting and ordering away for what he and Mother thought we children should grow up with. They bought first for the future.

Besides the bookcase in the livingroom, which was always called "the library," there were the encyclopedia tables and dictionary stand under windows in our diningroom. Here to help us grow up arguing around the diningroom

---

From a set of three lectures delivered at Harvard University in April 1983, to inaugurate the William E. Massey lecture series, and later published in One Writer's Beginnings *(1984).*

1. Fairy tale.

table were the Unabridged Webster, the Columbia Encyclopedia, Compton's Pictured Encyclopedia, the Lincoln Library of Information, and later the Book of Knowledge. And the year we moved into our new house, there was room to celebrate it with the new 1925 edition of the Britannica, which my father, his face always deliberately turned toward the future, was of course disposed to think better than any previous edition.

5   In "the library," inside the mission-style bookcase with its three diamond-latticed glass doors, with my father's Morris chair and the glass-shaded lamp on its table beside it, were books I could soon begin on—and I did, reading them all alike and as they came, straight down their rows, top shelf to bottom. There was the set of Stoddard's Lectures, in all its late nineteenth-century vocabulary and vignettes of peasant life and quaint beliefs and customs, with matching halftone illustrations: Vesuvius erupting, Venice by moonlight, gypsies glimpsed by their campfires. I didn't know then the clue they were to my father's longing to see the rest of the world. I read straight through his other love-from-afar: the Victrola Book of the Opera, with opera after opera in synopsis, with portraits in costume of Melba, Caruso, Galli-Curci, and Geraldine Farrar,[2] some of whose voices we could listen to on our Red Seal records.

My mother read secondarily for information; she sank as a hedonist into novels. She read Dickens in the spirit in which she would have eloped with him. The novels of her girlhood that had stayed on in her imagination, besides those of Dickens and Scott and Robert Louis Stevenson,[3] were *Jane Eyre, Trilby, The Woman in White, Green Mansions, King Solomon's Mines.*[4] Marie Corelli's[5] name would crop up but I understood she had gone out of favor with my mother, who had only kept *Ardath* out of loyalty. In time she absorbed herself in Galsworthy, Edith Wharton, above all in Thomas Mann of the *Joseph* volumes.[6]

St. Elmo[7] was not in our house; I saw it often in other houses. This wildly popular Southern novel is where all the Edna Earles in our population started coming from. They're all named for the heroine, who succeeded in bringing a dissolute, sinning roué and atheist of a lover (St. Elmo) to his knees. My mother was able to forgo it. But she remembered the classic advice given to rose growers on how to water their bushes long enough: "Take a chair and *St. Elmo.*"

To both my parents I owe my early acquaintance with a beloved Mark Twain. There was a full set of Mark Twain and a short set of Ring Lardner in

2. Nellie Melba (1861–1931), Enrico Caruso (1837–1921), Amelita Galli-Curci (1889–1964), Farrar (1882–1967), all opera stars.

3. Charles Dickens (1812–1870), Sir Walter Scott (1771–1832), Robert Louis Stevenson (1850–1894), all novelists.

4. Novels: *Jane Eyre* (1847), by Charlotte Brontë; *Trilby* (1894), by George du Maurier (1834–1896); *The Woman in White* (1859), by Wilkie Collins (1824–1889); *Green Mansions* (1904), by William Henry Hudson (1841–1922); and *King Solomon's Mines* (1885), by Sir H. Rider Haggard (1856–1925).

5. Pen name of Mary Mills Mackay (1855–1924), popular and prolific British novelist.

6. John Galsworthy (1867–1933), British novelist; Edith Wharton (1862–1937), American novelist; Thomas Mann (1875–1955), German novelist.

7. Novel (1866) by American author Augusta Jane Evans (1835–1909).

our bookcase,[8] and those were the volumes that in time united us all, parents and children.

Reading everything that stood before me was how I came upon a worn old book without a back that had belonged to my father as a child. It was called *Sanford and Merton*. Is there anyone left who recognizes it, I wonder? It is the famous moral tale written by Thomas Day in the 1780s, but of him no mention is made on the title page of *this* book; here it is *Sanford and Merton in Words of One Syllable* by Mary Godolphin. Here are the rich boy and the poor boy and Mr. Barlow, their teacher and interlocutor, in long discourses alternating with dramatic scenes—danger and rescue allotted to the rich and the poor respectively. It may have only words of one syllable, but one of them is "quoth." It ends with not one but two morals, both engraved on rings: "Do what you ought, come what may," and "If we would be great, we must first learn to be good."

This book was lacking its front cover, the back held on by strips of pasted paper, now turned golden, in several layers, and the pages stained, flecked, and tattered around the edges; its garish illustrations had come unattached but were preserved, laid in. I had the feeling even in my heedless childhood that this was the only book my father as a little boy had had of his own. He had held onto it, and might have gone to sleep on its coverless face: he had lost his mother when he was seven. My father had never made any mention to his own children of the book, but he had brought it along with him from Ohio to our house and shelved it in our bookcase.

My mother had brought from West Virginia that set of Dickens; those books looked sad, too—they had been through fire and water before I was born, she told me, and there they were, lined up—as I later realized, waiting for *me*.

I was presented, from as early as I can remember, with books of my own, which appeared on my birthday and Christmas morning. Indeed, my parents could not give me books enough. They must have sacrificed to give me on my sixth or seventh birthday—it was after I became a reader for myself—the ten-volume set of Our Wonder World. These were beautifully made, heavy books I would lie down with on the floor in front of the diningroom hearth, and more often than the rest volume 5, *Every Child's Story Book,* was under my eyes. There were the fairy tales—Grimm, Andersen, the English, the French, "Ali Baba and the Forty Thieves"; and there was Aesop and Reynard the Fox; there were the myths and legends, Robin Hood, King Arthur, and St. George and the Dragon, even the history of Joan of Arc; a whack of *Pilgrim's Progress* and a long piece of *Gulliver*.[9] They all carried their classic illustrations. I located myself in these pages and could go straight to the stories and pictures I loved; very often "The Yellow Dwarf" was first choice, with Walter Crane's Yellow Dwarf in full color making his terrifying appearance flanked by turkeys.[10] Now that volume is as worn and backless and hanging apart as my father's poor *Sanford and*

10

8. Twain, pen name of Samuel Langhorne Clemens (1835–1910); Lardner (1885–1933). Both were American novelists.

9. *The Pilgrim's Progress* (1678), novel by John Bunyan; *Gulliver's Travels* (1726), novel by Jonathan Swift.

10. Fairy tale illustrated by Crane (1845–1915), an illustrator of children's books.

Merton. The precious page with Edward Lear's "Jumblies"[11] on it has been in danger of slipping out for all these years. One measure of my love for *Our Wonder World* was that for a long time I wondered if I would go through fire and water for it as my mother had done for Charles Dickens; and the only comfort was to think I could ask my mother to do it for me.

I believe I'm the only child I know of who grew up with this treasure in the house. I used to ask others, "Did you have *Our Wonder World?*" I'd have to tell them The Book of Knowledge could not hold a candle to it.

I live in gratitude to my parents for initiating me—and as early as I begged for it, without keeping me waiting—into knowledge of the word, into reading and spelling, by way of the alphabet. They taught it to me at home in time for me to begin to read before starting to school. I believe the alphabet is no longer considered an essential piece of equipment for traveling through life. In my day it was the keystone to knowledge. You learned the alphabet as you learned to count to ten, as you learned "Now I lay me" and the Lord's Prayer and your father's and mother's name and address and telephone number, all in case you were lost.

15   My love for the alphabet, which endures, grew out of reciting it but, before that, out of seeing the letters on the page. In my own story books, before I could read them for myself, I fell in love with various winding, enchanting-looking initials drawn by Walter Crane at the heads of fairy tales. In "Once upon a time," an "O" had a rabbit running it as a treadmill, his feet upon flowers. When the day came, years later, for me to see the Book of Kells,[12] all the wizardry of letter, initial, and word swept over me a thousand times over, and the illumination, the gold, seemed a part of the word's beauty and holiness that had been there from the start.

Learning stamps you with its moments. Childhood's learning is made up of moments. It isn't steady. It's a pulse.

In a children's art class, we sat in a ring on kindergarten chairs and drew three daffodils that had just been picked out of the yard; and while I was drawing, my sharpened pencil and the cup of the yellow daffodil gave off whiffs just alike. That the pencil doing the drawing should give off the same smell as the flower it drew seemed a part of the art lesson—as shouldn't it be? Children, like animals, use all their senses to discover the world. Then artists come along and discover it the same way, all over again. Here and there, it's the same world. Or now and then we'll hear from an artist who's never lost it.

In my sensory education I include my physical awareness of the *word.* Of a certain word, that is; the connection it has with what it stands for. At around age six, perhaps, I was standing by myself in our front yard waiting for supper, just at that hour in a late summer day when the sun is already below the horizon and the risen full moon in the visible sky stops being chalky and begins to take on light. There comes the moment, and I saw it then, when the moon goes from flat to round. For the first time it met my eyes as a globe. The word "moon"

11. Narrative poem about creatures called Jumblies who went to sea in a sieve.
12. Illustrated Irish manuscript of the four Gospels from the eighth or ninth century.

came into my mouth as though fed to me out of a silver spoon. Held in my mouth the moon became a word. It had the roundness of a Concord grape Grandpa took off his vine and gave me to suck out of its skin and swallow whole, in Ohio.

This love did not prevent me from living for years in foolish error about the moon. The new moon just appearing in the west was the rising moon to me. The new should be rising. And in early childhood the sun and moon, those opposite reigning powers, I just as easily assumed rose in east and west respectively in their opposite sides of the sky, and like partners in a reel they advanced, sun from the east, moon from the west, crossed over (when I wasn't looking) and went down on the other side. My father couldn't have known I believed that when, bending behind me and guiding my shoulder, he positioned me at our telescope in the front yard and, with careful adjustment of the focus, brought the moon close to me.

The night sky over my childhood Jackson[13] was velvety black. I could see the   20
full constellations in it and call their names; when I could read, I knew their myths. Though I was always waked for eclipses, and indeed carried to the window as an infant in arms and shown Halley's Comet[14] in my sleep, and though I'd been taught at our diningroom table about the solar system and knew the earth revolved around the sun, and our moon around us, I never found out the moon didn't come up in the west until I was a writer and Herschel Brickell, the literary critic, told me after I misplaced it in a story. He said valuable words to me about my new profession: "Always be sure you get your moon in the right part of the sky."

My mother always sang to her children. Her voice came out just a little bit in the minor key. "Wee Willie Winkie's" song was wonderfully sad when she sang the lullabies.

"Oh, but now there's a record. She could have her own record to listen to," my father would have said. For there came a Victrola record of "Bobby Shafftoe" and "Rock-a-Bye Baby,"[15] all of Mother's lullabies, which could be played to take her place. Soon I was able to play her my own lullabies all day long.

Our Victrola stood in the diningroom. I was allowed to climb onto the seat of a diningroom chair to wind it, start the record turning, and set the needle playing. In a second I'd jumped to the floor, to spin or march around the table as the music called for—now there were all the other records I could play too. I skinned back onto the chair just in time to lift the needle at the end, stop the record and turn it over, then change the needle. That brass receptacle with a hole in the lid gave off a metallic smell like human sweat, from all the hot needles that were fed it. Winding up, dancing, being cocked to start and stop the record, was of course all in one the act of *listening*—to "Overture to *Daughter of the Regiment,*" "Selections from *The Fortune Teller,*" "Kiss Me Again," "Gypsy

---

13. Jackson, Mississippi, where Welty grew up.
14. Comet named after Edmund Halley (1656–1742), English astronomer.
15. "Wee Willie Winkie," nursery rhyme (1841) in which sleep is personified; "Bobby Shafftoe," traditional sea chantey (c. 1750); "Rock-a-Bye Baby" (1884), words from *Mother Goose's Melodies* (1765).

Dance from *Carmen*," "Stars and Stripes Forever," "When the Midnight Choo-Choo Leaves for Alabam," or whatever came next.[16] Movement must be at the very heart of listening.

Ever since I was first read to, then started reading to myself, there has never been a line read that I didn't *hear*. As my eyes followed the sentence, a voice was saying it silently to me. It isn't my mother's voice, or the voice of any person I can identify, certainly not my own. It is human, but inward, and it is inwardly that I listen to it. It is to me the voice of the story or the poem itself. The cadence, whatever it is that asks you to believe, the feeling that resides in the printed word, reaches me through the reader-voice. I have supposed, but never found out, that this is the case with all readers—to read as listeners—and with all writers, to write as listeners. It may be part of the desire to write. The sound of what falls on the page begins the process of testing it for truth, for me. Whether I am right to trust so far I don't know. By now I don't know whether I could do either one, reading or writing, without the other.

25   My own words, when I am at work on a story, I hear too as they go, in the same voice that I hear when I read in books. When I write and the sound of it comes back to my ears, then I act to make my changes. I have always trusted this voice.

16. *Daughter of the Regiment*, opera (1840) by the Italian composer Gaetano Donizetti; *The Fortune Teller*, operetta (1898) by the American Victor Herbert; "Kiss Me Again," song from Herbert's *Mlle. Modiste* (1905); *Carmen*, opera (1875) by the French composer Georges Bizet; "Stars and Stripes Forever," march (1897) by the American John Philip Sousa; "When the Midnight Choo-Choo Leaves for Alabam," popular song (1912) by the American Irving Berlin.

MLA CITATION

Welty, Eudora. "One Writer's Beginnings." 1983. *The Norton Reader: An Anthology of Nonfiction*. Ed. Melissa A. Goldthwaite et al. 14th ed. New York: Norton, 2016. 877–82. Print.

QUESTIONS

1. In the opening paragraphs Eudora Welty speaks of what she later calls her "sensory education." What does she mean? What examples does she give?

2. Throughout her essay Welty lists the titles of books that she and her mother read. What is the effect of these lists? Have you read any of the books? Or books like them? How important were they to you?

3. Welty concludes her essay by talking of the writer's voice—of "testing it for truth" and "trust[ing] this voice" (paragraphs 24 and 25). What meanings does she give the key words "truth" and "trust"?

4. Welty grew up before television and computers. How might today's technology affect a child's "sensory education"? Write an essay comparing a modern child's sensory education with Welty's.

VLADIMIR NABOKOV *Good Readers and Good Writers*

"HOW TO BE A GOOD READER" or "Kindness to Authors"—something of that sort might serve to provide a subtitle for these various discussions of various authors, for my plan is to deal lovingly, in loving and lingering detail, with several European masterpieces. A hundred years ago, Flaubert[1] in a letter to his mistress made the following remark: *Comme l'on serait savant si l'on connaissait bien seulement cinq à six livres:* "What a scholar one might be if one knew well only some half a dozen books."

In reading, one should notice and fondle details. There is nothing wrong about the moonshine of generalization when it comes *after* the sunny trifles of the book have been lovingly collected. If one begins with a ready-made generalization, one begins at the wrong end and travels away from the book before one has started to understand it. Nothing is more boring or more unfair to the author than starting to read, say, *Madame Bovary,* with the preconceived notion that it is a denunciation of the bourgeoisie. We should always remember that the work of art is invariably the creation of a new world, so that the first thing we should do is to study that new world as closely as possible, approaching it as something brand new, having no obvious connection with the worlds we already know. When this new world has been closely studied, then and only then let us examine its links with other worlds, other branches of knowledge.

Another question: Can we expect to glean information about places and times from a novel? Can anybody be so naive as to think he or she can learn anything about the past from those buxom best-sellers that are hawked around by book clubs under the heading of historical novels? But what about the masterpieces? Can we rely on Jane Austen's[2] picture of landowning England with baronets and landscaped grounds when all she knew was a clergyman's parlor? And *Bleak House,*[3] that fantastic romance within a fantastic London, can we call it a study of London a hundred years ago? Certainly not. And the same holds for other such novels in this series. The truth is that great novels are great fairy tales—and the novels in this series are supreme fairy tales.

Time and space, the colors of the seasons, the movements of muscles and minds, all these are for writers of genius (as far as we can guess and I trust we guess right) not traditional notions which may be borrowed from the circulating library of public truths but a series of unique surprises which master artists

---

A lecture Vladimir Nabokov delivered to his undergraduate class at Cornell University, where he taught from 1948 to 1959; published in Lectures on Literature *(1980). Nabokov is known especially for his novels, which include* Lolita *(1955) and* Pale Fire *(1962) among others.*

1. Gustave Flaubert (1821–1880), French novelist, author of *Madame Bovary.*

2. British novelist (1775–1817).

3. Novel (1853) by Charles Dickens that alternates scenes in London with the country and includes a satire on the British judicial system.

have learned to express in their own unique way. To minor authors is left the ornamentation of the commonplace: these do not bother about any reinventing of the world; they merely try to squeeze the best they can out of a given order of things, out of traditional patterns of fiction. The various combinations these minor authors are able to produce within these set limits may be quite amusing in a mild ephemeral way because minor readers like to recognize their own ideas in a pleasing disguise. But the real writer, the fellow who sends planets spinning and models a man asleep and eagerly tampers with the sleeper's rib, that kind of author has no given values at his disposal: he must create them himself. The art of writing is a very futile business if it does not imply first of all the art of seeing the world as the potentiality of fiction. The material of this world may be real enough (as far as reality goes) but does not exist at all as an accepted entirety: it is chaos, and to this chaos the author says "go!" allowing the world to flicker and to fuse. It is now recombined in its very atoms, not merely in its visible and superficial parts. The writer is the first man to map it and to name the natural objects it contains. Those berries there are edible. That speckled creature that bolted across my path might be tamed. That lake between those trees will be called Lake Opal or, more artistically, Dishwater Lake. That mist is a mountain—and that mountain must be conquered. Up a trackless slope climbs the master artist, and at the top, on a windy ridge, whom do you think he meets? The panting and happy reader, and there they spontaneously embrace and are linked forever if the book lasts forever.

5   One evening at a remote provincial college through which I happened to be jogging on a protracted lecture tour, I suggested a little quiz—ten definitions of a reader, and from these ten the students had to choose four definitions that would combine to make a good reader. I have mislaid the list, but as far as I remember the definitions went something like this. Select four answers to the question what should a reader be to be a good reader:

1. The reader should belong to a book club.
2. The reader should identify himself or herself with the hero or heroine.
3. The reader should concentrate on the social-economic angle.
4. The reader should prefer a story with action and dialogue to one with none.
5. The reader should have seen the book in a movie.
6. The reader should be a budding author.
7. The reader should have imagination.
8. The reader should have memory.
9. The reader should have a dictionary.
10. The reader should have some artistic sense.

The students leaned heavily on emotional identification, action, and the social-economic or historical angle. Of course, as you have guessed, the good reader is one who has imagination, memory, a dictionary, and some artistic sense—which sense I propose to develop in myself and in others whenever I have the chance.

Incidentally, I use the word *reader* very loosely. Curiously enough, one cannot *read* a book: one can only reread it. A good reader, a major reader, an active and creative reader is a rereader. And I shall tell you why. When we read a book for the first time the very process of laboriously moving our eyes from left to right, line after line, page after page, this complicated physical work upon the book, the very process of learning in terms of space and time what the book is about, this stands between us and artistic appreciation. When we look at a painting we do not have to move our eyes in a special way even if, as in a book, the picture contains elements of depth and development. The element of time does not really enter in a first contact with a painting. In reading a book, we must have time to acquaint ourselves with it. We have no physical organ (as we have the eye in regard to a painting) that takes in the whole picture and then can enjoy its details. But at a second, or third, or fourth reading we do, in a sense, behave towards a book as we do towards a painting. However, let us not confuse the physical eye, that monstrous masterpiece of evolution, with the mind, an even more monstrous achievement. A book, no matter what it is—a work of fiction or a work of science (the boundary line between the two is not as clear as is generally believed)—a book of fiction appeals first of all to the mind. The mind, the brain, the top of the tingling spine, is, or should be, the only instrument used upon a book.

Now, this being so, we should ponder the question how does the mind work when the sullen reader is confronted by the sunny book. First, the sullen mood melts away, and for better or worse the reader enters into the spirit of the game. The effort to begin a book, especially if it is praised by people whom the young reader secretly deems to be too old-fashioned or too serious, this effort is often difficult to make; but once it is made, rewards are various and abundant. Since the master artist used his imagination in creating his book, it is natural and fair that the consumer of a book should use his imagination too.

There are, however, at least two varieties of imagination in the reader's case. So let us see which one of the two is the right one to use in reading a book. First, there is the comparatively lowly kind which turns for support to the simple emotions and is of a definitely personal nature. (There are various sub-varieties here, in this first section of emotional reading.) A situation in a book is intensely felt because it reminds us of something that happened to us or to someone we know or knew. Or, again, a reader treasures a book mainly because it evokes a country, a landscape, a mode of living which he nostalgically recalls as part of his own past. Or, and this is the worst thing a reader can do, he identifies himself with a character in the book. This lowly variety is not the kind of imagination I would like readers to use.

So what is the authentic instrument to be used by the reader? It is impersonal imagination and artistic delight. What should be established, I think, is an artistic harmonious balance between the reader's mind and the author's mind. We ought to remain a little aloof and take pleasure in this aloofness while at the same time we keenly enjoy—passionately enjoy, enjoy with tears and shivers—the inner weave of a given masterpiece. To be quite objective in these matters is of course impossible. Everything that is worthwhile is to some extent subjective. For instance, you sitting there may be merely my dream, and I may be your nightmare. But what I mean is that the reader must know when and where to curb his imagination and this he does by trying to get clear the specific world the author places at his disposal. We must see things and hear things, we must visualize the rooms, the clothes, the manners of an author's people. The color of Fanny Price's eyes in *Mansfield Park*[4] and the furnishing of her cold little room are important.

10   We all have different temperaments, and I can tell you right now that the best temperament for a reader to have, or to develop, is a combination of the artistic and the scientific one. The enthusiastic artist alone is apt to be too subjective in his attitude towards a book, and so a scientific coolness of judgment will temper the intuitive heat. If, however, a would-be reader is utterly devoid of passion and patience—of an artist's passion and a scientist's patience—he will hardly enjoy great literature.

Literature was born not the day when a boy crying wolf, wolf came running out of the Neanderthal valley with a big gray wolf at his heels: literature was born on the day when a boy came crying wolf, wolf and there was no wolf behind him. That the poor little fellow because he lied too often was finally eaten up by a real beast is quite incidental. But here is what is important. Between the wolf in the tall grass and the wolf in the tall story there is a shimmering go-between. That go-between, that prism, is the art of literature.

Literature is invention. Fiction is fiction. To call a story a true story is an insult to both art and truth. Every great writer is a great deceiver, but so is that arch-cheat Nature. Nature always deceives. From the simple deception of propagation to the prodigiously sophisticated illusion of protective colors in butterflies or birds, there is in Nature a marvelous system of spells and wiles. The writer of fiction only follows Nature's lead.

Going back for a moment to our wolf-crying woodland little woolly fellow, we may put it this way: the magic of art was in the shadow of the wolf that he deliberately invented, his dream of the wolf; then the story of his tricks made a good story. When he perished at last, the story told about him acquired a good lesson in the dark around the camp fire. But he was the little magician. He was the inventor.

There are three points of view from which a writer can be considered: he may be considered as a storyteller, as a teacher, and as an enchanter. A major writer combines these three—storyteller, teacher, enchanter—but it is the enchanter in him that predominates and makes him a major writer.

15   To the storyteller we turn for entertainment, for mental excitement of the simplest kind, for emotional participation, for the pleasure of traveling in some remote region in space or time. A slightly different though not necessarily higher mind looks for the teacher in the writer. Propagandist, moralist, prophet—this

4. Novel (1814) by Jane Austen.

is the rising sequence. We may go to the teacher not only for moral education but also for direct knowledge, for simple facts. Alas, I have known people whose purpose in reading the French and Russian novelists was to learn something about life in gay Paree or in sad Russia. Finally, and above all, a great writer is always a great enchanter, and it is here that we come to the really exciting part when we try to grasp the individual magic of his genius and to study the style, the imagery, the pattern of his novels or poems.

The three facets of the great writer—magic, story, lesson—are prone to blend in one impression of unified and unique radiance, since the magic of art may be present in the very bones of the story, in the very marrow of thought. There are masterpieces of dry, limpid, organized thought which provoke in us an artistic quiver quite as strongly as a novel like *Mansfield Park* does or as any rich flow of Dickensian sensual imagery. It seems to me that a good formula to test the quality of a novel is, in the long run, a merging of the precision of poetry and the intuition of science. In order to bask in that magic a wise reader reads the book of genius not with his heart, not so much with his brain, but with his spine. It is there that occurs the telltale tingle even though we must keep a little aloof, a little detached when reading. Then with a pleasure which is both sensual and intellectual we shall watch the artist build his castle of cards and watch the castle of cards become a castle of beautiful steel and glass.

MLA CITATION

Nabokov, Vladimir. "Good Readers and Good Writers." 1980. *The Norton Reader: An Anthology of Nonfiction*. Ed. Melissa A. Goldthwaite et al. 14th ed. New York: Norton, 2016. 883–87. Print.

QUESTIONS

1. Make a list of the qualities that Vladimir Nabokov believes "good readers" should have; then make a list of the qualities he believes "good writers" should have. Do they match? Why or why not?

2. Nabokov, as he points out in the conclusion to his essay (paragraphs 14–16), considers the writer from three points of view: as storyteller, as teacher, and as enchanter. He has not, however, organized his essay by these points of view. Where and how does he discuss each one? Why does he consider the last the most important?

3. How would Eudora Welty (pp. 877–82) do on Nabokov's quiz? Give what you think would be her answers and explain, using information from her essay, what you think her reasons would be.

4. Take Nabokov's quiz (paragraph 5). Write an essay in which you explain your "right" answers (as Nabokov sees "good readers") and defend your "wrong" ones.

NORTHROP FRYE   *The Motive for Metaphor*

FOR THE PAST TWENTY-FIVE YEARS I have been teaching and studying English literature in a university. As in any other job, certain questions stick in one's mind, not because people keep asking them, but because they're the questions inspired by the very fact of being in such a place. What good is the study of literature? Does it help us to think more clearly, or feel more sensitively, or live a better life than we could without it? What is the function of the teacher and scholar, or of the person who calls himself, as I do, a literary critic? What difference does the study of literature make in our social or political or religious attitude? In my early days I thought very little about such questions, not because I had any of the answers, but because I assumed that anybody who asked them was naïve. I think now that the simplest questions are not only the hardest to answer, but the most important to ask, so I'm going to raise them and try to suggest what my present answers are. I say try to suggest, because there are only more or less inadequate answers to such questions—there aren't any right answers. The kind of problem that literature raises is not the kind that you ever "solve." Whether my answers are any good or not, they represent a fair amount of thinking about the questions. As I can't see my audience, I have to choose my rhetorical style in the dark, and I'm taking the classroom style, because an audience of students is the one I feel easiest with.

There are two things in particular that I want to discuss with you. In school, and in university, there's a subject called "English" in English-speaking countries. English means, in the first place, the mother tongue. As that, it's the most practical subject in the world: you can't understand anything or take any part in your society without it. Wherever illiteracy is a problem, it's as fundamental a problem as getting enough to eat or a place to sleep. The native language takes precedence over every other subject of study: nothing else can compare with it in its usefulness. But then you find that every mother tongue, in any developed or civilized society, turns into something called literature. If you keep on studying "English," you find yourself trying to read Shakespeare and Milton. Literature, we're told, is one of the arts, along with painting and music, and, after you've looked up all the hard words and the Classical allusions and learned what words like imagery and diction are supposed to mean, what you use in understanding it, or so you're told, is your imagination. Here you don't seem to be in quite the same practical and useful area: Shakespeare and Milton, whatever their merits, are not the kind of thing you must know to hold any place in society at all. A person who knows nothing about literature may be an ignoramus, but many people don't mind being that. Every child realizes that literature is taking him in a different direction from the immediately useful, and a good many children complain loudly about this. Two questions I want to deal with, then, are, first: what is the relation of English as the mother tongue to English

Originally delivered as a speech and then included in literary theorist Northrop Frye's The Educated Imagination *(1964), a book on the teaching of literature.*

as a literature? Second: What is the social value of the study of literature, and what is the place of the imagination that literature addresses itself to, in the learning process?

Let's start with the different ways there are of dealing with the world we're living in. Suppose you're shipwrecked on an uninhabited island in the South Seas. The first thing you do is to take a long look at the world around you, a world of sky and sea and earth and stars and trees and hills. You see this world as objective, as something set over against you and not yourself or related to you in any way. And you notice two things about this objective world. In the first place, it doesn't have any conversation. It's full of animals and plants and insects going on with their own business, but there's nothing that responds to you: it has no morals and no intelligence, or at least none that you can grasp. It may have a shape and a meaning, but it doesn't seem to be a human shape or a human meaning. Even if there's enough to eat and no dangerous animals, you feel lonely and frightened and unwanted in such a world.

In the second place, you find that looking at the world, as something set over against you, splits your mind in two. You have an intellect that feels curious about it and wants to study it, and you have feelings or emotions that see it as beautiful or austere or terrible. You know that both these attitudes have some reality, at least for you. If the ship you were wrecked in was a Western ship, you'd probably feel that your intellect tells you more about what's really there in the outer world, and that your emotions tell you more about what's going on inside you. If your background were Oriental, you'd be more likely to reverse this and say that the beauty or terror was what was really there, and that your instinct to count and classify and measure and pull to pieces was what was inside your mind. But whether your point of view is Western or Eastern, intellect and emotion never get together in your mind as long as you're simply looking at the world. They alternate, and keep you divided between them.

The language you use on this level of the mind is the language of consciousness or awareness. It's largely a language of nouns and adjectives. You have to have names for things, and you need qualities like "wet" or "green" or "beautiful" to describe how things seem to you. This is the speculative or contemplative position of the mind, the position in which the arts and sciences begin, although they don't stay there very long. The sciences begin by accepting the facts and the evidence about an outside world without trying to alter them. Science proceeds by accurate measurement and description, and follows the demands of the reason rather than the emotions. What it deals with is there, whether we like it or not. The emotions are unreasonable: for them it's what they like and don't like that comes first. We'd be naturally inclined to think that the arts follow the path of emotion, in contrast to the sciences. Up to a point they do, but there's a complicating factor.

That complicating factor is the contrast between "I like this" and "I don't like this." In this Robinson Crusoe life I've assigned you,[1] you may have moods of complete peacefulness and joy, moods when you accept your island and

5

1. Reference to *Robinson Crusoe* (1719), a novel by Daniel Defoe about a man shipwrecked on an island.

everything around you. You wouldn't have such moods very often, and when you had them, they'd be moods of identification, when you felt that the island was a part of you and you a part of it. That is not the feeling of consciousness or awareness, where you feel split off from everything that's not your perceiving self. Your habitual state of mind is the feeling of separation which goes with being conscious, and the feeling "this is not a part of me" soon becomes "this is not what I want." Notice the word "want": we'll be coming back to it.

So you soon realize that there's a difference between the world you're living in and the world you want to live in. The world you want to live in is a human world, not an objective one: it's not an environment but a home; it's not the world you see but the world you build out of what you see. You go to work to build a shelter or plant a garden, and as soon as you start to work you've moved into a different level of human life. You're not separating only yourself from nature now, but constructing a human world and separating it from the rest of the world. Your intellect and emotions are now both engaged in the same activity, so there's no longer any real distinction between them. As soon as you plant a garden or a crop, you develop the conception of a "weed," the plant you don't want in there. But you can't say that "weed" is either an intellectual or an emotional conception, because it's both at once. Further, you go to work because you feel you have to, and because you want something at the end of the work. That means that the important categories of your life are no longer the subject and the object, the watcher and the things being watched: the important categories are what you have to do and what you want to do—in other words, necessity and freedom.

One person by himself is not a complete human being, so I'll provide you with another shipwrecked refugee of the opposite sex and an eventual family. Now you're a member of a human society. This human society after a while will transform the island into something with a human shape. What that human shape is, is revealed in the shape of the work you do: the buildings, such as they are, the paths through the woods, the planted crops fenced off against whatever animals want to eat them. These things, these rudiments of city, highway, garden, and farm, are the human form of nature, or the form of human nature, whichever you like. This is the area of the applied arts and sciences, and it appears in our society as engineering and agriculture and medicine and architecture. In this area we can never say clearly where the art stops and the science begins, or vice versa.

The language you use on this level is the language of practical sense, a language of verbs or words of action and movement. The practical world, however, is a world where actions speak louder than words. In some way it's a higher level of existence than the speculative level, because it's doing something about the world instead of just looking at it, but in itself it's a much more primitive level. It's the process of adapting to the environment, or rather of transforming the environment in the interests of one species, that goes on among animals and plants as well as human beings. The animals have a good many of our practical skills: some insects make pretty fair architects, and beavers know quite a lot about engineering. In this island, probably, and certainly if you were alone, you'd have about the ranking of a second-rate animal. What makes our practical life really human is a third level of the mind, a level where consciousness and practical skill come together.

This third level is a vision or model in your mind of what you want to con- 10 struct. There's that word "want" again. The actions of man are prompted by desire, and some of these desires are needs, like food and warmth and shelter. One of these needs is sexual, the desire to reproduce and bring more human beings into existence. But there's also a desire to bring a social human form into existence: the form of cities and gardens and farms that we call civilization. Many animals and insects have this social form too, but man knows that he has it: he can compare what he does with what he can imagine being done. So we begin to see where the imagination belongs in the scheme of human affairs. It's the power of constructing possible models of human experience. In the world of the imagination, anything goes that's imaginatively possible, but nothing really happens. If it did happen, it would move out of the world of imagination into the world of action.

We have three levels of the mind now, and a language for each of them, which in English-speaking societies means an English for each of them. There's the level of consciousness and awareness, where the most important thing is the difference between me and everything else. The English of this level is the English of ordinary conversation, which is mostly monologue, as you'll soon realize if you do a bit of eavesdropping, or listening to yourself. We can call it the language of self-expression. Then there's the level of social participation, the working or technological language of teachers and preachers and politicians and advertisers and lawyers and journalists and scientists. We've already called this the language of practical sense. Then there's the level of imagination, which produces the literary language of poems and plays and novels. They're not really different languages, of course, but three different reasons for using words.

On this basis, perhaps, we can distinguish the arts from the sciences. Science begins with the world we have to live in, accepting its data and trying to explain its laws. From there, it moves towards the imagination: it becomes a mental construct, a model of a possible way of interpreting experience. The further it goes in this direction, the more it tends to speak the language of mathematics, which is really one of the languages of the imagination, along with literature and music. Art, on the other hand, begins with the world we construct, not with the world we see. It starts with the imagination, and then works towards ordinary experience: that is, it tries to make itself as convincing and recognizable as it can. You can see why we tend to think of the sciences as intellectual and the arts as emotional: one starts with the world as it is, the other with the world we want to have. Up to a point it is true that science gives an intellectual view of reality, and that the arts try to make the emotions as precise and disciplined as sciences do the intellect. But of course it's nonsense to think of the scientist as a cold unemotional reasoner and the artist as somebody who's in a perpetual emotional tizzy. You can't distinguish the arts from the sciences by the mental processes the people in them use: they both operate on a mixture of hunch and common sense. A highly developed science and a highly developed art are very close together, psychologically and otherwise.

Still, the fact that they start from opposite ends, even if they do meet in the middle, makes for one important difference between them. Science learns more and more about the world as it goes on: it evolves and improves. A physicist today knows more physics than Newton[2] did, even if he's not as great a scientist. But literature begins with the possible model of experience, and what it produces is the literary model we call the classic. Literature doesn't evolve or improve or progress. We may have dramatists in the future who will write plays as good as *King Lear,* though they'll be very different ones, but drama as a whole will never get better than *King Lear. King Lear* is it, as far as drama is concerned; so is *Oedipus Rex,* written two thousand years earlier than that,[3] and both will be models of dramatic writing as long as the human race endures. Social conditions may improve: most of us would rather live in nineteenth-century United States than in thirteenth-century Italy, and for most of us Whitman's celebration of democracy makes a lot more sense than Dante's *Inferno.*[4] But it doesn't follow that Whitman is a better poet than Dante: literature won't line up with that kind of improvement.

So we find that everything that does improve, including science, leaves the literary artist out in the cold. Writers don't seem to benefit much by the advance of science, although they thrive on superstitions of all kinds. And you certainly wouldn't turn to contemporary poets for guidance or leadership in the twentieth-century world. You'd hardly go to Ezra Pound, with his fascism and social credit and Confucianism and anti-semitism. Or to Yeats, with his spiritualism and fairies and astrology. Or to D. H. Lawrence, who'll tell you that it's a good thing for servants to be flogged because that restores the precious current of blood-reciprocity between servant and master. Or to T. S. Eliot, who'll tell you that to have a flourishing culture we should educate an élite, keep most people living in the same spot, and never disestablish the Church of England.[5] The novelists seem to be a little closer to the world they're living in, but not much. When Communists talk about the decadence of bourgeois culture, this is the kind of thing they always bring up. Their own writers don't seem to be any better, though; just duller. So the real question is a bigger one. Is it possible that literature, especially poetry, is something that a scientific civilization like ours will eventually outgrow? Man has always wanted to fly, and thousands of years ago he was making sculptures of winged bulls and telling stories about people who flew so high on artificial wings

---

2. Isaac Newton (1642–1727), English mathematician and physicist.

3. *King Lear,* tragedy (c. 1607), by Shakespeare; *Oedipus Rex,* tragedy (first performed 429 B.C.E.) by Sophocles.

4. Walt Whitman (1819–1892), American poet; Dante Alighieri (1265–1321), Italian poet; the *Inferno* is the first part of his *Divine Comedy* (c. 1302).

5. Pound (1885–1972), American-born poet, supported Mussolini's fascist regime in Italy and the right-wing economic doctrine of social credit. William Butler Yeats (1865–1939), Irish poet and dramatist; see, for example, his prose work *A Vision.* Lawrence (1885–1930), British author; see his short story "The Prussian Officer." Eliot (1888–1965), American-born poet who emigrated to England.

that the sun melted them off.[6] In an Indian play fifteen hundred years old, *Sakuntala,* there's a god who flies around in a chariot that to a modern reader sounds very much like a private aeroplane. Interesting that the writer had so much imagination, but do we need such stories now that we have private aeroplanes?

This is not a new question: it was raised a hundred and fifty years ago by   15
Thomas Love Peacock,[7] who was a poet and novelist himself, and a very brilliant one. He wrote an essay called *Four Ages of Poetry,* with his tongue of course in his cheek, in which he said that poetry was the mental rattle that awakened the imagination of mankind in its infancy, but that now, in an age of science and technology, the poet has outlived his social function. "A poet in our times," said Peacock, "is a semi-barbarian in a civilized community. He lives in the days that are past. His ideas, thoughts, feelings, associations, are all with barbarous manners, obsolete customs, and exploded superstitions. The march of his intellect is like that of a crab, backwards." Peacock's essay annoyed his friend Shelley,[8] who wrote another essay called *A Defence of Poetry* to refute it. Shelley's essay is a wonderful piece of writing, but it's not likely to convince anyone who needs convincing. I shall be spending a good deal of my time on this question of the relevance of literature in the world of today, and I can only indicate the general lines my answer will take. There are two points I can make now, one simple, the other more difficult.

The simple point is that literature belongs to the world man constructs, not to the world he sees; to his home, not his environment. Literature's world is a concrete human world of immediate experience. The poet uses images and objects and sensations much more than he uses abstract ideas; the novelist is concerned with telling stories, not with working out arguments. The world of literature is human in shape, a world where the sun rises in the east and sets in the west over the edge of a flat earth in three dimensions, where the primary realities are not atoms or electrons but bodies, and the primary forces not energy or gravitation but love and death and passion and joy. It's not surprising if writers are often rather simple people, not always what we think of as intellectuals, and certainly not always any freer of silliness or perversity than anyone else. What concerns us is what they produce, not what they are, and poetry, according to Milton,[9] who ought to have known, is "more simple, sensuous and passionate" than philosophy or science.

The more difficult point takes us back to what we said when we were on that South Sea island. Our emotional reaction to the world varies from "I like this" to "I don't like this." The first, we said, was a state of identity, a feeling that everything around us was part of us, and the second is the ordinary state of consciousness, or separation, where art and science begin. Art begins as soon as

6. Allusion to the Greek myth of Icarus, who flew too close to the sun on wings made of wax by his father, Daedalus.

7. British author (1785–1866).

8. Percy Bysshe Shelley (1792–1822), British poet.

9. John Milton (1608–1674), British poet; from a prose work, *Tractate of Education.*

"I don't like this" turns into "this is not the way I could imagine it." We notice in passing that the creative and the neurotic minds have a lot in common. They're both dissatisfied with what they see; they both believe that something else ought to be there, and they try to pretend it is there or to make it be there. The differences are more important, but we're not ready for them yet.

At the level of ordinary consciousness the individual man is the center of everything, surrounded on all sides by what he isn't. At the level of practical sense, or civilization, there's a human circumference, a little cultivated world with a human shape, fenced off from the jungle and inside the sea and the sky. But in the imagination anything goes that can be imagined, and the limit of the imagination is a totally human world. Here we recapture, in full consciousness, that original lost sense of identity with our surroundings, where there is nothing outside the mind of man, or something identical with the mind of man. Religions present us with visions of eternal and infinite heavens or paradises which have the form of the cities and gardens of human civilization, like the Jerusalem and Eden of the Bible, completely separated from the state of frustration and misery that bulks so large in ordinary life. We're not concerned with these visions as religion, but they indicate what the limits of the imagination are. They indicate too that in the human world the imagination has no limits, if you follow me. We said that the desire to fly produced the aeroplane. But people don't get into planes because they want to fly; they get into planes because they want to get somewhere else faster. What's produced the aeroplane is not so much a desire to fly as a rebellion against the tyranny of time and space. And that's a process that can never stop, no matter how high our Titovs and Glenns[10] may go.

For each of these six talks I've taken a title from some work of literature, and my title for this one is "The Motive for Metaphor," from a poem of Wallace Stevens.[11] Here's the poem:

> You like it under the trees in autumn,
> Because everything is half dead.
> The wind moves like a cripple among the leaves
> And repeats words without meaning.
>
> In the same way, you were happy in spring,
> With the half colors of quarter-things,
> The slightly brighter sky, the melting clouds,
> The single bird, the obscure moon—
>
> The obscure moon lighting an obscure world
> Of things that would never be quite expressed,
> Where you yourself were never quite yourself
> And did not want nor have to be,

10. Gherman S. Titov, Russian astronaut, first man to make a multi-orbital flight (1961); John H. Glenn, American astronaut, first American to make an orbital flight (1962), later became a senator from Ohio.

11. American poet (1879–1955).

> Desiring the exhilarations of changes:
> The motive for metaphor, shrinking from
> The weight of primary noon,
> The A B C of being,
>
> The ruddy temper, the hammer
> Of red and blue, the hard sound—
> Steel against intimation—the sharp flash,
> The vital, arrogant, fatal, dominant X.

What Stevens calls the weight of primary noon, the A B C of being, and the dominant X is the objective world, the world set over against us. Outside literature, the main motive for writing is to describe this world. But literature itself uses language in a way which associates our minds with it. As soon as you use associative language, you begin using figures of speech. If you say this talk is dry and dull, you're using figures associating it with bread and breadknives. There are two main kinds of association, analogy and identity, two things that are like each other and two things that are each other. You can say with Burns,[12] "My love's like a red, red rose," or you can say with Shakespeare:

> Thou that art now the world's fresh ornament
> And only herald to the gaudy spring.

One produces the figure of speech called the simile; the other produces the figure called metaphor.

In descriptive writing you have to be careful of associative language. You'll find that analogy, or likeness to something else, is very tricky to handle in description, because the differences are as important as the resemblances. As for metaphor, where you're really saying "this *is* that," you're turning your back on logic and reason completely, because logically two things can never be the same thing and still remain two things. The poet, however, uses these two crude, primitive, archaic forms of thought in the most uninhibited way, because his job is not to describe nature, but to show you a world completely absorbed and possessed by the human mind. So he produces what Baudelaire[13] called a "suggestive magic including at the same time object and subject, the world outside the artist and the artist himself." The motive for metaphor, according to Wallace Stevens, is a desire to associate, and finally to identify, the human mind with what goes on outside it, because the only genuine joy you can have is in those rare moments when you feel that although we may know in part, as Paul says, we are also a part of what we know.[14]

20

---

12. Robert Burns (1759–1796), Scottish poet.
13. Charles Baudelaire (1821–1867), French poet.
14. Allusion to 1 Corinthians 13.9–10: "For we know in part, and we prophecy in part. But when that which is perfect is come, then that which is in part shall be done away with."

MLA CITATION

Frye, Northrop. "The Motive for Metaphor." 1964. *The Norton Reader: An Anthology of Nonfiction*. Ed. Melissa A. Goldthwaite et al. 14th ed. New York: Norton, 2016. 888–95. Print.

QUESTIONS

1. At what point in his essay does Northrop Frye come to explain the meaning of his title? What is his conception of the motive for metaphor? Why does he wait to explain it?

2. Frye describes three kinds of English, or, rather, he describes one English and three uses to which we put it. What are they?

3. Frye describes metaphor, forcibly, as nonsense (paragraph 20). How, then, do we make sense of it?

4. Why, according to Frye, doesn't literature improve the way science does? What happens to old science? Read Thomas S. Kuhn's "The Route to Normal Science" (pp. 829–37), and do additional research if necessary. Then write an essay in which you compare the fates of old literature and old science.

NGŪGĪ WA THIONG'O *Decolonizing the Mind*

I WAS BORN into a large peasant family: father, four wives and about twenty-eight children. I also belonged, as we all did in those days, to a wider extended family and to the community as a whole.

We spoke Gīkūyū[1] as we worked in the fields. We spoke Gīkūyū in and outside the home. I can vividly recall those evenings of storytelling around the fireside. It was mostly the grown-ups telling the children but everybody was interested and involved. We children would re-tell the stories the following day to other children who worked in the fields picking the pyrethrum[2] flowers, tea-leaves or coffee beans of our European and African landlords.

The stories, with mostly animals as the main characters, were all told in Gīkūyū. Hare, being small, weak but full of innovative wit and cunning, was

Published in Decolonizing the Mind: The Politics of Language in African Literature *(1986), an essay collection that Ngũgĩ wa Thiong'o describes as his "farewell to English as a vehicle for any of [his] writings." The Kenyan novelist, playwright, and social critic has been a pioneer of African literature and a critic of colonialism. Although his first novels were composed in English, Ngũgĩ now writes in Gĩkũyũ, often translating his own work into English.*

1. Language spoken by the Kikuyu people, the majority of Kenyans.
2. Type of chrysanthemum, often used as an insecticide or for medicinal purposes.

our hero. We identified with him as he struggled against the brutes of prey like lion, leopard, hyena. His victories were our victories and we learned that the apparently weak can outwit the strong. We followed the animals in their struggle against hostile nature—drought, rain, sun, wind—a confrontation often forcing them to search for forms of co-operation. But we were also interested in their struggles amongst themselves, and particularly between the beasts and the victims of prey. These twin struggles, against nature and other animals, reflected real-life struggles in the human world.

Not that we neglected stories with human beings as the main characters. There were two types of characters in such human-centered narratives: the species of truly human beings with qualities of courage, kindness, mercy, hatred of evil, concern for others; and a man-eat-man two-mouthed species with qualities of greed, selfishness, individualism and hatred of what was good for the larger co-operative community. Co-operation as the ultimate good in a community was a constant theme. It could unite human beings with animals against ogres and beasts of prey, as in the story of how dove, after being fed with castor-oil seeds, was sent to fetch a smith working far away from home and whose pregnant wife was being threatened by these man-eating two-mouthed ogres.

There were good and bad story-tellers. A good one could tell the same story over and over again, and it would always be fresh to us, the listeners. He or she could tell a story told by someone else and make it more alive and dramatic. The differences really were in the use of words and images and the inflection of voices to effect different tones.   5

We therefore learned to value words for their meaning and nuances. Language was not a mere string of words. It had a suggestive power well beyond the immediate and lexical meaning. Our appreciation of the suggestive magical power of language was reinforced by the games we played with words through riddles, proverbs, transpositions of syllables, or through nonsensical but musically arranged words. So we learned the music of our language on top of the content. The language, through images and symbols, gave us a view of the world, but it had a beauty of its own. The home and the field were then our pre-primary school but what is important, for this discussion, is that the language of our evening teach-ins, and the language of our immediate and wider community, and the language of our work in the fields were one.

And then I went to school, a colonial school, and this harmony was broken. The language of my education was no longer the language of my culture. I first went to Kamaandura, missionary run, and then to another called Maanguuū run by nationalists grouped around the Gĩkũyũ Independent and Karinga Schools Association. Our language of education was still Gĩkũyũ. The very first time I was ever given an ovation for my writing was over a composition in Gĩkũyũ. So for my first four years there was still harmony between the language of my formal education and that of the Limuru peasant community.

It was after the declaration of a state of emergency over Kenya in 1952 that all the schools run by patriotic nationalists were taken over by the colonial regime and were placed under District Education Boards chaired by Englishmen. English became the language of my formal education. In Kenya, English became more than a language: it was *the* language, and all the others had to bow before it in deference.

Thus one of the most humiliating experiences was to be caught speaking Gĩkũyũ in the vicinity of the school. The culprit was given corporal punishment—three to five strokes of the cane on bare buttocks—or was made to carry a metal plate around the neck with inscriptions such as I AM STUPID or I AM A DONKEY. Sometimes the culprits were fined money they could hardly afford. And how did the teachers catch the culprits? A button was initially given to one pupil who was supposed to hand it over to whoever was caught speaking his mother tongue. Whoever had the button at the end of the day would sing who had given it to him and the ensuing process would bring out all the culprits of the day. Thus children were turned into witch-hunters and in the process were being taught the lucrative value of being a traitor to oneʼs immediate community.

10   The attitude to English was the exact opposite: any achievement in spoken or written English was highly rewarded; prizes, prestige, applause; the ticket to higher realms. English became the measure of intelligence and ability in the arts, the sciences, and all the other branches of learning. English became *the* main determinant of a childʼs progress up the ladder of formal education.

As you may know, the colonial system of education in addition to its apartheid racial demarcation had the structure of a pyramid: a broad primary base, a narrowing secondary middle, and an even narrower university apex. Selections from primary into secondary were through an examination, in my time called Kenya African Preliminary Examination, in which one had to pass six subjects ranging from Maths to Nature Study and Kiswahili.[3] All the papers were written in English. Nobody could pass the exam who failed the English language paper no matter how brilliantly he had done in the other subjects. I remember one boy in my class of 1954 who had distinctions in all subjects except English, which he had failed. He was made to fail the entire exam. He went on to become a turn boy[4] in a bus company. I who had only passes but a credit in English got a place at the Alliance High School, one of the most elitist institutions for Africans in colonial Kenya. The requirements for a place at the University, Makerere University College, were broadly the same: nobody could go on to wear the undergraduate red gown, no matter how brilliantly they had performed in all the other subjects unless they had a credit—not even a simple pass!—in English. Thus the most coveted place in the pyramid and in the system was only available to the holder of an English language credit card. English was the official vehicle and the magic formula to colonial elitedom.

Literary education was now determined by the dominant language while also reinforcing that dominance. Orature (oral literature) in Kenyan languages stopped. In primary school I now read simplified Dickens and Stevenson alongside Rider Haggard. Jim Hawkins, Oliver Twist, Tom Brown[5]—not Hare, Leopard and Lion—were now my daily companions in the world of imagina-

3. Swahili, a major East African language.

4. Someone who brings in customers; a tout.

5. Charles Dickens (1812–1870), British novelist, author of *Oliver Twist*; Robert Louis Stevenson (1850–1894), Scottish novelist, creator of Jim Hawkins in *Treasure*

tion. In secondary school, Scott and G. B. Shaw vied with more Rider Haggard, John Buchan, Alan Paton, Captain W. E. Johns.[6] At Makerere I read English: from Chaucer to T. S. Eliot with a touch of Grahame Greene.[7]

Thus language and literature were taking us further and further from ourselves to other selves, from our world to other worlds.

What was the colonial system doing to us Kenyan children? What were the consequences of, on the one hand, this systematic suppression of our languages and the literature they carried, and on the other the elevation of English and the literature it carried? To answer those questions, let me first examine the relationship of language to human experience, human culture, and the human perception of reality.

Language, any language, has a dual character: it is both a means of communication and a carrier of culture. Take English. It is spoken in Britain and in Sweden and Denmark. But for Swedish and Danish people English is only a means of communication with non-Scandinavians. It is not a carrier of their culture. For the British, and particularly the English, it is additionally, and inseparably from its use as a tool of communication, a carrier of their culture and history. Or take Swahili in East and Central Africa. It is widely used as a means of communication across many nationalities. But it is not the carrier of a culture and history of many of those nationalities. However in parts of Kenya and Tanzania, and particularly in Zanzibar,[8] Swahili is inseparably both a means of communication and a carrier of the culture of those people to whom it is a mother-tongue.

Language as communication has three aspects or elements. There is first what Karl Marx[9] once called the language of real life, the element basic to the whole notion of language, its origins and development: that is, the relations people enter into with one another in the labor process, the links they necessarily establish among themselves in the act of a people, a community of human beings, producing wealth or means of life like food, clothing, houses. A human community really starts its historical being as a community of cooperation in production through the division of labor; the simplest is between man, woman and child within a household; the more complex divisions are between branches of production such as those who are sole hunters, sole gatherers of fruits or sole workers in metal. Then there are the most complex divisions such as those in modern factories where a single product, say a shirt or a

15

Island; H. Rider Haggard (1856–1925), British adventure novelist; Brown, chief character in *Tom Brown's Schooldays* in the novel by Thomas Hughes.

6. Sir Walter Scott (1771–1832), Scottish poet and novelist; George Bernard Shaw (1856–1950), Irish-born playwright; Buchan (1875–1940), Scottish adventure novelist, author of *The Thirty-Nine Steps*, and also governor general of Canada; Paton (1903–1988), South African novelist; Johns (1893–1968), British writer, famous for the Biggles stories for boys.

7. Geoffrey Chaucer (c. 1343–1400), English poet, author of *The Canterbury Tales*; Eliot (1888–1965), American-born poet; Greene (1904–1991), British novelist.

8. Island off the east coast of Africa; part of Tanzania since 1964.

9. German political philosopher (1818–1883).

shoe, is the result of many hands and minds. Production is co-operation, is communication, is language, is expression of a relation between human beings and it is specifically human.

The second aspect of language as communication is speech and it imitates the language of real life, that is communication in production. The verbal signposts both reflect and aid communication or the relation established between human beings in the production of their means of life. Language as a system of verbal signposts makes that production possible. The spoken word is to relations between human beings what the hand is to the relations between human beings and nature. The hand through tools mediates between human beings and nature and forms the language of real life: spoken words mediate between human beings and form the language of speech.

The third aspect is the written signs. The written word imitates the spoken. Where the first two aspects of language as communication through the hand and the spoken word historically evolved more or less simultaneously, the written aspect is a much later historical development. Writing is representation of sounds with visual symbols, from the simplest knot among shepherds to tell the number in a herd or the hieroglyphics among the Agĩkũyũ gicaandi[10] singers and poets of Kenya, to the most complicated and different letter and picture writing systems of the world today.

In most societies the written and the spoken languages are the same, in that they represent each other: what is on paper can be read to another person and be received as that language, which the recipient has grown up speaking. In such a society there is broad harmony for a child between the three aspects of language as communication. His interaction with nature and with other men is expressed in written and spoken symbols or signs which are both a result of that double interaction and a reflection of it. The association of the child's sensibility is with the language of his experience of life.

20   But there is more to it: communication between human beings is also the basis and process of evolving culture. In doing similar kinds of things and actions over and over again under similar circumstances, similar even in their mutability, certain patterns, moves, rhythms, habits, attitudes, experiences and knowledge emerge. Those experiences are handed over to the next generation and become the inherited basis for their further actions on nature and on themselves. There is a gradual accumulation of values which in time become almost self-evident truths governing their conception of what is right and wrong, good and bad, beautiful and ugly, courageous and cowardly, generous and mean in their internal and external relations. Over a time this becomes a way of life distinguishable from other ways of life. They develop a distinctive culture and history. Culture embodies those moral, ethical and aesthetic values, the set of spiritual eyeglasses, through which they come to view themselves and their place in the universe. Values are the basis of a people's identity, their sense of particularity as members of the human race. All this is carried by language. Language as culture is the collective memory bank of a people's experience in

10. Agĩkũyũ, another term for Kikuyu, the group that forms the majority of the Kenyan population; gicaandi, a particular Kenyan song genre.

history. Culture is almost indistinguishable from the language that makes possible its genesis, growth, banking, articulation and indeed its transmission from one generation to the next.

Language as culture also has three important aspects. Culture is a product of the history which it in turn reflects. Culture in other words is a product and a reflection of human beings communicating with one another in the very struggle to create wealth and to control it. But culture does not merely reflect that history, or rather it does so by actually forming images or pictures of the world of nature and nurture. Thus the second aspect of language as culture is as an image-forming agent in the mind of a child. Our whole conception of ourselves as a people, individually and collectively, is based on those pictures and images which may or may not correctly correspond to the actual reality of the struggles with nature and nurture which produced them in the first place. But our capacity to confront the world creatively is dependent on how those images correspond or not to that reality, how they distort or clarify the reality of our struggles. Language as culture is thus mediating between me and my own self; between my own self and other selves; between me and nature. Language is mediating in my very being. And this brings us to the third aspect of language as culture. Culture transmits or imparts those images of the world and reality through the spoken and the written language, that is through a specific language. In other words, the capacity to speak, the capacity to order sounds in a manner that makes for mutual comprehension between human beings is universal. This is the universality of language, a quality specific to human beings. It corresponds to the universality of the struggle against nature and that between human beings. But the particularity of the sounds, the words, the word order into phrases and sentences, and the specific manner, or laws, of their ordering is what distinguishes one language from another. Thus a specific culture is not transmitted through language in its universality but in its particularity as the language of a specific community with a specific history. Written literature and orature are the main means by which a particular language transmits the images of the world contained in the culture it carries.

Language as communication and as culture are then products of each other. Communication creates culture: culture is a means of communication. Language carries culture, and culture carries, particularly through orature and literature, the entire body of values by which we come to perceive ourselves and our place in the world. How people perceive themselves affects how they look at their culture, at their politics and at the social production of wealth, at their entire relationship to nature and to other beings. Language is thus inseparable from ourselves as a community of human beings with a specific form and character, a specific history, a specific relationship to the world.

So what was the colonialist imposition of a foreign language doing to us children?

The real aim of colonialism was to control the people's wealth: what they produced, how they produced it, and how it was distributed; to control, in other words, the entire realm of the language of real life. Colonialism imposed its control of the social production of wealth through military conquest and subsequent political dictatorship. But its most important area of domination was the mental universe of the colonized, the control, through culture, of how people perceived themselves and their relationship to the world. Economic and political control can never be complete or effective without mental control. To control a people's culture is to control their tools of self-definition in relationship to others.

25   For colonialism this involved two aspects of the same process: the destruction or the deliberate undervaluing of a people's culture, their art, dances, religions, history, geography, education, orature and literature, and the conscious elevation of the language of the colonizer. The domination of a people's language by the languages of the colonizing nations was crucial to the domination of the mental universe of the colonized.

Take language as communication. Imposing a foreign language, and suppressing the native languages as spoken and written, were already breaking the harmony previously existing between the African child and the three aspects of language. Since the new language as a means of communication was a product of and was reflecting the "real language of life" elsewhere, it could never as spoken or written properly reflect or imitate the real life of that community. This may in part explain why technology always appears to us as slightly external, *their* product and not *ours*. The word "missile" used to hold an alien faraway sound until I recently learnt its equivalent in Gīkūyū, *ngurukuhī* and it made me apprehend it differently. Learning, for a colonial child, became a cerebral activity and not an emotionally felt experience.

But since the new, imposed languages could never completely break the native languages as spoken, their most effective area of domination was the third aspect of language as communication, the written. The language of an African child's formal education was foreign. The language of the books he read was foreign. The language of his conceptualization was foreign. Thought, in him, took the visible form of a foreign language. So the written language of a child's upbringing in the school (even his spoken language within the school compound) became divorced from his spoken language at home. There was often not the slightest relationship between the child's written world, which was also the language of his schooling, and the world of his immediate environment in the family and the community. For a colonial child, the harmony existing between the three aspects of language as communication was irrevocably broken. This resulted in the disassociation of the sensibility[11] of that child from his natural and social environment, what we might call colonial alienation. The alienation became reinforced in the teaching of history, geography, music, where bourgeois Europe was always the center of the universe.

The disassociation, divorce, or alienation from the immediate environment becomes clearer when you look at colonial language as a carrier of culture.

Since culture is a product of the history of a people which it in turn reflects, the child was now being exposed exclusively to a culture that was a

---

11. Echo of T. S. Eliot's famous phrase "dissociation of sensibility," a break from the past, when thought and feeling were unified.

product of a world external to himself. He was being made to stand outside himself to look at himself. *Catching Them Young* is the title of a book on racism, class, sex, and politics in children's literature by Bob Dixon. "Catching them young" as an aim was even more true of a colonial child. The images of his world and his place in it implanted in a child take years to eradicate, if they ever can be.

Since culture does not just reflect the world in images but actually, through those images, conditions a child to see that world a certain way, the colonial child was made to see the world and where he stands in it as seen and defined by or reflected in the culture of the language of imposition.   30

And since those images are mostly passed on through orature and literature it meant the child would now only see the world as seen in the literature of his language of adoption. From the point of view of alienation, that is of seeing oneself from outside oneself as if one was another self, it does not matter that the imported literature carried the great humanist tradition of the best Shakespeare, Goethe, Balzac, Tolstoy, Gorky, Brecht, Sholokhov,[12] Dickens. The location of this great mirror of imagination was necessarily Europe and its history and culture and the rest of the universe was seen from that center.

But obviously it was worse when the colonial child was exposed to images of his world as mirrored in the written languages of his colonizer. Where his own native languages were associated in his impressionable mind with low status, humiliation, corporal punishment, slow-footed intelligence and ability or downright stupidity, non-intelligibility and barbarism, this was reinforced by the world he met in the works of such geniuses of racism as a Rider Haggard or a Nicholas Monsarrat;[13] not to mention the pronouncement of some of the giants of western intellectual and political establishment, such as Hume (". . . The negro is naturally inferior to the whites. . . ."), Thomas Jefferson (". . . The blacks . . . are inferior to the whites on the endowments of both body and mind. . . ."), or Hegel[14] with his Africa comparable to a land of childhood still enveloped in the dark mantle of the night as far as the development of self-conscious history was concerned. Hegel's statement that there was nothing harmonious with humanity to be found in the African character is representative of the racist images of Africans and Africa such a colonial child was bound to encounter in the literature of the colonial languages. The results could be disastrous.

12. William Shakespeare (1564–1616), English playwright; Johann Wolfgang von Goethe (1749–1832), German novelist and playwright; Honoré de Balzac (1799–1850), French novelist; Leo (Count Lev Nikolayevich) Tolstoy (1828–1910), Russian novelist; Maxim Gorky (1868–1936), Russian dramatist; Bertolt Brecht (1898–1956), German dramatist; Mikhail Aleksandrovich Sholokhov (1905–1984), Russian novelist.

13. Monsarrat's *The Tribe That Lost Its Head* (1956) was this British novelist's satirical look at British colonialism and the African independence movement.

14. David Hume (1711–1776), Scottish philosopher; Jefferson (1743–1826), third U.S. president, 1801–1809; Georg Wilhelm Friedrich Hegel (1770–1831), German philosopher.

MLA CITATION

Thiong'o, Ngũgĩ wa. "Decolonizing the Mind." 1986. *The Norton Reader: An Anthology of Nonfiction.* Ed. Melissa A. Goldthwaite et al. 14th ed. New York: Norton, 2016. 896–903. Print.

QUESTIONS

1. The last paragraphs of Ngũgĩ wa Thiong'o's essay contain the names of many classic and contemporary European writers. Why do you think he chose to include them? Can you relate their inclusion to the way Ngũgĩ chooses to present himself in this essay?

2. What literary writers did you read in secondary school? What values were your teachers (or school) imparting in selecting those writers in particular?

3. Ngũgĩ experienced a particularly stark contrast between the values contained within the oral stories of his family and the written English of school. Discuss the different value systems. Have you noticed differences between what your extended family values and what your school seemed to want you to value?

4. Imagine an English class for a bilingual or bicultural community. Write a paper justifying the ideal balance between texts from the second language or culture (in translation or not) and English.

VIRGINIA WOOLF   *In Search of a Room of One's Own*

I
T WAS DISAPPOINTING not to have brought back in the evening some important statement, some authentic fact. Women are poorer than men because—this or that. Perhaps now it would be better to give up seeking for the truth, and receiving on one's head an avalanche of opinion hot as lava, discolored as dish-water. It would be better to draw the curtains; to shut out distractions; to light the lamp; to narrow the enquiry and to ask the historian, who records not opinions but facts, to describe under what conditions women lived, not throughout the ages, but in England, say in the time of Elizabeth.[1]

For it is a perennial puzzle why no woman wrote a word of that extraordinary literature when every other man, it seemed, was capable of song or son-

From Chapter 3 of Virginia Woolf's A Room of One's Own (1929), a long essay that began as lectures given at Newnham College and Girton College, women's colleges at Cambridge University, in 1928. In Chapter 1, Woolf advances the proposition that "a woman must have money and a room of her own if she is to write fiction." In Chapter 2, she describes a day spent at the British Museum (now the British Library) looking for information about the lives of women.

1. Elizabeth I, queen from 1558 to 1603.

net. What were the conditions in which women lived, I asked myself; for fiction, imaginative work that is, is not dropped like a pebble upon the ground, as science may be; fiction is like a spider's web, attached ever so lightly perhaps, but still attached to life at all four corners. Often the attachment is scarcely perceptible; Shakespeare's plays, for instance, seem to hang there complete by themselves. But when the web is pulled askew, hooked up at the edge, torn in the middle, one remembers that these webs are not spun in midair by incorporeal creatures, but are the work of suffering human beings, and are attached to grossly material things, like health and money and the houses we live in.

I went, therefore, to the shelf where the histories stand and took down one of the latest, Professor Trevelyan's *History of England*. Once more I looked up Women, found "position of," and turned to the pages indicated. "Wife-beating," I read, "was a recognised right of man, and was practised without shame by high as well as low. . . . Similarly," the historian goes on, "the daughter who refused to marry the gentleman of her parents' choice was liable to be locked up, beaten and flung about the room, without any shock being inflicted on public opinion. Marriage was not an affair of personal affection, but of family avarice, particularly in the 'chivalrous' upper classes. . . . Betrothal often took place while one or both of the parties was in the cradle, and marriage when they were scarcely out of the nurses' charge." That was about 1470, soon after Chaucer's time. The next reference to the position of women is some two hundred years later, in the time of the Stuarts. "It was still the exception for women of the upper and middle class to choose their own husbands, and when the husband had been assigned, he was lord and master, so far at least as law and custom could make him. Yet even so," Professor Trevelyan concludes, "neither Shakespeare's women nor those of authentic seventeenth-century memoirs, like the Verneys and the Hutchinsons, seem wanting in personality and character." Certainly, if we consider it, Cleopatra must have had a way with her; Lady Macbeth, one would suppose, had a will of her own; Rosalind, one might conclude, was an attractive girl. Professor Trevelyan is speaking no more than the truth when he remarks that Shakespeare's women do not seem wanting in personality and character. Not being a historian, one might go even further and say that women have burnt like beacons in all the works of all the poets from the beginning of time—Clytemnestra, Antigone, Cleopatra, Lady Macbeth, Phèdre, Cressida, Rosalind, Desdemona, the Duchess of Malfi, among the dramatists; then among the prose writers: Millamant, Clarissa, Becky Sharp, Anna Karenina, Emma Bovary, Madame de Guermantes—the names flock to mind, nor do they recall women "lacking in personality and character." Indeed, if woman had no existence save in the fiction written by men, one would imagine her a person of the utmost importance; very various; heroic and mean; splendid and sordid; infinitely beautiful and hideous in the extreme; as great as a man, some think even greater.[2] But this is woman in fiction. In fact, as Professor Trevelyan points out, she was locked up, beaten and flung about the room.

2. "It remains a strange and almost inexplicable fact that in Athena's city, where women were kept in almost Oriental suppression as odalisques or drudges, the stage

A very queer, composite being thus emerges. Imaginatively she is of the highest importance; practically she is completely insignificant. She pervades poetry from cover to cover; she is all but absent from history. She dominates the lives of kings and conquerors in fiction; in fact she was the slave of any boy whose parents forced a ring upon her finger. Some of the most inspired words, some of the most profound thoughts in literature fall from her lips; in real life she could hardly read, could scarcely spell, and was the property of her husband.

5   It was certainly an odd monster that one made up by reading the historians first and the poets afterwards—a worm winged like an eagle; the spirit of life and beauty in a kitchen chopping up suet. But these monsters, however amusing to the imagination, have no existence in fact. What one must do to bring her to life was to think poetically and prosaically at one and the same moment, thus keeping in touch with fact—that she is Mrs. Martin, aged thirty-six, dressed in blue, wearing a black hat and brown shoes; but not losing sight of fiction either—that she is a vessel in which all sorts of spirits and forces are coursing and flashing perpetually. The moment, however, that one tries this method with the Elizabethan woman, one branch of illumination fails; one is held up by the scarcity of facts. One knows nothing detailed, nothing perfectly true and substantial about her. History scarcely mentions her. And I turned to Professor Trevelyan again to see what history meant to him. I found by looking at his chapter headings that it meant—

"The Manor Court and the Methods of Open-field Agriculture . . . The Cistercians and Sheep-farming . . . The Crusades . . . The University . . . The House of Commons . . . The Hundred Years' War . . . The Wars of the Roses . . . The Renaissance Scholars . . . The Dissolution of the Monasteries . . . Agrarian and Religious Strife . . . The Origin of English Seapower . . . The Armada . . ." and so on. Occasionally an individual woman is mentioned, an Elizabeth, or a Mary; a queen or a great lady. But by no possible means could middle-class women with nothing but brains and character at their command have taken part in any one of the great movements which, brought together, constitute the historian's view of the past. Nor shall we find her in any collection of

should yet have produced figures like Clytemnestra and Cassandra, Atossa and Antigone, Phèdre and Medea, and all the other heroines who dominate play after play of the 'misogynist' Euripides. But the paradox of this world where in real life a respectable woman could hardly show her face alone in the street, and yet on the stage woman equals or surpasses man, has never been satisfactorily explained. In modern tragedy the same predominance exists. At all events, a very cursory survey of Shakespeare's work (similarly with Webster, though not with Marlowe or Jonson) suffices to reveal how this dominance, this initiative of women, persists from Rosalind to Lady Macbeth. So too in Racine; six of his tragedies bear their heroines' names; and what male characters of his shall we set against Hermione and Andromaque, Bérénice and Roxane, Phèdre and Athalie? So again with Ibsen; what men shall we match with Solveig and Nora, Hedda and Hilda Wangel and Rebecca West?"—F. L. LUCAS, *Tragedy*, pp. 114–15 [Woolf's note].

anecdotes. Aubrey[3] hardly mentions her. She never writes her own life and scarcely keeps a diary; there are only a handful of her letters in existence. She left no plays or poems by which we can judge her. What one wants, I thought—and why does not some brilliant student at Newnham or Girton supply it?—is a mass of information; at what age did she marry; how many children had she as a rule; what was her house like; had she a room to herself; did she do the cooking; would she be likely to have a servant? All these facts lie somewhere, presumably, in parish registers and account books; the life of the average Elizabethan woman must be scattered about somewhere, could one collect it and make a book of it. It would be ambitious beyond my daring, I thought, looking about the shelves for books that were not there, to suggest to the students of those famous colleges that they should re-write history, though I own that it often seems a little queer as it is, unreal, lop-sided; but why should they not add a supplement to history? calling it, of course, by some inconspicuous name so that women might figure there without impropriety? For one often catches a glimpse of them in the lives of the great, whisking away into the background, concealing, I sometimes think, a wink, a laugh, perhaps a tear. And, after all, we have lives enough of Jane Austen; it scarcely seems necessary to consider again the influence of the tragedies of Joanna Baillie upon the poetry of Edgar Allan Poe; as for myself, I should not mind if the homes and haunts of Mary Russell Mitford[4] were closed to the public for a century at least. But what I find deplorable, I continued, looking about the bookshelves again, is that nothing is known about women before the eighteenth century. I have no model in my mind to turn about this way and that. Here am I asking why women did not write poetry in the Elizabethan age, and I am not sure how they were educated; whether they were taught to write; whether they had sitting-rooms to themselves; how many women had children before they were twenty-one; what, in short, they did from eight in the morning till eight at night. They had no money evidently; according to Professor Trevelyan they were married whether they liked it or not before they were out of the nursery, at fifteen or sixteen very likely. It would have been extremely odd, even upon this showing, had one of them suddenly written the plays of Shakespeare, I concluded, and I thought of that old gentleman, who is dead now, but was a bishop, I think, who declared that it was impossible for any woman, past, present, or to come, to have the genius of Shakespeare. He wrote to the papers about it. He also told a lady who applied to him for information that cats do not as a matter of fact go to heaven, though they have, he added, souls of a sort. How much thinking those old gentlemen used to save

3. John Aubrey (1626–1697), whose biographical writings were published posthumously as *Brief Lives*.
4. Austen (1775–1817), English novelist; Baillie (1762–1851), Scottish dramatist and poet; Poe (1809–1849), American poet and short-story writer; Mitford (1787–1855), English novelist and essayist.

one! How the borders of ignorance shrank back at their approach! Cats do not go to heaven. Women cannot write the plays of Shakespeare.

Be that as it may, I could not help thinking, as I looked at the works of Shakespeare on the shelf, that the bishop was right at least in this; it would have been impossible, completely and entirely, for any woman to have written the plays of Shakespeare in the age of Shakespeare. Let me imagine, since facts are so hard to come by, what would have happened had Shakespeare had a wonderfully gifted sister, called Judith, let us say. Shakespeare himself went, very probably—his mother was an heiress—to the grammar school, where he may have learnt Latin—Ovid, Virgil and Horace—and the elements of grammar and logic. He was, it is well known, a wild boy who poached rabbits, perhaps shot a deer, and had, rather sooner than he should have done, to marry a woman in the neighborhood, who bore him a child rather quicker than was right. That escapade sent him to seek his fortune in London. He had, it seemed, a taste for the theatre; he began by holding horses at the stage door. Very soon he got work in the theatre, became a successful actor, and lived at the hub of the universe, meeting everybody, knowing everybody, practicing his art on the boards, exercising his wits in the streets, and even getting access to the palace of the queen. Meanwhile his extraordinarily gifted sister, let us suppose, remained at home. She was as adventurous, as imaginative, as agog to see the world as he was. But she was not sent to school. She had no chance of learning grammar and logic, let alone of reading Horace and Virgil. She picked up a book now and then, one of her brother's perhaps, and read a few pages. But then her parents came in and told her to mend the stockings or mind the stew and not moon about with books and papers. They would have spoken sharply but kindly, for they were substantial people who knew the conditions of life for a woman and loved their daughter—indeed, more likely than not she was the apple of her father's eye. Perhaps she scribbled some pages up in an apple loft on the sly, but was careful to hide them or set fire to them. Soon, however, before she was out of her teens, she was to be betrothed to the son of a neighboring woolstapler. She cried out that marriage was hateful to her, and for that she was severely beaten by her father. Then he ceased to scold her. He begged her instead not to hurt him, not to shame him in this matter of her marriage. He would give her a chain of beads or a fine petticoat, he said; and there were tears in his eyes. How could she disobey him? How could she break his heart? The force of her own gift alone drove her to it. She made up a small parcel of her belongings, let herself down by a rope one summer's night and took the road to London. She was not seventeen. The birds that sang in the hedge were not more musical than she was. She had the quickest fancy, a gift like her brother's, for the tune of words. Like him, she had a taste for the theatre. She stood at the stage door; she wanted to act, she said. Men laughed in her face. The manager—a fat, loose-lipped man—guffawed. He bellowed something about poodles dancing and women acting—no woman, he said, could possibly be an actress.[5] He hinted—you can imagine what. She could get no training in her craft. Could

5. In the Elizabethan theater boys played women's parts.

she even seek her dinner in a tavern or roam the streets at midnight? Yet her genius was for fiction and lusted to feed abundantly upon the lives of men and women and the study of their ways. At last—for she was very young, oddly like Shakespeare the poet in her face, with the same grey eyes and rounded brows—at last Nick Greene the actor-manager took pity on her; she found herself with child by that gentleman and so—who shall measure the heat and violence of the poet's heart when caught and tangled in a woman's body?—killed herself one winter's night and lies buried at some cross-roads where the omnibuses now stop outside the Elephant and Castle.[6]

That, more or less, is how the story would run, I think, if a woman in Shakespeare's day had had Shakespeare's genius. But for my part, I agree with the deceased bishop, if such he was—it is unthinkable that any woman in Shakespeare's day should have had Shakespeare's genius. For genius like Shakespeare's is not born among laboring, uneducated, servile people. It was not born in England among the Saxons and the Britons. It is not born today among the working classes. How, then, could it have been born among women whose work began, according to Professor Trevelyan, almost before they were out of the nursery, who were forced to it by their parents and held to it by all the power of law and custom? Yet genius of a sort must have existed among women as it must have existed among the working classes. Now and again an Emily Brontë or a Robert Burns blazes out and proves its presence.[7] But certainly it never got itself on to paper. When, however, one reads of a witch being ducked, of a woman possessed by devils, of a wise woman selling herbs, or even of a very remarkable man who had a mother, then I think we are on the track of a lost novelist, a suppressed poet, of some mute and inglorious Jane Austen,[8] some Emily Brontë who dashed her brains out on the moor or mopped and mowed about the highways crazed with the torture that her gift had put her to. Indeed, I would venture to guess that Anon, who wrote so many poems without signing them, was often a woman. It was a woman Edward Fitzgerald,[9] I think, suggested who made the ballads and the folk-songs, crooning them to her children, beguiling her spinning with them, or the length of the winter's night.

This may be true or it may be false—who can say?—but what is true in it, so it seemed to me, reviewing the story of Shakespeare's sister as I had made it, is that any woman born with a great gift in the sixteenth century would certainly have gone crazed, shot herself, or ended her days in some lonely cottage outside the village, half witch, half wizard, feared and mocked at. For it needs little skill in psychology to be sure that a highly gifted girl who had tried to use her gift for poetry would have been so thwarted and hindered by other people, so tortured and pulled asunder by her own contrary instincts, that she must

6. Prominent landmark in London, south of the Thames.

7. Woolf's examples are Brontë (1818–1848), the English novelist, and Burns (1759–1796), the Scottish poet.

8. Woolf alludes to Thomas Gray's "Elegy Written in a Country Churchyard": "Some mute inglorious Milton here may rest."

9. Poet and translator (1809–1883) of the *Rubáiyát of Omar Khayyám*.

have lost her health and sanity to a certainty. No girl could have walked to London and stood at a stage door and forced her way into the presence of actor-managers without doing herself a violence and suffering an anguish which may have been irrational—for chastity may be a fetish invented by certain societies for unknown reasons—but were none the less inevitable. Chastity had then, it has even now, a religious importance in a woman's life, and has so wrapped itself round with nerves and instincts that to cut it free and bring it to the light of day demands courage of the rarest. To have lived a free life in London in the sixteenth century would have meant for a woman who was poet and playwright a nervous stress and dilemma which might well have killed her. Had she survived, whatever she had written would have been twisted and deformed, issuing from a strained and morbid imagination. And undoubtedly, I thought, looking at the shelf where there are no plays by women, her work would have gone unsigned. That refuge she would have sought certainly. It was the relic of the sense of chastity that dictated anonymity to women even so late as the nineteenth century. Currer Bell, George Eliot, George Sand,[10] all the victims of inner strife as their writings prove, sought ineffectively to veil themselves by using the name of a man. Thus they did homage to the convention, which if not implanted by the other sex was liberally encouraged by them (the chief glory of a woman is not to be talked of, said Pericles,[11] himself a much-talked-of man), that publicity in women is detestable. Anonymity runs in their blood. The desire to be veiled still possesses them. They are not even now as concerned about the health of their fame as men are, and, speaking generally, will pass a tombstone or a signpost without feeling an irresistible desire to cut their names on it, as Alf, Bert or Chas. must do in obedience to their instinct, which murmurs if it sees a fine woman go by, or even a dog, Ce chien est à moi.[12] And, of course, it may not be a dog, I thought, remembering Parliament Square, the Sieges Allee and other avenues; it may be a piece of land or a man with curly black hair. It is one of the great advantages of being a woman that one can pass even a very fine negress without wishing to make an Englishwoman of her.

10   That woman, then, who was born with a gift of poetry in the sixteenth century, was an unhappy woman, a woman at strife against herself. All the conditions of her life, all her own instincts, were hostile to the state of mind which is needed to set free whatever is in the brain. But what is the state of mind that is most propitious to the act of creation, I asked. Can one come by any notion of the state that furthers and makes possible that strange activity? Here I opened the volume containing the Tragedies of Shakespeare. What was Shakespeare's state of mind, for instance, when he wrote *Lear* and *Antony and Cleopatra*? It was certainly the state of mind most favorable to poetry that there has ever existed. But Shakespeare himself said nothing about it. We only know casually

10. Pseudonyms of Charlotte Brontë (1816–1855), English novelist; Mary Ann Evans (1819–1880), English novelist; and Amandine Aurore Lucie Dupin, Baronne Dudevant (1804–1876), French novelist.

11. Athenian statesman (d. 429 B.C.E.).

12. French for "That dog is mine."

and by chance that he "never blotted a line."[13] Nothing indeed was ever said by the artist himself about his state of mind until the eighteenth century perhaps. Rousseau perhaps began it.[14] At any rate, by the nineteenth century self-consciousness had developed so far that it was the habit for men of letters to describe their minds in confessions and autobiographies. Their lives also were written, and their letters were printed after their deaths. Thus, though we do not know what Shakespeare went through when he wrote *Lear,* we do know what Carlyle went through when he wrote the *French Revolution;* what Flaubert went through when he wrote *Madame Bovary;* what Keats was going through when he tried to write poetry against the coming of death and the indifference of the world.

And one gathers from this enormous modern literature of confession and self-analysis that to write a work of genius is almost always a feat of prodigious difficulty. Everything is against the likelihood that it will come from the writer's mind whole and entire. Generally material circumstances are against it. Dogs will bark; people will interrupt; money must be made; health will break down. Further, accentuating all these difficulties and making them harder to bear is the world's notorious indifference. It does not ask people to write poems and novels and histories; it does not need them. It does not care whether Flaubert finds the right word or whether Carlyle scrupulously verifies this or that fact. Naturally, it will not pay for what it does not want. And so the writer, Keats, Flaubert, Carlyle, suffers, especially in the creative years of youth, every form of distraction and discouragement. A curse, a cry of agony, rises from those books of analysis and confession. "Mighty poets in their misery dead"[15]—that is the burden of their song. If anything comes through in spite of all this, it is a miracle, and probably no book is born entire and uncrippled as it was conceived.

But for women, I thought, looking at the empty shelves, these difficulties were infinitely more formidable. In the first place, to have a room of her own, let alone a quiet room or a sound-proof room, was out of the question, unless her parents were exceptionally rich or very noble, even up to the beginning of the nineteenth century. Since her pin money, which depended on the good will of her father, was only enough to keep her clothed, she was debarred from such alleviations as came even to Keats or Tennyson or Carlyle,[16] all poor men, from a walking tour, a little journey to France, from the separate lodging which, even if it were miserable enough, sheltered them from the claims and tyrannies of their families. Such material difficulties were formidable; but much worse were the immaterial. The indifference of the world which Keats and Flaubert and other men of genius have found so hard to bear was in her case not indifference but hostility. The world did not say to her as it said to them,

13. As recorded by his contemporary Ben Jonson in *Timber, or Discoveries Made upon Men and Matter.*
14. Jean-Jacques Rousseau (1712–1778), whose *Confessions* were published posthumously.
15. From the poem "Resolution and Independence" by William Wordsworth.
16. John Keats (1795–1821) and Alfred, Lord Tennyson (1809–1892), English poets; Thomas Carlyle (1795–1881), Scottish essayist.

Write if you choose; it makes no difference to me. The world said with a guf-faw, Write? What's the good of your writing? Here the psychologists of Newnham and Girton might come to our help, I thought, looking again at the blank spaces on the shelves. For surely it is time that the effect of discourage-ment upon the mind of the artist should be measured, as I have seen a dairy company measure the effect of ordinary milk and Grade A milk upon the body of the rat. They set two rats in cages side by side, and of the two one was fur-tive, timid and small, and the other was glossy, bold and big. Now what food do we feed women as artists upon? I asked, remembering, I suppose, that dinner of prunes and custard.[17] To answer that question I had only to open the eve-ning paper and to read that Lord Birkenhead is of opinion—but really I am not going to trouble to copy out Lord Birkenhead's opinion upon the writing of women. What Dean Inge says I will leave in peace. The Harley Street specialist may be allowed to rouse the echoes of Harley Street with his vociferations without raising a hair on my head. I will quote, however, Mr. Oscar Browning,[18] because Mr. Oscar Browning was a great figure in Cambridge at one time, and used to examine the students at Girton and Newnham. Mr. Oscar Browning was wont to declare "that the impression left on his mind, after looking over any set of examination papers, was that, irrespective of the marks he might give, the best woman was intellectually the inferior of the worst man." After saying that Mr. Browning went back to his rooms—and it is this sequel that endears him and makes him a human figure of some bulk and majesty—he went back to his rooms and found a stable-boy lying on the sofa—"a mere skeleton, his cheeks were cavernous and sallow, his teeth were black, and he did not appear to have the full use of his limbs. . . . 'That's Arthur' [said Mr. Brown-ing]. 'He's a dear boy really and most high-minded.'" The two pictures always seem to me to complete each other. And happily in this age of biography the two pictures often do complete each other, so that we are able to interpret the opinions of great men not only by what they say, but by what they do.

But though this is possible now, such opinions coming from the lips of important people must have been formidable enough even fifty years ago. Let us suppose that a father from the highest motives did not wish his daughter to leave home and become writer, painter or scholar. "See what Mr. Oscar Brown-ing says," he would say; and there was not only Mr. Oscar Browning; there was the *Saturday Review*; there was Mr. Greg[19]—the "essentials of a woman's being," said Mr. Greg emphatically, "are that *they are supported by, and they*

17. In Chapter 1, Woolf contrasts the lavish dinner—partridge and wine—she ate as a guest at a men's college at Cambridge University with the plain fare—prunes and custard—served at a women's college.

18. In Chapter 2, Woolf lists the fruits of her day's research on the lives of women, which include Lord Birkenhead's, Dean Inge's, and Mr. Oscar Browning's opinions of women; she does not, however, quote them. Harley Street, where fashionable medical doctors in London have their offices.

19. Mr. Greg does not appear on Woolf's list (see preceding note).

minister to, men"—there was an enormous body of masculine opinion to the effect that nothing could be expected of women intellectually. Even if her father did not read out loud these opinions, any girl could read them for herself; and the reading, even in the nineteenth century, must have lowered her vitality, and told profoundly upon her work. There would always have been that assertion—you cannot do this, you are incapable of doing that—to protest against, to overcome. Probably for a novelist this germ is no longer of much effect; for there have been women novelists of merit. But for painters it must still have some sting in it; and for musicians, I imagine, is even now active and poisonous in the extreme. The women composer stands where the actress stood in the time of Shakespeare. Nick Greene, I thought, remembering the story I had made about Shakespeare's sister, said that a woman acting put him in mind of a dog dancing. Johnson repeated the phrase two hundred years later of women preaching.[20] And here, I said, opening a book about music, we have the very words used again in this year of grace, 1928, of women who try to write music. "Of Mlle. Germaine Tailleferre one can only repeat Dr. Johnson's dictum concerning a woman preacher, transposed into terms of music. 'Sir, a woman's composing is like a dog's walking on his hind legs. It is not done well, but you are surprised to find it done at all.'"[21] So accurately does history repeat itself.

Thus, I concluded, shutting Mr. Oscar Browning's life and pushing away the rest, it is fairly evident that even in the nineteenth century a woman was not encouraged to be an artist. On the contrary, she was snubbed, slapped, lectured and exhorted. Her mind must have been strained and her vitality lowered by the need of opposing this, of disproving that. For here again we come within range of that very interesting and obscure masculine complex which has had so much influence upon the woman's movement; that deep-seated desire, not so much that *she* shall be inferior as that *he* shall be superior, which plants him wherever one looks, not only in front of the arts, but barring the way to politics too, even when the risk to himself seems infinitesimal and the suppliant humble and devoted. Even Lady Bessborough, I remembered, with all her passion for politics, must humbly bow herself and write to Lord Granville Leveson-Gower:[22] ". . . notwithstanding all my violence in politics and talking so much on that subject, I perfectly agree with you that no woman has any business to meddle with that or any other serious business, farther than giving her opinion (if she is ask'd)." And so she goes on to spend her enthusiasm where it meets with no obstacle whatsoever upon that immensely important subject,

20. Johnson's opinion is recorded in James Boswell's *The Life of Samuel Johnson, L.L.D.* Woolf, in her tale of Judith Shakespeare, imagines the manager bellowing "something about poodles dancing and women acting."

21. *A Survey of Contemporary Music*, Cecil Gray, p. 246 [Woolf's note].

22. Henrietta, countess of Bessborough (1761–1821); Lord Granville Leveson Gower, first Earl Granville (1773–1846). Their correspondence, edited by Castalia Countess Granville, was published as his *Private Correspondence, 1781 to 1821*, in 1916.

Lord Granville's maiden speech in the House of Commons. The spectacle is certainly a strange one, I thought. The history of men's opposition to women's emancipation is more interesting perhaps than the story of that emancipation itself. An amusing book might be made of it if some young student at Girton or Newnham would collect examples and deduce a theory—but she would need thick gloves on her hands, and bars to protect her of solid gold.

15   But what is amusing now, I recollected, shutting Lady Bessborough, had to be taken in desperate earnest once. Opinions that one now pastes in a book labelled cock-a-doodle-dum and keeps for reading to select audiences on summer nights once drew tears, I can assure you. Among your grandmothers and great-grandmothers there were many that wept their eyes out. Florence Nightingale shrieked aloud in her agony.[23] Moreover, it is all very well for you, who have got yourselves to college and enjoy sitting-rooms—or is it only bed-sitting-rooms?—of your own to say that genius should disregard such opinions; that genius should be above caring what is said of it. Unfortunately, it is precisely the men or women of genius who mind most what is said of them. Remember Keats. Remember the words he had cut on his tombstone. Think of Tennyson;[24] think—but I need hardly multiply instances of the undeniable, if very unfortunate, fact that it is the nature of the artist to mind excessively what is said about him. Literature is strewn with the wreckage of men who have minded beyond reason the opinions of others.

And this susceptibility of theirs is doubly unfortunate, I thought, returning again to my original enquiry into what state of mind is most propitious for creative work, because the mind of an artist, in order to achieve the prodigious effort of freeing whole and entire the work that is in him, must be incandescent, like Shakespeare's mind, I conjectured, looking at the book which lay open at *Antony and Cleopatra*. There must be no obstacle in it, no foreign matter unconsumed.

For though we say that we know nothing about Shakespeare's state of mind, even as we say that, we are saying something about Shakespeare's state of mind. The reason perhaps why we know so little of Shakespeare—compared with Donne or Ben Jonson or Milton[25]—is that his grudges and spites and antipathies are hidden from us. We are not held up by some "revelation" which reminds us of the writer. All desire to protest, to preach, to proclaim an injury, to pay off a score, to make the world the witness of some hardship or grievance was fired out of him and consumed. Therefore his poetry flows from him free and unimpeded. If ever a human being got his work expressed completely, it was Shakespeare. If ever a mind was incandescent, unimpeded, I thought, turning again to the bookcase, it was Shakespeare's mind.

23. See *Cassandra*, by Florence Nightingale, printed in *The Cause*, by R. Strachey [Woolf's note]. Florence Nightingale (1820–1910), English nurse and philanthropist.
24. Keats's epitaph reads "Here lies one whose name was writ in water." Tennyson was notably sensitive to reviews of his poetry.
25. John Donne (1572–1631), Jonson (1572–1637), and John Milton (1608–1674), English poets and, in contrast to Shakespeare, all learned men.

MLA CITATION

Woolf, Virginia. "In Search of a Room of One's Own." 1929. *The Norton Reader: An Anthology of Nonfiction*. Ed. Melissa A. Goldthwaite et al. 14th ed. New York: Norton, 2016. 904–14. Print.

QUESTIONS

1. At the beginning of her essay, Virginia Woolf wonders about the conditions in which women lived that made it difficult, if not impossible, for them to produce literature (paragraph 2). What does she reveal about those conditions in the course of her essay?

2. Throughout her essay Woolf supplies many examples of the obstacles faced by women writers. Choose two or three that you find particularly effective and explain why they are effective.

3. How does the phrase "A Room of One's Own" suggest a solution to the problems Woolf has enumerated for women writers?

4. What obstacles face writers in the twenty-first century? How do those obstacles vary based on the writer's background or identity? Write an essay, based on research and/or interviews, in which you argue the extent to which Woolf's argument is still relevant for a specific twenty-first-century population.

MICHAEL CHABON   *Kids' Stuff*

FOR AT LEAST THE FIRST FORTY YEARS of their existence, from the Paleozoic pre-Superman era of *Famous Funnies* (1933) and *More Fun Comics* (1936), comic books were widely viewed, even by those who adored them, as juvenile: the ultimate greasy kids' stuff. Comics were the literary equivalent of bubble-gum cards, to be poked into the spokes of a young mind, where they would produce a satisfying—but entirely bogus—rumble of pleasure. But almost from the first, fitfully in the early days, intermittently through the fifties, and then starting in the mid-sixties with increasing vigor and determination, a battle has been waged by writers, artists, editors, and publishers to elevate the medium, to expand the scope of its subject matter and the range of its artistic styles, to sharpen and increase the sophistication of its language and visual grammar, to probe and explode the limits of the sequential panel, to give free rein to irony, tragedy, autobiography, and other grown-up-type modes of expression.

Originally the keynote address at the 2004 ComicCon (the largest comic book convention in the Western Hemisphere) and later published in Maps and Legends: Reading and Writing along the Borderlands (2009), *a collection of essays by Michael Chabon.*

Also from the first, a key element—at times the central element—of this battle has been the effort to alter not just the medium itself but the public perception of the medium. From the late, great Will Eisner's lonely insistence, in an interview with the *Baltimore Sun* back in 1940 (*1940!*), on the artistic credibility of comics, to the nuanced and scholarly work of recent comics theorists, both practitioners and critics have been arguing passionately on behalf of comics' potential to please—in all the aesthetic richness of that term—the most sophisticated of readers.

The most sophisticated, that is, of *adult* readers. For the adult reader of comic books has always been the holy grail, the promised land, the imagined lover who will greet the long-suffering comic-book maker, at the end of the journey, with open arms, with acceptance, with approval.

A quest is often, among other things, an extended bout of inspired madness. Over the years this quest to break the chains of childish readership has resulted, like most bouts of inspired madness, in both folly and stunning innovation. Into the latter category we can put the work of Bernard Krigstein or Frank Miller, say, with their attempts to approximate, through radical attack on the conventions of panel layouts, the fragmentation of human consciousness by urban life; or the tight, tidy, miniaturized madness of Chris Ware.[1] Into the former category—the folly—we might put all the things that got Dr. Frederic Wertham[2] so upset about EC Comics in the early fifties, the syringe-pierced eyeballs and baseball diamonds made from human organs; or the short-lived outfitting of certain Marvel titles in 1965 with a label that boasted "A Marvel Pop Art Production"; or the hypertrophied, tooth-gnashing, blood-letting quote-unquote heroes of the era that followed Miller's *The Dark Knight Returns*. An excess of the desire to appear grown up is one of the defining characteristics of adolescence. But these follies were the inevitable missteps and overreaching in the course of a campaign that was, in the end, successful.

5   Because the battle has now, in fact, been won. Not only are comics appealing to a wider and older audience than ever before, but the idea of comics as a valid art form on a par at least with, say, film or rock and roll is widely if not quite universally accepted. Comics and graphic novels are regularly reviewed and debated in *Entertainment Weekly*, the *New York Times Book Review*, even in the august pages of the *New York Review of Books*. Ben Katchor won a MacArthur Fellowship, and Art Spiegelman a Pulitzer Prize.[3]

But the strange counterphenomenon to this indisputable rise in the reputation, the ambition, the sophistication, and the literary and artistic merit of

1. Krigstein (1919–1990), comic book artist and painter famous for his daring and varied styles; Miller (b. 1957), comic book artist and film director known for *Batman: The Dark Knight Returns*; Ware (b. 1967), comic book artist best known for his Acme Library Novelty Series.

2. Psychiatrist and crusader against comic books (1895–1981). His *Seduction of the Innocent* (1954) led to a congressional investigation of comics as a dangerous influence on adolescents.

3. Katchor (b. 1951), first comic book artist to win a MacArthur Genius Grant; Spiegelman (b. 1948), best known for his graphic memoir, *Maus* (1986), which recounts his father's experience during the Holocaust.

many of our best comics over the past couple of decades, is that over roughly the same period comics readership has declined. Some adults are reading better comics than ever before; but fewer people overall are reading any—far fewer, certainly, than in the great sales heyday of the medium, the early fifties, when by some estimates[4] as many as 650 million comic books were sold annually (compared to somewhere in the neighborhood of 80 million today). The top ten best-selling comic books in 1996, primarily issues making up two limited series, Marvel's *Civil Wars* and DC's *Infinite Crisis*, were all superhero books, and, like the majority of superhero books in the post–*Dark Knight*, post-*Watchmen* era, all of them dealt rather grimly, and in the somewhat hand-wringing fashion that has become obligatory, with the undoubtedly grown-up issues of violence, freedom, terrorism, vigilantism, political repression, mass hysteria, and the ambivalent nature of heroism. Among the top ten best-selling titles in 1960 (with an aggregate circulation, for all comics, of 400 million) one finds not only the expected *Superman* and *Batman* (decidedly sans ambivalence) but *Mickey Mouse, Looney Tunes*, and the classic sagas of *Uncle Scrooge*. And nearly the whole of the list for that year, from top to bottom, through *Casper the Friendly Ghost* (#14) and *Little Archie* (#25) to *Felix the Cat* (#47), is made up of kids' stuff, more or less greasy.

To recap—Days when comics were aimed at kids: huge sales. Days when comics are aimed at adults: not so huge sales, and declining.

The situation is more complicated than that, of course. Since 1960 there have been fundamental changes in a lot of things, among them the way comics are produced, licensed, marketed, and distributed. But maybe it is not too surprising that for a while now, fundamental changes and all, some people have been wondering: what if there were comic books for children?

Leaving aside questions of creator's rights, paper costs, retail consolidation, the explosive growth of the collector market, and direct-market sales, a lot of comic-book people will tell you that there is simply too much competition for the kid dollar these days and that, thrown into the arena with video games, special-effects-laden films, the Internet, iPods, etc., comics will inevitably lose out. I find this argument unconvincing, not to mention a cop out. It is, furthermore, an example of our weird naïveté, in this generation, about how sophisticated we and our children have become vis-à-vis our parents and grandparents, of the misguided sense of retrospective superiority we tend to display toward them and their vanished world. As if in 1960 there was not a *ton* of cool stuff besides comic books on which a kid could spend his or her considerably less constricted time and considerably more limited funds. In the early days of comics, in fact, unlike now, a moderately adventuresome child could find all kinds of things to do that were not only fun (partly because they took place with no adult supervision or mediation), but absolutely free. The price of fun doesn't get any more competitive than that.

I also refuse to accept as explanation for anything the often-tendered argument that contemporary children are more sophisticated, that the kind of comics that pleased a seven-year-old in 1960 would leave an ultracool kid of

10

---

4. See, for example, www.comichron.com [Chabon's note].

today snickering with disdain. Even if we accept this argument with respect to "old-fashioned" comics, it would seem to be invalidated by the increasing sophistication of comic books over the past decades. But I reject its very premise. The supposed sophistication—a better term would be *knowingness*—of modern children is largely, I believe, a matter of style, a pose which they have adapted from and modeled on the rampant pose of knowingness, of being wised up, that characterizes the contemporary American style, and has done at least since the late fifties–early sixties heyday of *Mad* magazine (a publication largely enjoyed, from the beginning, by children). Even in their irony and cynicism there is something appealingly insincere, maladroit, and, well, *childish* about children. What is more, I have found that even my own children, as knowing as they often like to present themselves, still take profound pleasure in the old comics that I have given them to read. My older son has still not quite recovered from the heartbreak he felt, when he was seven, reading an old "archive edition" of *Legion of Superheroes,* at the tragic death of Ferro Lad.

Children did not abandon comics; comics, in their drive to attain respect and artistic accomplishment, abandoned children. And for a long time the lovers and partisans of comics were afraid, after so many years of struggle and hard work and incremental gains, to pick up that old jar of greasy kid stuff again, and risk undoing all the labor of so many geniuses and revolutionaries and ordinary, garden-variety artists. Comics have always been an arriviste art form, and all upstarts are to some degree ashamed of their beginnings. But shame, anxiety, the desire to preserve hard-won gains—such considerations no longer serve to explain the disappearance of children's comics. The truth is that comic-book creators have simply lost the habit of telling stories to children. And how sad is that?

When commentators on comics address this question, in the hope of encouraging publishers, writers, and artists to produce new comic books with children in mind, they usually try formulating some version of the following simple equation: create more child readers now, and you will find yourselves with more adult readers later on. Hook them early, in other words. But maybe the equation isn't so simple after all. Maybe what we need, given the sophistication of children (if we want to concede that point) and the competition for their attention and their disposable income (which has always been a factor), is not simply *more* comics for kids, but more *great* comics for kids.

Easy, I suppose, for me to say. So although I am certain that there are many professional creators of comics—people with a good ear and a sharp eye for and a natural understanding of children and their enthusiasms—who would be able to do a far better job of it, having thrown down the finned, skintight gauntlet, I now feel obliged to offer, at the least, a few tentative principles and one concrete suggestion on how more great comics for kids might be teased into the marketplace, even by amateurs like me. I have drawn these principles, in part, from my memories of the comics I loved when I was young, but I think they hold true as well for the best and most successful works of children's literature.

1) Let's not tell stories that we think "kids of today" might like. That is a route to inevitable failure and possible loss of sanity. *We should tell stories that*

we would have liked as kids. Twist endings, the unexpected usefulness of unlikely knowledge, nobility and bravery where it's least expected, and the sudden emergence of a thread of goodness in a wicked nature, those were the kind of stories told by the writers and artists of the comic books that I liked.

2) Let's tell stories that, over time, build up an intricate, involved, involving mythology that is also accessible and comprehensible at any point of entry. The *intricacy*, the accretion of lore over time, should be both inventive and familiar, founded in old mythologies and fears but fully reinterpreted, reimagined. It will demand, it will ache, to be mastered by a child's mythology-mastering imagination. The *accessibility* will come from our making a commitment to tell a full, complete story, or a complete piece of a story, in every issue. This kind of layering of intricate lore and narrative completeness was a hallmark of the great "Superman-family" books (*Adventure, Jimmy Olsen, Superboy*) under the editorship of Mort Weisinger.[5]

3) Let's cultivate an unflagging readiness as storytellers to retell the same stories *with endless embellishment.* Anybody who thinks that kids get bored by hearing the same story over and over again has never spent time telling stories to kids. The key, as in baroque music, is repetition with *variation.* Again the Mort Weisinger–edited *Superman* books, written by unflagging story-tellers like Edmond Hamilton and Otto Binder,[6] were exemplary in this regard. The proliferation of theme and variation there verges, at times, on sheer, splendid madness.

4) Let's blow their little minds. A mind is not blown, in spite of whatever Hollywood seems to teach, merely by action sequences, things exploding, thrilling planetscapes, wild bursts of speed. Those are all good things; but a mind is blown when something that you always feared but knew to be impossible turns out to be true; when the world turns out to be far vaster, far more marvelous or malevolent than you ever dreamed; when you get proof that everything is connected to everything else, that everything you know is wrong, that you are both the center of the universe and a tiny speck sailing off its nethermost edge.

So much for my principles: here is my concrete suggestion. If it seems a little obvious, or has already been tried and failed, then I apologize. But I cannot help noticing that in the world of children's *literature,* an overwhelming preponderance of stories are stories *about* children. The same is true of films for children: the central characters are nearly always a child, or a pair or group of children. Comic books, however, even those theoretically aimed at children, are almost always about adults or teenagers. Doesn't that strike you as odd? I suggest that a publisher should try putting out a truly thrilling, honestly observed and remembered, richly imagined, involved and yet narratively straight-forward comic book for children, *about children.*

5. Weisinger (1915–1978), editor of the DC Comic *Superman* series; served as story editor for the 1950s Superman television show.

6. Hamilton (1904–1977), science fiction writer who, in his work for DC Comics, specialized in stories for Batman and Superman; Binder (1911–1974), writer of Captain Marvel comics for Fawcett and several classic Superman storylines for DC.

My oldest son is ten now, and he likes comic books. In 1943, if you were a ten-year-old, you probably knew a dozen other kids your age who were into Captain Marvel and the Submariner and the Blue Beetle. When I was ten, in 1973, I knew three or four. But in his class, in his world, my son is all but unique; he's the only one he knows who reads them, studies them, seeks to master and be worthy of all the rapture and strangeness they still contain. Now, comic books are so important to me—I have thought, talked, and written about them so much—that if my son did not in fact like them, I think he would be obliged to loathe them. I have pretty much *forced* comics on my children. But those of us who grew up loving comic books can't afford to take this hand-crafted, one-kid-at-a-time approach anymore. We have to sweep them up and carry them off on the flying carpets of story and pictures on which we ourselves, in entire generations, were borne aloft, on carpets woven by Curt Swan and Edmond Hamilton, Jack Kirby and Stan Lee, Chris Claremont and John Byrne.[7] Those artists did it for us; we who make comics today have a solemn debt to pass it on, to weave bright carpets of our own. It's our duty, it's our opportunity, and I really do believe it will be our pleasure.

7. Swan (1920–1996), comic book artist best known for drawing Superman comics, often written by Hamilton. Kirby (1917–1994), comic book artist, and Lee (b. 1922), writer, are best known for their collaboration at Marvel Comics. Claremont (b. 1950) and Byrne (b. 1950) collaborated on the *X-Men* series.

MLA CITATION

Chabon, Michael. "Kids' Stuff." 2004. *The Norton Reader: An Anthology of Nonfiction.* Ed. Melissa A. Goldthwaite et al. 14th ed. New York: Norton, 2016. 915–20. Print.

QUESTIONS

1. Michael Chabon's essay contrasts the comic book writer's desire for respect with the diminishing audience for comics. Discuss the relationships that link artistic sophistication to both public respect and sales. Do you find Chabon's explanation persuasive? Is he missing something?

2. This essay begins with statistics about the readership of comics, moves to narrative about the evolution of the form, and ends with a manifesto on how to get more kids to read comics. Analyze how each section builds on the others. How does Chabon make the transition from one to another?

3. Chabon is clearly passionate about comics. Choose a passage in which he most effectively conveys that passion, and analyze why it works.

4. Write your own list of principles for how to get kids to love something that you loved as a kid. What elements go into making a comic (or a video game, toy, collectible, or cartoon) great?

SCOTT McCLOUD   from *Understanding Comics*

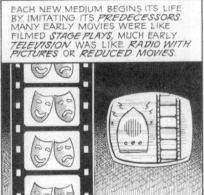

From Understanding Comics: The Invisible Art *(1993), a graphic book that gives a history of comics and cartooning.*

WORDS AND PICTURES IN COMBINATION MAY NOT BE MY *DEFINITION* OF COMICS, BUT THE COMBINATION HAS HAD *TREMENDOUS INFLUENCE* ON ITS *GROWTH.*

com·ics (kom'iks) **n.** ...a form, used with a singular... Juxtaposed pictori... ...er images in deliberate... ...ence, intended to conve... ...n and/or to produ... response in the... **2:** Superheroes... costumes, fight... villains who want... ...e world, in violent s... ...pulse...

A HUGE RANGE OF HUMAN EXPERIENCES CAN BE *PORTRAYED* IN COMICS THROUGH EITHER WORDS OR PICTURES.

AS A RESULT-- AND DESPITE ITS MANY *OTHER* POTENTIAL USES -- COMICS HAVE BECOME *FIRMLY IDENTIFIED* WITH THE ART OF *STORYTELLING.*

AND *INDEED,* WORDS AND PICTURES HAVE *GREAT* POWERS TO TELL STORIES WHEN CREATORS FULLY EXPLOIT THEM *BOTH.*

DADA
BIOGRAPHY · HORROR
ROMANCE · SURREALISM
BLANK VERSE · HISTORICAL FICTION
EPIC POETRY · FOLK TALES
SOCIAL ALLEGORY · EROTICA
ADAPTATIONS · MYSTERY · RELIGIOUS TOPICS
STREAM OF CONSCIOUSNESS
SATIRE

SEQUENTIAL ART

AND SO FAR, WE'VE ONLY SEEN THE *TIP OF THE ICEBERG!*

AS CHILDREN, WE "SHOW AND TELL" *INTERCHANGEABLY,* WORDS AND IMAGES COMBINING TO TRANSMIT A *CONNECTED SERIES OF IDEAS.*

IT'S GOT ONE OF *THESE* THINGS.

THE DIFFERENT WAYS IN WHICH WORDS AND PICTURES CAN *COMBINE* IN COMICS IS VIRTUALLY *UNLIMITED.*

BUT LET'S TRY TO BREAK IT DOWN INTO SOME DISTINCT *CATEGORIES.*

PERHAPS THE MOST *COMMON* TYPE OF WORD/PICTURE COMBINATION IS THE *INTER-DEPENDENT,* WHERE WORDS AND PICTURES GO *HAND IN HAND* TO CONVEY AN IDEA THAT NEITHER COULD CONVEY *ALONE.*

MEANWHILE...

DID ANYONE *SEE* YOU?

THIS IS ALL I NEED TO *STOP* HIM!

I ASK YOU, DOES THIS GUY LOOK LIKE A *C.E.O.* TO *YOU?*?

"AND JUST *GUESS* WHO DROVE UP IN BOB'S TRUCK AN HOUR LATER!"

HEY, MARGE!

OH, MY GOD!

HE'S LYING.

UH-HUH.

"AFTER COLLEGE, I PURSUED A CAREER IN *HIGH FINANCE*"

HURRY UP, WILLYA?!

INTERDEPENDENT COMBINATIONS AREN'T ALWAYS AN *EQUAL BALANCE* THOUGH AND MAY FALL *ANYWHERE* ON A SCALE BETWEEN TYPES ONE AND TWO.

GENERALLY SPEAKING, THE MORE IS SAID WITH *WORDS,* THE MORE THE PICTURES CAN BE FREED TO GO EXPLORING AND *VICE VERSA.*

$$\frac{P}{W}$$

$$\frac{W}{P}$$

IN COMICS AT ITS *BEST*, WORDS AND PICTURES ARE LIKE *PARTNERS* IN A *DANCE* AND EACH ONE TAKES TURNS *LEADING*.

WHEN *BOTH* PARTNERS TRY TO LEAD, THE COMPETITION CAN *SUBVERT* THE OVERALL GOALS...

YOW!

...THOUGH A LITTLE *PLAYFUL COMPETITION* CAN SOMETIMES PRODUCE *ENJOYABLE RESULTS*.

BUT WHEN THESE PARTNERS EACH *KNOW* THEIR ROLES--

--AND *SUPPORT* EACH OTHER'S *STRENGTHS*--

--COMICS CAN MATCH *ANY* OF THE ART FORMS IT DRAWS SO MUCH OF ITS STRENGTH FROM.

MLA CITATION

McCloud, Scott. *Understanding Comics.* 1993. *The Norton Reader: An Anthology of Nonfiction.* Ed. Melissa A. Goldthwaite et al. 14th ed. New York: Norton, 2016. 921–26. Print.

QUESTIONS

1. Scott McCloud announces in his title that he wants to help the reader understand comics. What features of comics does McCloud explain? How do the features of the comic strip form itself aid in that explanation?

2. Choose a frame in which you think word and image work well together, and analyze why they do so. Use one or more of McCloud's categories of analysis.

3. Using the categories that McCloud introduces in the second half of this selection, analyze how a comic strip in your local newspaper works. If relevant, suggest how it might work even better.

SUSAN SONTAG   *A Century of Cinema*

CINEMA'S HUNDRED YEARS appear to have the shape of a life cycle: an inevitable birth, the steady accumulation of glories, and the onset in the last decade of an ignominious, irreversible decline. This doesn't mean that there won't be any more new films one can admire. But such films will not simply be exceptions; that's true of great achievement in any art. They will have to be heroic violations of the norms and practices which now govern moviemaking everywhere in the capitalist and would-be capitalist world—which is to say, everywhere. And ordinary films, films made purely for entertainment (that is, commercial) purposes, will continue to be astonishingly witless; already the vast majority fail resoundingly to appeal to their cynically targeted audiences. While the point of a great film is now, more than ever, to be a one-of-a-kind achievement, the commercial cinema has settled for a policy of bloated, derivative filmmaking, a brazen combinatory or re-combinatory art, in the hope of reproducing past successes. Every film that hopes to reach the largest possible audience is designed as some kind of remake. Cinema, once heralded as *the* art of the twentieth century, seems now, as the century closes numerically, to be a decadent art.

Perhaps it is not cinema which has ended but only cinephilia—the name of the distinctive kind of love that cinema inspired. Each art breeds its fanatics.

Written in 1995 for the German newspaper Frankfurter Rundschau *and published in shortened form in the* New York Times Magazine *(1996); later reprinted in a small circulation American journal* Parnassus *(1997) and, with editorial changes, in Susan Sontag's collection of essays* Where the Stress Falls *(2001).*

The Arrival of a Train at La Ciotat Station, 1895.

The love movies aroused was more imperial. It was born of the conviction that cinema was an art unlike any other: quintessentially modern; distinctively accessible; poetic and mysterious and erotic and moral—all at the same time. Cinema had apostles (it was like religion). Cinema was a crusade. Cinema was a world view. Lovers of poetry or opera or dance don't think there is *only* poetry or opera or dance. But lovers of cinema could think there was only cinema. That the movies encapsulated everything—and they did. It was both the book of art and the book of life.

As many have noted, the start of moviemaking a hundred years ago was, conveniently, a double start. In that first year, 1895, two kinds of films were made, proposing two modes of what cinema could be: cinema as the transcription of real, unstaged life (the Lumière brothers) and cinema as invention, artifice, illusion, fantasy (Méliès).[1] But this was never a true opposition. For those first audiences watching the Lumière brothers' *The Arrival of a Train at La Ciotat Station*, the camera's transmission of a banal sight was a fantastic experience. Cinema began in wonder, the wonder that reality can be transcribed with such magical immediacy. All of cinema is an attempt to perpetuate and to reinvent that sense of wonder.

Everything begins with that moment, one hundred years ago, when the train pulled into the station. People took movies into themselves, just as the public cried out with excitement, actually ducked, as the train seemed to move toward *them*. Until the advent of television emptied the movie theatres, it was from a weekly visit to the cinema that you learned (or tried to learn) how to strut, to smoke, to kiss, to fight, to grieve. Movies gave you tips about how to be attractive, such as . . . it looks good to wear a raincoat even when it isn't raining. But whatever you took home from the movies was only a part of the larger experience of losing yourself in faces, in lives that were *not* yours—which is the more inclusive form of desire embodied in the movie experience. The strongest experience was simply to surrender to, to be transported by, what was on the screen. You wanted to be kidnapped by the movie.

5   The prerequisite of being kidnapped was to be overwhelmed by the physical presence of the image. And the conditions of "going to the movies"

1. Lumière brothers, Auguste (1864–1948) and Louis Jean (1862–1954), French inventors who in 1895 patented and demonstrated the Cinématographe, the first device for photographing, printing, and projecting films; Georges Méliès (1861–1938), early French experimenter with motion pictures, the first to film fictional narratives.

secured that experience. To see a great film only on television isn't to have really seen that film. (This is equally true of those made for TV, like Fassbinder's *Berlin Alexanderplatz* and the two *Heimat* films of Edgar Reitz.)[2] It's not only the difference of dimensions: the superiority of the larger-than-you image in the theatre to the little image on the box at home. The conditions of paying attention in a domestic space are radically disrespectful of film. Since film no longer has a stan-

Nana, 1926.

dard size, home screens can be as big as living room or bedroom walls. But you are still in a living room or a bedroom, alone or with familiars. To be kidnapped, you have to be in a movie theatre, seated in the dark among anonymous strangers.

No amount of mourning will revive the vanished rituals—erotic, ruminative—of the darkened theatre. The reduction of cinema to assaultive images, and the unprincipled manipulation of images (faster and faster cutting) to be more attention-grabbing, have produced a disincarnated, lightweight cinema that doesn't demand anyone's full attention. Images now appear in any size and on a variety of surfaces: on a screen in a theatre, on home screens as small as the palm of your hand or as big as a wall, on disco walls and mega-screens hanging above sports arenas and the outsides of tall public buildings. The sheer ubiquity of moving images has steadily undermined the standards people once had both for cinema as art at its most serious and for cinema as popular entertainment.

In the first years there was, essentially, no difference between cinema as art and cinema as entertainment. And *all* films of the silent era—from the masterpieces of Feuillade, D. W. Griffith, Dziga Vertov, Pabst, Murnau, King Vidor[3] to the most formula-ridden melodramas and comedies—look, are, better than most of what was to follow. With the coming of sound, the image-making

2. Rainer Werner Fassbinder (1946–1982) and Reitz (b. 1932), both German film directors.

3. Louis Feuillade (1873–1925), French film director who developed short adventure films and screen serials in the period around World War I; Griffith (1875–1948), American film director who innovated cross-cutting, close-ups, long shots, and flashbacks in such films as *The Birth of a Nation* (1915); Vertov (Denis Arkadyevich Kaufman, 1896–1954), Soviet film director who developed the "film-eye" theory, which made the camera operate as an instrument much like the human eye; Georg Wilhelm Pabst (1885–1967), Austrian film director who developed "montage" in such works as *The Joyless Street* (1925) and *The Threepenny Opera* (1931); Friedrich Wilhelm Murnau (1889–1931), German film director whose works include *Nosferatu* (1922), *The Last Laugh* (1924), and *Sunrise* (1927); Vidor (1894–1982), American film director who created *The Crowd*

Napoleon, 1927.

lost much of its brilliance and poetry, and commercial standards tightened. This way of making movies—the Hollywood system—dominated filmmaking for about twenty-five years (roughly from 1930 to 1955). The most original directors, like Erich von Stroheim and Orson Welles,[4] were defeated by the system and eventually went into artistic exile in Europe—where more or less the same quality-defeating system was in place with lower budgets; only in France were a large number of superb films produced throughout this period. Then, in the mid-1950s, vanguard ideas took hold again, rooted in the idea of cinema as a craft pioneered by the Italian films of the early postwar era. A dazzling number of original, passionate films of the highest seriousness got made with new actors and tiny crews, went to film festivals (of which there were more and more), and from there, garlanded with festival prizes, into movie theatres around the world. This golden age actually lasted as long as twenty years.

It was at this specific moment in the hundred-year history of cinema that going to movies, thinking about movies, talking about movies became a passion among university students and other young people. You fell in love not just with actors but with cinema itself. Cinephilia had first become visible in the 1950s in France: its forum was the legendary film magazine *Cahiers du Cinéma*

(1928) and later *The Citadel* (1938), the black-and-white scenes of *The Wizard of Oz* (1939), *The Fountainhead* (1949), and *War and Peace* (1956).
4. Stroheim (1885–1957), German filmmaker, best known for *Greed* (1925); Welles (1915–1985), American film director, best known for *Citizen Kane* (1941).

The 400 Blows, 1959.

(followed by similarly fervent magazines in Germany, Italy, Great Britain, Sweden, the United States, Canada). Its temples, as it spread throughout Europe
and the Americas, were the cinematheques and film clubs specializing in films
from the past and directors' retrospectives. The 1960s and early 1970s were
the age of feverish moviegoing, with the full-time cinephile always hoping to
find a seat as close as possible to the big screen, ideally the third row center.
"One can't live without Rossellini," declares a character in Bertolucci's *Before
the Revolution* (1964)—and means it.

   Cinephilia—a source of exultation in the films of Godard and Truffaut and
the early Bertolucci and Syberberg; a morose lament in the recent films of Nanni
Moretti[5]—was mostly a Western European affair. The great directors of "the
other Europe" (Zanussi in Poland, Angelopoulos in Greece, Tarkovsky and
Sokurov in Russia, Jancsó and Tarr in Hungary) and the great Japanese
directors (Ozu, Mizoguchi, Kurosawa, Naruse, Oshima, Imamura) have
tended not to be cinephiles, perhaps because in Budapest or Moscow or Tokyo

5. Jean-Luc Godard (b. 1930), French film director known for *Breathless* (1959), among
others; François Truffaut (1932–1984), French director whose films include *The 400
Blows* (1959), *Day for Night* (1973), and *The Last Métro* (1980); Bernardo Bertolucci (b.
1940), Italian filmmaker whose work includes *Last Tango in Paris* (1973) and *The Last
Emperor* (1987); Hans-Jurgen Syberberg (b. 1935), German director and critic, known
for his *Parsifal* (1988) and his book *Hitler: A Film from Germany* (1982), for which Sontag wrote the English preface; Moretti (b. 1953), Italian filmmaker, best known for
Caro Diario (Dear diary, 1993).

Persona, 1967.

or Warsaw or Athens there wasn't a chance to get a cinematheque education. The distinctive thing about cinephile taste was that it embraced both "art" films and popular films. Thus, European cinephilia had a romantic relation to the films of certain directors in Hollywood at the apogee of the studio system: Godard for Howard Hawks, Fassbinder for Douglas Sirk. Of course, this moment—when cinephilia emerged—was also the moment when the Hollywood studio system was breaking up. It seemed that moviemaking had re-won the right to experiment; cinephiles could *afford* to be passionate (or sentimental) about the old Hollywood genre films. A host of new people came into cinema, including a generation of young film critics from *Cahiers du Cinéma*; the towering figure of that generation, indeed of several decades of filmmaking anywhere, was Jean-Luc Godard. A few writers turned out to be wildly talented filmmakers: Alexander Kluge in Germany, Pier Paolo Pasolini in Italy. (The model for the writer who turns to filmmaking actually emerged earlier, in France, with Pagnol in the 1930s and Cocteau in the 1940s; but it was not until the 1960s that this seemed, at least in Europe, normal.) Cinema appeared to be reborn.

10   For some fifteen years there was a profusion of masterpieces, and one allowed oneself to imagine that this would go on forever. To be sure, there was always a conflict between cinema as an industry and cinema as an art, cinema as routine and cinema as experiment. But the conflict was not such as to make impossible the making of wonderful films, sometimes within and sometimes outside of mainstream cinema. Now the balance has tipped decisively in favor of cinema as an industry. The great cinema of the 1960s and 1970s has been thoroughly repudiated. Already in the 1970s Hollywood was plagiarizing and banalizing the innovations in narrative method and editing of successful new European and ever-marginal independent American films. Then came the catastrophic rise in production costs in the 1980s, which secured the worldwide reimposition of industry standards of making and distributing films on a far more coercive, this time truly global, scale. The result can be seen in the melancholy fate of some of the greatest directors of the last decades. What place is there today for a maverick like Hans Jurgen Syberberg, who has stopped mak-

Breathless, 1959.

ing films altogether, or for the great Godard, who now makes films about the history of film on video? Consider some other cases. The internationalizing of financing and therefore of casts was a disaster for Andrei Tarkovsky[6] in the last two films of his stupendous, tragically abbreviated career. And these conditions for making films have proved to be as much an artistic disaster for two of the most valuable directors still working: Krzysztof Zanussi (*The Structure of Crystals, Illumination, Spiral, Contract*) and Theo Angelopoulos (*Reconstruction, Days of '36, The Travelling Players*). And what will happen now to Béla Tarr (*Damnation, Satantango*)? And how will Aleksandr Sokurov (*Save and Protect, Days of Eclipse, The Second Circle, Stone, Whispering Pages*) find the money to go on making films, his sublime films, under the rude conditions of Russian capitalism?[7]

Predictably, the love of cinema has waned. People still like going to the movies, and some people still care about and expect something special, necessary from a film. And wonderful films are still being made: Mike Leigh's *Naked*, Gianni Amelio's *Lamerica*, Hou Hsiao-hsien's *Goodbye South, Goodbye*, and

6. Soviet film director (1932–1986), whose work was censored at home but won acclaim in the West. His *Katok i skripka* (*The Steamroller and the Violin*, 1960) won a prize at the New York Film Festival, and his first full-length feature film, *Ivanovo detstvo* (*Ivan's Childhood*, 1962), established his international reputation.

7. Zanussi (b. 1939), Polish film director; Angelopoulos (b. 1935), Greek film director; Tarr (b. 1955), Hungarian filmmaker; Sokurov (b. 1951), Russian filmmaker who in 1997 produced the award-winning *Mat i syn* (*Mother and Son*).

Abbas Kiarostami's *Close-Up* and Koker trilogy. But one hardly finds anymore, at least among the young, the distinctive cinephilic love of movies, which is not simply love of but a certain *taste* in films (grounded in a vast appetite for seeing and re-seeing as much as possible of cinema's glorious past). Cinephilia itself has come under attack, as something quaint, outmoded, snobbish. For cinephilia implies that films are unique, unrepeatable, magic experiences. Cinephilia tells us that the Hollywood remake of Godard's *Breathless* cannot be as good as the original. Cinephilia has no role in the era of hyperindustrial films. For by the very range and eclecticism of its passions, cinephilia cannot help but sponsor the idea of the film as, first of all, a poetic object; and cannot help but incite those outside the movie industry, like painters and writers, to want to make films, too. It is precisely this that must be defeated. That has been defeated.

If cinephilia is dead, then movies are dead. . . . no matter how many movies, even very good ones, go on being made. If cinema can be resurrected, it will only be through the birth of a new kind of cine-love.

MLA CITATION

Sontag, Susan. "A Century of Cinema." 1995. *The Norton Reader: An Anthology of Nonfiction*. Ed. Melissa A. Goldthwaite et al. 14th ed. New York: Norton, 2016. 927–34. Print.

QUESTIONS

1. Susan Sontag summarizes one hundred years of film history, from 1895 to 1995. Diagram her periodization of this history. Locate her moviegoing period (she was born in 1933) and yours on it. Which of the older films Sontag mentions have you seen? If you have seen other films made before you began going to the movies, name some of them. How did you see them—in a film-studies course, for example, or on your own?

2. What is Sontag's definition of a "cinephile"? Are you one? Why or why not?

3. Sontag expresses strong opinions about contemporary films: they are "astonishingly witless," "bloated, derivative," "a brazen combinatory or re-combinatory art" (paragraph 1), and reduced to "assaultive images, and the unprincipled manipulation of images (faster and faster cutting) to be more attention-grabbing" (paragraph 6). At the same time, they are "disincarnated, lightweight," and don't "demand anyone's full attention" (paragraph 6). Using at least three contemporary films that you have seen, write an essay in which you agree, disagree, or both with her charges.

Philip Kennicott *How to View Art: Be Dead Serious about It, but Don't Expect Too Much*

1. Take Time

THE BIGGEST CHALLENGE when visiting an art museum is to disengage from our distracted selves. The pervasive, relentless, all-consuming power of time is the enemy. If you are thinking about where you have to be next, what you have left undone, what you could be doing instead of standing in front of art, there is no hope that anything significant will happen. But to disengage from time has become extraordinarily complicated. We are addicted to devices that remind us of the presence of time, cellphones and watches among them, but cameras too, because the camera has become a crutch to memory, and memory is our only defense against the loss of time.

The raging debate today about whether to allow the taking of pictures inside the museum usually hinges on whether the act of photographing is intrusive or disruptive to other visitors; more important, the act is fundamentally disruptive to the photographer's experience of art, which is always fleeting. So leave all your devices behind. And never, ever make plans for what to do later in a museum; if you overhear people making plans for supper, drinks or when to relieve the baby sitter, give them a sharp, baleful look.

Some practical advice: If you go an hour before closing time, you won't have to worry about what time it is. Just wait until the guards kick you out. Also: If you have only an hour, visit only one room. Anything that makes you feel rushed, or compelled to move quickly, will reengage you with the sense of busy-ness that defines ordinary life. This is another reason that entrance fees are so pernicious: They make visitors mentally "meter" the experience, straining to get the most out of it, and thus re-inscribe it in the workaday world where time is money, and money is everything.

2. Seek Silence

Always avoid noise, because noise isn't just distracting, it makes us hate other people. If you're thinking about the mind-numbing banality of the person next to you, there's little hope that you will be receptive to art. In a museum, imagine that you have a magnetic repulsion to everyone else. Move toward empty space. Indulge your misanthropy.

That's not always easy. Too many museums have become exceptionally   5
noisy, and in some cases that's by design. When it comes to science and history museums, noise is often equated with visitor engagement, a sign that people are enjoying the experience. In art museums, noise isn't just a question of bad

Published in the Washington Post *(2014), where Philip Kennicott is an art and architecture critic.*

manners but a result of the celebrity status of certain artworks, such as the *Mona Lisa*, which attracts vast and inevitably tumultuous throngs of visitors to the Louvre. But any picture that attracts hordes of people has long since died, a victim of its own renown, its aura dissipated, its meaning lost in heaps of platitudes and cant. Say a prayer for its soul and move on.

Seek, rather, some quiet corner of the museum full of things no one else seems to care about. Art that is generally regarded as insipid (19th-century American genre paintings) or hermetic (religious icons from the Byzantine world) is likely to feel very lonely, and its loneliness will make it generous. It may be poor, but it will offer you everything it has.

3. STUDY UP

One of the most deceptive promises made by our stewards of culture over the past half century is: You don't need to know anything to enjoy art. This is true only in the most limited sense. Yes, art can speak to us even in our ignorance. But there's a far more powerful truth: Our response to art is directly proportional to our knowledge of it. In this sense, art is the opposite of popular entertainment, which becomes more insipid with greater familiarity.

So study up. Even 10 minutes on Wikipedia can help orient you and fundamentally transform the experience. Better yet, read the old cranks of art history, especially the ones who knew how to write and have now become unfashionable (Kenneth Clark, Ernst Gombrich).[1] When visiting special exhibitions, always read the catalogue, or at least the main catalogue essay. If you can't afford the catalogue, read it in the gift shop.

Rules for the gift shop: Never buy anything that isn't a book; never "save time" for the gift shop because this will make you think about time; never take children, because they will associate art with commerce.

10   Many museums have public education programs, including tours through the galleries with trained docents. Always shadow a docent tour before joining one. If the guide spends all his or her time asking questions rather than explaining art and imparting knowledge, do not waste your time. These faux-Socratic dialogues are premised on the fallacy that all opinions about art are equally valid and that learning from authority is somehow oppressive. You wouldn't learn to ski from someone who professed indifference to form and technique, so don't waste your time with educators who indulge the time-wasting sham of endless questions about what you are feeling and thinking.

4. ENGAGE MEMORY

The experience of art is ephemeral, and on one level we have to accept that. But beyond the subjective experience, art is also something to be studied and debated. Unfortunately, unlike most things we study and debate, art is difficult to summarize and describe. Without a verbal description of what you have seen, you may feel as if nothing happened during your visit. You may even feel

1. Clark (1903–1983), British author and former director of the National Gallery in London; Gombrich (1909–2001), art historian and author of *The Story of Art* (1950).

you can't remember anything about it, as if it was just a wash of images with nothing to hold on to.

But even if the actual experience of art is difficult to retain and remember, the names of the artists, the countries in which they worked, the years they lived and were active, and a host of other things are easily committed to memory. Some museum educators, who know these things, will tell you this kind of detail doesn't matter; they are lying. Always try to remember the name of and at least one work by an artist whom you didn't know before walking into the museum.

When trying to remember individual art works, make an effort to give yourself a verbal description of them. Perhaps write it in a notebook. The process of giving a verbal description will make details of the work more tangible, and will force you to look more deeply and confront your own entrenched blindness toward art. If your description feels clichéd, then go back again and again until you have said something that seems more substantial. If all else fails, simply commit the visual details of the work to memory, its subject matter, or general color scheme, or surface texture. Turn away from the work and try to remember it; turn back and check your mental image against the work itself. This isn't fun. In fact, it can be exhausting. That means you're making progress in the fight against oblivion.

5. Accept Contradiction

Art must have some utopian ambition, must seek to make the world better, must engage with injustice and misery; art has no other mission than to express visual ideas in its own self-sufficient language. As one art lover supposedly said to another: Monet, Manet,[2] both are correct.

Susan Sontag[3] once argued "against interpretation" and in favor of a more   15
immediate, more sensual, more purely subjective response to art; but others argue, just as validly, that art is part of culture and embodies a wide range of cultural meanings and that our job is to ferret them out. Again, both are correct.

The experience of art always enmires us in contradictions. I loathe figurative contemporary art except when I don't; ditto on abstraction. When looking at a painting, it's often useful to try believing two wildly contradictory things: That it is just an object, and an everyday sort of object; and that it is a phenomenally radical expression of human subjectivity. Both are correct.

Art is inspiring and depressing, it excites and enervates us, it makes us more generous and more selfish. A love-hate relationship with an artist, or a great work of art, is often the most intense and lasting of all relationships. After years of spending time in art museums, I've come to accept that I believe wildly contradictory and incompatible things about art. The usual cliché about this realization would be that by forcing us to confront contradiction, art makes us more

2. Oscar-Claude Monet (1840–1926) French impressionist painter; Édouard Manet (1832–1883), early modern French painter, known for bridging realist and impressionist art movements.

3. American filmmaker and author of fiction, nonfiction, and plays (1933–2004); see "A Century of Cinema," pp. 927–34.

human. But never trust anyone who says that last part: "art makes us more human." That's meaningless.

Rather, by forcing us to confront contradiction, art makes us ridiculous, exposes our pathetic attempts to make sense of experience, reveals the fault lines of our incredibly faulty knowledge of ourselves and the world. It is nasty, dangerous stuff, and not to be trifled with.

Some practical advice: If you feel better about yourself when you leave a museum, you're probably doing it all wrong.

MLA CITATION

Kennicott, Philip. "How to View Art: Be Dead Serious about It, but Don't Expect Too Much." 2014. *The Norton Reader: An Anthology of Nonfiction.* Ed. Melissa A. Goldthwaite et al. 14th ed. New York: Norton, 2016. 935–38. Print.

QUESTIONS

1. Philip Kennicott claims, "Our response to art is directly proportional to our knowledge of it" (paragraph 7). Do you agree? Why or why not? How important is study to the appreciation of art?

2. Kennicott uses the form of a list to guide readers in how to view art. Which of his five directives do you think is most important? Least important? Is there anything you would add to his list?

3. In paragraph 3, Kennicott cautions art viewers about feeling rushed, about anything that "will reengage you with the sense of busy-ness that defines ordinary life." Tim Kreider in "The 'Busy' Trap" (pp. 380–84) also warns against busy-ness. According to each of these authors, why is busy-ness a problem?

4. Use the form of a list to write a "how to" essay on a subject about which you could be considered an expert.

AARON COPLAND   *How We Listen*

E ALL LISTEN TO MUSIC according to our separate capacities. But, for the sake of analysis, the whole listening process may become clearer if we break it up into its component parts, so to speak. In a certain sense we all listen to music on three separate planes. For lack of a better terminology, one might name these: (1) the sensuous plane, (2) the expressive plane, (3) the sheerly musical plane. The only advantage to be gained from mechanically splitting up the listening process into these hypothetical planes is the clearer view to be had of the way in which we listen.

The simplest way of listening to music is to listen for the sheer pleasure of the musical sound itself. That is the sensuous plane. It is the plane on which

From Aaron Copland's classic guide, What to Listen for in Music *(1957).*

we hear music without thinking, without considering it in any way. One turns on the radio while doing something else and absentmindedly bathes in the sound. A kind of brainless but attractive state of mind is engendered by the mere sound appeal of the music.

You may be sitting in a room reading this book. Imagine one note struck on the piano. Immediately that one note is enough to change the atmosphere of the room—proving that the sound element in music is a powerful and mysterious agent, which it would be foolish to deride or belittle.

The surprising thing is that many people who consider themselves qualified music lovers abuse that plane in listening. They go to concerts in order to lose themselves. They use music as a consolation or an escape. They enter an ideal world where one doesn't have to think of the realities of everyday life. Of course they aren't thinking about the music either. Music allows them to leave it, and they go off to a place to dream, dreaming because of and apropos of the music yet never quite listening to it.

Yes, the sound appeal of music is a potent and primitive force, but you must not allow it to usurp a disproportionate share of your interest. The sensuous plane is an important one in music, a very important one, but it does not constitute the whole story.

There is no need to digress further on the sensuous plane. Its appeal to every normal human being is self-evident. There is, however, such a thing as becoming more sensitive to the different kinds of sound stuff as used by various composers. For all composers do not use that sound stuff in the same way. Don't get the idea that the value of music is commensurate with its sensuous appeal or that the loveliest sounding music is made by the greatest composer. If that were so, Ravel would be a greater creator than Beethoven.[1] The point is that the sound element varies with each composer, that his usage of sound forms an integral part of his style and must be taken into account when listening. The reader can see, therefore, that a more conscious approach is valuable even on this primary plane of music listening.

The second plane on which music exists is what I have called the expressive one. Here, immediately, we tread on controversial ground. Composers have a way of shying away from any discussion of music's expressive side. Did not Stravinsky[2] himself proclaim that his music was an "object," a "thing," with a life of its own, and with no other meaning than its own purely musical existence? This intransigent attitude of Stravinsky's may be due to the fact that so many people have tried to read different meanings into so many pieces. Heaven knows it is difficult enough to say precisely what it is that a piece of music means, to say it definitely, to say it finally so that everyone is satisfied with your explanation. But that should not lead one to the other extreme of denying to music the right to be "expressive."

My own belief is that all music has an expressive power, some more and some less, but that all music has a certain meaning behind the notes and that

5

---

1. Maurice Ravel (1875–1937), French composer; Ludwig van Beethoven (1770–1827), German composer.
2. Igor Stravinsky (1882–1971), Russian-born American composer.

that meaning behind the note constitutes, after all, what the piece is saying, what the piece is about. This whole problem can be stated quite simply by asking, "Is there a meaning to music?" My answer to that would be, "Yes." And "Can you state in so many words what the meaning is?" My answer to that would be, "No." Therein lies the difficulty.

Simple-minded souls will never be satisfied with the answer to the second of these questions. They always want music to have a meaning, and the more concrete it is the better they like it. The more the music reminds them of a train, a storm, a funeral, or any other familiar conception the more expressive it appears to be to them. This popular idea of music's meaning—stimulated and abetted by the usual run of musical commentator—should be discouraged wherever and whenever it is met. One timid lady once confessed to me that she suspected something seriously lacking in her appreciation of music because of her inability to connect it with anything definite. That is getting the whole thing backward, of course.

10   Still, the question remains, How close should the intelligent music lover wish to come to pinning a definite meaning to any particular work? No closer than a general concept, I should say. Music expresses, at different moments, serenity or exuberance, regret or triumph, fury or delight. It expresses each of these moods, and many others, in a numberless variety of subtle shadings and differences. It may even express a state of meaning for which there exists no adequate word in any language. In that case, musicians often like to say that it has only a purely musical meaning. They sometimes go farther and say that *all* music has only a purely musical meaning. What they really mean is that no appropriate word can be found to express the music's meaning and that, even if it could, they do not feel the need of finding it.

But whatever the professional musician may hold, most musical novices still search for specific words with which to pin down their musical reactions. That is why they always find Tchaikovsky[3] easier to "understand" than Beethoven. In the first place, it is easier to pin a meaning-word on a Tchaikovsky piece than on a Beethoven one. Much easier. Moreover, with the Russian composer, every time you come back to a piece of his it almost always says the same thing to you, whereas with Beethoven it is often quite difficult to put your finger right on what he is saying. And any musician will tell you that that is why Beethoven is the greater composer. Because music which always says the same thing to you will necessarily soon become dull music, but music whose meaning is slightly different with each hearing has a greater chance of remaining alive.

Listen, if you can, to the forty-eight fugue themes of Bach's *Well Tempered Clavichord.*[4] Listen to each theme, one after another. You will soon realize that each theme mirrors a different world of feeling. You will also soon realize that the more beautiful a theme seems to you the harder it is to find any word that will describe it to your complete satisfaction. Yes, you will certainly know whether it is a gay theme or a sad one. You will be able, in other words, in your

3. Peter Ilyich Tchaikovsky (1840–1893), Russian composer.
4. Work composed by Johann Sebastian Bach (1685–1750) in which forty-eight themes are presented by themselves and then elaborated in three voices.

own mind, to draw a frame of emotional feeling around your theme. Now study the sad one a little closer. Try to pin down the exact quality of its sadness. Is it pessimistically sad or resignedly sad; is it fatefully sad or smilingly sad?

Let us suppose that you are fortunate and can describe to your own satisfaction in so many words the exact meaning of your chosen theme. There is still no guarantee that anyone else will be satisfied. Nor need they be. The important thing is that each one feel for himself the specific expressive quality of a theme or, similarly, an entire piece of music. And if it is a great work of art, don't expect it to mean exactly the same thing to you each time you return to it.

Themes or pieces need not express only one emotion, of course. Take such a theme as the first main one of the *Ninth Symphony,*[5] for example. It is clearly made up of different elements. It does not say only one thing. Yet anyone hearing it immediately gets a feeling of strength, a feeling of power. It isn't a power that comes simply because the theme is played loudly. It is a power inherent in the theme itself. The extraordinary strength and vigor of the theme results in the listener's receiving an impression that a forceful statement has been made. But one should never try to boil it down to "the fateful hammer of life," etc. That is where the trouble begins. The musician, in his exasperation, says it means nothing but the notes themselves, whereas the nonprofessional is only too anxious to hang on to any explanation that gives him the illusion of getting closer to the music's meaning.

Now, perhaps, the reader will know better what I mean when I say that music does have an expressive meaning but that we cannot say in so many words what that meaning is.

The third plane on which music exists is the sheerly musical plane. Besides the pleasurable sound of music and the expressive feeling that it gives off, music does exist in terms of the notes themselves and of their manipulation. Most listeners are not sufficiently conscious of this third plane.

• • •

Professional musicians, on the other hand, are, if anything, too conscious of the mere notes themselves. They often fall into the error of becoming so engrossed with their arpeggios and staccatos that they forget the deeper aspects of the music they are performing. But from the layman's standpoint, it is not so much a matter of getting over bad habits on the sheerly musical plane as of increasing one's awareness of what is going on, in so far as the notes are concerned.

When the man in the street listens to the "notes themselves" with any degree of concentration, he is most likely to make some mention of the melody. Either he hears a pretty melody or he does not, and he generally lets it go at that. Rhythm is likely to gain his attention next, particularly if it seems exciting. But harmony and tone color are generally taken for granted, if they are thought of consciously at all. As for music's having a definite form of some kind, that idea seems never to have occurred to him.

It is very important for all of us to become more alive to music on its sheerly musical plane. After all, an actual musical material is being used. The intelligent

5. Composed by Beethoven.

listener must be prepared to increase his awareness of the musical material and what happens to it. He must hear the melodies, the rhythms, the harmonies, the tone colors in a more conscious fashion. But above all he must, in order to follow the line of the composer's thought, know something of the principles of musical form. Listening to all of these elements is listening on the sheerly musical plane.

20   Let me repeat that I have split up mechanically the three separate planes on which we listen merely for the sake of greater clarity. Actually, we never listen on one or the other of these planes. What we do is to correlate them—listening in all three ways at the same time. It takes no mental effort, for we do it instinctively.

Perhaps an analogy with what happens to us when we visit the theater will make this instinctive correlation clearer. In the theater, you are aware of the actors and actresses, costumes and sets, sounds and movements. All these give one the sense that the theater is a pleasant place to be in. They constitute the sensuous plane in our theatrical reactions.

The expressive plane in the theater would be derived from the feeling that you get from what is happening on the stage. You are moved to pity, excitement, or gayety. It is this general feeling, generated aside from the particular words being spoken, a certain emotional something which exists on the stage, that is analogous to the expressive quality in music.

The plot and plot development is equivalent to our sheerly musical plane. The playwright creates and develops a character in just the same way that a composer creates and develops a theme. According to the degree of your awareness of the way in which the artist in either field handles his material will you become a more intelligent listener.

It is easy enough to see that the theatergoer never is conscious of any of these elements separately. He is aware of them all at the same time. The same is true of music listening. We simultaneously and without thinking listen on all three planes.

25   In a sense, the ideal listener is both inside and outside the music at the same moment, judging it and enjoying it, wishing it would go one way and watching it go another—almost like the composer at the moment he composes it; because in order to write his music, the composer must also be inside and outside his music, carried away by it and yet coldly critical of it. A subjective and objective attitude is implied in both creating and listening to music.

What the reader should strive for, then, is a more *active* kind of listening. Whether you listen to Mozart or Duke Ellington,[6] you can deepen your understanding of music only by being a more conscious and aware listener—not someone who is just listening, but someone who is listening *for* something.

6. Wolfgang Amadeus Mozart (1756–1791), Austrian composer; Edward Kennedy ("Duke") Ellington (1899–1974), American jazz composer and band leader.

MLA CITATION

Copland, Aaron. "How We Listen." 1957. *The Norton Reader: An Anthology of Nonfiction.* Ed. Melissa A. Goldthwaite et al. 14th ed. New York: Norton, 2016. 938–42. Print.

QUESTIONS

1. List Aaron Copland's "three planes" of listening to music and explain what each entails. Are these three planes comprehensive? Is there another you would add?

2. In paragraphs 21–24, Copland uses the experience of going to the theater to illustrate his three planes of listening. Can you think of other artistic experiences that can be divided up into different "planes"? To what extent would the planes be the same as Copland's?

3. Copland uses classical music as examples in his explanation of the way humans listen to music. Write an essay about the ways you listen to another kind of music: folk, rap, jazz, hip-hop, pop, or rock.

MICHAEL HAMAD   *Song Schematics*

A S A KID, I saw random shapes in my head when I listened to music. They were mostly large, abstract geometric patterns, usually either blue or yellow in color, that floated around and interacted with some unseen gravitational force; other times I saw things that looked like gears or pulleys. Last year, after two decades of studying music theory, I stumbled into this weird visual language to explain what I hear. I call these drawings "schematics" because (as far as I can tell) they look like wiring diagrams.

My schematics are all drawn in real time (though I'll go back and add details, fix bad handwriting, and so on). They're also proportional. This one, of Phish playing "Chalk Dust Torture" in Camden, New Jersey, is roughly fourteen minutes long, so if you look at the exact center of the schematic, you're seeing what happens at minute seven. Creating these schematics is a form of meditation; when I'm drawing, I'm hearing the music, but I'm also thinking about other stuff: family, work, whatever. I think about my bad posture and the thickness of writing utensils. Sometimes I'll hear music that's not coming through my headphones. That's a strange feeling. Other times I'll listen to one piece of music and look at a schematic of something else, and I'll hear both. Mostly, though, I watch random ideas surface and disappear, and then I return directly to the music.

If you make music theory something fascinating to look at, will more people become interested in learning about it? I hope so. I've done more than a hundred of these in less than a year. Improvisational rock—the Grateful Dead, Phish, Umphrey's McGee—works best, but I want to see what a Katy Perry song looks like, or *Revolver*.[1] There's work to be done.

Printed in the music issue of the Believer (2014), *"a magazine of interviews, essays, and reviews" published by McSweeney's.*

1. Grateful Dead, rock band formed in 1965; Phish, rock band formed in 1983; Umphrey's McGee, rock band formed in 1997; Katy Perry (b. 1984), American singer-songwriter; *Revolver*, Beatles album released in 1966.

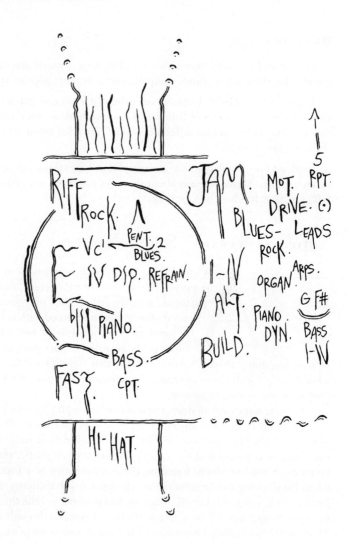

GENERAL

ARROWS = *tendencies, directions, or leanings in the music*

(.) = *major structural moments in the piece (to my ears)*

KEY = *tonal center, indicated by a capital letter (E, G, etc.)*

MODE = *the pitch collection used within a certain key*

I, II, III, ETC. = *harmonic function, or the gravity of certain chords next to each other within a certain key*

PENT = *a pentatonic (five-note) pitch collection or melody*

BLUES-ROCK = *improvisation using the blues-rock collection of pitches*

PROG = *the existence of a chord progression (it doesn't mean "progressive rock.")*

VC = *verse/chorus (1, 2, etc.); vocals are present*

ARPS = *arpeggios (instrument is usually indicated)*

MOT = *a recurring motif or melodic fragment*

^5, ^7, ETC. = *indication that a certain scale degree within the key is being emphasized melodically*

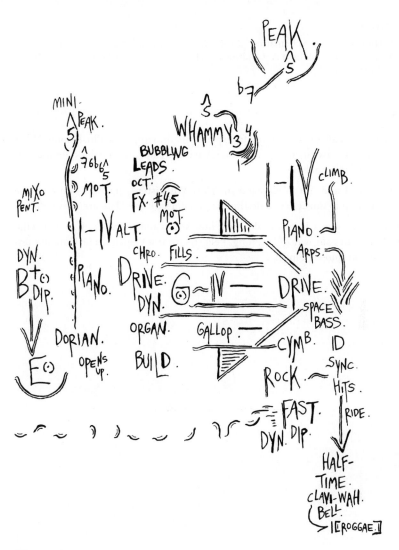

Dynamics

DYN DIP = *"dynamic dip" or a drop in volume or intensity*
BUILD = *A gradual increase in dynamics or intensity.*
DRIVE = *maintaining a pretty much full-throttle dynamics/intensity level*
GALLOP = *DRIVE on acid (you'll know it when you hear it)*
PEAK = *you'll know it when you hear it*

Percussion

FILLS = *the drummer plays outside the usual beat, adding intensity*

HITS = *two or more players lock together on a rhythmic or melodic riff*
SYNC HITS = *two or more instruments cooperate in some syncopated fashion*

Tone/Color

OCT = *the guitarist is playing in octaves*
FX = *the guitarist hits some sort of effects pedal*

Michael Hamad

MLA CITATION

Hamad, Michael. "Song Schematics." 2014. *The Norton Reader: An Anthology of Nonfiction*. Ed. Melissa A. Goldthwaite et al. 14th ed. New York: Norton, 2016. 943–45. Print.

QUESTIONS

1. Michael Hamad provides a key to explain his drawing of a Phish song. What categories does he use to analyze the song? Are there categories he does not use that would be helpful to include?

2. Both Hamad and Aaron Copland in "How We Listen" (pp. 938–42) describe ways of listening to music. How do their approaches differ? How are they similar?

3. Write an essay in which you describe how you listen to music. Use a specific song to illustrate your way of listening. Feel free to use Copland's or Hamad's terminology if you find it helpful.

PHILOSOPHY AND RELIGION

LANGSTON HUGHES *Salvation*

I WAS SAVED FROM SIN when I was going on thirteen. But not really saved. It happened like this. There was a big revival at my Auntie Reed's church. Every night for weeks there had been much preaching, singing, praying, and shouting, and some very hardened sinners had been brought to Christ, and the membership of the church had grown by leaps and bounds. Then just before the revival ended, they held a special meeting for children, "to bring the young lambs to the fold." My aunt spoke of it for days ahead. That night I was escorted to the front row and placed on the mourners' bench[1] with all the other young sinners, who had not yet been brought to Jesus.

My aunt told me that when you were saved you saw a light, and something happened to you inside! And Jesus came into your life! And God was with you from then on! She said you could see and hear and feel Jesus in your soul. I believed her. I had heard a great many old people say the same thing and it seemed to me they ought to know. So I sat there calmly in the hot, crowded church, waiting for Jesus to come to me.

The preacher preached a wonderful rhythmical sermon, all moans and shouts and lonely cries and dire pictures of hell, and then he sang a song about the ninety and nine safe in the fold, but one little lamb was left out in the cold.[2] Then he said: "Won't you come? Won't you come to Jesus? Young lambs, won't you come?" And he held out his arms to all us young sinners there on the mourners' bench. And the little girls cried. And some of them jumped up and went to Jesus right away. But most of us just sat there.

A great many old people came and knelt around us and prayed, old women with jet-black faces and braided hair, old men with work-gnarled hands. And the church sang a song about the lower lights are burning, some poor sinners to be saved. And the whole building rocked with prayer and song.

From The Big Sea (1940), *Langston Hughes's account of his early life.*

1. Place in the front of the church where potential converts sat during an evangelical service.
2. "The Ninety and Nine" mentioned in this paragraph and "Let the Lower Lights Be Burning," in the next, are the titles of famous evangelical hymns collected by Ira Sankey.

5   Still I kept waiting to *see* Jesus.

Finally all the young people had gone to the altar and were saved, but one boy and me. He was a rounder's[3] son named Westley. Westley and I were surrounded by sisters and deacons praying. It was very hot in the church, and getting late now. Finally Westley said to me in a whisper: "God damn! I'm tired o' sitting here. Let's get up and be saved." So he got up and was saved.

Then I was left all alone on the mourners' bench. My aunt came and knelt at my knees and cried, while prayers and songs swirled all around me in the little church. The whole congregation prayed for me alone, in a mighty wail of moans and voices. And I kept waiting serenely for Jesus, waiting, waiting—but he didn't come. I wanted to see him, but nothing happened to me. Nothing! I wanted something to happen to me, but nothing happened.

I heard the songs and the minister saying: "Why don't you come? My dear child, why don't you come to Jesus? Jesus is waiting for you. He wants you. Why don't you come? Sister Reed, what is this child's name?"

"Langston," my aunt sobbed.

10   "Langston, why don't you come? Why don't you come and be saved? Oh, Lamb of God! Why don't you come?"

Now it was really getting late. I began to be ashamed of myself, holding everything up so long. I began to wonder what God thought about Westley, who certainly hadn't seen Jesus either, but who was now sitting proudly on the platform, swinging his knickerbockered legs and grinning down at me, surrounded by deacons and old women on their knees praying. God had not struck Westley dead for taking his name in vain or for lying in the temple. So I decided that maybe to save further trouble, I'd better lie, too, and say that Jesus had come, and get up and be saved.

So I got up.

Suddenly the whole room broke into a sea of shouting, as they saw me rise. Waves of rejoicing swept the place. Women leaped in the air. My aunt threw her arms around me. The minister took me by the hand and led me to the platform.

When things quieted down, in a hushed silence, punctuated by a few ecstatic "Amens," all the new young lambs were blessed in the name of God. Then joyous singing filled the room.

15   That night, for the last time in my life but one—for I was a big boy twelve years old—I cried. I cried, in bed alone, and couldn't stop. I buried my head under the quilts, but my aunt heard me. She woke up and told my uncle I was crying because the Holy Ghost had come into my life, and because I had seen Jesus. But I was really crying because I couldn't bear to tell her that I had lied, that I had deceived everybody in the church, and I hadn't seen Jesus, and that now I didn't believe there was a Jesus any more, since he didn't come to help me.

---

3. Loafer or someone who is frequently drunk.

MLA CITATION

Hughes, Langston. "Salvation." 1940. *The Norton Reader: An Anthology of Nonfiction.*
    Ed. Melissa A. Goldthwaite et al. 14th ed. New York: Norton, 2016. 947–48.
    Print.

QUESTIONS

1. Langston Hughes describes how he lost his faith in Jesus at the age of twelve. How did the grown-ups in his life contribute to the experience?

2. Hughes was twelve "going on thirteen" (paragraph 1) when the event he describes in first-person narration took place. How careful is he to restrict himself to the point of view of a twelve-year-old child? How does he ensure that we, as readers, understand things that the narrator does not?

3. Write a first-person narrative in which you describe a failure—yours or someone else's—to live up to the expectations of parents or other authority figures.

BARACK OBAMA   *Eulogy for Clementa Pinckney*

GIVING ALL PRAISE AND HONOR TO GOD. (Applause.)
        The Bible calls us to hope. To persevere, and have faith in things not seen.
        "They were still living by faith when they died," Scripture tells us. "They did not receive the things promised; they only saw them and welcomed them from a distance, admitting that they were foreigners and strangers on Earth."

We are here today to remember a man of God who lived by faith. A man who believed in things not seen. A man who believed there were better days ahead, off in the distance. A man of service who persevered, knowing full well he would not receive all those things he was promised, because he believed his efforts would deliver a better life for those who followed.

To Jennifer, his beloved wife; to Eliana and Malana, his beautiful, wonderful daughters; to the Mother Emanuel family and the people of Charleston, the people of South Carolina.   5

I cannot claim to have the good fortune to know Reverend Pinckney well. But I did have the pleasure of knowing him and meeting him here in South Carolina, back when we were both a little bit younger. (Laughter.) Back when

On June 17, 2015, a twenty-one-year-old shooter entered Mother Emanuel African Methodist Episcopal Church in Charleston, South Carolina, and murdered nine people, including the senior pastor, Reverend Clementa Pinckney, also a state senator. President Barack Obama delivered this eulogy for Reverend Pinckney on June 26, 2015.

I didn't have visible grey hair. (Laughter.) The first thing I noticed was his graciousness, his smile, his reassuring baritone, his deceptive sense of humor—all qualities that helped him wear so effortlessly a heavy burden of expectation.

Friends of his remarked this week that when Clementa Pinckney entered a room, it was like the future arrived; that even from a young age, folks knew he was special. Anointed. He was the progeny of a long line of the faithful—a family of preachers who spread God's word, a family of protesters who sowed change to expand voting rights and desegregate the South. Clem heard their instruction, and he did not forsake their teaching.

He was in the pulpit by thirteen, pastor by eighteen, public servant by twenty-three. He did not exhibit any of the cockiness of youth, nor youth's insecurities; instead, he set an example worthy of his position, wise beyond his years, in his speech, in his conduct, in his love, faith, and purity.

As a senator, he represented a sprawling swath of the Low country,[1] a place that has long been one of the most neglected in America. A place still wracked by poverty and inadequate schools; a place where children can still go hungry and the sick can go without treatment. A place that needed somebody like Clem. (Applause.)

10   His position in the minority party meant the odds of winning more resources for his constituents were often long. His calls for greater equity were too often unheeded, the votes he cast were sometimes lonely. But he never gave up. He stayed true to his convictions. He would not grow discouraged. After a full day at the capitol, he'd climb into his car and head to the church to draw sustenance from his family, from his ministry, from the community that loved and needed him. There he would fortify his faith, and imagine what might be.

Reverend Pinckney embodied a politics that was neither mean, nor small. He conducted himself quietly, and kindly, and diligently. He encouraged progress not by pushing his ideas alone, but by seeking out your ideas, partnering with you to make things happen. He was full of empathy and fellow feeling, able to walk in somebody else's shoes and see through their eyes. No wonder one of his senate colleagues remembered Senator Pinckney as "the most gentle of the forty-six of us—the best of the forty-six of us."

Clem was often asked why he chose to be a pastor and a public servant. But the person who asked probably didn't know the history of the AME church. (Applause.) As our brothers and sisters in the AME church know, we don't make those distinctions. "Our calling," Clem once said, "is not just within the walls of the congregation, but . . . the life and community in which our congregation resides." (Applause.)

He embodied the idea that our Christian faith demands deeds and not just words; that the "sweet hour of prayer"[2] actually lasts the whole week long— (applause)—that to put our faith in action is more than individual salvation,

---

1. Low country region of South Carolina comprises the southern coast of the state and its islands, including the city of Charleston. Its economy was once dependent on plantations that grew rice and indigo.
2. "The Sweet Hour of Prayer" is a traditional hymn.

it's about our collective salvation; that to feed the hungry and clothe the naked and house the homeless is not just a call for isolated charity but the imperative of a just society.

What a good man. Sometimes I think that's the best thing to hope for when you're eulogized—after all the words and recitations and résumés are read, to just say someone was a good man. (Applause.)

You don't have to be of high station to be a good man. Preacher by thirteen. Pastor by eighteen. Public servant by twenty-three. What a life Clementa Pinckney lived. What an example he set. What a model for his faith. And then to lose him at forty-one—slain in his sanctuary with eight wonderful members of his flock, each at different stages in life but bound together by a common commitment to God.

Cynthia Hurd. Susie Jackson. Ethel Lance. DePayne Middleton-Doctor. Tywanza Sanders. Daniel L. Simmons. Sharonda Coleman-Singleton. Myra Thompson. Good people. Decent people. God-fearing people. (Applause.) People so full of life and so full of kindness. People who ran the race, who persevered. People of great faith.

To the families of the fallen, the nation shares in your grief. Our pain cuts that much deeper because it happened in a church. The church is and always has been the center of African American life—(applause)—a place to call our own in a too often hostile world, a sanctuary from so many hardships.

Over the course of centuries, black churches served as "hush harbors" where slaves could worship in safety; praise houses where their free descendants could gather and shout hallelujah—(applause)—rest stops for the weary along the Underground Railroad; bunkers for the foot soldiers of the Civil Rights Movement. They have been, and continue to be, community centers where we organize for jobs and justice; places of scholarship and network; places where children are loved and fed and kept out of harm's way, and told that they are beautiful and smart—(applause)—and taught that they matter. (Applause.) That's what happens in church.

That's what the black church means. Our beating heart. The place where our dignity as a people is inviolate. When there's no better example of this tradition than Mother Emanuel—(applause)—a church built by blacks seeking liberty, burned to the ground because its founder sought to end slavery, only to rise up again, a Phoenix from these ashes. (Applause.)

When there were laws banning all-black church gatherings, services happened here anyway, in defiance of unjust laws. When there was a righteous movement to dismantle Jim Crow, Dr. Martin Luther King Jr. preached from its pulpit, and marches began from its steps. A sacred place, this church. Not just for blacks, not just for Christians, but for every American who cares about the steady expansion—(applause)—of human rights and human dignity in this country; a foundation stone for liberty and justice for all. That's what the church meant. (Applause.)

We do not know whether the killer of Reverend Pinckney and eight others knew all of this history. But he surely sensed the meaning of his violent act. It was an act that drew on a long history of bombs and arson and shots fired at churches, not random, but as a means of control, a way to terrorize and oppress. (Applause.) An act that he imagined would incite fear and recrimination; violence and suspicion. An act that he presumed would deepen divisions that trace back to our nation's original sin.

Oh, but God works in mysterious ways. (Applause.) God has different ideas. (Applause.)

He didn't know he was being used by God. (Applause.) Blinded by hatred, the alleged killer could not see the grace surrounding Reverend Pinckney and that Bible study group—the light of love that shone as they opened the church doors and invited a stranger to join in their prayer circle. The alleged killer could have never anticipated the way the families of the fallen would respond when they saw him in court—in the midst of unspeakable grief, with words of forgiveness. He couldn't imagine that. (Applause.)

The alleged killer could not imagine how the city of Charleston, under the good and wise leadership of Mayor Riley—(applause)—how the state of South Carolina, how the United States of America would respond—not merely with revulsion at his evil act, but with big-hearted generosity and, more importantly, with a thoughtful introspection and self-examination that we so rarely see in public life.

25   Blinded by hatred, he failed to comprehend what Reverend Pinckney so well understood—the power of God's grace. (Applause.)

This whole week, I've been reflecting on this idea of grace. (Applause.) The grace of the families who lost loved ones. The grace that Reverend Pinckney would preach about in his sermons. The grace described in one of my favorite hymnals—the one we all know: Amazing grace, how sweet the sound that saved a wretch like me. (Applause.) I once was lost, but now I'm found; was blind but now I see. (Applause.)

According to the Christian tradition, grace is not earned. Grace is not merited. It's not something we deserve. Rather, grace is the free and benevolent favor of God—(applause)—as manifested in the salvation of sinners and the bestowal of blessings. Grace.

As a nation, out of this terrible tragedy, God has visited grace upon us, for he has allowed us to see where we've been blind. (Applause.) He has given us the chance, where we've been lost, to find our best selves. (Applause.) We may not have earned it, this grace, with our rancor and complacency, and shortsightedness and fear of each other—but we got it all the same. He gave it to us anyway. He's once more given us grace. But it is up to us now to make the most of it, to receive it with gratitude, and to prove ourselves worthy of this gift.

For too long, we were blind to the pain that the Confederate flag stirred in too many of our citizens. (Applause.) It's true, a flag did not cause these murders. But as people from all walks of life, Republicans and Democrats, now acknowledge—including Governor Haley,[3] whose recent eloquence on the subject is worthy of praise—(applause)—as we all have to acknowledge, the flag has

3. Nikki R. Haley (b. 1972), governor of South Carolina.

always represented more than just ancestral pride. (Applause.) For many, black and white, that flag was a reminder of systemic oppression and racial subjugation. We see that now.

Removing the flag from this state's capitol would not be an act of political correctness; it would not be an insult to the valor of Confederate soldiers. It would simply be an acknowledgment that the cause for which they fought—the cause of slavery—was wrong—(applause)—the imposition of Jim Crow after the Civil War, the resistance to civil rights for all people was wrong. (Applause.) It would be one step in an honest accounting of America's history; a modest but meaningful balm for so many unhealed wounds. It would be an expression of the amazing changes that have transformed this state and this country for the better, because of the work of so many people of goodwill, people of all races striving to form a more perfect union. By taking down that flag, we express God's grace. (Applause.)

But I don't think God wants us to stop there. (Applause.) For too long, we've been blind to the way past injustices continue to shape the present. Perhaps we see that now. Perhaps this tragedy causes us to ask some tough questions about how we can permit so many of our children to languish in poverty, or attend dilapidated schools, or grow up without prospects for a job or for a career. (Applause.)

Perhaps it causes us to examine what we're doing to cause some of our children to hate. (Applause.) Perhaps it softens hearts toward those lost young men, tens and tens of thousands caught up in the criminal justice system—(applause)—and leads us to make sure that that system is not infected with bias; that we embrace changes in how we train and equip our police so that the bonds of trust between law enforcement and the communities they serve make us all safer and more secure. (Applause.)

Maybe we now realize the way racial bias can infect us even when we don't realize it, so that we're guarding against not just racial slurs, but we're also guarding against the subtle impulse to call Johnny back for a job interview but not Jamal. (Applause.) So that we search our hearts when we consider laws to make it harder for some of our fellow citizens to vote. (Applause.) By recognizing our common humanity by treating every child as important, regardless of the color of their skin or the station into which they were born, and to do what's necessary to make opportunity real for every American—by doing that, we express God's grace. (Applause.)

For too long—

AUDIENCE: For too long!

THE PRESIDENT: For too long, we've been blind to the unique mayhem that gun violence inflicts upon this nation. (Applause.) Sporadically, our eyes are open: When eight of our brothers and sisters are cut down in a church basement, twelve in a movie theater, twenty-six in an elementary school. But I hope we also see the thirty precious lives cut short by gun violence in this country every single day; the countless more whose lives are forever changed—the survivors crippled, the children traumatized and fearful every day as they walk to school, the husband who will never feel his wife's warm touch, the entire communities whose grief overflows every time they have to watch what happened to them happen to some other place.

The vast majority of Americans—the majority of gun owners—want to do something about this. We see that now. (Applause.) And I'm convinced that by acknowledging the pain and loss of others, even as we respect the traditions and ways of life that make up this beloved country—by making the moral choice to change, we express God's grace. (Applause.)

We don't earn grace. We're all sinners. We don't deserve it. (Applause.) But God gives it to us anyway. (Applause.) And we choose how to receive it. It's our decision how to honor it.

None of us can or should expect a transformation in race relations overnight. Every time something like this happens, somebody says we have to have a conversation about race. We talk a lot about race. There's no shortcut. And we don't need more talk. (Applause.) None of us should believe that a handful of gun safety measures will prevent every tragedy. It will not. People of goodwill will continue to debate the merits of various policies, as our democracy requires— this is a big, raucous place, America is. And there are good people on both sides of these debates. Whatever solutions we find will necessarily be incomplete.

40   But it would be a betrayal of everything Reverend Pinckney stood for, I believe, if we allowed ourselves to slip into a comfortable silence again. (Applause.) Once the eulogies have been delivered, once the TV cameras move on, to go back to business as usual—that's what we so often do to avoid uncomfortable truths about the prejudice that still infects our society. (Applause.) To settle for symbolic gestures without following up with the hard work of more lasting change—that's how we lose our way again.

It would be a refutation of the forgiveness expressed by those families if we merely slipped into old habits, whereby those who disagree with us are not merely wrong but bad; where we shout instead of listen; where we barricade ourselves behind preconceived notions or well-practiced cynicism.

Reverend Pinckney once said, "Across the South, we have a deep appreciation of history—we haven't always had a deep appreciation of each other's history." (Applause.) What is true in the South is true for America. Clem understood that justice grows out of recognition of ourselves in each other. That my liberty depends on you being free, too. (Applause.) That history can't be a sword to justify injustice, or a shield against progress, but must be a manual for how to avoid repeating the mistakes of the past—how to break the cycle. A roadway toward a better world. He knew that the path of grace involves an open mind—but, more importantly, an open heart.

That's what I've felt this week—an open heart. That, more than any particular policy or analysis, is what's called upon right now, I think—what a friend of mine, the writer Marilynne Robinson, calls "that reservoir of goodness, beyond, and of another kind, that we are able to do each other in the ordinary cause of things."

That reservoir of goodness. If we can find that grace, anything is possible. (Applause.) If we can tap that grace, everything can change. (Applause.)

45   Amazing grace. Amazing grace.

(Begins to sing)—Amazing grace—(applause)—how sweet the sound, that
saved a wretch like me; I once was lost, but now I'm found; was blind but now
I see. (Applause.)

Clementa Pinckney found that grace.

Cynthia Hurd found that grace.

Susie Jackson found that grace.

Ethel Lance found that grace.   50

DePayne Middleton-Doctor found that grace.

Tywanza Sanders found that grace.

Daniel L. Simmons Sr. found that grace.

Sharonda Coleman-Singleton found that grace.

Myra Thompson found that grace.   55

Through the example of their lives, they've now passed it on to us. May we
find ourselves worthy of that precious and extraordinary gift, as long as our
lives endure. May grace now lead them home. May God continue to shed His
grace on the United States of America. (Applause.)

MLA CITATION

Obama, Barack. "Eulogy for Clementa Pinckney." 2015. *The Norton Reader:An
        Anthology of Nonfiction*. Ed. Melissa A. Goldthwaite et al. 14th ed. New York:
        Norton, 2016. 949–55. Print.

QUESTIONS

1. Barack Obama notes that despite Reverend Pinckney's achievements, he lived
without "high station" (paragraph 15). What do you think he wants to communicate
to his audience with this observation, and how does it help you understand what
he means by calling Pinckney "a good man"?

2. Read Martin Luther King Jr.'s "Letter from Birmingham Jail" (pp. 806–19), and
compare how King and Obama speak to their audiences about the history of racism in the United States. What factors might account for the similarities and
differences?

3. At several points in his eulogy, Obama calls on his audience to take action.
What forms of action does he recommend? What forms of action do you think
might help fight racism on your campus or in your community?

4. Look up the lyrics and listen to several recordings of one of the hymns referred
to in this eulogy ("Sweet Hour of Prayer" or "Amazing Grace"), and write an essay
discussing the appropriateness of the reference in this eulogy.

CHRISTOPHER HITCHENS *When the King Saved God*

AFTER SHE WAS ELECTED the first female governor of Texas, in 1924, and got herself promptly embroiled in an argument about whether Spanish should be used in Lone Star schools, it is possible that Miriam A. "Ma" Ferguson did *not* say, "If the King's English was good enough for Jesus Christ, it's good enough for the children of Texas." I still rather hope that she did. But then, verification of quotations and sources is a tricky and sensitive thing. Abraham Lincoln lay dying in a room full of educated and literate men, in the age of the wireless telegraph, and not far from the offices of several newspapers, and we *still* do not know for sure, at the moment when his great pulse ceased to beat, whether his secretary of war, Edwin Stanton, said, "Now he belongs to the ages" or "Now he belongs to the angels."

Such questions of authenticity become even more fraught when they involve the word itself becoming flesh; the fulfillment of prophecy; the witnessing of miracles; the detection of the finger of God. Guesswork and approximation will not do: the resurrection cannot be half true or questionably attested. For the first 1,500 years of the Christian epoch, this problem of "authority," in both senses of that term, was solved by having the divine mandate wrapped up in languages that the majority of the congregation could not understand, and by having it presented to them by a special caste or class who alone possessed the mystery of celestial decoding.

Four hundred years ago, just as William Shakespeare was reaching the height of his powers and showing the new scope and variety of the English language, and just as "England" itself was becoming more of a nation-state and less an offshore dependency of Europe, an extraordinary committee of clergymen and scholars completed the task of rendering the Old and New Testaments into English, and claimed that the result was the "Authorized" or "King James" version. This was a fairly conservative attempt to stabilize the Crown and the kingdom, heal the breach between competing English and Scottish Christian sects, and bind the majesty of the King to his devout people. "The powers that be," it had Saint Paul saying in his Epistle to the Romans, "are ordained of God." This and other phrasings, not all of them so authoritarian and conformist, continue to echo in our language: "When I was a child, I spake as a child"; "Eat, drink, and be merry"; "From strength to strength"; "Grind the faces of the poor"; "salt of the earth"; "Our Father, which art in heaven." It's near impossible to imagine our idiom and vernacular, let alone our liturgy, without them. Not many committees in history have come up with such crystalline prose.

King James I, who brought the throne of Scotland along with him, was the son of Mary, Queen of Scots, and knew that his predecessor, Queen Elizabeth I,

Published in Vanity Fair *(2011), a magazine that covers fashion, current events, and culture.*

The title page of the New Testament in the first edition of the King James Bible, published by Robert Barker ("Printer to the King's most Excellent Maiestie") in 1611.

had been his mother's executioner. In Scotland, he had had to contend with extreme Puritans who were suspicious of monarchy and hated all Catholics. In England, he was faced with worldly bishops who were hostile to Puritans and jealous of their own privileges. Optimism, prosperity, and culture struck one note—Henry Hudson was setting off to the Northwest Passage, and Shakespeare's Globe Theater was drawing thoughtful crowds to see those dramas of power and legitimacy *Othello, King Lear,* and *The Tempest*—but terror and insecurity kept pace. Guy Fawkes and his fellow plotters, believed to be in league with the Pope, nearly succeeded in blowing up Parliament in 1605. Much of London was stricken with visitations of the bubonic plague, which, as Bishop Lancelot Andrewes (head of the committee of translators) noted with unease, appeared to strike the godly quite as often as it smote the sinner. The need was for a tempered version of God's word that engendered compromise and a sense of protection.

Bishop Andrewes and his colleagues, a mixture of clergymen and classi-   5
cists, were charged with revisiting the original Hebrew and Greek editions of the Old and New Testaments, along with the fragments of Aramaic that had found their way into the text. Understanding that their task was a patriotic and "nation-building" one (and impressed by the nascent idea of English Manifest

Destiny, whereby the English people had replaced the Hebrews as God's chosen), whenever they could translate any ancient word for "people" or "tribe" as "nation," they elected to do so. The term appears 454 times in this confident form of "the King's English." Meeting in Oxford and Cambridge college libraries for the most part, they often kept their notes in Latin. Their conservative and consensual project was politically short-lived: in a few years the land was to be convulsed with civil war, and the Puritan and parliamentary forces under Oliver Cromwell would sweep the head of King Charles I from his shoulders. But the translators' legacy remains, and it is paradoxically a revolutionary one, as well as a giant step in the maturing of English literature.

Imagining the most extreme form of totalitarianism in his *Nineteen Eighty-Four* dystopia, George Orwell[1] depicted a secret class of occult power holders (the Inner Party clustered around Big Brother) that would cement its eternal authority by recasting the entire language. In the tongue of "Newspeak," certain concepts of liberty and conscience would be literally impossible to formulate. And only within the most restricted circles of the regime would certain heretical texts, like Emmanuel Goldstein's manifesto, still be legible and available. I believe that Orwell, a strong admirer of the Protestant Reformation and the poetry of its hero John Milton,[2] was using as his original allegory the long struggle of English dissenters to have the Bible made available in a language that the people could read.

Until the early middle years of the 16th century, when King Henry VIII began to quarrel with Rome about the dialectics of divorce and decapitation, a short and swift route to torture and death was the attempt to print the Bible in English. It's a long and stirring story, and its crux is the head-to-head battle between Sir Thomas More and William Tyndale[3] (whose name in early life, I am proud to say, was William Hychyns). Their combat fully merits the term "fundamental." Infuriating More, Tyndale whenever possible was loyal to the Protestant spirit by correctly translating the word *ecclesia* to mean "the congregation" as an autonomous body, rather than "the church" as a sacrosanct institution above human law. In English churches, state-selected priests would merely incant the liturgy. Upon hearing the words "Hoc" and "corpus" (in the "For this is my body" passage), newly literate and impatient artisans in the pews would mockingly whisper, "Hocus-pocus," finding a tough slang term for the religious obfuscation at which they were beginning to chafe. The cold and righteous More, backed by his "Big Brother" the Pope and leading an inner party of spies and inquisitors, watched the Channel ports for smugglers risking everything to import sheets produced by Tyndale, who was forced to do his translating

---

1. English novelist and essayist (1903–1950); see "Shooting an Elephant" (pp. 750–55) and "Politics and the English Language" (pp. 510–19).

2. English poet and author of *Paradise Lost* (1603–1674).

3. More (1478–1535), author of *Utopia* and Lord Chancellor of England, was executed by Henry VIII for opposing Henry's separating England from the Roman Catholic Church; Tyndale (c. 1494–1536), first translator of the Bible into English.

and printing from exile. The rack and the rope were not stinted with dissenters, and eventually Tyndale himself was tracked down, strangled, and publicly burned. (Hilary Mantel's masterpiece historical novel, *Wolf Hall*, tells this exciting and gruesome story in such a way as to revise the shining image of "Saint" Thomas More, the "man for all seasons," almost out of existence. High time, in my view. The martyrdoms he inflicted upon others were more cruel and irrational than the one he sought and found for himself.)

Other translations into other languages, by Martin Luther himself, among others, slowly entered circulation. One of them, the so-called Geneva Bible, was a more Calvinist and Puritan English version than the book that King James commissioned, and was the edition which the Pilgrim Fathers, fleeing the cultural and religious war altogether, took with them to Plymouth Rock. Thus Governor Ma Ferguson was right in one respect: America was the first and only Christian society that could take an English Bible for granted, and never had to struggle for a popular translation of "the good book." The question, rather, became that of exactly *which* English version was to be accepted as the correct one. After many false starts and unsatisfactory printings, back in England, the Anglican conclave in 1611 adopted William Tyndale's beautiful rendering almost wholesale, and out of their zeal for compromise and stability ironically made a posthumous hero out of one of the greatest literary dissidents and subversives who ever lived.

Writing about his own fascination with cadence and rhythm in *Notes of a Native Son,* James Baldwin[4] said, "I hazard that the King James Bible, the rhetoric of the store-front church, something ironic and violent and perpetually understated in Negro speech . . . have something to do with me today; but I wouldn't stake my life on it." As a child of the black pulpit and chronicler of the Bible's huge role in the American oral tradition, Baldwin probably was "understating" at that very moment. And, as he very well knew, there had been times when biblical verses *did* involve, quite literally, the staking of one's life. This is why the nuances and details of translation were (and still are) of such huge moment. For example, in Isaiah 7:14 it is stated that, "behold, a virgin shall conceive, and bear a son, and shall call his name Immanuel." This is the scriptural warrant and prophecy for the impregnation of the Virgin Mary by the Holy Ghost. But the original Hebrew wording refers only to the pregnancy of an *almah,* or young woman. If the Hebrew language wants to identify virginity, it has other terms in which to do so. The implications are not merely textual. To translate is also to interpret; or, indeed, to lay down the law. (Incidentally, the American "Revised Standard Version" of 1952 replaced the word "virgin" with "young woman." It took the Fundamentalists until 1978 to restore the original misreading, in the now dominant "New International Version.")

Take an even more momentous example, cited by Adam Nicolson in his very fine book on the process, *God's Secretaries.* In the First Epistle to the Corinthians, Saint Paul reminds his readers of the fate that befell many backsliding

10

4. American writer (1924–1987); see "Stranger in the Village" (pp. 251–60).

pre-Christian Jews. He describes their dreadful punishments as having "happened unto them for ensamples," which in 1611 was a plain way of conveying the word "example" or "illustrative instance," or perhaps "lesson." However, the original Greek term was *typoi*, which by contrast may be rendered as "types" or "archetypes" and suggests that Jews were to be eternally punished for their special traits. This had been Saint Augustine's[5] harsh reading, followed by successive Roman Catholic editions. At least one of King James's translators wanted to impose that same collective punishment on the people of Moses, but was overruled. In the main existing text, the lenient word "ensamples" is given, with a marginal note in the original editions saying that "types" may also be meant. The English spirit of compromise at its best.

Then there are seemingly small but vital matters of emphasis, in which Tyndale did not win every round. Here is a famous verse which one might say was central to Christian teaching: "This is my Commandment, that you love one another, as I have loved you. / Greater love hath no man than this, that a man lay down his life for his friends." That's the King James version, which has echoed in the heads of many churchgoers until their last hour. Here is how the verse read when first translated by Tyndale: "This is my Commandment, that you love together as I have loved you. / Greater love than this hath no man, than that a man bestow his life for his friends."

I do not find that the "King's English" team improved much on the lovely simplicity of what they found. Tyndale has Jesus groping rather appealingly to make a general precept or principle out of a common bond, whereas the bishops and scholars are aiming to make an iron law out of love. In doing so they suggest strenuous martyrdom ("lay down," as if Jesus had been a sacrifice to his immediate circle only). Far more human and attractive, surely, is Tyndale's warm "bestow," which suggests that a life devoted to friendship is a noble thing in itself.

Tyndale, incidentally, was generally good on the love question. Take that same Epistle of Paul to the Corinthians, a few chapters later. For years, I would listen to it in chapel and wonder how an insipid, neuter word like "charity" could have gained such moral prestige. The King James version enjoins us that "now abideth faith, hope and charity, these three; but the greatest of these is charity." Tyndale had put "love" throughout, and even if your Greek is as poor as mine you will have to admit that it is a greatly superior capture of the meaning of that all-important original word *agape*. It was actually the frigid clerical bureaucrat Thomas More who had made this into one of the many disputations between himself and Tyndale, and in opting to accept his ruling it seems as if King James's committee also hoped to damp down the risky, ardent spontaneity of unconditional love and replace it with an idea of stern duty. Does not the notion of compulsory love, in any form, have something grotesque and fanatical about it?

Most recent English translations have finally dropped More and the King and gone with Tyndale on this central question, but often at the cost of making "love" appear too husky and sentimental. Thus the "Good News Bible" for

5. Christian philosopher and theologian (354–430 C. E.).

American churches, first published in 1966: "Love never gives up; and its faith, hope and patience never fail." This doesn't read at all like the outcome of a struggle to discern the essential meaning of what is perhaps our most numinous word. It more resembles a smiley-face Dale Carnegie[6] reassurance. And, as with everything else that's designed to be instant, modern, and "accessible," it goes out of date (and out of *time*) faster than Wisconsin cheddar.

Though I am sometimes reluctant to admit it, there really *is* something   15 "timeless" in the Tyndale/King James synthesis. For generations, it provided a common stock of references and allusions, rivaled only by Shakespeare in this respect. It resounded in the minds and memories of literate people, as well as of those who acquired it only by listening. From the stricken beach of Dunkirk[7] in 1940, faced with a devil's choice between annihilation and surrender, a British officer sent a cable back home. It contained the three words "but if not . . ." All of those who received it were at once aware of what it signified. In the Book of Daniel, the Babylonian tyrant Nebuchadnezzar tells the three Jewish heretics Shadrach, Meshach, and Abednego that if they refuse to bow to his sacred idol they will be flung into a "burning fiery furnace." They made him an answer: "If it be so, our god whom we serve is able to deliver us from the burning fiery furnace, and he will deliver us out of thy hand, o King. / *But if not*, be it known unto thee, o king, that we will not serve thy gods, nor worship the golden image which thou hast set up."

A culture that does not possess this common store of image and allegory will be a perilously thin one. To seek restlessly to update it or make it "relevant" is to miss the point, like yearning for a hip-hop Shakespeare. "Man is born unto trouble as the sparks fly upward," says the Book of Job. Want to try to improve that for Twitter? And so bleak and spare and fatalistic—almost non-religious— are the closing verses of Ecclesiastes that they were read at the Church of England funeral service the unbeliever George Orwell had requested in his will: "Also when they shall be afraid of that which is high, and fears shall be in the way, and the almond tree shall flourish, and the grasshopper shall be a burden, and desire shall fail: because man goeth to his long home. . . . Or ever the silver cord be loosed, or the golden bowl be broken, or the pitcher be broken at the fountain, or the wheel broken at the cistern. / Then shall the dust return to the earth as it was."

At my father's funeral I chose to read a similarly non-sermonizing part of the New Testament, this time an injunction from Saint Paul's Epistle to the Philippians: "Finally, brethren, whatsoever things are true, whatsoever things are honest, whatsoever things are just, whatsoever things are pure, whatsoever things are lovely, whatsoever things are of good report; if there be any virtue, and if there be any praise, think on these things."

6. American author (1888–1955) of the best-selling self-help book *How to Win Friends and Influence People.*

7. Site of British resistance and retreat against the German army during World War II from May to June 1940.

As much philosophical as spiritual, with its conditional and speculative "ifs" and its closing advice—always italicized in my mind since first I heard it—to *think* and reflect on such matters: this passage was the labor of men who had wrought deeply with ideas and concepts. I now pluck down from my shelf the American Bible Society's "Contemporary English Version," which I picked up at an evangelical "Promise Keepers" rally on the Mall in Washington in 1997. Claiming to be faithful to the spirit of the King James translation, it keeps its promise in this way: "Finally, my friends, keep your minds on whatever is true, pure, right, holy, friendly and proper. Don't ever stop thinking about what is truly worthwhile and worthy of praise."

Pancake-flat: suited perhaps to a basement meeting of A.A., these words could not hope to penetrate the torpid, resistant fog in the mind of a 16-year-old boy, as their original had done for me. There's perhaps a slightly ingratiating obeisance to gender neutrality in the substitution of "my friends" for "brethren," but to suggest that Saint Paul, of all people, was gender-neutral is to rewrite the history as well as to rinse out the prose. When the Church of England effectively dropped King James, in the 1960s, and issued what would become the "New English Bible," T. S. Eliot[8] commented that the result was astonishing "in its combination of the vulgar, the trivial and the pedantic." (Not surprising from the author of *For Lancelot Andrewes*.) This has been true of every other stilted, patronizing, literal-minded attempt to shift the translation's emphasis from plangent poetry to utilitarian prose.

20   T. S. Eliot left America (and his annoyingly colorless Unitarian family) to seek the traditionalist roots of liturgical and literary tradition in England. Coming in the opposite direction across the broad Atlantic, the King James Bible slowly overhauled and overtook the Geneva version, and, as the Pilgrim-type mini-theocracies of New England withered away, became one of the very few books from which almost any American could quote something. Paradoxically, this made it easy to counterfeit. When Joseph Smith[9] began to fabricate his Book of Mormon, in the late 1820s, "translating" it from no known language, his copy of King James was never far from his side. He plagiarized 27,000 words more or less straight from the original, including several biblical stories lifted almost in their entirety, and the throat-clearing but vaguely impressive phrase "and it came to pass" is used at least 2,000 times. Such "borrowing" was a way of lending much-needed "tone" to the racket. Not long afterward, William Miller[10] excited gigantic crowds with the news that the Second Coming of Jesus would occur in 1843. An associate followed up with an 1844 due date. These disappointed prophecies were worked out from marginal notes in Miller's copy of the King James edition, which he quarried for apocalyptic evidence. (There had always been those, from the earliest days, when it was being decided which

---

8. American poet and writer (1888–1965).

9. Founder of the Church of Jesus Christ of Latter-day Saints (1805–1844).

10. American preacher (1782–1849) whose prophecy about Jesus's second coming in 1844 eventually led to the foundation of the Seventh-day Adventists and Advent Christians.

parts of the Bible were divinely inspired and which were not, who had striven to leave out the Book of Revelation. Martin Luther himself declined to believe that it was the work of the Holy Spirit. But there Christianity still is, well and truly stuck with it.) So, of the many Christian heresies which were born in the New World and not imported from Europe, at least three—the Mormons, or Latter-Day Saints; the Millerites, or Seventh-Day Adventists; and their schismatic product the Jehovah's Witnesses—are indirectly mutated from a pious attempt to bring religious consensus to Jacobean England.

Not to over-prize consensus, it does possess certain advantages over randomness and chaos. Since the appearance of the so-called "Good News Bible," there have been no fewer than 48 English translations published in the United States. And the rate shows no sign of slackening. Indeed, the trend today is toward what the trade calls "niche Bibles." These include the "Couples Bible," "One Year New Testament for Busy Moms," "Extreme Teen Study Bible," "Policeman's Bible," and—somehow unavoidably—the "Celebrate Recovery Bible." (Give them credit for one thing: the biblical sales force knows how to "be fruitful and multiply.") In this cut-price spiritual cafeteria, interest groups and even individuals can have their own customized version of God's word. But there will no longer be a culture of the kind which instantly recognized what Lincoln meant when he spoke of "a house divided." The gradual eclipse of a single structure has led, not to a new clarity, but to a new Babel.

Those who opposed the translation of the Bible into the vernacular—rather like those Catholics who wish the Mass were still recited in Latin, or those Muslims who regard it as profane to render the Koran out of Arabic—were afraid that the mystic potency of incantation and ritual would be lost, and that daylight would be let in upon magic. They also feared that if God's word became too everyday and commonplace it would become less impressive, or less able to inspire awe. But the reverse turns out to have been the case, at least in this instance. The Tyndale/King James translation, even if all its copies were to be burned, would still live on in our language through its transmission by way of Shakespeare and Milton and Bunyan and Coleridge, and also by way of beloved popular idioms such as "fatted calf" and "pearls before swine." It turned out to be rather more than the sum of its ancient predecessors, as well as a repository and edifice of language which towers above its successors. Its abandonment by the Church of England establishment, which hoped to refill its churches and ended up denuding them, is yet another demonstration that religion is manmade, with inky human fingerprints all over its supposedly inspired and unalterable texts. Ma Ferguson was right in her way. She just didn't know how many Englishmen and how many Englishes, and how many Jesus stories and Jesuses, there were to choose from.

MLA CITATION

Hitchens, Christopher. "When the King Saved God." 2011. *The Norton Reader: An Anthology of Nonfiction*. Ed. Melissa A. Goldthwaite et al. 14th ed. New York: Norton, 2016. 956–63. Print.

QUESTIONS

1. Why do you think Christopher Hitchens opens with two examples of what people might or might not have said? How does Hitchens's first paragraph prepare readers for his argument?

2. Hitchens provides both historical context and examples of translations he claims were made for political reasons. How much of the information Hitchens provides here was new to you? Provide examples.

3. Compare a verse or selection in two or more translated texts. You may use different translations of the Bible or, perhaps, a poem from another language that has been translated into English in different ways. Write an essay in which you compare and contrast the different translations, showing the significance of different word choices.

LEON WIESELTIER *Ring the Bells*

FOR A LONG TIME I did not hear the beauty of church bells; or more accurately, I did not wish to hear it. They sounded only like Christianity, which in my early years was a vexing triumphalist sound—the pealing of history, from which my honor as a Jew required me to recoil. When the tintinnabulations of the Church of St. Francis Xavier on Avenue O reached my ears, they brought the message that I was a member of a minority. I was not acquainted with the liturgical schedule of the church, with the practical reason for the ringings—though I might have surmised, based on my own experience of the aesthetically nullifying effects of the repetitions of ritual, that Christians who heard the bells religiously, in their ancient role as a signaling device, also did not attend to their beauty. When the bells sounded, it was a time for prayer, not for music. Art demands detachment, but religion forbids it. (There is an old joke about two jazz musicians walking along a street when a huge bell falls out of a church steeple and crashes disastrously behind them. "What was that?" one asks, with alarm. "F sharp," the other replies.)

Still, no soul is only Jewish or only Christian, and eventually the beauty got to me. And then I had another problem. It happened in graduate school, when life is slow enough for spiritual incidents. I was loitering in the magnificent little cloister at Magdalen College. It was a late afternoon in an Oxford autumn, and the yellow spears of the waning sun were landing in the severe stone geometries of the place and striking the walls like friendly lightning. Suddenly I heard the harmonies of a choir rehearsing evensong—a piece by Byrd,[1] I

Published in the New Republic (2008), a Washington-based journal of politics and cultural criticism, where Leon Wieseltier was literary editor from 1983 to 2014.

1. William Byrd (c. 1540–43–1623), English Renaissance composer of church music.

later learned—in an adjoining chapel. Fixed by the lights and the sounds, I was overcome, and elated by, an unfamiliar contentment, and I thought: this is Christian beauty and I want it. I was shocked by the thought. I remember thinking also that we, I mean the Jews, have nothing like this. This was another variety of minoritarian torment. Soon the joy passed, perhaps because the singing ceased, and my confusion passed with it. As I strolled home along Addison's Walk,[2] I got it clear in my mind that Christianity may in some of its expressions be beautiful, but beauty is not Christian. Religious or cultural or national definitions of beauty are conceptual mistakes. So I returned, you might say, to my senses. And the next day I returned to Magdalen to consult the chapel schedule, so that I might hear the choir again.

I was reminded of the evolution of my relationship to the ravishments of other traditions when I read about the controversy at Harvard about the broadcast of the Muslim call to prayer in Harvard Yard. It was sounded from the steps of Widener Library—where a great Jewish scholar once spent many decades in the groundbreaking study of early Islamic philosophy—for several days during Islam Awareness Week. (Is anybody not aware of Islam?) The sound of the adhan[3] in the quads startled many people, and provoked ferocious opposition. An editorial in the *Crimson*[4] denounced it as an infringement upon the liberty of others, who were forced to listen to an affirmation of a faith in which they do not believe. What troubled the eloquent authors of the editorial was the text of the summons, which included the words "I bear witness that there is no lord except God" and "I bear witness that Mohammed is the Messenger of God." "This puts the adhan in a different class of expression than, say, the sounding of church bells or the displaying of a menorah," they maintained, "because it publicly advances a theological position." Indeed it does, though it is important to add that almost all of the alleged victims of this aural coercion could not understand a word of it. For all they knew, they were listening to a recipe for kanafi.[5] And the menorah is, in its fiery silence, a religious symbol of a religious holiday, even if most American Jews prefer to think of the occasion historically or commercially. Is the sight of it, therefore, an optical coercion? As for church bells, see above. Moreover, the secular integrity of the setting was long ago surrendered. In the middle of it stands an imposing Christianish chapel, which, despite its hospitality to people of all faiths, could never be mistaken for a synagogue or a mosque. Years ago I was among a company of Jews—I think it included the dean of the faculty, though I may be mistaken— who festively carried a Torah through Harvard Yard, and this was no more "halacha[6] at Harvard" than the adhan is "sharia at Harvard." Even before there was multiculturalism, there was respect for human variety and pleasure in it.

2. Footpath around a small island in the River Cherwell on the grounds of Magdalen College, Oxford. Named for the author Joseph Addison (1672–1719).

3. Call to worship for Muslims.

4. Harvard University's student-run newspaper.

5. Middle Eastern dessert.

6. Guide to all aspects of Jewish life based on interpretations of the Bible.

An open civil space will always be cacophonous. There will be affirmation and alienation, sometimes even within a single individual; and there will be indifference, which is in its way one of the accomplishments of pluralism. When I was at college, the arrival of spring was reliably announced by the defiant blasting of "Sympathy for the Devil" from dorm-room loudspeakers turned toward the campus. I did not share the theological position that it advanced, but I was exhilarated. In a Dionysian frenzy I played frisbee until dark.

There are also other controversies of diversity at Harvard: one of the university gyms has been restricted for six hours a week for the use of Muslim women whose religious observance does not permit them to work out in the company of men. As a matter of principle, this troubles me—I believe in integration, and in the challenges that the experience of integration presents to the insularity of traditional identities (Woodrow Wilson once remarked that the purpose of a college education is to make a man as much unlike his father as possible), and the customization of places according to identity can be carried to absurd and unfair lengths; but these Muslim women would not be at Harvard if they, too, did not in some way believe in integration, and it seems humane to allow their abs some respite from the pressure. But the adhan, like the church bells, sounds magnificently American to me. Indeed, the ringing of the bells began, long before democracy, in a proto-democratic moment, in 313, when the Edict of Milan established the "Peace of the Church" and the persecution of Christians in the Roman Empire came to an end, and Christians could be summoned publicly to prayer. And who was Constantine compared to Lincoln? As I write, the bells of Lincoln's church across the street from my office are chiming, and sweetening yet another hour of this Jew's day.

MLA CITATION

Wieseltier, Leon. "Ring the Bells." 2008. *The Norton Reader: An Anthology of Nonfiction*. Ed. Melissa A. Goldthwaite et al. 14th ed. New York: Norton, 2016. 964–66. Print.

QUESTIONS

1. Leon Wieseltier takes a commonplace urban occurrence—the ringing of church bells—and turns it into a meditation on diversity. Do you think he succeeds? Why or why not?

2. Wieseltier includes different perspectives on whether religious symbols (both auditory and visual) should be allowed on college campuses. What is Wieseltier's position on this question? What is yours? What factors influence your answer?

3. What should be the place of religious symbols on a college campus? Choose a specific example with which you have experience, and write an editorial for your college newspaper that shows your position.

HENRY DAVID THOREAU *Where I Lived, and What I Lived For*

WHEN I FIRST took up my abode in the woods, that is, began to spend my nights as well as days there, which, by accident, was on Independence day, or the fourth of July, 1845, my house was not finished for winter, but was merely a defence against the rain, without plastering or chimney, the walls being of rough weather-stained boards, with wide chinks, which made it cool at night. The upright white hewn studs and freshly planed door and window casings gave it a clean and airy look, especially in the morning, when its timbers were saturated with dew, so that I fancied that by noon some sweet gum would exude from them. To my imagination it retained throughout the day more or less of this auroral character, reminding me of a certain house on a mountain which I had visited the year before. This was an airy and unplastered cabin, fit to entertain a travelling god, and where a goddess might trail her garments. The winds which passed over my dwelling were such as sweep over the ridges of mountains, bearing the broken strains, or celestial parts only, of terrestrial music. The morning wind forever blows, the poem of creation is uninterrupted; but few are the ears that hear it. Olympus[1] is but the outside of the earth every where.

The only house I had been the owner of before, if I except a boat, was a tent, which I used occasionally when making excursions in the summer, and this is still rolled up in my garret; but the boat, after passing from hand to hand, has gone down the stream of time. With this more substantial shelter about me, I had made some progress toward settling in the world. This frame, so slightly clad, was a sort of crystallization around me, and reacted on the builder. It was suggestive somewhat as a picture in outlines. I did not need to go out doors to take the air, for the atmosphere within had lost none of its freshness. It was not so much within doors as behind a door where I sat, even in the rainiest weather. The Harivansa[2] says, "An abode without birds is like a meat without seasoning." Such was not my abode, for I found myself suddenly neighbor to the birds; not by having imprisoned one, but having caged myself near them. I was not only nearer to some of those which commonly frequent the garden and the orchard, but to those wilder and more thrilling songsters of the forest which never, or rarely, serenade a villager,—the wood-thrush, the veery, the scarlet tanager, the field-sparrow, the whippoorwill, and many others.

From Henry David Thoreau's book Walden *(1854), an account of his life in a small cabin on Walden Pond, outside the village of Concord, Massachusetts; in* Walden *Thoreau not only describes his life in the woods but also develops a philosophy for living.*

1. Mountain where the Greek gods dwell.
2. Fifth-century epic poem about the Hindu god Krishna.

I was seated by the shore of a small pond, about a mile and a half south of the village of Concord and somewhat higher than it, in the midst of an extensive wood between that town and Lincoln, and about two miles south of that our only field known to fame, Concord Battle Ground;[3] but I was so low in the woods that the opposite shore, half a mile off, like the rest, covered with wood, was my most distant horizon. For the first week, whenever I looked out on the pond it impressed me like a tarn high up on the side of a mountain, its bottom far above the surface of other lakes, and, as the sun arose, I saw it throwing off its nightly clothing of mist, and here and there, by degrees, its soft ripples or its smooth reflecting surface was revealed, while the mists, like ghosts, were stealthily withdrawing in every direction into the woods, as at the breaking up of some nocturnal conventicle. The very dew seemed to hang upon the trees later into the day than usual, as on the sides of mountains.

This small lake was of most value as a neighbor in the intervals of a gentle rain storm in August, when, both air and water being perfectly still, but the sky overcast, mid-afternoon had all the serenity of evening, and the wood-thrush sang around, and was heard from shore to shore. A lake like this is never smoother than at such a time; and the clear portion of the air above it being shallow and darkened by clouds, the water, full of light and reflections, becomes a lower heaven itself so much the more important. From a hill top near by, where the wood had been recently cut off, there was a pleasing vista southward across the pond, through a wide indentation in the hills which form the shore there, where their opposite sides sloping toward each other suggested a stream flowing out in that direction through a wooded valley, but stream there was none. That way I looked between and over the near green hills to some distant and higher ones in the horizon, tinged with blue. Indeed, by standing on tiptoe I could catch a glimpse of some of the peaks of the still bluer and more distant mountain ranges in the north-west, those true-blue coins from heaven's own mint, and also of some portion of the village. But in other directions, even from this point, I could not see over or beyond the woods which surrounded me. It is well to have some water in your neighborhood, to give buoyancy to and float the earth. One value even of the smallest well is, that when you look into it you see that earth is not continent but insular. This is as important as that it keeps butter cool. When I looked across the pond from this peak toward the Sudbury meadows, which in time of flood I distinguished elevated perhaps by a mirage in their seething valley, like a coin in a basin, all the earth beyond the pond appeared like a thin crust insulated and floated even by this small sheet of intervening water, and I was reminded that this on which I dwelt was but *dry land*.

5   Though the view from my door was still more contracted, I did not feel crowded or confined in the least. There was pasture enough for my imagination. The low shrub-oak plateau to which the opposite shore arose, stretched

3. Site of the famous Battle of Concord, April 19, 1775, considered the start of the American Revolution.

away toward the prairies of the West and the steppes of Tartary,[4] affording ample room for all the roving families of men. "There are none happy in the world but beings who enjoy freely a vast horizon,"—said Damodara,[5] when his herds required new and larger pastures.

Both place and time were changed, and I dwelt nearer to those parts of the universe and to those eras in history which had most attracted me. Where I lived was as far off as many a region viewed nightly by astronomers. We are wont to imagine rare and delectable places in some remote and more celestial corner of the system, behind the constellation of Cassiopeia's Chair, far from noise and disturbance. I discovered that my house actually had its site in such a withdrawn, but forever new and unprofaned, part of the universe. If it were worth the while to settle in those parts near to the Pleiades or the Hyades, to Aldebaran or Altair,[6] then I was really there, or at an equal remoteness from the life which I had left behind, dwindled and twinkling with as fine a ray to my nearest neighbor, and to be seen only in moonless nights by him. Such was that part of creation where I had squatted;—

> "There was a shepherd that did live,
>   And held his thoughts as high
> As were the mounts whereon his flocks
>   Did hourly feed him by."[7]

What should we think of the shepherd's life if his flocks always wandered to higher pastures than his thoughts?

Every morning was a cheerful invitation to make my life of equal simplicity, and I may say innocence, with Nature herself. I have been as sincere a worshipper of Aurora[8] as the Greeks. I got up early and bathed in the pond; that was a religious exercise, and one of the best things which I did. They say that characters were engraven on the bathing tub of king Tching-thang[9] to this effect: "Renew thyself completely each day; do it again, and again, and forever again." I can understand that. Morning brings back the heroic ages. I was as much affected by the faint hum of a mosquito making its invisible and unimaginable tour through my apartment at earliest dawn, when I was sitting with door and windows open, as I could be by any trumpet that ever sang of fame. It was Homer's[10] requiem; itself an Iliad and Odyssey in the air, singing its own wrath and wanderings. There was something cosmical about it; a standing

---

4. Region that includes what is today northern Pakistan.

5. One of the many names of Krishna, the Hindu god.

6. Cassiopeia's Chair, the Pleiades, and the Hyades are constellations; Aldebaran and Altair are stars.

7. Lines from "The Shepherd's Love for Philladay," from Thomas Evan's *Old Ballads* (1810).

8. Goddess of dawn.

9. Confucius (551–479 B.C.E.), Chinese philosopher.

10. Greek epic poet (eighth century B.C.E.), author of the *Odyssey* and the *Iliad*.

advertisement, till forbidden, of the everlasting vigor and fertility of the world. The morning, which is the most memorable season of the day, is the awakening hour. Then there is least somnolence in us; and for an hour, at least, some part of us awakes which slumbers all the rest of the day and night. Little is to be expected of that day, if it can be called a day, to which we are not awakened by our Genius, but by the mechanical nudgings of some servitor, are not awakened by our own newly-acquired force and aspirations from within, accompanied by the undulations of celestial music, instead of factory bells, and a fragrance filling the air—to a higher life than we fell asleep from; and thus the darkness bear its fruit, and prove itself to be good, no less than the light. That man who does not believe that each day contains an earlier, more sacred, and auroral hour than he has yet profaned, has despaired of life, and is pursuing a descending and darkening way. After a partial cessation of his sensuous life, the soul of man, or its organs rather, are reinvigorated each day, and his Genius tries again what noble life it can make. All memorable events, I should say, transpire in morning time and in a morning atmosphere. The Vedas[11] say, "All intelligences awake with the morning." Poetry and art, and the fairest and most memorable of the actions of men, date from such an hour. All poets and heroes, like Memnon,[12] are the children of Aurora, and emit their music at sunrise. To him whose elastic and vigorous thought keeps pace with the sun, the day is a perpetual morning. It matters not what the clocks say or the attitudes and labors of men. Morning is when I am awake and there is a dawn in me. Moral reform is the effort to throw off sleep. Why is it that men give so poor an account of their day if they have not been slumbering? They are not such poor calculators. If they had not been overcome with drowsiness they would have performed something. The millions are awake enough for physical labor; but only one in a million is awake enough for effective intellectual exertion, only one in a hundred millions to a poetic or divine life. To be awake is to be alive. I have never yet met a man who was quite awake. How could I have looked him in the face?

We must learn to reawaken and keep ourselves awake, not by mechanical aids, but by an infinite expectation of the dawn, which does not forsake us in our soundest sleep. I know of no more encouraging fact than the unquestionable ability of man to elevate his life by a conscious endeavor. It is something to be able to paint a particular picture, or to carve a statue, and so to make a few objects beautiful; but it is far more glorious to carve and paint the very atmosphere and medium through which we look, which morally we can do. To affect the quality of the day, that is the highest of arts. Every man is tasked to make his life, even in its details, worthy of the contemplation of his most elevated and critical hour. If we refused, or rather used up, such paltry information as we get, the oracles would distinctly inform us how this might be done.

11. Sacred texts that contain hymns, incantations, and rituals from ancient India.

12. Son of Aurora, the goddess of dawn, and a mortal, Memnon was king of the Ethiopians; he was slain by Achilles while fighting the Greeks in Troy. When he died, his mother's tears formed the morning dew.

I went to the woods because I wished to live deliberately, to front only the essential facts of life, and see if I could not learn what it had to teach, and not, when I came to die, discover that I had not lived. I did not wish to live what was not life, living is so dear, nor did I wish to practise resignation, unless it was quite necessary. I wanted to live deep and suck out all the marrow of life, to live so sturdily and Spartan-like as to put to rout all that was not life, to cut a broad swath and shave close, to drive life into a corner, and reduce it to its lowest terms, and, if it proved to be mean, why then to get the whole and genuine meanness of it, and publish its meanness to the world; or if it were sublime, to know it by experience, and be able to give a true account of it in my next excursion. For most men, it appears to me, are in a strange uncertainty about it, whether it is of the devil or of God, and have *somewhat hastily* concluded that it is the chief end of man here to "glorify God and enjoy him forever."

Still we live meanly, like ants; though the fable tells us that we were long   10
ago changed into men;[13] like pygmies we fight with cranes;[14] it is error upon error, and clout upon clout, and our best virtue has for its occasion a superfluous and evitable wretchedness. Our life is frittered away by detail. An honest man has hardly need to count more than his ten fingers, or in extreme cases he may add his ten toes, and lump the rest. Simplicity, simplicity, simplicity! I say, let your affairs be as two or three, and not a hundred or a thousand; instead of a million count half a dozen, and keep your accounts on your thumb nail. In the midst of this chopping sea of civilized life, such are the clouds and storms and quicksands and thousand-and-one items to be allowed for, that a man has to live, if he would not founder and go to the bottom and not make his port at all, by dead reckoning, and he must be a great calculator indeed who succeeds. Simplify, simplify. Instead of three meals a day, if it be necessary eat but one; instead of a hundred dishes, five; and reduce other things in proportion. Our life is like a German Confederacy, made up of petty states, with its boundary forever fluctuating, so that even a German cannot tell you how it is bounded at any moment. The nation itself, with all its so called internal improvements, which, by the way, are all external and superficial, is just such an unwieldy and overgrown establishment, cluttered with furniture and tripped up by its own traps, ruined by luxury and heedless expense, by want of calculation and a worthy aim, as the million households in the land; and the only cure for it as for them is in a rigid economy, a stern and more than Spartan simplicity of life and elevation of purpose. It lives too fast. Men think that it is essential that the *Nation* have commerce, and export ice, and talk through a telegraph, and ride thirty miles an hour, without a doubt, whether *they* do or not; but whether we should live like baboons or like men, is a little uncertain. If we do not get our sleepers, and forge rails, and devote days and nights to the work, but go to tinkering upon our *lives* to improve *them*, who will build railroads? And if railroads are not built, how shall we get to heaven in season? But if we stay at home

13. In a Greek fable Aeacus asks Zeus to increase a scanty population by turning ants into men.

14. From the *Iliad* by Homer, in which the Trojans are represented as the cranes.

ınd mind our business, who will want railroads? We do not ride on the railroad; it rides upon us. Did you ever think what those sleepers are that underlie the railroad? Each one is a man, an Irishman, or a Yankee man. The rails are laid on them, and they are covered with sand, and the cars run smoothly over them. They are sound sleepers, I assure you. And every few years a new lot is laid down and run over; so that, if some have the pleasure of riding on a rail, others have the misfortune to be ridden upon. And when they run over a man that is walking in his sleep, a supernumerary sleeper in the wrong position, and wake him up, they suddenly stop the cars, and make a hue and cry about it, as if this were an exception. I am glad to know that it takes a gang of men for every five miles to keep the sleepers down and level in their beds as it is, for this is a sign that they may sometime get up again.

Why should we live with such hurry and waste of life? We are determined to be starved before we are hungry. Men say that a stitch in time saves nine, and so they take a thousand stitches to-day to save nine to-morrow. As for *work*, we haven't any of any consequence. We have the Saint Vitus' dance,[15] and cannot possibly keep our heads still. If I should only give a few pulls at the parish bell-rope, as for a fire, that is, without setting the bell, there is hardly a man on his farm in the outskirts of Concord, notwithstanding that press of engagements which was his excuse so many times this morning, nor a boy, nor a woman, I might almost say, but would forsake all and follow that sound, not mainly to save property from the flames, but, if we will confess the truth, much more to see it burn, since burn it must, and we, be it known, did not set it on fire,—or to see it put out, and have a hand in it, if that is done as handsomely; yes, even if it were the parish church itself. Hardly a man takes a half hour's nap after dinner, but when he wakes he holds up his head and asks, "What's the news?" as if the rest of mankind had stood his sentinels. Some give directions to be waked every half hour, doubtless for no other purpose; and then, to pay for it, they tell what they have dreamed. After a night's sleep the news is as indispensable as the breakfast. "Pray tell me any thing new that has happened to a man any where on this globe,"—and he reads it over his coffee and rolls, that a man has had his eyes gouged out this morning on the Wachito River;[16] never dreaming the while that he lives in the dark unfathomed mammoth cave of this world, and has but the rudiment of an eye himself.

For my part, I could easily do without the post-office. I think that there are very few important communications made through it. To speak critically, I never received more than one or two letters in my life—I wrote this some years ago—that were worth the postage. The penny-post is, commonly, an institution through which you seriously offer a man that penny for his thoughts which is so often safely offered in jest. And I am sure that I never read any memorable news in a newspaper. If we read of one man robbed, or murdered, or killed by accident, or one house burned, or one vessel wrecked, or one steamboat

---

15. Nervous disorder marked by jerky, spasmodic movements that occurs in cases of rheumatic fever involving the connective tissue of the brain.

16. In southern Arkansas.

blown up, or one cow run over on the Western Railroad, or one mad dog killed, or one lot of grasshoppers in the winter,—we never need read of another. One is enough. If you are acquainted with the principle, what do you care for a myriad instances and applications? To a philosopher all *news*, as it is called, is gossip, and they who edit and read it are old women over their tea. Yet not a few are greedy after this gossip. There was such a rush, as I hear, the other day at one of the offices to learn the foreign news by the last arrival, that several large squares of plate glass belonging to the establishment were broken by the pressure,—news which I seriously think a ready wit might write a twelvemonth or twelve years beforehand with sufficient accuracy. As for Spain, for instance, if you know how to throw in Don Carlos and the Infanta, and Don Pedro and Seville and Granada, from time to time in the right proportions,—they may have changed the names a little since I saw the papers,—and serve up a bull-fight when other entertainments fail, it will be true to the letter, and give us as good an idea of the exact state of ruin of things in Spain as the most succinct and lucid reports under this head in the newspapers: and as for England, almost the last significant scrap of news from that quarter was the revolution of 1649; and if you have learned the history of her crops for an average year, you never need attend to that thing again, unless your speculations are of a merely pecuniary character. If one may judge who rarely looks into the newspapers, nothing new does ever happen in foreign parts, a French revolution not excepted.

What news! how much more important to know what that is which was never old! "Kieou-he-yu (great dignitary of the state of Wei) sent a man to Khoung-tseu to know his news. Khoung-tseu caused the messenger to be seated near him, and questioned him in these terms: What is your master doing? The messenger answered with respect: My master desires to diminish the number of his faults, but he cannot come to the end of them. The messenger being gone, the philosopher remarked: What a worthy messenger! What a worthy messenger!" The preacher, instead of vexing the ears of drowsy farmers on their day of rest at the end of the week,—for Sunday is the fit conclusion of an ill-spent week, and not the fresh and brave beginning of a new one,—with this one other draggle-tail of a sermon, should shout with thundering voice,—"Pause! Avast! Why so seeming fast, but deadly slow?"

Shams and delusions are esteemed for soundest truths, while reality is fabulous. If men would steadily observe realities only, and not allow themselves to be deluded, life, to compare it with such things as we know, would be like a fairy tale and the Arabian Nights' Entertainments. If we respected only what is inevitable and has a right to be, music and poetry would resound along the streets. When we are unhurried and wise, we perceive that only great and worthy things have any permanent and absolute existence,—that petty fears and petty pleasures are but the shadow of the reality. This is always exhilarating and sublime. By closing the eyes and slumbering, and consenting to be deceived by shows, men establish and confirm their daily life of routine and habit every where, which still is built on purely illusory foundations. Children, who play life, discern its true law and relations more clearly than men, who fail to live it worthily, but who think that they are wiser by experience, that is, by failure. I have read in a Hindoo book, that "There was a king's son, who, being expelled in infancy from his native city, was brought up by a forester, and, growing up to maturity in that state, imagined himself to belong to the barbarous race with which he lived. One of his father's ministers having discovered him, revealed to him what he was, and the misconception of his character was removed, and he knew himself to be a prince. So soul," continues the Hindoo philosopher, "from the circumstances in which it is placed, mistakes its own character, until the truth is revealed to it by some holy teacher, and then it knows itself to be *Brahme*."[17] I perceive that we inhabitants of New England live this mean life that we do because our vision does not penetrate the surface of things. We think that that *is* which *appears* to be. If a man should walk through this town and see only the reality, where, think you, would the "Mill-dam"[18] go to? If he should give us an account of the realities he beheld there, we should not recognize the place in his description. Look at a meeting-house, or a court-house, or a jail, or a shop, or a dwelling-house, and say what that thing really is before a true gaze, and they would all go to pieces in your account of them. Men esteem truth remote, in the outskirts of the system, behind the farthest star, before Adam and after the last man. In eternity there is indeed something true and sublime. But all these times and places and occasions are now and here. God himself culminates in the present moment, and will never be more divine in the lapse of all the ages. And we are enabled to apprehend at all what is sublime and noble only by the perpetual instilling and drenching of the reality that surrounds us. The universe constantly and obediently answers to our conceptions; whether we travel fast or slow, the track is laid for us. Let us spend our lives in conceiving then. The poet or the artist never yet had so fair and noble a design but some of his posterity at least could accomplish it.

15   Let us spend one day as deliberately as Nature, and not be thrown off the track by every nutshell and mosquito's wing that falls on the rails. Let us rise early and fast, or break fast, gently and without perturbation; let company come and let company go, let the bells ring and the children cry,—determined to make a day of it. Why should we knock under and go with the stream? Let us not be upset and overwhelmed in that terrible rapid and whirlpool called a dinner, situated in the meridian shallows. Weather this danger and you are safe, for the rest of the way is down hill. With unrelaxed nerves, with morning vigor, sail by it, looking another way, tied to the mast like Ulysses. If the engine whistles, let it whistle till it is hoarse for its pains. If the bell rings, why should we run? We will consider what kind of music they are like. Let us settle ourselves, and work and wedge our feet downward through the mud and slush of opinion, and prejudice, and tradition, and delusion, and appearance, that alluvion which covers the globe, through Paris and London, through New York and Boston and Concord, through church and state, through poetry and philosophy and religion, till we come to a hard bottom and rocks in place, which we can call *reality*, and say, This is, and no mistake; and then begin, having a

17. Supreme soul, the essence of all being, in Hinduism.

18. Dam built in 1635 in the town of Concord on the site of an Indian fishing weir.

point d'appui,[19] below freshet and frost and fire, a place where you might found a wall or a state, or set a lamp-post safely, or perhaps a gauge, not a Nilometer,[20] but a Realometer, that future ages might know how deep a freshet of shams and appearances had gathered from time to time. If you stand right fronting and face to face to a fact, you will see the sun glimmer on both its surfaces, as if it were a cimeter,[21] and feel its sweet edge dividing you through the heart and marrow, and so you will happily conclude your mortal career. Be it life or death, we crave only reality. If we are really dying, let us hear the rattle in our throats and feel cold in the extremities; if we are alive, let us go about our business.

Time is but the stream I go a-fishing in. I drink at it; but while I drink I see the sandy bottom and detect how shallow it is. Its thin current slides away, but eternity remains. I would drink deeper; fish in the sky, whose bottom is pebbly with stars. I cannot count one. I know not the first letter of the alphabet. I have always been regretting that I was not as wise as the day I was born. The intellect is a cleaver; it discerns and rifts its way into the secret of things. I do not wish to be any more busy with my hands than is necessary. My head is hands and feet. I feel all my best faculties concentrated in it. My instinct tells me that my head is an organ for burrowing, as some creatures use their snout and fore-paws, and with it I would mine and burrow my way through these hills. I think that the richest vein is somewhere hereabouts; so by the divining rod and thin rising vapors I judge; and here I will begin to mine.

19. Reference point.
20. Gauge placed in the Nile River in ancient times to measure the rise of the water.
21. Saber with a curved blade, usually spelled "scimitar."

MLA CITATION

Thoreau, Henry David. "Where I Lived, and What I Lived For." 1854. *The Norton Reader: An Anthology of Nonfiction*. Ed. Melissa A. Goldthwaite et al. 14th ed. New York: Norton, 2016. 967–75. Print.

QUESTIONS

1. Henry David Thoreau's title might be rephrased as two questions: "Where did I live?" and "What did I live for?" What answers does Thoreau give to each?

2. Throughout this essay Thoreau poses questions—for example, "Why is it that men give so poor an account of their day if they have not been slumbering?" (paragraph 7) or "Why should we live with such hurry and waste of life?" (paragraph 11). To what extent does he answer these questions? Why might he leave some unanswered or only partially answered?

3. Thoreau is known for his aphorisms (short, witty nuggets of wisdom). Find one you like and explain its relevance for living today.

4. If you have ever chosen to live unconventionally at some point in your life, write about your decision, including the reasons and the consequences.

VIRGINIA WOOLF   *The Death of the Moth*

OTHS THAT FLY by day are not properly to be called moths; they do not excite that pleasant sense of dark autumn nights and ivy-blossom which the commonest yellow-underwing asleep in the shadow of the curtain never fails to rouse in us. They are hybrid creatures, neither gay like butterflies nor sombre like their own species. Nevertheless the present specimen, with his narrow hay-colored wings, fringed with a tassel of the same color, seemed to be content with life. It was a pleasant morning, mid-September, mild, benignant, yet with a keener breath than that of the summer months. The plough was already scoring the field opposite the window, and where the share had been, the earth was pressed flat and gleamed with moisture. Such vigor came rolling in from the fields and the down beyond that it was difficult to keep the eyes strictly turned upon the book. The rooks too were keeping one of their annual festivities; soaring round the tree tops until it looked as if a vast net with thousands of black knots in it had been cast up into the air; which, after a few moments sank slowly down upon the trees until every twig seemed to have a knot at the end of it. Then, suddenly, the net would be thrown into the air again in a wider circle this time, with the utmost clamor and vociferation, as though to be thrown into the air and settle slowly down upon the tree tops were a tremendously exciting experience.

The same energy which inspired the rooks, the ploughmen, the horses, and even, it seemed, the lean bare-backed downs, sent the moth fluttering from side to side of his square of the window-pane. One could not help watching him. One was, indeed, conscious of a queer feeling of pity for him. The possibilities of pleasure seemed that morning so enormous and so various that to have only a moth's part in life, and a day moth's at that, appeared a hard fate, and his zest in enjoying his meagre opportunities to the full, pathetic. He flew vigorously to one corner of his compartment, and, after waiting there a second, flew across to the other. What remained for him but to fly to a third corner and then to a fourth? That was all he could do, in spite of the size of the downs, the width of the sky, the far-off smoke of houses, and the romantic voice, now and then, of a steamer out at sea. What he could do he did. Watching him, it seemed as if a fiber, very thin but pure, of the enormous energy of the world had been thrust into his frail and diminutive body. As often as he crossed the pane, I could fancy that a thread of vital light became visible. He was little or nothing but life.

Yet, because he was so small, and so simple a form of the energy that was rolling in at the open window and driving its way through so many narrow and intricate corridors in my own brain and in those of other human beings, there was something marvellous as well as pathetic about him. It was as if someone

The title essay of Virginia Woolf's collection The Death of the Moth, and Other Essays *(1942), compiled after her death in 1941.*

had taken a tiny bead of pure life and decking it as lightly as possible with down and feathers, had set it dancing and zig-zagging to show us the true nature of life. Thus displayed one could not get over the strangeness of it. One is apt to forget all about life, seeing it humped and bossed and garnished and cumbered so that it has to move with the greatest circumspection and dignity. Again, the thought of all that life might have been had he been born in any other shape caused one to view his simple activities with a kind of pity.

After a time, tired by his dancing apparently, he settled on the window ledge in the sun, and, the queer spectacle being at an end, I forgot about him. Then, looking up, my eye was caught by him. He was trying to resume his dancing, but seemed either so stiff or so awkward that he could only flutter to the bottom of the window-pane; and when he tried to fly across it he failed. Being intent on other matters I watched these futile attempts for a time without thinking, unconsciously waiting for him to resume his flight, as one waits for a machine, that has stopped momentarily, to start again without considering the reason of its failure. After perhaps a seventh attempt he slipped from the wooden ledge and fell, fluttering his wings, on to his back on the window sill. The helplessness of his attitude roused me. It flashed upon me that he was in difficulties; he could no longer raise himself; his legs struggled vainly. But, as I stretched out a pencil, meaning to help him to right himself, it came over me that the failure and awkwardness were the approach of death. I laid the pencil down again.

The legs agitated themselves once more. I looked as if for the enemy against 5
which he struggled. I looked out of doors. What had happened there? Presumably it was midday, and work in the fields had stopped. Stillness and quiet had replaced the previous animation. The birds had taken themselves off to feed in the brooks. The horses stood still. Yet the power was there all the same, massed outside indifferent, impersonal, not attending to anything in particular. Somehow it was opposed to the little hay-colored moth. It was useless to try to do anything. One could only watch the extraordinary efforts made by those tiny legs against an oncoming doom which could, had it chosen, have submerged an entire city, not merely a city, but masses of human beings; nothing, I knew, had any chance against death. Nevertheless after a pause of exhaustion the legs fluttered again. It was superb this last protest, and so frantic that he succeeded at last in righting himself. One's sympathies, of course, were all on the side of life. Also, when there was nobody to care or to know, this gigantic effort on the part of an insignificant little moth, against a power of such magnitude, to retain what no one else valued or desired to keep, moved one strangely. Again, somehow, one saw life, a pure bead. I lifted the pencil again, useless though I knew it to be. But even as I did so, the unmistakable tokens of death showed themselves. The body relaxed, and instantly grew stiff. The struggle was over. The insignificant little creature now knew death. As I looked at the dead moth, this minute wayside triumph of so great a force over so mean an antagonist filled me with wonder. Just as life had been strange a few minutes before, so death was now as strange. The moth having righted himself now lay most decently and uncomplainingly composed. O yes, he seemed to say, death is stronger than I am.

MLA CITATION

Woolf, Virginia. "The Death of the Moth." 1942. *The Norton Reader: An Anthology of Nonfiction*. Ed. Melissa A. Goldthwaite et al. 14th ed. New York: Norton, 2016. 976–77. Print.

QUESTIONS

1. Trace the sequence in which Virginia Woolf comes to identify with the moth. How does she make her identification explicit? How is it implicit in the language she uses to describe the moth?

2. Choose one of the descriptions of a small living creature or creatures in Annie Dillard's "Sight into Insight," below, and compare it with Woolf's description of the moth. Does a similar identification take place in Dillard's essay? If so, how; if not, why not?

3. Henry David Thoreau, in "The Battle of the Ants" (pp. 770–72), also humanizes small living creatures. How do his strategies differ from Woolf's?

4. Write two descriptions of the same living creature, one using Woolf's strategies, the other using Thoreau's. Or, alternatively, write an essay in which you analyze the differences between them.

ANNIE DILLARD   *Sight into Insight*

WHEN I WAS SIX OR SEVEN YEARS OLD, growing up in Pittsburgh, I used to take a penny of my own and hide it for someone else to find. It was a curious compulsion; sadly, I've never been seized by it since. For some reason I always "hid" the penny along the same stretch of sidewalk up the street. I'd cradle it at the roots of a maple, say, or in a hole left by a chipped-off piece of sidewalk. Then I'd take a piece of chalk and, starting at either end of the block, draw huge arrows leading up to the penny from both directions. After I learned to write I labeled the arrows "SURPRISE AHEAD" or "MONEY THIS WAY." I was greatly excited, during all this arrowdrawing, at the thought of the first lucky passerby who would receive in this way, regardless of merit, a free gift from the universe. But I never lurked about. I'd go straight home and not give the matter another thought, until, some months later, I would be gripped by the impulse to hide another penny.

There are lots of things to see, unwrapped gifts and free surprises. The world is fairly studded and strewn with pennies cast broadside from a gener-

Originally published in Harper's Magazine *(1974), an American monthly covering politics, society, culture, and the environment; included in Annie Dillard's Pulitzer Prize–winning book,* Pilgrim at Tinker Creek *(1974).*

ous hand. But—and this is the point—who gets excited by a mere penny? If you follow one arrow, if you crouch motionless on a bank to watch a tremulous ripple thrill on the water, and are rewarded by the sight of a muskrat kit paddling from its den, will you count that sight a chip of copper only, and go your rueful way? It is very dire poverty indeed for a man to be so malnourished and fatigued that he won't stoop to pick up a penny. But if you cultivate a healthy poverty and simplicity, so that finding a penny will make your day, then, since the world is in fact planted in pennies, you have with your poverty bought a lifetime of days. What you see is what you get.

Unfortunately, nature is very much a now-you-see-it, now-you-don't affair. A fish flashes, then dissolves in the water before my eyes like so much salt. Deer apparently ascend bodily into heaven; the brightest oriole fades into leaves. These disappearances stun me into stillness and concentration; they say of nature that it conceals with a grand nonchalance, and they say of vision that it is a deliberate gift, the revelation of a dancer who for my eyes only flings away her seven veils.

For nature does reveal as well as conceal: now-you-don't-see-it, now-you-do. For a week this September migrating red-winged blackbirds were feeding heavily down by Tinker Creek at the back of the house. One day I went out to investigate the racket; I walked up to a tree, an Osage orange, and a hundred birds flew away. They simply materialized out of the tree. I saw a tree, then a whisk of color, then a tree again. I walked closer and another hundred blackbirds took flight. Not a branch, not a twig budged: the birds were apparently weightless as well as invisible. Or, it was as if the leaves of the Osage orange had been freed from a spell in the form of redwinged blackbirds; they flew from the tree, caught my eye in the sky, and vanished. When I looked again at the tree, the leaves had reassembled as if nothing had happened. Finally I walked directly to the trunk of the tree and a final hundred, the real diehards, appeared, spread, and vanished. How could so many hide in the tree without my seeing them? The Osage orange, unruffled, looked just as it had looked from the house, when three hundred red-winged blackbirds cried from its crown. I looked upstream where they flew, and they were gone. Searching, I couldn't spot one. I wandered upstream to force them to play their hand, but they'd crossed the creek and scattered. One show to a customer. These appearances catch at my throat; they are the free gifts, the bright coppers at the roots of trees.

It's all a matter of keeping my eyes open. Nature is like one of those line drawings that are puzzles for children: Can you find hidden in the tree a duck, a house, a boy, a bucket, a giraffe, and a boot? Specialists can find the most incredibly hidden things. A book I read when I was young recommended an easy way to find caterpillars: you simply find some fresh caterpillar droppings, look up, and there's your caterpillar. More recently an author advised me to set my mind at ease about those piles of cut stems on the ground in grassy fields. Field mice make them; they cut the grass down by degrees to reach the seeds at the head. It seems that when the grass is tightly packed, as in a field of ripe grain, the blade won't topple at a single cut through the stem; instead, the cut stem simply drops vertically, held in the crush of grain. The mouse severs the bottom again and again, the stem keeps dropping an inch at a time, and finally the head is low enough for the mouse to reach the seeds. Meanwhile the mouse is positively littering the field with its little piles of cut stems into which, presumably, the author is constantly stumbling.

If I can't see these minutiae, I still try to keep my eyes open. I'm always on the lookout for ant lion traps in sandy soil, monarch pupae near milkweed, skipper larvae in locust leaves. These things are utterly common, and I've not seen one. I bang on hollow trees near water, but so far no flying squirrels have appeared. In flat country I watch every sunset in hopes of seeing the green ray. The green ray is a seldom-seen streak of light that rises from the sun like a spurting fountain at the moment of sunset; it throbs into the sky for two seconds and disappears. One more reason to keep my eyes open. A photography professor at the University of Florida just happened to see a bird die in midflight; it jerked, died, dropped, and smashed on the ground.

I squint at the wind because I read Stewart Edward White: "I have always maintained that if you looked closely enough you could *see* the wind—the dim, hardly-made-out, fine débris fleeing high in the air." White was an excellent observer, and devoted an entire chapter of *The Mountains* to the subject of seeing deer: "As soon as you can forget the naturally obvious and construct an artificial obvious, then you too will see deer."

But the artificial obvious is hard to see. My eyes account for less than 1 percent of the weight of my head; I'm bony and dense; I see what I expect. I once spent a full three minutes looking at a bullfrog that was so unexpectedly large I couldn't see it even though a dozen enthusiastic campers were shouting directions. Finally I asked, "What color am I looking for?" and a fellow said, "Green." When at last I picked out the frog, I saw what painters are up against: the thing wasn't green at all, but the color of wet hickory bark.

The lover can see, and the knowledgeable. I visited an aunt and uncle at a quarter-horse ranch in Cody, Wyoming. I couldn't do much of anything useful, but I could, I thought, draw. So, as we all sat around the kitchen table after supper, I produced a sheet of paper and drew a horse. "That's one lame horse," my aunt volunteered. The rest of the family joined in: "Only place to saddle that one is his neck"; "Looks like we better shoot the poor thing, on account of those terrible growths." Meekly, I slid the pencil and paper down the table. Everyone in that family, including my three young cousins, could draw a horse. Beautifully. When the paper came back it looked as though five shining, real quarter horses had been corralled by mistake with a papier-mâché moose; the real horses seemed to gaze at the monster with a steady, puzzled air. I stay away from horses now, but I can do a creditable goldfish. The point is that I just don't know what the lover knows; I just can't see the artificial obvious that those in the know construct. The herpetologist asks the native, "Are there snakes in that ravine?" "Nosir." And the herpetologist comes home with, yessir, three bags full. Are there butterflies on that mountain? Are the bluets in bloom, are there arrowheads here, or fossil shells in the shale?

10   Peeping through my keyhole I see within the range of only about 30 percent of the light that comes from the sun; the rest is infrared and some little

ultraviolet, perfectly apparent to many animals, but invisible to me. A night-mare network of ganglia, charged and firing without my knowledge, cuts and splices what I do see, editing it for my brain. Donald E. Carr[1] points out that the sense impressions of one-celled animals are *not* edited for the brain: "This is philosophically interesting in a rather mournful way, since it means that only the simplest animals perceive the universe as it is."

A fog that won't burn away drifts and flows across my field of vision. When you see fog move against a backdrop of deep pines, you don't see the fog itself, but streaks of clearness floating across the air in dark shreds. So I see only tat-ters of clearness through a pervading obscurity. I can't distinguish the fog from the overcast sky; I can't be sure if the light is direct or reflected. Everywhere darkness and the presence of the unseen appalls. We estimate now that only one atom dances alone in every cubic meter of intergalactic space. I blink and squint. What planet or power yanks Halley's Comet out of orbit? We haven't seen it yet; it's a question of distance, density, and the pallor of reflected light. We rock, cradled in the swaddling band of darkness. Even the simple darkness of night whispers suggestions to the mind. This summer, in August, I stayed at the creek too late.

Where Tinker Creek flows under the sycamore log bridge to the tear-shaped island, it is slow and shallow, fringed thinly in cattail marsh. At this spot an astonishing bloom of life supports vast breeding populations of insects, fish, reptiles, birds, and mammals. On windless summer evenings I stalk along the creek bank or straddle the sycamore log in absolute stillness, watching for musk-rats. The night I stayed too late I was hunched on the log staring spellbound at spreading, reflected stains of lilac on the water. A cloud in the sky suddenly lighted as if turned on by a switch; its reflection just as suddenly materialized on the water upstream, flat and floating, so that I couldn't see the creek bot-tom, or life in the water under the cloud. Downstream, away from the cloud on the water, water turtles smooth as beans were gliding down with the current in a series of easy, weightless push-offs, as men bound on the moon. I didn't know whether to trace the progress of one turtle I was sure of, risking sticking my face in one of the bridge's spider webs made invisible by the gathering dark, or take a chance on seeing the carp, or scan the mudbank in hope of seeing a muskrat, or follow the last of the swallows who caught at my heart and trailed it after them like streamers as they appeared from directly below, under the log, flying upstream with their tails forked, so fast.

But shadows spread and deepened and stayed. After thousands of years we're still strangers to darkness, fearful aliens in an enemy camp with our arms crossed over our chests. I stirred. A land turtle on the bank, startled, hissed the air from its lungs and withdrew to its shell. An uneasy pink here, an unfath-omable blue there, gave great suggestion of lurking beings. Things were going on. I couldn't see whether that rustle I heard was a distant rattlesnake, slit-eyed, or a nearby sparrow kicking in the dry flood debris slung at the foot of a willow. Tremendous action roiled the water everywhere I looked, big action, inexplicable. A tremor welled up beside a gaping muskrat burrow in the bank

---

1. American research chemist and science journalist (1903–1986).

and I caught my breath, but no muskrat appeared. The ripples continued to fan upstream with a steady, powerful thrust. Night was knitting an eyeless mask over my face, and I still sat transfixed. A distant airplane, a delta wing out of nightmare, made a gliding shadow on the creek's bottom that looked like a stingray cruising upstream. At once a black fin slit the pink cloud on the water, shearing it in two. The two halves merged together and seemed to dissolve before my eyes. Darkness pooled in the cleft of the creek and rose, as water collects in a well. Untamed, dreaming lights flickered over the sky. I saw hints of hulking underwater shadows, two pale splashes out of the water, and round ripples rolling close together from a blackened center.

At last I stared upstream where only the deepest violet remained of the cloud, a cloud so high its underbelly still glowed, its feeble color reflected from a hidden sky lighted in turn by a sun halfway to China. And out of that violet, a sudden enormous black body arced over the water. Head and tail, if there was a head and tail, were both submerged in cloud. I saw only one ebony fling, a headlong dive to darkness; then the waters closed, and the lights went out.

15   I walked home in a shivering daze, up hill and down. Later I lay open-mouthed in bed, my arms flung wide at my sides to steady the whirling darkness. At this latitude I'm spinning 836 miles an hour round the earth's axis; I feel my sweeping fall as a breakneck arc like the dive of dolphins, and the hollow rushing of wind raises the hairs on my neck and the side of my face. In orbit around the sun I'm moving 64,800 miles an hour. The solar system as a whole, like a merry-go-round unhinged, spins, bobs, and blinks at the speed of 43,200 miles an hour along a course set east of Hercules. Someone has piped, and we are dancing a tarantella until the sweat pours. I open my eyes and I see dark, muscled forms curl out of water, with flapping gills and flattened eyes. I close my eyes and I see stars, deep stars giving way to deeper stars, deeper stars bowing to deepest stars at the crown of an infinite cone.

"Still," wrote Van Gogh[2] in a letter, "a great deal of light falls on everything." If we are blinded by darkness, we are also blinded by light. Sometimes here in Virginia at sunset low clouds on the southern or northern horizon are completely invisible in the lighted sky. I only know one is there because I can see its reflection in still water. The first time I discovered this mystery I looked from cloud to no-cloud in bewilderment, checking my bearings over and over, thinking maybe the ark of the covenant[3] was just passing by south of Dead Man Mountain. Only much later did I learn the explanation: polarized light from the sky is very much weakened by reflection, but the light in clouds isn't polarized. So invisible clouds pass among visible clouds, till all slide over the mountains; so a greater light extinguishes a lesser as though it didn't exist.

2. Vincent van Gogh (1853–1890), Dutch Postimpressionist painter.
3. Repository for the stone tablets of the Ten Commandments, carried by the ancient Israelites during their desert wanderings.

In the great meteor shower of August, the Perseid, I wail all day for the shooting stars I miss. They're out there showering down committing hara-kiri in a flame of fatal attraction, and hissing perhaps at last into the ocean. But at dawn what looks like a blue dome clamps down over me like a lid on a pot. The stars and planets could smash and I'd never know. Only a piece of ashen moon occasionally climbs up or down the inside of the dome, and our local star without surcease explodes on our heads. We have really only that one light, one source for all power, and yet we must turn away from it by universal decree. Nobody here on the planet seems aware of this strange, powerful taboo, that we all walk about carefully averting our faces, this way and that, lest our eyes be blasted forever.

Darkness appalls and light dazzles; the scrap of visible light that doesn't hurt my eyes hurts my brain. What I see sets me swaying. Size and distance and the sudden swelling of meanings confuse me, bowl me over. I straddle the sycamore log bridge over Tinker Creek in the summer. I look at the lighted creek bottom: snail tracks tunnel the mud in quavering curves. A crayfish jerks, but by the time I absorb what has happened, he's gone in a billowing smoke screen of silt. I look at the water; minnows and shiners. If I'm thinking minnows, a carp will fill my brain till I scream. I look at the water's surface: skaters, bubbles, and leaves sliding down. Suddenly, my own face, reflected, startles me witless. Those snails have been tracking my face! Finally, with a shuddering wrench of the will, I see clouds, cirrus clouds. I'm dizzy, I fall in.

This looking business is risky. Once I stood on a humped rock on nearby Purgatory Mountain, watching through binoculars the great autumn hawk migration below, until I discovered that I was in danger of joining the hawks on a vertical migration of my own. I was used to binoculars, but not, apparently, to balancing on humped rocks while looking through them. I reeled. Everything advanced and receded by turns; the world was full of unexplained foreshortenings and depths. A distant huge object, a hawk the size of an elephant, turned out to be the browned bough of a nearby loblolly pine. I followed a sharp-shinned hawk against a featureless sky, rotating my head unawares as it flew, and when I lowered the glass a glimpse of my own looming shoulder sent me staggering. What prevents the men at Palomar[4] from falling, voiceless and blinded, from their tiny, vaulted chairs?

I reel in confusion: I don't understand what I see. With the naked eye I can see two million light-years to the Andromeda galaxy. Often I slop some creek water in a jar, and when I get home I dump it in a white china bowl. After the silt settles I return and see tracings of minute snails on the bottom, a planarian or two winding round the rim of water, roundworms shimmying, frantically, and finally, when my eyes have adjusted to these dimensions, amoebae. At first the amoebae look like *muscae volitantes*, those curled moving spots you seem to see in your eyes when you stare at a distant wall. Then I see the amoebae as drops of water congealed, bluish, translucent, like chips of sky in the bowl. At length I choose one individual and give myself over to its idea of an

20

4. Astronomical observatory in California.

evening. I see it dribble a grainy foot before it on its wet, unfathomable way. Do its unedited sense impressions include the fierce focus of my eyes? Shall I take it outside and show it Andromeda, and blow its little endoplasm? I stir the water with a finger, in case it's running out of oxygen. Maybe I should get a tropical aquarium with motorized bubblers and lights, and keep this one for a pet. Yes, it would tell its fissioned descendants, the universe is two feet by five, and if you listen closely you can hear the buzzing music of the spheres.

Oh, it's mysterious, lamplit evenings here in the galaxy, one after the other. It's one of those nights when I wander from window to window, looking for a sign. But I can't see. Terror and a beauty insoluble are a riband of blue woven into the fringe of garments of things both great and small. No culture explains, no bivouac offers real haven or rest. But it could be that we are not seeing something. Galileo[5] thought comets were an optical illusion. This is fertile ground: since we are certain that they're not, we can look at what our scientists have been saying with fresh hope. What if there are *really* gleaming, castellated cities hung up-side-down over the desert sand? What limpid lakes and cool date palms have our caravans always passed untried? Until, one by one, by the blindest of leaps, we light on the road to these places, we must stumble in darkness and hunger. I turn from the window. I'm blind as a bat, sensing only from every direction the echo of my own thin cries.

I chanced on a wonderful book called *Space and Sight,* by Marius Von Senden. When Western surgeons discovered how to perform safe cataract operations, they ranged across Europe and America operating on dozens of men and women of all ages who had been blinded by cataracts since birth. Von Senden collected accounts of such cases; the histories are fascinating. Many doctors had tested their patients' sense perceptions and ideas of space both before and after the operations. The vast majority of patients, of both sexes and all ages, had, in Von Senden's opinion, no idea of space whatsoever. Form, distance, and size were so many meaningless syllables. A patient "had no idea of depth, confusing it with roundness." Before the operation a doctor would give a blind patient a cube and a sphere; the patient would tongue it or feel it with his hands, and name it correctly. After the operation the doctor would show the same objects to the patient without letting him touch them; now he had no clue whatsoever to what he was seeing. One patient called lemonade "square" because it pricked on his tongue as a square shape pricked on the touch of his hands. Of another post-operative patient the doctor writes, "I have found in her no notion of size, for example, not even within the narrow limits which she might have encompassed with the aid of touch. Thus when I asked her to show me how big her mother was, she did not stretch out her hands, but set her two index fingers a few inches apart."

For the newly sighted, vision is pure sensation unencumbered by meaning. When a newly sighted girl saw photographs and paintings, she asked, "'Why do they put those dark marks all over them?' 'Those aren't dark marks,' her

---

5. Galileo Galilei (1564–1642), Italian astronomer and mathematician.

mother explained, 'those are shadows. That is one of the ways the eye knows that things have shape. If it were not for shadows, many things would look flat.' 'Well, that's how things do look,' Joan answered. 'Everything looks flat with dark patches.'"

In general the newly sighted see the world as a dazzle of "color-patches." They are pleased by the sensation of color, and learn quickly to name the colors, but the rest of seeing is tormentingly difficult. Soon after his operation a patient "generally bumps into one of these color-patches and observes them to be substantial, since they resist him as tactual objects do. In walking about it also strikes him—or can if he pays attention—that he is continually passing in between the colors he sees, that he can go past a visual object, that a part of it then steadily disappears from view; and that in spite of this, however he twists and turns—whether entering the room from the door, for example, or returning back to it—he always has a visual space in front of him. Thus he gradually comes to realize that there is also a space behind him, which he does not see."

The mental effort involved in these reasonings proves overwhelming for many patients. It oppresses them to realize that they have been visible to people all along, perhaps unattractively so, without their knowledge or consent. A disheartening number of them refuse to use their new vision, continuing to go over objects with their tongues, and lapsing into apathy and despair.

On the other hand, many newly sighted people speak well of the world, and teach us how dull our own vision is. To one patient, a human hand, unrecognized, is "something bright and then holes." Shown a bunch of grapes, a boy calls out, "It is dark, blue and shiny. . . . It isn't smooth, it has bumps and hollows." A little girl visits a garden. "She is greatly astonished, and can scarcely be persuaded to answer, stands speechless in front of the tree, which she only names on taking hold of it, and then as 'the tree with the lights in it.'" Another patient, a twenty-two-year-old girl, was dazzled by the world's brightness and kept her eyes shut for two weeks. When at the end of that time she opened her eyes again, she did not recognize any objects, but "the more she now directed her gaze upon everything about her, the more it could be seen how an expression of gratification and astonishment overspread her features; she repeatedly exclaimed: 'Oh God! How beautiful!'"

I saw color-patches for weeks after I read this wonderful book. It was summer; the peaches were ripe in the valley orchards. When I woke in the morning, color-patches wrapped round my eyes, intricately, leaving not one unfilled spot. All day long I walked among shifting color-patches that parted before me like the Red Sea and closed again in silence,[6] transfigured, wherever I looked back. Some patches swelled and loomed, while others vanished utterly, and dark marks flitted at random over the whole dazzling sweep. But I couldn't sustain the illusion of flatness. I've been around for too long. Form is condemned to an eternal danse macabre with meaning: I couldn't unpeach the peaches. Nor can I remember ever having seen without understanding; the color-patches of

25

6. According to the book of Exodus in the Bible, the Red Sea parted for the Israelites and closed over the Egyptians pursuing them.

infancy are lost. My brain then must have been smooth as any balloon. I'm told I reached for the moon; many babies do. But the color-patches of infancy swelled as meaning filled them; they arrayed themselves in solemn ranks down distance which unrolled and stretched before me like a plain. The moon rocketed away. I live now in a world of shadows that shape and distance color, a world where space makes a kind of terrible sense. What Gnosticism[7] is this, and what physics? The fluttering patch I saw in my nursery window—silver and green and shape-shifting blue—is gone; a row of Lombardy poplars takes its place, mute, across the distant lawn. That humming oblong creature pale as light that stole along the walls of my room at night, stretching exhilaratingly around the corners, is gone, too, gone the night I ate of the bittersweet fruit, put two and two together and puckered forever my brain. Martin Buber[8] tells this tale: "Rabbi Mendel once boasted to his teacher Rabbi Elimelekh that evenings he saw the angel who rolls away the light before the darkness, and mornings the angel who rolls away the darkness before the light. 'Yes,' said Rabbi Elimelekh, 'in my youth I saw that too. Later on you don't see these things anymore.' "

Why didn't someone hand those newly sighted people paints and brushes from the start, when they still didn't know what anything was? Then maybe we all could see color-patches too, the world unraveled from reason, Eden before Adam gave names. The scales would drop from my eyes; I'd see trees like men walking; I'd run down the road against all orders, hallooing and leaping.

Seeing is of course very much a matter of verbalization. Unless I call my attention to what passes before my eyes, I simply won't see it. If Tinker Mountain erupted, I'd be likely to notice. But if I want to notice the lesser cataclysms of valley life, I have to maintain in my head a running description of the present. It's not that I'm observant; it's just that I talk too much. Otherwise, especially in a strange place, I'll never know what's happening. Like a blind man at the ball game, I need a radio.

30　　　When I see this way I analyze and pry. I hurl over logs and roll away stones; I study the bank a square foot at a time, probing and tilting my head. Some days when a mist covers the mountains, when the muskrats won't show and the microscope's mirror shatters, I want to climb up the blank blue dome as a man would storm the inside of a circus tent, wildly, dangling, and with a steel knife claw a rent in the top, peep, and, if I must, fall.

But there is another kind of seeing that involves a letting go. When I see this way I sway transfixed and emptied. The difference between the two ways of seeing is the difference between walking with and without a camera. When I walk with a camera I walk from shot to shot, reading the light on a calibrated meter. When I walk without a camera, my own shutter opens, and the moment's light prints on my own silver gut. When I see this second way I am above all an unscrupulous observer.

It was sunny one evening last summer at Tinker Creek; the sun was low in the sky, upstream. I was sitting on the sycamore log bridge with the sunset at

7. Promise of secret knowledge of the divine.
8. Jewish religious philosopher (1878–1965).

my back, watching the shiners the size of minnows who were feeding over the muddy sand in skittery schools. Again and again, one fish, then another, turned for a split second across the current and flash! the sun shot out from its silver side. I couldn't watch for it. It was always just happening somewhere else, and it drew my vision just as it disappeared: flash! like a sudden dazzle of the thinnest blade, a sparking over a dun and olive ground at chance intervals from every direction. Then I noticed white specks, some sort of pale petals, small, floating from under my feet on the creek's surface, very slow and steady. So I blurred my eyes and gazed toward the brim of my hat and saw a new world. I saw the pale white circles roll up, roll up, like the world's turning, mute and perfect, and I saw the linear flashes, gleaming silver, like stars being born at random down a rolling scroll of time. Something broke and something opened. I filled up like a new wineskin. I breathed an air like light; I saw a light like water. I was the lip of a fountain the creek filled forever; I was ether, the leaf in the zephyr; I was flesh-flake, feather, bone.

When I see this way I see truly. As Thoreau[9] says, I return to my senses. I am the man who watches the baseball game in silence in an empty stadium. I see the game purely; I'm abstracted and dazed. When it's all over and the white-suited players lope off the green field to their shadowed dugouts, I leap to my feet, I cheer and cheer.

But I can't go out and try to see this way. I'll fail, I'll go mad. All I can do is try to gag the commentator, to hush the noise of useless interior babble that keeps me from seeing just as surely as a newspaper dangled before my eyes. The effort is really a discipline requiring a lifetime of dedicated struggle; it marks the literature of saints and monks of every order east and west, under every rule and no rule, discalced[10] and shod. The world's spiritual geniuses seem to discover universally that the mind's muddy river, this ceaseless flow of trivia and trash, cannot be dammed, and that trying to dam it is a waste of effort that might lead to madness. Instead you must allow the muddy river to flow unheeded in the dim channels of consciousness; you raise your sights; you look along it, mildly, acknowledging its presence without interest and gazing beyond it into the realm of the real where subjects and objects act and rest purely, without utterance. "Launch into the deep," says Jacques Ellul,[11] "and you shall see."

The secret of seeing, then, is the pearl of great price. If I thought he could teach me to find it and keep it forever I would stagger barefoot across a hundred deserts after any lunatic at all. But although the pearl may be found, it may not be sought. The literature of illumination reveals this above all: although it comes to those who wait for it, it is always, even to the most practiced and adept, a gift and a total surprise. I return from one walk knowing where the killdeer nests in the field by the creek and the hour the laurel blooms. I return from the same walk a day later scarcely knowing my own name. Litanies hum

35

9. Henry David Thoreau (1817–1862), American writer; see "Where I Lived, and What I Lived For" (pp. 967–75) and "The Battle of the Ants" (pp. 770–72).

10. Shoeless, as in the order of the Discalced Carmelites.

11. French Protestant theologian and critic of technology (1912–1994).

in my ears; my tongue flaps in my mouth, *Alim non,* alleluia! I cannot cause light; the most I can do is try to put myself in the path of its beam. It is possible, in deep space, to sail on solar wind. Light, be it particle or wave, has force: you rig a giant sail and go. The secret of seeing is to sail on solar wind. Hone and spread your spirit till you yourself are a sail, whetted, translucent, broadside to the merest puff.

When her doctor took her bandages off and led her into the garden, the girl who was no longer blind saw "the tree with the lights in it." It was for this tree I searched through the peach orchards of summer, in the forests of fall and down winter and spring for years. Then one day I was walking along Tinker Creek thinking of nothing at all and I saw the tree with the lights in it. I saw the backyard cedar where the mourning doves roost charged and transfigured, each cell buzzing with flame. I stood on the grass with the lights in it, grass that was wholly fire, utterly focused and utterly dreamed. It was less like seeing than like being for the first time seen, knocked breathless by a powerful glance. The flood of fire abated, but I'm still spending the power. Gradually the lights went out in the cedar, the colors died, the cells unflamed and disappeared. I was still ringing. I had been my whole life a bell, and never knew it until at that moment I was lifted and struck. I have since only very rarely seen the tree with the lights in it. The vision comes and goes, mostly goes, but I live for it, for the moment when the mountains open and a new light roars in spate through the crack, and the mountains slam.

MLA CITATION

Dillard, Annie. "Sight into Insight." 1974. *The Norton Reader: An Anthology of Nonfiction.* Ed. Melissa A. Goldthwaite et al. 14th ed. New York: Norton, 2016. 978–88. Print.

QUESTIONS

1. Annie Dillard often uses several examples to support a general claim. In paragraph 3, for instance, she writes, "nature is very much a now-you-see-it, now-you-don't affair" and follows with "[a] fish flashes, then dissolves" and "the brightest oriole fades into leaves." Locate other examples of this technique, marking the general statements and examples that accompany them. What purpose does this technique serve? In what kinds of writing is it appropriate, in what kinds inappropriate?

2. How does the kind of seeing Dillard describes at the end of her essay differ from the kind of seeing she describes at the beginning?

3. Take one of Dillard's general statements and come up with supporting examples of your own.

4. Dillard says, "I see what I expect" (paragraph 8). Write a description of something familiar, paying attention to how you "edit" your seeing. Then write a parallel description of it as if you were seeing it "unedited," as Dillard tries to see "color-patches" like the newly sighted do (paragraph 27).

PLATO   *The Allegory of the Cave*

ND NOW, I SAID, let me show in a figure how far our
nature is enlightened or unenlightened: Behold! human
beings living in an underground den, which has a
mouth open toward the light and reaching all along
the den; here they have been from their childhood,
and have their legs and necks chained so that they
cannot move, and can only see before them, being prevented by the chains from
turning round their heads. Above and behind them a fire is blazing at a distance, and between the fire and the prisoners there is a raised way; and you
will see, if you look, a low wall built along the way, like the screen which mari-
onette players have in front of them, over which they show the puppets.

I see.

And do you see, I said, men passing along the wall carrying all sorts of
vessels, and statues and figures of animals made of wood and stone and various materials, which appear over the wall? Some of them are talking, others
silent.

You have shown me a strange image, and they are strange prisoners.

Like ourselves, I replied; and they see only their own shadows, or the shad-   5
ows of one another, which the fire throws on the opposite wall of the cave?

True, he said; how could they see anything but the shadows if they were
never allowed to move their heads?

And of the objects which are being carried in like manner they would only
see the shadows?

Yes, he said.

And if they were able to converse with one another, would they not suppose that they were naming what was actually before them?

Very true.   10

And suppose further that the prison had an echo which came from the
other side, would they not be sure to fancy when one of the passers-by spoke
that the voice which they heard came from the passing shadow?

No question, he replied.

To them, I said, the truth would be literally nothing but the shadows of
the images.

That is certain.

And now look again, and see what will naturally follow if the prisoners are   15
released and disabused of their error. At first, when any of them is liberated
and compelled suddenly to stand up and turn his neck round and walk and look
toward the light, he will suffer sharp pains; the glare will distress him and he
will be unable to see the realities of which in his former state he had seen the
shadows; and then conceive some one saying to him, that what he saw before was

From the Republic, *a dialogue in ten books written by Plato in the early years of his Academy,
a school he founded (c. 380* B.C.E.) *to give a philosophical education to men embarking on
political careers. In this section Socrates questions Glaucon, a student.*

an illusion, but that now, when he is approaching nearer to being and his eye is turned toward more real existence, he has a clearer vision—what will be his reply? And you may further imagine that his instructor is pointing to the objects as they pass and requiring him to name them—will he not be perplexed? Will he not fancy that the shadows which he formerly saw are truer than the objects which are now shown to him?

Far truer.

And if he is compelled to look straight at the light, will he not have a pain in his eyes which will make him turn away to take refuge in the objects of vision which he can see, and which he will conceive to be in reality clearer than the things which are now being shown to him?

True, he said.

And suppose once more, that he is reluctantly dragged up a steep and rugged ascent, and held fast until he is forced into the presence of the sun himself, is he not likely to be pained and irritated? When he approaches the light his eyes will be dazzled and he will not be able to see anything at all of what are now called realities.

20   Not all in a moment, he said.

He will require to grow accustomed to the sight of the upper world. And first he will see the shadows best, next the reflections of men and other objects in the water, and then the objects themselves; then he will gaze upon the light of the moon and the stars and the spangled heaven; and he will see the sky and the stars by night better than the sun or the light of the sun by day?

Certainly.

Last of all he will be able to see the sun, and not mere reflections of him in the water, but he will see him in his own proper place, and not in another; and he will contemplate him as he is.

Certainly.

25   He will then proceed to argue that this is he who gives the season and the years, and is the guardian of all that is in the visible world, and in a certain way the cause of all things which he and his fellows have been accustomed to behold?

Clearly, he said, he would first see the sun and then reason about him.

And when he remembered his old habitation, and the wisdom of the den and his fellow-prisoners, do you not suppose that he would felicitate himself on the change, and pity them?

Certainly, he would.

And if they were in the habit of conferring honors among themselves on those who were quickest to observe the passing shadows and to remark which of them went before, and which followed after, and which were together; and who were therefore best able to draw conclusions as to the future, do you think that he would care for such honors and glories, or envy the possessors of them? Would he not say with Homer,

Better to be the poor servant of a poor master,

and to endure anything, rather than think as they do and live after their manner?

Yes, he said, I think that he would rather suffer anything than entertain 30
these false notions and live in this miserable manner.

Imagine once more, I said, such an one coming suddenly out of the sun to
be replaced in his old situation; would he not be certain to have his eyes full of
darkness?

To be sure, he said.

And if there were a contest, and he had to compete in measuring the shadows with the prisoners who had never moved out of the den, while his sight was
still weak, and before his eyes had become steady (and the time which would
be needed to acquire this new habit of sight might be very considerable) would
he not be ridiculous? Men would say of him that up he went and down he
came without his eyes; and that it was better not even to think of ascending;
and if any one tried to loose another and lead him up to the light, let them only
catch the offender, and they would put him to death.

No question, he said.

This entire allegory, I said, you may now append, dear Glaucon, to the pre- 35
vious argument; the prison-house is the world of sight, the light of the fire is
the sun, and you will not misapprehend me if you interpret the journey upwards
to be the ascent of the soul into the intellectual world according to my poor
belief, which, at your desire, I have expressed—whether rightly or wrongly God
knows. But, whether true or false, my opinion is that in the world of knowledge the idea of good appears last of all, and is seen only with an effort; and,
when seen, is also inferred to be the universal author of all things beautiful and
right, parent of light and of the lord of light in this visible world, and the immediate source of reason and truth in the intellectual; and that this is the power
upon which he who would act rationally either in public or private life must
have his eye fixed.

I agree, he said, as far as I am able to understand you.

Moreover, I said, you must not wonder that those who attain to this beatific
vision are unwilling to descend to human affairs; for their souls are ever has-
tening into the upper world where they desire to dwell; which desire of theirs
is very natural, if our allegory may be trusted.

Yes, very natural.

And is there anything surprising in one who passes from divine contem-
plations to the evil state of man, misbehaving himself in a ridiculous manner; if, while his eyes are blinking and before he has become accustomed to
the surrounding darkness, he is compelled to fight in courts of law, or in
other places, about the images or the shadows of images of justice, and is
endeavoring to meet the conceptions of those who have never yet seen absolute justice?

Anything but surprising, he replied. 40

Any one who has common sense will remember that the bewilderments of
the eyes are of two kinds, and arise from two causes, either from coming out
of the light or from going into the light, which is true of the mind's eye, quite
as much as of the bodily eye; and he who remembers this when he sees any
one whose vision is perplexed and weak, will not be too ready to laugh; he will
first ask whether that soul of man has come out of the brighter life, and is

unable to see because unaccustomed to the dark, or having turned from darkness to the day is dazzled by excess of light. And he will count the one happy in his condition and state of being, and he will pity the other; or, if he have a mind to laugh at the soul which comes from below into the light, there will be more reason in this than in the laugh which greets him who returns from above out of the light into the den.

That, he said, is a very just distinction.

MLA CITATION

Plato. "The Allegory of the Cave." 380 B.C.E. *The Norton Reader: An Anthology of Nonfiction.* Ed. Melissa A. Goldthwaite et al. 14th ed. New York: Norton, 2016. 989–92. Print.

QUESTIONS

1. Plato uses Socratic dialogue, a question-and-answer form in which characters discuss moral and philosophical problems, usually with a philosopher-teacher instructing a student. Locate the key questions the teacher poses, and answer them in your own terms. Are your answers similar to those of Glaucon, the student? Why or why not?

2. Plato begins with an analogy (or allegory) in which he likens human knowledge to visual sight in an underground den. Locate Plato's interpretation of this allegory. What points does he derive from it?

3. Write an allegory in which you characterize some aspect of human existence, and embed your interpretation within your essay.

JESUS   *Parables of the Kingdom*

THE TEN VIRGINS

Then shall the kingdom of heaven be likened unto ten virgins, which took their lamps, and went forth to meet the bridegroom.

And five of them were wise, and five were foolish.

They that were foolish took their lamps, and took no oil with them:

But the wise took oil in their vessels with their lamps.

5   While the bridegroom tarried, they all slumbered and slept.

And at midnight there was a cry made, Behold, the bridegroom cometh; go ye out to meet him.

Then all those virgins arose, and trimmed their lamps.

And the foolish said unto the wise, Give us of your oil; for our lamps are gone out.

From Jesus's teachings, as written in Matthew 25 and Luke 15, King James Bible (1611).

But the wise answered, saying Not so; lest there be not enough for us and you: but go ye rather to them that sell, and buy for yourselves.

And while they went to buy, the bridgroom came; and they that were ready 10 went in with him to the marriage: and the door was shut.

Afterward came also the other virgins, saying, Lord, Lord, open to us.

But he answered and said, Verily I say unto you, I know you not.

Watch therefore, for ye know neither the day nor the hour wherein the Son of man cometh.

THE TEN TALENTS

For the kingdom of heaven is as a man travelling into a far country, who called his own servants, and delivered unto them his goods.

And unto one he gave five talents,[1] to another two, and to another one; to every man according to his several ability; and straightway took his journey.

Then he that had received the five talents went and traded with the same, and made them other five talents.

And likewise he that had received two, he also gained other two.

But he that had received one went and digged in the earth, and hid his 5 lord's money.

After a long time the lord of those servants cometh, and reckoneth with them.

And so he that had received five talents came and brought other five talents, saying, Lord, thou deliveredst unto me five talents: behold, I have gained beside them five talents more.

His lord said unto him, Well done, thou good and faithful servant: thou hast been faithful over a few things, I will make thee ruler over many things: enter thou into the joy of thy lord.

He also that had received two talents came and said, Lord, thou deliverdst unto me two talents: behold, I have gained two other talents beside them.

His lord said unto him, Well done, good and faithful servant; thou hast 10 been faithful over a few things, I will make thee ruler over many things: enter thou into the joy of thy lord.

Then he which had received the one talent came and said, Lord, I knew thee that thou art an hard man, reaping where thou hast not sown, and gathering where thou hast not strawed:

And I was afraid, and went and hid thy talent in the earth: lo, there thou hast that is thine.

His lord answered and said unto him, Thou wicked and slothful servant, thou knewest that I reap where I sowed not, and gather where I have not strawed:

Thou oughtest therefore to have put my money to the exchanges, and then at my coming I should have received mine own with usury.

1. Middle Eastern coins.

15 Take therefore the talent from him, and give it unto him which hath ten talents.

For unto every one that hath shall be given, and he shall have abundance: but from him that hath not shall be taken away even that which he hath.

And cast ye the unprofitable servant into outer darkness: there shall be weeping and gnashing of teeth.

When the Son of man shall come in his glory, and all the holy angels with him, then shall he sit upon the throne of his glory:

And before him shall be gathered all nations: and he shall separate them one from another, as a shepherd divideth his sheep from the goats:

20 And he shall set the sheep on his right hand, but the goats on the left.

Then shall the King say unto them on his right hand, Come, ye blessed of my Father, inherit the kingdom prepared for you from the foundation of the world:

For I was an hungred, and ye gave me meat: I was thirsty, and ye gave me drink: I was a stranger, and ye took me in:

Naked, and ye clothed me: I was sick, and ye visited me: I was in prison, and ye came unto me.

Then shall the righteous answer him, saying, Lord, when saw we thee an hungred, and fed thee? or thirsty, and gave thee drink?

25 When saw we thee a stranger, and took thee in? or naked, and clothed thee?

Or when saw we thee sick, or in prison, and came unto thee?

And the King shall answer and say unto them, Verily I say unto you, Inasmuch as ye have done it unto one of the least of these my brethren, ye have done it unto me.

Then shall he say also unto them on the left hand, Depart from me, ye cursed, into everlasting fire, prepared for the devil and his angels:

For I was an hungred, and ye gave me no meat: I was thirsty, and ye gave me no drink.

30 I was a stranger, and ye took me not in: naked, and ye clothed me not: sick, and in prison, and ye visited me not.

Then shall they also answer him, saying, Lord, when saw we thee an hungred, or athirst, or a stranger, or naked, or sick, or in prison, and did not minister unto thee?

Then shall he answer them, saying, Verily I say unto you, Inasmuch as ye did it not to one of the least of these, ye did it not to me.

And these shall go away into everlasting punishment: but the righteous into life eternal.

THE PRODIGAL SON

And he said, A certain man had two sons;

And the younger of them said to his father, Father, give me the portion of goods that falleth to me. And he divided unto them his living.

And not many days after that, the younger son gathered all together, and took his journey into a far country, and there wasted his substance with riotous living.

And when he had spent all, there arose a mighty famine in that land; and he began to be in want.

And he went and joined himself to a citizen of that country; and he sent him into his fields to feed swine. 5

And he would fain have filled his belly with the husks that the swine did eat; and no man gave unto him.

And when he came to himself, he said, How many of my father's hired servants have bread enough and to spare, and I perish with hunger!

I will arise and go to my father, and will say unto him, Father, I have sinned against heaven, and before thee,

And am no more worthy to be called thy son; make me as one of thy hired servants.

And he arose, and came to his father. But when he was yet a great way off, his father saw him, and had compassion, and ran, and fell on his neck, and kissed him. 10

And the son said unto him, Father, I have sinned against heaven, and in thy sight, and am no more worthy to be called thy son.

But the father said to his servants, Bring forth the best robe, and put it on him; and put a ring on his hand, and shoes on his feet.

And bring the fatted calf, and kill it; and let us eat, and be merry.

For this, my son, was dead, and is alive again; he was lost, and is found. And they began to be merry.

Now his elder son was in the field; and as he came and drew nigh to the house, he heard music and dancing. 15

And he called one of the servants, and asked what these things meant.

And he said unto him, Thy brother is come; and thy father hath killed the fatted calf, because he hath received him safe and sound.

And he was angry, and would not go in; therefore came his father out, and entreated him.

And he, answering, said to his father, Lo, these many years do I serve thee, neither transgressed I at any time thy commandment; and yet thou never gavest me a kid, that I might make merry with my friends.

But as soon as this, thy son, was come, who hath devoured thy living with harlots, thou hast killed for him the fatted calf. 20

And he said unto him, Son, thou art ever with me, and all that I have is thine.

It was meet that we should make merry, and be glad; for this, thy brother, was dead, and is alive again; and was lost, and is found.

MLA CITATION

Jesus. "Parables of the Kingdom." 1611. *The Norton Reader: An Anthology of Nonfiction.* Ed. Melissa A. Goldthwaite et al. 14th ed. New York: Norton, 2016. 992–95. Print.

QUESTIONS

1. Many parables end with a moral explicitly stated. What explicit lessons does Jesus append to his parables?

2. Is it possible to deduce more than one moral from a biblical parable? Think of additional or alternative morals that you might draw from one of Jesus' parables.

3. Write a parable that, while using narrative form, has a moral or lesson embedded within it.

Zen Parables

MUDDY ROAD

Tanzan and Ekido were once traveling together down a muddy road. A heavy rain was still falling.

   Coming around a bend, they met a lovely girl in a silk kimono and sash, unable to cross the intersection.

   "Come on, girl," said Tanzan at once. Lifting her in his arms, he carried her over the mud.

   Ekido did not speak again until that night when they reached a lodging temple. Then he no longer could restrain himself. "We monks don't go near females," he told Tanzan, "especially not young and lovely ones. It is dangerous. Why did you do that?"

5   "I left the girl there," said Tanzan. "Are you still carrying her?"

A PARABLE

Buddha told a parable in a sutra:

   A man traveling across a field encountered a tiger. He fled, the tiger after him. Coming to a precipice, he caught hold of the root of a wild vine and swung himself down over the edge. The tiger sniffed at him from above. Trembling, the man looked down to where, far below, another tiger was waiting to eat him. Only the vine sustained him.

   Two mice, one white and one black, little by little started to gnaw away the vine. The man saw a luscious strawberry near him. Grasping the vine with one hand, he plucked the strawberry with the other. How sweet it tasted!

LEARNING TO BE SILENT

The pupils of the Tendai school used to study meditation before Zen entered Japan. Four of them who were intimate friends promised one another to observe seven days of silence.

Translations from Zen Flesh, Zen Bones: A Collection of Zen and Pre-Zen Writings *(1957) compiled by Paul Reps and Nyogen Senzaki. Zen Buddhists use parables, called* koans, *as a means to enlightenment.*

On the first day all were silent. Their meditation had begun auspiciously, but when night came and the oil lamps were growing dim one of the pupils could not help exclaiming to a servant: "Fix those lamps."

The second pupil was surprised to hear the first one talk. "We are not supposed to say a word," he remarked.

"You two are stupid. Why did you talk?" asked the third.

"I am the only one who has not talked," concluded the fourth pupil. 5

MLA CITATION

Zen Parables. "Muddy Road," "A Parable," "Learning to Be Silent." 1957. *The Norton Reader: An Anthology of Nonfiction*. Ed. Melissa A. Goldthwaite et al. 14th ed. New York: Norton, 2016. 996–97. Print.

QUESTIONS

1. Although some parables end with an explicitly stated moral, Zen parables often do not. Which parables include an explicit lesson? Which require the reader to deduce a lesson?

2. Is it possible to deduce more than one moral from a Zen parable? Try writing two different lessons that you might draw from one Zen parable.

3. Write a Zen-like parable that uses narrative form, includes two characters, and ends with a surprising lesson.

AUTHOR BIOGRAPHIES

Edward Abbey (1927–1989)
American essayist, novelist, and self-described "agrarian anarchist." Born in Pennsylvania, Abbey lived in the Southwest from 1948, when he began his studies at the University of New Mexico, until his death. He took as his most pervasive theme the beauty of the Southwestern desert and the ways it has been despoiled by government, business, and tourism. Abbey's novels include *Fire on the Mountain* (1963), *Good News* (1980), and *The Monkey Wrench Gang* (1975), which is credited with helping to inspire the radical environmentalist movement. He published several collections of essays, among them *Abbey's Road* (1979), *Beyond the Wall: Essays from the Outside* (1984), *One Life at a Time, Please* (1988), and, most famously, *Desert Solitaire* (1968), drawing on his years as a ranger in the national parks of southern Utah. See also abbeyweb.net.

Roger Angell (b. 1920)
American sportswriter and essayist. The son of a *New Yorker* fiction editor and the stepson of *New Yorker* essayist E. B. White, Angell became the *New Yorker's* fiction editor and made a name for himself as the "Poet Laureate of Baseball" for his witty and lyrical essays about the national pastime, which have appeared regularly in the *New Yorker* since 1962. His many collections of baseball writing include *Season Ticket: A Baseball Companion* (1988) and *Game Time: A Baseball Companion* (2004); his autobiography, *Let Me Finish* (2006), describes a boyhood dominated by the literary world and baseball. See also newyorker .com/contributors/roger-angell.

Maya Angelou (1928–2014)
American memoirist, poet, essayist, and playwright. Born Marguerite Ann Johnson in St. Louis, Angelou attended public schools in Arkansas and California before studying music and dance. In her lifetime, she worked as a cook, streetcar conductor, singer, actress, dancer, teacher, and director, with her debut film *Down in the Delta* (1998).

Author of numerous volumes of poetry (her *Complete Collected Poems* was published in 1994) and ten plays (stage, screen, and television), Angelou may be best known for *I Know Why the Caged Bird Sings* (1969), the first volume of her autobiography and one of the most influential accounts of the African American woman's experience in contemporary literature. Angelou published her seventh and final volume of autobiography, *Mom & Me & Mom*, in 2013. See also mayaangelou.com.

Gloria Anzaldúa (1942–2004)
American poet and writer. Anzaldúa was born to Mexican American parents and worked on the family ranch in southern Texas until attending Pan American University as the first woman from her family to enter college. She received an M.A. in English from the University of Texas, Austin, and embarked on a career as a writer, college instructor, independent scholar, and social activist. Her most ambitious work, *Borderlands/La Frontera: The New Mestiza* (1987), examines "border women" like herself who grew up estranged from both their Mexican Indian heritage and also the Anglo-American society that considers them outsiders. Her other works include the anthology *This Bridge Called My Back* (co-edited with Cherríe Moraga, 1981), *Making Face, Making Soul/Haciendo Caras* (1990), and *La Prieta* (1997), an autobiographical essay written in her characteristic "Spanglish," a mixture of Spanish and English. See also poetryfoundation.org/ bio/gloria-e-anzaldua.

Isaac Asimov (1920–1992)
American biochemist, science writer, and novelist. Born in Russia, Asimov was educated in the United States and received a Ph.D. in biochemistry from Columbia University. In 1949 he became a member of the faculty at the School of Medicine, Boston University, where he taught biochemistry. Asimov wrote or edited more than 500 books on topics as diverse as mathematics, astronomy, physics, chemistry, biology, geography,

mythology, and Shakespeare; his science fiction works include some of the most famous and influential in that genre, particularly the short story collection *I, Robot* (1950) and the *Foundation Trilogy* of novels (1951, 1952, 1953). Among his many works of nonfiction are *The Intelligent Man's Guide to Science* (1965), *Lecherous Limericks* (1976), *The Road to Infinity* (1979), the memoir *In Joy Still Felt* (1980), and *Asimov's Guide to the Bible*, Volumes I and II (1981). See also asimovonline.com.

James Baldwin (1924–1987)
American essayist, novelist, and social activist. Baldwin was born in Harlem, became a minister at fourteen, and grew to maturity in an America plagued by racism and homophobia. He moved to Paris in 1948 believing that only outside the United States could he be read as "not merely a Negro; or, even, merely a Negro writer." Both his first published novel, *Go Tell It on the Mountain* (1953), and his first play, *The Amen Corner* (1955), are autobiographical explorations of race and identity. Although he would write other plays, Baldwin concentrated his energies on essays and novels such as *Giovanni's Room* (1956) and *Another Country* (1962). His stories are collected in *Going to Meet the Man* (1965), and his essay collections, including *Notes of a Native Son* (1955) and *The Fire Next Time* (1963), demonstrate Baldwin's skills as a social critic. See also egs.edu/library/james-baldwin/biography.

Dan Barber (b. 1969)
American chef, restauranteur, and food writer. A graduate of both Tufts University, where he earned a B.A. in English, and the French Culinary Institute, Barber has combined cooking and writing throughout his career. He is a multiple winner of the prestigious James Beard Award (including Best Chef: New York City in 2006, and Outstanding Chef of the United States in 2009). Barber has become a leading voice in the local foods movement; his articles about food's origins, the consequences of certain food choices, and the sustainability of modern food production have appeared in the *New York Times*, *Gourmet*, and *Food & Wine*. His book *The Third Plate* was published in 2014. Barber is chef and co-owner of Blue Hill in Manhattan and Blue Hill at Stone Barns in Pocantico Hills, New York. See also bluehillfarm.com.

Dennis Baron (b. 1944)
American scholar of linguistics and communication. Baron was educated at Brandeis University, Columbia University, and the University of Michigan; he then taught high school English in New York City, and since 1975 has been a professor of English and linguistics at the University of Illinois. Baron's works of scholarship include *Grammar and Good Taste: Reforming the American Language* (1982), *The English-Only Question: An Official Language for Americans?* (1990), and most recently *A Better Pencil: Readers, Writers, and the Digital Revolution* (2009), which discusses culture-wide shifts in the way we read and write since the computer age. Baron blogs at *The Web of Language* and is on *Twitter*. See also illinois.edu/blog/view/25.

Dan Barry (b. 1958)
American journalist and author. Born in New York City, Barry earned degrees from St. Bonaventure University and New York University before starting his career as a journalist. While working for the *Providence Journal* in 1992 he shared a Pulitzer Prize for his reporting on a state banking crisis. Since 1995 he has worked for the *New York Times*, where he has written on topics ranging from the 9/11 attacks and Hurricane Katrina to baseball, bowling, and junk food. Barry is the author of three books: *Pull Me Up: A Memoir* (2004); *City Lights* (2007), a collection of his "About New York" columns in the *Times*; and *Bottom of the 33rd: Hope, Redemption, and Baseball's Longest Game* (2001), a winner of the 2012 PEN/ESPN Award for Literary Sports Writing. See also danbarryonline.com.

Lynda Barry (b. 1956)
American cartoonist and author. Born in Wisconsin, Barry grew up in Seattle and attended Evergreen State College in Olympia, Washington, where she began to draw comic strips. Without her knowledge, a friend and fellow cartoonist, Matt Groening (the creator of *The Simpsons*), launched her career by publishing Barry's strips in the *University of Washington Daily*. Since then her weekly comic strip, *Ernie Pook's Comeek*, has appeared in more than fifty publications; her many books include such collections as *The Fun House* (1987) and *Down the Street* (1989); the illustrated novels *The Good Times Are Killing Me* (1988) and *Cruddy* (1999); and *What It Is* (2008), a

graphic novel that is part memoir and part how-to guide for creating graphic novels. Barry's most recent work is *Syllabus: Notes from an Accidental Professor* (2014). See also drawnandquarterly.com/author/lynda-barry.

Alison Bechdel (b. 1960)
American cartoonist. Bechdel was born and raised in Lock Haven, Pennsylvania, and attended Simon's Rock College and Oberlin University, where she earned her B.A. degree. In 1983 she began her long-running comic strip *Dykes to Watch Out For*, first published in the feminist weekly *Womannews*. Over the next twenty-five years, *Dykes* evolved from a single panel to a multi-panel strip featuring a growing cast of characters and a complex web of relationships. Her best-selling graphic memoir *Fun Home* (2006) was adapted into the Tony award–winning musical play (2015); Bechdel followed it with *Are You My Mother?: A Comic Drama* (2012), another commercial and critical success. In 2014 Bechdel received a MacArthur Fellowship. She presently lives, draws, and blogs in Vermont. See also dykestowatchoutfor.com.

Caroline Bird (1915–2011)
American journalist, public-relations specialist, and writer. Bird attended Vassar College, graduated from the University of Toledo, and received her M.A. from the University of Wisconsin. She worked as a researcher at *Newsweek* and *Fortune* in the 1940s, then moved into public relations, which she left after twenty years to write books that tracked the challenges faced by the women of her generation: *The Invisible Scar* (1966), a study of the lingering effects of the Great Depression; *Born Female: The High Cost of Keeping Women Down* (1968); *Enterprising Women: Their Contribution to the American Economy, 1776–1976* (1976); *Second Careers: New Ways to Work after Fifty* (1992); and *Lives of Our Own: Secrets of a Salty Old Woman* (1995). Her best-known book, *The Case against College* (1975), argues that college is, for many students, an overpriced waste of time. See also specialcollections.vassar.edu/collections/manuscripts/findingaids/bird_caronline.html.

Eula Biss (b. c. 1977)
American nonfiction writer. Upon graduating from Hampshire College, Biss moved to New York City, where she taught in public schools for several years before leaving to earn an M.F.A. degree in the University of Iowa's nonfiction writing program. Since then she has published three books: *The Balloonists* (2002), a collection of autobiographical prose poems; *Notes from No Man's Land* (2009), a volume of essays about race in America; and *On Immunity: An Inoculation* (2014), an exploration of vaccination, vampires, and the value we place on health. Acknowledging the influence of poets Adrienne Rich and Sylvia Plath, Biss has written: "I count that as one of the reasons why I tend to think of personal narrative—particularly when it concerns the body or domesticity—as a perfectly viable space for intellectual exploration." See also eulabiss.net.

Tom Bissell (b. 1974)
American journalist and author. After graduating from Michigan State University in 1996 with a degree in English, Bissell served as a Peace Corps volunteer in Uzbekistan; he then turned to the travel writing that made his name as a journalist. In addition to his widely anthologized short stories and feature articles, Bissell has published a number of books, including *Chasing the Sea: Lost among the Ghosts of Empire in Central Asia* (2003), *God Lives in St. Petersburg: and Other Stories* (2005), and *The Disaster Artist* (2013), co-written with Greg Sestero. His 2010 book, *Extra Lives: Why Video Games Matter*, stems from Bissell's deep involvement with video games; he has written scripts for six games, including *Gears of War: Judgment* (2013). See also grantland.com/contributors/tom-bissell.

Jaswinder Bolina (b. 1978)
American poet and essayist. Bolina's parents immigrated to the United States from northern India and he was born and grew up in Chicago. He earned a B.A. in philosophy from Loyola University Chicago before going on to the University of Michigan for his M.F.A. in creative writing and Ohio University for his Ph.D. in English. In his poems and essays, Bolina brings to light and challenges the hidden premises behind any too-easy understandings of the world, or of words. Bolina's poems have been collected in the volumes *Carrier Wave* (2006) and *Phantom Camera* (2012), as well as the chapbook *The Tallest Building in America* (2014). He teaches in the M.F.A. Program in Creative Writing at the University of Miami. See also jaswinderbolina.com.

Mark Bowden (b. 1951)
American journalist, author, and screen-writer. A native of St. Louis, Bowden earned his B.A. at Loyola University Maryland. In addition to his twenty-four years as a staff writer for the *Philadelphia Inquirer*, Bowden has written what he calls "deep journalism" for many other publications, including the *New Yorker*, the *Atlantic*, *Sports Illustrated*, and *Rolling Stone*. "Nothing will ever replace language as the medium of thought," he writes, "so nothing will replace the well-written, originally reported story, or the well-reasoned essay." His book about a failed military intervention in Somalia, *Black Hawk Down* (1999), earned him a national reputation and was made into a film in 2001. His ten other books range in subject from modern warfare to professional sports; the most recent is *The Finish: The Killing of Osama bin Laden* (2012). See also theatlantic.com/author/mark-bowden.

David Brooks (b. 1961)
Canadian-born essayist and news commentator. Brooks was born in Toronto, grew up in New York City, and graduated from the University of Chicago in 1983 with a degree in history. Presently a columnist for the *New York Times* and commentator on *PBS NewsHour*, he was previously a writer and editor for the *Wall Street Journal* and then the senior editor of the *Weekly Standard*. Brooks is the author of *Bobos in Paradise: The New Upper Class and How They Got There* (2000) and *On Paradise Drive: How We Live Now (and Always Have) in the Future Tense* (2004). Brooks himself reports that he was politically liberal before "coming to my senses" as a young man; since then he has frequently broken with fellow conservatives by espousing moderate views on social issues. See also nytimes.com/column/david-brooks.

DeNeen Brown
American journalist. Brown, presently a staff writer at the *Washington Post*, is known for covering a broad array of topics, from the problems caused by urban gentrification to the politics and events taking place in Washington, D.C., and Maryland. As the *Post*'s Canada bureau chief, she traveled throughout the Arctic regions to report on indigenous peoples and the effects of climate change. Brown is the recipient of numerous awards for her investigative journalism. Her essay "First Person Singular: Sometimes It Is

about You" is included in the anthology *Telling True Stories: A Nonfiction Writers' Guide* (2007). See also washingtonpost.com/people/deneen-l-brown.

Nicholas Carr (b. 1959)
American journalist and author. Carr received his B.A. from Dartmouth College and an M.A. in English from Harvard University, where he was executive editor of the *Harvard Business Review*. After nearly two decades as a management consultant, Carr published his first book, *Does IT Matter? Information Technology and the Corrosion of Competitive Advantage* (2004), earning him a reputation as a contrarian in an age of great excitement about technological change. *The Big Switch: Rewiring the World, from Edison to Google* (2008) and *The Shallows: What the Internet Is Doing to Our Brains* (2010) both argue that the explosion of innovation in information technology is already having widespread and unforeseen effects—not necessarily for the better—on commerce, culture, and human intelligence. His most recent book is *The Glass Cage: Automation and Us* (2014). See also nicholasgcarr.com.

Michael Chabon (b. 1963)
American novelist and essayist. Born in Pittsburgh, Chabon grew up there and in Columbia, Maryland. He was educated at Carnegie Mellon University, the University of Pittsburgh, and the University of California, Irvine, where he received an M.F.A. in creative writing. The commercial and critical success of his first novel, *The Mysteries of Pittsburgh* (1988), written as his master's thesis, was followed by his second novel, *Wonder Boys* (1995). *The Amazing Adventures of Kavalier & Clay* (2000), a Pulitzer Prize winner, features Chabon's characteristic themes: family ties, a search for Jewish identity, and a fascination with "lowbrow" genre fiction and comic books. Subsequent books have included the novel *The Yiddish Policemen's Union* (2007) and most recently *Telegraph Avenue* (2012). See also michaelchabon.com.

Julia Child (1912–2004)
American chef, author, and TV personality. Born Julia McWilliams, she grew up in Pasadena, California, and earned her B.A. in English at Smith College. While serving with the Office of Strategic Services (precursor to the CIA) in Ceylon during the Second World War, she met her husband, Paul Cushing

Child, an OSS colleague. After the war he joined the U.S. State Department and was posted to Paris, where Julia Child studied cooking at Le Cordon Bleu and co-authored *Mastering the Art of French Cooking* (1961), an immediate best-seller. In 1963 she debuted television's first cooking show, *The French Chef*, which ran for ten years and made Julia Child a household name. In addition to her many books about food and cooking, her posthumously published memoir, *My Life in France* (2006), became the basis for Meryl Streep's Oscar-nominated portrayal of Child in the film *Julie & Julia*. See also pbs.org/food/julia-child.

Judith Ortiz Cofer (b. 1952)
American novelist, poet, and essayist. Born in Hormigueros, Puerto Rico, Cofer spent much of her childhood traveling between her Puerto Rican home and Paterson, New Jersey. Educated at Augusta College, Florida Atlantic University, and Oxford University, Cofer is professor emerita of English and creative writing at the University of Georgia. *Silent Dancing* (1990) reflects her ongoing efforts to explore her bicultural and bilingual roots as a member of what she calls "the Puerto Rican diaspora." Her other books include *The Latin Deli: Prose and Poetry* (1995), *Woman in Front of the Sun: On Becoming a Writer* (2000), *The Meaning of Consuelo* (2003), the young adult novel *Call Me Maria* (2006), and *A Love Story Beginning in Spanish: Poems* (2005). See also judithortizcofer.english.uga.edu.

Aaron Copland (1900–1990)
American composer, conductor, and writer. Born and raised in Brooklyn, Copland studied music theory and practice in Paris in the early 1920s, then returned to New York to compose, organize concert series, publish American scores, and further the cause of the American composer. His experiments with adapting jazz to classical composition gradually led Copland to develop a distinctly American style. He incorporated American folk songs and legends into many of his works, including three ballet scores: *Billy the Kid* (1938), *Rodeo* (1942), and *Appalachian Spring* (1944), winner of the Pulitzer Prize. His other popular works include *Lincoln Portrait* (1942), for narrator and orchestra; *Fanfare for the Common Man* (1942); and *Connotations for Orchestra* (1962). An avid reader throughout his long life, he also wrote music criticism and essays. In his later years Copland was celebrated as "the Dean of American Music." See also coplandhouse.org.

William Cronon (b. 1954)
American environmental historian. Born in Connecticut and raised in Wisconsin, Cronon was a double major in history and English at the University of Wisconsin. After winning a Rhodes scholarship and completing a degree at Oxford University, Cronon earned a Ph.D. from Yale University, where he taught for over a decade. He later returned to the University of Wisconsin, where he teaches American environmental history and the history of the American West. His books, all of which concern the way humans shape the natural world and are in turn shaped by it, include *Changes in the Land: Indians, Colonists, and the Ecology of New England* (1983), *Nature's Metropolis: Chicago and the Great West* (1991), *Under an Open Sky: Rethinking America's Western Past* (1992), and *Uncommon Ground: Rethinking the Human Place in Nature* (1995). See also williamcronon.net.

Amy Cunningham (b. 1955)
American journalist and essayist. Cunningham studied English at the University of Virginia and has been a freelance writer since she graduated in 1977. She has written on yoga, meditation, spirituality, feminism, and healthy living for magazines such as *Glamour*, *Mademoiselle*, *Parenting*, and the *Washington Post Sunday Magazine*, as well as for several online journals. She has also written a blog, "ChatteringMind," for the website Beliefnet.com. See also chatteringmind.com.

Edwidge Danticat (b. 1969)
Haitian American author. Raised for much of her childhood by an aunt and uncle in Port-au-Prince, Haiti, Danticat was educated in French and began writing in her native Creole when she was only nine years old. At twelve she joined her immigrant parents in Brooklyn; within two years she published her first work in English. After earning a B.A. at Barnard College and an M.F.A. in creative writing from Brown University, she turned her thesis into her first novel, *Breath, Eyes, Memory* (1994). The themes of that novel—Haitian identity, the immigrant experience, mothers and daughters—have informed her work ever

since. In 2009 Danticat was granted a MacArthur Fellowship. She has published more than fifteen books, including novels and collections of both short stories and essays. Her most recent novel is *Claire of the Sea Light* (2013). See also newyorker.com/contributors/edwidge-danticat.

Debra Dickerson (b. 1960)
American lawyer and essayist. Raised in St. Louis, Missouri, Dickerson earned degrees from the University of Maryland and Harvard Law School. She has been an officer in the U.S. Air Force, a senior editor at *U.S. News and World Report*, and a lawyer for the NAACP Legal Defense Fund. She is presently a Senior Fellow at the New American Foundation in Washington, D.C. Her writing has appeared in the *New Republic*, the *New York Times*, and the *Nation*, among other periodicals; she is also a blogger for *Mother Jones*. Her books, focusing on the role of race in American life, include the memoir *An American Story* (2000) and *The End of Blackness* (2004). See also debradickerson.com.

Joan Didion (b. 1934)
American novelist, essayist, and screenwriter. A native of California, Didion studied at the University of California at Berkeley. After winning *Vogue* magazine's Prix de Paris contest for excellence in writing, she began working for the magazine, and left in 1963, the year her first novel, *Run River*, was published. Since then, she has written five more novels, most recently *The Last Thing He Wanted* (1996). The essays collected in *Slouching Towards Bethlehem* (1968) and *The White Album* (1979) captured the spirit of the 1960s and 1970s, respectively, and put Didion in the forefront of American essayists. Her recent works of nonfiction include *Fixed Ideas: America since 9.11* (2003) and *The Year of Magical Thinking* (2005), winner of the National Book Award. *We Tell Ourselves Stories in Order to Live* (2006) collects her first seven volumes of nonfiction. See also vanityfair.com/culture/2011/10/joan-didion-201110.

Annie Dillard (b. 1945)
American nature writer, poet, and novelist. Born in Pittsburgh, Pennsylvania, Dillard received her B.A. and M.A. from Hollins College. She has published books that range from the poetry of her first

book, *Tickets for a Prayer Wheel* (1974), to the nature meditation *Holy the Firm* (1977), the memoir *An American Childhood* (1987), the literary theory in *Living by Fiction* (1982), the essay collection *Teaching a Stone to Talk* (1982), and the novels *The Living* (1992) and *The Maytrees* (2007). In her Pulitzer Prize–winning nonfiction narrative *Pilgrim at Tinker Creek* (1974), Dillard recounts years she spent living in seclusion in the natural world, much like Henry David Thoreau. In *The Writing Life* (1989) she muses on her life's work—"to examine all things intensely and relentlessly." See also anniedillard.com.

Frederick Douglass (1818–1895)
American abolitionist, orator, journalist, and memoirist. Born a slave in Maryland, Douglass learned at a young age how to read and write, even though it was against the law to teach literacy to a slave. In 1836 he escaped from his master and fled to the North with Anna Murray, also a freed slave, whom he later married. Douglass soon became an important orator in the abolitionist movement and, with the publication of his first autobiography, *A Narrative of the Life of Frederick Douglass* (1845), an international spokesman for freedom. Douglass founded the antislavery newspaper the *North Star* in 1847 and actively recruited black soldiers to join the Union Army at the outbreak of the Civil War. He continued his autobiography in *My Bondage and My Freedom* (1855) and *Life and Times of Frederick Douglass* (1881, rev. 1892). See also loc.gov/collection/frederick-douglass-papers/about-this-collection.

Brian Doyle (b. 1956)
American essayist, editor, and author. Born in New York City, Doyle received his B.A. from the University of Notre Dame in 1978. He worked on various magazines and newspapers in Chicago and Boston, and since 1991 has edited the University of Portland's *Portland Magazine*. A prolific writer of essays, stories, and the prose poems he calls "proems," Doyle has published ten books, including the essay collection *Spirited Men* (2004), about male musicians and writers; *The Wet Engine* (2005), about "hearts and how they work and do not work and get repaired and patched, for a while"; and *The Grail* (2006), about a year in an Oregon vineyard. His most recent book is *The Plover* (2015).

See also orionmagazine.org/contributor/ brian-doyle.

David James Duncan (b. 1952)
American novelist, essayist, and environmental activist. Born in Portland, Oregon, and educated at Portland State University, Duncan is best known for his two best-selling novels, *The River Why* (1983) and *The Brothers K* (1992), both of which center around his passion for fly-fishing and wilderness. Duncan's other books include *River Teeth* (1996), a volume of short stories; *My Story as Told by Water* (2001), a memoir; and most recently *God Laughs and Plays: Churchless Sermons in Response to the Preachments of the Fundamentalist Right* (2006). A student of Eastern spiritual traditions, Duncan advocates "direct, small-scale compassion-activism" in response to threats to the natural environment. See also davidjamesduncan.com.

David Eagleman (b. 1971)
American neuroscientist and writer. Born in New Mexico, Eagleman studied literature at Rice University before earning his Ph.D. in neuroscience at Baylor College of Medicine, where he now directs both the Laboratory for Perception and Action and the Initiative on Neuroscience and Law. In his scientific work, he studies how the brain processes sensory input to create what he calls "a temporally unified picture of the world." Eagleman's collection of short speculative fictions, *Sum: Forty Tales from the Afterlives* (2009), was an international best-seller; it explores the viewpoint he calls "Possibilianism." He followed this with *Wednesday Is Indigo Blue: Discovering the Brain of Synesthesia* (co-authored with Richard Cytowic, 2009), *Why the Net Matters: How the Internet Will Save Civilization* (2010), and *Incognito: The Secret Lives of the Brain* (2011). Eagleman is also the writer and host of the PBS television series *The Brain* (2015). See also eagleman.com.

Lars Eighner (b. 1948)
American writer. Born in Corpus Christi, Texas, Eighner attended the University of Texas at Austin, where he now lives. A self-described "skeptical Democrat," Eighner has worked in hospitals and drug-crisis programs despite ongoing struggles with illness and homelessness. His book *Travels with Lizbeth* (1993), which describes his three years of surviving on the streets with his dog, was a best-seller. He has also published *Elements of Arousal* (1994), a how-to guide on writing gay erotica, and the comic novel *Pawn to Queen Four* (1995), about the gay subculture of a Texas town. See also larseighner.com.

Nora Ephron (1941–2012)
American journalist, director, and screenwriter. Born in New York City, Ephron grew up in Beverly Hills, California, the daughter of two screenwriters. Soon after graduating from Wellesley College in 1962, she began writing for the *New York Post, Esquire*, the *New York Times Magazine*, and *New York* magazine. In the mid-1970s she turned from journalism to screenplays and was nominated for three Academy Awards for best original screenplay, for *Silkwood* (1983), *When Harry Met Sally* (1989), and *Sleepless in Seattle* (1993). In the 1990s she began directing films, including *You've Got Mail* (1998), *Lucky Numbers* (2000), and *Julie & Julia* (2009). Her books include the novel *Heartburn* (1996) and the essay collections *Wallflower at the Orgy* (1970), *Crazy Salad* (1975), *Scribble, Scribble: Notes on the Media* (1978), and *I Remember Nothing: and Other Reflections* (2010). See also imdb.com/name/nm0001188.

David Epstein
American journalist and author. Epstein earned his B.S. degree in environmental science and astronomy at Columbia University; he also holds master's degrees from Columbia in both environmental science and journalism. After a stint as a crime reporter for the *New York Daily News*, he wrote for *Sports Illustrated*, where he produced award-winning articles on the abuse of steroids, the particular dangers of heart failure faced by athletes, and painkiller addiction in sports. His first book, *The Sports Gene: Inside the Science of Extraordinary Athletic Performance* (2013), explores the role of genetics in the making of top-flight athletes. See also thesportsgene.com.

M. F. K. Fisher (1908–1992)
American gastronome and food writer. Born in Albion, Michigan, Mary Frances Kennedy grew up in Whittier, California, and attended the University of California, Berkeley, where she met her first husband, Alfred Young Fisher. The couple spent the early years of their marriage

in France; it was in Dijon, which she would later describe as "the gastronomical capital of the world," that she became immersed in the culinary arts that would be her lifelong passion. Not long after returning to the United States she wrote her first book about food and the art of living well, *Serve It Forth* (1937). Among the many books that followed, the best known are *Consider the Oyster* (1941), *The Art of Eating* (1954), and two memoirs, *The Gastronomical Me* (1943) and *Long Ago in France* (1991). See also mfkfisher.com.

Frances FitzGerald (b. 1940)
American journalist and author. FitzGerald was born in New York City to a prominent political family; her father was a deputy director of the CIA, her mother an ambassador to the United Nations. Since graduating from Radcliffe College in 1962, FitzGerald has worked as a freelance journalist and regularly contributes to such publications as the *New Yorker*, the *Nation*, *Rolling Stone*, and the *New York Review of Books*. Her reporting in Vietnam at the height of the war there in 1966 resulted in her first book, *Fire in the Lake: The Vietnamese and the Americans in Vietnam* (1972); it won both the Pulitzer Prize and the National Book Award for nonfiction. Her later books include *America Revised: History Schoolbooks in the Twentieth Century* (1979), *Way Out There in the Blue: Reagan, Star Wars, and the End of the Cold War* (2000), and *Vietnam: Spirits of the Earth* (2002). See also newyorker.com/contributors/frances-fitzgerald.

Franklin Foer
American journalist. Born into a family of writers, Foer began his own career in journalism soon after graduating from Columbia University. He has written extensively for such publications as *Slate* and *New York* magazine, and has published two books: *How Soccer Explains the World* (2004) and *Jewish Jocks* (co-edited with Marc Tracy, 2012). Foer is probably best known for his work with the *New Republic*, a century-old political journal, for which he was managing editor from 2006 to 2010. When a new owner acquired the magazine in 2012, he persuaded Foer to resume his former post; two years later Foer was forced out and more than half the staff resigned in protest. Before leaving the *New Republic*, Foer edited a volume celebrating the magazine's 100 years, *Insurrections of the Mind* (2014). See also @FranklinFoer on *Twitter*.

Benjamin Franklin (1706–1790)
American statesman, inventor, writer, and diplomat. Born in Boston, Franklin was apprenticed at twelve to his brother, a printer. He resettled in Philadelphia and at twenty-four was editor and publisher of the *Pennsylvania Gazette*. In 1733 he began writing *Poor Richard's Almanack*, a collection of aphorisms and advice. Retiring from business at forty-two to devote himself to study and research, he soon found himself involved in colonial politics. From 1757 until 1763 he represented the colonies in England. He served on the committee appointed to draft the Declaration of Independence and later was both minister to France and delegate to the Paris peace conference that officially concluded the Revolutionary War. Revered as "the First American," late in his life he became an advocate for the abolition of slavery. His posthumously published *Autobiography* is a classic memoir. See also britannica.com/biography/Benjamin-Franklin.

Joey Franklin (b. 1980)
American essayist. Franklin grew up in Beaverton, Oregon, and after a two-year stint as a Mormon missionary in Japan he earned a B.A. in English at Brigham Young University, an M.A. in creative nonfiction at Ohio University, and a Ph.D. in literature and creative writing from Texas Tech University. A specialist in creative nonfiction, Franklin professes an interest in "memory, identity, and self-representation." His essays have appeared in *American Literary Review*, *Gettysburg Review*, and the *Writer's Chronicle*; many of these are collected in his first book, *My Wife Wants You to Know I'm Happily Married* (2015). Franklin teaches creative writing at Brigham Young University. See also joey-franklin.blogspot.com.

Ian Frazier (b. 1951)
American essayist and humorist. Born in Hudson, Ohio, Frazier studied at Western Reserve Academy and Harvard University, where he worked as a humorist at the satirical *Harvard Lampoon*. Since his graduation from Harvard in 1973 many of his humorous pieces have appeared first in the *New Yorker* and then been collected in such volumes as *Dating Your Mom* (1986), *Coyote v. Acme* (1996), and *Lamentations of the*

Father (2008). Frazier's best-known work of nonfiction is *Great Plains* (1989)—like his works *Family* (1994) and *On the Rez* (2000), it is based on both extensive research and his own experiences after moving to Montana in 1982. Since relocating with his family to the East Coast he has published *Gone to New York: Adventures in the City* (2005) as well as his most recent book, the best-selling *Travels in Siberia* (2010). See also us .macmillan.com/author/ianfrazier.

David H. Freedman (b. 1954)
American journalist and author. Born in Boston, Freedman studied for two years at Northwestern University before deciding he'd be better off "learning what to write about rather than how to write it." He transferred to Oberlin College and earned a bachelor's degree in physics. Since then Freedman's writing, primarily about science, technology, and business, has appeared in a wide range of publications, including *Science, Discover, Scientific American, Forbes, Wired*, and the *Atlantic*, where he is now a contributing editor. Freedman's immersion in science has led him to become skeptical about the reliability of scientific findings and especially of science journalism. Increasingly he focuses on health care and medical science. The latest of his five books, *Wrong: Why Experts Keep Failing Us—and How to Know When Not to Trust Them* (2010) grew out of his 2010 *Atlantic* article, "Lies, Damned Lies, and Medical Science." See also fatandskinner.org.

Northrop Frye (1912–1991)
Canadian literary critic and educator. A graduate of the University of Toronto's Victoria College and Oxford University, Frye served as a member of the faculty at Victoria College from 1939 until his death. A specialist in Renaissance and Romantic literature, he launched his career with *Fearful Symmetry* (1947), which led to a radical reevaluation of the works of English poet William Blake. His best-known work, *Anatomy of Criticism* (1957), represents his lifelong project: to make the criticism of literature as rigorously systematic as science. The critic's chief task, he argues, is not to evaluate a work of literature but to discern the archetypes that inform the work. Frye would go on to write more than forty books that apply his theories to subjects ranging from Shakespeare's comedies and Milton's epics to Canadian culture and the Bible as literature. See also

thecanadianencyclopedia.ca/en/article/northrop-frye.

Paul Fussell (1924–2012)
American literary and cultural historian. Born in Pasadena, California, Fussell was twice decorated for his service in the U.S. Army in World War II, earned a Ph.D. at Harvard University, and taught at Connecticut College and University of Pennsylvania. Fussell's early books dealt with poetic theory and eighteenth-century literature. With the publication of *The Great War and Modern Memory* (1975), a National Book Award winner, Fussell became better known as a critic of the glorification of war in popular culture. In *Class: A Guide through the American Status System* (1983), he reveals a sharp eye for the nuances of social class. Fussell also edited *The Norton Book of Travel* (1987) and *The Norton Book of Modern War* (1990). See also nyti .ms1E2Am2Q.

Henry Louis Gates Jr. (b. 1950)
American scholar and literary critic. Born and raised in West Virginia, Gates was educated at Yale and Cambridge Universities. Now a professor at Harvard University, Gates edits African American literature, composes literary criticism, and writes for general audiences. He has created a number of television documentaries, including "African American Lives" (2006), and his essays have appeared in the *New Yorker, Newsweek, Sports Illustrated*, and the *New York Times*. Gates's many books include *Figures in Black: Words, Signs, and the "Racial" Self* (1987); *The Signifying Monkey* (1988), winner of the National Book Award; *Colored People* (1994), his best-selling autobiography; *Wonders of the African World* (1999); and most recently *The Henry Louis Gates Jr. Reader* (2012), a collection of his writings. Gates is the general co-editor of *The Norton Anthology of African American Literature* (3rd ed. 2014). See also aaas.fas.harvard .edu/people/henry-louis-gates-jr.

Atul Gawande (b. 1965)
American surgeon, teacher, and essayist. Born in Brooklyn to Indian immigrant parents, Gawande grew up in Athens, Ohio. He earned his B.A. at Stanford University, studied at Oxford University as a Rhodes Scholar, and then earned his M.D. from Harvard Medical School. In addition to scholarly studies published in the *New England Journal*

of Medicine, his articles about health care and the medical profession have appeared frequently in *Slate* and the *New Yorker*. Gawande's four books, including *Complications: A Surgeon's Notes on an Imperfect Science* (2002), and *The Checklist Manifesto: How to Get Things Right* (2009), have been widely praised for the clarity with which they illuminated a complex, technical subject for a general readership. His most recent book is *Being Mortal: Medicine and What Matters in the End* (2014). See also gawande.com.

Roxane Gay (b. 1974)
American writer and commentator. Born in Omaha, Nebraska, Gay earned an M.A. at the University of Nebraska at Lincoln, and a Ph.D. in rhetoric and technical communications from Michigan Technological University, and is now a professor of English at Purdue University. Her short stories and essays have appeared in such publications as *Time*, *McSweeney's*, and the *Nation*, as well as in a broad range of anthologies, from *Best Sex Writing* (2012) to *Best American Mystery Stories* (2014). Her books include *Ayiti* (2011), a short-story collection; *An Untamed State* (2014), a novel; and *Bad Feminist* (2014), a volume of essays that discusses the difficulties of being a woman in a world without perfect role models. Gay is also the founder of Tiny Hardcore Press. See also roxanegay.com.

A. Bartlett Giamatti (1938–1989)
American scholar and author. Born in Boston and raised in South Hadley, Massachusetts, Giamatti spent much of his life at Yale University. There he earned his bachelor's and doctorate degrees, was a professor of English, and began his tenure as Yale's youngest-ever president in 1978. Eight years later he left Yale and turned to his first love: baseball. Giamatti was named president of the National League in 1986 and commissioner of Major League Baseball in 1989. Just five months after assuming his dream job, he died suddenly of a heart attack at age fifty-one. Author of eight books, Giamatti published influential scholarly volumes such as *Play of Double Senses: Spenser's Faerie Queene* (1975) and books about the role of academia in American culture such as *The University and the Public Interest* (1981). His lyrical essays about baseball are collected in *A Great and Glorious Game* (1998). See also baseballlibrary.com.

Malcolm Gladwell (b. 1963)
Canadian journalist and essayist. Born in England and raised in Canada, Gladwell graduated from the University of Toronto in 1984 and soon began his career as a journalist, writing for various publications including the *Washington Post*. Since joining the staff of the *New Yorker* in 1996, he has contributed articles on an array of topics, from the "science of shopping" to highway safety to the SAT to mammography. His books, all international best-sellers, include *The Tipping Point: How Little Things Can Make a Big Difference* (2000), *Blink: The Power of Thinking without Thinking* (2005), *Outliers: The Story of Success* (2008), *What the Dog Saw* (2009), and most recently *David and Goliath: Underdogs, Misfits, and the Art of Battling Giants* (2013). See also gladwell.com.

Thomas Goetz (b. 1968)
American author and health care entrepreneur. Goetz holds a B.A. degree from Bates College, a master's degree in public health from the University of California, Berkeley, and a master's degree in American literature from the University of Virginia. At *Wired* magazine, where he was a longtime executive editor, he wrote articles about genomics, medical technology, and behavior change that have been widely anthologized; his popular TED talk about redesigning medical data led up to his co-founding of Iodine, "a health technology company with the mission of turning medical research data into clear and actionable tools for ordinary people to make better decisions about their health." Goetz is the author of two books: *The Decision Tree: Taking Control of Your Health in the New Era of Personalized Medicine* (2010) and *The Remedy* (2014), which chronicles the story of the battle against tuberculosis. See also thomasgoetz.com.

JJ Goode (b. 1981)
American food and travel writer. Goode grew up in New Jersey eating supermarket mac and cheese, frozen pizza, and tuna noodle casserole. He is a graduate of Vassar College, where he studied psychology because, he says, he was afraid of taking writing classes. Now Goode writes about every aspect of food and drink: pancakes and pasta, salsa and sushi, cocktails and coffee. He has written for the *New York Times*, *Gourmet*, *Bon Appétit*, *Saveur*, and many other publications. He has co-authored several

cookbooks, including *Truly Mexican* (2011) and *Tacos, Tortas, and Tamales* (2012), both with Roberto Santibanez; *Pok Pok: Food and Stories from the Streets, Homes, and Roadside Restaurants of Thailand* (2013) with Andy Ricker; *A Girl and Her Pig* (2012); and most recently *A Girl and Her Greens* (2015).

Stephen Jay Gould (1941–2002)

American paleontologist, essayist, and educator. Raised in New York City, Gould graduated from Antioch College and received a Ph.D. from Columbia University in 1967. He then joined the faculty of Harvard University as a professor of geology and zoology and taught courses in paleontology, biology, and the history of science. Gould demystified science for lay readers in the essays he wrote for a regular column in *Natural History* magazine; many of these were collected in *Ever Since Darwin* (1977), *Hen's Teeth and Horse's Toes* (1983), and *Eight Little Piggies* (1993). Gould's *The Mismeasure of Man* (1981), which questioned traditional ways of testing intelligence, won the National Book Critics Circle Award for essays and criticism. A renowned neo-Darwinian, Gould championed the theory of evolution throughout his career; his last book on this subject, *The Structure of Evolutionary Theory*, appeared in 2002. See also amnh.org/science/bios/gould.

Gerald Graff (b. 1937)

American scholar and author. Born and raised in Chicago, Graff went on to earn his B.A. in English from the University of Chicago. After receiving his doctorate in English and American literature from Stanford University, he taught at a number of universities before settling at the University of Illinois at Chicago, where he has taught writing and literature since 2000. Graff has authored books such as *Literature against Itself* (1979) and *Professing Literature: An Institutional History* (1987) that champion what he calls "literature's rational, discursive qualities"; his books critiquing American intellectual culture include *Clueless in Academe: How Schooling Obscures the Life of the Mind* (2004). Most recently, Graff and his wife, writer Cathy Birkenstein, have co-authored *"They Say/I Say": The Moves That Matter in Academic Writing* (2014). See also geraldgraff.com.

David Halberstam (1934–2007)

American journalist, historian, and author. Halberstam grew up in Yonkers, New York, and earned a B.A. at Harvard University, where he began his career in journalism as managing editor of the *Harvard Crimson*. He is known for his Pulitzer Prize–winning reporting on the Vietnam War for the *New York Times*, as well as his book *The Best and the Brightest* (1972), regarded as a masterpiece of historical analysis. Halberstam's twenty-two books, mainly about politics and war, also include a novel, *The Children* (1999), and a number of books on sports, including *Playing for Keeps* (1999), a profile of basketball legend Michael Jordan, and *The Education of a Coach* (2005), about New England Patriots coach Bill Belichick. Halberstam was completing the research for *The Glory Game: How the 1958 NFL Championship Changed Football Forever* (2008) when he was killed in an automobile accident. See also achievement.org/autodoc/page/hal.0bio-1.

Michael Hamad (b. 1972)

American music critic and visual artist. Hamad holds a master's degree in music theory from the Hartt School and a doctorate in musicology from Brandeis University. As a staff music writer for the *Hartford Courant*, he covers popular music, jazz, "and whatever else sounds interesting." Hamad is also a guitarist and a visual artist who has devised a unique way of visually reimagining music in the form of "schematics"—assemblages of words and symbols, created in real time, that graph his aural experience in two or even three dimensions. Hamad's artwork has appeared in the *Village Voice*, the *Believer*, and the *New York Times*. See also setlistschematics.tumblr.com.

Stephen Hawking (b. 1942)

British physicist and author. Born in Oxford and raised in London, Hawking earned his B.A. at Oxford University and his Ph.D. at Cambridge University, where for three decades he held the professorship of mathematics once held by Sir Isaac Newton. Hawking is a renowned theoretical physicist; his work has contributed greatly to the modern scientific understanding of cosmology, quantum gravity, and black holes. In addition to a wealth of highly specialized scientific publications, his *A Brief History of Time* (1988) introduced millions of readers to contemporary ideas about the physical universe. *The Grand Design* (2010), co-written with American physicist Leonard

Mlodinow, discusses attempts to combine Einstein's theory of general relativity with quantum physics to create a "Theory of Everything." Hawking has recently published a memoir, *My Brief History* (2013). See also hawking.org.uk.

Christopher Hitchens (1949–2011)
British American journalist, author, and commentator. The son of an officer in the British Royal Navy, Hitchens was born in England and grew up on naval bases. He attended Oxford University and was drawn to the political left of the 1960s; in the ensuing decades he would continue to call himself a Marxist, but he resisted orthodoxies of any kind and often took positions that confounded his friends and allies. Hitchens's journalism was published in the *New Statesman*, *Vanity Fair*, and *Slate*; it was his long association with the *Nation* that led him to move to the United States, where he eventually became a U.S. citizen. Once called "a gadfly with gusto," Hitchens became best known for his outspoken, confrontational atheism. He wrote, co-wrote, or edited more than forty books; *God Is Not Great: How Religion Poisons Everything* (2007) was a major bestseller. See also vanityfair.com/contributor/christopher-hitchens.

Langston Hughes (1902–1967)
American poet, playwright, and fiction writer. Born in Joplin, Missouri, Hughes grew up in the American Midwest before coming to New York City to attend Columbia University. Appalled by the racial discrimination there, he left Columbia to pursue his own writing, especially the "jazz poetry" that became his hallmark. After a period of travel and living abroad, he returned to the United States to complete his B.A. at Pennsylvania's Lincoln University. He returned to New York and soon emerged as a key figure in the Harlem Renaissance of the 1920s and 1930s, beginning with his collection of poems, *The Weary Blues*, in 1926. In his lifetime he would publish sixteen more volumes of poetry as well as two novels, seven collections of short stories, twenty-six plays, and seven works of nonfiction, including the memoir *The Big Sea* (1940). See also poetryfoundation.org/bio/langston-hughes.

Zora Neale Hurston (1891–1960)
American anthropologist, folklorist, and writer. A central figure of the Harlem Renaissance of the 1920s and 1930s,

Hurston was born in Notasulga, Alabama, and grew up in Eatonville, Florida, the daughter of a Baptist preacher and a seamstress. She attended Howard University and in 1928 received a B.A. from Barnard College, where she studied anthropology and developed an interest in black folk traditions and in oral history. Hurston's writing draws on her knowledge of folklore and uses a vigorous, rhythmical, direct prose style that influenced many later American writers. Her works include the play *Mule Bone: A Comedy of Negro Life in Three Acts* (1931), written with Langston Hughes; the novel *Their Eyes Were Watching God* (1937); her autobiography, *Dust Tracks on a Road* (1942); as well as her *Collected Stories* (1995) and *Collected Plays* (2008). See also zoranealehurston.com.

T. H. Huxley (1825–1895)
English biologist and educator. Born in a village near London, Huxley had little formal education but immersed himself in the burgeoning scientific literature of his day. Through apprenticeships he learned enough about the practice of medicine to sign on as a surgeon's mate aboard the HMS *Rattlesnake*. During the ship's four-year voyage of discovery, Huxley studied marine invertebrates; the papers he wrote and illustrated with his own drawings won him a fellowship in the prestigious Royal Society when he returned to England in 1850. In the ensuing years, Huxley presided over numerous scientific institutions and became known as "Darwin's bulldog" for his vigorous defense of Charles Darwin's theory of human evolution, first published in 1871. In his own book *Evidence as to Man's Place in Nature* (1863), Huxley had already set out the terms of the debate that would roil the scientific world for decades. See also aleph0.clarku.edu/Huxley.

Molly Ivins (1944–2007)
American newspaper columnist and essayist. Born in California and raised in Houston, Texas, Ivins received a B.A. from Smith College and an M.A. in journalism from Columbia University. She worked on the staffs of the *Houston Chronicle*, the *Minneapolis Tribune*, the *Texas Observer*, the *New York Times*, and the *Dallas Times Herald*; she became nationally famous as a syndicated political columnist at the *Fort Worth Star-Telegram*. An unapologetic liberal, Ivins used humor to address serious issues and

delighted especially in exposing politics at its worst. Her collections include *Molly Ivins Can't Say That, Can She?* (1991) and *You Got to Dance with Them What Brung You* (1998). Her books include *Shrub: The Short but Happy Political Life of George W. Bush* (2000), *Bushwhacked: Life in George W. Bush's America* (2003), and *Who Let the Dogs In? Incredible Political Animals I Have Known* (2004). See also mollyivins.com.

Leslie Jamison
American novelist and essayist. Jamison was born in Washington, D.C., and grew up in Los Angeles. She earned a B.A. in English at Harvard University, studied in the Writer's Workshop at the University of Iowa, and is currently working on a Ph.D. in English literature at Yale University, where she is investigating addiction narratives. Her own writing has appeared in such publications as *Harper's Magazine*, *Oxford American*, the *Believer*, and the *New York Times Book Review*, where she is a columnist. Her first novel, *The Gin Closet* (2010), was named one of the best books of the year by the *San Francisco Chronicle*. *The Empathy Exams* (2014), a collection of essays that explores responses to both our own pain and the pain of others, was published in 2014 and immediately hailed as a literary triumph. See also lesliejamison.com.

Thomas Jefferson (1743–1826)
American lawyer, architect, and writer; governor of Virginia (1779–1781), secretary of state to George Washington (1789–1793), vice president to John Adams (1797–1801), and third president of the United States (1801–1809). A learned man of significant accomplishments in many fields, Jefferson became a lawyer and was elected to Virginia's House of Burgesses, where he argued the cause of American independence. After completing his second term as president of the United States, he founded the University of Virginia, designing both the buildings and the curriculum. A fluent stylist, Jefferson authored Virginia's Statute of Religious Freedom and wrote books on science, religion, architecture, and even Anglo-Saxon grammar. He is best known for writing the Declaration of Independence; his preliminary drafts were edited by a committee that included Benjamin Franklin and John Adams before Jefferson prepared the final revision. See also monticello.org.

Jesus (c. 4 B.C.E.–c. 30 C.E.)
Jesus of Nazareth, first-century spiritual teacher. The central, foundational figure of the Christian religion, worshipped by most Christians as the Son of God and the Messiah, Jesus spent his brief public career in Palestine, preaching to his fellow Jews a message of repentance, conversion, and loving-kindness. Jesus' life and teachings are known principally through the four canonical gospels of the New Testament, written and assembled by his followers in the decades after his execution in Jerusalem by the Roman authorities. One of his favorite teaching devices was the parable, a literary form with a long history, used extensively in the rabbinical tradition. The parables of Jesus, despite their seeming simplicity and grounding in the world of everyday experience, often convey subtle, highly nuanced moral and spiritual teachings that have intrigued scholars and lay believers alike for two millennia. See also rc.net/wcc/parables.htm.

Jeffrey Owen Jones (1944–2007)
American journalist, educator, and screenwriter/producer. Born in Manhattan and raised in Westport, Connecticut, Jones attended Williams College and went on to earn a master's degree from Middlebury College. As a young intern for *Time* magazine in 1965, Jones was sent to interview Bob Dylan, who soon immortalized Jones as the clueless reporter in "Ballad of a Thin Man": "Something is happening here / and you don't know what it is / do you, Mr. Jones?" After a period of writing and directing films in Spain, he returned to Williams to teach Spanish; he later taught film and animation at the Rochester Institute of Technology. Jones was awarded an Emmy Award in 1997 in recognition of his work as a producer of educational videos for CBS. He and journalist Peter Meyer co-wrote *The Pledge: A History of the Pledge of Allegiance* (2010). See also nme.com/news/bob-dylan/32804.

Garrison Keillor (b. 1942)
American radio host, humorist, and essayist. Born in Anoka, Minnesota, Keillor graduated from the University of Minnesota in 1966. He is the creator and host of the popular weekly NPR radio program *A Prairie Home Companion*, a live revue featuring comic skits, spoof advertisements, nationally renowned musicians, and Keillor's trademark monologues, "the news from Lake

Wobegon." *The Writer's Almanac*, Keillor's daily NPR radio program, highlights literary history, especially poetry. He has contributed humorous stories to the *New Yorker*, the *Atlantic*, and Salon .com, and is the author of many books, including *Happy to Be Here* (1981), *Homegrown Democrat* (2004), the best-selling *Lake Wobegon* series, and most recently *Life among the Lutherans* (2009) and *Pilgrims: A Wobegon Romance* (2009). See also prairiehome.publicradio.org.

John Fitzgerald Kennedy (1917–1963)
American author, politician, and thirty-fifth president of the United States. Born in Brookline, Massachusetts, Kennedy graduated from Harvard University and developed his senior thesis into the best-selling *Why England Slept* (1940). He received the Navy and Marine Corps Medal for his service in World War II. At twenty-nine Kennedy was elected to the U.S. House of Representatives; six years later he narrowly won a seat in the U.S. Senate, representing Massachusetts. His book *Profiles in Courage* (1956), detailing notable instances of political integrity by U.S. senators, won the Pulitzer Prize and added to his growing fame. In 1960 his eloquence and poise in televised debates against Richard Nixon helped Kennedy win the presidency. His inaugural address, calling for all citizens' participation in the affairs of their nation, is one of the best-known speeches in American history. On November 22, 1963, Kennedy was assassinated in Dallas, Texas. See also jfklibrary.org.

Philip Kennicott (b. 1966)
American music and architecture critic. Kennicott grew up in Schenectady, New York, attended Deep Springs College, and graduated from Yale University with a degree in philosophy. He began his career in journalism as the classical music critic for the *Detroit News* before moving on to the *St. Louis Post-Dispatch* and then the *Washington Post*, where he now serves as chief art and architecture critic. His articles about classical music have appeared in the *New Republic* and *Gramophone*. In addition to music, he has written on a broad array of topics, including gun control, Abraham Lincoln, and the U.S. Holocaust Memorial Museum. His essay "Smuggler," first published in the *Virginia Quarterly Review*, was selected for *Best American Essays* (2015). In 2013 Kennicott was awarded the Pulitzer Prize

for criticism in recognition of "his eloquent and passionate essays on art and the social forces that underlie it." See also philipkennicott.com.

Martin Luther King Jr. (1929–1968)
American clergyman and civil rights leader. By the age of twenty-six, the Atlanta-born King had completed his undergraduate education, finished divinity school, and received a Ph.D. in religion from Boston University. In 1956 King took a public stand to support blacks boycotting segregated buses in Montgomery, Alabama, marking his entry into the civil rights struggle. Soon he became a major figure in the civil rights movement, advocating nonviolent protest in the spirit of Jesus' teachings and Mahatma Gandhi's principles of passive resistance. In 1963, Birmingham, Alabama, one of the most segregated cities in the South, became the focal point for violent racial confrontations; 2,400 civil rights workers, King among them, were jailed, occasioning his now-famous "Letter from Birmingham Jail." In 1964, at thirty-five, he became the youngest-ever recipient of the Nobel Peace Prize. King was assassinated on April 4, 1968, in Memphis, Tennessee. See also thekingcenter.org.

Stephen King (b. 1947)
American fiction writer. Born in Portland, Maine, King grew up fascinated with horror comics and began writing macabre tales while still a teenager. Not long after graduating with a degree in English from the University of Maine in 1970, he began his first novel, *Carrie* (1973), a best-selling supernatural thriller soon followed by *Salem's Lot* (1975), *The Shining* (1977), and the serialized fantasy *The Dark Tower: The Gunslinger* (1977–1981). Today King is a publishing phenomenon; his fifty-four novels, six nonfiction books, and ten collections of short stories have sold more than 500 million copies worldwide. Even after sustaining severe injuries in a 1999 road accident, he has managed to fulfill his daily quota of 2,000 words. See also stephenking.com.

Maxine Hong Kingston (b. 1940)
American memoirist and novelist. Born in Stockton, California, to a Chinese immigrant family, Kingston grew up in a culture in which English was a second language; friends and relatives regularly gathered at her family's laundry to tell

stories in Chinese and reminisce about their native country. After graduating from the University of California at Berkeley, Kingston taught school in California and Hawaii and began publishing poetry, stories, and articles in magazines such as the *New Yorker, New West, Ms.,* and the *New York Times Magazine.* Her best-known works, *The Woman Warrior: Memoirs of a Girlhood among Ghosts* (1976) and the National Book Award–winning *China Men* (1980), combine memoir, family legends, and fiction. She has also published three novels, including *Tripmaster Monkey: His Fake Book* (1989), and a volume of poems, *I Love a Broad Margin to My Life* (2011). Kingston is a professor emerita of English, at the University of California, at Berkeley. See also poetryfoundation.org/ bio/maxine-hong-kingston.

Jonathan Kozol (b. 1936)
American author, educator, and social activist. Born in Boston, Kozol was educated at Harvard University and, as a Rhodes Scholar, Oxford University. He taught in Boston-area public schools, an experience he described in his first book, the nonfictional *Death at an Early Age* (1967), a National Book Award winner. His interest in education reform, theories of learning, and social justice have informed all of his twelve books, including *Rachel and Her Children: Homeless Families in America* (1988), *Savage Inequalities: Children in America's Schools* (1991), *Amazing Grace: The Lives of Children and the Conscience of a Nation* (1995), *Letters to a Young Teacher* (2007), and *Fire in the Ashes: Twenty-Five Years Among the Poorest Children in America* (2012). His most recent book is a memoir, *The Theft of Memory: Losing My Father One Day at a Time* (2015). See also jonathankozol.com.

Tim Kreider (b. 1967)
American essayist and cartoonist. Kreider grew up in Baltimore, where he went to public schools before attending Johns Hopkins University's Writing Seminars program. For twelve years his satirical cartoons ran in the *Baltimore City Paper* and other alternative weeklies; these have been collected in three volumes as *The Pain—When Will It End?* (2004), *Why Do They Kill Me?* (2005), and *Twilight of the Assholes* (2011). His cartoons and essays—about politics, books, movies, and life in general—have appeared in many periodi-

cals, including *Men's Journal,* the *Comics Journal,* and the *New York Times.* Kreider's most recent book is a collection of essays and cartoons called *We Learn Nothing* (2012). See also timkreider.com.

Elisabeth Kübler-Ross (1926–2004)
Swiss American psychologist. Born and educated in Switzerland, Kübler-Ross came to the United States in 1958 to continue her medical studies. She discovered her life's mission when, assigned to a psychiatric hospital, she was appalled by the treatment of dying patients. Her first book, *On Death and Dying* (1969), expressed her outrage and outlined the Five Stages of Grief that made her international reputation. She devoted the rest of her life to understanding the psychology of death, improving care for the terminally ill, and supporting the hospice movement. Her twenty-three books include *On Children and Death* (1983), *AIDS: The Ultimate Challenge* (1987), *The Wheel of Life: A Memoir of Living and Dying* (1997), and, with David Kessler, *On Grief and Grieving: Finding the Meaning of Grief through the Five Stages of Loss* (2005). See also ekrfoundation.org.

Thomas S. Kuhn (1922–1996)
American physicist, philosopher, and historian. Educated at Harvard University, where he earned a Ph.D. in physics, Kuhn was a specialist in the history and philosophy of science. The author of *The Copernican Revolution* (1957) and *The Essential Tension: Selected Studies in Scientific Tradition and Change* (1977), he taught the history of science at Harvard from 1948 to 1956, when he moved to the University of California at Berkeley. Kuhn is perhaps best known for *The Structure of Scientific Revolutions* (1962; 1970; 1996), in which he argued that scientific understanding is determined by frameworks or "paradigms" that periodically are shown to be outmoded and are replaced in "paradigm shifts." Before his death, Kuhn was Laurance S. Rockefeller Professor of Philosophy at the Massachusetts Institute of Technology. Much of his later work is collected in *The Road since Structure: Philosophical Essays, 1970–1993* (2000). See also plato .stanford.edu/entries/thomas-kuhn.

Jhumpa Lahiri (b. 1967)
American short-story writer and novelist. Lahiri was born in London to Bengali Indian immigrant parents who, when

she was three years old, moved the family to the United States and settled in Kingston, Rhode Island. She earned her B.A. from Barnard College; at Boston University she earned three master's degrees and a Ph.D. in Renaissance Studies. Her short stories were collected in *The Interpreter of Maladies* (1999), a winner of the 2000 Pulitzer Prize. In her second story collection, *Unaccustomed Earth* (2008), as well as her novels *The Namesake* (2003) and *The Lowland* (2013), Lahiri continues to focus on the experience of Indian immigrants and their children. See also jhumpalahiri.net.

Chang-rae Lee (b. 1965)
American novelist. When he was three, Lee and his family left South Korea for the United States, settling in Westchester, New York. He received his B.A. from Yale in 1987 and spent a year as an equities analyst before pursuing his M.F.A. at the University of Oregon. Beginning with *Native Speaker* (1995), Lee's five novels all explore various aspects of identity—race, ethnicity, and "Americanness." *A Gesture Life* (1999) focuses on a Japanese American former medic who recalls treating "comfort women"—Korean women forced to have sex with Japanese soldiers in World War II. *The Surrendered* (2011), set in the Korean War, was a Pulitzer Prize finalist. Lee's most recent novel, *On Such a Full Sea* (2014), features a Chinese American fish farmer living in a dystopian Baltimore—"B-Mor." See also newyorker.com/contributors/chang-rae-lee.

Annie Leonard (b. 1964)
American environmental activist and filmmaker. A native of Seattle, Leonard earned a bachelor's degree from Barnard College and a master's degree in city and regional planning from Cornell University. Her career has been devoted to promoting sustainability and curbing the excesses of consumerism, particularly the common practice of using poor countries as a dumping ground for the garbage and hazardous waste produced by rich countries. This work led her to create an animated documentary film, *The Story of Stuff* (2007), about the life cycle of material goods—manufacture, distribution, use, and disposal. She has now created a series of "Story of" films, including *The Story of Cap and Trade* (2009), *The Story of Electronics* (2010), and *The Story of Solutions* (2013). Her book version of *The Story of Stuff* came

out in 2010. In 2014 she was named executive director of Greenpeace USA. See also storyofstuff.org.

Michael Lewis (b. 1960)
American journalist and author. Born in New Orleans, Lewis earned a B.A. in art history at Princeton University and an M.A. in economics at the London School of Economics. His work in the financial industry provided the background for his first book, *Liar's Poker: Rising through the Wreckage on Wall Street* (1989). Since then Lewis has produced thirteen more nonfiction bestsellers that shed light on the inner workings of a particular industry. *The New New Thing* (2000), for example, tells the story of Silicon Valley's rise to tech dominance; *Moneyball: The Art of Winning an Unfair Game* (2003) describes the "sabermetric" approach to creating a winning pro baseball team; and Lewis's latest book, *Flash Boys* (2014), functions as an indictment of Wall Street's use of modern electronic securities trading. See also michaellewiswrites.com.

Alan Lightman (b. 1948)
American physicist, author, and humanitarian. As a Memphis, Tennessee, high school student, Lightman won both science fairs and literary awards; he studied physics at Princeton University and earned his Ph.D. in theoretical physics from the California Institute of Technology. Lightman has made fundamental contributions to the field of astrophysics while also writing poems, short stories, and essays on science appearing in journals as *Harper's Magazine*, *Granta*, *Smithsonian*, *Story*, and the *New Yorker*. His many books include the novels *Einstein's Dreams* (1993), an international best-seller; *The Diagnosis* (2000), a National Book Award finalist; and *Mr g* (2012), a history of creation narrated by God himself. Lightman currently teaches the humanities at the Massachusetts Institute of Technology. In 2003 he founded the Harpswell Foundation to help develop a new generation of women leaders in Cambodia and elsewhere in the developing world. See also cmsw.mit.edu/alan-lightman.

Abraham Lincoln (1809–1865)
American lawyer, orator, legislator, and sixteenth president of the United States. Born in Kentucky, Lincoln was largely self-made and self-taught. In 1830 his family moved to Illinois, where Lincoln

prepared himself for a career in law. In 1834 he was elected to the first of four terms in the Illinois state legislature, and in 1847, to the U.S. Congress. Elected president in 1860, Lincoln guided the Union through the Civil War while pressing for passage of the Thirteenth Amendment (1865), which outlawed slavery "everywhere and forever" in the United States. His most famous speech, the Gettysburg Address (1863), was delivered at the site of one of the Civil War's bloodiest battles. Shortly after his reelection and with the war drawing to a close, Lincoln gave his Second Inaugural Address (1865), an eloquent appeal for reconciliation and peace. He was assassinated a little more than a month later. See also whitehouse.gov/1600/presidents/abrahamlincoln.

Teresa Lust (b. 1964)
American chef, food writer, and editor. Lust grew up in Yakima, Washington, and earned a B.S. degree in biology at Washington State University before earning her master's degree in liberal studies at Dartmouth College. Her first book, *Pass the Polenta: And Other Writings from the Kitchen, with Recipes* (1998), is a blend of memoir, thoughts about food and its meaning in our lives, and the recipes of her Italian immigrant grandmother, for whom food was family, love, and life itself. A professional chef and an Italian teacher, Lust is also the translator of Italian author Alessandra Lavagnino's novel *Librarians of Alexandria: A Tale of Two Sisters* (2006). See also eatyourbooks.com/authors/8168/teresa-lust.

Niccolò Machiavelli (1469–1527)
Italian statesman and political philosopher. An aristocrat who held public office while Florence was a republic, Machiavelli fell from favor when the Medici family returned to power in 1512. He was tortured during a brief imprisonment; upon his release he retired to a life of studying philosophy and wrote the treatises that would become seminal works of modern political science. Machiavelli's most famous work, *The Prince* (1513), not published until after his death, has exerted considerable literary and political influence within the Western tradition. Because *The Prince* is such a clear-eyed, unsentimental description of the politics of his era, the term "Machiavellian" has come to mean manipulative, deceitful, and amoral. In fact, Machiavelli himself was a trusted civil servant and an admired philosopher. See also egs.edu.library/niccolo-machiavelli/biography.

Nancy Mairs (b. 1943)
American poet and essayist. Mairs was born in Long Beach, California, and grew up in Boston. Married at nineteen, she completed her B.A. at Wheaton College, had a child, and earned M.F.A. and Ph.D. degrees from the University of Arizona. The personal difficulties that inform her writing include a near-suicidal bout of agoraphobia and anorexia, and the later discovery that she was afflicted with multiple sclerosis. She found salvation both in writing and in Roman Catholicism, to which she converted in her thirties. Her first book was a collection of poems, *In All the Rooms in the Yellow House* (1984). The eight books of essays and memoirs Mairs has written since include *Plaintext: Deciphering a Woman's Life* (1986), *Carnal Acts* (1990), *Waist-High in the World: A Life among the Nondisabled* (1996), *Voice Lessons: On Becoming a (Woman) Writer* (1997), and, most recently, *A Dynamic God: Living an Unconventional Catholic Faith* (2007). See also nancymairs.com.

Scott McCloud (b. 1960)
American cartoonist and comics theorist. McCloud was born in Boston, Massachusetts, and earned a B.F.A. in illustration at Syracuse University. The creator of the science fiction/superhero comic book series *Zot!*, McCloud has also done the artwork for many issues of *Superman* as well as his own *Destroy!!*, which he describes as "a deliberately over-the-top, oversized single-issue comic book, intended as a parody of formulaic superhero fights." In 1993, he published *Understanding Comics*, a scholarly work on the definition, history, and methodology of comics, done entirely in comics form; it is widely considered one of the definitive works on the subject. He followed this study with *Reinventing Comics* (2000) and *Making Comics* (2006). See also scottmcloud.com.

Jane McGonigal (b. 1977)
American game designer and author. McGonigal grew up in New Jersey and earned a B.A. in English from Fordham University. Even before she had gone on to complete her doctorate in performance studies from the University of California, Berkeley, she had designed commercial video games such as *I Love Bees* (2004)

and *Last Call Poker* (2005). Now known for alternative-reality games like *World Without Oil* (2007), McGonigal believes that gaming, particularly massively multiplayer online gaming, can help to make the world a better place by generating and focusing collective human intelligence for the common good. She is the author of *Reality Is Broken: Why Games Make Us Better and How They Can Change the World* (2011). McGonigal's most recent game is *SuperBetter* (2012), the product of her efforts to relieve the symptoms of a concussion she suffered in 2009; the game's working title was *Jane the Concussion-Slayer.* See also janemcgonigal.com.

Bill McKibben (b. 1960)
American environmentalist and nature writer. Born in Lexington, Massachusetts, McKibben attended Harvard University, where he was president of the *Harvard Crimson* newspaper. He then worked as a staff writer at the *New Yorker*, which serialized his first book, *The End of Nature* (1989), an introduction to climate change and a plea for a reformed attitude to nature. Since then he has written about an array of environmental topics, earning him *Time* magazine's description as "the world's best green journalist." McKibben's books include *Hope, Human and Wild: True Stories of Living Lightly on the Earth* (1995); *Deep Economy: The Wealth of Communities and the Durable Future* (2007), an attempt to envision a more localized and more sustainable economic system; *Eaarth: Making a Life on a Tough New Planet* (2010), about the inevitability of climate change; *The Global Warming Reader* (2011); and most recently *Oil and Honey: The Education of an Unlikely Activist* (2013). See also billmckibben.com.

John McPhee (b. 1931)
American nonfiction author. McPhee was born in Princeton, New Jersey, and educated at Princeton University and Cambridge University. He began his writing career at *Time* magazine; since 1965 he has been a staff writer for the *New Yorker*, which has serialized many of his thirty-two books. His first book, *A Sense of Where You Are* (1965), profiled then-college basketball player Bill Bradley. His subsequent books include *Encounters with the Archdruid* (1971), a portrait of Sierra Club founder David Brower; *Coming into the Country*, a look at life in

Alaska; and *Annals of the Former World* (1998), a tetralogy about geology, which was awarded the Pulitzer Prize. His most recent book is *Silk Parachute* (2010). For decades he has taught a creative writing course, "The Literature of Fact," at Princeton. See also johnmcphee.com.

Jessica Mitford (1917–1996)
Anglo-American memoirist, journalist, and social activist. Born into one of England's most famous aristocratic families, "Decca" Mitford had little formal education but read widely; she would later describe her privileged upbringing in the memoir *Daughters and Rebels* (1960). She emigrated to the United States in 1939, eventually marrying a prominent civil rights lawyer. During the 1960s she established herself as an investigative reporter with a talent for social criticism. Her study of the American funeral industry, *The American Way of Death* (1963, 1998), was followed by *The Trial of Dr. Spock* (1969), *Kind and Unusual Punishment: The Prison Business* (1973), and *The American Way of Birth* (1992). Her memoir *A Fine Old Conflict* (1977) recounts her youthful enthusiasm for and subsequent disillusionment with the Communist party; *The Making of a Muckraker* (1979) describes her career as a journalist. See also peterysussman.com/decca.

Leonard Mlodinow (b. 1954)
American physicist, author, and screenwriter. Born in Chicago to Holocaust-survivors, Mlodinow showed an early aptitude for mathematics and eventually earned his doctorate in physics at the University of California at Berkeley. Much of his scientific career has been devoted to tackling difficult mathematical problems in quantum mechanics, the forefront of modern-day physics. Among the science books he has written for the general reader are *The Drunkard's Walk: How Randomness Rules Our Lives* (2008) and most recently *Subliminal: How Your Unconscious Mind Rules Your Behavior* (2012). A much-sought-after co-author, Mlodinow has teamed up with British physicist Stephen Hawking on two books: *A Briefer History of Time* (2005) and *The Grand Design* (2010). In *The War of the Worldviews* (2011), Mlodinow and Deepak Chopra address "the big questions" from their respective scientific and spiritual perspectives. Mlodinow has also written television screenplays for

Star Trek: The Next Generation and *Mac-Gyver*. See also onbeing.org.

N. Scott Momaday (b. 1934)

American poet, novelist, and artist. Born into the Kiowa tribe of Oklahoma, Momaday grew up on several Indian reservations in the American Southwest. After earning a B.A. at the University of New Mexico and a Ph.D. at Stanford University, he has taught poetry and Native oral tradition at a number of universities and designed the graduate program in Indian Studies at the University of California at Berkeley. Momaday's Pulitzer Prize–winning novel *House Made of Dawn* (1968) was a breakthrough not only for him but for American Indian writers in general. Momaday has written several volumes of poetry, most recently *Again the Far Morning: New and Selected Poems* (2011); the autobiographical works *The Names: A Memoir* (1976) and *The Man Made of Words: Essays, Stories, Passages* (1997); and collections of Kiowa folktales, including *The Way to Rainy Mountain* (1969) and *Four Arrows & Magpie: A Kiowa Story* (2006). See also poets .org/poetsorg/poet/n-scott-momaday.

Toni Morrison (b. 1931)

American author and teacher. Born to working-class parents and raised in Lorain, Ohio, Morrison received her undergraduate education at Howard University before completing her master's degree at Cornell University. She worked as an editor for a decade before beginning to publish her own writing, much of which centers on the complexities of race and gender. Her first novel, *The Bluest Eye* (1970), centered upon a black child's yearning to be white; her fifth, *Beloved* (1987), about the agonizing choices faced by a mother fleeing slavery, won the Pulitzer Prize. After the publication of *Jazz* (1992) Morrison received the 1993 Nobel Prize for literature. The most recent of her eleven novels are *Home* (2012) and *God Help the Child* (2015). Morrison held teaching positions at Howard, Yale, and Rutgers Universities before moving to Princeton University, where she is currently a fellow in the Council of the Humanities. See also tonimorrisonsociety.org.

John Muir (1838–1914)

American naturalist, preservationist, and writer. Muir's family emigrated from Scotland to the United States in 1849 and settled in Wisconsin. An avid student of nature, Muir studied geology and botany at the University of Wisconsin, though he left without taking a degree. As a young man, Muir traveled widely in the western United States to study its flora and fauna. He became a vocal advocate for what was then called "preservationism," co-founding the Sierra Club in 1882 to promote the protection of wilderness areas from development. Muir's efforts are largely responsible for the creation of Yosemite National Park; in 1976 the California Historical Society voted him "The Greatest Californian." His writings, which celebrate wilderness and extol the natural beauty of the American West, include such classics as *The Mountains of California* (1894) and *My First Summer in the Sierra* (1911). See also sierraclub.org/john_muir_exhibit.

Vladimir Nabokov (1899–1977)

Russian American poet, novelist, and educator. Born to a wealthy and prominent St. Petersburg family that barely escaped the 1917 revolution in Russia, Nabokov was educated at Cambridge University. He settled into the Russian émigré communities of Germany and later France, becoming known as a poet, novelist, and critic. In 1940 Nabokov came to the United States, where he taught literature at Wellesley College and Cornell University, and published four more novels and numerous essays, stories, and poems. He became an international celebrity and literary icon in 1958, when his controversial novel *Lolita* (1955) was finally published in America. With the earnings from *Lolita* Nabokov retired from teaching and moved to Switzerland to devote himself to writing such classic novels as *Pale Fire* (1962) and *Ada* (1969), as well as translating his early Russian novels into English. See also nabokov.com.

Gloria Naylor (b. 1950)

American fiction writer and essayist. Naylor was born in New York City to parents from Southern sharecropping families who, wanting better opportunities for their daughter, stressed reading and urged her to keep a journal from an early age. She earned her B.A. from Brooklyn College and began writing her first novel, *The Women of Brewster Place* (1982), winner of the National Book Award for Best First Novel. She then earned an M.A. in Afro-American studies from Yale University and resumed her career as a novelist known for her portrayals of black women.

Her books include *Linden Hills* (1985), *Mama Day* (1988), *Bailey's Café* (1992), and *The Men of Brewster Place* (1998). Naylor's most recent work, *1996*, was published in 2005. See also aalbc.com/authors/gloria.html.

Marion Nestle (b. 1936)
American nutritionist and author. Nestle holds three degrees from the University of California, Berkeley, including a doctorate in molecular biology. Much of her long scholarly career has been spent at New York University, where she teaches nutrition, food studies, and public health. She has served as senior nutrition policy advisor for the Department of Health and Human Services. In her research, Nestle studies food from both a scientific and a socioeconomic viewpoint, with emphasis on the role of marketing on food choice, obesity, and food safety. Her seven books include *Food Politics: How the Food Industry Influences Nutrition and Health* (2002), *Safe Food: The Politics of Food Safety* (2010), and most recently *Why Calories Count: From Science to Politics* (2012). Her column "Food Matters" appears in the *San Francisco Chronicle*. See also foodpolitics.com.

Judith Newman (b. 1961)
American journalist and author. Newman grew up in Scarsdale, New York; she earned a B.A. from Wesleyan University and an M.A. in English and comparative literature from Columbia University. As a freelance journalist, Newman has written on a wide range of subjects—entertainment, beauty, sex, relationships, books, science, and popular culture—for more than fifty periodicals, including *Vogue*, *Vanity Fair*, *Allure*, *Harper's Magazine*, the *Wall Street Journal*, and the *New York Times*. Her article "I Have Seen Cancers Disappear," which first ran in *Discover*, was chosen for *Best American Science and Nature Writing* (2002). Newman's books include *Parents from Hell: Unexpurgated Tales of Good Intentions Gone Awry* (1995) and a memoir, *You Make Me Feel Like an Unnatural Woman: Diary of a New (Older) Mother* (2004), which detailed the travails of giving birth (to twins) after "seven years of science." See also judithnewman.com.

Ngũgĩ wa Thiong'o (b. 1938)
Kenyan novelist, playwright, and social critic. Born in what was then British East Africa, Ngũgĩ grew up amid colonialism, revolution, and the emergence of independent Kenya in 1963. His first novel, *Weep Not, Child* (1964), and his second, *A Grain of Wheat* (1967), depict the Mau Mau Uprising against the British. His 1977 play, *Ngaahika Ndeenda*, written in his native Gĩkũyũ and translated by the author as *I Will Marry When I Want* (1982), was critical of the Kenyan government, resulting in Ngũgĩ's yearlong imprisonment. He has since lived in self-imposed exile in the United States and is currently a professor of comparative literature at the University of California at Irvine. His books include *Decolonising the Mind* (1986), which argues for the use of native languages; *Wizard of the Crow* (2006), a novel; and *Dreams in a Time of War: A Childhood Memoir* (2010). See also ngugiwathiongo.com.

Michelle Nijhuis (b. 1974)
American science journalist and author. A graduate of Reed College with a degree in biology, Nijhuis (pronounced NYE-house) now describes herself as a "lapsed biologist." She began her career in journalism as an intern at *High Country News*, where she is now a contributing editor. Her articles about conservation and climate change have appeared in many publications, including *Audubon*, *Orion*, *Smithsonian*, and *National Geographic*. Nijhuis has won awards for articles on white-nose syndrome in bats, the human-assisted migration of threatened species, and the "doubt industry's" attempts to thwart the work of legitimate scientists. Her work has appeared in *Best American Science Writing* (2003) and *Best American Science and Nature Writing* (2009 and 2013); she is also the co-editor, with journalist Thomas Hayden, of *The Science Writers' Handbook* (2013). After living in rural Colorado for fifteen years, she and her family now live in White Salmon, Washington. See also michellenijhuis.com.

Joyce Carol Oates (b. 1937)
American author. Born in Lockport, New York, Oates attended a one-room schoolhouse and was the first in her family to complete high school before earning a scholarship to Syracuse University, where she graduated as valedictorian. She went on to earn an M.A. from the University of Wisconsin at Madison and was a Ph.D. candidate at Rice University when she decided instead to devote her energies to writing. Since then she has written over

100 books, including more than fifty novels; dozens of short-story, essay, and memoir collections; and eleven volumes of poetry. Her countless honors include two O. Henry Awards for short stories, a National Book Award for the novel *them* (1969), and a host of Pulitzer Prize nominations, notably for the novel *Blonde* (2001) and her most recent short-story collection, *Lovely, Dark, Deep* (2015). Her latest novel is *Jack of Spades* (2015). See also web.usfca.edu/jco.

Barack Obama (b. 1961)
American author, politician, and forty-fourth president of the United States. Born in Honolulu to an American mother and a Kenyan father, Obama grew up in Hawaii and Indonesia before earning degrees at Columbia University and the Harvard Law School. He worked as a community organizer in Chicago and taught constitutional law at the University of Chicago Law School. Before his election to the U.S. presidency, he served in the Illinois State Senate and the U.S. Senate. Obama is the author of two books: his memoir, *Dreams from My Father* (1995), and a political manifesto, *The Audacity of Hope* (2006). His keynote speech at the 2004 Democratic National Convention catapulted him to national attention; his speech at Cairo University, soon after his inauguration, marked a "new beginning" in U.S. relations with the rest of the world. In 2009 Obama was awarded the Nobel Peace Prize. See also barackobama.com.

George Orwell (1903–1950)
Pen name of Eric Blair, English journalist, essayist, novelist, and social critic. Born in India and educated in England, Orwell was an officer in the Indian Imperial Police in Burma (1922–1927), an experience he later recounted in the novel *Burmese Days* (1934). In 1927 he went to Europe to pursue his career as a writer. His first book, *Down and Out in Paris and London* (1933), depicts his years of poverty and struggle while working as a dishwasher and day laborer. Orwell's experiences fighting in the Spanish Civil War are the subject of the memoir *Homage to Catalonia* (1938). Of his seven novels, the satiric *Animal Farm* (1945) and the dystopian *Nineteen Eighty-Four* (1949), both indictments of totalitarianism, have become classics. Orwell, one of the most polished and respected stylists in the English language, published

five collections of essays, including *Shooting an Elephant and Other Essays* (1950). See also george-orwell.org.

Henry Petroski (b. 1942)
American engineer, author, and educator. A New York City native, Petroski received his bachelor's degree from Manhattan College and his doctorate in mechanics from the University of Illinois at Urbana-Champaign. Currently he teaches civil engineering and history at Duke University, specializing in failure analysis. Having a particular knack for explaining engineering to the nonspecialist, Petroski delights in revealing the technological complexity behind everyday objects like pencils and toothpicks. He is a frequent contributor to the magazines *American Scientist* and *Prism*; his dozen books include *To Engineer Is Human: The Role of Failure in Successful Design* (1985); *The Pencil: A History of Design and Circumstance* (1990); *Invention by Design: How Engineers Get from Thought to Thing* (1996); a memoir, *Paperboy: Confessions of a Future Engineer* (2002); and *The Essential Engineer: Why Science Alone Will Not Solve Our Global Problems* (2010). His most recent book is *The House with Sixteen Handmade Doors: A Tale of Architectural Choice and Craftsmanship* (2014). See also cee.duke.edu/faculty/henry-petroski.

Jo-Ann Pilardi (b. 1941)
American philosopher and educator. Pilardi earned her B.A. in English at Duquesne University, her M.A. in philosophy at Pennsylvania State University, and her Ph.D. in humanities at Johns Hopkins University. A longtime activist in the women's liberation movement, Pilardi helped to develop the Women's Studies Program at Maryland's Towson University, where today she is professor emerita of Philosophy and Women's Studies. Her works include *Simone de Beauvoir Writing the Self: Philosophy Becomes Autobiography* (1999), "Domestic Hospitality: Self, Other, and Community" in *Feminism and Hospitality: Gender in the Host/Guest Relationship* (2010), and "From 'Alien' to 'Guest': A Philosophical Scrutiny of the Bush Administration's Guest Worker Initiative" in *Radical Philosophy Today: Philosophy against Empire* (2006). See also towson.edu/womensstudies/popup/pilardi.htm.

Plato (c. 428–c. 348 B.C.E.)

Greek philosopher, mathematician, and teacher. Born to an aristocratic family, probably in Athens, Plato was among the most ardent students of the philosopher Socrates. After Socrates was executed in 399 B.C.E., Plato is believed to have traveled throughout the Mediterranean before returning in the 380s to found the Academy, the Western world's first formally constituted institution of higher learning. Most of Plato's known writings are dialogues featuring Socrates in vigorous pursuit of the truth of human existence through tireless questioning. The best known of these Socratic dialogues, the *Republic*, probes the nature of justice, the relationship between the individual and society, and the ideal "forms" that are, Plato believed, the ultimate reality beyond the world we experience with our senses. Plato remains enormously influential; his teachings were carried on by his student Aristotle, and indeed all of Western philosophy has been called "footnotes to Plato." See also plato.stanford.edu.

Michael Pollan (b. 1955)

American author, environmental journalist, and educator. The son of two writers, Pollan was educated at Bennington College, Oxford University, and Columbia University, where he earned his M.A. in English. Pollan's first book, *Second Nature: A Gardener's Education* (1991), sets the template for a career focused mainly on food—not only as a source of nutrition and pleasure for the individual but also as a critical factor in science, economics, politics, and culture. An outspoken critic of modern industrial agriculture, he has explored these themes in numerous articles and in books such as *The Botany of Desire: A Plant's-Eye View of the World* (2001), *In Defense of Food: An Eater's Manifesto* (2005), *The Omnivore's Dilemma: A Natural History of Four Meals* (2006), and *Food Rules: An Eater's Manual* (2009). Pollan is a professor of journalism at the University of California at Berkeley. See also michaelpollan.com.

Joe Posnanski (b. 1967)

American sports journalist. Posnanski grew up in South Euclid, North Carolina, and attended the University of North Carolina in Charlotte, where he studied English. His journalism career began as a reporter for the *Charlotte Observer*; he then moved on to the *Cincinnati Post*, the *Augusta Chronicle*, and the *Kansas City Star*, where he was twice named Sports Columnist of the Year. In 2009 he became a senior writer for *Sports Illustrated*. Since 2013 he has been the national columnist for NBC Sports. Posnanski's passionate writing about sports of every kind is steeped in a deep knowledge of sports lore and minutiae. His four books include *The Soul of Baseball: A Road Trip through Buck O'Neil's America* (2007), *Paterno* (2012), and most recently *The Secret of Golf: The Story of Tom Watson and Jack Nicklaus* (2015). Posnanski's award-winning blog is called *Joe Blog*. See also joeposnanski.com.

Anna Quindlen (b. 1953)

American journalist and novelist. Born in Philadelphia, Quindlen graduated from Barnard College and immediately began writing for the *New York Post*. Three years later she moved to the *New York Times*, where she would eventually win a Pulitzer Prize for the regular column she once described as "taking things personally for a living." These columns have been collected in *Living Out Loud* (1988) and *Thinking Out Loud* (1993). After twenty years Quindlen left the *Times* to devote herself to writing fiction and has since published six novels, including *Object Lessons* (1991); *One True Thing* (1994), which was made into a movie in 1998; *Black and Blue* (1998); *Blessings* (2002); *Every Last One* (2010); and most recently *Still Life with Bread Crumbs* (2014). *How Reading Changed My Life* (1998) is her memoir about the importance of reading. See also annaquindlen.net.

Tasneem Raja (b. 1982)

American journalist. Born in Camden, New Jersey, Raja is a graduate of the school of journalism at the University of California at Berkeley. Raja was an interactive journalism producer at the *Bay Citizen* and a features reporter at the *Chicago Reader* before joining *Mother Jones*, where, in addition to her work as interactive editor on the magazine's web productions, she wrote articles on anything and everything—from presidential politics to the National Weather Service's psychedelic maps of Hurricane Sandy, with particular attention to new media and the often-second-class role of women in the tech industry. The business magazine *Fast Company* named her "one of the smartest people on *Twitter*." In 2014 she became digital editor of National Public Radio's Code Switch Team, which focuses on "overlapping themes of race, ethnicity and culture, how they play out in our lives and communities, and how all of this is shifting." See also npr.org/sections/codeswitch.

Tom Regan (b. 1938)
American philosopher and teacher. Born in Pittsburgh, Regan earned his B.A. at Thiel College in Pennsylvania and his Ph.D. in philosophy from the University of Virginia. He has spent most of his career teaching philosophy at North Carolina State University, where he is now professor emeritus. His research in theoretical and applied ethics led him to the teachings of Mohandas Gandhi, whom Regan credits for his interest in the ethical treatment of animals. Today Regan is regarded as one of the leading intellectuals in the animal rights movement. His works include *All That Dwell Therein: Essays on Animal Rights and Environmental Ethics* (1982); *The Case for Animal Rights* (1983, 1985, 2004); his autobiography, *The Bird in the Cage: A Glimpse of My Life* (1991); *Empty Cages: Facing the Challenge of Animal Rights* (2004); and *A Better Life and Other Pittsburgh Stories* (2014), a volume of short fiction. See also tomregan.info.

Adrienne Rich (1929–2012)
American poet and essayist. Born in Baltimore, Maryland, Rich grew up reading and writing poetry from an early age. She published her first volume of poems, *A Change of World* (1951), even before completing her B.A. at Radcliffe College. Her many subsequent collections, reflecting her emergence as a fiercely outspoken feminist, include *Snapshots of a Daughter-in-Law* (1963), the National Book Award–winning *Diving into the Wreck* (1974), *The Fact of a Doorframe: Poems Selected and New, 1950–1984* (1984), *Midnight Salvage* (1999), and *Tonight No Poetry Will Serve: Poems 2007–2010* (2011). Her essays have been collected in several volumes, including *Arts of the Possible: Essays and Conversations* (2001), *Poetry and Commitment* (2007), and *A Human Eye: Essays on Art in Society* (2009). The recipient of many honors, Rich was awarded the National Book Foundation's 2006 Medal for Distinguished Contribution to American Letters. See also poetryfoundation.org/bio/adrienne-rich.

Richard Rodriguez (b. 1944)
American essayist and teacher. Born in San Francisco to Mexican American immigrant parents, Rodriguez learned to speak English in a Catholic grammar school in Sacramento, California, and went on to earn a B.A. from Stanford University and an M.A. from Columbia University. Once a doctoral candidate in English literature at the University of California at Berkeley, Rodriguez opted instead to pursue his own path as a teacher, journalist, and author. He now works for the Pacific News Service and is a regular guest on *PBS NewsHour*. In *Hunger of Memory: The Education of Richard Rodriguez* (1982), he recounts his sometimes painful assimilation into mainstream American society. His next two books, *Days of Obligation: A Letter to My Mexican Father* (1992) and *Brown: The Last Discovery of America* (2002), further explore the tensions between his Mexican and his American selves. His most recent book is *Darling: A Spiritual Autobiography* (2013). See also "Regarding Mystery: An Interview with Richard Rodriguez" at parisreview.org.

Mike Rose (b. 1944)
American educator and author. Born to Italian immigrant parents in Altoona, Pennsylvania, Rose grew up in Los Angeles. Because of an administrative error at his high school, he was placed in the "vocational track" for academic underachievers; a teacher discovered the error, and Rose went on to excel as a student, earning his B.A. from Loyola University and a Ph.D. in education from UCLA. Rose has made a career of championing the academic potential of the poor and underprivileged. A teacher for forty years, he is presently a professor at the UCLA Graduate School of Education and Information Studies. His many books include *Lives on the Boundary* (1989), which argues that poor preparation, not lack of intelligence, hampers most underachieving students; *The Mind at Work: Valuing the Intelligence of the American Worker* (2004); *Back to School: Why Everyone Deserves a Second Chance at Education* (2012); and *Why School?: Reclaiming Education for All of Us* (2014). See also mikerosebooks.com.

Scott Russell Sanders (b. 1945)
American novelist, essayist, and teacher. Born in Memphis, Tennessee, and

educated at Brown and Cambridge Universities, Sanders has spent his teaching career at Indiana University at Bloomington, where he is professor of English. The author of four novels, two short-story collections, and seven children's books, he is best known for his nature writing and his personal essays. Among his many books are *Wilderness Plots: Tales about the Settlement of the American Land* (1983, 2007); *The Paradise of Bombs* (1987), a collection of essays about violence in the United States; *Staying Put: Making a Home in a Restless World* (1994); *The Force of Spirit* (2000), a collection of meditations on family and the passage of time; *A Private History of Awe* (2006), a spiritual memoir; *A Conservationist Manifesto* (2009); and most recently *Divine Animal* (2014), a novel. See also scottrussellsanders.com.

Chief Seattle (c. 1780–1866)
Native American leader. Seattle (also Seathl or Sealth) was chief of the Suquamish, Duwamish, and allied Salish tribes of the Pacific Northwest. He was baptized a Roman Catholic in 1848 and, foreseeing the unstoppable influx of whites, became an advocate of peace. Local settlers honored him and his work by naming their town Seattle, an Anglicization of Si'ahl (his name in his native language, Lushootseed). His famous address is a reply to an offer to buy over two million acres of Indian land around Puget Sound, proffered in 1854 by Isaac Stevens, governor of the newly created Washington Territory. (No authenticated translation of the speech exists; the most common version was first published thirty-three years after the fact.) Because of Seattle's example, his people avoided the bloody warfare that afflicted the territory from 1855 until 1870. See also suquamish.nsn.us./historyculture .aspx.

David Sedaris (b. 1956)
American humorist and author. Born in Johnson City, New York, Sedaris grew up in Raleigh, North Carolina. He attended both Western Carolina University and Kent State University before graduating from the School of the Art Institute of Chicago. While working odd jobs in Raleigh, New York City, and Chicago, a lucky encounter with radio host Ira Glass led to the National Public Radio broadcast of Sedaris reading "SantaLand Diaries," his hilarious memoir of work-

ing as an elf assistant to a department-store Santa. An immediate hit with listeners, Sedaris became a regular contributor to Glass's *This American Life* program on NPR, recounting ostensibly autobiographical tales of his upbringing, his struggles with work and with drugs, and much else. These pieces have been collected in nine best-selling books, from *Barrel Fever* (1994) to *Let's Explore Diabetes with Owls* (2013). Sedaris presently lives in England. See also davidsedarisbooks.com.

Peter Singer (b. 1946)
Australian author, philosopher, and ethicist. Born in Melbourne, Australia, to Austrian parents fleeing Nazi persecution, Singer was educated at Melbourne University and at England's Oxford University. Throughout his subsequent academic career, during which he has held professorships in England, Australia, and the United States, Singer has generated controversy and even outrage for his application of utilitarianism— "the greatest good of the greatest number"—to a wide variety of ethical issues, ranging from euthanasia and abortion to economic justice and animal rights. A prolific author, Singer's principal works include *Animal Liberation* (1975), *Practical Ethics* (1979), *How Are We to Live?: Ethics in an Age of Self-Interest* (1993), *Rethinking Life and Death* (1994), and most recently *The Most Good You Can Do: How Effective Altruism Is Changing Ideas about Living Ethically* (2015). He is currently a professor of bioethics at Princeton University. See also princeton.edu/~psinger.

Rebecca Skloot (b. 1972)
American science journalist and author. Skloot grew up in Portland, Oregon, and attended Portland Community College to become a veterinary technician; she then earned a B.S. in biology from Colorado State University and an M.F.A. in creative nonfiction from the University of Pittsburgh. Her more than 200 feature articles and essays have appeared in such publications as *Discover, O: The Oprah Magazine*, the *New York Times Magazine*, and *Popular Science*, where she is a contributing editor. Skloot's first book, *The Immortal Life of Henrietta Lacks* (2010), the story of a line of cells taken from an unwitting subject and used in cutting-edge biological research, is a case study in social class, race relations, and modern

science. A publishing phenomenon, the book took ten years to research and write, was a number-one *New York Times* best-seller, and has been translated into more than twenty-five languages. See also rebeccaskloot.com.

Gwendolyn Ann Smith

American activist and journalist. Smith has written the "Transmissions" column for the *Bay Area Reporter* since 2000, and is the managing editor for Genderfork, an online forum for the transgender community. A transgender woman herself, Smith initiated Transgender Day of Remembrance (November 20) as an annual memorial to victims of anti-transgender hatred and violence. See also genderfork.com.

Susan Sontag (1933–2004)

American writer, art critic, and filmmaker. Born in New York City, Sontag grew up in Tucson, Arizona, and Los Angeles. After graduating from high school at fifteen, she started classes at the University of California at Berkeley, later earning philosophy degrees from the University of Chicago and Harvard University and studying further at Oxford University and the University of Paris. Sontag's collection of essays *Against Interpretation* (1966) staked out her place as a serious intellectual, just as *Trip to Hanoi* (1968) established her reputation as a political and cultural critic. After a near-fatal bout with breast cancer, she wrote *Illness as Metaphor* (1978), followed by *AIDS and Its Metaphors* (1988). Sontag considered herself foremost a novelist; her novels include *The Volcano Lover* (1992) and the National Book Award–winning *In America* (2001). Her last collection of essays, *Where the Stress Falls*, appeared in 2001. See also susansontag.com.

Elizabeth Cady Stanton (1815–1902)

American abolitionist and women's rights activist. Born in Johnstown, New York, she excelled academically at Johnstown Academy, but because of her sex, was barred from nearby Union College. She married the prominent abolitionist Henry B. Stanton, and the two spent their honeymoon at the World's Anti-Slavery Convention in London. In 1848 Stanton joined Lucretia Mott and others to organize the first American convention for women's rights, held in Seneca Falls, New York, where Stanton presented her draft of the "Declaration of Sentiments and Resolutions," now seen as a founding document of modern feminism. Three years later she was introduced to Susan B. Anthony, who became her lifelong friend and colleague; together they founded the National Woman Suffrage Association in 1869. Stanton spent the rest of her life campaigning for women's suffrage and legislation that would make divorce laws more favorable to women. See also nps.gov/wori/learn/historyculture/elizabeth-cady-stanton.htm.

Brent Staples (b. 1951)

American journalist and essayist. Born in Chester, Pennsylvania, Staples earned his B.A. from Widener University and his Ph.D. in psychology from the University of Chicago. After several years teaching college psychology, he began his career in journalism with a brief stint at the *Chicago Sun-Times* before joining the *New York Times* in 1983. Staples has often written about the role of race in American culture, striving to broaden the consideration of the "black experience"—an expression he says he despises—beyond stereotypes of poverty and crime. A list of his recent *New York Times* articles includes topics as diverse as plagiarism, gardening, and urban wildlife. In 1990 he joined the *Times* editorial board. His memoir, *Parallel Time: Growing Up in Black and White*, was published in 1994. See also @BrentNYT on *Twitter*.

Wallace Stegner (1909–1993)

American historian, novelist, and environmentalist. Stegner was born in Lake Mills, Iowa, and had an itinerant upbringing in Montana, Utah, and Saskatchewan. He studied at the University of Utah and the University of Iowa, where he earned a doctorate in 1935. He taught at the University of Utah, the University of Wisconsin, and Harvard University before settling at Stanford University, where he established the creative writing program that now bears his name. His thirteen novels include *Angle of Repose* (1971), winner of the Pulitzer Prize, and *The Spectator Bird* (1977), winner of the National Book Award. Stegner also published six short-story collections and sixteen works of nonfiction, including *Mormon Country* (1942), a history of Utah; *Wolf Willow* (1962), an autobiography; and *On the Teaching of Creative Writing* (1982). See also wallacestegner.org.

Sandra Steingraber (b. 1959)
American biologist, poet, and essayist. A native of Illinois, Steingraber received her B.A. in biology from Illinois Wesleyan University, her M.A. in English from Illinois State University, and her Ph.D. in biology from the University of Michigan. Since a near-fatal bout with bladder cancer when she was in her twenties, Steingraber has devoted her career to exploring the connections between the environment and human health. Her first book was a volume of intimately personal poems, *Post-Diagnosis* (1995). In *Living Downstream: An Ecologist Looks at Cancer and the Environment* (1997), she examines the links between industrial chemicals and increased risks of cancer; following its publication, Steingraber was hailed as "the new Rachel Carson" by the Sierra Club. Her most recent book is *Raising Elijah: Protecting Our Children in an Age of Environmental Crisis* (2011). Steingraber currently teaches at Ithaca College. See also steingraber .com.

Jonathan Swift (1667–1745)
Anglo-Irish poet, satirist, and cleric. Born to English parents who resided in Ireland, Swift studied at Trinity College, Dublin, and then moved to London in 1689. There he became part of the literary and political worlds, beginning his career by writing political pamphlets in support first of the Whigs, then the Tories. Swift earned a master's degree at Oxford University before returning to Ireland. Ordained in the Church of Ireland in 1695, he was appointed dean of St. Patrick's Cathedral, Dublin, in 1713 and held the post until his death. One of the master satirists of the English language, he wrote several scathing attacks on extremism and anti-Irish bigotry, including *The Battle of the Books* (1704), *A Tale of a Tub* (1704), and *A Modest Proposal* (1729), but he is probably best known for the imaginative worlds he created in *Gulliver's Travels* (1726). See also britannica.com/ biography/Jonathan-Swift.

Paul Theroux (b. 1941)
American novelist, essayist, and travel writer. Born in Medford, Massachusetts, Theroux earned a B.A. at the University of Massachusetts before teaching in Malawi as a Peace Corps volunteer, and at Uganda's Makerere University and the University of Singapore. Since then he has lived mainly in England when not traveling all over the world— by train whenever possible. Theroux's novels include *Waldo* (1967), *Saint Jack* (1973), *The Mosquito Coast* (1981), and *Dr. Slaughter* (1984), each made into a movie. He is best known for his travel books, particularly *The Great Railway Bazaar: By Train through Asia* (1975), *The Old Patagonian Express: By Train through the Americas* (1979), *Riding the Iron Rooster* (1988), *The Happy Isles of Oceania* (1992), *Dark Star Safari* (2002), *A Dead Hand: A Crime in Calcutta* (2009), and most recently the novel *Mr. Bones* (2014). See also paultheroux.com.

Henry David Thoreau (1817–1862)
American philosopher, essayist, naturalist, and poet. A graduate of Harvard University, Thoreau worked at a number of jobs—schoolmaster, house painter, employee in his father's pencil factory— before becoming a writer. He befriended Emerson and joined the Transcendental Club, contributing frequently to its journal, the *Dial*. Drawn to the natural world, he wrote his first book, *A Week on the Concord and Merrimac Rivers* (1849), about a canoe trip with his brother. Thoreau's abolitionist stance against slavery led to his arrest for refusing to pay the Massachusetts poll tax (an act of protest against the Mexican War, which he viewed as serving the interests of slaveholders). His essay defending this act, "Civil Disobedience" (1849), his book on the solitary life, *Walden* (1854), and his speech "A Plea for Captain John Brown" (1859) are classics of American literature. See also thoreausociety.org.

Sallie Tisdale (b. 1957)
American nurse and essayist. Born in Eureka, California, Tisdale earned a nursing degree from the University of Portland in 1983. She has worked as a registered nurse and taught at Reed College, Northwestern University, and New York University. A largely self-taught writer on health and medical issues, Tisdale has contributed to the *Antioch Review*, *Tricycle*, *Harper's Magazine*, and the *New Yorker*. "I am really a generalist," she writes, "drawn to a variety of subjects and points of view, but memoir and the first-person essay are the core of all I do." Her books include *The Sorcerer's Apprentice: Tales of the Modern Hospital* (1986), *Lot's Wife* (1988), *Talk Dirty to Me* (1994), *The Best Thing I Ever Tasted: The Secret of Food* (2000), and *Women of the Way: Discovering 2,500 Years of*

Buddhist Wisdom (2006). She is a contributing editor at *Harper's Magazine* and *Salon*. See also sallietisdale.com.

Lad Tobin (b. 1953)
American educator and author. After earning degrees at Earlham College, the University of Chicago, and the University of New Hampshire, Tobin embarked on a lifelong career as a college writing teacher. A specialist in composition theory and creative nonfiction, he currently teaches at Boston College, where he was the founder and longtime director of the first-year writing program. His autobiographical essays, which have appeared in the *Sun*, the *Rumpus*, *Utne Reader*, and *Fourth Genre*, usually focus on how in midlife he has rediscovered his adolescent memories, hobbies, and obsessions. Tobin is also the author of numerous articles and two books—*Writing Relationships: What Really Happens in the Composition Class* (1991) and *Reading Student Writing: Confessions, Meditations, and Rants* (2004)—about teaching writing. He encourages his students to follow Grace Paley's advice: "You write from what you know but you write into what you don't know." See also thesunmagazine.org/author/lad-tobin.

Sojourner Truth (c. 1797–1883)
American abolitionist and women's rights activist. Born into slavery as Isabella Baumfree in Swartekill, New York, Truth she escaped to freedom with her infant daughter in 1826, just a year before slavery was abolished in New York State, and then won a court battle to free one of her sons—the first such legal victory of a black woman over a white man. In 1843, declaring that "the Spirit calls me, and I must go," she adopted the name Sojourner Truth and became an itinerant preacher, condemning the institution of slavery. The famed abolitionist William Lloyd Garrison encouraged her to dictate her memoirs, which he then published as *The Narrative of Sojourner Truth: A Northern Slave* in 1850. A year later, while attending the Women's Rights Convention in Akron, Ohio, she extemporaneously delivered the speech that became known as "Ain't I a Woman?" See also sojournertruth.org.

Mark Twain (1835–1910)
Pen name of Samuel Clemens, American journalist, novelist, and humorist. Twain grew up in Hannibal, Missouri, beside the river that he would later immortalize in the memoir *Life on the Mississippi* (1883) and in *The Adventures of Huckleberry Finn* (1885), regarded by many as one of the greatest American novels. First apprenticed as a printer, he was by turns a riverboat pilot, a Confederate soldier (for two weeks), a gold prospector, and a journalist. His short story "The Celebrated Jumping Frog of Calaveras County" (1867) made him famous; during his lifetime he was enormously popular, lecturing widely to great acclaim and publishing a flood of articles, essays, stories, and novels. Many of his books, including the memoir *Roughing It* (1872) and the novel *The Adventures of Tom Sawyer* (1876), are classics. William Faulkner called Twain "the father of American literature." See also cmgww.com/historic/twain.

Fred Vogelstein (b. 1962)
American journalist and author. A native of New York City, Vogelstein holds a degree in political science from Pomona College and was a fellow at Columbia University's Graduate School of Business. He has been a staff writer for the *Wall Street Journal*, *New York Newsday*, and *U.S. News and World Report*, as well as senior editor covering the tech industry for *Fortune* magazine; currently he is a contributing editor at *Wired*. Vogelstein's career as a business journalist has coincided with the rise of the internet. Much of his reporting covers digital media; the intensely competitive tech industry; and the rapidly evolving ways that technology is transforming business, media, and society. His first book, *Dogfight: How Apple and Google Went to War and Started a Revolution* (2013), is a glimpse beyond Silicon Valley's gadgets into the personalities and competing visions that will shape society's future. See also fredvogelstein.com.

Alice Walker (b. 1944)
American poet, novelist, essayist, and social activist. Born to a sharecropping family in rural Georgia, Walker attended Spelman College and Sarah Lawrence College, where she wrote her first book of poems, *Once* (1968). As an editor for *Ms. Magazine*, Walker championed a revival of interest in the work of Zora Neale Hurston before receiving widespread fame for her third novel, *The Color Purple* (1982), winner of both the Pulitzer Prize and the National Book Award. Her subsequent novels include *The Temple of My Familiar* (1989) and *Possessing the*

Secret of Joy (1992). Walker's nonfiction includes the essay collection In Search of Our Mothers' Gardens: Womanist Prose (1983) and Chicken Chronicles: A Memoir (2011). Her most recent book is a collection of poems, The World Will Follow Joy (2013). She lives in San Francisco, where she runs the publishing company Wild Tree Press. See also alicewalkersgarden.com.

David Foster Wallace (1962–2008)
American novelist and nonfiction writer. Born in Ithaca, New York, Wallace grew up in Champaign and Urbana, Illinois, the son of two college professors. He earned a B.A. in English and philosophy at Amherst College; his English thesis would become his first novel, The Broom of the System (1987). He went on to earn an M.F.A. in creative writing at the University of Arizona. His second novel, Infinite Jest (1996), showcases Wallace's penchant for experimental metafiction, baroque language, ironic detachment, and layered footnotes. Wallace's ten books include the short-story collections Brief Interviews with Hideous Men (1999) and Oblivion (2004), and the essay collections A Supposedly Fun Thing I'll Never Do Again (1997) and Consider the Lobster (2005). Wallace received a MacArthur Fellowship in 1997. His third novel, The Pale King, was unfinished when he took his own life in 2008. See also thehowlingfantods.com/dfw.

Eudora Welty (1909–2001)
American writer, critic, and photographer. Born and raised in Jackson, Mississippi, Welty became one of the South's leading literary voices. After graduating from the University of Wisconsin in 1929 and studying for a year at Columbia University's School of Business, she returned to Jackson and became a publicity agent for the Works Progress Administration, a New Deal social agency. With the help of Robert Penn Warren and Cleanth Brooks, she published several short stories that launched her literary career. Best known for her masterly short fiction—her Collected Stories came out in 1982—Welty's work includes such novellas and novels as The Robber Bridegroom (1942) and The Optimist's Daughter (Pulitzer Prize, 1972); two volumes of photographs; and an acclaimed collection of critical essays, The Eye of the Story (1978). Three lectures delivered at Harvard University in April 1983 were published as One Writer's Beginnings (1984). See also eudorawelty.org.

E. B. White (1899–1985)
American poet, journalist, editor, and essayist. Elwyn Brooks White was born in Mount Vernon, New York. Just three years after graduating from Cornell University in 1921, he began a sixty-year career on the staff of the New Yorker, contributing poems and articles and serving as a discreet and helpful editor. Among his many books, three written for children earned him lasting fame: Stuart Little (1945), Charlotte's Web (1952), and The Trumpet of the Swan (1970). Renowned for his graceful prose, White revised and edited William Strunk's text The Elements of Style (1919, 1959), a classic guide to writing still widely known as "Strunk and White." The collection Essays of E. B. White was published in 1977; a year later White was awarded a Pulitzer Prize for a lifetime of literary achievement. See also britannica.com/biography/E-B-White.

Leon Wieseltier (b. 1952)
American journalist and author. A native of Brooklyn, New York, Wieseltier was educated at the Yeshiva of Flatbush, Columbia University, Oxford University, and Harvard University. He was the longtime literary editor of the New Republic, and is currently a contributing editor and critic for the Atlantic. Passionate in his view about politics and culture, Wieseltier has been called one of the "ideas men of the liberal intelligentsia," yet some of his positions, such as his staunch support of the Iraq War, have made him a maverick of the left. Among his books of fiction and nonfiction are Against Identity (1996), a critique of modern ideas about the self, and Kaddish (2000), a personal exploration of the Jewish prayers of mourning. In 2013, Wieseltier was awarded the $1-million Dan David Prize for "a foremost writer and thinker who confronts and engages with the central issues of our times." See also theatlantic.com/author/leon-wieseltier.

Chris Wiewiora (b. 1987)
Born in Buckhannon, West Virginia, Wiewiora grew up in Orlando, Florida, and earned his B.A. in English at the University of Central Florida, where he served as an editor at the Florida Review. His essay "The Gift of Nothing" led to his acceptance in the M.F.A. at Iowa State University's Creative Writing and Envi-

ronment Program, where he was managing editor of *Flyway*; the essay, first published in *Stymie*, has since been cited as "Notable" in *Best American Sports Writing* (2012). Wiewiora has held a variety of jobs, one of which, a pizza tosser, led to his essay "This Is Tossing," which was published in the literary magazine *MAKE* as well as the anthology *Best Food Writing* (2013). See also chriswiewiora.com.

Patricia Williams (b. 1951)
American legal scholar and critic. Williams received her B.A. from Wellesley College and her J.D. from Harvard Law School. Currently a professor at Columbia Law School, she is a leading proponent of critical race theory, which argues that race is a principal determinant in the legal system and in culture generally. Her monthly column, "Diary of a Mad Law Professor," appears in the *Nation*. Her books include *The Alchemy of Race and Rights: Diary of a Law Professor* (1991), *The Rooster's Egg* (1995), *Seeing a Color-Blind Future: The Paradox of Race* (1997), and *Open House: Of Family, Friends, Food, Piano Lessons, and the Search for a Room of My Own* (2004). Williams also co-edited *The Blind Goddess: A Reader on Race and Justice* (2011). She has received a MacArthur Fellowship, along with numerous other honors. See also thenation.com/authors/patricia-j-williams.

Terry Tempest Williams (b. 1955)
American poet, nature writer, and environmental activist. Born to a Mormon family in Corona, California, Williams grew up surrounded by the vast desert landscape of Utah; she holds degrees in both English and environmental education from the University of Utah. Her first book, *Pieces of White Shell: A Journey to Navajoland* (1984), is a personal exploration of Native American myths. Her much-reprinted essay, "The Clan of One-Breasted Women," became the final section of the autobiographical *Refuge: An Unnatural History of Family and Place* (1991). Her subsequent books include *An Unspoken Hunger: Stories from the Field* (1994), *Red: Passion and Patience in the Desert* (2001), *The Open Space of Democracy* (2004), and most recently *When Women Were Birds* (2012). Williams is a frequent contributor to the *New York Times*, the *New Yorker*, *Orion*, and other publications. She is a columnist at the *Progressive*. See also coyoteclan.com.

Tom Wolfe (b. 1931)
American journalist, essayist, and novelist. A native of Richmond, Virginia, Wolfe earned a B.A. at Washington and Lee University and a Ph.D. in American studies from Yale. Working as a traditional journalist at the *Washington Post* and the *New York Herald Tribune*, Wolfe started to utilize techniques derived from narrative fiction, creating what became known as "the New Journalism." Books such as *The Kandy-Kolored Tangerine-Flake Streamline Baby* (1965), *The Electric Kool-Aid Acid Test* (1968), and *From Bauhaus to Our House* (1981) established his reputation as a witty social critic and historian of popular culture. Wolfe's National Book Award–winning chronicle of the American space program, *The Right Stuff* (1979), was made into a popular film. His satiric novels—*Bonfire of the Vanities* (1987), *A Man in Full* (1998), *I Am Charlotte Simmons* (2005), and most recently *Back to Blood* (2012)—aim to depict the breadth of American society. See also tomwolfe.com.

Virginia Woolf (1882–1941)
English novelist, critic, and essayist. The London-born daughter of the eminent philosopher Sir Leslie Stephen, Woolf was mainly self-educated through access to her father's substantial library. For decades she was at the center of the Bloomsbury Group, a celebrated collection of artists, scholars, and writers that included both Woolf and her husband, socialist writer Leonard Woolf. Together, the Woolfs founded and operated the Hogarth Press, whose publications included many of her works. A foremost modernist, Woolf employed psychological insight, lyricism and experimental literary techniques in her fiction; her nine novels include the now-classic *Mrs. Dalloway* (1925), *To the Lighthouse* (1927), and *The Waves* (1931). Her numerous essays are collected in four volumes; they include *A Room of One's Own* (1929), a historical investigation of women and creativity; and *Three Guineas* (1938), philosophical dialogues that explore issues of war and feminism. See also www.virginiawoolfsociety.co.uk/vw_res.biography.htm.

William Zinsser (1922–2015)
American journalist, writer, editor, and educator. Born in New York City, Zinsser graduated from Princeton University and then served in the army for two

years at the end of World War II. In 1946 he joined the staff of the *New York Herald Tribune*, eventually becoming an editorial writer. A freelancer throughout the 1960s, Zinsser contributed to *Life*, *Look*, the *New York Times Magazine*, and other publications. In the 1970s he joined the English faculty at Yale University, where he taught nonfiction writing and edited the alumni magazine. Zinsser's nineteen books range in subject from travel to jazz to baseball, but he is best known for *On Writing Well* (1976, 1998), a classic guide to clear, economical nonfiction writing, as well as the memoir *Writing Places: The Life Journey of a Writer and Teacher* (2009). His award-winning columns from the *American Scholar* have been collected in *The Writer Who Stayed* (2012). See also williamzinsserwriter .com.

CREDITS

CHRONOLOGICAL INDEX

Genres Index

CULTURAL ANALYSIS

NATURE WRITING

Op-Eds

Parables

Profile of a Person

PROFILE OF A PLACE

PROPOSALS

REPORTAGE

RHETORICAL MODES INDEX

Narrating

Exemplifying

CLASSIFYING AND DIVIDING

EXPLAINING A PROCESS

COMPARING AND CONTRASTING

DEFINING

ANALYZING CAUSE AND EFFECT

THEMATIC INDEX

Gender and Sexuality

LIFE AND DEATH

POP CULTURE

RACE AND ETHNICITY

RELIGION AND SPIRITUALITY

WORK

INDEX